Brief Contents

Achieve for *Principles of Economics*

Engage Every Student

Achieve is a comprehensive set of interconnected teaching and assessment tools. It incorporates the most effective elements from Macmillan's market-leading solutions in a single, easy-to-use platform. Our resources were co-designed with instructors and students, using a foundation of learning research and rigorous testing.

Everything You Need in a Single Learning Path

Achieve is an online learning system that supports students and instructors at every step, from the first point of contact with new content to demonstrating mastery of concepts and skills. Powerful resources including an integrated e-book, robust homework, and a wealth of interactives create an extraordinary learning resource for students.

Learning Objectives Provide Powerful Insights

Every asset you can assign in Achieve is tagged to a learning objective. Insights and reporting help instructors and students understand how they are performing against objectives, enabling more efficient and effective interventions.

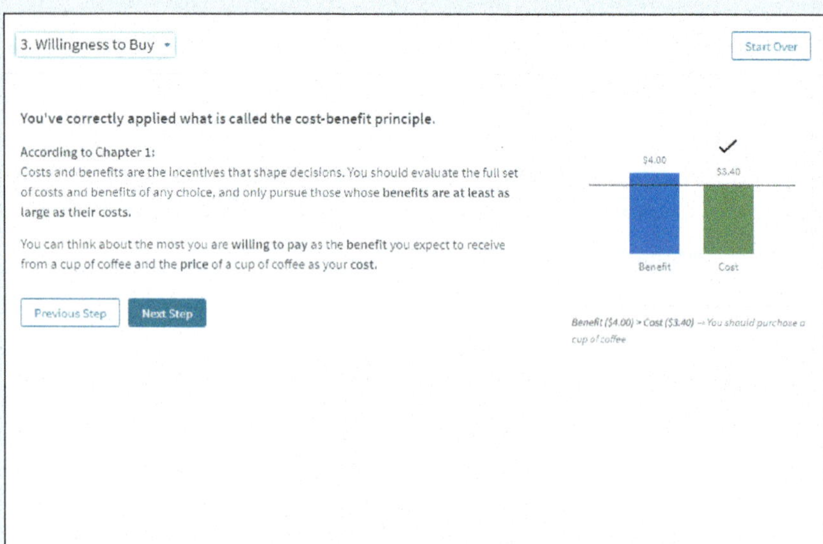

Interactive Decision Points Decision Points activities allow students to explore their own decision-making process and how economic principles and thinking can inform their decisions. Students work step-by-step through decision-making scenarios, receiving feedback about how economic principles did (or did not) play into their choices. Decision Points help students apply economic insights to their everyday lives.

Instructor Activity Guides The guides provide instructors with a structured plan to facilitate an activity that encourages student engagement in both face-to-face and remote learning courses. Each guide is based on a single topic and allows students to participate through questions, group work, presentations, and/or simulations. The guide displays the activity type, estimated prep and class time, implementation instructions, suggestions for remote implementation where applicable, and Learning Objectives and Bloom's level for ease of use. Our Instructor Activity Guides encourage engagement from a Pre-Class Reflection question to prime student interest and offer follow-up iClicker questions to measure comprehension.

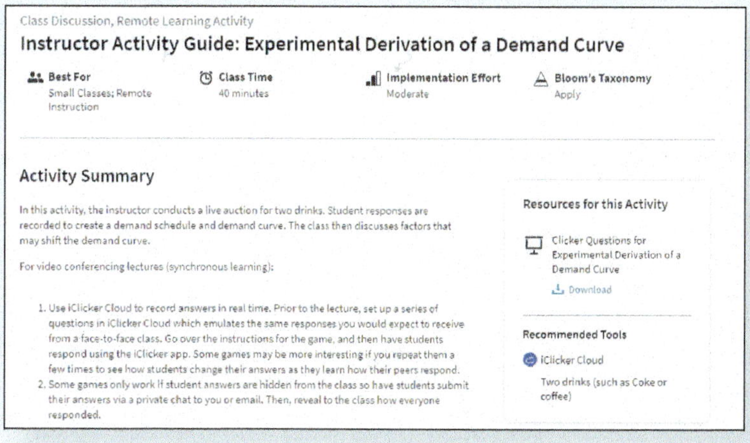

Interactive E-Book The Achieve e-book allows students to highlight and take notes; instructors can choose to assign sections of the e-book as part of their course assignments.

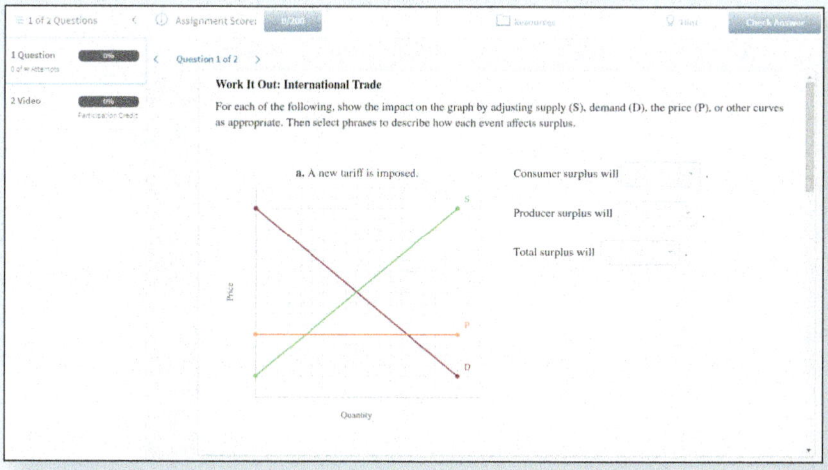

Work It Out These skill-building activities pair sample end-of-section problems with targeted feedback and video explanations to help students solve problems step by step. This approach allows students to work independently, tests their comprehension of concepts, and prepares them for class and exams.

End-of-Chapter Questions Developed by economists active in the classroom, these multistep problems are paired with rich feedback for incorrect and correct responses that guide students through the process of problem solving. These questions also feature our user-friendly graphing tool, designed so students focus entirely on economics and not on how to use the application.

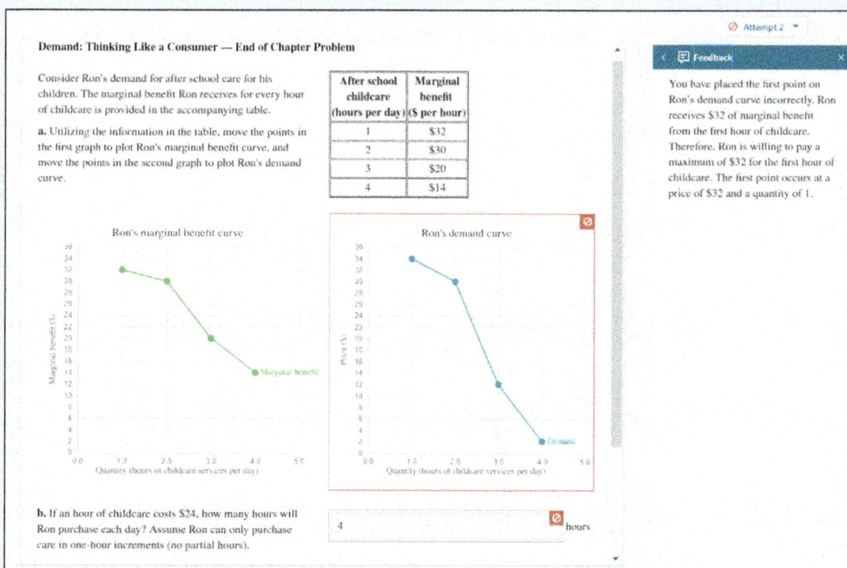

Practice Quizzes Designed to be used as a study tool, these quizzes feature questions from the Test Bank and allow for multiple attempts as students familiarise themselves with content.

Powerful Support for Instructors

Test Bank This comprehensive Test Bank contains multiple-choice and short-answer questions to help instructors assess students' comprehension, interpretation, and ability to synthesise.

Lecture Slides These brief, interactive, and visually interesting slides are designed to hold students' attention in class with graphics and animations demonstrating key concepts and real-world examples.

Clicker Slides These slides contain questions to incorporate active learning in the classroom. Students can participate by using the iClicker app on their smartphone or laptop.

iClicker Integration With Achieve's seamless integration with iClicker, you can help any student participate—in the classroom or virtually. iClicker's attendance feature gets students in class, then instructors can choose from flexible polling and quizzing options to engage, check understanding, and get feedback from students in real time. iClicker also allows students to participate using laptops, mobile devices, or iClicker remotes—whichever each student prefers. Additionally, we offer Instructor Activity Guides and book-specific iClicker question slides within Achieve to make the most out of your class time. It's no surprise that over a decade after being founded by educators, iClicker still leads the market. And thousands of instructors continue to give every student a voice with our simple, award-winning student engagement solutions.

Instructor's Resource Manual The Instructor's Resource Manual offers instructors teaching materials and tips to enhance the classroom experience, along with chapter objectives, outlines, and a breakdown of the large library of MRU videos.

Gradebook Assignment scores are collected into a comprehensive Gradebook providing instructors reporting on individuals and overall course performance.

LMS Integration LMS Integration is included so that all students' scores in Achieve can easily integrate into a school's learning management system and that an instructor's Gradebook and roster are always in sync.

Customer Support Our Achieve Client Success Specialist Team—dedicated platform experts—provides collaboration, software expertise, and consulting to tailor each course to fit your instructional goals and student needs. Start with a demo at a time that works for you to learn more about how to set up your customised course.

PRINCIPLES of ECONOMICS

Richard Holden

University of New South Wales

Betsey Stevenson

University of Michigan

Justin Wolfers

University of Michigan

macmillan learning

Executive Vice President, General Manager: Charles Linsmeier
Vice President, Social Sciences and High School: Shani Fisher
Senior Executive Program Manager: Carolyn Merrill
Development Manager: Lukia Kliossis
Sales and Marketing Director: Katie Thorn
Marketing Manager, Australia/New Zealand: Fiona McNeill
Executive Marketing Manager: Scott Guile
Marketing Assistant: Claudia Cruz
Executive Director, Digital Workflow Strategy: Noel Hohnstine
Associate Director, Digital Content: Joshua Hill
Editorial Assistant: Amanda Nava
Senior Director, Content Management Enhancement: Tracey Kuehn
Executive Managing Editor: Michael Granger
Senior Lead Content Project Manager: Kerry O'Shaughnessy
Senior Workflow Project Manager: Jennifer Wetzel
Production Supervisor: Brianna Lester
Director of Design, Content Management: Diana Blume
Senior Design Services Manager: Natasha A. S. Wolfe
Interior Design: Kevin Kall and Dirk Kaufman
Senior Cover Design Manager: John Callahan
Cover Design: Dirk Kaufman
Art Manager: Matthew McAdams
Illustration Coordinator: Janice Donnola
Illustrations: Network Graphics
Executive Permissions Editor: Robin Fadool
Media Project Manager: Andrew Vaccaro
Composition: Lumina Datamatics, Inc.
Printing and Binding: Lakeside Book Company

ISBN-13: 978-1-319-51175-3
ISBN-10: 1-319-51175-9

Printed in the United States of America
1 2 3 4 5 6 28 27 26 25 24 23

Macmillan Learning
120 Broadway
25th Floor
New York, NY 10271
macmillanlearning.co.uk

Dedication

With thanks to those in previous generations who inspired, educated, and raised us.

In awe of those in the next generation—you are better, faster, and smarter.

And with inspiration from introductory students who are about to learn that economics will give you superpowers—our hope is that you'll use those superpowers to create a more joyful world.

About the Authors

Richard Holden

Richard Holden is Professor of Economics at UNSW Business School, director of the Economics of Education Knowledge Hub @UNSWBusiness, co-director of the New Economic Policy Initiative, and President of the Academy of the Social Sciences in Australia. Prior to that he was on the faculty at the University of Chicago and the Massachusetts Institute of Technology.

Richard's research focuses on contract theory, organisational economics, law and economics, and political economy. He has written on topics including: network capital, political districting, the boundary of the firm, incentives in organisations, mechanism design, voting rules, and blockchain.

Richard has published in top general interest journals such as the *Quarterly Journal of Economics,* the *American Economic Review* and the *Review of Economic Studies.* He is currently editor of the *Journal of Law and Economics,* and is the founding director of the Herbert Smith Freehills Inititative on Law & Economics at UNSW.

He is a Fellow of the Econometric Society, a Fellow of the Academy of the Social Sciences in Australia, a Distinguished Fellow of the Luohan Academy, and a Senior Academic Fellow at the e61 Institute.

His research has been featured in press articles in *The New York Times, The Financial Times, The Economist,* and *The New Republic.* Richard appears regularly as a media commentator, and has published opinion pieces in outlets including *The Australian Financial Review, The Australian, The New York Times, The New Republic,* and *The Sydney Morning Herald.* He also writes a weekly column called Vital Signs for *The Conversation.*

Richard earned a BEc(Hons) and the University Medal from the University of Sydney, and an AM and a PhD in economics from Harvard University.

Betsey Stevenson is a professor of economics and public policy at the University of Michigan. Her research focuses on the impact of public policies on the labour market, and explores women's labour market experiences, the economic forces shaping the modern family, and the role of subjective well-being data for public policy. She serves on the Executive Committee of the American Economic Association, and is also a research associate with the National Bureau of Economic Research, a fellow of the Institute for Economic Research in Munich, a visiting associate professor of economics at the University of Sydney, and a research fellow with the Centre for Economic Policy Research in London. She served as a member of the Council of Economic Advisers from 2013 to 2015, where she advised President Obama on social policy, labour market, and trade issues. She also served as the chief economist of the U.S. Department of Labor from 2010 to 2011. Betsey is an occasional editorialist for Bloomberg, and a trusted presence in the public debate about economics and public policy. She earned a BEc and BMath from Wellesley College and an AM and PhD in economics from Harvard University.

Betsey Stevenson and Justin Wolfers

Justin Wolfers is a professor of economics and public policy at the University of Michigan. He has done research in both macroeconomics and applied microeconomics topics, having explored unemployment and inflation, the power of prediction markets, the economic forces shaping the modern family, discrimination, and happiness. He is a research associate with the National Bureau for Economic Research, a fellow of the Brookings Institution, a fellow of the Peterson Institute for International Economics, a research fellow with the Centre for Economic Policy Research in London, a fellow of the Institute for Economic Research in Munich, a visiting professor of economics at the University of Sydney, and an international research fellow at the Kiel Institute for the World Economy in Germany. He has been an editor of the Brookings Papers on Economic Activity, a board member on the Committee on the Status of Women in Economics, a member of the Panel of Advisors of the U.S. Congressional Budget Office, among many other board and advisory positions. He is currently a contributing columnist for *The New York Times*, and has written about economic issues in numerous other outlets. He is frequently quoted in the media on economic policy and relied upon to provide unbiased assessments of the current state of the macroeconomy. Justin earned a BEc(Hons) and the University Medal from the University of Sydney and an AM and PhD in economics from Harvard University.

A Fresh Perspective on Economics

A slow-motion revolution has transformed economics. We've moved beyond the widget factory—the standardised set of business interactions involving inputs, outputs, and pricing decisions—towards a social science that can speak to the decisions we make in every aspect of our lives. Successive cohorts of economists have transformed the field so that it has greater relevance and a closer relationship to actual human behaviour, making it more meaningful to more people. This is no longer your parents' economics.

This transformation presents a once-in-a-generation teaching opportunity. More than ever before, we have the capacity to deliver a compelling introductory economics class that will deliver an extraordinary return on our students' investment in the field.

This opportunity requires a textbook that works with instructors to showcase how economics has become *broader,* and we show that it is more relevant to a larger, more diverse population of students. It has to show that economics has become more *useful* for the ordinary business of life, and our students delight in seeing the relevance of economic tools to the real-world decisions they face. We believe that by focusing on *intuition,* we can reorient students to seeing themselves as economic actors poised to apply the lessons they're learning throughout their lives.

Our fresh perspective gives us an opportunity to write in a voice that students actually want to read. If you've ever had the pleasure of reading one of those popular economics books that takes readers on a joyous romp through our field, you'll quickly understand why millions of people spend their weekends reading them. Podcast rankings and bestseller lists reveal a latent demand for an approach that supplies some of the same magic. We aim to bring that sense of delight and discovery to your introductory economics class.

Economics can provide students with a toolkit of extraordinary breadth, usefulness, and insight. It's a toolkit they can use to better understand and navigate their world, empowering them to make better decisions in the many different roles they'll play in the economy, their communities, and their careers—indeed, in every aspect of their lives.

For economics instructors, the opportunity is larger still, giving us the capacity to transform individual lives and entire communities. Our goal is for every single student who turns the page to do more than remember—to use(!)—what they've learned, every day, for the rest of their lives. We aim to show them the power and transformative potential in the lessons they're about to absorb.

We each have that one class that we remember from college. It's the class you look back on as having somehow caused your synapses to fire differently, that sparked new neural connections, and provided a clarity that felt like it allowed you to see beyond the horizon. It might have been the class that inspired you to study economics—or maybe it was a subject that, though it seemed tangential to your studies at the time, you've found yourself drawing on every day since. We want Principles of Economics to be *that class* for each of our students, and for each of yours.

Richard Holden

Betsey Stevenson

Justin Wolfers

Broadly Applicable

We're part of a generation that has come to understand economics as a set of tools, rather than a specific set of interactions in traditional markets. In our research, we've analysed marriage and divorce, women's changing role in the labour market, happiness, elections, unemployment, and inequality. This broad approach enables us to show students that the economic tools they're learning can be used to study families, education, and health as well as business strategy, political economy, finance, and economic policy. This greater relevance means that studying economics has a bigger payoff for more students across a wider range of interests and career ambitions, including those who have traditionally been deterred from the field. The result is a more diverse set of students, higher enrollments, and greater momentum in the major.

Tobin Rogers/Hill Street Studios/Blend Images/Getty Images

How will you allocate your limited attention? *See Chapter 1.*

Extraordinarily Useful

In our experience, students identify with economics when economics identifies with them. And so on every page we show how it applies to the real-world decisions they'll face in their lives. The theory of supply comes to life when students see themselves not just as potential suppliers but also as suppliers of their labour, their savings, and even their attention. The theory of comparative advantage that animates international trade is more broadly a theory of task allocation that students can use now to inform their choice of major, and later as managers assigning responsibilities among their staff. Likewise, the net present value framework we use to teach future CEOs how to make investment decisions applies equally to our students' decisions to invest in their education, their health, and their careers. The value of the economic toolkit becomes immediately obvious when students can start using it straight away—and when they can see themselves applying it through the rest of their lives.

Oleksiy Maksymenko Photography/Alamy Stock Photo

Vacuum or cook? *See Chapter 6.*

Refreshingly Intuitive

This broader and more useful scope requires us to shift perspectives, from thinking about our students as spectators who watch the economic action unfold, to preparing them for the important roles they'll play as economic actors. That means emphasising economic intuition so that they learn to see the world through an economics lens. We do this by doing more, with less. Rather than overstuff each lesson with technical detail, we focus on the foundational ideas. For faculty, this means teaching the same economic ideas that you use every day. For students, it means working through these ideas again and again, to build familiarity and competence. In time, the muscle that connects theory with reality grows stronger, and something magical happens as students start to recognise economic forces all around them. This transforms the relationship that our students have with economics: They report that it changes from just another subject of classroom study to a whole new way of thinking that they find themselves using every day.

Adam Crowley/AGE Fotostock

Should you keep or sell your textbooks? *See Chapter 3.*

Build a Solid Foundation

If you want to build something that lasts, start with a solid foundation. This means stripping economics back to its foundational ideas, and then showing the power and reach of those ideas.

Four Core Principles. Endless Applications.

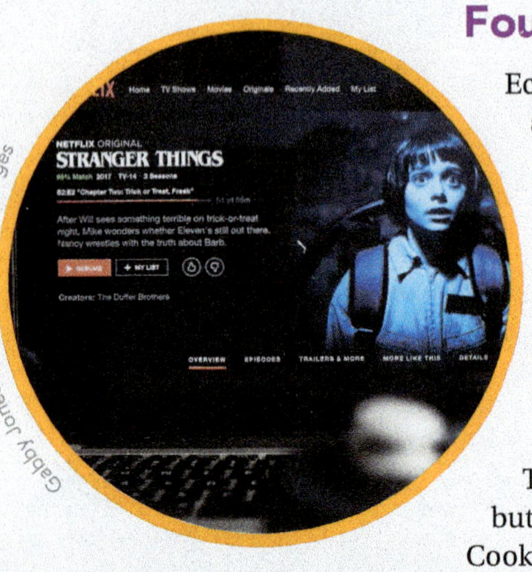

Gabby Jones/Bloomberg/Getty Images

Should you stream one more episode? *See Chapter 1.*

Economists know that the core principles of economics can be applied broadly, to just about any decision. Our goal is for students to walk out of the principles course thinking the same way. In Chapter 1, we introduce students to the four core principles that are the foundation of economic reasoning:

- The *marginal principle:* Ask "one more?" instead of "how many?"
- The *cost-benefit principle:* Compare the relevant costs and benefits
- The *opportunity cost principle:* Remember to consider the opportunity costs
- The *interdependence principle:* Take account of the broader effects of your decisions

Throughout the book, we show students how these four core principles form a simple but powerful framework for making even the most mundane decisions (Walk or drive? Cook or takeaway?). We then return to them throughout the book, to show students how these basic tools can be scaled up to larger decisions, with higher stakes (Spend or save? Make or buy? Work or school?). These ideas recur in every chapter of the book, showing students the unity and power of the economic approach. In our experience, students have a much easier time understanding new concepts when they see them built from the same core principles. Along the way, they develop vital "muscle memory," learning to apply these core ideas to any new economic question they face. Over time, they'll naturally come to "think like an economist."

Economic Intuition Begins with the Basics

Ian G Dagnall/Alamy Stock Photo

What happens to the demand and supply of lifeguards in the summertime? *See Chapter 4.*

The concepts of supply and demand are the foundational framework for much of economics, which is why it's essential that students master this material. We walk students patiently through these topics, dedicating a full chapter to demand, then supply, and finally equilibrium. This breakdown of topics aligns with the way most instructors already teach, taking several lectures to work through this foundational material even as most textbooks rush through it all in a single chapter. Our deliberate approach supports students with clear, familiar examples and plenty of opportunities to practise drawing and shifting curves, helping them build a deeper and more intuitive understanding of the ideas behind the curves. By the time they're through the first few chapters, the urge to find an equilibrium is practically a reflex. This sets them up for success in later chapters, where they'll apply the supply and demand framework to new problems and adapt it to account for specific market failures.

From Fundamentals to "One Economics"

By mastering the four core principles and the basics of supply and demand, students learn to apply the tools of economics to just about any decision they face. We leverage this foundation as later chapters delve into more advanced topics. In each case, we follow a recipe that students will find familiar, initially focusing on individual choices, then aggregating them to yield demand and supply curves, and ultimately market outcomes. We work through the principles to discover a series of "rational rules"—such as producing until marginal revenue equals marginal cost, hiring until wages equal the marginal revenue product of labour, or consuming until the marginal benefit of a dollar of spending today is equal to the marginal benefit of spending a dollar-plus-interest tomorrow. This approach also sets students up for a thoroughly modern treatment of macroeconomics, which is built from these microeconomic foundations. The payoff is that our students study "one economics," which they can apply to whatever new issues interest them.

Ann Kirby-Payne

Which social app will you use? *See Chapter 2.*

Useful Economics for the Real World

While most students won't become professional economists, they are all economic actors who will manage their careers and their families, play active roles in their communities, and perhaps run their own businesses. We show students that economics gives them a valuable toolkit that will make them more effective decision makers in almost any role they choose. For example, we introduce comparative advantage as a framework for efficiently allocating household tasks, and then move on to show how it can be used to organise teams, businesses, and other organisations before finally discussing it as a driver of international trade. Our analysis of the relative efficiency of markets concludes with case studies of how managers and nonprofits use internal markets to harness market forces. A broader framing of externalities makes the policies used to solve them relevant not only to governments looking to reduce environmental harm, but also to managers looking to fix misaligned incentives in the workplace. In analysing private information, we show that you should be wary of sellers who know something you don't, and what you can do to avoid getting ripped off. And when buyers know something you don't, we show that often you won't get the customers you want, and what you can do about it. The macroeconomic framework we introduce to forecast consumption yields concrete advice about when to save, how to form a saving plan, and how to stick to it. Our study of labour markets reveals how employers can tweak wages and incentives to get the most out of their employees, and how workers can leverage their comparative advantage to be more efficient (and better compensated). The material on uncertainty applies as much to managing your household portfolio as it does to managing your business assets. This broad reach makes economics more inviting to a more diverse group of students from a range of backgrounds, each with different plans for the future.

JAMES ROSS/EPA-EFE/Shutterstock

How can a nonprofit use market forces to better feed Australia's hungry? *See Chapter 6.*

Teaching Modern Economics

Economics has changed dramatically over recent decades, but economics textbooks have not. We integrate the insights of today's economics into the curriculum to show students an approach to economics that reflects the reality they see and that addresses the problems that modern economists are focused on.

Every Decision is an Economic Decision

Should you drive, walk, or take the bus? Which tasks should you do yourself and which should you delegate? Will you get a job or do postgraduate study? Our treatment of economics follows the lead of modern researchers, relentlessly applying economic analysis to "the ordinary business of everyday life." Throughout this book, students are challenged to apply a decision-making framework derived from core economic principles to the countless choices they face each day.

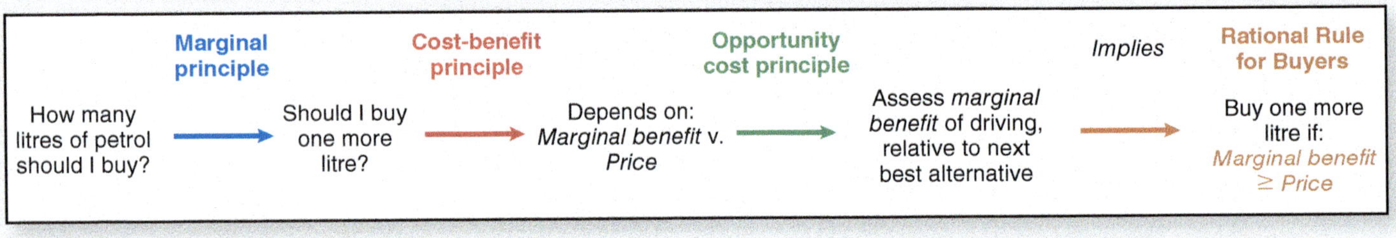

The four core principles of economics are translated into active decision-making tools that are applied throughout the text.

From Market Structure to Business Strategy

The field of industrial organisation has reinvented itself over recent decades, creating a disconnect between how economists think about market structure and what has continued to be taught to introductory students. We eliminate this disconnect by reorienting the analysis of market structure to emphasise business strategy. Instead of a passive description of the market structure that managers inherit, we shift focus toward an active understanding of how businesses shape their competitive environment by strategically shaping the incentives of their competitors, potential entrants, suppliers, and customers. Consistent with the understanding of modern industrial organisational economists, this means putting less emphasis on discrete market structures, and more emphasis on the deeper economic forces that managers confront: Market power, the threat of new entrants, product positioning, incomplete contracts with suppliers and customers, and strategic interactions.

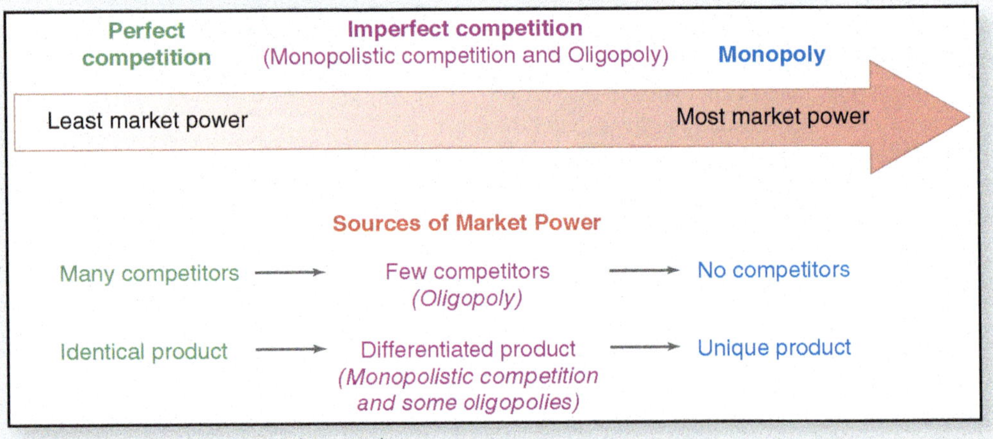

Modern economists look beyond four distinct market structures to see a continuum of market power.

A Deep Dive into Decision Making

Our focus is on giving students modern tools they can use to make better decisions. Our chapter on private information analyses how best to make decisions when others know something that you don't. Our chapter on game theory provides a toolkit for figuring out what to do when your best choice depends on what someone else does, and their best choice depends on what you do. Our chapter on uncertainty helps students make better choices across states of nature. For instance, we integrate insights from behavioural economics throughout the book so that students learn to counter the psychological biases that might lead them to make bad choices.

A product manager at Kellogg's decides where to position their new breakfast cereal on a continuum from sweet to nutritious.

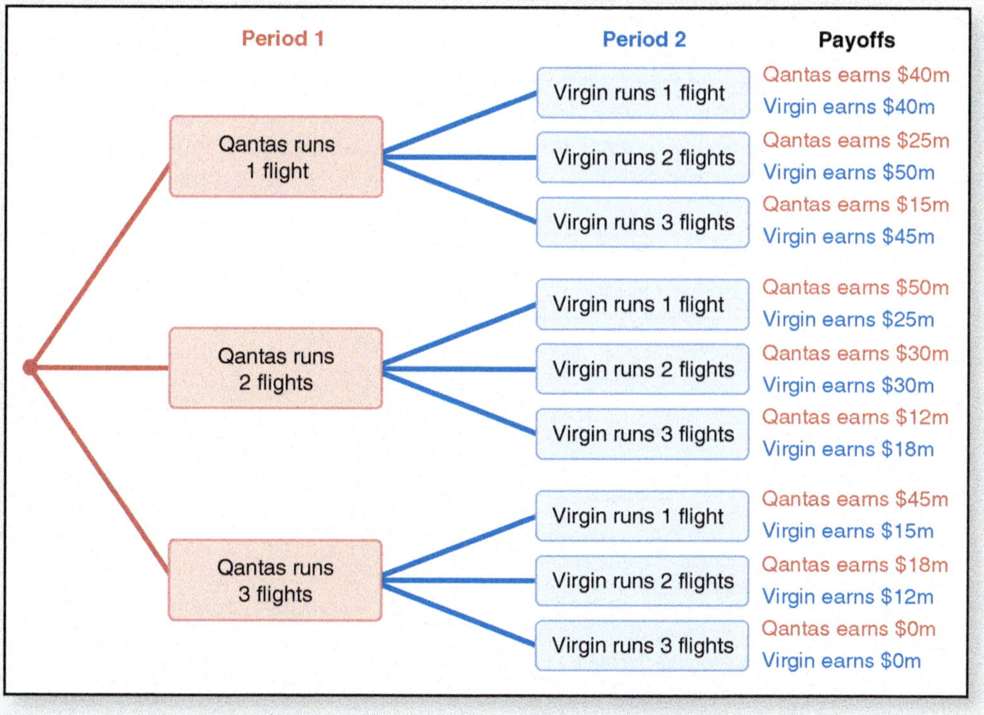

Prune your game tree down until you get to the best decision.

Micro Foundations of Macroeconomics

Whether economists are looking at microeconomic or macroeconomic topics, our method is the same: Focus on individual decisions, such as those that our students will actually face, explore the factors that shape those decisions, and aggregate them to illustrate market outcomes. This sharp focus on micro foundations—which includes separate chapters analysing consumption, investment, the financial sector, and the influence of the global economy—helps students see the connections between their personal choices and the broader economy. It allows us to put the student front and center, confronting them with the decisions they'll face in their own lives as consumers, managers, investors, stockholders or bondholders, and importers or exporters, while helping them pull it all together to understand the forces impacting the macroeconomy.

How much did your bedhead contribute to GDP?

A Flexible Approach to Business Cycle Models

Our analysis of business cycles follows the approach and language that policy makers use to analyse macroeconomic fluctuations. We begin by providing students with a stylized version of the basic framework that Reserve Bank policy makers use to interpret the business cycle, using the *IS* curve to explain spending decisions, together with an *MP* curve that describes monetary policy and the influence of the financial sector. We add a modern Phillips curve to explain inflation, and finally bring the pieces together

Organisational note: *As discussed on page 741, different economists like to examine business cycles from slightly different perspectives. Much like viewing a concert, you can see things differently depending on where you sit. Now that you've been introduced to business cycles, it's time for you—or more likely, your instructor—to choose your seat for the show. If your instructor wants you to see the economy from the same perspective as the RBA does, they'll direct you to read Chapters 30 and 31 (perhaps with Chapter 32 as a capstone). If your instructor recommends a more traditional view, then read Chapter 33. And if they want you to really appreciate the role of aggregate expenditure, they might recommend you start with the appendix. Remember that you'll still be able to see the whole show, no matter where you sit.*

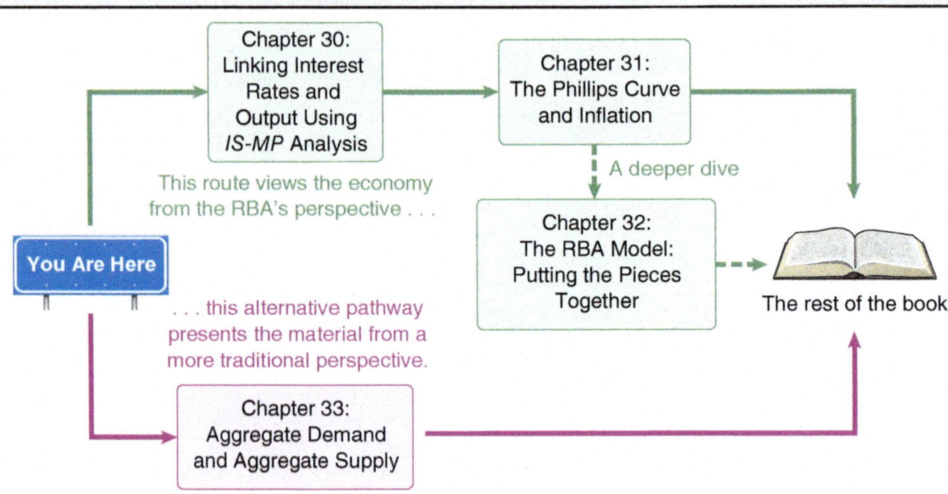

Two separate paths, but they lead to the same place.

into a complete general equilibrium model. The result is an approach that echoes and is reinforced by media reports of ongoing policy debates. Of course, we also recognize that many instructors may wish to teach using the more traditional Aggregate Demand and Aggregate Supply model, which is why we provide full coverage of this perspective as well. This two-track approach allows you to pick the path for teaching business cycles that works best for you and your students. Either path will lead your students to the same destination—a clear understanding of business cycles—and prepare them for a thorough understanding of how monetary policy and fiscal policy can be used to counter the effects of the business cycle.

Applications That Keep It Real

As instructors, we know that the best way for students to learn is to involve them with the content, and we've worked hard to demonstrate that students' lives already involve—and will always involve—real economic decisions.

EVERYDAY Economics **Would you rather live in the United States or in Australia?**

Australia has instituted a 38-hour workweek, requiring employers to pay overtime to compensate for any extra hours worked. By contrast, in the United States the typical workweek is 40 hours. Australia also requires that employees have access to substantial paid vacation time, paid sick leave, and paid parental leave. None of these are required in the United States. Add it all up, and over the course of a year, a typical Australian employee works 100 fewer hours than their American counterpart. That's the equivalent of two and a half fewer workweeks! But this comes at a cost. The average income in Australia—that is, GDP per person—is 9% lower than it is in the United States. Which would you prefer: more money, or more time off? ■

Michele Jackson/Alamy Stock Photo

Australians have more time to sit in cafés than Americans do, but less money to spend in them.

▲ **Everyday Economics** No widgets, no lemonade stands. We invite students to apply their economic toolkit to the sorts of situations they face—from salary negotiations to the division of labour in their home. By asking themselves "what would I do?" students naturally come to a deeper understanding of the economic principles involved.

Interpreting the DATA **Global trade is rising because of declining trade costs.**

International trade—both exports and imports—has been a growing share of the Australian economy throughout the entire postwar period (Figure 1). This trend—sometimes called "globalisation"—has transformed the economy. And it's largely due to declining trade costs.

Figure 1 | Imports and Exports Are a Rising Share of the Australian Economy

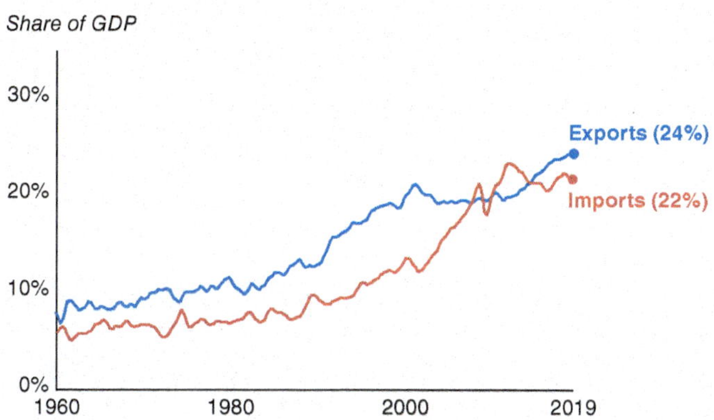

Data from: Australian Bureau of Statistics.

▲ **Interpreting the Data** When data were scarce, the role of economic theory was to fill in the missing pieces when the relevant facts were unavailable. But today, facts are cheap and data are abundant—perhaps even overwhelming. As a result, today's students will use economic theory instead as a framework for interpreting these data. These brief features show students how to interpret real-world observations through an economic lens. The goal is to help students build confidence in using economic theory to transform data into insight.

Do the Economics

Answers: a. Don't let yesterday's $60 sunk cost lead you to go to a party you won't enjoy. b. Walk out. You've already paid for the ticket and can't get the money back, so the $15 is a sunk cost you should ignore. c. The problem says that you would prefer to be with your friends, so go to the Gold Coast! The $599 nonrefundable package is a sunk cost.

It is easy to fall for the sunk-cost fallacy. Think about the following scenarios:

a. Yesterday you rented a costume for $60 to go to your friends annual "come as your favourite Superhero" party. But today you're feeling sick, and as you're getting dressed to go to the party, you realise that you won't enjoy it. Do you head to the party?

b. You paid $15 for movie tickets. But 30 minutes into the film, you've seen enough: The acting is terrible, the plot is predictable, and the jokes are cringe-worthy. Do you stay for the last hour?

c. You found a great deal for the summer holidays: a $599 package deal to the Whitsundays. You immediately buy the package and tell your friends about it. Unfortunately, by the time they call, tickets are sold out. Instead, your friends decide to drive to the Gold Coast, where you can all stay for free with your best friend's uncle. You would prefer to be with your friends, but the $599 package deal is nonrefundable. Do you go to the Whitsundays? ■

▲ **Do the Economics** For economics to be useful, students must practise using it. Embedded directly into the text narrative, these brief exercises confront students with real-life scenarios and challenge them to "do economics," by analysing the underlying logic of each situation, and helping them work through the solutions. Through this process, students will come to see economics as a verb—an active process of applying economics to understand the world and inform their choices.

Tools That Prepare and Engage

To help students to learn and apply economic concepts, we've worked hard to think like students. Our study tools meet students where they are, giving them the support they'll need to master the material. Integrated features prepare students for the road ahead, support students while they read, and provide practical tools for review. When students feel supported, they feel motivated to succeed.

It Helps to Have a Navigation System

It can be all too easy for students to get lost in the economic woods, focusing only on the trees right in front of them. We provide tools to help students both see the road ahead and pan back to see the bigger picture so that they can synthesise what they're learning as they move through the course.

▶ **The big picture** Each part of the book opens with a simple graphic organiser that illuminates the broad pathway ahead, outlining key learning objectives for each chapter and previewing the questions that students will be answering as they move through the content. Students never wander into "uncharted territory," but instead arrive at each new topic fully prepared, with a broad view of the terrain and a plan for navigating it.

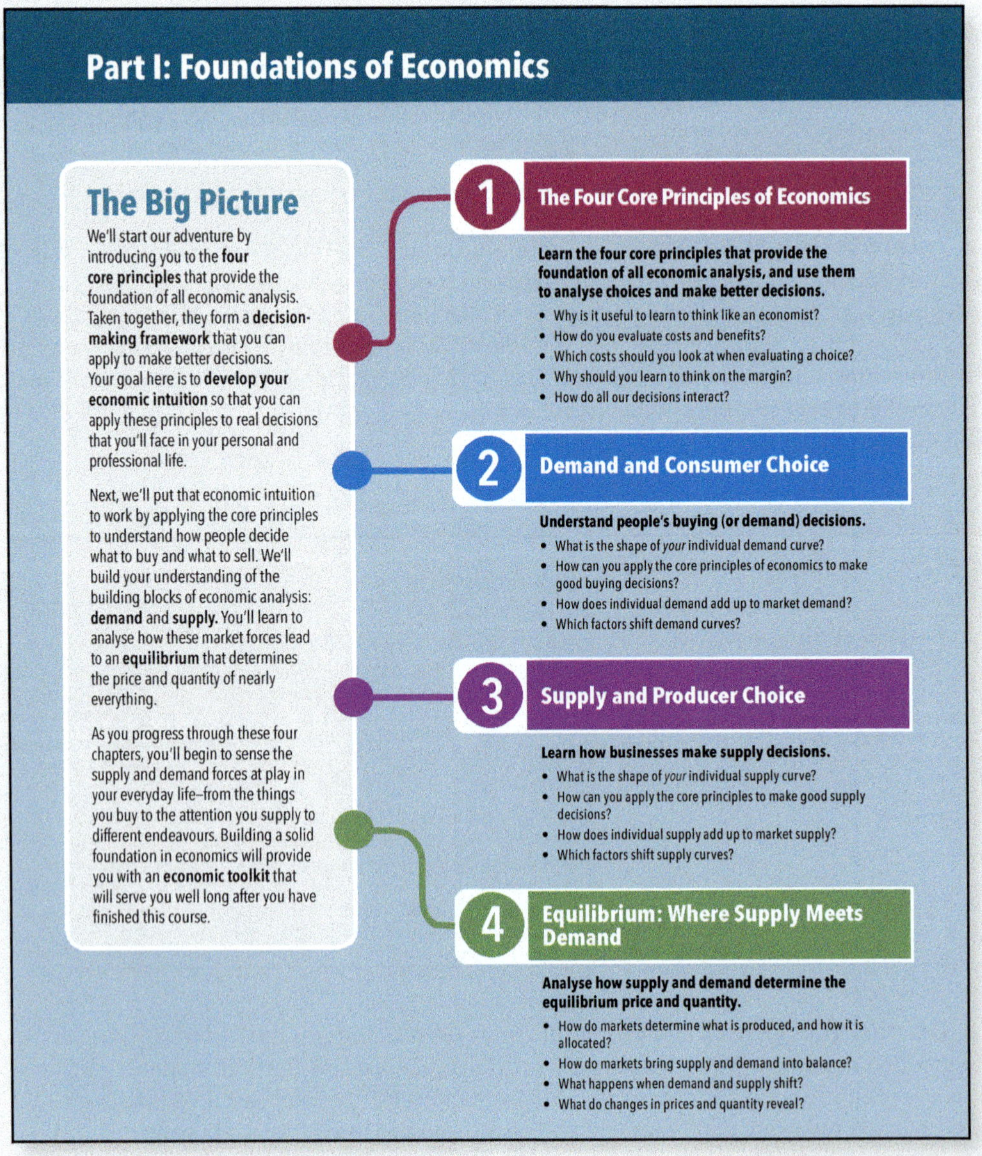

Part I: Foundations of Economics

The Big Picture

We'll start our adventure by introducing you to the **four core principles** that provide the foundation of all economic analysis. Taken together, they form a **decision-making framework** that you can apply to make better decisions. Your goal here is to **develop your economic intuition** so that you can apply these principles to real decisions that you'll face in your personal and professional life.

Next, we'll put that economic intuition to work by applying the core principles to understand how people decide what to buy and what to sell. We'll build your understanding of the building blocks of economic analysis: **demand** and **supply.** You'll learn to analyse how these market forces lead to an **equilibrium** that determines the price and quantity of nearly everything.

As you progress through these four chapters, you'll begin to sense the supply and demand forces at play in your everyday life–from the things you buy to the attention you supply to different endeavours. Building a solid foundation in economics will provide you with an **economic toolkit** that will serve you well long after you have finished this course.

1 The Four Core Principles of Economics

Learn the four core principles that provide the foundation of all economic analysis, and use them to analyse choices and make better decisions.

- Why is it useful to learn to think like an economist?
- How do you evaluate costs and benefits?
- Which costs should you look at when evaluating a choice?
- Why should you learn to think on the margin?
- How do all our decisions interact?

2 Demand and Consumer Choice

Understand people's buying (or demand) decisions.

- What is the shape of *your* individual demand curve?
- How can you apply the core principles of economics to make good buying decisions?
- How does individual demand add up to market demand?
- Which factors shift demand curves?

3 Supply and Producer Choice

Learn how businesses make supply decisions.

- What is the shape of *your* individual supply curve?
- How can you apply the core principles to make good supply decisions?
- How does individual supply add up to market supply?
- Which factors shift supply curves?

4 Equilibrium: Where Supply Meets Demand

Analyse how supply and demand determine the equilibrium price and quantity.

- How do markets determine what is produced, and how it is allocated?
- How do markets bring supply and demand into balance?
- What happens when demand and supply shift?
- What do changes in prices and quantity reveal?

◀ **The road ahead** Each chapter opens with a list of defined learning objectives and a short story that piques student curiosity.

CHAPTER 3

Supply and Producer Choice

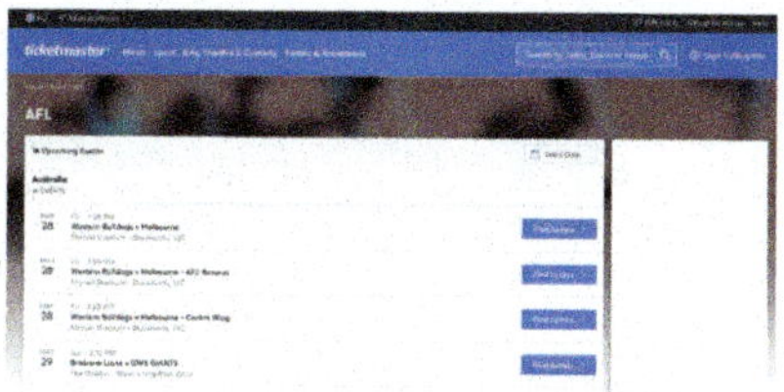

How much would you sell your seat for?

Just as your day is filled with decisions about what to buy, you also have to decide what to sell. After all, everything that is bought is also sold. While you might not think of yourself as a seller if you aren't (yet!) managing a business, you are already managing one very important small business: Your Own Undertaking (or Y.O.U., for short). YOU are already making very important supply decisions. You may have sold concert tickets on StubHub; perhaps you have also sold furniture or a big ticket item, like an old car. You may hold a part-time job, where you sell your labour in return for an hourly wage.

You also supply things in transactions that don't involve money. Your household is like a small business, and you might produce cooking and cleaning services in return for similar services from your family or housemates. You probably supply child care, transport, and advice to those you love. You also supply camaraderie to your friends, an audience to online advertisers, and your attention to this important chapter on supply.

In this chapter, we'll dig into *supply*—the decisions that we make as sellers. The structure of this chapter largely parallels our analysis of demand. We'll start with individual decisions and apply the core principles of economics to help guide you to make good supply decisions. Next, we'll pan back and assess total market supply, which is the sum of these individual decisions. We'll then explore how changing market conditions shift supply.

There's a lot to cover with supply—the global economy consists of millions of businesses producing and selling a dazzling array of goods. But the same logic underpins every business decision. Let's start by putting ourselves into the shoes of a manager, trying to decide how much to produce and sell.

Chapter Objective

To understand how businesses make selling or supply decisions.

3.1 Individual Supply: What You Sell, at Each Price
Discover the shape of your business's individual supply curve.

3.2 Your Decisions and Your Individual Supply Curve
Apply the core principles to make good supply decisions.

3.3 Market Supply: What the Market Sells
Add up individual supply to discover market supply.

3.4 What Shifts Supply Curves?
Understand what factors shift supply curves.

3.5 Shifts versus Movements Along Supply Curves
Distinguish between movements along a supply curve and shifts in supply curves.

▼ **Every roadmap needs landmarks** Before students dig into any new topic, we remind them of their learning objective, helping them to focus on the most important takeaways as they read.

3.2 Your Decisions and Your Individual Supply Curve

Learning Objective *Apply the core principles to make good supply decisions.*

▼ **Marginal reminders** Short, simple tools help students to both preview and review topics, providing practical pedagogical support.

Five factors shift the market supply curve:

1. Input prices
2. Productivity and technology
3. Prices of related outputs
4. Expectations
5. The type and number of sellers

. . . and not a change in price.

Don't Just Summarise . . . Synthesise

Effective studying isn't just repetition—it requires students to unpack what they've learned, repackage it with what they already knew, and test themselves on how well they understand it all. We've developed a set of tools to help students not just review and recall, but understand and apply what they've learned.

▶ **Tying It Together** At the end of each chapter, students are invited to think comprehensively about what they have learned. Rather than simply summarising or concluding the chapter, these thoughtfully composed sections show students how to synthesise new information with prior knowledge—a crucial component of understanding and retention.

Tying It Together

I bet you've noticed some similarities between this chapter, which analysed supply and seller's decisions, and the previous chapter, which analysed demand and buyer's decisions. There's a good reason for this—the forces driving supply and demand are very closely related. This is best illustrated by a simple thought experiment involving a brief detour to Mars.

But let's start on Earth. Think about a simple transaction, such as when you pull into my petrol station and buy 30 litres of petrol for $45. (You probably won't be surprised to know that I don't actually own a petrol station, but let's pretend for a moment that I do.) If you're like most economics students, you'll analyse this by noting that you are buying petrol and I am selling petrol. Consequently, we can analyse this transaction by exploring your demand for petrol and my supply of petrol.

Now consider how a Martian—who understands neither money nor petrol—might view the same transaction. They might think that I am trying to buy your cash and you are willing to sell it to me. How will I pay for your cash? Why, with petrol, of course. Viewed this way, I am the buyer who has a demand for your cash, and you are the seller who is willing to supply it to me if I'm willing to pay you enough litres of petrol. While the Martian's perspective seems funny, there's a certain logic to it.

Neither the Martian's nor the Earthling's interpretation is wrong. You are just as much a buyer of petrol as you are a seller of cash. And I am just as much a seller of petrol as a buyer of cash. When you think about it this way, it's no surprise that the same principles that animate our study of demand are also essential to understanding supply.

This similarity makes learning supply and demand a lot easier. In reality, there's only

◀ **Built-in study guide** We've systematically used the headings in this book to embed a simple but effective study tool right into the reading experience. Glancing at the coloured and boldfaced headings before reading the chapter provides a useful preview; rereading them afterward enables students to thoroughly review and check their understanding of each topic.

Producer Surplus

Consumer surplus tells us about the gains from trade that buyers get. But buyers aren't the only ones who benefit from a transaction; sellers also gain something. When you gain economic surplus from *selling* something, economists refer to it as **producer surplus,** because you're earning that surplus in your role as a producer. You gain producer surplus when you sell something at a higher price than the marginal costs you incur.

Producer surplus is the price, less the marginal cost. Let's analyse what happens when you walk into a Levi's store to buy a pair of jeans for $100, but this time, we'll focus on the producer's perspective. For Levi's, the marginal benefit of selling you those jeans is the $100 price you paid for them. And the marginal cost is the $70 worth of extra denim, thread, and labour it took to make that extra pair of jeans. Levi's is thrilled to get $100 in return for $70 worth of denim, thread and labour. It's thrilled because producing and selling those jeans made Levi's $30 better off. This $30 is the producer surplus that Levi's gains from this transaction.

Producer surplus describes the gain a producer gets from selling something at a higher price than is necessary for them to want to supply the item, which is its marginal cost. More generally, the producer surplus a seller gains from a transaction is the price they receive less the marginal cost. And so, you can measure it as:

$$\text{Producer surplus} = \text{Price} - \text{Marginal cost}$$

Producer surplus is the area above the supply curve and below the price. So far, we've figured out the producer surplus from Levi's selling you one pair of jeans. What about the total producer surplus from all the jeans sold by all producers? The producer surplus from any individual transaction is the price less marginal cost. This leads to a simple graphical representation: Total producer surplus in a market is *the area below the price and above the supply curve, out to the quantity sold,* as shown in Figure 2.

To see why, recall from Chapter 3 that the supply curve is also the seller's marginal cost curve. This means that each point on the supply curve reveals a seller's marginal cost. And so for any given sale, a seller gains producer surplus equal to the price, less their marginal cost, and the marginal cost is the height of the supply curve. Add this producer surplus up across all jeans sold, and you'll end up adding the entire area above the supply curve and below the price, out to the quantity sold.

You earn producer surplus on all but your last sale. As a seller, your producer surplus is the difference between the price and your marginal costs. But the

Producer surplus is the price, less the marginal cost.
Producer surplus is the area above the supply curve and below the price.
You earn producer surplus on all but your last sale.

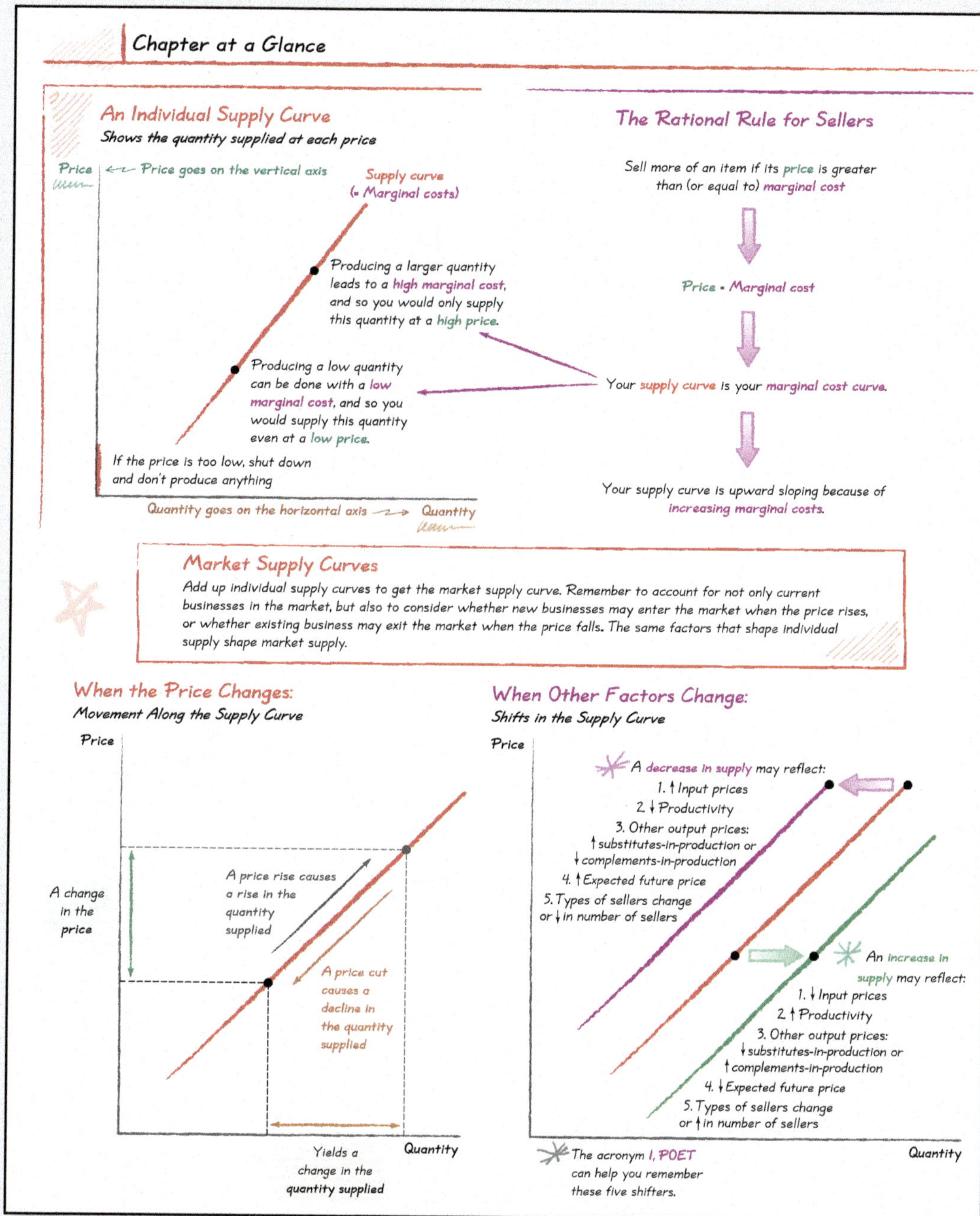

◀ **Chapter at a Glance** These innovative, visual summaries offer a clear overview of the key topics in each chapter, providing useful guidance for study and review.

▶ **Questions for discussion and assessment** Each chapter ends with a full set of discussion questions and problems, aligned to chapter learning objectives.

Discussion and Review Questions

Learning Objective 2.1 *Discover the shape of your individual demand curve.*

1. You just took an Uber from home to campus for the first time and were willing to pay $13 for the trip. It was so much easier than driving yourself that you are willing to pay $21 for the same trip tomorrow. Have you violated the law of demand? Why or why not?

Learning Objective 2.2 *Apply the core principles of economics to make good demand decisions.*

2. Do you use water for things that are beyond what is necessary to sustain life? What if the price of water in your home tripled? How would you respond? Are there activi-

Learning Objective 2.5 *Distinguish between movements along a demand curve and shifts in demand curves.*

6. Find the flaw in reasoning in the following statement: "An increase in the cost of oil will cause the price of a plane ticket to increase. This increase in price will cause a decrease in demand for airline travel and a leftward shift in the demand curve."

Study Problems

Learning Objective 2.1 *Discover the shape of your individual demand curve.*

Practise the Process of Graphing

Compare the usual static presentation of many textbook graphs with the dynamic process that instructors actually use to teach this material, and it becomes clear: An economics graph is not a static object for students to look at and memorise; it's something students need to *work through*. That's why we've reimagined these graphs in a way that emphasises the *process* of graphing.

Figure 3 | **The Consequences of Imports**

If there is no international trade:

No-trade equilibrium occurs where: **Quantity demanded by domestic buyers** equals **quantity supplied by domestic sellers**, resulting in 100 million shirts sold at a price of $20.

When we allow imports:

Step 1 The price of imported goods declines to the **world price**.

Step 2 At this new price, check the **domestic supply curve** to find that the **quantity supplied by domestic sellers declines**, and check the **domestic demand curve** to find the **quantity demanded by domestic buyers rises**.

Step 3 **Imports** make up the difference between domestic demand and domestic supply.

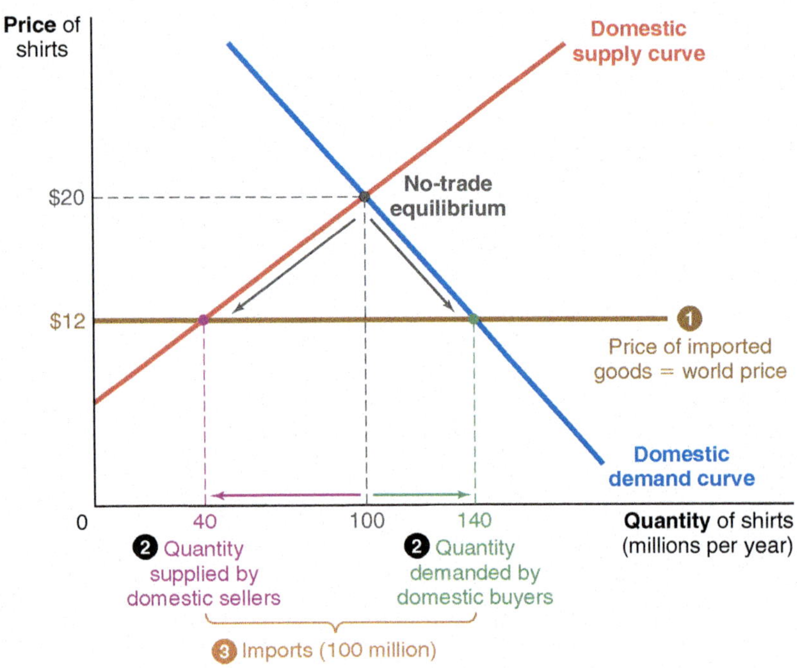

When we allow imports:

Step 1: The price of imports = the world price of $12, *a price cut*.

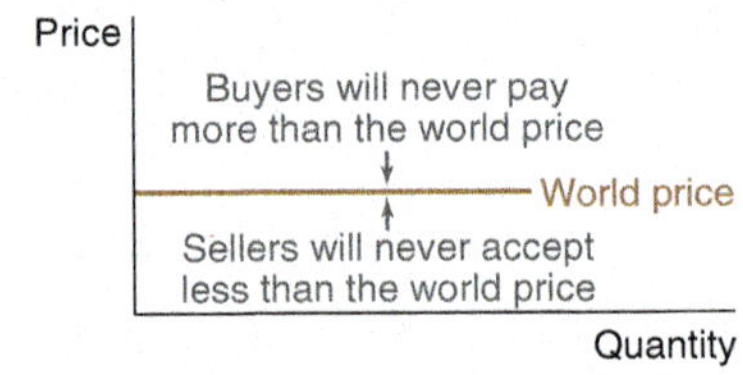

Step 2: At this new price:
a) The quantity supplied by domestic sellers *declines* (to 40 million shirts)
b) The quantity demanded by domestic buyers *rises* (to 140 million shirts)

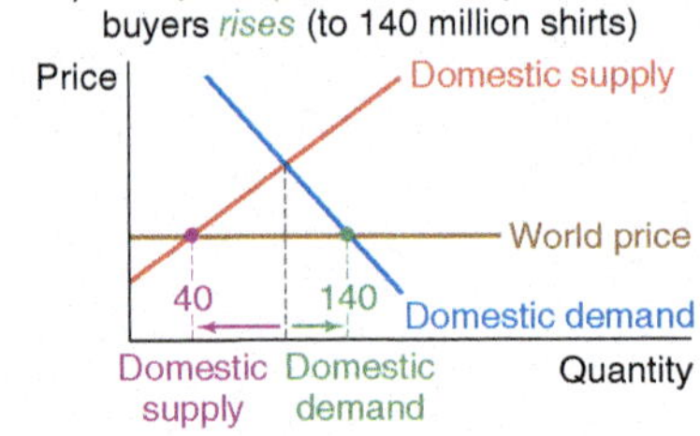

Step 3: The difference is made up by imports (= 140m − 40m = 100 million shirts)

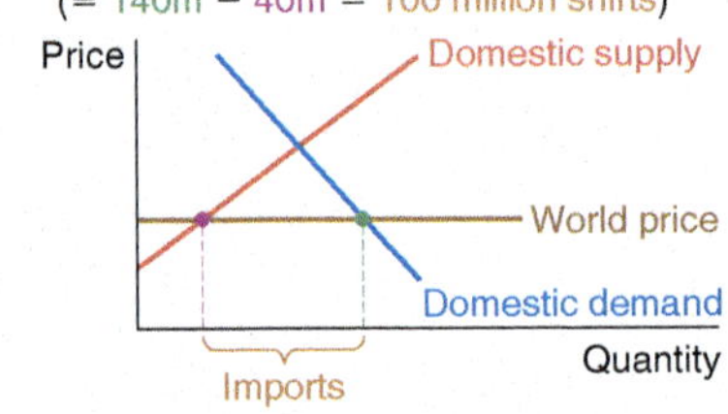

▲ **Step-by-step breakdowns of key graphs** We crack the curves open by breaking economics graphs down into carefully formulated steps.

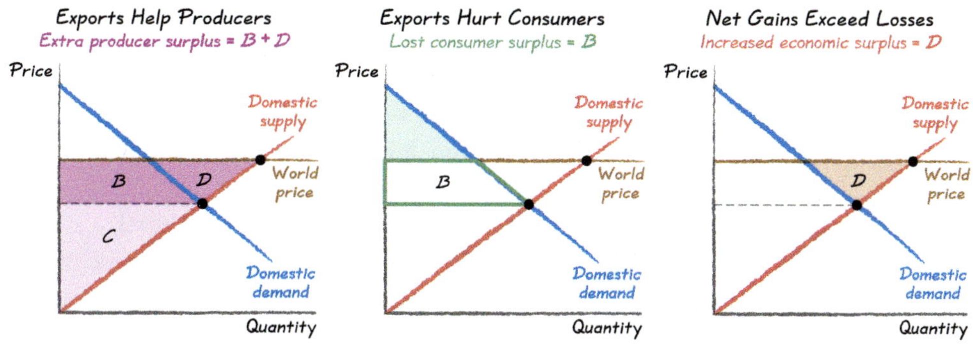

▲ **Casual graphs model good economics habits** We encourage students to embrace the process of graphing—to see themselves doodling in the margins—by sketching thumbnail graphs in the margins, on the backs of envelopes, or wherever they prefer to thoughtfully doodle. These graphs model the process of transforming an idea that's described verbally in the text into its graphical counterpart.

Suppose Australia institutes a ban on trans fats, a cheap but unhealthy ingredient used in fast food. What effect does this have on the market for hot chips?

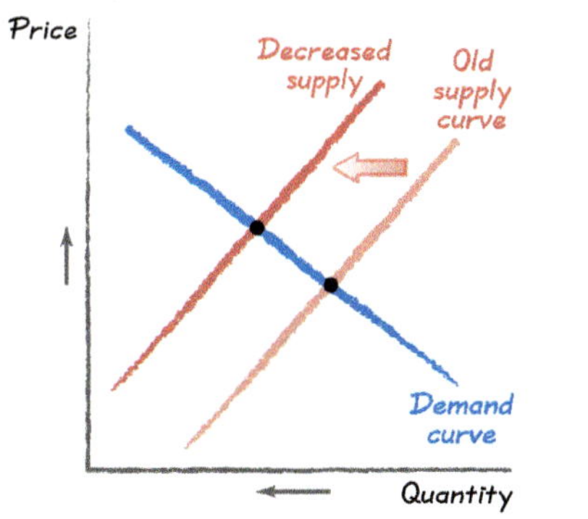

Higher cost of input
→ A decrease in supply

Result: Higher price, lower quantity.

Before a cyclone in tropical North Queensland, people stock up on essential supplies such as food and water. How will this affect the market for groceries?

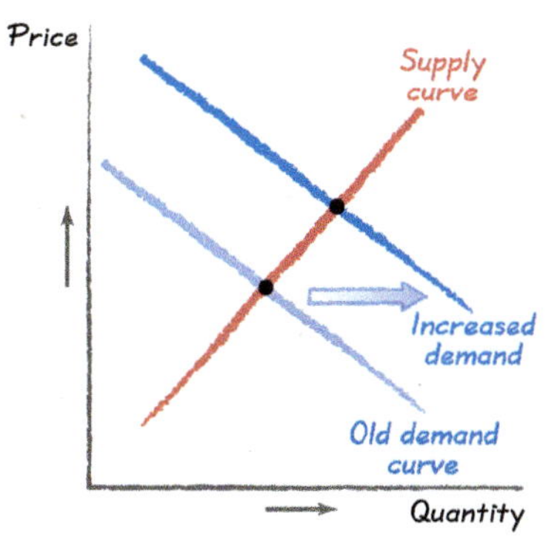

Consumers prefer greater quantities
→ An increase in demand

Result: Higher price, higher quantity.

Coal is burned to produce electricity. What happens in the market for electricity when the price of coal decreases?

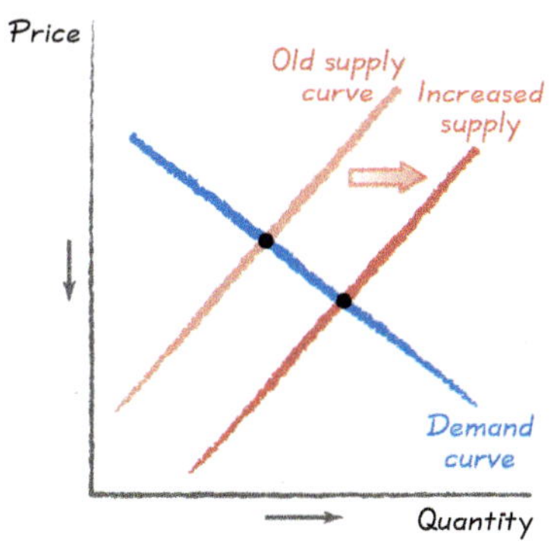

Lower cost of input
→ An increase in supply

Result: Lower price, higher quantity.

▲ **Practise, practise, practise** Through constant repetition, students will come to think graphically whenever they encounter new economic questions.

Acknowledgments

In some sense this book started more than 20 years ago. Richard was a second-year undergraduate at the University of Sydney and Justin was in his honours year. Richard was pretty confident that he knew a lot of economics. Then he met Justin. He's been on a journey to catch up ever since. He still hopes to some day.

Justin and Betsey finished their PhDs at Harvard in 2001 and Richard started in 2002. They were taught how to be professional economists by many of the same people: Greg Mankiw, Larry Katz, Claudia Goldin, Oliver Hart, Philippe Aghion, Jeremy Stein, Andrei Shleifer, Ed Glaeser, Elhanan Helpman, Drew Fudenberg, Jerry Green, and numerous others.

We all think about economics the same way, even though our research covers some different areas. We've all seen how thinking like an economist can help us make better decisions in our own lives—personal and professional. And we all have a passion for communicating ideas to our students and in the media.

Richard is mainly Australian and a bit American (he lived there for 10 years). Betsey is mainly American and a bit Australian. And Justin is still making up his mind (but has the most Australian accent of the three of us).

Our textbook family has a nontraditional form, and at various points, Chuck Linsmeier, Shani Fisher, and Carolyn Merrill have sat at the head of the table. We're grateful for your wise counsel, big-picture leadership, and the inspiring values you provided. Lukia Kliossis has been an extraordinary development editor who has shepherded us through this adaptation from the start to the finish line, and she made sure that every page sparkles. Joshua Hill is that rare talent who is both an economist and expert of pedagogy, and in his wizard-like ways has conjured up much of the ecosystem within which the book lies. We are also grateful to our marketing team, led by Scott Guile, Clay Bolton, and Stephanie Ellis—and their Australian counterparts, Katie Thorn, Chelsea Clugtson, Alex Chamoun, and Fiona McNeill, who were world-class advocates for our text so it can support instructors and students in Australian undergraduate courses. We're fortunate to have had such a talented production and design team for our book, and owe a debt of gratitude to Catherine Woods, Tracey Kuehn, Lisa Kinne, Robin Fadool, Jennifer Wetzel, Lawrence Guerra, Jason Perkins, Andrew Vaccaro, Diana Blume, Natasha Wolfe, Matt McAdams, Janice Donnola, Ron Weikart, John Callahan, Dirk Kaufman, and Kevin Kall. The entire mind-boggling process of production was expertly coordinated by Kerry O'Shaughnessy. And a very special thanks to our copyeditor, Judith Bamber, and proofreader, Angela Dennis. Your amazing attention to detail—and extra sets of Australian eyes—did not go unnoticed.

An extraordinary group of colleagues and friends read chapters in detail and generously offered their expertise on subject matter and pedagogy: Jeff Borland, Chris Edmond, Bruce Preston, Isobel Dixon-Holden, Scott French, Leonora Risse, Aarti Singh, Marian Vidal-Fernandez, Jordi Vidal-Robert, and Andrew Wait. DJ Thornton provided exceptional research assistance, great advice, and invaluable perspective.

In addition to our textbook family, we also have domestic families. Balancing it all is a juggling act that we couldn't have pulled off without the love, support and understanding of Patricia Gruber, Sean Manuel, Cherith Harkness, Jill Benevides, Ellen Goodman, Helen and Gordon Stevenson, and Rosalind Dixon. The love and joy that Matilda and Oliver (Justin and Betsey) and Isobel and Hartley (Richard) provide fuel us every day. We hope that their patience in listening to us discuss economics at dinner means that they're learning to use economics to make good decisions in their own lives. Finally, Richard wouldn't have become an economist without two people who are no longer with us, but will always be with him: Stephen Salsbury and Alberto Alesina. Hugs.

We express our deep appreciation to the many reviewers who provided invaluable feedback as we developed this project.

Sindy Abadie, *Southwest Tennessee Community College*

Dorian Abreu, *Hunter College*

Haydory Akbar Ahmed, *Missouri State University*

Seemi Ahmad, *Dutchess Community College*

Jason Aimone, *Baylor University*

Basil Al-Hashimi, *Mesa Community College, Red Mountain Campus*

Samuel Allen, *Virginia Military Institute*

Shahina Amin, *The University of Northern Iowa*

Lian An, *University of North Florida*

Giuliana Campanelli Andreopoulos, *William Paterson University*

Elena Antoniadou, *Emory University*

Anna Antus, *North Hennepin Community College*

Hannah Apps, *Kalamazoo College*

Ramses Armendariz, *Indiana University, Kelley School of Business*

Luke Armstrong, *Lee College*

Becca Arnold, *San Diego Mesa College*

Sonia Asare, *Capital Community*

Daniel Asfaw, *Indiana University* and *Purdue University Indianapolis*

Ioanna Avgeri, *ONCAMPUS Amsterdam*

Collins Ayoo, *Carleton University*

Sahar Bahmani, *University of Wisconsin at Parkside*

Diana Bajrami, *College of Alameda*

Gyanendra Baral, *Oklahoma City Community College*

Leah Barnhard, *Wichita State University*

James E. Bathgate, *Western Nevada College*

Hamid Bastin, *Shippensburg University*

Clare Battista, *California Polytechnic State University–San Luis Obispo*

Leon Battista, *University of Bridgeport*

Klaus G. Becker, *Texas Tech University*

Christina Beers, *Ohio University*

Susan M. Bell, *Seminole State College of Florida*

Audrey Benavidez, *Del Mar College*

Cynthia Benelli, *Santa Barbara City College*

Janine Bergeron, *Southern New Hampshire University*

Prasun Bhattacharjee, *East Tennessee State University*

Amrita Bhattacharya, *Southern Illinois University, Carbondale*

David Black, *University of Toledo*

Lane Boyte-Eckis, *Troy University*

Elizabeth Breitbach, *University of South Carolina*

Joseph Brignone, *Brigham Young University*

Stacey Brook, *University of Iowa*

Bruce Brown, *Cal Poly Pomona*

Dave Brown, *Penn State University*

Joseph Bucci, *Chestnut Hill College*

Bill Burrows, *Lane Community College*

Randall Campbell, *Mississippi State University*

James Carden, *University of Mississippi*

Valbona Cela, *Tri-County Technical College*

Stephanie Cellini, *George Washington University*

Rik Chakraborti, *University of Wyoming*

Jieun Chang, *Southwestern Oklahoma State University*

David Chaplin, *Northwest Nazarene University*

June Charles, *North Lake College*

Anoshua Chaudhuri, *San Francisco State University*

Nan-Ting Chou, *University of Louisville*

Shih-Hsien Chuang, *Northwest Missouri State University*

Dmitry Chulkov, *Indiana University Kokomo*

Marcelo Clerici-Arias, *Stanford University*

Kevin Cochrane, *Colorado Mesa University*

Bradley Collins, *Blue Ridge Community College*

Gregory Colson, *University of Georgia*

Larry Cook, *University of Toledo*

Jeremy Cook, *Wheaton College*

Patrick Crowley, *Texas A&M University, Corpus Christi*

Berg Cui, *Indiana University*

John Cullis, *Iowa State University*

Mark Cullivan, *San Diego State University*

Scott Cunningham, *Baylor University*

Chifeng Dai, *Southern Illinois University*

Sonia Dalmia, *Grand Valley State University*

Manabendra Dasgupta, *University of Alabama at Birmingham*

Andrew Davis, *Acadia University*

Stephen Davis, *Southwest Minnesota State University*

Dale R. DeBoer, *University of Colorado, Colorado Springs*

Juan DelaCruz, *Lehman College*

Cornelia Denvir, *Ulster County Community College*

Satis Devkota, *University of Minnesota, Morris*

Paramita Dhar, *Central Connecticut State University*

Liang Ding, *Macalester College*

Veronika Dolar, *Suny College at Old Westbury*

David Dupuis, *Université de Sherbrooke*

Eva Dziadula, *University of Notre Dame*

Finley Edwards, *Baylor University*

Renee Edwards, *Houston Community College*

Sherine El Hag, *California State University, Dominguez Hills*

Harold W. Elder, *University of Alabama*

Scott Elliott, *Hocking College*

Harry Ellis, Jr., *University of North Texas*

Tisha L.N. Emerson, *Baylor University*

Michael Enz, *Roanoke College*

Jonathan Ernest, *Clemson University*

Mark Evers, *Southern Utah University* and *University of Denver*

Terry Eyland, *Bishop's University*

Elena Falcettoni, *University of Minnesota*

Mohammadmahdi Farsiabi, *Wayne State University*

Irene R. Foster, *The George Washington University*

Jennifer Fowler, *Belmont University*

David Franck, *Francis Marion University*

Tracey Freiberg, *St. John's University*

Scott French, *University of New South Wales*

Matthew Friedman, *University of Wisconsin, Madison*

Florencia Gabriele, *Emmanuel College*

Mary N. Gade, *Oklahoma State University*

Cynthia L. Gamez, *El Paso Community College*

Guanlin Gao, *Chaminade University of Honolulu*

Phillip Garner, *Dixie State University*

Karl Geisler, *Idaho State University*

Pedro Gete, *Georgetown University*

Linda Ghent, *Eastern Illinois University*

Shankar Ghimire, *Western Illinois University*

Alex Gialanella, *New England College*

Otis Gilley, *Louisiana Tech University*

Rob Girtz, *Black Hills State University*

Gregory Givens, *University of Alabama*

Christian G. Glupker, *Grand Valley State University*

Malcolm Gold, *Avila University*

Terri Gonzales-Kreisman, *Delgado Community College*

Richard Gosselin, *Houston Community College*

David Gray, *University of Ottawa*

Natalia Gray, *Southeast Missouri State University*

Joanne Guo, *University of Bridgeport*

Jason Gurtovoy, *Embry-Riddle Aeronautical University*

David Harris, *Benedictine College*

Darcy Hartman, *The Ohio State University*

William Hawkins, *Yale University*

Megharanji Hazra, *Towson University*

Jessica Hennessey, *Furman University*

Ryan Herzog, *Gonzaga University*

Joshua Hess, *University of South Carolina*

Wayne R. Hickenbottom, *University of Texas at Austin*

Paul M. Holmes, *Ashland University*

Jim Hornsten, *Northwestern University*

Indrit Hoxha, *Penn State University, Harrisburg*

Yu Hsing, *Southeastern Louisiana University*

Kuang-Chung Hsu, *University of Central Oklahoma*

Brian Hurst, *San Jose State University*

Taurean Hutchinson, *Susquehanna University*

Jennifer Imazeki, *San Diego State University*

Nuria Quella Isla, *Stony Brook University*

Miren Ivankovic, *Anderson University* and *Clemson University*

Jesse Jacobs, *Fort Hays State University*

Michael Jones, *University of Cincinnati*

George Jones, *University of Wisconsin Rock County*

Troy Joseph, *Carleton University*

George A. Jouganatos, *California State University, Sacramento*

Steve Kaifa, *County College of Morris*

Serkan Kalman, *The College of New Jersey*

Lillian Kamal, *University of Hartford*

Alice Louise Kassens, *Roanoke College*

Nargess Kayhani, *Mount Saint Vincent University*

Hossein S. Kazemi, *Stonehill College*

Sukanya Kemp, *University of Akron*

Zafar Dad Khan, *University of Virginia's College at Wise*

Frank W. Kim, *Point Loma Nazarene University*

Hyeongwoo Kim, *Auburn University*

Jongsung Kim, *Bryant University*

Janice Rye Kinghorn, *Miami University*

Richard Kirk, *Georgia State University Perimeter College*

Audrey Kline, *University of Louisville*

Colin Knapp, *Penn State University*

Mikhail Kouliavtsev, *Stephen F. Austin State University*

Catherine S. Krause, *University of New Mexico*

Santosh Kumar, *Sam Houston State University*

Dan LaFave, *Colby College*

Ghislaine Lang, *San Jose State University*

Susan Laury, *Georgia State University*

Daniel Lawson, *Oakland Community College*

Nhan Le, *Alma College*

Tuan Viet Le, *West Virginia Wesleyan College*

Jim Lee, *Texas A&M University, Corpus Christi*

Michael Leonard, *Kwantlen Polytechnic University*

Hank Lewis, *Lone Star College, University Park*

Willis Lewis, *Winthrop University*

Zhen Li, *Albion College*

Carlos Liard, *Central Connecticut State University*

Sung Soo Lim, *Calvin College*

Bo Liu, *Southern New Hampshire University*

Haiyong Liu, *East Carolina University*

Ira T. Lovitch, *Mount Saint Mary's University, Los Angeles*

Heather Luea, *Vanderbilt University*

Rotua Lumbantobing, *Western Connecticut State University*

Gennady Lyakir, *Fashion Institute of Technology*

Rita Madarassy, *Santa Clara University*

Mark Maier, *Glendale Community College*

Svitlana Maksymenko, *University of Pittsburgh*

C. Lucy Malakar, *Lorain County Community College*

Khawaja Mamun, *Sacred Heart University*

Abir Mandal, *University of Kansas*

Emily Marshall, *Dickinson College*

Ladan Masoudie, *University of Southern California*

Robert McComb, *Texas Tech University*

Clinton McCully, *Northern Virginia Community College*

Eric McDermott, *University of Illinois, Urbana-Champaign*

Steven McMullen, *Hope College*

Lois McWhorter, *University of the Cumberlands*

Shah Mehrabi, *Montgomery College*

Saul Mekies, *Kirkwood Community College* and *University of Iowa*

Diego Mendez-Carbajo, *Illinois Wesleyan University*

Lewis Metcalf, *Parkland College*

Charles Meyrick, *Housatonic Community College*

Meghan Hennessy Mihal, *St. Thomas Aquinas College*

Jeanette Milius, *Iowa Western Community College*

Edward Millner, *Virginia Commonwealth University*

Phillip Mixon, *Troy University*

Lavinia Moldovan, *Mount Royal University*

Mark Monsky, *Wake Technical Community College*

Sucharita Mukherjee, *College of Saint Benedict*

Yolunda Nabors, *Tennessee Technological University*

Ronald C. Necoechea, *Roberts Wesleyan College*

Lindsey Nagy, *Muhlenberg College*

ABM Nasir, *North Carolina Central University*

Augustine C. Nelson, *University of Miami*

Nicolas Nervo, *Tarrant County College*

Charles Newton, *Houston Community College*

Mihai Nica, *University of Central Oklahoma*

Alexandra Nica, *University of Iowa*

Jelena Nikolic, *Northeastern University*

Dmitri Nizovtsev, *Washburn University*

Lindsay Noble Calkins, *John Carroll University*

Claudette Nyang'oro, *Miami Dade College*

Scott Ogawa, *Northwestern University*

Gokcen G. Ogruk-Maz, *Texas Wesleyan University*

David J. O'Hara, *Metropolitan State University*

Nur M. Onvural, *Pfeiffer University*

Wafa Hakim Orman, *University of Alabama in Huntsville*

Jinhwan Oh, *Ewha Womans University*

Sheyi Oladipo, *SUNY College at Old Westbury*

Grace Onodipe, *Georgia Gwinnett College*

Catherine R. Pakaluk, *The Catholic University of America*

Debashis Pal, *University of Cincinnati*

Maria Papapavlou, *San Jacinto College*

Darshak Patel, *University of Kentucky*

Lourenco Paz, *Baylor University*

Nicholas D. Peppes, *St. Louis Community College*

Timothy Perri, *Appalachian State University*

Matthew Pham, *The Ohio State University*

Julien Picault, *UBC Okanagan*

Brennan Platt, *Brigham Young University*

Sanela Porca, *University of South Carolina Aiken*

Ashley Provencher, *Siena College*

Sarah Quintanar, *University of Arkansas at Little Rock*

Reza M. Ramazani, *Saint Michael's College*

Surekha K.B. Rao, *Indiana University Northwest*

Christian Raschke, *Sam Houston State University*

Jack Reardon, *University of Wisconsin, Eau Claire*

Tracy L. Regan, *Boston College*

Agne Reizgeviciute, *California State University, Chico*

Sam Richardson, *Boston College*

Leonora Risse, *Royal Melbourne Institute of Technology*

Christopher Roark, *University of Chicago*

Amanda Ross, *University of Alabama*

Wes Routon, *Georgia Gwinnett College*

Moumita Roy, *Bloomsburg University*

Jeffrey Rubin, *Rutgers University*

Stefan Ruediger, *Arizona State University*

Melissa M. Rueterbusch, *Mott Community College*

Malkiat Sandhu, *University of California, Silicon Valley Extension*

Chandini Sankaran, *Boston College*

Naveen Sarna, *Northern Virginia Community College*

George Sarraf, *University of California Irvine*

Edward Sayre, *University of Southern Mississippi*

Edward Scahill, *University of Scranton*

Mark Scanlan, *Stephen F. Austin State University*

Helen Schneider, *University of Texas at Austin*

Heather A. Schumacker, *Salt Lake Community College*

Armine Shahoyan, *Tulane University*

Alexandra Shiu Nicolay, *McLennan Community College*

Jonathan Silberman, *Oakland University*

Joe Silverman, *San Diego State University*

Aarti Singh, *University of Sydney*

Harmeet Singh, *Texas A&M University, Kingsville*

Catherine Skura, *Sandhills Community College*

Anastasia Smith, *Pfeiffer University*

Deanna Smith, *Missouri State University, West Plains*

Joseph Sobieralski, *Southwestern Illinois College*

Katherine Sobota, *Bowling Green State University*

Mario Solis-Garcia, *Macalester College*

Robert Sonora, *Fort Lewis College*

Carolyne Soper, *Central Connecticut State University*

Nicole Soto, *Southern New Hampshire University*

Forrest Spence, *University of Notre Dame*

Richard Stahnke, *University of Maryland*

Kalina Staub, *University of North Carolina, Chapel Hill*

Josh Staveley-O'Carroll, *Babson College*

Andrew Stephenson, *Georgia Gwinnett College*

Jeffrey Stewart, *University of Dayton*

Edward Strafaci, *Wagner College*

Jacqueline Strenio, *Southern Oregon University*

Carolyn Fabian Stumph, *Purdue University Fort Wayne*

Peter Summers, *High Point University*

Meiping (Aggie) Sun, *Fordham University*

Timothy Sweeney, *Metropolitan Community College, Omaha*

Andre Switala, *Boston University*

Philip Szmedra, *Georgia Southwestern State University*

Vera Tabakova, *East Carolina University*

Raul Tadle, *California State University, Sacramento*

Ariuntungalag Taivan, *University of Minnesota Duluth*

Shelley Tapp, *Wayland Baptist University*

Michael Tasto, *Southern New Hampshire University*

Mark L. Tendall, *Stanford University*

Vitaly Terekhov, *Marianopolis College*

William Thralls, *Johnson & Wales University, North Miami*

Angela K. Thurman, *Tarrant County College*

James Tierney, *Penn State University*

Edward J. Timmons, *Saint Francis University*

Susanne Toney, *Savannah State University*

Richard Tontz, *California State University, Northridge*

Jill A. Trask, *Tarrant County College, Southeast Campus*

Yulya Truskinovsky, *Wayne State University*

Phillip Tussing, *Houston Community College*

Tate Twinam, *University of Washington, Bothell*

Nathaniel Udall, *Wharton County Junior College*

Veronica Udeogalanya, *Medgar Evers College*

Don Joseph Paredes Uy-Barreta, *Hult International Business School*

Vicar S. Valencia, *Indiana University South Bend*

Ross S vanWassenhove, *University of Houston*

Sam Vegter, *Western Piedmont Community College*

Angelino Viceisza, *Spelman College*

Marian Vidal-Fernandez, *University of Sydney*

Jordi Vidal-Robert, *University of Sydney*

Norma Vite-Leon, *Marianopolis College*

Rubina Vohra, *New Jersey City University*

Lucia Vojtassak, *University of Calgary*

Annie Voy, *Gonzaga University*

Cheryl Wachenheim, *North Dakota State University*

William A. Walsh, *University of Alabama*

Qingbin Wang, *Johnson & Wales University*

Yaqin Wang, *Youngstown State University*

Yongqing Wang, *University of Wisconsin–Milwaukee at Waukesha*

Kaycee Chandler Washington, *Collin College*

Andrew Wait, *University of Sydney*

Wendy Wasnich, *Ashland University*

Kristine West, *St. Catherine University*

Elizabeth M. Wheaton, *Southern Methodist University*

Katie Wick, *Abilene Christian University*

A. Williams, *Gateway Community College*

Amanda L. Wilsker, *Georgia Gwinnett College*

Allison Witman, *University of North Carolina Wilmington*

Jim R. Wollscheid, *University of Arkansas, Fort Smith*

Kelvin Wong, *Arizona State University*

Jadrian Wooten, *Penn State University*

Sonia Worrell Asare, *Capital Community College*

Deborah Amelia Wright, *Southeastern Community College*

Sheng Xiao, *Westminster College*

Travis Yates, *Penn State University*

Janice Yee, *Worcester State University*

James Yoo, *California Baptist University*

Anthony Zambelli, *Cuyamaca College*

George Zestos, *Christopher Newport University*

Fang Zhang, *California State University, Fullerton*

Oleksandr (Alex) Zhylyevskyy, *Iowa State University*

Organisation of This Book

Learn the four principles of economics that create a decision-making framework to help you better understand demand, supply, and equilibrium and build a solid foundation for economic analysis.

Use supply and demand analysis to measure market responsiveness, examine the effects of government intervention, evaluate welfare, and understand the gains from trade.

Apply the economic lens to explore the consequences of global trade, examine market failures that arise from externalities, analyse the labour market, and assess inequality and poverty.

Move beyond perfect competition and learn how managers make strategic decisions in imperfectly competitive markets.

Learn about the role of risk and information and develop strategies for decision making when information is limited.

Contents

A Quick Review of Graphs

You'll see a lot of graphs in the pages ahead—don't let it scare you. You encounter graphs every time you scroll through your news feed: charts for election results, opinion polls, sales figures, health outcomes, and just about anything else. Apps on your phone might supply you with graphs to show how many steps you took last week, how much you spent over the past month on different types of goods, or how many books you read last year. When you were applying to university, you probably consulted graphs that showed the range of entrance exam scores for first-year students at universities you were eyeing to see how you measured up.

We live in a time when data is cheap and plentiful, and so many aspects of our lives are quantified. Graphs make sifting through all of it a lot easier. Economics can make you a more effective user of all of that data. To start, here's a quick refresher to walk you through some familiar graphs, with useful tips on how to read them. Along the way, we'll remind you of some of the basic tools and language you'll use to work through them.

Graphs That Break Down Numbers

Figure 1 | **Breaking Down Average Household Spending**

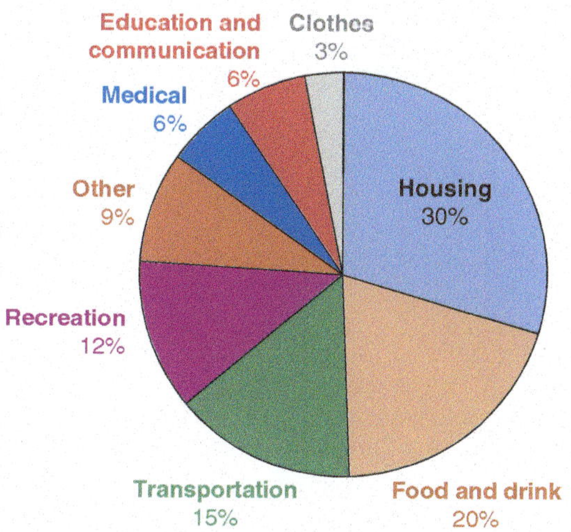

Data from: Australian Bureau of Statistics.

◀ Pie Charts When you want to break down a total into its component slices, **pie charts** can provide an easy way to show each of the parts that comprise the whole.

Figure 2 | **The Australian Income Distribution**

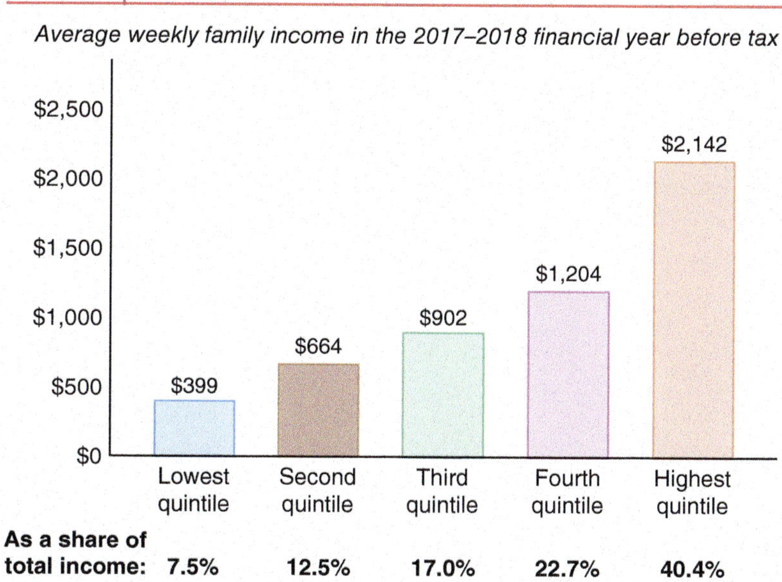

Data from: Australian Bureau of Statistics.

◀ Analysing Distributions When you want to see how an economic statistic—say, income—is distributed across the population, it can be helpful to divide the data up into smaller, equal-sized segments. In economics you'll come across lots of data that has been broken down into fifths, segments that we call **quintiles.** This breakdown reveals the dispersion in outcomes across the population—a fact often obscured by measures like the median or mean. Bar charts like this one use quintiles to show that the poorest fifth of the population get by with an average weekly income of less than $400, while the richest fifth enjoys an average weekly income of over $2,000.

Graphs That Show Comparisons

Most of the graphs you encounter are designed to *visualise* numbers, give them scale, and provide opportunities to make *comparisons.*

Figure 3 | Highly Educated People Earn More Money

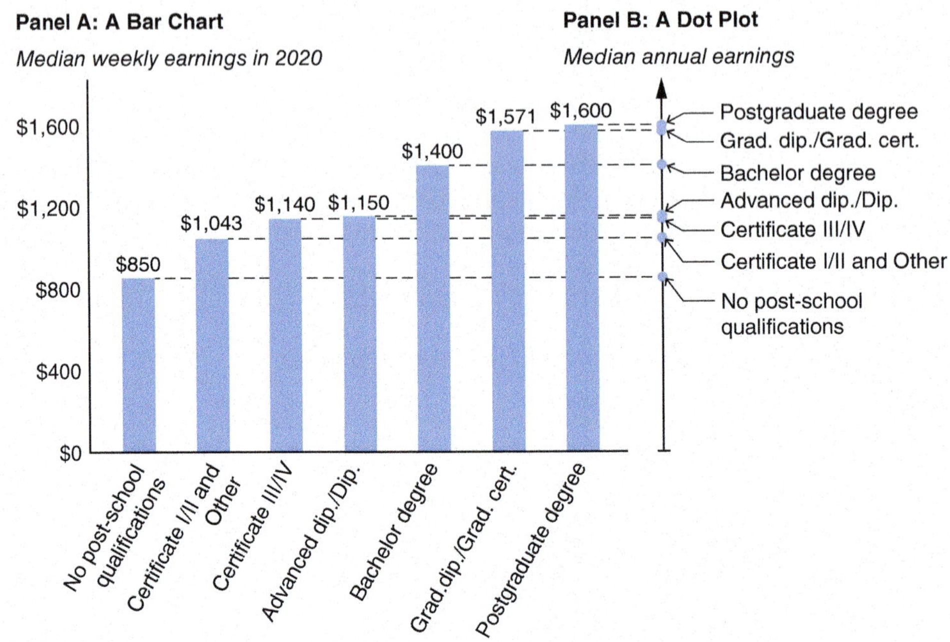

Data from: Australian Bureau of Statistics.

▲ **Bar Chart and Dot Plot** Sometimes you'll want to compare data for different categories. One of the most common ways to visualise and compare data across different categories is with a bar chart. For example, a **bar chart** can show you, for particular levels of education, the median earnings of the person with that amount of education. Each bar in Panel A represents a category of education—like an Advanced Diploma or Diploma—and the height of the bar shows the median earnings of a person with that level of education. It's easy to see that people with more education generally have higher earnings.

An even simpler way to represent data across categories is with a **dot plot,** as shown in Panel B. A dot plot shows different values for different groups, plotting the data along a single axis to show how different variables rank along a particular scale. Instead of the height of the bars showing you the median earnings of each education category, there is a dot on the dot plot. Both bar charts and data plots can be used to show the same information, so which way do you prefer to see the data?

▼ Time-Series Graphs Often, you'll want to look at how a certain indicator or data point changes over time. Plot time on the horizontal axis and your data (in this case, the share of GDP to workers) along the vertical axis, and voila:

A boring spreadsheet of numbers like this:

	A	B
1	Year	Share of GDP to workers
2	Sep-1960	49.77%
3	Dec-1960	49.96%
4	Mar-1961	50.92%
5	Jun-1961	50.86%
6	Sep-1961	51.22%
7	Dec-1961	51.70%
8	Mar-1962	51.54%
9	Jun-1962	52.48%
10	Sep-1962	52.89%

. . . becomes a clear **time-series graph.** The years become the horizontal axis, now for column B, plot the data along the vertical axis for each year and connect the dots. You now have a pretty graph that makes it much easier to take in the big finding—the share of GDP to workers has declined over recent decades.

Figure 4 | **Labour's Share of GDP Has Declined Over Recent Decades**

Data from: Australian Bureau of Statistics.

Graphs That Show Relationships

In economics, we are concerned not just with numbers describing different outcomes, but with *relationships* between different outcomes. The **coordinate system** enables you to display two sets of data on a single graph. This simple setup forms the skeleton of many of the graphs you will encounter in economics; it's also one that you're probably familiar with from high school maths class. You can plot one measure on the horizontal axis, and a second measure on the vertical, so each data point shows a pair of outcomes for an individual person, state, or country.

Figure 5 | **People in High-Income Countries Are More Satisfied with Their Lives**

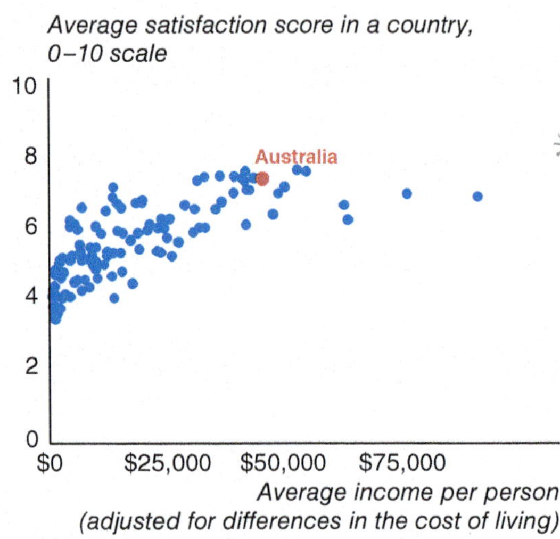

* *Remember: Scatterplots show all the underlying data and so reveal the shape of the relationship between two variables.*

▲ Scatterplot You can plot individual data points on a coordinate graph to create a **scatterplot.** This simple graph helps you to see the range of responses and observe whether any patterns emerge. For example, we can plot the average happiness of people in a country and each country's average income. Americans rated their level of life satisfaction on average to be about 7 on a scale of 1–10; and their average annual income is about $56,000 per person. The black dot below represents those two numbers—it shows the average level of happiness *and* income for people in Australia. The other dots represent other countries' averages. Looking at all the dots, you can see that richer countries are generally happier countries. There's a relationship there.

Figure 6 | **Lukia's Demand for Avocados Depends on the Price**

How many avocados does Lukia buy each week?

Price of avocados	Quantity of avocados
$0.50	5
$1.00	4
$1.50	3
$2.00	2
$2.50	1

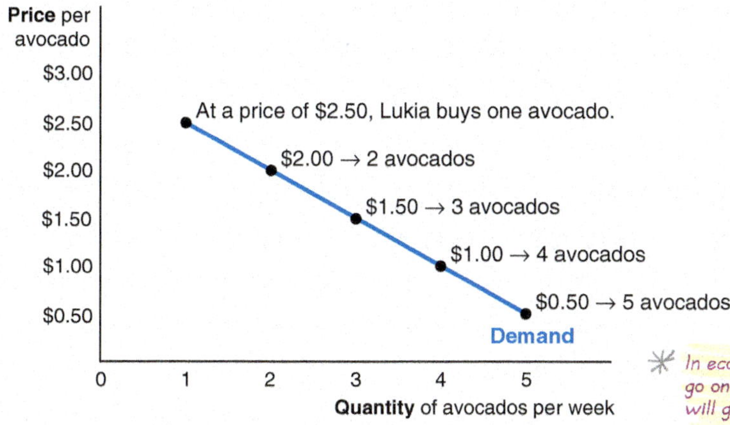

In economics, price will always go on the vertical axis; quantity will go on the horizontal.

▲ **The stylised graphs of economics** One thing you'll graph a lot in economics is the relationship between the price of stuff and the quantity of stuff people will buy or sell at different prices. The **demand curve,** a fundamental tool in economics, shows the quantity of stuff that people will buy at different prices. The demand curve always shows price on the vertical axis and quantity on the horizontal axis.

The demand curve will almost always slope down from top left to bottom right, reflecting the idea that when something becomes cheaper, people buy more of it. For example, when avocados are priced at $2.50 each, Lukia will only buy one. But when they are on sale for $0.50, she'll buy five, and eat avocado toast all week long.

This graph demonstrates a **negative relationship** between quantity and price—you can see this because the line tilts downward as you look from left to right. If the line tilted upward from left to right, you'd be looking at a **positive relationship.**

In economics you'll want to look at not just the direction of the line, but the steepness of it. This is called the **slope.** You calculate the slope along a straight line by looking at two points on the line, and dividing the vertical change by the horizontal change. In simple terms, it's *rise over run.* In mathematical terms, it's

$$\text{Slope} = \frac{\text{Change in the value on the vertical axis}}{\text{Change in value on the horizontal axis}} = \frac{\Delta y}{\Delta x} = \frac{\text{rise}}{\text{run}}$$

Hint: The little triangle (Δ) is the Greek symbol delta. It's used as a shorthand for "change" – in this case, a change in value.

In the chapters ahead, you'll see lots of stylised graphs like this. We'll take the time to walk you through each one, and provide a quick refresher on how to do all the calculations that come up in this book as we get to them.

A Relationship Is Not The Same Thing as Cause and Effect

Sometimes you'll look at a graph, and you'll see a very clear relationship between two variables. For example, if you compare healthcare expenditures over time with clothing and footwear expenditures in the same time period, you'll see a clear relationship:

Figure 7 | **Healthcare and Clothing Expenditures Are Highly Correlated**

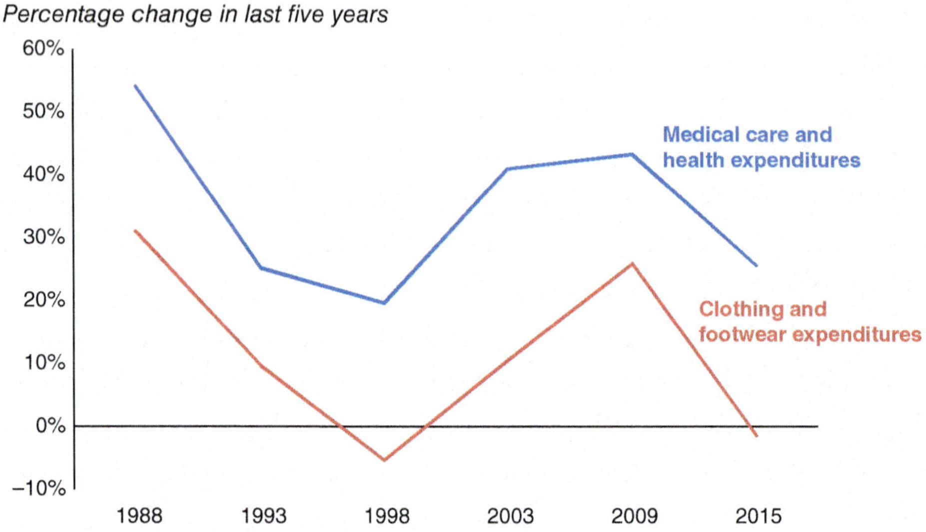

You probably wouldn't infer that spending on healthcare leads people to buy more clothing. Lots of variables are related, but that doesn't mean that one causes the other. There are other **omitted variables** that are related to both of these outcomes.

It's also possible to think you've identified a cause-and-effect relationship, but to get it backward. If you compared clothing and footwear expenditures with, say, time students spend in school, you would probably conclude that people tend to buy more clothing and footwear during the holiday shopping season. But if you'd conclude that people shop more before the holidays to buy more clothing and footwear, you've **reversed the causality.**

Both cases should make you wary about drawing conclusions whenever you look at data, be it in a textbook like this one or a news story: The fact that two things are related, or correlated, doesn't mean one causes the other. As the saying goes, "correlation does not imply causation."

PART I:
Foundations of Economics

Part I: Foundations of Economics

The Big Picture

We'll start our adventure by introducing you to the **four core principles** that provide the foundation of all economic analysis. Taken together, they form a **decision-making framework** that you can apply to make better decisions. Your goal here is to **develop your economic intuition** so that you can apply these principles to real decisions that you'll face in your personal and professional life.

Next, we'll put that economic intuition to work by applying the core principles to understand how people decide what to buy and what to sell. We'll build your understanding of the building blocks of economic analysis: **demand** and **supply.** You'll learn to analyse how these market forces lead to an **equilibrium** that determines the price and quantity of nearly everything.

As you progress through these four chapters, you'll begin to sense the supply and demand forces at play in your everyday life—from the things you buy to the attention you supply to different endeavours. Building a solid foundation in economics will provide you with an **economic toolkit** that will serve you well long after you have finished this course.

1 The Four Core Principles of Economics

Learn the four core principles that provide the foundation of all economic analysis, and use them to analyse choices and make better decisions.

- Why is it useful to learn to think like an economist?
- How do you evaluate costs and benefits?
- Which costs should you look at when evaluating a choice?
- Why should you learn to think on the margin?
- How do all our decisions interact?

2 Demand and Consumer Choice

Understand people's buying (or demand) decisions.

- What is the shape of *your* individual demand curve?
- How can you apply the core principles of economics to make good buying decisions?
- How does individual demand add up to market demand?
- Which factors shift demand curves?

3 Supply and Producer Choice

Learn how businesses make supply decisions.

- What is the shape of *your* individual supply curve?
- How can you apply the core principles to make good supply decisions?
- How does individual supply add up to market supply?
- Which factors shift supply curves?

4 Equilibrium: Where Supply Meets Demand

Analyse how supply and demand determine the equilibrium price and quantity.

- How do markets determine what is produced, and how it is allocated?
- How do markets bring supply and demand into balance?
- What happens when demand and supply shift?
- What do changes in prices and quantity reveal?

CHAPTER 1

The Four Core Principles of Economics

I remember being where you are now—at the start of my first university economics class. For me it was the first economics class I had ever taken. I definitely remember not knowing what to expect. I didn't know anyone who was "an economist," I didn't know anyone who had done economics at university, and I wasn't really clear what the subject was even about. What I definitely didn't expect was that the course would change my life. It gave me a set of tools to help me make sense of things ranging from personal financial decisions to government policy. And even though I've spent every year since learning economics (and that's quite a lot of years now), I'm amazed at how much I learned in that first introductory class.

Monkey Business Images/Shutterstock

Every economist starts out right where you are.

While some parts of that class came naturally to me, other parts seemed foreign. But as I kept studying economics I realised that it doesn't have to be complicated. In fact, the best economists and clearest thinkers I know make economics seem simple, but powerful.

At its heart, economics is just a small set of ideas—or *principles*—that you can apply over and over. It took me longer than I'd like to admit to fully understand the power and reach of these principles. But it needn't take you that long. That's why I wrote the book that you're reading right now: I want to teach you these powerful principles, and I want you to learn how to *use* them. I believe that everyone can benefit from the clarity that economic tools bring. And I hope that by the end of this chapter, you'll have mastered what it took me so long to learn: that economics is built upon four core principles that can be used to provide insight into just about any problem worth thinking about.

I invested much of my adult life learning this, and I still reckon it was worth it. For you, it's just one chapter, so it's a much better investment (and by the end of the chapter you should be able to explain why that is). Let's dig in.

Chapter Objective

Learn the four core principles that provide the foundation of all economic analysis, and use them to analyse choices and make better decisions.

1.1 A Principled Approach to Economics
Understand economics as a way of thinking, grounded in a set of broadly applicable principles that you'll find useful "in the ordinary business of life."

1.2 The Cost-Benefit Principle
The Cost-Benefit Principle: Costs and benefits are the incentives that shape decisions. You should evaluate the full set of costs and benefits of any choice, and only pursue those whose benefits are at least as large as their costs.

1.3 The Opportunity Cost Principle
The Opportunity Cost Principle: The true cost of something is the next best alternative you must give up to get it. Your decisions should reflect this opportunity cost, rather than just the out-of-pocket financial costs.

1.4 The Marginal Principle
The Marginal Principle: Decisions about quantities are best made incrementally. You should break "how many" decisions down into a series of smaller, or marginal, decisions.

1.5 The Interdependence Principle
The Interdependence Principle: Your best choice depends on your other choices, the choices others make, developments in other markets, and expectations about the future. When any of these factors change, your best choice might change.

1.1 A Principled Approach to Economics

Learning Objective *Understand economics as a way of thinking, grounded in a set of broadly applicable principles that you'll find useful "in the ordinary business of life."*

Economics is not just about money, nor is it just about business or even government policy—though it can be helpful for understanding each of these. Rather, it's a way of thinking, and the economic approach can also help you understand politics, families, careers, and just about every aspect of your life. The economic toolkit that will help you better manage your money, your employees, and your business will also help you better manage your time, your energy, and your relationships. It'll provide you with guidance as you make both small decisions such as whether to walk out of a bad movie (you should), and the big ones, such as whether to buy a new car (it depends). Once you learn to think like an economist, you'll find yourself constantly discovering new ways in which it can be useful.

Ultimately all of economics is built on a small set of principles that together define what it means to "think like an economist." If you learn these core principles, you'll be able to do this too. Following this principled approach means that rather than memorising facts about the economy, you'll learn a systematic approach to thinking about the world.

The Economic Approach

One famous definition of economics describes it as the study of people "in the ordinary business of life." I like this definition because it hints at the idea that the same principles that you might use to analyse business decisions will also be useful for analysing the decisions that arise in everyday life. But rather than memorising this specific definition, I want you to learn to *do* economics. That's what this chapter is all about. Think about economics as a toolkit, and this chapter as an introduction to actively using these tools.

We're going to start with the four core principles that comprise the foundation upon which all economic reasoning is based. They aren't about any specific market or any particular decision. Rather, they define an approach to analysing individual decisions and how they interact. Wrap your head around these ideas and connect them to the difficult choices you confront, and you'll be *doing economics*. You'll be translating basic economic principles into carefully considered actions. As you learn to employ the tools of the economist's trade, you'll quickly see how these principles can help you make better choices in both your personal life and your professional life. Internalise these principles, and you'll find yourself *doing economics* every single day.

Think of the task ahead this way: In this chapter, you'll learn the four core principles of economics. The rest of your study of economics will be about applying them. It's an approach that'll guide you through both *microeconomics,* in which you'll study individual decisions and their implications for specific markets, as well as *macroeconomics,* in which you'll trace through their broader implications across the whole economy.

Gabby Jones/Bloomberg via Getty Images

Should you stream one more episode? It's an economic decision.

A Systematic Framework for Making Decisions

The atom is the basic unit of matter, and so physicists begin by trying to understand the atom, and from that, build their insights into the functioning of our physical world. Biologists start with the cell, the basic building block of all living things, and build from there to understand how different organisms live. And for economists, individual decisions—choices—are the foundation of all economic forces. Your decisions, and those of others, collectively determine what's made, who gets it, and whether it yields fair outcomes. Because these broad economic outcomes are the product of many individual choices, economic analysis always begins by focusing on individual decisions.

This is where the four core principles come in. Together, they provide a systematic framework for analysing individual decisions. In particular, through the rest of this chapter, we'll see that whenever economists evaluate a decision:

- We consider the costs and benefits of a choice. (The *cost-benefit principle*.)
- Before making a choice, we consider the alternatives, asking: "Or what?" (The *opportunity cost principle*.)
- We think at the margin, always asking whether a bit more or a bit less of something would be an improvement. (The *marginal principle*.)
- We are particularly attuned to understanding how different decisions depend on each other. (The *interdependence principle*.)

Sounds straightforward, right? The challenge is going to be applying these ideas—which we'll analyse through the rest of this chapter—to the wide array of decisions you'll face in your life.

This systematic approach provides insight into just about every decision you face. Going shopping? Apply the core principles of economics, and you'll likely make better choices about what to buy. Trying to decide whether to do further study? We'll see that the core principles can help you sort out whether that's a good idea. Thinking of starting your own business? Apply these principles to figure out whether that's your best choice. Settling down, and trying to decide how many children you should have? Again, apply these principles.

If you get in the habit of thinking about economics through the core principles, you'll develop a sharper understanding and make better decisions. Speaking of which, you now face an important decision: You have to decide whether to keep reading, or not. I would like to think that my past students would agree that the benefit of learning to think like an economist far exceeds the cost. And as you're about to discover, when the benefits exceed the costs, the first of these principles tells you that it's a choice worth making. So keep reading!

1.2 The Cost-Benefit Principle

Learning Objective *The Cost-Benefit Principle: Costs and benefits are the incentives that shape decisions. You should evaluate the full set of costs and benefits of any choice, and only pursue those whose benefits are at least as large as their costs.*

Nerida Kyle is a 23-year-old economics graduate who is about to start her first full-time job, working in Human Resources in Brisbane. She likes her new apartment, but there's no good public transport near it, and she's too far from work to bike or walk. Nerida figures that she'll need to buy a car to get to work because the only other alternative is to get an Uber each way, and that's going to cost her $30 a day. But before she heads out car shopping, she finds herself wondering: Is buying a car really my best choice?

The **cost-benefit principle** says that costs and benefits are the *incentives* that shape decisions. This principle suggests that before you make any decision, you should:

- Evaluate the full set of costs and benefits associated with that choice.
- Pursue that choice, only if the benefits are at least as large as the costs.

cost-benefit principle Costs and benefits are the incentives that shape decisions. You should evaluate the full set of costs and benefits of any choice, and only pursue those whose benefits are at least as large as their costs.

This principle says that Nerida should buy a car only if it yields benefits that are at least as large as the costs. Because the balance of costs and benefits define Nerida's incentive to buy the car, this principle is sometimes best remembered by its conclusion: *incentives matter.*

The *cost-benefit principle* isn't just relevant when deciding whether to purchase a car—it is relevant for literally any choice that you might consider. Look around, and you'll see that decisions people make—where to buy groceries, whether to study economics, and what career to pursue—reflect their incentives, as they weigh the balance of costs and benefits.

Although it may seem obvious to do something only if the benefits exceed the costs, following the *cost-benefit principle* can be more challenging than it sounds. The trick is to think broadly but precisely about what constitutes a cost or benefit.

Quantifying Costs and Benefits

The hardest part of analysing costs and benefits can be figuring out how to compare very different aspects of a decision. Let's think about a simpler choice: You walk into a coffee shop and have to decide whether to buy a coffee. The chalkboard above the counter says that the price of coffee is $4.

The *cost-benefit principle* says that you should buy the coffee if the benefit is at least as large as the cost. The cost is pretty easy to quantify: It's the $4 you'll have to fork over. The benefits, however, are harder to measure. After all, how do you quantify the rich aroma of freshly ground coffee, the earthy richness of the first sip, and the caffeine-fuelled jolt that follows?

How do you compare these benefits with $4? It may seem like that old expression—that you can't compare apples and oranges. But actually, with a little work, you can.

willingness to pay In order to convert nonfinancial costs or benefits into their monetary equivalent, ask yourself: "What is the most I am willing to pay to get this benefit (or avoid that cost)?"

Convert costs and benefits into dollars by evaluating your willingness to pay. There's a simple trick that economists use: We convert each cost and benefit into its money equivalent. And that's easier than you may think: Simply assess your **willingness to pay.** That is, ask yourself: What is the most that you would be willing to pay in order to obtain a particular benefit or to avoid a particular cost?

Let's use this approach to quantify the benefits of coffee. Are you willing to pay $5 for it? If not, how about $4? Maybe $3? How about just $2? Maybe only $1? If you don't like coffee, you probably aren't willing to pay anything. If the most you are willing to pay is $5, then this is the dollar value of the benefits you receive from that coffee. You should always ask yourself about your willingness to pay before you look at the price. After all, you are simply trying to quantify the benefit you get from buying a coffee, and that benefit depends on how delicious it is to you, not the price on the menu.

Let's say that, like me, you are willing to pay up to $5 for a good cup of coffee. This doesn't mean that you actually want to pay $5—of course you would prefer to pay a lower price, and you're happy to see that it only costs $4. Now that you've answered the willingness-to-pay question, you have now quantified both the benefit ($5) and the cost ($4) of coffee in the same units (money). With costs and benefits in the same unit, it's easy to apply the *cost-benefit principle*. In this case, the benefit exceeds the cost, so you should buy that coffee.

pixproviderAB/E+/Getty Images

Money is just a tool for measuring value.

Money is the measuring stick, not the objective. Some people worry that converting costs and benefits into their monetary equivalents reflects an unhealthy obsession among economists with money, or a belief that money is the only thing that matters. But that's wrong. Money is simply a common measuring stick that allows you to compare a wide variety of costs and benefits, taking account of *both* financial *and* nonfinancial aspects of a decision. Economists are no more obsessed with money than architects are obsessed with millimetres; these are just how we take our measurements.

Converting costs and benefits into their monetary equivalents, will allow you to take account of a wide variety of nonfinancial issues. For example, you can factor in the degree of satisfaction you get from a cup of coffee, and the value of your time or effort in getting to the café. Any consequence of your choices can be a cost or benefit, as long as it has meaning to you.

Interpreting the DATA **What's the benefit you get from Google?**

What is the benefit to you from having access to Google? Even though the price of using Google is $0, the benefit from having all of the world's information at your fingertips is much larger.

One way of answering this is to think about living without Google. Instead of Googling for answers, you would have to head to the library to answer most questions. Researchers have shown that, on average, students could find answers to questions 15 minutes faster using an internet search than a library (not factoring in the time saved from convenience). Once you factor in the number of searches people do, and put a value on the time saved, Google's chief economist reckons these benefits from using Google add up to around $650 per year for the average person. Google illustrates an important point: The benefit you get from something can be unrelated to the price you pay. ■

The cost-benefit principle isn't selfish—if you aren't. At first glance, it may seem like the *cost-benefit principle* says you should make selfish decisions. According to this view, doing something nice—such as buying your friend a coffee—is all cost and no benefit. But this reasoning is wrong, and it comes from defining costs and benefits too narrowly. A careful cost-benefit analysis takes into account both the financial and nonfinancial aspects of a decision. Your innate generosity is an important nonfinancial aspect to consider. If you enjoy buying your friend a coffee—perhaps you like seeing them happy, or maybe you enjoy their company—then this is an important benefit that you need to account for.

Monkey Business Images/Shutterstock

The cost-benefit principle isn't just about you.

How can you quantify this benefit? As with other nonfinancial benefits, you should think in terms of your willingness to pay: How much are you willing to pay so that your friend can enjoy a coffee? The more you enjoy doing nice things like this, the more you are willing to pay for it. Similarly, the benefit of donating time or money to a nonprofit will be high if the cause means a lot to you. You need to include these unselfish motivations in your cost-benefit calculations.

The key to using the *cost-benefit principle* properly is to think broadly about the *full* set of costs and benefits involved in your choices. When you account for your unselfish motivations, the *cost-benefit principle* will lead you to make unselfish choices.

Maximise Your Economic Surplus

When you follow the *cost-benefit principle*, every decision you make will yield larger benefits than costs. The difference between the benefits you enjoy and the costs you incur is called your **economic surplus,** and it is a measure of how much your decision has improved your well-being. Making good decisions is all about maximising your economic surplus.

economic surplus The total benefits minus total costs flowing from a decision. It measures how much a decision has improved your well-being.

Follow the cost-benefit principle, and your choices will increase your economic surplus. In fact, you generate economic surplus every time you make a decision using the *cost-benefit principle*. Consider again what happened when you bought a cup of coffee: As a buyer, you gained something worth \$5 to you (remember, that's your willingness to pay for it), and in exchange, you transferred something worth only \$4 (your money). This simple act of exchange generated an extra \$1 worth of benefits to you! That's your economic surplus.

Now think about the same transaction from the perspective of the seller—the person who owns the café. If a cup of coffee costs \$1 to make, then they have exchanged something worth \$1 to them (some coffee beans, perhaps some milk and sugar, and a few minutes of a barista's time) for something worth \$4 (your money), generating \$3 of economic surplus for them. Both buyer and seller are better off.

Let's consider a more important example: Opera Australia might offer you a job paying \$75,000 per year, but you love the arts so much that you would have accepted the job even if it paid less, say \$60,000. If so, your new job yields you an economic surplus of \$15,000. Of course, if Opera Australia's managers are following the *cost-benefit principle*, they offered you the job because they believe that you will generate benefits for them that exceed the \$75,000 per year that they are offering to pay you. Perhaps by finding some great new performers, you are expected to generate an extra \$150,000 per year in new revenue, generating \$75,000 in economic surplus for them. The *cost-benefit principle* ensures that both you and Opera Australia make choices that generate additional economic surplus, and avoid those that reduce your economic surplus.

Both buyers and sellers benefit from voluntary exchange. In each of the above examples, both the buyer and seller benefited from the transaction, with each earning an economic surplus. If buyers and sellers always follow the *cost-benefit principle*, then each will choose to trade only if the benefits to them are at least as large as their costs. This ensures that all transactions will yield an economic surplus. This idea of both sides benefiting from a voluntary exchange lies at the heart of all economic transactions.

This insight should shape how you think about economic transactions. Often non-economists think about the economy like a sporting competition—that if you gain, I lose. It's a cute analogy—but it's wrong. It's often more useful to think of economic transactions as being more like cooperation than competition. The café owner has something you really want (coffee), and you have something they really want (money). By cooperating, you can make each other better off. Similarly, you may have something Opera Australia really wants (the ability to identify great performers, and in doing so you might generate \$150,000 in new revenue for them) and they have something you want (a fun job and a good salary). Both buyers and sellers benefit from voluntary exchange, as long as they each follow the *cost-benefit principle*.

Juice Images/Alamy

Sellers get money, buyers get the stuff they want. Both are better off.

Focus on Costs and Benefits, Not How They're Framed

The *cost-benefit principle* says that you should make choices based on the underlying costs and benefits of the choice you face, rather than how they are described, or *framed*. But sellers will often try to make this difficult.

For instance, whenever a shirt is on sale, the price tag will show both the sale price and the original price. However, the amount of money you "save" is irrelevant. Instead, you need to ask yourself a simple question: Do the benefits of this shirt outweigh the cost (the sale price)? Similarly, many restaurants include one outrageously expensive item on the menu, even though no one orders it. (Lobster, anyone?) This overpriced lobster makes everything else on the menu look cheap by comparison. The restaurant hopes that with the money you "saved" by not ordering lobster, you'll be tempted to order an extra item, such as an entree or dessert. And some people do succumb to this temptation. This is a mistake: Your choice of food should depend on costs and benefits, and not on something irrelevant, such as whether there's an overpriced lobster on the menu.

Following the advice of the *cost-benefit principle* can be harder than it sounds. For instance, how would you respond to the following scenario?

Do the Economics

You're the CEO of a large but struggling insurance company. Sales have fallen, and you need to cut costs in order to avoid losing money this year. You anticipate needing to fire 6,000 of your employees. Your management team has been exploring alternatives to this drastic action. During your Monday morning meeting, they suggest two possible plans:

- *Plan A:* Saves 2,000 jobs.
- *Plan B:* Has a one-in-three chance of saving all 6,000 jobs, but a two-in-three chance of saving no jobs at all.

Which plan would you choose?

Plan A ☐ Plan B ☐

You arrive back at work on Tuesday, and your management team tells you that they have figured out a new set of alternatives to consider. They present the following two different alternatives:

- *Plan 1:* Will result in the certain loss of 4,000 jobs.
- *Plan 2:* Has a two-in-three chance of losing all 6,000 jobs, but a one-in-three chance of losing no jobs.

Which plan would you choose?

Plan 1 ☐ Plan 2 ☐

As the manager of your own life, you are going to confront high-stakes decisions just like this one.

Let's now turn from using your gut to make decisions, to rigorously applying the cost-benefit principle. If you compare the choices you were offered on Monday with those offered on Tuesday, you will soon realise: They are identical! They were simply framed differently. That's right: Since the total number of jobs at stake is 6,000, Plan A, which saves 2,000 jobs, is the same as Plan 1, which loses 4,000 jobs. Similarly, a one-in-three chance of saving 6,000 jobs in Plan B is the same as a one-in-three chance of losing no jobs in Plan 2.

So, if you chose Plan A on Monday, you also should have chosen Plan 1 on Tuesday, and if you chose Plan B on Monday, you also should have chosen Plan 2 on Tuesday. However, it's possible that your choices between Monday and Tuesday were not consistent. If so, you're not alone.

In fact, around 80% of people choose Plan A when offered a choice between Plans A and B, and about 80% of people choose Plan 2 when offered a choice between Plans 1 and 2. This means that most people change their decision depending on how it is described. And that's a mistake. ■

Framing effects can lead you astray. This is an example of a broader problem. Psychologists have documented that small differences in how alternatives are described, or framed, can lead people to make different choices. This phenomenon is

framing effect When a decision is affected by how a choice is described, or framed. You should avoid letting framing effects alter your own decisions.

known as the **framing effect.** But while the framing effect is common, it is not rational, and you don't want your decision making to be this arbitrary. If you want to make good decisions that aren't affected by how your choices are described, you should follow the *cost-benefit principle*. That is, you should evaluate the full set of costs and benefits of each alternative and only pursue those whose benefits are at least as large as their costs.

If you rigorously followed the *cost-benefit principle*, laying out the pros and cons of each plan, you would've ended up with an analysis like that in Figure 1.

Figure 1 | **Costs and Benefits of Each Plan**

	Monday's alternatives		Tuesday's alternatives	
	Plan A	**Plan B**	**Plan 1**	**Plan 2**
Benefit	Save 2,000 jobs	One-in-three chance to save 6,000 jobs	Save 2,000 jobs*	One-in-three chance to save 6,000 jobs*
Cost	Lose 4,000 jobs*	Two-in-three chance to lose 6,000 jobs*	Lose 4,000 jobs	Two-in-three chance to lose 6,000 jobs

*Remember: If you do nothing, your firm will lose 6,000 jobs.

When you articulate your costs and benefits this clearly, you're less likely to fall prey to framing effects.

Applying the Cost-Benefit Principle

Let's return to the decision we started with: Should Nerida buy a car or simply take an Uber to work every day? Since she's trying to decide what to do over the next year, she should consider the costs and benefits that accrue over that year. Here are the costs she came up with:

- She can buy a 5-year-old Toyota Corolla for $12,000, which she could sell for $10,000 after using it for the year.
- She expects to drive 10 kilometres to and from work, 5 days a week, for 47 weeks per year (she takes 4 weeks annual leave and there are public holidays as well), and she anticipates getting 15 kilometres per litre. Petrol currently sells for $1.29 per litre.
- Comprehensive Insurance, registration, and a CTP Green Slip costs $1,900 per year.
- She anticipates spending another $1,000 per year on servicing/repairs.
- Parking costs $10 per day.

The benefit of buying a car will be the Uber fares that she doesn't have to pay. Each time she avoids taking an Uber to or from work, she'll save $15 in fares. Over the course of a year, this will add up to $7,050. (For now, let's say that this is the only benefit she gets from owning a car, because she can borrow her roommate's car on the weekends.)

Figure 2 tallies up the costs and benefits. This is a useful exercise, highlighting just how expensive the total costs of driving are. Once Nerida considers all the hidden costs, the total cost of having her own car for one year adds up to more than $7,650! This annual cost is larger than the $7,050 benefit of not having to pay for an Uber each day. So while it feels decadent, Nerida takes an Uber to and from work every day. And this earns just over $600 worth of economic surplus—not a bad return for doing a few quick calculations!

Figure 2 | **The Costs and Benefits of Car Ownership**

Costs (Costs associated with buying and maintaining a car and driving to and from work for a year)		**Benefits** (Savings from not taking an Uber)	
Cost of the car: $12,000 purchase price minus $10,000 resale value	$2,000	*Uber fare savings:* $15 per trip × 2 trips per day × 5 days per week × 47 weeks per year	$7,050
Petrol costs: 10 kilometres × 2 trips per day × 5 days per week × 47 weeks = 4,700 kilometres. Because she gets 15 kilometres per litre, she'll need 4,700 kilometres / 15 kilometres per litre = 313.33 litres, which cost a total of $1.29 per litre × 313.33 litres.	$404.20		
Parking costs: $10 per day × 5 days per week × 47 weeks per year	$2,350		
Insurance and registration	$1,900		
Services and repairs	$1,000		
Total annual costs	$7,654.20	*Total annual benefits*	$7,050

EVERYDAY Economics

The true cost of car ownership

Are you surprised by how expensive car ownership is? In fact, for many people, it's even more costly than this. You won't make the right decision about whether to buy a car unless you account for the full set of costs and benefits associated with owning a car. To help you, the RACV website has a useful calculator to figure out the total cost of owning a car. Click through to www.racv.com.au/on-the-road/buying-a-car/car-running-costs.html and calculate what it'll cost you. The results might surprise you. ■

Calculate costs and benefits, relative to your next best alternative. Let's pause to notice something important about how Nerida calculated her costs and benefits. She's comparing buying a car with taking an Uber to work instead. That is, she's comparing one possibility—driving to work—with its *next best alternative,* which is taking an Uber. In fact, this is exactly the type of thinking that lies at the heart of our next principle: the *opportunity cost principle*. It's an important principle because it'll help you count your costs and benefits properly.

1.3 The Opportunity Cost Principle

Learning Objective *The Opportunity Cost Principle: The true cost of something is the next best alternative you must give up to get it. Your decisions should reflect this opportunity cost, rather than just the out-of-pocket financial costs.*

Nerida has enjoyed a fair bit of success in her first three years of work. She has also noticed that many of the executives she admires have advanced degrees. In the long run, she might be even more successful if she studied for a Master of Business Administration (MBA). But is it worth it? The *cost-benefit principle* tells her that a good decision requires comparing the relevant benefits and costs. The benefits of an MBA are better career prospects. Indeed, careful studies show that MBAs earn around 10% more than comparable university graduates. But what are the costs?

Opportunity Costs Reflect Scarcity

The most obvious cost of an MBA is tuition, which is about $42,000 per year for two years. But this isn't the only cost. For instance, if Nerida pursues an MBA full time, she'll have to quit her job. The more Nerida thinks about it, the more she realises that some costs aren't always obvious. And so she is left wondering: How can you be sure that your decisions reflect your true costs and benefits?

opportunity cost The true cost of something is the next best alternative you have to give up to get it.

The opportunity cost of something is the next best alternative you have to give up. Your decisions should reflect your **opportunity cost,** rather than just out-of-pocket costs, because the true cost of something is what you must give up to get it. This principle reminds you that whether you are deciding how to spend your money, your time, or anything else, you should think about its alternative uses. It tells you to assess the consequences of your choice relative to the *best* of your alternatives. The principle forces you to focus on the real *trade-offs* you face, and in doing so you will make better decisions. The *opportunity cost principle* is such a fundamental part of economic thinking that when economists say "costs," we really mean opportunity costs.

Let's now see how thinking about opportunity costs might lead you to assess your decisions differently.

People who haven't studied economics tend to think about the cost of something as the out-of-pocket financial cost—how much money they have to take out of their back pocket to pay for it. But this can be very misleading. For instance, studying economics in the library until closing time every day doesn't lead to any extra out-of-pocket costs. If this were the right way to think about costs, then you would be in the library studying economics whenever it's open, since the benefit (learning more economics, which helps you make better decisions) surely offsets the out-of-pocket cost of zero. But this ignores other important costs. Your time is scarce, and so each hour spent studying economics has an opportunity cost, because it's an hour that you can't spend studying psychology, marketing, history, or maths. It's also an hour you can't spend sleeping, working, or just enjoying life. You should only study another hour of economics if it yields benefits that are at least as large as those of the best of these alternatives.

The *opportunity cost principle* leads you to focus on the true trade-offs you face. If you make one choice (studying economics until 3 A.M.), what is the best alternative that you're forced to give up? Just as the *opportunity cost principle* can help you better allocate your time (as in this example), it can help you better allocate your scarce money, attention, and resources.

The opportunity cost principle highlights the problem of scarcity. If you ever think that a choice involves no costs, think again. Even if there's no out-of-pocket cost, there's always an opportunity cost. The logic is simple: Whenever you choose to do something, you are implicitly choosing not to do something else. Deciding to watch a movie? That's a decision not to spend two hours preparing for class. The forgone opportunity to pursue an activity is the opportunity cost that you need to consider.

scarcity The problem that resources are limited.

This opportunity cost arises because of a fundamental economic problem: **scarcity.** Your resources are limited—that is, they're scarce. It's not just that you have limited income, but you also have limited time (only 24 hours in a day), limited attention, and limited willpower. Any resources you spend pursuing one activity leaves fewer resources to pursue others. Scarcity implies that you always face a trade-off. Whenever you use any scarce resource—your time, money, attention, willpower, or other resource—there's an opportunity cost.

EVERYDAY Economics The opportunity cost is the road not taken

The *opportunity cost principle* even informs some poetry. Consider the last stanza of the poem "The Road Not Taken," by the great American poet Robert Frost:

I shall be telling this with a sigh
Somewhere ages and ages hence:
Two roads diverged in a wood, and I—
I took the one less traveled by,
And that has made all the difference.

Frost's traveller has come to a fork in the road, and faces a stark choice: which path to take. What is the opportunity cost of taking one path? The opportunity cost is the road not taken. Frost's traveller takes "the one less traveled by," and when he says that this "has made all the difference," he is comparing it to his next best alternative. You can think of the *opportunity cost principle* as asking you to consider "the road not taken." ■

Calculating Your Opportunity Costs

Remember, the opportunity cost of something is what you give up to get it. So, if you want to make sure that you are evaluating your opportunity cost correctly, you should ask yourself two questions:

1. What happens if you pursue your choice?
2. What happens under your next best alternative?

That's it. Now, let's apply this principle to figuring out the true opportunity cost of pursuing an MBA.

1. *What happens if Nerida pursues an MBA?*
   If Nerida pursues an MBA, she'll quit her job, pay tuition, pay for rent and meals and spend a lot of time studying. These consequences are listed in the first column of Figure 3.
2. *What happens if Nerida pursues her next best alternative?*
   Nerida's next best alternative is to keep working in her current job. If she chooses this route, she won't have to pay tuition, she'll earn $70,000 per year, she'll still have to pay for rent and meals, and she'll spend her days working. These consequences are listed in the second column of Figure 3.

Figure 3 | **The Opportunity Costs of Pursuing an MBA (per year)**

Costs of her choice	–	Costs of her next best alternative	=	Opportunity cost
If Nerida pursues an MBA		*If she continues to work full time instead*		*The cost of an MBA, relative to working full time*
Tuition costs $42,000		She won't pay tuition		$42,000 tuition
She quits her job		She earns $70,000 from her job		+ $70,000 in forgone income
Rent and meals cost $40,000		Rent and meals cost $40,000		+ No opportunity cost (She has to pay for housing and food whether or not she pursues an MBA)
10 hours per day studying		10 hours per day at work		+ No opportunity cost (She works 10 hours per day either way)
				= $112,000 per year in total opportunity cost

If the opportunity cost of something is what you must give up to get it, then it's the difference between the consequences of making that choice and the consequences of the next best alternative. And so the opportunity cost of pursuing an MBA—shown in the final column of Figure 3—is equal to the first column minus the second column. We've found that the opportunity cost of pursuing an MBA is $112,000 per year, and so a two-year program comes at a cost of $224,000. This analysis reveals that Nerida should pursue an MBA only if the benefit exceeds the total opportunity cost of $224,000.

Your analysis has revealed four important lessons about opportunity costs:

Lesson one: Some out-of-pocket costs are opportunity costs. The first cost that Nerida thought about was the $42,000 per year cost of tuition. Obviously this is an out-of-pocket cost. It is also an opportunity cost—she has to pay tuition if she pursues an MBA, but she wouldn't incur this expense if she pursued her next best alternative, which is continuing in her current job.

Lesson two: Opportunity costs need not involve out-of-pocket financial costs. But focusing too much on out-of-pocket financial costs might lead you to miss important opportunity costs. For instance, one of the biggest costs of pursuing an MBA is the salary that you forgo when you leave your job. Nerida is currently earning $70,000 per year, so going without this salary is a substantial opportunity cost!

Lesson three: Not all out-of-pocket costs are real opportunity costs. Paying too much attention to out-of-pocket financial costs can also lead you to think about factors that aren't actually relevant opportunity costs. For instance, if Nerida pursues an MBA, she'll have to pay $40,000 per year for rent and meals. But this isn't a cost that should be associated with getting your MBA, since even if you didn't pursue an MBA, you would still have to pay for food and housing. If the expense is the same, and if you have to pay for it under either alternative, then it's not an opportunity cost.

Lesson four: Some nonfinancial costs are not opportunity costs. There are also nonfinancial costs of pursuing an MBA. For instance, Nerida will have to work hard, studying 10 hours per day. But in her current job, Nerida also works hard for 10 hours per day. Thus, relative to her next best alternative, the hard work demanded by an MBA program isn't an opportunity cost.

EVERYDAY Economics

The true cost of university

You now have the tools you need to assess the true cost of your own university experience. I bet you thought about the cost of university before applying, and you probably looked up numbers on the university's website. If you are eligible for HECS/HELP you might have also realised that tuition costs are not paid up front, but over time as an "income-contingent" loan. If you are an overseas student you would have realised that your fees need to be paid right away. But you were probably missing an important part of the puzzle. That website probably listed the cost of things such as tuition, and may have given some estimates of rent or on-campus housing costs—a list that is surprisingly unhelpful for evaluating the true opportunity cost of attending university.

For that, you need to know: If you weren't attending university, what would be different? It's true that you wouldn't be paying tuition, so that's an opportunity cost. But you would surely continue to eat, so the cost of food isn't an opportunity cost. The same goes for the cost of rent—although on-campus accommodation might be cheaper than renting off campus. University websites seem to manage to omit the biggest cost of going to university, which is that if you weren't studying, you would probably be working and earning tens of thousands of dollars. Those forgone earnings are an important opportunity cost that you need to consider.

Yes, going to university involves a large opportunity cost. But hopefully applying the *opportunity cost principle* to your decisions while you're in university will help you make sure that the benefit of your university education exceeds the cost. ■

The "Or What?" Trick

Here's a simple trick to ensure that you are always applying the *opportunity cost principle* correctly: Whenever you pose a question, the word "OR" should be in the middle of your sentence. That is, when Nerida asks, "Should I get an MBA?" she is only asking half the question. She needs to add: "OR keep working?" The "OR" part of this sentence forces you to consider your alternatives, which is at the heart of the *opportunity cost principle*. So remember, always ask: "Or what?" Sometimes you'll find that you can list more than one alternative. When this happens, just remember that the opportunity cost is the best of these alternatives. So you have a choice: Use this simple trick, OR sometimes make bad choices.

Andy Dean Photography/Shutterstock

In order to make a good decision, you always have to ask "Or what?," comparing your choice to its next best alternative.

Do the Economics

What are the opportunity costs of each of the following choices?

- *Should you hang out with your friends on Saturday afternoon?*
  Or what? Or should you study for Tuesday's exam?
- *Should you devote a lot of time to an extracurricular activity and aim for a top leadership position?*
  Or what? Or should you study a lot more and aim for great marks.
- *Should you do an unpaid internship this summer?*
  Or what? Or should you continue waiting tables?
- *Should you hire your best friend to work in your family business?*
  Or what? Or should you hire someone else?
- *Should you invest your savings in the stock market, where your savings can grow a lot in value over the long run, but where they can also fall in value?*
  Or what? Or should you invest your savings in the bank, where the value of your savings will stay roughly the same?
- *Should your online store export its goods, selling them to people overseas?*
  Or what? Or sell them only to people domestically instead?
- *Should you spend all of your income?*
  Or what? Or should you save some of your income, to spend it in the future?

Your actual answers to these questions are unique to you, but they still make up some of the biggest costs you'll face. That's why you're learning the tools of economics, so that you can make better decisions for your own unique life. ■

How Entrepreneurs Think About Opportunity Cost

The *opportunity cost principle* is also critical to how entrepreneurs evaluate whether or not to start a business. Just as you shouldn't be overly focused on out-of-pocket costs, entrepreneurs know to look beyond their business revenues and financial costs. They also understand that starting a new business imposes some hard-to-see opportunity costs. The "Or what?" approach makes these costs clearer. Starting a new business requires confronting the following two questions:

- *Should you start a new business or stay in your current job?*

  Starting a new business means quitting your job and thus, giving up your regular salary. These *forgone earnings* are the opportunity cost of an entrepreneur's time.
- *Should you invest your money in the new business or leave it in the bank?*

  Investing your money in your business means not investing it in the bank, and so not earning interest. This *forgone interest* is the opportunity cost of an entrepreneur's capital.

So when you are thinking about starting a new business, it isn't enough just to figure out whether you'll earn a financial profit. Starting a business is only a good idea from a financial perspective if the benefit it yields—those financial profits—are large enough to offset the opportunity cost of the income you forgo by investing both your time and your money into this business, rather than your next best alternative.

You Should Ignore Sunk Costs

Sometimes when you've spent a lot of time or money on a project, you may think: "I can't stop now; I've already put so much into this project." But this is a mistake. When the time, effort, and other costs you put into the project cannot be reversed, they are referred to as **sunk costs.** And good decision makers ignore sunk costs. Why? The *opportunity cost principle* asks you to compare the consequences of your choice with the consequences of the next best alternative. Since sunk costs can't be reversed, you'll incur those costs under either scenario, which means that they are not opportunity costs. Thus, you should ignore sunk costs.

sunk cost A cost that has been incurred and cannot be reversed. A sunk cost exists whatever choice you make, and hence it is not an opportunity cost. Good decisions ignore sunk costs.

Unfortunately, many of us find it hard to ignore sunk costs in our everyday lives. Have you ever seen anyone stay in an unhappy relationship because they've already spent so much time working on it? Or perhaps you've seen someone stay in a university degree, job, or career that they hate, figuring that it's the right thing to do, given how much time and effort they have put into it. Sometimes corporate executives make similar mistakes, throwing good money after bad, in the hope that an investment project will eventually pay off.

Do the Economics

It is easy to fall for the sunk-cost fallacy. Think about the following scenarios:

a. Yesterday you rented a costume for $60 to go to your friends annual "come as your favourite Superhero" party. But today you're feeling sick, and as you're getting dressed to go to the party, you realise that you won't enjoy it. Do you head to the party?

b. You paid $15 for movie tickets. But 30 minutes into the film, you've seen enough: The acting is terrible, the plot is predictable, and the jokes are cringe-worthy. Do you stay for the last hour?

c. You found a great deal for the summer holidays: a $599 package deal to the Whitsundays. You immediately buy the package and tell your friends about it. Unfortunately, by the time they call, tickets are sold out. Instead, your friends decide to drive to the Gold Coast, where you can all stay for free with your best friend's uncle. You would prefer to be with your friends, but the $599 package deal is nonrefundable. Do you go to the Whitsundays? ■

Answers: a. Don't let yesterday's $60 sunk cost lead you to go to a party you won't enjoy. b. Walk out. You've already paid for the ticket and can't get the money back, so the $15 is a sunk cost you should ignore. c. The problem says that you would prefer to be with your friends, so go to the Gold Coast! The $599 nonrefundable package is a sunk cost.

Applying the Opportunity Cost Principle

The *opportunity cost principle* is an incredibly powerful tool that can help you better understand all sorts of decisions. The following examples illustrate just how important it is in explaining the decisions that people make.

The economy went bust in 2020, but with premium films like *Mulan* debuting online, Disney Plus boomed.

Why do people watch more movies during an economic downturn?

During the 2008 recession, the movie business boomed. And during the pandemic, streaming services enjoyed record profits. Why? The most important cost of seeing a movie isn't the price of the ticket or streaming service. Instead, it's the opportunity cost of your time. The movie takes two hours, and you could spend this time doing something else. Perhaps you could be working instead of seeing the movie. But when the economy is weak, there are fewer jobs, and there is often less work to do, and so the opportunity cost of your time is lower. Or perhaps the alternative to the movie is going to a party. But fewer people throw parties when the economy is weak, and even fewer threw them during the pandemic when parties were both dangerous and often prohibited by local laws. So your alternative to going to a party during a recession might be a night watching television. Because the opportunity cost of time is lower during an economic downturn (especially one caused by a pandemic!), people choose to watch more movies. In fact, a weak economy is often good news for the movie industry.

Why not get married as soon as you turn 16? Many high school students get involved in romantic relationships, but very few get married at age 16. Why? The choice you face is: Should I get married or keep searching for a better match? At age 16, you may have had only a couple of romantic entanglements, and so the possibility that later on you'll meet someone who's an even better match is pretty high. That is, the opportunity cost of marriage—the opportunity to search for an even better partner—is high. By your twenties and thirties, you have more life experience and have met people from many spheres of life. While there's always the possibility that you'll find someone even better later on, the opportunity cost of getting married is likely to be much lower.

Distribution of Age at First Marriage

Share of first marriages in 2018 occuring in each age bracket

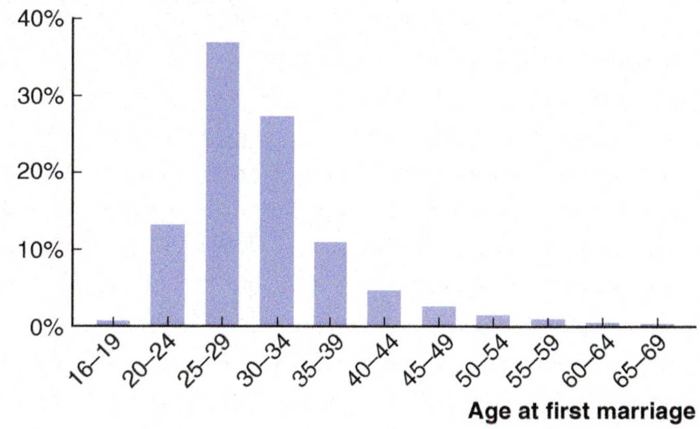

Data from: Australian Bureau of Statistics.

Why do people with terminal illnesses want unproven experimental drugs? Most people are unwilling to take unproven experimental drugs, because they fear that the drugs will do more harm than good. But people with terminal illnesses sometimes plead with their doctors to be allowed to be part of a new medical trial. Why? For healthy people, the choice they face is between taking part in a risky experiment and continuing with their healthy, happy lives. For those with terminal illnesses, the alternative to the risky experiment is continued illness and probable death. Due to this lower opportunity cost, people with severe illnesses are willing to take risks that others are not.

Why I don't eat free muffins. During your career, you might find yourself in early-morning business meetings, in which they try to tempt you with a tray of muffins (and sometimes some fruit, for decoration). These are usually pretty tasty and they're free, but I never eat them. Why? In order to stay healthy, I try to limit myself to only one indulgence each day. So I face a choice: should I eat the muffin or enjoy some ice cream tonight? And I love ice cream. So while the financial cost of the muffin is $0, it's still too expensive, because the opportunity cost of a muffin is an even more delicious bowl of ice cream.

Why are there fewer stay-at-home mums? In 1978, more than half of all mothers stayed out of the labour force. Since then, things have changed, and the most recent data suggest that just under 40% of mums stay at home. Why? Most mothers face a choice between staying at home and working for pay. Over recent decades, there has been a sharp rise in women's wages, and since 1978, the annual earnings of a typical full-time female worker rose by nearly $29,000 (after adjusting for inflation), even as male earnings grew by a little over $19,000. Consequently, the opportunity cost of being a stay-at-home mum has risen. As this opportunity cost has risen, fewer women have chosen to stay at home. Instead, more women are now choosing to combine motherhood and working for increasingly better pay.

Mothers in the Labour Force

Share of mothers with youngest child aged 0–5 who are either unemployed or not looking for work

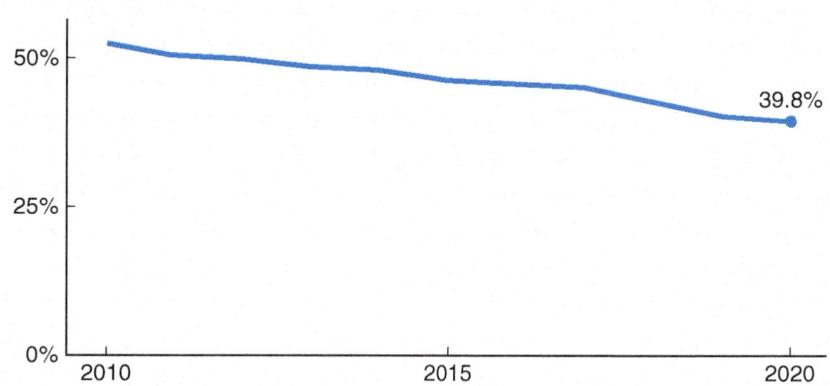

Data from: Australian Bureau of Statistics.

The Production Possibility Frontier

production possibility frontier Shows the different sets of output that are attainable with your scarce resources.

Sometimes you'll find it useful to visualise your opportunity costs. That's what the **production possibility frontier** (PPF) is for—it maps out the different sets of output that are attainable with your scarce resources. It illustrates the trade-offs—that is, the opportunity costs—you confront when deciding how best to allocate scarce resources like your time, money, raw inputs, or production capacity.

The production possibility frontier illustrates your alternative outputs. Let's see how this applies to your study time. If you have three hours per night to study, you can allocate that time between studying economics and studying psychology. Perhaps each extra hour per night you devote to studying economics will raise your econ mark by 8 points, while allocating that time to studying psychology instead will boost your psych mark by only 4 points.

Effectively you're the CEO of a grades-producing factory whose inputs are study time and whose outputs are marks. You can devote your factory's resources to boosting your econ or psych scores to varying degrees. At one extreme, you could spend all three hours studying economics, which would raise your econ mark by 24 points (and psych by nothing). At the other extreme, you could spend all three hours studying psychology, which would boost your psych mark by 12 points (and econ by nothing). In between there's a bunch of other possibilities for allocating your study time, each of which corresponds to a point on your production possibility frontier. Together, these points form a frontier, shown in Figure 4 as a straight line (although in many other cases, your production possibilities frontier may be a bowed-out curve). We call this a *frontier*, because it describes the most that you can produce given your current circumstances. If you waste your resources, or use them inefficiently, you won't even hit this frontier, and you'll end up producing less of each output than you otherwise could.

Figure 4 | The Production Possibility Frontier

You have 3 hours per night to devote to studying either economics (where each hour will boost your mark by 8 points) or psychology (where each hour will boost your mark by 4 points). The **production possibility frontier** shows what you can produce with alternative allocations of your time.

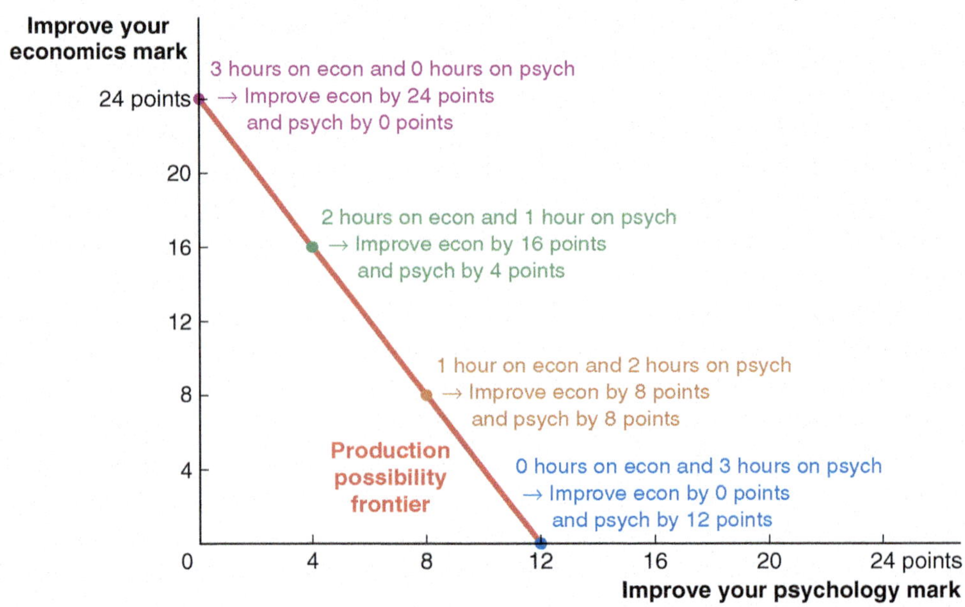

Moving along your production possibility frontier reveals your opportunity costs. When you're on your production possibility frontier, you can't produce more of one output unless you produce less of the other. Moving along your production possibility frontier highlights this opportunity cost: Every hour you devote to studying psychology (which boosts your psych mark by 4 points) is one less hour you can devote to economics (which would have boosted your econ mark by 8 points). As a result, the opportunity cost of adding 4 more points to your psych mark is earning 8 fewer points on econ.

Productivity gains shift your production possibility frontier outward. So, what if you want to produce more than is possible with your production possibility frontier? Well, you'll have to change something. One way to do that is to discover new production techniques that allow you to do more with the same amount of inputs. For example, if you uncover more effective study habits (my advice: reading the text before class is much more productive than cramming weeks later) you might be able to increase the mark boost that comes from each hour you spend studying. This increase in productivity shifts out your production possibility frontier. But even if you get better at studying psych and econ, your resources are still limited; and so there's still an opportunity cost to your time.

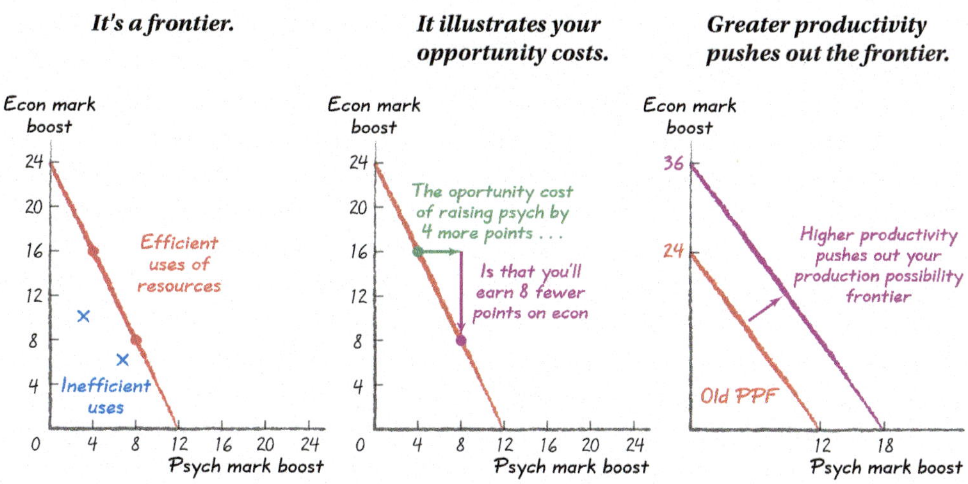

Recap: Evaluating Either/Or Decisions

Let's take a breath, and take stock. The two principles that we have studied so far provide useful guidance whenever you are trying to decide whether or not to do something—such as whether to get an MBA, whether to get married, whether to go to a movie, and whether to look for a job. Since you either choose to do these things or not, we call these "either/or" choices. The *cost-benefit principle* says: Do it if the benefits are at least as large as the costs. But what are the costs? The *opportunity cost principle* says that the true cost of something is the best alternative you give up to get it. Taken together, these principles say: You should pursue your choice if it yields benefits that are at least as large as the opportunity cost, which is your next best alternative.

But many choices are "how many" rather than "either/or" choices. Consider some examples: How many classes should you take? How many workers should you hire? How many children should you have? When you face "how many" questions, you'll need to use one more core principle, the marginal principle, which will allow you to simplify even incredibly complicated "how many" choices into a series of much simpler "either/or" choices. This will help you answer a much wider range of questions, since you've already figured out how to make good "either/or" choices.

Applying the Marginal Principle: Once you have broken a problem into a series of marginal choices, apply the *cost-benefit principle*. The *marginal principle* is useful for "how many" decisions, but not for "either/or" choices.

1.4 The Marginal Principle

Learning Objective *The Marginal Principle: Decisions about quantities are best made incrementally. You should break "how many" decisions down into a series of smaller, or marginal, decisions.*

Let's revisit Nerida, a few years after business school. She has decided to combine her entrepreneurial savvy with her love of food by opening an Italian restaurant. She has already chosen a location and remodelled it. Next she needs to decide how many workers to hire. The benefit of hiring a larger staff is that she'll serve more meals, leading to higher revenue. But this also means higher costs—because more staff means a higher wage bill and selling more meals means buying more fresh produce. As with so many things, there's a trade-off. So, Nerida wonders just how many workers she should hire.

marginal principle Decisions about quantities are best made incrementally. You should break "how many" questions into a series of smaller, or marginal decisions, weighing marginal benefits and marginal costs.

marginal benefit The extra benefit from one extra unit (of goods purchased, hours studied, etc.).

marginal cost The extra cost from one extra unit.

The **marginal principle** says that decisions about quantities are best made incrementally. Whenever you face a decision about how many of something to choose (such as, "How many workers should I hire?"), it is always easier to break it into a series of smaller, or marginal, decisions (such as, "Should I hire one more worker?").

The *marginal principle* suggests that you evaluate whether the extra benefit from hiring one more worker exceeds the extra cost of that extra worker. We call the extra benefit you get from one more worker the **marginal benefit;** the extra cost of that worker is called the **marginal cost.** Applying the *cost-benefit principle* to this marginal choice, you should hire one more worker only if the marginal benefit exceeds the marginal cost.

As Figure 5 illustrates, this is a process that you should apply iteratively: After you've decided to hire that extra worker, you should compare the marginal cost and benefit of hiring *another* worker. Again, if the marginal benefit exceeds the marginal cost, you should hire that person, too. Then you should ask whether it is worth hiring yet another worker. And so it continues, as you work your way through a series of straightforward "either/or" choices, until eventually you decide against hiring any more workers.

When Is the Marginal Principle Useful?

Whenever you have to decide "how many" of something to choose, you should use the *marginal principle* to break your decision into a series of smaller marginal choices. However, there are some decisions that are not "how many" questions, but rather "either/or" questions. For instance, when Nerida was deciding whether to open her restaurant, she faced an "either/or" decision, so the *marginal principle* was not relevant. But sometimes we'll find that even choices that seem like "either/or" choices have "how many" questions lurking within. For instance, Nerida wasn't just deciding whether to open a restaurant, but also how big it should be, and so she found the *marginal principle* useful when she decided how many square metres of retail space to lease.

The bottom line: First determine what type of choice you face. If you face a "how many" choice, you should break it down into a series of smaller marginal decisions. You know that you have broken a decision into its smallest components when you are left with only "either/or" choices to make. Then, apply the *cost-benefit principle* and the *opportunity cost principle* to each of these simpler "either/or" choices.

Figure 5 Applying the Marginal Principle

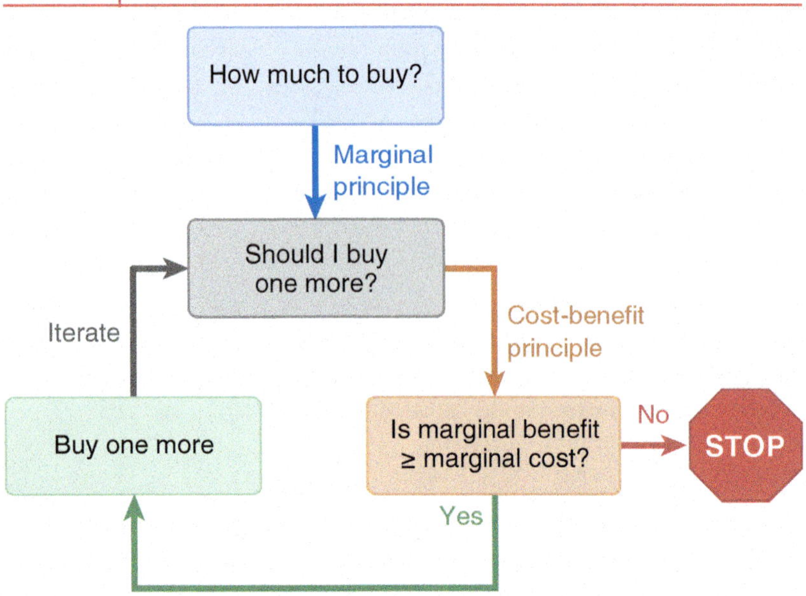

Do the Economics

Can you apply the *marginal principle* to simplify the following decisions?

- *How many workers should I hire?*
  Simplifies to: Should I hire one more worker?
- *How many pairs of shoes should I buy?*
  Simplifies to: Should I buy one more pair of shoes?
- *How many classes should I take?*
  Simplifies to: Should I take one more class this semester?
- *How many children should I have?*
  Simplifies to: Should I have one more child?
- *Should I marry my current partner?*
  This is an either-or question, and so can't be further simplified.
- *How many hours per week should I work?*
  If you are in a job where you can change your hours of work, then you should ask: Should I work one more hour?
  If you can't change the number of hours you work, then this is an either-or question (should I get a second job?), and can't be further simplified. ■

Now we have figured out how to restate any "how many" choice as an "either/or" marginal choice. But remember, deciding "how many" actually requires answering a *series* of these marginal "either/or" questions. Every time you ask one of these marginal questions and the answer is yes, you should ask it again. And if the answer is yes, ask it yet again. You should keep asking until the answer is no. In fact, that is the essence of the most powerful application of the *marginal principle*, as we will learn in the next section.

Using the Rational Rule to Maximise Your Economic Surplus

The *marginal principle* provides a simple rule of thumb that will help you maximise your economic surplus (the difference between your total benefits and total costs). Here's the rule:

The **Rational Rule:** *If something is worth doing, keep doing it until your marginal benefits equal your marginal costs.*

Rational Rule If something is worth doing, keep doing it until your marginal benefits equal your marginal costs.

The logic of this rule is straightforward. You know from the *cost-benefit principle* that whenever the benefits of a choice exceed the costs, it is a good choice. And when you apply the *marginal principle*, you don't analyse the "how many" choice all at once ("How many workers should I hire?"). Instead, you analyse a series of simpler "either/or" choices ("Should I hire one more worker?"). The *marginal principle* tells you to keep hiring, as long as the marginal benefit of each worker exceeds the marginal cost. But you should stop hiring just before the marginal cost becomes larger than the marginal benefit. When does this occur? In most cases, this crossing point occurs right when the marginal benefit is equal to the marginal cost. (In the remaining cases—when the marginal benefit and marginal cost are never exactly equal—you should keep hiring as long as the marginal benefit exceeds the marginal cost.)

The Rational Rule says to keep going until marginal benefit equals marginal cost. Let's apply this reasoning to a decision you face at the start of each semester: how many classes to take. The *marginal principle* says to break up this "how many" choice into a series of "either/or" choices. Should you take one class? The benefit of the first class is surely greater than the cost. So you should definitely take that class. Given that you are taking one class this semester, should you take a second? If the marginal benefit of this extra class exceeds the marginal cost, you should. And the same logic holds for a third class and a fourth (and possibly more). In fact, you should keep increasing your course load as long as the marginal benefit of each extra class is at least as large as the marginal cost. But at some point—usually when you are thinking about whether to take a fifth or a sixth class—the marginal benefit of an extra class will be too low or the marginal cost is just too high (perhaps because the opportunity cost of one more class is constant sleep deprivation). And if the marginal cost of that extra class is greater than the marginal benefit, you shouldn't take that extra class.

Following the Rational Rule leads to good decisions. Some people find the *Rational Rule* confusing—why would you want to set your marginal benefits equal to your marginal costs? After all, don't you simply want to maximise your economic surplus—the difference between the benefits you enjoy and the costs you incur? It turns out that if you follow the *Rational Rule*, your choices will maximise your economic surplus. Why? Let's try to provide Nerida with some insight as she tries to figure out how many workers to hire.

If the marginal benefit of hiring one more worker exceeds the marginal cost, then hiring an additional worker will increase your economic surplus. Since the marginal benefit of this extra worker exceeds their marginal cost, hiring them will boost your total benefit by more than it boosts your total cost. Thus, hiring this extra worker will raise your economic surplus (which is the difference between the total benefits you enjoy and the total costs you incur). If you always hire more workers when the marginal benefits are greater than the marginal costs, you will increase your economic surplus, which moves you ever closer to the point at which your economic surplus is at its highest possible level.

If the marginal benefit of hiring one more worker is less than the marginal cost, then hiring an additional worker will lower your economic surplus. If you did hire this worker, they would raise your total costs by more than they would raise your total benefits, and so hiring them would lower your economic surplus. Hiring (or keeping) a worker whose marginal benefit is less than their marginal cost will move you further away from the point at which your economic surplus is maximised.

You maximise your economic surplus right at the point where the marginal cost of hiring the last worker equals the marginal benefit. So, hiring more workers will increase your economic surplus as long as the marginal benefit exceeds the marginal cost. But at some point, the marginal benefit of an additional worker will be less than the marginal cost. When this happens, hiring that worker would reduce your economic surplus. So, at what point do you stop hiring? Right when the marginal benefit equals the marginal cost. At this point, you have increased your economic surplus as much as possible, right up to the point where hiring another worker would reduce your economic surplus.

Do the Economics

Let's now apply the *Rational Rule* to helping Nerida figure out the number of workers to hire. In each row of Figure 6, she has written down her projections of her total costs and total benefits, according to the different staffing levels she is considering. She considers as few as two staff (in the first row), to as many as seven (in the final row). Each staffing level is noted in the first column. The second column shows the number of meals that Nerida anticipates selling, and this increases as she hires more staff.

What are the implications of this? On the benefit side, the more meals she sells each week, the greater the revenue she earns. On average, each meal sells for about $25, and so her weekly revenue will be $25, multiplied by the number of meals served.

Figure 6 | **Nerida's Weekly Costs and Benefits Depend on the Number of Staff**

Number of workers	Meals served	Total benefits (Revenue = $25 × number of meals)	Marginal benefit (Change in total benefit from hiring an extra server)	Total costs ($10 per meal food costs + $300 per server + $500 rent + $1,000 for Nerida's time)	Marginal cost (Change in total cost from hiring an extra server)	Profit or economic surplus (Total benefits less total costs)
2	160	$4,000		$3,700		$300
3	210	$5,250	$1,250	$4,500	$800	$750
4	250	$6,250	$1,000	$5,200	$700	$1,050
5	280	$7,000	$750	$5,800	$600	$1,200
6	300	$7,500	$500	$6,300	$500	$1,200
7	310	$7,750	$250	$6,700	$400	$1,050

Profit is maximised when marginal benefit = marginal cost → 6 workers

Maximum profit ← $1,200

Marginal benefit equals marginal cost

This total revenue, which is her total benefit, is shown in the third column. On the cost side, running a restaurant is an expensive business. She pays $500 per week in rent. Also, as an entrepreneur, she has to consider the opportunity cost of her own time, which is $1,000 per week. Each part-time server she hires costs $300 per week, and each extra meal that is prepared costs $10 in raw ingredients. The sum of these costs is her total cost, and the total costs associated with each staffing level are shown in the fifth column.

While Nerida has worked out her total costs and benefits, the *marginal principle* suggests that we focus on her marginal benefits, rather than her total benefits. The marginal benefit to Nerida of hiring an additional worker, shown in the fourth column, is the extra revenue that she will earn from that worker. For example, the marginal benefit of hiring the third worker is simply the total benefit from hiring three workers, minus the total benefit from hiring two workers, or $5,250 – $4,000 = $1,250 per week. We can do similar calculations for each extra staff member, and these marginal benefit calculations are shown in the fourth column. We also need to work out Nerida's marginal costs, which are the extra costs that come with hiring each extra worker (and from making the extra meals they serve). For instance, adding a third worker and increasing the number of meals Nerida serves causes her total costs to rise from $3,700 per week in the first row, to $4,500 per week in the next row, for a marginal cost of $800. When we do similar marginal cost calculations for each additional staff member, we arrive at the numbers shown in the sixth column.

Now, let's apply the *Rational Rule*. Notice that hiring that third worker brings an additional (or marginal) benefit of $1,250 per week, and an additional (or marginal) cost of $800 per week. Because the marginal benefits exceed the marginal costs, Nerida is definitely better off hiring that third worker. But should she also hire a fourth worker? And what about a fifth worker after that? The *Rational Rule* is useful: Keep hiring workers until the marginal benefits are equal to the marginal costs. In this case, Nerida's marginal benefits and costs are equal when she hires six workers. And so the rule says: Hire six workers.

Does this make sense? You can check the final column, which calculates her economic surplus, which in this case is her economic profit—her total benefits less total costs. Looking down this column, the highest profit Nerida can earn is $1,200. She can earn this profit if she hires either five or six workers. The *Rational Rule* led Nerida to hire six workers, which is the choice that yields the (equal) highest profits. Great news!

You might notice that the *Rational Rule* recommends that you keep hiring until the marginal benefit is equal to the marginal cost, which occurred when she hired six workers. But hiring that sixth worker whose marginal benefit was exactly equal to their marginal cost neither raised nor lowered her economic surplus. So while the rule told Nerida to hire six workers, she would have earned the same profit had she hired only five people. In practice, the important point is to stop hiring just before your marginal cost becomes larger than your marginal benefit. ■

Applying the Rational Rule

The *marginal principle* is particularly useful precisely because it is so practical. As you study economics, you will see that the *Rational Rule* is applicable to just about every choice you make. Indeed, it describes how people like Nerida actually run their businesses. The problem is that most people don't know in advance exactly what the costs and benefits will be for each alternative they face. So how do they make decisions?

Businesses experiment at the margin to learn their marginal costs and benefits. Nerida needs to decide how many workers to hire, but in reality, she isn't sure whether she would be better off hiring two workers or three. So she experiments with different business decisions. She starts by hiring two workers. And then, as an experiment, she tries hiring one more person, to figure out whether that boosts her benefits by more than it boosts her costs. If it does—that is, if the marginal benefit exceeds the marginal cost—she'll declare that experiment a success, and keep that extra person on payroll permanently. If the costs exceed the benefits, she'll eventually let that person go or fail to replace a worker who quits.

For Nerida, hiring the third worker yields $1,250 extra revenue, which more than offsets the $800 in extra costs. She then continues her experimenting, hiring a fourth person; when that also raises her profits, she'll experiment further, hiring a fifth and sixth person, and then a seventh. With each experiment, she focuses on the changes in costs and benefits that occur; these are her marginal costs and marginal benefits. When she tries adding a seventh worker, she finds that her costs rise by $400, but her revenue only rises by $250. Because this experiment reveals that her marginal cost exceeds the marginal benefit (and hence that the seventh person reduces her total profit), she declares that experiment a failure, and won't keep a seventh worker on permanently.

Notice that in this process of judging her experiments as successes or failures, Nerida is following the *Rational Rule*: If hiring additional staff is worth doing, she'll keep doing it until her marginal benefits equal her marginal costs. And by using this rule, she experiments her way to the point where her profits are maximised.

Do the Economics

Now, it's your turn to apply the *Rational Rule* to make decisions. Remember to think about the relevant marginal costs and marginal benefits. Consider yourself in the following roles:

- *As a consumer: How many cups of coffee should you buy today?*

  Keep buying coffee until the marginal benefit (your willingness to pay for that last cup of coffee) is equal to the marginal cost (the price and, if it's late, how much it would stand in the way of getting a good night's rest).

- *As a producer: How many tonnes of coffee should you produce?*

  Keep producing coffee until the marginal benefit of producing an extra tonne (the wholesale price you can sell it for) is equal to the marginal cost of producing another tonne.

- *As a worker: How many hours should you work as a barista?*

  Keep working until the marginal benefit (your hourly wage) is equal to the marginal cost of working (the value of the marginal hour of leisure time that you are missing).

- *As an investor: How much should you invest in a new chain of speciality coffee shops?*

  Keep investing until the marginal benefit (your return on the last dollar invested) is equal to the marginal cost. (This includes the opportunity cost of that last dollar: How else could you invest that dollar, and how could you spend it now?)
- *As an export company: How many tonnes of coffee should you export?*

  Keep exporting until the marginal benefit (the price you can get for the coffee overseas) is equal to the marginal cost (the price at which domestic producers will sell you one more tonne, plus the price of shipping it overseas).
- *As a job-seeker: How many coffee shops should you send your résumé to?*

  Keep sending job applications until the marginal benefit (the value of the increased chance of finding a job) is equal to the marginal cost of an application (the time and hassle of filling out one more application).
- *As an employer: How many workers should you hire?*

  Keep hiring until the marginal benefit of an extra worker (the rise in revenues you get from selling more coffee) is equal to the marginal cost (the wages of that last worker and the cost of that extra coffee). ■

sumire8/Shutterstock

They may all look the same, but that doesn't mean that the marginal benefit of each bean is the same.

Recap: The marginal principle creates a structure to simplify complicated "how many" questions. Each of these examples involves thinking about making decisions in very different economic roles. Yet all of the answers follow a parallel structure. The power of the *marginal principle* is that it creates a common structure in all decisions in which you choose "how many," and it simplifies an otherwise complicated decision. The best choices—the ones that maximise your economic surplus—all follow the same pattern, as described by the *Rational Rule*: Choose the quantity where the marginal benefit equals the marginal cost. That way, you will maximise your economic surplus.

By now, we've come a long way in developing the skills you need to think like an economist. It's all about learning to identify the key issues underpinning any choice. The *cost-benefit principle* asks you to identify the relevant costs and benefits of a decision. The *opportunity cost principle* asks you to identify your true opportunity costs. And the *marginal principle* asks you to identify the marginal choices that make up any "how many" decision. Now, let's turn to the final principle, which involves identifying the many different ways that your decisions affect and are affected by other decisions.

1.5 The Interdependence Principle

Learning Objective *The Interdependence Principle: Your best choice depends on your other choices, the choices others make, developments in other markets, and expectations about the future. When any of these factors change, your best choice might change.*

Nerida's restaurant is doing well, and she's thinking about opening earlier so that she can also serve lunch. She's aware that the likely success of the lunch shift—and hence whether it's worth pursuing—depends on a range of other factors. First of all, it depends on *her other decisions.* Nerida has also been thinking about offering cooking classes, but she doesn't have enough bandwidth to succeed at both new projects. Second, it depends on the *decisions made by others within her market.* If the other Italian restaurant in town opens for lunch, it's unlikely that there will be enough customers for her to break even serving lunch. As such, her best choice depends on the choices of her rivals. On the flip side, if more people eat out rather than bring lunch from home, then perhaps it will be profitable. And so her best choice also depends on the choices her potential customers make. Third, it depends on *developments in other markets.* If Adidas opens a new Australian headquarters nearby, that will mean more foot traffic (pun not intended), and more potential lunchtime customers. But she'll have to compete with Adidas for workers, and so it might also mean that she'll have to pay higher wages. Fourth, it depends on her *expectations about the future.* She expects the economy to expand next year, and that means more customers with more money in their pockets, which could potentially make her lunch service very profitable.

As Nerida thinks harder about all of this, she sees that the economy—and indeed, her life—is rife with interdependencies. Her best decision depends on many factors, and as these other factors change, so does her best course of action. Indeed, all choices are interdependent, and they both shape—and are shaped by—the choices that you and others make, both now and in the future.

interdependence principle Your best choice depends on your other choices, the choices others make, developments in other markets, and expectations about the future. When any of these factors change, your best choice might change.

This is the **interdependence principle,** which recognises that your best choice depends on your other choices, the choices others make, developments in other markets, and expectations about the future. When any of these factors changes, your best choice might change. There are four types of interdependencies you'll need to think about:

1. Dependencies between each of your individual choices
2. Dependencies between people or businesses in the same market
3. Dependencies between markets
4. Dependencies through time

These four different types of interdependencies can be illustrated by thinking about how you choose your classes. First, if you take an economics class, you won't be able to take some other class that is scheduled at the same time.

Second, if another student takes the last spot in a popular class, then you will have to take a different class. That is, your decisions about which classes to take also depend on the choices of others in the same "market."

Third, if you believe (as I do!) that the falling cost and increasing capacity of data-crunching computers means that the skills you learn in introductory economics—which include how to interpret those data—have become more valuable, then your best decision in one market (which class to take) depends on outcomes in other markets (the growing availability of data).

And fourth, your decision to study economics today changes the set of classes you have met the prerequisites for, affecting the courses you can take next year. For example, completing introductory economics will enable you to take more advanced economics courses in the future, whereas those classes wouldn't be an option if you didn't take this class. Thus, the best course to take this year depends on what classes you expect to take in the future.

The broader point is that the best choice for you—such as which classes you take this semester—will depend on many other factors. If any of these other factors change, then your best choice might change, too. Let's explore these four different types of dependencies in greater detail.

Interdependency One: Dependencies Between Your Own Choices

Since you have *limited resources,* every choice you make affects the resources available for every other decision. This interdependence follows from the many different constraints you face. Consider the following examples:

- You have a budget constraint due to *limited income,* and so the amount of money available to spend on entertainment depends on how much you spend on food.

- You have *limited time* because there are only 24 hours in a day, and so the amount of time available to study for economics depends on how much time you spend studying psychology.
- You have *limited attention,* so the amount of attention you give your economics lecture depends on whether you allow yourself to be distracted by your smartphone.
- You have *limited production capacity* because you only have one factory, and so the number of production lines available to produce electric cars depends on how many are producing regular cars.
- You have *limited wealth* to invest, and so the amount you invest in a new start-up depends on how much you invest in stocks and bonds.

Tobin Rogers/Hill Street Studios//Blend Images/Getty Images

How you spend your limited attention will affect your marks.

In these cases, the interdependence follows from limited income, time, attention, production capacity, and wealth. Before moving on, ponder how other constraints, such as limited energy, limited cognitive capacity, and limited willpower will create other interdependencies between your choices.

Interdependency Two: Dependencies Between People (or Businesses)

The choices made by other economic actors—people, businesses, governments, or other groups—shape the choices available to you. In many cases, this arises because you're competing for *society's scarce resources.* The more others get, the less that's left over for you. Consequently, your best choice depends on the choices that others make.

When people compete for scarce resources, they typically do so in a market. And so you'll more easily see these interdependencies by focusing on how buyers or sellers compete. For instance, if Atlassian hires the best software engineers in Sydney, it will be hard for a Sydney-based start-up to find talented employees. And so a start-up's hiring outcomes depend on those made by Atlassian, because they're competing *buyers* in the labour market. Alternatively, if your classmate is hired by Atlassian, that's one less job for you to get. In this case, your outcome depends on your classmate's because you're competing *sellers* in the labour market.

To get a sense of these interdependencies, it's useful to start by identifying the relevant market. It's an approach that applies well beyond traditional markets, as the following examples show:

- Your ability to date the most interesting person in your class depends on the other people they might date in your class.
  You're competing "buyers" in the dating market.
- Whether your vote sways the next election depends on whether my vote offsets yours.
  We're competing "sellers" in the market for votes.
- Whether your parents attend your younger brother's Tuesday evening debate depends on whether they're attending your sister's Tuesday evening soccer game.
  Your siblings are competing "buyers" in the market for parental attention.
- Whether the local council adopts your new policy proposal depends on whether they prefer my alternative proposal.
  We're competing "sellers" in the marketplace of ideas.

Understanding these interdependencies between competitors in a market is a critical first step. In the next chapter, we'll push these ideas further, analysing the forces of supply and demand in greater detail.

Interdependency Three: Dependencies Between Markets

Choices are also interdependent across *different markets*. In particular, changes in prices and opportunities in one market affect the choices you might make in other markets. For instance:

- Rising interest rates in the credit market make it more expensive to get a mortgage, which might lead you not to buy a home.
  Your choice in the housing market depends on the credit market.
- When demand for housing falls, entrepreneurs often convert existing homes into something else, such as child care centres, making it easier for you to find child care.
  Your choice in the child care market depends on the housing market.
- If you live in an area with many high-quality, low-cost child care options, you may be more likely to return to work soon after becoming a parent.
  Your choice in the labour market depends on the market for child care.
- When both spouses work, households are more likely to need two cars.
  Your choice in the car market depends on the labour market.

So you can see that there are dependencies running all the way from the credit market to the housing market, to the child care market, to the labour market. If you ignore the *interdependence principle*, you could be tempted to just consider each market in isolation. But as these examples demonstrate, this can risk missing a large part of the story, because changes in these other markets shape your costs and benefits, and can thereby change which option is your best choice.

Interdependency Four: Dependencies Over Time

As a consumer, you always face the option of buying something tomorrow, rather than buying it today. And similarly, as an executive, you get to choose when to produce goods and when to bring them to market. Likewise, investors, employers, and workers all get to decide when to invest, hire, and work. These alternatives mean that your choices always reflect a trade-off across time: Is it better to act today or tomorrow? As expectations about the future change, the terms of this trade-off change, and so your best choice might change.

Your choices are also linked through time by the investments you make. For instance, if you invest in a new factory, in your education, or in getting fit, this expands your choices in the future, as these investments give you the opportunity to produce more, get a better job, or enjoy better health, respectively. Because your future depends so heavily on the choices you make today, you need to be sure to take account of these connections. And so the investment choices you'll want to make today depend on your expectations about the future.

What Else?

The big idea behind the *interdependence principle* is to ask, "What else?" And this leads to two types of "what else?" questions. The first asks: *What else* might my decision affect? Every decision has ripple effects, and you'll need to assess them all in order to count the full set of costs and benefits that'll follow. The second "what else?" question asks: *What else* might affect my decision? The answer will help you figure out all the ways in which your costs and benefits—and hence your best choice—might change if other factors change.

Tying It Together

OK, that's it. The economic method, boiled down to four core principles. Think I'm kidding? I'm not. Really. Thinking like an economist is simply a matter of applying the core principles to the world around you. And that's why it is so important that you understand these core principles. As you read the rest of this book, don't be afraid to come back to this chapter for a refresher.

Using the Core Principles in Practice

It's time to 'fess up: I presented the four core principles of economics in the order that is easiest to learn. But when you confront a problem, you need to think through the principles in a different order. Here's the four-step process you should work through:

Step one: First, use the *marginal principle* by breaking "how many" choices down into simpler marginal choices. Ask yourself whether you would be better off doing a bit more of something, or a bit less.

Step two: Then apply the *cost-benefit principle* by assessing the relevant costs and benefits. Since you're analysing a marginal question, this says you need to assess whether the marginal benefit exceeds the marginal cost.

Step three: To evaluate all the relevant costs and benefits, you'll need to apply the *opportunity cost principle* and ask, "Or what?" This ensures that you take full account of what you give up when you make a choice. You should focus on the relevant opportunity costs, not just financial out-of-pocket costs.

Step four: The *interdependence principle* helps you identify how changes in other factors—in your own choices, other people, other markets, and expectations about the future—might lead you to make a different decision.

Want to remember this order? Just think "MCOI," which stands for Marginal, then Cost-benefit, Opportunity cost, and Interdependence. It's a recipe worth remembering, because you'll see it again and again throughout this book, so it is best to learn it now. The rest of your study of economics is really about applying this recipe to a range of interesting social and economic contexts. As you proceed through each chapter in this book, we'll study the decisions that you'll make in your various roles as an economic actor—as a buyer, a seller, a worker, a boss, an entrepreneur, an investor, an importer, or an exporter. The value of our systematic approach is that in each chapter the method will be the same, and it will quickly become familiar: I'll ask you to put yourself in the shoes of that economic actor and apply the core principles of economics so that you can figure out how to make the best decisions possible. With some practice, you'll be able to use the core principles to ensure that you make good decisions in every sphere of your life.

Zarya Maxim Alexandrovich/Shutterstock

Imagine walking in someone else's shoes.

To predict what others will do, put yourself in their shoes. The core principles of economics that we've outlined in this chapter aren't just useful for helping you make good decisions. They can also be used for the equally important task of understanding and even predicting the decisions of others: your customers, competitors, employees, suppliers, and even friends and family.

The key to forecasting how they'll respond is the **someone else's shoes technique.** The idea behind putting yourself in someone else's shoes is to allow yourself to have an empathetic understanding of how someone else views the world. In movies like *Freaky Friday,* mother and daughter have to switch bodies to learn to understand each other, but you can do it by mentally putting yourself in someone else's shoes.

someone else's shoes technique By mentally "trading places" with someone so that you understand their objectives and constraints, you can forecast the decisions they will make.

That's the essence of the someone else's shoes technique. If you want to forecast the decisions that someone else will make, then you should mentally put yourself in their

Now that you're at the end of your first chapter, let me give you a study tip that you can use throughout this book. If you've only got 10 minutes and want to review the key ideas from a chapter, go back, quickly flip through it, and you'll discover that **the bold headings that look like this are a built-in study guide.** If you re-read only those headings, you'll get all the key points. Or if you want my "cheat sheet," turn the page.

shoes, and try to figure out what decision you would make, if you faced their incentives. Putting yourself in someone else's shoes is all about empathy, and it's important to account for that person's preferences and the constraints that they face. It's likely that they are trying to make good decisions. And so these four core principles can help you better understand and predict the decisions that they will make.

Principles in short. And finally, a memory trick. If you find it hard to remember all the detail that you've read in this chapter, relax. It all boils down to asking four questions that are so simple you need just a few words. Always ask:

- One more? (*The marginal principle*)
- Does the benefit beat the cost? (*The cost-benefit principle*)
- Or what? (*The opportunity cost principle*)
- What else? (*The interdependence principle*)

Chapter at a Glance

The Cost-Benefit Principle

Costs and benefits are the incentives that shape decisions. You should evaluate the full set of costs and benefits of any choice you face, and only pursue those whose benefits are at least as large as their costs.

That is, incentives matter!

The difference between benefits and costs is your economic surplus. If your costs and benefits cannot be directly compared, evaluate them in terms of your willingness to pay for them.

Don't let the framing of a choice–that is, how it's described–affect your cost-benefit analysis.

The Opportunity Cost Principle

The true cost of something is the next best alternative you must give up to get it. Your decisions should reflect this opportunity cost, rather than just the out-of-pocket financial costs.

Good decisions focus on opportunity cost, rather than direct financial costs.

Make sure that whenever you consider a decision, you ask, "Or what?" For example: "Should I get an MBA?" Or what? "Or stay in my current job?" The "or" part highlights your opportunity cost.

Sunk costs are not opportunity costs, and so they should be ignored.

The Marginal Principle

Decisions about quantities are best made incrementally.

Break "how many" decisions down into a series of smaller, or marginal, decisions.

For example, instead of asking: "How many workers should I hire?" ask: "Should I hire one more person?" Answering this requires comparing the "extra" or marginal benefits of that extra person with the "extra" or marginal costs incurred.

Following the Rational Rule will maximise your economic surplus: *If something is worth doing, keep doing it until your marginal benefits equal your marginal costs.*

The Interdependence Principle

Your best choice depends on your other choices, the choices others make, developments in other markets, and expectations about the future. When any of these factors change, your best choice might change.

Consider four kinds of interdependence:

1. Dependencies between your own choices
2. Dependencies between people/firms in a market
3. Dependencies between markets
4. Dependencies through time

Apply the core principles, in this order:

The marginal principle	→	The cost-benefit principle	→	The opportunity cost principle	→	The interdependence principle
Address "marginal" questions, instead of "how many" questions		Assess the marginal costs and benefits		Which costs? The opportunity costs		Take account of broader effects of your decisions

To forecast the decisions others make, put yourself in someone else's shoes. If you had their objectives and constraints, what decision would you make?

Key Concepts

cost-benefit principle, 5
economic surplus, 7
framing effect, 10
interdependence principle, 26
marginal benefit, 20
marginal cost, 20
marginal principle, 20
opportunity cost, 12
production possibility frontier, 18
Rational Rule, 21
scarcity, 12
sunk cost, 16
someone else's shoes technique, 29
willingness to pay, 6

Discussion and Review Questions

Learning Objective 1.2 *The Cost-Benefit Principle*

1. Consider the following statement: "Economists always put things into monetary terms; as a result, economics can most appropriately be called the study of money."

   Is this true or false? Briefly explain your reasoning.

2. Use the cost-benefit principle to evaluate the following:

   a. You are about to buy a calculator for $10, and the salesperson tells you that the model you want to buy is on sale for $5 at the store's other branch, which is a 20 minute drive away. Would you make the trip?

   b. You are about to buy a laptop for $2,000 and the salesperson tells you that the model you want to buy is on sale for $1,995 at the store's other branch, which is a 20 minute drive away. Would you make the trip?

   c. Did you make the same choice in both cases? Should you have? Do you think this is how people actually choose?

Learning Objective 1.3 *The Opportunity Cost Principle*

3. During the economic downturn of 2008–2009, the unemployment rate increased to nearly 10% in the United States. At the same time, the price of higher education tuition and the number of higher education enrollees increased. Using the opportunity cost principle, explain why more people would enroll in higher education during this time period even as the price of higher education increased.

4. A friend once remarked that longer movies were a better deal than shorter movies because the ticket price was the same in both cases. Therefore, the longer movie provided more benefit for the same cost as a shorter movie. Using the opportunity cost principle, evaluate your friend's statement.

Learning Objective 1.4 *The Marginal Principle*

5. In 2016, the top-selling pharmaceutical drug in the world was AbbVie's Humira, which is used for the treatment of several common, chronic conditions. The majority of its profits are derived from treatment of the most common diseases, so why does AbbVie develop drugs for rare diseases instead of investing all of its resources towards drugs for common diseases? Use the marginal principle to briefly explain your answer.

Learning Objective 1.5 *The Interdependence Principle*

6. You are a preschool teacher but are considering quitting your job to start a day-care facility of your own. Describe four types of dependencies that will affect your decision, with at least one example for each.

Study Problems

Learning Objective 1.2 *The Cost-Benefit Principle*

1. Ivan has inherited his grandmother's vintage car which he values at $45,000. He decides that he might be willing to sell it so he posts it on carsales.com.au for $55,000. Samantha is interested and willing to pay up to $72,000. Would Ivan and Samantha want to voluntarily engage in trade? How much economic surplus is created for both of them as a result of this exchange? What is the total economic surplus?

2. It's Sunday, and you are considering whether you should go out to dinner at a restaurant with your friend. The meal is expected to cost you $40, and the restaurant charges a 10% surcharge on Sundays. An Uber will cost you $10 to get there. You value the restaurant meal at $20. You enjoy your friend's company and are willing to pay $30 just to spend an evening with her. If you did not go out to the restaurant, you would eat at home using groceries that cost you $16. How much are the benefits and costs associated with going out to dinner with your friend? Should you go out to dinner with your friend?

Learning Objective 1.3 *The Opportunity Cost Principle*

3. It is a beautiful afternoon and you are considering taking a leisurely stroll through the park. There are several other activities you had considered doing instead. The value you would have received from each of the activities is provided in the table below.

Alternative activities	Value
Streaming a movie	$5
Taking a nap	$8
Chatting with your best friend	$13
Reading a new book	$15

What is the opportunity cost to you of taking the stroll through the park?

4. Suppose you have exams in economics and astronomy tomorrow, and you only have four hours left to study. The accompanying table provides the combinations of time spent studying economics and astronomy and your expected exam scores.

Hours spent studying economics	Economics exam score	Hours spent studying astronomy	Astronomy exam score
0	60	0	70
1	80	1	83
2	90	2	87
3	95	3	90
4	98	4	92

a. Draw a production possibilities frontier to illustrate your study options. What is the opportunity cost, in terms of your marks, of studying one extra hour for economics or one extra hour for astronomy?

b. If your goal is to maximise your combined exam scores, how many hours should you spend studying each subject?

c. Your laptop dies and refuses to start up. All your notes and class materials are saved on its hard drive. How do your production possibilities change? Illustrate in your graph from part (a).

5. Your niece is deciding whether or not to open a lemonade stand. She expects to sell 20 cups of lemonade for $1 per cup. She has already made a sign that cost her $10 and will have $15 worth of additional costs for cups and lemonade mix if she decides to open the stand. If your niece decides to open the lemonade stand, how much profit will she earn? Should she open the lemonade stand? What kind of cost is the $10 spent on the lemonade stand sign?

Learning Objective 1.4 *The Marginal Principle*

6. Aliyah is preparing to expand her IT consulting company. The current market rate for IT professionals is $78,000 per year. Each employee she hires will also require a computer and equipment that costs $6,000 per employee annually. Hiring more employees means that Aliyah can provide consulting services to more clients each year. Each client Aliyah has will pay her $10,000 per year.

The number of clients Aliyah can take on depends on the number of workers she hires as shown in the accompanying table. What is the marginal cost and marginal benefit of hiring each worker? Using the Rational Rule to maximise her economic surplus, how many workers should Aliyah hire?

Number of workers	Clients per year
0	0
1	11
2	20
3	27
4	32

7. Neal likes coffee. At the local coffee shop, the price of a cup of coffee is $3.50. Neal's total benefits from drinking coffee is provided in the accompanying table. What is Neal's marginal benefit of consuming each cup of coffee? How many cups should he consume each day?

Quantity of coffee	Total benefits
1	$8
2	$14
3	$18
4	$20
5	$21

Learning Objective 1.5 *The Interdependence Principle*

8. Consider your decision to read this textbook on economics. Identify which of the four core principles of economics is most relevant for the following aspects of that decision.

a. Reading this textbook will help establish a solid foundation for understanding concepts you will learn in more advanced economics courses.

b. Reading this textbook will require time and effort, but doing so will help you improve your mark in this course.

c. The time you will spend reading this textbook could instead be used to study for your chemistry exam.

d. Each extra page that you read and each practice problem that you complete will help you increase your understanding of the material.

9. For each of the following, indicate how you might apply the four core principles of economics.

a. You are considering whether you should vote in the next election.

b. You watch a beautiful sunset from the back porch of your home.

c. Should you major in economics or philosophy?

d. Should you and your spouse purchase a second vehicle?

Demand and Consumer Choice

CHAPTER 2

Waring Abbott/Michael Ochs Archives/Getty Images

Some decisions are sweeter than others.

Scientists have identified a part of the brain that fires up every time you evaluate a possible buying decision. Think about how busy that part of your brain must be. Every time you look at a menu, a price tag, or an advertisement, it fires up, asking: Is this a good deal? Should I buy? If so, how many? Sometimes the answer is no, you shouldn't buy. Sometimes the answer is yes, and you'll make a purchase—perhaps a $2 cookie. And sometimes you'll make a life-changing decision such as choosing to buy a car or a house. But collectively, even the small decisions add up to a big deal—they're a large chunk of the millions of dollars you will probably spend over your lifetime.

In this chapter, we'll develop a deeper understanding of demand—the decisions that we make as buyers. We'll start by studying individual demand, zooming in and focusing on the decisions that you make as an individual consumer trying to decide how much of a product to buy. We'll apply the core principles of economics that we developed in Chapter 1 to guide you towards making better buying decisions.

Next we'll pan back and analyse market demand, which managers use to project how much of a product the market as a whole will buy at each price. Because total market-wide demand is simply the sum of the individual demand choices made by millions of buyers, you'll find that your deeper understanding of individual demand will help you better understand market demand. We'll then explore how changing market conditions shift market demand.

By the end of this chapter, you'll understand the key factors that drive the millions of purchasing decisions that underpin much of our economy. Let's get started.

Chapter Objective

Understand people's buying, or demand, decisions.

2.1 Individual Demand: What You Want, at Each Price

Discover the shape of your individual demand curve.

2.2 Your Decisions and Your Demand Curve

Apply the core principles of economics to make good demand decisions.

2.3 Market Demand: What the Market Wants

Add up individual demand to discover market demand.

2.4 What Shifts Demand Curves?

Understand what factors shift demand curves.

2.5 Shifts versus Movements Along Demand Curves

Distinguish between movements along a demand curve and shifts in demand curves.

2.1 Individual Demand: What You Want, at Each Price

Learning Objective *Discover the shape of your individual demand curve.*

It's Monday morning, and Darren is driving to the office. He notices his petrol tank is nearly empty. The nearby service station typically offers the best prices, and right now, its sign says $1.40 per litre. So Darren faces a decision: How much petrol should he buy?

You face decisions like this every day. At your favorite clothing store, jeans might be on sale, and you have to decide whether to buy another pair or make do with your existing jeans. On your way to class, you probably walked past a coffee shop and had to decide whether to buy a coffee or save your money for other uses. Every time you see a price tag, you face the same question: At this price, what quantity should you buy?

Let's dig deeper into Darren's purchases of petrol. Darren was recently surveyed about his petrol-buying habits and Figure 1 shows both the survey form and Darren's responses (in purple).

Figure 1 | **A Survey of an Individual's Petrol Demand**

Name: *Darren*

We are interested in understanding next year's demand for petrol.
What quantity of petrol do you expect to purchase per week next year:

If the price is $1.80 per litre?	*5 litres*
If the price is $1.60 per litre?	*10 litres*
If the price is $1.40 per litre?	*15 litres*
If the price is $1.20 per litre?	*25 litres*
If the price is $1.00 per litre?	*35 litres*

Each row of Figure 1 asks Darren how much petrol on average he would buy per week, at different prices. The first row shows that when the price of petrol is $1.80 per litre, he is willing to buy only 5 litres of petrol per week, on average. The last row shows that when the price is as low as $1.00 per litre, he plans to buy 35 litres per week. This isn't meant too literally: Darren doesn't just top up his car in 5 litre increments, rather, he's thinking about how the petrol price changes how much he'll drive, and hence how often he'll need to fill his tank. His answers reflect the amount of petrol he thinks he'll buy over the course of the year, averaged out per week.

An Individual Demand Curve

individual demand curve A graph, plotting the quantity of an item that someone plans to buy, at each price.

You know the old saying: "A picture is worth a thousand words"? Well, this is one of those cases. You can plot Darren's answers in the table above so that you turn those numbers into a picture that summarises his buying plans. This graph is called his **individual demand curve,** and it plots the quantity that he plans to buy at each price. This chapter will use graphs to understand and summarise demand. If your graphing skills are a bit rusty, don't worry; we'll proceed slowly. (You may also find it useful to read the Graphing Review.)

The line in Figure 2 illustrates Darren's individual demand curve for petrol. Each dot corresponds with one of Darren's responses to the petrol survey shown in Figure 1. For instance, Darren said that if the price of petrol is $1.80 per litre, he plans to buy 5 litres per week. This point is plotted in the top left of Figure 2; simply look across from the price of $1.80 (on the vertical axis) to the quantity of 5 litres of petrol (on the horizontal axis), and you can see this first response, graphed as the first point. Likewise, Darren said that if the price of petrol is $1.60 per litre, he plans to buy 10 litres of petrol per week, and this is the next point plotted on Figure 2. You can see each of his responses plotted as a point in Figure 2.

There are also many different prices that Darren wasn't asked about. For instance, he wasn't asked how he would respond to a petrol price of $1.50. A straight line between the $1.40 and $1.60 dots provides a reasonable estimate, suggesting that he would buy 12.5 litres. This line connecting the dots is Darren's individual demand curve, showing the quantity he will demand at each price.

You can remember what an individual demand curve is just by analysing the words. "Individual" means we are referring to one person, "demand" means it's about buying decisions, and "curve" means we are graphing it (and sometimes these curves are straight lines). That's it: Your individual demand curve is a graph summarising your buying plans, and how they vary with the price.

Figure 2 | Graphing an Individual Demand Curve

Darren's Individual Demand Curve

How much petrol is he willing to buy at each price?

(A) **Price** is on the vertical axis, and **quantity demanded** is on the horizontal axis.

(B) When the price is **$1.80 per litre**, Darren will purchase just **5 litres** of petrol per week. An individual demand curve also illustrates how the quantity demanded changes as the price changes. If the price falls to **$1.60 per litre**, the quantity he demands will rise to **10 litres** per week. At a price of **$1.40**, he will buy **15 litres**, and so on.

(C) The **individual demand curve** shows the quantity of petrol per week that Darren is willing to buy, at each price. The individual demand curve is downward sloping: The lower the price, the higher the quantity demanded.

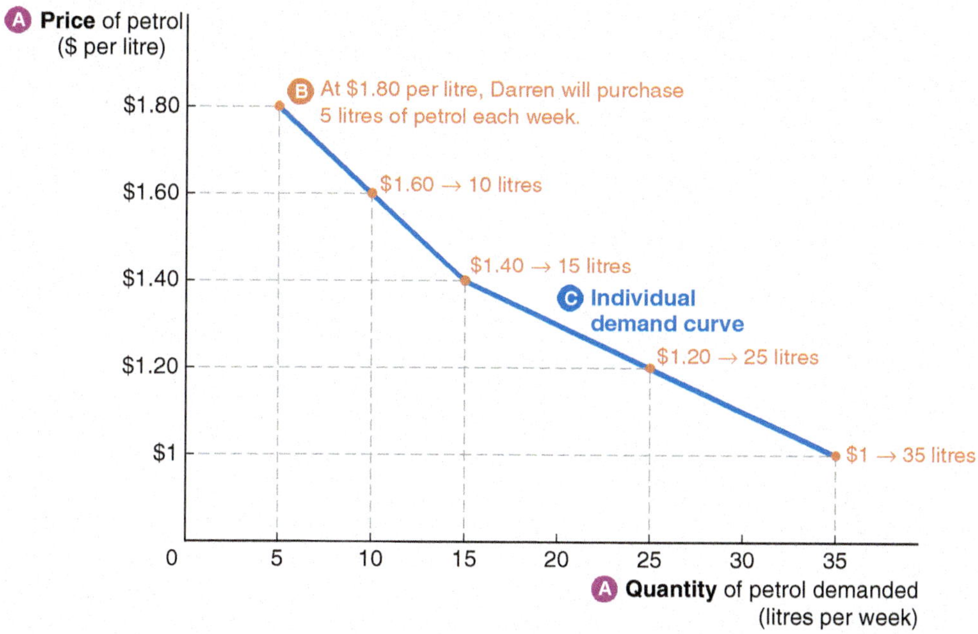

Graphing conventions. Be careful to always use the same conventions when graphing demand curves. Price always goes on the vertical axis, and the quantity demanded goes on the horizontal axis. (I remember this as "P's before Q's," so that as I look from left to right, or from top to bottom, I label P's—the price—before labeling Q's—the quantity.) Don't forget to label the units on both axes. In this case, the price of petrol is measured in dollars per litre. The quantity of petrol demanded is measured in litres per week.

Some students ask why price goes on the vertical axis and quantity goes on the horizontal axis. There's no good answer—it's because economists have graphed demand curves in this way for so long that it's now a convention that everyone follows. By following these established conventions, we can all speak the same, consistent language.

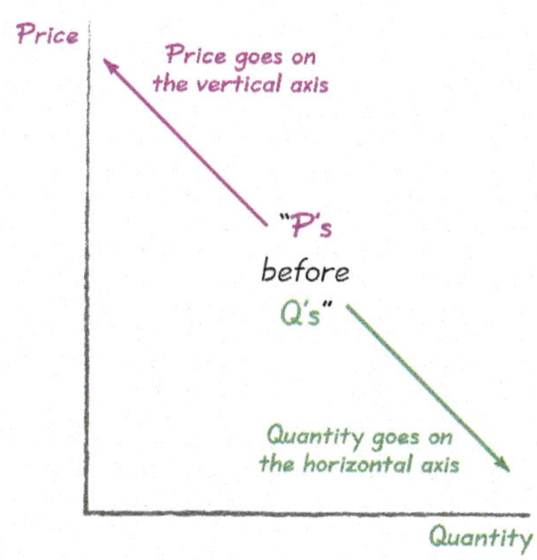

An individual demand curve holds other things constant. The demand curve shown in Figure 2 plots Darren's buying plans, given current economic conditions. But if something important were to change—say, if he lost his job—then his buying plans would change, and so his individual demand curve would change, too. In order to acknowledge this, economists say that a particular demand curve is graphed, **"holding other things constant."** We know that things other than price can influence your demand—your demand for petrol might change if you bought a more fuel-efficient car—and the *interdependence principle* reminds us not to forget these connections! But first, we want to consider what happens when the price—and only the price—changes. So when we "hold other things constant," we're really just pushing aside changes in those other factors for now, so that we can focus on understanding how demand is affected by the price.

"holding other things constant" A commonly used qualifier noting your conclusions may change if some factor that you haven't analysed changes. (In Latin, it's *ceteris paribus*.)

The individual demand curve is downward-sloping. Notice that Darren's individual demand curve is downward-sloping: It starts high on the left, and as you move to the right, it heads downward. Downward-sloping demand means that as the price gets lower, the quantity demanded gets larger. When petrol costs less, people buy more of it. Or you can think about it the other way around: If petrol costs more, people buy less of it.

Remember: Your individual demand curve is a graph summarising your buying plans, and how they vary with the price.

Discover your individual demand curve. Whenever you see a price tag and pause to decide whether to make a purchase and, if so, how many items to buy, you are considering the quantity you will demand at that price. If you graphed these thoughts, you would plot your individual demand curve. Let's delve into this idea in a bit more detail, and explore your individual demand curve for jeans.

Do the Economics

Executives at Levi's want to understand their customers better. So they've asked their marketing team to figure out the individual demand curve for jeans of customers like you.

Marketing executives often run surveys to learn about demand for their product, and the Levi's jeans survey, in Panel A of Figure 3, is an example. Go ahead and take the survey. Next, turn to Panel B below and plot your responses. When you're done, you've just discovered your individual demand curve for jeans.

Figure 3 | **Discover Your Individual Demand Curve**

Panel A:

Levi's is interested in understanding how many pairs of jeans you will buy over the next five years. Holding other things constant, how many pairs of jeans do you expect to purchase:

Price of jeans ($ per pair)	Quantity of jeans
If jeans cost $150?	
If jeans cost $125?	
If jeans cost $100?	
If jeans cost $75?	
If jeans cost $50?	
If jeans cost $25?	

Panel B: Your Individual Demand Curve

How many pairs of jeans do you expect to purchase at each price?

To graph your individual demand curve, plot the data from your responses to the Levi's jeans survey.

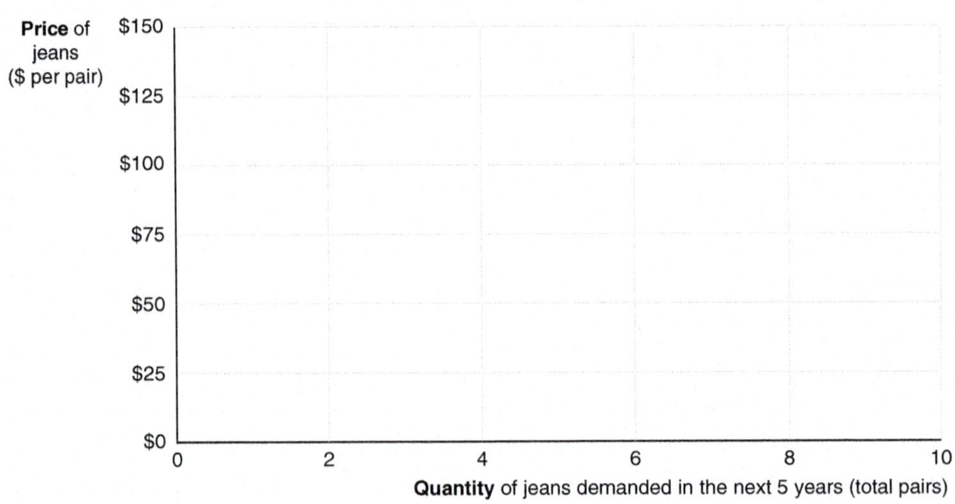

Even though I haven't seen your graph, I'm willing to bet that you just plotted a downward-sloping individual demand curve! ■

The Law of Demand

Okay, so we've figured out that your individual demand curve for jeans is downward-sloping. And Darren's individual demand curve for petrol was also downward-sloping. If we repeat the same exercise for other goods, you'll quickly discover that your individual demand curve for petrol, ice cream, concert tickets—or just about anything else—is also downward-sloping.

Economists have asked similar questions about thousands of goods over hundreds of years, and we keep seeing the same pattern: The quantity demanded is higher when the price is lower. You've probably seen the same pattern in your daily life: If something is cheaper, you buy more of it. And if it's more expensive, you buy less of it (holding other things—like quality!—constant). This is such a pervasive pattern that economists call the tendency for the quantity demanded to be higher when the price is lower the **law of demand.**

law of demand The tendency for quantity demanded to be higher when the price is lower.

That's it—we've figured out your individual demand curve. It's simply a graph that describes the quantity you will demand at each price. It's useful, because it allows businesses to forecast how customers like you will respond to different prices. And since the law of demand suggests that you'll demand a larger quantity when the price is low, your demand curve is downward-sloping.

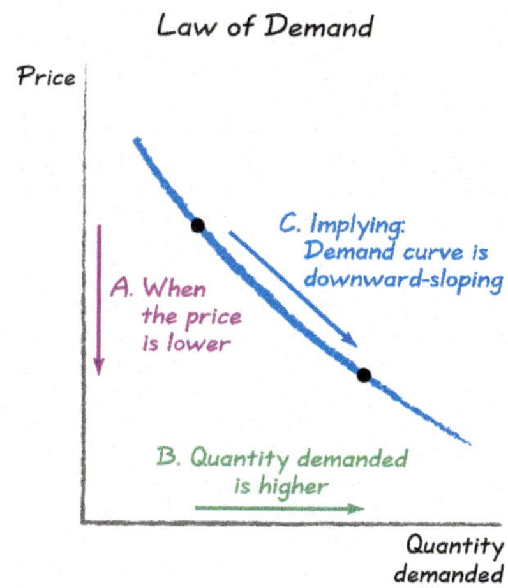

Now that you know how to construct your individual demand curve, let's explore how you can apply the core principles of economics to make better demand decisions.

2.2 Your Decisions and Your Demand Curve

Learning Objective *Apply the core principles of economics to make good demand decisions.*

So far, we've focused on the actual buying decisions that people make. Let's turn to the harder question: What are the best buying choices you can make? The core principles of economics can provide useful guidance. As we go through each principle, you'll get a deeper sense of the various factors that shape individual demand curves.

Choosing the Best Quantity to Buy

Let's start by exploring what's behind Darren's individual demand curve. In a follow-up interview, he provided some insight into his preferences. Darren can only buy petrol in 5L pre-filled cans from the petrol station. Darren starts by thinking about all of the possible uses he has for a can of petrol and prioritises them. He does this by thinking about the benefits he gets from each alternative use. Because dollars is the measuring stick by which we assess benefits, he puts a dollar value on these benefits that summarises how much he's willing to pay for each possible use of a can of petrol. Figure 4 gives his explanations for how he'll use each can of petrol and the benefit each use has for him.

Focus on your marginal benefits. Each row shows one of Darren's uses for each additional can of petrol. He's listed them in order of his priority—from the uses that deliver the largest benefit to him to those that deliver the least benefit. When he thinks about these benefits, he's not just thinking about the dollars involved. He's thinking about his benefits broadly, such as the benefits of saving time, of seeing his parents, or of taking a relaxing drive to unwind. And in each case, he's comparing them to his next best alternative.

Remember: The additional benefit you get from buying one additional item is called its *marginal benefit.*

Darren is thinking about the additional benefit of one more can of petrol—that is, the *marginal benefit.* When Darren thinks about the different ways he can use an extra can of petrol, he's really thinking about the marginal benefit he gets from each can of petrol, and this is shown in the final column of Figure 4, "Marginal benefit."

Figure 4 | Darren's Uses for Petrol

Priority	Darren's thoughts	Marginal benefit
1 (Highest Priority)	If I buy only one can of petrol per week, I'll use it to do my weekly shopping at the Coles in the next suburb over. The alternative is to shop at my local supermarket, which is more expensive. Going to Coles instead saves me $9 each week.	$9.00
2	If I buy a second can of petrol, I'll also drive to work every day. I prefer this to catching the bus. The time and money saved add up to a $8 benefit.	$8.00
3	A third can of petrol allows me to visit my parents more often. I could call them instead, but I prefer seeing them. There's no financial benefit to this, but there's a benefit nonetheless, because I love my parents. Putting a number on this is hard, but I'm willing to pay up to $7 for the can of petrol required for this visit.	$7.00
4	With a fourth can of petrol, I can drive to hang out with my friends during the weekend. I could get a ride instead, since all of my friends live nearby, but it's nice to have the flexibility that driving gives me. I get about $6.50 in benefit from this.	$6.50
5	A fifth can allows me to drive to the gym twice a week. But I could jog there instead, which is a good warm-up. Saving time is useful, but given that I have to warm up anyway, the benefit of driving to the gym is worth only $6.	$6.00
6	If I buy a sixth can of petrol, I'll use it to do my weekly errands. But I don't really mind walking around town to do these errands. The benefit of driving to do errands is only $5.50.	$5.50
7 (Lowest Priority)	If I buy a seventh can, I'll use it to take a scenic drive when I need some quiet time. But I'm nearly as happy taking quiet time at home, so the benefit of this option is pretty low. Perhaps this can yields a benefit as small as $5.	$5.00

Do the Economics

Let's return to Darren as he was driving towards the petrol station. He noticed that petrol is selling for $1.40 per litre (well, actually for 139.9c per litre) and he's trying to decide how much to buy. Remember that Darren can only buy petrol in 5 litre cans, so at $1.40 per litre, each can costs $7. What is your advice?

paoarqi/Stock Editorial/Getty Images

OK, so petrol is never *exactly* $1.40 per litre.

- *Should he buy a first can of petrol?*

  Yes. According to Figure 4, Darren will use this can to shop at Coles, which yields him a marginal benefit of $9, which is greater than the $7 it will cost him.

- *OK, so continue: Should he buy a second can of petrol at $7? (Hint: You should ask: What are the benefits? What will this cost?)*

  The second can of petrol yields a $8 marginal benefit, which is greater than the marginal cost of $7. Sounds like a good deal.

- *And should he buy a third can?*

  The third can is a close call. It yields $7 of marginal benefits, which is slightly more than the marginal cost (which is actually $6.995). But the marginal benefit exceeds the marginal cost, so Darren should buy this third can.

- *What about a fourth can?*

  The fourth can yields a $6.50 marginal benefit, and it's not worth spending $7 to get a $6.50 marginal benefit.

- *And a fifth? A sixth?*

  Similar logic suggests that Darren shouldn't buy a fifth or sixth can either: In each case they yield a marginal benefit less than the $7 marginal cost of a can of petrol.

- *Bottom line: What quantity of petrol should he buy at 139.9c per litre?*

  Darren should buy 3 cans, or equivalently, 15 litres of petrol.

Notice that your advice is based solely on comparing the price of a can of petrol with the *marginal benefit* that Darren gets from it. In fact, whenever you need to figure out your demand for any good, you should follow the same logic, comparing the price with your marginal benefit. This is why economists say that understanding demand is all about understanding marginal benefits. ■

Apply the core principles to make good buying decisions. Darren's approach to buying petrol seems pretty sensible. In fact, he's implicitly relying on the core principles of economics. You'll want to apply the same logic when you're making your own demand decisions, whether you're deciding how many pairs of jeans to purchase, how many shares of Google to invest in, or how many workers to hire. Let's see how.

The *marginal principle* says that you should break "how many" questions into a series of smaller marginal choices. Darren's clearly thinking this way, considering each additional, or marginal, can of petrol separately, and how he would use it. It means that he's ready to analyse the simpler question of whether to buy just one more can of petrol. And indeed, we just evaluated whether to buy a first, then a second, then a third and a fourth can of petrol when the price was $1.40.

For each of these marginal decisions, Darren's best choice depends on the *cost-benefit principle*, which says: Yes, he should buy that additional can of petrol if its benefit exceeds the cost. The cost of an additional can of petrol is simply its price. The benefit of an additional can is called its marginal benefit.

And notice that when Darren evaluates his marginal benefits, he applies the *opportunity cost principle*, asking: "Or what?" He doesn't just ask about the benefits of driving to Coles; he compares it to the next best alternative, which is doing his shopping nearby. It's only by comparing driving to Coles with the next best alternative that he figures out that the marginal benefit of the first can of petrol is $9. He does something similar in each row of Figure 4. Here's a chance to test yourself: Go back and underline the "or what?"—the next best alternative that he identifies on each row. (Answer: It's the second sentence of each row.)

The Rational Rule for Buyers

Working systematically through the core principles—as shown in Figure 5—leads to the conclusion that Darren should keep buying additional cans of petrol as long as the marginal benefit is greater than (or equal to) the price.

Figure 5 | **Rational Rule for Buyers**

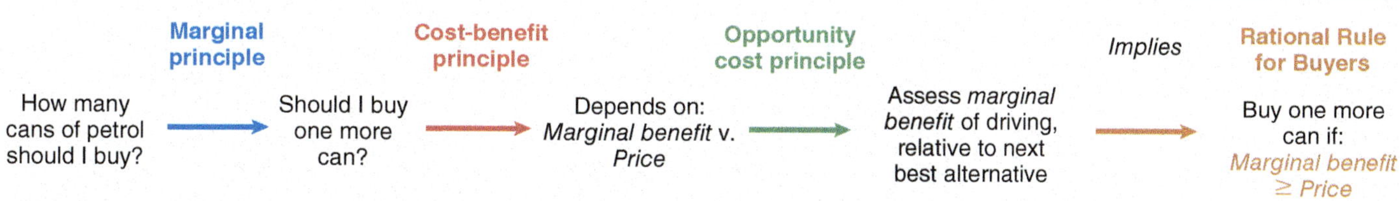

We've uncovered a pretty powerful rule, which you can apply to *any* buying decision:

The Rational Rule for Buyers: *Buy more of an item if the marginal benefit of one more is greater than (or equal to) the price.*

The Rational Rule for Buyers Buy more of an item if the marginal benefit of one more is greater than (or equal to) the price.

The *Rational Rule for Buyers* puts together the advice from three of the four core principles in one sentence. You should think at the margin, comparing the marginal benefit of one more item with the marginal cost (in this case, the price), and evaluate these costs and benefits relative to your next best alternative. You can apply this rule to your real-world buying decisions. For instance, it says to Darren: You should buy another can of petrol if it yields a marginal benefit greater than or equal to its price.

You might be wondering what role the *interdependence principle* plays in all this. It's already there in Darren's reasoning: His decisions depend on the availability of the bus, his desire to go to the gym, and even his love for his parents! For now, we're focusing only on the effects of different prices, holding these other things constant. But when we return to the *interdependence principle* later in this chapter, we'll see that if these other things were to change, so would his plans.

Follow the Rational Rule for Buyers to maximise your economic surplus. The *Rational Rule for Buyers* is good advice. Why? If buying one more can of petrol yields marginal benefits for Darren that exceed the price he pays, then he is better off. That is, he'll enjoy greater economic surplus—which is the difference between his total benefits and total costs—because this purchase will boost his total benefits by more than it boosts his total costs. And that's the reason why you'll want to follow this rule in your own life.

In fact, you want to take *every* opportunity to make those purchases that will make you better off, and take a pass on any purchases that will make you worse off. If you relentlessly follow the *Rational Rule for Buyers* and buy more petrol (and more food and more clothes and so on) for as long as the marginal benefits are at least as large as the price, then by taking every opportunity to boost your economic surplus, you'll succeed at maximising your economic surplus.

> To maximise your economic surplus, keep applying the Rational Rule for Buyers, continuing to buy until:
>
> Price = Marginal benefit

(You might wonder why this rule says its marginal benefit is *exactly equal* to the price. Truth is, this decision doesn't make a difference, because buying that last item will make you neither better off nor worse off. Still, I say you should continue to buy up to, *and including*, the point when marginal benefit equals price, because it'll make the rest of your analysis a bit simpler.)

Keep buying until price equals marginal benefit. If you follow the *Rational Rule for Buyers*, you'll keep buying more petrol until the marginal benefit of the last can you buy is *equal* to the price. Why? The rule suggests you keep buying cans of petrol as long as the marginal benefit of each can is at least as high as the price. Consequently, you will stop buying more petrol just before the marginal benefit of the next can falls below the price—which occurs when the *marginal benefit equals price.*

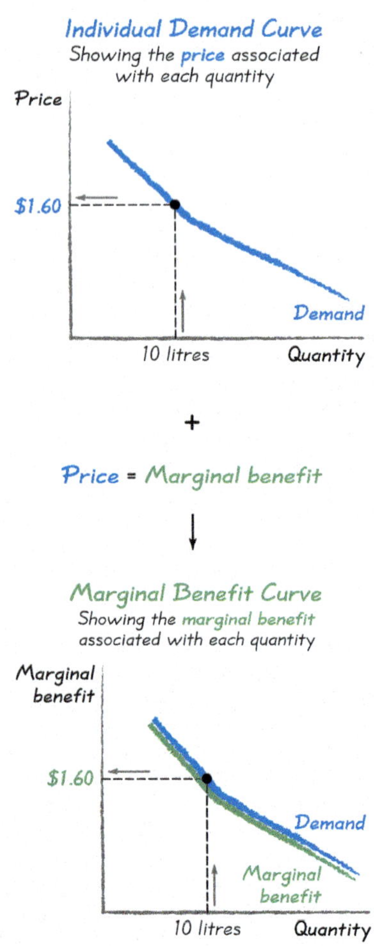

You might recognise this insight. Recall the *Rational Rule* from Chapter 1, which said: "If something is worth doing, keep doing it until your marginal benefits equal your marginal costs." We're simply adapting this rule to when you're buying stuff, and so the marginal cost of an extra can of petrol or pair of jeans is simply the price. As such, adapting the *Rational Rule* to your role as a buyer says you should keep buying until:

Price = Marginal benefit

Your demand curve is also your marginal benefit curve. Hopefully you can now see why economists say that understanding demand requires remembering just one phrase: *Price equals marginal benefit.*

This reveals a new perspective for thinking about demand: Your demand curve is also your marginal benefit curve. Think about it: Your demand curve illustrates the *price* at which you will buy each quantity of petrol. If you keep buying until *price equals marginal benefit,* then the same curve illustrates the *marginal benefit* of each can of petrol.

Your demand curve reveals your marginal benefits. This yields an important insight for managers. It's likely that you'll want to know how much your customers benefit from your products. You could commission an expensive survey to find out. But there's a cheaper way to do this: Your customers' demand curves are also their marginal benefit curves, and so you can also learn about their marginal benefits by just observing their buying patterns. For instance, if Darren buys two cans of petrol when the price is $8 per can, then you can infer that the marginal benefit to Darren of that second can is $8.

Let's summarise. Demand is all about marginal benefits. Indeed, your demand curve *is* your marginal benefit curve. Consequently, understanding demand is really about understanding marginal benefits.

Diminishing marginal benefit explains why your demand curve is downward-sloping. Economists have studied the marginal benefits of many different items, and discovered a general tendency towards **diminishing marginal benefit.** That is, the marginal benefit of each additional item is smaller than the marginal benefit of the previous item.

diminishing marginal benefit Each additional item yields a smaller marginal benefit than the previous item.

Let's get delicious about this, and focus on ice cream. (Yum!) One or two scoops are scrumptious. A third scoop still tastes pretty good. By the fourth, you're getting tired of all that sugar. And a fifth scoop will make you feel sick. (Believe me.) As you eat more ice cream, the marginal benefit of another scoop keeps getting smaller.

And a similar pattern follows for other goods. Take Darren's demand for petrol. He planned to use his first can of petrol for his high marginal benefit activities (shopping), his second can would go to a slightly lower benefit activity (driving to work), and each successive can is used for a lower priority trip. As a result, each extra can yields a successively lower marginal benefit.

If you think about most of the things you buy in a year, I bet you'll agree that you get diminishing marginal benefits from not just extra scoops of ice cream, or litres of petrol, but also pairs of jeans, concert tickets, pairs of headphones, and just about everything you buy. (If you want to point out that there are exceptions to this rule—for instance, your second shoe yields a larger marginal benefit than your first shoe—I'll agree, as long as you agree that these exceptions are rare.)

Diminishing marginal benefits is an important phenomenon because it means that each extra purchase yields a lower marginal benefit, and hence your marginal benefit curve is downward-sloping. And since your marginal benefit curve is also your demand curve, this means that your demand curve is downward-sloping. That is, if extra scoops of ice cream, cans of petrol, or pairs of jeans yield a lower marginal benefit, you'll only buy them if the price is lower. And that's why your individual demand curve is downward-sloping.

Recap: Individual demand reflects marginal benefits. We've covered a lot of ground, so let's take a breather and recap. So far, we've been focused on individual demand—the buying decisions that you as an individual will make. We began with the individual demand curve, which summarises the quantity you demand at each price.

We then turned to the more difficult question: What are the best buying choices you can make? This led us to the *Rational Rule for Buyers*, which says to keep buying more of an item as long as the marginal benefit of one more is greater than (or equal to) its price. This process helps us see why people, like Darren, are willing to pay less for each additional item, like each additional can of petrol, since the marginal benefit from each additional item is declining. As a result, we saw that individual demand curves are downward-sloping.

See the Connections

Follow the *Rational Rule for Buyers* → *Price = Marginal benefit* (The Rational Rule, applied to buyers) → Your demand curve is your marginal benefit curve → Your demand curve is downward-sloping because of diminishing marginal benefits

How Realistic Is This Theory of Demand?

By this point you might be thinking: *Is this realistic? Does anyone really act this way?* And maybe it is a bit unrealistic to say that when you're shopping, you're actually thinking deeply about your marginal benefits. Good point. But these are still important ideas, for two reasons.

Thinking through the core principles provides useful advice and helpful forecasts. First, the *Rational Rule for Buyers* provides useful advice to *you*. As you learn to apply this rule to your everyday buying decisions, you'll find yourself making better decisions.

Second, these rules will often provide a useful way for you to understand, and even predict, how other people will act. This is the "someone else's shoes" technique discussed in Chapter 1. If you want to know how someone else will act, put yourself in their shoes and ask: What would you do if you were in their shoes? Presumably, you would try to make the best decisions possible, so you would try to follow the *Rational Rule for Buyers*. In fact, store owners have long known that diminishing marginal benefits is an important factor in determining sales—that is one reason you often see specials like: "Buy one, get the second half-price."

As buyers experiment, they may come to act as if they follow the core principles. Still, it's likely that people don't act *exactly* as this theory suggests, at least not right away. But people generally do (and should!) buy more of those goods with higher marginal benefits and lower prices. And even though most people aren't thinking through the exact calculations that we've outlined, they may follow a different process to the same outcome.

People move closer and closer to making their very best decisions as they gain more experience. Perhaps you got overexcited when you visited Costco for the first time and bought a 5-litre tub of mayonnaise, only to see it spoil. But next time you hit the store you'll make savvier choices. Through the process of experimenting—buying different goods and different amounts of goods—people find out what works best for them. As a result, people will often end up making choices *as if* they made the calculations that our theories predict they should make. This is going to be a really useful insight, as we now turn to analysing how buyers—as a group—combine to make up market demand.

2.3 Market Demand: What the Market Wants

Learning Objective *Add up individual demand to discover market demand.*

We've focused so far on the buying decisions of individuals. Now it's time to pan back and take a broad view, analysing *market demand*—the purchasing decisions of all buyers taken as a whole. As a manager, you'll find this broad view useful because it's total market demand that tells you how much business is up for grabs. And of course, it's not just businesses that need to know market demand: Nonprofits seeking donations, universities seeking applicants, and YouTubers seeking subscribers all benefit from being able to estimate market demand for what they're selling. In each case, you're interested in assessing the total quantity demanded—across all people—at each price. The **market demand curve** provides exactly this information: It plots the total quantity of a good demanded by the market (that is, across all potential buyers), at each price.

market demand curve A graph plotting the total quantity of an item demanded by the entire market, at each price.

From Individual Demand to Market Demand

Let's explore how real-world managers estimate the market demand curve for their products. As we'll see, individual demand curves are the building blocks of market demand.

Market demand is the sum of the quantity demanded by each person. Lets go back to doing things in terms of litres now rather than 5L cans. For each price per litre, the market demand curve illustrates the total quantity demanded by the market. This means you'll need to figure out the total quantity demanded when the price is \$1, then \$1.20, then \$1.40, and so on. At each specific price, the total quantity of petrol demanded is simply the sum of the quantity that each potential consumer will demand at that price.

Managers sometimes use survey data to figure out their market demand curves. One way to get this information is to survey your potential customers. In fact, there's a simple four-step process that many managers follow to estimate the market demand curve for their products.

Step one: Survey your customers, asking each person the quantity they will buy at each price. When Darren was surveyed about his petrol-purchasing behaviour (in Figure 1), it was as part of a broader survey that was sent to a representative sample of 200 potential customers, asking each of them about the quantity of petrol they plan to buy at each price. Their responses are shown in Panel A, on the left of Figure 6, with each person's response shown in a different column. I've only shown you the responses of the first two people to respond—Darren and Brooklyn—but in the full spreadsheet, there are another 198 columns.

Figure 6 From Individual Demand to Total Market Demand

Panel A: Individual Demand | **Panel B: Total Market Demand**

Step 1: Run a survey								**Step 2**	**Step 3**	**Projection**
Price ($ per litre)	Darren's demand		Brooklyn's demand		… 198 other people …			Total demand across 200 people	Scale up to represent 20 million people	Total market demand
$1	35	+	20	+	…	=		20,000 litres	× 100,000	= 2.0 billion litres
$1.20	25	+	15	+	…	=		18,000 litres	× 100,000	= 1.8 billion litres
$1.40	15	+	10	+	…	=		16,000 litres	× 100,000	= 1.6 billion litres
$1.60	10	+	5	+	…	=		14,000 litres	× 100,000	= 1.4 billion litres
$1.80	5	+	0	+	…	=		12,000 litres	× 100,000	= 1.2 billion litres

Step two: For each price, add up the total quantity demanded by your customers. *For each price*, you should add up the quantity demanded by each person in the survey. The top row shows that when the price is $1 per litre, Darren demands 35 litres, Brooklyn demands 20 litres, and you also need to add up the quantities demanded by each of the other 198 potential customers who were surveyed. This is calculated on the full spreadsheet, and it adds up to 20,000 litres.

I repeated these calculations for each price from $1 to $1.80—once for each row—and the results are shown in the first column of Panel B, presented on the right of Figure 5. This is where you can see that at a price of $1 per litre, the survey respondents would collectively buy 20,000 litres of petrol, and at $1.20 per litre, this would fall to 18,000 litres.

To add up demand, you add the quantity demanded by each individual at each price (and not the price each individual pays at each quantity).

Step three: Scale up the quantities demanded by the survey respondents so that they represent the whole market. If the total market for petrol consisted of just the 200 people we surveyed, then these numbers would represent the market demand. But in reality, there are around 20 million potential customers in Australia. The idea of market research is that our survey of 200 people is intended to be representative of those 20 million potential customers. This means that the total quantity demanded by the entire population will be one hundred thousand times larger than the total quantity demanded by the 200 survey respondents. Thus, you need to scale up the quantities so that they represent the whole market. (This works well if the 200 people in your survey are representative of the broader population of 20 million Australians.)

In practice, this means that when the price of petrol is $1 per litre, and the 200 people surveyed collectively say that they would buy a total of 20,000 litres of petrol, you can project that the entire market of 20 million consumers would buy 2 billion litres of petrol (that is, 2000 million) per week. Consequently, the projected market demand at each price, shown in the final column of Figure 6, is one hundred thousand times the total quantity demanded by our survey respondents.

The market demand curve plots the total quantity demanded by the market at each price. Okay, now that we've figured out the total quantity demanded by the market, at each price, all that remains is to draw the market demand curve.

Step four: Plot the total quantity demanded by the market at each price, yielding the market demand curve. The graphing conventions for *market* demand curves are the same as when graphing *individual* demand curves: Price is on the vertical axis, and quantity on the horizontal axis. For each price listed in the first column in Figure 6, you plot the corresponding total quantity demanded by the market, which is listed in the last column. Each row in the table is represented by a purple dot in Figure 7. We then connect these dots to arrive at our estimate of the market demand curve for petrol in Australia. In fact, this figure is quite similar to the statistical estimates of demand curves that major petrol executives actually rely on.

Figure 7 | Estimating Market Demand

To calculate the market demand curve for all of Australia:

Step 1: Survey a representative sample of the market, asking each person **the quantity they will buy at each price**. (Shown in Figure 6.)

Step 2: For each price, add up the **total quantity demanded by the people surveyed**.

Step 3: To make projections about the **total quantity demanded by the entire market**, scale up the quantities demanded by the survey respondents so that they represent the whole market. We have 200 survey respondents representing 20 million consumers, and so we project that the quantity demanded by the entire population will be **one hundred thousand times larger**.

Step 4: Plot the **total quantity demanded by the entire market** at each price to get the **market demand curve**.

1 Price ($ per litre)	2 Total quantity demanded by 200 survey respondents (litres per week)	3 Projection: Total market demand by 20 million consumers (litres per week)
$1.80	12,000	× 100,000 = 1.2 billion
$1.60	14,000	× 100,000 = 1.4 billion
$1.40	16,000	× 100,000 = 1.6 billion
$1.20	18,000	× 100,000 = 1.8 billion
$1	20,000	× 100,000 = 2.0 billion

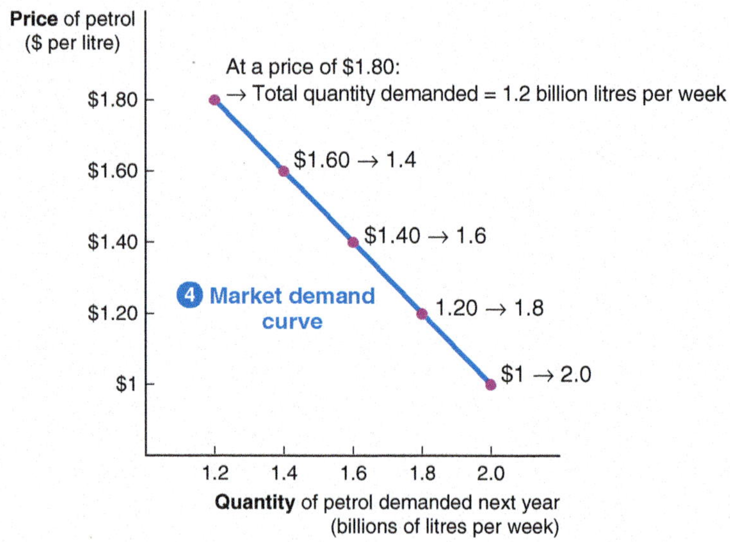

The Market Demand Curve Is Downward-Sloping

Market demand curves obey the "law of demand": The total quantity demanded is higher when the price is lower.

We've seen (in Figure 7) that the market demand curve in the petrol market is downward-sloping. Executives in virtually every industry have estimated the market demand curves for their products, and time and again, they have found that the total quantity demanded by the market tends to be higher when the price is lower. That is, market demand curves obey the law of demand: The total quantity demanded is higher when the price is lower.

Your understanding of this *market*-wide phenomenon follows directly from your understanding of *individual* demand curves. The market demand curve is built by adding up individual demand at each price, and so it inherits many of the characteristics of those individual demand curves. In particular, since lower petrol prices induce most people to increase the quantity of petrol they demand, lower prices lead the total quantity demanded by the market—that is, the sum of the quantities demanded across all individuals—to increase.

Prices change demand for both new and old customers. Petrol station owners report that there are two reasons why lower prices yield an increase in market demand. First, when prices are low, their current customers buy more petrol. Second, petrol station owners report that lower prices help them get new customers, as the lower cost of driving encourages some people to buy a car. These two aspects of demand—changing demand among existing customers and extra demand from new customers—are important parts of market demand for most goods.

This is why you have to consider the demand of all *potential* customers when estimating demand, rather than just looking at current customers, since changes in price can change who your customers are.

Movements Along the Demand Curve

Managers find the market demand curve to be useful, because it shows them how the market price shapes the total quantity demanded across all buyers. To forecast the total quantity demanded, simply locate the price on the vertical axis, look straight across until you hit the demand curve, and then look straight down to the quantity axis for your answer. Figure 7 shows that at a price of $1.60, the total quantity of petrol demanded by the market is 1.4 billion litres per week. To figure out what will happen if the price falls to $1.20, find the new price on the vertical axis, this time looking across from a price of $1.20 until you hit a new point on the demand curve. Then look down to the quantity axis, which says that the new quantity of petrol demanded is 1.8 billion litres of petrol. Just as the law of demand suggests, a fall in price led to a rise in the quantity demanded, from 1.4 billion to 1.8 billion litres per week.

Movement Along the Demand Curve

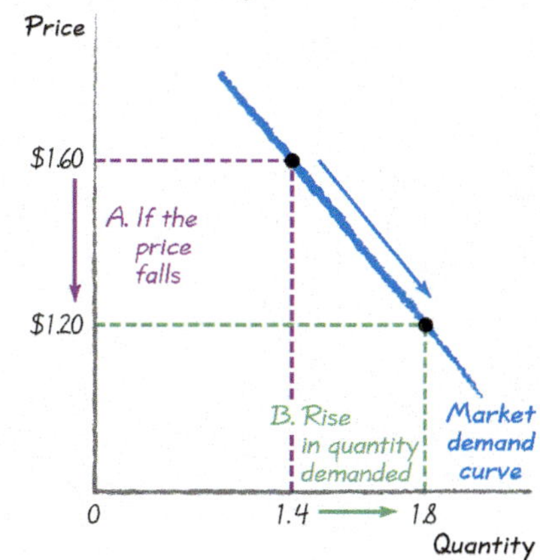

Did you notice that the price change led the market to move from one point on the demand curve, to another point along the same curve? In fact, whenever you're assessing the consequences of a price change—when nothing else is changing (recall we are holding other things constant)—you'll always compare different points along the *same* demand curve. That is, price changes cause movement *along* a fixed demand curve. After all, the demand curve summarises the entire relationship between price and the quantity demanded. We will use very specific language to make what we are talking about clear: A change in price causes a **movement along the demand curve,** yielding a **change in the quantity demanded.** Yes, I know this sounds unwieldy, but it will help keep things straight. Trust me.

movement along the demand curve A price change causes movement from one point on a fixed demand curve to another point on the same curve.

change in the quantity demanded The change in quantity associated with movement along a fixed demand curve.

2.4 What Shifts Demand Curves?

Learning Objective *Understand what factors shift demand curves.*

So far, we've analysed how the quantity demanded varies with the price of a good, *holding other things constant.* We've used three of the four core principles—the *opportunity cost principle*, the *cost-benefit principle*, and the *marginal principle*—to uncover some powerful ideas about demand, such as the *Rational Rule for Buyers*.

But what happens when factors other than the price change? For that, we're going to need to bring in the fourth principle.

The Interdependence Principle and Shifting Demand Curves

The *interdependence principle* reminds you that a buyer's best choice also depends on many other factors beyond price, and when these other factors change, so might their demand decisions. For instance, the quantity of petrol you'll buy (at any given price) might change when you get a pay raise, the amount of traffic increases, or the price of alternatives

shift in the demand curve A movement of the demand curve itself.

increase in demand A shift of the demand curve to the right.

decrease in demand A shift of the demand curve to the left.

such as catching the bus falls. When you're no longer holding these other things constant, the demand curve may shift. When the demand curve itself moves, we refer to it as a **shift in the demand curve.** Because your demand curve is also your marginal benefit curve, any factor that changes your marginal benefits will shift your demand curve.

As Figure 8 illustrates, a rightward shift is an **increase in demand,** because at each and every price, the quantity demanded is higher. A leftward shift is a **decrease in demand,** because the quantity demanded is lower at each and every price.

Figure 8 | Shifts in the Demand Curve

Panel A: An Increase in Demand

Ⓐ An **increase in demand shifts the demand curve to the right**, leading to a higher quantity demanded at each and every price.

Panel B: A Decrease in Demand

Ⓑ A **decrease in demand shifts the demand curve to the left**, leading to a lower quantity demanded at each and every price.

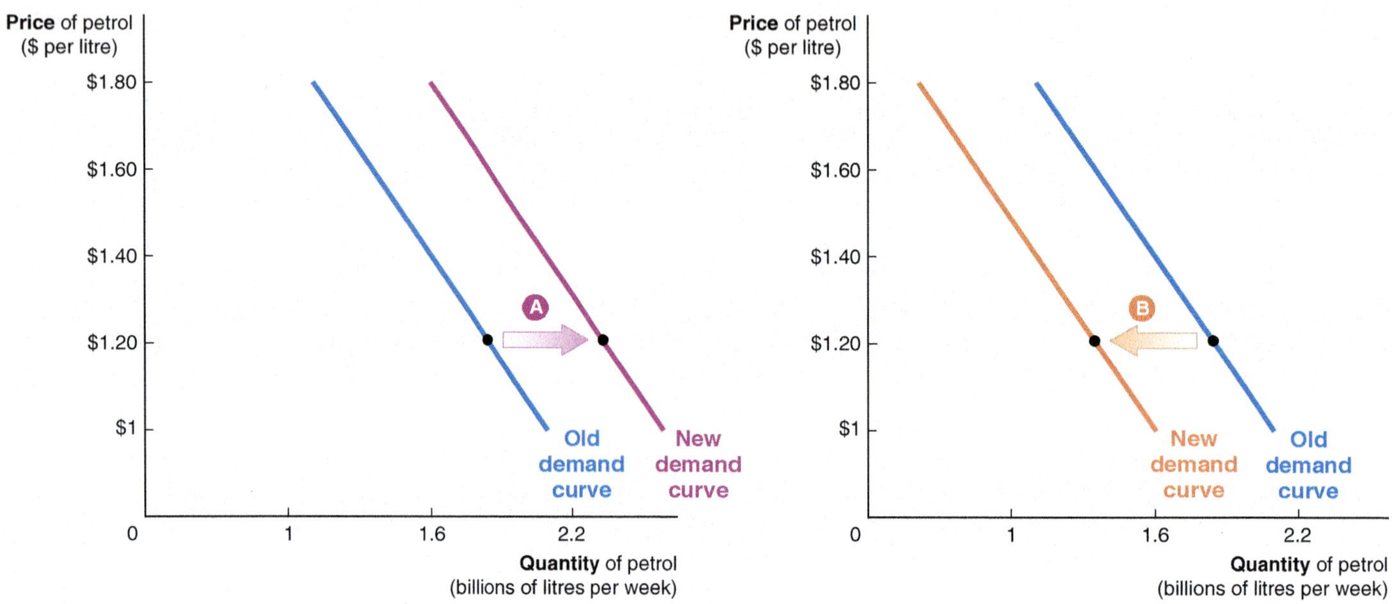

Six Factors Shifting the Demand Curve

Six factors shift the market demand curve:
1. Income
2. Preferences
3. Prices of related goods
4. Expectations
5. Congestion and network effects
6. The type and number of buyers

. . . but not a change in price.

The *interdependence principle* reminds you that buying choices depend on many other factors, and when those other factors shift, so will people's buying plans, thereby shifting the demand curve. But what are these other factors? They are:

1. Income
2. Preferences
3. Prices of related goods
4. Expectations
5. Congestion and network effects

} Shifts individual demand and hence market demand

6. The type and number of buyers ⟶ Only shifts market demand

Changes in any of the first five of these factors shift individual demand curves, and because the market demand curve is built up from individual demand curves, they shift the market demand curve. The final factor—the type and number of buyers—only shifts market demand curves.

Let's now evaluate how each of these six factors can lead to a shift in demand.

Demand shifter one: Income. All of your individual choices are interdependent, since you only have a limited amount of income to spend. Money you spend on petrol is money that you can't spend on clothes. But when your income is higher, you can afford to buy a larger quantity of both. Thus, at each and every price level, you can buy a larger quantity of petrol (and clothes), causing your demand curve to shift to the right—which we call an increase in demand. If your income were to fall, then you would probably choose to buy less petrol at each and every price, shifting your demand curve to the left—and that's called a decrease in demand.

If your demand for a good increases when your income is higher, we call it a **normal good.** Most goods are normal goods. But there are also exceptions, called **inferior goods,** where demand decreases when income rises. "Inferior" goods aren't bad; they're simply those goods you buy less of when your income is higher. For instance, when you're at university and struggling with a limited income, you might take the bus a lot, but when you get your first full-time job, you might buy your own car. Since the higher income in your first job reduced your demand for bus rides, we conclude that bus rides are an inferior good. Typically, inferior goods are those where you're "making do," and when your income rises, you'll switch to a higher-quality but more expensive alternative, instead.

normal good A good for which higher income causes an increase in demand.

inferior good A good for which higher income causes a decrease in demand.

Can you think of other examples of normal and inferior goods? One simple trick is to think about how your buying patterns will change when you start earning a lot more money. Try it; it's fun! Personally, I've noticed that as my income has risen, I eat more restaurant meals but less fast food; I take more Ubers and less public transport; and sport jackets have replaced hoodies in my wardrobe. Hence, for me, restaurant meals, Ubers, and sport jackets are normal goods, but fast food, public transport, and hoodies are inferior goods.

xiaorui/Shutterstock

An inferior good that provides superior comfort.

Interpreting the DATA — Which retailers do well in a recession?

The distinction between normal and inferior goods can be pretty useful in practice. For instance, economists studying retail stores in the United States have found that rising income led to more purchases at Target and fewer at Walmart. Somewhat cheekily (but entirely accurately) they concluded that "shopping at Target is perfectly normal, but shopping at Walmart is not."

The fact that Walmart sells inferior goods (in the economist's sense) is not necessarily bad news for Walmart: During the 2008–2009 recession associated with the Financial Crisis, average income fell. This boosted demand for goods from Walmart because Walmart sells a lot of inferior goods. Meanwhile, Target, which sells mainly normal goods, experienced a decrease in demand. Figure 9 shows that the recession, which increased the demand for Walmart's goods, led its stock price to rise, while the decrease in demand for Target's goods led the value of its stock to fall by about 40%. ■

Figure 9 | Normal and Inferior Goods

Normal and Inferior Goods

A In 2007, **Target's stock price** was much higher than **Walmart's**.

B The **U.S. economy entered a recession** in December 2007, and average incomes fell.

C **Walmart** sells **inferior goods**, so a decline in average income raised its sales, and so its **stock price rose**.

D **Target** sells **normal goods**, so falling average income led to a decrease in demand, and so its **stock price fell**.

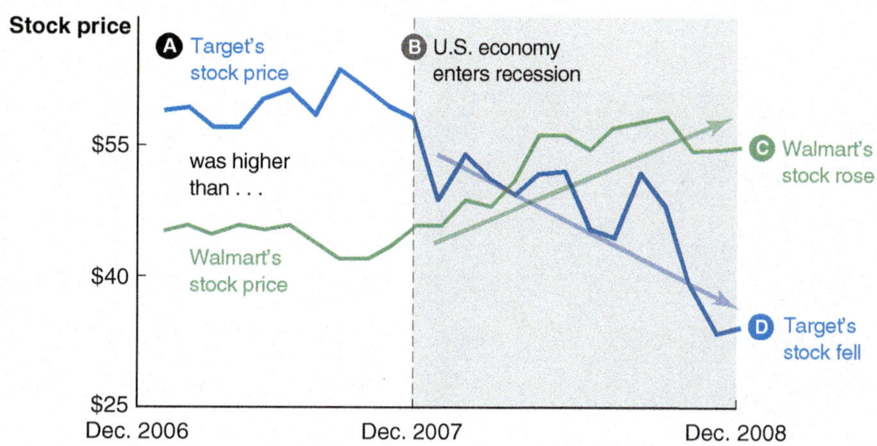

Demand shifter two: Your preferences. Changes in your preferences can shift your demand curve. What if Darren had a baby? His entire consumption bundle might change as he considered his new needs. Would he want to drive to work more so that he could rush home if the baby got sick? Or would he take the bus more so that he could enjoy a few minutes of rest? In fact, there are large numbers of marketers trying to figure out how to take advantage of the changes in people's demand due to life events like getting married or having a baby.

Companies spend billions of dollars each year attempting to influence our preferences through advertising. If Pepsi somehow convinces you that it's better than Coke, this will increase your demand for Pepsi and decrease your demand for Coke. *Social pressure* can also shift your demand curve. For instance, rising environmental awareness has decreased demand for so-called "gas-guzzlers" (making Hummer stretch limos less socially acceptable in many quarters) shifting the demand curve to the left. Preferences are also affected by fashion cycles, such as the fads that increased demand for Ugg boots and Crocs in the early 2000s, thereby shifting demand curves to the right. Of course when people came to their senses and these fads ended, demand fell, and the curve shifted to the left!

Demand shifter three: Prices of related goods. Your choices are also interdependent across different goods. For instance, your demand for meat pies is closely related to your demand for tomato sauce. If the price of tomato sauce rises, you'll buy fewer bottles of tomato sauce *and* fewer meat pies. Consequently, the higher cost of tomato sauce causes a decrease in your demand for meat pies, shifting your demand curve for meat pies to the left. When the higher price of one good decreases your demand for another good, we call them **complementary goods.** Typically, complementary goods "go well together." That is, tomato sauce is a complement to a meat pie, just like a new smartphone case is a complement to your new smartphone. Similarly, cars are a complement to petrol because you need both petrol and a car to drive, and so cheaper cars lead more people to drive, and this increases the demand for petrol, shifting the demand curve to the right.

complementary goods Goods that go together. Your demand for a good will decrease if the price of a complementary good rises.

substitute goods Goods that replace each other. Your demand for a good will increase if the price of a substitute good rises.

In contrast, **substitute goods** replace each other. Walking, cycling, ride-sharing, and catching the bus are all substitutes for driving. If the price of bus tickets doubles, you might start driving to work instead of catching the bus, increasing your demand for petrol. Your demand for any good will increase if the price of its substitutes rises. (And your demand will decrease if the price of substitutes falls.)

EVERYDAY Economics How you can have an influence—indirectly

If you think about substitutes and complements, you sometimes can influence things that are otherwise out of your direct control. For instance, your parents might want you to spend more time studying, but feel powerless to make you do this. However, crafty parents encourage studying by encouraging complements to studying and discouraging substitutes. And so parents often help their kids pay for textbooks, laptops, and desk chairs (complements to studying), but not parties or video games (which are substitutes for study).

Likewise, employers want their workers to focus at work, so they strategically provide free coffee, which is a complement to focused work, and they often block access to Facebook, which is a substitute.

Or think about gifts between significant others on Valentine's Day. Fancy dinners are a common gift, but a membership to an online dating site is less common. Think you can explain this in terms of complements and substitutes? ■

Miguel Candela/SOPA Images/ZUMA Wire/Alamy

New phone? You're probably going to buy a new case, too.

Demand shifter four: Expectations. As a consumer, you get to choose not only what to buy, but also when to buy it. Your choices are linked through time. This simple insight can help you save money, and along the way, shift your demand curves. Think about your reaction when you drive past a petrol station charging super high prices. If you believe that this high price is only temporary, you might put off filling your tank for a few days, decreasing today's demand for petrol. Conversely, if you believe petrol prices are going to rise further, you should probably fill up right away, increasing today's demand. That is, your expectations about future petrol prices can shift your demand curve to the left or to the right.

This insight is really an example of the logic of substitutes: Petrol purchased tomorrow is a substitute for petrol purchased today, and a higher price for this substitute increases demand for petrol purchased today, while a lower price decreases it.

EVERYDAY Economics — How thinking about the future saves you money

Uber's surge-pricing feature generates a lot of controversy. It automatically boosts the price of a ride so that it'll be two or three times higher during peak hours, as an incentive to get more drivers on the road. Some riders work around this and save some money by planning their day a bit more carefully. Instead of calling for a ride during a peak period—say, straight after a concert gets out—you could hang out with your friends for a bit and get a ride home an hour later, when the rush is over and the price has returned to normal.

Notice what's happening here: Your expectations about a lower price later tonight lead to a decline in your demand for Ubers right now. That's because a ride home later tonight is a substitute for a ride home right now, and a lower price of the substitute decreases your demand. It's an example of a more general idea: You can save a few dollars by making sure you think about future prices before you buy. ■

network effect When a good becomes more useful because other people use it. If more people buy such a good, your demand for it will also increase.

congestion effect When a good becomes less valuable because other people use it. If more people buy such a product, your demand for it will decrease.

Demand shifter five: Congestion and network effects. The usefulness of some products—and hence your demand for them—is also shaped by the choices that other people make. Think about social-networking websites. Many Australian university students use Facebook, Instagram, or Snapchat, but in China, WeChat is the most popular social media platform. This is an example of a **network effect**—where a product or service becomes more useful to you as more people use it. If a product is more useful, it yields greater marginal benefits, increasing your demand. Network effects have important business implications: Signing up a few early adopters makes your product more valuable to other customers, increasing the demand for your product, leading more customers to adopt the product, and making it even more valuable again. In these markets, winning the early rounds of competition is critical to your business's long-run success.

By contrast, some products become less valuable when more people use them, and this reverse case is called a **congestion effect.** For example, your demand for driving on a particular road declines if many others are also using that road, since more cars create congestion and traffic. Likewise, your demand for a particular formal dress might decrease if someone else is wearing it.

Denis Charlet/AFP/Getty Images

Love it or hate it? Depends on who else is using it.

EVERYDAY Economics — What determines the language we speak, the computer programs we use, and the cars we drive?

Network and congestion effects are everywhere. For instance, while you have probably complained about Microsoft Word, many university students still use it, mainly to ensure that they can share files with others. Or think about the demand for learning languages. Most Australian schools teach English rather than French. This isn't because English is the more beautiful language; it is simply the most useful language, given that most people in Australia speak English. In France, the reverse occurs (in terms of the primary language taught. Of course, most students in France learn English as well, and some students in Australia learn French as well as English).

The types of cars that people buy are also interdependent. City-dwellers sometimes buy SUVs, but not because they plan to go off-road driving. Instead, they worry that because there are so many other large cars on the road, they now need to drive a large car to stand a reasonable chance of surviving an accident. Thus, the choices made by other people in Australia increase your demand for Facebook, Microsoft Word, large cars, and learning English, but decrease your demand for WeChat, Open Office, learning French, and compact cars. ■

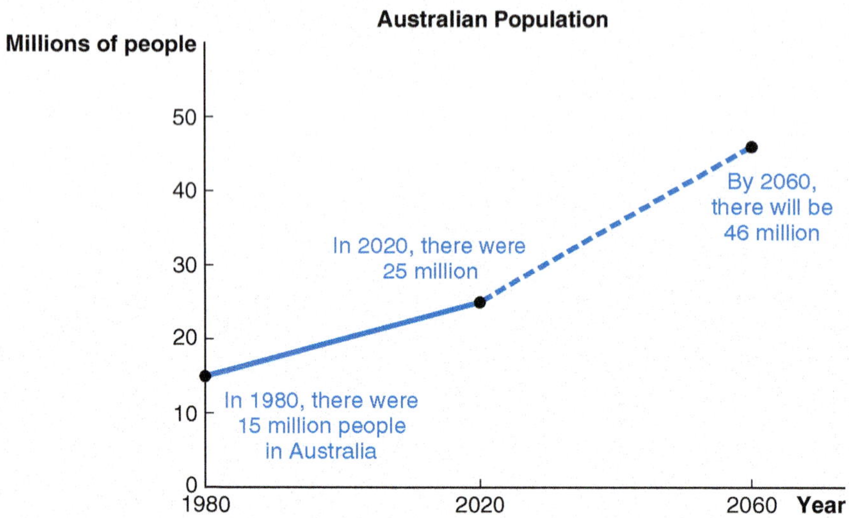

2019 data from: Australian Bureau of Statistics.

Demand shifter six: Type and number of buyers. So far, we have analysed the five factors that shift individual demand curves. Because market demand is the sum of individual demand, each of the factors that shift individual demand also shift market demand. In addition, if the composition of the market changes through demographic composition or type of buyers in the market, then market demand will also change. For instance, the baby boom that followed World War II initially led to an increase in the demand for baby clothes. As this cohort progressed through their lives, there was an increase in the demand for schoolbooks, then for university education, and subsequently for houses, cars, and child care. Over the next decade, these aging Baby Boomers will cause demand for health care and nursing homes to rise. But there's another sizeable cohort—the Millennials born between 1981 and 1996—and their preferences and life stages will shape market demand in Australia.

Additionally, market demand is shaped by the number of buyers. If the number of potential buyers rises then there are more individual demand curves to add up when calculating market demand. Thus, an increase in the number of potential buyers shifts the market demand curve to the right. Over short periods of time, increases in population are relatively unimportant, as the Australian population grows by only about 1% each year. But over longer periods, this can add up. The Australian population has increased by more than 70% since 1980, and this alone has nearly doubled the quantity demanded in most markets. The Australian population is expected to increase by another 80% between 2020 and 2060. The dependence of demand curves on market size partly explains why many business owners are in favour of increased immigration: More people means increased demand for their firm's products.

Another critical factor increasing market size is international trade and the opening of new foreign markets. For instance, the opening of the Chinese economy means that there are now more than one billion Chinese consumers for exporters to serve, which potentially represents an enormous shift in demand.

Recap: When things other than price change, your demand curve may shift. To recap, changes in market conditions affect your demand decisions. These changes reflect the *interdependence principle* at work: Your best choices depend on many factors, and when these factors change, so will your best buying decisions. The five factors that shift individual demand curves—your income, your preferences, the prices of other goods, your expectations, and network and congestion effects—are all factors that can change your marginal benefit. Because your marginal benefit curve is your demand curve, shifts in these factors can shift your demand curve. Keep these factors in mind as we now turn to reviewing the distinction between movements along the demand curve versus shifts of the demand curve.

2.5 Shifts versus Movements Along Demand Curves

Learning Objective *Distinguish between movements along a demand curve and shifts in demand curves.*

It can be tricky to figure out when to look for movements along the demand curve versus shifts in that curve. But it's essential if you are going to correctly forecast the consequences of changing economic conditions. Here's a simple rule of thumb: *If the only thing that's changing is the price, then you're thinking about a movement along the demand curve. But when other market conditions change, you need to think about shifts in the demand curve.*

Movements Along the Demand Curve

To see why changes in price are different from changes in other factors, let's revisit Darren after the price of petrol changes. This price change won't lead Darren to change his answers to the survey in Figure 1. That survey already described his plans to change the quantity of petrol he uses if the price changes. Likewise, his individual demand curve—which simply plotted his answers to that survey—will be unchanged. And if individual demand curves don't shift following a price change, then neither will the market demand curve. The logic is simply this: A demand curve is a plan for how to respond to different prices, and if buyers' plans haven't shifted, then the market demand curve hasn't shifted.

When the price changes, you are analysing a movement along the demand curve. When other factors change, the demand curve may shift.

Indeed, managers find the demand curve to be useful precisely because they can use it to assess the consequences of a price change. For instance, Panel A in Figure 10

Figure 10 | **Movement Along the Demand Curve versus Shifts in the Demand Curve**

Panel A—When the Price Changes:
Movement Along the Demand Curve

(A) A change in price, from $1.60 to $1.20 per litre.
(B) Causes a movement along the demand curve,
(C) Leading to a change in the quantity demanded, raising the quantity demanded from 1.4 to 1.8 billion litres per week.

Panel B—When Other Factors Change:
Shifts in the Demand Curve

(A) A decrease in demand shifts the demand curve to the left, decreasing the quantity at each and every price.

(B) An increase in demand shifts the demand curve to the right, increasing the quantity at each and every price.

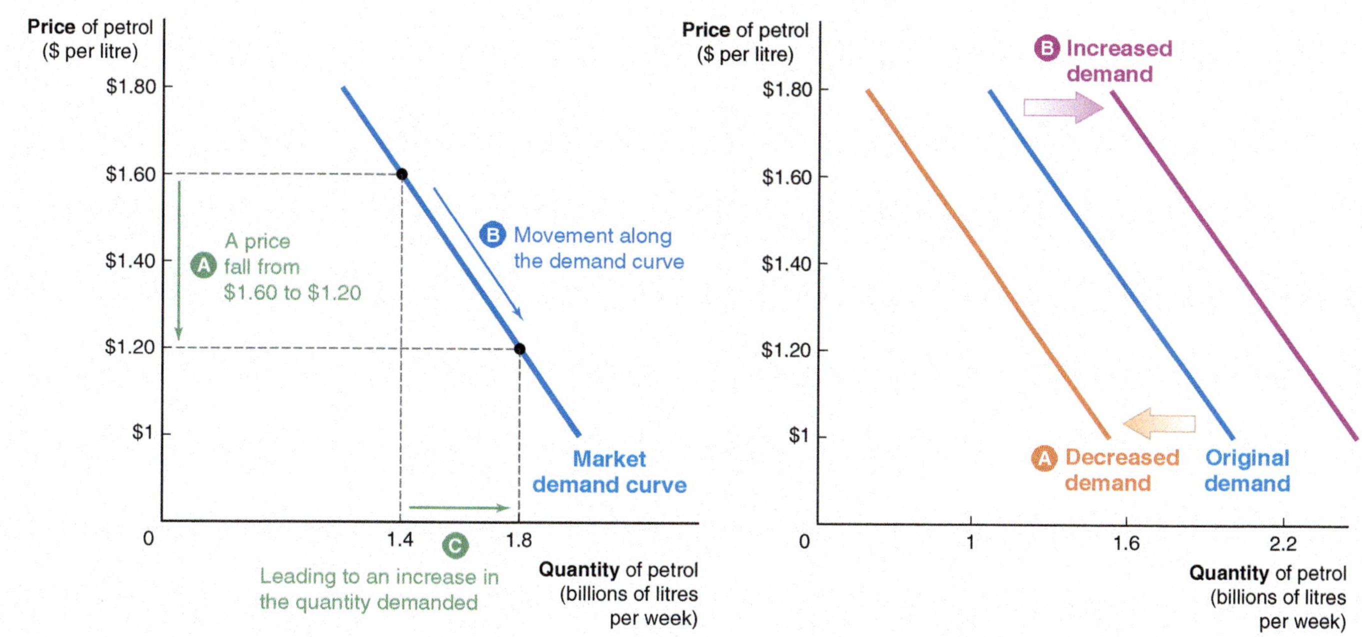

shows that when the price of petrol is $1.60, the total quantity demanded will be 1.4 billion litres per week, and when the price of petrol falls to $1.20, the quantity demanded will rise to 1.8 billion litres. As you can see, this price change leads to a movement along the demand curve. And this analysis shows that a lower price leads to an increase in the quantity demanded.

Shifts in Demand

But if other factors change—factors other than the price—then Darren might revise his buying plans. For instance, changes in things like Darren's income, his preference for driving, the price of alternatives such as Uber, his expectations about future petrol prices, or the number of other drivers creating traffic could all lead him to decide to change how much petrol he'll buy even if the price doesn't change. When these factors change the quantity that Darren demands at a given price, they lead to a shift in his demand curve.

To figure out whether a change in market conditions will shift the demand curve, ask yourself: Has something changed that would cause you to give different answers to a survey about the quantity you'll demand at each price? If so, then this will shift your demand curve. The right-hand panel of Figure 10 illustrates an increase in demand, which causes the demand curve to shift to the right, and also a decrease in demand, which causes it to shift to the left.

Of course, not every change in market conditions will cause the demand curve to shift. To figure out which ones will matter, apply the *interdependence principle.* If something is unconnected to your buying decisions, then it won't change your buying plans—which is the quantity you demand at a given price—and so it won't shift your individual demand curve. Put simply, if your answers to the survey about your demand plans haven't changed, then your demand hasn't shifted. But if they do change, then it is connected, and this dependence may change things. To make it easy to think about what could shift the demand curve, remember the six demand shifters: Income, Preferences, Prices of related goods, Expectations, Congestion and network effects, and the Type and number of buyers. Finally, let me give you a hint that'll help you memorise these six factors: Rearrange the first letter of each of them, and it'll spell out PEPTIC, which should make this lesson a bit easier to digest.

Things that shift the demand curve are **PEPTIC:**
Preferences
Expectations
Price of related goods
Type and number of buyers
Income
Congestion and network effects

Tying It Together

We have studied demand from two perspectives. We started with the individual demand decisions that you make, and then considered total market demand for a product, across all buyers. These two perspectives are each important, although for different reasons. Managers want to know how much people will buy at each price. This is exactly what the market demand curve reveals. Consumers want to know how to make the best choices given their limited income, and this is what our study of individual demand addresses. Because these individual demand curves are the building blocks of the market demand curve, these questions are fundamentally intertwined.

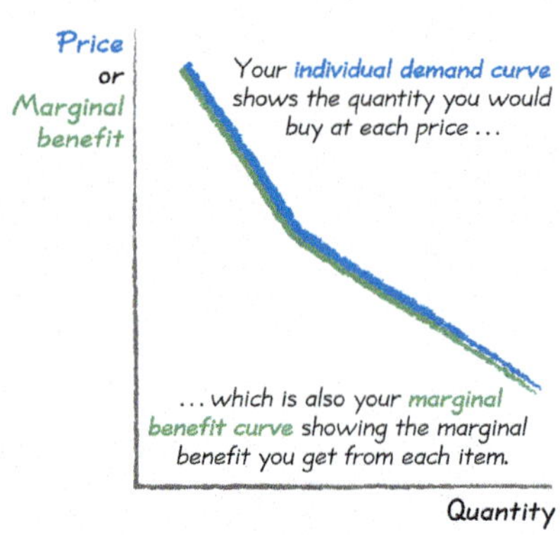

Individual Demand

The most common question you'll face as a buyer is: "How much should I buy?" The *Rational Rule for Buyers* distills the core economic principles down to one simple piece of advice: *Buy more of an item if the marginal benefit of one more is greater than (or equal to) the price.* Follow this advice consistently, and you'll keep buying until your marginal benefit equals the price. In turn, your individual demand curve is your marginal benefit curve. And the tendency towards diminishing marginal benefits means that your marginal benefit curve—and hence your demand curve—is downward-sloping. You can see why economists say that understanding demand is all about understanding marginal benefits.

There's also a more general idea at work here. In Chapter 1, we introduced the *Rational Rule*, which simply says: *If something is worth doing, keep doing it until the marginal benefit equals the marginal cost.* The *Rational Rule for Buyers* is just the application of this rule to your buying decisions, where the marginal cost of buying something is the price. Throughout your study of economics, we'll discover that whenever you are trying to figure out how to make optimal choices—whether in your role as a buyer, seller, worker, boss, entrepreneur, investor, or anything else—the relevant rule will turn out to be an application of the *Rational Rule*. That's the advantage of our principles-based approach: It highlights the similarities of good decision making across very different contexts. Stay tuned; we'll see more of this in future chapters.

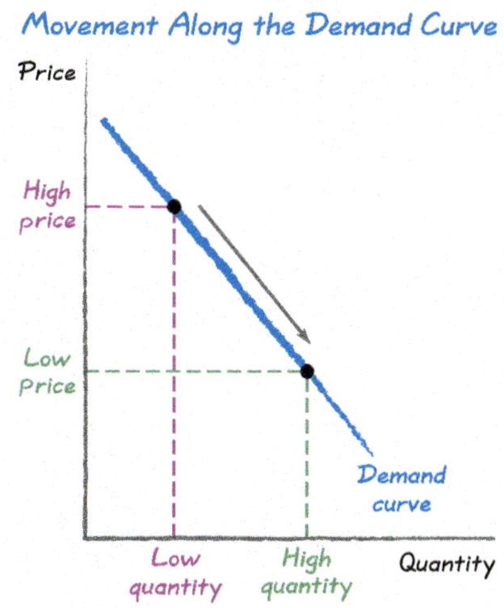

Market Demand

Managers find the market demand curve to be useful because it allows them to forecast how changing economic conditions will affect the quantity they will sell. When the price changes, this causes *a movement along the market demand curve,* and hence changes in the total *quantity demanded.* Because the demand curve is downward-sloping, a lower price will raise the total quantity demanded, and a higher price will reduce the total quantity demanded.

But there are also several factors that shift your demand curve. An *increase* in demand is a rightward shift of the demand curve at each and every price, while a *decrease* in demand is a leftward shift.

The *interdependence principle* leads us to six key factors that shift demand curves. These include changes in:

- *Income*: Higher income increases the demand for normal goods, but decreases the demand for inferior goods.
- *Preferences*: Demand for particular goods can increase or decrease as your desire for those goods changes. Preferences can be changed by trends, advertising, changing lifestyles, and countless other factors. Advertisers will try to increase your demand for their products. Social pressure can also shift demand curves.
- *Prices of related goods*: Demand will increase if the price of substitute goods rises, or the price of complementary goods falls. Demand will decrease if the price of substitute goods falls, or the price of complementary goods rises.
- *Expectations*: If prices are expected to rise, today's demand will increase; if prices are expected to fall, today's demand will decrease.
- *Congestion and network effects*: If a good with network effects becomes more popular, demand will increase. If a good with congestion effects becomes more popular, demand will decrease.
- *Type and number of buyers*: Demand will increase due to population growth, immigration, or access to new international markets. Demographic change can also shift demand. This factor only affects market demand curves, not individual demand.

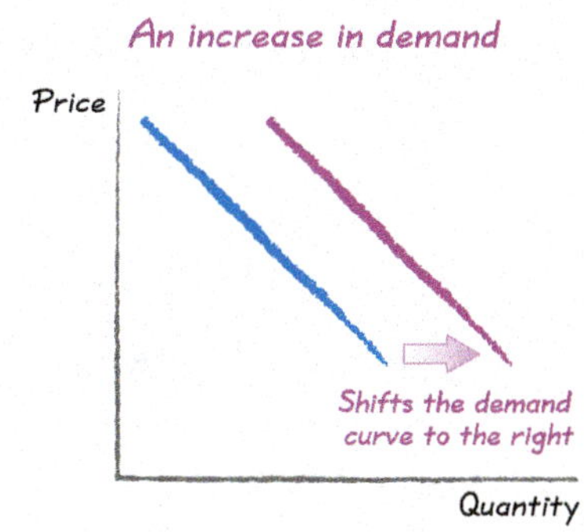

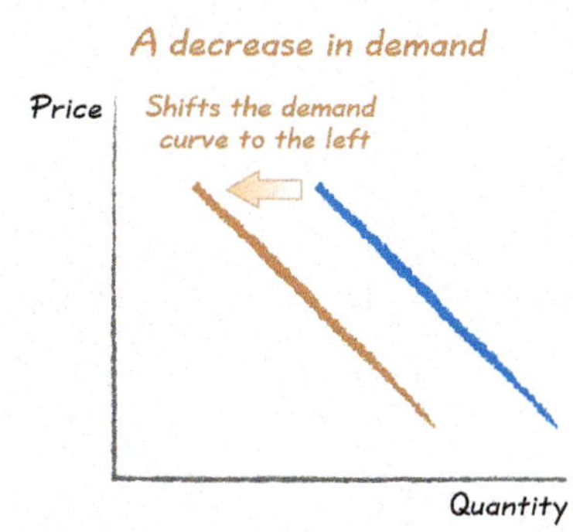

This chapter focused on consumers and how marginal benefits shape demand. In the next chapter, we'll turn our focus to businesses, and how the marginal costs of production affect supply.

Chapter at a Glance

An Individual Demand Curve

Shows the quantity demanded at each price.

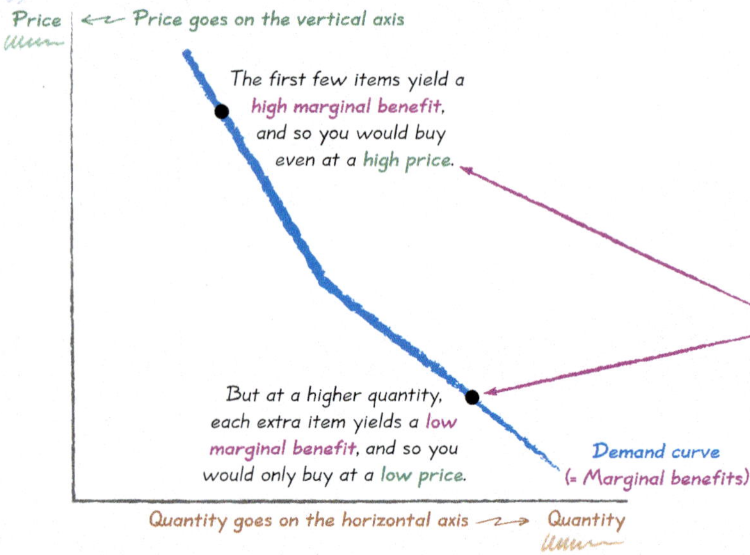

The Rational Rule for Buyers

Buy more of an item if its marginal benefit is greater than (or equal to) the price

⇩

Price = Marginal benefit

⇩

Your demand curve is your marginal benefit curve.

⇩

Your demand curve is downward sloping because of diminishing marginal benefits.

Market Demand Curves

1. Survey a representative sample of the market, asking people the quantity they will buy at each price.
2. For each price, add up the total quantity demanded by the people surveyed.
3. Scale up the quantities demanded by the people surveyed, so that they represent the entire market.
4. Plot the total quantity demanded by the market, against price.

When the Price Changes:

Movement Along the Demand Curve

When Other Factors Change:

Shifts in the Demand Curve

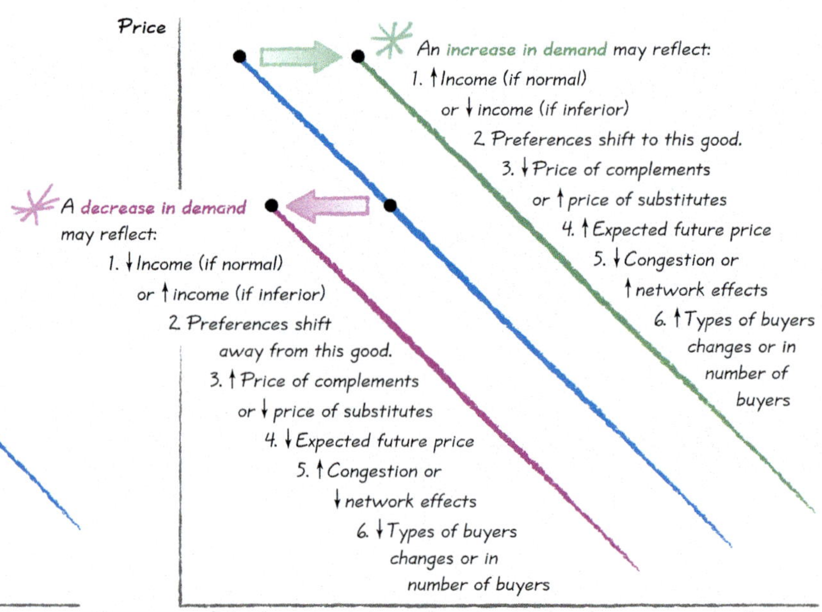

The acronym PEPTIC can help you remember these six shifters.

Key Concepts

change in the quantity demanded, 47
complementary goods, 50
congestion effect, 51
decrease in demand, 48
diminishing marginal benefit, 43
"holding other things constant," 37
increase in demand, 48
individual demand curve, 36
inferior good, 49
law of demand, 39
market demand curve, 44
movement along the demand curve, 47
network effect, 51
normal good, 49
The Rational Rule for Buyers, 41
shift in the demand curve, 48
substitute goods, 50

Discussion and Review Questions

Learning Objective 2.1 *Discover the shape of your individual demand curve.*

1. You just took an Uber from home to campus for the first time and were willing to pay $13 for the trip. It was so much easier than driving yourself that you are willing to pay $21 for the same trip tomorrow. Have you violated the law of demand? Why or why not?

Learning Objective 2.2 *Apply the core principles of economics to make good demand decisions.*

2. Do you use water for things that are beyond what is necessary to sustain life? What if the price of water in your home tripled? How would you respond? Are there activities that you would change or stop doing? Briefly explain. Does your demand for water obey the law of demand?

Learning Objective 2.3 *Add up individual demand to discover market demand.*

3. A team of analysts at Amazon is researching the viability of producing a smart watch. How might they estimate potential demand for their smart watch? What kinds of factors would the analysts want to keep in mind to create the most accurate estimates?

Learning Objective 2.4 *Understand what factors shift demand curves.*

4. For each of the following goods or services, indicate whether you think they are normal or inferior goods for most consumers. Briefly explain your reasoning.
   a. The newest iPhone
   b. 10-year-old used cars
   c. Dental services

5. When Sony released the PlayStation 4, it was reported that it was making a loss of $65 on every console. However, Sony expected to make this up with sales of online play subscriptions (PS+) and increased royalties from video games. Use the concepts described in this chapter to help explain this strategy.

Learning Objective 2.5 *Distinguish between movements along a demand curve and shifts in demand curves.*

6. Find the flaw in reasoning in the following statement: "An increase in the cost of oil will cause the price of a plane ticket to increase. This increase in price will cause a decrease in demand for airline travel and a leftward shift in the demand curve."

Study Problems

Learning Objective 2.1 *Discover the shape of your individual demand curve.*

1. Deliveroo, a food delivery service, has recently expanded to your area. The accompanying table contains the number of deliveries per month that you demand at various delivery prices. Use this information to plot your individual demand curve. Describe the slope of your individual demand curve.

Price	Deliveries
$10	2
$7	4
$5	6
$4	8
$2	10
$1	12

Learning Objective 2.2 *Apply the core principles of economics to make good demand decisions.*

2. Consider Rob's demand for after-school care for his children. The marginal benefit Rob receives for every hour of child care is provided in the accompanying table. Using the Rational Rule for Buyers, if an hour of child care costs $24, how many hours would Rob purchase each day? What about for $18 per hour? Draw Rob's marginal benefit curve and his demand curve.

Hours of after school child care	Marginal benefit (per hour)
1	$32
2	$30
3	$20
4	$14

3. Kathy is attending university in Canberra. Each year she returns home to visit her family and friends in Melbourne. Kathy's annual demand curve for plane tickets from Canberra to Melbourne is provided in the accompanying graph. How much benefit does Kathy receive from each trip home? If the price of a round-trip ticket is $300, how many trips should Kathy take?

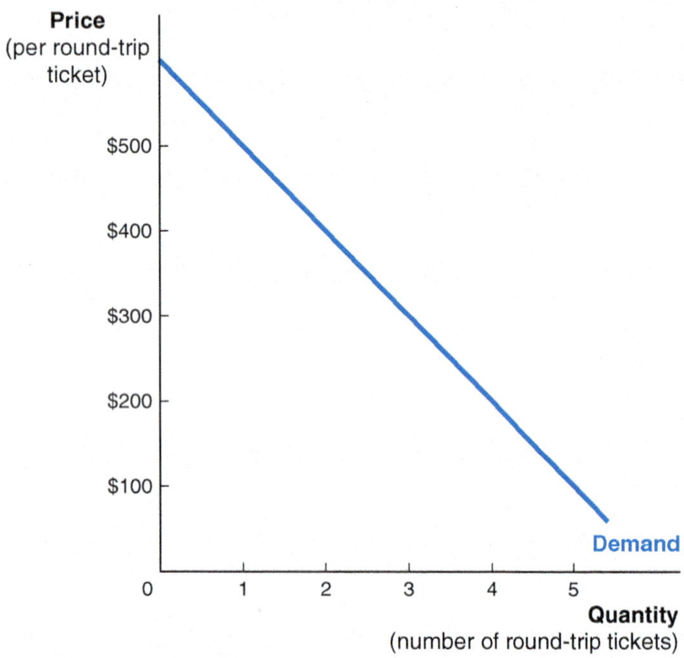

Learning Objective 2.3 *Add up individual demand to discover market demand.*

4. The marginal benefit received for each litre of petrol consumed per week for Ang, Tony, and Gianna is provided in the accompanying table. On the same graph, plot each of their individual demand curves. Assuming these are the only people in the market, graph the market demand curve for petrol.

Litres consumed per week	Ang's marginal benefit	Tony's marginal benefit	Gianna's marginal benefit
1	$7	$4	$8
2	$5	$3	$6
3	$3	$2	$4
4	$1	$1	$2

5. You own the only pharmacy in the small town of Wonomboville, which has 40,000 residents. You would like to get a sense of what the local demand is for seasonal allergy medicine so you can determine how many packages to keep in stock and what price to charge. You conduct a survey of four residents of Wonomboville, asking them about the quantity of allergy medicine they would buy each allergy season at various prices. Their responses are shown in the accompanying table. Estimate and graph the demand for the *entire* town of Wonomboville.

Price	Lee	June	Carlotta	Eric
$8	8	5	6	9
$10	6	4	5	5
$12	4	3	4	3
$14	2	2	2	1
$18	0	1	1	0

Learning Objective 2.4 *Understand what factors shift demand curves.*

6. For each of the following pairs of goods, identify whether they are substitutes or complements and use a graph to illustrate how the change described impacts the markets for both goods or services.

   a. Petrol and SUVs: The price of petrol increases.

   b. Taking a train or plane between Canberra and Melbourne: The price of airfare increases.

   c. A smartphone and an Optus data plan: The price of a monthly data plan increases.

7. Consider the market demand curve for the Samsung Galaxy smartphone. For each of the following, assess whether it would cause a rightward shift in the demand curve, a leftward shift in the demand curve, or no change in the demand curve.

   a. Batteries in Samsung smartphones begin to spontaneously combust.

   b. Apple decides to increase the price of the newest iPhone by 10%.

   c. Samsung increases the price of the Galaxy by 10%.

8. According to a 2018 article in the *Wall Street Journal,* proposed tariffs on imported steel could cause the price to consumers of new cars to increase by as much as $300. Use a graph to illustrate the impact of this on the current demand curve for new cars in the United States.

9. As part of the marketing team at Virgin Australia, you must develop a strategy to increase demand for flights between Brisbane and Sydney. You examine the data from previous flights and determine that the existing

demand for flights between the two cities is as given in the following table.

Price per flight	Quantity demanded per day
$200	1,200
$300	1,100
$400	1,000
$500	900
$600	800
$700	700

a. However, your team launches a viral advertising campaign that is so successful that all existing consumers increase their willingness to pay by $100, and 50 new customers demand flights at every price. Fill in the following table to show the new quantity demanded at each price following the advertising campaign.

Price per flight	Quantity demanded per day after the advertising campaign
$200	1,350
$300	
$400	
$500	
$600	
$700	

b. Use a graph to illustrate both the initial demand curve and the new demand curve from part (a).

Learning Objective 2.5 *Distinguish between movements along a demand curve and shifts in demand curves.*

10. Illustrate graphically how each of the following events will impact the demand for cups of coffee and explain why demand changes.

a. Average hourly wages increase in Australia.

b. NSW Fair Trading requires all cafés to post warnings to consumers of the cancer-causing components of coffee.

c. Cafés increase the price of coffee in order to pay their baristas more.

CHAPTER

3

Supply and Producer Choice

Just as your day is filled with decisions about what to buy, you also have to decide what to sell. After all, everything that is bought is also sold. While you might not think of yourself as a seller if you aren't (yet!) managing a business, you are already managing one very important small business: Your Own Undertaking (or Y.O.U., for short). YOU are already making very important supply decisions. You may have sold concert tickets on StubHub; perhaps you have also sold furniture or a big ticket item, like an old car. You may hold a part-time job, where you sell your labour in return for an hourly wage.

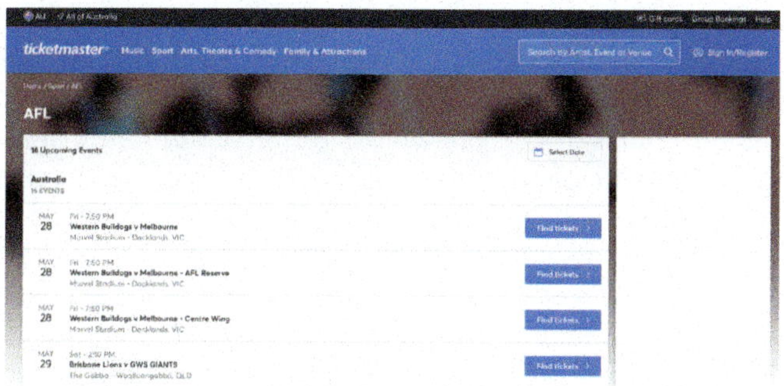

How much would you sell your seat for?

You also supply things in transactions that don't involve money. Your household is like a small business, and you might produce cooking and cleaning services in return for similar services from your family or housemates. You probably supply child care, transport, and advice to those you love. You also supply camaraderie to your friends, an audience to online advertisers, and your attention to this important chapter on supply.

In this chapter, we'll dig into *supply*—the decisions that we make as sellers. The structure of this chapter largely parallels our analysis of demand. We'll start with individual decisions and apply the core principles of economics to help guide you to make good supply decisions. Next, we'll pan back and assess total market supply, which is the sum of these individual decisions. We'll then explore how changing market conditions shift supply.

There's a lot to cover with supply—the global economy consists of millions of businesses producing and selling a dazzling array of goods. But the same logic underpins every business decision. Let's start by putting ourselves into the shoes of a manager, trying to decide how much to produce and sell.

Chapter Objective

To understand how businesses make selling or supply decisions.

3.1 Individual Supply: What You Sell, at Each Price
Discover the shape of your business's individual supply curve.

3.2 Your Decisions and Your Individual Supply Curve
Apply the core principles to make good supply decisions.

3.3 Market Supply: What the Market Sells
Add up individual supply to discover market supply.

3.4 What Shifts Supply Curves?
Understand what factors shift supply curves.

3.5 Shifts versus Movements Along Supply Curves
Distinguish between movements along a supply curve and shifts in supply curves.

3.1 Individual Supply: What You Sell, at Each Price

Learning Objective *Discover the shape of your business's individual supply curve.*

Shannon has been working hard for the past few weeks, preparing for her company's annual planning summit. She joined BP's management training program straight out of university and has spent the past few years working as a business analyst in the strategy division. BP is a major producer and seller of petrol (among other fuels and products), and the planning summit brings together the heads of every major business unit to formulate production and sales plans for the next year. Shannon impressed her boss enough that she's been picked to present the division's analysis.

Killua X/Shutterstock

A refinery transforms crude oil into petrol.

Understandably, she's nervous, as the decisions that are made at the planning summit will ripple throughout the company. The head of the retail division will use these plans to coordinate sales targets across hundreds of petrol stations. The engineers who run the Kwinana refinery in Western Australia—the large plant that transforms crude oil into petrol—will use the decisions as the basis for setting their production schedules. And the logistics division—which buys the crude oil needed by the refineries and which also imports refined fuel from overseas—will start making purchasing plans. Shannon also knows that impressing the company's senior executives will be critical to her own career prospects.

The question on the planning summit's agenda is one that is central to all businesses: *Given the price of our product, what quantity should we supply?* The stakes are high, because the right decision can be the difference between a healthy profit and a big loss.

At the summit, Shannon gives a presentation outlining how the company should respond if next year's petrol price is high. Because a high petrol price would make selling more petrol profitable, she recommends that the company ramp up production. Her presentation is quite specific, outlining exactly how much BP should increase production, depending on how much prices rise.

She then turns to more pessimistic scenarios, assessing how the company should respond to low petrol prices. If the price of petrol is low, she recommends cutting back the quantity of petrol it produces and sells. Her presentation makes clear that the lower the petrol price falls, the greater the cutbacks required, and hence the lower the quantity they would supply. Finally, she concludes that if the petrol price is sufficiently low, the best way to minimise losses would be to halt production entirely and produce no petrol. While this would be a hard decision to make, it would help BP survive until petrol prices rose again.

Shannon's presentation details how the ideal quantity to produce and sell varies, depending on the price. Indeed, because price is a critical factor determining any company's profitability, businesses often find it useful to plan for a variety of different scenarios. Figure 1 shows the memo that Shannon distributed after the meeting, describing her company's supply plans for next year. Each bullet point in Shannon's memo shows the quantity of petrol she recommends that BP supply, at each price.

Figure 1 | BP's Supply Plan

Memo

TO: All department heads—Refining, Retail, and Logistics units
FROM: Shannon David, Business planning division
SUBJECT: Petrol Supply Plans

This memo summarises the production and sales plans that we agreed upon in last week's planning summit. Specifically, we decided:

- If the petrol price is $1 per litre, we will produce 100 million litres per week.
- If the petrol price is $1.20 per litre, we will produce 130 million litres per week.
- If the petrol price is $1.40 per litre, we will produce 160 million litres per week.
- If the petrol price is $1.60 per litre, we will produce 190 million litres per week.
- If the petrol price is $1.80 per litre, we will produce 220 million litres per week.
- If the petrol price is below $1 per litre, all production will shut down, so we will produce zero litres per week.

Please use these numbers as the basis for setting next year's plans for your division. These production and sales plans are based on our current understanding of market conditions, which may change; if so, we will revisit these numbers.

An Individual Supply Curve

individual supply curve A graph plotting the quantity of an item that a business plans to sell at each price.

While Shannon has written the plan up as a memo, economists find it more convenient to represent these plans in a simple graph, called an individual supply curve. An **individual supply curve** is a graph of the quantity that a business plans to sell at each price; it summarises a business's selling plans. You can graph an individual supply curve for anything that you might sell—goods, services, your time, anything!—you just need to think about the quantity you'd sell at each price.

An individual supply curve graphs your selling plans. Figure 2 graphs the individual supply curve for Shannon's company, plotting the supply plans she outlined point by point in her memo. The graphing conventions for supply curves are the same as for demand curves: Price goes on the vertical axis, and quantity is on the horizontal axis. (Remember: "P's before Q's.")

Figure 2 | An Individual Supply Curve

BP's Individual Supply Curve:
How much petrol is it willing to supply at each price?

- **A** When the price is **$1 per litre**, BP plans to sell just **100 million litres** per week. An individual supply curve also illustrates how the quantity a business will supply changes as the price changes. If the price rises to **$1.20 per litre**, the quantity supplied will rise to **130 million litres** per week, and at a price of **$1.40 per litre**, it will rise to **160 million litres**, and so on.
- **B** At very low prices—below $1 per litre—BP will stop producing petrol, and so the quantity supplied is zero.
- **C** The **individual supply curve** shows the quantity of petrol that BP is willing to sell, at each price. It is an upward-sloping curve: the higher the price, the higher the quantity supplied.

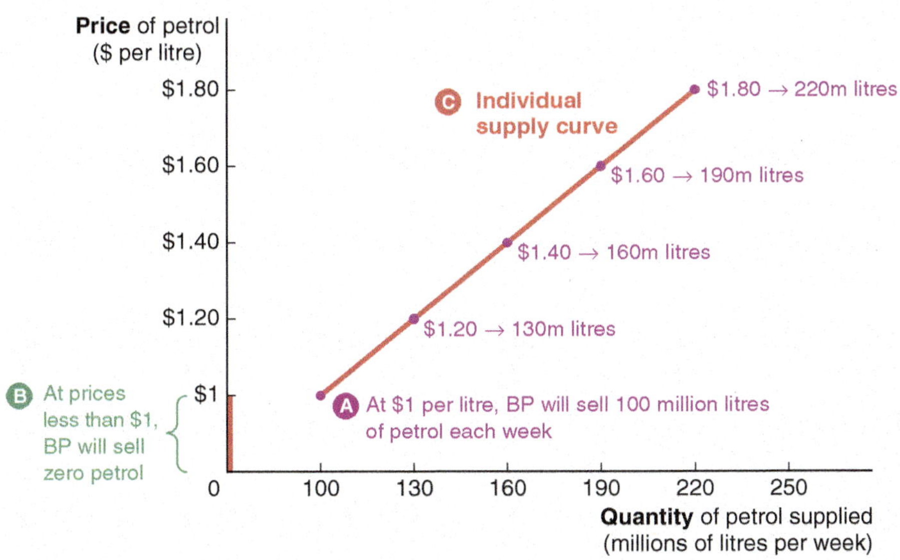

Each bullet point in Shannon's memo represents a separate point on her company's individual supply curve. The first bullet point says that at a price of $1 per litre, BP plans to produce 100 million litres of petrol per week. This point is plotted at the lower left of Figure 2— simply look across from the price of $1 (on the vertical axis) to the quantity of 100 million litres of petrol (on the horizontal axis), and you'll find it graphed as the first point. The next bullet point in the memo is plotted as the next point to the right: When the price rises to $1.20 per litre, BP plans to increase the quantity supplied to 130 million litres of petrol per week. Each subsequent point shows that as the price rises, the quantity BP plans to supply also rises, all the way up to the final point, where a price of $1.80 per litre leads Shannon to recommend that BP supply 220 million litres of petrol per week. Finally, we connect these dots in order to estimate the quantity supplied at prices in between those mentioned in Shannon's memo. This line is BP's individual supply curve, and it illustrates the quantity the company will supply, at each price.

Notice the last bullet point in Shannon's memo: It says that when the price falls below $1, the company should supply zero petrol. Why? For any company, there's a point where the price is sufficiently low that your best choice is to minimise your losses by temporarily shutting down operations until the price rises again. This is illustrated by the vertical red line on the far left of Figure 2, which shows that if the price is between $0 and $0.99, BP plans to supply zero litres of petrol.

Adam Crowley/AGE Fotostock

Which should you keep, and which should you sell?

An individual supply curve holds other things constant. The supply curve shown in Figure 2 plots the amount of petrol BP will supply at different prices, given current economic conditions. But if something important were to change—say, the price of crude oil rose, or the wages of refinery workers fell—BP would change its plans, and those new plans would result in a new supply curve. This is why we say that an individual supply curve shows the quantity of petrol that a company is willing to sell at each price, *holding other things constant*. Of course, the *interdependence principle* reminds us that things other than price can influence supply. But for now, we're "holding other things constant," so that we can focus on what happens when the price—and only the price—changes. Stay tuned though, because later in this chapter we'll analyse how shifts in these other factors can cause the supply curve to shift.

The individual supply curve is upward-sloping. Notice that the individual supply curve in Figure 2 rises upward as you look from left to right. It is *upward-sloping* because at higher petrol prices, BP plans to supply a larger quantity. This makes sense—if each litre brings a higher price, selling extra litres of petrol will be more profitable, and so BP should do more of it. (I'll call this supply curve "upward-sloping" even though it's vertical for prices below $1, because eventually higher prices led to a larger quantity supplied.)

Not all businesses go through the careful planning process that BP does. But even so, each of them still has an individual supply curve. After all, every business must choose what quantity to supply when the price changes. When you graph these choices, the resulting individual supply curve illustrates the extent to which a higher price leads to a larger quantity supplied.

Do the Economics

Just as BP is making supply decisions, you are also making important supply decisions in your everyday life. Let's work through an example, and discover the shape of your individual supply curve.

At the end of this year, you'll probably have several used university textbooks. And once you've passed your exams, you'll have to choose which books to keep and which to sell to next year's students. As such, you are a supplier in the market for university textbooks. For each book, you'll have to decide whether it is worth selling, given the price. If the book is uninteresting or if it is for a class that's not relevant for your future

Figure 3 | Discover Your Individual Supply Curve

Panel A: Amazon Textbook Buyback Survey

Amazon is interested in understanding how many of your used textbooks you will sell at the end of the year. Other things being equal, how many of your current textbooks do you expect to sell?

Price of used textbooks	Quantity of used textbooks you will sell this year
If the price is $5 per book	
If the price is $10 per book	
If the price is $20 per book	
If the price is $40 per book	
If the price is $60 per book	
If the price is $80 per book	
If the price is $100 per book	

Panel B: Your Individual Supply Curve

How many used textbooks are you willing to sell at each price?

To graph your individual supply curve, plot the data from your responses to the Amazon Textbook Buyback Survey.

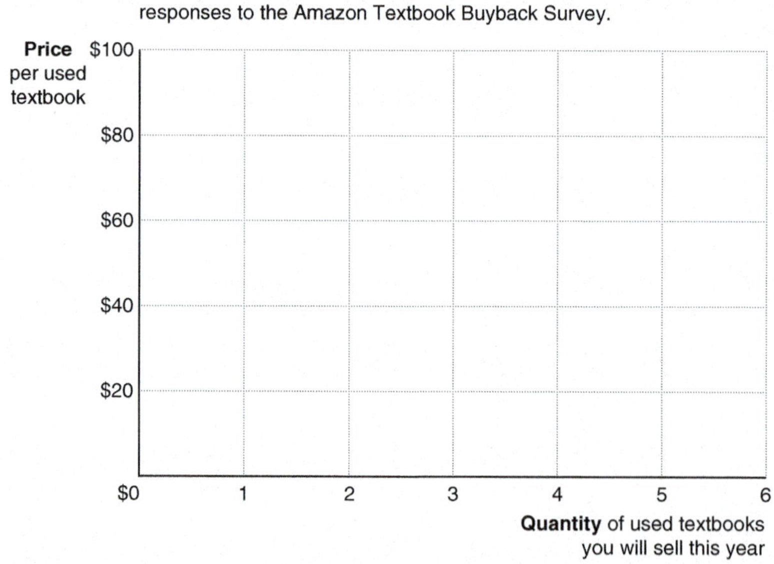

work, you are likely to sell it, even if you can only get a few dollars for it. But if it's a book that you'll need to refer to for next year's classes or later in your career, then you will be more reluctant to sell it. In fact, you may be happy to keep many of your books. But if you can get a high enough price, you'll go ahead and sell them. So the quantity of used textbooks you supply depends on the price.

Amazon launched a textbook buyback scheme, and their senior executives are trying to figure out what price they will need to offer sellers like you. One way for them to assess market conditions is to run a simple survey, like the one shown on the left in Panel A of Figure 3.

Go ahead and fill in your answers, describing your supply plans: How many second-hand textbooks will you re-sell at the end of the year, if you're offered a price of $5 per book? What if the price is $10, $20, $30, $40, or even higher? Now, take the data from Panel A and plot your responses in the figure in Panel B. You have discovered your individual supply curve for textbooks. When Amazon's executives analyse your individual supply curve, they will notice that the higher the price they offer, the larger the quantity that you will supply. That is, they'll discover that individual supply curves for used textbooks are upward-sloping. ■

The Law of Supply

You've now seen that BP will supply more petrol when the price of petrol is high. Likewise, you will supply more used textbooks when their price is high. In fact, economists have studied supply decisions in thousands of different markets and they have found that there's a general tendency for the quantity supplied to be higher when the price is higher. It's an intuitive idea: If you can sell something for a higher price, you'll sell more of it (holding other things constant). This is such a general principle that economists call it the **law of supply.** This law means that supply curves are upward-sloping, because higher prices are associated with larger quantities.

law of supply The tendency for the quantity supplied to be higher when the price is higher.

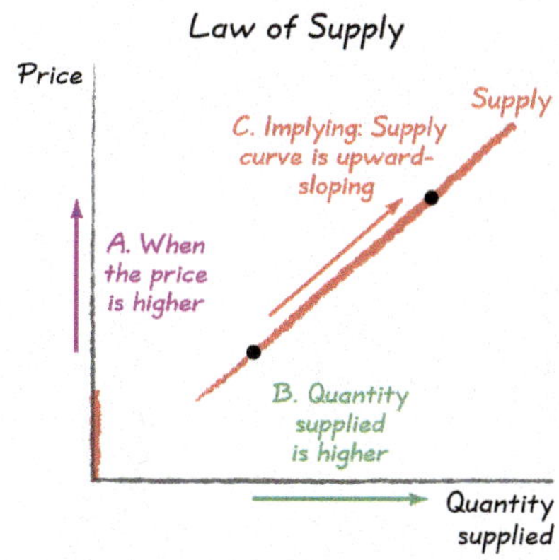

You are a supplier. Let's continue thinking about the supply decisions of our favourite business, Y.O.U., Incorporated. It turns out that YOU are making supply decisions every day. You are a supplier whenever you offer something in exchange for something else. And so figuring out your role as a supplier means answering two simple questions: What are you supplying? And in exchange for what?

If you are selling your old mobile phone, then you are a supplier of mobile phones. Or if you are selling concert tickets you can't use, you are a supplier of concert tickets. You are also a supplier when you offer services, instead of "stuff." If you have a job, you are a supplier of labour to your employer. Your economics instructor is a supplier of educational services.

Asking, "In exchange for what?" tells us about the price. Sometimes the price is some amount of cash—say, if you listed your mobile phone for $100 on eBay, or your on-campus job pays $25 per hour. But the price isn't always measured in dollars. For instance, you might offer to help your friend with their economics homework, on the understanding that they will help you with your psychology. Here, you are supplying your services as an economics tutor. And there is a price attached to your help, even though it's not measured in dollars: You are hoping for a certain amount of psychology tutoring in return. When you start to think like this, you'll see that you are making important supply decisions every day of your life. Even though many of these don't look like standard business decisions, you can learn to make better decisions by following the same logic that managers use when figuring out how to make good supply choices. Let's now turn to exploring that logic, working through Shannon's thoughts as she analyses the best supply decisions for BP.

Hero Images/Getty Images

Your tutor is a supplier—of academic help.

3.2 Your Decisions and Your Individual Supply Curve

Learning Objective *Apply the core principles to make good supply decisions.*

So far, we've learned how to summarise your supply plans using an individual supply curve. But where do these plans come from? Let's step back to see how Shannon prepared her analysis. We'll start by digging into the best pricing decisions for BP, and then turn to how to use the core principles to guide the choice of what quantity to produce at each price.

Setting Prices in Competitive Markets

A central part of any management role is understanding your competitive environment, and Shannon has analysed BP's position carefully. It operates in a fiercely competitive market in which there are lots of refineries around the world producing petrol and supplying the Australian market. Those refineries are all trying to sell their petrol through thousands of petrol stations around the country—and the main product they sell—petrol—is pretty much identical. Consumers are just as happy purchasing petrol refined by BP as they are purchasing petrol refined by any other firm, because BP petrol is neither better nor worse than petrol from Caltex, Mobil, or Shell.

perfect competition Markets in which 1) all firms in an industry sell an identical good; and 2) there are many buyers and sellers, each of whom is small relative to the size of the market.

Shannon has discovered that BP operates in a market characterised by **perfect competition,** which is the special case in which 1) all firms in the market are selling an identical good; and 2) there are many sellers and many buyers, each of whom is small relative to the size of the market. This has important implications for BP's price-setting strategy.

Perfectly competitive firms are price-takers, following the market price. When you're operating in a perfectly competitive market, your best strategy is to charge a price that is pretty much identical to whatever your competitors are charging. And so when the prevailing market price of petrol is $1.40 per litre, Shannon recommends that BP follow along, also selling its petrol for around $1.40.

Here's why. BP could try charging a bit more than the market price, but if you charge $1.45 when your competitors sell an identical product for $1.40, you'll quickly lose all your customers. Alternatively, BP could try to undercut its competitors, selling its petrol for $1.35 per litre instead. But this doesn't make sense either. Because BP is small relative to the entire refinery industry, it can expand production and still continue to sell a higher quantity of petrol at the market price of $1.40 per litre. So the only effect of charging a price below the market price will be to reduce the profits you earn on each litre of petrol you produce.

price-taker Someone who decides to charge the prevailing price and whose actions do not affect the prevailing price.

Consequently, managers in perfectly competitive markets don't spend a lot of time strategising about price, because their best price is the market price. This makes them **price-takers,** which means they take the market price as given and just follow along. Likewise, when you're a buyer in a perfectly competitive market—say, when you're buying petrol—you're acting as a price-taker, because you take the price as given, and decide what quantity to buy.

Not all markets are perfectly competitive. Of course, not all businesses operate in perfectly competitive markets, and so this advice isn't for everyone. If you operate in a market with only a handful of buyers or a handful of sellers, it's likely that you can have an important influence on the price. If this describes your industry, we'll analyse how best to set prices when we learn about *market power*—a key concept in microeconomics.

But for the rest of this chapter—and indeed, throughout our analysis of supply, demand, and equilibrium—we'll focus on perfectly competitive markets in which buyers and sellers are price-takers. Partly this is because nearly all markets involve some degree of competition, and so this is a natural foundation on which to build your understanding. We'll learn how perfectly competitive markets work, and along the way we'll build the analytical foundation you'll need when you later turn to focusing on imperfectly competitive markets. It's also to help simplify your introduction to economics. If all this talk of perfectly and imperfectly competitive markets seems a bit hazy now, don't worry, stick with microeconomics and we'll explore it more directly later when we learn about market power. But for now, realise that focusing on price-takers simplifies things, because then you can analyse the question of what quantity to produce separately from the question of what price to set.

Some of you might question whether the Australian petrol market is really all that competitive. In fact, once you start thinking about it, you might wonder whether any markets in Australia are very competitive! Australia has four major banks, two major supermarket chains, and three main telecommunications providers. There is a lot of concentration in many markets in Australia. But it is really useful to have a benchmark of perfect competition in mind against which to assess different markets, even if a given market doesn't perfectly fit the definition of "perfect" competition.

Choosing the Best Quantity to Supply

Since BP operates in a perfectly competitive market, Shannon focuses her attention on the question of what quantity to supply at any given price. She has a vast spreadsheet listing information about the costs of producing more or less petrol. But how can she transform this information into a concrete plan?

Apply the core principles to your supply decisions. It's time to put yourself in Shannon's shoes and apply the core principles, so that you can figure out the plan that'll yield the largest possible profit for BP. We'll start by figuring out what quantity to supply when the price of petrol is $1.40 per litre. If you repeat this step for the whole range of prices, you will have mapped out BP's whole supply curve.

So let's start by analysing how many litres of petrol BP should produce when the price is $1.40. I've included the core principles in Figure 4 below, to remind you how they might help you here.

Figure 4 | Applying the Core Economic Principles to Your Supply Decisions

Principle		The Idea		Applying the Principle
The marginal principle	→	Decisions about quantities are best made incrementally. Break "how many" questions into a series of smaller, or marginal, decisions.	→	Should I supply one more litre of petrol?
The cost-benefit principle	→	Costs and benefits are the incentives that shape decisions. You should evaluate the full set of costs and benefits of any choice, and only pursue those whose benefits are at least as large as their costs.	→	Is the price you get for the extra litre of petrol at least as large as the marginal cost? If so, then yes, you want to supply it.
The opportunity cost principle	→	The true cost of something is the next best alternative you must give up to get it. Your decisions should reflect this opportunity cost, rather than just the out-of-pocket financial costs.	→	Ask, "Or what?" If my business weren't producing this petrol, how else could we use our resources? This principle helps you figure out what to count as marginal costs.
The interdependence principle	→	Your best choice depends on your other choices, the choices others make, developments in other markets, and expectations about the future. When any of these factors change, your best choice might change.	→	"Holding other things constant" means we'll put aside these other factors for now and will return to them later.

Thinking at the margin means asking: Should you produce one more? The *marginal principle* says that decisions about quantities are best made incrementally, and that you should break "how many" questions into a series of smaller marginal choices. Instead of asking "how many" litres of petrol to produce, ask: *Should I produce one more litre of petrol?*

Compare marginal benefit and marginal cost. The answer depends on the *cost-benefit principle*, which says: Yes, you should produce that additional litre of petrol if the benefit of that extra litre exceeds the cost. That is, your decision *depends on the balance of marginal benefits and marginal costs.*

Of course, it's a bit unrealistic to think that a refinery manager who's responsible for making millions of litres of petrol per day will analyse her production litre by litre. She might think instead in terms of whether to expand annual production of petrol by 10 million extra litres. But we'll persist in asking whether to produce just one more litre because it points to the important insight—one confirmed by many leading managers—that smart supply decisions focus on marginal benefits and marginal costs.

Rawpixel.com/Shutterstock

Someday, you will learn to love spreadsheets.

The *marginal benefit* to your firm of producing an additional litre of petrol is simply the amount of money you'll get for it. If the price of petrol is $1.40, then the marginal benefit to BP of producing another litre of petrol is $1.40. That is, in a perfectly competitive market, your marginal benefit is the market price.

What about the *marginal cost*—that is, the extra cost from producing one extra litre of petrol? Turning back to her spreadsheets, Shannon sees that she has detailed data on the quantities of crude oil and other inputs, such as chemical additives, that will be needed in order to expand production, as well as the overtime hours it'll require.

Your marginal costs include variable costs but exclude fixed costs. As you think about what expenses to include in your calculation of marginal cost, you should apply the *opportunity cost principle*, asking "Or what?" You shouldn't just calculate the cost of producing another litre of petrol, you should compare it to the next best alternative, which is not expanding production.

If BP expands production, it'll have to buy more crude oil, more chemical additives, and pay its workers to work overtime. In the next best alternative—in which BP doesn't expand production—it won't need to buy this extra oil, extra chemicals, or pay these extra wages. As such, these are all opportunity costs—they're costs that BP incurs when it expands production, but wouldn't incur otherwise. These are called **variable costs,** because they *vary* with the quantity of output you produce. Your marginal costs are your additional variable costs.

variable costs Those costs—like labour and raw materials—that vary with the quantity of output you produce.

Shannon's spreadsheets also show that BP incurs a range of other costs. For instance, there's the cost of the refinery structures and equipment. But these pose no opportunity cost, because BP would have to pay for its building and equipment even if it pursued its next best alternative of not expanding production. The same is true for the land that it uses and the money BP pays its top managers, because producing another litre of petrol doesn't require more land or another CEO. These are all examples of **fixed costs** that don't change when you vary the quantity of output you produce. Because you have to pay your fixed costs whether or not you expand your production, they're not part of the opportunity cost of producing more petrol. Your fixed costs are irrelevant to your marginal cost.

fixed costs Those costs that don't vary when you change the quantity of output you produce.

Bottom line: As you calculate your marginal cost, make sure that it reflects only the variable costs that you'll incur from producing extra petrol, and that you're excluding all fixed costs.

The Rational Rule for Sellers in Competitive Markets

It's time to put all of this advice together. We've worked through the core principles—as summarised in the flowchart below—and that led us to the conclusion that BP should keep selling additional litres of petrol as long as the price is greater than (or equal to) the marginal cost.

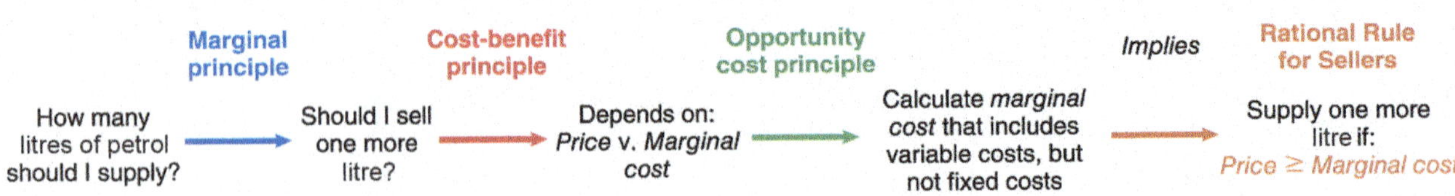

In fact you've uncovered a pretty powerful rule, which you can apply to *any* selling decision (in perfectly competitive markets):

The **Rational Rule for Sellers in Competitive Markets:** *Sell one more item if the price is greater than (or equal to) the marginal cost.*

Rational Rule for Sellers in Competitive Markets Sell one more item if the price is greater than (or is equal to) the marginal cost.

The *Rational Rule for Sellers* puts together the advice from three of the four principles in one sentence. It takes the big question facing managers about what quantity to sell, and reminds you to think at the margin, assessing whether to sell one more item by comparing your marginal benefit (in this case, the price you'll get) with the marginal cost, recognising that you should tally up your additional variable costs because they're the only true opportunity cost of expanding production.

Managers in competitive markets apply this rule to their real-world supply decisions. For instance, it says to Shannon that BP should expand production if the price of petrol exceeds marginal cost. Indeed, BP should keep expanding production for as long as the price continues to be at least as large as marginal cost.

Follow the Rational Rule for Sellers to maximise your profits. The *Rational Rule for Sellers* is good advice because it'll lead you to expand production whenever it'll boost your profits. After all, if the price of that extra litre of petrol exceeds the marginal cost, then producing and selling that extra litre will lead BP's revenues to rise by at least as much as their costs. As a result, BP's profit—which is its revenues minus its costs—will rise. Indeed, if you relentlessly follow the *Rational Rule for Sellers*—so that you take every opportunity to supply goods when the price is at least as high as your marginal cost—you'll produce the quantity that earns your firm the largest possible profit. It's the fact that this rule maximises your profits that makes it good advice for aspiring managers to follow.

To maximise your profits, keep applying the Rational Rule for Sellers, continuing to produce until:

Price = Marginal cost

(And if you're wondering why the *Rational Rule for Sellers* says to still sell an item even when its price is *exactly equal* to it marginal cost, realise that doing so will neither increase nor decrease your profits. It says to continue to sell up to, *and including*, the point when price equals marginal cost, only because it'll make the rest of your analysis a bit simpler.)

Keep selling until price equals marginal cost. If you follow this rule consistently, you'll continue to raise the quantity you supply until the point at which the marginal cost of the last litre is equal to the price. Why? Just as the *Rational Rule for Buyers* tells you to keep buying until your marginal benefit is equal to your marginal cost (which is the price), the *Rational Rule for Sellers* tells you to keep selling litres of petrol until your marginal benefit (the price) is equal to your marginal cost. That means you raise the quantity of petrol supplied as long as the price of each additional litre is at least as high as the marginal cost. Consequently, you should stop increasing the quantity of petrol you supply just before the marginal cost exceeds the price—which occurs in competitive markets when the *price equals marginal cost.*

You might recognise this insight as applying the *Rational Rule* from Chapter 1, which said: "If something is worth doing, keep doing it until your marginal benefits equal your marginal costs." When you're a supplier in a competitive market, the marginal benefit of selling an additional item is the price. As such, adapting the rule to your role as a supplier in a competitive market says you should expand production until:

Price = Marginal cost

Your supply curve is also your marginal cost curve. At this point, it should be clear why economists say that understanding supply is all about understanding marginal costs.

In fact, this reveals a new perspective for thinking about supply: Your firm's individual supply curve is also its marginal cost curve. After all, your individual supply curve plots the *price* associated with each specific quantity of petrol you might supply. If you keep selling until *price equals marginal cost,* then the same curve illustrates the *marginal cost* associated with each litre of petrol.

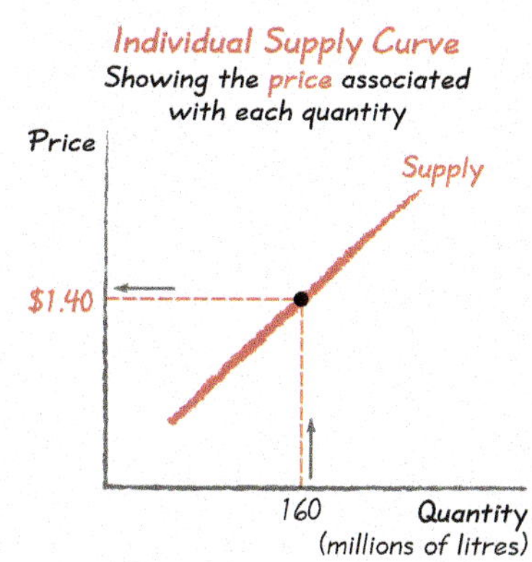

\+

Price = Marginal cost

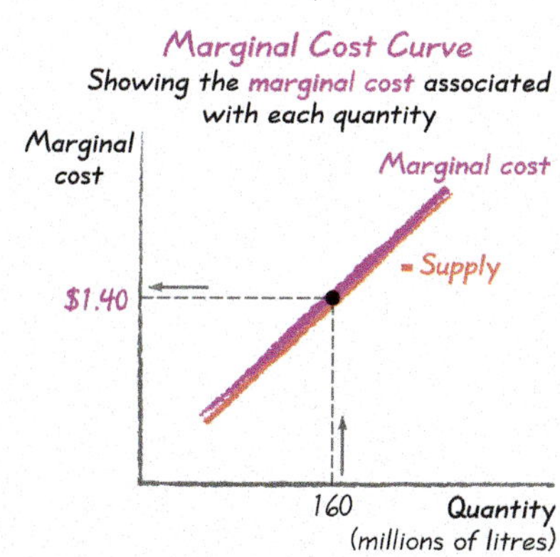

Your supply curve reveals your marginal costs. This yields an important insight. As an executive, you might want to compare your company's marginal costs to those of your rivals. Or perhaps as an analyst tracking the industry, you might be interested in understanding a business's cost structure. Or as a policy maker, you might need to better understand the costs of certain activities. You could try asking, but most companies will refuse to divulge this proprietary information, particularly if they're worried that you'll use it to gain a competitive edge. But don't let that stop you. As long as a company follows the *Rational Rule for Sellers*, its individual supply curve is also its marginal cost curve. And this means that you can also learn about its marginal costs just by observing its selling patterns. For instance, if a rival refinery supplies exactly 160 million litres of petrol when the price is $1.40, then you can infer that the marginal cost of producing that final litre must be roughly $1.40.

Let's summarise: Supply is all about marginal costs. Indeed, your supply curve is your marginal cost curve. Consequently, understanding supply is really about understanding marginal costs, and this insight sets the stage for the rest of this chapter.

Rising Marginal Cost Explains Why Your Supply Curve Is Upward-Sloping

Recall that the law of supply says that the quantity supplied tends to be higher when the price is higher. That is, it says the supply curve is upward-sloping. But what makes the supply curve upward-sloping?

> Supply curves are upward-sloping because of rising marginal costs due to:
> 1. diminishing marginal product
> 2. rising input costs.

For companies that follow the *Rational Rule for Sellers*, the supply curve is also their marginal cost curve. This implies that the supply curve must be upward-sloping because the marginal cost curve is upward-sloping. And why is that? Because, at some point as you increase the quantity you produce, the marginal cost of producing an extra litre of petrol rises. This increasing marginal cost reflects bottlenecks that arise when you try to expand production.

Diminishing marginal product leads to rising marginal costs. Expanding your production requires increasing your use of inputs, like labour. The extra output you get from an additional unit of input—like hiring one more worker—is called the **marginal product** of that input. Most firms find that at some point, hiring additional workers yields smaller and smaller increases in output. That is, they experience **diminishing marginal product,** which occurs when the marginal product of an input declines as you use more of it. (Note that diminishing marginal product doesn't mean that extra inputs will *reduce* your output. Rather, it says that the extra output produced by the next worker you hire won't be quite *as large* as the extra output produced by the previous worker you hired.)

marginal product The increase in output that arises from an additional unit of an input, like labour.

diminishing marginal product The marginal product of an input declines as you use more of that input.

In the short run, diminishing marginal product can occur when some of your inputs are fixed. Extra workers around a fixed office space can make it crowded and noisy, making it hard for anyone to get anything done. In a factory, extra workers might spend more time waiting for others to finish using equipment. A farmer can sow more seed, but with a fixed plot of land, that'll lead the plants to become overcrowded and many won't survive.

In the longer run, you can expand production by increasing all your inputs—hiring more workers, buying more equipment and more land. But the new workers you hire will have less experience and so will take longer to get things done. It'll be hard to find new land that's as fertile or well-located as your existing land. Expanding your company's research and development team won't boost your output by much if new ideas become harder to find. And managing a large workforce can become unwieldy, creating coordination problems as your company's top management is stretched thin. Whatever the cause, the result is that at some point, adding extra inputs won't produce as much extra output, and so your marginal costs will rise.

EVERYDAY Economics — The diminishing marginal product of homework

You've probably experienced diminishing marginal product while writing a paper for a class. The first day's work might be super productive; you gather your research, put your notes together, and start on a rough draft. On the second day, you expand on a few sections, improve your draft, and work out the inconsistencies. On the third day, you're starting with a pretty good paper, and while you can find ways to improve it, you're not making it much better. You could keep working on it forever, and each day you could probably find another small way to improve it. But you're experiencing diminishing marginal product as the amount that each successive day's work will boost your mark gets smaller and smaller. At some point the marginal product of an additional day's work on the paper is so low that you're better off just handing it in and catching up on your other subjects. ■

Rising input costs also lead to rising marginal costs. There's a second reason why your marginal costs might rise as you increase production: The cost of your inputs might rise. As you buy more of an input, its opportunity cost—what it could be used for instead—rises. You may be required to pay time and a half in order to get your staff to work overtime. Or perhaps you'll need to offer higher wages to attract more workers. It may also become harder to find workers or other inputs, raising search costs. Or perhaps inputs can only be found further away, raising transportation costs. The result is that at some point the rising costs of your inputs might lead your marginal costs to rise.

Recap: Individual supply reflects marginal costs. We've come a long way in understanding supply, so let's take stock. We've focused on individual supply—the selling decisions that an individual business makes. We described how an upward-sloping individual supply curve maps out your production plans, summarising the quantity you will supply at each price.

We then turned to asking: What are the best supply decisions you can make? This led us to the *Rational Rule for Sellers in Competitive Markets*, and if you follow it, you'll keep selling until price equals marginal cost. And diminishing marginal product and rising input costs explain why marginal costs are increasing, which explains why businesses are willing to supply a larger quantity only when prices are higher. As a result, supply curves tend to be upward-sloping.

See the Connections

Follow the *Rational Rule for Sellers in Competitive Markets* → *Price = Marginal cost* (*The Rational Rule*, applied to sellers) → Your supply curve is your marginal cost curve → Your supply curve is upward-sloping because of rising marginal costs

How Realistic Is This Theory of Supply?

By now, you may be scratching your head and asking: Do managers really behave this way? At a large firm like BP, they probably do—graduates with skills like Shannon's are in high demand, particularly by larger and more sophisticated businesses. But what about other companies?

As sellers experiment, they may come to act as if they follow the core principles. Many other businesses—particularly smaller businesses—can't or won't engage in such deep analytics. But chances are they do something simpler instead. They experiment with the right quantity to produce—producing a bit more or a bit less this week to see how it affects their profits. And this process of experimenting leads their managers to continue to make better decisions, until they've eventually discovered the quantity that maximises their profits. The *Rational Rule for Sellers* is valuable, because it provides a more direct path to figuring out the quantity that will maximise profits in a competitive market. But ultimately the managers who experiment their way to the profit-maximising outcome will end up making exactly the same supply choices as if they were following this rule. So if you need to figure out what choices a manager will make, the *Rational Rule for Sellers* will provide a pretty good forecast.

Survival of the fittest will weed out bad managers. There's also an evolutionary force that makes the *Rational Rule for Sellers* particularly relevant. There are lots of different rules of thumb that a manager could use instead. But many of these alternative rules lead managers to make bad decisions, and their companies eventually go out of business. You can think of this as a version of "survival of the fittest." The result is that those rules of thumb that lead to decisions that yield outcomes similar to the *Rational Rule for Sellers*—that is, that get close to maximising their profits—will survive, while those that yield worse decisions will die out. And so whether intentionally or by accident, the businesses that survive make decisions *as if* they were following the *Rational Rule for Sellers*.

Thinking through the principles provides useful advice and helpful forecasts. The *Rational Rule for Sellers* is important for two reasons. First, it provides useful advice to you. Managers who understand the rule are successful because it guides them to make the decisions that'll earn their businesses the largest possible profit. Talk to managers you admire, and you'll discover that they keep a laser-like focus on their marginal costs when making supply decisions, just as the rule suggests.

It's also useful for a second reason: If you need to forecast the supply decisions of a savvy manager, it's a good bet that they are thinking through the *Rational Rule for Sellers* and focusing on marginal costs. And if your competitors or suppliers don't want to reveal their marginal costs to you, you can still infer what they are by analysing their supply decisions. Since their individual supply curve is their marginal cost curve, their supply decisions reveal their marginal costs. This is going to be a useful insight as we turn to analysing how sellers as a group combine to shape market supply.

3.3 Market Supply: What the Market Sells

Learning Objective *Add up individual supply to discover market supply.*

So far, we've focused on the supply decisions of an individual firm. Now it's time to analyse *market supply*—the total quantity of an item supplied across all firms in the market. Just as your company's individual supply curve illustrates the quantity that an individual business will supply at each price, the **market supply curve** plots the total quantity that the entire market—including all producers—will supply, at each price.

market supply curve A graph plotting the total quantity of an item supplied by the entire market, at each price.

From Individual Supply to Market Supply

Just as we built market demand curves by adding up individual demand, we build market supply curves by adding up the individual supply curves of all potential suppliers.

Market supply is the sum of the quantity supplied by each seller. For each price, the market supply curve illustrates the total quantity supplied by the market. This means that you'll need to figure out the total quantity supplied when the price is $1, then $1.20, then $1.40, and so on. To find the total quantity supplied at a given price, simply add up the quantity supplied by each individual supplier.

There's a shortcut you can use if all the suppliers are quite similar. For example, if there are 10 refineries making the same supply decisions as BP, then at any given price, the quantity supplied will be 10 times the quantity BP supplies. This relationship between individual and market supply is shown in Figure 5. Because the market supply curve is built from individual supply curves, the same factors that shape individual supply, such as rising marginal costs, also shape market supply.

How market analysts estimate supply curves. Estimating market supply curves in the real world is somewhat more complicated, as suppliers are not typically identical to each other. As such, when you want to assess market supply, you'll need to figure out how much each potential supplier will supply at any given price. For example, we already know

Figure 5 | **The Market Supply Curve for Petrol in Australia**

Market supply plots the total quantity supplied across all sellers, at each price.

A **Individual supply** refers to the quantity an individual business will supply at each price. Plotting these numbers yields the **individual supply curve**.

B The market consists of **10 similar suppliers**, and so the total quantity supplied by the market at any given price will be 10 times larger.

C Plotting the **market supply** at each price yields the **market supply curve**.

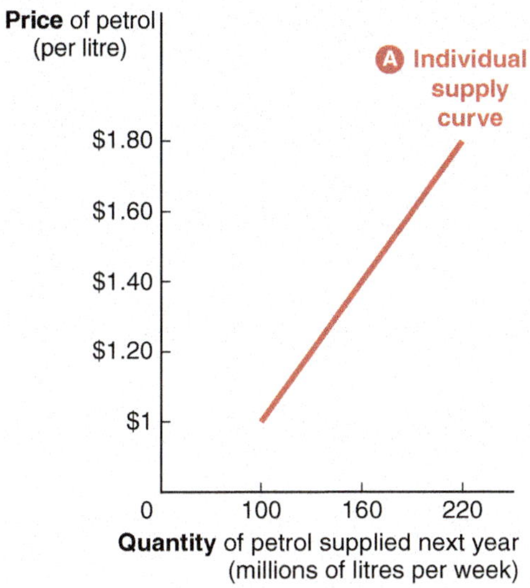

	A Individual supply	×	B Number of suppliers	=	C Market supply
Price (per litre)	**Quantity supplied per individual business** (millions of litres per week)		**Number of sellers in the market**		**Total quantity supplied** (millions of litres per week)
$1.80	220	×	10	=	2,200
$1.60	190	×	10	=	1,900
$1.40	160	×	10	=	1,600
$1.20	130	×	10	=	1,300
$1	100	×	10	=	1,000

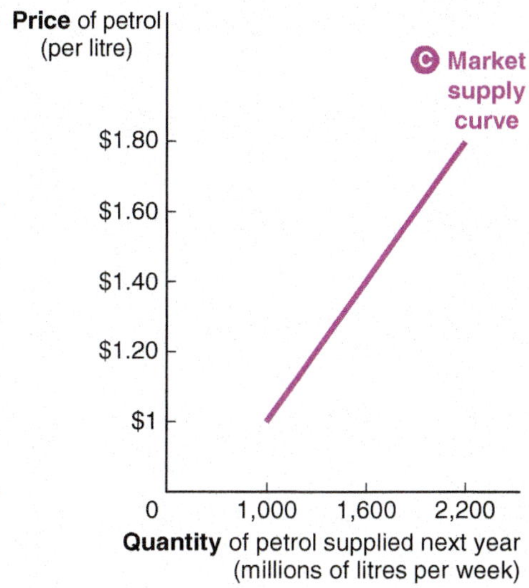

that BP produces 160 million litres of petrol when the price of petrol is $1.40, but how many other businesses are producing petrol? And how much will they each supply when the price is $1.40? Just as you can get a sense of market demand from surveying a subset of potential buyers, you can estimate market supply by surveying a sample of businesses, asking how much they will each supply at any given price. A comprehensive survey can illustrate how different segments of the market will increase the quantity supplied as the price changes. The tricky part is that you have to survey not only those businesses that are currently supplying petrol, but also those businesses that might enter the market when the price is high.

The Market Supply Curve Is Upward-Sloping

The market supply curve in Figure 5 shows that a higher price of petrol leads to a higher total quantity of petrol to be supplied, and hence the market supply curve is upward-sloping. Economists have found that in virtually every market the higher the price, the greater the quantity supplied. That is, the market supply curve obeys the law of supply.

There are two reasons that a higher price leads to a larger quantity supplied to the market:

Reason one: A higher price leads individual businesses to supply a larger quantity. When the price of the good your business sells is higher, you'll supply a larger quantity. Indeed, this is exactly what the individual supply curve shows. And because the market supply curve is built by adding up individual supply at each price, it inherits many of the characteristics of those individual supply curves, including their upward slope.

Reason two: A higher price means more businesses are supplying their goods and services; a lower price means fewer businesses are doing so. There's a second dynamic to consider: A higher price means that it's more profitable to be a supplier in your industry. And that's the sort of signal that leads existing firms to expand into your market, or new entrepreneurs to start new businesses. As a result, a higher price leads to more suppliers, leading to a larger quantity supplied.

On the flip side, a lower price means fewer businesses will be profitable, and thus fewer businesses will be willing to supply their goods and services. And that, in turn, helps explain why a lower price leads to a smaller total quantity being supplied.

As you evaluate market supply, make sure that your analysis accounts for both the choices that existing businesses make and also for whether new businesses will enter the market or existing businesses will exit.

Movements Along the Supply Curve

Movement Along the Supply Curve

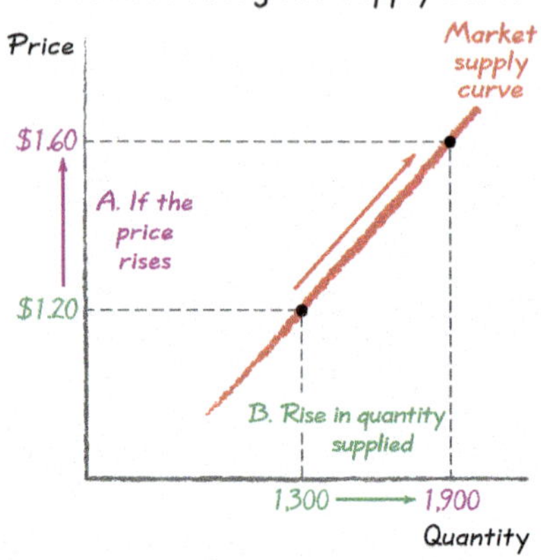

movement along the supply curve A price change causes movement from one point on a fixed supply curve to another point on the same curve.

change in the quantity supplied The change in quantity associated with movement along a fixed supply curve.

Managers find the market supply curve to be useful because it aggregates and summarises the behaviour of their competitors, showing the total quantity supplied across all sellers. To forecast the total quantity supplied in your market, simply locate the price on the vertical axis, then look across until you hit the supply curve, and finally look straight down to the quantity axis for your answer. The market supply curve shown on the right of Figure 5 shows that at $1.20 per litre, the market supplies 1,300 million litres of petrol. To figure out what happens when the price rises to $1.60, find $1.60 on the vertical axis, look across to where it hits the market supply curve, and then look down at the horizontal axis to see that the new quantity of petrol supplied is 1,900 million litres. Just as the law of supply suggests, a higher price led to a rise in the quantity supplied from 1,300 million to 1,900 million litres per week.

Notice that a price change led to a movement from one point on the market supply curve to another point along the same curve. That is, a price change causes movement from one point on a fixed supply curve to another point on the same curve. We use very specific terminology to keep this clear: A change in prices causes **movement along the supply curve** yielding a **change in the quantity supplied.** (This is just like demand, where a change in price causes movement along the demand curve yielding a change in the quantity demanded.) That insight covers the effects of price changes. Our next task is to evaluate how other changes will shift the supply curve.

3.4 What Shifts Supply Curves?

Learning Objective *Understand what factors shift supply curves.*

So far we've considered how the quantity supplied varies with the price of a good, *holding other things constant.* We applied the *opportunity cost principle,* the *cost-benefit principle,* and the *marginal principle,* and discovered the *Rational Rule for Sellers in Competitive Markets,* which helps you figure out how the quantity you supply should vary with the price. Now it's time to bring in the *interdependence principle* and ask: What happens when factors other than price change?

The Interdependence Principle and Shifting Supply Curves

The *interdependence principle* reminds you that your best choice as a seller depends on many other factors beyond price, and when these other factors change, so might your supply decisions. For instance, if the price of crude oil—which is an input into petrol—rises, Shannon would recommend that BP revise its supply plans. She would also revise BP's supply plans if the engineering division discovers more efficient production processes, or if it becomes more profitable to shift to a different line of business.

In each of these cases, the quantity that BP is willing to supply at any given price has changed. They're each examples of changing conditions leading sellers to revise their supply plans, and their new plans create a new supply curve. When the supply curve moves, we refer to it as a **shift in the supply curve.** Because your supply curve is also your marginal cost curve, any factor that changes your marginal costs will shift your supply curve.

As Figure 6 illustrates, a rightward shift is an **increase in supply,** because at each and every price, the quantity supplied is higher. A leftward shift is a **decrease in supply,** because the quantity supplied is lower at each and every price.

shift in the supply curve A movement of the supply curve itself.

increase in supply A shift of the supply curve to the right.

decrease in supply A shift of the supply curve to the left.

Figure 6 | **Shifts in the Supply Curve**

Panel A: An Increase in Supply

Ⓐ An **increase in supply shifts the supply curve to the right**, leading to a higher quantity supplied at each and every price.

Panel B: A Decrease in Supply

Ⓑ A **decrease in supply shifts the supply curve to the left**, leading to a lower quantity supplied at each and every price.

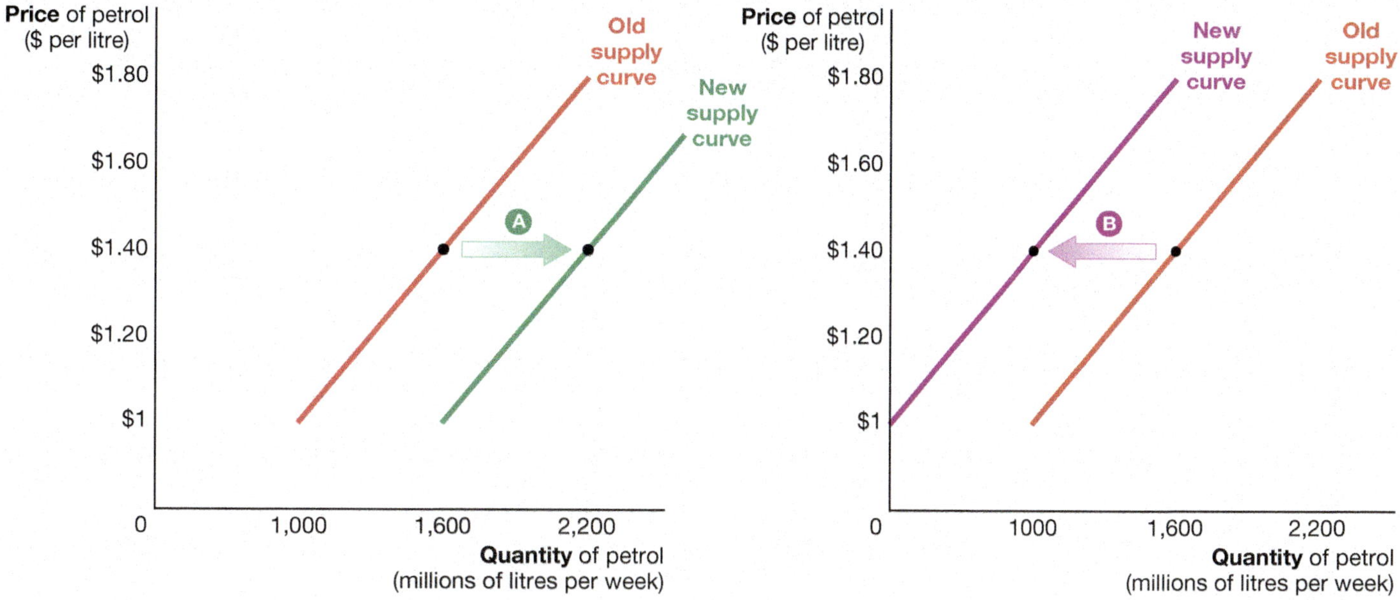

Five Factors Shifting the Supply Curve

The *interdependence principle* tells us that suppliers' choices depend on many other factors, and when those other factors shift, so will their selling plans, thereby shifting the supply curve. The key factors that cause the supply curve to shift are:

1. Input prices
2. Productivity and technology
3. Prices of related outputs
4. Expectations
5. The type and number of sellers

(Factors 1–4: Shift individual supply and hence market supply. Factor 5 → Only shifts market supply)

Changes in any of the first four of these factors shift individual supply curves, and because the market supply curve is built up from individual supply curves, these factors shift the market supply curve, too. The fifth and final factor—the type and number of sellers—only shifts the market supply curve.

As we now turn to analysing how each of these factors leads to a shift in supply, a recurrent theme will be that any factor that changes marginal costs—including opportunity costs—will cause a shift in supply.

> Five factors shift the market supply curve:
> 1. Input prices
> 2. Productivity and technology
> 3. Prices of related outputs
> 4. Expectations
> 5. The type and number of sellers
>
> . . . and not a change in price.

Supply shifter one: Input prices. The *interdependence principle* reminds us that the choices other businesses make affect your decisions. When your suppliers

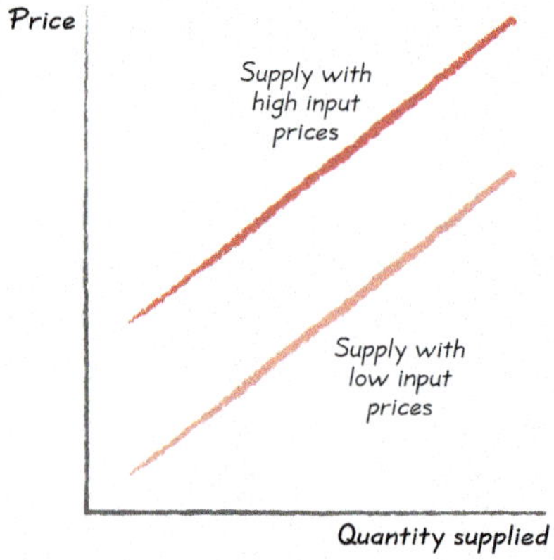

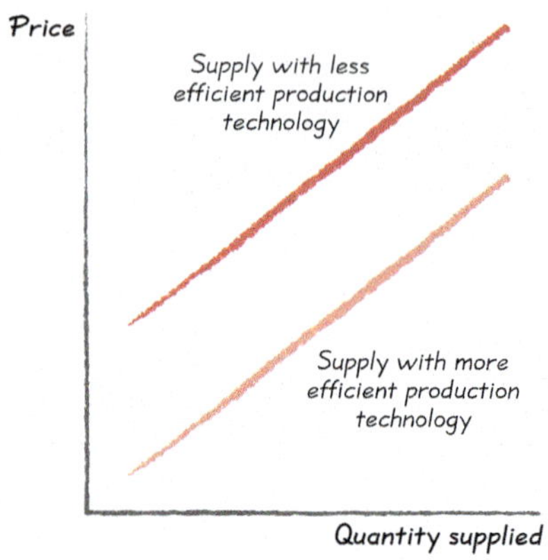

change the prices of your inputs, they change your marginal costs, and this will shift your supply curve.

For instance, refineries have two key inputs: crude oil and labour. If the price of either of these inputs rises, then so will BP's marginal cost of producing each additional litre. And that in turn lowers the quantity BP is willing to supply at any given price. Another way to say this is that a rise in marginal costs causes the price associated with any point on the supply curve to rise, because the marginal cost curve is the supply curve. This change is a leftward (or upward) shift in BP's supply curve. Likewise, a decline in input costs will shift BP's supply curve to the right (or downward).

More generally, changes in any input price will cause your supply curve to shift—whether it's a change in the price of a crude input like oil or a change in the hourly wage you pay your workers. There's also a global dimension to this: If your inputs are purchased internationally, then changes in the foreign exchange rate will also affect your costs, shifting your supply curve.

Supply shifter two: Your business's productivity and technology. Productivity growth—when businesses figure out how to produce more output with fewer inputs—is a key force reducing marginal costs through time. And because your supply curve is also your marginal cost curve, higher productivity leads to an increase in supply, shifting the supply curve to the right. For instance, if BP adopts new refinery processes that allow it to produce the same amount of petrol with fewer workers or less crude oil, this will reduce its marginal costs. Because new production techniques will only be adopted if they reduce costs, this process of ongoing improvement generally lowers costs, shifting the supply curve to the right.

This productivity growth is often driven by technological change, including the invention of new types of machinery or the adoption of new management techniques. The *interdependence principle* is critical to these shifts, because disruptive technological change is often due to developments in other industries. For instance, the internet was first developed as a military communications network, but it has since revolutionised production, sales, and distribution in industries as diverse as music, media, travel, and manufacturing. Productivity gains may also reflect your business's investments in research and development. There's also a natural tendency for productivity to rise through time due to learning by doing, as managers learn what does and doesn't work, thereby discovering further efficiencies. This is one reason that businesses grow over time—as they become more efficient, their supply curve shifts to the right.

Supply shifter three: Prices of related outputs. The *interdependence principle* also emphasises the connections between different markets. As a supplier, your decisions are interdependent because there are many different lines of business you could engage in. For instance, BP can use its oil refineries to produce petrol or to produce alternative products such as diesel fuel. If the price of diesel fuel rises enough, it will be more profitable for BP to produce diesel than to produce petrol. This will lead BP to switch some production from petrol to diesel, shifting its petrol supply curve to the left. When the price increase of one good (like diesel) decreases your supply of another (like petrol), we call them **substitutes-in-production.** Typically, substitutes-in-production arise when you can use your resources to produce alternative goods (like petrol versus diesel). This is the *opportunity cost principle* at work, as a higher price of diesel raises the opportunity cost of producing petrol. This higher marginal cost of producing petrol (remember: marginal cost includes opportunity costs, and not just out-of-pocket costs) causes BP to decrease its supply of petrol.

substitutes-in-production Alternative uses of your resources. Your supply of a good will decrease if the price of a substitute-in-production rises.

By contrast, goods that are **complements-in-production** are usually produced together. For instance, asphalt—the surface used to make our roads—is a natural byproduct of refineries. Consequently, if the price of asphalt rises, it becomes more profitable to operate a refinery, even if the price of petrol remains unchanged. As a result, an increase in the price of complements-in-production, like asphalt, leads BP to increase its supply of petrol. You can think of the extra revenues from asphalt as

complements-in-production Goods that are made together. Your supply of a good will increase if the price of a complement-in-production rises.

effectively lowering the marginal cost of producing petrol, shifting the supply curve to the right.

A warning: Don't confuse the complements that shift demand curves (products that you might *consume* together such as a meat pie and tomato sauce) with complements-in-production which shift supply curves (these are products you might *produce* together, such as petrol and asphalt). Likewise, don't confuse the substitutes that shift demand curves (goods you might *consume* as a substitute for each other, like buying a pizza instead of a meat pie), with substitutes-in-production which shift supply curves (which are alternative uses of resources you use for production, like producing diesel instead of petrol).

Bottom line: Supply will increase (shift to the right) if the prices of goods that are substitutes-in-production fall or if the prices of complements-in-production rise. And, supply will decrease (shift to the left) if the prices of substitutes-in-production rise or the prices of complements-in-production fall.

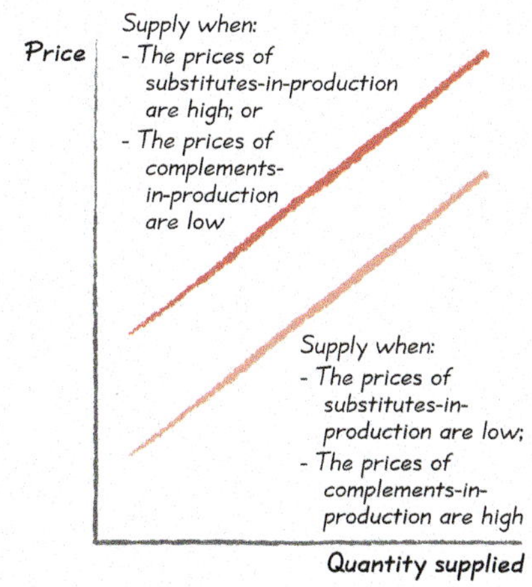

Supply shifter four: Expectations. Recall from the *interdependence principle* that your decisions are linked through time. In the short run, if you expect the price of your product to rise next year, you can increase your profits by storing it and selling it next year. This will decrease your supply this year (shifting your supply curve to the left) and increase your supply next year (shifting next year's supply curve to the right). You can see this as an application of the *opportunity cost principle*, as the opportunity cost of selling your goods this year is not selling them next year. And so expectations of higher petrol prices in the future raises the opportunity cost of supplying petrol this year, leading to a decrease in this year's supply. Of course, this only matters for goods that can be stored, and so future price changes will cause a shift in the supply of petrol (which is storable), but not fresh fish (which isn't).

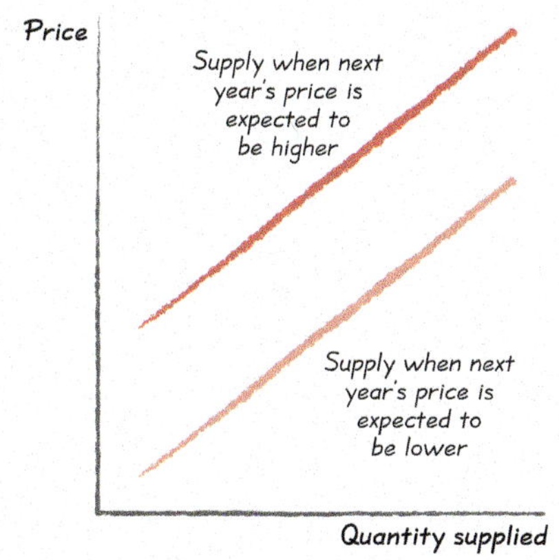

When goods are storable, your decisions about how much to *produce* this year can be separated from your decisions about the quantity to *supply* for sale. This distinction is particularly important when you expect prices to change. For instance, when BP expects a higher petrol price next year, it will increase production this year, but decrease its supply this year, storing unsold petrol to sell later at a higher price. Next year when the higher price arrives, it will increase both its production and supply.

If BP expects higher prices to persist in the long run, it will buy more equipment and hire more workers, which will increase both its production and its supply. Thus, the expectation of higher prices will decrease supply only in the short term; in the long run, businesses will invest in expanding capacity, increasing supply.

Supply shifter five: The type and number of sellers. The final supply shift to consider is the type and number of sellers. Because the market supply adds up the total amount supplied by all the sellers in a market, if those sellers change so will the market supply curve. If the market is composed of different types of businesses then the composition of market supply will change.

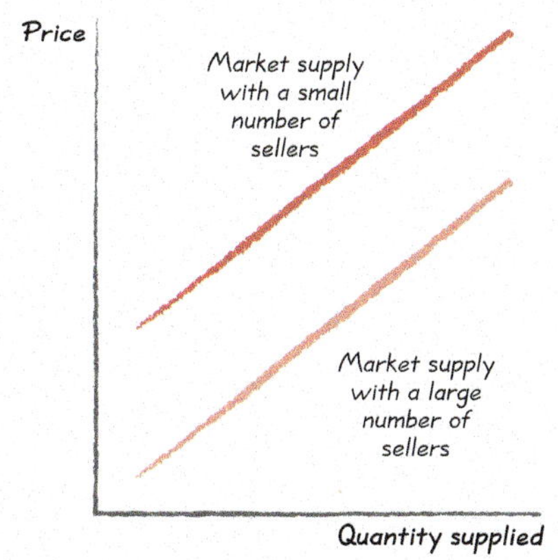

If new businesses enter the market, then the supply from these new businesses needs to be added to the market supply. As new businesses enter the market, they increase the total quantity supplied at each price, shifting the supply curve to the right. Similarly, if businesses shut their doors, exiting the market, the supply curve will shift to the left. Because the entry and exit decisions of businesses are driven by expected future profits, any factor that changes expected future profits will change the number of suppliers in the market and thereby shift the market supply curve.

It's worth noting that the first four shifters of supply impact market supply because they shift individual supply curves. Each factor that leads your business to increase supply will likely also lead your competitors to increase supply. Because the market supply curve is simply the sum of individual supply curves, each of these factors will also shift the market supply curve. However, the fifth shifter—the type and number of sellers—doesn't involve shifts of individual supply curves. Changes in the type and number of sellers shift only the market supply curve.

Recap: When things other than price change, your supply curve may shift. Let's recap. Your individual supply curve is your marginal cost curve, so anything that shifts your marginal costs will shift your supply curve. Indeed, each of the four factors that shift individual supply curves are relevant because they change your marginal costs. Changes in the prices of your inputs and your business's productivity both directly change your marginal costs. Changes in the prices of alternative outputs (that is, of substitutes-in-production and complements-in-production) and expectations about future prices also shift your marginal costs, by changing the opportunity cost of what you're producing and when you sell it.

Because the market supply curve is built from individual supply curves, these four factors shift the market supply curve, too. You can usually figure out the direction of the shift by remembering that any increase in marginal costs leads to a decrease in supply (shifting the curve to the left), while a decrease in marginal costs leads to an increase in supply (shifting the curve to the right). The fifth and final factor—the type and number of sellers—also shifts the market supply curve, but not individual supply curves. It'll be worth keeping these factors in mind as we now return to exploring the distinction between movements along the supply curve versus shifts of the supply curve.

3.5 Shifts versus Movements Along Supply Curves

Learning Objective *Distinguish between movements along a supply curve and shifts in supply curves.*

You'll find supply curves to be useful tools for analysing how changing market conditions shape the quantity that businesses supply. The key will be to distinguish between *movements along* a supply curve and *shifts in* a supply curve. Here's a simple rule of thumb:

> *If the only thing that's changing is the price, then you're thinking about a movement along the supply curve. But when other market conditions change, you need to think about shifts in the supply curve.*

Movements Along the Supply Curve

The reason that the supply curve doesn't shift following a price change is because the supply curve already summarises how much a business will change the quantity it supplies if the price changes. Think back to Shannon's memo (way back in Figure 1), in which she laid out the quantity she recommends BP supply at each price. A price change won't lead her to revise her memo—after all, the point of that memo was to lay out a plan for how BP should respond to different prices. And because BP's individual supply curve simply plots the plans outlined in Shannon's memo, if these plans don't shift, neither will its individual supply curve.

And if individual supply curves don't shift following a price change, then neither will the market supply curve. The point is that a market supply curve summarises the plans of how all potential suppliers respond to different prices, and so if none of their individual plans shift, then the market supply curve won't shift.

Indeed, managers find the supply curve to be useful precisely because they can use it to assess the consequences of a price change. For instance, Panel A in Figure 7 shows that when the price of petrol is $1.20, the total quantity supplied by the market is 1.3 billion litres per week. And it also shows that when the price of petrol is $1.60, the quantity supplied rises to 1.9 billion litres per week. As you can see, this price change leads to a movement along the supply curve. And this analysis shows that a higher price leads to a rise in the quantity supplied.

Figure 7 | **Movement Along a Supply Curve, and Shifts in the Supply Curve**

Panel A: When the Price Changes:
Movement Along the Supply Curve

Ⓐ A **change in price**, from $1.20 to $1.60 per litre.
Ⓑ Causes a **movement along the supply curve**.
Ⓒ Leading to a **change in the quantity supplied**, raising the quantity supplied from 1.3 to 1.9 billion litres per week.

Panel B: When Other Factors Change:
Shifts in the Supply Curve

Ⓐ A **decrease in supply** shifts the supply curve to the left, decreasing the quantity at each and every price.
Ⓑ An **increase in supply** shifts the supply curve to the right, increasing the quantity at each and every price.

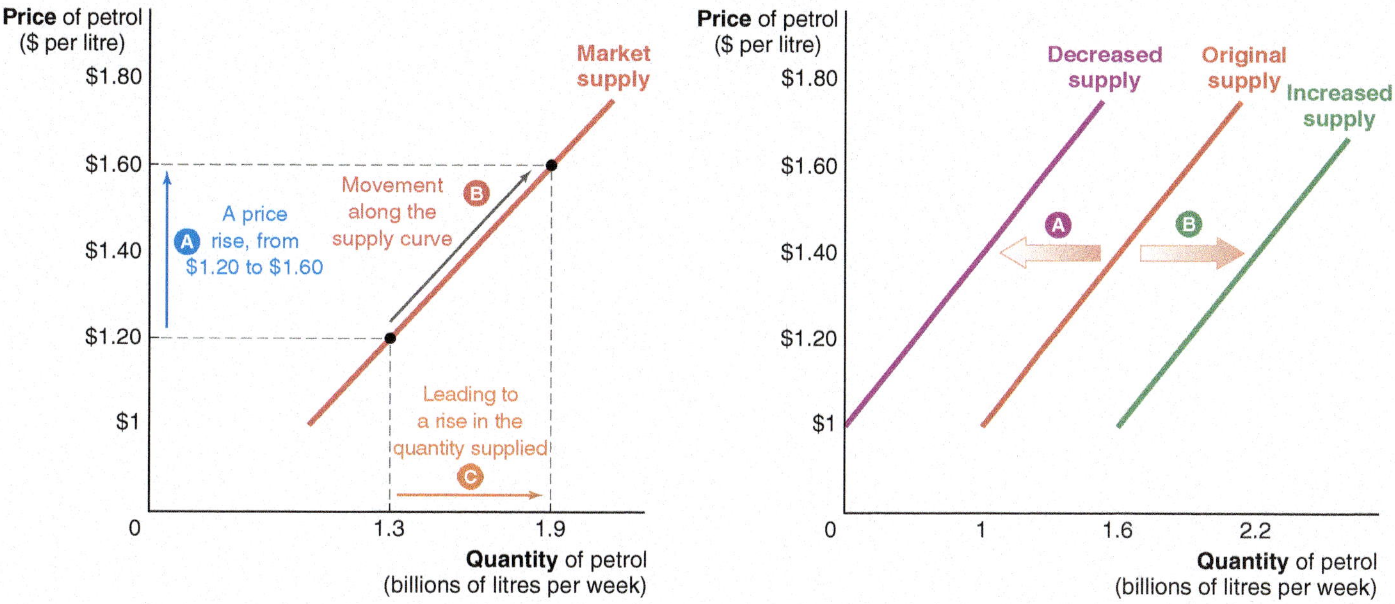

Shifts in Supply

But when other factors change—factors other than price—then you should revisit your plans about the quantity you'll supply at each price. For example, a change in the price of BP's inputs, in its productivity, its other options for production, or its expectations about future prices would lead Shannon to revise BP's supply plans. These factors will change the quantity that BP supplies at any given price, and as a result, they'll shift the supply curve. In order for a specific change in market conditions to shift your supply curve, it'll have to change your supply plans.

Remember that your supply curve is also your marginal cost curve, and so anything that changes your marginal costs will shift your supply curve. As you think about whether your costs have changed, make sure to think about both your out-of-pocket costs and your opportunity costs. If your marginal costs and hence your supply plans shift, then your supply curve will shift, as shown in Panel B of Figure 7. Lower marginal costs make it profitable to sell a larger quantity at any given price, and so will lead to an increase in supply, shifting the supply curve to the right. By contrast, higher marginal costs mean that it's no longer profitable to produce as large a quantity at any given price, and so will lead to a decrease in supply, shifting the supply curve to the left.

Shifts in supply are all about the *interdependence principle*: Your best supply decisions depend on many other factors, and when those factors change, so will your supply curve. The easy way to assess which factors cause the supply curve to shift is to remember the five supply shifters described in the last section: Input prices; Productivity and technology; Other opportunities and the price of related outputs; Expectations; and Type and number of sellers. And here's a hint that'll help you remember all five of these: Their first letters spell out I, POET. So when it comes to memorising the five factors that shift the supply curve, just remember you're a poet and then you'll know it.

Tying It Together

I bet you've noticed some similarities between this chapter, which analysed supply and seller's decisions, and the previous chapter, which analysed demand and buyer's decisions. There's a good reason for this—the forces driving supply and demand are very closely related. This is best illustrated by a simple thought experiment involving a brief detour to Mars.

But let's start on Earth. Think about a simple transaction, such as when you pull into my petrol station and buy 30 litres of petrol for $45. (You probably won't be surprised to know that I don't actually own a petrol station, but let's pretend for a moment that I do.) If you're like most economics students, you'll analyse this by noting that you are buying petrol and I am selling petrol. Consequently, we can analyse this transaction by exploring your demand for petrol and my supply of petrol.

Now consider how a Martian—who understands neither money nor petrol—might view the same transaction. They might think that I am trying to buy your cash and you are willing to sell it to me. How will I pay for your cash? Why, with petrol, of course. Viewed this way, I am the buyer who has a demand for your cash, and you are the seller who is willing to supply it to me if I'm willing to pay you enough litres of petrol. While the Martian's perspective seems funny, there's a certain logic to it.

Neither the Martian's nor the Earthling's interpretation is wrong. You are just as much a buyer of petrol as you are a seller of cash. And I am just as much a seller of petrol as a buyer of cash. When you think about it this way, it's no surprise that the same principles that animate our study of demand are also essential to understanding supply.

This similarity makes learning supply and demand a lot easier. In reality, there's only one set of principles governing the decisions you make as both a buyer and a seller. In our analysis of both supply and demand decisions, we used the same four core principles of economics to analyse how to make good decisions. Figure 8 highlights how these same foundations lead to some striking parallels between making good decisions as a seller and making good decisions as a buyer. It also highlights crucial differences, the most important of which is that we usually consider demand to be motivated by a desire by consumers to maximise economic surplus, while businesses on the supply side are trying to maximise profits.

Figure 8 | The Parallels Between Demand and Supply

	Demand	Supply
Your objective	Maximise economic surplus, which is the difference between the benefit you get and the price you pay.	Maximise profits, which is the difference between your revenues and your costs.
To decide on your quantity, follow the:	Rational Rule for Buyers: Buy one more item if the marginal benefit exceeds (or is equal to) the price.	Rational Rule for Sellers in Competitive Markets: Sell one more item if the price exceeds (or is equal to) the marginal cost.
Implying that:	Your demand curve is your marginal benefit curve.	Your supply curve is your marginal cost curve.
Curve slopes	Demand curves slope down. Because of diminishing marginal benefit.	Supply curves slope up. Because of increasing marginal cost.
The market	The market demand curve is the sum of the quantity each individual consumer demands, at each particular price.	The market supply curve is the sum of the quantity each individual business supplies, at each particular price.
A rise in price causes	A movement along the demand curve, reducing the quantity demanded.	A movement along the supply curve, raising the quantity supplied.
A fall in price causes	A movement along the demand curve, raising the quantity demanded.	A movement along the supply curve, reducing the quantity supplied.
Curves are shifted by	Shifts in demand curves are caused by changes in: • Income • Preferences • Prices of substitutes or complements • Expectations • Congestion or network effects • The type and number of consumers (shifts market demand only) . . . and not by a change in market price.	Shifts in supply curves are caused by changes in: • Input prices • Productivity and technology • Prices of substitutes-in-production and complements-in-production • Expectations • The type and number of sellers (shifts market supply only) . . . and not by a change in market price.

Chapter at a Glance

An Individual Supply Curve

Shows the quantity supplied at each price

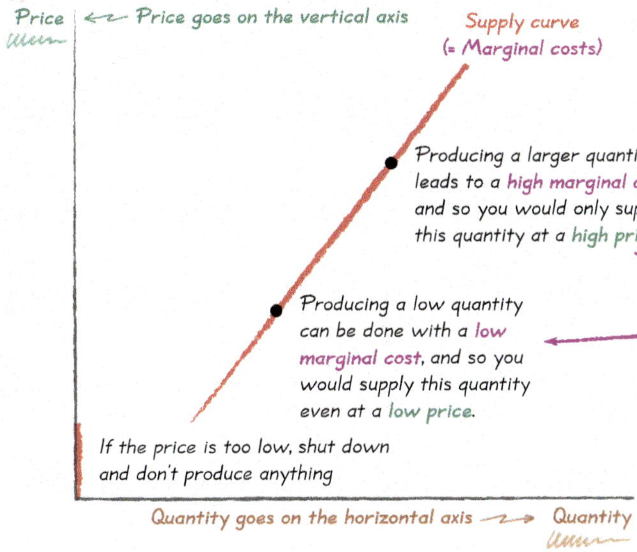

The Rational Rule for Sellers

Sell more of an item if its price is greater than (or equal to) marginal cost

Price = Marginal cost

Your supply curve is your marginal cost curve.

Your supply curve is upward sloping because of increasing marginal costs.

Market Supply Curves

Add up individual supply curves to get the market supply curve. Remember to account for not only current businesses in the market, but also to consider whether new businesses may enter the market when the price rises, or whether existing business may exit the market when the price falls. The same factors that shape individual supply shape market supply.

When the Price Changes:

Movement Along the Supply Curve

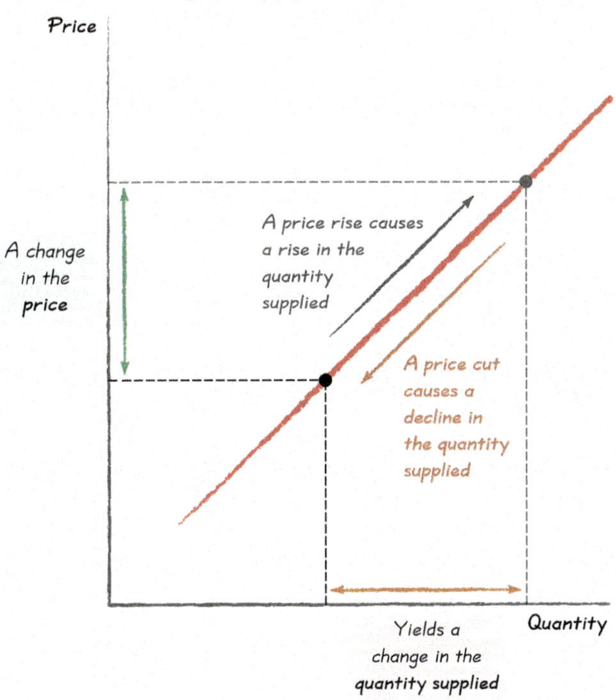

When Other Factors Change:

Shifts in the Supply Curve

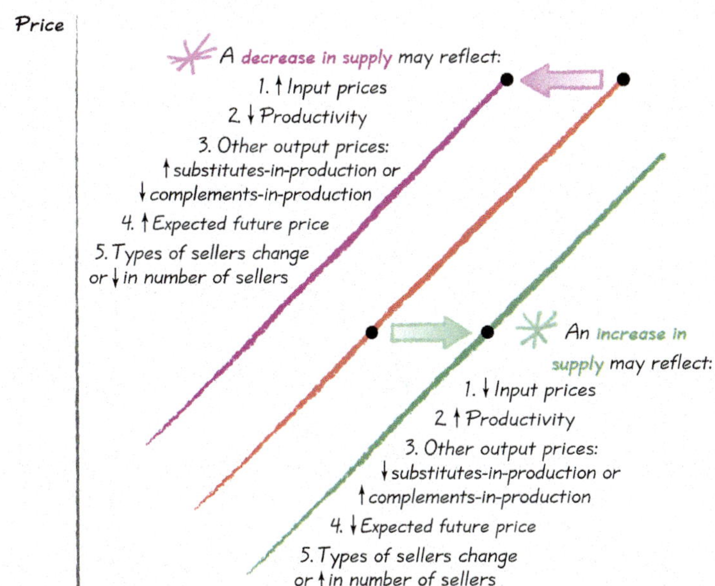

The acronym I, POET can help you remember these five shifters.

Key Concepts

Discussion and Review Questions

Learning Objective 3.1 *Discover the shape of your business's individual supply curve.*

1. Most people don't manage a business, however nearly everyone acts as a seller in some context. Give some examples of how you operate as a seller in your everyday life.
2. Workers act as sellers of their time in the labour market in return for some wage. Let's discover your individual supply curve for labour. For each hourly wage rate provided in the accompanying table, determine how many hours you would be willing to work each week. Then, plot your individual supply curve for labour. Are there wage rates at which you would not be willing to work at all? Use the concept of opportunity cost to briefly explain your reasoning.

Hourly wage rate	Hours willing to work each week
$10	
$20	
$30	
$40	

3. You've probably come across locations along the highway where there's a Caltex petrol station on one side of the road and a Shell petrol station on the other. The two petrol stations are often selling us petrol at exactly the same price. Why is this occurring?

Learning Objective 3.2 *Apply the core principles to make good supply decisions.*

4. Determine which of the four core principles should be applied in the following decisions and explain how to apply them.
   a. Your boss has offered to pay you for up to five hours of overtime today. You've already been working for 10 hours and are deciding if you want to stay another hour.
   b. A local DHL manager is trying to decide whether to pay for a new truck and driver to supply a larger quantity of package deliveries each day.

Learning Objective 3.3 *Add up individual supply to discover market supply.*

5. What is wrong with the following statement?
   The market supply for natural gas is the sum of all prices that natural gas producers are willing and able to sell at for every quantity.

Learning Objective 3.4 *Understand what factors shift supply curves.*

6. Maria is an executive at the a2 Milk Company. Using the interdependence principle, explain why and how she should change production plans if one of her milk suppliers cut the price they charge a2 by 20%. What about if workers, through their union, demand a 12% across-the-board pay raise?

Learning Objective 3.5 *Distinguish between movements along a supply curve and shifts in supply curves.*

7. What impact does the decision to enroll at university have on your individual supply curve for labour while you are at university? Does it cause a shift in the supply curve or a movement along the supply curve? Draw a graph to illustrate your decision.

Study Problems

Learning Objective 3.1 *Discover the shape of your business's individual supply curve.*

1. You have landed a job as an analyst working for a company that is selling a new environmentally friendly single cup coffee maker. Using the accompanying supply plan, draw your company's individual supply curve. Does your company's supply curve follow the law of supply?

Price	Quantity supplied (thousands)
$100	0
$150	500
$200	1,000
$250	1,500
$300	2,000
$350	2,500
$400	3,000

2. Thomas is the general manager for a local automated car wash. The market he operates in is perfectly competitive: Every car wash in the area is charging $14 for a car wash, which is also the marginal cost per wash. What will happen to Thomas's profits if he changes his price to $16. Why? What about a price of $10? What is his profit-maximising price?

3. Edith is the owner and manager of a small coffee shop that employs three workers who use the shop's one coffee machine to make and serve coffee to paying customers. Business has begun to pick up; lines are getting longer every day in her shop. On a busy morning, she sees her employees scrambling to take orders, get cups, fill coffee from the coffee machine, and serve customers in a timely manner. She thinks that if she hires three more employees, she'll be able to sell twice as much coffee. Do you think she's likely to be right? Why or why not?

Learning Objective 3.2 *Apply the core principles to make good supply decisions.*

4. Boeing is a producer of aircraft. Determine whether each of the following are fixed costs or variable costs for Boeing. Then, determine if they should be included in the marginal cost of producing an additional plane.

   a. The manufacturing plant used to produce the aircraft

   b. The labour used to produce the aircraft

   c. The seats that are installed in each aircraft

5. Mike, a manufacturer of generic medications, is deciding how much to charge retailers for their generic paracetamol. The marginal cost for each bottle is provided in the accompanying table. If the price of a bottle is $7.75, how many thousand bottles would Mike produce each day? What about if the price is $9.00 per bottle? Use the Rational Rule for Sellers in Competitive Markets to help explain why the values are different. Finally, draw Mike's individual supply curve.

Quantity of paracetamol (thousand bottles)	**Marginal cost** (per bottle)
1	$6.00
2	$7.00
3	$7.75
4	$8.25
5	$9.00
6	$9.50

Learning Objective 3.3 *Add up individual supply to discover market supply.*

6. Suppose there are four petrol stations in your neigbourhood. The quantity of petrol that each one is willing to supply per week at various prices is provided in the accompanying table. Determine the quantity supplied for the entire market at each price, and graph the market supply curve. Illustrate on your graph what happens to the supply curve when the price rises from $1.40 to $1.80.

Price per litre	Station A	Station B	Station C	Station D
$1.80	8,000	5,000	6,000	9,000
$1.60	6,000	4,000	5,000	5,000
$1.40	4,000	3,000	4,000	3,000
$1.20	2,000	2,000	2,000	1,000
$1	0	1,000	1,000	0

Learning Objective 3.4 *Understand what factors shift supply curves.*

7. You have recently been hired by Qantas to work in its strategy division. For each of the following, illustrate how Qantas's supply curve for airline flights will be affected, by drawing a graph showing any changes.

   a. The price of jet fuel falls.

   b. Innovative new software allows Qantas to more efficiently allocate its aircraft.

   c. Qantas has just signed a new enterprise bargaining agreement (EBA) that raises the hourly wage it pays to its employees.

8. When Dell adopted a "lean production" process—a management tool that reduces inefficiencies without reducing production—it became one of the world's largest computer manufacturers. What impact did the adoption of lean production techniques have on Dell's individual supply curve for computers? Use a graph to help illustrate your answer.

Learning Objective 3.5 *Distinguish between movements along a supply curve and shifts in supply curves.*

9. Briefly explain whether each of the following represents a shift in supply or a change in quantity supplied. Use a graph to illustrate your answer.

   a. An increase in the use of corn in the production of ethanol has raised the cost of corn to farmers who use it as livestock feed.

   b. Speculators in world iron ore markets push the price of iron ore up, leading Australian iron-ore companies to expand production.

CHAPTER

4

Equilibrium: Where Supply Meets Demand

Scene one: Utter chaos. It's the Sydney Stock Exchange in the 1980s—back when markets were "open outcry" and before all trades were made on computers. Traders on the floor of the exchange are packed in close to each other, raising their hands, shouting. Their eyes grow weary as they watch stock prices rise and fall. But even though they're shouting, they aren't fighting. Above the din, you hear someone yell: "I'll buy five thou' at four-forty."

Joelle Icard/Getty Images

After studying economics for a while, you will start to see supply and demand curves everywhere.

Scene two: An upscale coffee shop. It even has a view of the beach and free Wi-Fi. This looks like a nice place to relax and enjoy a latte or herbal tea, and so you walk in. The barista greets you with a warm smile and asks: "What can I get you?"

Scene three: It's 2 A.M., and you're still awake. You've been searching for hours, and the web pages are starting to blur. But you know that if you persist, you'll find an online store offering a great deal on the new television you want.

Scene four: Justin Bieber's right Yeezy, tossed into the audience during a concert, is up for auction on eBay. The first bid comes in at around $10,000. There are five days left before the bidding ends, and the shoe will go to the highest bidder. That's five days for you to consider how much of a belieber you are and whether you'd pay your right leg to own his right shoe.

These stories are all about the same thing: markets, the interaction of supply and demand. Buyers and sellers come together in a market, and your job in this chapter is to analyse how the forces of supply and demand interact in markets. The last two chapters have given you a solid foundation for assessing the choices that both buyers and sellers make. Our task now is to bring both sides together, embedding all of this within a complete supply-and-demand framework. It's a valuable framework that's essential for understanding the business world, and a whole lot more. You'll use it to forecast what gets bought and sold, what the prices of various products will be, and how these outcomes change when economic conditions change. Indeed, it's such a powerful framework that it'll guide much of the rest of your study of economics.

Chapter Objective

Analyse how supply and demand determine the equilibrium price and quantity.

4.1 Understanding Markets
Survey the central role that markets play in our society, determining what is produced, how, by whom, and who gets it.

4.2 Equilibrium
Analyse how markets bring supply and demand into balance.

4.3 Predicting Market Changes
Assess the consequences of shifts in demand and supply, and how changes in prices and quantities reveal whether demand or supply changed.

4.1 Understanding Markets

Learning Objective *Survey the central role that markets play in our society, determining what is produced, how, by whom, and who gets it.*

Imagine that it's your job to organise society. It's much harder than you might think. For instance, you have to decide which goods get produced. Given that a typical supermarket stocks around 40,000 items, and Amazon sells more than 10 million different items, this might take forever. And that's only the beginning. You also have to decide who will produce each of these goods, where to produce them, and how they'll be made. You'll need to buy enough raw materials and make sure you've hired workers with the right skills, each equipped with the right tools. Somehow, you want to ensure that each good is produced in the most efficient way possible by the lowest-cost supplier. Once you've made these production decisions, you still need to decide how to allocate these goods, figuring out who gets what. Making good allocation decisions requires understanding who would really value which goods. There's no point, for instance, in giving a meat pie to a vegetarian.

Thankfully, this isn't how we organise our society. There's no central planner telling each of us what to do, or what we each get. Instead, we rely on markets to organise what is produced, how it's produced, and how it's allocated. In place of the central plans used in **planned economies** like Cuba and the former Soviet Union (and to a lesser degree, China), the **market economies** in Australia, New Zealand, much of the Asia Pacific region, Europe, and North America are organised around markets. Instead of central plans, there are prices, and these prices provide incentives and information. For instance, if you really want a hybrid car, you'll be willing to pay a higher price for one. In turn, the prospect of selling hybrid cars for more money than nonhybrid alternatives provides an incentive for Toyota to produce the Prius, their best-selling hybrid.

planned economy Centralised decisions are made about what is produced, how, by whom, and who gets what.

market economy Each individual makes their own production and consumption decisions, buying and selling in markets.

Markets transform your desires into a price that you're willing to pay. This price provides a profit signal that motivates firms to produce and supply desired products.

What Is a Market?

market A setting bringing together potential buyers and sellers.

A **market** is any setting that brings together potential buyers and sellers. We often refer to sellers as "suppliers" and buyers as "demanders." Armed with this definition, you'll see that markets are everywhere, organising most of what we do. When you buy a coffee, you're a buyer (demander) in the coffee market. Indeed, whenever you spend money buying something, there's a good chance that you're acting as a demander of consumer goods or services.

Markets are everywhere. But there are many other economic roles that you'll also play, beyond "consumer." For instance, as a worker, you're a supplier in the labour market, selling your hard work for an hourly wage. If you run your own business, you might end up as a buyer in the labour market, buying the hard work of your employees. When you take out a home loan or small business loan, you're on the demand side in the market for credit. When you put your savings in the bank, you're a supplier of credit, supplying your savings to the bank, which will lend them to other borrowers. You're also embedded in a global market, and your purchase of an imported laptop from China sets off a chain of transactions in which the retailer selling the computer trades Australian dollars for Chinese yuan in the foreign exchange market, and then uses those yuan to purchase the laptop in China.

Each of these transactions involves a buyer and a seller meeting in a market. And in each case, there's a price that plays a central role, whether it's the price of a coffee, the wage earned by a worker, the interest rate on a loan or a savings account, or a foreign exchange rate.

Take an expansive view of markets. Modern economists believe that markets play an even larger role in your life beyond simply what you buy and sell. This expansive view of economics requires a creative understanding of what the relevant "prices" are. For instance, as a voter, you're a supplier in the market for votes. These votes aren't literally bought and sold, but you're more likely to vote for the politician who promises the policies you want. And so the price in the market for votes is the set of policies that a politician promises. The higher this price—that is, the better the set of promises that a politician makes—then the more likely it is that you'll supply your vote to that politician.

Krivosheev Vitaly/Shutterstock

A long-dead philosopher once said, "Teach a parrot the terms 'supply and demand' and you've got an economist." He was only half-joking.

Someday you may also be in the marriage market, open to the possibility that the right boyfriend or girlfriend will become your husband or wife. In this market, the "price" is the promise you make about how much love and support you'll offer, and the effort you'll put into helping run your joint household. The higher the price you offer—that is, the more you appear to be a terrific catch—the more likely your demand for a spouse will be met by a willing supplier. But as much as the market metaphor may help you understand dating markets, I still suggest calling your partner "sweetie" rather than "supplier."

There's also a market for marks in university courses. I don't mean to suggest that your lecturer is corrupt. Instead, students are on the demand side for marks, and lecturers are on the supply side. The "price" for good marks is good performance on quizzes, papers, and exams. As we'll see, when there's a lot of demand in a market, prices tend to be higher. This means that when there are a lot of students trying to earn an "HD" (that is, demand is high), it will require more hard work (that is, the price will be high).

When you think creatively, you'll start to see markets everywhere. Your introduction to economics will involve close study of the markets for consumer products, labour, machinery, land, financing, government bonds, foreign currencies, and more. But there are also markets for information, health, education, friends, influence, ideas, and even love. Armed with this broader notion of markets, you'll come to see just how pervasive markets forces are. That's why the core principles of economics can help you make better decisions across nearly all domains of your life.

How Markets Are Organised

There are many different ways in which buyers and sellers meet, and each of them counts as a market. A few examples are illustrated in Figure 1. In some cases, like in a coffee shop, prices are *posted*, and you simply pay the price, grab your latte, and go. Alternatively, perhaps you've participated in an *auction*, where the price you paid depends on how much the other bidders forced you to raise your bid on Justin Bieber's right shoe. Or consider the raucous *financial market* that was the floor of the Sydney Stock Exchange in the 1980s. Prices changed second by second as millions of dollars were won and lost, as traders bought and sold shares in big companies. These days, trading on stock markets around the world is automated, and happens through Bloomberg terminals and other devices. That's just a more efficient way to match the supply of and demand for shares in Apple or Facebook, or even old-economy companies like General Electric. Increasingly, markets are migrating *online*, and so shopping for your next television might involve comparing prices across dozens of websites. While each of these settings seems very different—brick-and-mortar stores versus internet stores, bidding versus posted prices, a coffee shop versus a trading pit—they're all markets because they bring buyers and sellers together. And in each case, the price is determined by the forces of supply and demand.

In each of these cases, outcomes are determined by the forces of supply and demand, so we can use the same economic framework to understand all of them. Indeed, the power of economic analysis is that supply and demand are the key forces shaping outcomes in many different kinds of markets. But there's also an important qualification: The supply and demand curves that we've studied so far are most appropriate for analysing markets that are characterised by *perfect competition*. Recall that perfect competition involves many buyers and many sellers of an identical good, and each of these buyers is small relative to the whole market. In this chapter, we'll work towards an understanding of how supply and demand interact in perfectly competitive markets. In reality, many markets are not

Figure 1 | **Various Markets**

martin berry/Alamy Stock Photo

Posted prices at a café

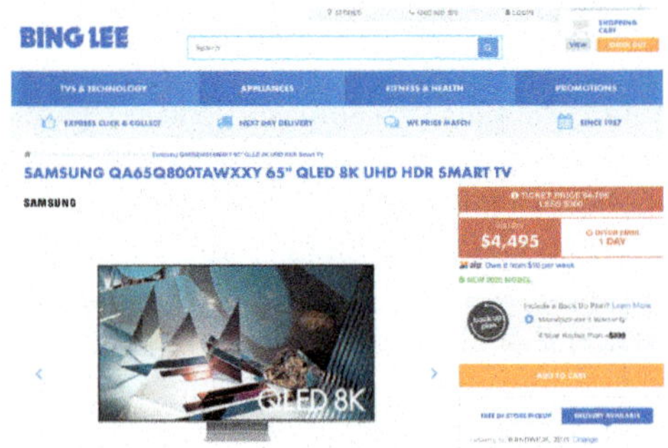

Online prices for a new TV

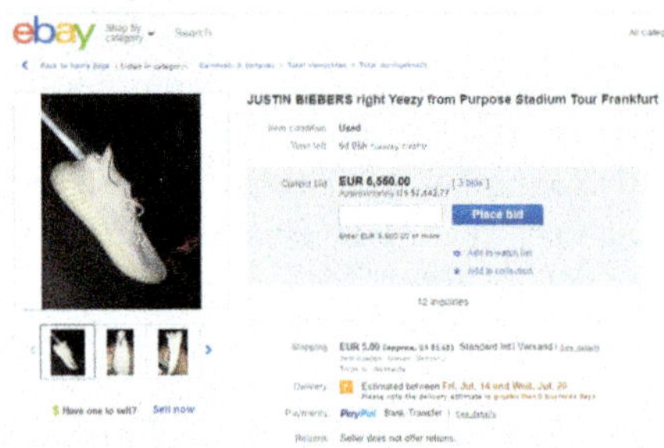

Justin's right shoe, selling at auction

DreamPictures/RGB Ventures/Alamy Stock Photo

Floor of the Sydney Stock Exchange

perfectly competitive. And so in later chapters, we'll see how some of our conclusions can change depending on the degree of competition in the market. But for now, let's see how perfectly competitive markets operate.

4.2 Equilibrium

Learning Objective *Analyse how markets bring supply and demand into balance.*

equilibrium The point at which there is no tendency for change. A market is in equilibrium when the quantity supplied equals the quantity demanded.

equilibrium price The price at which the market is in equilibrium.

equilibrium quantity The quantity demanded and supplied in equilibrium.

You may have encountered the term **equilibrium** in your science classes. Scientists refer to equilibrium as a stable situation with no tendency to change; this occurs when competing forces balance each other. The same idea applies in economics. A market is in equilibrium when the quantity supplied is equal to the quantity demanded. In equilibrium, every seller who wants to sell an item can find a buyer, and every buyer can find a willing seller. Because of this balancing, there's no tendency for the market price to change when a market is in supply-equals-demand equilibrium. There's only one price at which the quantity supplied equals the quantity demanded. This is referred to as the **equilibrium price.** The resulting quantity is called the **equilibrium quantity.**

Supply Equals Demand

The building blocks of our analysis will be market demand and supply curves. As you know, market demand and supply curves summarise the purchasing and producing decisions of all the participants in the market. The equilibrium occurs at the point at which the market supply and demand curves cross, because this is the point at which the quantity supplied equals the quantity demanded. You will see this most clearly by working through an example, and Figure 2 reintroduces the data on the market demand for petrol (which should be familiar from Chapter 2) and data on the market supply (from Chapter 3).

Figure 2 | Supply and Demand

The Market for Petrol in Australia

Equilibrium occurs where the supply curve cuts the demand curve.

Ⓐ The **quantity of petrol demanded at each price** is listed in the table, and graphed as the downward-sloping **demand curve**.

Ⓑ The **quantity of petrol supplied at each price** is listed in the next column of the table, and graphed as the upward-sloping **supply curve**.

Ⓒ Supply-equals-demand **equilibrium** occurs where the supply and demand curves meet. This yields an **equilibrium price** of $1.40, and an **equilibrium quantity** of 1.6 billion litres of petrol that´s produced and purchased each week. There is no shortage or surplus in equilibrium.

Ⓓ At **any price below the equilibrium price**, such as $1.20, the quantity demanded exceeds the quantity supplied, yielding a **shortage**.

Ⓔ At **any price higher than the equilibrium price**, such as $1.60, the quantity supplied exceeds the quantity demanded, yielding a **surplus**.

Price	Ⓐ Quantity demanded	Ⓑ Quantity supplied	Quantity supplied minus quantity demanded
$1.20	1.8	1.3	Ⓓ −0.5 (a shortage)
$1.40	1.6	1.6	Ⓒ Equilibrium: No shortage or surplus
$1.60	1.4	1.9	Ⓔ +0.5 (a surplus)

Note: All quantities are billions of litres per week.

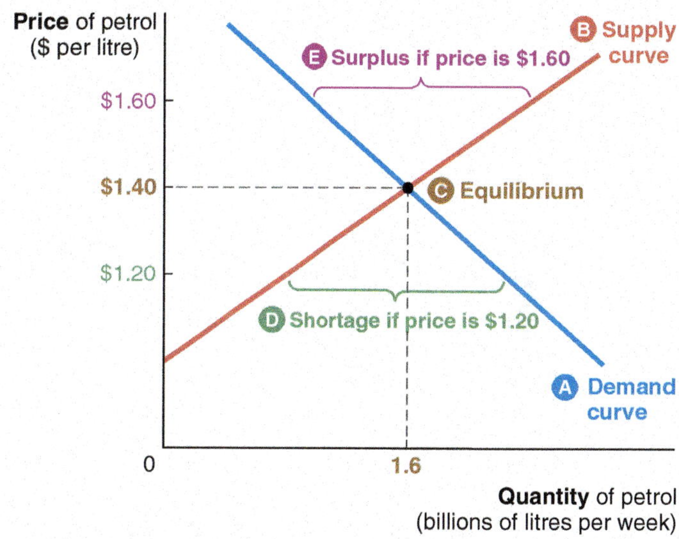

The table lists both the quantity demanded at each price and the quantity supplied at each price. Graphing the price against the quantity demanded yields the downward-sloping market demand curve shown on the right. Likewise, graphing the price against the quantity supplied yields the upward-sloping market supply curve.

Now that we've graphed the relevant data, it's time to figure out the equilibrium. Equilibrium occurs at the point where the quantity demanded is equal to the quantity supplied, and this occurs where the curves cross. Check both the graph and the table, and you'll see that when the price is $1.40 per litre, then 1.6 billion litres of petrol are demanded each week, and 1.6 billion litres are supplied. Consequently, the equilibrium price of petrol is $1.40 per litre, and at that price, the equilibrium quantity of petrol produced each week is 1.6 billion litres. Markets have a tendency to move towards equilibrium, and once they find it, prices and quantities stop changing—at least until something disturbs the market.

Recap: Equilibrium reflects both supply and demand. You've covered a lot of ground since you started studying economics, so let's review how we got here. In the chapter on demand, we discovered how to summarise the behaviour of many individual buyers with a downward-sloping market demand curve. Likewise, the actions of many individual sellers lead to an upward-sloping market supply curve. Markets tend to move towards equilibrium, which occurs at the point where the supply and demand curves cross.

When you stop to think about it, it's pretty amazing. The seemingly chaotic actions of many buyers and sellers in competitive markets can be summarised neatly into demand and supply curves. And the resulting market outcomes can be predicted by calculating the supply-equals-demand equilibrium. Your graphical analysis also makes it clear that market equilibrium is determined in equal measure by *both* supply and demand. Any analysis that omits either side of the market will be incomplete. While this might sound obvious right now, you'll be surprised at how often you hear even so-called experts talk about supply (and marginal costs) but forget demand (and marginal benefits), or vice-versa.

EVERYDAY Economics **Why is water cheap, while diamonds are expensive?**

AlmarinaStudio/Shutterstock

Rashid Valitov/Shutterstock

Diamonds or water: Which is more valuable?

Water is essential for human survival. Not only is it delicious and refreshing, but it also sustains all life. If you don't drink enough water, you'll die. And yet water is extremely cheap. Contrast this with diamonds, which sparkle beautifully, but are inessential for human survival and yet incredibly expensive. What's up with that? Your analysis of supply and demand yields two important lessons that are at the core of resolving this paradox.

Prices are determined by both supply and demand: If you think it's surprising that water can be both essential and cheap, you're probably only thinking about the demand (or marginal benefit) side. For instance, you figure that if something is essential, people must be willing to pay a lot for it. But prices are determined by *both* supply and demand. And when you think about the supply (or marginal cost) side, you'll notice that water is also plentiful and costs little to produce, while diamonds are scarce and expensive to mine.

Prices are determined at the margin: Okay, so prices are determined by both supply and demand; so far so good. Now recall that your demand curve is your *marginal* benefit curve, while the supply curve is your *marginal* cost curve. That is, when you think about your demand for water, you need to think about your marginal benefit, not total benefit. The total benefit of all your water consumption is extraordinarily high—it sustains your life. But if the price of water rose, you probably wouldn't reduce the amount of water you drink. Instead, you might take shorter showers or water your lawn less often. Thus, the "marginal" litre of water you buy is quite inessential. And so your willingness to pay for a litre of water is low, because the marginal litre brings little marginal benefit. But if water ever were to become so scarce that the marginal litre would save you from dehydration, your willingness to pay for one more litre of water may be so high as to make water more valuable than diamonds. ■

Getting to Equilibrium

So far, we've described equilibrium as the point at which there's no tendency for change. It's also important because markets tend to move towards the point of supply-equals-demand equilibrium. As a result, you can use your analysis of equilibrium to predict whether prices are likely to rise or fall.

shortage When the quantity demanded exceeds the quantity supplied.

Shortages lead the price to rise. Let's begin by thinking about what happens when the price is below the equilibrium level. Figure 2 demonstrates that when petrol is only $1.20 per litre, a **shortage** will result: The quantity of petrol demanded (1.8 billion litres per week) far exceeds the quantity supplied (1.3 billion litres). There are too many people chasing too little petrol, leading to shortages. As a result, individual petrol stations find themselves selling out of petrol, or facing long queues of desperate customers. How will suppliers and demanders respond to this shortage?

Start by putting yourself in the shoes of your local petrol station owner. You know that at a price of $1.20, you will sell out of petrol. You also know that if you raise your price to $1.21, you'll still sell all your petrol (check Figure 2; there's still a shortage), and so raising your price means raising your profits. Raising your price to $1.22 will raise your profits even further, and you will still sell all your petrol. As long as the shortage persists, you'll keep marking up your price.

Petrol customers are also a critical part of the process of pushing the price towards equilibrium. If you're a customer who's worried about a petrol shortage, you might tell a petrol station owner that you're willing to pay 1 cent per litre above her posted price of $1.22 to avoid missing out, and so the price rises to $1.23. As this process continues, the price will keep rising until the petrol shortage is eliminated, which occurs when the price is $1.40.

surplus When the quantity demanded is less than the quantity supplied.

Surpluses lead the price to fall. A similar process operates in the reverse direction when the price is above its equilibrium. Figure 2 shows that when petrol is $1.60 per litre, a **surplus** results as the quantity of petrol supplied far exceeds the quantity demanded. Petrol station owners, trying to sell off their unsold petrol, will charge lower prices in the hope of attracting more customers. With enough competition, repeated rounds of discounting will push the price down to $1.40 per litre, eliminating this surplus.

Figure 3 illustrates that when supply and demand are out of step, the forces of competition push markets towards the equilibrium price, thereby eliminating any shortages or surpluses. Economists emphasise this equilibrium point because it can help you figure out whether prices are headed up or down. And it's only when a market reaches equilibrium that supply and demand will be in balance, and so there will be no tendency for the price to change.

Figure 3 | How Markets Approach Equilibrium

There are two forces pushing markets towards equilibrium:

Ⓐ When **the price is above the equilibrium price**: A **surplus** leads to discounts, which **push the price down**.

Ⓑ When **the price is below the equilibrium price**: A **shortage** leads to mark ups, which **push the price up**.

Ⓒ Only when **supply equals demand** is the price stable and the market in equilibrium.

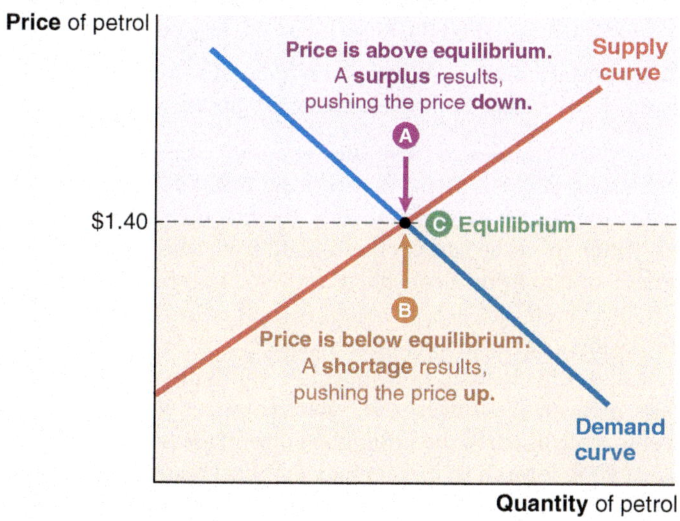

Figuring Out Whether Markets Are in Equilibrium

How can you tell whether a market is in a supply-equals-demand equilibrium? A simple diagnostic is to check whether prices are changing. Whenever the price is rising, that's a sign that at the current price, the quantity demanded exceeds the quantity supplied. And if the price is falling, it's likely that the quantity supplied exceeds the quantity demanded. If prices are free to adjust, then eventually these markets will be drawn to their equilibrium.

But sometimes, this process of price adjustment might be slow, or the price isn't free to change. And so this excess demand or supply will spill over into other domains. The next case study examines what happens when a market is not in equilibrium.

EVERYDAY Economics Smart parking meters

Have you ever driven around for what seemed like hours, looking for a place to park? The problem is that the number of parking spaces is relatively fixed, and during busy times, the quantity of spots demanded exceeds this fixed supply. What you're experiencing is a parking market that's stuck out of equilibrium. And the price can't rise to eliminate this shortage, because that would require reprogramming all the parking meters.

People respond in different ways to this problem. You might keep circling the block, effectively queuing for the next spot that comes up. Another possibility is to alter your plans for the evening by starting your night with dinner at a restaurant that offers valet parking. Yet another alternative—one that's quite common in the neighbourhood of big concerts or sporting events—is that you'll find someone who will let you park in their driveway for $20. But each of these are pretty costly fixes—mere Band-Aids for the problem. When the price can't change, the shortage of parking spots can persist.

Is there a better solution? The city of San Francisco thinks so, and it has experimented with one possibility: charging higher prices to park in the most overcrowded areas during busy times, and lower prices during less popular times. The program seems to have worked: Since it began, the number of people "cruising" for a spot has fallen by about 30%. ■

The problem of insufficient parking spaces highlights the three symptoms of a market out of equilibrium, which is also known as *disequilibrium:*

Symptom one: Queuing. When you're driving around looking for a spot, you're effectively queuing—waiting in line—for the next available spot. The extra time you spend in the queue raises the effective price you're paying because it'll cost you both time and money to get a spot.

Symptom two: Bundling of extras. When you bought dinner just so you could get the valet to park your car, you were effectively buying extras (that dinner) so you could get the thing you wanted (the parking spot), and this effectively raises the price you're paying to park.

Symptom three: A secondary market. When you parked in someone else's driveway, you found a way around the "official" market for parking spots.

Each of these symptoms serves to raise the "effective price," even when the price charged by sellers can't directly rise. These three symptoms of disequilibrium are not just about parking spaces—they occur in many markets. For instance, when a new videogame console is released, you'll often see gamers queuing to snag a scarce console. You'll find videogame stores that'll only sell you a console if you also buy a bunch of extra games that they bundle with it. And you'll find people reselling their consoles at a hefty markup on secondary markets like eBay or Facebook Marketplace.

If the problem is a surplus instead of a shortage, you'll observe similar symptoms, although in reverse—in a way that lowers the "effective price." For instance, sellers may queue to meet buyers—such as when the unemployed, who are potential sellers of labour, queue for a chance at a job interview. Buyers may demand "extras" be bundled for free, such as when savvy car buyers can get the dealership to throw in an upgrade. And prices will be lower on the secondary market, such as when tickets to unpopular sporting events sell below face value on StubHub.

4.3 Predicting Market Changes

Learning Objective *Assess the consequences of shifts in demand and supply, and how changes in prices and quantities reveal whether demand or supply changed.*

So far, we've seen that the intersection of market supply and demand curves determines the equilibrium price and quantity. We're now going to harness this powerful insight to predict how prices will change when economic conditions change.

Shifts in Demand

The market demand curve summarises people's current buying plans, but if those plans shift, then so will the market demand curve. As you likely recall from your study of demand in Chapter 2, there are several factors that shift demand, including income, preferences, the price of related goods, expectations, congestion and network effects, and the type and number of buyers. But remember: A change in the price will not cause a shift in demand.

Any change that leads you (or others) to buy a larger quantity at each price is an *increase in demand,* shifting the demand curve to the right. And if the change leads

Factors that shift demand curves:

1. Income increases demand for normal goods and decreases demand for inferior goods
2. Preferences including advertising and social pressure
3. Prices of complements and substitutes
4. Expectations
5. Congestion and network effects
6. The type and number of buyers

... but *not* a change in price.

people to buy a smaller quantity at each price, it's a *decrease in demand,* shifting the demand curve to the left. Again, don't confuse these *shifts in the demand curve* with a *movement along the demand curve* due to a change in price, which leads to a *change in the quantity demanded.*

Figure 4 illustrates how the market equilibrium changes when the demand curve shifts. The original or old equilibrium in this market—shown as the black dot—occurs when petrol sells for $1.40 per litre, and 1.6 billion litres of petrol are sold each week. But following a shift in demand, the market will move to a new equilibrium.

Figure 4 | Shifts in the Demand Curve

Shifts in demand cause price and quantity to move in the same direction.

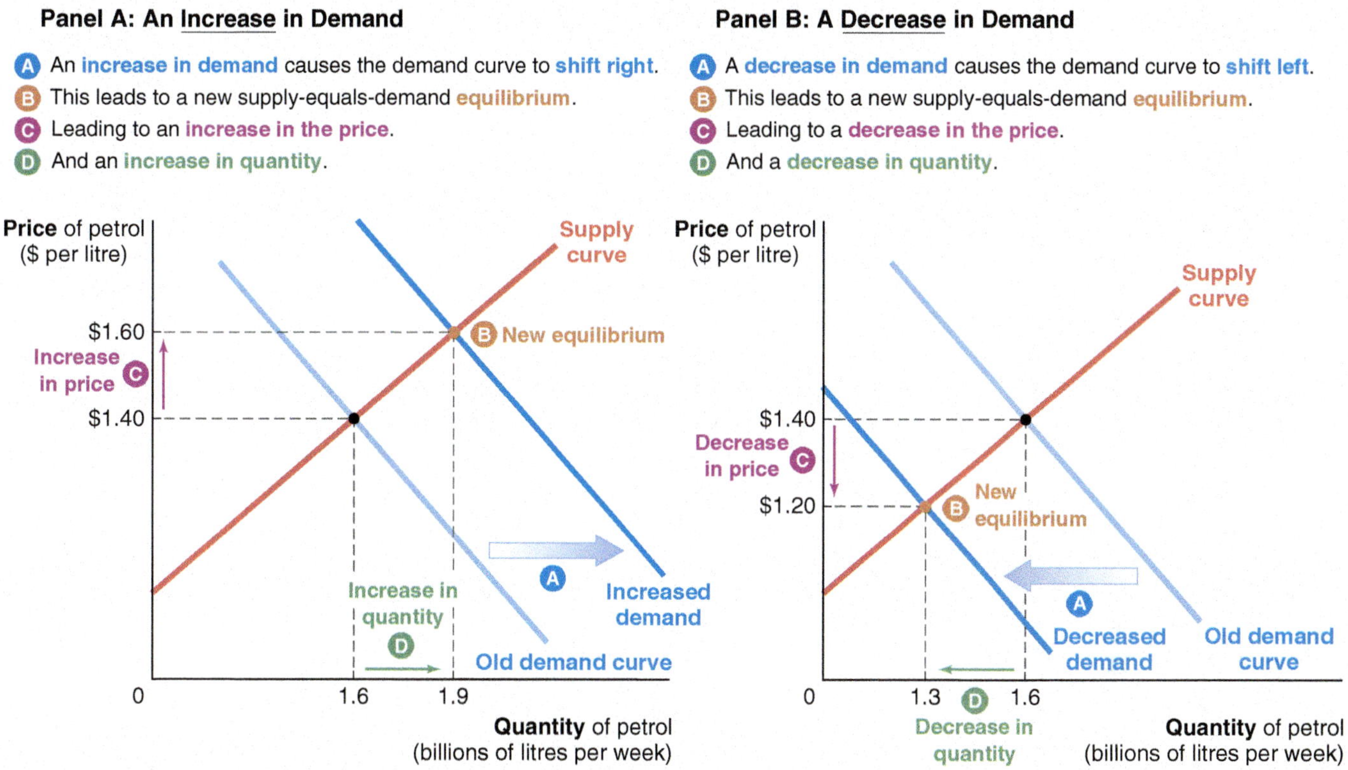

An increase in demand leads to a higher price and a larger quantity.

Panel A shows the consequences of an increase in demand, which is a shift of the demand curve to the right. The new equilibrium occurs at the point where this new demand curve intersects the supply curve, and you can read off the new equilibrium price ($1.60) and quantity (1.9 billion litres). This new equilibrium price is higher than in the old equilibrium ($1.60, compared with $1.40), as is the new equilibrium quantity (1.9 billion litres, compared with 1.6 billion). What's causing this change? An increase in demand means that buyers want to buy more at the old price of $1.40, but sellers don't want to supply any more. If the price didn't change, a shortage would result. But the prospect of a shortage leads the price to be bid up to $1.60, and that higher price is the incentive that leads suppliers to increase the quantity they supply as they move along their supply curve. The end result is that *an increase in demand causes an increase in both the price and quantity.*

A decrease in demand leads to a lower price and a smaller quantity.

Panel B shows that the opposite shift has the opposite effect. It shows a decrease in demand, which shifts the demand curve to the left, moving the market to a new equilibrium where this new demand curve cuts the supply curve. Comparing the new equilibrium to the old one, you'll see that this decrease in demand causes a reduction in both the equilibrium price (to $1.20 per litre) and quantity (to 1.3 billion litres). Again, pause to reflect on why this happens. There's decreased demand, but at the old price of $1.40, no change in supply. If the price didn't change, a surplus would result. The prospect of a surplus leads the price to be bid down to $1.20, and that lower price is the incentive that leads suppliers to decrease the quantity they supply as they move along their supply curve. The end result is that *a decrease in demand causes a decrease in both the price and quantity.*

Demand shifts lead price and quantity to move in the same direction. Notice that the equilibrium price and quantity both increase following an increase in demand, and they both decrease following a decrease in demand. And so in both cases, *shifts in demand cause price and quantity to change in the same direction.* As we're about to see, that's not true for shifts in supply.

Shifts in Supply

Factors that shift supply curves:

1. Input prices
2. Productivity and technology
3. Other opportunities and the prices of related outputs
4. Expectations
5. The type and number of sellers

... but *not* a change in price.

The market supply curve summarises managers' current selling plans, and if those plans shift, then so will the market supply curve. As you recall from your study of supply in Chapter 3, there are several factors that shift supply, including input prices, productivity and technology, other opportunities and the prices of related outputs, expectations, and the type and number of sellers. But remember: A change in the price will not cause a shift in supply.

A shift that increases the quantity suppliers plan to sell at each price is an *increase in supply,* and it shifts the supply curve to the right. The opposite—a *decrease in supply*—shifts the curve to the left. As we explore the consequences of shifts in the supply curve, be sure not to confuse them with *movements along the supply curve,* which occur when businesses change their quantity supplied in response to a change in price.

Figure 5 illustrates the consequences of shifts in supply. Once again, the original or old equilibrium in this market occurs when petrol sells for $1.40 per litre and 1.6 billion litres of petrol are produced. But if there's a shift in supply, the market will move to a new equilibrium.

Figure 5 | Shifts in the Supply Curve

Shifts in supply cause price and quantity to move in opposite directions.

Panel A: An Increase in Supply

A. An increase in supply causes the supply curve to shift right.
B. This leads to a new supply-equals-demand equilibrium.
C. Leading to a decrease in the price.
D. And an increase in quantity.

Panel B: A Decrease in Supply

A. A decrease in supply causes the supply curve to shift left.
B. This leads to a new supply-equals-demand equilibrium.
C. Leading to an increase in the price.
D. And a decrease in quantity.

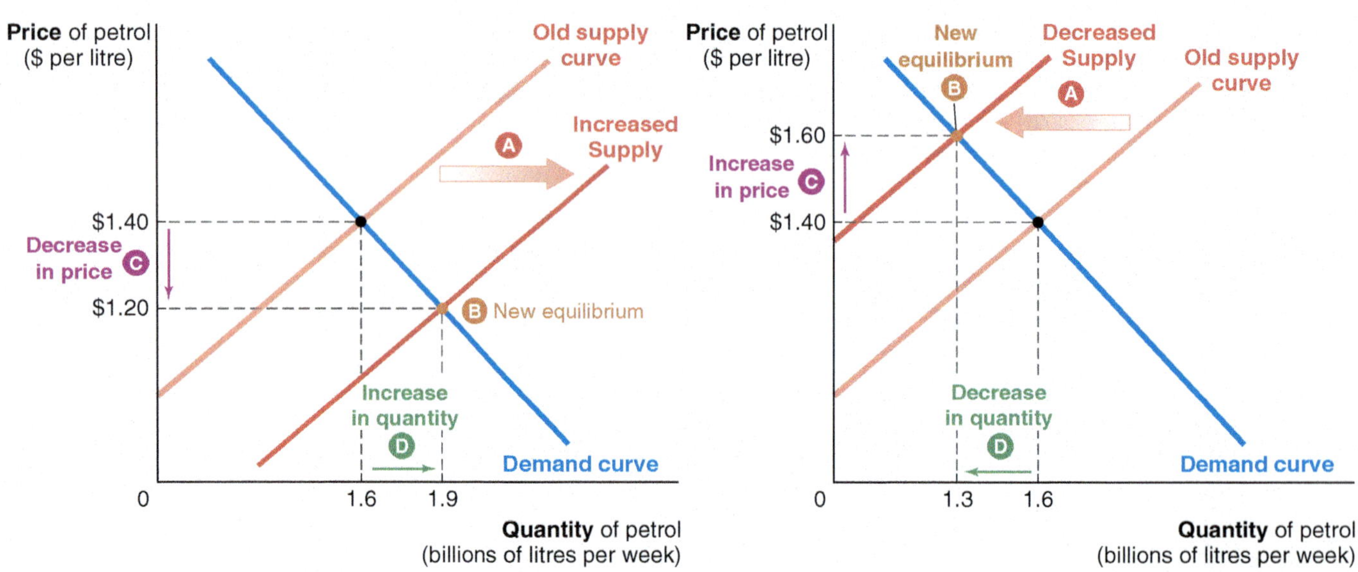

An increase in supply leads to a lower price and a larger quantity. Panel A shows an increase in supply, when the supply curve shifts to the right. The new equilibrium occurs at the point where this new supply curve cuts the demand curve, and it results in a new equilibrium price (of $1.20) and quantity (of 1.9 billion litres). This new equilibrium price is lower than in the old equilibrium ($1.20, compared with $1.40), and the new quantity is larger (1.9 billion litres, compared with 1.6 billion). To see what's going on, realise that an increase in supply means that managers want to sell more at the old price of $1.40, but buyers don't want to demand any more. If the price didn't change, this increase in supply would lead to a surplus. And this is what causes the price to be bid down to $1.20. That lower price is the incentive that leads buyers to increase the quantity they demand as they move along their demand curve. The end result is that *an increase in supply causes a decrease in price and an increase in quantity.*

A decrease in supply leads to a higher price and a smaller quantity. Panel B shows that the opposite shift has the opposite effect. It shows a decrease in supply, which shifts the supply curve to the left, moving the market to a new equilibrium where this new supply curve cuts the demand curve. Comparing the new equilibrium to the old one, you'll see that this decrease in supply causes an increase in the equilibrium price (to $1.60 per litre) and a decrease in the quantity (to 1.3 billion litres). Again, pause to reflect on why this happens. There's decreased supply, but no change in demand. If the price didn't change from $1.40, this decreased supply would lead to a shortage. The prospect of this shortage leads the price to be bid up to $1.60, and that higher price is the incentive that leads buyers to decrease the quantity they demand as they move along their demand curve. The end result is that *a decrease in supply causes an increase in the price and a decrease in quantity.*

Supply shifts lead price and quantity to move in opposite directions. Notice that an increase in supply causes the price to fall and the quantity to rise, while a decrease in supply causes the price to rise and the quantity to fall. That is, *a shift in supply causes price and quantity to move in opposite directions.* By contrast, your analysis of demand shifts revealed that *a shift in demand causes price and quantity to move in the same direction.* As you work through further examples, you can use these rules to check your analysis.

A shift in *supply* causes price and quantity to move in opposite directions. A shift in *demand* causes price and quantity to move in the same direction.

Predicting Market Outcomes

Congratulations! You have now built the foundations of a powerful framework for predicting market outcomes. The study of buyers that you began in Chapter 2 tells you which factors shape and shift the demand curve. Likewise, your study of sellers that you began in Chapter 3, tells you about the supply side. Now, when you put these together, you can predict how markets will respond to changing economic conditions. This simple supply-and-demand framework is the most powerful predictive device I know.

Okay, let's practice actually applying the supply-and-demand approach, by analysing a few real-world business questions. When you work through these examples, you should use the following simple three-step recipe that will help you predict real-world market outcomes.

Step one: Is the supply or demand curve shifting (or both)?
Remember that any change affecting buyers or their marginal benefits will shift the demand curve, while any change affecting sellers or their marginal costs will shift the supply curve.

Step two: Is that shift an increase, shifting the curve to the right? Or is it a decrease, shifting the curve to the left?
An increase in marginal benefit is an increase in demand, while an increase in marginal cost creates a decrease in supply.

Step three: How will prices and quantities change in the new equilibrium?
Compare the old equilibrium with the new equilibrium.

Let's see how the three-step recipe works, using a few simple examples.

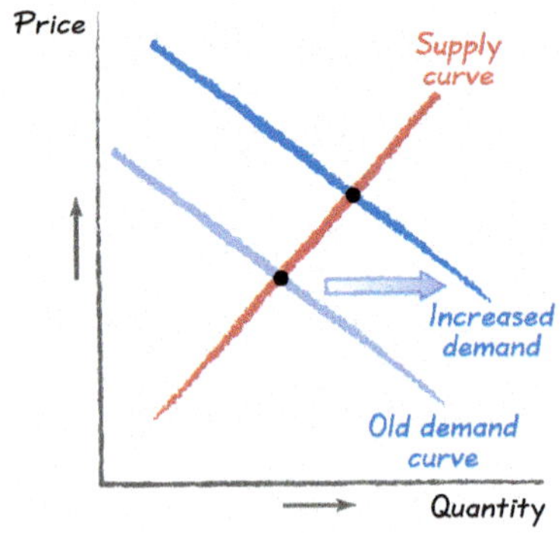

Example one: *A major retailer announces plans to install charging stations for electric cars in 50 parking spaces in 12 major metropolitan areas in Australia. How will this affect the demand for electric cars?*

Step one: Because *buyers* of electric cars will have greater access to charging stations while running errands, the convenience—and therefore marginal benefit—of owning an electric car will be higher so this will *shift the demand curve.*

Step two: The increased convenience will *increase* demand for electric cars, *shifting the demand curve to the right.*

Step three: At the new equilibrium, this increased demand will *raise both the price and quantity* of electric vehicles. This is good news for electric car manufacturers.

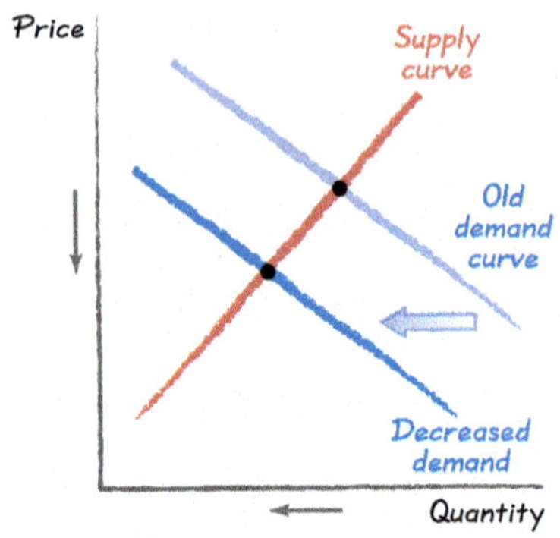

Example two: *Amazon announces that it is developing technology to deliver orders to customers within 60 minutes. Owners of local brick-and-mortar stores want to know how this will affect their companies' sales.*

Step one: Since the people who normally buy from their local stores will have a closer substitute for buying goods that they want quickly, this will *shift the demand curve.*

Step two: These buyers will find buying from Amazon to be more attractive, making them less likely to buy from local brick-and-mortar stores. This is a *decrease* in demand for goods from local stores, *shifting the demand curve to the left.*

Step three: Reduced demand will lead to a new equilibrium with both a *lower price and a lower quantity.* This is bad news for local stores.

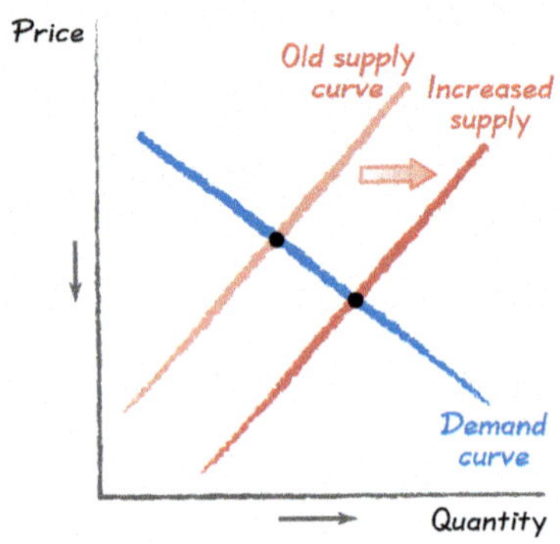

Example three: *The federal government announces a plan to fund research that will eventually lower the cost of the batteries used in hybrid cars. The head of Toyota's hybrid vehicle division wants to know how these innovations will affect the hybrid car market.*

Step one: Since the new manufacturing technologies will affect the *seller's* marginal cost of producing each hybrid car, this will *shift the supply curve.*

Step two: Because these cheaper batteries will reduce the cost of an important input into making hybrid cars, it will lower their marginal costs. Lower marginal costs lead to an *increase* in supply, *shifting the supply curve to the right.*

Step three: This increased supply will mean a *lower price* and *higher quantity* of hybrid cars sold—a welcome development for those who would like to see more "green" vehicles on the roads.

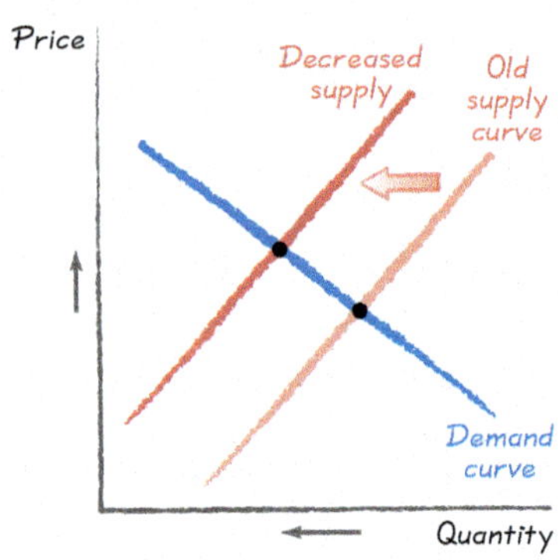

Example four: *Due to a drought in Queensland, farmers face rising costs for water. Macadamia farming is a water-intensive process. How will the drought affect the market for macadamias?*

Step one: Since water is an input into macadamia farming, the scarcity of the input will increase the *seller's* marginal cost of producing macadamias, which will *shift the supply curve.*

Step two: Because the marginal cost of producing macadamias will rise, supply will *decrease, shifting the supply curve to the left.*

Step three: This decrease in supply will lead to a new equilibrium involving a *higher price and lower quantity* of macadamias.

Do the Economics

Think you've got this business of predicting outcomes all figured out? Here's your chance to check, as you work through a dozen more examples.

If some Australian states lower the legal driving age, what will be the effect on the market for cars?

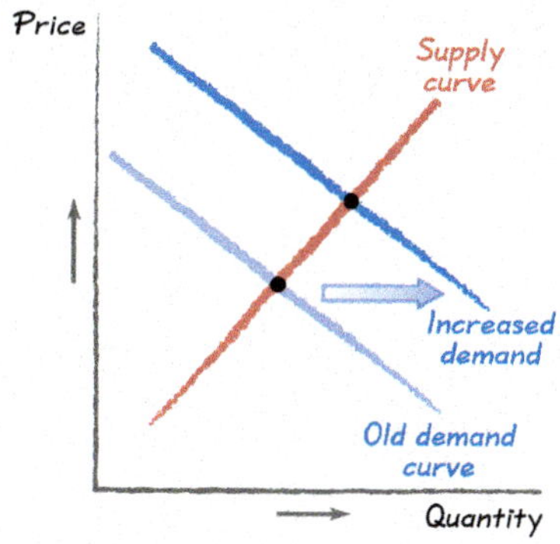

More consumers
→ An increase in demand

Result: Higher price, higher quantity.

Fishermen can now use a "fishfinder" to locate schools of fish in the ocean. How might this affect the market for fish?

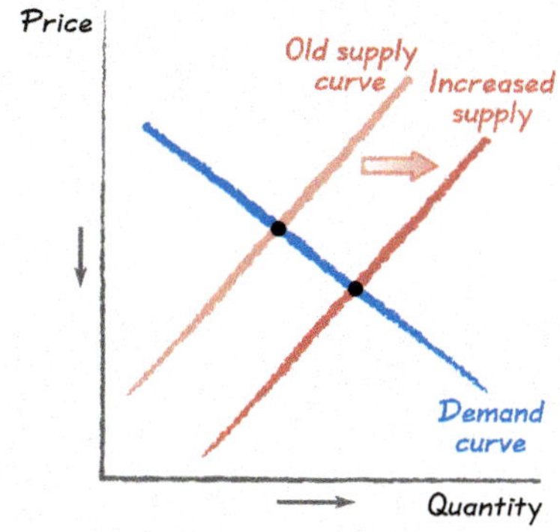

Greater productive efficiency
→ An increase in supply

Result: Lower price, higher quantity.

Sony reduced the price of its latest PlayStation videogame console. What effect will this have on the market for competing consoles such as the Xbox?

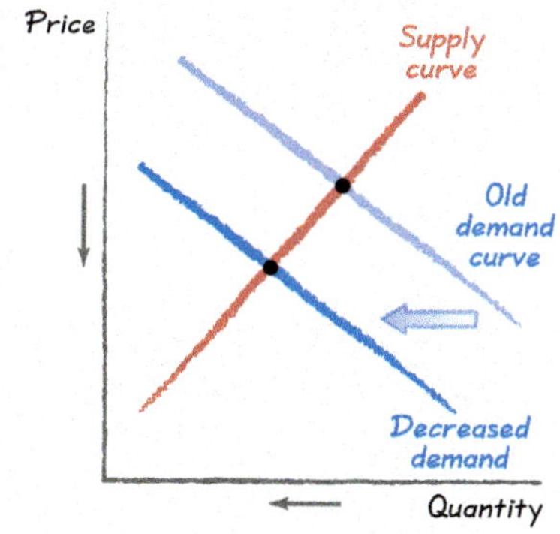

Lower price of substitute goods
→ A decrease in demand

Result: Lower price, lower quantity.

Suppose Australia institutes a ban on trans fats, a cheap but unhealthy ingredient used in fast food. What effect does this have on the market for hot chips?

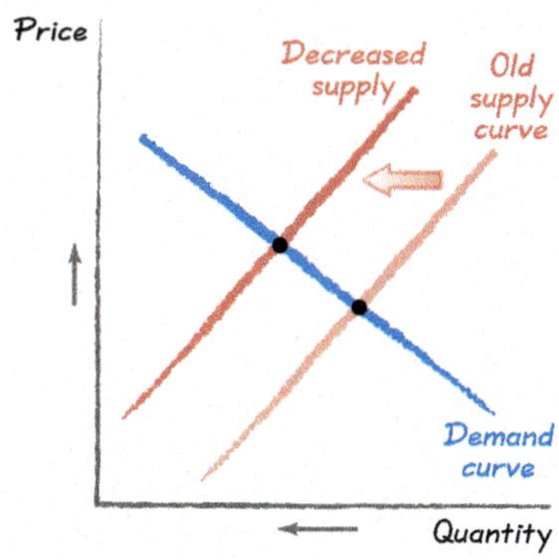

Higher cost of input
→ A decrease in supply

Result: Higher price, lower quantity.

Before a cyclone in tropical North Queensland, people stock up on essential supplies such as food and water. How will this affect the market for groceries?

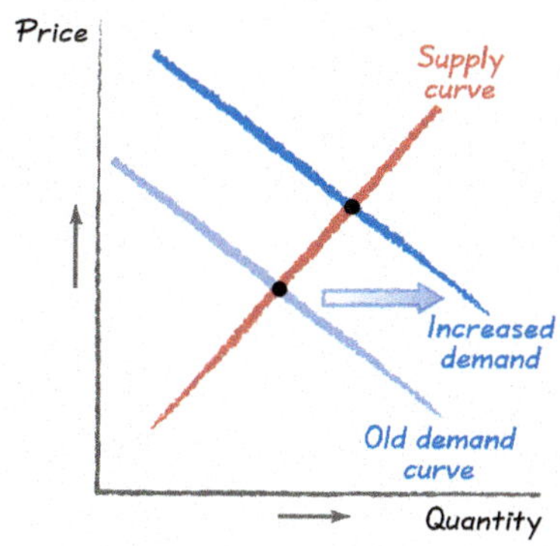

Consumers prefer greater quantities
→ An increase in demand

Result: Higher price, higher quantity.

Coal is burned to produce electricity. What happens in the market for electricity when the price of coal decreases?

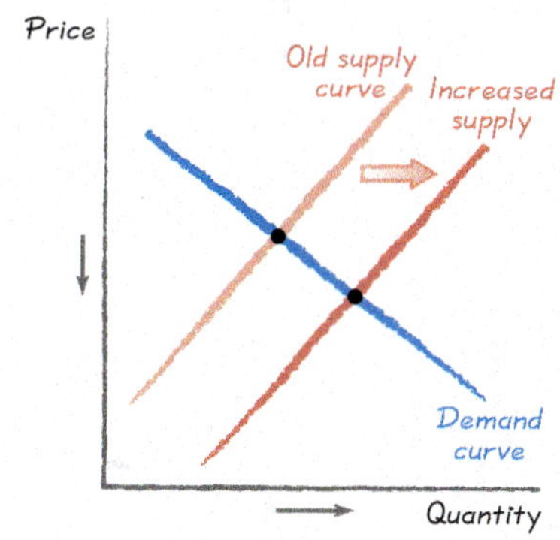

Lower cost of input
→ An increase in supply

Result: Lower price, higher quantity.

How did decreasing petrol prices affect the market for fuel-efficient hybrids?

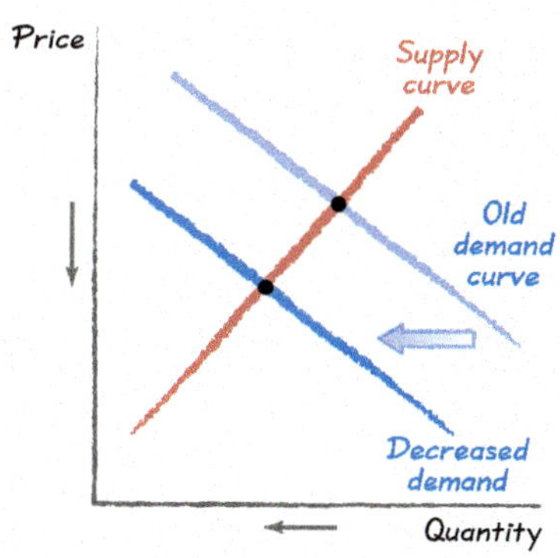

Lower price of a substitute (less fuel-efficient cars)
→ A decrease in demand

Result: Lower price, lower quantity.

Increasingly, corn is being turned into biofuel instead of being used as food. What has this done to the market for corn as a food?

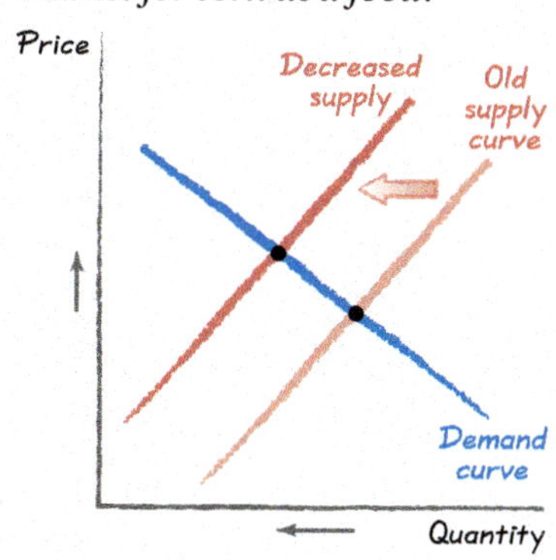

Biofuel and feed corn are substitutes-in-production
→ A decrease in supply

Result: Higher price, lower quantity.

A Chinese whitegoods company plans to start selling fridges in Australia. What will be the effect on the market for fridges in Australia?

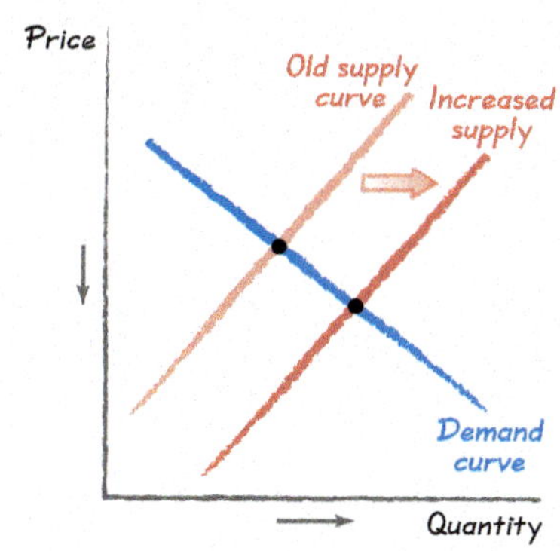

More sellers in the market
→ An increase in supply

Result: Lower price, higher quantity.

Incomes fell during the last recession. How did this affect the market for luxury jewellery?

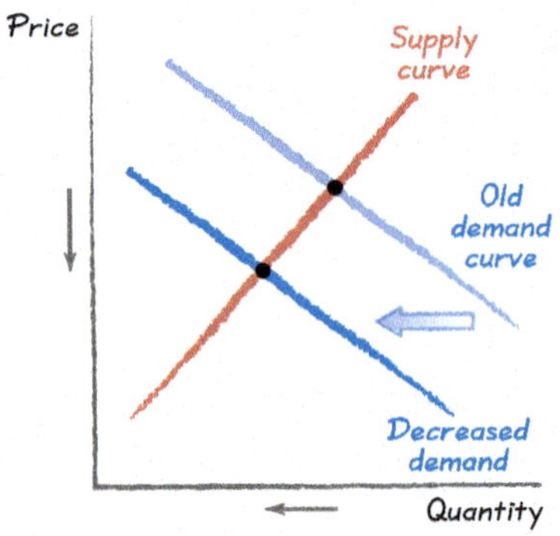

Lower incomes
→ A decrease in demand (since luxury jewellery is a normal good)

Result: Lower price, lower quantity.

It was found that certain types of plastic water bottles release harmful chemicals. What happened in the market for metal water bottles?

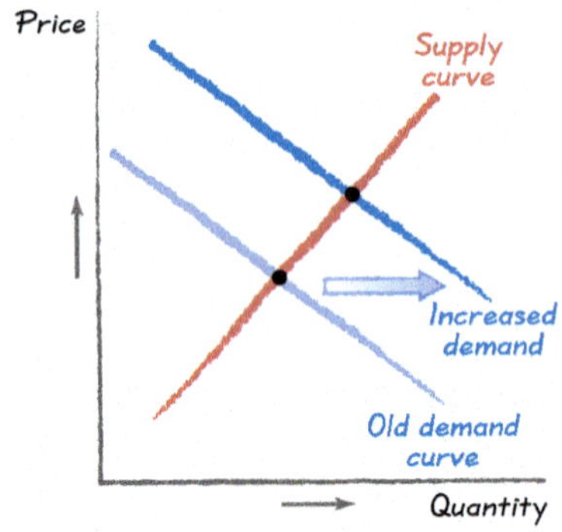

Consumer tastes shifted
→ An increase in demand

Result: Higher price, higher quantity.

During the Irish potato famine in the 1840s, much of the potato crop was destroyed. What was the effect on the market for potatoes?

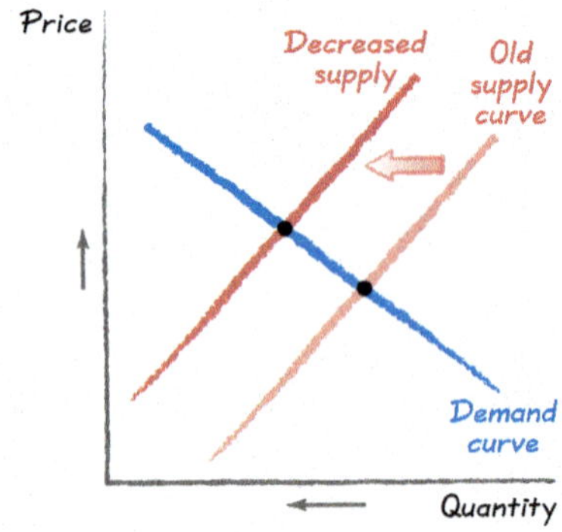

Decreased productivity of farms
→ A decrease in supply

Result: Higher price, lower quantity. ■

Recap: Summary of the consequences of shifting supply and demand. Let's summarise where we are so far. Figure 6 sums up what we've learned from analysing shifts in supply and demand.

Figure 6 | **Consequences of Shifts in Demand or Supply**

	Effect on equilibrium quantity	Effect on equilibrium price
Increase in demand (Example: The effect of investment banker bonuses on designer clothing sales)	Rises	Rises
Decrease in demand (Example: The effect of increased violence in Bali on tourism there)	Falls	Falls
Increase in supply (Example: The effect of more efficient battery production on hybrid cars)	Rises	Falls
Decrease in supply (Example: The effect of higher oil prices on the petrol market)	Falls	Rises

Shifts in demand cause price and quantity to move in the same direction

Shifts in supply cause price and quantity to move in opposite directions

When Both Supply and Demand Shift

So far, we've analysed what happens when *either* supply or demand shifts. But what happens when *both* curves shift at the same time? Fortunately, the same rules still hold, and when more than one curve shifts, you can simply add up the effects. Let's see how with an example.

In 2020 the Australian fresh produce market was hit by two big changes: because of the coronavirus pandemic the Australian economy entered a severe recession, and the supply of many vegetables fell because of severe drought. A recession reduces the incomes of fresh produce consumers, which causes a decrease in their demand for such food. Drought decreases supply for farmers. What's the likely impact of these simultaneous shifts on the market for fresh produce?

Let's begin by considering each of these shifts separately. When you have more than one shock, you can start by looking at each shift separately and then adding up the effects.

Consider the first shift. The recession caused a decrease in the demand for fresh produce at each price. This decrease in demand lowers the equilibrium quantity and price. (You can check this with a quick supply-and-demand sketch, or by looking up at the second row of Figure 6.) The second shift is a decrease in the supply of fresh produce. This shift lowers the equilibrium quantity but raises the equilibrium price. (Again, confirm this with a quick sketch.) Finally, add up each of these effects. Both of these shifts lower the equilibrium quantity. The effect on the price is a bit trickier: While the first shift (the decrease in demand) suggests the price will fall, the second shift (the decrease in supply) suggests it will rise. The total change in the price is therefore unclear. Thus, the combined effect of these two shifts is that quantity *will* fall, but the price could *either* rise or fall.

In fact, when supply and demand both shift, your conclusion will often be "it depends." That's because a change in supply might cause the price or quantity to move in one direction, and then the change in demand can cause it to move in the opposite direction. The total effect depends on which shift has the biggest impact.

The effect of two shifts can depend on which curve shifts the most. Figure 7 illustrates this point, by showing two extreme cases. Case 1 shows what happens when the demand shift is much bigger than the shift in supply. Case 2 shows the opposite extreme, with a small shift in demand and a much bigger shift in supply. Just as we predicted, the equilibrium quantity declines in both cases. But in Case 1, the price of fresh produce falls, while in Case 2, the price of fresh produce rises. This follows the prediction that the price can either rise or fall, and it shows that the outcome depends on whether the shift in demand or shift in supply dominates. (In fact, the price might even stay the same if the two effects exactly offset each other.)

Figure 7 | Shifts in Supply and Demand

When Both Supply and Demand Curves Shift

*Analyse two extreme cases: Case 1—A **big** demand shift with a **small** supply shift.*
*Case 2—A **small** demand shift with a **big** supply shift.*

Ⓐ A **decrease** in both supply and demand causes **both curves to shift left**.

Ⓑ This leads to a new supply-equals-demand **equilibrium**.

Implications depend on whether it's a big shift in supply and a small shift in demand, or a small shift in supply and a big shift in demand.

Ⓒ The **price could rise or fall**: It falls in Case 1, but rises in Case 2.

Ⓓ And a **decrease in quantity** occurs in either scenario.

Case 1: A Big Shift in Demand and a Small Shift in Supply | **Case 2: A Small Shift in Demand and a Big Shift in Supply**

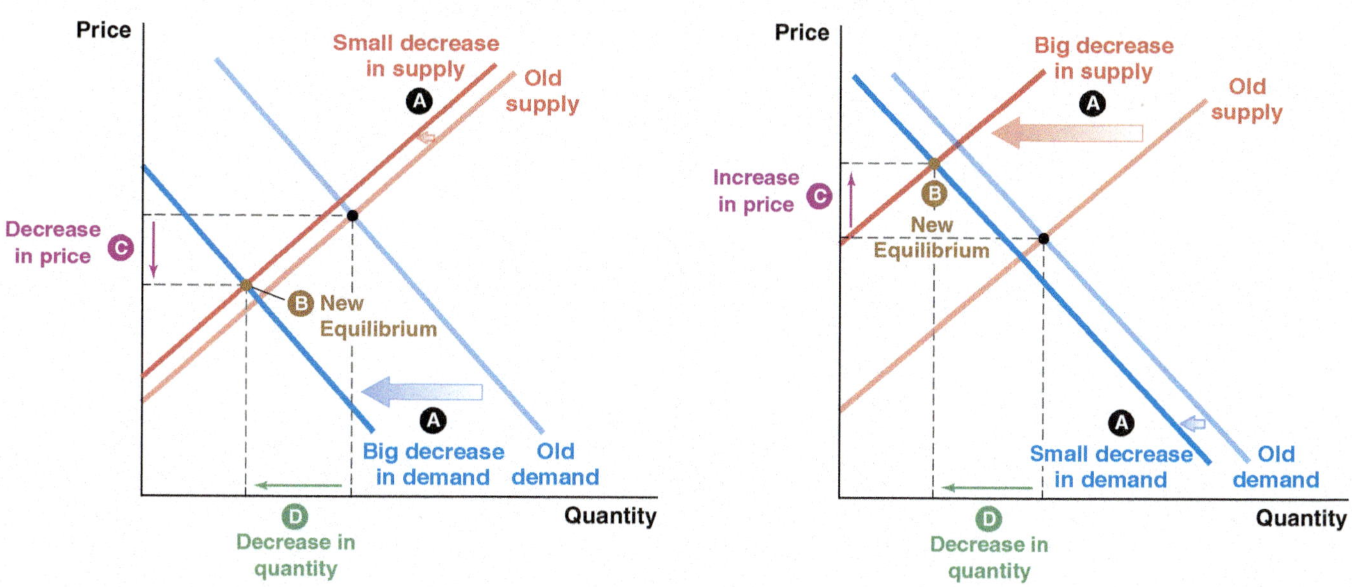

Use the morning-evening method to work out the effects of two curves shifting. So far we've analysed what happens when demand and supply both decrease. You're now in a position to analyse all the different cases in which there are simultaneous shifts that lead both supply and demand to either increase or decrease. Figure 8 shows how to work through each possibility, and introduces a shortcut you might find helpful, called the *morning-evening method.*

Here's the idea. Analysing two curves shifting on the same day can get messy. Instead, it can be simpler to think about it *as if* the demand curve shifts in the morning and the supply curve shifts in the evening. (The order doesn't really matter.) This way you can just think about one shift at a time. And to find out the total change over the course of the day, simply add up the morning effect and the evening effect.

Let's try it, starting with the first row of Figure 8: What happens when there's an increase in both demand and supply? To be concrete, think about the market for lifeguards in the summer, which is flooded with new buyers as pools open for the season (increasing demand) and new suppliers as students become available (increasing supply).

Ian G Dagnall/Alamy Stock Photo

Summertime means overtime; wintertime means out of work.

Start with the morning, when the increase in demand leads to an increase in the quantity of lifeguards hired, and an increase in the price they're paid (that is, their wage). Next, evaluate the changes that occur in the evening. An increase in supply will lead to an increase in quantity, and a decrease in price. Finally, to evaluate what happened over the day as a whole, simply add up what happened in the morning and the evening. The quantity rose in the morning and rose again in the evening, so it must have risen over the day as a whole. But the effect on the price is a bit thornier: It rose in the morning and fell in the evening. Over the whole day, the change in the price is unclear—it might have risen or fallen, depending on whether the demand shift had a bigger or smaller effect than the supply shift. In fact, this analysis provides an accurate diagnosis of how the market for lifeguards changes in the summer: The quantity rises, while the price can either rise or fall.

The second row of Figure 8 asks you to work through the implications of an increase in demand, combined with a decrease in supply, while the third row asks you to work out what happens when demand decreases but supply increases. You should work through each of these examples for yourself, following the logic discussed above. The fourth row shows the final possibility—a decrease in demand and a decrease in supply—which is exactly what happened in the fresh produce example we discussed above (and illustrated in Figure 7).

Figure 8 | When Both Supply and Demand Curves Shift

	Morning	*Evening*	Total effect (*Morning* + *Evening*)	
	Effect of demand shock	Effect of supply shock	Effect on equilibrium price	Effect on equilibrium quantity
Increase in demand and increase in supply	↑P, ↑Q	↓P, ↑Q	It depends (↑P + ↓P)	Rises (↑Q + ↑Q)
Increase in demand and decrease in supply	↑P, ↑Q	↑P, ↓Q	Rises (↑P + ↑P)	It depends (↑Q + ↓Q)
Decrease in demand and increase in supply	↓P, ↓Q	↓P, ↑Q	Falls (↓P + ↓P)	It depends (↓Q + ↑Q)
Decrease in demand and decrease in supply	↓P, ↓Q	↑P, ↓Q	It depends (↓P + ↑P)	Falls (↓Q + ↓Q)

Bottom line: When more than one curve shifts, you can consider the implications first of one shift, and then of the other and then add them together. And don't be surprised if your prediction for changes in price or quantity is, "It depends."

Interpreting Market Data

So far, we've used supply and demand to help you *predict* the consequences of changing market conditions. Let's now turn to an alternative way of thinking, in which supply and demand are diagnostic tools to help you *diagnose* what is happening in the economy. In order to do this, you need to remember two key rules:

Rule one: If prices and quantities move in the same direction, then the demand curve has definitely shifted. (It's possible that the supply curve may also have shifted.)

Rule two: If prices and quantities move in opposite directions, then the supply curve has definitely shifted. (It's possible that the demand curve may also have shifted.)

Notice that while these rules can tell you if a particular curve shifted, each comes with a parenthetic aside ("It's possible . . .") that is there to remind you that you shouldn't read this as evidence that the other curve didn't shift.

Armed with these rules, let's work through some examples of how changes in prices and quantities are important clues that'll help you figure out what's driving changing market conditions.

Interpreting the DATA — How did the advent of e-books change the publishing industry?

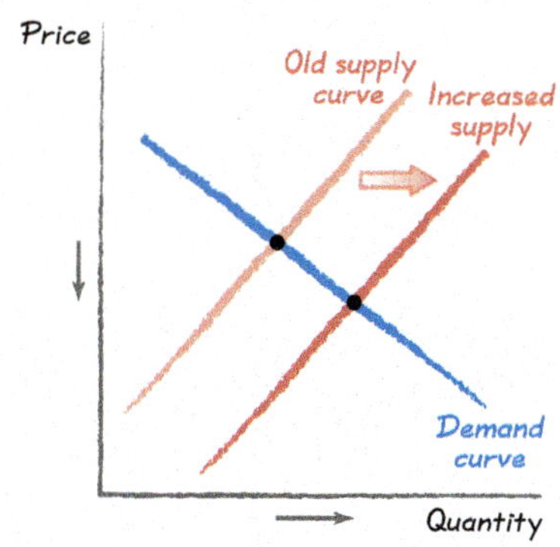

Electronic book readers, such as the Amazon Kindle, have given consumers the choice to buy the latest bestseller either as a printed book or as an e-book. In response, the quantity of most bestsellers sold rose (summing across electronic and paper editions), while the average price paid per book fell. What do these price and quantity changes tell us?

Because price and quantity moved in opposite directions, we can infer that this reflects a shift in the supply curve, and the fact that the quantity rose implies that supply increased. Why? An e-book can be produced at a much lower marginal cost (there's no expensive paper or binding or warehousing or shipping), and a decline in marginal costs will increase supply. ■

Interpreting the DATA — Why do house sales boom during spring and summer, but house prices don't?

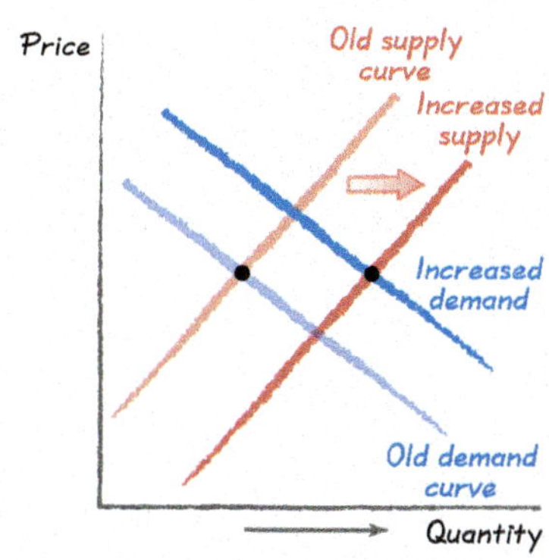

Every spring, and on into the summer, the quantity of houses sold rises dramatically, but the price of housing doesn't change much. What do these market movements tell us?

It's easy to see why many buyers want to move in the warmer seasons—work is typically slower, and their kids won't have to change schools during the school year. Consequently, the demand for housing increases. But if this were the whole story, then housing prices would typically rise in the spring and summer, when in reality they're usually flat. This suggests that there is also an increase in supply. In fact, this makes sense: Many people trying to buy a new house are also trying to sell their old house. Consequently, both supply and demand increase in these seasons. Both of these forces lead to an increase in the quantity sold. And because the increase in supply is roughly equal to the increase in demand, the pressure on housing prices to rise (due to increasing demand) is offset by pressure on them to fall (due to increasing supply). ■

Interpreting the DATA How did 9/11 affect the market for New York office space?

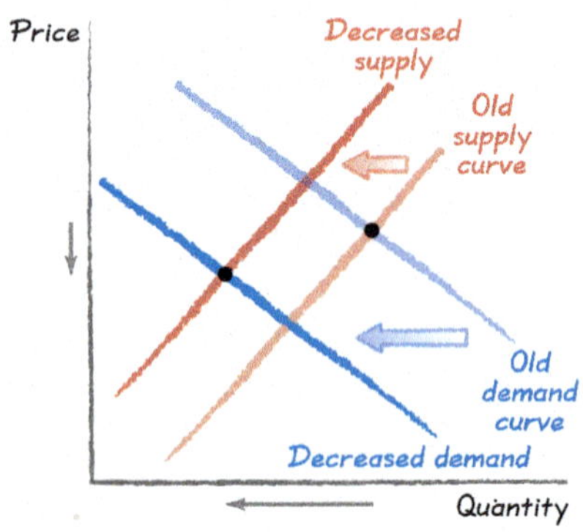

The terrorist attacks that toppled the World Trade Center on September 11, 2001, had a chilling effect on countries around the world as well as the U.S. economy. Consider the market for New York office space. The destruction of the Twin Towers reduced the available supply of office space, shifting the supply curve to the left. If this were all that happened, we would expect the price of office space to rise, and the quantity to fall. But over ensuing months, the price of office space actually fell. What do these changes tell us?

Because price and quantity moved in the same direction, we can infer that the demand for New York office space also declined. It is likely that this decrease was due to the perception that New York was now a less safe location for an office building, and some businesses chose to locate elsewhere as a result. ■

Tying It Together

Let's review how far we have come. In Chapter 1, you read about four core principles of economics, and we made the promise that these principles would be the key ingredients of any economic analysis. Since then, we've applied these principles to a key market, the market for petrol.

We began in Chapter 2 by considering the demand side—focusing on potential buyers of petrol. It turns out that the amount of petrol that any individual is willing to buy depends on the price of petrol, and this relationship is summarised by their individual demand curve. By adding up the demand of many consumers, we arrived at the market demand curve, which summarises the total quantity of petrol demanded by the market at each potential price.

In Chapter 3, we turned to the supply side, analysing potential sellers of petrol. The quantity of petrol that a seller is willing to sell depends on the price of petrol, and this relationship is also neatly summarised, this time by their supply curves. Adding up supply across different sellers yields the market supply curve.

Finally, in this chapter, we've seen how these market demand and supply curves reveal the market equilibrium, and how the market will tend to move towards producing the equilibrium quantity at the equilibrium price. It is this price that acts as the signal for some people to buy and others to sell, and hence determines what gets made, by whom, and to whom it is sold.

You've now covered an enormous amount of ground. In particular, you've developed a complete framework that you can use to analyse any competitive market, whether it's the market for petrol, food, housing, or indeed anything else.

This supply-and-demand framework is very important. So if you feel unsure about any of this, go back and read these chapters again. Truly. It's important. In fact, it is the basis of almost all economic analysis. The rest of economics comes down to developing these ideas in two directions. First, we'll apply these insights to other important markets, such as the markets for labour, capital, and housing. And second, we'll refine our analysis so that you can gain greater insight into the real world, where markets are not always perfectly competitive.

Chapter at a Glance

Getting to Equilibrium

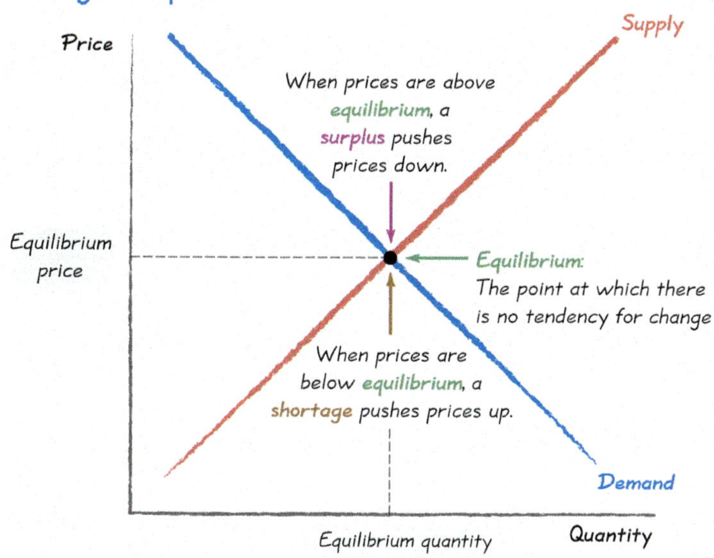

Is it a shortage or a surplus?

With a surplus: Prices are falling, discounting may occur, sellers may queue to find buyers, and sometimes extras get bundled for "free."

With a shortage: Prices are rising, buyers may queue to meet sellers, and sometimes there are secondary markets and/or "bundling" of unnecessary costly extras.

Three-step recipe when market conditions change

Step 1: Is the supply or demand curve shifting (or both)?

Step 2:. Is that shift an increase (shifting the curve to the right) or a decrease (shifting the curve to the left)?

Step 3: How will prices and quantities change in the new equilibrium?

Shifts in Demand

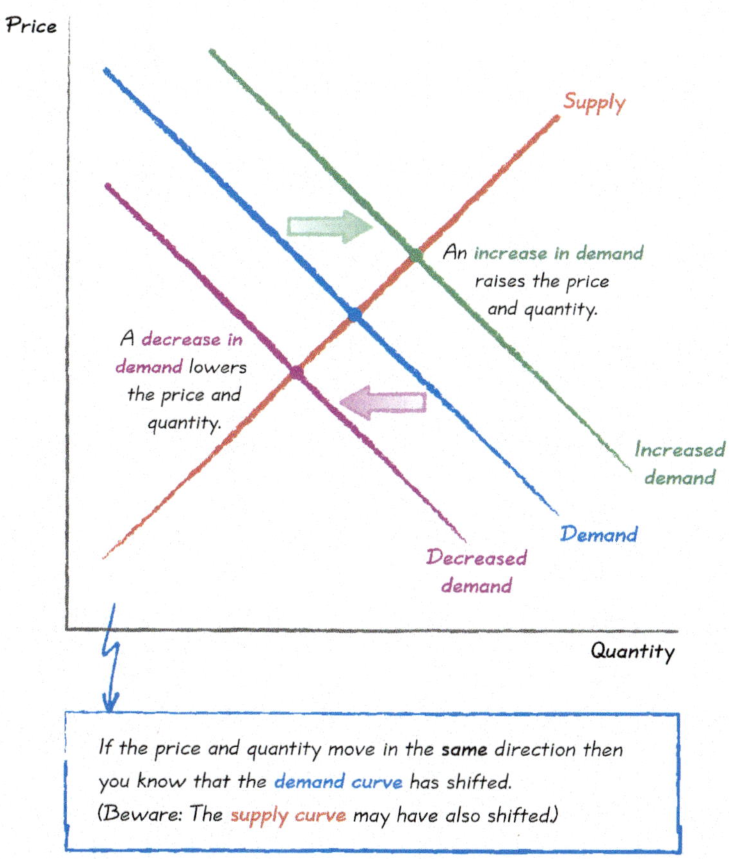

If the price and quantity move in the **same** direction then you know that the demand curve has shifted.
(Beware: The supply curve may have also shifted.)

Shifts in Supply

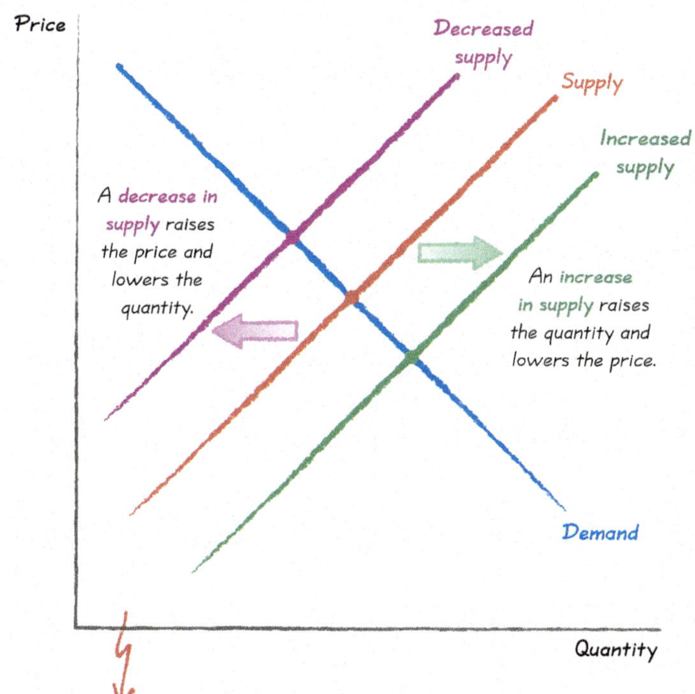

If the price and quantity move in **opposite** directions then you know that the supply curve has shifted.
(Beware: The demand curve may have also shifted.)

Key Concepts

equilibrium, 88
equilibrium price, 88
equilibrium quantity, 88
market, 86
market economy, 86
planned economy, 86
shortage, 90
surplus, 90

Discussion and Review Questions

Learning Objective 4.1 *Survey the central role that markets play in our society, determining what is produced, how, by whom, and who gets it.*

1. Provide some examples of markets in which you participated, or will participate in, today. How often were you a buyer/demander? How often were you the seller/supplier? How would a change in price have affected your choices?
2. Provide some examples of markets that don't use currency to pay for goods and services.
3. Explain how looking for someone to marry is like a market. How is a marriage market similar to a labour market?

Learning Objective 4.2 *Analyse how markets bring supply and demand into balance.*

4. If the average price of petrol is $1.40 per litre in your neighbourhood, and petrol is a perfectly competitive market, explain what might happen and why in your neighbourhood if the price of petrol dropped to $0.50 overnight? What if it jumped up to $5 per litre overnight?
5. Movie stars such as Nicole Kidman, Hugh Jackman, Russell Crowe, and Cate Blanchett are paid millions of dollars per movie, which can take as much as six months of full-time work for an actor, while doctors and nurses earn considerably less over the same time period. Briefly explain why.

Learning Objective 4.3 *Assess the consequences of shifts in demand and supply, and how changes in prices and quantities reveal whether demand or supply changed.*

6. Higher average incomes increase the demand for preventative dental visits. Explain why this will lead the quantity supplied of dental visits to increase, but supply will not increase.
7. Suppose the supply of green tea increases; why is it that equilibrium price and equilibrium quantity move in opposite directions?

Study Problems

Learning Objective 4.1 *Survey the central role that markets play in our society, determining what is produced, how, by whom, and who gets it.*

1. You are the coordinator of a not-for-profit organisation that distributes donated items to three local homeless shelters. What is the most efficient way to allocate your supplies to meet demand at different locations? Which of these best represent a planned approach and which best represent a market approach?
   a. Divide the donations evenly among the three shelters.
   b. Ask shelters to submit their requests, and decide what to send where based on their answers.
   c. Offer each shelter a virtual "budget" and have them bid on different items.
2. You purchased a ticket to the musical *Hamilton* through a verified reseller for $457.00. When your ticket arrives, you see the face value printed on it is $259.00. Based on this transaction, is the face-value price being charged by the show's producers above, below, or equal to the equilibrium price? How do you know?

Learning Objective 4.2 *Analyse how markets bring supply and demand into balance.*

3. Consider the following data from the market demand and supply for apartments.

Rent per week	Quantity demanded	Quantity supplied
$800	5,000	23,000
$700	8,000	20,000
$600	11,000	17,000
$500	14,000	14,000
$400	17,000	11,000
$300	20,000	8,000

   The average weekly rent for apartments is currently $400. At this price, how many apartments will be rented in this market? Is the market currently in equilibrium, experiencing a shortage, or experiencing a surplus? What do you expect to happen to the average rent? What is the equilibrium rent and quantity in the market?
4. When you arrive at the petrol station, there is a line of cars wrapped around the block waiting for petrol, so you go to the petrol station down the road, only to find another line of cars! You join the queue and end up waiting over an hour just to get to the bowser and then are told that they've run out of petrol. Is this market in equilibrium? Why or why not?

Learning Objective 4.3 *Assess the consequences of shifts in demand and supply, and how changes in prices and quantities reveal whether demand or supply changed.*

5. During the height of the coronavirus pandemic in Australia, the federal government urged all Australians to arrange to have their flu shots in April, three months before the usual peak flu season. There was such an enormous take-up of the flu vaccine that by the end of April, some GPs had waiting lists hundreds of people long, with only enough vaccinations to immunise a fraction of their patients. Some GPs didn't receive any vaccinations at all. Use a supply and demand diagram to illustrate the impact of this event on the market for flu vaccines in Australia. What impact will this have on the equilibrium price and equilibrium quantity in the Australian vaccine market?

6. In each of the following examples, determine how supply or demand shift and how the equilibrium price and quantity change.

   a. Smartphones: Microchips used in smartphones have become more powerful and less costly to produce.

   b. ALS medical research funds: The ALS ice bucket challenge goes viral, leading to more awareness around the benefits and needs of ALS research.

7. Australia has an ageing population, indeed over 1/3 of Australians are over the age of 55. The healthcare sector is made up of almost 25% older workers, and at the same time, demand for health care is expected to increase in the coming years.

   a. Given that the average retirement age is 65, what do you think will happen to the supply and demand of healthcare workers in the next 10 to 20 years?

   b. Illustrate the changes you have outlined above in a demand and supply diagram with the number of healthcare workers on the horizontal axis, and price (wage) on the vertical axis.

   c. Based on your diagram, forecast what will happen to the equilibrium wage for healthcare workers as a result of the shift/s.

8. Show in a diagram the effect on the demand curve, the supply curve, the equilibrium price, and the equilibrium quantity of each of the following events.

   a. The market for gold in Australia: A campaign against unethical gold mining has reduced the use of gold in jewellery production and increased the use of other metals such as silver AND import restrictions limit the amount of gold that can be imported into Australia.

   b. The market for international airline tickets: Incomes decline due to a recession AND Emirates adds more Australian cities to its list of international flight destinations.

9. In each of the following scenarios, explain the changes in either supply or demand that would result. If the initial equilibrium price were yet to change, indicate whether a surplus or a shortage would result. Given this, what do you expect will subsequently happen to the price of the good?

   a. *In the market for paper:* New advances in recycling technology reduce the cost of producing paper made from recycled materials.

   b. *In the market for lightbulbs:* Philips Electronics Australia, one of the largest suppliers of light bulbs, decides to discontinue producing light bulbs.

   c. *In the market for Gold Coast hotels:* A weeks-long period of torrential rain causes tourists to cancel their hotel room reservations and go on holiday elsewhere.

10. For each of the following observations, determine whether supply, demand, or both shifted and how.

   a. Over the last decade, the price of hybrid electric vehicles decreased, while the number of hybrid vehicles sold increased.

   b. During summer, the number of daily flights between Melbourne and Brisbane increases, as does the price of a ticket.

   c. From July to October in Australia, personal certified practising accountants (CPAs) see a dramatic increase in their number of billable hours, but the average hourly rate of a CPA remains the same.

PART II:
Analysing Markets

Part II: Analysing Markets

The Big Picture

You've mastered the basic tools of demand, supply, and equilibrium—now it's time to put them to work. In the chapters ahead, we'll use them to **analyse markets.** We'll learn to quantify how responsive buyers and sellers are to changing market conditions, by calculating a measure of responsiveness called **elasticity.**

We'll see how to extend your supply and demand analysis to take account of the effects of government policies like **taxes, price controls, and quantity regulations**, assessing the consequences of those actions on the quantities that are sold and the prices that buyers pay and sellers receive.

We'll then learn how to use supply and demand curves to **evaluate welfare,** illustrating how they can help policy makers figure out which policies will do the most to improve people's well-being. We'll also evaluate when supply and demand will lead to **efficient** outcomes and when they will lead to **market failure.**

Finally, we'll bring everything together to demonstrate how market forces help reallocate stuff to better uses, and how prices help coordinate economic activity. We'll also see how you can get more done when you focus on your **comparative advantage** and do the activities in which you have the lowest opportunity cost. The result is that trade between buyers and sellers makes them both better off, generating **gains from trade.**

5 Elasticity: Measuring Responsiveness

Measure how much quantities demanded and supplied respond to changing market conditions.

- How much less do people buy when prices go up? How much more do people buy when prices go down?
- How does elasticity shape your total revenue and your business strategy?
- How responsive is demand to changes in income, and to the prices of other goods?
- By how much does the quantity supplied respond to price changes?

6 Taxes, Price Controls, and Quantity Regulations

Forecast the consequences of government policies.

- What happens when the government taxes something?
- Why do economists say it doesn't matter whether you tax buyers or sellers?
- What happens to the quantity sold when the government sets minimum or maximum prices?
- What happens to the prices buyers and sellers pay when the government regulates quantities?
- How are taxes, price regulations, and quantity regulations the same? How are they different?

7 Welfare Economics: Market Efficiency and Market Failure

Analyse how markets affect economic welfare.

- How do economists evaluate welfare and economic efficiency?
- How can you measure the gains to buyers and the gains to sellers?
- How efficient are competitive markets?
- What are the costs of market failure?
- What are the limitations of economic efficiency in policy analysis?

8 Comparative Advantage and Gains from Trade

Examine how markets generate gains from trade.

- What do markets do?
- How can you best allocate tasks to ensure they're done with the lowest opportunity cost?
- What is comparative advantage and why does it allow more to be produced?
- What role do prices play in coordinating economic activity?
- How can you harness market forces in your own life?

Elasticity: Measuring Responsiveness

CHAPTER 5

In 2004, Qantas, Australia's leading airline, established a low-cost subsidiary called "Jetstar." The company describes their strategy this way: "Jetstar's mission is to offer low fares to enable more people to fly to more places, more often."

Fabrizio Gandolfo/SOPAImages/LightRocket/Getty Images

When—and where—does price matter most? Jetstar knows.

In practice, Qantas was responding to the entry of Virgin into the Australian market. Virgin targeted people travelling for leisure more than business travellers, and this put Qantas under competitive pressure. If Qantas had lowered their prices across the board, they would have taken a big profit hit.

By launching Jetstar they were able to segment the market into two parts: business travellers and others willing to pay for better service, and leisure travellers who are typically very cost-conscious. This strategy allowed Qantas to effectively charge different prices to different parts of the market, by offering a premium product (Qantas flights) and a low-cost product (Jetstar flights).

That is why Jetstar tends to fly to holiday destinations like Ballina (near Byron Bay), Coolangatta (near the Gold Coast), and Honolulu. It has fewer flights on routes like Sydney-Melbourne which are dominated by business travellers, and on some routes (like Sydney-Perth) Jetstar has no flights at all.

Since 2004, Jetstar has carried more than 250 million passengers on flights, and now flies to 85 destinations. They must be doing something right!

As Jetstar's success demonstrates, good business decisions are based on understanding precisely how responsive buyers and sellers are to changing prices. And so in this chapter, we'll explore how companies like Jetstar measure whether buyers and sellers will respond a lot, or a little, to changing prices.

We will start by analysing the responsiveness of buyers, and then turn to the responsiveness of sellers. Along the way, we'll also assess how to measure the effects of changing market conditions like changes in income or the prices of other goods.

Chapter Objective

Measure how much quantities demanded and supplied respond to changing market conditions.

5.1 Price Elasticity of Demand
Measure the responsiveness of the quantity demanded to price changes, using the price elasticity of demand.

5.2 How Businesses Use Demand Elasticity
Understand how demand elasticity shapes your total revenue and your business strategy.

5.3 Other Demand Elasticities
Assess the responsiveness of demand to income, and to the prices of other goods.

5.4 Price Elasticity of Supply
Measure the responsiveness of the quantity supplied to price changes, using the price elasticity of supply.

5.1 Price Elasticity of Demand

Learning Objective *Measure the responsiveness of the quantity demanded to price changes, using the price elasticity of demand.*

The law of demand tells us that when the price falls, the quantity demanded will rise. But as Jetstar's management understand, the important question is: By how much? Whether cutting the price of airline tickets leads to a lot more customers, or only a few more, determines whether or not Jetstar's low-fare strategy is a good one. It all depends on how responsive buyers are to prices. That's why our first task is to figure out how to measure this responsiveness.

Measuring Responsiveness of Demand

price elasticity of demand A measure of how responsive buyers are to price changes. It measures the percent change in quantity demanded that follows from a 1% price change.

$$\text{Price elasticity of demand} = \frac{\text{Percent change in quantity demanded}}{\text{Percent change in price}}$$

The **price elasticity of demand** measures how responsive buyers are to price changes. Specifically, it measures by what percent the quantity demanded will change in response to a 1% price change.

To measure the price elasticity of demand, observe how the quantity demanded responds to a price change. That responsiveness is measured by the ratio of the *percent change in quantity demanded* to the *percent change in price* as you move along the demand curve. That is:

$$\text{Price elasticity of demand} = \frac{\text{Percent change in quantity demanded}}{\text{Percent change in price}}$$

For example, cutting the price of petrol by 10% typically leads to an increase in the quantity demanded of about 2.5%. Putting these numbers together reveals that the price elasticity of petrol is about −0.25 (= 2.5% rise in the quantity demanded/10% fall in the price = 2.5%/−10%). Notice that the price elasticity of demand is a negative number because cutting the price raises the quantity demanded. In fact, when it comes to movements along the demand curve, the law of demand tells us that price and quantity changes always move in the opposite direction: When the price goes up, the quantity demanded goes down, and when the price goes down, the quantity demanded goes up.

Absolute value focuses on the magnitude of the price elasticity of demand. Economists often want to focus on the magnitude of the price elasticity of demand. To do this, they use what mathematicians call the absolute value, which simply means ignore the negative sign. Thus, the absolute value of the price elasticity of demand is the price elasticity of demand with the negative sign dropped. It can be expressed using the absolute value symbol, which is two straight lines: $|elasticity|$. It's useful because an elasticity of −2.5 means a bigger percent change in demand than would occur if the elasticity was −0.25. Focusing on absolute value makes it easier to talk about the magnitude of the change: $|-2.5| = 2.5$ and $|-0.25| = 0.25$, and since 2.5 is bigger than 0.25, when we talk about elasticity in absolute value terms, we can say simply that a larger elasticity means a larger percent change in the quantity demanded.

Do the Economics

When Uber cut the price of a ride in Sydney by 15%, it found that the quantity of rides demanded rose by 30%. What is the absolute value of the price elasticity of demand for Uber rides?

$$\text{Absolute value of the price elasticity of demand} = \left|\frac{+30\%}{-15\%}\right| = |-2| = 2 \blacksquare$$

When quantity is very responsive, demand is elastic. What Uber found was that riders were very responsive to prices. When it cut prices, the quantity of rides demanded rose by an even greater percentage. When buyers are very responsive to price, economists describe their demand as elastic. Specifically, we say that demand is **elastic** whenever the absolute value of the percent change in quantity demanded is larger than the absolute value of the percent change in price. This also means that the absolute value of the price elasticity of demand is greater than 1.

elastic When the absolute value of the percent change in quantity is larger than the absolute value of the percent change in price, which means that the absolute value of the price elasticity is greater than 1.

When demand is elastic, price increases also lead to large changes in the quantity demanded. Take Matilda, for example; she lives and works in a suburb where she can walk to work. But she prefers to drive to the supermarket. And she likes to take road trips on the weekend, to go hiking in a national park, or to spend a day at the beach an hour away. When the price of petrol rises, however, the cost of that day at the beach becomes a bit too high, and when the price of petrol goes even higher, those other road trips start to look pretty expensive, too. After all, she can hang out with friends that live close by, go for a run in her neighbourhood, or go for a swim at the community pool. All of this means that when the price of petrol increases, the quantity of petrol Matilda demands falls by a lot.

When quantity is very unresponsive, demand is inelastic. Oliver lives in a dense city where he can walk, ride a bike, or take public transport to most of the places he wants to go. However, he needs his car to get to his job in the suburbs. He doesn't use it for much else. When the price of petrol rises, he doesn't have much choice but to keep buying petrol to get to work, and when the price falls, he doesn't feel the need to drive anywhere else. As such, the quantity of petrol Oliver demands is not very responsive to changes in price.

When buyers are not very responsive to price changes, economists describe their demand as **inelastic.** Specifically, we say that demand is inelastic whenever the absolute value of the percent change in quantity demanded is smaller than the absolute value of the percent change in price. This also means that the absolute value of the price elasticity of demand is smaller than 1.

inelastic When the absolute value of the percent change in quantity is smaller than the absolute value of the percent change in price, which means that the absolute value of the price elasticity is less than 1.

When the absolute value of the price elasticity of demand is exactly equal to 1 it is neither elastic nor inelastic. Some economists refer to this as *unit elastic,* so that it has a name. But the important thing to note is simply that this is the dividing line between elastic and inelastic.

Elastic demand curves are relatively flatter than inelastic demand curves. Figure 1 shows an example of both an inelastic demand curve like Oliver's (in purple), as well as an elastic demand curve like Matilda's (in green). One of the first things you might notice is that *an elastic demand curve is relatively flat,* while *an inelastic demand curve is relatively steep.* Whenever two demand curves pass through the same point, the demand curve that's flatter at that point is the more elastic demand curve. This is because when demand is elastic, the quantity demanded is relatively responsive. In contrast, when demand is inelastic, the quantity demanded is relatively unresponsive.

It's important to note that elasticity is not, however, the same thing as slope. The slope of the demand curve—remember, slope is rise over run—is equal to the change in price divided by the change in quantity. Elasticity is given by the *percent* change in quantity divided by the *percent* change in price. As a result, while linear demand curves, like the one shown in Figure 1, have the same slope all along the curve, the elasticity will differ along the curve.

There are two extreme cases when the slope clearly reveals elasticity. When the demand curve is completely horizontal it means that the price elasticity of demand is infinite—any change in price leads to an infinite change in quantity. Economists call this **perfectly elastic** demand. When the demand curve is completely vertical it means that the price elasticity of demand is zero—no matter what the change in price, the total quantity demanded is unchanged. Economists call this **perfectly inelastic** demand.

perfectly elastic When any change in price leads to an infinitely large change in quantity.

perfectly inelastic When quantity does not respond at all to a price change.

Figure 1 | **Price Elasticity of Demand**

The same change in price can cause a different change in quantity, depending on the elasticity.

A fall in the price of petrol will cause the quantity demanded to rise. By how much depends on whether buyers have:

A **Inelastic demand**: Buyers are not very responsive to price, so the **quantity demanded rises only a little**.

B **Elastic demand**: Buyers are very responsive to price, and so the **quantity demanded rises by a lot**.

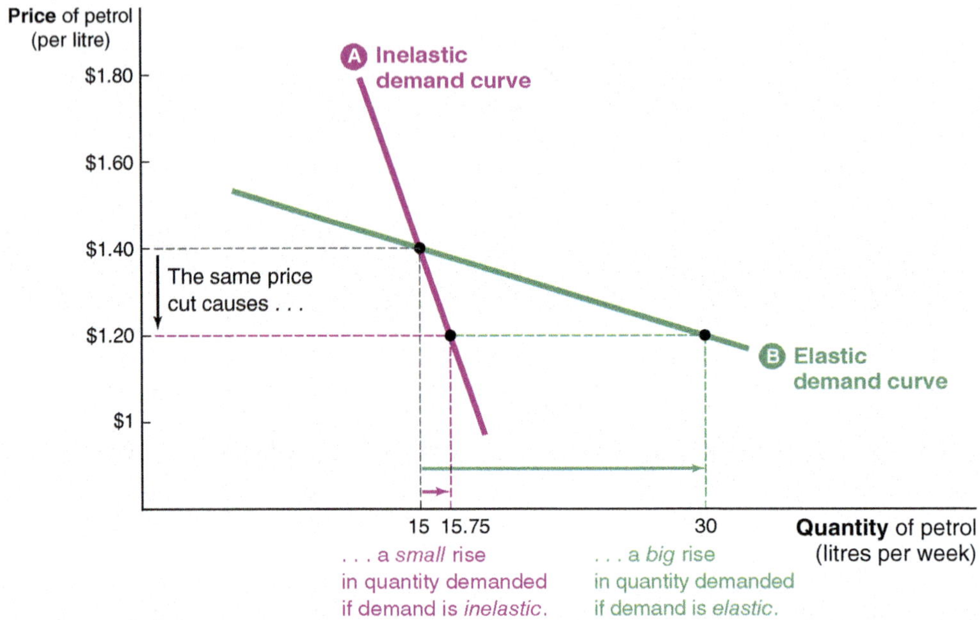

Interpreting the DATA — Why the minimum wage debate is all about elasticity

Australia has the second-highest national minimum wage in the world. In 2020, it was $19.84 per hour or $753.80 per 38 hour week (before tax). Casual employees covered by the national minimum wage also get a 25% casual loading. There are often debates about the level of the minimum wage; you may have strong opinions on it yourself. Labour activists argue that higher wages will help the poor by helping them earn more. On the other side, business lobbyists argue that a higher minimum wage will hurt the poor by causing employers to employ fewer low-wage workers.

In Australia, the Fair Work Commission (FWC) sets the level of the minimum wage. When announcing a 3% increase in the minimum wage in 2019, FWC President Justice Ian Ross said: "We are satisfied that the level of increase we have decided upon will not lead to any adverse inflationary outcome nor will it have any measurable negative impact on employment." That last statement, regarding a "negative impact on employment" is all about the price elasticity of demand for labour.

To understand the importance of the price elasticity of demand, you must first realise that in the labour market, workers are suppliers who supply their labour. Employers are therefore buyers, who demand the labour of workers. What's the price employers pay? The wage. So an increase in the minimum wage is an increase in the price that buyers of minimum wage labour must pay. The price elasticity of demand therefore tells us how much the quantity of labour demanded will change when there is an increase in its price.

Some who argue against raising the minimum wage claim that it would cause employers to fire lots of workers. This argument boils down to saying that employer's demand for labour is very elastic. If this is true, a modest rise in the price of labour (remember, the price of labour is the wage!) leads to a large decline in the quantity of labour demanded. In this case, getting higher wages for the lucky few who still have jobs may not be worth the cost of losing so many jobs (and some even say that it won't cost any jobs).

By contrast, many of those arguing for a higher minimum wage believe that very few people would lose their jobs. They're claiming that the quantity of labour demanded would not respond much to a higher minimum wage—in other words, that labour demand is very inelastic. By this view, raising the minimum wage will lead to the loss of a small number of jobs.

So the minimum wage debate isn't simply about being for or against workers. Whether you think it is a good idea to raise the minimum wage will partly depend on whether you think the demand for labour is elastic or inelastic. Did you know you were arguing about elasticity? What are your thoughts? Do you think the demand for labour at a wage of $19.84 per hour is elastic or inelastic? Your answer to that question may be your best guide to deciding whether you support raising the minimum wage. ■

Recap: The spectrum from perfectly inelastic to perfectly elastic demand. Figure 2 summarises the difference between perfectly inelastic, inelastic, elastic, and perfectly elastic demand. As you read through this table, test yourself on what each of these concepts means.

Figure 2 | Inelastic and Elastic Demand

	Definition	Which means . . .	Implies	Graphically
Perfectly inelastic demand	|*% change in quantity*| is zero for any |*% change in price*|	The quantity demanded is unchanged for any change in price.	*Absolute value of the price elasticity of demand = 0*	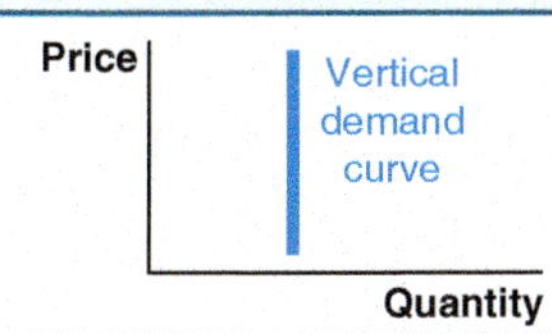
Inelastic demand	|*% change in quantity*| is smaller than |*% change in price*|	The quantity demanded is relatively unresponsive to a change in price.	*Absolute value of the price elasticity of demand < 1*	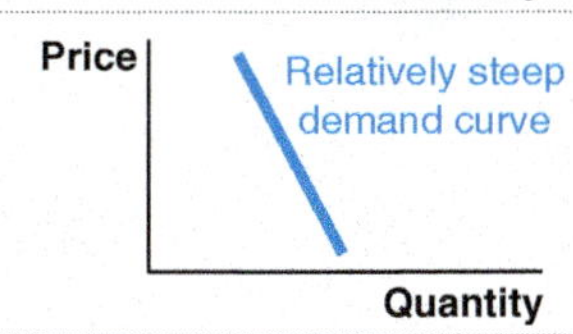
Elastic demand	|*% change in quantity*| is larger than |*% change in price*|	The quantity demanded is relatively responsive to a change in price.	*Absolute value of the price elasticity of demand > 1*	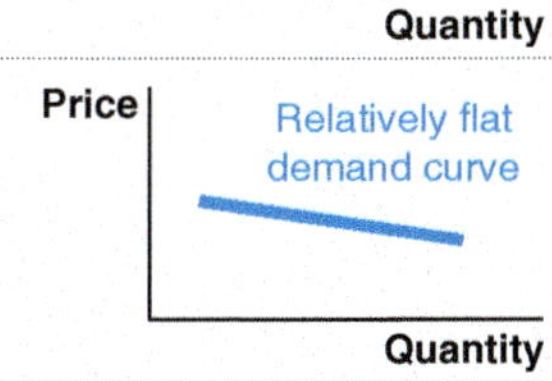
Perfectly elastic demand	|*% change in quantity*| is infinite for any |*% change in price*|	The quantity demanded is infinitely responsive to a change in price.	*Absolute value of the price elasticity of demand = ∞*	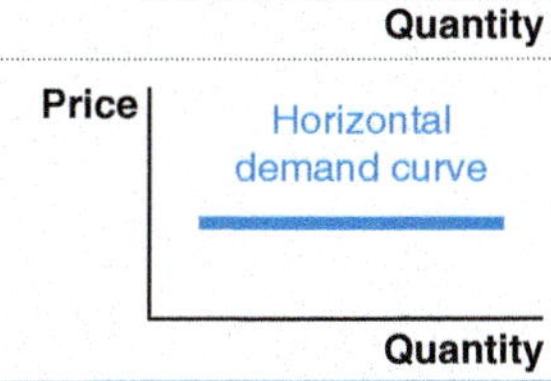

Determinants of the Price Elasticity of Demand

You now know that demand for some goods and services (including the demand for workers) may respond a lot or a little (or somewhere in between) to price changes. And you know that the price elasticity of demand measures this responsiveness. Perhaps you are wondering why the responsiveness of demand to price changes is high for some products and low for others.

Recall that the *opportunity cost principle* tells you that to figure out the benefits of buying something, you need to compare it to the next best alternative. It follows that price elasticity of demand is all about how good that next best alternative is—in other words, it reflects the extent to which there are good *substitutes* available for the marginal purchase.

The price elasticity of demand reflects the availability of substitutes. It is larger:

1. When there are more competing products
2. For specific brands rather than broad categories
3. For things that aren't necessities
4. When consumers search more
5. When there's more time to adjust

Elasticity is all about substitutability. Recall that Oliver has inelastic demand for petrol, because he has no alternative way to get to work other than driving. Since he doesn't have a good substitute available, his marginal benefit from the litres of petrol necessary to get to work is very high, and so he will continue to buy enough petrol for his commute even if the price rises sharply.

Oliver derives little benefit from other uses of petrol. In fact, parking is such a hassle in his neighbourhood that once he's found a spot on Friday after work, he doesn't want to move his car again until he leaves for work on Monday morning. For Oliver, driving is not a good substitute for walking, and so even if the price of petrol falls sharply, it won't induce him to buy more.

Because Oliver doesn't have close substitutes for his transportation choices, Oliver's marginal benefit from the last litre of petrol he consumes—the one that gets him home from work on Friday—is quite high, but the marginal benefit he gets from the next litre is pretty low. As a result, if the price were to fall or rise, he's unlikely to change the quantity he demands by much, if at all. Thus, Oliver's demand for petrol is *inelastic*.

Matilda, on the other hand, has a lot of good substitutes for her current uses of petrol. When the price of petrol rises, she realises that hanging out with her friends in her own suburb is a pretty good substitute for driving one hour to spend the weekend at the beach, so she will cut back on her petrol purchases. Similarly, when the price of petrol falls, she is more likely to find that driving for an extra weekend away will pass the cost-benefit test, and so she'll increase the quantity of petrol she purchases. When you are close to indifferent between two options—like Matilda is—small differences in the price can lead you to make very different choices. Thus, Matilda's demand for petrol is *elastic*.

Bottom line: The availability of substitutes determines the price elasticity of demand. We'll now take a look at five determinants of the price elasticity of demand, but you'll quickly see that these determinants are simply factors that help explain what kind of substitutes you are likely to have.

Demand elasticity factor one: More competing products mean greater elasticity. The more competing products there are, the more likely you are to find a close substitute. As a result, you'll be more price sensitive when you are shopping at large Woolworths supermarket than at a small convenience store. Why? A typical Woolworths stocks around 20,000 different products. All of those different products mean that you'll be more likely to find a good substitute if the price of your first choice has gone up. So if the price of Quilton 3-ply toilet paper rises, you might buy Sorbent Silky White instead. But when you are at the convenience store, your only other option might be Scott Essential 2-ply toilet tissue. Because the Sorbent is a closer substitute to the Quilton, a small rise in the price of Quilton will lead more people to make the switch at Woolworths than at the convenience store.

As you think about competing products, remember to think broadly. For instance, managers at Jetstar know that demand is more elastic when their customers have the option of flying on Qantas or Virgin instead. But they have also found that demand is more elastic for shorter flights such as between Sydney and Canberra, for which driving is a reasonable substitute.

Demand elasticity factor two: Specific brands tend to have more elastic demand than categories of goods. Because specific brands tend to have more close substitutes, demand for these goods is typically more elastic than demand for broad categories of goods. For example, there are many close substitutes for Carman's Classic Fruit & Nut Muesli, and so when the price goes up many people will substitute to a different breakfast cereal (or other breakfast item). As a result, demand for Carman's Classic Fruit & Nut Muesli is quite elastic. By contrast, consumers are less responsive to price changes in the overall category of breakfast cereals. Demand is less elastic because the alternatives—eating something other than cereal, such as yogurt or toast—are quite different.

chris24/Alamy Stock Photo

There are plenty of substitute cereals—*if* you're willing to accept a substitute.

Demand elasticity factor three: Necessities have less elastic demand. Things that you really can't do without are things that you will keep buying even as the price rises. What makes something a necessity? A necessity is something where there isn't a good substitute available and doing without isn't a good option. Food is a necessity. What is the alternative to food? To go hungry. That's not a viable alternative, and it helps explain why demand is inelastic for food staples like eggs, rice, pasta, fruits, and vegetables. Restaurant meals, however, are not a necessity for most people. Why? Because eating at home is a good substitute. Not surprisingly, Figure 3 shows that restaurant meals have more elastic demand than staple foods you might eat at home. However, what's a necessity for one person might not be for another. For example, if you don't have access to a kitchen, restaurant meals might be more of a necessity for you.

Figure 3 Price Elasticity of Demand for Consumer Goods

	Absolute Value of the Price Elasticity of Demand	
Rice and pasta	0.1	Very Inelastic
Eggs	0.2	
Water	0.3	
Public transportation	0.4	
Fruits and vegetables	0.8	
Shellfish	0.9	
Breakfast cereal	1.0	
Citrus fruits	1.1	
Cakes and cookies	1.2	
Sauces and seasonings	1.9	
Restaurant meals	2.0	Very Elastic

Demand elasticity factor four: Consumer search makes demand more elastic. When consumers are willing to search a lot for a low-cost alternative for something, demand for that product is more elastic. Why? Because the more you search for a good deal, the more likely you are to find an acceptable, lower-priced substitute. If stores raise their price, customers actively searching are more likely to find a good alternative. Therefore, those who are most willing to search will be more responsive to price changes.

EVERYDAY Economics **Should you search harder for bargains on perishable or storable goods?**

Should you spend more time looking for bargains on perishable goods like fresh fish, or storable goods like laundry detergent? The answer is storable goods. Think about it: If you get a $1 discount on fish, then you can save a dollar on tonight's dinner. But if you find laundry detergent that is $1 cheaper, you can stock up, buying half a dozen bottles of detergent. Sure, it'll be enough to last you for months, and you'll have to find a place to store it, but buying six bottles means that you'll save $6 instead of $1.

Since customers tend to stock up when they see a good price on a storable good, demand for storable goods tends to be much more elastic than for perishable goods. And this is still due to substitutability: Today's low price on detergent is a substitute not just for buying it at a higher price today, but also for buying detergent next month. ■

Demand elasticity factor five: Demand gets more elastic over time. On any given day, many of your decisions about what to purchase are difficult to change. For instance, if you take a road trip and the price of petrol goes up when you are headed home, you're probably going to buy the petrol you need to get home regardless of any price rise (even if it's large!). You might buy less petrol once you get back home, but you'll still face constraints like needing to get to work or owning a car that isn't very fuel-efficient. In the very short run, it's hard to change how much petrol you buy.

But if petrol prices stay higher, you'll adjust your plans over time so you drive even less. You might figure out public transport options. Eventually, you may replace your car with a more fuel-efficient one. You may even consider moving closer to work or school so that you can drive less. And so over time, the same price change will lead to a bigger change in the quantity demanded. This happens because as time passes, you will tend to have more options to choose from, which is another way of saying that more substitutes become available. More substitutes mean more elastic demand, so over time, demand tends to become more elastic. As a result, demand is more elastic in the long run than in the short run. But how long is the long run? It depends on when more substitutes become available. If you were already planning to upgrade your car next month, the long run for you is a month. But for someone locked into a two-year lease on a car, the long run may be two years.

Elasticity will differ by person, product, and price. All of the factors affecting the price elasticity of demand boil down to whether there are good substitutes for what you want to buy. We described Carman's muesli as having a lot of close substitutes because most people find that switching to another breakfast cereal doesn't make them that much less happy. But if you really love Carman's muesli more than any other breakfast food, then there may not be close substitutes available for you. Your preferences across the available alternatives determine your elasticity of demand. Ultimately, elasticity varies according to who you are, what product you're considering, what the price is, and how quickly you need to respond.

Your price elasticity of demand also differs depending on where you are on your demand curve. For instance, if you need to drive to go to work, but you like to drive on the weekends as well, then you might have highly inelastic demand when prices are high and you are only buying petrol to get to work. But if prices fall enough, your demand might become more elastic as you start buying petrol for leisure trips outside of work.

Even though elasticities differ across people, products, and prices, they can be compared because they're all measuring the same thing: how responsive the percent change in quantity demanded is, relative to the percent change in the price.

Do the Economics

Do you think demand is elastic or inelastic for the following goods?

a. Flowers on Valentine's Day
b. Health care
c. Smith's potato chips
d. Electricity
e. Apple iPads ■

Answer: a. Demand for flowers is price inelastic around Valentine's Day, since price is unlikely to be a good excuse not to buy flowers for your partner; b. Demand for health care is inelastic, since there are few good substitutes for medical care when you are sick; c. Demand for Smith's potato chips is highly elastic because there are many other snack foods—including other brands of potato chips—that people can choose from; d. Electricity has few substitutes and has fairly inelastic demand in the short run; e. Apple iPads have fairly elastic demand, because there are other ways to access information and entertainment.

Calculating the Price Elasticity of Demand

So far, you have seen that to measure elasticity, you need the percent change in quantity demanded and the percent change in price. With these two numbers, you are easily able to calculate the price elasticity of demand by dividing the percent change in quantity demanded by the percent change in price.

But what if you need to calculate the percent change in quantity demanded and the percent change in price? It seems easy enough, but you'll quickly notice an annoying problem—the normal way you think about calculating the percent change depends on where you start. For instance, when quantity goes from 100 to 150, it's a 50% increase. But if it goes back from 150 to 100 it's a 33% decrease. That's an annoying problem because if the percent change depends on the starting point, then elasticity will depend on the starting point. Since we want a consistent measure of elasticity between two points, we need a measure that doesn't depend on the starting point.

The problem isn't related to elasticity, but rather to how we calculate the percent change in price and quantity. Economists often use a special method called the midpoint formula which measures the percent change between any two points relative to a baseline *midway* between those two points. Let's see how we calculate it.

Use the midpoint formula to calculate the percent changes in price and quantity. To calculate the percent change in quantity between any two points, Q_2 and Q_1, divide the difference between the two points by the average of the two points. Thus, the formula for calculating the percent change in quantity is:

$$\text{Percent change in quantity} = \frac{Q_2 - Q_1}{(Q_2 + Q_1)/2} \times 100$$

Similarly, to calculate the percent change in price between any two prices, divide the difference between them by the average of the two price points. Thus the midpoint formula for calculating the percent change in price is:

$$\text{Percent change in price} = \frac{P_2 - P_1}{(P_2 + P_1)/2} \times 100$$

Once you have calculated the percent change in quantity demanded and percent change in price using the midpoint formula, you are ready to calculate the price elasticity of demand given what you already know—it is simply the percent change in quantity demanded divided by the percent change in price.

There's a bit of math involved with the midpoint formula. So when you're trying to calculate an elasticity using the midpoint formula, a calculator can come in handy. And because economists don't always use the midpoint formula, we'll try to be clear about when we want you to use it.

Neirfy/Shutterstock

I'm sorry I couldn't afford flowers this Valentine's Day; they were too expensive. Please be mine?

Do the Economics

The New York City Parks Department learned an important lesson about elasticity when it decided to increase the price of using city-owned tennis courts. Residents used to pay $100 for a seasonal permit, which allowed them to play on any city-owned court. City managers thought that if they raised the price to $200, they would sell nearly as many permits, while increasing their revenue. However, the price increase led the quantity of permits demanded to drop from 12,774 down to 7,265. Calculate the absolute value of the price elasticity of demand for New York tennis permits using the midpoint formula.

Step one: *What was the percent change in the price?*

$$\text{Percent change in price} = \frac{200 - 100}{(200 + 100)/2} \times 100 = \frac{100}{150} \times 100 = +67\%$$

Step two: *How much did the quantity demanded change as a percent, in response?*

$$\text{Percent change in quantity} = \frac{7{,}265 - 12{,}774}{(7{,}265 + 12{,}774)/2} \times 100$$

$$= \frac{-5{,}509}{10{,}020} \times 100 = -55\%$$

Step three: *Calculate the elasticity:*

$$\text{Absolute value of the price elasticity of demand} = \left| \frac{\text{Percent change in quantity}}{\text{Percent change in price}} \right|$$

$$= \left| \frac{-55\%}{+67\%} \right| = 0.8 \quad \blacksquare$$

Now that you know how to calculate the price elasticity of demand, let's turn to understanding how you will use it.

5.2 How Businesses Use Demand Elasticity

Learning Objective *Understand how demand elasticity shapes your total revenue and your business strategy.*

The price elasticity of demand is a critical factor determining how managers set their business strategy. So far you've seen how to measure the price elasticity of demand. As a manager, you will want to use the price elasticity of demand for your product to forecast the likely consequences of any change in price. If you rearrange the formula for price elasticity of demand, you see that:

$$\text{Percent change in quantity demanded} = \text{Price elasticity of demand} \times \text{Percent change in price}$$

For instance, the price elasticity of demand for eggs is around –0.2. Based on this, you can project the likely consequences of a change in the price of eggs. If the price of eggs were to rise by 10%, you can forecast that the quantity of eggs demanded will decline by around 2%:

total revenue The total amount you receive from buyers, which is calculated as price × quantity.

$$\text{Percent change in quantity demanded} = -0.2 \times 10\% = -2\%$$

Knowing the price elasticity of demand for your product allows you to forecast how price changes will affect your revenues and profits. Our next task is to explore how the price elasticity of demand shapes your revenues and therefore your decisions.

Figure 4 | **Total Revenue**

Your total revenue is the amount you receive from buyers, which is calculated as price × quantity. Remember, the area of a rectangle is the height (price) times the base (quantity).

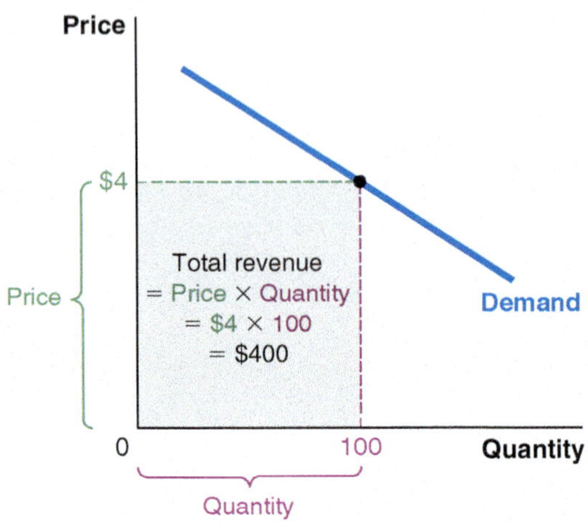

Elasticity and Revenue

If the market price for eggs is going up by 10% and the quantity sold declines by 2%, what does that mean for total revenue? **Total revenue** is the total amount you receive from buyers, which equals price times quantity:

$$\text{Total revenue} = \text{Price} \times \text{Quantity}$$

Total revenue is shown graphically in Figure 4. It's the rectangle created by price times quantity. So in the example shown, if at a price of $4, a coffee shop sells 100 cups of coffee, their total revenue is equal to $4 × 100 = $400.

Since a change in price leads to a change in the quantity demanded in the opposite direction, the impact on total revenue will depend on the relative magnitudes of the two changes. The price elasticity of demand tells you whether the percent change in price is larger than the percent change in

Figure 6 shows estimates of the income elasticity of demand for various goods. As you might expect, demand for health expenditures, petrol, and houses all increase with income, but their income elasticities are small. In contrast, demand for aeroplane tickets and new cars is highly sensitive to income, and both goods have a large income elasticity of demand.

The income elasticity of demand is negative for inferior goods. The goods you buy less of when your income goes up are inferior goods. These are often goods like two-minute noodles; you buy them to "make do" when your income is low, but upgrade to something better when your income is higher. Because the quantity of inferior goods you consume moves in the opposite direction to your income, their income elasticity of demand is negative. Figure 6 shows that processed fruits and vegetables have a negative income elasticity of demand. As people's incomes rise, they tend to switch to fresh fruits and vegetables instead.

Figure 6 | **Income Elasticity of Demand for Various Goods**

	Income Elasticity of Demand
Processed fruits and vegetables	−0.3
Electricity	0.0
Organic fruit	0.2
Health expenditures	0.4
Homeownership	0.5
Petrol	0.5
New cars	1.7
Aeroplane tickets	1.8

5.4 Price Elasticity of Supply

Learning Objective *Measure the responsiveness of the quantity supplied to price changes, using the price elasticity of supply.*

So far we've focused on how responsive *buyers* are to changes in prices. But you also know that the prices *sellers* face matter for their decisions. The law of supply tells you that when the price rises, the quantity supplied will also rise. As with buyers, we want to be able to measure by how much sellers will respond, and understand what drives whether their response is likely to be small or large.

Measuring Responsiveness of Supply

The **price elasticity of supply** measures how responsive *sellers* are to price changes. Specifically, it measures by what percent the quantity supplied will increase following a 1% price change. The larger this percent change in quantity supplied, the more responsive sellers are to price changes.

price elasticity of supply A measure of how responsive sellers are to price changes. It measures the percent change in quantity supplied that follows from a 1% price change.

$$\text{Price elasticity of supply} = \frac{\text{Percent change in quantity supplied}}{\text{Percent change in price}}$$

To measure the price elasticity of supply, observe how the quantity supplied responds to a price change. Specifically, you can measure the price elasticity of supply as the ratio of the *percent change in quantity supplied* to the *percent change in price* as you move along your supply curve. That is:

$$\text{Price elasticity of supply} = \frac{\text{Percent change in quantity supplied}}{\text{Percent change in price}}$$

For instance, when the price of petrol rises by about 20%, the quantity supplied typically rises by about 2%. Putting these numbers together reveals that the price elasticity of supply of petrol is 0.1 (=2% rise in quantity supplied/20% rise in the price).

Do the Economics

When demand for Uber rides increases—for example when it rains, when a concert or sporting event ends, or during busy commuting times—Uber responds by raising prices. If you've ever used Uber, you probably know this as surge pricing. The argument for surge pricing is not just that it reduces the quantity of rides demanded (think back

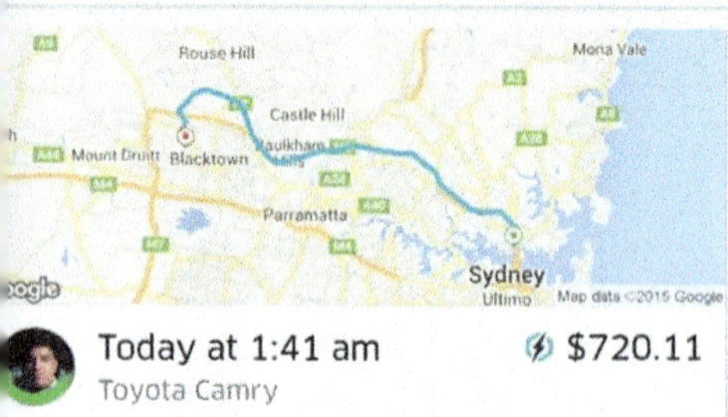

The $720 fare for a 40-minute ride.

to our earlier estimate of the absolute value of the price elasticity of demand for Uber rides) but also that the higher prices increase the quantity of rides supplied by drivers.

For example, on New Year's Eve in Sydney, demand for rides skyrocketed. In response, Uber increased prices by 80%. This price increase led to a 100% increase in Uber drivers supplying rides. Use the percent change in the price and the percent change in the quantity supplied to calculate the price elasticity of supply for Uber rides:

$$\text{Price elasticity of supply} = \frac{+100\%}{+80\%} = 1.25$$

In fact, at "super peak" times, prices surged by as much as 800%, leading some people who didn't check their app carefully (perhaps because of their New Year's Eve celebrations) to pay as much as $720 for a 40-minute ride! ■

Price elasticity of supply is positive. You'll notice that the price elasticity of supply is a positive number. That's because changes in price lead to changes in quantity supplied in the same direction as you move along a supply curve: Raising the price increases the quantity supplied, while lowering the price reduces the quantity supplied. Just as with the price elasticity of demand (and every other elasticity as well), a bigger absolute value of the price elasticity of supply means that the quantity is more responsive to price changes. However, since the price elasticity of supply is positive, there's no need to take the absolute value.

Quantity is relatively unresponsive when supply is inelastic. Airports are a nightmare during school holidays. Even if you book your flight months in advance, you're likely to find that tickets are more expensive than they are for other times. And if you don't book ahead of time, you may find that flights are sold out. Often there are quite a lot of people who have been bumped off an oversold plane or who are struggling to get rebooked if they missed a connecting flight. With all this extra demand and higher prices, why don't airlines just add more flights? The answer is that many airlines simply don't have the ability to sell very many more tickets in response to higher prices.

Airports, not airlines, control how many flights can go out of each gate, and there are a limited number of gates available. Many airports operate at near capacity much of the year, making it hard to add extra flights at busy times. Airlines could fly larger planes, but where would they get the bigger planes for just a week or two? And their supply of pilots and flight attendants is limited, as safety laws limit the hours crewmembers can work. In short, it is really difficult for airlines to increase the quantity of flights supplied by much in response to higher prices at busy times of the year.

When suppliers can't increase the quantity supplied by much in response to higher prices, economists describe their supply as *inelastic*. Just as with the price elasticity of demand, we say that supply is inelastic whenever the magnitude of the percent change in quantity supplied is smaller than the percent change in price. This means that supply is inelastic if the price elasticity of supply is smaller than 1. As Figure 7 shows, this corresponds with a relatively steep supply curve.

Quantity is relatively responsive when supply is elastic. Marcus runs a catering business out of what used to be a restaurant. The space is more than he currently needs, but he couldn't find anything smaller at a lower price. With the economy improving, more people want to host catered events, and the prices that he can charge are rising. These higher prices make it profitable for him to expand, so he quickly hires more people to help in the kitchen, and he is grateful that the kitchen has room to expand. He doubles his bookings right away and is considering leasing an even bigger space for the coming year if prices continue to rise.

When suppliers like Marcus are very responsive to price, economists describe their supply as *elastic*. Just as with the absolute value of the price elasticity of demand, we say that supply is elastic whenever the magnitude of the percent change in quantity supplied is larger than the percent change in price. This means that supply is elastic if the price elasticity of supply is larger than 1.

Perfectly elastic and inelastic supply represent the extremes. As with demand, there are two extreme cases. When the supply curve is completely horizontal it means that the price elasticity of supply is infinite—any change in price leads to an infinite change in quantity supplied. Economists call this *perfectly elastic supply.* When the supply curve is completely vertical it means that the price elasticity of supply is zero—no matter what the change is in price, the total quantity supplied is unchanged. Economists call this *perfectly inelastic supply.*

For any two supply curves passing through the same point, the supply curve that is relatively flatter at that point will have more elastic supply at that point than the supply curve that is relatively steeper. Figure 7 summarises the difference between perfectly inelastic, inelastic, elastic, and perfectly elastic supply. As you read through this table, test yourself on what each of these concepts means.

Figure 7 | Inelastic and Elastic Supply

	Definition	Which means . . .	Implies	Graphically
Perfectly inelastic supply	*% change in quantity supplied* is zero for any *% change in price*	The quantity supplied is unchanged for any change in price.	*Price elasticity of supply = 0*	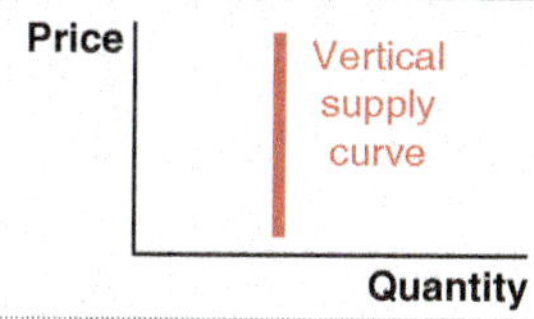
Inelastic supply	*% change in quantity supplied* is smaller than *% change in price*	The quantity supplied is relatively unresponsive to a change in price.	*Price elasticity of supply < 1*	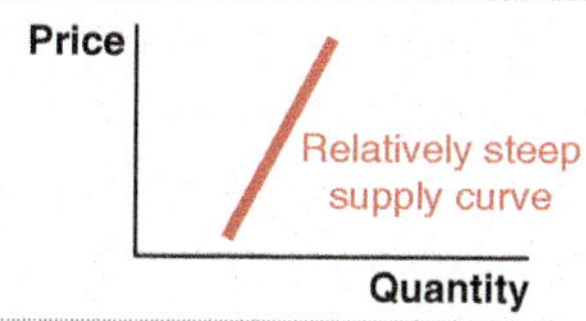
Elastic supply	*% change in quantity supplied* is larger than *% change in price*	The quantity supplied is relatively responsive to a change in price.	*Price elasticity of supply > 1*	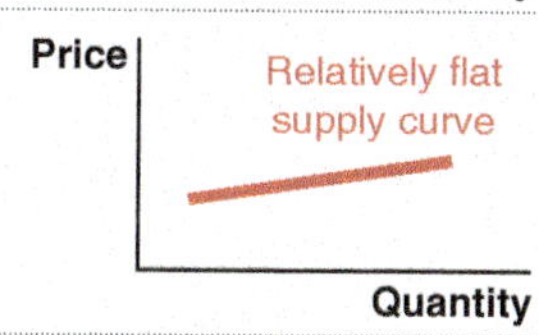
Perfectly elastic supply	*% change in quantity supplied* is infinite for any *% change in price*	The quantity supplied is infinitely responsive to a change in price.	*Price elasticity of supply = ∞*	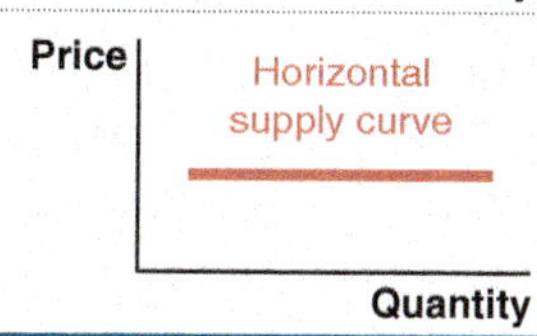

Determinants of the Price Elasticity of Supply

The price elasticity of supply reflects how willing businesses are to increase the quantity supplied in response to a higher price. To assess this, put yourself in the shoes of a supplier, and think about how you would respond to a higher price. If you increase your production, your profits will likely rise, but by how much depends on how rapidly your marginal costs rise. And that, in turn, depends on how *flexible* your business can be.

Price elasticity of supply is all about flexibility. Your business's flexibility is the underlying determinant of your price elasticity of supply. It describes how easily and cheaply you can mobilise resources to expand production when prices rise, and how easily you can cut your expenses or repurpose your resources when the price falls. *The more flexible you are, the greater your price elasticity of supply will be.*

The price elasticity of supply reflects the flexibility of firms to increase or decrease the quantity supplied. It is larger:

1. For firms that store inventories
2. When inputs are easily available
3. For firms with extra capacity
4. When firms can easily enter and exit the market
5. When there's more time to adjust

Recall how hard it is for airlines to respond to an increase in ticket prices at the holidays. An airline such as Qantas typically lacks the flexibility to adjust the supply of airline tickets because it doesn't have much flexibility to add more workers, more planes, or more flights. Similarly, when prices fall, Qantas is equally inflexible. It could fly its planes less full, but that yields very little savings because it is still paying for the aeroplane, flight attendants, fuel, and airport. And it can't easily repurpose its planes to other tasks, because what else can you use a 787 Dreamliner for? If Qantas cuts back on the number of flights without repurposing its planes, it has to pay for storage of the plane; it's also likely that it has an enterprise bargaining agreement that will make it hard to cut back on staff. Both of these factors reduce the cost savings from cutting back on flights. All of this inflexibility means that the supply of flights is relatively inelastic.

By contrast, recall that Marcus easily expands his business when prices rise because he has a lot of flexibility in how he runs his catering business. When the price he gets for catered food rises, he finds it easy to buy more raw ingredients, hire more staff, and make more food. The extra space in his kitchen means that he doesn't face capacity constraints. Likewise, if the price of his goods were to fall, he can simply cut back on production. It's not a big deal, because he can simply order less from his suppliers. His staff are mostly hourly workers, so he can easily cut their hours as well. All of this flexibility means that the supply of catered meals is relatively elastic.

Bottom line: *Flexibility* determines the price elasticity of supply. It's an idea that underpins each of the following five determinants of the price elasticity of supply.

Supply elasticity factor one: Inventories make supply more elastic. If your business's product is easily stored, then you can use inventories to provide the flexibility to respond quickly to price changes. For instance, oil refineries can immediately dial up supply by selling stored inventories of petrol when the price is high. They can also dial it back down by stockpiling inventories when the price is low. As a result, the quantity supplied can respond rapidly to price changes, yielding more elastic supply.

Inventories provide flexibility by breaking the link between production and supply. They allow you to adjust the quantity you supply, even if it is difficult to adjust your production. But it's a form of flexibility that not all companies have. A refinery can get away with selling petrol that it manufactured a month ago. But if a catering company tried that with their sandwiches, the health department would shut them down.

Supply elasticity factor two: Easily available variable inputs make supply elastic. If the variable inputs you need to expand production are easily available, then your supply will be more elastic. This is because you'll be able to increase production swiftly in response to a price rise. For instance, Marcus's catering company can easily hire more workers and buy more supplies when the price of catered meals rises. As a result, he has the flexibility to increase the quantity he supplies in response to a price rise. By contrast, while it's easy for airlines to buy more fuel, it's harder to get more pilots or more planes. The problem is not that these inputs are impossible to get, but rather that the extra cost involved makes expanding production not worthwhile.

It's also important to think about reallocating your existing resources, because that can give you greater flexibility to respond to changes in the prices of specific products. For example, if the price of flights between Perth and Brisbane rises, Qantas could reallocate its resources, shifting the planes, pilots, and fuel from other routes to flying between Perth and Brisbane instead. By contrast, we've seen that if the price of all airline tickets were to rise, it would be difficult for Qantas to expand its total number of flights, because this would require more pilots and planes. As a result, supply in narrow categories like Perth-to-Brisbane flights is often relatively elastic, even as the supply of broader categories—like airline tickets generally—is relatively inelastic.

Supply elasticity factor three: Extra capacity makes supply elastic. Sometimes a business has fixed inputs, such as a factory in which it manufactures goods or an office for its workers. Marcus's catering business has a kitchen in which his workers prepare meals. In the short run, these fixed inputs provide a constraint on a business's ability to expand production. That means that if a business is already using its fixed input at full capacity, it will be difficult to respond even if a business can easily access more of its variable inputs. If, on the other hand, it has extra capacity, then its supply will be more elastic.

One of the reasons that Marcus's catering company can easily adjust production as prices change is that he has a larger kitchen than he needs. This extra capacity gives him the flexibility to respond to higher prices by hiring more kitchen staff and catering more events. But there's a point at which he'll use up this extra capacity, and once he runs out of kitchen space, he won't be able to increase production—at least not without a costly investment in renting a new kitchen. At that point, his price elasticity of supply will become inelastic.

It's worth thinking broadly about what capacity constraints might limit your flexibility. For instance, a key constraint on airlines is that they need an airport gate to load and unload their passengers. And there are only a fixed number of gates in each city, meaning that many airlines can only sell more tickets by buying bigger planes.

Supply elasticity factor four: Easy entry and exit make supply more elastic. So far, we have focused on how existing businesses can change production in response to changing prices. However, the quantity supplied in the market is also a function of the number of suppliers. When the price rises, new businesses may enter the market, and when it falls some businesses may exit. Market supply will be more elastic when it is easier for businesses to enter or exit a market.

The flexibility to freely enter the catering market is one of the key reasons that supply is quite elastic. If you want to start a catering company, you'll need cooking skills, business know-how, a kitchen, and around $100,000 to cover startup costs. It's not easy, but there are enough people with these skills and assets that when prices rise, you'll see people start new catering companies. The entry of new businesses leads to a rise in the total quantity supplied at a higher price.

By contrast, it is rare to see new airlines start in response to high prices. After all, a single Boeing 787 costs about $125 million, and you'll probably need a few of those to get started. And who's got that sort of cash lying around?

Supply elasticity factor five: Over time, supply becomes more elastic. Supply adjustments often take time, and so the quantity supplied will adjust by a lot more over a period of several years than it will over several days. As a result, the price elasticity of supply is typically larger when you're looking over a longer time horizon.

Think about how the influence of each of the factors listed above varies over time. How do managers respond after a price rise? That afternoon, the only way to increase the quantity supplied is to run down your inventories. Over the next few days, you might think about how to expand your production. In the longer run, you can also expand your capacity by building a new factory. And in the long run, high prices will lure new businesses into the market. The result is that the price elasticity of supply may be quite small in the short run, but it is typically much larger over the long run. How long does it take to get the full adjustment? Again, it depends. You can set up a new catering business relatively quickly, so the long run for catering may be only a year. Building new oil refineries takes much longer, and so the long run for petrol can be more than a decade.

Calculating the Price Elasticity of Supply

Just like with the price elasticity of demand, it's useful to have a consistent measure of the price elasticity of supply between two points. To do this, we once again need to use the midpoint formula to calculate the percent changes in price and quantity. As a refresher, to calculate the percent change in quantity between any two points, Q_2 and Q_1, divide the difference between the two points by the average of the two points. Thus, the formula for calculating the percent change in quantity is:

$$\text{Percent change in quantity supplied} = \frac{Q_2 - Q_1}{(Q_2 + Q_1)/2} \times 100$$

Similarly, to calculate the percent change in price between any two prices, divide the difference between them by the average of the two price points. Thus the formula for calculating the percent change in price is:

$$\text{Percent change in price} = \frac{P_2 - P_1}{(P_2 + P_1)/2} \times 100$$

Basically, the midpoint formula you learned for demand works equally well for supply and it's just as useful.

Once you've calculated the percent change in quantity and percent change in price using the midpoint formula, you're ready to calculate the price elasticity of supply given what you already know—it is simply the percent change in quantity supplied divided by the percent change in price.

Do the Economics

Let's calculate the change in Uber drivers supplying rides when the price rises using the midpoint formula. Usually an Uber driver can expect to earn $150 driving a 6-hour shift. But surge pricing on particularly busy nights means that Uber drivers can expect to earn $210 driving a 6-hour shift. Typically, there are 200 drivers on the road, but surge pricing leads that to rise to 300 drivers. Calculate the price elasticity of supply of Uber drivers using the midpoint formula.

Step one: *What was the percent change in the price?*

$$\text{Percent change in price} = \frac{210 - 150}{(210 + 150)/2} \times 100 = \frac{60}{180} \times 100 = 33\%$$

Step two: *How much did the quantity supplied change as a percent, in response?*

$$\text{Percent change in quantity} = \frac{300 - 200}{(300 + 200)/2} \times 100 = \frac{100}{250} \times 100 = 40\%$$

Step three: *Calculate the elasticity:*

$$\text{Price elasticity of supply} = \frac{\text{Percent change in quantity}}{\text{Percent change in price}} = \frac{+40\%}{+33\%} = 1.2$$ ■

Tying It Together

This chapter was about the calculations that businesses make every day as they experiment with their prices and other factors to maximise their profits. If you lower your prices, will total revenue go up or down? Should you try introducing a new product at a lower price point, or will that cannibalise the sales of your other products? Where should you open your next store so as to get the mix of customers most likely to be receptive to your products? Should you pursue a high- or low-price strategy? It's not enough to know how sensitive demand for your product is to its own price. You also need to know how sensitive demand will be to the prices of other products and to household incomes.

Answering these questions requires numbers. It's not enough to know whether sales will go up or down; real businesses need to know by how much. And that's what elasticity does: It allows you to forecast how much quantities will change under different market conditions.

Every elasticity is about the same thing—measuring the responsiveness of quantity to various changes in market conditions. We've really introduced only one concept in this chapter: Elasticity measures the percent change in quantity following a 1% change in some other factor. And this means that you only need to remember one formula:

$$\text{Elasticity} = \frac{\text{Percent change in quantity}}{\text{Percent change in some other factor}}$$

That other factor could be the price of your good, the price of another good, or income. (And if there were other factors you thought mattered, you could also calculate their elasticities, too.)

In every case, the bigger the number in absolute value, the more elastic the good is, which means it's more responsive. For the price elasticity of demand and supply, you saw that whether the elasticity (in absolute value terms) is bigger or smaller than 1 tells you something important—whether the percent change in quantity will be bigger or smaller than the percent change in price.

For the cross-price elasticity of demand and the income elasticity of demand, whether the elasticity is positive or negative tells you something important about the type of good it is. But underneath it all, elasticity is just about one big idea: measuring how responsive people's decisions are to changing conditions.

Chapter at a Glance

Elasticity: Measures the responsiveness of quantity to changes in other factors.

$$= \frac{\text{Percent change in quantity}}{\text{Percent change in some other factor}}$$

A larger elasticity (in absolute value) means greater responsiveness

Demand Elasticity

Price elasticity of demand: A measure of how responsive buyers are to price changes.

$$= \frac{\text{Percent change in the quantity demanded}}{\text{Percent change in price}}$$

Elastic demand: The quantity **demanded** is relatively responsive to a change in price.

Inelastic demand: The quantity **demanded** is relatively unresponsive to a change in price.

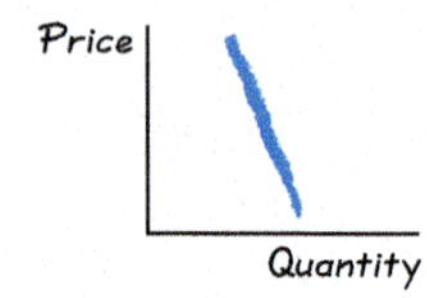

Knowing whether price elasticity of demand is elastic or inelastic can help a business maximise revenue.

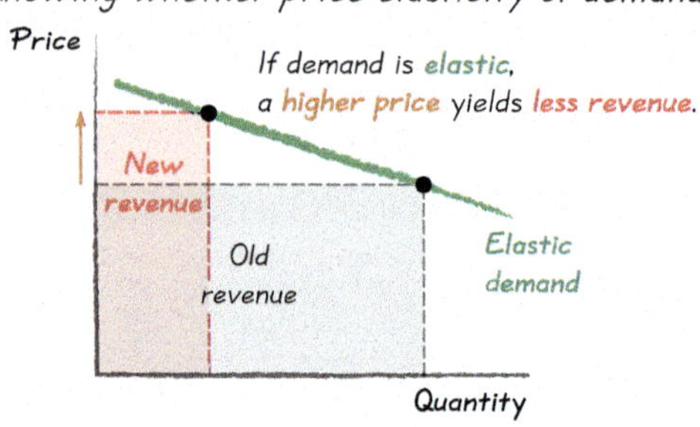

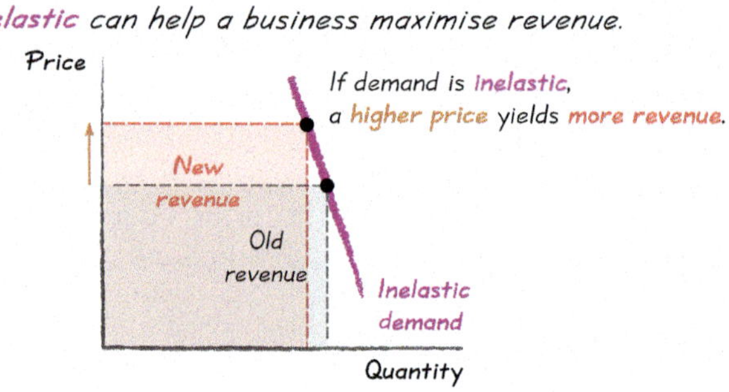

Demand is more elastic when good substitutes exist:

- Markets with many competing products
- Specific brands, rather than broad categories
- Necessities
- Goods where search is less costly
- Long time horizon

Supply Elasticity

Price elasticity of supply: A measure of how responsive sellers are to price changes.

$$= \frac{\text{Percent change in the quantity supplied}}{\text{Percent change in price}}$$

Elastic supply: The quantity **supplied** is relatively responsive to a change in price.

Inelastic supply: The quantity **supplied** is relatively unresponsive to a change in price.

Supply is more elastic when firms have flexibility

- Products are easily stored
- Additional inputs are available
- Businesses have extra capacity
- Market entry and exit are easy
- Long time horizon

Other Demand Elasticities

Cross-price elasticity: A measure of how responsive the demand of one good is to price changes of another.

$$= \frac{\text{Percent change in the quantity demanded}}{\text{Percent change in the price of another good}}$$

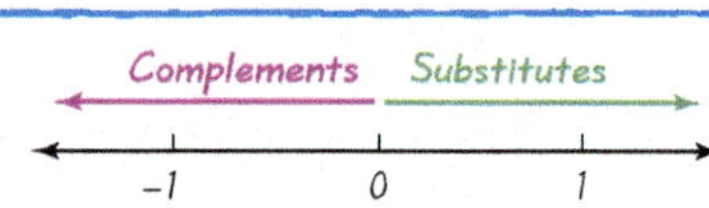

Cross-price elasticity

Income elasticity: A measure of how responsive the demand for a good is to changes in income.

$$= \frac{\text{Percent change in the quantity demanded}}{\text{Percent change in income}}$$

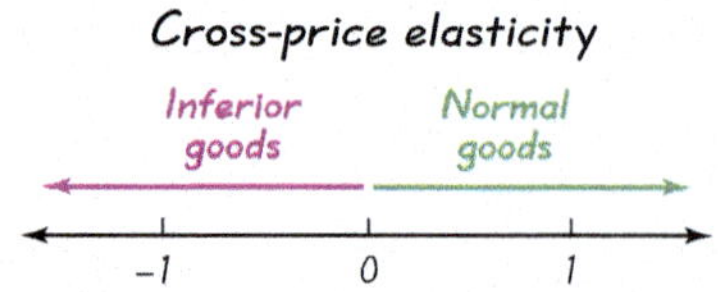

Income elasticity of demand

Key Concepts

cross-price elasticity of demand, 122
elastic, 111
income elasticity of demand, 124
inelastic, 111
perfectly elastic, 111
perfectly inelastic, 111
price elasticity of demand, 110
price elasticity of supply, 125
total revenue, 118

Discussion and Review Questions

Learning Objective 5.1 *Measure the responsiveness of the quantity demanded to price changes, using the price elasticity of demand.*

1. Provide some examples of goods or services that you purchase that have relatively inelastic demand. How would you respond to a 10% increase in price? Are there any goods that you would consider perfectly inelastic?
2. What impact has access to the internet on smartphones had on the price elasticity of demand for items from Harvey Norman or Dymocks? What are some strategies these companies could take to combat any negative impacts?

Learning Objective 5.2 *Understand how demand elasticity shapes your total revenue and your business strategy.*

3. You are a pricing manager at a pharmaceutical company. The CEO of the company calls a meeting of all managers to explain that it is critical to increase revenue soon or you may have to start laying off employees. You know that the absolute value of the price elasticity of your leading patented drug is about 0.5. What are some possible changes you could suggest to the CEO to increase revenue?

Learning Objective 5.3 *Assess the responsiveness of demand to income, and the prices of other goods.*

4. What are some examples of pairs of goods or services you purchase that are complements or substitutes? Would their cross-price elasticity be positive or negative, and why? What would happen to your purchasing decisions if the price of one of the goods decreased by 50%?
5. What are some examples of things you purchase that have positive or negative income elasticities? How would your purchase decisions change if your income rose by 20%?

Learning Objective 5.4 *Measure the responsiveness of the quantity supplied to price changes, using the price elasticity of supply.*

6. Consider two different companies. The first has a relatively inelastic supply curve; the second has a relatively elastic supply curve. What factors might lead to the difference in supply elasticities between these two businesses? Can you envision an example for each type of company?

Study Problems

Learning Objective 5.1 *Measure the responsiveness of the quantity demanded to price changes, using the price elasticity of demand.*

1. In 2011, Cyclone Yasi led banana production in Queensland to fall by 30%. Queensland produces nearly all of Australia's bananas. One month after the cyclone, prices at Coles and Woolworths roughly doubled to \$5.99/kg. What does this tell you about the price elasticity of demand for bananas?
2. The EpiPen is a life-saving device used by people with severe allergies. The Australian distributor of the EpiPen raised its price by nearly 25% per year for nearly a decade. For each price increase of 25%, would quantity demanded change by more or less than 25%?
3. Europe has eight different companies selling devices similar to the EpiPen. If these devices were available in the Australian market, what would happen to the price elasticity of demand for the EpiPen?

Learning Objective 5.2 *Understand how demand elasticity shapes your total revenue and your business strategy.*

4. Suppose the toll for crossing the Sydney Harbour Bridge in a car is \$4 and you read a newspaper report that less revenue is being generated than analysts expect. What type of additional information would you need to know in order to determine if the toll should be increased or decreased to maximise revenue?
5. Suppose an experiment is conducted that provides the data in the accompanying table. What is the price elasticity of demand for using the toll road when the price falls from \$4 to \$3 (use the midpoint method). Is it elastic or inelastic? Finally, calculate the change in toll revenue when the toll rate changes. Which rate should the toll road charge if the government wants more toll revenue?

Toll rate	Number of vehicles using the tollway per day
\$4	10,000
\$3	12,000

6. People differ in their willingness to pay for air travel and airlines would like to charge different prices to different people. Airlines typically attempt to divide passengers into two types: leisure travellers and business travellers. Suppose that an airline is charging $400 per return ticket for all passengers on flights between Sydney and Melbourne, The accompanying tables provide information on quantity demanded for air travel for leisure travellers and business travellers.

Leisure travellers

Price per ticket	Quantity of tickets per flight
$400	100
$500	50

Business travellers

Price per ticket	Quantity of tickets per flight
$400	100
$500	90

Using the midpoint method, calculate and describe the price elasticity of demand for both types of passengers if the airline increases prices to $500. Calculate the change in total revenue for each group.

Learning Objective 5.3 *Assess the responsiveness of demand to income, and the prices of other goods.*

7. The average price of petrol in the United States rose by 17% between 2007 and 2008. The number of extremely large, "gas-guzzling" vehicles called Hummers sold in the United States fell by 50% over the same period. Use these values to calculate the cross-price elasticity between petrol and Hummers.

8. We often observe that items such as different brands of paracetamol, petrol, and tomato sauce are typically priced the same, particularly when consumers can find these goods in close proximity to each other (such as at petrol stations on opposite sides of the street, or products next to each other on the same grocery store shelf). What does this indicate about the cross-price elasticity of demand for the different brands of the same product? Would you expect the cross-price elasticity to be relatively large or small in magnitude? Positive or negative?

9. In September 2020, Netflix increased its monthly price for new subscribers by $1 for its basic plan and $2 for its standard plan. In response, someone commented on social media: "So tired of being a student. Can't wait until I have a stable job and won't have a meltdown cause Netflix raised their price by $1." What does this statement indicate about the income elasticity of demand for Netflix for this student? Is it normal or inferior?

Learning Objective 5.4 *Measure the responsiveness of the quantity supplied to price changes, using the price elasticity of supply.*

10. The accompanying table shows how many Veggie Delite with Avo sandwiches Subway might be willing to sell each day at two different prices. Using the midpoint formula, calculate the price elasticity of supply when price increases from $8.95 to $9.50. Is the price elasticity of supply relatively elastic or inelastic? Suppose that Subway wishes to analyse what happens annually instead of daily. What would happen to its estimated supply curve; would it become relatively steeper or flatter?

Price per sandwich	Quantity supplied
$8.95	200,000
$9.50	210,000

CHAPTER

6

Taxes, Price Controls, and Quantity Regulations

When you were offered your first job, you may have been offered pay at the minimum wage. This isn't a wage determined by supply and demand—it's a wage set by the government. Employers are prohibited from hiring anyone at a lower wage even if you would be willing to work for less.

Martin Berry/Alamy Stock Photo

Would you do this job for less than minimum wage?

It's just one example of the way government policy can change prices in the market. So far we have focused on market forces, analysing how supply and demand determine the quantity and price at which goods are sold. Supply and demand play an important role in determining the quantity and price of any product, but there is another important factor influencing many market outcomes: the laws, regulations, and taxes set by the government. Every day you buy or sell goods in which the government has had an influence in the market.

Government policy may play a role in determining the number of apartments available for you to rent, how much you have to pay for them, and whether you can build a new home or open a business where you want. Taxes impact your take-home pay and how much the goods and services you purchase cost. Government policy can even shape the most personal of decisions, such as whether to get married and how many kids to have, by changing the relevant costs and benefits.

Government doesn't stop the forces of supply and demand—the core principles that provide the foundation of all economic analysis still apply. But, by shaping costs and benefits, government policy can change the decisions that sellers and buyers make, ultimately changing the quantities sold and the prices that buyers pay and sellers receive. While you may have views about whether a particular government action is a good idea or not, our goal in this chapter is simply to assess what various government actions do to quantity demanded, quantity supplied, and prices. Specifically, we'll assess how the three tools that the government uses—taxes, policies limiting prices that can be charged, and policies limiting the quantities that can be bought or sold—change market outcomes and prices.

Chapter Objective

Forecast the consequences of government policies.

6.1 How Taxes and Subsidies Change Market Outcomes
Assess how taxes shape supply, demand, and equilibrium outcomes.

6.2 Price Regulations
Evaluate the full set of consequences of price ceilings and price floors.

6.3 Quantity Regulations
Analyse the consequences of quantity regulations.

6.1 How Taxes and Subsidies Change Market Outcomes

Learning Objective *Assess how taxes shape supply, demand, and equilibrium outcomes.*

kunchit jantana/Shutterstock

Sweet and bubbly and subject to government intervention.

I bet that you drink sugar-sweetened drinks like soft drinks, juices, energy drinks, or bubble tea—at least now and again. Most Australians do, and some do so a lot. Adolescent males consume on average more than a litre per day of these drinks, making up more than 10% of their daily energy needs. It's no secret that these sugary drinks are not good for us. It's not just that it'll rot your teeth, it can also lead to heart disease, diabetes, and high blood pressure.

Sugary drinks are the biggest source of added sugar in most people's diets. As a result, the World Health Organization has implored governments to help cut the consumption of sugary drinks. That's why many countries and many cities in the United States have introduced special taxes on sugar-sweetened beverages, although the idea remains controversial in Australia. The idea behind these "soft drink taxes" is to drive up the price of sugary drinks so people will drink fewer of them.

These policies have sparked lots of debate about the government's role in both driving up prices of sugary drinks for consumers and driving down sales and prices received by beverage manufacturers. That's in fact exactly what taxes typically do—they tend to reduce the quantity demanded and the quantity supplied of the taxed good as buyers pay more and sellers receive less. Why the difference between the price buyers pay and the price sellers receive? Because the government takes a cut in the form of a tax.

You and your friends may disagree about whether this policy makes people better off. Some argue that people should have the right to buy as many sugary drinks as they want at market prices—in essence deciding for themselves how much to drink. Others argue that people are overconsuming sugary drinks because they aren't fully taking into account the negative effects on their health later in life and on the health care system.

We'll focus on evaluating these arguments in later chapters. For now, our goal is to understand how the tax changes the quantity sold and the prices buyers pay and sellers receive. Let's see how all this works by analysing a tax on sugary beverages that came into effect in Philadelphia, in the United States, in 2017.

A Tax on Sellers

In 2017, Philadelphia introduced a tax on sellers of sugar-sweetened beverages of 1.5 U.S. cents per ounce, which is about 0.05 U.S. cents per litre. (We'll be talking in terms of U.S. dollars a fair bit in this chapter, because after all, the tax was introduced in the United States. If you want to convert any example to Australian dollars, a rough guideline is to multiply the U.S. dollars by 1.3.) The way the tax works is that when you buy a 600ml bottle of soft drink, you'll pay whatever price the seller posts and you don't have to worry about the tax. The seller keeps whatever you pay minus the new tax, because they're responsible for sending the tax to the government. This is a tax on sellers because if you buy a 600ml soft drink, the seller needs to send \$0.30 (\$0.0005 per litre × 600ml) to the government.

A tax on sellers shifts the supply curve. The tax represents a marginal cost to sellers because it's an additional cost they must pay for each unit they sell. You learned in Chapter 3 that the supply curve is the marginal cost curve. Therefore, when marginal costs increase, the supply curve shifts. This is the *interdependence principle* in action, illustrating how the choices of others—in this case, the government—affect your decisions.

Figure 1 shows the market for soft drinks in Philadelphia. Before the tax is implemented, the supply curve intersects the demand curve at 1.4 million bottles of 600ml soft drinks sold per week, at an equilibrium price of \$1.10 per bottle. (I know these numbers look really

Figure 1 | Effects of Taxing Soft Drink Sellers in Philadelphia

If a new tax on sellers of $0.30 is introduced:

(A) The supply curve shifts up $0.30 (the amount of the tax), as measured on the vertical axis. The tax raises the marginal cost for sellers by $0.30, so they will only sell if the price is $0.30 higher for each bottle of soft drink.

(B) Equilibrium occurs at the point where the new supply curve meets the demand curve.

(C) The quantity of soft drinks purchased each week falls from 1.4 million bottles to 1.2 million bottles.

(D) The price buyers pay after the tax rises by $0.20 (from $1.10 to $1.30).

(E) The price sellers receive after the tax falls by $0.10 (from $1.10 to $1.00).

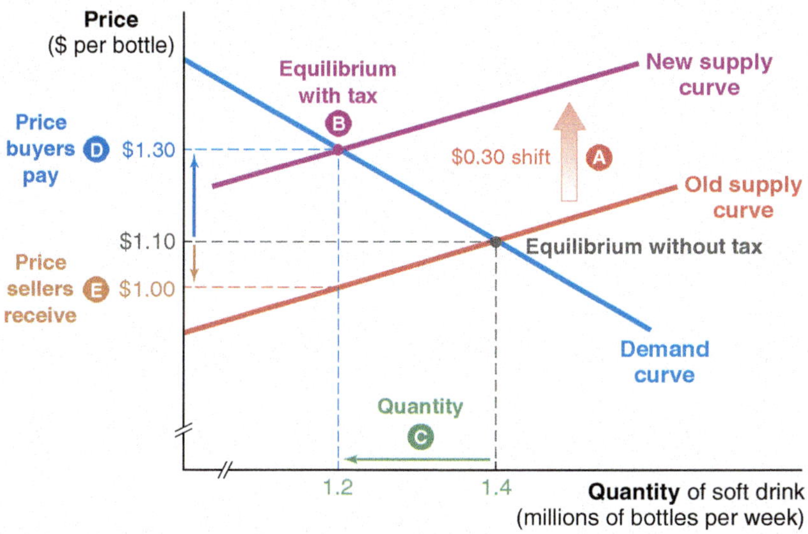

low compared to what you would pay at a convenience store in Australia, but they're the actual U.S. numbers—and they introduced the tax—so we're going to stick with them.) Philadelphia's soft-drink tax adds $0.30 to the marginal cost of a 600ml bottle of soft drink, causing supply to decrease. Typically, we describe a decrease in supply as shifting the supply curve to the left. In this case, you might find it easier to think about the supply curve shifting up by the amount of the increase in marginal costs. Since the supply curve is the marginal cost curve, if marginal costs are $0.30 higher, then the supply curve must shift $0.30 up.

The tax leads to a decline in the quantity sold. The shift in supply results in the new supply curve intersecting the demand curve at a lower quantity demanded. The quantity of soft drink sold declines from 1.4 million bottles per week to 1.2 million bottles. The end result is that higher soft drink prices lead to lower soft drink sales because each bottle of soft drink costs consumers more.

The tax increases the price buyers pay and decreases the price sellers receive. The new price of $1.30 is the price you pay at the register for a 600ml bottle of soft drink, but it isn't the amount that sellers keep, since they have to send the government $0.30 per bottle in taxes. Thus, Figure 1 shows that at the new equilibrium, the price buyers pay for the soft drink rises from $1.10 to $1.30, an increase of $0.20. But sellers, who have to send $0.30 per soft drink to the government, only keep $1.00 ($1.30 minus $0.30), a fall of $0.10 from the equilibrium price without taxes of $1.10.

Both buyers and sellers bear the economic burden of the tax on sellers. There is an important distinction between who is assigned by the government to send a tax payment and who ultimately bears its burden. The **statutory burden** of a tax describes the burden of being assigned by the government the responsibility of sending a tax payment. But if you want to know who experiences a greater loss as a result of the tax, you should focus instead on the **economic burden,** which describes the burden created by the change in after-tax prices faced by buyers and sellers as a result of the tax.

statutory burden The burden of being assigned by the government to send a tax payment.

economic burden The burden created by the change in after-tax prices faced by buyers and sellers.

In Philadelphia, the statutory burden is entirely a tax on sellers—after all, they are responsible for sending in the full payment to the government. However, buyers and sellers each bear some of the economic burden. Even though the tax is \$0.30, the price sellers get to keep after they send in the tax payment is only \$0.10 less than the pre-tax equilibrium price of \$1.10. Buyers of soft drinks—like you—make up the difference because you pay \$0.20 more per soft drink than you would without the tax.

Effectively then, buyers and sellers are sharing the economic burden of the soft drink tax. In our example, buyers bear a larger share of the economic burden of a soft drink tax. Economists have estimated the economic burden of soft drink taxes and have found that about two-thirds of a tax on soft drink tends to fall on consumers. **Tax incidence** describes the division of the economic burden of a tax between buyers and sellers.

tax incidence The division of the economic burden of a tax between buyers and sellers.

A Tax on Buyers

Instead of taxing soft drink sellers, the government could change the statutory burden and levy a tax on soft drink buyers. Practically, the way this typically works is that stores post the price without the tax, you pay the tax as you check out, and the store does you the convenience of mailing in the tax. But it's just that, a convenience. You may not realise it, but when the government levies a tax on buyers, the buyer is responsible for submitting the payment to the government if the store doesn't do it for them.

So what happens if we switch the statutory burden to buyers? The price posted at store is the before-tax price and reflects what the store receives without the tax. Buyers, however, have to pay that price plus the \$0.30 per soft drink tax when they get to the register.

A tax on buyers shifts the demand curve. In Chapter 2, you learned that the demand curve is the marginal benefit curve. A tax of \$0.30 reduces the marginal benefit of buying a soft drink by \$0.30, because that soft drink now comes with a 30-cent tax obligation. As such, a tax on buyers causes a decrease in demand. This is the *interdependence principle* in action, showing how the choices of others—in this case, the government—affect your decisions. Typically, we describe a decrease in demand as shifting the demand curve to the left. But when you're analysing a tax, you might find it easier to think about the demand curve shifting down by the amount of the tax. The reason that the demand curve in Figure 2 shifts down by \$0.30 is that buyers will only be willing to purchase the same quantity as before if the pre-tax price is \$0.30 lower.

The tax leads to a decline in the quantity sold. Following the shift in demand, the new demand curve intersects the supply curve at a lower quantity supplied. The quantity of soft drink sold declines from 1.4 million bottles per week to 1.2 million and the price that sellers charge for each bottle declines from \$1.10 to \$1.00. But the price buyers pay is both the price the store charges and the tax payment they must make. So buyers now pay \$1.30 (the new store price of \$1.00 plus an additional \$0.30 tax), which is \$0.20 cents per soft drink more than the \$1.10 they paid before the tax.

The tax increases the price buyers pay and decreases the price sellers receive. Let's unpack what's happening with the price a bit more. Figure 2 shows that the sellers' price declines from \$1.10 to \$1.00 per soft drink. Thus, the price received by sellers has fallen by \$0.10 per soft drink. Meanwhile, the price buyers pay has risen, from \$1.10 per soft drink to \$1.30 (that is, \$1.00 per soft drink plus the \$0.30 tax), and so the after-tax cost of a 600ml soft drink has risen by \$0.20.

Buyers and sellers bear the economic burden of a tax on buyers. The statutory burden is simple: This is a tax levied on buyers. But what about the economic burden? We've found that a tax on buyers of \$0.30 per soft drink raises the price buyers pay for soft drinks (including taxes) by \$0.20 per soft drink. In turn, the price sellers receive has declined by \$0.10 per soft drink, from \$1.10 to \$1.00. Thus, buyers and sellers share the economic burden of this tax (albeit unevenly).

Figure 2 | Effects of Taxing Soft Drink Buyers in Philadelphia

If a new tax on buyers is introduced:

A The **demand curve** shifts down **$0.30** (the amount of the tax), as measured on the vertical axis. The tax reduces the marginal benefit for buyers by $0.30, so at any given quantity buyers will now be willing to buy soft drinks only if the before-tax price is $0.30 per bottle lower.

B **Equilibrium** occurs at the point where the new demand curve meets the supply curve.

C The **quantity of soft drinks** purchased **falls** from **1.4 million** bottles per week to **1.2 million** bottles per week.

D The **price buyers pay** after the tax **rises** by $0.20 (from $1.10 to **$1.30**).

E The **price sellers receive** after the tax **falls** by $0.10 (from $1.10 to **$1.00**).

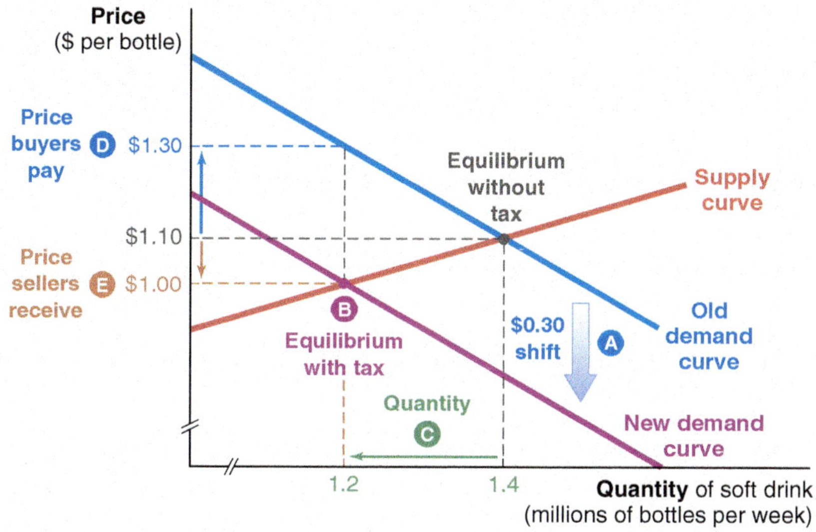

The Statutory Burden and Tax Incidence

We've just uncovered a startling result: Whether the new soft drink tax is levied on buyers or sellers, it has the same economic effect! Go back and compare the previous two examples. Taxing sellers $0.30 per soft drink (as in Figure 1) led the equilibrium quantity of soft drinks to decline from 1.4 million bottles of soft drink per week to 1.2 million. The price paid by buyers rose from $1.10 to $1.30 per bottle, while the price received by sellers (after they've paid their tax obligations) fell from $1.10 to $1.00. Placing the statutory burden on buyers instead (as in Figure 2) also led the equilibrium quantity of bottles of soft drink sold to decline from 1.4 million bottles per week to 1.2 million. And it also led the cost to the buyer (that is, the price paid inclusive of the tax obligation) to rise from $1.10 per bottle to $1.30, while the price sellers received fell from $1.10 per bottle to $1.00. The numbers are identical! That is, a soft drink tax has exactly the same effects, whether it is assigned to buyers or sellers! This isn't a coincidence, it's a general insight about all taxes, so let me reinforce this: *It doesn't matter whether the buyer or seller is assigned by the government to send in the tax; the end result is exactly the same.*

The fact that it doesn't matter whether you levy a tax on buyers or sellers is a surprising finding that holds for all taxes. And just to be clear, I'm not saying that taxes don't matter. When the government levies a tax, buyers buy less, sellers sell less, and prices are higher for buyers and lower for sellers. What is irrelevant, however, is whether the tax is levied on buyers or sellers. The tax matters, but who has the statutory burden turns out not to matter at all!

Tim Allen/Alamy Stock Photo

It doesn't matter whether it is the buyer or the seller who puts the money into the tax jar.

It doesn't matter who puts the money into the tax jar. Here's a simple metaphor that might help explain this surprising finding. You've just picked out an ice-cold Coke, and you walk to the counter inside a convenience store to pay. A "tax jar" is sitting on the counter. You pull $1.30 out of your pocket to pay for the Coke.

If the seller is assigned the statutory burden, you hand the seller $1.30. The seller, being responsible for submitting the tax, puts $0.30 of this into the "tax jar" and the remaining $1 into their cash register. If instead you're assigned the statutory burden as the buyer, then what changes? You still pull the same $1.30 out of your pocket. The only thing that changes is that this time, you're the one who puts the $0.30 into the "tax jar," and you hand the shopkeeper the remaining $1.00 to put into their cash register. In both cases, the same $1.30 comes out of the buyer's pocket, the same $1.00 goes into the shopkeeper's cash register, and the same $0.30 goes into the tax jar. That is, the transactions among buyer, seller, and government are inherently the same, irrespective of whether the tax is assigned to buyers or sellers.

This yields a surprising conclusion: Neither buyers nor sellers should care about who has the statutory burden, because a change in the statutory burden doesn't affect the economic burden they each face.

EVERYDAY Economics **Who pays for your Superannuation?**

Superannuation is a program in Australia that provides you with retirement income. To fund the program, employers pay 9.5% (at present) of your wages into an individual superannuation account on your behalf.

With real wages in Australia (wages adjusted for inflation in consumer prices) fairly flat since 2013, and with the 9.5% "Superannuation Guarantee Levy" due to rise in increments to 12% by 2025, there has been a lot of public debate about the effect of the increase. Some people argue that if wages aren't rising much anyway, then at least the increase in superannuation gives workers something. Other people argue that forcing employers to pay more superannuation means wage rises will be even lower.

How would things change if the law changed so employers no longer had to pay the 9.5% superannuation, and instead workers were assigned to foot the whole bill? Or what if employers paid half and workers paid half? Each of these alternatives would change the statutory burden of these taxes.

But as we've already established, the economic burden doesn't depend on whether a tax is levied on the buyer of labour (your employer) or the seller (you). The outcome in terms of wages and workers employed won't change. What would change would be the amount of pay you see on your pay slip (since right now you don't see what your employer pays, but you do see what you are paying). Research shows that workers tend to bear most of the economic burden from superannuation, because labour supply is fairly inelastic. This means that an increase in the superannuation guarantee to 12% will, all else equal, tend to lower wage rises that otherwise might have occurred. Workers are just trading wages today for retirement savings in the future. ■

The Economic Burden of Taxes

City officials in Philadelphia argued that a soft drink tax would raise needed revenue from the beverage industry to fund education. But others argued that these taxes would hurt consumers since a soft drink tax will raise the price consumers pay for soft drinks. These are arguments about tax incidence: Who is going to bear the economic burden of the tax—soft drink suppliers or soft drink buyers?

Tax incidence depends on the price elasticity of demand and supply. Tax incidence depends on your ability to avoid taxes—the more that you can avoid the tax, the less of it you will pay (and thus the lower your economic burden). The way to avoid a tax is to not buy or sell things that are taxed. In Chapter 5, you learned that the price elasticity of demand tells you how responsive buyers are to price changes and the price elasticity of supply tells you how responsive sellers are to price changes. Since taxes cause prices to change, it makes sense that the price elasticities of demand and supply determine who is best able to avoid a tax. Let's explore this separately for buyers and sellers.

Sellers bear a smaller share of the economic burden when supply is relatively elastic. If you're a seller, the only way to avoid a tax hike is to supply a smaller quantity. Importantly, sellers experience a tax hike as a reduction in the after-tax price they receive. Sellers avoid a tax by decreasing the quantity they supply as the after-tax price they receive falls. If you owned a soft drink company, what would you do if you were taxed? Remember that the key to the elasticity of supply is how flexible the seller is. Can you easily switch to making another, nonsugary drink? Or producing a different type of product? The more flexibility sellers have to use their resources to do something differently, the more elastic the price elasticity of supply.

Figure 3 shows two graphs, each starting from the same market equilibrium prior to the tax being introduced and each adding the same 30-cent tax on soft drinks. The difference between the two graphs is that supply is relatively elastic on the left and is more inelastic on the right. For the same tax added to the market, the price sellers receive will fall by less when supply is relatively more elastic (as shown at left in Figure 3). In contrast, when supply is relatively more inelastic (as shown at right in Figure 3), sellers bear more of the economic burden of the tax and therefore see a *larger* decline in the after-tax price. The larger the price elasticity of supply, the more sellers avoid the economic burden of the tax. *And so the more elastic a seller's supply curve is, the smaller their share of the economic burden.*

Figure 3 | Price Elasticity and Tax Incidence

Ⓐ When the tax is introduced, the supply curve shifts up until it lies $0.30 (the amount of the tax) higher, as measured on the vertical axis.

Ⓑ When demand is relatively inelastic and supply is relatively elastic, the price for buyers goes up by a lot and they bear a larger share of the tax incidence.

Ⓒ When demand is relatively elastic and supply is relatively inelastic, the price for buyers goes up by only a small amount and sellers bear a larger share of the tax incidence.

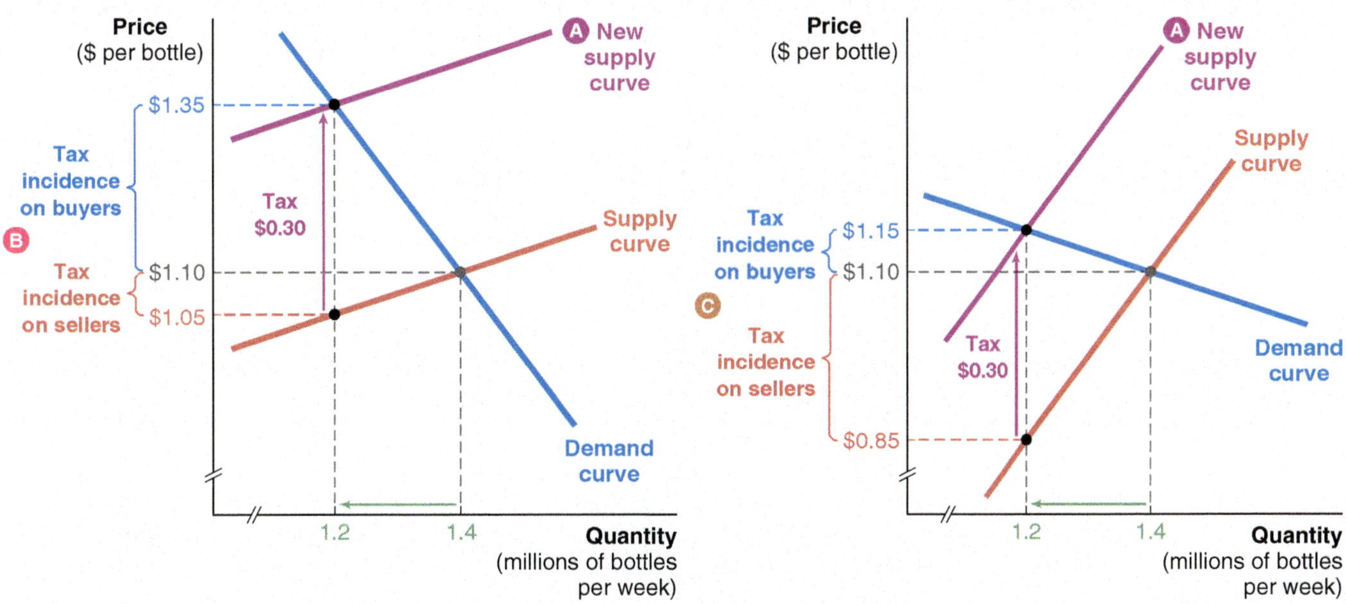

Buyers bear a smaller share of the economic burden when demand is relatively elastic. As a consumer, you can avoid a soft drink tax by buying fewer soft drinks. In fact, you won't pay any soft drink tax if you don't buy any soft drink. The more you reduce the quantity you demand in response to a tax-induced price hike, the more you are effectively avoiding the tax, leaving sellers to pay more. Your price elasticity of demand—that is, your responsiveness to an increase in price—is determined by the substitutes available to you. What would you do if the price of soft drinks went up? Would you switch to a nonsugary beverage?

The left side of Figure 3 shows demand that is inelastic relative to supply. In this case, buyers are not very responsive to changes in price relative to sellers. As a result, a larger share of the economic burden falls on buyers. So if you are an advocate representing the interests of consumers, an important question to ask when analysing the likely impact of a soft drink tax is, how willing are consumers to give up soft drinks?

The more consumers are willing to switch to unsweetened tea, water, and maybe diet soft drinks, the more elastic their demand curve is. And when demand is relatively elastic, as in the right side of Figure 3, their share of the tax incidence will be smaller. Recall that both figures show the same $0.30 tax being added to the market, but the price increase that buyers face differs substantially. The price increase buyers face is lower when demand is relatively more elastic.

Recap: The factor that is more elastic will have a smaller share of the economic burden. In the end, the full amount of the tax will get sent to the government, and the question is where did the money really come from. When the price elasticity of demand is large relative to the price elasticity of supply, then buyers bear a smaller share of the economic burden. In this case, the money is coming from sellers who have to lower their prices by more to keep customers. By contrast, if the price elasticity of supply is larger, then the share of the economic burden paid by sellers is smaller. In this case, the money is coming from buyers who pay higher prices rather than giving up a lot of consumption. The end result is that whichever factor is more elastic bears less of the economic burden of the tax. The underlying logic is that you can "get out of the way" of taxes by changing the quantities you buy or sell. And whoever has the largest elasticity "gets out of the way" more effectively.

When it comes to soft drinks, buyers' demand is relatively more inelastic than sellers' supply. Researchers have shown that buyers typically bear about two-thirds of the economic burden of the tax, while sellers bear a third. Why? It essentially comes down to tastes. People like sugary drinks and therefore don't find other substitutes quite as good; sellers, on the other hand, have a bit more flexibility to sell other products.

A Three-Step Recipe for Evaluating Taxes

Let's step back and see that to analyse these taxes we followed the same three-step recipe for predicting market outcomes that you used to find market equilibriums in Chapter 4. When you're analysing a new tax, ask these three questions:

Step one: *Is the supply or demand curve shifting?*
Remember that any change affecting buyers or their marginal benefits will shift the demand curve, while any change affecting sellers or their marginal costs will shift the supply curve. (Although given what you've learned about the economic burden of a tax, it really doesn't matter which curve shifts!)

Step two: *Is that shift an increase in taxes, shifting the curve to the left? Or is it a decrease in taxes, shifting the curve to the right?*
Taxes will typically shift the supply or the demand curve to the left because they are a cost that reduces the marginal benefit for consumers when they are assigned the statutory burden of a tax and raises the marginal cost for sellers when they are the ones who are assigned to send in the tax. A decrease in marginal benefit is a decrease in demand (a shift to the left or down). On the supply side, an increase in marginal cost causes a decrease in supply (a shift to the left or up).

Step three: *How will prices and quantities change in the new equilibrium?*
Compare the pre-tax equilibrium with the post-tax equilibrium. There is one complication to remember with taxes: There are really two prices—the price the buyer pays and the price the seller receives. Remember that these prices are after taxes. So you'll need to be careful to identify which of these prices you're thinking about.

Now you can practice following this recipe by working out what will happen with a tax on petrol.

Do the Economics

For many years (from 2001) the tax on petrol in Australia (called "excise") was frozen. In 2014 the Abbott government reintroduced indexation so that the tax on fuel would go up twice each year based on the Consumer Price Index. Let's look at what happens if the excise goes up by $0.05 per litre. Sellers pay this tax directly to the government, meaning the tax is already incorporated into the price you see when you drive by the petrol station. How does this affect market outcomes?

Let's work through the three-step recipe to find out.

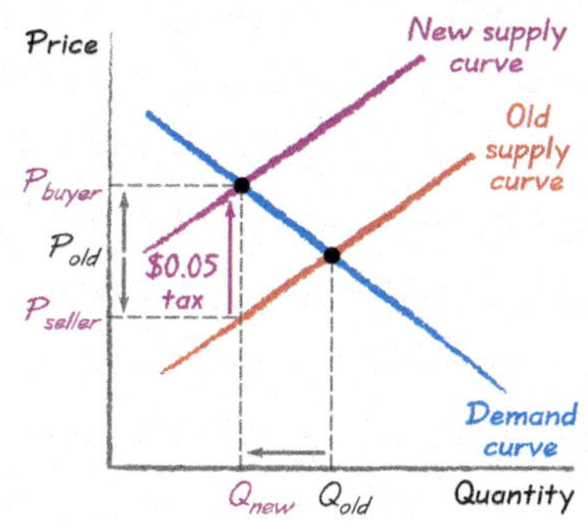

Step one: *Is the supply or demand curve shifting?*

The supply curve shifts because the tax is paid by sellers.

Step two: *Is that shift an increase in taxes, shifting the curve to the left? Or is it a decrease in taxes, shifting the curve to the right?*

An extra tax on sellers will raise their marginal costs, since they have a new expense for each additional litre sold: the money they need to send to the government. And higher marginal costs decrease supply, shifting the supply curve to the left (up). Because the tax is $0.05 per litre, the supply curve shifts left (up) until it lies $0.05 higher as measured on the vertical axis.

Step three: *How will prices and quantities change in the new equilibrium?*

The quantity of petrol sold will decrease, the price sellers receive after the tax will fall, and the price buyers pay will increase. ■

Analysing Subsidies

So far we've considered taxes, but what if instead of charging a tax, the government were to give a subsidy? A **subsidy** is a payment made by the government to those who make a specific choice. For example, the Australian government provides a subsidy (depending on household income) for child care. The government uses subsidies to try to encourage the consumption of certain goods and services, such as child care.

subsidy A payment made by the government to those who make a specific choice.

It turns out that you can use the same three-step recipe you just learned to analyse a tax, to understand how quantity demanded, quantity supplied, and price will change when the government offers a subsidy. One way to think about a subsidy is as a negative tax since it operates just like a tax, but with the opposite sign. Subsidies increase the quantities demanded and supplied, and they tend to lower the price buyers pay and increase the price sellers receive. And just like a tax, the outcomes don't depend on the statutory assignment of the subsidy.

To see what happens with a subsidy, let's consider child care in more detail. Governments around the world want to ensure that kids receive good early childhood education and that parents are able to work. As a result, they often offer a range of subsidies to parents to help them manage the costs of child care, and policy makers have debated whether to increase these subsidies further.

Consider a proposal to pay parents of young children an additional $3,000 subsidy for child care, on top of what they already receive from various government programs. When the director of a child care centre asks you to predict the likely outcomes for the number of children seeking slots in the child care market, you now know how to respond: Work through the three-step recipe we developed to analyse a tax change.

The first step is to ask: *Is the demand or supply curve shifting?* Since the subsidy will be given to parents who put their children in child care, the subsidy will shift the demand curve. At each price, parents' willingness to put their child in child care will be higher. This is because parents will receive care and a $3,000 payment from the government when they choose to put their kid in child care. So the marginal benefit of using child care has gone up.

Notice that we are analysing this as an "either/or" question—parents can either put their child in professional child care or keep them at home. Because many parents have to pay weekly or even monthly for a place at a child care centre, this is a reasonable simplification.

The second step is to ask: *Is this shift an increase in subsidies, shifting the curve to the right? Or is it a decrease in subsidies, shifting the curve to the left?* A subsidy to consumers always increases demand by raising consumers' marginal benefit by the amount of the subsidy. Parents will be more willing to purchase child care at any given price, because the "effective price"—after the subsidy—is lower. Another way to think about it is that they are willing to pay more because each child care place will come with a $3,000 payment. So it adds $3,000 to the marginal benefit of putting a child in child care. The demand curve shifts to the right or up by the amount of the subsidy as shown in Figure 4.

Figure 4 | Effects of Subsidising Child Care

If a new subsidy is introduced:

- **A** The **subsidy** increases the willingness of parents to purchase child care. At any given quantity, they will still be willing to purchase child care even if the before-subsidy price is $3,000 higher. This **shifts the demand curve right** until it lies **$3,000 higher**, as measured on the vertical axis. (This is a subsidy for buyers, so the supply curve is unaffected.)
- **B** **Equilibrium** occurs where the new demand curve intersects with the supply curve.
- **C** The **quantity of child care** purchased **rises** from **1.3 million** children to **1.5 million** children in child care.
- **D** **Sellers now receive $12,000 per child** in care, **an increase of $2,000 per child** (= $12,000 – $10,000).
- **E** **Parents now pay $9,000** after receiving the $3,000 subsidy from the government. The price consumers pay including the subsidy has therefore fallen by $1,000 (= $10,000 – $9,000). Note that buyers and sellers share the benefit of this subsidy to buyers.

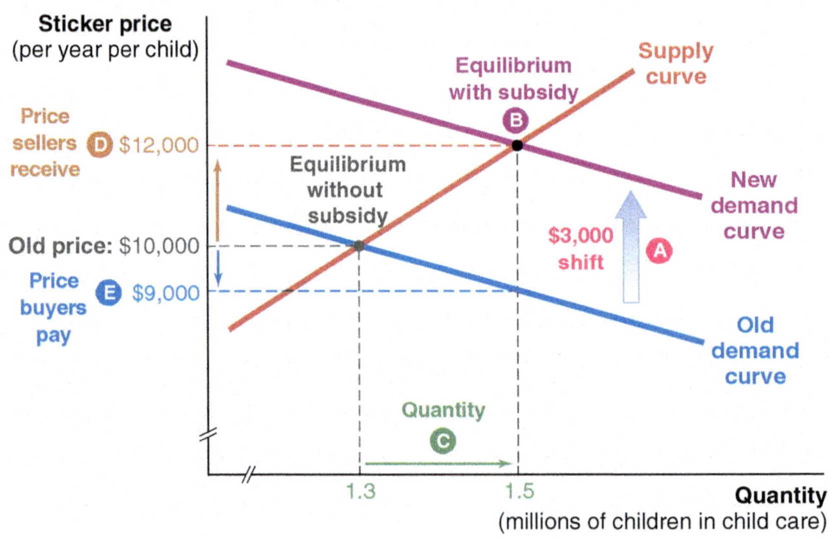

The third step is to ask: *How will prices and quantities change in the new equilibrium?* The demand curve shifts right and intersects the supply curve at a higher quantity supplied of child care. The result is a higher price for child care providers. Prior to the subsidy, parents paid $10,000 a year for child care. The after-subsidy demand curve intersects the supply curve at the higher price of $12,000 per year. As a result, child care suppliers receive an increase of $2,000 per year. Parents pay $12,000 to the child care suppliers, but receive a $3,000 payment. As such, the price parents pay after the subsidy falls from $10,000 per year to $9,000 per year.

Just as with the economic burden of taxes, the economic benefit of subsidies is shared between buyers and sellers. In this case, the price child care providers receive goes up by $2,000, while the after-subsidy cost to parents falls by $1,000.

What determines the distribution of the subsidy between buyers and sellers? I bet you guessed it: the price elasticities of demand and supply. When demand is more elastic relative to supply, buyers capture less of a subsidy. Sellers capture more of the subsidy when their supply is inelastic. When supply is relatively more inelastic it means that a larger increase in price is needed to induce sellers to increase the quantity supplied to the level that buyers want. The opposite is true when demand is more inelastic relative to supply. If buyers have only a small change in their quantity demanded, then they will be able to capture more of the subsidy. In the extreme, when the price elasticity of demand is zero—meaning that a subsidy leads to no change in demand, then buyers will capture the entire subsidy. But if supply is completely inelastic, the opposite happens. In short, just like the elastic factor gets out of the way of taxes, the elastic factor gets out of the way of subsidies.

Just like with taxes, it doesn't matter who gets the subsidy. What if the government paid the subsidy to child care providers instead so that each child care provider received a payment from the government of $3,000 per child enrolled? Just like with taxes, the economic burden, or in this case we should say economic benefit, of subsidies is determined not by the statutory burden—who is assigned to get the subsidy, but by price elasticities of demand and supply. That means that we'd get the exact same outcome if the government sent the subsidy payments to child care providers instead of sending them to parents. A subsidy sent to providers would shift the supply curve to the right or down by the amount of the subsidy and the outcome would be exactly the same: The new equilibrium quantity would be higher, buyers would pay less, and sellers would receive more in total, including the subsidy. *Whether it's a tax or a subsidy, it's the laws of supply and demand, not the laws set by government that determine who bears the economic burden of a tax and who gets the benefit of a subsidy.*

Now that we've dealt with how taxes shape economic behaviour, let's move on to another way in which governments try to reshape market outcomes: regulating prices directly.

6.2 Price Regulations

Learning Objective *Evaluate the full set of consequences of price ceilings and price floors.*

Sometimes, what might seem to some like an excessively high or low price can lead people to try to persuade the government to pass regulations to control the price. When the government sets a maximum price, this is referred to as setting a **price ceiling.** The opposite of a price ceiling is a **price floor,** which is when the government sets a minimum price.

price ceiling A maximum price that sellers can charge.

price floor A minimum price that sellers can charge.

Let's start with price ceilings and how they impact the housing market.

Price Ceilings: When Regulation Forces Lower Prices

The rent is too high! It's a common rallying cry that leads residents to pressure policy makers to do something to control housing prices. Many large cities in the United States have some form of price ceiling on housing, often referred to as rent control. (Australia hasn't had rent control since World War II, but during the coronavirus pandemic some people argued that it should be reintroduced.) The price ceilings may be an upper limit on the amount some landlords can charge in monthly rent or the amount by which they can raise the rent for an existing tenant. Let's take a look at how price ceilings affect market outcomes in the rental market.

The first thing to note is that when price ceilings are above the equilibrium price, they don't have any effect. When a price ceiling prevents the market from reaching the equilibrium price because the highest price that sellers can charge is set below the equilibrium price, economists refer to it as a **binding price ceiling.**

binding price ceiling A price ceiling that prevents the market from reaching the market equilibrium price, meaning that the highest price sellers can charge is set below the equilibrium price.

Since there aren't rent control laws in Australia, we're going to discuss rent control in the United States. You've probably seen some examples of rent control watching U.S. television shows, and it's a really useful example of how price ceilings work, and what negative effects they can have.

Price ceilings lower prices, but cause shortages. Kate is a 28-year-old journalist in Cleveland, Ohio. She writes about city politics for Cleveland's local newspaper and often appears on local television. Since graduating from journalism school, she has worked for local newspapers across the country and now is eager to cover national news. After months of networking and applying for jobs, she has landed her dream job as an on-air reporter for one of the biggest news networks in the United States, CNN. However, the job is based in New York City, where finding an apartment is notoriously difficult.

New York City has imposed price ceilings in its housing rental market. We can use the supply-and-demand framework to figure out the likely consequences. Let's begin by analysing the market for studio apartments in Manhattan. Figure 5 shows the demand and supply curves for these apartments. As you know, equilibrium occurs where the curves cross, which is at a rent of $3,000 per month; at this equilibrium price, there are 1 million studio apartments available to rent, matched by 1 million renters. Note that a price ceiling is only binding if it is below the equilibrium price of $3,000. For example, if the government set a price ceiling of $4,000, the equilibrium price of $3,000 would be charged and the price ceiling would have no effect.

Now consider the consequences of imposing a price ceiling of $2,000 per month, which is shown as the horizontal line in Figure 5. The supply curve tells you that at this

Figure 5 | Rent Control and the Market for New York City Apartments

If a price ceiling is imposed:

- (A) **Without any regulation, equilibrium** would mean that **1 million apartments** are rented at **$3,000 per month.**
- (B) The **price ceiling** establishes a maximum rent of **$2,000 per month.**
- (C) **Suppliers** are willing to rent **950,000 apartments** at this price.
- (D) **Consumers** demand **1.1 million apartments** at this price.
- (E) This leads to a **shortage of 150,000 apartments.**

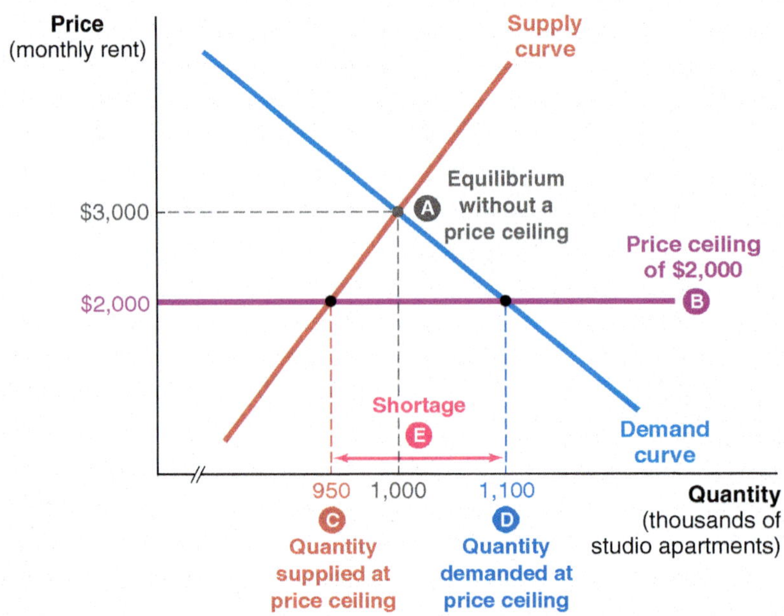

price, the quantity supplied will be 950,000 apartments—less than the million units that are supplied at the equilibrium. The demand curve tells you that at this price, the quantity demanded will be 1.1 million apartments—more than the million units that are demanded at the equilibrium. The difference between the quantity demanded and quantity supplied is a *shortage*: There are 150,000 people looking for an apartment who can't find one at this lower price. Kate is one of them; she has spent weeks looking for an apartment and can't find anything. However, she is determined to work for CNN. So she decides to accept the job offer, rent an apartment outside the city, and undertake an arduous commute to CNN's New York office by train each day.

Although rent control hurts outsiders like Kate by creating a shortage, it benefits the incumbents who live in rent-controlled apartments—at least up to a point. Ben and Jessica are a young couple living together in a rent-controlled studio apartment on the Upper West Side of New York, within walking distance of Central Park. The lower rent has helped them save money and live in an upscale neighbourhood that they would not have been able to afford otherwise. But now that they're ready to have children, they realise they don't have enough space for loud, energetic toddlers. They have to move, but they're worried that if they leave their current apartment, they may not be able to find another apartment in New York City. The shortage caused by rent control applies as equally to them as it does to Kate. After a lot of fruitless searching, they decide to move out of New York City.

There are unintended consequences of price controls. Because rent control results in people who can't find apartments, landlords know that they'll be able to find other tenants easily. As a result, landlords are often less responsive to requests for repairs. They think that even if their current tenants are unhappy, there are thousands of other people willing to take over their lease. Indeed, there's no incentive for a landlord to do anything to improve an apartment if they can't charge a higher price for a nicer place. The "bargain" of a rent-controlled apartment may be partially "undone" by tenants paying for their own upkeep.

Thomas Koehler/Getty Images

The owner of a rent-controlled apartment has little incentive to repair it.

Rent control may also change how landlords select their tenants. When there's a binding price ceiling, there will be dozens of responsible tenants hoping to get each apartment. The landlord may then allocate the apartment on some arbitrary basis, perhaps renting it only to family or friends, or those who share their political beliefs or have some other connection to the landlord. Some landlords may even illegally reject tenants based on race, ethnicity, family status, religion, or sex.

Rent control may also change how potential renters behave. In their rush to find a rent-controlled apartment, some might offer real estate agents bribes to learn about vacant apartments. Others might offer the legal alternative to bribes, "finders' fees," while yet others might spend their weekends trolling nearby buildings for an opening. A black market sometimes emerges in which those who are lucky enough to get a rent-controlled apartment then unofficially sublease it at a higher price. In each case, the effect is the same: The total price of the apartment—when you include bribes, finders' fees, and the cost of hassle or unofficial subleases—rises above the regulated $2,000 per month.

EVERYDAY Economics

Are anti-price gouging laws a good idea?

When Uber introduced surge pricing, economists cheered, while many riders jeered. In fact, the idea of raising prices at moments of high demand is so off-putting that some countries have laws prohibiting such temporary price increases, particularly during weather emergencies. These laws ban "price gouging." But is this a good idea?

Supplies like water, bread, and petrol can all quickly disappear in the face of a big hailstorm or bush fire, and it can also be impossible to get a taxi. It simply isn't possible for everyone to get as much as they want at the original prices. Those who support anti-price-gouging laws argue that raising prices only benefits businesses because businesses are limited to whatever inventory they have on hand, therefore supply is pretty inelastic. They also argue that price gouging hurts the poor, who are the least able to purchase necessities at higher prices.

Those who argue to allow price gouging point out that anti-price-gouging laws are a form of a price ceiling. That means they do two things: They lead to a decrease in the quantity supplied and an increase in the quantity demanded, thus creating shortages. For example, price ceilings during weather emergencies might encourage consumers at the front of the queue to overbuy at normal prices—for example, buying an extra loaf of bread "just in case"—exacerbating the shortage. Think about what happened to toilet paper supplies during the early days of the coronavirus pandemic in Australia! Critics of anti-price-gouging laws also argue that allowing prices to rise will lead to an increase in the quantity supplied, even during a natural disaster. They believe that higher prices will encourage enterprising individuals to find a way to get more supply to where it's needed.

What do you think? (Hint: Notice that this debate depends a lot on the short-run price elasticities of demand and supply during a storm.) ■

William West/AFP/Getty Images

Price ceilings: Promising you won't get ripped off on something that's out of stock anyway.

Price ceilings lead to shortages in many markets. To summarise: A binding price ceiling can lead to shortages and queuing. Search costs, finders' fees, bribes, and a black market may raise the total cost to buyers above the price ceiling. These outcomes are not specific to big city apartment markets, but rather are the likely consequences of demanders and suppliers confronted by a price ceiling. Here are other instances of price ceilings:

- "Usury laws," which prevent payday loan companies from charging excessively high interest rates. These laws prevent exploitation of borrowers, but they mean that sometimes companies will refuse to make any loans at all if they can't charge high enough interest rates.
- Taxi fares, which are often set by the local government. When fares are set too low, it can be hard to get a cab (think of a Saturday night or a rainstorm).
- Price ceilings on food and toiletries in Venezuela created a shortage of these essentials and led to a large black market for these goods.

Interpreting the DATA — Why is there a shortage of kidney donors?

Jade Chen is a 40-year-old Sydneysider who is in end-stage renal failure. With only 6% kidney function, she is being kept alive by an intensive and uncomfortable course of dialysis. While Jade is currently very sick, if she receives a kidney transplant, she can resume a healthy life. Unfortunately, she can't find a kidney donor. She's not alone: There are around 1,700 people in Australia waiting for kidneys, 12,000 people on dialysis, and chronic kidney disease was the underlying cause of 3,600 deaths in 2018.

But these are all preventable deaths. Each of us is born with two kidneys, yet you only need one. If you donate one, your remaining kidney simply gets stronger and takes over the work of the kidney you donated. Giving your spare kidney to someone like Jade is both cheap and fairly safe. So why is there a kidney shortage?

For starters, it is illegal to receive money in exchange for donating an organ. In effect, Australian law sets a price ceiling on kidneys of $0. This price ceiling means that there is very little incentive for any of the millions of people walking around with a "spare" kidney to supply one. Consequently, the quantity of kidneys supplied at this $0 price ceiling is less than the quantity demanded, leading to a severe shortage, just as supply-and-demand analysis predicts.

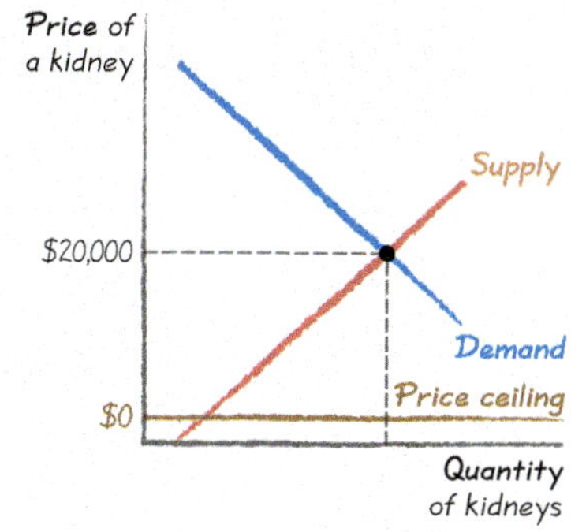

The *cost-benefit principle* suggests only donating a kidney if the benefit exceeds the cost. The cost of donating your kidney includes a few days or even weeks off work, the chance of experiencing a health complication during the donation process, and a somewhat higher chance of kidney failure later in life. Since there's no monetary benefit, your sense of fulfillment from helping someone return to health has to equal or exceed the costs in order for you to want to donate your kidney. As a result, many kidney donations today are between family members.

Economists Gary Becker and Julio Elias have calculated that if donors were paid as little as $20,000 for their efforts, the current kidney shortage could be eliminated. And that's a small charge, relative to the fact that a kidney could give someone like Jade both a higher-quality and longer life. In fact, these same economists have valued these benefits to people like Jade at over $700,000.

So why do governments the world over ban the selling of organs like kidneys? One word: repugnance. People find the idea of paying for organs repugnant because it "commodifies" our essential humanity. They fear that people could be induced to donate a kidney for $20,000 only if they were poor and desperate or didn't understand the risks. Moreover, they are concerned that a market for kidneys may make existing volunteers less likely to donate, since their valuable kidney donation may now seem less altruistic.

What do you think? ■

Price Floors: When Regulation Forces Higher Prices

The opposite of a price ceiling is a price floor, which sets a minimum price that can be charged. The first thing to note is that when a price floor is set below the equilibrium price, it doesn't have any effect. When a price floor prevents the market from reaching the equilibrium price because the lowest price that sellers can charge is set above the equilibrium price, economists refer to it as a **binding price floor.**

binding price floor A price floor that prevents the market from reaching the equilibrium price, meaning that the lowest price that sellers can charge is above the equilibrium price.

Governments have different reasons for setting binding price floors. Sometimes they are trying to raise prices in order to help sellers. For example, the minimum wage is a price floor—it's a minimum price that can be charged for an hour of work. Governments typically set minimum wages in order to raise the wages received by the lowest-wage workers. The fact that the quantity demanded declines is an undesirable side effect. Other times, governments are explicitly trying to reduce the quantity sold. For example, many governments have set minimum prices for alcohol in order to reduce alcohol consumption.

These two goals reflect the fact that a price floor does two things: It raises prices and it lowers the quantity sold.

Let's take a look at a price floor for alcohol, to apply what you've learned about how to analyse a price regulation.

Reduce the quantity of alcohol consumed by setting a minimum price. Excessive alcohol consumption imposes high costs on society in the form of health issues, crime, and public disturbances. Not surprisingly then, governments are often under pressure to adopt policies to try to encourage people to drink less. One policy option some governments have tried is to set a minimum price for alcoholic drinks.

A minimum price is a price floor—it prevents alcohol from being sold at a lower price even if the market equilibrium price would be lower. Many provinces in Canada have had price regulations on alcohol and some states in the United States regulate alcohol prices. Most recently, Scotland adopted a clear price floor for alcohol that effectively sets a minimum price for a can of beer at $2.00. What's the likely effect of such a policy?

The first step to analysing a price regulation is to ask whether the regulation is binding. Figure 6 shows the market for beer with an equilibrium price of $1 per can of beer. Since the price floor establishes a minimum price of $2.00 a can, the price floor is binding and determines the price.

Figure 6 | Scotland's Price Floor on Alcohol

If a price floor is imposed:

Ⓐ Without any regulation, supply-equals-demand **equilibrium** would mean that **15 billion cans of beer** would be sold per year at a price of **$1.00 per can.**

Ⓑ The **price floor** establishes a **minimum price of $2.00 per can.**

Ⓒ **Consumers** demand **13 billion cans** per year at this price.

Ⓓ **Suppliers** are willing to sell **17 billion cans** per year at this price.

Ⓔ This yields a **surplus of 4 billion cans** of beer per year—meaning that producers would be willing to produce and sell up to 4 billion more cans of beer at this price but they are prevented from doing so by the government.

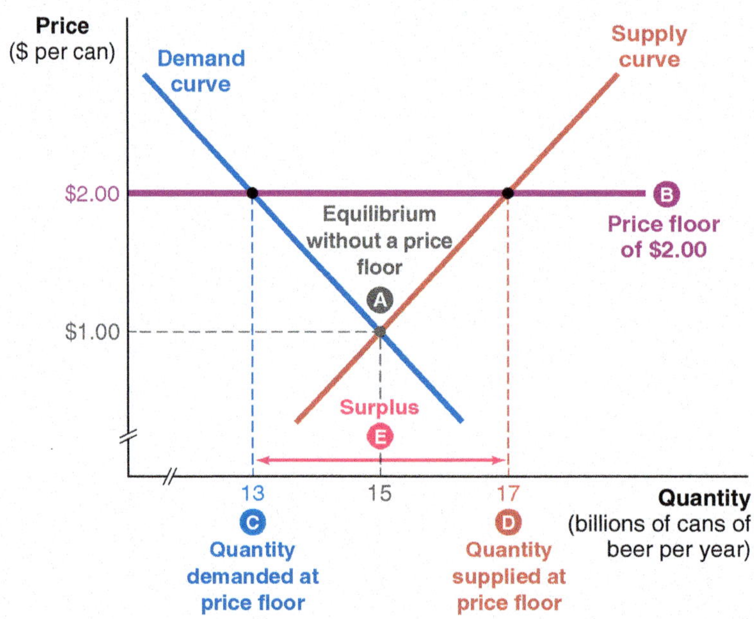

At the higher price established by the price floor, the quantity demanded is less than the quantity supplied. With a binding price floor, the quantity produced will be equal to the minimum of the quantity demanded and the quantity supplied at the regulated price. Figure 6 shows that at a price of $2.00 the quantity demanded falls to 13 billion cans per year from the equilibrium quantity of 15 billion cans per year. However, at this higher price, the desired quantity supplied rises to 17 billion cans. The difference, 4 billion cans, is a potential surplus.

What happens to the surplus? In a perfectly competitive market, sellers can sell all they want at the equilibrium price. When the government imposes a binding price floor, that is no longer true. Some sellers won't find anyone to buy their product and as a result may try to illegally sell on the black market at prices below the price floor. Alternatively, it may just result in sellers fighting over market share and some sellers exiting the market.

One form of surplus that you are probably familiar with is unemployment. Unemployment will occur when more people want to work at the wages that businesses are paying than can find work at those wages—that is, there is a surplus of workers. The minimum wage establishes a price floor, and as you have seen, when the price floor is binding, the quantity supplied (people looking for jobs that pay the minimum wage) will exceed the quantity demanded (employers willing to hire people at the minimum wage). The gap between the two leads to some people spending time unemployed until they are able to snag one of the available jobs.

EVERYDAY Economics **Why do farmers like price floors?**

Farmers around the world often lobby their government to put price floors on agricultural products. Why? As you've already seen, price floors increase the price, which boosts businesses' profit margins. But this higher price lowers the quantity demanded. Farmers get a higher price, but sell less. So why do they want the government to establish price floors? The answer is that they typically lobby their government for two things: to set a price floor for their product and to promise to buy up any surplus. In this way, farmers typically get to have their cake and eat it too—they sell less to consumers at higher prices and then sell the remaining surplus to the government at the same high prices. And this means that consumers lose twice: They pay more at the store and then they pay more in taxes so the government can afford to buy up all the surplus. What does the government do with the surplus it buys? Some of the surplus is sent to food banks and domestic charities and some of it is sent overseas as a form of foreign aid. ■

6.3 Quantity Regulations

Learning Objective *Analyse the consequences of quantity regulations.*

Just as the government might set the maximum or minimum price for the market, it can also set a **quantity regulation**—a maximum or minimum quantity that can be sold. A **mandate** requires you to buy or sell a minimum amount of a good. A health insurance mandate requires consumers to purchase private health insurance. This happens in Australia for people earning over a certain income, otherwise they need to pay additional taxes. A housing mandate occurs when developers want to build new housing and they are told that they must also build (hence, supply) a certain amount of low-income housing. A binding mandate—meaning that without the mandate the equilibrium quantity would be lower—on buyers, increases the quantity buyers demand. A binding mandate on sellers increases the quantity sellers supply. In both cases, the amount of the good or service sold increases to the mandated amount.

quantity regulation A minimum or maximum quantity that can be sold.

mandate A requirement to buy or sell a minimum amount of a good.

Quotas set a limit on the maximum quantity of a good that can be sold. Quotas can be on buyers—for instance, many countries around the world that have legalised marijuana limit the amount that people can buy per day. These limits are designed to reduce the quantity sold by reducing demand. Quotas, however, are more frequently placed on suppliers. For instance, New South Wales has a taxi quota; a cab is legal only if its owner holds a "plate," and only about 6,000 were on issue in early 2020. Consequently, even during rush hour, you won't see more than 6,000 taxis on the roads all across NSW. Of course, taxis now have competitors like Uber. To understand what motivated Uber to enter the market and how they changed the market for rides, you need to understand what a quota on sellers does to the quantity supplied and the prices charged. So let's take a closer look at a quota in the housing market, and then we'll look at what happened in the taxi market.

quota A limit on the maximum quantity of a good that can be sold.

Quotas

Whenever you drive around a quiet, leafy neighbourhood, it usually isn't that way by chance. Often, zoning laws explain why there are houses with backyards instead of apartment buildings. Zoning laws articulate the type and quantity of housing that can be built in an area. Most Australian suburbs have zoning laws. The result is usually less housing and higher prices. Why? Because zoning laws effectively impose quotas, limiting the number of housing units that can be built. Let's use the supply-and-demand framework to see why this happens.

Sydney is a city with zoning regulations that limit the development of housing. Figure 7 illustrates the consequences of housing quotas in Sydney, showing the supply and demand curves for housing in Sydney. If there were no government regulation, then you would expect the supply-equals-demand equilibrium to occur, and there would be 280,000 housing units in Sydney, selling for $700,000 each.

Figure 7 | Zoning Laws and the Sydney Housing Market

If a maximum quantity is imposed on sellers:

- **A** If there were no regulation, then supply-equals-demand **equilibrium** would lead to **280,000 houses** being sold at a price of $700,000 each.
- **B** **Zoning laws** impose a **maximum quantity of 120,000 houses**.
- **C** **Suppliers** are willing to sell this quantity if the **price is at least $400,000**.
- **D** **Buyers** are willing to pay up to **$1,000,000** for these houses.
- **E** If the quantity regulation is imposed on sellers, then **competition** among buyers will push the price up to **$1,000,000**.

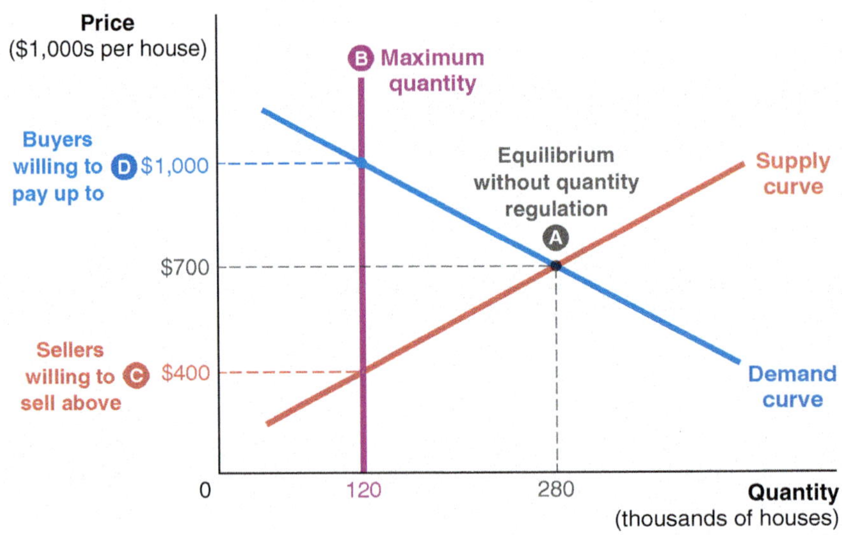

Quotas raise prices. Figure 7 shows that zoning restricts development to a maximum of 120,000 houses. Because consumers want to purchase more housing and sellers want to sell more housing, the quota will be binding—meaning that the quota will determine the quantity sold. Suppliers are willing to supply a quantity of 120,000 houses as long as the price is at least $400,000 per house. You can see this in Figure 7 by looking at the intersection of the supply curve with the maximum quantity, which occurs at a price of $400,000 per house.

However, with only 120,000 houses available, buyers are willing to pay up to $1,000,000 for these houses. You can see this in Figure 7 by looking at the intersection of the demand curve with the maximum quantity. If sellers sell houses for less than $1,000,000, there will be more buyers than sellers. Because buyers can demand as much housing as they want, but sellers are limited to selling only the 120,000 houses, buyers will compete with each other for the limited available housing, bidding up the price until it reaches $1,000,000, where the quantity demanded is equal to the maximum quantity that can be supplied due to the zoning regulation. Even though sellers would be willing to sell for less, competition among buyers for scarce goods leads buyers to pay higher prices.

Due to zoning laws, homeowners in Sydney can sell their houses for $300,000 more than they could without the laws (prices rose from $700,000 without the quota to $1,000,000 with the quota), and they enjoy a less crowded environment. However, fewer people are able to afford to live in Sydney, and those who do have to pay more for housing.

This has a direct effect on people like Indira, who would like to move to Sydney. Indira is a software engineer living in Perth, who would like to accept a job offer at Atlassian's headquarters in Sydney to advance her career. Due to zoning restrictions, she can't find a house in the area in her price range. So she stays in Perth and works remotely for Atlassian. This arrangement allows her to keep enjoying lower-cost housing, but it also makes it harder for her to bond with her colleagues, limiting her ability to make new contributions and get promoted.

EVERYDAY Economics

How Uber undermined government taxi quotas

Quotas set by the government limit taxis in many cities. As you've just seen, a quota that restricts supply leads to higher prices and a lower quantity sold. You also saw that suppliers would be willing to sell for less—meaning that the marginal cost of providing another taxi ride is well below the price in the market with quotas. That gap between price and marginal cost creates an incentive for potential sellers to find a way around the regulation. Uber did just that. They entered the market as an alternative business—ride sharing—and they argued that ride-sharing businesses weren't covered by the government quantity regulations.

Researchers have shown that the supply of drivers in a city rose by as much as 50% and that incomes for taxi drivers fell as prices paid for rides fell on average. So part of what ride-sharing companies did was undermine regulations that limited supply and therefore drove prices down. But there was another effect that pushed prices in the other direction—ride-sharing companies improved the technology matching potential riders to potential drivers. You no longer have to stand in the rain hoping to hail a taxi, but you can stay where it's dry and look for a ride on your phone. The technological change increased the productivity of drivers—they spend more time driving people and less time looking for people to drive—and by improving the marginal benefit of a ride, the technological change increased demand from consumers. ■

Quotas are quite common. Analysing quantity regulations can be useful for understanding an enormous array of government regulations, since quantity restrictions are quite common beyond what you might think of as "traditional" markets. Consider the following quotas:

- Immigration quotas effectively limit the supply of workers;
- China lets families have a maximum of three children;
- Trade quotas limit the number of certain goods that can enter a country, and customs regulations limit what kind and how many souvenirs you can bring back from abroad;
- The Australian government has capped the number of medical residents, or doctors in training, that it funds;
- Environmental regulations often limit the quantity of pollutants that firms can release;

- During droughts, Australian governments limit when people can water their gardens;
- Transport for NSW limits the number of hours truck drivers can work each week.

In each of these cases, the restrictions reduce the quantity of each activity.

Compare price and quantity regulation. Let's summarise the steps we've taken to analyse a quantity regulation, and compare it with a price regulation. The first step is the same in both cases: Begin by figuring out if the regulation is binding. Does it establish a maximum quantity below (or a minimum quantity above) the equilibrium? If the regulation isn't binding, it won't affect market outcomes. But if it is binding, you need to determine the new price and quantity.

With price regulation, the new price will be the regulated price, and you need to find the quantity sold at that price. The quantity sold is determined by the forces of supply and demand and is the minimum of the quantity demanded or the quantity supplied. With quantity regulation, the quantity is determined by the regulation and the forces of supply and demand determine the price. With a quota on sellers, the resulting price will be determined by what buyers are willing to pay for the limited quantity available. A quota on buyers, however, will lead to the price at which suppliers are willing to supply the restricted quantity that buyers demand.

Tying It Together

In Chapter 4, we saw that the market forces of supply and demand lead to an outcome where all buyers can buy what they want at the posted price, and all sellers can sell what they want at the posted price. In practice, however, buyers and sellers aren't the only actors in the market: Government policy also shapes how much is bought and sold. The three forms of government regulation we looked at in this chapter—taxes, price regulations, and quantity regulations—are all tools at the government's disposal to change outcomes.

Taxes, price regulations, and quantity regulations can all be used to achieve the same policy objectives. But each policy typically hurts some constituencies in the process of helping others, and different policies yield different distributional outcomes. For example, you saw that Scotland is reducing the quantity of alcohol consumed by setting a price floor. Other countries tax alcohol to achieve a similar effect—lowering the amount of alcohol consumed by raising the price that buyers pay and lowering the price that sellers receive. Governments also directly limit the quantity of alcohol that people can purchase. For example, people under the age of 18 cannot purchase alcohol in Australia and businesses are often prohibited from selling to inebriated people. Both of these policies limit the quantity of alcohol demanded in the market. Governments also restrict the quantity supplied by limiting the quantity of businesses that can sell alcohol by requiring liquor licences.

A government can choose any of these policies to achieve a policy goal of lowering the quantity of alcohol consumed. However, the three policies have different distributional effects across buyers and sellers. With the price floor in Scotland, sellers will receive a higher price and buyers will pay a higher price. This means that while businesses may struggle to gain market share in Scotland (remember, the quantity demanded is below the desired quantity supplied), the ones that succeed make a nice profit selling at prices well above their marginal cost. When the government uses a tax, the price suppliers receive falls relative to equilibrium. Suppliers sell less and the price they keep after taxes is lower. It's no wonder businesses prefer price floors over taxes. Notice that taxes raise the after-tax price for buyers while lowering the price sellers receive because they also raise revenue for the government to fund public services.

Not surprisingly, almost everyone hates taxes, even if they like the government services the revenue funds.

What about quotas? When the government restricts supply, the lucky sellers who are able to succeed in the market are able to charge higher prices, so like a price floor, sellers benefit more from restrictions that limit supply. However, if the government effectively limits demand, the quantity consumed will decline and so will the price.

In this chapter, we didn't ask whether the various government policies we examined were a good idea or not. In Chapter 7, we'll take a deeper look at the benefits generated in the economy for buyers and for sellers. And then in Chapter 10, you'll see what happens when markets fail to generate as many benefits as are possible for buyers and sellers. Government policy is sometimes a response to pressure from people who are looking out for their own interest and sometimes a desire to correct a market failure. Once you have these tools under your belt, you'll be better able to decide whether a particular government intervention in the economy is a good idea or not.

Chapter at a Glance

Three Types of Government Intervention:

The statutory burden of a tax or subsidy does not determine **economic burden**. The price elasticities of demand and supply determine the economic burden.

Quantity: Taxes reduce the quantity sold, while subsidies increase the quantity sold.

Prices: The economic burden describes how prices change as a result of a tax. It is determined by the price elasticities of supply and demand. Buyers and sellers tend to share the burden, with buyers paying more after a tax and sellers receiving less after a tax. Subsidies lead to lower prices for buyers and higher prices for sellers.

1. Taxes

A Tax on Sellers

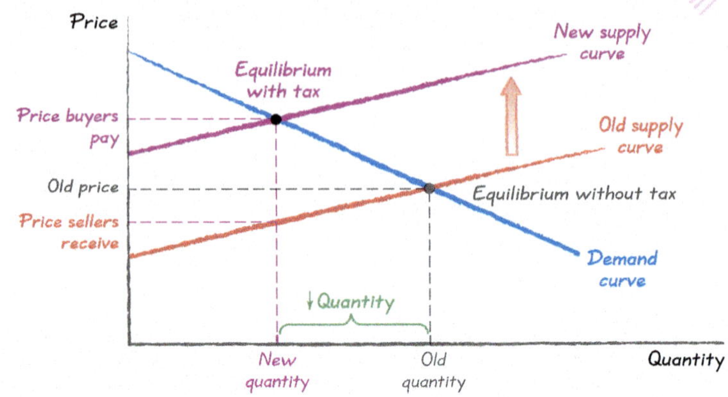

Price ceiling: A maximum price that sellers can charge. ⇨ **Shortage**

Price floor: A minimum price that sellers can charge. ⇨ **Surplus**

Quantity: Both price ceilings and price floors reduce the quantity sold.

Prices: Price ceilings keep prices low, benefiting some buyers. Buyers tend to prefer price ceilings. Price floors keep prices high, benefiting some suppliers.

2. Price Regulation

A Price Ceiling

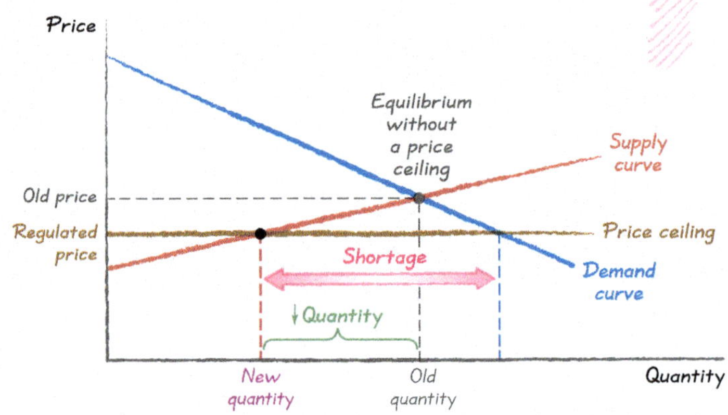

Quantity regulation: A minimum or maximum quantity that can be sold.

Quantity: Quotas reduce the quantity sold, while mandates increase the quantity sold.

Prices: Prices with quotas and mandates are determined by the forces of supply and demand. A quota that limits the quantity sellers can sell results in higher prices. A quota that limits the quantity buyers demand results in lower prices.

3. Quantity Regulation

A Quota

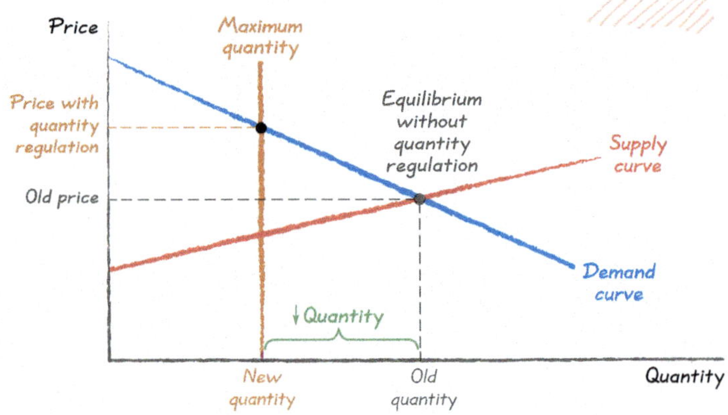

Taxes, price regulations, and quantity regulations can all achieve the same policy objective.

The **three types of government intervention** shown in these three graphs can achieve the same quantity reduction. The new quantity is the same across the tax, price ceiling, and quota. Distributional consequences across buyers and sellers differ.

Key Concepts

Discussion and Review Questions

Learning Objective 6.1 *Assess how taxes shape supply, demand, and equilibrium outcomes.*

1. You are planning a summer holiday and are about to book a hotel room online for $149 a night. However, when you get to the reservation screen, you are informed that you will be charged an additional $30 a night in various taxes that you have to pay to the hotel. Between you and the hotel, who do you think is carrying the larger share of the economic burden of the taxes? What ultimately determines whether you or the hotel bear the majority of the economic burden?

Learning Objective 6.2 *Evaluate the full set of consequences of price ceilings and price floors.*

2. Provide a real-world example of a price ceiling. How could the price ceiling result in a shortage?
3. Provide a real-world example of a price floor. How could the price floor result in a surplus?

Learning Objective 6.3 *Analyse the consequences of quantity regulations.*

4. Provide a real-world example of a quantity regulation. Under what circumstances will it impact market outcomes?

Study Problems

Learning Objective 6.1 *Assess how taxes shape supply, demand, and equilibrium outcomes.*

1. Consider the market for movie tickets shown in the accompanying graph. What is the equilibrium price and quantity? Illustrate graphically what happens to the supply curve if the government imposes a $4 per ticket tax on movie theatres. Identify the amount consumers now pay for a ticket and the amount cinemas get to keep. How is the economic burden shared?

   Show on the graph what happens if instead, the government imposes a $4 per ticket tax on movie goers. Identify the amount consumers now pay for a ticket and the amount cinemas get to keep. How is the economic burden shared? Compare your answer from when the statutory burden was on cinemas. What impact does the statutory burden of a tax have on the tax incidence? Who bears the economic burden and why?

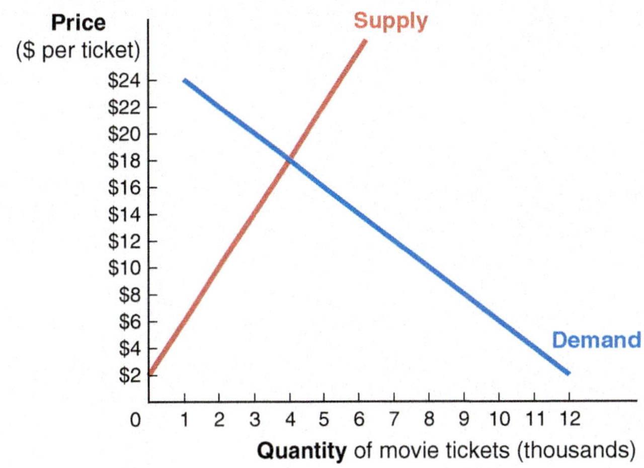

2. Unlike many countries, Australia does not subsidise agricultural production (it does provide some assistance for seasonal variability and droughts, though). By contrast, the U.S. government provides subsidies for a variety of agricultural products.

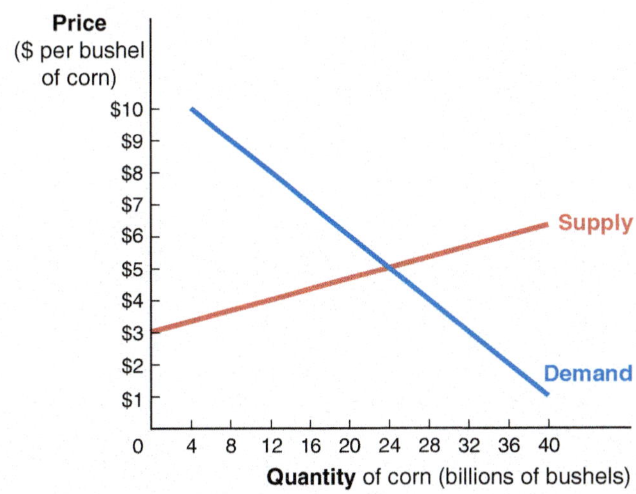

   In the absence of government involvement, what is the equilibrium price and quantity in the market for corn if the demand and supply for corn is as given in the accompanying graph. If the government offers a $2 per unit subsidy to the suppliers of corn, what happens to the price consumers pay inclusive of the subsidy? What price will suppliers receive, inclusive of the subsidy? Use a graph to illustrate the effect of this subsidy.

Learning Objective 6.2 *Evaluate the full set of consequences of price ceilings and price floors.*

3. Since there isn't really any rent control in Australia any more, data on the market demand and market supply of rental apartments in a small university town in the U.S. is provided in the accompanying table.

Rent (per week)	Quantity demanded	Quantity supplied
$500	5,000	13,000
$450	8,000	12,000
$400	11,000	11,000
$350	14,000	10,000
$300	17,000	9,000

Suppose that in order to assist tenants, the local government imposed a price ceiling (rent control) on apartments at $300 per unit. Would this create a shortage or a surplus? Of how many units? With the price ceiling in place, what would we expect to happen to the quality of rental apartments that are available?

4. The accompanying graph depicts a market for labour.

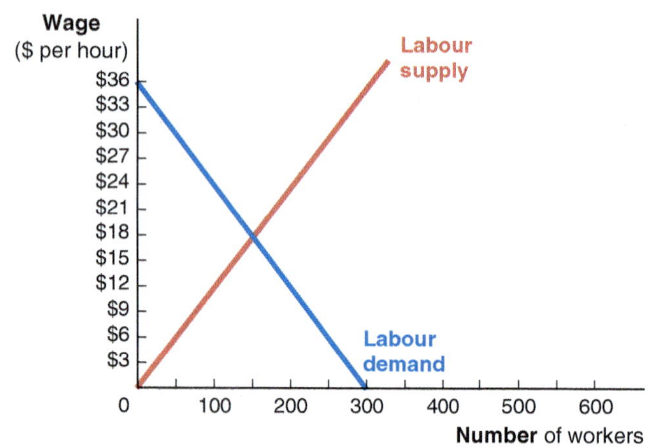

What is the equilibrium wage and equilibrium quantity of workers that will be hired in this particular labour market? Suppose the government imposes a minimum wage in this market at $12 per hour. What would happen in this market as a result of the new minimum wage? Suppose that the government decides to increase the minimum wage to $30 (an $18 increase). What would happen in this market as a result of the increase in the minimum wage?

Learning Objective 6.3 *Analyse the consequences of quantity regulations.*

5. Australia produced a little more than 2.4 million tonnes of iron ore a day in 2018. If market supply and demand for iron ore is as given in the accompanying graph, show what happens if the government imposes a maximum quota of 1.8 million tonnes per day. What will happen to the price of iron ore in this market?

One of the main uses for iron ore is to produce steel. Suppose that cars become significantly less prevalent in the market, due to a push for sustainability and environmental consciousness. As a result, what would happen to the demand curve for iron ore? Is it possible that the quantity restriction imposed by the government will no longer become relevant in this market?

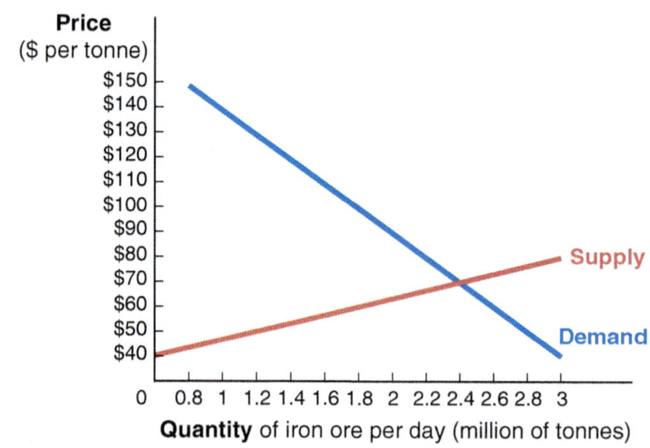

6. A paper in a leading medical journal reported that the Australian Government would implement annual increases in tobacco excise taxes of 12.5%, starting in 2016 and running through to and including 2020. This would increase the cost of a pack of cigarettes to $40, one of the highest prices for cigarettes in the world. Public health experts consider increasing the cost of cigarettes to be one of the most effective ways to reduce tobacco use.

a. What might be some of the unintended consequences of such a tax?

b. If lower-income Australians tend to smoke more than higher-income Australians, is such a tax fair in your view?

c. In 2019 the cigarette tax in Australia produced about $17 billion in government revenue. What do you think are the best uses of that revenue?

CHAPTER 7

Welfare Economics: Market Efficiency and Market Failure

Onfokus/iStock/Getty Images

Ride-sharing changed more than just transportation.

Most parents warn their children never to get in a stranger's car. These days they likely also warn their kids not to meet up with random strangers from the internet. Yet every time you open your Uber app, you literally summon strangers from the internet to get in their car. It shows just how much change Uber has wrought.

Talk to your driver, and you'll discover that Uber has also created a whole new model of work. Drivers decide where and when they want to work, and for how long. They don't answer to a boss, and they each provide their own workplace. But this freedom comes with a cost, as drivers aren't covered by the federal laws that protect most other workers, including minimum-wage laws, and worker's compensation, athough these things may be changing in some jurisdictions.

Uber is also disruptive. It has led to a huge decline in business for taxi drivers. Existing taxi companies are finding it hard to recruit new drivers, and they're losing customers hand over fist.

All of this has led to a fierce policy debate about whether Uber is a good thing. Not everyone is convinced that it is, and at various points, local governments in many countries have restricted or even outright banned the ride-sharing company.

It's a debate in which economic arguments loom large. But how can we tell whether allowing ride-share services like Uber is good for a community? How do economists weigh the gains to riders against the cost to taxi drivers? Should we just trust that the market is delivering what people want?

This chapter introduces the tools of welfare economics, which you'll use to assess how different outcomes affect economic well-being. We'll start with an overview of how economists evaluate public policies. We'll calculate economic surplus, and use this to assess the efficiency of markets. Then we'll take a look at how markets can fail, and use these tools to assess the costs of market failure. Finally, we'll join the debate about the appropriate role of economic efficiency in policy analysis.

Chapter Objective

Analyse how markets affect economic welfare.

7.1 Evaluating Public Policies
Learn how to evaluate welfare and economic efficiency.

7.2 Measuring Economic Surplus
Measure the economic surplus generated in a market.

7.3 Market Efficiency
Assess the efficiency of markets.

7.4 Market Failure and Deadweight Loss
Measure the costs of market failure.

7.5 Beyond Economic Efficiency
Evaluate the limitations of economic efficiency in policy analysis.

7.1 Evaluating Public Policies

Learning Objective *Learn how to evaluate welfare and economic efficiency.*

Should we raise the minimum wage? Should the petrol excise be higher? Should tertiary education be free? Should the speeding limit be higher? Should we reduce barriers to trading with China? Should Uber be legal? Each of these questions brings intense political debate. As a voter, a taxpayer, a community activist, or a business stakeholder—and possibly even as a policy adviser, policy maker, or politician—you're going to play a key role in that debate.

Positive and Normative Policy Analysis

Your contribution will be most valuable if it's based on careful analysis. Typically this means that you should conduct your analysis in two distinct stages:

Stage one: Positive analysis describes what is going to happen. The first stage of analysis is to ask: *What is going to happen if we adopt this policy?* This calls for a purely objective analysis, describing and forecasting the effects of the policy. For instance, you can use the supply-and-demand framework to predict the likely consequences of raising the minimum wage. You can use it to forecast the number of people who'll get a pay raise, to estimate how much their pay will increase, to assess the effects on the profitability of employers, and to predict how many jobs businesses will eliminate due to these higher wages. An in-depth analysis might even detail the characteristics of those who'll gain and lose from such a policy. This type of inquiry, an assessment that describes what is happening or predicts what will happen, is called **positive analysis**.

positive analysis Describes what *is* happening, explaining why, or predicting what will happen.

Stage two: Normative analysis assesses what should happen. The second step asks: *Which is the better outcome, and what policy should the government adopt?* Answering this question requires a value judgement about which outcome is better. In the first step, economists merely describe likely effects. The second step requires making a judgement. What should be done? Whenever you opine on what should happen—whenever you use words like *should* or *ought*—you're doing **normative analysis**, because your conclusions rest on normative, or value judgements.

normative analysis Prescribes what *should* happen, which involves value judgements.

Think about the minimum wage: Should it be raised or not? Positive analysis is helpful, because it lays out the likely consequences of the policy, outlining who'll gain, who'll lose, and what the stakes are for all concerned. But to assess whether the policy is worth pursuing, you need to evaluate whether the gains to some people outweigh the losses to others, and that requires a value judgement. It depends on how you weigh the benefits of higher wages for low-wage workers against the costs of lower profits for employers and the pain of unemployment for those who lose their jobs. Whatever view you hold, I bet that at least one of your classmates has a different set of values, and so comes to the opposite conclusion.

Do the Economics

Which of the following claims involve positive analysis, and which reflect normative analysis?

a. Higher taxes on petrol will lead people to use public transport more frequently.

b. University fees should be lower so that students from less affluent families can afford it.

c. The average single Australian taxpayer pays around 23.6% of their income in income taxes.

d. Income taxes are too high and the federal government should cut them.
e. A leading forecaster expects the Australian dairy industry to produce more than $4 billion of output next year.
f. Australia should spend more of the federal budget on foreign aid. ■

Answer: a, c, and e are positive analysis, and b, d, and f involve normative analysis.

Efficiency and Equity

If you're going to take a position in policy debates advocating what the government *should* do, then you're going to need a way to judge which policy yields better outcomes. That is, we need a way to evaluate how a policy affects *welfare*. Fortunately you've already developed the building blocks that can be helpful for this kind of normative analysis.

The efficiency criterion favours the outcome that yields the most economic surplus. Recall that **economic surplus** measures the benefits that follow from a decision, less the costs you incur. It measures the gains generated whenever something is bought or sold. Economists often evaluate policies using the criterion of **economic efficiency,** which says that the more economic surplus that's generated, the better the outcome. When economists describe an outcome as more efficient, they mean that it yields more economic surplus. At the extreme, the **efficient outcome** yields the largest possible economic surplus. The underlying logic is that economic surplus measures the size of the economic pie, and a bigger slice of pie is always better.

economic surplus The total benefits minus total costs flowing from a decision.

economic efficiency An outcome is more economically efficient if it yields more economic surplus.

efficient outcome The efficient outcome yields the largest possible economic surplus.

Efficient outcomes won't make everyone happy. Increasing economic efficiency rarely makes everyone happy, because most policies help some people and harm others. Economic efficiency simply assesses whether economic surplus rises, and this can only occur if the gains in economic surplus to those who are helped are larger than the declines in surplus among those who are harmed. But even if a policy is efficient, some people might be harmed, and those who are harmed aren't going to be happy.

For instance, the laws that allow Uber to operate in your city probably raise economic surplus, even as they harm taxi drivers who now face more competition, and owners of taxi plates who have seen the value of their asset drop. Economic surplus is higher because, overall, the benefits to Uber drivers and passengers outweigh the harm suffered by taxi drivers. But that argument is little solace to those taxi drivers who lose their livelihood.

Efficient outcomes hold the potential to make everyone better off. Relying on economic efficiency implicitly involves some difficult value judgements. In this case, it embeds the judgement that the harm done to taxi drivers is a reasonable price to pay for the benefits to Uber's drivers and customers. Perhaps you agree with this judgement, and perhaps you don't.

One argument for focusing on efficiency is that whenever economic surplus rises it's *possible* for those who benefit to compensate those who were harmed, and to do so in a way that ensures everyone's better off. This is just the idea that with a bigger pie it's always possible to slice it in a way that ensures everyone gets a bigger slice. In practice, this might mean levying a small tax on Uber's drivers and customers, and sending the proceeds to the taxi drivers who were hurt by this policy.

Equity is also important (but ignored by efficiency). In reality, it's rare for new policies to compensate the people they harm. Thus, the argument that it's *possible* to make everyone better off is just that, a *possibility.* The reality is that policies change both the level of economic surplus and the distribution of that surplus.

Consequently, real-world policy debates are rarely just about efficiency. They also focus on **equity,** which is about assessing whether a policy will yield a fair distribution of economic benefits. When you evaluate both efficiency and equity, you'll account for both the size of the pie, and how it's sliced.

equity An outcome yields greater equity if it results in a fairer distribution of economic benefits.

7.2 Measuring Economic Surplus

Learning Objective *Measure the economic surplus generated in a market.*

We've just seen that economic surplus plays an important role in economic policy debates. And so if you want to influence these debates, you'll need to know how to measure economic surplus. That's our next task.

Consumer Surplus

consumer surplus The economic surplus you get from buying something; Consumer surplus = Marginal benefit – Price

When you gain economic surplus from *buying* something, economists refer to it as **consumer surplus,** because you're earning that surplus in your role as a consumer. You gain consumer surplus when you buy something for a cheaper price than the marginal benefit you get from it.

Your marginal benefit is your willingness to pay for these jeans.

Consumer surplus is your marginal benefit, less the price. Let's take an everyday example. You're at the shopping centre looking for new jeans, and you find the perfect pair of Levi's, although the price tag is missing. After trying them on, you decide you're willing to pay up to \$160 for them. You ask the sales assistant to look up the price and learn some good news: The price is only \$100. It's good news, because you were willing to pay up to \$160 for the jeans, but you got them for only \$100. It's like you're \$60 ahead! That \$60 gain is the consumer surplus you get from this transaction.

Consumer surplus describes the gain from buying something at a price below the highest price you were willing to pay (which is your marginal benefit). It's the marginal benefit you'll get from those jeans, less the price you pay. You can see it graphically in Figure 1, and you can measure it as:

$$\text{Consumer surplus} = \text{Marginal benefit} - \text{Price}$$

Figure 1 | Consumer Surplus

Ⓐ Your **consumer surplus** from *a single purchase* is the difference between your marginal benefit and the price.

Ⓑ The **total consumer surplus** *across all buyers* is the area under the demand curve above the price.

Ⓒ This is the **area of a triangle** = $\frac{1}{2}$ **Base × Height.**

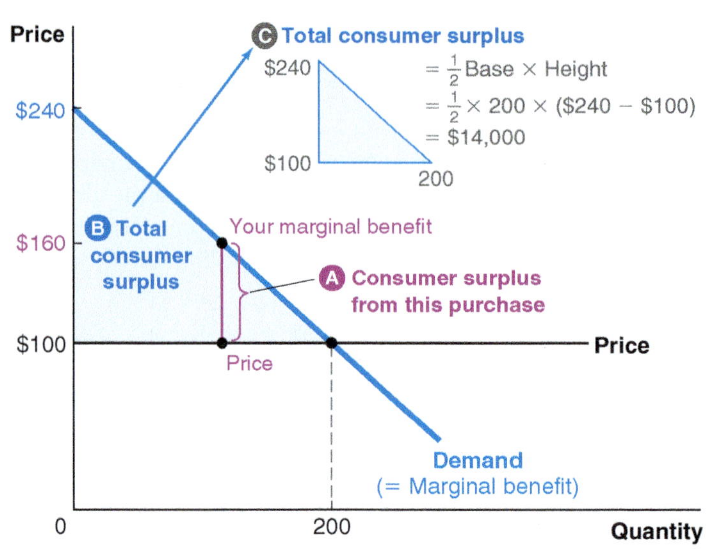

Consumer surplus is the area below the demand curve and above the price. So far, we've analysed the consumer surplus of a single transaction—it's the marginal benefit you get, less the price you pay. What about the consumer surplus of all purchases in a market? Let's take a look at the market demand curve.

Figure 1 shows the market demand curve for jeans. Recall from Chapter 2 that the demand curve is the marginal benefit curve. This means that each point on the demand curve reveals an individual buyer's marginal benefit. And so for any individual purchase, the consumer surplus gained is the marginal benefit (which is given by the height of the demand curve) less the price. You can see the consumer surplus from your single purchase shown as the difference between the point on the demand curve where the marginal benefit is equal to $160 minus the price of $100. Add up this gain for each pair of jeans sold, and you'll end up with the entire area under the demand curve and above the price, out to the quantity purchased. This reveals that total consumer surplus in a market is *the area under the demand curve and above the price, out to the quantity sold.*

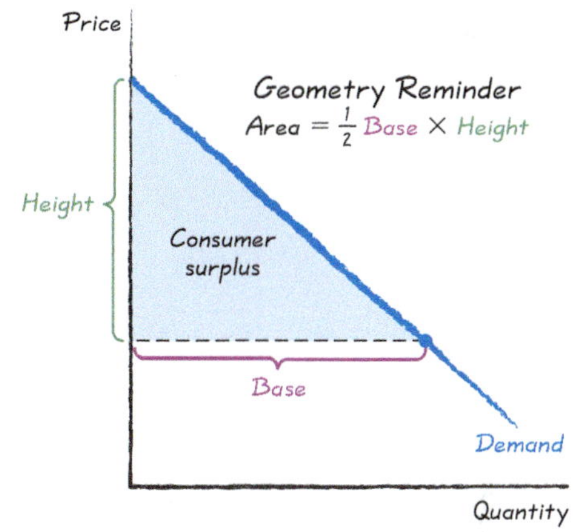

The area of a triangle is half the base, times the height. This is the moment you thought might never arrive: High school geometry will be useful. Here's why: When the demand curve is a straight line, consumer surplus is a right-angled triangle. So figuring out total consumer surplus means figuring out the area of that triangle, which is half the base, times the height.

Do the Economics

What's the consumer surplus of a song? Let's try to work it out. Take Rihanna's song "Work," which she sang with Drake. She sold 10 million copies of this song for roughly $1.29 a copy. If half the people who bought this song said in a survey that they would have been willing to pay at least $2.29 for it, then we have two points on the demand curve for this song. If we connect these two points to get an estimate of the demand curve for this song, we'll discover that the demand curve cuts the vertical axis at $3.29.

Consumer surplus is the area under the demand curve and above the price, out to the quantity sold. Zoom in on that triangle:

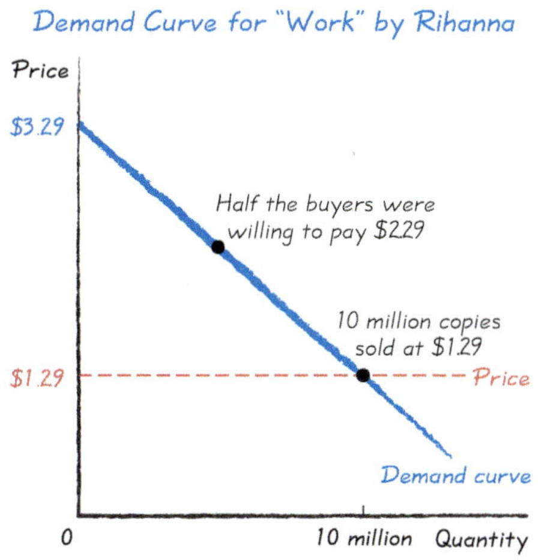

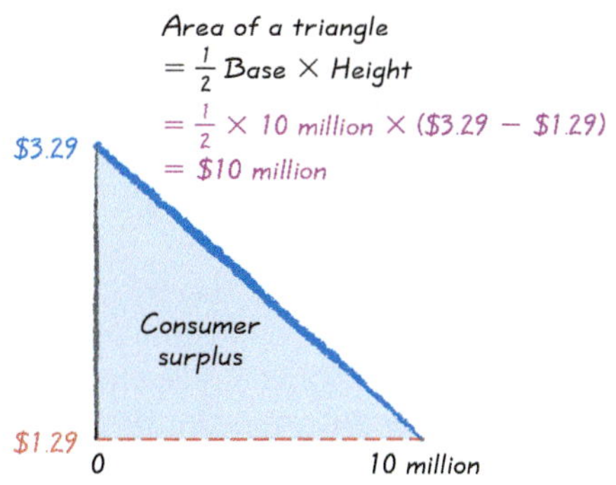

That's it. Rihanna's song created around $10 million in consumer surplus for her fans. Thanks, Rihanna! ■

You earn consumer surplus on all but your last purchase. Some students are puzzled by the idea that consumer surplus is the *difference* between their marginal benefit and the price, while the *Rational Rule for Buyers* (introduced in Chapter 2) says to keep buying until price *equals* marginal benefit. But there's no contradiction. The *Rational Rule* tells you to keep buying jeans until the marginal benefit *of the last pair* is equal to the price. If you bought four pairs, then your fourth and last pair yields a marginal benefit equal to their $100 price tag. That means you won't earn any consumer surplus on that last pair. But the marginal benefit from your first pair is likely much higher—you don't have to wear shorts! Perhaps your marginal benefit was $160 for that first pair, exceeding the $100 price, and therefore, yielding a healthy consumer surplus. Likewise, you also may earn consumer surplus on the second and third pair you buy. The point is, even if you earn no consumer surplus on the *last* item you purchase, you'll likely earn consumer surplus from *all of your preceding purchases.*

You enjoy a lot of consumer surplus in your life. Consumer surplus is important because the price you pay for something is often a poor indicator of the benefits you get from it. Consider water. Because it's so cheap, your marginal litre of water is probably used for something pretty unnecessary, like running the tap while brushing your teeth.

But how much would you be willing to pay for the roughly 3 litres a day you need to stay alive? Thousands of dollars, right? Yet your water bill shows that you pay only a few cents for it. The fact that water is cheap doesn't mean that it's not valuable; rather, it means that you're enjoying thousands of dollars of water-related consumer surplus.

The same idea applies to health care. Antibiotics that sell for only a few dollars can prevent a simple infection from becoming life threatening. The vaccinations you got as a baby protect you from polio, tetanus, and hepatitis, yet they cost your parents very little. And if you've ever had a friend or relative survive a life-saving operation, you've probably enjoyed a lot of surgery-related consumer surplus. Even if the surgery cost thousands, that price is small relative to the benefit of saving a loved one.

Each of these examples shows that you'll enjoy a lot of consumer surplus in your life. Indeed, that's a theme we'll continue to explore in the next case study.

SolStock/E+/Getty Images

Not every use of water saves your life.

Interpreting the DATA **Consumer surplus on the internet**

Perhaps you started your day by checking your e-mail. Maybe you skimmed Instagram, Facebook, Snapchat, or Twitter. Hopefully you looked up the weather forecast before heading out. You might have listened to Spotify on the way to class. While you (hopefully!) didn't look at your phone during class, when it ended you may have used Google to look up a troubling concept. And later in the evening, you might have used TripAdvisor to choose where to get dinner, and checked Google Maps for directions. Or maybe it's a quiet night, so you headed home to browse BuzzFeed, read the news, and then watch videos on YouTube. How much did you pay to use each of these sites?

Nothing. Nada. $0.

If you used the price to measure the economic importance of your favourite websites, you'd infer that they're worth nothing. But that would be a mistake. It's a mistake, because it fails to account for the enormous consumer surplus that a good website generates.

To measure this consumer surplus, think about how much you would pay each year to have access to Google. Likewise, you can evaluate your willingness to pay for

Wikipedia, TikTok, and all the other internet services to figure out the marginal benefit you get from your favourite websites. The consumer surplus you get from them is this marginal benefit, less the price, which is $0.

Economists have made such calculations, considering different ways of measuring the marginal benefit people get from these services. They've looked at how much people used to spend on internet access when it was a newer, more expensive technology; at how much people used to pay for non-internet based substitutes like encyclopedias; at how much time people spend on the internet; and at what people say they would have to be paid to give up access to internet services. While estimates vary, one reasonable estimate is that access to the internet collectively brings the average person around $3,500 per year worth of consumer surplus. Consumer surplus reveals that these websites are extremely valuable, even though most of this value isn't reflected in their low or nonexistent price. ■

Producer Surplus

Consumer surplus tells us about the gains from trade that buyers get. But buyers aren't the only ones who benefit from a transaction; sellers also gain something. When you gain economic surplus from *selling* something, economists refer to it as **producer surplus,** because you're earning that surplus in your role as a producer. You gain producer surplus when you sell something at a higher price than the marginal costs you incur.

producer surplus The economic surplus you get from selling something; Producer surplus = Price – Marginal cost.

Producer surplus is the price, less the marginal cost. Let's analyse what happens when you walk into a Levi's store to buy a pair of jeans for $100, but this time, we'll focus on the producer's perspective. For Levi's, the marginal benefit of selling you those jeans is the $100 price you paid for them. And the marginal cost is the $70 worth of extra denim, thread, and labour it took to make that extra pair of jeans. Levi's is thrilled to get $100 in return for $70 worth of denim, thread and labour. It's thrilled because producing and selling those jeans made Levi's $30 better off. This $30 is the producer surplus that Levi's gains from this transaction.

Producer surplus describes the gain a producer gets from selling something at a higher price than is necessary for them to want to supply the item, which is its marginal cost. More generally, the producer surplus a seller gains from a transaction is the price they receive less the marginal cost. And so, you can measure it as:

$$\text{Producer surplus} = \text{Price} - \text{Marginal cost}$$

Producer surplus is the area above the supply curve and below the price. So far, we've figured out the producer surplus from Levi's selling you one pair of jeans. What about the total producer surplus from all the jeans sold by all producers? The producer surplus from any individual transaction is the price less marginal cost. This leads to a simple graphical representation: Total producer surplus in a market is *the area below the price and above the supply curve, out to the quantity sold,* as shown in Figure 2.

To see why, recall from Chapter 3 that the supply curve is also the seller's marginal cost curve. This means that each point on the supply curve reveals a seller's marginal cost. And so for any given sale, a seller gains producer surplus equal to the price, less their marginal cost, and the marginal cost is the height of the supply curve. Add this producer surplus up across all jeans sold, and you'll end up adding the entire area above the supply curve and below the price, out to the quantity sold.

You earn producer surplus on all but your last sale. As a seller, your producer surplus is the difference between the price and your marginal costs. But the *Rational Rule for Sellers in Competitive Markets* (in Chapter 3) says to keep selling until price equals marginal cost. At first glance, this might confuse you into thinking that you won't earn any producer surplus if you follow this rule. But that's not right. Instead, realise that the *Rational Rule* says to keep selling *until* price equals marginal cost. This means that

Figure 2 | **Producer Surplus**

A **Producer surplus** from *a single sale* is the difference between the price the seller receives and the marginal cost.

B The **total producer surplus** *across all sellers* is the area above the supply curve below the price out to the quantity sold.

C This is the **area of a triangle** = $\frac{1}{2}$ **Base** × **Height.**

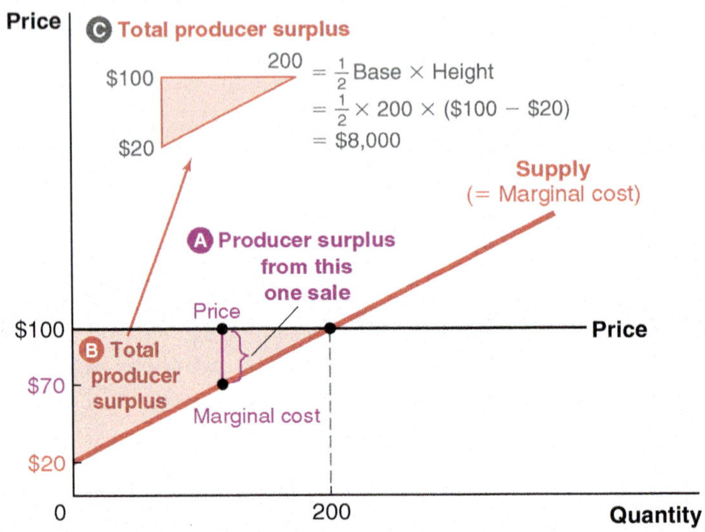

price is equal to marginal cost only for the last (or marginal) pair of jeans you sell. With an upward-sloping marginal cost curve, the marginal cost of every other pair of jeans you make is lower, and so you'll earn a healthy producer surplus on all but the last pair of jeans you sell.

EVERYDAY Economics **The producer surplus of work**

My first job was coaching cricket and I loved it. I got to play cricket and improve my own game, while passing on whatever I knew about how to play a game I loved. The pay was also great. Here's what I never told the business who hired me—I would have done it for half the pay. Have you ever had a job that you would have done for less than you were actually paid? If so, then you earned producer surplus at your job.

Here's the logic: As a worker, you're a supplier, selling your labour, and your hourly wage is the price you're selling it at. What's the relevant marginal cost? Applying the *opportunity cost principle*, it's the value of your next best use of that hour. If the wage exceeds how much you value this alternative use of your time, then you're earning producer surplus.

During the coronavirus pandemic, many countries imposed lockdowns in order to keep the virus under control. This resulted in millions of jobs being moved away from the office to be done from home. During this time, one survey found that one-in-three Australians would take a pay cut to work from home after Covid restrictions were lifted. This means we can infer that about one-third of Australians were receiving a larger producer surplus from being able to work from home than they would have received working in the office! ■

Voluntary Exchange and Gains from Trade

Next time you go shopping, pay attention to how polite everyone is. When I last bought a pair of jeans, I handed over my money and said to the seller, "thank you," and the seller said to me "thank you." We now understand why. I said thank you, because the store gave me a pair of jeans that I valued at more than what I paid. I was grateful to gain some consumer surplus. And the seller said thank you because I gave them money that they value more than the stitched denim they were handing over. They were grateful to gain some producer surplus. This is more than just politeness—it reveals a deeper economic truth: Voluntary transactions create *both* consumer and producer surplus. This means both the buyer and the seller gain from trade. The big idea here is that buying or selling goods and services isn't a zero-sum game in which one person wins at the other person's expense. Instead, trade is a win-win situation, creating gains for *both* the buyer and the seller. That's why economists talk about *the gains from trade.*

Voluntary exchange ensures both buyer and seller enjoy gains from trade. Trade generates gains for both the buyer and the seller because it's based on **voluntary exchange,** where buyers and sellers exchange money for goods only if they both want to. And you only want to buy or sell stuff if it'll make you better off.

voluntary exchange Buyers and sellers exchange money for goods only if they both want to.

Think about it: As a buyer following the *cost-benefit principle*, you'll only buy a pair of jeans if the marginal benefit you receive is at least as large as the price you pay. That is, you'll only buy something if it yields consumer surplus. Likewise, a supplier following the *cost-benefit principle* will only sell jeans if the price is at least as large as their marginal cost. That is, suppliers only produce stuff if they expect it'll generate producer surplus. And so voluntary exchange ensures that both buyer and seller enjoy gains from trade (or at least that neither is made worse off).

This leads to an underappreciated perspective. You might be used to thinking about markets as being mostly about *competition.* But voluntary exchange generates economic surplus for both buyers and sellers, and so perhaps it's more useful to think about markets as facilitating *cooperation.* Just as your purchase of Levi's jeans helps boost its bottom line, Levi's production of jeans has also helped you line your bottom!

This doesn't mean that consumers and producers share equally in the gains from trade. But even if the gains are unequal, as long as both buyers and sellers are well-informed and follow the *cost-benefit principle*, neither will engage in a trade that makes them worse off.

Economic surplus is marginal benefit less marginal cost. Let's put the pieces together. The economic surplus generated by a transaction is the sum of consumer surplus enjoyed by the buyer (the marginal benefit, less the price) and the producer surplus accruing to the seller (the price, less the marginal cost). Add them up, and the economic surplus generated by a transaction is the marginal benefit less the marginal cost:

$$\begin{aligned}\text{Economic surplus} &= \underbrace{\text{Consumer surplus}}_{\text{Marginal benefit} - \text{Price}} + \underbrace{\text{Producer surplus}}_{\text{Price} - \text{Marginal cost}} \\ &= \text{Marginal benefit} - \text{Marginal cost}\end{aligned}$$

For instance, when you buy a pair of jeans that brings you \$160 worth of benefit, and it cost Levi's only \$70 worth of denim, cotton, and labour, the transaction creates \$90 in economic surplus.

Economic surplus is the area between the demand and supply curves. Total economic surplus, or gains from trade, across a whole market is the consumer surplus triangle (the area below the demand curve and above the price) plus the producer surplus triangle (the area above the supply curve and below the price). Add them up and you'll discover that *economic surplus is the area between the demand and supply curves, to the left of the quantity bought and sold,* as shown in Figure 3.

Alternatively, you can think of the economic surplus from a single transaction as being the marginal benefit less the marginal cost. Add this up across all items purchased, and it's the difference between marginal benefits (the demand curve) and marginal cost (the supply curve) across all items bought and sold. And that's why economic surplus is the area between the demand (or marginal benefit) curve and the supply (or marginal cost) curve, out to the total quantity.

Figure 3 | Economic Surplus

Ⓐ **Economic surplus** of *a single transaction* is the marginal benefit, less the marginal cost.
Ⓑ **Economic surplus** is the area between the demand and supply curves.
Ⓒ Economic surplus gained from all transactions:
= ***Consumer surplus*** + ***Producer surplus***.
= ***Marginal benefit*** − ***Marginal cost***.

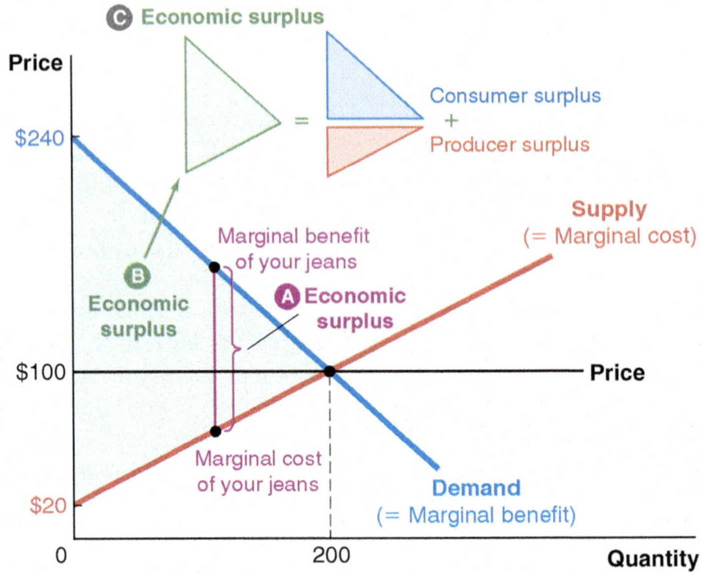

Okay, so now you should have a good sense of how to measure economic surplus—it's the marginal benefit to the buyer less the marginal cost to the seller. This means that on a graph, it's the area between the demand and supply curves, to the left of the quantity sold.

Now let's use these tools to assess the efficiency of markets.

7.3 Market Efficiency

Learning Objective *Assess the efficiency of markets.*

Markets are the central organising institution of our lives. They determine what products are made, how much is produced, who makes what, who gets what, and what the price will be. Markets determine your income and what you can afford to buy. It isn't always this way. In centrally planned economies like Cuba, North Korea, and to an extent China, the government decides what gets made, and who gets what.

It's time to ask: Are markets a good idea? Why should markets play such a central role in our lives? The main argument is that markets yield more efficient outcomes. That is, markets create the largest possible amount of economic surplus by providing efficient answers to three key questions: (1) who makes what; (2) who gets what; and (3) how much gets bought and sold? Let's explore how markets answer each of these questions.

Question One: Who Makes What?

Think about the supply side of the economy: Millions of businesses produce a dizzying array of products. How do we know which businesses should produce which products? Which firms should produce a lot, and which should produce only a little? Who should be in business, and who should go kaput? While it's nearly impossible for any individual to find the best answer, a well-functioning market can figure it all out. Let's explore how.

Efficient production minimises costs. **Efficient production** occurs when we produce a given level of output at the lowest possible cost. This requires allocating production so that each item is produced at the lowest marginal cost.

efficient production Producing a given quantity of output at the lowest possible cost, which requires producing each good at the lowest marginal cost.

Consider two important suppliers in the market for strawberries. Beerenberg is a large family-owned farm in South Australia, while Australian Strawberry Distributors (ASD) have a large industrial (also family-owned) farm in Victoria. The marginal cost curve of each farm is shown in Figure 4, along with the current price of strawberries, which is $12 per kilo. You may have heard of Beerenberg before, maybe you've seen their jams and chutneys on the shelf at your local supermarket or in a restaurant.

Figure 4 | **Which Firm Should Supply How Much?**

(A) When the price is $12, **Beerenberg supplies 300,000 kilos** and **ASD supplies 700,000 kilograms**.

(B) If Beerenberg produces a larger share, **total costs will rise** because **Beerenberg will produce these extra strawberries at a marginal cost > $12**, even as ASD's marginal costs are < $12.

(C) If ASD produces a larger share, **total costs will rise**, because **ASD will produce those extra strawberries at a marginal cost > $12**, even as Beerenberg's marginal cost is < $12.

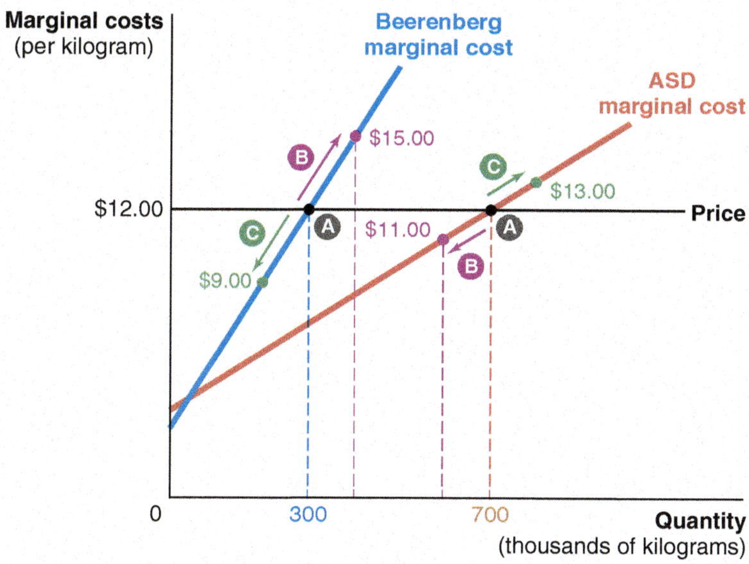

A business's marginal cost curve is also its individual supply curve, and so when the price is $12 per kilo, ASD supplies 700,000 kilos of strawberries, and Beerenberg supplies 300,000 kilos. This is efficient production, because there's no way to produce 1 million kilos of strawberries at a lower cost. That is, supply and demand lead to efficient production.

To see this, consider the alternatives.

What if you ask Beerenberg to produce a greater number of strawberries and ASD to produce fewer? The total cost of producing those 1 million strawberries will rise. It'll cost Beerenberg more than $12 per kilo to produce those extra strawberries (perhaps as much as $15 per kilo) even though ASD had previously produced those extra strawberries at a marginal cost of less than $12 per kilo (perhaps as low as $11). So this alternative is inefficient, because it raises the total cost of producing these 1 million kilos of strawberries.

Alternatively, what if you ask Beerenberg to produce fewer strawberries and ASD to produce more? That's also inefficient. The problem is that when ASD produces more strawberries, its marginal cost exceeds $12 per kilo (perhaps it's as high as $13), while Beerenberg could have produced those extra strawberries at a marginal cost below $12 (perhaps as low as $9). And so this alternative plan is also costlier.

Putting the pieces together, we've discovered that any production plan other than the one caused by the forces of supply and demand would raise costs. Amazingly enough, supply and demand lead Beerenberg and ASD to divvy up total production in such a way as to ensure that it occurs at the lowest possible cost! This is how competitive markets lead to efficient production in which each item is produced at the lowest possible cost.

Markets distribute production across firms in a way that minimises costs. It's worth pausing to think about how amazing this is. The farmers at ASD and Beerenberg probably don't know each other, and indeed, it's unlikely they've ever even been in touch. Neither has an interest in ensuring that 1 million kilograms of strawberries is produced as cheaply as possible. Instead, each of them pursues their own self-interest, choosing the production levels that maximise their own profits. Yet this self-interest leads these businesses to split production in a way that ensures that together they produce the industry's total output at the lowest possible cost.

In sum, perfectly competitive markets ensure efficient production so that every good is produced by the supplier who can do so at the lowest possible marginal cost.

Question Two: Who Gets What?

Let's now turn to the demand side of the economy. There are millions of people who all want to consume the myriad products the economy produces. Who should get what? To take just one example: Who should get a lot of strawberries, and who should get just a few? Intuitively, we want the strawberries to go to people who will really value them. After all, there's no point in sending strawberries to people who despise them.

efficient allocation Allocating goods to create the largest economic surplus, which requires that each good goes to the person who'll get the highest marginal benefit from it.

Efficient allocation maximises benefits. An **efficient allocation** occurs when goods are allocated to create the largest economic surplus from them, which requires that each good goes to the person who gets the highest marginal benefit from it (at least as measured by how much they are willing to pay).

Consider two strawberry buyers, Gabrielle and Peter, who like to buy directly from strawberry farms. Their marginal benefit curves are shown in Figure 5. Remember, these marginal benefit curves are also their individual demand curves, and so when the price is $12, Peter will buy 0.7 kilograms of strawberries, and Gabrielle will buy 0.3 kilograms.

Figure 5 | **Who Should Get How Much?**

(A) When the price is $12, Peter buys 0.7 kilos of strawberries, and Gabrielle buys 0.3 kilograms.

(B) Giving Peter fewer and Gabrielle more is a bad idea because Peter forgoes strawberries with a marginal benefit > $12, but Gabrielle only gets < $12 marginal benefit from extra strawberries.

(C) Giving Peter more and Gabrielle fewer is also a bad idea, because Peter gets < $12 marginal benefit from extra strawberries, but Gabrielle forgoes strawberries yielding > $12 marginal benefit.

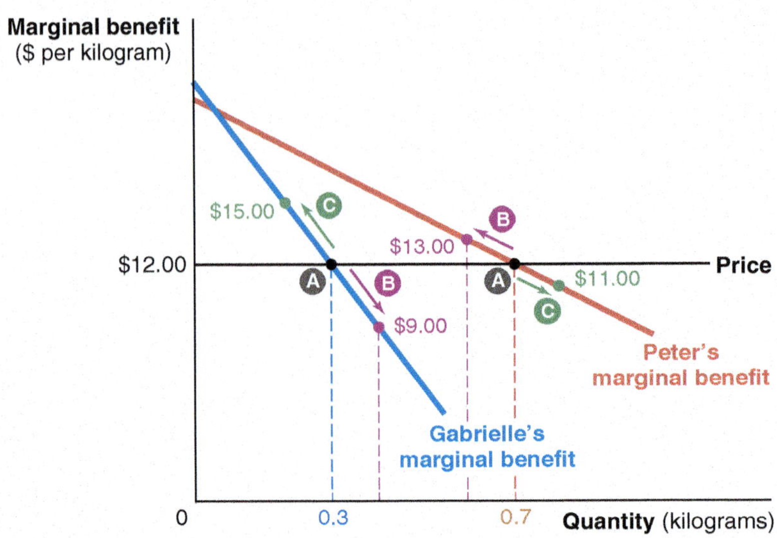

This is an efficient allocation, because each strawberry is going to the person with the highest marginal benefit, ensuring that they generate the largest economic surplus. That is, supply and demand leads to an efficient allocation.

To see this, consider alternative allocations.

You could give Gabrielle some of Peter's strawberries. But that will decrease economic surplus, because the extra benefit to Gabrielle is less than the forgone benefit to Peter. The reason is that Gabrielle's marginal benefit from extra strawberries is less than $12 (perhaps as low as $9), while Peter is forgoing strawberries from which he would get a marginal benefit that's greater than $12 (perhaps as high as $13).

Alternatively, you could try to give Peter some of Gabrielle's strawberries, but this will also decrease economic surplus, because Peter's marginal benefit from getting extra strawberries is less than $12 (say, $11), while Gabrielle will forgo strawberries from which she would get a marginal benefit that's greater than $12 (perhaps $15).

We've discovered that the forces of supply and demand lead Gabrielle and Peter to divvy up these strawberries in a way that ensures each strawberry goes to the person who'll get the highest marginal benefit from it (at least as measured in terms of willingness to pay). Any other allocation would reduce the total amount of economic surplus. It follows that competitive markets lead to an efficient allocation of goods in which each item ends up being sold to the person who'll get the highest marginal benefit from it.

Markets allocate goods to those with the highest marginal benefit. This is an extraordinary outcome. Neither Gabrielle nor Peter know each other, and indeed, they've never even spoken. But by each pursuing their own self-interest, they've ensured that each strawberry is allocated to the person who would enjoy the highest marginal benefit from it. This same logic applies to how markets allocate billions of strawberries (and countless other items) across millions of buyers—the competitive market will allocate them to the people with the highest marginal benefit. As each buyer pursues their own self-interest, the market allots each strawberry to the person who gets the largest marginal benefit, at least as measured by their willingness to pay.

Question Three: How Much Gets Bought and Sold?

So far we've seen that whatever quantity of goods is produced, competitive markets lead to *efficient production,* which means those goods are produced at the lowest overall cost. Competitive markets also lead to *efficient allocation,* which means those goods are allocated to the people who get the largest marginal benefit from them.

Our final step is to analyse the quantity of goods that is bought and sold. We'll assess whether the forces of supply and demand lead to the **efficient quantity,** which is the quantity that produces the largest possible economic surplus.

efficient quantity The quantity that produces the largest possible economic surplus.

The Rational Rule for Markets says to produce until marginal benefit equals marginal cost. Let's start by figuring out the efficient quantity of strawberries: How many strawberries will produce the largest possible economic surplus for society as a whole? Since this is a "how many" question, the *marginal principle* says to focus on the simpler question: "Should we produce one more strawberry?" Next, apply the *cost-benefit principle*, which says that yes, an extra strawberry will increase economic surplus, as long as the marginal benefit is at least as large as the marginal cost.

Put the pieces together, and we get the following very helpful rule.

The **Rational Rule for Markets:** *To increase economic surplus, produce more of an item if the marginal benefit of one more is greater than (or equal to) its marginal cost.*

Rational Rule for Markets Produce more of a good if its marginal benefit is greater than (or equal to) its marginal cost.

It follows that we'll get the largest possible economic surplus if the market keeps producing until marginal benefit equals marginal cost. That is, the efficient quantity occurs where:

$$\text{Marginal benefit} = \text{Marginal cost}$$

Supply and demand produce the surplus-maximising quantity. There is no one in charge of the market; yet somehow the forces of supply and demand naturally produce this surplus-maximising quantity. Recall that equilibrium occurs where supply equals demand. In a well-functioning market, the supply curve is also the marginal cost curve, and the demand curve is also the marginal benefit curve. And so supply-equals-demand equilibrium occurs at the point where marginal benefit equals marginal cost. As Figure 6 illustrates, this is the point that creates the largest possible economic surplus.

Figure 6 | **What Quantity Yields the Most Surplus**

A At quantities less than the equilibrium, the **marginal benefit to buyers** of another unit **exceeds the marginal cost to sellers**.

B At quantities greater than the equilibrium, the **marginal cost to sellers exceeds the marginal benefit to buyers**.

C Therefore, the **equilibrium quantity** creates the **largest possible economic surplus**.

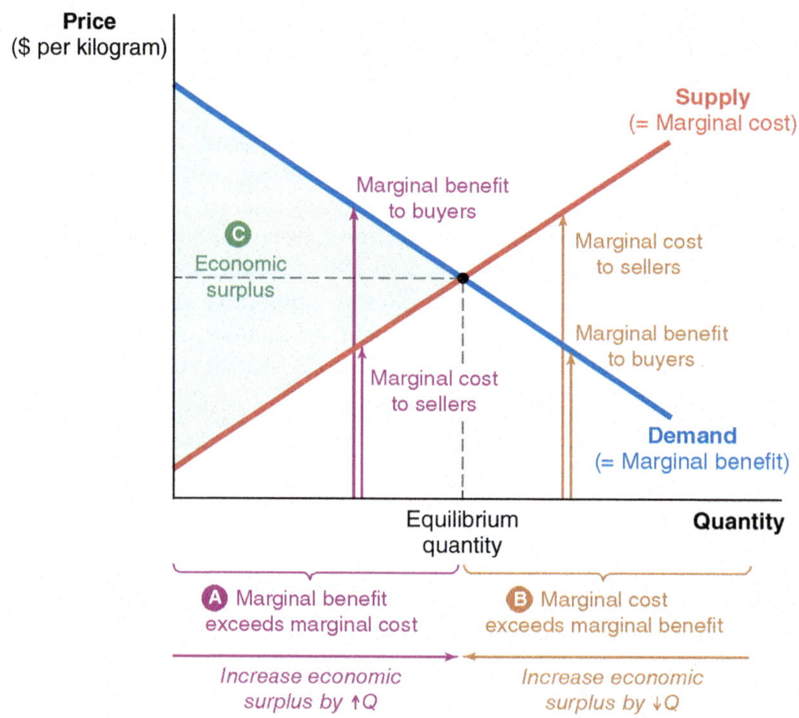

To see why, realise that if sellers produce less than the equilibrium quantity, the marginal benefit to buyers exceeds the marginal cost to sellers, and so we could increase economic surplus by increasing production. On the flipside, if sellers produce more than the equilibrium quantity, the marginal cost to sellers exceeds the marginal benefit to buyers, and so we could increase economic surplus by decreasing production.

It follows that the quantity that maximises economic surplus is also the equilibrium quantity that results from the forces of supply and demand. That is, competitive markets lead to the *efficient quantity* of any good.

It's as if all economic activity is being directed by an invisible hand. Let's put all of this together, because it's a pretty extraordinary finding. Organising our economy—deciding who makes what, who gets what, and how much to make of each good—is a task of astonishing difficulty. It's so difficult that no committee of expert economists could ever figure out how to do all of this efficiently.

Yet millions of buyers and sellers, guided by nothing but their own self-interest, end up doing what an expert committee cannot. They produce the quantity that maximises the total amount of economic surplus. They ensure that this quantity is produced at the lowest marginal cost. And they ensure that each good goes to the person who draws the largest marginal benefit from it, as revealed by their willingness to pay. The market achieves an efficient outcome, despite the fact that no market participant is trying to achieve that goal. Instead, as each person pursues their independent self-interest, they guide the market towards an efficient outcome. As Adam Smith, who was one of the founders of economics, noted, it is as if all economic activity is guided by an "invisible hand."

7.4 Market Failure and Deadweight Loss

Learning Objective *Measure the costs of market failure.*

At this point, you might be wildly enthusiastic about markets. After all, we've established that competitive markets yield efficient outcomes, which means they generate the largest possible economic surplus. But there's a critically important caveat: Our supply and demand curves represent well-informed buyers and sellers interacting in a well-functioning market with perfect competition. But the world doesn't always work this way.

Market Failure

In reality, supply and demand don't always work as smoothly as we'd like.

Market failure occurs when the forces of supply and demand lead to an inefficient outcome. Market failures are common, and their frequency and severity should temper your enthusiasm for market forces.

market failure When the forces of supply and demand lead to an inefficient outcome.

There are five main sources of market failure. Let's explore why they arise and how they change market outcomes.

Sources of market failure:

1. Market power
2. Externalities
3. Information problems
4. Irrationality
5. Government regulations

Market failure one: Market power undermines competitive pressures. The problem of *market power* arises when markets don't meet the perfectly competitive ideal of many sellers selling identical products. Instead, most markets are dominated by only a handful of companies. For instance, nearly every major breakfast cereal in Australia is made by Kellogg's, Nestlé, or Sanitarium. The cereals they sell all differ to some degree. Sellers exploit this limited competition by charging higher prices, and this leads consumers to buy a smaller quantity. The result is that market power leads to underproduction as businesses with market power tend to produce less than the efficient quantity. We'll analyse market power in greater detail in Chapter 14.

Market failure two: Externalities create side effects. The problem of *externalities* arises whenever the choices that buyers and sellers make have side effects on others.

For instance, many utilities produce electricity by burning coal, which has side effects including smog, acid rain, and greenhouse gases. You (and many others) are affected by these side effects even if you don't buy or sell coal, or electricity produced from coal. When suppliers don't take sufficient account of these side effects, they'll produce more coal and hence more pollution than is in society's best interests. More generally, businesses tend to produce more than the efficient quantity of products with negative side effects.

Externalities aren't always negative. Some activities have side effects that help other people—such as when your flu shot not only protects you from getting sick but also prevents others from getting sick because you won't infect them with the virus. If people don't take account of these positive side effects, they'll do fewer of these helpful activities than are in society's best interests. We'll explore these insights further in Chapter 10.

Susan Norwood/Alamy

Even if you don't litter, you feel the side effects of it.

Market failure three: Information problems undermine trust. The problem of *private information* can arise when you're worried that the people you're doing business with know something you don't. For instance, if a seller knows more about the quality of the used car they're selling than you do, you might wonder why they're selling it.

Your fears about what they're hiding might lead you not to buy that second-hand car. It's an example of how private information can undermine trust, leading people to buy or sell less than the efficient quantity, a phenomenon we'll explore in Chapter 20.

Market failure four: Irrationality leads to bad decisions. The problem of *irrationality* is that sometimes people make decisions that aren't in their best interests. If buyers don't systematically follow the *Rational Rule for Buyers*, their demand decisions may no longer reflect their marginal benefits, and so an efficient allocation is unlikely. And if suppliers don't systematically follow the *Rational Rule for Sellers*, their supply decisions may not be driven by their marginal costs, and so efficient production is unlikely.

In fact, psychologists and behavioural economists have documented many ways in which people systematically make mistakes. We've analysed some of them in Chapter 1, and we will explore more of them in Chapter 19.

Market failure five: Government regulations impede market forces. The problem posed by *government regulations* is that they can impede market forces. As you've already seen in Chapter 6, taxes on buying or selling stuff leads a lower quantity to be bought or sold. Likewise, regulating the price sellers can charge or limiting the quantity they can sell also changes the quantity sold. Sometimes these government regulations exist to combat the market failures listed above, such as environmental regulations that try to prevent overpollution. But sometimes government regulations create their own distortions, pushing the market away from the efficient quantity.

Deadweight Loss

deadweight loss How far economic surplus falls below the efficient outcome; Deadweight loss = Economic surplus at the efficient quantity − Actual economic surplus.

The costs of market failure can be measured by calculating how much it reduces economic surplus. That's the idea behind **deadweight loss,** which is the difference between the largest possible economic surplus (which occurs at the efficient quantity), and the actual level of economic surplus:

$$\text{Deadweight loss} = \text{Economic surplus at efficient quantity} - \text{Actual economic surplus}$$

Economic surplus and deadweight loss focus on marginal benefits and marginal costs. Calculating deadweight loss requires you to measure economic surplus at two points—at the efficient quantity and at the actual quantity. And so before continuing, it's worth remembering that the economic surplus in any given transaction is:

$$\text{Economic surplus} = \text{Marginal benefit} - \text{Marginal cost}$$

Often when we measure economic surplus, we use a shortcut: If the demand curve corresponds with marginal benefits, and the supply curve corresponds with marginal costs, then economic surplus is the area between the demand and supply curves. We'll avoid that shortcut now, because market failure can make the demand curve a poor measure of marginal benefits, or it can make the supply curve a poor measure of marginal costs. And so in what follows, we'll focus directly on the marginal benefit and marginal cost curves. And because the economic surplus of any individual transaction is the difference between marginal benefit and marginal cost curves, the *economic surplus in the entire market is the area between the marginal benefit and marginal cost curves, out to the quantity.*

Producing less than the efficient quantity creates deadweight loss. Figure 7 returns to the strawberry market, but this time, there's a market failure, which means that the actual quantity of strawberries bought or sold—shown as the vertical line—is less than the efficient quantity. For now, we'll put aside the reason for this market failure—what matters is figuring out the consequences for economic surplus.

Start by measuring the economic surplus at the efficient quantity. To find the efficient quantity, follow the *Rational Rule for Markets*, which says to keep increasing the quantity until marginal cost equals marginal benefit. That is, the efficient quantity is where

Figure 7 | Underproduction Creates Deadweight Loss

Ⓐ Market failure leads the **actual quantity** produced to be less than the **efficient quantity**.

Ⓑ This yields **actual economic surplus** equal to the area below the marginal benefit curve and above the marginal cost curve, out to this actual quantity.

Ⓒ **Deadweight loss** shows how much greater economic surplus could have been, if the efficient quantity were produced.

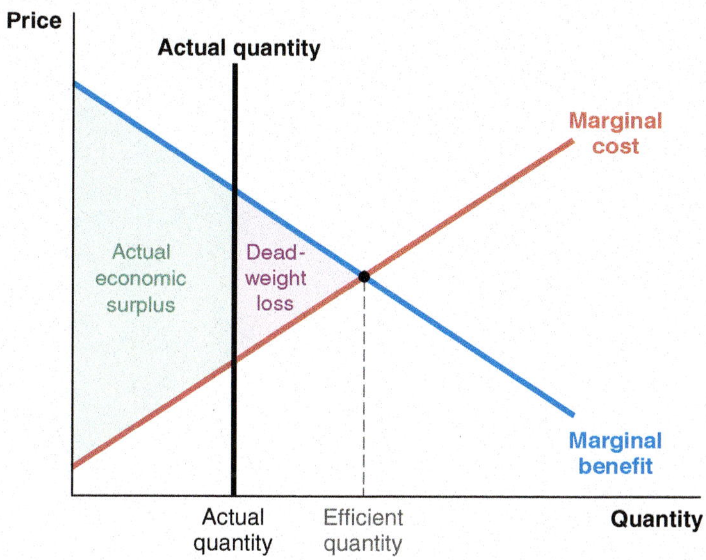

the marginal cost and marginal benefit curves cross. The corresponding economic surplus is the area between these curves, out to the efficient quantity. In Figure 7, it's the entire triangle—including both the green and purple parts—shaped like this one: . Because this is the efficient quantity, this is the largest possible economic surplus for this market.

Next, evaluate the economic surplus when market failure leads a smaller actual quantity to be sold. The corresponding economic surplus is the area between the marginal benefit and marginal cost curves, out to this smaller actual quantity. In Figure 7, it's the green trapezoid shaped like this one: .

Deadweight loss measures economic surplus lost due to this market failure, and so measures how far this actual economic surplus falls short of the larger economic surplus that occurs at the efficient quantity. As such, it's the lost economic surplus due to the actual quantity falling short of the efficient quantity—and this is shown as the smaller purple triangle shaped like this: . This deadweight loss triangle reflects the failure to execute potentially advantageous transactions, as increasing the quantity would yield marginal benefits that exceed marginal costs.

Finally, notice that the deadweight loss from underproduction is shaped like an arrowhead, pointing toward the efficient quantity.

Producing more than the efficient quantity also creates deadweight loss. Next, consider the possibility that a market failure leads to overproduction, with the actual quantity exceeding the efficient quantity. Again, we'll put aside the question of precisely what market failure causes this, but just note that the actual quantity is shown as a vertical line in Figure 8.

The efficient quantity, as before, is the quantity at which marginal cost and marginal benefit are equal. The corresponding economic surplus—which is the largest possible economic surplus—is shaded in orange, and looks like this triangle: .

But in this case, market failure leads a larger quantity to be produced. Notice that once production exceeds the efficient quantity, the marginal benefit of these extra strawberries is *less* than the marginal cost. That is, this extra production actually reduces economic

Figure 8 | **Overproduction Creates Deadweight Loss**

Ⓐ Market failure leads the **actual quantity** produced to be greater than **efficient quantity**.

Ⓑ The **largest possible economic surplus** is the area below the marginal benefit curve and above the marginal cost curve, out to the efficient quantity.

Ⓒ **Deadweight loss** shows how much economic surplus is destroyed by producing more than the efficient quantity.

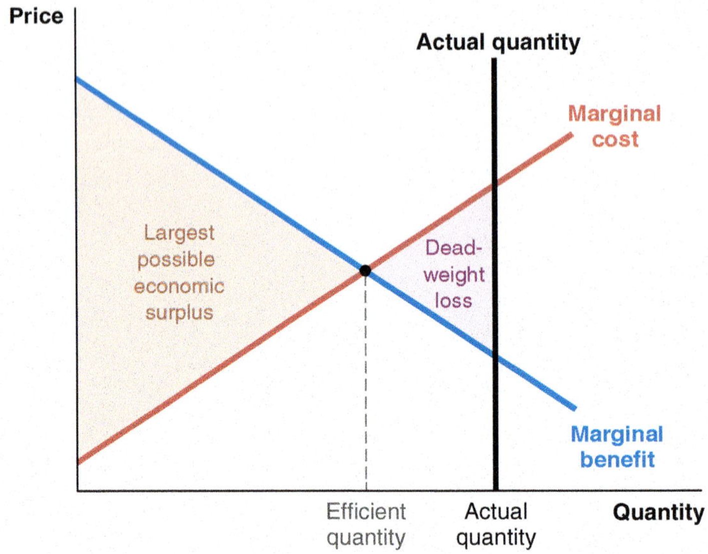

surplus. It's not that these strawberries are bad, it's that the extra cost to produce them exceeds the marginal benefits people derive from them.

These extra goods reduce economic surplus by an amount equal to the difference between their marginal costs and marginal benefits. Thus, the deadweight loss due to overproduction is the area between the marginal cost and marginal benefit curves, from the efficient quantity out to the actual quantity. It's the purple triangle shaped like this one: ◀.

Deadweight loss looks like an arrowhead pointed at the efficient quantity. Here's a simple trick that'll help you keep all this straight. Notice that when there's underproduction (as in Figure 7), the deadweight loss—which looks like this ▶—appears to be an arrowhead pointing at the efficient quantity. And when there's overproduction (as in Figure 8), the deadweight loss—which looks like this ◀—also appears to be an arrowhead pointing at the efficient quantity. In both cases, it appears as the arrowhead from the actual quantity, pointing to the efficient quantity. It's like the graph is trying to give you advice: The economy will do better if we move this way.

Quantities rather than prices are essential to measuring deadweight loss. Notice that we calculated deadweight loss based on the marginal cost and benefit curves, and the actual *quantity* produced. None of our calculations depended on what happened to the *price*. That is because deadweight loss measures the consequences of producing a *quantity* that's larger or smaller than the efficient quantity. Once the quantity has been determined, the *price* only redistributes economic surplus. For instance, a higher price for strawberries means that strawberry buyers pay more—which reduces their consumer surplus—but in equal measure, strawberry sellers receive more, which increases their producer surplus. The buyer's loss is the seller's gain, and the net effect is that total amount of economic surplus, which is shared by buyers and sellers, remains unchanged.

Bottom line: It's the quantity that determines the total amount of economic surplus, and hence the deadweight loss. You only need to analyse the price if you want to figure out whether it's buyers or sellers who enjoy that economic surplus.

Market Failure versus Government Failure

It's time to step back, to analyse what all this means for one of the biggest economic, political, and, indeed, philosophical debates of our time: How much of a role should market forces play in our society? And how much of a role is there for the government?

The efficiency of well-functioning markets points to the importance of market forces. We discovered that well-functioning competitive markets can do extraordinary things: They ensure that each good or service is produced by the business that can do so at the lowest possible marginal cost (that's the idea of *productive efficiency*), that each good goes to the person who'll get the highest marginal benefit from it (that's the idea of *allocative efficiency*), and that we'll produce the quantity of each good that yields the largest possible economic surplus (that is, the *efficient quantity*). All told, well-functioning markets lead to the *efficient outcome,* which means they produce the largest possible economic surplus. This finding is the most persuasive case for organising our society around markets.

Market failure points to an important role for government. While this sounds good in theory, the reality is that *market failure* is common. And that means that markets will produce somewhat worse outcomes than in the ideal case, yielding costly deadweight loss. That, in turn, provides a powerful argument for the government to play a role, because well-designed policies can limit market failure, yielding more efficient outcomes that reduce deadweight loss.

There's a lot of debate about how big that role should be. In some cases, government can improve things by helping organise and regulate markets. For example, food safety standards ensure that no one sells peanut butter tainted with salmonella. In others, it'll use taxes, subsidies, and quantity regulations to correct market failures. For example, the government taxes smoking and subsidises flu shots for the elderly. And sometimes the government will provide what the market can't—such as when the government provides national security and social welfare programs.

Government failure limits the extent to which we should rely on government. The existence of market failure doesn't necessarily suggest that government will do a better job. That's because of another problem, **government failure,** which exists when government policies lead to worse outcomes. Often this arises because politicians and bureaucrats make choices that aren't in the public interest.

government failure When government policies lead to worse outcomes.

Politicians are often motivated to make the choices that will improve their reelection chances, rather than those that'll improve efficiency or equity. That leads them to be overly responsive to voters who are politically organised and not to those who stay quiet. They're more responsive to those who give big campaign donations than to those who don't. And they'll often choose whatever's popular rather than what's right. The result is that government responses to existing market failures can actually make things worse.

The problem of government failure may be even worse in nondemocratic countries, where a royal family or a dictator doesn't need to worry that really bad policies will lead them to lose an election. As such, they're free to focus on enriching themselves and their cronies without facing any electoral consequences.

Government failure isn't just about politicians, as government bureaucrats also face incentives that may lead them to do things that are not in the public's interest. If the people who head government agencies want to expand their empires, they'll often wind up creating a sprawling and bloated bureaucracy that fails to provide efficient services. Some bureaucrats become too friendly with those they regulate, and start to act in the best interests of that industry, rather than the broader public. And poorly paid bureaucrats don't have much of an incentive to work hard, be efficient, or even make the best decisions.

The point is that just as market failure is pervasive, so is government failure. And that means that the question of whether our society would be better off with a greater emphasis on market forces versus a more forceful government comes down to whether the losses caused by market failure exceed those caused by government failure. On this score, there are no hard and fast rules, and your judgement likely varies across different policies, on different issues, in different markets, with different branches of government, and in different times and places.

7.5 Beyond Economic Efficiency

Learning Objective *Evaluate the limitations of economic efficiency in policy analysis.*

When you get involved in economic policy debates—advocating for one position or another—your arguments will move beyond purely positive analysis, to normative analysis. And that means that you need to figure out a way to assess whether one outcome is better than another.

One criteria that many economists use is that of *economic efficiency.* By this view, we should choose the outcome that yields the larger economic surplus. Even though this approach is common in economics, you may not find it entirely satisfying.

Critiques of Economic Efficiency

Focusing on economic efficiency can sound like a version of the argument that we should always choose the largest possible pie. While that might sound like it's a good idea, realise that it implicitly embeds some very strong value judgements that have led many people to criticise the focus given to economic efficiency. So before you decide whether to evaluate an economic policy on efficiency grounds, make sure you think through the following three critiques.

Critique one: Distribution matters, and so it's also important to account for equity. First, a focus on economic efficiency means trying to obtain the largest possible economic surplus, irrespective of who it goes to. But most people believe the *distribution* of economic benefits also matters. That's why in reality, most economists look beyond efficiency, and also analyse the **distributional consequences** of new policies—meaning who gets what—and assess whether that outcome seems fair or equitable. This critique says that it's not just the size of the pie that matters, but also how it's sliced.

distributional consequences Who gets what.

Critique two: Willingness to pay reflects ability to pay, not just marginal benefit. Recall that economic surplus is the marginal benefit, less the marginal cost. And so maximising economic surplus requires ensuring that each good goes to the person with the largest possible marginal benefit. So far, so good. But realise that economists often equate marginal benefits with your willingness to pay. So economic surplus is built on the idea that if you're willing to pay more for a slice of pie than I am, then we can infer that you derive a greater marginal benefit from that slice, and so you should get it.

But this raises what I call the Kim Kardashian problem. There's one slice of pie left, and you really want it—you love pie! Given that you love pie, you argue that it makes sense for you to get it. But Kardashian counters that it would be more efficient for her to get it. Let's do the math: You love pie, and so you're willing to pay up to $12 for that last slice, which is a lot of money for you. Kardashian is an incredibly wealthy celebrity. Even though she won't enjoy eating pie as much as you will, she's willing to pay $50 for the last slice—after all, she has so much money, why not spend it on pie? Economic surplus is built on the idea that Kardashian is right—the fact that she's willing to pay more than you are means that there's a greater economic surplus from her getting that last slice. The problem here is that how much you are willing to pay for pie partly reflects how much you like pie, and partly it reflects your ability to pay.

Chris Weeks/Getty Images

This is why she has a greater willingness to pay.

Critique three: The means matter, not just the ends. Economic efficiency is all about *outcomes.* But some people think that what matters more is the *process.* For instance, if you made the apple pie, perhaps you deserve a bigger slice. Or perhaps what matters more is equality of opportunity rather than outcomes. If everyone had a chance to make an apple pie, why should those who actually made pie be forced to share with others? Or perhaps what matters is the process by which you decided how to cut that apple pie: Was it democratic or dictatorial? Or perhaps you believe that everyone has a right to have some pie.

Whatever your beliefs, the point is that people don't always judge the desirability of an approach purely by the outcomes it creates. Often, the process matters, too. But judgements based on economic efficiency focus only on the consequences of a policy, and not on the process that led to that outcome.

Use economic efficiency cautiously. None of this is to say that you should ignore economic efficiency. Rather, that you should use it carefully, aided by a clear sense of precisely what it means. And so your normative analysis may involve analysing economic efficiency, but you might also choose to emphasise other ethical considerations, too.

Indeed, real-world policy debates typically reflect not only a technical evaluation of economic efficiency and deadweight loss, but also analysis of distributional and equity consequences, and broader notions of fairness. Few arguments are won just by describing what'll happen to economic surplus.

Tying It Together

It's time to pull all these threads together and return to the debate about whether the government should allow ride-sharing companies like Uber to operate. You'll see that the tools you've developed in this chapter provide a powerful lens for analysing public policies.

The first stage of our analysis involves positive analysis, asking: What *is* going to happen when we ban or when we allow Uber? That means analysing what'll happen to the employment and wages of both taxi drivers and of Uber drivers; assessing whether Uber has increased the total quantity of rides; evaluating how much people have to pay for a ride; and accounting for nonfinancial costs and benefits such as whether Uber has reduced the typical wait time to get a ride home. Careful analysis has found that wages and employment of taxi drivers have fallen; employment of Uber drivers has risen, and they enjoy more flexible work hours. The overall number of rides has risen, and wait times have fallen. Your positive analysis tells you who gains from ride-sharing (Uber drivers and their customers), and who loses (taxi drivers), and by how much.

Balancing these competing interests requires a normative analysis, which assesses which is the better outcome and what policy the government *should* adopt. You might start by asking whether economic surplus increased. You know the quantity of rides went up, but in order to assess whether total economic surplus rose or fell, you'll need to know why. The answer is that market failure, government failure, and technological change have all played a role in this rapidly shifting market.

Let's start with market failure. When taxis first started out, passengers didn't know whether their driver would be safe or reckless. Government responded by regulating taxis to ensure that only qualified drivers could offer rides. That made taxi licences valuable.

That sparked a form of government failure. Here's the problem: Existing taxis earn more when they face fewer competitors. And so taxi owners pressured the government to prevent new taxi drivers and new taxi companies from entering the market. Government officials relented, restricting the supply of taxis. This artificial restriction on supply led the quantity of rides to be less than the efficient quantity, creating deadweight loss.

Sometimes market forces work to undo the inefficiencies created by government failure. In this case, that's what Uber did. It's not technically a taxi company, and so it found a way to skirt these regulations. As a result, the entry of Uber increased the quantity of rides toward the efficient quantity, thereby raising economic surplus. Of course, Uber also adds to congestion on the road, so it's possible that there are now too many rides! In that case, economic surplus would be higher with some limitations on Uber.

Technological change also played an important role as ride-sharing apps provide efficient routing using GPS, they allow drivers to use a car that might otherwise sit in their driveway, and they permit drivers to flexibly schedule their shifts for when their opportunity costs are lowest. These changes all reduce the marginal cost of producing a ride. Lower marginal costs lead to a rise in the efficient quantity of rides. If there were no increase in the quantity supplied, this would have led to an even larger gap between the actual quantity and the efficient quantity of rides, creating even more deadweight loss.

All told, Uber likely increased the total amount of economic surplus and that's why many economists tend to view ride-sharing as a good outcome. However, economic surplus doesn't have to be your only criteria in a normative analysis. You might have concern about distributional effects of Uber or concerns about the fairness of undercutting the full-time profession of taxi drivers. Ultimately, your opinion will depend on how you value the gains to the winners relative to the losses for the losers. While reasonable people might bring different values to this discussion, weighing these costs and benefits differently, your analysis of economic surplus provides you with an important tool with which to begin crafting your view.

Chapter at a Glance

Evaluating Public Policies

Positive Analysis: Describes what **is** happening, explaining why, or predicting what will happen.
Normative Analysis: Prescribes what **should** happen, which involves value judgements.

Policies can be evaluated using the criteria of:

Economic Efficiency: An outcome is more economically efficient if it yields more Economic Surplus.

Equity: An outcome yields greater equity if it results in a fairer distribution of economic benefits.

Measuring Economic Surplus

Economic Surplus: The benefit of an action, less the cost. Economic surplus = Marginal benefit − Marginal cost	=	**Consumer Surplus:** The economic surplus you get from buying something. Consumer surplus = Marginal benefit − Price	+	**Producer Surplus:** The economic surplus you get from selling something. Producer surplus = Price − Marginal cost

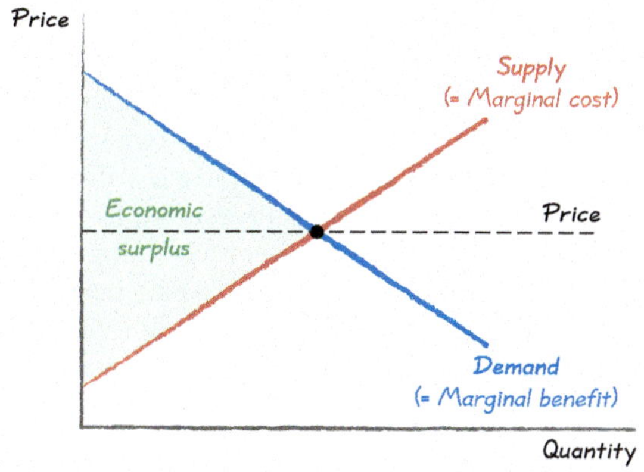

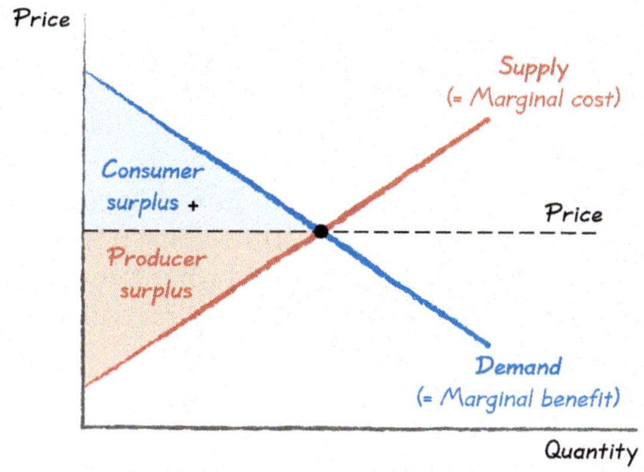

Market Efficiency

Efficient Outcome: The efficient outcome yields the largest possible Economic Surplus.
Markets create efficient outcomes by:

1. Efficient Production	**2. Efficient Allocation**	**3. Efficient Quantity**
Producing a given quantity of output at the lowest possible cost, which requires producing each good at the lowest marginal cost.	Allocating goods to create the largest Economic Surplus, which requires that each good goes to the person who'll get the highest marginal benefit from it.	The quantity that produces the largest possible Economic Surplus. **The Rational Rule for Markets:** Produce more of a good if its marginal benefit is greater than (or equal to) the marginal cost.

Measuring the Costs of Market Failure

Market failure: When the forces of supply and demand lead to an inefficient outcome.
Deadweight loss: How far Economic Surplus falls below the Efficient Outcome.
Deadweight loss = Economic surplus at efficient quantity − Actual economic surplus
Government failure: When government policies lead to worse outcomes.

Key Concepts

Discussion and Review Questions

Learning Objective 7.1 *Learn how to evaluate welfare and economic efficiency.*

1. Think of an important policy issue and provide an example of both a positive economic statement and a normative economic statement related to that policy.
2. If an outcome is economically efficient, does this mean that everybody involved benefits? Provide an example to briefly explain your reasoning.

Learning Objective 7.2 *Measure the economic surplus generated in a market.*

3. Think of something you've purchased in the last few days. How much consumer surplus did you get from the purchase? Use the Rational Rule for Buyers to explain why you purchased that quantity. How much producer surplus do you think the seller got and what is the total economic surplus? Use the Rational Rule for Sellers to explain why the seller sold the item to you.

Learning Objective 7.3 *Assess the efficiency of markets.*

4. There are dozens of laptop manufacturers around the world. Does the idea of efficient production mean that there should only be one laptop manufacturer making laptops at the lowest marginal cost?
5. Use the Rational Rule for Markets to explain why the equilibrium quantity in a market maximises the market's total economic surplus.

Learning Objective 7.4 *Measure the costs of market failure.*

6. Why do markets sometimes fail to generate efficient outcomes?
7. Can you think of any examples of markets that fail? Explain why that market failure does not mean that government control will necessarily lead to a better outcome.

Study Problems

Learning Objective 7.1 *Learn how to evaluate welfare and economic efficiency.*

1. Identify each of the following statements as either a positive statement or a normative statement:
   - **a.** Raising taxes on pollution emissions will result in some factories closing.
   - **b.** The federal government should tax pollution to address climate change.
   - **c.** An increase in the petrol excise will reduce the amount that people drive and therefore cause a reduction in air pollution.
   - **d.** If the federal income tax is increased, workers will decide to increase the number of hours they work each year.
2. Sean is a TAFE student and has been saving up money from his job waiting tables at a restaurant for weeks to see the musical *Hamilton*. He is willing to pay $255 for a ticket. Anca has seen *Hamilton* five times already, but wants to see it again before heading to Europe for a month. She is willing to pay $800 for a ticket. There is one ticket left, and the seller is charging $250. Does Sean or Anca buying the ticket lead to a more economically efficient outcome?

Learning Objective 7.2 *Measure the economic surplus generated in a market.*

3. You are planning a move across town. Doing your research you find that the average rate of a removalist company is $150 per hour for two removalists (van included). The marginal benefit you receive from each hour of the two removalists' time (and van) is listed in the accompanying table.

Hours of movers' time	Marginal benefit
1 hour	$500
2 hours	$380
3 hours	$300
4 hours	$150
5 hours	$100
6 hours	$50
7 hours	$0

   - **a.** For how many hours should you hire the removalists? How much consumer surplus do you receive?

b. Now suppose that instead of paying per hour, a removalist company offers a flat rate of $900 for two removalists plus a van for an eight-hour day. Would you hire the removalists? How has your consumer surplus changed?

4. If the weekly demand curve for petrol is as provided in the following graph, then how much consumer surplus would consumers receive if the market price for petrol was $1.40 per litre? What about for a price of $1.00 per litre?

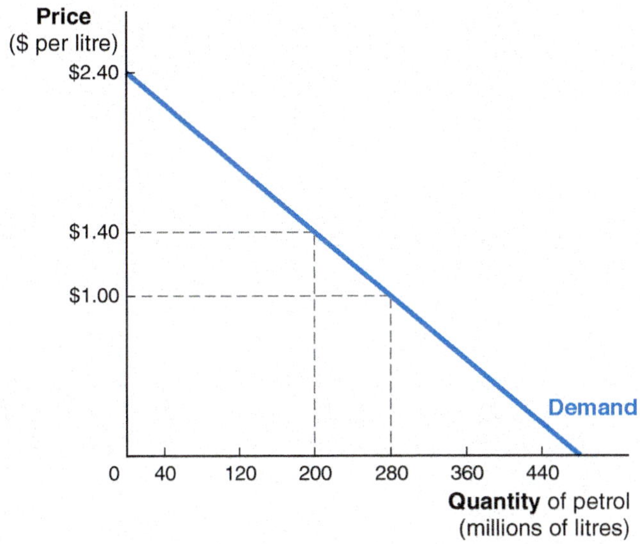

5. Last year the average price for an airline ticket was $400, but the average price dropped to $350 this year due to a decrease in the demand for flights. The accompanying table contains information on the supply of air travel.

Airfare (price per ticket)	Quantity supplied (millions of seats)
$0	0
$175	35
$350	70
$400	80
$575	115
$750	150

Draw the supply curve and use it to calculate producer surplus last year and producer surplus this year. How did producer surplus change?

Learning Objective 7.3 *Assess the efficiency of markets.*

6. Consider the market for Atlantic salmon. Petuna, Tasmania's smallest salmon farm, and Huon Aquaculture, a large corporate supplier, are both producers of Atlantic salmon. The marginal cost curves for both firms are shown in the accompanying graph.

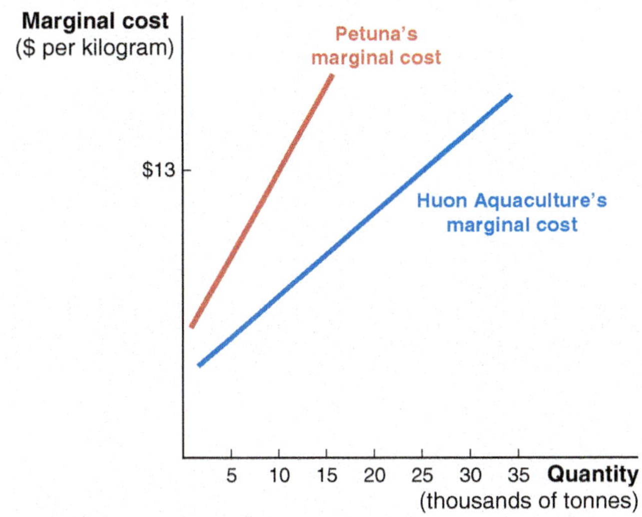

If the market price is $13 per kilo of salmon, how many kilos of salmon would Petuna supply? What about Huon Aquaculture? How many total kilos would they collectively supply? Is this allocation the most productively efficient way to produce this quantity of salmon?

7. Now, consider two people in the market for Atlantic salmon, Reagan and Cheryl. The marginal benefit curves for both individuals are shown in the accompanying graph.

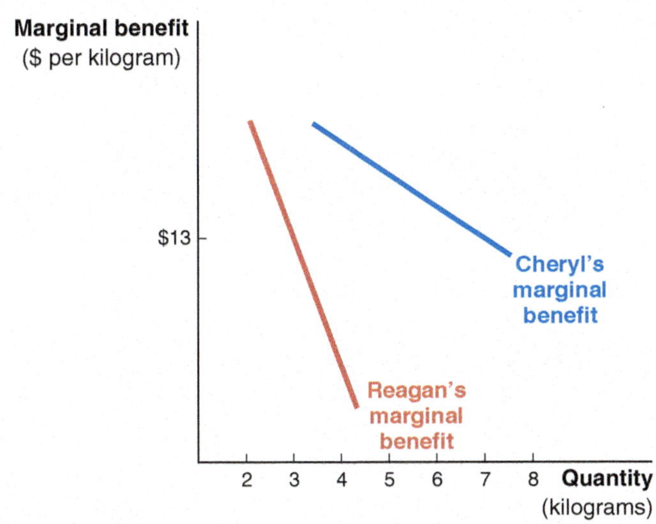

If the market price is $13 per kilo of salmon. How many kilos would Reagan purchase? How many kilos would Cheryl? How many total kilos will they collectively purchase? Is this allocation the most allocatively efficient way to distribute this quantity of Atlantic salmon?

8. Fei, Morgan, and Lakesha are all in the market for new Levi's jeans. The marginal benefit for each pair of jeans per year for each of them is provided in the following table:

Quantity	Fei	Morgan	Lakesha
1	$170	$80	$180
2	$120	$64	$150
3	$64	$48	$110
4	$40	$32	$64
5	$30	$16	$50

If a pair of Levi's jeans is on sale for $64, how many pairs of jeans will each person purchase? How much consumer surplus does each of them receive from the last pair of jeans purchased? How much consumer surplus will each of them receive for each of the pairs they buy at a price of $64? How much do they receive collectively?

Learning Objective 7.4 *Measure the costs of market failure.*

9. A study done by University of Minnesota economist, Joel Waldfogel, estimated the difference in the actual monetary value of gifts received and how much the recipient would have been willing to pay to buy them on their own. The results suggested that the average receiver's valuation was approximately 90% of the actual purchase price.
   a. In 2018, it was estimated that the average amount spent on Christmas gifts in Australia was $1,325. Based on the estimate from the Waldfogel study, how much of this would be considered a deadweight loss?
   b. In 2018, there were approximately 19 million people in Australia above the age of 18. Assuming that each individual purchased $1,325 worth of gifts, what is the size of the total deadweight loss associated with gift giving in Australia?

10. Consider the national market for child care in the accompanying graph.

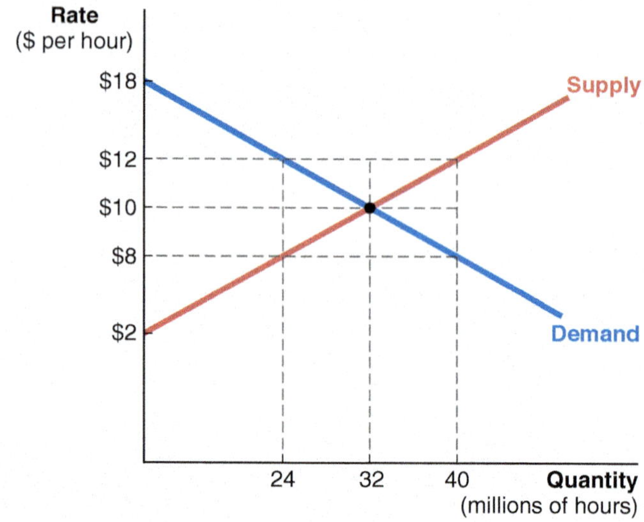

   a. At 32 million hours, what is the size of total economic surplus in this market? Label the area representing total economic surplus on the graph.
   b. At 24 million hours, what is the size of total economic surplus in this market? Label the area representing total economic surplus on the graph.
   c. Is total economic surplus at 24 million hours larger or smaller than at 32 million hours? Label the area on the graph representing the difference in economic surplus. What is this area called?
   d. Between 24 million hours and 32 million hours, which of the following is true? The marginal benefit to households exceeds the marginal cost to child care providers or the marginal cost to child care providers exceeds the marginal benefit to households.
   e. Repeat parts b–d for 40 million hours instead of 24 million hours.
   f. What is the efficient quantity of hours in this market?

CHAPTER 8

Comparative Advantage and Gains from Trade

Why stay in a hotel when you can rent someone's treehouse for the weekend?

Luciana Rinaldi/Shutterstock

Airbnb has done something extraordinary. If you've got a spare room, or if you're not using your house for a weekend, you can post a few photos on their website, and with any luck, you'll find someone who wants to rent it. And if you're travelling, you can find a vast array of bedrooms, houses, and even houseboats, castles, and treehouses to rent.

All those spare rooms and houses always existed, but they weren't previously being supplied to a rental market. Airbnb has persuaded homeowners to become suppliers in a new market for short-term accommodation. Similarly, travellers have always visited new cities, but they used to stay in hotels. Airbnb has also convinced travellers to forgo hotels to become buyers in the market for short-term accomodation in people's homes. By creating a new market, Airbnb has created new possibilities.

As a result, there are honeymooners staying in a castle in the French countryside, tourists staying on a sugarcane farm near Cairns, a family enjoying a week in a treehouse, and a 20-something at a conference staying with two baristas in Melbourne. None of these people knew each other last week, yet today they're sending each other money and staying in each other's homes. And they're all enjoying gains from trade: The travellers gain an interesting place to stay, and their hosts gain a welcome boost to their incomes.

The true star of this story is not Airbnb's management, but the market that Airbnb has created. It brings together different people, in different places, each with different needs and different assets. The market coordinates all of this activity, allocating the honeymooners to the castle and the family to the treehouse.

This story is not unique. Far from it. Markets are everywhere. You interact with them so often that sometimes you forget how pervasive they are. Indeed, markets are arguably the dominant force organising our lives today.

And so in this chapter, we ask: What do markets do for us? The key idea is that markets are all about harvesting the gains from trade that make each of us better off. We'll begin by describing gains from trade. Then we'll see how comparative advantage generates these gains. And finally, we'll explore the key role that prices play in coordinating economic activity, and how managers can harness market forces to make better choices. Let's get started.

Chapter Objective

Learn how markets generate gains from trade.

8.1 Gains from Trade
Understand the role of markets in reallocating resources to better uses.

8.2 Comparative Advantage
Use comparative advantage to allocate tasks to those with the lowest opportunity cost.

8.3 Prices Are Signals, Incentives, and Information
Understand the role that prices play in coordinating economic activity.

8.4 How Managers Can Harness Market Forces
Be ready to harness market forces in your own life.

8.1 Gains from Trade

Learning Objective *Understand the role of markets in reallocating resources to better uses.*

gains from trade The benefits that come from reallocating resources, goods, and services to better uses.

What exactly is it that markets do? Here's the big idea. You have some stuff. Other people have other stuff. They want some of your stuff more than you do. You want some of their stuff more than they do. So you swap some of your stuff for some of their stuff. Hey, presto! You're both better off, because now you both have stuff you want more. These benefits you get from reallocating stuff to its better uses are called the **gains from trade.**

And that's what markets do: They reallocate stuff—resources, goods, and services—to better uses, generating gains from trade. That's it. It's a simple idea, but it's also amazingly powerful.

Obviously I've simplified, so let's connect the dots a bit more. Of course you don't directly trade your stuff for someone else's. Instead, you buy and sell goods and services using money. But money is just a convenience that allows you to engage in more complicated trades. When you sell an hour of your labour to your employer for $20, and then use that $20 to buy food, you've effectively traded your time for food. You gain from this trade because you want that food more than you want another hour of time to do something else. In fact, everyone gains. Your employer gains because the work you did for them boosted their profits and now they can buy more stuff, just as the grocery store owner that sold you the food also gains, because they can spend your $20 to buy goods that they value more highly.

When I say that markets allocate "stuff," think about that idea broadly—they allocate all sorts of resources, goods, and services, including time. When people buy and sell their labour, they're using markets to allocate people to tasks and tasks to people. Let's explore this idea a bit further, as we turn our attention to how markets create gains from trade by effectively allocating tasks. We'll start with a simple but delicious task: cooking dinner.

8.2 Comparative Advantage

Learning Objective *Use comparative advantage to allocate tasks to those with the lowest opportunity cost.*

Should you cook dinner tonight, or should your roommate? It's a seemingly small decision, and the stakes are pretty low. But you'll have to make this decision at dinner time for a lot of the days in your life. That makes the stakes (or should I say steaks) seem a bit higher. And you don't just have to figure out who'll cook. Every day, you make dozens of other decisions, deciding who should clean the house, shop for groceries, or pay the bills. The underlying question in each case is the same: How best to allocate these tasks?

When you go to work as a manager, you'll face similar questions. How do you divide tasks among team members? Who should be in charge of organising meetings and ensuring the team meets deadlines? Who should be in charge of getting feedback from other divisions? Who should give the big presentation to a client? These management questions are the same ones you face as a household manager: How best to allocate these tasks?

Now think about the whole economy. There are literally billions of tasks performed in all sorts of organisations across Australia. Each task could be performed by any one of millions of workers who each have different skills, and in some instances, the task could also be completed by a machine. The economic management question facing the country is similar to the question you confront as the manager of your company or your household: How best to allocate these tasks?

Whether you're responsible for running your household, your company, or the whole economy, you'll need to figure out how best to allocate different tasks. Whatever task you're thinking about, you'll want to get it done at the lowest possible cost (if the work is of the same quality). As such, your goal should be to allocate each task to the lowest-cost producer. There's one big idea that can help you do this: comparative advantage.

Introducing Comparative Advantage

Let's start with a simple case, analysing how two roommates, Helen and Jamie, should allocate tasks around their home. It's a pretty stylised example, but stick with me, because it'll yield an insight that applies equally well whether you're the manager of your household, your company, or the economy.

Helen and Jamie want to figure out how best to assign their household tasks. For now, we'll focus on just two tasks, cooking and vacuuming. Like good economists, they start with the data:

- Helen says that she can vacuum their house in four hours, or she can make a meal in two hours.
- Jamie says that vacuuming their house also takes him four hours, but it takes him only one hour to make a meal.

So how should they assign these tasks?

Absolute advantage tells you who's best at a task, but not who should do the task. Before I tell you how Helen wants to allocate tasks, let's look closely at her argument. Helen argues that Jamie should do both the cooking and the vacuuming because he is better at all household chores than her. After all, Jamie can make meals in less time than she can, and she's no faster at vacuuming. *If* we measured costs in terms of time spent, she's got a point—each chore costs Jamie less or equal time than it costs Helen. Helen's argument is based on the idea that economists call **absolute advantage,** which is the ability of one person to do a task using fewer inputs than someone else.

absolute advantage The ability to do a task using fewer inputs.

But Helen's conclusion is flawed because she's not thinking about opportunity costs.

Comparative advantage is all about opportunity cost. The *opportunity cost principle* reminds you that the true cost of something is what you must give up to get it. To figure out the true cost of Helen or Jamie vacuuming the house, you need to ask, "Or what?" Jamie can vacuum the house, *or* spend that time making meals. That's why the opportunity cost of Jamie vacuuming is the number of meals he could have otherwise cooked. Likewise, if Helen vacuums the house, the opportunity cost is the number of meals she could otherwise have made. You should focus on opportunity cost because you want to minimise what you have to give up to get the task done—which is what opportunity cost measures.

To get the most output with your given inputs, you should allocate each task to the person with the lowest opportunity cost. That's such an important point that I'm going to say it again: You should allocate each task to the person who can do it at the lowest opportunity cost. This seemingly straightforward idea is so important that economists have a specific term for it: The person with the lower opportunity cost of completing a particular task has a **comparative advantage** at that task. It's *comparative* because opportunity cost *compares* what you can produce if assigned one task with what you would produce if you spent that time on another task. And it's an *advantage,* because a lower opportunity cost means that you give up less to get a task done and so it's more efficient for you to do that task.

comparative advantage The ability to do a task at a lower opportunity cost.

When each person in a group—a household, a business or the economy—focuses on the task for which they have a comparative advantage, the group will produce more. This larger economic pie is due to the gains from trade from reallocating or trading tasks. If Helen and Jamie want to produce more—or if they want more free time—they should assign the vacuuming to whoever has a comparative advantage in vacuuming, and whoever has a comparative advantage in cooking should cook. And so we now turn to asking: Who has a comparative advantage in each task?

Calculate the opportunity cost of each task. The top panel of Figure 1 shows how long it takes Jamie or Helen to vacuum the house, or produce one meal. But to find out who has a comparative advantage in vacuuming, you'll need to focus instead on *opportunity costs.* The opportunity cost of doing a task is the output you could produce in your next best alternative task. You can calculate it as follows:

$$\text{Opportunity cost of a task} = \frac{\text{Hours this task takes}}{\text{Hours required to produce alternative output}}$$

Figure 1 | Evaluating Opportunity Costs

Productivity: *How long does it take to:*

	Vacuum the house	Produce one meal
Jamie	4 hours	1 hour
Helen	4 hours	2 hours

↓

Evaluate the opportunity cost: *What does each person forgo to:*

	Vacuum the house	Produce one meal
Jamie	4 meals	Vacuuming $\frac{1}{4}$ of the house
Helen	2 meals	Vacuuming $\frac{1}{2}$ of the house

The opportunity cost of vacuuming the house is lower for Helen	The opportunity cost of producing a meal is lower for Jamie
↓	↓
Helen has a comparative advantage in vacuuming	Jamie has a comparative advantage in producing meals

You can see this formula in action, as follows:

- Jamie takes four hours to vacuum the house, but if he spent that time cooking instead, he would have four more hours to devote to cooking, during which he would produce one meal per hour. And so for Jamie, vacuuming the house comes at an opportunity cost of 4 hours/1 hour per meal = 4 meals.
- Helen takes four hours to vacuum the house, but if she spent that time cooking instead, she would have four more hours to devote to cooking, during which she would produce a meal every two hours. Thus, for Helen, vacuuming the house comes at an opportunity cost of 4 hours/2 hours per meal = 2 meals.

The lower panel of Figure 1 shifts the focus from the rate of production to opportunity costs. The left column shows the opportunity cost for each person of vacuuming the house, in terms of meals they could make instead. Comparing Helen's and Jamie's opportunity costs reveals that Helen has a comparative advantage at vacuuming, because vacuuming the house costs her fewer forgone meals than if Jamie were to do the job. (The opportunity cost of vacuuming the house is only two meals for Helen, versus four meals for Jamie.)

Okay, so now let's figure out who has a comparative advantage in cooking, by seeing who can make a meal at the lowest opportunity cost:

- Jamie takes only an hour to make a meal, but if he spent that time cleaning instead, he would have one more hour to vacuum at a rate of one house every four hours. Thus for Jamie, one meal comes at an opportunity cost of vacuuming 1 hour/4 hours per house = ¼ of the house.
- Helen takes two hours to make a meal, but if she spent that time cleaning instead, she would have two more hours to vacuum at a rate of one house every four hours. Thus, for Helen, one meal comes at an opportunity cost of vacuuming 2 hours/4 hours per house = ½ of the house.

Comparing these (in the right column) reveals that Jamie has a comparative advantage at producing meals because each meal costs him less in forgone vacuuming than it costs Helen (the opportunity cost of producing another meal is that Jamie won't vacuum only one-quarter of the house, compared with half the house for Helen).

Everyone has a comparative advantage. Notice that, in an absolute sense, Helen is better at neither cooking nor vacuuming than Jamie. That is, Helen lacks an absolute advantage at any task. But even though Helen isn't better at any household task, she can still help her household produce more. After all, her household is better off assigning her to some task than to nothing at all. That's why the *opportunity cost principle* is so central here—it ensures that you think about all of the possible uses of Helen's time. And it shows that Helen will make the biggest contribution if she's assigned to the task that she's least bad at relative to Jamie.

It's often most intuitive to think of comparative advantage in exactly these terms: You have a comparative advantage in the task that you're least bad at. Everyone has a comparative advantage in something, even if they don't have an absolute advantage in anything, because everyone must be least bad at something as long as people have different opportunity costs.

A three-step recipe identifies who has a comparative advantage in each task. You're going to want to identify who has a comparative advantage in other situations, so let's take a step back and walk through the three steps we've followed:

Step one: Determine how long each task would take each person (as in the top panel of Figure 1). This measures the cost of producing each good, *in hours.*

Step two: Convert this into a measure of *opportunity cost,* by calculating how much of the alternative good you could have produced in that time.

Step three: Evaluate who has a *comparative advantage* at each task by assessing who can produce each good at the lowest opportunity cost.

You can use this three-step recipe to identify comparative advantage in any domain.

Do the Economics

Amanda and Zara are partners in a small suburban law office. They have to decide how to assign the work that they're getting. Amanda can write a will in three hours, or an employment contract in six hours. Zara is slower, and it takes her nine hours to write a will, and nine hours to write an employment contract.

Step one: Measure the cost of producing each good *in hours.*

Productivity: *How long does it take to:*

	Write a will	Write an employment contract
Amanda	3 hours	6 hours
Zara	9 hours	9 hours

Step two: Calculate the *opportunity cost* of producing each good.

a. Evaluate the opportunity cost for Amanda and Zara to produce a will. (Hint: You're making comparisons *across* tasks, so you compute it by comparing numbers *across* a row.)

b. Evaluate the opportunity cost for Amanda and Zara to produce an employment contract.

Evaluate the opportunity cost: *What does each forgo to:*

	Write a will	Write an employment contract
Amanda	A will takes Amanda 3 hours, and in that time she could otherwise write ___ employment contracts	An employment contract takes Amanda 6 hours, and in that time she could otherwise write ___ wills
Zara	A will takes Zara 9 hours, and in that time she could otherwise write ___ employment contracts	An employment contract takes Zara 9 hours, and in that time she could otherwise write ___ wills

Answer: a. Amanda: ½, Zara: 1; b. Amanda: 2, Zara: 1; c. Amanda; d. Zara

Step three: Evaluate who has a *comparative advantage* by assessing who has the lowest opportunity cost for each task.

c. Who has a comparative advantage in writing wills? (Hint: You're trying to figure out who's *down* for the task, so look *down* that column to find who has the lowest opportunity cost.)

d. Who has a comparative advantage in writing employment contracts? ■

Rearranging who does what creates more stuff. There's a big payoff from thinking in terms of comparative advantage: Simply by rearranging who does what, *you can produce more stuff with the same inputs.* All you need to do is reallocate the tasks so that we each do more of those tasks where we each hold a comparative advantage, and less of the other tasks.

This logic says that Jamie should reallocate time from vacuuming to cooking, and Helen should reallocate time from cooking to vacuuming. Figure 2 illustrates what'll happen if they follow this advice.

Figure 2 | Gains from Trade Due to Comparative Advantage

Reallocate *tasks* according to comparative advantage to increase output

If Helen and Jamie each reallocate four more hours per week to their comparative advantage (and four fewer hours to the other task) . . .

	Vacuuming	Meals produced
Jamie	*4 fewer hours vacuuming* → House gets vacuumed 1 fewer time	*4 more hours cooking* → 4 more meals
Helen	*4 more hours vacuuming* → House gets vacuumed 1 more time	*4 fewer hours cooking* → 2 fewer meals
Total	House still gets vacuumed as often	2 more meals each week

In this example, Jamie reallocates four hours each week from vacuuming to cooking, which will mean the house gets vacuumed one fewer time, but he'll make four more meals per week. And if Helen reallocates four hours each week from making meals to vacuuming, she'll produce two fewer meals per week, but she'll make sure the house gets vacuumed one more time. Add it up, and as the bottom row shows, their household now produces two extra meals each week and the house still gets vacuumed. Specialising according to comparative advantage has made both Helen and Jamie better off—there are two more nights each week when they'll eat at home, rather than having to pay for a takeaway.

Where do these extra meals come from? It's not from working harder—Helen and Jamie are simply reallocating the tasks each does around the house, and so neither of them is working longer hours on household chores. And in this example, it's not that they're each getting better at the tasks they've been assigned (although that could also happen). Rather, this extra stuff is the dividend from rearranging their household tasks according to comparative advantage. That's the power of comparative advantage: By ensuring each task is done at the lowest opportunity cost, you produce more in the same amount of time.

This extra output is called the gains from *trade,* because Helen can only get her meals made at the lowest opportunity cost by trading tasks with Jamie, and Jamie can only get the vacuuming done at the lowest opportunity cost by trading tasks with Helen.

specialisation Focusing on specific tasks.

Trading allows people to reallocate tasks so that more output is produced with a lower opportunity cost. And this leads to **specialisation** in which people focus on specific tasks, spending more of their time on what they're relatively good at, and less of their time doing other stuff.

Comparative Advantage in Action

Don't get lost in the details. Instead, focus on the big idea here, which is that you can produce more if you use comparative advantage to assign tasks. You should assign each task to the person who can do it at the lowest opportunity cost. This is an idea that you can apply well beyond the simple examples we've explored so far.

Use comparative advantage to assign workers to tasks. Shrewd managers use comparative advantage to figure out how to assign their workers to different jobs:

- Your dentist probably doesn't clean your teeth or take your X-rays. Instead, most dentists allocate these tasks to their hygienist, which frees them up to do more complicated (and expensive!) procedures on another patient.
- Your pet's veterinarian probably leaves nail trimming to an assistant, so they can focus their time on medical exams and treatment.
- Senior lawyers rarely draft legal motions. Instead, they assign those tasks to junior lawyers or paralegals, which frees up the senior lawyer to do the more profitable work of having fancy lunches in order to get more clients.
- Your hairdresser probably doesn't wash your hair. Instead, hairdressers typically allocate that task to an assistant, so that they can do more high-paying tints, highlights, or colouring jobs.
- Chef Shannon Bennett is the best cook in his kitchen at the famed Vue de Monde in Melbourne—but that doesn't mean he does the cooking. A restaurateur and executive chef, Bennett's time is best spent overseeing his business: working with local vendors, planning menus, creating new dishes, and training staff on how to prepare them.

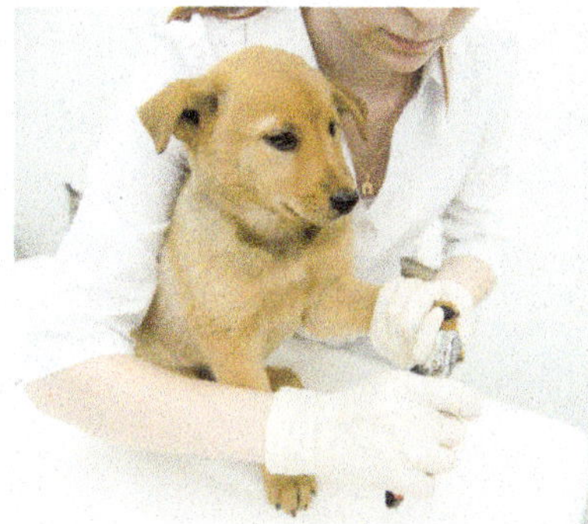
Ermolaev Alexander/Shutterstock

While both your vet and their assistant know how to trim your puppy's nails, only one of them has a comparative advantage.

In each case, the idea is that you should delegate tasks whenever you can delegate them to someone with a lower opportunity cost. And the upside is that it'll free you up to spend more time on those tasks where you hold a comparative advantage.

EVERYDAY Economics **Should the best drummer play the drums?**

It's been reported that when John Lennon was asked "Is Ringo Starr the best drummer in the world?" he responded that "he's not the best drummer in The Beatles!" He may be right because their bassist, Paul McCartney, was also a superb drummer. And this makes me think that The Beatles were also savvy economists, using comparative advantage to assign tasks. After all, if the opportunity cost of having McCartney play drums was losing him as a bass guitarist, that's too high a price to pay. Comparative advantage says that you don't necessarily want the best drummer playing drums, because you also need to think about their opportunity cost. ■

Ron Howard/Redferns/Getty Images

"He's not the best drummer in The Beatles."

Markets Facilitate Gains from Trade

So far we've found that Helen and Jamie are both better off—they produce more—if they hold a household meeting and divvy up their household tasks according to comparative advantage. But this simple story points to a broader lesson that extends well beyond assigning tasks to your roommates.

Markets offer the opportunity to specialise according to comparative advantage. Even if Helen and Jamie are no longer roommates, the logic of comparative advantage still applies. This logic says that they'll both be better off if each task is assigned to the person who can do it at the lowest opportunity cost. That might mean that Helen occasionally drops by Jamie's house to vacuum, and Jamie repays the favour by sending Helen home with some of his pre-prepared meals. As we've seen, trading tasks like this makes them both better off.

This logic also works even if Helen and Jamie don't know each other. And this is where markets come in: Markets help strangers exploit the gains from trade that come from specialising according to comparative advantage. After all, the logic of comparative advantage tells Helen to do more of the tasks where her opportunity cost is low, and to rely on others for tasks where she has a higher opportunity cost. That logic will lead her to start a company that'll vacuum people's living rooms for them. And when she's hungry, she'll use some of her profits to buy food from someone who can make delicious meals at a lower opportunity cost than she can. Who knows, she may even buy meals made by some guy called Jamie.

Likewise, the logic of comparative advantage tells Jamie to do more of those tasks where his opportunity cost is low, and rely on others for tasks where he has a high opportunity cost. That's why he'll partner with a delivery network to sell his favourite recipes to people too busy to do elaborate food prep. And when his floors get dirty, he'll see if there's a business that can get his vacuuming done. He might even end up a customer of his old friend Helen.

The gains from trade are just as great in this market-based exchange as they are when Helen and Jamie are roommates. And the incentive to do this is just as great, because when Helen and Jamie each focus on those tasks where they hold a comparative advantage, together they get more done. That is, there are gains from trade.

Comparative advantage explains why there are gains from trade in markets. Indeed, our simple story is an abridged version of a real-world business success story, in which Helen is Helen Greiner. As an undergraduate student she was so inspired by R2-D2 in *Star Wars* that she focused her studies on robotics and artificial intelligence. It led her to start the company iRobot, which makes the Roomba, a $500 robot that'll vacuum your house for you. Helen's robots are so efficient that they can vacuum your home at a lower opportunity cost than you can. And even though you don't know Helen, you can still trade with her. Pay her company $500, and in return the robot she helped invent will do your vacuuming, allowing you to spend the hours you save on those tasks where you have a comparative advantage.

David Paul Morris/Bloomberg/Getty Images

Helen Greiner, co-founder of iRobot Corp.

Likewise, Jamie is a stand-in for Jamie Oliver, the British celebrity cook sometimes known as "The Naked Chef." He, too, is specialising in tasks where he holds a comparative advantage. In 2015, he partnered with HelloFresh, a service that delivers recipes and all necessary ingredients directly to your door, so you can enjoy preparing delicious meals without having to do the meal planning and food shopping. Even though you don't know Jamie, for a reasonable weekly fee, he'll send you his meal kits, saving you time that you can spend on activities where you hold a comparative advantage.

The beauty of all this is that markets allow you to trade tasks with both Helen and Jamie, so that you can spend less time on tasks like cleaning and cooking where your opportunity cost is high, and more time on tasks where you hold a comparative advantage. And because each task—vacuuming the living room, making dinner, and studying economics—is being done at its lowest possible opportunity cost, you're each better off. The big idea here is that people following their comparative advantage creates gains from trade.

Axel Heimken/picture-alliance/dpa/AP Images

Jamie Oliver, celebrity chef.

Comparative advantage explains why people specialise. And so this simple story about Helen and Jamie is not just about two happy roommates. Rather, it's a metaphor for the entire economy. It's a metaphor that explains why each of us specialises in the specific tasks for which we hold a comparative advantage—those with leadership skills work as managers, number-crunchers work as business analysts, and empathetic people work in human resources. Each of us uses the money we make to buy stuff that's made by people who have a comparative advantage in those tasks—buying cars designed by skilled engineers, restaurant meals from expert chefs, and education from dedicated teachers.

In turn, all of this comparative advantage-driven specialisation ensures that each product is made at the lowest opportunity cost, which ensures there are gains from all this trade.

Do more of what you're relatively good at, and less of the other stuff. Comparative advantage boils down to one key piece of advice: Do more of what you're *relatively* good at, and less of the other stuff. This simple advice explains why:

- It pays to get your shirts professionally pressed: The opportunity cost of wrestling with an iron is time you could spend working toward your next promotion.
- Few executives make their own lunch: The opportunity cost of spending 10 minutes making a sandwich is simply too high when you have an empire to run.
- Busy families buy pre-cut vegetables: The opportunity cost of chopping vegetables is time busy parents could spend with their kids.
- Politicians let lobbyists draft bills for them: The opportunity cost of drafting legislation is time that an ambitious politician can spend wooing voters.
- Actors don't do their own stunts: Even though no one is tougher than Dwayne "The Rock" Johnson, he doesn't do his own stunts, because the opportunity cost of The Rock breaking a bone is much greater than it is for his cousin, Tanoai Reed, who works as his stunt double.
- AirTasker is so successful: If you're busy, you can't afford the time to assemble your new Ikea furniture. But through AirTasker, you can find someone who has a comparative advantage in building furniture, and hire them to do it for you.

s_bukley/Newscom

Only one of them is Dwayne Johnson. The other has a lower opportunity cost of stunt work.

In each of these cases, the market plays an important role in helping people focus on the tasks for which they have a comparative advantage: It provides you with pressed shirts, a busy executive with lunch, a harried family with pre-cut vegetables, politicians with pre-written bills, actors with stunt doubles, and someone to build your Ikea furniture for you. The time and energy you save on tasks other people do is time you can allocate to tasks for which you do have a comparative advantage.

Interpreting the DATA: How shifting comparative advantage explains changes in family life

Comparative advantage can explain some of the most important social changes of the past century, including the changing nature of work, families, and relationships. Let me explain.

Most couples have two broad sets of tasks to manage: the task of earning money, and housework. Historically, housework was a full-time job, and the opportunity cost of doing this work was the forgone earnings from not pursuing a career. Comparative advantage suggests that whether the couple assigns the housework to the man or the woman depends on who can do it at the lowest opportunity cost.

Back in your grandparents' day, discrimination kept women's wages down. As a result, each hour of housework came with a lower opportunity cost for your grandmother than for your grandfather, because it meant forgoing an hour of low-paid work. That's why so many women of that era were homemakers, while their husbands pursued their careers.

As the twentieth century progressed, social and economic changes led more women to go to university. More education led to higher potential wages for women, increasing the opportunity cost of staying home. As the logic of comparative advantage suggests, this led more women to enter the workforce.

What happened to housework, then? A parallel development—the invention of new household appliances—led families to reorganise their domestic priorities. Here's why: Your washing machine has a comparative advantage at laundry, your dishwasher has a comparative advantage at washing dishes, and the Roomba has a comparative advantage at vacuuming. Your microwave oven means that industrial kitchens can churn out easily reheated meals at a lower opportunity cost than any homemaker. As a result, your parents' generation does a lot less housework than their parents did, because they employ a small army of domestic robots to wash, clean, and cook, instead. Your generation will do even less, as online services make it easier for you to outsource and automate chores like paying your bills.

In turn, these robots mean that the opportunity cost of pursuing a career has fallen—the housework will still get done!—and so in many more households today, both parents work. They're following the dictates of comparative advantage, doing what they're relatively good at—working in their job—and relying on others (including domestic robots!) to do the other stuff. ■

Oleksiy Maksymenko Photography/Alamy

The Roomba: Helping people worldwide focus on their comparative advantage.

Comparative Advantage Drives International Trade

Comparative advantage explains how you benefit from specialising in some tasks and trading with others. This also means that comparative advantage explains why we trade with people who live in other countries, and hence it explains *international trade.*

To see why, let's return to the story of Helen and Jamie. We began this chapter by analysing a simple example of two roommates who'll both be better off if they trade tasks. As we discovered, they're both better off when Helen takes more responsibility for vacuuming the house, and Jamie does more of the cooking. The same logic applies to the real-world Helen Greiner and Jamie Oliver. In the real world it means that Helen will buy tasty meals designed by Jamie, by purchasing them from HelloFresh. And Jamie will buy a Roomba designed by Helen, to vacuum his house. These choices are driven by the now-familiar logic that says trading—either trading tasks in a household, or trading meals for robots in the market—enables Helen and Jamie to get their cooking and cleaning done at the lowest opportunity cost.

We trade with foreigners for the same reason we trade with locals. Now let's add one more wrinkle: Helen Greiner is American, while Jamie Oliver is British. When Jamie buys a Roomba, it's an export from an American firm to a British buyer. And if Helen buys one of Jamie's meal kits, it's an export from a British-German partnership (Jamie is British; HelloFresh is German) to an American. This international trade between an American and a Brit makes them both better off, creating gains from trade.

By this telling, the gains from trade created by comparative advantage are the reason for international trade. Those gains from trade are an incentive for people all around the world to focus on what they're best at, and rely on others for the other stuff. And the result will be that tasks will be allocated to the people who can do them at the lowest opportunity cost—even when that person happens to live overseas. We'll study international trade in greater depth in Chapter 9. But even now it should be clear that when comparative advantage drives you to trade with someone—and even if that person is living overseas—you'll both end up better off.

EVERYDAY Economics **The international trade controversy in my life**

I used to do my own taxes every July. But then I got offered the chance to teach an executive education course at an overseas university. So I switched from spending a week in July doing my taxes to teaching executive education, and I hired a tax accountant. Financially, I was better off, because I paid the accountant less than I was paid for teaching my course. And the accountant was happy to have an additional client. By my telling, this is comparative advantage creating gains from trade.

Now think about how this might play out in terms of the politics of international trade. To do so, you'll have to allow me to declare myself to be an independent country. Let's call it the Republic of Nerdonia, population one.

Critics of international trade will argue that it has wrought extraordinary havoc upon Nerdonia. This once-proud republic used to have a thriving financial-services sector (my tax preparation), but this seemingly lucrative sector has collapsed. It was destroyed by "offshoring" (the foreign-based accountant). All Nerdonia has to show for it is a huge bilateral trade deficit with the accountant (the deficit arises because I pay them every July, but they buy nothing from me).

Every word of this argument makes trade sound terrible, and every word is true (although exaggerated for effect). But I still think this trade was worthwhile, and my accountant agrees. The critics have overlooked two untold stories that are central to the logic of comparative advantage. First, Nerdonia now has an emerging education industry (the new course I teach), and that's only possible because of trade with the accountant. And second, too often the trade debate only focuses on the production side of the economy, effectively asking who's doing the tax preparation. But this misses the consumption side, which is where the gains are. I consume and enjoy the fruits of my accountant's labour every time I get my tax refund, and I enjoy some small splurges from the remainder of my executive education earnings. ■

Recap: Comparative advantage is about reallocating resources to their better uses. You've now come a long way in uncovering what markets are all about. The economy largely consists of some people selling stuff they've made, and others buying it. We now see why they do this—they're reallocating tasks according to comparative advantage. And all this trade generates gains from trade, which make both buyer and seller better off.

This should lead you to think differently about markets. Rather than thinking about them as a zero-sum competition in which your gain is my loss, the logic of comparative advantage shows how they can enable a win-win outcome for both buyer and seller. If that now seems obvious, then you're well on your way to becoming an economist. You won't meet an economist who doesn't believe in the power of comparative advantage. But it just might be the hardest idea for non-economists to believe.

I began this chapter by saying that markets reallocate stuff to better uses. And we've seen how markets reallocate a valuable resource—such as your time—to a better use, which is performing those tasks for which you hold a comparative advantage. You might wonder how it is that markets figure out where each resource is most valuable. That's where prices come in, and our next task is to explore the role that prices play in coordinating economic activity.

8.3 Prices Are Signals, Incentives, and Information

Learning Objective *Understand the role that prices play in coordinating economic activity.*

Organising our economy is a colossal logistical challenge. Each business needs access to the right inputs. Those inputs need to arrive at the right time. They need to be combined in just the right way to be transformed into useful products. And those products need to go to the right people. Markets do an extraordinary job of organising all of this. But how?

A price is:

1. A signal
2. An incentive
3. A bundle of information

The answer is prices. They play three central roles. First, a price is a rapid-fire signal, sending messages that are heard around the globe. Second, a price is an incentive, inducing people to make better choices. And third, prices aggregate information, incorporating the judgements that motivate the thousands of buying and selling decisions that push the price up or down. Prices guide nearly every decision we make, helping to organise and coordinate economic activity.

Role One: A Price Is a Signal

ildi_papp/Depositphotos

It's pronounced "keen-wah," and it's delicious.

Quinoa has been called the "miracle grain of the Andes." Its small rice-like seeds are grown almost exclusively on the plains of the Andes mountains in Peru and Bolivia, and it's so nutritious that NASA feeds it to astronauts. In recent years, health-conscious Westerners have discovered quinoa and what was considered peasant food for centuries is now on the menu at healthy salad places, trendy cafés, and fancy restaurants. Stop by any grocery store and you'll find quinoa salads, quinoa breakfast cereals, quinoa granola bars, quinoa crackers, and even quinoa-based pasta.

The recent quinoa fad is the biggest change to ever hit this market. But it's all happening far away from the farmers who are high in the Andes mountains, cut off from news about the rest of the world. How do they learn about food trends in Australia? And how do Australian gourmands communicate their new love for quinoa to the farmers in Peru and Bolivia?

They communicate through the price. The sharp increase in demand led the price of quinoa to more than triple in just a few years. That skyrocketing price is a *signal,* creating a line of communication between buyers and sellers.

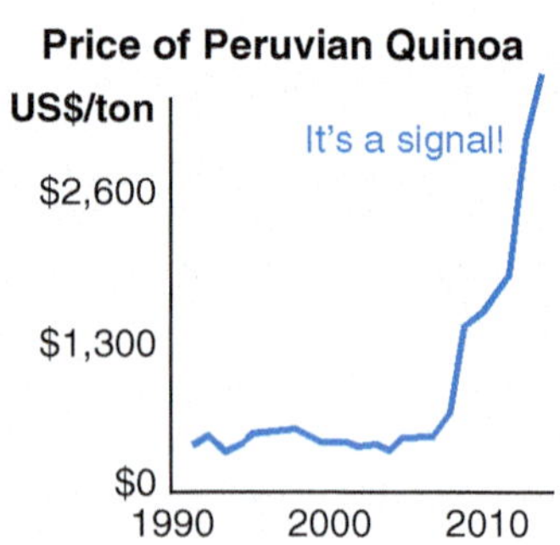

The price is a signal to potential suppliers. Potential suppliers may not otherwise know much about what's happening on the demand side of the market. Peruvian and Bolivian farmers may know little about Australian food trends, but they know the price of quinoa. When the price skyrockets, it sends these farmers a very clear message: "Quinoa is now more valuable—grow more quinoa!" More generally, a price tells potential suppliers how much buyers value their products, because it reveals the buyer's marginal benefit, or willingness to pay.

The price is a signal to potential buyers. Potential buyers may not otherwise know what is happening on the supply side of the market. Few Australians pay much attention to agricultural developments in the Andes, and so you're probably unaware of how difficult it is for Peruvian farmers to expand quinoa production. But you do look at the prices when you're at a restaurant or grocery store. And when the price of quinoa rises, it sends potential buyers like you a clear message: "Quinoa is scarce—buy less of it!" More generally, the price tells potential buyers about how expensive it is for sellers to produce more of a product, as it reveals the seller's marginal cost.

These signals help coordinate better outcomes. Price signals help coordinate the extraordinary chain of events that puts quinoa on your plate. Some of your quinoa might come from a Peruvian farmer who expands his production. And some might come from a Bolivian family that cuts back and eats more Argentinian-grown wheat instead. That quinoa might get to you on a Norwegian container ship that'll transport it to Australia. All of this occurs even if you don't know anyone in Peru, Bolivia, Argentina, or Norway.

It takes an extraordinary degree of coordination to get that quinoa to you. Prices are what make this miracle of global coordination possible. Price allows for the rapid-fire transmission of signals that are equally well understood in English, Spanish, Norwegian, and Quechua (the language spoken in the Andes).

Role Two: A Price Is an Incentive

So far I've described prices as providing a valuable line of communication between buyers and sellers. People respond to these signals because prices serve another role: A price is an *incentive.* The incentive is straightforward: A high price is an incentive for buyers to cut back a bit, just as it's an incentive for suppliers to expand production.

A high price is an incentive for suppliers to produce more. For *suppliers,* a high price is an incentive to increase production, because it creates new profit opportunities. The high price of quinoa is an incentive for farmers in the Andes to switch from growing corn to growing quinoa, which is what spurred them to quadruple their production of quinoa. This high price is an incentive for Bolivians to leave their mining jobs to return to their rural villages to farm quinoa. It's also an incentive stimulating innovation, and scientists at a Peruvian university have developed a variety of quinoa that will grow in coastal areas. A high price is an incentive with global influence, and it has led farmers in Western Australia's Wheatbelt to experiment with growing quinoa. Geneticists around the world are hard at work mapping the quinoa genome that will help them genetically engineer new high-yielding varieties. This extraordinary mobilisation occurs because the high price is an incentive for producers to increase the quantity they supply.

A high price is an incentive for buyers to consume less. For potential *buyers,* a high price raises the opportunity cost of consuming quinoa, creating an incentive to consume less. This incentive has far-reaching effects. It has led many Peruvian and Bolivian families to switch from eating quinoa to alternative grains like wheat, which are now relatively more affordable. South American farmers no longer use quinoa as chicken feed. And you might have noticed your serve of quinoa salad has become a little smaller at your local café. Each of these groups is conserving quinoa, because the high price is an incentive for potential buyers to decrease the quantity they demand.

Mark J. Barrett/Alamy

No quinoa for you.

A price provides an incentive for strangers to cooperate. The end result is that the quinoa that was once reserved for a South American chicken is now being served at your local café. This occurs even though South American chickens neither know you, nor particularly care about you. Rather, the South American chicken farmer is moved to consume less, allowing your local café to sell you that quinoa as a salad. This all happens due to the incentives embedded in the price of quinoa.

Role Three: A Price Aggregates Information

A price also aggregates information. Learn how to interpret what it's saying, and you'll make better decisions. The clearest example of this involves **prediction markets,** in which people trade contracts whose payoffs are linked to whether an uncertain event occurs. For instance, there are prediction markets where you can buy a share that'll be worth $1 if the Australian Labor Party (ALP) wins the next election (and nothing otherwise). They're called prediction markets, because their price effectively communicates a prediction. For instance, if the price of that ALP stock is $0.60, you can think of this as the market forecasting that the ALP has (roughly) a 60 percent chance of winning.

prediction markets Markets whose payoffs are linked to whether an uncertain event occurs.

The process of buying and selling aggregates information. Prediction markets yield useful forecasts because prices aggregate information. For instance, someone in Queensland who sees a lot of yard signs and bumper stickers supporting the ALP might buy stock, while someone in South Australia who saw the candidate give a bad speech might sell it. Good polling numbers might lead more people to buy the stock, while rising unpopularity might lead others to sell it. And so it goes on.

Through this process, the price will come to reflect—or aggregate—all of this information. Careful studies have shown that prediction markets yield more accurate forecasts than public opinion polls, statistical models, or televised experts. This means that you can quickly become an expert on politics without ever reading *Crikey*—simply follow political prediction markets online.

Market prices broadcast useful information. The same idea applies in other markets, and there are many financial prices that yield valuable business intelligence. The price of financial contracts linked to decisions yet to be made by the Reserve Bank of Australia reveals the odds that interest rates will rise. The price of futures contracts—where a buyer agrees to purchase a commodity like oil, wheat, or natural gas at a specific time in the future—is effectively a bet on the future price of these commodities. Tracking the price of these contracts can provide useful intel about future disruptions to your input costs. In financial markets, traders bet on whether inflation will be high or low, and so the price of these securities (they're called "inflation swaps") can yield useful inflation forecasts. While some of these financial products might seem a bit obscure, the broader idea is that because prices aggregate information, they provide you with useful business intelligence.

EVERYDAY Economics **Use markets to pick a better fantasy football team**

Sports-betting markets are effectively prediction markets, because a bet on your favourite team is the same as buying a security that'll only pay off if your team wins. The prices in these markets—the betting odds—aggregate information from thousands of betters, who have studied just about every conceivable detail about each team. As a result, studies have shown them to be incredibly accurate. And that's your opportunity: Use these prices as an aid while choosing your fantasy football team, and you'll effectively be drawing on the expertise of thousands of sports-mad betters. ■

8.4 How Managers Can Harness Market Forces

Learning Objective *Be ready to harness market forces in your own life.*

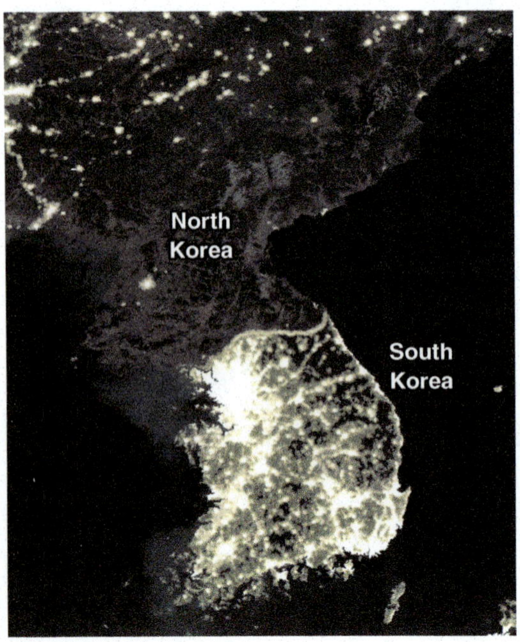

Satellite images of North and South Korea illustrate the power of market forces.

When Japanese troops in Korea surrendered at the end of World War II, it set in motion a remarkable natural experiment. The Soviet Union accepted the surrender in the north of the country, and administered the region that came to be known as North Korea. The United States accepted the surrender in the south, and set up the region now known as South Korea. These terms of surrender would later have enormous economic implications. Soviet influence led North Korea to set up a centrally planned economy, in which government officials decided who made what, who got what, and how much was made. By contrast, the United States set up a market economy in South Korea, and instead of a centralised government bureaucracy directing economic activity, it was left to market forces.

This natural experiment in market forces yielded rather extraordinary results. Both Koreas were equally poor in the immediate aftermath of the war. Today, the average annual income in market-oriented South Korea is about \$36,000 per year. That's about 20 times greater than in the centrally planned North Korea, where average income is about \$1,800 per person and people are often hungry. Market forces have allowed South Koreans to explore and exploit gains from trade, and this has made them enormously better off.

There's no more striking way to see this difference than the photos that NASA takes from space. As satellite photos show, South Korea is brightly lit and pulsating with activity, while North Korea is dark, as if nothing is happening.

The lesson from the Korean peninsula seems to be that if you're going to be the CEO of a country, it's far better for your people if you operate like South Korea—using market forces to allocate your scarce resources—than North Korea, where all choices are made by centralised managers.

Internal Markets Allocate Resources

The extraordinary success of South Korea, harnessing the power of market forces, has lessons for the management of individual companies. Some companies have figured out how to use the lessons from market economies to develop new internal markets that help them.

That's the idea behind **internal markets,** which are markets that managers set up *within* their organisation so that different divisions can buy and sell scarce resources. Just as regular markets efficiently allocate scarce resources to better uses, internal markets can help your company, nonprofit, or government agency allocate scarce resources to better uses.

internal markets Markets within a company to buy and sell scarce resources.

The internal operations of most large companies more closely resemble North Korea than South Korea. A typical CEO—much like the leader of North Korea—holds an enormous amount of centralised power, and uses that power to direct all activity within the company. A CEO—again, much like North Korea's supreme leader—heads a vast bureaucracy, and together with their deputies, formulates long-term plans that guide the broader enterprise and decides how best to deploy workers and machinery among their alternative uses.

The knowledge problem means that managers can't get the information they need. Foodbank Australia is a nonprofit—the largest network of food banks in Australia. It solicits food donations from large companies like Arnott's or even supermarkets like Coles and Woolworths, and then allocates that food to more than 2600 charities around the country providing more than 77 million meals a year to struggling Australians. Their good work means that thousands of families will be able to eat tonight.

The logistics of getting this right are complicated. To see why, put yourself in the shoes of an executive at Foodbank's Sydney headquarters. You've just been sent a truckload of fruit to distribute, and you want to send it to the region that'll get the largest benefit from it. To figure out where this is, you'll need to know the marginal benefit of a truckload of fruit for each of your (over) 2600 charities. Calling all 2600 charities would take forever, and even then, you've got no guarantee they'll provide accurate information.

This is an example of the **knowledge problem,** which is that the knowledge or information you need to make a good decision may be so broadly dispersed that it's not available to any individual decision maker. Think of this knowledge as being like a treasure map. The problem is that many people have a few small shreds of the map—a meals-on-wheels service in Adelaide may know the marginal benefit *it* would get from another truckload of fruit, just as the breakfast program at a Gold Coast school knows *its* marginal benefit. But no one has access to the whole map—what each food bank's marginal benefit is—making it impossible to navigate a path to the best outcome. Without access to this dispersed information, the executives at headquarters have no way to identify the best use for that truckload of fruit.

knowledge problem When knowledge needed to make a good decision is not available to the decision maker.

Markets solve the knowledge problem. Foodbank Australia might be better off if they took a leaf from the book of the largest network of food banks in the United States, Feeding America. Feeding America realised that they could harness market forces to help them allocate their food to a vast number of locations. After all, if markets allocate stuff to its better uses, they figured that an internal market could help them allocate food to where it would be most useful. They set up an internal market for allocating donated food. Here's how it works: When a new truckload of food arrives, all food banks can bid for it in an internal eBay-style auction. This means that the food banks that really need fruit can bid more for fruit. Because the highest bidder wins the

JAMES ROSS/EPA-EFE/Shutterstock

At Foodbank Australia, an internal market determines what food they're serving at this food bank.

auction, each truckload of donated food goes to a food bank that really needs it. To ensure that all food banks can compete for the food on a level playing field, they don't bid using real money, but rather an artificial currency issued by Feeding America.

This internal market avoids the knowledge problem, because it doesn't rely on a centralised decision maker knowing what's best or rely on personal relationships that may lead some regional food banks to do better than others. Instead, it relies on each regional food bank knowing its own marginal benefit and bidding accordingly. To continue the treasure map analogy: You don't need the whole map if there's someone at each navigation point telling you where to go next. Feeding America has discovered that the forces of supply and demand can allocate the donated food more efficiently than their managers can. The result is that less food is wasted, more people get fed, and because donors know their food is finding needy families, they're more willing to donate.

Use internal markets to allocate scarce resources. Feeding America's success points to a lesson that you should remember when you're a manager: You might be able to harness the power of markets to help you do a better job.

For instance, at Google, when computer resources were scarce, the executive team didn't ask managers to decide whether the Gmail team was more deserving than the YouTube or Chrome teams. Instead, managers allocated computer processing time, disk space, and memory by setting up an internal market so that the different product teams could compete to buy the space they needed. NASA has tried something similar. When NASA sent a spacecraft to Saturn, it had to figure out how to allocate the scarce resources of weight, electric power, data transmission, and budget across the different teams conducting scientific experiments. Rather than rely on the judgement of managers, it set up an internal market in which the scientists could trade the resources they needed.

EVERYDAY Economics

Getting into the classes you want

Many university students have experienced the frustration of wanting to take a particular class, only to discover that it is full. Can you think of a way to use internal markets to make sure that you get into the classes you value the most? Several leading international business and law schools have a solution. They allocate scarce slots in popular classes with an internal market. Each student is given the same amount of Monopoly money to use to buy and sell spots in popular classes. The more you want to be in a particular class, the more you'll bid, leading each spot to be allocated to the student who values it most. ■

Internal prediction markets can improve your forecasts. Another type of internal market—an internal prediction market—can be helpful whenever you need an accurate forecast. For instance, managers at Ford need accurate forecasts of the number of each type of car they'll sell each week. Traditionally they relied on forecasts put together by their internal analysts. But when Ford set up a prediction market and allowed its employees to bet on the outcome, the market yielded forecasts that were 25% more accurate.

Likewise Google's managers need to forecast things like how many people will use Gmail, whether a project will be completed on time, and what its competitors will do. When Google set up its own prediction markets, the prices yielded remarkably accurate forecasts about these critically important business issues. Experiments at other companies such as HP, Intel, Nokia, and Siemens yielded similar findings.

Tying It Together

This chapter is about understanding what markets do. And what they do best is reallocate resources to better uses. That reallocation generates gains from trade. What's the source of these gains from trade? We make more stuff when we use comparative advantage to reallocate tasks to their lowest-cost producer. The result is an extraordinary degree of specialisation, in which prices play a central role in coordinating economic activity.

We can see all of this by following the story of a particular good through the economy, from start to finish. Here's what happened when Nobel laureate Milton Friedman gazed with wonder upon a single pencil, musing about the extraordinary economic journey it took to your desk:

> *Look at this lead pencil. There's not a single person in the world who could make this pencil . . .*
>
> *The wood . . . comes from a tree . . . To cut down that tree, it took a saw. To make the saw, it took steel. To make steel, it took iron ore. This black center . . . comes from some mines in South America. This red top up here, this eraser, a bit of rubber, probably comes from Malaya, where the rubber tree isn't even native! It was imported from South America by some businessmen with the help of the British government. This brass ferrule? I haven't the slightest idea where it came from. Or the yellow paint! Or the paint that made the black lines. Or the glue that holds it together.*
>
> *Literally thousands of people cooperated to make this pencil. People who don't speak the same language, who practice different religions, who might hate one another if they ever met!*

Milton Friedman with his remarkable pencil.

Next time you pick up a pencil, you really should marvel at the extraordinary path that it has taken to you. And marvel also at the incredibly low price: If you buy a dozen pencils, they'll cost you about 30 cents each.

These two marvels are linked. The pencil follows an extraordinary path because every single part of the pencil is produced by people who specialise in the narrow task for which they hold a comparative advantage. Markets reallocate stuff to better uses, and in this case, they reallocate the tasks that go into making a pencil to those who can do them at the lowest opportunity cost.

The extraordinary symphony of productive effort that led to the production of Milton Friedman's pencil was conducted by the price system, which signals what is needed, provides an incentive to act, and aggregates the information needed to decide how to act.

So if you're ever stuck in an exam trying to remember what markets do, just look at the pencil you're writing with.

Chapter at a Glance

Gains from Trade: The benefits that come from reallocating resources, goods, and services to better uses.

Comparative Advantage: The ability to do a task at a lower **opportunity cost**. Use comparative advantage to allocate tasks to those with the lowest opportunity cost.
(*Absolute Advantage:* The ability to do a task using fewer inputs.)

A three-step recipe identifies who has a comparative advantage in each task:

#1. Determine how long the task would take each person. This measures the cost of producing each good, **in hours**.

Productivity: *How long does it take to complete:*

	Task A	Task B
Person 1	___ hours	___ hours
Person 2	___ hours	___ hours

#2. Convert this into a measure of **opportunity cost**, by calculating how much of the alternative good you could have produced in that time.

Evaluate the opportunity cost: *What does each forgo to complete:*

	Task A	Task B
Person 1	Task A takes Person 1 ___ hours, and in that time they could otherwise complete ___ of Task B	Task B takes Person 1 ___ hours, and in that time they could otherwise complete ___ of Task A
Person 2	Task A takes Person 2 ___ hours, and in that time they could otherwise complete ___ of Task B	Task B takes Person 2 ___ hours, and in that time they could otherwise complete ___ of Task B

#3. Evaluate who has a **comparative advantage** at each task by assessing who can do each task or produce each good at the lowest opportunity cost.

Prices play three central roles

1. **A price is a signal**, providing a valuable line of communication between buyers and sellers.
2. **A price is an incentive**, inducing people to make better choices.
3. **A price aggregates information**, incorporating the judgements that motivate the thousands of buying and selling decisions that push the price up or down.

Harnessing Market Forces

Internal markets: Markets within a company to buy and sell scarce resources. →	Use internal markets to allocate scarce resources.
Knowledge problem: When the knowledge needed to make a good decision is not available to an individual decision maker. →	Markets solve the knowledge problem.
Prediction markets: Markets whose payoff is linked to whether an uncertain event occurs. →	Prediction markets aggregate information.

Key Concepts

absolute advantage, 187
comparative advantage, 187
gains from trade, 186
internal markets, 199
knowledge problem, 199
prediction markets, 197
specialisation, 190

Discussion and Review Questions

Learning Objective 8.1 *Understand the role of markets in reallocating resources to better uses.*

1. How has the emergence of ride-sharing apps like Ola and Uber created gains from trade that didn't exist before?

Learning Objective 8.2 *Use comparative advantage to allocate tasks to those with the lowest opportunity cost.*

2. Think of your current roommate(s) or people you have lived with in the past, and provide an example of a household task that you have an absolute advantage completing and a household task you have a comparative advantage completing. Would it be better for your household if you specialised in the task for which you have an absolute advantage, or the task for which you have a comparative advantage? Explain your reasoning.
3. Explain how you can apply the three-step recipe of identifying comparative advantages to completing a group project.
4. Use comparative advantage to explain why you don't produce everything you consume. For example, why do you buy a T-shirt from Target instead of making it yourself? Or why do you buy groceries instead of growing your own food?
5. Use the opportunity cost principle to describe what you gain from specialising in your chosen (or to be chosen) profession.
6. Use the ideas of comparative advantage and specialisation to explain why, over the last several decades, the number of manufacturing jobs have decreased in Australia and increased in other countries such as China.

Learning Objective 8.3 *Understand the role that prices play in coordinating economic activity.*

7. You manage a farm equipment supply store in rural Queensland. Explain how you could use the price of soybean futures as a signal, an incentive, and as a source of information to help make better business decisions. For example, what does the future price of soybeans tell you about whether you should increase your supply of soybean equipment or shift your stock toward sugarcane equipment?
8. Go to an online predictions market (searching online should find you a number of them quickly) and make a prediction based on the prices you find. What information does the price tell you? How confident are you in this prediction and why?

Learning Objective 8.4 *Be ready to harness market forces in your own life.*

9. Provide an example of a knowledge problem that has impacted a company or an organisation. Describe how setting up an internal market would help better allocate resources to solve the knowledge problem.
10. You are a director at a game studio. The CEO emailed you asking for the most accurate chances of the game making its release date. How could you use a predictions market to answer the CEO's question?

Study Problems

Learning Objective 8.1 *Understand the role of markets in reallocating resources to better uses.*

1. Explain the gains from trade that arise for both buyers and sellers in the following transactions:
   a. Neighbours Jordan and Chelsea are both working parents. They are able to hire a single babysitter to care for both of their toddlers for 75% of what they would collectively have to pay two separate babysitters.
   b. Elijah decides that his family should eat more healthy meals, but they are short on time. He buys a subscription that sends healthy preplanned meals to his home three times a week.
   c. Bailey accepts an extra shift at work and hires a cleaning service to clean her apartment.

Learning Objective 8.2 *Use comparative advantage to allocate tasks to those with the lowest opportunity cost.*

2. You and your friend Olivia are both volunteers at a dog rescue. The shelter supervisor asks the two of you to clean out kennels and haul bags of dog food from the donation area to storage. You know from your last time volunteering that you can clean out 10 kennels in an hour or move 5 bags of dog food. Olivia can clean out 6 kennels in an hour or move 6 bags of dog food. Olivia suggests that you split the tasks equally. Answer the following questions to determine if Olivia is making the best decision.
   a. Who has an absolute advantage in doing each task?
   b. What are Olivia's opportunity costs of doing each task?
   c. What are your opportunity costs of doing each task?
   d. Who has a comparative advantage in doing each task?

e. Who should do each task to minimise the amount of time you both spend?

f. Was Olivia's suggestion the best possible way to allocate your time? Why or why not?

3. You're working on a team-based homework assignment with a partner, Deidre, that consists of an essay and graphing questions. You can write an essay answer in 15 minutes while Deidre takes 20 minutes to write an essay of similar quality. You can answer a graphing question in 30 minutes and it also takes Deidre 30 minutes.

a. What are you and your partner's opportunity cost of answering essay questions and of finishing graphing questions?

b. Use the opportunity cost principle to determine each of your comparative advantages.

c. If you each agree to spend one more hour on the task for which you hold a comparative advantage, and one less hour on the other task, what will happen to your joint output?

4. As the manager at a local florist, you supervise two employees, Anita and Jerome. There are two tasks that need to be completed: floral arrangements and flower delivery. It takes Anita 30 minutes to finish one floral arrangement and it takes her 40 minutes to make one delivery. It takes Jerome 10 minutes to finish one floral arrangement and it takes him 30 minutes to make one delivery.

a. Who has an absolute advantage in each task?

b. What are Anita and Jerome's opportunity costs of making floral arrangements? What is each of their opportunity costs of making one delivery?

c. Who has a comparative advantage in floral arrangements? What about deliveries?

d. Suppose, initially, Jerome and Anita each spent 4 hours each day doing floral arrangements and 2 hours each day doing deliveries. If you changed their tasks so that each individual did nothing but the task for which they had a comparative advantage, how many more floral arrangements would your store make, and how many more deliveries?

5. Imagine that it takes an average Australian miner 10 hours to mine a tonne of coal and 20 hours to mine a tonne of manganese. It takes the average South African miner 4 hours to mine a tonne of coal and 12 hours to mine a tonne of manganese.

a. Create a table to show how productive each miner is in a day.

b. For each miner, calculate the opportunity cost of mining a tonne of coal and a tonne of manganese.

c. In what task does each miner have a comparative advantage?

d. Which resource will each country import? How about export?

e. Explain how markets provide the opportunity for the mining companies to specialise and earn gains from trade.

6. In 2017, Ecuador's biggest export was crude (unprocessed) petroleum, 63% of which it exported to the United States, and Ecuador's biggest import was refined (processed) petroleum, of which 70% was imported from the United States. What does this tell you about the countries' comparative advantages in extracting petroleum and refining petroleum?

Learning Objective 8.3 *Understand the role that prices play in coordinating economic activity.*

7. Over a six-month period in 2007, the price of corn increased by almost 70% as a result of increased demand for ethanol biofuel.

a. What signal does the dramatic price increase give buyers and farmers?

b. How does the price change impact buyers' and farmers' incentives?

c. How do you think buyers and farmers responded to the dramatic price increase?

8. Between 2016 and 2017, Nintendo produced 2.3 million NES Classic Edition mini consoles that sold out almost immediately as they arrived at stores. The retail price of the mini console was $99.95. However, if you were to check eBay at the time, you would see that people were buying the units for $400 each from scalpers. Describe what signal this price sends to both scalpers and people buying the consoles to play them. How does the high price change their incentives?

9. Large airlines sometimes engage in fuel hedging as a way to avoid wild changes in jet fuel prices. To fuel hedge, an airline purchases a futures contract from an oil company that states they will purchase a set quantity of jet fuel at a specific price in the future regardless of what the actual market price is in the future. What do you expect to happen to the price of jet fuel in the future if the price of a fuel hedge decreases? Why?

Learning Objective 8.4 *Be ready to harness market forces in your own life.*

10. You're working as a paid intern on a small team of four software developers: Each member of the team faces different deadlines and requires your support at different times. You only have 38 hours per work week to offer. How could the company set up an internal market to ensure that your time is best allocated among the four team members each month?

PART III:

Applications and Policy Issues

Part III: Applications and Policy Issues

The Big Picture

You've spent a lot of time building up your economic muscles—now it's time to flex them. In the chapters ahead, we'll put your economic toolkit to work, analysing the most important economic forces that will shape your life, make news headlines, and spark family arguments.

We'll dig into the effects of **globalisation** by evaluating the costs and benefits of **international trade.** We'll consider climate change as an example of a broader problem in which **side effects** create a conflict between private interest and society's interests.

We'll explore what determines your wage and how many jobs are available by evaluating the **demand for labour,** the **supply of labour,** and the effects of **labour market regulations.** And then we'll turn to assessing the broader social issues of **income inequality,** and the incidence of **poverty,** and assess the government's role in income **redistribution.**

These are big issues, and they shape both your everyday life and the lives of those around you. Learn to deal with them effectively, and you'll be better equipped to deal with the messy reality of our world.

9 International Trade

Understand the consequences of global trade.

- Why do we trade with people in other countries?
- Who gains from international trade? Who loses?
- What are arguments for and against international trade?
- What are the effects of trade policy?
- How does globalisation shape your life?

10 Externalities and Public Goods

Explore what happens when your choices have side effects on others.

- When is there conflict between private interest and society's interests, and why do these conflicts lead to inefficient outcomes?
- How can we solve these conflicts?
- Why do problems arise when people can't be excluded from using something?

11 The Labour Market

Learn to make good decisions as both an employer and a worker and understand how wages are determined.

- What determines the wages people are paid and the number of people employed?
- How do employers decide how many workers to hire?
- How do workers decide how much to work?
- How does the labour market respond to changing economic conditions?

12 Why Wages Vary: Workers, Jobs, Institutions, and Discrimination

Understand why wages vary.

- What skills do employers want from workers?
- Why should you consider doing a job that other people hate?
- How do government regulations affect your wage?
- What role does discrimination play in the labour market?
- How can smart managers spur their staff to work harder?

13 Inequality, Poverty, and Social Insurance

Understand inequality, poverty, the tools government uses to address them, and the trade-off between efficiency and equity.

- How much economic inequality is there in Australia?
- How prevalent is poverty, and what are its implications?
- How does the government affect inequality and poverty?
- What are the arguments for and against income redistribution?

CHAPTER 9

International Trade

Turn your shirt inside out and look at the tag. No, not the washing instructions—look at the tag that tells you where it was made. What does it say? Most likely it says, "Made in China," or perhaps Vietnam, Bangladesh, or Indonesia. Now try your jeans. Even if they're Rip Curl—what could be more Australian?—most are not actually made in Australia. If you own an iPhone, the design was American, but the phone was likely assembled in China. Keep looking around you: at your laptop, your TV. You'll quickly discover that many of your possessions are made in another country.

Betsey Stevenson and Justin Wolfers

UGG Australia, Made in China

Now imagine your future career. If you become a movie star, you'll be famous all around the world. If you're an accountant, you might work for a company with offices all around the globe. If you're a programmer, your app will be sold in dozens of countries. If you're in advertising, your best clients might be multinationals, and your slogan will be heard worldwide. If you go into finance, you might buy and sell foreign companies. And if you're running a business, you'll be more successful if you think about the whole world as your market, rather than just Australia.

The point is that economic opportunities extend across national borders. Trade barriers have fallen, transportation has improved, and electronic networks make communication easier. As a result, the world is now more interconnected than ever, and globalisation is one of the most important forces in your lifetime. It's time to explore how this will shape your life. Why do we do all this international trade? Who's gaining? Who's getting hurt by it? There's a lot of fear about international trade, but as you read on, hopefully you'll see it as a source of opportunity.

Chapter Objective

Understand the consequences of global trade.

9.1 Comparative Advantage is the Foundation of International Trade
Discover why we trade with people in other countries.

9.2 How International Trade Shapes the Economy
Use supply and demand to assess the consequences of international trade.

9.3 The Debate About International Trade
Evaluate the arguments for and against international trade.

9.4 International Trade Policy
Understand how and why governments shape international trade.

9.5 Effects of Globalisation
Illustrate how globalisation shapes your life.

9.1 Comparative Advantage is the Foundation of International Trade

Learning Objective *Discover why we trade with people in other countries.*

What drives people in different countries to trade with each other? As a buyer, why do you buy goods imported from other countries? As a manager, why would you buy raw materials from foreign rather than domestic producers? As a producer, why would you sell your output to foreigners rather than just locals?

import To buy goods or services from foreign sellers.

export To sell goods or services to foreign buyers.

The most obvious reason to buy goods from abroad is that you can get a better deal. You will choose to **import**—that is, buy goods or services from foreign sellers—when foreign products are cheaper than their Australian-made equivalents.

Likewise, Australian businesses choose to **export**—that is, sell their goods or services to foreign buyers—when they can get a better price than if they just sold them in Australia. Indeed, many businesses find more people willing to pay a high price for their products when they supply them to the global market comprising all 8 billion people on the planet, rather than just the 26 million Australians in their domestic market.

Comparative Advantage and International Trade

You can get a better deal by trading with foreigners for the same reason that you get a better deal by trading with people within your country. The reason is *comparative advantage.*

You have a comparative advantage in a task if you can complete it at a lower opportunity cost than someone else. Instead of making everything yourself, you should specialise in those activities where you have a comparative advantage, because this means your opportunity cost is lower than others. And you should rely on your trading partners for the other stuff, where their opportunity costs are lower.

When we each specialise according to our comparative advantage, we're each doing more of what we're relatively good at and trading with others so we're buying the things they're relatively good at. The result is that we can both end up better off. Specialising according to comparative advantage means that we can produce more together than we can apart. (This should all be familiar from the first half of Chapter 8. If it's not, go back and read it right now. The idea of comparative advantage is so important to international trade that I'll wait here until you're done.)

Geography is irrelevant. This idea of assigning tasks to those with the lowest opportunity cost is no less persuasive if the people with the lowest opportunity cost happen to live in another country. After all, an international border is just an arbitrary invisible line. So the same logic and calculations that suggest you'll be better off if you trade with other Australians also suggest that you'll be better off if you trade with foreigners who happen to be on the other side of that invisible line.

Comparative advantage drives international trade. This logic says that we choose to import and export for the same reasons we do business with other Australians: Specialising according to comparative advantage can give us both more stuff. The only thing that's different about international trade is the scope and scale of specialisation that's possible when there are 8 billion people scattered around the world to trade with.

It leads Australians to export those goods where their opportunity costs are low and to import goods for which their opportunity costs are high. This is why, for example, computer scientists and engineers in America design the iPhone, while Chinese factory workers manufacture them. And both sides gain when trade is driven by comparative advantage, as this division of labour leads to lower iPhone prices globally and better-designed smartphones for the Chinese.

Does comparative advantage really drive international trade? Some of this might seem a bit far-fetched. After all, do people really make the sort of comparative advantage calculations we outlined in Chapter 8 before deciding whether to import or export goods?

The answer is yes, but in a much simpler way. All you need to do is look at the price tag. When you shop for shirts, the *cost-benefit principle* tells you to pay careful attention to the price. And in a competitive market, the price is equal to marginal cost. (Yep, that's the *marginal principle* at work again.) This means that when you compare the price of an imported shirt with the price of the domestically produced shirt, you're effectively comparing their marginal costs. The *opportunity cost principle* reminds you that marginal cost should include all relevant opportunity costs. This means that when you compare the price of domestic versus imported shirts, you're effectively comparing the opportunity cost of each—and this is exactly what the idea of comparative advantage suggests you should do.

By looking for the lower-priced shirt, you're effectively evaluating which shirt was made at the lowest opportunity cost. And when you buy that cheaper shirt, you're buying from the manufacturer who has a comparative advantage in shirt-making.

Anan Kaewkhammul/Alamy

The price tag will tell you a lot about your comparative advantage.

What Gets Traded?

Comparative advantage yields a pretty stark piece of advice: Produce what you're good at and buy what you aren't. Applied to international trade, this says to export the stuff you can produce at the lowest opportunity cost, and import the other stuff. In reality, that advice is a bit too stark, because there's one more factor to consider: trade costs.

Trade costs determine whether it's worth buying or selling internationally. **Trade costs** are the extra costs—aside from the price—incurred as a result of buying or selling your goods internationally rather than domestically. For instance, buying a car from Japan involves shipping costs. You might also have to pay an extra tax to the Australian government on imports, or a tax to a foreign government for exports. The *opportunity cost principle* reminds you to consider the full set of costs—not just the out-of-pocket financial expenses. And so trade costs also include the hassle of working across language barriers, trading across different time zones, dealing with foreign laws, and adapting to different ways of doing business.

trade costs The extra costs incurred as a result of buying or selling internationally, rather than domestically.

The *cost-benefit principle* says that trade is only worthwhile if the benefit exceeds the cost. This means that you should only import a good if the price you can get it for from another country is sufficiently far below the local price as to offset the associated trade costs. Likewise, you should only export a good if the price you'll get for it in another country is sufficiently far above your local price as to offset the export-related trade costs.

Trade costs determine how important international trade is in your sector. It follows that it's unlikely to ever be worth importing or exporting products with high trade costs. On the flip side, there's a lot of international trade in products with low trade costs. And so trade costs determine whether international trade is likely to be a big factor in your market.

For example, trade costs associated with digital music are virtually zero—Spotify simply exports bits and bytes—and so there's a huge amount of international trade in music. Clothes are more expensive to trade, but they're still easily sent in massive container ships, which explains why your shirt was probably imported. However, it's prohibitively expensive to get a cavity filled in another country (think of the flight costs), and it's virtually impossible to transport a house. Consequently there's almost no international trade in dental services, and no international trade in houses.

Do the Economics

Which of the following goods or services are traded internationally? (Hint: Think about the relevant trade costs.)

☐ Land	☐ Wheat	☐ Flowers
☐ Coffee beans	☐ A hot cup of coffee	☐ Sandwiches
☐ Laptops	☐ Cloud computing	☐ Surveillance equipment
☐ A haircut	☐ Hair gel	☐ Hairdressing scissors
☐ Cars	☐ Bikes	☐ Taxi rides
☐ Bowling shoes	☐ Bowling alleys	☐ An afternoon bowling ■

Answer: Coffee beans, laptops, cars, bowling shoes, wheat, cloud computing, hair gel, bikes, flowers, surveillance equipment, hairdressing scissors

Trade costs don't just determine what is traded. As the next case study shows, they also determine how much is traded. Indeed, declining trade costs are responsible for one of the most important economic trends of your lifetime.

Interpreting the DATA **Global trade is rising because of declining trade costs.**

International trade—both exports and imports—has been a growing share of the Australian economy throughout the entire postwar period (Figure 1). This trend—sometimes called "globalisation"—has transformed the economy. And it's largely due to declining trade costs.

Figure 1 **Imports and Exports Are a Rising Share of the Australian Economy**

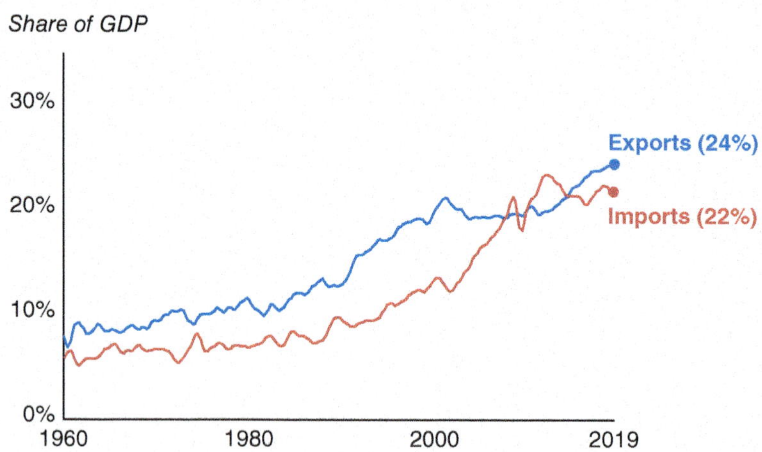

Data from: Australian Bureau of Statistics.

Australia has brokered trade agreements with a number of countries that have eliminated extra taxes (called tariffs) imposed on trading with them. Some of these trade agreements have also reduced the red tape that often hinders exporters.

The standardisation of shipping containers dramatically decreased the cost of shipping goods overseas, and ongoing improvements in air travel reduced transport costs. The increased adoption of English has made international transactions run more smoothly, and an increasingly global business culture makes it easier to do business across borders.

The internet has made global communication much cheaper and quicker, which has fuelled greater international trade in services. For instance, the financial industry is becoming more globalised as computers link banks and financial networks at lightning speed. And it's now easy for foreign radiologists to read X-rays taken in Australia.

As trade costs fall, companies trade more intermediate inputs, creating global supply chains. For instance, Barbie is produced by a global supply chain. Her plastic limbs and hair are made by workers in Taiwan and Japan; she's assembled in Indonesia, Malaysia, and China; and she was designed and marketed in the United States. International trade allows Barbie to be manufactured and sold more inexpensively, while allowing workers in each country to contribute what they do best. ■

She has seen the world.

Choosing Your Trading Partners: Sources of Comparative Advantage

It's a good bet that trade costs will continue to fall, making international trade an even more important force through your career. This more integrated global marketplace will create new opportunities for you to exploit your comparative advantage. Which raises the question: What *is* your comparative advantage, and what strategic choices can you make to enhance it?

Economists have identified three factors that shape your comparative advantage: relatively abundant inputs, specialised skills, and the benefits of mass production. Let's examine each in detail.

Sources of comparative advantage:

1. Abundant inputs
2. Specialised skills
3. Mass production

Source one: Abundant inputs—Take advantage of what you have, to get what you want. New Zealand has lots of land, and so New Zealand farmers can raise sheep cheaply to export wool. Canada has ample forests, and so Canadian foresters export wood and related products like paper. Saudi Arabia has abundant oil, which is an essential input into the petrol that Saudi refineries export. France has ideal soil for growing grapes, leading French winemakers to export wine. Australia has a lot of precious metals, and so mining companies export iron ore and gold. Each of these examples reflects a comparative advantage that is due to the relative abundance of the necessary inputs compared to their trading partners.

Some of this relative abundance of inputs is simply a matter of climate, geography, and natural resources. But people, businesses, and countries can shape their advantages through strategic investments. For instance, the Australian Government's large investments into schools and universities have helped create the relative abundance of highly educated workers that led to Australia's comparative advantage in scientific fields, such as medical research.

This focus on abundant inputs suggests that international trade is all about exporting products made with resources you have a lot of, and importing products made with resources that are scarce. Importantly, it is *relative* abundance of inputs that matters—whether you have more or less labour relative to capital, land, or sunshine than your trading partners.

The more your trading partner differs from you, the larger the gains from trade will be. If your trading partner has very different resources—whether they're worker skills, machinery, natural resources, or climate—it's likely they'll also have very different opportunity costs, leading to gains from trade.

Interpreting the DATA — What inputs are relatively abundant in Australia?

As a savvy manager, you should specialise in making and exporting products that rely on inputs that are relatively abundant near you. And you'll find likely customers in areas where those inputs are relatively scarce. On the flip side, you should import those goods that require inputs that are relatively scarce near you. And you'll typically get the best deal if you import them from a country where those inputs are relatively abundant.

So which inputs are abundant, and which are scarce in Australia relative to other countries? Compared to Australia, Indonesia doesn't have abundant land. (Indonesia has over 10 times the population of Australia, but only a quarter of the landmass!) Compared to countries such as China, India, and Bangladesh, Australia doesn't have particularly abundant labour. This might leave you thinking that because our businesses

Abundant Skilled Labour

Share of adults 25+ with tertiary education

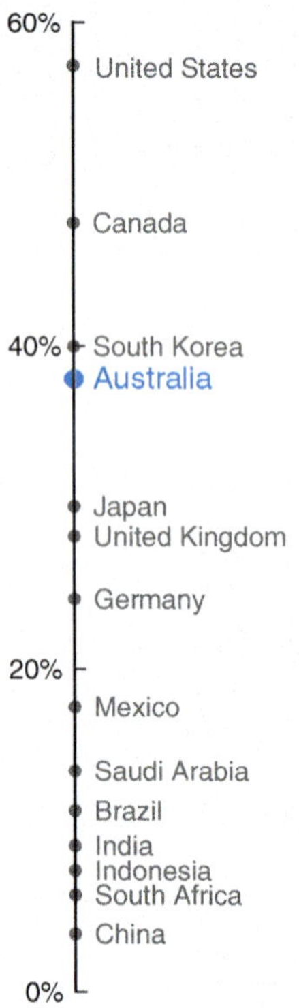

Data from: World Bank.

use state-of-the-art machinery, Australia has relatively abundant capital. But studies have found that Australia exports goods that are slightly *less* capital intensive than its imports. So what abundant inputs drive our comparative advantage?

The answer is a specific category of labour: *highly educated* workers. Australia has a much higher share of workers with some university education compared to other countries. In turn, this means that our comparative advantage is in producing skill-intensive goods, such as scientific and medical instruments, trucks, and computer software. This is good news for smart university students: You're Australia's comparative advantage!

By contrast, because less-educated workers are *relatively* scarce in Australia, we have a comparative disadvantage in mass manufacturing. This explains why Australians import toys, footwear, and clothing from businesses in China and Indonesia where wage costs are lower. (Although, as we will discuss later in this chapter, these workers sometimes face arduous working conditions and there are often concerns about exploitation.) ■

Source two: Develop a specialised skill. Businesses in Switzerland, France, and Australia have roughly similar access to capital and skilled labour. Yet the Swiss are the world's best watchmakers, the French produce the greatest cheese, and Australians make terrific spreads (hello Vegemite), which pair nicely with some French cheese! In each case, skilled artisans produce watches, cheese, or Vegemite in a way that their foreign counterparts can't match. Your unique skills, production methods, or expertise can be an important source of comparative advantage.

As they say, practice makes perfect: If you—or a country or a business—focus on a particular product for a long time, you'll likely discover new production techniques that lower your costs. This comparative advantage gets stronger over time, as you produce more and learn more. Economists refer to this as "learning by doing," and it explains how a long-term investment in a specific industry can pay off. As a manager, you'll discover that the more you produce, the more efficient you'll become, which will lead you to sell and hence produce more, creating more opportunities to learn, further reinforcing your comparative advantage.

Source three: Exploit the benefits of mass production. Ikea sells millions of Billy bookcases each year to buyers all around the world. It sells so many of them because the Billy bookcase is so cheap. And the Billy bookcase is so cheap because Ikea sells so many of them. This virtuous cycle arises because of the benefits of mass production (which are sometimes called *economies of scale*).

Billy the bookcase and his creator, Ronnie the robot.

When you're producing millions of bookcases, you can invest in creating incredibly specialised production lines that are much more efficient. For instance, rather than hiring skilled woodworkers to make the Billy, Ikea has programmed specialised robots to do most of the work, and they can work 24 hours a day, 7 days a week. The automated production line is so efficient that it makes a new bookcase every five seconds. In addition, Ikea produces so much furniture that it's one of the world's largest purchasers of wood. This gives it substantial bargaining power, which it uses to demand cheaper wood, further lowering its input costs. Put it all together, and the opportunity cost of producing another bookcase is lower for Ikea than for any other business. These lower opportunity costs due to the benefits of mass production can be another enduring source of comparative advantage, particularly for large producers.

EVERYDAY Economics **Using comparative advantage at home**

The same big idea that drives international trade—comparative advantage—also explains why you trade tasks with your roommates to make your household run more efficiently. It's simple: You want to allocate each task to the person who has a comparative advantage. And thinking about the sources of comparative advantage can help.

Who should do the weekly shopping? The idea that *abundant inputs* creates comparative advantage suggests that you should assign that task to the housemate who owns a car, because they have a relative abundance of the necessary capital equipment. Who should be responsible for IT around the house—making sure the Wi-Fi works, and that the stereo can pair with everyone's phones? Assign that task to whoever has developed a *specialised skill* in computer networking. As they get used to troubleshooting, they'll develop even more expertise. And what about cooking dinner? Anyone can cook spaghetti, so perhaps anyone could have a comparative advantage here. True, but since it's just as easy to make spaghetti for four as it is for one, the *benefits of mass production* create a comparative advantage for whoever is already cooking for themselves to cook for the whole household. The same ideas that guide successful global businesses can also guide your household. Allocating tasks according to comparative advantage will make your household more efficient, and it'll make sure you get your shopping, technology, and meals dealt with at the lowest possible opportunity cost. ■

Now that we've explored how comparative advantage drives international trade, it's time to explore how international trade reshapes supply and demand.

9.2 How International Trade Shapes the Economy

Learning Objective *Use supply and demand to assess the consequences of international trade.*

International trade reshapes the forces of supply and demand in Australia, and so our next task is to assess how it changes outcomes in the various markets in which you'll do business.

The World Market

Let's start with the shirt you're wearing right now. I'll bet that it began life in a foreign factory, probably in a country with a lot of low-wage workers. (Go ahead and check the label. I'll wait. . . . Was I right?) Your shirt then joined millions of other shirts for the journey to Australia in one of the huge container ships that links the shirt market in Australia with those in China, Bangladesh, Indonesia, and the rest of the world.

World supply and world demand determine the world price. The market for shirts is a truly global market. Thousands of manufacturers around the world compete to sell their shirts to billions of potential buyers located in just about every country on Earth. When shirts are traded internationally, the price is determined by the interactions of all the buyers and sellers around the world. That is, the price is determined in the *world market* by the intersection of world supply and world demand shown in Figure 2. *World supply* describes the total quantity of shirts produced by all manufacturers in the world at each price. Similarly, *world demand* describes the total quantity of shirts demanded across all shirt buyers in

Figure 2 | The World Market

Ⓐ **World supply** is the total quantity of shirts supplied by all sellers around the world.
Ⓑ **World demand** is the total quantity of shirts demanded by all buyers around the world.
Ⓒ **Equilibrium** occurs in the world market when world supply equals world demand.
Ⓓ The **world price** is the price that shirts are bought and sold for on the world market.

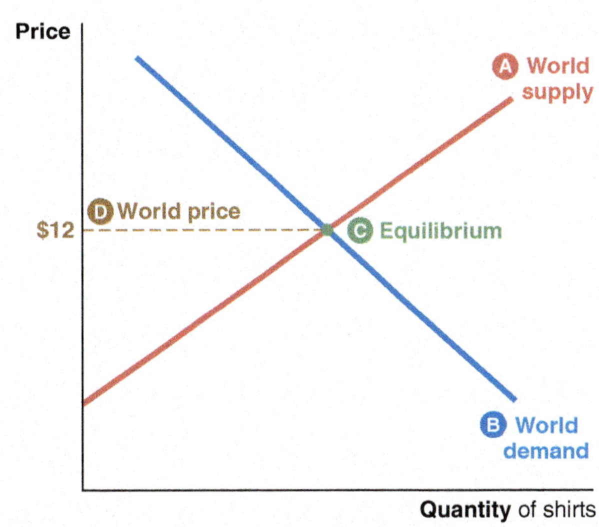

world price The price that a product sells for in the global market.

every country, at each price. World demand and world supply jointly determine the **world price,** which is the price that a traded good sells at in the world market. This world price is the price that consumers pay to buy imported shirts, and the price that producers can get for exporting their shirts.

When Australia is a small player, take the world price as given. Realise that Australia is only a relatively small player in the global shirt market. This means that the actions of Australian importers and exporters won't influence the world price much. That is, in the world market, Australian buyers and sellers are *price-takers,* which means that they can take the world price as given. (Only those who are big players relative to world supply or world demand need to think about how their decisions change the world price.)

The Effects of Imports

domestic demand curve Shows the quantity of a good that all domestic consumers added together plan to buy, at each price.

domestic supply curve Shows the quantity of a good that all domestic suppliers added together plan to sell, at each price.

Let's now explore how international trade shapes the domestic market. We'll need some new terminology to do this. The **domestic demand curve** illustrates the quantity of goods that domestic buyers—that is, all Australians taken together—plan to buy at each price. Likewise, the **domestic supply curve** illustrates the quantity of goods that domestic producers plan to sell at each price. These curves, which are shown in Figure 3, will be familiar from our earlier study of supply and demand. But we now need to be clear that these curves refer only to Australian buyers and Australian sellers.

Figure 3 | The Consequences of Imports

If there is no international trade:

No-trade equilibrium occurs where: Quantity demanded by domestic buyers equals quantity supplied by domestic sellers, resulting in 100 million shirts sold at a price of $20.

When we allow imports:

Step 1 The price of imported goods declines to the world price.

Step 2 At this new price, check the domestic supply curve to find that the quantity supplied by domestic sellers declines, and check the domestic demand curve to find the quantity demanded by domestic buyers rises.

Step 3 Imports make up the difference between domestic demand and domestic supply.

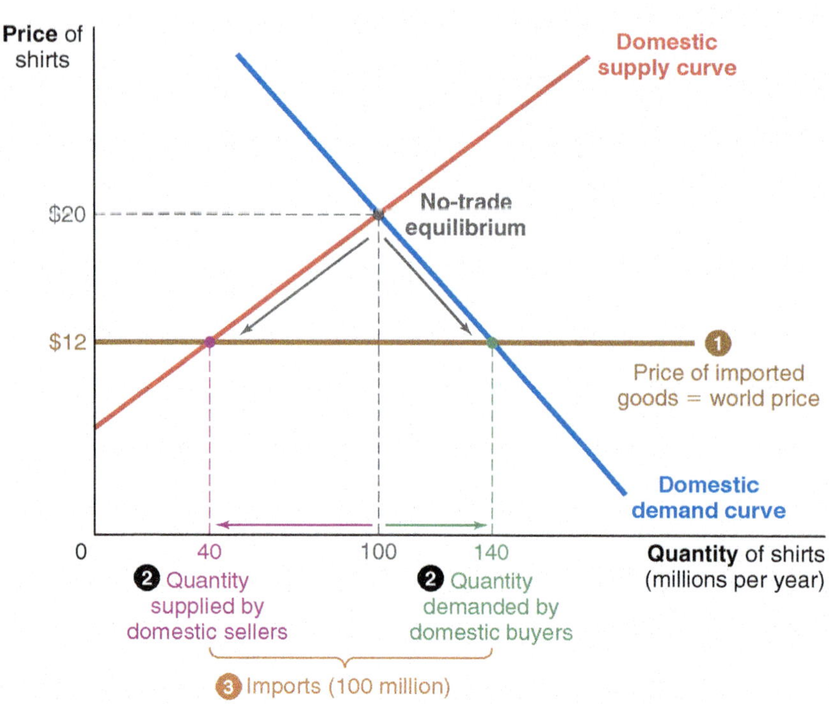

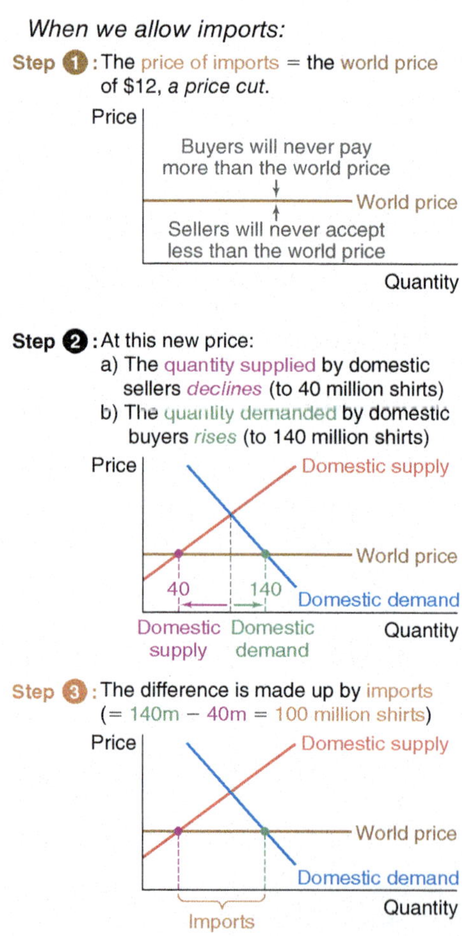

Evaluate the equilibrium when there's no trade. To set a baseline of comparison, we'll start by assessing the likely outcomes if there were no trade. As before, it's all about where supply meets demand. In the absence of international trade, the equilibrium price is determined by the intersection of the domestic demand and supply curves. In Figure 3, these curves intersect when shirts sell for $20.

David Ewing/Moment/Getty Images

Your shirt is arriving.

Evaluate how imports shape domestic markets. To see what happens when we allow for the possibility of international trade, we'll follow a simple three-step recipe:

Step one: *What will be the price of a traded good?*

When the domestic market is linked to the world market through trade, you have new options to consider. For instance, international trade gives buyers the option to import shirts at the world price of $12. As a result, you'll never pay a seller more than $12 for a shirt. Likewise, international trade means that sellers always have the option to export their shirts at the world price of $12. This means they'll never accept less than $12 per shirt. And so if buyers never pay more than $12, and sellers never sell for less than $12, the equilibrium price must be $12. *For traded goods, the price is equal to the world price.*

Step two: *At this new price, what quantities will be demanded and supplied by domestic buyers and sellers?*

To find the responses of Australians to this new lower price, consult their domestic demand and domestic supply curves. Begin by locating the new price, $12, on the vertical axis in Figure 3, and then look across until you hit the supply curve. Look down, and you'll see that domestic sellers will supply 40 million shirts when they can get $12 per shirt. And what quantity will domestic buyers purchase? Look across from the $12 price until you hit the domestic demand curve, then look down, and you'll see that domestic buyers will demand 140 million shirts.

Step three: *What quantity will be traded?*

Notice that when goods are traded internationally, there can be a large gap between the quantity demanded by domestic buyers and the quantity supplied by domestic sellers. International trade makes up the difference, with imports filling the gap between the quantity demanded by domestic buyers and the quantity supplied by domestic sellers.

Imports lead to lower prices, less domestic production, and more domestic consumption. Putting the pieces together, we've found that when buyers import goods:

- The price declines to the world price.
- This lower price leads to a lower quantity supplied by domestic sellers, but a higher quantity demanded by domestic buyers.
- Imports fill the gap between the quantity demanded and the quantity supplied.

Our simple three-step recipe gives you a forecast about what's likely to happen as a result of importing foreign shirts. But do imports make you better off? As we'll see, the answer depends on whether you're a consumer or producer of shirts.

See the Connections

What are the effects of imports? → The price is lower (= world price). → *At this lower price:* The quantity demanded by domestic buyers is higher. And the quantity supplied by domestic sellers is lower. → Imports make up the difference between the quantity demanded by domestic buyers and the quantity supplied by domestic sellers.

Imports Raise Economic Surplus

Australian consumers gain when they import their shirts, because they get lower prices. But Australian producers lose, because foreign competition forces them to lower their prices or lose customers. The *cost-benefit principle* suggests that policy makers should make decisions about trade policy based on whether the gains exceed the losses.

To assess the balance of these competing effects, we'll compare the increase in consumer surplus that buyers gain with the decrease in producer surplus that sellers lose. That's the exercise we perform in Figure 4. This figure may look complicated at first glance, but by proceeding slowly, you'll see that it's actually pretty intuitive.

Start by assessing economic surplus when there's no international trade to set a baseline. In this case, the no-trade equilibrium occurs where the domestic supply and demand curves cross. Remember that domestic buyers earn consumer surplus when they get to buy a shirt at a price that is lower than their marginal benefit. Because the domestic demand curve shows these marginal benefits, the total consumer surplus they earn is the area below the domestic demand curve, but above the price. This is triangle labeled area A in Figure 4. Domestic suppliers earn producer surplus when the price is above their marginal cost. Because the domestic supply curve reflects each producer's marginal costs, the total producer surplus that they earn is the area that's above the domestic supply curve and below the price. This is the large triangle of area $B+C$.

So the total economic surplus with no trade is the area $A+B+C$. That's the baseline. What happens when we allow imports?

Figure 4 | **The Welfare Consequences of Allowing Imports**

Effects of Imports on Economic Surplus

	No trade	Free trade	Difference
Consumer surplus	A	$A+B+D$	$B+D$
Producer surplus	$B+C$	C	$-B$
Total surplus	$A+B+C$	$A+B+C+D$	$+D$

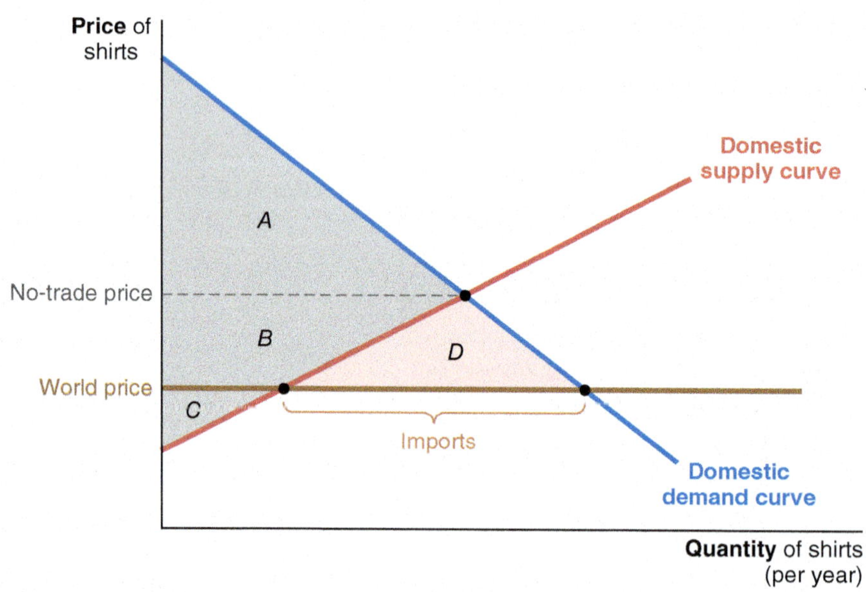

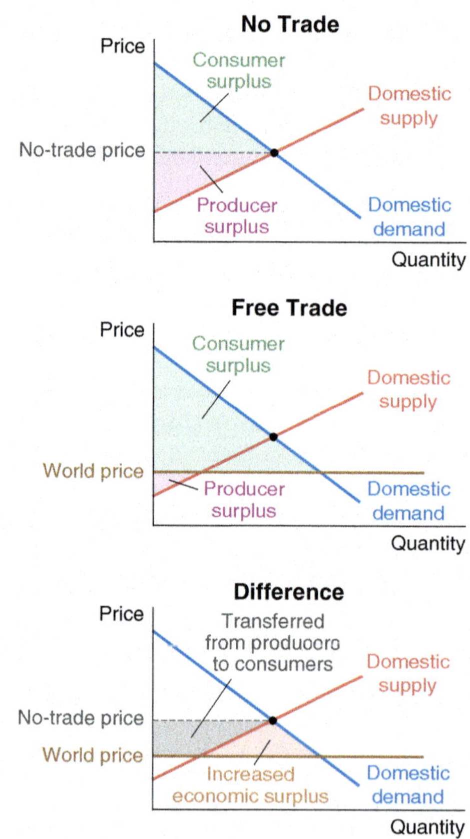

Cheap imports raise consumer surplus. Allowing imports leads domestic buyers to pay a lower price, and at this lower price they buy a larger quantity of these cheap shirts. As a result, the consumer surplus of domestic consumers rises. Graphically, consumer surplus is the area below the demand curve but above the price buyers pay, which is now the world price, and so consumer surplus is the large triangle $A+B+D$. You can see why domestic consumers are happier: The lower price of shirt imports raises their consumer surplus—from area A to the larger area, $A+B+D$.

Domestic producers lose producer surplus due to foreign competition. Domestic producers are worse off because a lower world price means that they have to sell their shirts at lower prices, and as a result, they no longer find it profitable to sell as many shirts. Graphically, producer surplus is the area above their domestic supply curve but below the price they now charge, which is now the lower world price. You can now see why producers are less happy: The lower price of shirts reduces their producer surplus—from area $B+C$ to the smaller area C.

The benefits exceed the costs, and imports raise total economic surplus. So far, we've seen that imports raise the consumer surplus enjoyed by Australian consumers and lower the producer surplus earned by Australian producers. What's the net effect?

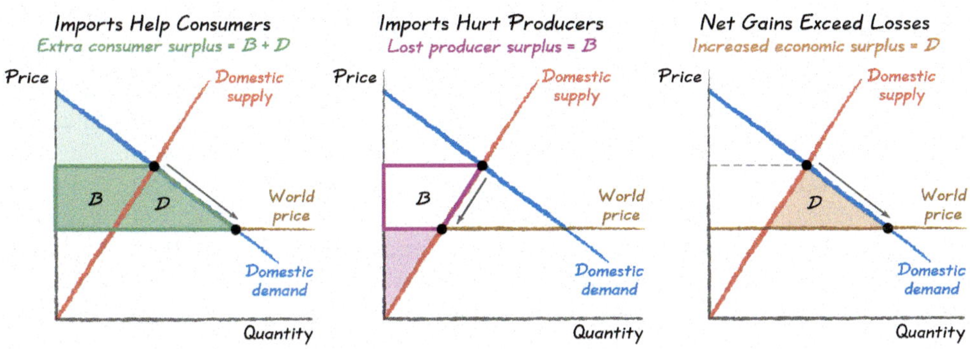

We've figured out that consumers gain , while producers lose a smaller amount, . This means that taken together, Australians—when we take account of their roles as both consumers and producers—gain economic surplus from importing, and this net gain is the area 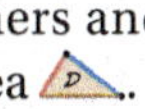.

Many people are surprised to hear economists say that imports are good for Australians. Often, this is because when they think about "the economy," they're thinking about producers—the factories, businesses, and workers who lose some economic surplus. But it's important not to forget consumers, who derive an even larger benefit from buying cheaper goods.

The gains to buyers from allowing imports exceed the losses to sellers. There's a neat intuition underlying all of this. The main effect of imports is to lower the price of shirts, and if Australian producers wanted to, they could sell just as many shirts as before, just as Australian consumers could buy just as many as before. Indeed, if Australians didn't change how many shirts they bought or produced, then the economic surplus gained by Australian buyers due to international trade lowering prices would exactly equal the economic surplus lost by Australian producers due to these lower prices. But when the price falls, Australian suppliers *minimise their losses* by supplying fewer cheap shirts, while Australian buyers *amplify their gains* by buying more cheap shirts, often from international sellers. (Imports fill the gap between the decreased production by Australian sellers and the increased purchases by Australian consumers.) The net effect is that the amplified gains to buyers outweigh the minimised losses to sellers, and so imports lead Australians—taken as a whole—to enjoy more economic surplus.

Recap: The consequences of allowing imports. It's time to summarise what we've learned about imports. It's always best to start with what happens to the price. Cheap foreign competitors cause the price of goods we import to fall. Buyers respond by raising the quantity they demand, while sellers respond by reducing the quantity they supply, with imports filling the difference. The lower price increases the consumer surplus of buyers, and decreases the producer surplus of sellers. And because buyers amplify their gains and sellers minimise their losses, the net effect is for total economic surplus to increase.

Okay, that's the effect of imports. Now it's time to apply the same approach to analysing the market for exports.

The Effects of Exports

Australia has a lot of land compared to other countries with dense populations, although some of it is not arable. Take Indonesia for example, they have over 10 times the Australian population, but only a quarter of the land! Our abundance of land has led to a thriving farming industry which goes back generations. One of Australia's largest exports to this day is meat. To keep things simple in this example, let's just consider beef. Figure 5 shows the domestic demand and supply curves for beef. If there were no trade, the equilibrium would occur where these curves cross. At a price of $18 per kilo, the 1 million tonnes of beef demanded by domestic buyers exactly matches the 1 million tonnes of beef supplied by domestic sellers. But what happens when Australian farmers like Australian Good Meat and AACo also export their beef?

Evaluate how exports shape domestic markets. Let's work through our three-step recipe:

Step one: *What will be the price of a traded good?*

Internationally, there's a lot of demand for beef, and the world price is $24 per kilo. This means that sellers will not sell beef to domestic Australian buyers for less than the $24 per kilo they can get by selling in the world market. Likewise, international trade means that domestic Australian buyers have the option to import beef from foreign sellers such as the Japanese company Starzen Co. for $24 per kilo, and so they will never pay domestic sellers more than $24 per kilo. If suppliers will never sell for less than $24 per kilo, and buyers will never pay more than $24 per kilo, the equilibrium price must be $24 per kilo. *For traded goods, the price is equal to the world price.*

Step two: *At this new price, what quantities will be demanded and supplied by domestic buyers and sellers?*

Begin by locating the new price, $24 per kilo, on the vertical axis, and then look across until you hit the demand curve. Look down, and you'll see that domestic buyers will demand 800,000 tonnes of beef at $24 per kilo. And what quantity will domestic producers sell? Look across from the $24 per kilo price until you hit the domestic supply curve, then look down, and you'll see that domestic sellers will supply 1.4 million tonnes of beef.

Step three: *What quantity will be traded?*

While domestic supply and domestic demand are not equal, the market is still in equilibrium, because of exports to foreign buyers who make up the difference. If domestic suppliers produce 1.4 million tonnes of beef and domestic buyers purchase only 800,000 tonnes of beef, then the difference is made up by the 600,000 tonnes of beef that are exported each year.

Exports lead to higher prices, more domestic production, and less domestic consumption. We've now figured out the effects of exports. When domestic sellers export their goods:

Figure 5 | The Consequences of Exports

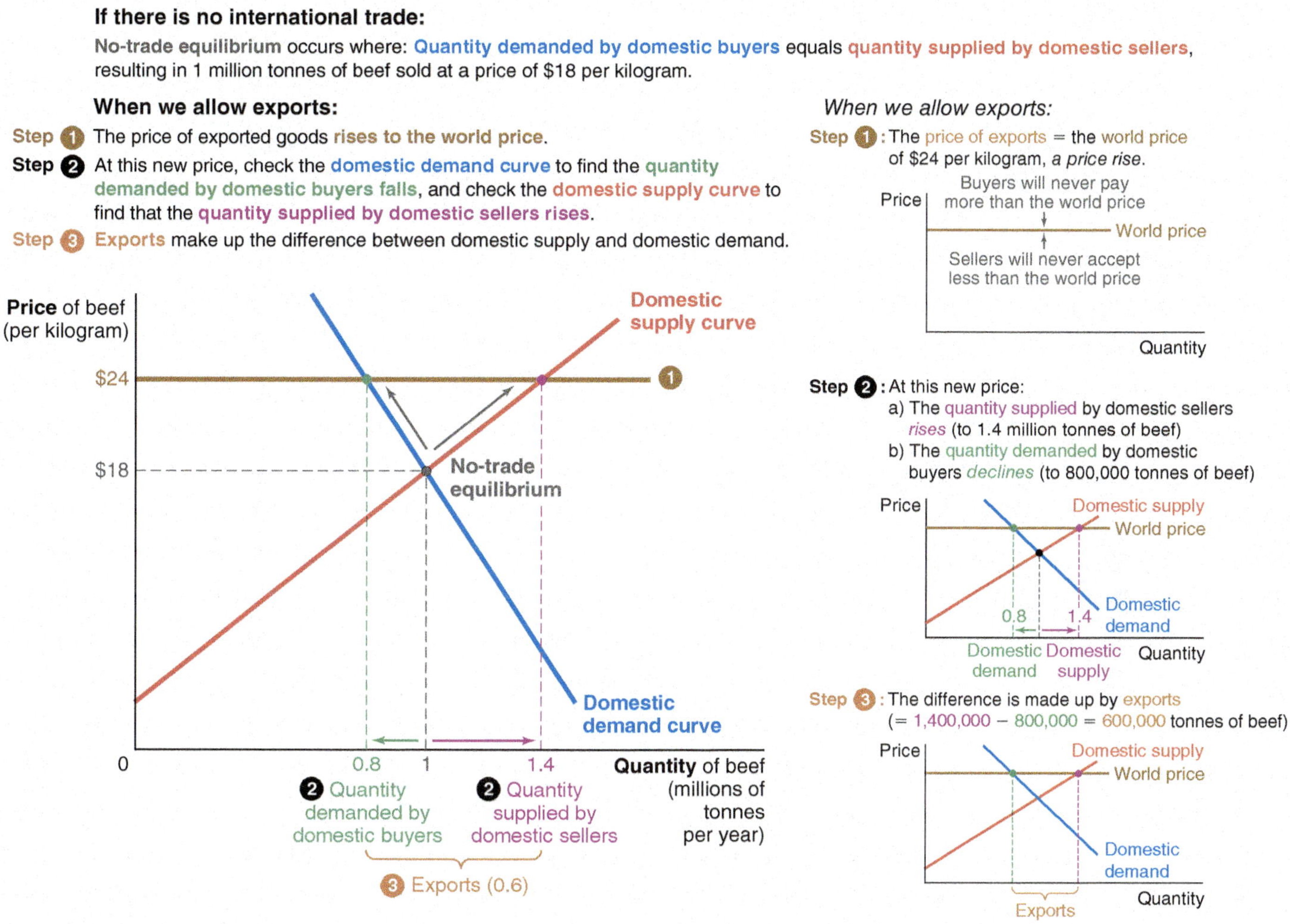

- The price rises to the world price.
- This higher price leads to a higher quantity supplied by domestic sellers but a lower quantity demanded by domestic buyers.
- Exports fill the gap between the quantity supplied and the quantity demanded.

This tells us how exports reshape the forces of supply and demand. But do exports make you better off? Your view likely depends on whether you're a buyer or seller of beef.

See the Connections

What are the effects of exports? → The price is higher (= world price). → *At this higher price:* The quantity demanded by domestic buyers is lower. And the quantity supplied by domestic sellers is higher. → Exports make up the difference between the quantity demanded by domestic buyers and the quantity supplied by domestic sellers.

Exports Raise Economic Surplus

Previously, we worked out that imports raise the total economic surplus of Australians. What about exports? They also raise the economic surplus of Australians. To see why, let's keep working our way through the market for beef, in Figure 6.

Figure 6 | The Welfare Consequences of Allowing Exports

Effects of Exports on Economic Surplus

	No trade	Free trade	Difference
Consumer surplus	$A+B$	A	$-B$
Producer surplus	C	$B+C+D$	$B+D$
Total surplus	$A+B+C$	$A+B+C+D$	$+D$

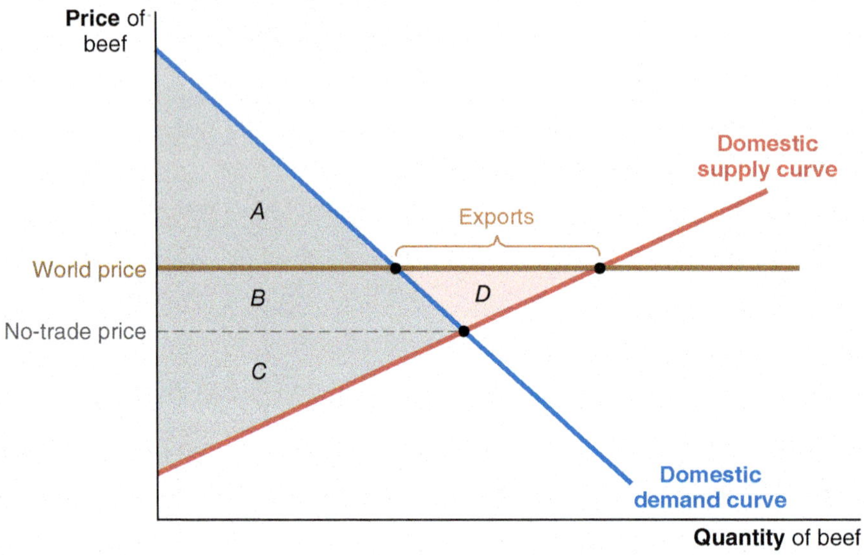

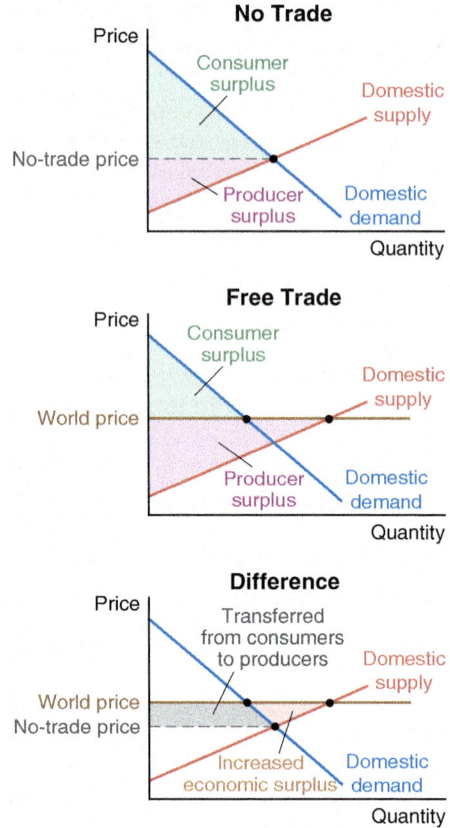

Start by assessing economic surplus when there's no international trade to set a baseline. With no international trade in beef, equilibrium occurs where the domestic supply and demand curves cross. At this no-trade price, buyers earn consumer surplus equal to area $A+B$, while domestic sellers earn a producer surplus equal to area C. Okay, so the total economic surplus with no trade is equal to area $A+B+C$. How does it change when we allow exports?

More expensive exports raise producer surplus. Allowing exports raises the price that domestic sellers get for their beef, which leads them to sell a larger quantity. As a result, producer surplus rises. Graphically, producer surplus is the area above the domestic supply curve but below the new higher price, which is now the world price, and so it is area $B+C+D$. Domestic producers are happy to have the opportunity to export because the higher price of beef raises their producer surplus—from area C to the larger area $B+C+D$.

Domestic consumers lose consumer surplus due to foreign competition. Domestic buyers are worse off because they now have to compete with buyers in other countries, and so the price they pay rises to the higher world price, which also causes them to reduce the quantity they demand. Graphically, consumer surplus is the area below the demand curve, but above this higher price, and so it is area A. Exports make domestic consumers less happy because the higher price of beef reduces their consumer surplus—from area $A+B$, when there is no trade, to the smaller area A.

The benefits exceed the costs, and exports raise total economic surplus. So far we've seen that exports raise the producer surplus earned by Australian suppliers and lower the consumer surplus enjoyed by Australian consumers. What's the net effect?

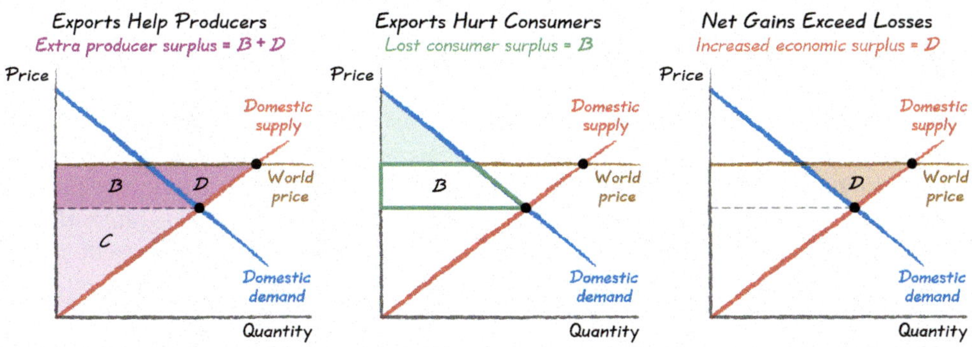

We've figured out that domestic producers gain , while domestic consumers lose a smaller amount, 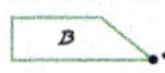. This means that taken together, Australians—when we take account of their roles as producers and consumers—gain economic surplus from exporting, and this net gain is shown as area 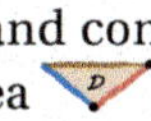.

Recap: The consequences of allowing exports. Okay, now let's summarise what we've learned about exports. We'll begin by analysing what happens to the price. We export those goods that foreign buyers are willing to pay a lot more for, and this leads the price of goods that we export to rise. That higher price leads domestic sellers to raise the quantity they supply, while domestic buyers reduce the quantity they demand. Exports fill the gap between domestic supply and domestic demand. The higher price increases the producer surplus of sellers, and decreases the consumer surplus of domestic buyers. And because sellers amplify their gains by selling more beef at the higher price, while buyers minimise their losses by purchasing a smaller quantity, the net effect is for total economic surplus to increase.

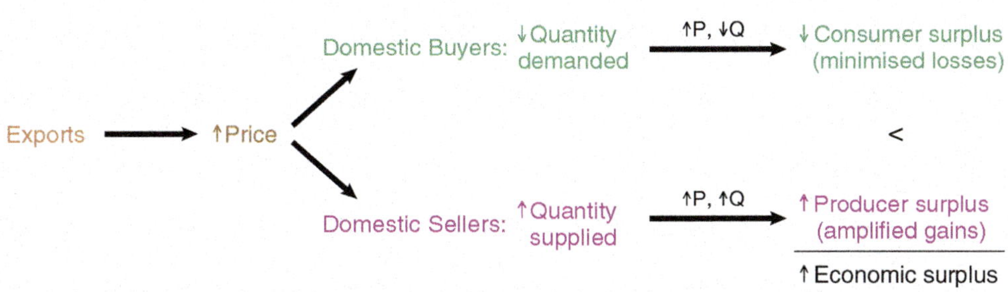

Who Wins, and Who Loses? The Politics of International Trade

We've covered a lot of ground, but now you're well positioned to forecast how changing trade patterns will impact your market. I've summarised our key findings in Figure 7.

Figure 7 | The Effects of International Trade

	Effects of allowing	
Effects on:	**Imports**	**Exports**
Domestic price	↓	↑
Quantity supplied by domestic businesses	↓	↑
Quantity demanded by domestic consumers	↑	↓
Consumer surplus (of Australian consumers)	↑ (a lot)	↓ (a bit)
Producer surplus (of Australian producers)	↓ (a bit)	↑ (a lot)
Total economic surplus (in Australia)	↑	↑

Some students try to memorise this whole table. I have a simpler trick: Whenever you face a trade-related question, first think about the reason anyone imports or exports stuff—to get a better price. You import to get a lower price on stuff you buy, and you export to get a higher price on stuff you sell. Get this right, and the rest should be straightforward. Supply-and-demand analysis tells you that higher prices lead domestic buyers to reduce the quantity they demand and domestic sellers to increase the quantity they supply. (Lower prices lead to the opposite.) The consequences for consumer and producer surplus make sense if you simply remember that consumers like low prices while producers prefer high prices.

International trade increases economic surplus, but not everyone wins. So far, we've seen that trade increases the economic surplus enjoyed by Australians. That's the argument in support of trade. We've analysed goods such as beef, which Australian businesses export, and shirts, which Australians import. In both cases, the free flow of goods and services across national borders raises the total economic surplus enjoyed by Australians. We'd see the same thing if we performed the analysis for any other country. The implication is that international trade raises the living standards of *both* Australians *and* our trading partners. And it does so both when we are the exporters and when we are the importers.

But trade doesn't just expand the pie; it also redistributes it. And that means that not everyone gains. Whether you will personally gain or lose from lower prices for shirts (or higher prices for beef) depends on whether you're a buyer or a seller of shirts (or beef). These mixed effects are critical to understanding the political debate about trade, because people often advocate for what's in their personal interest, rather than what's in the best interest of the country as a whole.

Import-competing businesses oppose international trade. The people arguing most vehemently against international trade are typically those who stand to lose from it. This is why business leaders in industries that have to compete with imports—such as Australian clothing manufacturers—often lobby for fewer imports. The workers in these businesses might be worried about their jobs, leading them to also argue against free trade.

Beyond import-competing businesses, there are also people hurt by the fact that they now have to compete with foreign buyers to purchase Australian-made products. For instance, when Australian businesses export their beef, it raises the price, which hurts domestic buyers of beef. So people in Brisbane who don't want to pay higher prices for beef might protest against free trade in beef.

Exporters and import-dependent businesses support international trade. Similar logic says that the groups most likely to lobby strongly in favour of free trade are those who gain from the ability to compete in foreign markets. This is why export-oriented businesses like Australian Good Meat and AACo would be likely to support efforts to open up new markets overseas. The other big supporters of trade are Australian businesses that import cheaper raw materials such as oil, steel, machinery, and software.

Consumers are rarely an active voice in this debate, but perhaps they should be. After all, it's likely that you also benefit from trade in the form of cheaper shirts, mobile phones, and laptops. But consumers often don't realise that these gains are the result of international trade. Even if they did realise this, they aren't organised into effective lobby groups, and so their voice is often absent from the political debate.

Do the Economics

For each of the following developments, figure out the effect on the price, and hence whether domestic buyers gain or lose, and whether domestic sellers gain or lose:

a. A new type of container ship cuts the cost of shipping cars to Australia in half.
b. Sweden refuses to buy lobsters exported from Victoria.
c. A trade deal makes it easier for Australian farmers to sell beef in Japan.
d. Imports of cheap manufactured goods from China increase.
e. Technology makes it possible for Indian radiologists to read the X-rays of Australian patients. ■

Answer: a. ↓, win, lose; b. ↓, win, lose; c. ↑, lose, win; d. ↓, win, lose; e. ↓, win, lose

9.3 The Debate About International Trade

Learning Objective *Evaluate the arguments for and against international trade.*

Let's now turn to assessing the arguments that are most frequently used in the often-heated debates about whether international trade is good for Australians.

Five Arguments for Limiting International Trade

Our supply-and-demand analysis showed that both importing and exporting raise the economic surplus of Australians. But it left out some important details that lead some to argue that there are specific cases where government should consider restraining international trade. The proponents of limiting international trade raise five major arguments. As we evaluate each argument we'll then turn to the counterarguments. It's up to you to judge which you find most convincing.

Arguments for limiting international trade:
1. Protecting national security
2. Helping infant industries
3. Preventing unfair competition
4. Enforcing minimum standards
5. Saving jobs

Argument one: National security requires that we produce strategically important goods ourselves. International trade makes countries more reliant on one another, but this may not be a good thing if other countries don't have our best interests at heart. This suggests that it may be critical to our national security for strategically important goods like pharmaceuticals to be made domestically. This has become particularly salient since the coranavirus pandemic. Some people make a similar argument for high-tech fields with security implications, like cryptography. An even broader interpretation suggests that we also need to protect domestic sources of food, so that we can still eat if today's trading partners become tomorrow's enemies.

The counterargument is that that these concerns are often overstated. For example, dozens of countries export food and other essentials, and it's unlikely that Australia will get into a massive trade dispute (or war) with all of them at once. The national security argument is often cited by industries.

Argument two: Protection can help infant industries develop. The infant industry argument suggests that governments can help create new industries by shielding fledgling businesses from international competition. For instance, Brazil banned imports of computers for many years, hoping that new Brazilian businesses—infants—would spring up to meet demand, and through time, they would develop efficient production methods. They hoped that once these businesses had learned enough to be globally competitive, they could allow international trade to resume.

But the infant industry often fails to grow up. Brazil's computer manufacturers never became as efficient as American businesses like Dell. All that Brazil got for its efforts was high computer prices and several inefficient computer businesses that eventually went bust. This example illustrates the critique that it can be difficult for governments to identify which industries are likely to mature well if shielded from competition. A related problem is that as infant industries grow, their political power also increases, leading them to pressure governments to keep renewing their "temporary" assistance.

Argument three: Anti-dumping laws prevent unfair competition. Another argument suggests that trade policy should be used to shield domestic businesses from unfair competition. For instance, sometimes a foreign company will temporarily charge extremely low prices—effectively "dumping" their goods on the Australian market—so that that they can drive their Australian competitors out of business. If successful, this would lead to less competition and higher prices in the long run, which would be bad for Australian consumers. Anti-dumping laws try to prevent this.

Opponents argue that in practice it's hard to figure out if foreign businesses are dumping their goods to drive out Australian competitors, or if they're efficient producers offering great prices. Whatever the reality, local businesses will try to convince the government that cheap imports represent unfair competition. Sometimes those local businesses are right, and anti-dumping laws serve their purpose. But frequently, these foreign businesses simply hold a comparative advantage that allows them to produce at a lower cost.

Argument four: Trade shouldn't be a way to skirt regulations. Australia's voters have agreed, through the laws passed by their elected officials, that businesses must meet certain minimum standards. For example, Australian factories can't employ children, they must pay workers at least award wages, they must meet environmental standards, and they must follow certain safety precautions to protect both workers and consumers.

These standards drive costs up, but we get something in return—namely, safer products, a cleaner environment, and a marketplace that treats everyone fairly. Trade provides a way to get around these social agreements. For instance, we strictly regulate how Australian factories dispose of environmentally sensitive waste. But buying goods produced by dirty factories abroad is just as bad for the environment. By this view, it makes sense to restrict some kinds of trade to preserve the rules society has agreed upon. The argument is that if we prevent unsafe or unethical practices at home, we often want to also hold foreign businesses to the same standards.

Opponents argue that the labour or environmental standards that are appropriate for a rich country like Australia are not appropriate for poorer nations. They fear that restricting trade with poor countries can create even more poverty.

Argument five: Foreign competition may lead to job losses. Possibly the most common argument against free trade comes from workers who are concerned that foreign competition will cost them their jobs. Our earlier analysis suggests that workers in import-competing sectors are right to be concerned, because greater openness to trade leads those firms that lack a comparative advantage to shrink and lay off workers.

Australia has generally reduced tariffs and other barriers to imports very substantially since the 1990s. But prior to that we had large barriers to imports of textiles, clothing and footwear, motor vehicles, and many household appliances like fridges. These propped up local jobs while they were in place, but hurt Australian consumers through higher prices. When they were removed, workers moved into other sectors and consumers benefited from lower prices.

Many of those workers in import-competing sectors whose jobs are destroyed can and do retrain and find new jobs. This suggests that opening up to international trade will have only a temporary effect on unemployment. Indeed, Figure 8 shows that there is no relationship between how much a country imports and its unemployment rate.

Workers who worry about their jobs counter that the "temporary" adjustments caused by trade last for a long time. And they've got a point. There's evidence that the tremendous growth of the Chinese manufacturing sector, and the associated rise in Chinese exports, has reduced employment and wages in the Australian manufacturing sector. And it doesn't yet seem like many of these lost jobs have been replaced by jobs in other sectors, even many years later. So while trade might only have a temporary effect on unemployment, this "temporary" effect may last long enough to be virtually permanent for some people.

Figure 8 | Unemployment Is Not Related to Imports

Each point shows imports and unemployment for a separate country.

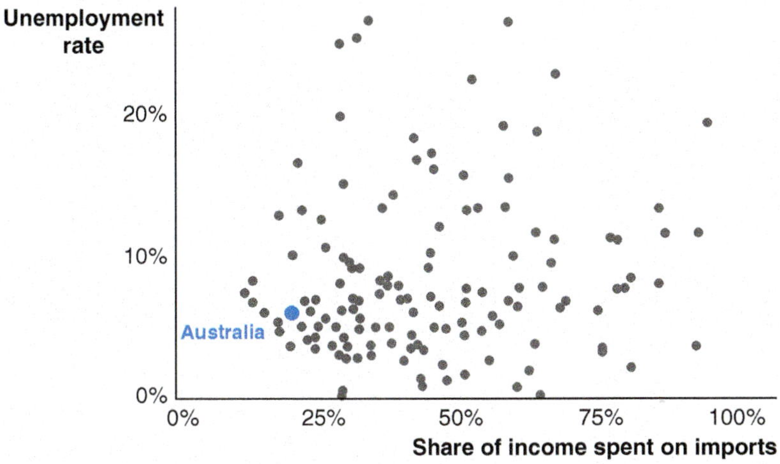

Data from: World Bank.

An Intuitive Approach to the International Trade Debate

As you've probably noticed, the economic argument in favour of international trade—which is based on comparative advantage leading to greater economic surplus—can be pretty technical. This has led economists to try to find better ways to make their point. The following parable provides a different perspective, highlighting the logical errors that sometimes creep into political debates about trade.

Marcelo Rudini/Alamy Stock Photo

This is one way of making trucks.

Harvesting a Western Australian truck crop? There are at least two ways to make trucks. The first involves assembly lines in Queensland, where skilled manufacturing workers—assisted by plenty of robots—transform steel into Volvo trucks. The second way is less well known, but perhaps more amazing: You can grow trucks in Western Australia.

Here's how. Buy wheat seeds, sow them, and water them. With enough care, you'll soon have a field full of wheat. Harvest this wheat, and put it on a boat headed into the Pacific Ocean. Wait a few months, and the ship will return with Hyundai trucks. Now just drive those trucks off the boat. Voila! You've harvested a crop of trucks that you grew from seeds. The fact that this happened because the cargo ship stopped in South Korea to trade wheat for trucks is beside the point. The trucks were the direct result of the efforts of farmers in Western Australia.

Both of these methods of making trucks employ plenty of Australian workers—in one case, it's manufacturing workers in Queensland; in the other, it's farm workers in Western Australia. And they each produce high-quality trucks. So why would we prefer one approach to the other? This question is central to the trade debate, because when people argue for protecting Australian industries from international competition, they're effectively arguing that we should build trucks in Queensland, and stop growing them in Western Australia. But that's inefficient. When there are different ways to make something, we typically let different producers compete with each other, letting buyers choose to buy from the lowest-cost producer. But if we force Australians to buy Queensland-made trucks, even if it's cheaper to grow them in Western Australia, then we'll end up paying more for our trucks. This efficiency loss is a major reason not to limit international trade.

David Gray/Bloomberg/Getty Images

Art Wager/E+/Getty Images

This is another: You can grow wheat and export it overseas, in return for new trucks.

9.4 International Trade Policy

Learning Objective *Understand how and why governments shape international trade.*

Your company's success in winning international business will depend on navigating the complex maze of government policies that foreign governments put in place to help protect their domestic businesses—your rivals!—from competition. So it's time to explore how countries regulate trade and how those regulations will affect your market conditions. We'll then turn to examining global trade agreements, which limit the ways that individual countries can protect their businesses.

Tools of Trade Policy

Managers of international businesses quickly learn that they need to compete in two domains. The first is the market, where you'll compete to produce the best goods at the lowest price. And second, you'll be forced to compete in the political marketplace, as your foreign rivals will lobby their governments to adopt policies that will protect them from having to compete with you. That's why our next task is to evaluate how international trade policies can affect your market.

tariff A tax on imported products.

Tariffs are a tax on imported goods. As **tariffs** are taxes on imported goods, they increase trade costs. We can use our domestic demand and supply curves to figure out the consequences of this higher trade cost.

For instance, what happens if the government imposes a $4 tariff on shirts? We already know what happens without the tariff: The equilibrium price will be equal to the world price of $12. This outcome is shown in grey in Figure 9.

Figure 9 | **The Effects of an Import Tariff**

1. Initially, the price of imported shirts is $12. A $4 tariff raises trade costs by $4, causing the **price to rise** to $16.
2. Due to this higher price: Domestic buyers **demand a lower quantity**. Domestic sellers **supply a higher quantity**.
3. Which means that with a tariff, **imports are lower**.
4. The tariff leads to: A **decrease in consumer surplus**, and a **smaller increase in producer surplus** and **government revenue**, thereby **decreasing total economic surplus**.

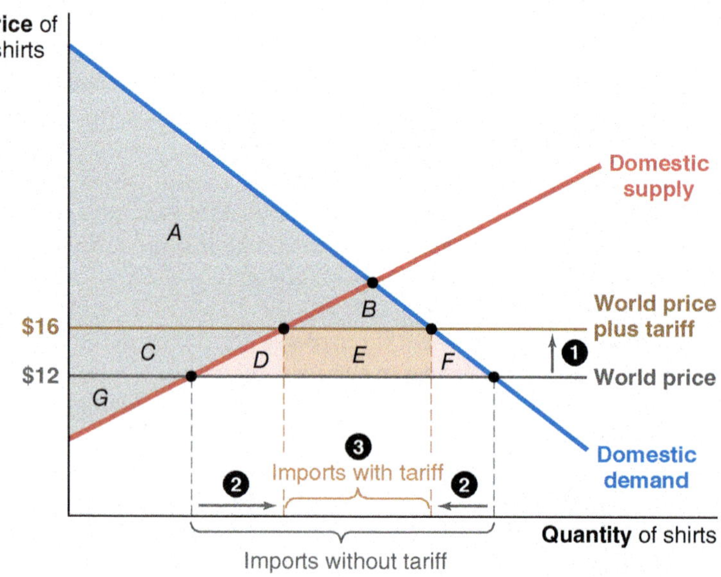

Welfare Effects of an Import Tariff

		No tariff	With tariff	Difference (4)
Consumer surplus	*Area below demand curve and above price*	A + B + C + D + E + F	A + B	−(C + D + E + F)
Producer surplus	*Area above supply curve and below price*	G	C + G	+C
Government surplus	*$4 per shirt times the number of shirts imported*	None	E	+E
Total surplus	*Sum of above*	A + B + C + D + E + F + G	A + B + C + E + G	−(D + F)

Let's use our three-step recipe to see the effects of adding a $4 tariff:

Step one: *What will the new price be?* This tariff adds $4 to the trade costs of importers. Because the world price of $12 is fixed, importers have to pay the world price of $12 plus the tariff of $4. Therefore, the price of shirts rises by $4, to $16.

Step two: *At this new price, what quantities will be demanded and supplied?* Consult the domestic supply and demand curves to discover that at the new higher price, the quantity demanded by domestic buyers is lower, while the quantity supplied by domestic suppliers is higher.

Step three: *What quantity will be traded?* Recall that imports make up the gap between the quantities demanded and supplied. Because this gap shrinks, imports fall.

A tariff on imports will:

1. ↑Price, which will:
2. ↓Quantity demanded by domestic buyers and ↑Quantity supplied by domestic sellers,
3. Causing ↓imports.

OK, so given these effects, who wins and who loses from a tariff?

Domestic buyers are unhappy because the higher price means they either pay an extra $4 per shirt or buy fewer shirts. Their consumer surplus is the area under the demand curve and above the price. Before the tariff, this was equal to the triangle made up of the areas $A+B+C+D+E+F$. After the tariff, this falls to area $A+B$. Thus, tariffs cause consumer surplus to fall by area $C+D+E+F$.

Domestic suppliers are happy because the higher price means higher profit margins on each shirt sold and they also sell an increased quantity. Producer surplus is the area above the supply curve and below the price. Without a tariff, this was area G. After the tariff, it is area $C+G$. Thus, tariffs cause producer surplus to rise by an amount equal to area C.

The *government* also gains because it collects $4 of revenue for each shirt imported. This total tax revenue is equal to the $4 tax (which is the height of rectangle E) times the total number of imports (the width of rectangle E). So the tariff yields tax revenue equal to the height times width—that is, the area of rectangle E.

Adding all this up, consumers lose $C+D+E+F$; producers gain C; and the government gains E. Hence, in total, a tariff will decrease the economic surplus of Australians by an amount equal to area $D+F$.

If you're worried that Figure 9 looks complicated, don't be. It's really not so bad. The charts below show how we built this figure. We started by analysing outcomes without a tariff. Then we analysed the case with a tariff, tracking consumer surplus, producer surplus, and government revenue. Finally, we looked to see what changed.

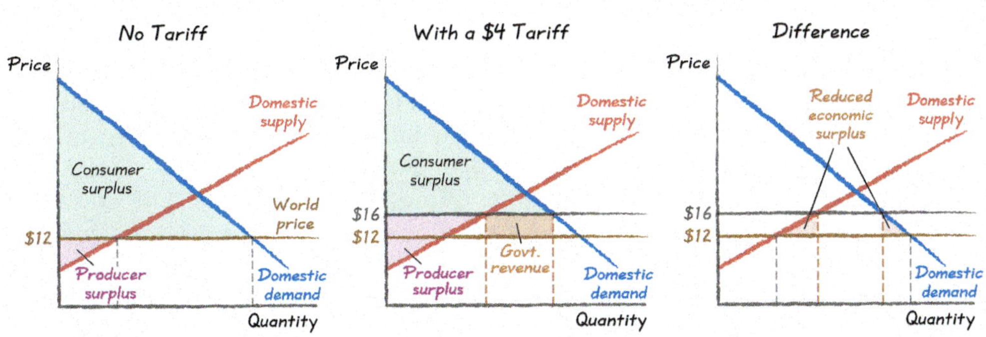

And the end result is worth all this work. We've found that taxing goods made in other countries actually reduces the total economic surplus of Australians! If this is surprising, here's the intuition: The extra government revenue isn't really a gain, because it's effectively paid by Australian consumers who now pay an extra $4 for each shirt they import. And so the tariff shifts money from one set of Australians (consumers) to another (the government). The tariff also raises the price of shirts, which distorts both the choices that consumers make (they'll buy fewer shirts) and the choices that producers make (they keep producing even when it's not efficient to do so).

Red tape is like a tariff because it raises costs, but it doesn't even raise revenue. Tariffs aren't the only tool that governments use to reduce

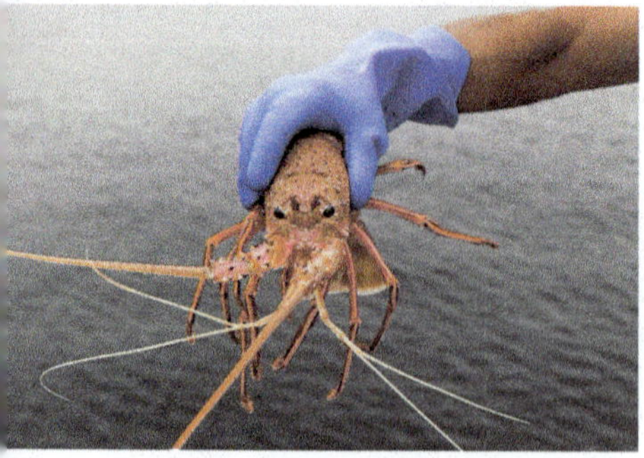

Given all the red tape, it's a miracle this lobster ever made it to China!

international trade. Consider what it takes to export lobster to China. Before you get started, you have to register with the Department of Agriculture as an exporter (that means paperwork), then the Department has to send off your details to the General Administration of Customs in China, which is only done once a quarter, and await their approval (which can take weeks, even months). Once you finally have approval to export lobster to China, you can airfreight your lobster which, upon arrival, will be screened extensively by customs. Make sure you write the product name, specifications, production date, shelf life, storage temperature, establishment registration number, exact destination, and the name and address of the Chinese distributor in both English and Chinese on your packaging, or it may not be accepted at customs. And if you do all of this, there's always the chance that customs officials take their time inspecting your product—in the past there have been times where customs has taken so long that the quality of the lobster has been compromised! Of course, if you get your lobster into China and to a distributor, they will most likely inspect it too before sending it anywhere!

All this red tape ultimately has the same effect as a tariff—it increases trade costs and so raises the price of Australian-produced lobster. The effect of this higher price is the same, whether it's caused by tariffs or red tape: It reduces the quantity demanded, raises the quantity supplied by domestic sellers, and therefore reduces international trade. But red tape is more inefficient than a tariff, because it doesn't even raise revenue for the government.

Import quotas have similar effects to tariffs, but don't raise revenue. Tariffs and red tape affect trade because they raise the price of foreign goods, reducing the quantity of international trade. However, setting an import quota would also have the same impact. An **import quota** limits the quantity of a good that can be imported. For instance, the $4 tariff on shirts in Figure 9 reduces imports to a quantity equal to the width of rectangle *E*. The government could achieve the exact same outcome—the same price and the same quantity demanded, supplied, and imported—if instead it imposed a quota limiting imports to this number. However with a quota, the government wouldn't raise revenue the way it does with tariffs (unless it auctioned off the scarce import licences).

import quota A limit on the quantity of a good that can be imported.

Exchange rate manipulation changes the price of your goods in foreign markets. Foreign governments can also give their companies a leg up by manipulating their exchange rate. Think about how this affects an Australian exporter, such as the winemaker Penfolds. A bottle of 2008 Penfolds Grange typically sells for A$1,000 (the "A$" symbol means "in Australian dollars"), and if it takes five Chinese yuan (China's currency) to buy one Australian dollar, then each bottle of wine will cost a Chinese buyer 5000 yuan. But if the Chinese government sets the exchange rate so that it takes six yuan to buy one Australian dollar, then the price of Penfold's Grange for a Chinese buyer rises to A$1,000×6 yuan per dollar = 6,000 yuan. In effect, China's exchange rate movement adds 1,000 yuan to the cost of each bottle of wine, making it less likely that Chinese consumers will buy Australian-made wine. Keeping the price of the yuan artificially low—the price of yuan is low when it takes more yuan to buy a dollar—makes Australian products more expensive for Chinese buyers.

The lower yuan also makes it cheaper for Australians to import goods from China. Consider a shirt that a Chinese business will sell for 60 yuan. When the exchange rate is 5 yuan per dollar, this sells for 60/5 = A$12. But when the exchange rate is pushed down to 6 yuan per dollar, it sells for A$10 instead. Thus, Australian producers in both exporting and import-competing industries lose business when China keeps its currency artificially low. On the flipside, Australian consumers gain from buying Chinese goods at lower prices. In the past, China's government has weakened its currency to increase its exports and reduce its imports, and this policy has been a subject of some controversy.

Current Trade Policy

We've come a long way in understanding the many ways that government policy can shape trade. Let's take a look at the current state of play.

Australian trade policy largely embraces free trade. While trade policy is still hotly debated, Australia still broadly encourages international trade. As shown in Figure 10, the average tariff charged on imports into Australia was only 2.2% in 2018, which is down from rates as high as 20% over 30 years ago. Australia has as few or fewer trade barriers than nearly all of our trading partners.

However, Australia has historically protected a few specific industries from foreign trade. Most notably, the manufacturing lobby was very successful in persuading the government to maintain high tariffs on clothing and textiles between 1970 and 2003, before the introduction of the Customs Tariff Amendment Bill.

Bottom line: Australia has largely embraced free trade. That conclusion holds even as the future is less clear, as politicians have argued both for aggressively increasing tariffs, and for eliminating them altogether.

Figure 10 | Average Tariff Rate Levied by Australia

Tariffs collected as a share of total imports

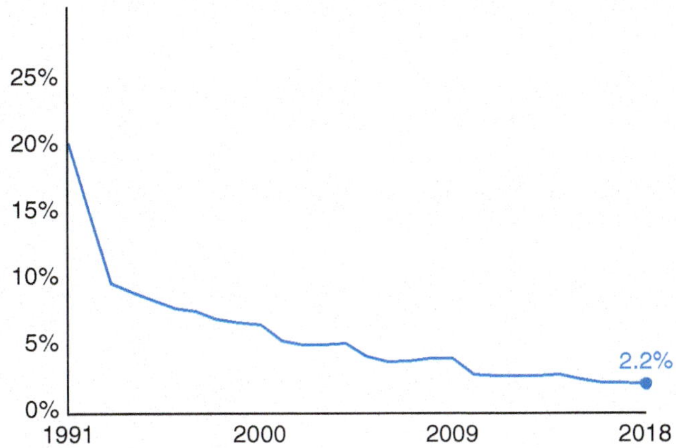

Data from: World Bank.

Australia has signed many free-trade agreements. Your fate as an exporter will depend partly on the trade policies adopted by the countries you're exporting to. Tariffs vary across products and across countries. The average tariff rates in the world's major economies, shown in Figure 11, are typically pretty low.

In many cases, you'll actually face lower tariffs than shown here, because Australia has negotiated free-trade agreements with numerous other countries. The first free-trade agreement Australia negotiated was with New Zealand in 1983. Since then we have signed agreements with a host of countries including: Singapore, the United States, Chile, eight countries in the ASEAN alliance, Malaysia, Korea, Japan, and China. While these are often called "free-trade agreements," it is more accurate to call them free-*er* trade agreements, since they typically reduce rather than eliminate trade barriers.

The World Trade Organization is a forum for global agreements to reduce trade barriers. Negotiating these trade agreements country by country is time-consuming. That's why large-scale multilateral (that is, many-country) trade agreements often make more sense. Today, nearly all countries are members of the World Trade Organization—or WTO, for short. The WTO provides a forum for these countries to jointly agree to reduce or eliminate trade barriers. It has played a major role in reducing trade barriers throughout the world.

WTO agreements also curtail the extent to which individual countries can put up trade barriers. They include two important principles. The first, called *most-favoured-nation status*, means that all member nations must treat all others equally—at least as well as the most favoured nation. (There is an exception for free-trade agreements.) And second, the *national treatment principle* means that imported goods and locally produced goods must be treated equally once they've entered a country. If your business is hurt by trade barriers that violate these principles, there may be a useful remedy.

Talks to further reduce trade barriers have been underway since the "Doha round"—named after the Middle Eastern city in which member countries agreed to another round of negotiations. These talks aimed to reduce tariffs on manufactured goods in many poor countries, in return for reduced farm subsidies in Australia and Europe. Unfortunately, the Doha round has remained deadlocked for many years. (Yawn.) But even if this round is a failure, past reductions in trade barriers have unleashed a torrent of international trade whose effects are felt throughout the world. Let's now turn to analysing how these international linkages shape your life.

Figure 11 | Average Tariff Rate

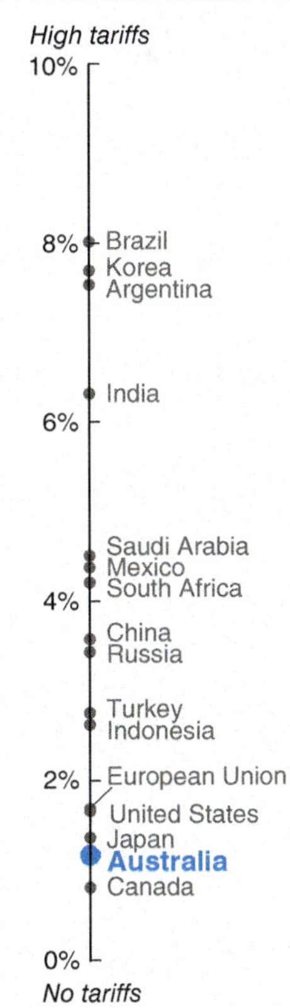

Data from: World Bank.

9.5 Effects of Globalisation

Learning Objective *Illustrate how globalisation shapes your life.*

globalisation The increasing economic, political, and cultural integration of different countries.

The *interdependence principle* reminds us that your economic life depends on decisions made by others, including those made by people all around the world. The increasing global integration of economies, cultures, political institutions, and ideas is called **globalisation.** Trade costs have declined because of lower trade barriers, closer political integration, improved telecommunications, electronic banking, the internet, and improved rail, sea, and air transportation. And this has led our lives to become increasingly connected with those of people living in other countries. But as much as globalisation is a trendy buzzword today, it's not actually new: International trade has been with us, and growing, for centuries.

Globalisation and the Labour Market

Imagine that you work for Atlassian, writing computer software that facilitates collaboration. Each product you and your team produce embodies some of your labour. And so every time the company's software is purchased in China, so is some of your labour. Effectively, you are selling some of your labour in China. Likewise, each shirt that you import from China embodies the labour of Chinese workers. And so even though Australian and Chinese *labourers* don't directly compete with each other (they're in different national labour markets), their *labour* does compete—it's just embodied in the goods that are traded between countries.

Figure 12 | Countries with Higher Wages Have Higher Productivity

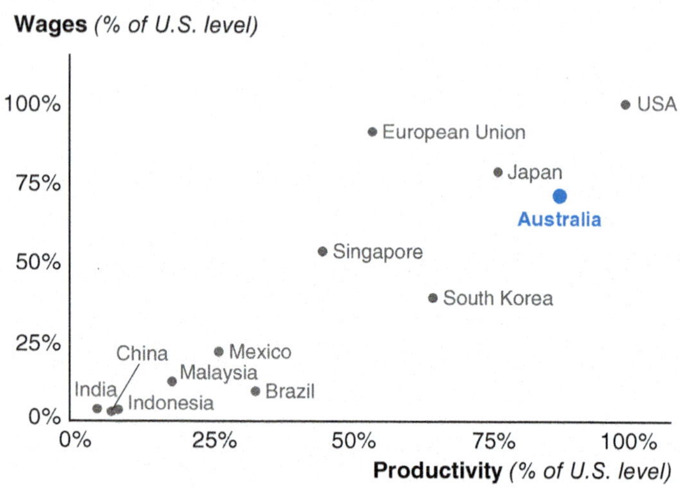

Data from: Ceglowski and Golub, "Just How Low Are China's Labour Costs?" *World Economy,* 30(4), 2007. Dolman, Parham, and Zheng, "Can Australia Match US Productivity Performance?", *Australian Government Productivity Commission,* 2007.

Productivity determines average wages. This leads some to worry that globalisation may force Australian wages down to the low levels seen in countries like China, India, or Indonesia. If all workers were similar, this might be a long-run consequence of international trade. And it would be disastrous for Australian workers. On average, Australian manufacturing workers earn A$26 (around US$20) per hour, compared to A$2.25 (US$1.69) in India, A$5.35 (US$4.11) in China, and A$5.28 (US$3.96) in Mexico. While in the United States, which has the highest productivity in the world, manufacturing workers earn US$39 on average (around A$50).

Fortunately, wages aren't going to be equalised anytime soon, because workers are not all the same. While the United States has the highest productivity in the world, Australia also has a very high productivity, at around 87% of the U.S. level on average. The productivity of an average Australian manufacturing worker is 10.5 times higher than that of their Chinese counterpart. This means that businesses are willing to pay Australian workers 10.5 times more. Figure 12 shows that countries with higher productivity tend to enjoy higher average wages. And while this is true in the manufacturing sector, Australia's high minimum wage laws mean that even with a lower productivity than the United States in other sectors, Australian wages tend to be higher than U.S. wages on average.

International trade is raising income inequality within Australia. Not all workers in a country benefit from international trade, as it raises some wages while lowering others. In particular, recall that Australia exports skill-intensive goods such as financial services and education. As trade costs fall, foreign demand for these goods increases. This also increases the demand for highly educated workers. Consequently, globalisation raises the incomes of highly educated workers in Australia, because it increases the demand for the stuff they make.

On the flip side, recall that because many of our trading partners have abundant low-skilled labour, they tend to export goods like clothing that use a lot of less-educated workers. As these countries engage in more trade, Australians will import more clothing. This decreases the demand for domestically produced clothing. In turn, this decreases the demand for the predominantly low-wage and less-educated workers in that industry, leading to even lower wages. More generally, globalisation reduces the wages of workers in import-competing sectors, and in Australia, these sectors tend to employ a lot of less-educated workers. Consequently, international trade probably explains some of the rising income inequality in Australia over recent decades. That said, inequality in Australia after taxes and transfers has remained relatively flat due to our strong social safety net.

International trade can have the same effect as immigration. There's an interesting implication of all this for immigration policy. The government currently restricts the number of foreigners immigrating to Australia to shield domestic workers from foreign competition. But even though foreign *labourers* can't enter Australia at will, foreign *labour* can—at least to the extent that it is embodied in imports produced by foreign workers. And so trade in goods can have the exact same effects that immigration otherwise might, serving as a source of competition for Australian labour.

Are foreign workers being exploited or offered opportunity? Opponents of globalisation often argue that it is exploitative. When you buy a shirt from China, it was probably made by someone earning less than $4 per hour, often in grim conditions—certainly far worse than would be legal in Australia. And so they might argue that it's immoral and exploitative to buy cheap shirts made under such bad conditions. Do you agree?

Before answering, consider the counterargument, which invokes the *opportunity cost principle*, to ask: "Or what?" If Australians stopped buying these shirts, what would happen to the workers that produce them? For many Chinese workers, it's likely that their next best alternative involves working for an even lower wage. While $2 per hour is a low wage for an Australian, for many people in rural China, it represents a big improvement in their quality of life.

This debate is especially relevant to debates about "fair trade" versus "free trade." Both sides argue that Australians should continue to trade with people in poor countries. But "fair trade" advocates argue that we should pay higher prices for imports—high enough to ensure a reasonable standard of living for the workers involved. They also argue that Australian negotiators should insist on including minimum labour standards as part of new trade agreements. They claim fair trade would yield better working conditions and higher incomes for foreign workers, though at the cost of higher prices in Australia.

But higher prices lead to a lower quantity demanded. So it's likely that the higher prices for fair-trade shirts would reduce the quantity demanded. And so these policies could destroy the jobs of the very people they aim to help. What are your thoughts on fair trade?

Tying It Together

The world is getting smaller. Countries have torn down trade barriers, trade costs have rapidly declined, and communication technology has dramatically improved. As a result, your life is more closely integrated with the rest of the globe than at any time in human history. This chapter has given you the tools to understand how international trade is reshaping our domestic markets. You're now equipped to recognise both the opportunities and the threats from globalisation.

There are some subtle but important differences in how economists view trade, compared to the general public. Here's some of what makes the economic perspective unique:

Trade is about cooperation, not competition. Trade is like a good marriage: Find the right partner, and you'll both be better off. The magic of voluntary exchange is that it makes both the buyer and the seller better off, no matter which country they're living in. But trade is often described in very different terms—as if it's a competition, and every time China wins, Australia loses.

This view of trade as a competition makes the mistake of viewing global business as a fight over a fixed pie. But trade is about reallocating tasks so that they're done more efficiently. Ultimately, it's about cooperation so that everyone gets more of what they want. The beauty of international trade is that if we can import apples more cheaply, we can bake a bigger apple pie.

People trade. Countries don't. When economists talk about trade, they talk about people, rather than countries. That's because people trade; countries don't. Australia doesn't buy shirts; individual Australians do. Trade is not war. It's millions of people cooperating with strangers they've never met, to get a better deal.

Trade is not just about business. Consumers matter too. When noneconomists think about "the economy," they tend to focus on businesses, such as the car manufacturer that relocated to another country. And they're right to be concerned, as many businesses are threatened by cheap imports. But when economists analyse the economy, they think about buyers as well as sellers. Cheap imports may threaten some jobs, but they also offer Australian workers a way to make their wages go further, which raises their living standards. The next time you replace your laptop or your mobile phone, or buy a nice piece of clothing at a good price, you're reaping the benefits of cheap imports.

Trade is an opportunity, and not just a threat. For the workers who might lose their jobs at the car manufacturer, the threat posed by international trade is very real. But just as some car manufacturers are closing, dozens of new office buildings are opening. Even as some businesses shrink, others find ways to profit from the opportunity to sell to a global marketplace of 8 billion people.

However, just as economic thinking about trade can provide clarity, there are also blind spots.

Trade is a threat, and not just an opportunity. Sometimes, the logic of the *cost-benefit principle* leads economists to focus too much on the bottom line. The bottom line is that trade expands the pie, but this misses the equally important fact that trade also redistributes it. If a worker in a foreign factory just got your slice of pie, you're likely to think that an economist who reminds you that it's a bigger pie just doesn't get it.

Trade causes disruption in the short run. Economists tend to focus on the long-run effects of things, while the short-run impacts might be quite different.

While trade may increase the size of the pie in the long run, reassigning people to different pie-making roles causes a lot of disruption in the short run. Economists may need to pay more attention to these short-run disruptions. After all, these temporary effects can last long enough—sometimes many years—that they're nearly permanent for the people involved.

Trade is not just about economics. Anxiety about globalisation is not just about economics. The closure of an auto plant is not just about lost jobs; it can also mean the death of a city, the end of a particular way of life, and the loss of local traditions. As the world becomes more integrated, local and national cultures are becoming more similar. And so globalisation is not just about the size of the pie, or even how we slice it, but also about the flavour of the pie.

Global integration will continue to be a major force throughout your life. As you think ahead toward your career, think about how best to position yourself to benefit from the enormous opportunities it will bring.

Chapter at a Glance

Comparative advantage drives international trade.

Sources of comparative advantage: Abundant inputs | Specialised skills | Mass production

Consequences of Imports

No Trade | Step 1: Domestic price = World price | Step 2: Domestic responses | Step 3: Imports fill the gap

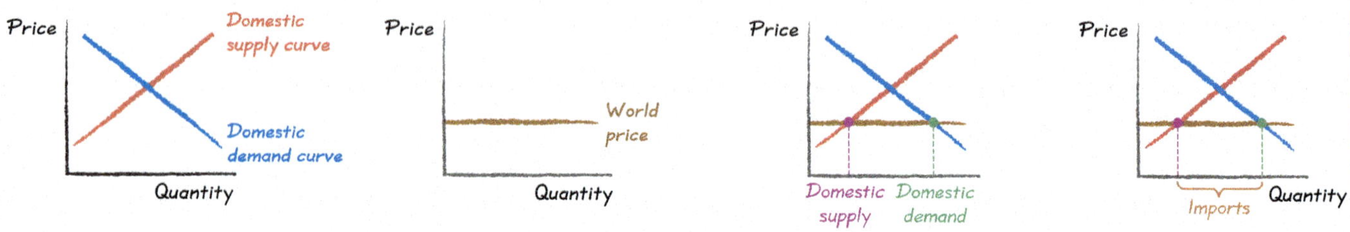

Imports → ↓Price

- Buyers: ↑Quantity demanded —↓P, ↑Q→ ↑Consumer surplus (amplified gains)
- >
- Sellers: ↓Quantity supplied —↓P, ↓Q→ ↓Producer surplus (minimised losses)

↑Economic surplus

Consequences of Exports

No Trade | Step 1: Domestic price = World price | Step 2: Domestic responses | Step 3: Exports fill the gap

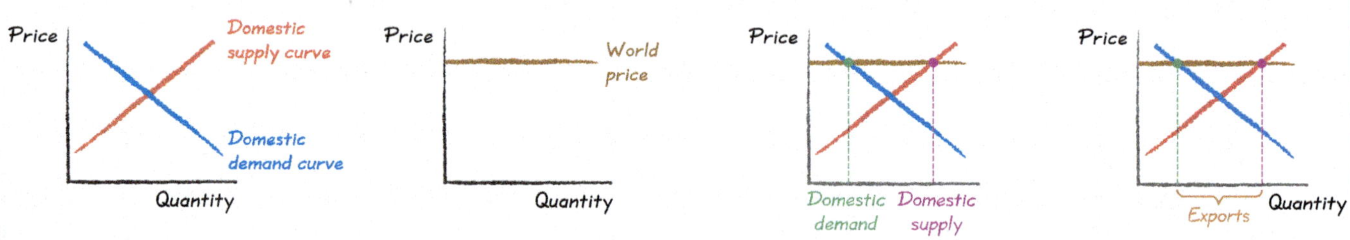

Exports → ↑Price

- Buyers: ↓Quantity demanded —↑P, ↓Q→ ↓Consumer surplus (minimised losses)
- <
- Sellers: ↑Quantity supplied —↑P, ↑Q→ ↑Producer surplus (amplified gains)

↑Economic surplus

Arguments for Limiting Trade

1. National security
2. Infant industry
3. Preventing unfair competition
4. Enforcing minimum standards
5. Saving jobs

Trade Policy Tools

1. Tariffs: a tax on imported products
2. Import quotas
3. Red tape
4. Exchange rate manipulation
5. Free-trade agreements (and the WTO)

Globalisation: The increasing economic, political, and cultural integration of different countries.

Key Concepts

domestic demand curve, 214	globalisation, 230	tariff, 226
domestic supply curve, 214	import, 208	trade costs, 209
export, 208	import quota, 228	world price, 214

Discussion and Review Questions

Learning Objective 9.1 *Discover why we trade with people in other countries.*

1. Meagan, a contractor, is hired to install cabinets in a new home and has to decide whether to build the cabinets herself or purchase them from a local cabinet shop. What role does comparative advantage play in her decision? Will your answer change if she has to purchase the cabinets from a foreign supplier? Please explain why this does or doesn't affect your answer.
2. Why do you think Colombia's key exports include coffee, flowers, bananas, and tropical fruits?
3. For each of the following, explain how it can be a source of comparative advantage and provide an example.
   a. Abundant inputs
   b. Specialised skills
   c. Mass production

Learning Objective 9.2 *Use supply and demand to assess the consequences of international trade.*

4. The North American Free Trade Agreement (NAFTA), signed in 1994, reduced trade barriers between the United States, Canada, and Mexico. NAFTA's supporters argued that by reducing trade barriers, consumer prices would be lower, and that increased trade would create more jobs in the United States. Briefly explain why this could occur.
5. In 2018, Bill Shorten, the ALP leader at that time, criticised the Trans-Pacific Partnership trade agreement as having a negative impact on jobs in Australia. In particular, he cited the impact on manufacturing jobs. In what ways might free-trade agreements have a negative impact on jobs in Australia?

Learning Objective 9.3 *Evaluate the arguments for and against international trade.*

6. For each of the following cases for limiting international trade, briefly explain the rationale for limiting trade and provide a possible counterargument. Which arguments do you find most compelling?
   a. National security requires we produce strategically important goods ourselves.
   b. Protection can help infant industries develop.
   c. Anti-dumping laws prevent unfair competition.
   d. Trade shouldn't be a way to avoid regulations.
   e. Foreign competition leads to job losses.

Learning Objective 9.4 *Understand how and why governments shape international trade.*

7. Small, open economies like Australia understand that they would be badly hurt by trying to raise tariff barriers. Large, relatively independent countries like the United States, operate under a potentially different political calculus. For instance, in January 2018 President Donald Trump imposed tariffs of 20%–50% on imported home washing machines. This prompted Whirlpool, which produces residential washing machines in the United States, to announce plans to hire 200 additional workers. Explain how the tariffs on imported washing machines would affect the price Whirlpool is able to charge and its quantity supplied of washing machines. Why would these changes cause Whirlpool to hire more workers?

   Two months later, President Trump imposed a 25% tariff on steel imports and a 10% tariff on aluminium imports. Whirlpool quickly felt the impact of these tariffs on their production costs. In June the U.S. Department of Labour estimated that the cost of producing washing machines had increased by 17%. Explain how the steel tariffs may affect Whirlpool's hiring plans.

Learning Objective 9.5 *Illustrate how globalisation shapes your life.*

8. Kemala is a factory worker in Indonesia, where she earns the equivalent of roughly A$1.30 per hour producing T-shirts to export to Australia. Some people argue that this wage is exploitative and unfair and others argue that she is a great example of the benefits of free trade. Explain the economic reasoning behind both sides of this argument using the principles of economic thinking.

Study Problems

Learning Objective 9.1 *Discover why we trade with people in other countries.*

1. For each of the following goods that are imported into Australia, identify which of the three sources of comparative advantage (abundant inputs, specialised skills, or mass production) accounts for that country's comparative advantage.
   a. Australia imported $7.18 billion worth of vehicles (mainly passenger cars) from Japan in 2019.

b. Australia imported $40 million worth of chocolate and cocoa-based products from Switzerland in 2019.

c. Australia imported $1.6 billion worth of footwear items from China in 2018.

Learning Objective 9.2 *Use supply and demand to assess the consequences of international trade.*

2. The majority of kiwifruit consumed in Australia is imported, much of it coming from New Zealand and Italy. The amount of kiwifruit that is imported increased from 14,000 tonnes in 1992 to 22,000 tonnes in 2020. Much of this increase can be attributed to a reduction in transportation costs associated with improved roads and storage technology.

Use a domestic supply and domestic demand graph to illustrate the impact of imports on the market for kiwifruit in Australia. Be sure to properly label all relevant curves. Label the market outcome prior to international trade and the predicted outcome with international trade. Label the price, quantity demanded, quantity supplied, and amount of imports. What happens to the price that consumers pay for kiwifruit and what impact will this have on consumer surplus? Use your graph to illustrate your answers.

3. In 2019, Australia was importing approximately 330,000 barrels of crude oil per day at an average price of $93 per barrel. The domestic demand and supply of crude oil in Australia is given by the graph below.

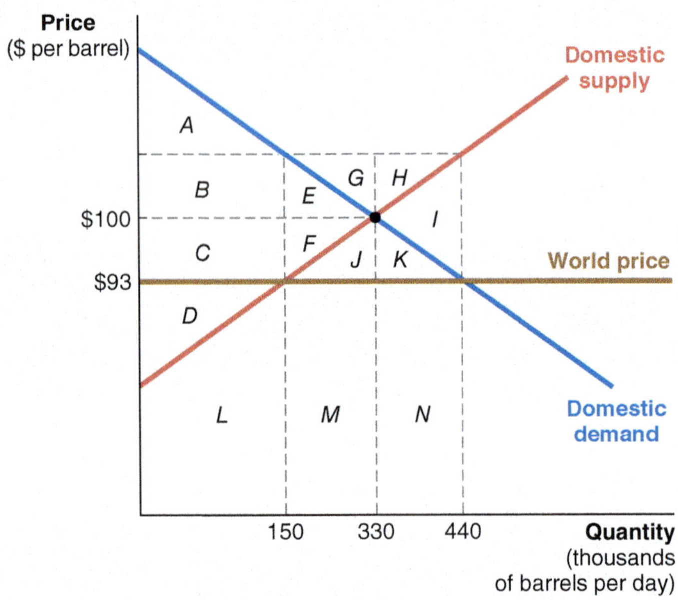

Use the letters and values in the graph to fill in the following table.

	Without trade	With trade
Quantity supplied domestically		
Quantity demanded domestically		
Quantity imported		
Area of consumer surplus		
Area of producer surplus		

4. Draw a domestic demand and domestic supply curve for apples in Australia using data given in the table below.

Price (per apple)	Quantity demanded domestically (millions of kilograms per year)	Quantity supplied domestically (millions of kilograms per year)
$0.15	930	758
$0.30	844	844
$0.45	758	930
$0.60	672	1016

a. Identify the equilibrium price and quantity without trade.

b. If the price at which apples are traded in the world market is $0.15 per apple higher than the domestic price, what is the world price?

c. If Australia allows international trade, how many apples will be produced domestically in Australia and how many apples will be purchased in Australia?

d. Will Australia import or export apples? How many?

e. Will consumer surplus rise or fall? What about producer surplus? And total economic surplus?

Learning Objective 9.3 *Evaluate the arguments for and against international trade.*

5. Australia imports a lot of cars, despite having had its own car industry. Each of the following statements are arguments some people could make for restricting imports of cars into Australia. For each statement, identify the threat to the Australian industry that the argument is trying to counter, and identify the opportunities that would be given up if the argument wins.

a. "Foreign manufacturers are offloading cars made with cheap foreign labour operating in unsafe and unhealthy factories. We must pass a law to prevent this exploitation."

b. "We need to foster the innovation of small car companies in Australia that could truly change the car industry. Allowing foreign electric vehicle manufacturers like Tesla to sell cars in Australia will squander any chance of creating those cars domestically."

Learning Objective 9.4 *Understand how and why governments shape international trade.*

6. Australia consumes and produces a lot of sugar. The Australian sugar industry is one of the few Aussie industries which still enjoys protection today.

The world price for sugar was around $0.26 per kilo at the start of 2019. Using the table below, figure out how much sugar would be demanded and supplied domestically at the world price. How much sugar would be imported into Australia?

Illustrate using a graph.

Price ($ per kilogram)	Quantity demanded domestically (millions of kilograms per year)	Quantity supplied domestically (millions of kilograms per year)
$ 0.12	3600	450
$ 0.26	3000	900
$ 0.40	2400	1350
$ 0.54	1800	1800

Show graphically how the price of sugar in Australia, imports, domestic consumer surplus, domestic producer surplus, and government revenue would change if Australia imposed a 6 cent tariff per pound of sugar.

7. Australia has historically imposed import tariffs (called an excise) on tobacco. Let's take a look at how these tariffs impact the market for tobacco. The domestic supply and domestic demand for tobacco are illustrated by the graph below.

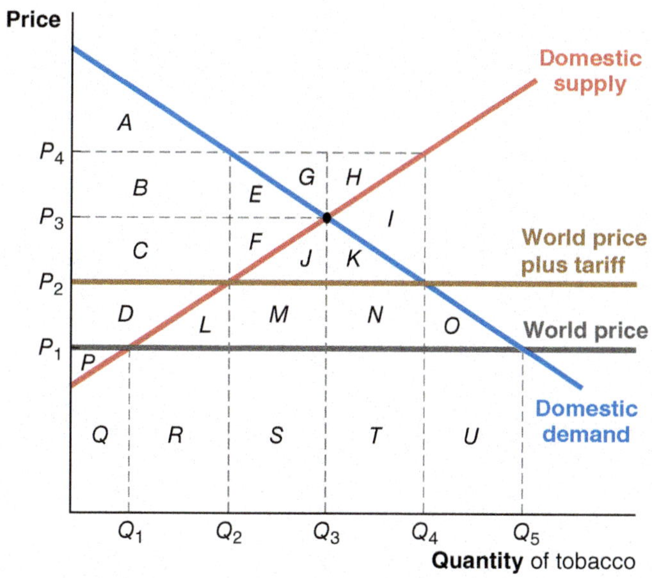

a. Use the letters and values in the graph to fill in the following table, comparing the outcomes of free trade and restricted trade.

	Without tariff	With import tariff	Difference
Price			
Quantity of domestic demand			
Quantity of domestic supply			
Imports			
Area of consumer surplus			
Area of producer surplus			
Area of government revenue			
Area of total economic surplus (including government)			

b. If the government decides to replace the tariff with a quota that will have the same effect on the market as the tariff, the quota should restrict imports to what quantity?

Learning Objective 9.5 *Illustrate how globalisation shapes your life.*

8. You are thinking of purchasing a new shirt for $5 that has a "Made in Indonesia" tag on it. You're shopping with a friend who mentions how terrible working conditions are for textile workers in Indonesia and says, "If they'd only charge $10 for their shirts, then all the sweatshop workers would be so much better off." Identify the possible flaw in this argument.

CHAPTER 10

Externalities and Public Goods

The Earth is heating up, causing glaciers to melt and the sea level to rise. This has disrupted global weather patterns, leading to more extreme weather events such as floods and droughts. As a result, thousands of species face extinction as their habitats disappear. Humanity faces related threats, as climate change has led to declining crop yields. Scientists have suggested that if nothing changes, whole cities will eventually be submerged under water.

airphoto.gr/Shutterstock

The costs of greenhouse gases are borne by everyone.

A leading cause of all this upheaval is rising greenhouse gases. To understand what's going on, realise that nature has blessed our planet with a blanket of greenhouse gases that insulates us from the extreme temperatures in outer space. The problem is that this blanket is getting thicker, which is warming the Earth. The rise in greenhouse gases over the past 150 years is mostly due to burning fossil fuels that release greenhouse gases into the atmosphere.

But beyond the science, economists see an even deeper cause of climate change, and it's rooted in a pervasive market failure. Here's the problem: Whenever one of us decides to burn fossil fuels, the ensuing pollution affects all of us. This means that no individual person bears the full consequences of their choice to use fossil fuels. Because people fail to account for the harm they do to the well-being of their fellow citizens, they burn more fossil fuels than is in our collective best interest.

This type of problem extends well beyond climate change. In this chapter we'll discover that when people don't face the full costs and benefits of their actions, they'll often make choices that ignore the interests of affected bystanders. Failing to resolve the tension between your private interest and society's interest can lead markets, communities, and corporations to make bad choices.

But these problems are not inevitable, and in the second half of this chapter, we'll dig into potential solutions, exploring ways in which you can change people's incentives so that they make decisions that better serve society's interests. The payoff is that you'll have a set of tools you can use to generate better outcomes for your community, your company, and your planet.

Chapter Objective

Explore what happens when your choices have side effects on others.

10.1 Identifying Externalities
Identify externalities and their consequences.

10.2 The Externality Problem
Analyse how externalities lead markets to produce inefficient outcomes.

10.3 Solving Externality Problems
Learn how to solve externality problems.

10.4 Public Goods and the Tragedy of the Commons
Understand how to solve externality problems that arise when people can't be excluded from using something.

10.1 Identifying Externalities

Learning Objective *Identify externalities and their consequences.*

Your decision to drive to work or to school isn't just about you because it also affects other people. Your car is powered by energy that creates pollution when it's produced. If it runs on petrol, your exhaust spits out noxious gases, stinking up the air that others breathe. When you drive, you create traffic, slowing down other people's commutes. Drivers are also a hazard to others, and car accidents kill over 1,100 Australians each year. Each kilometre you drive adds to the wear and tear on the roads, and you don't pay directly for those repairs, but rather, drivers and taxpayers as a whole are on the hook.

externality A side effect of an activity that affects bystanders whose interests aren't taken into account.

Driving is not just about you, because it involves an **externality**—a side effect on bystanders whose interests aren't fully taken into account. Externalities are important because they lead to *market failure*, producing inefficient outcomes that aren't in society's best interest. This failure arises when there are bystanders who are affected by your choices and who can't easily shape them. As a result, their interests are ignored or underweighted. The key insight of this chapter is that when people make decisions without facing the full consequences of their actions—that is, when externalities are involved—bad outcomes can result.

Types of Externalities

negative externality An activity whose side effects harm bystanders.

positive externality An activity whose side effects benefit bystanders.

An activity whose side effects *harm* bystanders is called a **negative externality.** For instance, the exhaust that spews from your tailpipe is a negative externality because it harms others who breathe in that pollution. Alternatively, some activities involve **positive externalities,** which are activities whose side effects *benefit* bystanders. For instance, when you get a Covid-19 vaccine, it prevents you from getting sick, *and* it also protects your friends and classmates, because if you don't get Covid-19, they're not at risk of catching it from you.

Negative externalities impose costs on others. The following examples of negative externalities illustrate how my choices have side effects that harm you (or other bystanders):

- If I stand up at a concert, you won't be able to see the stage.
- If I smoke near you, my secondhand smoke might cause you to get cancer.
- If I take antibiotics too often, a resistant bacterial strain is more likely to form that makes antibiotics less effective for you.
- If I choose to drive a big SUV instead of a small car, then you're more likely to sustain a life-threatening injury if our cars collide.
- If I'm disruptive during your economics class, you'll probably learn less.
- If I'm trolling on social media sites, you'll find them less pleasant and less useful.

Roman Rvachov/Shutterstock

When you stand up at a concert, you create a negative externality.

Negative externalities create problems because people often make decisions without taking full account of the costs that their choices impose on others. For example, internet trolls often think they're engaging in harmless fun because they're not thinking about others. But if they were forced to pay for the costs they impose on others, they might do something less annoying instead. When people fail to account for the costs their negative externalities impose, they do more of these activities than would be in society's best interest.

Positive externalities generate benefits for others. Positive externalities also affect bystanders, but with side effects that benefit others. The following examples illustrate some important positive externalities:

- When you plant a tree, it'll recycle carbon dioxide into oxygen, which improves air quality for everyone in your neighbourhood.

- When you buy a big-screen television for your living room, your roommates will also enjoy being able to watch movies.
- When you work hard and earn a pay rise, you'll pay more taxes, which fund better schools, parks, and other government services that benefit your community.
- When you discover a brilliant new scientific breakthrough, other entrepreneurs might use your idea to launch their own new products.
- When you prepare before your study group meeting, your friends will benefit from your insights.
- When you exercise regularly, you'll become healthier and your health insurer (or other taxpayers, through Medicare) will benefit because they'll likely spend less on your medical care.

Positive externalities sound like a good thing, since in each of these cases, your actions help other people. But they still lead to market failure because people typically make decisions without taking full account of the positive effects of their choices on bystanders. As a result, they'll do less of these socially useful activities than is in society's best interest. That means that even better outcomes could occur if the benefits to society were taken into account.

For example, when you decide whether to get a Covid vaccine, you might apply the *cost-benefit principle* and compare the cost of the shot with the benefit to you of a reduced chance of getting sick. Since the vaccine is free to the individual in Australia, there is no financial cost to getting vaccinated. But there is the risk of side effects, like blood clots. If you think you're not very likely to get the virus, you might decide not to be vaccinated, reasoning that the benefit *to you* doesn't exceed the risks of side effects. But that might not be the best choice for *your class*. After all, that shot will prevent *you* from getting sick and it also prevents *your classmates* from catching the virus from you. Even if the benefits don't outweigh the costs to you, the benefits to the rest of your class might mean that the benefits to you and to your class as a whole exceed the costs. Left to make the decision yourself, you might make the choice that's in your best interest, rather than what's in the total best interest. More generally, when people fail to account for the benefits associated with positive externalities, they do less of these activities than is in society's best interest.

Do the Economics

Think about all of the interactions involved in your economics class. When you go to class, prep your homework, work on group assignments, and study for and take exams, do your actions affect other people? Who? How? Do you take full account of their wishes? In other words: What are the externalities? ■

Answer: Here are some important externalities. If you're disruptive in class, you'll make it hard for your classmates to pay attention, which is a negative externality because they'll learn less. When you ask good questions in class, you push your instructor to be clearer, which is a positive externality benefiting your classmates. When you slack off on a group assignment, you force the rest of the group to work harder, which is a negative externality. When you study with your friends, you might help them understand a tough concept (like externalities), which is a positive externality. If a classmate cheats on an exam and gets a "distinction" or "high distinction" that they don't deserve, then if the class is curved, that's one less D or HD for you and your classmates to earn, which is a negative externality.

A price change is not an externality. Before we move on, let's clear up a potential misunderstanding: *A price change is not an externality.* For instance, consider what happens when the price of housing rises. Some people complain that higher house prices are a negative externality, because it makes life harder for new homebuyers. But they're only thinking about half the story. The full story is that the higher price will hurt a homebuyer who has to pay more, but that harm is exactly offset by a gain to the home seller, who'll get paid more for their house. Even if your dream home becomes so expensive that you're priced out of the market, some other shopper will buy it instead. A price change isn't an externality because once you total up the effects, it generates neither costs nor benefits. Price changes aren't an externality, but rather a *redistribution* between buyers and sellers.

There's another way to think about this. Externalities are about the side effects on people whose interests aren't taken into account. You might think that by bidding a high price in an auction for an apartment you impose an externality on other bidders. Either they don't win the auction, or they may have to pay a higher price if they do win. So you are affecting other people. But this is not an externality, because the market's price mechanism—in this instance the rules of the auction—mediates the transaction. Externalities are about side effects that aren't mediated by the market, which is why they cause market failure. By contrast, when prices rise and fall in response to the actions of buyers and sellers, you're seeing the mechanism by which markets work.

The Conflict Between Private Interest and Society's Interest

Externalities create tension between your personal or private interest and society's interest. Your *private interest* is all about the costs and benefits that you personally incur. But *society's interest* includes all costs and benefits, whether they accrue to you or to others. If your choices don't affect others, your private interest will correspond with society's interest. But when your actions affect bystanders—that is, when there are externalities—there's a conflict between your private interest and society's interest. And that conflict can lead markets to fail. To see why, let's explore how externalities shape the decisions that sellers and buyers make.

marginal private cost The extra cost paid by the seller from one extra unit.

external cost A cost imposed on bystanders.

marginal external cost The extra external cost imposed on bystanders from one extra unit.

marginal social cost All marginal costs, no matter who pays them = *Marginal private cost plus marginal external cost.*

Negative externalities create external costs. Let's start with the negative externality caused by the production of petrol. Refineries transform crude oil into more useful products, such as the petrol that fuels your car. In Chapter 3 on supply, you discovered how an oil refinery makes decisions about how much petrol to supply. Like all businesses, its supply decisions are guided by marginal cost, which is the extra cost associated with producing one more unit of output. The refinery applies the *cost-benefit principle* and only produces more when the price it can get for the additional petrol is at least as large as the marginal cost.

But sellers, like a refinery, are not focusing on all the marginal costs, they are focused only on the marginal costs they pay. Let's distinguish between two types of marginal costs. There's the extra costs that are paid for by the seller, which are called **marginal private costs.** Sellers pay close attention to marginal private costs—for a refinery these include any extra oil, labour, and electricity it uses—because they directly impact their bottom line. But they don't pay for the **external cost,** which is the harm that negative externalities such as pollution impose on bystanders. (They're called *external* costs, because they're imposed on people external to those that generated them.) Because suppliers don't pay external costs, they tend to ignore them when making supply decisions. However, each unit of a good produced with negative externalities has both marginal private costs and **marginal external costs**—which are the extra external costs imposed on bystanders from one extra unit.

In past chapters we've described a business's supply curve as its marginal cost curve, but when managers ignore marginal external costs, we need to be more precise: The supply curve is the marginal *private* cost curve. Yet from society's perspective, it doesn't really matter whether a cost is paid by the seller or imposed on bystanders. That means from society's perspective, the relevant marginal cost of an extra litre of petrol is the **marginal social cost,** which is the sum of the marginal private costs paid by the seller and the marginal external costs borne by bystanders:

$$\text{Marginal social cost} = \text{Marginal private cost} + \text{Marginal external cost}$$

Figure 1 illustrates the wedge that negative externalities can drive between the supply curve and the marginal social cost curve. Sellers are guided by their private marginal costs, and so the supply curve is also their private marginal cost curve. The marginal social cost also

Figure 1 | Negative Externalities

Negative externalities drive a wedge between the supply curve and the marginal social cost curve.

Ⓐ The supply curve is also the marginal private cost curve.

Ⓑ Marginal external costs are those extra costs borne by bystanders.

Ⓒ Marginal social cost = Marginal private cost + Marginal external cost. Hence the marginal social cost curve lies above the supply curve.

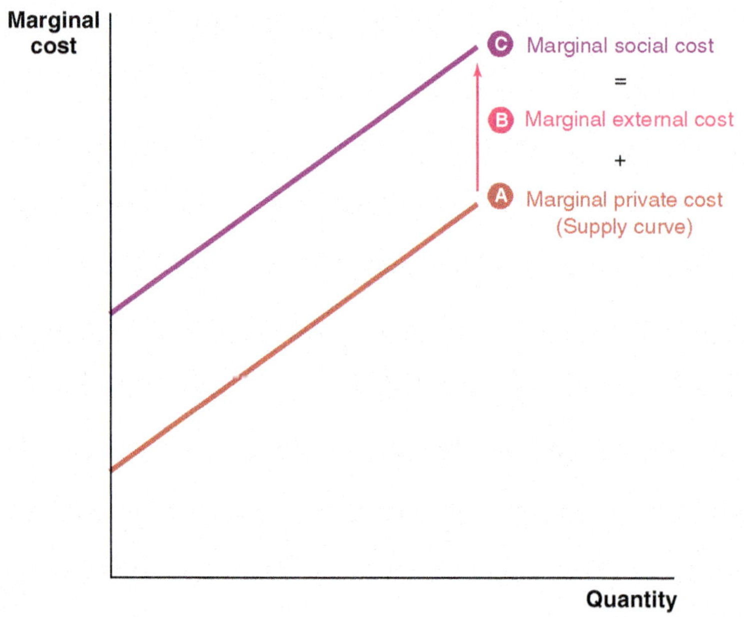

includes the marginal external cost. As a result, the marginal social cost curve lies above the supply curve, with the size of the wedge between them equal to the marginal external cost.

Positive externalities create external benefits. Let's turn to a parallel analysis when there are positive externalities. For example, when you decide whether or not to get a Covid vaccine, you are making a decision that has clear potential benefits and costs for you. If you get the jab, you'll be more protected from the virus, but you'll also take time out of your day, receive a not-so-pleasant jab, and with some vaccines there is a small chance of a life-threatening blood clot.

In Chapter 2 about demand, you discovered that buying decisions are guided by marginal benefits, which are the benefits you get from buying one more of something. But just like sellers, buyers' decisions are guided by the extra benefits that accrue to them, and these are called the **marginal private benefit.** These are the marginal gains that buyers enjoy from each unit they purchase. For a Covid vaccine, the marginal private benefit is the protection to your own health that the jab provides.

marginal private benefit The extra benefit enjoyed by the buyer from one extra unit.

The vaccine also creates benefits to others who are less likely to catch the virus from you. The protection that the vaccine offers those around you is an **external benefit,** the benefit that positive externalities create for bystanders. Each extra unit purchased of something with positive externalities has a **marginal external benefit**—the extra external benefit enjoyed by bystanders from the extra unit.

external benefit A benefit accruing to bystanders.

marginal external benefit The extra external benefit accruing to bystanders from one extra unit.

Because buyers don't enjoy marginal external benefits, they tend to ignore them, or undervalue them, when making demand decisions. To be clear, if you are a caring friend, you may consider the benefit that your vaccine provides your friends. After all, when you get the vaccine, they'll be less likely to catch the virus from you. But most people undervalue the benefits that accrue to other people, particularly people that they don't know well. This means that they don't consider them as much as they would if they were the ones personally enjoying them. Let's be honest, how much do you really consider the benefit to the strangers that you may contaminate on the bus?

marginal social benefit All marginal benefits, no matter who gets them = Marginal private benefit + marginal external benefit.

While previous chapters have described a buyers' demand curve as their marginal benefit curve, it's more precise to say that the demand curve corresponds with the buyers' marginal *private* benefits. But from society's perspective, a benefit is a benefit, whether it accrues to the buyer or to someone else. That's why the marginal benefit that's relevant to society as a whole is the **marginal social benefit,** which is the sum of the marginal benefit accruing to the buyer and the marginal external benefit:

$$\text{Marginal social benefit} = \text{Marginal private benefit} + \text{Marginal external benefit}$$

Figure 2 shows that positive externalities drive a wedge between the demand curve for vaccines and marginal social benefits. Buyers are guided by their private marginal benefits, and so the demand curve is also the private marginal benefit curve. But from society's perspective, there are also external benefits to consider. The marginal external benefits are included in marginal social benefits, which is why the marginal social benefit curve lies above the demand curve, and the wedge between them reflects the magnitude of the marginal external benefits.

So far, you've seen how externalities create a wedge between what's in society's best interest and what's in the best interests of sellers and buyers. Let's now turn to considering the problems that this wedge creates.

Figure 2 | Positive Externalities

Positive externalities drive a wedge between the demand curve and marginal social benefits.

A The **demand curve** is also the **marginal private benefit** curve.
B **Marginal external benefits** are those extra benefits accruing to bystanders.
C **Marginal social benefit** = **Marginal private benefit** + **Marginal external benefit**.
Hence the marginal social benefit curve lies above the demand curve.

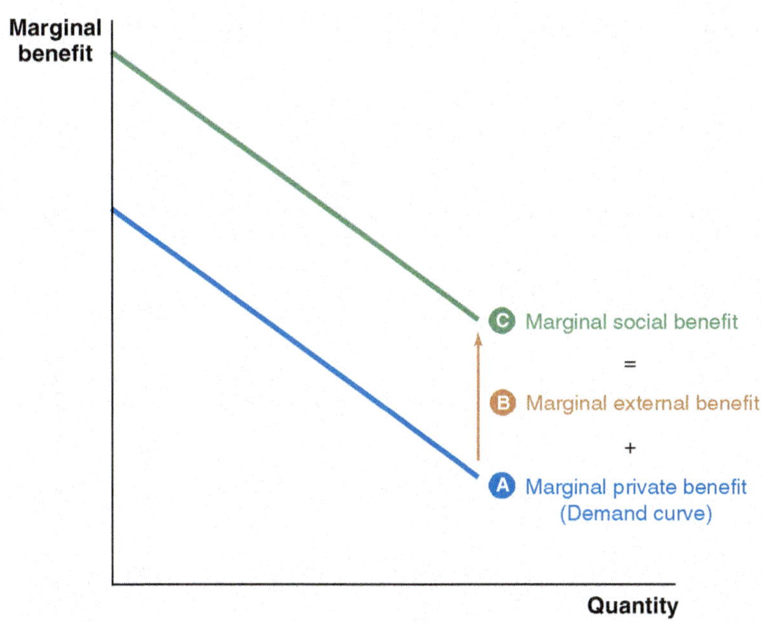

10.2 The Externality Problem

Learning Objective *Analyse how externalities lead markets to produce inefficient outcomes.*

A major theme of economics is that the forces of demand and supply often yield the best possible outcomes for society. This is such an important idea that we devoted Chapter 7 to it. It's time to add an important qualifier: The forces of supply and demand often yield the best possible outcomes *for buyers and sellers*. But when there are externalities, there's another set of stakeholders to consider—those bystanders whose well-being is affected by the choices that others make. Because market forces ignore the interests of these stakeholders, they'll typically fail to find the most efficient outcome in the presence of externalities.

If the market can't find the best outcome for society, then it's our job to find it. So let's go hunting for it.

The Rational Rule for Society

socially optimal outcome The outcome that is most efficient for society as a whole, including the interests of buyers, sellers, and bystanders.

We're trying to find the **socially optimal outcome,** which is the outcome that's most efficient for society as a whole, taking account of all the costs and all the benefits, whether they accrue to buyers, sellers, or bystanders. This means figuring out what quantity of a good will yield the largest possible economic surplus. When we're analysing the petrol market, it means asking: From society's perspective, how many litres of petrol should we produce?

It's time to apply the core principles of economics. Start by noticing that this is a "how many" question, so we should apply the *marginal principle,* which says to focus on the simpler question: Will society be better off if it produces one more litre of petrol?

goodluz/Shutterstock

The problem is that she's thinking about getting to work and not about the pollution she's creating.

Next, apply the *cost-benefit principle*. The benefit to society of producing one more litre of petrol is the marginal social benefit, and the cost to society is the marginal social cost. And so this principle says that society should produce another litre of petrol if the marginal social benefit exceeds the marginal social cost.

The *opportunity cost principle* will be useful in evaluating these costs and benefits. Marginal social cost is the marginal private cost plus the marginal external cost. You can read marginal private costs directly from a business's supply curve. What about marginal external costs? To find external costs, consider the opportunity costs for others, asking "or what?" An important opportunity cost of petrol is the forgone opportunity to have less pollution. Likewise, marginal social benefit includes the buyer's marginal private benefit—which you can read off their demand curve—and when there is a positive externality, you also need to add the corresponding marginal external benefit.

Produce until marginal social benefit equals marginal social cost. Finally, put all this together, and we get the following very helpful rule:

Rational Rule for Society Produce more of an item if its marginal social benefit is greater than (or equal to) the marginal social cost.

The **Rational Rule for Society:** *Produce more of an item as long as its marginal social benefit is at least as large as the marginal social cost.*

Following this rule suggests that society should keep producing petrol until it gets to the point where marginal social benefit no longer exceeds marginal social cost. That occurs when the marginal social benefit is equal to the marginal social cost. We've discovered something pretty remarkable—a simple way to find the socially optimal outcome. It occurs at the quantity where:

$$\text{Marginal social benefit} = \text{Marginal social cost}$$

I say this is remarkable because you've now uncovered something that even the collective intelligence of the markets won't (or at least not without a bit of help)—you've found the socially optimal outcome in the presence of externalities. The logic we've used should also feel pretty familiar, because it's just an application of the *Rational Rule* from Chapter 1, which says: If something is worth doing, keep doing it until your marginal benefits equal your marginal costs. But this time, we've adapted this rule to thinking about production from society's perspective, which means that our adapted rule equates marginal *social* benefit and marginal *social* cost.

Follow a three-step recipe to analyse externalities. At this point, we've developed all the tools we need to analyse externality problems. It's time to put the pieces together. We'll follow a simple three-step recipe:

Step one: Predict the *equilibrium* outcome to forecast what you think will happen.

Step two: Assess what *externalities* are involved.

Step three: Find the *socially optimal outcome* that is in society's best interest, and then compare this to the equilibrium forecast from the first step.

You can use this recipe to analyse both negative externalities (which is our next task), and positive externalities (which will follow straight after).

Consequences of Negative Externalities

Okay, let's apply this recipe to a real-world externality problem, focusing on the case of negative externalities in the market for petrol.

Step one: Predict the equilibrium outcome.

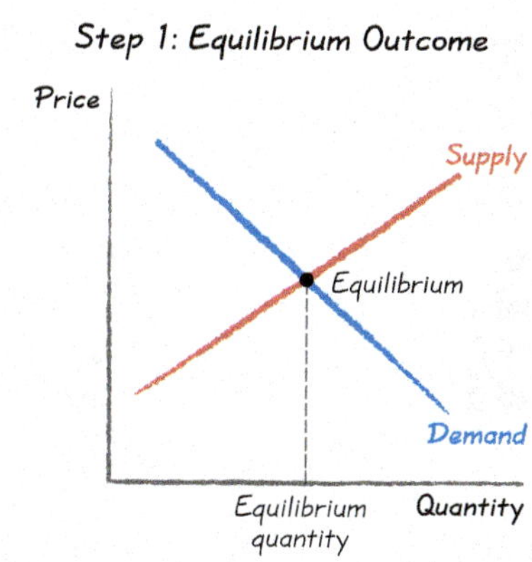

Your first step is to *predict* what will happen. Here, we return to using our old friends, supply and demand. The market outcome will be a supply-equals-demand equilibrium, which occurs where these two curves cross.

Notice that this equilibrium reflects only the decisions of buyers (via the demand curve, which reflects marginal private benefits) and sellers (through the supply curve, which reflects marginal private costs). The bystanders who have to live with the side effects of these choices play no role in determining this outcome. This gives the first hint that there may be a problem: We predict that market forces will lead to the same outcome whether the side effects of petrol are positive or negative, and whether these side effects are large, small, or nonexistent.

Step two: Assess the externalities.

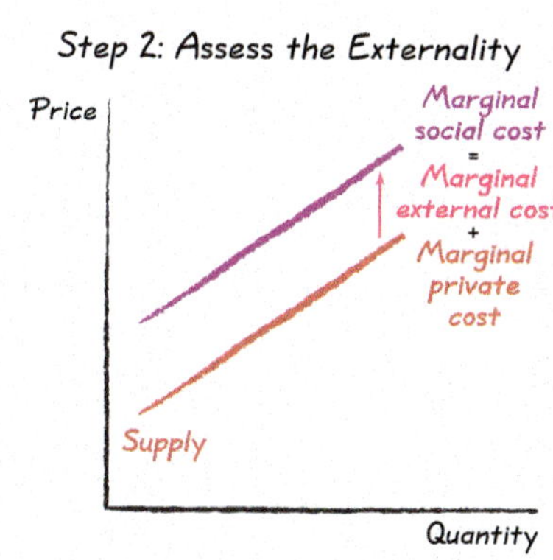

Next, assess whether you're dealing with positive or negative externalities, and how large those external effects are. You should consider all of the relevant side effects, and ask: Does petrol help or hurt bystanders? And by how much?

Each litre of petrol produced creates harm to bystanders by polluting the air. In addition, each litre of petrol has marginal external costs associated with the externalities caused by using the petrol.

A recent study measured the marginal external costs associated with each litre of petrol and it's about 55 cents. As a result, the marginal social cost of each litre of petrol produced—which is the marginal private cost plus this marginal external cost—is 55 cents per litre higher than the marginal private cost given by the supply curve. As Figure 3 illustrates, this means that the marginal social cost curve lies above the supply curve, with the wedge between them equal to the marginal external cost (in this case, of 55 cents). From society's perspective, the refinery's supply curve understates the marginal costs of producing more petrol, because it doesn't account for the marginal external costs.

Step three: Find the socially optimal outcome.

In step one, we analysed the supply-equals-demand equilibrium, which is our forecast of what is likely to happen, rather than what is in society's best interest.

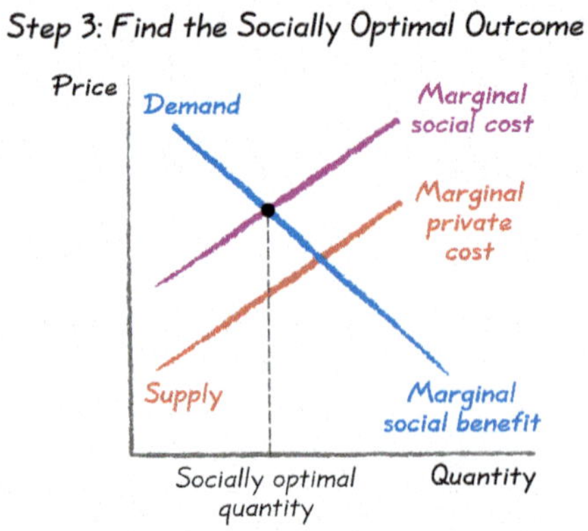

In step two, we saw how negative externalities interfere with the logic of the market, by driving a wedge between the supply curve (which determines outcomes) and the marginal social cost curve (which is relevant to figuring out what is in society's best interest). In the final step, we'll figure out what outcome is in society's best interest.

This is where the *Rational Rule for Society* is useful: It says that the socially optimal outcome occurs at the quantity where the marginal social benefit is equal to the marginal social cost. We've already seen that a negative externality leads the marginal social cost curve to lie above the supply curve. As long as there are no positive externalities (more on this below), the demand curve is also the marginal social benefit curve. And so the *Rational Rule for Society* says that the socially optimal outcome occurs where the marginal social cost curve crosses the demand curve.

Figure 3 | Negative Externalities Lead to Overproduction

Ⓐ The **equilibrium** outcome depends on supply (marginal private cost) and demand.
Ⓑ **Marginal social cost** = **marginal private cost** + **marginal external cost**, and so the marginal social cost curve lies above the supply curve.
Ⓒ The **socially optimal outcome** occurs where **marginal social cost** = **marginal social benefit**.
Ⓓ The **equilibrium quantity** is larger than the **socially optimal quantity**, and hence negative externalities yield **overproduction**.

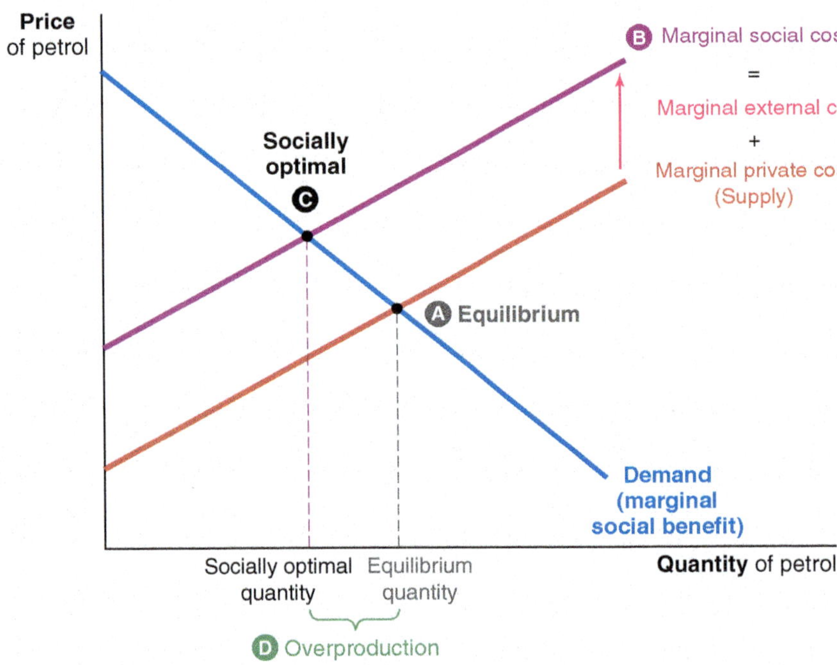

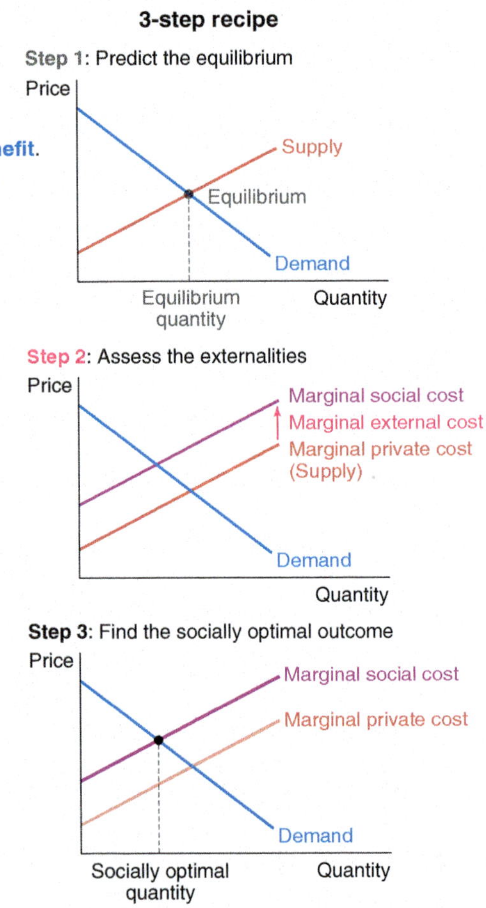

If people don't take account of the external costs of their actions, they'll pursue those actions too often.

Negative externalities lead to overproduction. Finally, compare your forecast of what will happen (the supply-equals-demand equilibrium) with what's in society's best interest (the socially optimal outcome). Figure 3 reveals that in the face of a negative externality, the equilibrium quantity of petrol produced will be higher than is socially optimal. More simply stated: *Goods that create negative externalities are overproduced.*

Here's the intuition: When businesses don't take account of the costs of the pollution they emit, they do more of it. This isn't just about petrol: The same logic shows that any product involving negative externalities will be overproduced. This intuition also hints at a policy solution: Try to find ways to make polluters bear all the costs of their actions—including the cost of pollution. These higher costs can counter the incentives that lead to the overproduction of products with negative externalities.

There is a socially optimal quantity of pollution. Notice that when we ask how much petrol production is socially optimal, we're also effectively asking how much petrol-related pollution is socially optimal. Even though we concluded that polluting products like petrol are overproduced, Figure 3 also shows that the socially optimal quantity of petrol is positive. In turn, this means that it's socially optimal for there to be some pollution.

Some people think this sounds kind of crazy. They reason that because pollution is bad, the best outcome for society must be to eliminate it. But their logic isn't quite right. If society could eliminate pollution *at no cost,* then their reasoning is right. But the reality is that cutting pollution is costly. It's costly because we can only cut pollution by also cutting those activities that cause pollution. Fossil fuels present a trade-off: They cause harmful pollution, but they also make life more convenient. The whole point of our analysis has been to find the right balance by taking into account all the costs and all the benefits of using fossil fuels.

The message of our analysis is that we should produce less petrol, which means polluting less. But it's one thing to say we should pollute *less,* and it's another to say we should *eliminate* pollution. Eliminating pollution would also require eliminating petrol. Are you willing to do that? Most people say no, suggesting that they believe some degree of pollution is an acceptable price for society to pay in order to enjoy the convenience of using petrol-powered cars. Our analysis shows that we don't need to eliminate petrol. Instead, we need to solve the deeper problem that refineries don't face the full costs associated with the production of petrol. Solve that, and we'll solve the overproduction of petrol.

Vadim Petrakov/Shutterstock

How much of this is in society's best interest?

EVERYDAY Economics **The hazards of splitting the bill**

You've probably noticed that going out to dinner with a group can get pretty expensive, particularly when you decide to split the bill. Blame negative externalities. To see why, put yourself in the shoes of a particularly calculating dining companion. Usually they will skip dessert, but they're smart enough to realise that when you're splitting the cost six ways, a $6 piece of cake will only add $1 to their share of the bill. That's their marginal private cost. From the group's perspective, the problem is that they're ignoring the marginal external cost, which is that their five dining companions will each have to pay another dollar each. The dessert is a negative externality for other people's wallets, boosting the bill. This example also highlights how caring about the people around you can reduce negative externalities: The more your friends care about you the more likely they'll be to consider the costs they're imposing on you.

Some economists invited people to lunch to find out how much people ignore the costs they impose on others. Some folks were told they would pay only for what they personally ordered, and they spent about $9 each, on average. But those folks who were told that the whole table would split the bill ended up spending about $13 each. And when the researchers said they would pay for everyone's lunch—which is the experimental equivalent of your boss paying for a corporate lunch—the average bill rose to $22 per person! ■

Consequences of Positive Externalities

Let's now turn to analysing the consequences of positive externalities, where the side effects of your actions *benefit* bystanders. We'll follow the same three-step recipe, but this time our focus is on the external benefits that products like a flu shot generate for bystanders.

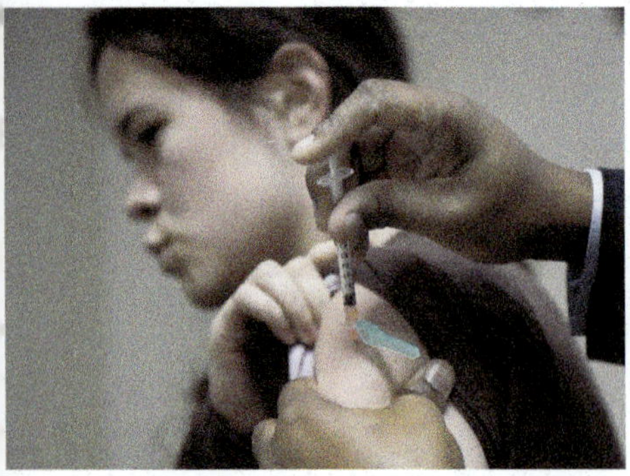

DON EMMERT/AFP/Getty Images

Instead of thinking about the pain, focus on the positive externality.

Markets yield too few positive externalities. In this real-world example, we'll focus on the market for flu shots. Big pharmaceutical companies like GlaxoSmithKline and Seqirus are the suppliers, while you are one of the millions of potential buyers who make up the demand side.

Step one: Predict the equilibrium outcome.

As usual, the equilibrium occurs where the demand and supply curves meet, as shown in the upper right-hand side graph in Figure 4.

Step two: Assess the externalities.

The demand curve only measures marginal *private* benefits. When around half of all Australians get a flu shot costing $15, we can infer that the benefit of the immunity it provides them and those that they care about is worth at least $15. But there's also a marginal external benefit: If you don't get the flu, then bystanders won't catch it from you. If this marginal external benefit is worth another $10, then the marginal *social* benefit curve lies $10 above the demand curve, as shown in the middle right-hand side graph of Figure 4.

Figure 4 Positive Externalities Lead to Underproduction

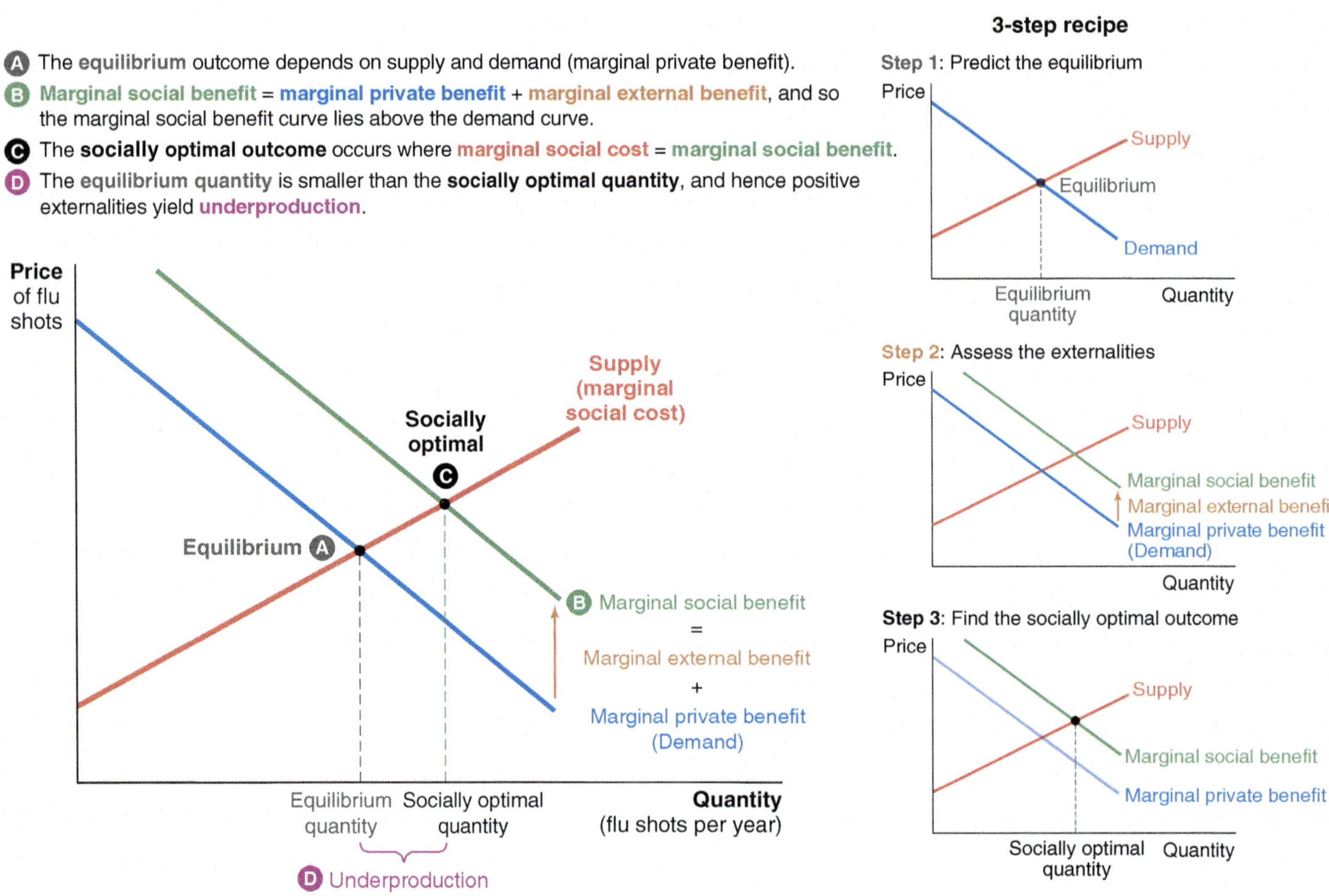

Step three: Find the socially optimal outcome.

Following the *Rational Rule for Society*, the socially optimal outcome occurs where the marginal social benefit equals the marginal social cost. In step two, we graphed the marginal social benefit curve. What about the marginal social costs?

The supply curve summarises marginal private costs. As long as there are no negative externalities, the supply curve is also the marginal social cost curve. Thus, the social optimum occurs where these two curves cross, as shown in the lower graph on the right-hand side of Figure 4.

Finally, let's look to the big picture in Figure 4. Compare your forecast of what will happen (the supply-equals-demand equilibrium) with what's in society's best interest (the socially optimal outcome). You'll discover that fewer people get flu shots than would be socially optimal. More simply stated: *Goods that create positive externalities are underproduced.*

Here's the intuition: When people don't take account of the marginal external benefits that their choices generate, they do less of it—in this case, buy fewer flu shots than is in society's best interest. This isn't just about flu shots: The broader point is that anything that generates positive externalities tends to be underproduced. As the following case study illustrates, you might recognise this pattern from your own life.

EVERYDAY Economics

Why you don't work out, eat healthily, study, or save enough

Positive externalities might just explain why you don't work out, eat healthily, study, or save enough. How? Psychologists view your mind as being engaged in an internal struggle between your current self and your future self. You can think of your current self as making decisions, and your future self as being like a "bystander" who is affected by the choices your present self makes.

Let's see how this shapes your decision about whether or not to go to the gym. Your current self considers the cost of working out, which includes the effort required to go to the gym and exercise. But the benefits of working out mainly accrue to your future self, who'll enjoy better health. This means that your current self sees little benefit to working out. The problem is that your current self considers benefits that accrue to your future self to be an externality, and so your current self doesn't take them into account. Because your current self makes all the decisions, you'll exercise less often than is optimal for the "society" of both your current and future self. This same logic applies to any activity where your current self bears the cost and your future self enjoys the benefit. That's why the same ideas might explain why you don't eat healthy food often enough, why you study too little, and why you don't save enough. ■

Recap: Positive and negative externalities, summarised. We've covered a lot of ground. Let's take a moment to pause and summarise what we've learned, shown in Figure 5.

Figure 5 | Summarising the Effects of Externalities

Type of externality	Your actions	Problem	Implication	An example
Negative externality	Harm others	Marginal private costs understate marginal social costs.	Overproduction	Polluters produce too much greenhouse gas.
Positive externality	Help others	Marginal private benefits understate marginal social benefits.	Underproduction	Too few people get immunisations.

You've now mastered the tools for identifying both positive and negative externalities, and analysing their consequences. In the next section, we'll explore how you can solve these externality problems to create better outcomes.

10.3 Solving Externality Problems

Learning Objective *Learn how to solve externality problems.*

Solutions to the externality problem rely on "internalising the externality":

1. Private bargaining
2. Fix the price: Corrective taxes and subsidies
3. Fix the quantity: Cap and trade
4. Laws, rules, and regulations
5. Government provision of public goods
6. Assign ownership rights

The externality problem can be summed up simply: Worse outcomes occur when people don't take into account the interests of bystanders. That's why our next task is to figure out how to fix this problem. We'll start by exploring four specific solutions: private bargaining, corrective taxes and subsidies that change the price, cap-and-trade programs that change the quantity, and regulations. In the subsequent section, which addresses the specific externality problems associated with public goods and common ownership, we'll explore two more solutions: government provision of public goods, and assigning ownership rights to individuals. As we explore each of these potential solutions, it'll become apparent that the most effective fix will depend on the setting.

All of these solutions share the same basic goal: To get buyers and sellers to act as if they're taking marginal external costs and benefits into account. In each case, the underlying idea is to realign incentives so that people take account of—that is, internalise—the effects of their actions on bystanders. That's why the big idea here is sometimes described as getting people to *internalise the externality.* Let's dive into how to do this by exploring each of these solutions in turn.

Solution One: Private Bargaining and the Coase Theorem

Private bargaining can sometimes solve externality problems. Here's how: Get all the interested parties in a room—make sure to include both the bystanders who are affected by an externality and those who cause it—and give them an opportunity to negotiate with each other. We've already seen that externality problems typically lead markets to fail to achieve the socially optimal outcome. This means that better outcomes are possible, and it's the prospect of that better outcome that'll give the people in the room an incentive to search for a creative bargain that'll make them all better off. Bargain creatively, and you'll discover that through side payments, strategic investments, and mergers, you can solve some common externality problems.

alarich/Deposit Photos

With the right side payment, they might not crank it all the way up.

Side payments can solve externalities. Often the solution will involve some kind of *side payment.* Here's the idea: If someone else's actions harm you, you can pay them to do something else instead. For instance, if your neighbour's loud music prevents you from sleeping, you could offer them $5 to turn it down. You'll benefit from this deal, because you'll only offer $5 if you value the quiet at least $5. And they'll also benefit, because they'll only accept your offer if that $5 is worth more to them than cranking up the volume. And so this deal—which involves a considerate action in exchange for a side payment—leaves you both better off. Of course, you might think this deal is unfair, because you feel you should have the right to some quiet at night. Even if it is unfair, it's often effective. More generally, if loud music—or any negative externality—harms you more than it helps those creating it, there's a price you'll be willing to pay that'll successfully induce them to make a more considerate choice.

With positive externalities, you follow a similar logic. If someone has the opportunity to make a choice that would benefit you, then you could pay them to do it. For instance, customers of Australian private health insurer AIA can earn a free Apple Watch over time by meeting certain physical activity targets recorded on the watch! AIA figures that more physically active customers are less likely to make health insurance claims. This private bargain involves AIA sharing some of the benefit of a positive externality with its clients, so as to give those clients an incentive to do more of it.

Coase Theorem If bargaining is costless and property rights are clearly established and enforced, then externality problems can be solved by private bargains.

The Coase Theorem explains why side payments work. These are both examples of an insight called the **Coase Theorem,** which says that when people can bargain costlessly and legal rights are clear and enforced—so that it's possible to enforce these agreements—then externality problems can be solved by private bargaining. For example, loud music benefits your head-banging neighbours, but when they're choosing the volume, they typically don't take account of the cost to your sleep. By paying your neighbour for quiet, you effectively raise the opportunity cost to them of playing loud music because that would mean forgoing your $5 side payment. You've given your neighbour an incentive to consider the broader costs of their actions.

Perhaps the most surprising implication of the Coase Theorem is that private bargaining can restore the socially optimal outcome. To see why, start by thinking about the largest side payment you should offer your neighbour to turn down their music. You should be willing to pay up to the amount of the marginal external cost they're imposing on you (perhaps less a cent, so you come out slightly ahead). Now put yourself in your neighbour's shoes. The cost of turning up the volume now includes both their private cost, plus an opportunity cost—the possibility of not getting the side payment you offered—that's equal to the marginal external cost. The possibility of losing that side payment effectively internalises the externality. That means that as your neighbour reaches for the volume dial, they're now forced to confront the full social cost of their choice, and so they'll choose the socially optimal outcome.

Importantly, this efficient outcome is achieved through *private* bargaining—without the need for new government intervention. By this view, government intervention isn't required, because the prospect of finding a more efficient outcome is enough of an incentive to get people to start bargaining. And when they start bargaining, they'll discover creative ways to get others to make more considerate choices and split the gains in a way that ensures everyone comes out ahead.

Do the Economics

Here are some other real-life externality problems. Can you think of creative private bargains—potentially involving side payments—that would internalise the externality?

a. Installing an alarm system reduces the chances of your home being broken into, which benefits your insurance company, because it'll make fewer payouts.

b. Opening a major department store within a shopping centre attracts more customers, which helps the nearby small businesses in the shopping centre.

c. When beekeepers keep their hives near apple orchards, their bees will pollinate the apples, increasing the output of the orchards.

d. When beekeepers are allowed to put their hives in orange groves, the sticky nectar in orange blossoms helps the bees produce more honey. ■

Answer: These are all examples of common practices in each industry: a. Insurance companies can charge you a lower price if you install an alarm system. b. Shopping centre owners like Westfield can charge lower rent to large "anchor stores" like department stores—effectively making a side payment to them—because the higher foot traffic allows them to charge higher rent to small businesses. c. Apple growers can pay beekeepers to put hives in their orchards because it increases their apple yield. d. Beekeepers can pay orange growers for the right to put their hives in orange groves because it increases their honey yield.

Strategic investments can solve externality problems. So far we've described private bargains as involving side payments. But sometimes it's also worth considering making *strategic investments*, which are just a different type of private bargain.

Consider the externality problem facing executives at Google, which makes most of its money from online advertising. From Google's perspective, the more people who have access to the internet, the better, because then it'll sell more ads, increasing its profits. But to the cable companies that provide internet service, this extra profit is a positive externality—they see Google as a bystander, and the extra profits Google earns are an external benefit of providing internet access. The result is that internet access is underprovided, relative to what would occur if Google's extra profits were taken into account. Can you think of a way for cable companies to internalise this externality?

Google did, and here's its answer: It is building high-speed wireless internet networks in sub-Saharan Africa and Southeast Asia to reach people outside of major cities. This investment internalises the externality that Google enjoys from more people being online, because it'll earn both the revenue that an internet provider would earn, as well as extra advertising revenue from having more people online.

Sunday Alamba/AP Images

Google has invested in making internet access more widespread, which increases the number of people viewing their advertisements.

Mergers can solve externality problems. There's an alternative type of private bargain that Google could have considered: a *merger*. If it merged with an internet service provider, then the new combined entity would make decisions about where to build wireless networks, taking account of both the direct revenues from providing internet service, and also the extra advertising revenue that Google will earn.

In fact, this is a key reason that companies are often involved in several lines of business. When there are externalities across different markets, it's profitable for a business to operate in each market, so that the people at headquarters can make decisions that internalise all the externalities involved.

Private bargaining can solve externality problems when bargaining costs are low. So far all of the examples of private bargaining have had a few things in common: In each case there were only a few parties to negotiate with, and so while bargaining wasn't costless, it wasn't very costly. And in these cases the stakes were high enough for the parties involved to make it worth incurring these costs. As the *cost-benefit principle* predicts, private bargaining is most likely to succeed when the benefits from solving the externality problem are high, and the costs of bargaining to find a solution are low.

It's nearly impossible to get all of the people affected by climate change together to bargain toward a solution.

When bargaining is difficult, externalities remain a problem. Private bargaining won't always work, particularly when it's difficult or costly to reach a bargain. For instance, consider the climate change problem. The total benefits to slowing climate change exceed the costs, and so *in theory,* there's a way in which those who would gain from lower greenhouse petrol levels could strike a bargain where they pay polluters to pollute less. The problem is that *in practice,* there's no way for billions of people spread all around the world to negotiate with millions of polluters headquartered in different countries. It may even be infeasible, because many of those who would benefit from addressing climate change are yet to be born, and so they can't bargain to protect their future Earth. That's why private bargaining isn't going to solve the climate change problem.

Indeed, many of our most important pressing environmental problems affect many people, and so the cost of bargaining is high. Moreover, while many environmental problems are important to society as a whole, the benefit to each individual from solving them is small. (How much would you, personally, be willing to pay to save the spotted owl from extinction?) In these cases, there's no hope that bargaining will solve externality problems. And when private bargaining can't solve externality problems, it's time to look for other solutions. That's what we'll explore next.

Solution Two: Corrective Taxes and Subsidies

An alternative approach focuses on using prices to change the incentives of buyers and sellers. The idea is to use taxes and subsidies to "correct" the market price in a way that leads people to internalise the marginal external costs and benefits of their actions.

corrective tax A tax designed to induce people to take account of the negative externalities they cause.

Corrective taxes can solve negative externalities. A **corrective tax** can induce people to take account of the negative externalities they create. The idea is that even if people ignore the external costs they impose on bystanders, they'll pay attention to a tax. Imposing a per-unit tax that's equal to the marginal external cost will effectively lead people to make choices *as if* they're accounting for the marginal external costs of their actions. (A corrective tax is sometimes also called a *Pigouvian tax,* after its founder, Mr. Pigou.)

To see how a corrective tax works, put yourself in the shoes of an oil refinery executive trying to decide how much petrol to produce. You'll focus on your company's marginal private costs, because that's what affects your bottom line, and you'll largely ignore the marginal external cost of the increased pollution (which is 75 cents a litre) because it doesn't affect your profits. But a tax equal to the 75-cents-per-litre marginal external cost will lead you to respond *as if* you were taking account of the marginal external costs. Thus, the tax effectively internalises the externality by making the costs of the negative externality internal to the supplier's cost-benefit calculations.

Figure 6 illustrates how this works. The left panel shows the problem of negative externalities, which is that the supply curve understates the true marginal social costs by an amount equal to the marginal external cost, which is 75 cents per litre. This should be familiar; it's the same as Figure 3 and shows the same result—that negative externalities lead to overproduction. The right panel shows how a corrective tax set equal to the 75-cents-per-litre marginal external cost solves this overproduction problem. When suppliers have to pay this tax, it raises the marginal private cost of producing petrol by 75 cents. This shifts the supply curve up by 75 cents (because a refinery executive will only be willing to supply any given quantity if the price is 75 cents higher to offset the higher taxes they pay). This new supply curve in the right panel now corresponds exactly with the marginal social cost curve in the left panel, and both of these curves meet the demand curve at the socially optimal quantity.

Figure 6 Corrective Taxes Solve the Problem of Negative Externalities

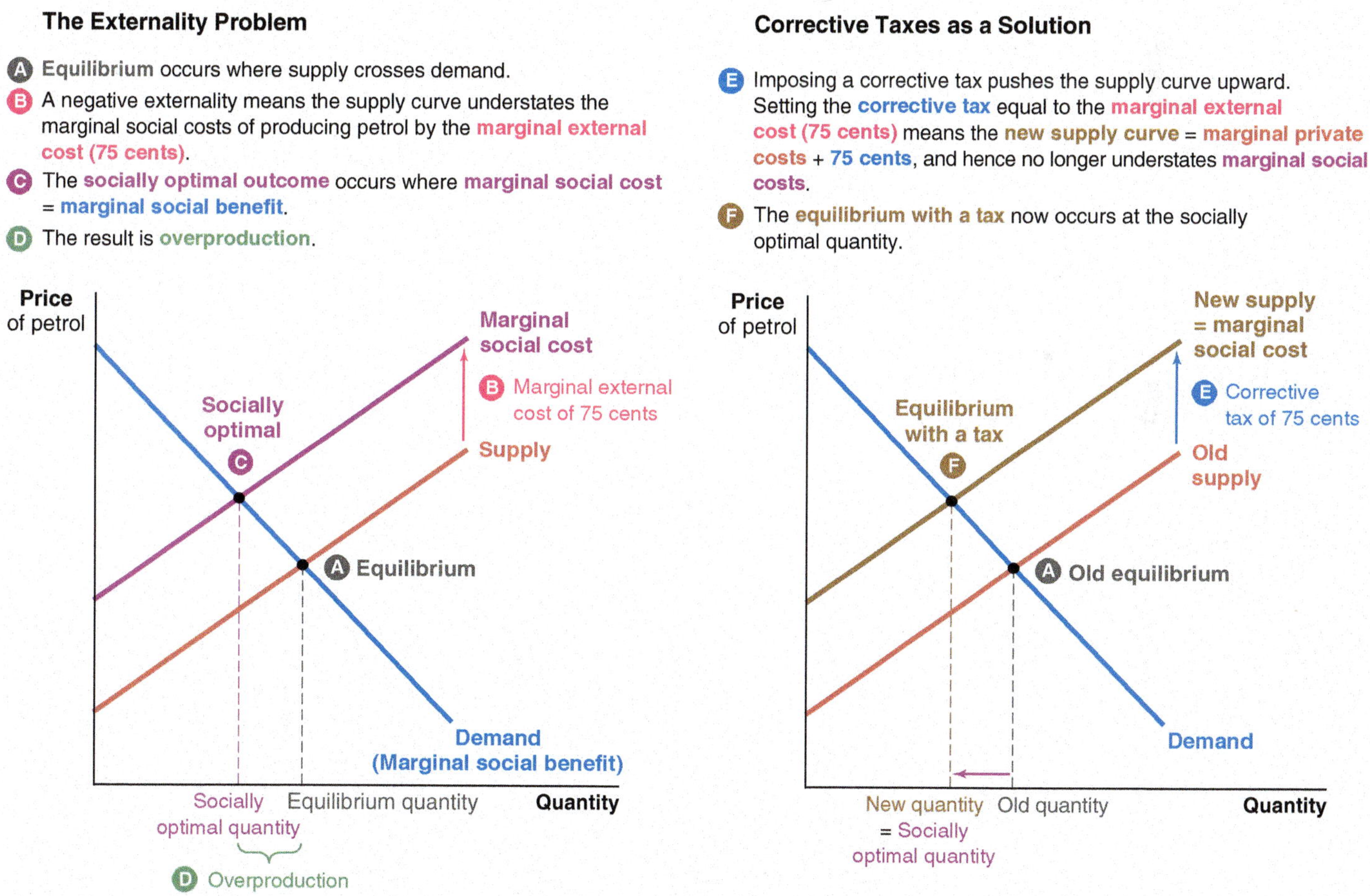

Imposing a tax equal to the marginal external cost leads suppliers to make choices based on their new marginal cost (their original marginal private cost plus the 75 cents per litre tax), which now coincides with the marginal social cost (the marginal private cost plus a 75 cents per litre marginal external cost). That is, the tax leads suppliers to act *as if* they care about both their private costs and external costs, leading them to internalise the externality.

You saw in Chapter 6 that when the government imposes taxes, the equilibrium quantity typically declines. In the case of a negative externality, the decline in the quantity is correcting the overproduction that occurs when external costs are ignored. You also saw in Chapter 6 that it doesn't matter whether the seller or buyer is asked to make the tax payment, the same outcome will occur. The same thing is true with corrective taxes—a tax on either buyers or sellers of petrol will lead the market to internalise the external costs.

Corrective taxes are widely used to solve externality problems. For instance, the government charges a cigarette excise of around $35 per pack, which leads smokers to internalise (some of) the marginal external costs due to secondhand smoke and the costs to the health care system of treating heart and lung disease. Likewise, in some families, you have to put a dollar into a "swear jar" each time you use a swear word, because using a swear word is perceived to be a negative externality on family members (although not all families are the same!). Road tolls are just a corrective tax by another name, and they lead fewer people to drive on those roads, countering the negative externality of congestion and wear and tear on the roads.

Atomazul/Alamy

A swearing tax is an incentive to reduce negative externalities.

Corrective subsidies can fix positive externalities. Subsidies can help people internalise the benefits of their actions to others. Just like corrective taxes, **corrective subsidies** are designed to induce people to take account of the positive externalities they cause. For instance, insurance companies will often subsidise your purchase of an alarm system for your house or car. They benefit from the fact that an alarm will reduce the chances of you having a theft. Since they want you to internalise this external benefit from the alarm system, they offer a subsidy. The logic of such subsidies is the same: If the problem of positive externalities is that people don't account for the marginal external benefits they confer on others, then a subsidy can act as the incentive spurring people to do more of them.

corrective subsidy A subsidy designed to induce people to take account of the positive externalities they cause.

Lawsuits, norms, and social sanctions are like corrective taxes. The logic of corrective taxes also underpins our legal system. This is easiest to see when you realise that the damages that courts award are effectively a corrective tax. The law provides you with a right to sue others whenever they harm you in specific ways. In the language of economics, those harms are a negative externality. And the threat of a lawsuit provides an incentive for people to consider the consequences of their actions on bystanders, thereby internalising the externality.

Beyond explicit taxes or the threat of lawsuits, norms and social sanctions can also act like corrective taxes. For instance, farting in a crowded elevator is pretty gross—gross enough that an economist would call it a negative externality. So why don't people do it more often? Try it and you'll discover you'll get a lot of dirty looks, and those dirty looks are sort of like a corrective tax. Similar social norms prevent people from littering, from talking during movies, and from being late for meetings.

iQoncept/Shutterstock

It's not a subsidy, but it helps.

A warm glow and social recognition are like corrective subsidies. Similarly, the warm glow that you feel when you help others is a lot like a corrective subsidy, countering the underprovision of positive externalities. For instance, there's no financial incentive to give blood, but if you do, the Red Cross will give you a sticker, and you'll enjoy the feeling of knowing that you did your part. Post about it on Instagram, and all those likes add up to a pretty healthy "subsidy" for doing the right thing.

Recap: Corrective taxes and subsidies fix distortions caused by market failures. If you're used to thinking about taxes and subsidies as distorting market outcomes, it's time to adjust your thinking. It's true that in otherwise well-functioning markets, taxes and subsidies distort market outcomes by driving a wedge between the price paid by buyers and that received by sellers. But when there's a market failure, corrective taxes or subsidies can offset the wedge between private and social costs or benefits, fixing a preexisting distortion.

Solution Three: Cap and Trade

The idea of corrective taxes is that changing *prices* can reduce the quantity of negative externalities produced, eliminating the overproduction problem. An alternative approach is to change the *quantity* of the harmful activity directly, through a quantity regulation. Recall from Chapter 6 that a *quota* is a limit on the maximum quantity of a good or service that can be sold.

When a quota is binding, it requires the quantity to be less than what it would be at the supply-equals-demand equilibrium. Figure 7 shows a binding quota in the market for petrol. The quota results in less petrol being produced, reducing the overproduction of a good that involves negative externalities. The best outcome from society's perspective occurs when you set the quantity cap equal to the socially optimal quantity.

Figure 7 | How Quotas Can Fix Negative Externalities

Ⓐ At the supply-equals-demand **equilibrium**, the quantity produced was higher than the socially optimal quantity, due to negative externalities

Ⓑ This can be solved by setting a **quota** (a maximum quantity).

Ⓒ If the quota is set to the socially optimal quantity, then the **socially optimal outcome** is what occurs.

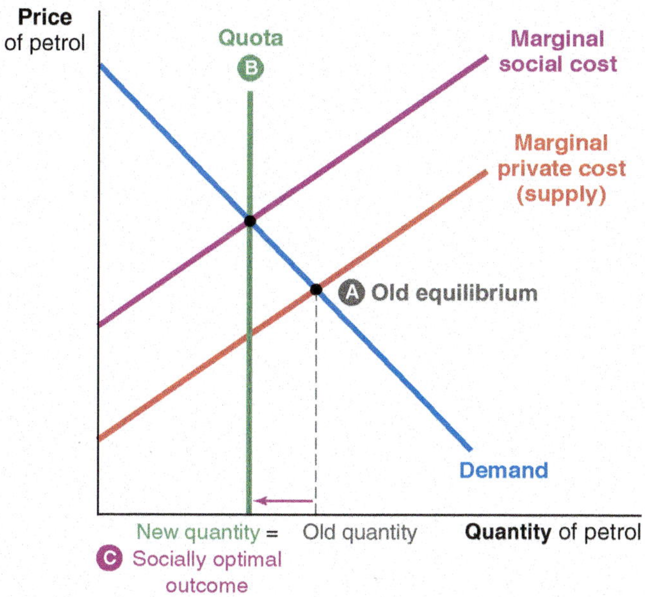

Your choice between quantity regulation and taxes depends on what you know. Any outcome you can achieve by changing prices (which is what corrective taxes do) can also be achieved by changing quantities (which is what quotas do). This illustrates the broader point you learned in Chapter 6, that the government can use any of its tools to get the same socially optimal quantity.

Your choice between corrective taxes or quantity regulation depends on the information you have. If you know the marginal external cost, then use it as the basis for setting your corrective tax and the market will find the socially optimal quantity. And if you know the socially optimal quantity instead, use that in setting your quota.

Increase efficiency by allowing businesses to trade their permits. When the government sets a quota, it has to determine not only the socially optimal quantity for the whole market to produce, but also how much each individual supplier is allowed to produce. One solution is to set a specific quantity cap for each company. But this can create inefficiencies if the government gives similar quotas to both inefficient and efficient companies. Unfortunately it's hard for the government to avoid this, because it can't easily identify which suppliers are efficient (and it's politically hard to set different caps for different businesses without favouritism or even corruption getting in the way).

Economists have figured out a way to solve this problem. Rather than impose fixed quantity caps for each individual business, the government can issue each business a number of permits, where each permit gives its holder the right to produce a certain quantity of output. The difference is that unlike a fixed quota for each producer, businesses can buy and sell—that is, trade—these permits. To see what this does, realise that if your business is more efficient than mine—that is, if your marginal costs are lower—you'll make a bigger profit from expanding production than I would. As a result, you value an extra permit more than me. That means there's a price at which I can sell you my permit that'll boost both your profits and mine. More generally, these trades are profitable only when a more efficient business buys permits from a less efficient business. Allowing businesses to trade these permits has the happy effect of letting the government correct the negative externality by setting a maximum quantity of output, while still allowing market forces to redistribute production toward more efficient producers and away from their inefficient rivals.

Governments use cap and trade to limit pollution. We've learned that there's an "optimal" amount of pollution and that quantity regulations like quotas can help get to the socially optimal quantity. We've also seen that quantity caps are more efficient when businesses can trade their permits so that market forces determine the best allocation across businesses. Now let's add another important role for market forces: If you want to ensure that there's an incentive for businesses to find innovative production techniques that create less pollution, then it's better to regulate how much they pollute, rather than how much they produce. When businesses face a cost of *polluting*, they will seek cheaper ways to produce their goods and services. This will lead them to find ways to pollute less because it will reduce their costs of production.

cap and trade A quantity regulation implemented by allocating a fixed number of permits, which can then be traded.

Combining these insights has led to policy proposals called **cap and trade.** The "cap" part is that the government regulates the quantity of negative externalities directly—setting a maximum quota or "cap" on the amount of pollution—such as the number of tonnes of sulfur dioxide that can be emitted. The "trade" part occurs when it implements this by issuing pollution permits which can be traded (which is why these are sometimes called *tradeable emissions permits*).

Each permit allows its holder to produce a specific quantity of pollution. Because different factories use different technologies, these permits are worth different amounts to different companies. The owner of a relatively "green" factory—which can produce a lot of output for each tonne of pollution it emits—will value these permits highly, because each permit gives them the right to expand production a lot. By contrast, the owner of "dirty" factory—one that uses a technology that spews a lot of sulfur dioxide per unit of output—won't value these permits as highly, because each permit only gives them the right to expand production a little bit. As a result, green companies will buy permits from dirty companies. The result is that the "cap" part of cap and trade will reduce total emissions, and the "trade" part will lead production to be concentrated among businesses that use cleaner technologies.

Cap-and-trade systems are critical to how we deal with environmental problems. For instance, cap and trade is central to the Kyoto Protocol, which is an international treaty that commits each country to cut back on harmful greenhouse gases. A limited number of permits to emit harmful greenhouse gases have been issued, and these are bought and sold on a global market.

A cap-and-trade system is like a corrective tax. If you think about a cap-and-trade system through the lens of the *opportunity cost principle*, you'll quickly see that it's a lot like a corrective tax. Why? A corrective tax raises the direct financial cost of producing more petrol. A cap-and-trade system works instead by raising the opportunity cost: If you pollute more, you'll need to use one of your permits, rather than selling it. This forgone revenue is an important opportunity cost, just like a corrective tax. Under either corrective taxes or cap and trade, polluting becomes costlier—either in terms of paying more tax, or by forgoing the possible revenue from selling your permit. The net effect of these higher financial or opportunity costs is that suppliers act as if they're considering the marginal external costs of their actions—effectively internalising the externality.

Both corrective taxes or subsidies and cap-and-trade systems attempt to harness the power of the market to solve externality problems as efficiently as possible. When that's not possible, we need to turn to laws, rules, and regulations instead.

Solution Four: Laws, Rules, and Regulations

Many of our laws exist to help solve problems caused by negative externalities. Noise restrictions outlaw disturbing your neighbours, speeding laws prevent you from endangering fellow motorists, zoning laws prevent you from constructing a building that will be an eyesore to your neighbours, and safety laws prevent employers from endangering their workers.

Do the Economics

Can you think of the externalities that the following types of laws help solve?

a. Laws banning smoking in public places.

b. Regulations known as Corporate Average Fuel Economy (CAFE) standards require car manufacturers to ensure the cars they make don't use too much petrol per kilometre.

c. The law that makes unsolicited "spam" calls to anyone on the "Do Not Call" list illegal.

d. School rules that require students to be up-to-date on their vaccines. ■

Answer: a. Exposure to secondhand smoke raises the risk of cancer. b. Enhanced fuel economy reduces petrol usage, and hence harmful emissions. c. A marketing call that you don't want costs you time. d. Each student's vaccination helps prevent an outbreak at school that can affect other students and teachers.

Company rules also target externalities. It's not just governments that use rules to help internalise externalities. Many corporations also have formal rules and codes of conduct to deal with externalities. For instance, some companies ban intra-office dating because it protects your co-workers from the negative externality of dealing with a messy breakup. Nearly all corporate IT departments require antivirus software, because it protects the whole network from viruses and hackers. Before the coronavirus pandemic Yahoo! banned working from home, based on the observation that informal hallway conversations often lead to positive externalities like new collaborations and new ideas.

The Golden Rule is about externalities. When you were growing up, your parents probably taught you the "Golden Rule"—to do unto others as you would like them to do unto you. The idea dates back to the New Testament, if not earlier, and nearly every religion has a similar teaching. The point is to take account of how your actions affect other people. In economic terms, your parents, like your religion, are urging you to internalise externalities.

EVERYDAY Economics **What do campaign spending limits, anti-doping rules, and school uniforms have in common?**

Sometimes what matters is not whether you're doing well, but whether you're doing better than others. For instance, in elections, if one candidate spends a lot on advertisements, their opponents will have to do the same just to keep up. In many sports, athletes feel compelled to take performance-enhancing drugs, because their opponents do. Disgraced cyclist Lance Armstrong, after admitting doping for all of his seven Tour de France victories, even compared taking such drugs with putting air in his bike's tyres. Relatedly, many students in schools where uniforms are not mandatory (like in many parts of the United States) feel a similar pressure to be at least as fashionable as their friends. Each of these is a zero-sum game, in which your gain comes at your opponent's expense. That is, your action yields a negative externality for those who you temporarily edge ahead of. We would all be better off if we could eliminate such contests. That is one reason for campaign spending limits, anti-doping rules, and the school uniforms that are typical in Australian schools. They are solutions to the same basic problem—preventing the negative externalities in these zero-sum contests. ■

Rules are a blunt instrument. Many rules lead to better outcomes. However, regulations can often blunt the forces of competition, which would otherwise ensure that only efficient firms survive. Thus, many economists prefer to use solutions that complement market forces—such as corrective taxes and subsidies, or cap and trade—and to use regulations only when those solutions aren't feasible.

This also reflects the fact that regulations are a blunt instrument. While it often makes sense to try to *reduce* certain negative externalities, sometimes it's only feasible to write a rule that will eliminate them altogether. ("Don't feed the ducks" is an easy-to-enforce rule, even though "Don't overfeed the ducks" is the goal.)

Other problems arise with poorly written regulations. Rules that specify how to achieve a given objective can lead to inefficiencies. For instance, laws requiring the use of energy-saving light bulbs sound like a good idea, but they're inefficient if people would rather reduce their energy use by running their air conditioners less often, instead of replacing all of their lights with expensive LEDs.

Moreover, regulations can reduce the incentive to innovate and discover new ways of reducing an externality. For example, environmental regulations that require factories to install industrial scrubbers to control polluting emissions provide no incentive to find an even more effective way of reducing emissions.

By now, you should have a useful sense of the first four solutions to externality problems, and the conditions under which it makes sense to use them. We're now going to turn to a specific set of externalities in greater detail, and we'll add two more solutions, which are tailored to the specific circumstances we'll study in the next section.

10.4 Public Goods and the Tragedy of the Commons

Learning Objective *Understand how to solve externality problems that arise when people can't be excluded from using something.*

Our final task is to focus on solving a specific type of externality problem, but before we can do that, we need to explore what makes these externalities special. Typically, when I own something—say, a new car—I can stop you from using it. I just lock the car. But special problems arise when a product is **nonexcludable,** which means that people cannot easily be excluded from using it. The specific problem this causes depends on one other characteristic: whether your using the good actually harms me. When something is **nonrival,** one person's enjoyment or use of it doesn't subtract from another person's enjoyment or use.

nonexcludable When someone cannot be easily excluded from using something.

nonrival good A good for which one person's use doesn't subtract from another's.

As we'll see, this can create externality problems that would undermine an otherwise viable business plan. Our last two solutions to externality problems—government provision of public goods and assigning ownership rights—will focus on solving externality problems that arise when something is nonrival, nonexcludable, or both nonrival and nonexcludable. Let's dive in to tackling these special externality problems.

Public Goods and the Free-Rider Problem

When people cannot be easily excluded from using something, a particular kind of externality problem called the **free-rider problem** can occur, in which someone can enjoy the benefits of something without bearing the costs. For instance, if you enjoy beautiful architecture, breathing clean air, or living free from the risk of smallpox, you are likely free-riding on the work of others. Beautiful architecture, clean air, and the eradication of disease are all nonexcludable—you can't prevent people who don't pay for them from enjoying their benefits. Free riders don't pay for the benefits they receive, and are therefore bystanders, enjoying positive externalities. As with other types of positive externalities, the market ignores the interests of bystanders, and as a result may underproduce the good, or even worse, fail to provide it at all.

free-rider problem When someone can enjoy the benefits of a good without bearing the costs.

With nonrival goods, free riders enjoy positive externalities without hurting others. If you clean your apartment, then your roommates will enjoy a tidy home, whether or not they helped. If you help plant flowers in your local park, other people will enjoy the benefits of spending time in a beautiful park even if they didn't help plant the flowers. And if you persuade the government to adopt smarter economic policies, local businesses will benefit, even if they didn't help in your lobbying effort. In each of these cases, the free rider—the roommates, park patrons, or business owners—benefit from your actions, even if they didn't contribute.

Importantly, note that in each of these examples, the benefits enjoyed by the free rider don't actually hurt you. You still get to enjoy your clean home, even if your roommate also enjoys it. You still get to enjoy the beautiful park. And better economic policy helps you, even if it also helps others. That is, consumption of clean homes, pretty flowers, and better economic policy are nonrival.

Whenever there are bystanders who benefit from your actions without contributing (that is, when something is nonexcludable), and when their benefits don't subtract from anyone else's (that is, when consumption is nonrival), then a positive externality results. As we saw earlier, activities involving positive externalities are underproduced, because buyers and sellers don't take account of the benefits to free riders.

When goods or services are rival and it's easy to exclude those who don't pay, there's no free-rider problem. To understand why nonrival goods are special, it's worth taking a look at their opposite. A **rival good** is one for which your use of it comes at someone else's expense. For instance, if you eat the cookie on the table, I can't. For businesses selling rival and easily excludable goods, the free-rider problem is never an issue. A bakery, for instance, simply won't give you a cookie if you don't pay. Because bakeries can easily exclude those who don't pay from benefiting from their goods, they don't need to worry about free riders. And because there are no externalities from your consuming a cookie (remember not to litter!), the right amount of cookies are sold in the market.

rival good A good for which your use of it comes at someone else's expense.

Public goods are nonrival goods afflicted by the free-rider problem. A nonrival good that is nonexcludable and hence subject to the free-rider problem is sufficiently important to have its own name: It's called a **public good.**

public good A nonrival good that is nonexcludable and hence subject to the free-rider problem.

The example of the national military gives you a hint as to why we call these public goods. Imagine that instead of a public (government-run) military, a private company offered to provide national security—keeping your country safe from foreign invaders—for the low price of $20 per person per month. This company would quickly discover that it couldn't exclude people who didn't pay from enjoying the benefits of living in a safe nation. As such, few people would choose to pay, and most would free-ride instead. This nonexcludability creates a free-rider problem so severe that it's unlikely that any private company would find it profitable to provide national security. National security is also nonrival—my enjoyment of our safety doesn't subtract from your enjoyment of it. Consequently, because national security is both nonexcludable and nonrival, it is a public good. The problem is that even though we all benefit from national security, the market will fail to provide it. This is why the government provides national security instead, devoting about one-fifth of the federal budget to this purpose.

Solution Five: Government Support for Public Goods

Public goods create positive externalities for people who don't contribute to them since they can't be excluded from enjoying the good. The heart of the free-rider problem is that businesses can't force people to contribute toward public goods they benefit from. And like positive externalities more generally, that means that the equilibrium quantity will be below the socially optimal quantity. This brings us to our fifth solution for externalities: Government can help pay for public goods. A simple solution to the underprovision of public goods is for the government to purchase public goods for everyone to use, paid for from tax revenues.

This is a powerful insight, as it explains why the military, police, and public parks are all paid for out of our taxes, rather than being (under) produced by private businesses. It also explains why the government funds so much scientific research. All are examples of public goods. Some people argue that having a literate population is also a public good, and hence this explains why governments fund public education, and why policies to improve the quality of education are often referred to as building "a clever country".

There are three facts about public goods you should know. A public good has a specific definition that you've already seen but to truly understand what a public good is, keep these three facts in mind:

Fact one: *Just because the government provides it, doesn't mean that it is a public good.*

The government provides many goods that are not actually public goods, in that they are either excludable, rival, or both. For instance, the government delivers mail through Australia Post. Mail delivery is both excludable (if you don't pay, you can't mail something) and rival (when the postal worker is at my house delivering a package, she isn't at your house).

Fact two: *Just because something is a public good doesn't mean that the government should fund it.*

Determining something is a public good is one thing; deciding whether or not the government should pay for it is another. Savvy policymakers apply the *cost-benefit principle*, making public investments for which social benefits exceed social costs, which means that the decision about whether the government should provide a public good will depend on both the good and the community. Some communities may really value parks, while others value research. Not surprisingly, then, there are often big political battles over which public goods the government should fund.

Fact three: *Just because the government should fund a public good, doesn't mean that the government should provide it.*

Juergen Held/travelstock44/Alamy Stock Photo

Is this spectacle at the socially optimal level?

Public goods like New Year's Eve fireworks on Sydney Harbour will be underprovided by the market. That is why it makes sense for the government to raise revenue to ensure that the socially optimal level is provided. However, this is not an argument for government employees to actually manufacture and light the fireworks, as the government could just as easily pay a private firm to do this instead.

Public goods can be provided by communities. Sometimes, public goods occur on a much smaller scale, but the same principles apply. Within your household, a TV in the living room is a public good. If you don't solve the free-rider problem, then you could end up living in a house without a TV. One solution is for the "local government" of you and your roommates to pitch in $100 each and jointly buy one for all of you to collectively enjoy. Similarly, a clean house is a public good, and the local government of you and your roommates may need to create a chore chart to ensure that the kitchen and bathrooms get regularly cleaned.

Other public goods are funded in more creative ways. For instance, while many newspaper websites have a "paywall" so that they can only be read by subscribers, the *Guardian* ask readers without a subscription for donations. You might get a pop-up message like this: "In these extraordinary times, millions rely on the *Guardian* for high-impact, independent journalism that stands for truth and integrity. With no shareholders or billionaire owner, we report on world events with accuracy, free from political and commercial influence. And unlike many others, we're committed to keeping our reporting open for all readers. Every contribution, however big or small, makes a difference. Support the *Guardian* from as little as $1. Thank you." And many schools get parents to voluntarily provide public goods, through the P&C Association—for example cooking sausages or running the cake stall at annual BBQs, coaching a debating or soccer team, or helping out in classroom reading or maths groups—by relying on the social norms of parental involvement.

Businesses try to turn public goods into club goods. A public good is nonexcludable and nonrival, but businesses have an incentive to try to find a way to make them excludable. For example, you could buy some land, build a road on it, set up a tollbooth, and only let people pass if they pay you. The road is now excludable, but still largely nonrival. Sure, there's wear and tear on the road, and too many people could cause congestion. But when there isn't much traffic, the marginal cost of a car is close to zero.

club good A good that is excludable, but nonrival in consumption.

Economists call these kinds of goods—ones that are excludable but nonrival in consumption—**club goods.** They are a type of local monopoly, and just like all monopolies left to their own devices, they charge a higher price, leading the quantity that they sell to be lower than the socially optimal quantity. What this means is that businesses often provide club goods, but they underprovide them.

Here's how club goods are relevant: Businesses try to solve the problem of public goods by figuring out how to exclude people. If they can figure out how to exclude people, they can turn a public good into a club good. For example, cable television figured out how to turn the public good of broadcast television into a club good by scrambling their signal so only paying customers can get it. However, cable television is a nonrival good, and this means that the marginal cost of an additional viewer is zero. As a result, there are lots of people for whom the price of cable TV is set higher than their marginal benefit, even though the marginal cost of providing them with cable TV is below their marginal benefit.

So while businesses can attempt to solve public-goods problems by creating ways to exclude nonpaying customers, they don't fully solve the problems inherent in public goods since they underprovide club goods.

Solution Six: Assign Ownership Rights for Common Resource Problems

So far we've considered situations in which nonrival goods are nonexcludable. Let's now consider what happens when rival goods are nonexcludable. Goods that are rival but nonexcludable are **common resources.** Common resources have private gains but shared costs. Once you catch a fish, you privately benefit from eating it, but the cost—the reduced number of fish left—is shared by everyone. By imposing a cost that falls on others, your fishing causes a negative externality. This brings us to the sixth solution for solving externalities—assigning property rights—but first, let's take a closer look at common resource problems through a simple parable that remains relevant today.

common resource A good that is rival and also nonexcludable.

tragedy of the commons The tendency to overconsume a common resource.

Common resources can lead to a tragedy of the commons. The **tragedy of the commons** dates back to when most towns had a central grassed area called the "commons." Shepherds who brought their sheep to graze on the commons benefited from this grass but didn't pay for the privilege. The problem is that when it costs nothing to graze sheep on the town commons, each shepherd does a lot of it. The result is a tragedy: The commons will be overgrazed and the grass will never grow back.

This tragedy of the commons occurs because people overconsume common resources. Just as with other negative externalities, we get too much of those activities where people don't pay for the full social cost of their actions. What makes this a tragedy is that everyone would be better off if we could agree to limit consumption of common resources.

Matthias Naumann/Alamy

If too many of them graze, the grass will never grow back.

The tragedy of the commons occurs whenever rival goods are nonexcludable. This parable still applies today, and it describes a broad range of negative externalities. For instance, just as shepherds overgrazed the town commons, fishermen are overfishing our oceans, and today, conservationists at the International Union for Conservation of Nature have found that more than half of all tuna species are at risk of extinction. The decline in the annual global catch of southern bluefin tuna illustrates the problem with overfishing today—there's fewer fish to catch tomorrow.

The Earth's atmosphere is also a common resource, and our polluting factories are destroying it for the rest of us. The tragedy of the commons is a parable well suited to understanding not only environmental issues, but also congestion problems. Traffic jams are a result of the tragedy of the commons, in which our highways are overused by drivers who don't pay for the extra congestion they cause. Likewise, the internet is a common resource, and spammers' overuse makes e-mail communication more difficult for everyone.

Annual Global Catch of Southern Bluefin Tuna

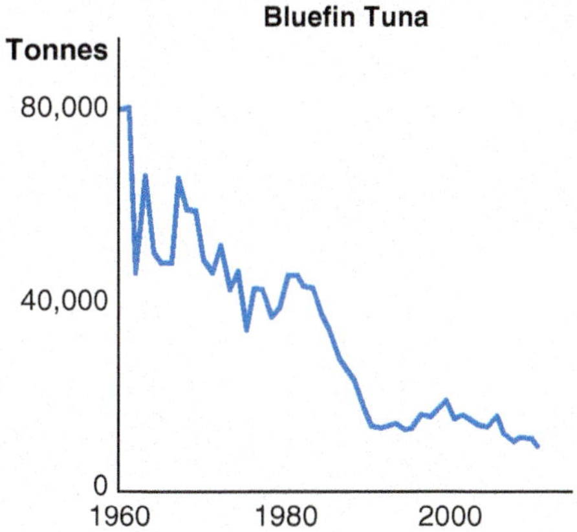

Data from: FAO.

Assign ownership rights to solve the tragedy of the commons. Our last solution to externality problems tells us how to solve situations involving a tragedy of the commons: assign ownership rights. The tragedy of the commons causes problems because when everyone owns something, they end up acting as if no one owns it. Ownership rights can help by facilitating successful private bargaining. The new owner of the commons might sell the right to graze to shepherds with limits on their maximum number of sheep. Importantly, that owner would be careful not to overgraze the common, because doing so would only undermine her ability to sell grazing rights again next year. The costs and benefits of grazing on the commons become the owner's costs and benefits, leading them to effectively internalise the externality.

Recap: Nonexcludable goods create externality problems. Let's summarise what we've learned about nonexcludable goods using the broader context of externalities. When you can't exclude nonpayers from using a good, there will be externalities. The type of externality depends on the type of good involved. When it's a nonrival good—so the free rider's enjoyment of it doesn't harm anyone else—then we have a public good, which yields positive externalities, and positive externalities are typically underproduced by the market. When it's a rival good, we get the tragedy of the commons, in which your use of a common resource means that there's less of it for others, which is a negative externality, leading to too much selfish behaviour.

	Rival	Nonrival
Excludable	Private goods • *Cookies* • *Cars*	Club goods • *Cable TV* • *Toll roads*
Nonexcludable	Common resources • *Fish* • *Public parks and beaches*	Public goods • *Defence* • *Scientific research*

Tying It Together

Six insights for dealing with externalities:

1. Don't intervene if you don't need to.
2. Complementing market forces is better than hindering them.
3. The right tool depends on what you're uncertain about.
4. Consider costs and benefits of regulations or public goods.
5. Target bad outcomes, not specific processes.
6. Ensure there's an incentive to innovate.

By now, you should recognise that whenever someone makes choices without taking account of the consequences for bystanders, bad outcomes may result. Specifically, we get too many negative externalities, which harm bystanders, and too few positive externalities, which help bystanders.

While climate change is one of the clearest examples of an externality problem, you should also recognise that externalities occur in every facet of your life. They shape outcomes not only within your natural environment, but also in your business, your workplace, your community, and even within yourself. As such, it's critical that you also learn to identify possible solutions. We've analysed private bargaining, corrective taxes and subsidies, quantity regulations and cap-and-trade systems, and government regulations—and when there's a nonexcludable good involved, direct provision of public goods, or assigning ownership rights to prevent the tragedy of the commons.

As we've assessed each of these tools, we've uncovered a few general principles for deciding which solutions work best. Let's put those insights together:

Insight one: *Don't intervene if you don't need to.*

If people can use private bargains to solve an externality problem, let them. This is most likely to succeed when transaction costs are small and the benefits to solving the problem are large. In the tragedy of the commons, assigning ownership rights facilitates private bargains between individuals.

Insight two: *Complementing market forces is better than hindering them.*

If you're going to intervene, solutions like corrective taxes and subsidies, or cap-and-trade programs complement market forces. This is usually better than regulations or government provision, which hinder market forces. That's because competition between suppliers helps ensure that output will be produced by those who can do so at a lower social cost, and competition between buyers ensures it will be allocated to those who value that output the most. Alternatively phrased, your analysis of externalities points to a better destination for society. Competition can find the most efficient path to get there.

Insight three: *The right tool depends on what you're uncertain about.*

Use corrective taxes (or subsidies) when you are more confident that you know the marginal external costs (or benefits), but use quantity restrictions like cap and trade when you are more confident about the socially optimal quantity.

Insight four: *Consider costs and benefits of regulations or public goods.*

When market-based solutions aren't possible, consider either regulations or direct provision of public goods, but only if the benefits exceed the costs.

Insight five: *Target outcomes, not specific processes.*

If you tell people what to do, they'll do it. But if you tell them what outcome to achieve, they might find more efficient ways to achieve it. For instance, we've analysed how either a tax on petrol or a quota on petrol usage would reduce emission of greenhouse gases. But if you care about reducing greenhouse gases, an even better solution would be a tax or a cap on greenhouse petrol emissions. Why? It could be that businesses have other lower-cost ways to reduce emissions of greenhouse gases than cutting back on petrol use.

Insight six: *Ensure there's an incentive to innovate.*

Relatedly, you want to ensure there's always a robust incentive for businesses to innovate and discover new ways to solve externality problems. Policies that tell businesses what you want to achieve give them scope to innovate by figuring out how. By contrast, regulations that tell them what to do, or taxes or caps on specific processes, reduce this incentive.

Let's summarise. Externalities are an example of a market failure, leading the forces of supply and demand to outcomes that aren't in society's best interest. That's the bad news. The good news is that, with a keen understanding of externalities, there are practical solutions that you can employ to generate better outcomes for everyone by inducing people to internalise the externality.

Chapter at a Glance

An externality is a side effect of an activity that affects bystanders whose interests aren't taken into account.

Follow the 3-step recipe to analyse externality problems.

Step 1: Predict the equilibrium outcome.

Step 2: Assess what externalities are involved.

Step 3: Find the socially optimal outcome and compare it to the equilibrium outcome.

Negative externalities have external costs that harm others. The **supply curve** understates **marginal social costs**, leading to **overproduction**

1: Predict the equilibrium outcome

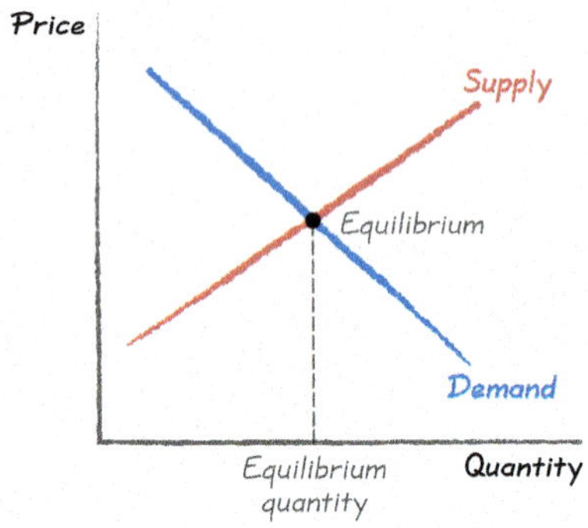

2. Assess the externalities

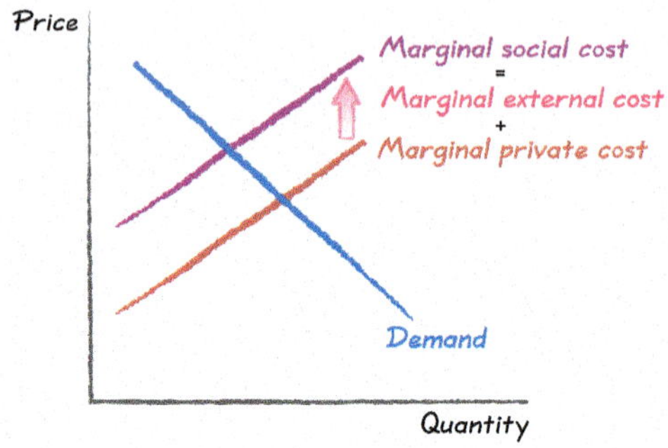

3. Find the socially optimal outcome

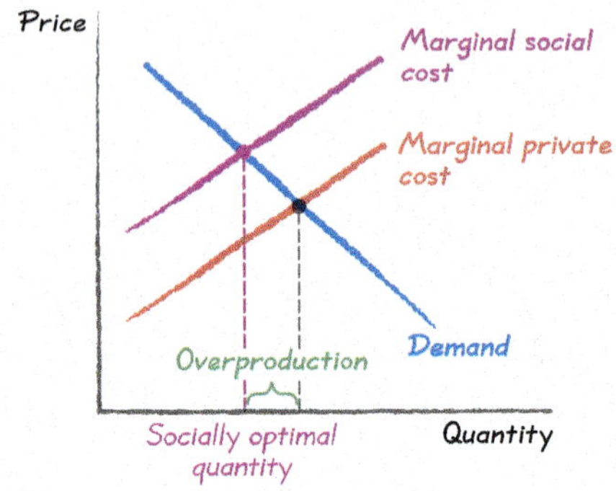

Positive externalities help others. The **demand curve** understates **marginal social benefits**, leading to **underproduction.**

1: Predict the equilibrium outcome

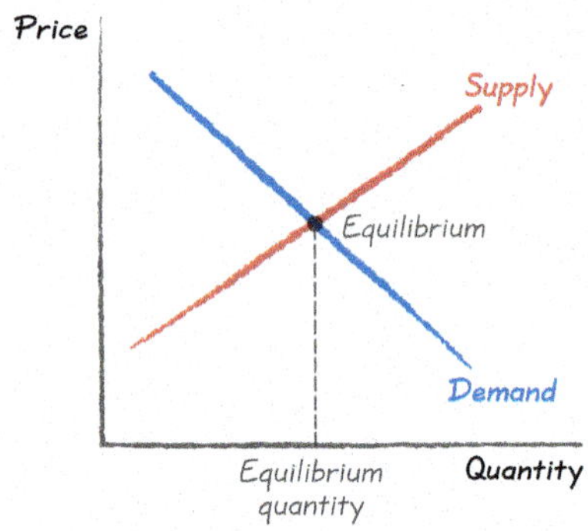

2. Assess the externalities

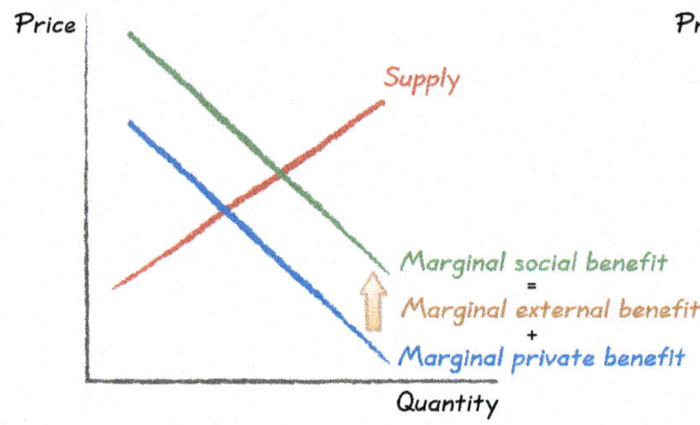

3. Find the socially optimal outcome

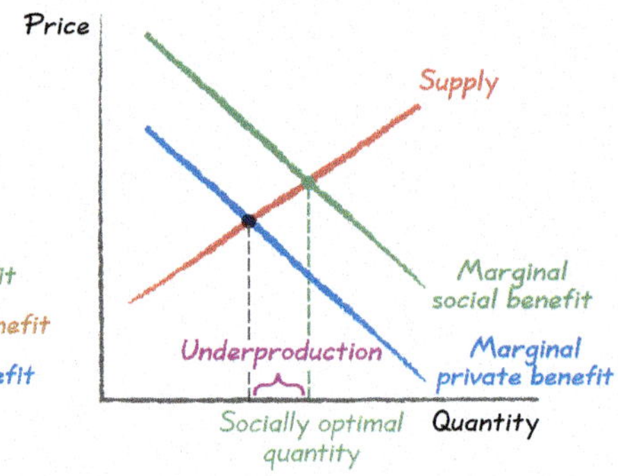

Solving externalities relies on "internalising the externality"

#1: Private bargaining (Coase Theorem)	• Works best when bargaining costs are low. • When bargaining is difficult, externalities remain a problem.
#2: Fix the price: Corrective taxes and subsidies	• Set a corrective tax equal to the external cost. • Set a corrective subsidy equal to the external benefit.
#3: Fix the quantity: Cap and trade	• Fix the quantity at the socially optimal level. • Allowing firms to trade their quantity caps improves efficiency.
#4: Laws, rules, and regulations	• Rules may be a blunt instrument and reduce competitive forces.
#5: Government support for public goods	• Because public goods are underprovided, one solution is for the government to purchase public goods for everyone, paid for from tax revenues.
#6: Assign ownership rights to solve the tragedy of the commons	• The tragedy of the commons occurs when rival goods are affected by free rider problems. Ownership rights help by facilitating successful private bargaining.

Key Concepts

cap and trade, 256
club good, 260
Coase Theorem, 250
common resource, 261
corrective subsidy, 254
corrective tax, 252
external benefit, 243
external cost, 242
externality, 240
free-rider problem, 258
marginal external benefit, 243
marginal external cost, 242
marginal private benefit, 243
marginal private cost, 242
marginal social benefit, 243
marginal social cost, 242
negative externality, 240
nonexcludable, 258
nonrival good, 258
positive externalities, 240
public good, 259
Rational Rule for Society, 244
rival good, 259
socially optimal outcome, 244
tragedy of the commons, 261

Discussion and Review Questions

Learning Objective 10.1 *Identify externalities and their consequences.*

1. For each of the following, identify and describe both a possible negative externality *and* a possible positive externality.
   a. You build a chicken coop in your suburban backyard.
   b. You get sick and go to a doctor. The doctor diagnoses you with a bacterial infection and prescribes you an antibiotic.
   c. An urban farmer installs a beehive to help pollinate their rooftop gardens.

Learning Objective 10.2 *Analyse how externalities lead markets to produce inefficient outcomes.*

2. The median earnings for a 25- to 34-year-old, full-time, year-round worker with only a high school education was $53,829 in 2016, while similar workers with an undergraduate degree (but no further education) earned $76,731, and as a result, they pay more income tax.
   a. Is there a private benefit to individuals who attend university and get an undergraduate degree?
   b. Is there an external benefit associated with an individual earning an undergraduate degree?
   c. Do you think that the private market—meaning without government support for students or universities—for university education would result in too many or too few people going to college relative to the socially optimal outcome?
   d. If you think that the private market would not result in the socially optimal outcome, what types of things could the government do in order to achieve a socially optimal outcome in the market for university education?

Learning Objective 10.3 *Solve externality problems.*

3. In 2019 three residents in Rokewood, Victoria brought a Supreme Court challenge against a planned 228-turbine wind farm, with each turbine being as much as 230m tall. The residents raised concerns about the wind farm preventing building on their own land and the impact on brolga breeding habitats. How could the wind farm developer could have utilised insights from the Coase Theorem to avoid its legal troubles?
4. A local school administrator observes an increase in the number of flu outbreaks in the public schools over the last two years. She is concerned that this is putting other children at risk, so she proposes that the government should subsidise flu shots in order to increase coverage rates.
   a. Are the administrator's concerns valid—are too few children getting flu shots—and will a subsidy lead to a more socially optimal quantity? Draw a graph to help analyse this policy.
   b. The school nurse suggests publishing a list of which kids did not get a flu shot, in the hope that public shaming will lead people to vaccinate their children. Is this strategy likely to work? Why or why not?
5. Provide an example of a positive and a negative externality not mentioned in the chapter for which social norms act like a corrective tax or subsidy.
6. The Nobel Prize–winning economist Oliver Hart once said, "If we know the marginal social cost [of pollution] emissions, a tax is better, but if we know the optimal quantity, cap and trade is better." Explain why this is true.

Learning Objective 10.4 *Understand how to solve externality problems that arise when people can't be excluded from using something.*

7. Provide an example of a public good and briefly describe how the good is both nonexcludable and nonrival. Will the market provide too much or too little of a public good? Why? Should the government fund and/or provide the public good? Could the community provide for the public good in some way besides directly through government?
8. Some goods are rival but nonexcludable; others are excludable but nonrival. Which of these pairs of

characteristics describes a "club good"? Which describes a common resource? What is the "tragedy of the commons" and how does it relate to the characteristics of a common resource?

9. A policy maker argues that congestion on the roads can be solved by private ownership of the roads. He argues that if the roads were privately owned, then the externality of congestion would be fully internalised and solved by the market. Discuss this by first explaining the externality problem that leads to congestion, and then explain whether the private market would deliver the efficient level of roads.

Study Problems

Learning Objective 10.1 *Identify externalities and their consequences.*

1. For each of the following examples, identify whether a positive or negative externality is present and whether there will be too little or too much of the activity relative to the socially optimal outcome.
   - **a.** Jerome has a beautifully landscaped front lawn with lots of colourful flowers.
   - **b.** Dave takes advantage of the low price of petrol to purchase an SUV that is not very fuel efficient.
   - **c.** Susan decides to walk to work instead of driving.
   - **d.** Anita decides to drink coffee on the bus while she rides to work and spills it on the person sitting next to her.

Learning Objective 10.2 *Analyse how externalities lead markets to produce inefficient outcomes.*

2. The graph below illustrates a market for cigarettes. Use it to answer the questions that follow.

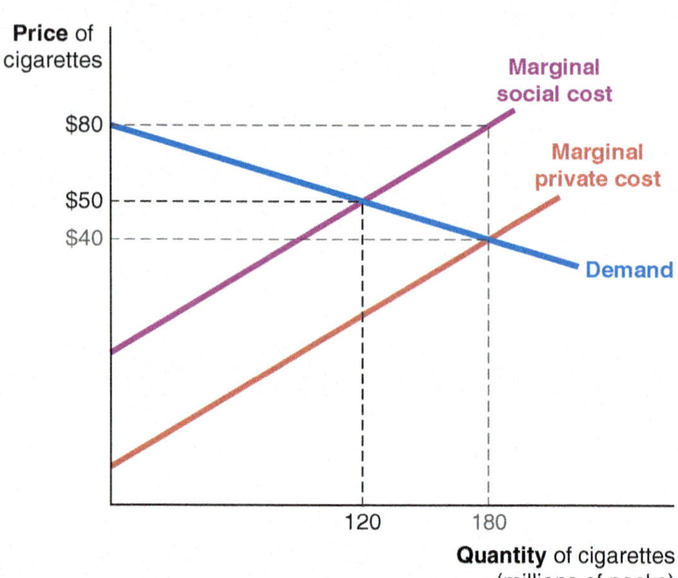

   - **a.** Based only on the graph, are there positive or negative externalities associated with cigarettes? Explain your answer.
   - **b.** Show the equilibrium price and quantity in this market.
   - **c.** What is the socially optimal quantity in this market?
   - **d.** According to the graph, what is the marginal external cost of a packet of cigarettes?

3. The graph below shows the market for house-painting services. Use it to answer the questions that follow.

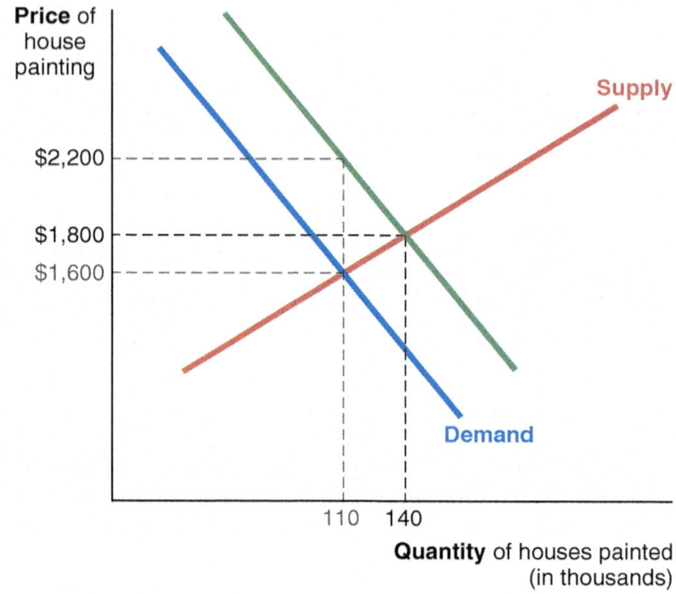

   - **a.** Painting the exterior of your house yields external benefits for your neighbours. Label the private marginal benefit and social marginal benefit curves and show the amount of the external benefit.
   - **b.** Show the equilibrium price and quantity.
   - **c.** What is the socially optimal quantity in this market?
   - **d.** Does the market produce too much or too little of this good relative to the socially optimal outcome? How much?

4. People experiencing a medical emergency experience better outcomes if someone near them has first aid training and can immediately begin providing assistance. As a result, first aid training and certification is required for jobs working with the elderly and with children. First aid training also benefits the trained person's friends and family. It even benefits strangers who live in the same community since it increases the chances that there is someone near them with first aid training when a medical emergency occurs.
   - **a.** Use a demand and supply graph to illustrate a hypothetical market for first aid training.
   - **b.** Will this market result in a socially optimal level of first aid training, more than the socially optimal level of consumption of first aid training, or less than the socially optimal level of first aid training?
   - **c.** Use your graph to label the socially optimal level of first aid training/certificates.

Learning Objective 10.3 *Solve externality problems.*

5. Refer to the graph in Study Problem 2 that shows the market for cigarettes. Suppose the government wants to eliminate inefficiency in this market by imposing a tax on each pack of cigarettes sold.

a. What is the amount of the per-pack tax that would result in the socially optimal level of consumption in this market?

b. A quota can also be used to solve the externality problem. What quantity should the government choose for the quota limit if its goal is to achieve the socially optimal outcome?

c. Why isn't the socially optimal quantity of cigarettes zero?

6. Each scenario below involves an externality. For each, identify the externality and explain whether it is "likely" or "not likely" that private bargaining will lead to a socially optimal outcome.

a. Conducting scientific research that is likely to spark other innovations.

b. Putting together an excellent music playlist.

c. Mowing your lawn in the middle of the night.

d. Producing steel that results in pollution affecting millions of residents in the surrounding area.

7. In order to curb CO_2 emissions, the government creates a cap-and-trade system for freight companies that use semi-trailer trucks to move freight. Some freight companies have already spent lots of money investing in low-emission trucks or even developing battery technologies to decrease emissions. Other companies have invested nothing to decrease their emissions. Explain how the cap-and-trade program, if implemented successfully, will decrease emissions.

8. Some economists argue that early child care generates an external benefit to society. Consider the following demand and supply graph for early childhood education.

a. How does the market equilibrium differ from what is best for society?

b. If the government were to provide a per-unit subsidy in this market in order to achieve the socially optimal outcome, how large a subsidy would the government need to provide?

c. How much in total would the government need to spend in this market each month to achieve a socially optimal outcome?

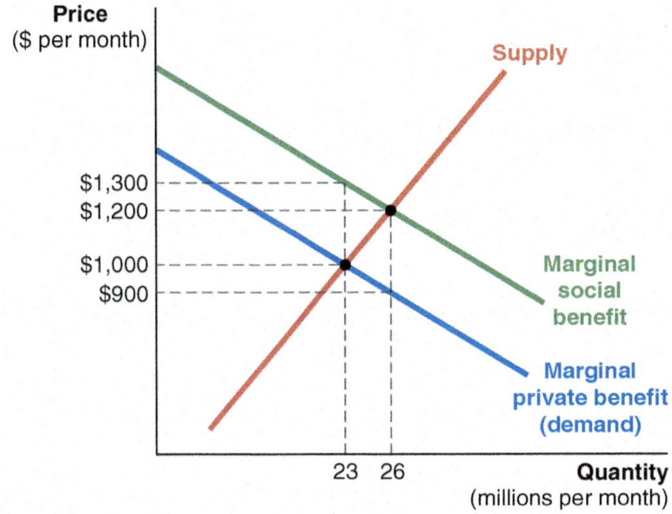

Learning Objective 10.4 *Understand how to solve externality problems that arise when people can't be excluded from using something.*

9. For each of the following, identify whether it is nonexcludable, nonrival, neither, or both and briefly explain your answer. Additionally, determine which would suffer from the free-rider problem.

a. A national forest with dozens of access points for hiking trails located along public roads and highways

b. Bouddi National Park

c. National defence

d. A train

10. There are effective vaccines for a number of infectious diseases, such as measles, mumps, and rubella. Most parents immunise their children with the "MMR" vaccine, but some "anti-vaxxers" maintain that vaccines are dangerous and refuse to vaccinate their children. The Australian government maintains that the best scientific evidence is that the vaccine is completely safe.

Beginning in 2016, the Australian government introduced a "No-jab, No-pay" policy which denies the Family Tax Benefit part A, Child Care Benefit, and the Child Care Rebate to parents who do not vaccinate their children.

a. Is the MMR vaccine a private good or a public good? Why?

b. Is the "No-Jab, No-Pay" policy a good one, and are there alternative policy interventions that you think would be preferable?

The Labour Market

CHAPTER 11

As a 19-year-old student at the University of Western Australia, Melanie Perkins taught fellow students how to use graphic design programs offered by Adobe and Microsoft, but she noticed how difficult and unintuitive these platforms were for most students: "People would have to spend an entire semester learning where the buttons were, and that seemed completely ridiculous."

Eóin Noonan/Sportsfile for Web Summit/Getty Images

Melanie Perkins founded Canva when she was just 24 years old.

Perkins also remembered her experience on her high school yearbook staff and how challenging it was to produce a polished yearbook. She wanted to make it easier for beginner designers to get professional results. So while she was still in university, she and now husband Cliff Obrecht started a website, Fusion Books, which allowed students to collaborate to design profile pages and articles and then print and deliver the yearbooks.

Fusion Books was successful and is still around today, but Perkins had a larger goal of creating a company that would allow users to "Design Anything"—from presentations and posters to restaurant menus—in a simple and easy-to-use interface. This was the founding of Canva—a design startup that today has an estimated value of US$15 billion.

But why was this startup so successful? Perkins realised that she needed to have the right team in place and this started with finding the right investors. After reportedly being turned down by more than 100 potential investors, she received an invite to pitch her idea at a Silicon Valley conference. At this conference, Perkins and Obrecht realised the value of networking—and they secured an invite to MaiTai, an exclusive gathering of kitesurfers and tech investors.

So kitesurfing became Perkins's new hobby and it paid off! Through this group, she connected with Lars Rasmussen, a co-founder of Google Maps. Rasmussen became Canva's tech advisor and helped Perkins and Obrecht bring ex-Google employee Cameron Adams on board as a third co-founder and Chief Product Officer. With the right team of co-founders in place, Canva's funding took off as they secured an initial venture capital funding of US$1.5 million in 2012. A year later, Canva went live.

Canva currently employs over 700 people. "As leader, I feel my job is to set the vision and goals for the company, and then work with everyone to empower them to dream big and crazy," says Perkins. Perkins is well on her way to building one of the world's most successful start-up unicorns as approximately 85% of Fortune 500 companies use Canva.

As Perkins's story shows, the labour market can play a big role is shaping your life story. You're likely to begin your career as a supplier of labour. You might even find your first job at a tech company like Canva. As your career progresses, you might gain responsibility for hiring (or one day own your own company like Perkins) and become a demander of labour. Each decision you make will shape your future and determine which skills you'll acquire.

Chapter Objective

Learn to make good decisions both as an employer and as a worker and understand how wages are determined.

11.1 The Labour Market: Supply and Demand at Work
Understand how wages and employment are determined by the forces of supply and demand.

11.2 Labour Demand: Thinking Like an Employer
Discover how employers decide how many workers to hire.

11.3 Labour Supply: How to Balance Work and Leisure
Decide how much time to devote to work versus leisure.

11.4 Changing Economic Conditions and Labour Market Equilibrium
Evaluate how the labour market will respond to changing economic conditions.

11.1 The Labour Market: Supply and Demand at Work

Learning Objective *Understand how wages and employment are determined by the forces of supply and demand.*

Africa Studio/Shutterstock

A great hair stylist can give you a great haircut. But what determines their wage?

What determines the price of a haircut? That's easy: supply and demand. Hair salons are suppliers, constantly looking to win new customers. You and I are on the demand side, trying to get the best haircut at the best price. The price of a haircut is determined by the intersection of the supply and demand curves, as shown in the left panel of Figure 1.

Okay, next question: What determines the wage paid to the hair stylist who gave you that haircut? Again, it's all about supply and demand. Instead of the market for hair*cuts,* we need to focus on the labour market for hair *stylists,* where people can buy or sell an hour of a hair stylist's time. So the labour market is like any other market, except the units on the price and quantity axes are a bit different. The price of an hour of a hair stylist's time is their *hourly wage*. And the quantities a salon buys are their *hours of work*. The rest should be familiar, as the wage of hair stylists is determined by the intersection of these labour supply and labour demand curves, as shown in the right panel of Figure 1.

Whose choices do these labour supply and labour demand curves represent? In most other markets, we think about businesses as suppliers and ordinary folks like you and me as demanders. But in the labour market, we switch places. As a worker, you're on the supply side, looking to sell your labour for the highest wage you can get. And businesses are on the demand side, looking to hire the best workers they can find at the lowest price possible.

Figure 1 | **The Market for Haircuts and the Labour Market for Hair Stylists**

Panel A: What Determines the Price of a Haircut? The Market for Haircuts

The price of a haircut is determined by the intersection of:

Ⓐ An upward-sloping **supply** curve (reflecting the decisions of hair salons); and

Ⓑ A downward-sloping **demand** curve (reflecting the decisions of hair salon customers).

Panel B: What Determines the Wage of Hair Stylists? The Labour Market for Hair Stylists

The wage of a hair stylist is determined by the intersection of:

Ⓐ An upward-sloping **labour supply** curve (reflecting the decisions of hair stylists); and

Ⓑ A downward-sloping **labour demand** curve (reflecting the decisions of hair salons).

Ⓒ The "price" in the labour market is an **hourly wage**, and the "quantity" is measured as **hours of work**.

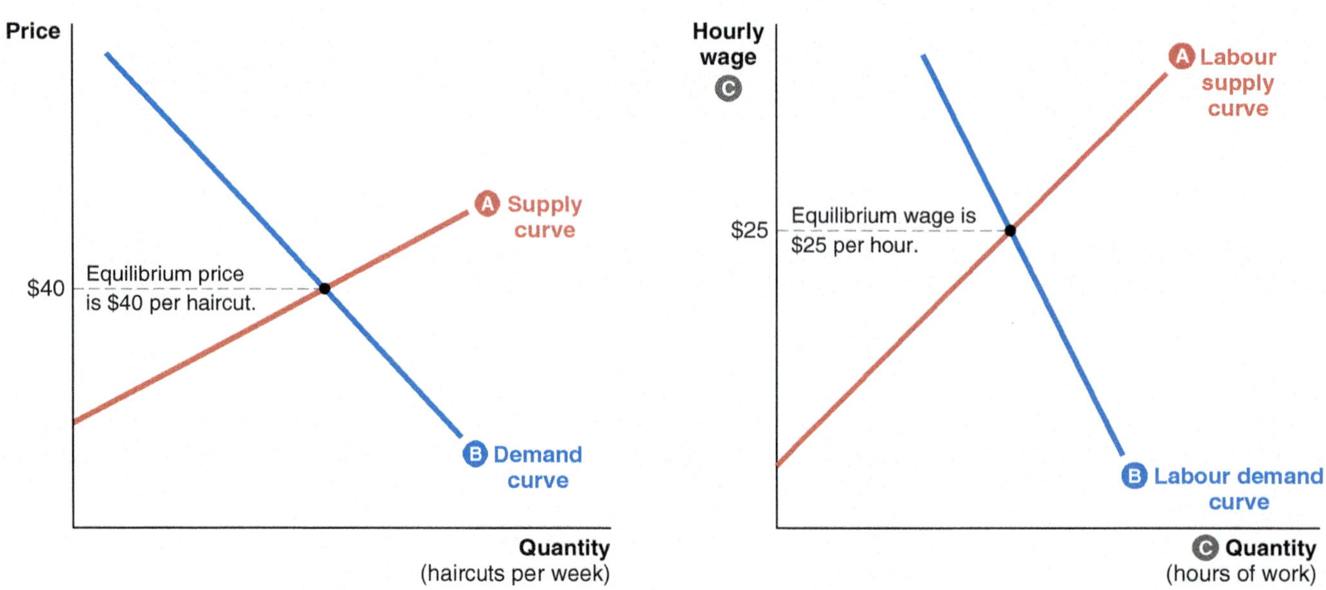

Let's think about why the labour supply curve is upward-sloping by analysing the decisions of Chris, a potential hair stylist. He has to choose whether to supply his labour as a hair stylist or do something else. If the wage for hair stylists is too low, he might take another job—maybe working as a skin care specialist, a veterinary assistant, or receptionist. Or perhaps he doesn't think it's worth giving up his time for work. (Notice the *opportunity cost principle* at work here—he's asking should I work another hour as a stylist, or what?) If the wage is higher, many hair stylists will work longer hours. (They're balancing things at the margin, à la the *marginal principle*.) And the higher the wage, the more people will want to work in hair salons rather than other retail establishments (you can see the *interdependence principle* here). Taken together, higher wages mean more people like Chris will seek out hair stylist work, either giving up more time to work, or forgoing other work opportunities. (That's the *cost-benefit principle*.) Thus, the quantity of hours supplied in the market for hair stylists typically rises with the wage. An upward-sloping labour supply curve is just the law of supply, applied to the labour market.

Remember:
Wage is the price of labour, so it goes on the vertical axis. Hours of work measures the quantity of labour, so that goes on the horizontal axis. (And don't forget to label the units on both axes.)

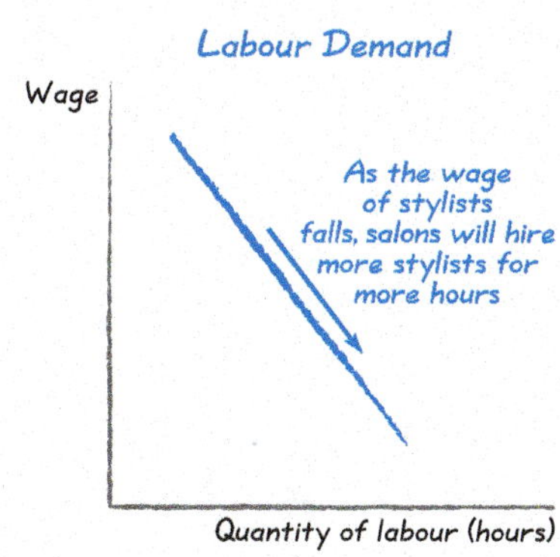

On the demand side, we find hair salons looking to hire hair stylists. If the wage is too high, they'll hire few hair stylists, which means they'll sell fewer haircuts. (This is the *opportunity cost principle* highlighting the consequences of less hiring.) On the other hand, if the wage is lower, salons might also find it profitable to remain open for longer hours—opening earlier in the morning, remaining open later at night, or opening on more days—so they can sell more haircuts. (Again, the *cost-benefit principle*.) Thus, the quantity of hours demanded in the market for hair stylists is typically higher when the wage is lower. (Managers calculate exactly how many more hours they demand by using the *marginal principle*.) The downward-sloping labour demand curve is just the law of demand, applied to the labour market. And all of these calculations will also be affected by changes in the cost of other inputs in the hair salon business, like rent for the salon (the *interdependence principle*).

We've described the broad contours of the labour market: Wages and employment are determined by the intersection of the downward-sloping labour demand curve and the upward-sloping labour supply curve. In the rest of this chapter, we'll focus on how you can apply the core principles of economics to making better decisions in the labour market. As a worker, you'll want to know how to make good labour supply decisions: how many hours you should work; which occupation to choose; and whether to work or pursue an alternative like more education. And as a future manager, you'll want to know how to make good labour demand decisions: how many workers you should hire and what wage to pay them. Let's begin with labour demand.

11.2 Labour Demand: Thinking Like an Employer

Learning Objective *Discover how employers decide how many workers to hire.*

Let's start with a business that you are probably already quite familiar with: Your local hair salon. Gabriela has been a successful hair stylist for years, not only managing a long list of clients who wait to see her, but also helping new stylists hone their skills and build their client base. For years her friends had been telling her to open her own salon. She knew she would love managing her own business, helping other stylists develop, and building an experience that her customers would be able to depend on. And so Head Area was born. Gabriela's not just her own boss; as a small business owner, she's now an employer. At first, she's unsure of herself, since she's never been an employer before. But then she realises that an employer is simply a buyer. In her daily life, she makes good buying decisions; the only difference now is that she's not buying jeans or some other consumer good—she's buying the time and effort of the hair stylists she hires. Gabriela studied how

FotoAndalucia/Shutterstock

Sellers in the market for stylists.

to make smart buying decisions when she studied economics in college. So all she needs to do is adapt that advice to the specific case of buying labour. (If the material on demand from Chapter 2 is rusty, now's a good time to take another look.)

How Many Workers Should You Hire at What Price?

Gabriela's first task is to figure out how many hair stylists to hire. Head Area is one of many employers in the area competing to hire from a large pool of qualified hair stylists. When there are lots of businesses looking to hire from a pool of many workers with similar skills, the labour market is *perfectly competitive.*

Remember:
In a perfectly competitive labour market, savvy employers pay the market wage.

- Why pay more if you can still get good people?
- But if you pay less, good workers will go to other firms.

In a competitive labour market, employers pay the market wage. As an employer in a perfectly competitive labour market, you'll find that there is a prevailing market wage that you'll need to pay to hire workers. Why? If you try paying any less than the market wage, you won't be able to hire anyone—they'll all go and work for your competitors instead. And because there are lots of workers available, Gabriela can hire as many workers as she needs at the market wage. So she decides to pay the market wage.

Apply the core principles of economics to figure out how many workers to hire. When you're a manager operating in a perfectly competitive labour market, the real choice you face is *how many* workers to hire. You should recognise this as a "how many" decision, and so the *marginal principle* suggests breaking this big decision into smaller marginal choices. Thus, the relevant question is whether to hire one more worker. And after that, ask again: Should you hire one more worker? And so on.

The *cost-benefit principle* says: Hire one more worker only if that extra worker yields a marginal benefit greater than the marginal cost incurred. And so Gabriela needs to figure out the marginal benefit and marginal cost of hiring one more worker.

To understand the marginal cost and benefit of hiring one more worker, invoke the *opportunity cost principle* and ask, "Or what?" You can hire that extra worker or keep your costs and production at current levels. Thus, we compare the marginal cost and marginal benefit of another worker to this baseline.

Calculate the marginal cost and benefit of another worker. The marginal cost of another worker is the increase in your business's costs due to hiring one more worker—which is simply the weekly wage you pay that worker. The marginal benefit is the extra revenue you'll earn. The extra output you produce from hiring an extra worker is called the **marginal product of labour.** Recall from Chapter 3 on supply that most businesses experience diminishing marginal product—meaning that at some point, hiring additional workers yields smaller and smaller increases in output.

marginal product of labour The extra production that occurs from hiring an extra worker.

Gabriela has calculated how many haircuts she can sell if she hires another stylist, but in order to decide whether hiring another stylist is worthwhile, she wants to measure this marginal benefit in terms of extra dollars of revenue, rather than extra haircuts. So she focuses on the **marginal revenue product,** which is the marginal product of labour (the extra output due to hiring one more worker), multiplied by the price she can sell that output for. The marginal revenue product is the extra revenue produced by hiring an additional worker. For example, if Gabriela hires one more stylist, she calculates that she can sell 40 more haircuts per week. If each haircut sells for $40, then the marginal revenue product of hiring that additional stylist is 40 extra haircuts times $40 per haircut, or $1600 per week.

marginal revenue product Measures the marginal revenue from hiring an additional worker. The marginal revenue product is equal to the marginal product of labour multiplied by the price of that product.

$$MRP_L = MP_L \times P$$

The Rational Rule for Employers

Okay, let's put all this together into advice Gabriela can use. She should hire one more worker if the marginal benefit exceeds the marginal cost. The marginal benefit is the marginal revenue product, which is the marginal product times the price. The marginal cost is the wage. Thus, she should hire one more worker if the marginal revenue product of labour is greater than (or equal to) the wage. We've just figured out the basic guideline that all smart managers follow:

The **Rational Rule for Employers:** *Hire additional workers as long as their marginal revenue product is greater than (or equal to) the wage.*

Rational Rule for Employers Hire more workers if the marginal revenue product is greater than (or equal to) the wage.

You'll notice that this looks a lot like the *Rational Rule for Buyers* that we covered in Chapter 2 on demand. That rule says to buy more of something if the marginal benefit of buying one more is greater than or equal to its price. As an employer, you're a buyer—buying the time and effort of your workers—so naturally, you follow a similar rule. In fact, the *Rational Rule for Employers* is simply the application of this rule to hiring workers: You should hire more workers as long as the marginal benefit to you—which is your marginal revenue product—is greater than or equal to the price, which is the wage you pay your workers.

Let's see how this rule works in practice.

Do the Economics

When Gabriela's hair salon first opened, she only employed one hair stylist and sold 40 haircuts per week. If she hired a second person, she would keep the hair salon open later each weekday. She thinks she might sell an extra 35 haircuts with a second hair stylist. If she were to hire a third person, she could also stay open on weekends, and she would have an extra hair stylist available during the busiest times. As a result, she thinks she would win some walk-in business from the salon nearby, and so she'll sell an extra 30 haircuts per week. A fourth hair stylist might allow her to have multiple hair stylists available much of the time, ensuring that no one has to wait very long for a haircut, so she'll sell another 25 haircuts per week. A fifth employee would allow her to stay open even later, and have even more stylists around some of the time. But the extra hours aren't that likely to be as popular, and it will be hard to keep that many stylists busy, so she thinks that she'll only sell another 20 haircuts per week. These numbers—which describe the *marginal product* of each extra stylist—are shown in the first two columns of Figure 2.

- Each haircut sells for $40. Can you figure out the *marginal revenue product* of each hair stylist?
- Each hair stylist is paid $1000 per week. How many hair stylists should Gabriela hire? (Hint: Compare the marginal revenue product in Column C and the wage in Column D.)

Figure 2 | **The Marginal Revenue Product of Each Worker at Head Area Salon**

(A) Number of hair stylists	(B) Marginal product (haircuts per week)	(C) Marginal revenue product (marginal product × $40 per haircut)	(D) Wage for a hair stylist ($ per week)
1	40	$1,600	$1,000
2	35	$1,400	$1,000
3	30	$1,200	$1,000
4	25	$1,000	$1,000
5	20	$800	$1,000

Keep hiring until: *wage equals marginal revenue product* → (row 4)

Marginal revenue product = Wage

The marginal revenue product of each hair stylist, which is shown in the third column, is the marginal product of each additional hair stylist (measured in haircuts), multiplied by the price of a haircut, which is $40. (Keep in mind that the marginal product reflects the additional number of haircuts that one more hair stylist makes possible for the entire salon, and not the specific number of haircuts that each stylist performs. In practice, a new hair stylist would likely split some of the existing work with the other hair stylists, in addition to selling more haircuts than would have been possible before.)

The *Rational Rule for Employers* says to keep hiring as long as the marginal revenue product of an additional worker is at least as large as their wage. The marginal revenue product of the first three hair stylists is greater than their wage, so Gabriela should hire them. For the fourth stylist, the marginal revenue product is exactly equal to the wage. Recall from earlier chapters that when the marginal cost of a decision is exactly equal to the marginal benefit, we'll assume that the person buys that last unit. The same thing is true for workers—the last worker brings in enough to cover their wages, and so Gabriela hires this fourth worker. Following this rule, we predict that Gabriela will hire four hair stylists. You can see why hiring a fifth hair stylist doesn't make any sense—they would add $800 to revenues but cost $1000, which reduces profits. ■

Following the Rational Rule for Employers will maximise your profits. Here's another reason why it's good business sense to follow the *Rational Rule for Employers*: It will lead your firm to the largest profits possible. In order to see this, let's return to Gabriela's hiring decisions at Head Area and analyse her profits.

Do the Economics

To maximise your profits, apply the Rational Rule for Employers, continuing to hire until:

Wage = Marginal revenue product

Let's analyse how Gabriela's total sales, revenue, costs, and profits depend on the number of hair stylists she hires. In Figure 3, the first two columns show that Gabriela's total output rises as she hires more hair stylists. This is calculated by adding up the data from Column B in Figure 2. You can now calculate Gabriela's:

- Total revenue: which is $40 times the number of haircuts sold
- Total costs: which are $1000 times the number of hair stylists hired
- Finally, calculate Gabriela's profits, which are her total revenue minus total costs.

Figure 3 | **Total Revenue, Costs, and Profits at Head Area Salon, per Week**

(A) Number of hair stylists	(B) Total output (haircuts per week)	(C) Total revenue ($40 price × total output)	(D) Total costs ($500 per hair stylist)	(E) Profit (total revenue less total costs)
1	40	$1,600	$1,000	$600
2	75	$3,000	$2,000	$1,000
3	105	$4,200	$3,000	$1,200
4	130	$5,200	$4,000	$1,200
5	150	$6,000	$5,000	$1,000

Using the *Rational Rule for Employers* leads you to the maximum profit. → (row 4)

← Maximum profit (row 4)

Gabriela's profit (shown in the last column) is at its highest level when she hires four workers. This is exactly what the *Rational Rule for Employers* told her to do. So following this rule led her to maximise her profits. (It's true that she could get the same profit with three workers, but note that the fourth worker brings in just enough to make it worthwhile to hire them, so she does.) ■

Labour demand is equal to the marginal revenue product of labour. As Gabriela discovered, following the *Rational Rule for Employers* leads to the greatest possible profit. So remember: *Keep hiring until the wage equals the marginal revenue product of the last worker hired.* This is why economists say that labour demand is all about understanding the marginal revenue product of labour.

In fact, your company's labour demand curve is the same thing as its marginal revenue product curve. Here's the logic. Your labour demand curve illustrates the wage at which you will buy each quantity of labour. The *Rational Rule for Employers* tells you to keep hiring until the wage equals the marginal revenue product of labour. And so the same curve illustrates how the marginal revenue product of labour varies with the quantity of labour demanded.

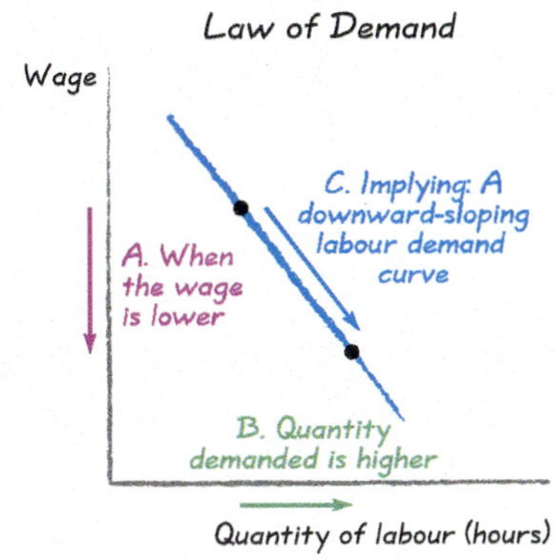

Labour demand is downward-sloping because of diminishing marginal product. Notice that your labour demand curve is downward-sloping: Employers demand a greater quantity of labour when the wage is lower. This is an example of the law of demand, which says that the lower the price of something, the larger the quantity demanded. In the labour market, this reflects diminishing marginal product: As Gabriela discovered, when you hire more workers, each additional worker is less productive than the previous one. Thus, the lower the wage, the greater the number of workers the *Rational Rule for Employers* will say to hire.

Analysing Labour Demand Shifts

Okay, let's take stock. We've figured out the key idea behind labour demand: You should keep hiring more workers until the marginal revenue product of the last worker hired is equal to the wage. Following this rule yields a labour demand curve, which is also your company's marginal revenue product curve, showing how the number of workers you hire declines as the market wage rises.

derived demand The demand for an input derives from the demand for the stuff that input produces.

Let's now turn to the *interdependence principle*, which reminds you that the best hiring decisions will also depend on outcomes in other markets. We can use our deeper understanding of hiring to forecast how labour demand shifts when economic conditions change. There are four important factors that shift labour demand curves. Let's explore them.

Labour demand shifter one: Changes in demand for your product. The labour market is different from the market for petrol, jeans, or other goods in one important respect: Employers hire workers because they're an input to production. In other words, unlike goods and services that you consume, demand for labour is not based on the desire to consume labour. Instead it is a result of the demand that your customers have for the stuff that your workers make. Economists call this a **derived demand,** because the demand for labour is derived from the demand for the stuff they make for you to sell. Gabriela's salon is translating her customers' demand for haircuts into her demand for hair stylists.

So what happens when the demand for what you sell increases? If it leads the price of your product to rise, then the marginal revenue product of all of your workers is higher. Why? Remember: Their marginal revenue product is their marginal product, times the price of what they make. If the price goes up, then so will the marginal revenue product. Figure 4 illustrates how an increase in demand for the product you sell will cause an increase in your business's labour demand, shifting the curve to the right.

Figure 4 | **Effects of an Increase in the Demand for Haircuts on the Labour Market for Hair Stylists**

Gabriela's **labour demand curve**, which is also her **marginal revenue product of labour curve**:

Ⓐ Marginal revenue product = Marginal product × Price. When the price of a haircut is $40, labour demand = $40 × marginal product.

Ⓑ When the price of a haircut rises to $60, this increase in demand for haircuts causes an **increase in the labour demand curve** for hair stylists, because the work hair stylists do is now more valuable.

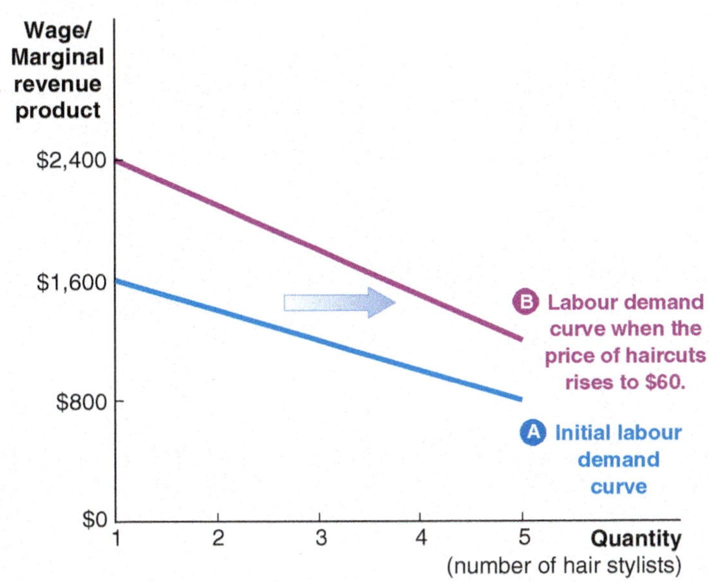

This insight also yields some useful advice when you think about your career: Pick an occupation and industry where you are confident that demand for what you produce will be robust for years to come. So while it makes sense to think about a career in medicine or computer science, those who work in manufacturing are finding that the demand for their services is waning.

Labour demand shifter two: Changes in the price of capital. The market for labour is also closely linked with the market for capital goods, such as business machinery. Workers and machines produce stuff together. Sometimes they complement each other, such as journalists working with computers to produce news stories. But sometimes they are in competition with each other, such as in a restaurant that either needs a person to take orders or a self-ordering kiosk. These two different types of relationships explain why a decline in the price of capital or the invention of a new technology can lead to either an increase in labour demand or a decrease in labour demand.

There are two forces at play here. First, there's a *scale effect*: When the price of capital goods (or any of your inputs) declines, your business can produce output more cheaply, so at a given price, you will sell a larger quantity. That is, you'll produce at a larger scale, which may require more workers, increasing your business's labour demand. Second, there's a *substitution effect* countering this: There are many tasks that can be done by either workers or machines. And so when the price of these machines falls, the demand for workers to do tasks that can be substituted for machines decreases.

Which force dominates determines whether labour and capital are complements or substitutes. If the scale effect dominates then labour and capital are *complements*, so a decrease in the price of capital will lead to a rightward shift of the labour demand curve. If the substitution effect dominates then labour and capital are *substitutes*, so a decrease in the price of capital will lead to a leftward shift of the labour demand curve.

How do you know which effect will dominate? It tends to differ by occupation. Typically, machinery can most readily substitute for routine tasks performed. Thus in occupations with many routine tasks—like many fast-food jobs—a decline in the price of capital tends to lead to a decrease in the demand for labour. High-skilled workers often do fewer routine tasks and so are more likely to be complements to capital equipment. Thus in labour markets for high-skilled workers—like computer scientists—a decline in the price of capital (like computers) tends to lead to an increase in the demand for their labour.

As you think about potential careers, you should be aware that there's been a long-run tendency for the price of business machinery to decline through time. And so you want to invest in jobs that will *complement* technology. Typically, these jobs require a university degree, which is one reason that the wages of university graduates have been rising so quickly compared to those without a university degree.

Labour demand shifter three: Better management and productivity gains. Improved management and technological changes that increase the productivity of labour mean that each of your workers can produce more per week. Since your labour demand curve is equal to the marginal revenue product of your workers, an increase in your workers' marginal product will increase your demand for labour as long as the

Figure 5 | Effects of an Increase in the Marginal Product of Stylists on the Labour Market for Stylists

Gabriela's **labour demand curve**, which is also her **marginal revenue product of labour curve**:

(A) Marginal revenue product = Marginal product × Price.
(B) When online booking increases the marginal product of each stylist, this leads to an increase in marginal revenue product which causes an **increase in the labour demand curve** for hair stylists.

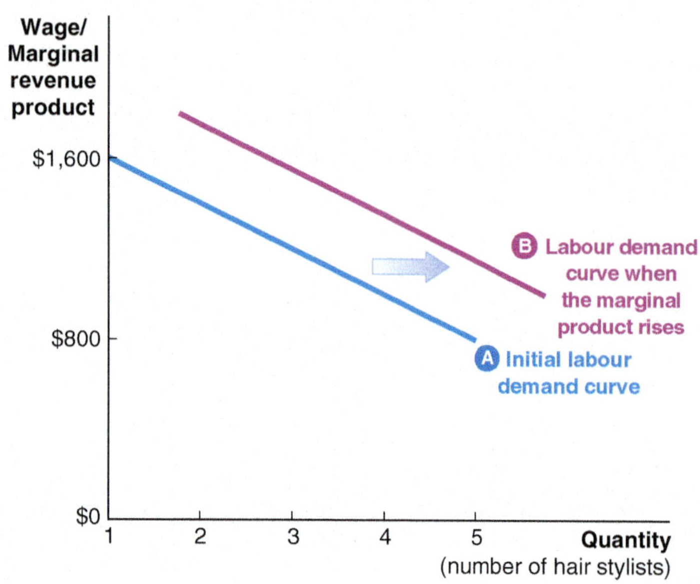

price of the product you are selling is unchanged. In other words, when each additional worker is generating more revenue for you, then you'll want to hire more workers. Figure 5 shows what happens when Gabriela makes a few management changes that increase her workers' productivity. For example, she may have adopted new technology that allows customers to book their appointments online, and this frees up her stylists from answering phones. This reduced time on the phone means that each stylist can produce more haircuts, and hence more revenue. This higher marginal revenue product leads to an increase in labour demand, shifting the curve upward and to the right.

Labour demand shifter four: Nonwage benefits, subsidies, and taxes. So far we've evaluated labour demand as if the only cost of hiring a worker is paying them their weekly wage. In reality, hiring workers can be much more expensive than just the wage, because many workers receive nonwage benefits from their employer and their employer makes contributions to benefits programs for them. When employers make hiring decisions they consider how much an extra worker will cost them taking account of all of the costs, not just the wage.

For instance, many workers receive super, paid days off, and other benefits from their employer. In addition, employers often have to pay "payroll taxes" for each worker. There are also some government programs that provide subsidies or tax cuts when employers hire workers. If any of these other costs change—for example, retirement becomes more expensive—the labour demand curve will shift. Specifically, if nonwage costs rise, then the labour demand associated with any given wage level will decrease, shifting labour demand to the left. If nonwage costs fall, then the labour demand associated with any given wage level will increase, shifting labour demand to the right.

The market labour demand curve shifts due to:

1. Changes in demand for your product
2. Changes in the price of capital
3. Better management techniques and productivity gains
4. Nonwage benefits, subsidies, and taxes

Will Robots Take Your Job?

If you are like most people, you have two big questions about work and technology. The first is: Will high wages increase the chance that workers will be replaced with machines? The second is: Will technology ultimately mean that the economy will run out of jobs for people? Let's tackle each of these questions.

Higher wages create an incentive to invest in capital. So far, we've been thinking about how higher wages will lead you to hire fewer people because fewer workers will have a marginal revenue product that is at least as high as the wage. But higher wages may also lead you to change *how* you produce that output, leading you to substitute machinery for labour. For example, as the market wages of fast-food workers rose, McDonald's installed self-service ordering kiosks. Because kiosks are a substitute for workers, installing these kiosks reduced McDonald's demand for workers. On the flip side, in regions where wages are low, McDonald's continues to use workers instead of this expensive machinery.

Joshua Lott/Bloomberg/Getty Images

May I take your order?

It often takes many years for businesses to change the ways they deploy capital, and so these effects often play out quite slowly. As a result of these long-run shifts in production methods, labour demand tends to be even more sensitive to wages in the long run than the marginal revenue product curve suggests. This insight—that the price elasticity of demand for most goods becomes more elastic over time as people gain more flexibility to adapt—should be familiar from Chapter 5, and it's just as true for the price elasticity of demand for workers.

Interpreting the DATA The long-run effects of the minimum wage

In Chapter 5 you learned about elasticity and specifically that the debate around how an increase in the minimum wage will affect jobs partially depends on how elastic you think the demand for labour is. A number of studies have found that changes in the minimum wage have little impact on the number of low-wage workers who are hired, suggesting that the demand for labour is pretty inelastic. Typically, these conclusions come from comparing the evolution of employment in an area that increases its minimum wage with employment in nearby states or countries that did not change their minimum wage. These studies tend to focus on the change in employment that occurs within a few months—or perhaps a year or two—after a change in the minimum wage.

However, recent studies have shown that, in the long run, higher minimum wages encourage businesses to slowly adopt innovative labour-saving technology and management practices. This suggests the long run negative employment effects of the minimum wage are likely larger than those we observe right after a minimum wage increase occurs. ■

Bert Hardy/Getty Images

Modern computers made the typing pool obsolete.

New technology helps the owners of the robots at the expense of workers. The rise of self-serve kiosks provides a useful metaphor representing the broader problem of robots replacing workers. If simple robots—in the form of kiosks—are replacing workers at McDonald's, you might wonder how long it'll be until more advanced robots take your job. Will the emergence of new labour-saving technologies mean fewer jobs in the economy of the future, making workers worse off?

One way to think about this is to imagine if McDonald's cashiers owned the order-taking robot. Would a McDonald's cashier like to have their robot do their work for them? Of course they would! Think about it: a cashier could go to school to develop new skills, look after their kids, or work on writing a great novel, all while collecting a paycheck from the "work" done by their robot. So from the perspective of the fast-food workers, the problem isn't that robots are doing the work they once did. Rather, the problem is that workers aren't getting paid for this work, and they aren't getting paid for this work because they don't own the robots. This ownership problem is the reason that new technology typically has led low-wage workers to lose, while the entrepreneurs who own businesses or robots gain.

Technology leads to the end of some jobs and the birth of others. The robot factories themselves need employees, and robots need to be serviced, so technological change also creates new jobs. As a result, even as new technologies often lead the demand for fast-food workers to fall, they may lead the demand for high-skilled engineers to increase. As old jobs die, new jobs are born. In the long run, the increased demand for higher-skilled, higher-paid jobs is probably a good thing. But in the short run, those people who lack the skills needed to succeed in a technologically advanced labour market may struggle to find a job.

The *interdependence principle* is key to seeing how the rise of robots will create new jobs far beyond the robot industry. Technological change boosts productivity, and this is a key reason that we can produce and consume so much more today than our grandparents could. Because we're producing more with less, demand for other goods and services grows. For example, the restaurant kiosks make restaurants more productive and that will increase the supply of fast food, shifting the supply curve to the right, and lowering the price. Because fast food becomes cheaper, there's more money left for consumers to spend on other stuff. The increased demand for other stuff leads to new jobs.

The implication: In occupations where robots are replacing workers, jobs are disappearing. But other jobs will emerge in other sectors. It follows that you want to avoid investing in a job that is at threat from the technologies of the future. Robots are good at routine tasks, and so this suggests avoiding occupations that mostly involve routine tasks, such as those involving data entry, driving, or mass production.

Median Annual Earnings, by Undergraduate Major
(10 years into career)

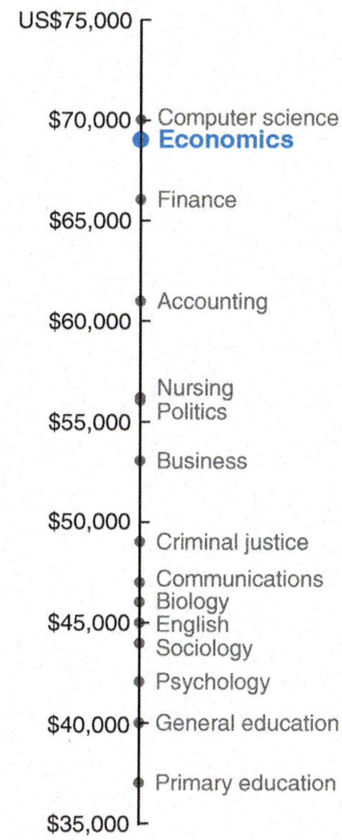

Data from: Hamilton Project.

EVERYDAY Economics Why studying economics is a good idea

The rise of new technologies is likely good news for economics students. Why? I'll quote Google's chief economist:

> If you are looking for a career where your services will be in high demand, you should find something where you provide a scarce, complementary service to something that is getting ubiquitous and cheap. So what's getting ubiquitous and cheap? Data. And what is complementary to data? Analysis.

What's the leading framework for analysing and interpreting data? Economics. Indeed, economics majors already earn more than most other majors. And as data becomes even more ubiquitous, your investment in understanding economics will become even more valuable. So keep reading, because studying economics is a great investment in your career. ■

11.3 Labour Supply: How to Balance Work and Leisure

Learning Objective *Decide how much time to devote to work versus leisure.*

Your **labour supply** is the time you spend working in the market. And work is going to be a big part of your life. Let's say that you work for 40 years before retiring at age 65, and for 48 weeks per year, you work a regular 38-hour week. Then you'll spend 72,960 hours, or over 4.3 million minutes, as a labour supplier! Given this, it's critical that you make smart labour supply choices.

labour supply The time you spend working in the market.

Your Individual Labour Supply: Allocating Your Time Between Labour and Leisure

How much time should you allocate to work? There are only 24 hours in each day. And it's up to you to decide how best to allocate them. So it's best to treat time as a scarce resource and make the best choices you can.

The opportunity cost of working is everything you do when you're not working. Every hour that you spend working is one less hour you have available for other things besides paid work. Economists call all this time "leisure" because it includes relaxing, hanging out with friends, or indulging your passions. But it also includes all sorts of unpaid work—like care-giving, taking classes and studying, making meals and cleaning your house—that few people think of as leisure. But we'll lump them all together (along with sleep!) and call it all leisure, to clearly distinguish that time from time spent in paid work.

The *opportunity cost principle* tells us that the cost of work is forgoing time spent doing other stuff. The implication is that choosing the number of hours you work is equivalent to choosing your hours of leisure. This is why economists describe labour supply as being about the choice between labour and leisure.

MartinPrescott/Getty Images

It may not look like leisure, but it's what he'd give up if he were working.

Choose how many hours to work by thinking at the margin. Deciding how many hours to work is clearly a "how many" choice. The *marginal principle* suggests that you break this decision up into a series of smaller, or marginal, questions, asking: Should I work one more hour?

This is one of those cases where the *marginal principle* might seem a bit unrealistic. After all, do you really get to decide whether to work one more hour? Sure, if you are self-employed—say, as a tutor or a babysitter—you often have direct control over your hours, and you can choose whether or not to accept more clients. But many jobs come with a fixed number of hours, such as office jobs that require you to work nine to five, five days per week. Even so, the *marginal principle* remains useful. For instance, if you want to work more hours you can look for a different job involving longer hours, or you could take on a second job. If you're paid hourly, you can sometimes take on overtime shifts. In many professions, you're paid a weekly salary that doesn't depend on how many hours you work. But even then, you can choose to work longer hours. While the payoff won't be a larger paycheck this week, your hard work will make it more likely that you'll get a raise or promotion, which increases your future income.

In short, when you consider all these different margins of adjustment, perhaps it does make sense to say that you choose the hours you work even if you aren't paid hourly. So the marginal question is relevant: Should you work one more hour?

The Rational Rule for Workers

The *cost-benefit principle* suggests that you weigh the cost and benefit of working one more hour. The benefit of working one more hour is the wage that you'll earn; the cost is the hour of leisure you'll do without. So the answer is: You should work one more hour if the wage is greater than the marginal benefit of leisure. In fact, this is the basis for a very useful rule:

Rational Rule for Workers Work one more hour as long as the wage is at least as large as the marginal benefit of another hour of leisure.

The **Rational Rule for Workers:** *Work one more hour as long as the wage is at least as large as the marginal benefit of another hour of leisure.*

If you follow this rule, you'll keep choosing more work and less leisure until the marginal benefit of one more hour of leisure is equal to the wage. Bottom line: Just as labour demand is all about your marginal revenue product, your labour supply is all about the marginal benefit of leisure.

The *Rational Rule for Workers* has some interesting implications for the shape of your labour supply curve. To see why, notice that it suggests that labour supply depends on two factors: the wage, and the marginal benefit of leisure. This means that there are two forces in play here. In fact, when the wage rises, there are two different effects, which work in opposite directions.

substitution effect Measures how people respond to a change in relative prices. A higher wage increases the returns to work relative to leisure, leading you to work more.

The substitution effect says that higher wages make work relatively more attractive. The **substitution effect** measures how people respond to a change in relative prices. When your wage goes up, the opportunity cost of an hour of leisure goes up. It's as if leisure becomes more expensive, because you'll have to give up more money to get an hour of leisure. This is called the substitution effect because higher wages are an incentive to substitute more work for less leisure. The substitution effect is why people work longer hours when their wages rise, and so it leads to an upward-sloping individual labour supply curve, as shown in Panel A of Figure 6.

income effect Measures how people's choices change when they have more income. A higher wage increases your income, leading you to choose more leisure and hence less work.

The income effect says higher income makes leisure more attractive. The **income effect** measures how people's choices change when they have more income. You learned in Chapter 2 that your demand for normal goods shifts to the right when your income rises. Because your demand curve is also your marginal benefit curve, this also means that your marginal benefit of normal goods goes up when your income increases. So what does this mean for leisure? For most people, leisure is a normal good, so a rise in income means an increase in the marginal benefit of leisure. Thus a higher wage—which boosts workers' incomes—will lead them to choose more leisure, which means working fewer hours.

There's another way of seeing this: A higher wage means that you have more income. What should you buy with your extra income? When your hourly wage rate rises, you don't need to work as many hours to buy the things you were purchasing before. Rather than spending your pay increase buying more stuff, you might spend it buying more leisure time. The somewhat counterintuitive result is that the income effect provides a reason for workers to cut their hours in response to a wage rise. The income effect leads to a downward-sloping labour supply curve, as shown in Panel B of Figure 6.

Figure 6 | Individual Labour Supply Curves

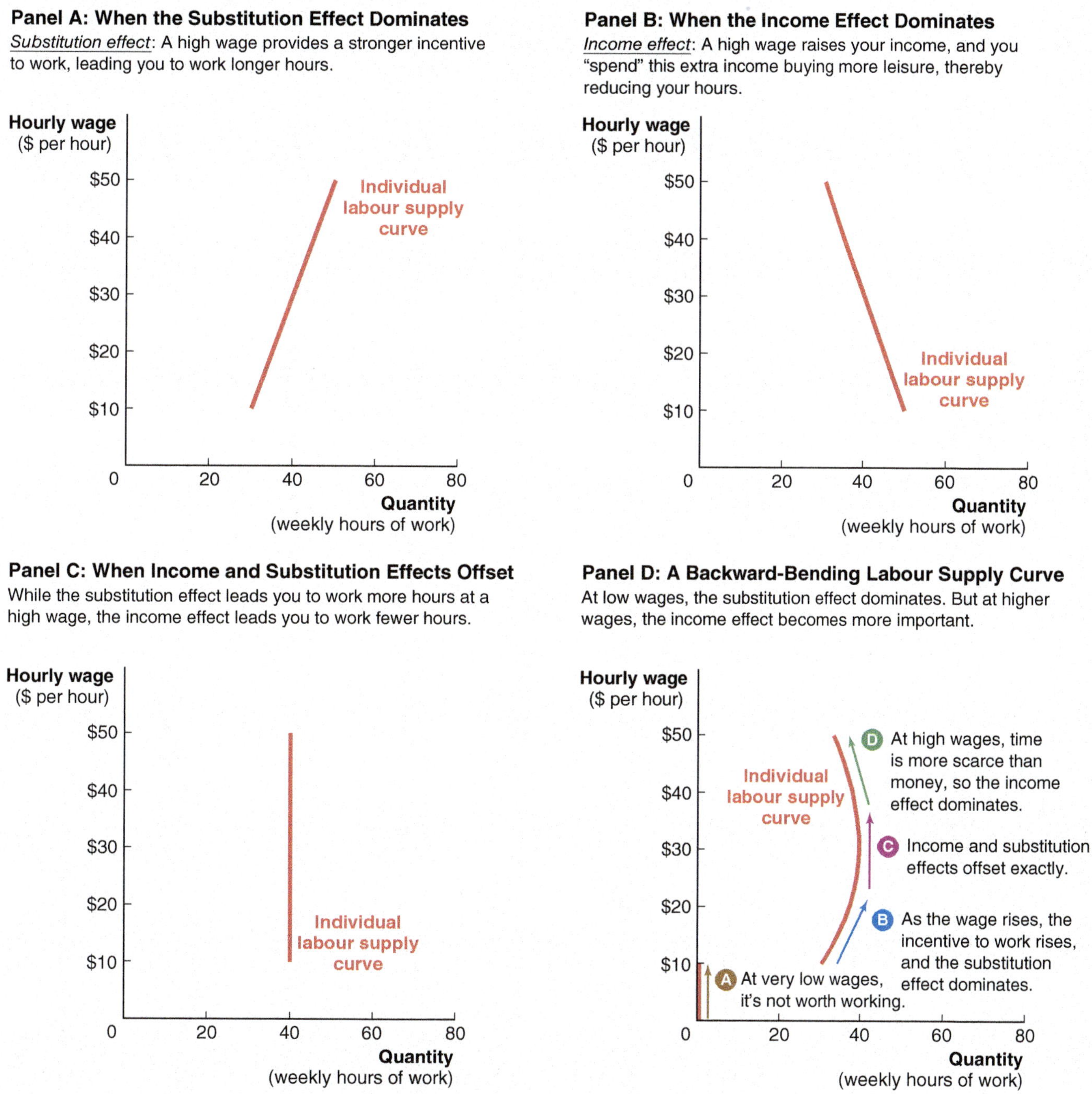

Your labour supply curve depends on the balance of income and substitution effects. Let's put these pieces together. The *Rational Rule for Workers* tells you to compare the marginal benefit of another hour of working (which is the wage you would earn) with the cost, which is the marginal benefit of the hour of leisure you would have to forgo. When the wage goes up, there are two effects: A higher wage raises the marginal benefit of working another hour (that's the substitution effect); and, because leisure is a normal good, it raises the marginal benefit of an extra hour of leisure (that's the income effect). These two forces push in opposite directions.

How do these two offsetting forces work in practice? If the substitution effect is dominant, then your individual labour supply curve is upward-sloping, as shown in Panel A of Figure 6. If the income effect is dominant, then your individual labour supply curve may be downward-sloping, as shown in Panel B. And if the two effects exactly offset each other, then your individual labour supply curve is vertical, as in Panel C. Or if the income effect becomes more important when your wage is higher, then your individual labour supply curve might change from upward-sloping when your wage is low, to vertical to downward-sloping when your wage is high—as shown in Panel D. People may have very differently shaped individual labour supply curves, depending on how they value money versus time.

Do the Economics

Let's discover *your* individual labour supply curve right now. Start by answering the labour supply survey in Panel A of Figure 7, which asks how many hours you would be willing to work each week if I offered you a different wage. As you respond, think about how income and substitution effects shape your answers. Then plot your responses in Panel B.

Figure 7 | **Discover Your Individual Labour Supply Curve**

Panel A: Your Individual Labour Supply

Think about your current part-time job. How many hours per week would you choose to work if I paid you:

Hourly wage rate	**Labour supply** (hours per week)
$1 per hour	
$20 per hour	
$40 per hour	
$80 per hour	
$120 per hour	
$160 per hour	
$200 per hour	

(Remember: You can't work more than 168 hours in a week, nor less than 0 hours.)

Panel B: Your Individual Labour Supply Curve

How many hours are you willing to work at each wage?

Plot your responses to discover your individual labour supply curve.

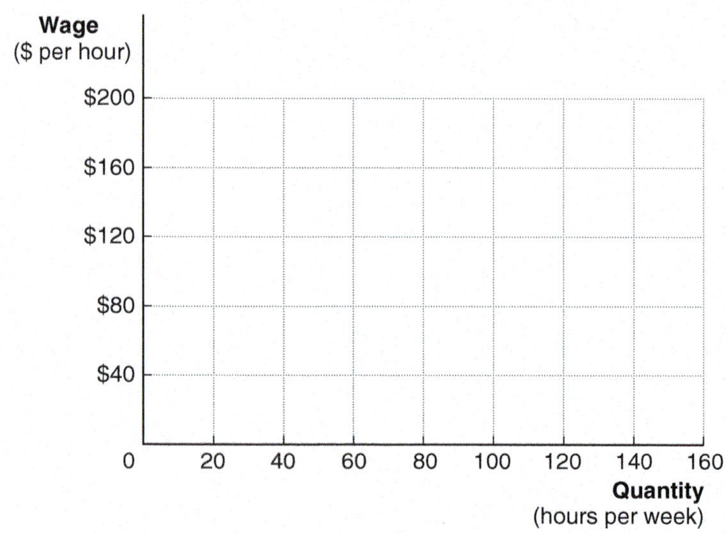

What did you discover? Many students figure that they won't work at all when the wage is too low. Eventually, when the wage is high enough, they find it worthwhile to work. As the wage rises further, some students decide to work more. But at some point, the wage is so high that some students opt to work fewer hours. Why? Because the higher wage means that they can still pay for the essentials if they work less, and they can use the extra time to increase their chances of succeeding in their studies. This is the income effect at work. If you followed this pattern, you may have sketched a backward-bending labour supply curve, as shown in Panel D of Figure 6. ■

The price elasticity of labour supply measures workers' responsiveness to wages. In Chapter 5 you discovered that the price elasticity of supply measures how responsive sellers are to changes in prices. We can adapt this idea to the labour market where you are supplying hours of your time and the relevant price is your wage. The wage elasticity of labour supply measures how the quantity of labour supplied responds to a change in the wage. Remember that when quantity is relatively unresponsive we describe supply as being inelastic. Few economists agree about the precise estimate of the elasticity of labour supply, but most economists agree that individual labour supply is relatively inelastic. Look back at your own estimates—how many more hours did you say you would work if you could earn $160 an hour? Was it less than twice as many hours as when the wage was $80? If so, your labour supply is relatively inelastic between $80 and $160 an hour. Let's take a look at the evidence on the shape of labour supply curves.

Interpreting the DATA **Does the individual labour supply curve slope up or down?**

The slope of the typical individual labour supply curve remains a matter of debate. Some economists have estimated the price elasticity of labour supply by looking at how people's working hours change when their after-tax wage changes. If Parliament passes an income tax cut, your after-tax wage rises, and people tend to work a little bit more. Most estimates suggest that it takes about a 10% after-tax wage increase to get people to work about 1–3% more. This evidence suggests that the labour supply curve is upward-sloping, but inelastic.

An alternative approach looks at differences in wage rates across people in different occupations. It turns out that the average number of hours worked is roughly the same among workers in high-paying occupations as it is for those in low-paying jobs. This evidence suggests that the labour supply curve is nearly vertical.

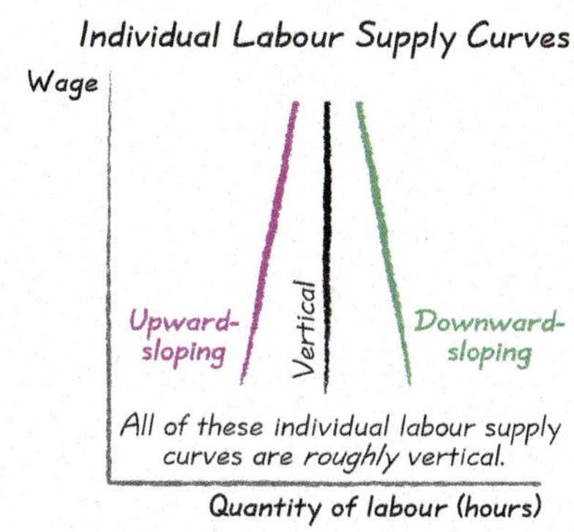

Finally, analysing wage changes over long periods of time yields a different story. Over the past century, wages have risen enormously, and the typical working week has declined, although by not a lot. This evidence that higher wages led to less work suggests that labour supply is downward-sloping.

While these different types of analyses point to qualitatively different conclusions, they're quantitatively similar. The common thread to all of these observations is that the effect of changing wages on individual labour supply is relatively small. So the individual labour supply curve is nearly vertical for most people. But remember that some people won't work at all if the wage is too low. In fact, higher wages raise the likelihood that people will work, which is the issue we'll now turn to. ■

The Extensive Margin: Choose Whether or Not to Work

Total labour supply depends not just on how many hours each worker decides to supply, but also on how many people are in the workforce. In fact, only around two-thirds of adults are either working or looking for work, and many of the remaining one-third are homemakers, retirees, or full-time students. So we now shift our focus from the *intensive margin* (which describes the number of hours each worker supplies—a measure of how intensively existing workers supply their labour) to the *extensive margin* (which describes the number of people in the workforce—a measure of the extent of work).

To do so, start by putting yourself in the shoes of someone trying to decide whether to join the workforce or not. While the *Rational Rule for Workers* focuses on how many hours you should work if you decide to work, the decision of whether to work is an either/or question, and so the *marginal principle* doesn't apply. Instead, start with the *cost-benefit principle*, which says to join the workforce if the benefits exceed the costs.

Consider the broad range of opportunity costs and benefits that come from working. The benefits of working include not only the wage that you'll earn, but also the nonwage benefits like super contributions that come with the job, along with the fact that today's work experience might help boost your future earnings.

To see the costs of work, apply the *opportunity cost principle*, and ask "or what?" This question can be quite illuminating. For those who don't have a compelling alternative use of their time, this opportunity cost might be quite small. But for parents with young

Median Annual Income, by Occupation

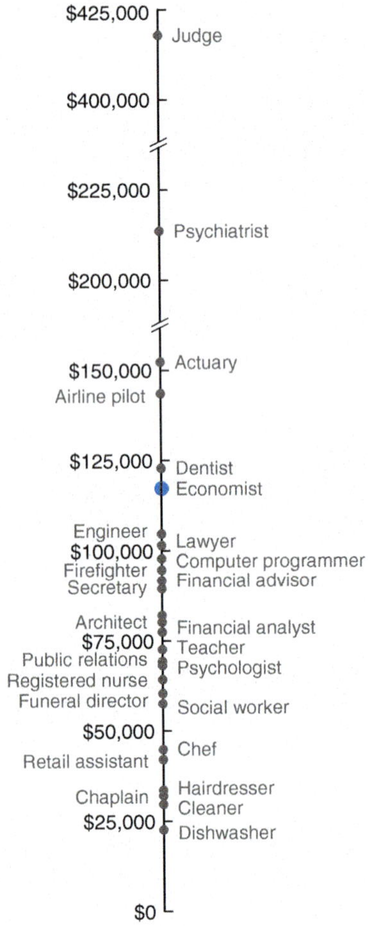

Data from: Australian Bureau of Statistics.

Want to look up the wages in 800 separate occupations? Try: https://www.abs.gov.au/statistics/labour/earnings-and-work-hours/employee-earnings/aug-2020#occupation

children, the opportunity cost of work is not staying home to raise their kids. For many older people, the opportunity cost is not enjoying their long-awaited retirement. And for students, the opportunity cost might be not taking a full course load. These higher opportunity costs explain why these groups are particularly likely to opt out of the workforce.

The cost of searching for a job, the expense of buying business-appropriate attire, the drudgery of a long commute to and from work, and the difficulty of arranging child care are all fixed costs associated with working. They can lead some people to choose not to work at all, rather than just working a few hours a week.

Higher wages lead more people to enter the labour force. The higher the wage is, the larger will be the share of the population for whom the benefits of joining the workforce exceed the costs. As a result, higher wages lead more people to decide to supply their labour to the market.

Okay, so far we've analysed your choice of whether or not to work, and, if so, how many hours to work. There's one more important choice you'll make: the type of job to have. This choice determines the specific labour market you'll supply your labour to.

Choosing Your Occupation

Do you remember when you were a kid and people asked you what you wanted to be when you grew up? If you were like many kids, you had a pretty narrow sense of possible occupations. Maybe you wanted to be a teacher, a firefighter, a doctor, or an athlete. In reality, there are actually hundreds of different occupations that you will ultimately choose among. How will you decide?

One of the first factors that you'll think about when choosing an occupation is your likely earnings. The figure to the left shows the enormous variation in average annual incomes earned across a variety of occupations. You need to know the wages in different occupations so you can make a good choice about which career to pursue.

Apply the cost-benefit principle to figure out the right occupation for you. The market wage will be a major factor influencing which occupation you choose. This is just the *cost-benefit principle* at work: The higher the income you'll earn, the greater the benefit from joining a specific occupation. Thus, wages act as an important signal, directing workers into different occupations. The higher the wage, the more people will join a specific occupation.

But while wages are an important factor in deciding your occupation, they shouldn't be the only one. Remember that the *cost-benefit principle* says that you should think broadly about the relevant costs and benefits.

Consider the Benefits

Do what you love: There is truth in this old adage. After all, your working life will probably take up 38 hours of each week of your life until you retire. If you hate what you do, it will be hard to really give it your all over that much time, not to mention that it'll probably make you quite unhappy. The trick is to find an occupation that matches your interests. If you love the ocean and find science interesting, then marine biologist might be the job for you. If you love meeting people, you might enjoy sales. If you love crunching numbers, become an analyst. When you love what you are doing, you're more likely to succeed. This isn't just pop psychology—it's serious economics: When you love your job, the effort required to succeed comes with a lower opportunity cost.

Ask about benefits: Will you get flexible hours, housing assistance, or the opportunity for further training? These benefits can make a lower-wage job more attractive—a fact well understood by people in the military.

Think about the future: The skills that you are accumulating today will sustain you throughout your professional life. So plan your career around developing skills that will continue to be valuable.

Follow your comparative advantage: Think about what you're good at—or what you can do at a lower opportunity cost—relative to other people. That's the career you're most likely to succeed in. And that success will lead you to a better wage trajectory.

Ask about the trajectory: Your starting salary is simply the beginning. In some occupations—such as medicine—there's low pay and long hours in the first few years on the job. After that, the big money flows. Don't just ask about your starting salary; find out what people are earning after a decade of work.

Consider the Costs

Evaluate the risks: Is this an occupation—such as musician or actor—in which only a few bright stars rise to the top and others earn very little? If so, don't fall into the trap of overestimating the odds of success.

Consider the volatility: If bonuses and commissions are a big part of the pay, will you still be able to get by if you have a bad year? Is your job at risk if the economy tanks? If so, can you deal with these risks?

Don't forget the hours: While your employer may technically be paying you for a 38-hour week, in some occupations the norm is that employees work much longer hours. Ask a corporate lawyer or management consultant, and you'll hear they often work 80 or even 100 hours per week. If the marginal benefit you get from extra leisure hours is high, this isn't the life for you.

Recap: Labour supply decisions involve whether you should work, how much you should work, and what you should do. You face three key labour supply decisions in your life. First, you have to decide whether to work. Second, you have to decide how many hours to work. And third, you have to decide what kind of work you should do. All of these decisions boil down to applying the *cost-benefit principle* and considering your opportunity costs. You may also find that the *interdependence principle* is relevant when the answer to any one of these questions might influence how you answer the other two.

So you now know how people like yourself think about how many hours to work, the decision to work, and what kind of occupation to pursue. Our next task is to put all of this together to think about labour supply in specific occupational labour markets, such as the market for hair stylists.

The Market Labour Supply Curve

In the first half of the chapter, you saw that the market labour demand curve is downward-sloping. What about the market labour supply curve? Market labour supply curves are upward-sloping—meaning that the higher the wage in a particular occupation, the more people there are willing to work in that occupation. There are three reasons that the market labour supply curve is upward-sloping:

Market labour supply depends on:

1. How many people decide to work
2. How many hours existing workers put in
3. Which occupations people choose

Reason one: New people may be induced to enter the workforce. Higher wages convince more people to work, rather than pursue alternatives, such as studying, retiring, or working as a homemaker. A higher wage for hair stylists may induce some people who weren't working to decide to look for a job as a stylist. For example, a parent who stopped working as a stylist to stay home with their kids might be induced to go back into the labour market if the wage for stylists is high.

Reason two: Existing workers may put in more hours. When wages go up, people already working in that occupation may increase the number of hours they work. You already know that this is likely to be a small effect, because while higher wages provide a greater incentive to work (the substitution effect), they also increase the demand for leisure (the income effect). So if the wages of hair stylists go up, on average the hours existing stylists work will go up a small amount.

Reason three: Some people may switch occupations. Remember that wages help shape which occupations people join. So if the wage of hair stylists increases, more people

Figure 8 | Market Labour Supply Curve for Hair Stylists

The market labour supply curve reflects three influences. When the wage is higher:

1: Existing hair stylists may choose to work more hours (the substitution effect), although some may work fewer hours (due to the income effect).
2: Students, retirees, or homemakers may return to the workforce.
3: People will choose to become hair stylists, rather than pursue other occupations.

Consequently, a higher wage is associated with a larger quantity of labour supplied, yielding an upward-sloping market labour supply curve.

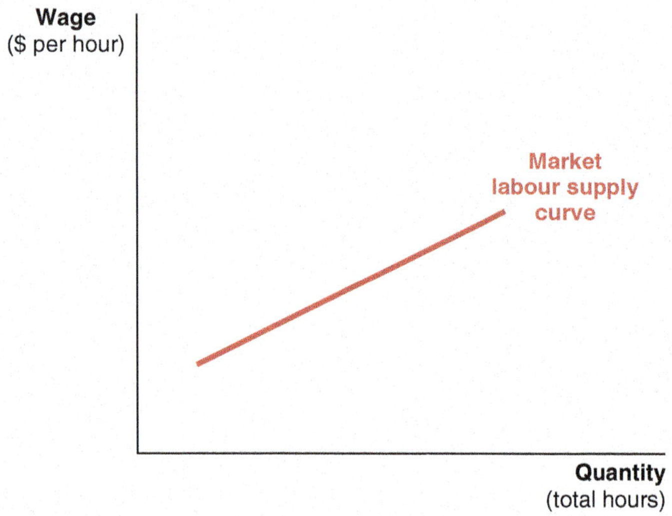

would apply for jobs as a stylist, rather than for jobs in retail or waiting tables. The ready supply of *potential* new hair stylists at this higher wage is large.

Putting all this together, these three reasons reflect three different types of decisions that people make:

- How many people decide to work,
- How many hours existing workers will put in, and
- Which occupations people choose.

The third decision is important enough to ensure that the market labour supply curve in almost every occupation is upward-sloping. This holds even if individual labour supply curves of existing workers aren't upward-sloping. Why? Even if a higher wage won't induce you to work more hours, or even if it won't induce many more people to work, it will induce others to enter your occupation in order to earn that higher wage. This ensures that the total quantity of hours supplied in the market for hair stylists—or any other occupation—rises with the wage, as suggested by the upward-sloping market labour supply curve shown in Figure 8.

Analysing Labour Supply Shifts

Let's now turn to using our deeper understanding of labour supply to forecast how changing economic conditions cause labour supply curves to shift. The key will be the *interdependence principle,* which reminds us that labour supply decisions are connected to other markets and to government policies. As we work through the four factors that shift labour supply curves, remember that an increase in labour supply shifts the curve to the right, while a decrease in labour supply will shift it to the left.

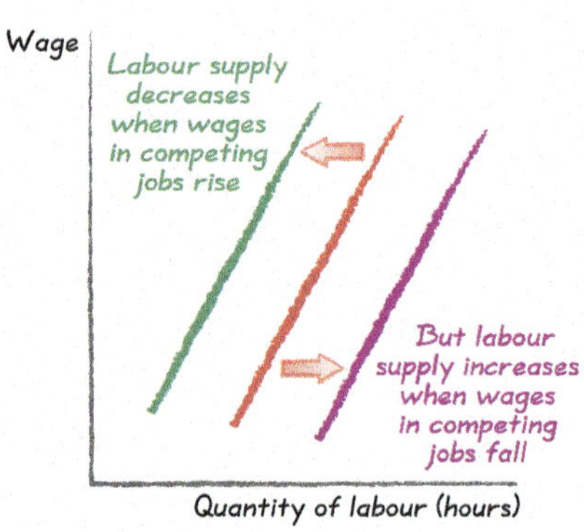

Labour supply shifter one: Changing wages in other occupations. The market for hair stylists is connected to the market for workers at skin-care salons. If wages for skin-care specialists rise, some hair stylists will look for work in the skin-care industry instead. Consequently, wage increases in jobs that compete for similar workers reduce the supply of labour, shifting the supply curve to the left. And if wages in these other occupations fall, skin-care workers will become hair stylists instead, increasing the available labour supply of hair stylists (shifting the labour supply curve of hair stylists to the right).

Labour supply shifter two: Changing number of potential workers. The total number of people in the labour market is a subset of the total number of people in a society. That means that when the population grows, so does potential labour supply. Population can grow because more people are born than are dying—which happens either because of an increase in births or an increase in life expectancy. The population can also grow through immigration. Population growth typically increases labour supply, while a decrease in the population decreases labour supply.

The age distribution of the population also matters. Few children or elderly people work. People are most likely to work in their 30s and 40s, so growth in the population in this age range boosts labour supply. But a shift in the age distribution toward retirement age—as is currently underway in Australia and other developed countries—leads to a decrease in labour supply, shifting the labour supply curve to the left, since fewer of these people work.

Labour supply shifter three: Changing benefits of not working. Remember that the decision to work or not work in the labour market is driven by comparing the wage with the forgone benefits of not working. So anything that changes the benefits of not working will shift the labour supply curve. For instance, the introduction of a government program like Youth Allowance will lead to a decrease in labour supply among young workers as more of them choose to pursue education. (And after those students graduate with degrees—such as in accounting—it will increase the labour supply of accountants.)

Anything that lowers the cost of child care will increase the labour supply of parents, by reducing their benefit of staying home and providing the care themselves. And if Parliament were to reduce pension payments to older Australians, then the labour supply of people over age 65 would likely increase.

Similarly, various government support programs aimed at helping people without a job—such as rent assist, family tax benefit, disability support, and other welfare programs administered by Centrelink—have an unintended side effect: They increase the opportunity cost of working. As a result, these programs induce some people to work less or not work at all, reducing labour supply. In some countries (including Australia), these benefits are so generous that taking a job may only increase your income by a tiny amount. The government tries to lessen the disincentive to work for certain benefits. For example, you can only receive JobSeeker (formerly Newstart Allowance) payments if you are actively looking for a job; and you can't get disability payments without certain certifications from a doctor or specialist. However the government sometimes also strengthens the disincentive to work. For example, you can't get rent assist payments unless you're already on another welfare payment; and you can't get a health care card unless you consistently have a low income.

Four factors that shift labour supply:

1. Changing wages in other occupations
2. Changing number of potential workers
3. Changing benefits of not working
4. Nonwage benefits, employment subsidies, and income taxes

Labour supply shifter four: Nonwage benefits, subsidies, and income taxes. So far we've described the wage as if it represents the total benefit to working. But in reality, there are other factors to consider, which is why workers focus on their after-tax total compensation, taking account of all nonwage benefits, taxes, and subsidies. For instance, most employers offer nonwage benefits such as super, annual leave, meals, and subsidised transportation. In addition, working provides you benefits when you retire through the pension or, if you become unemployed, through unemployment benefits. Some government programs—for example JobKeeper during the coronavirus pandemic—have also provided wage subsidies so that the government effectively supplements your income for each extra hour you work. These nonwage benefits and subsidies increase the benefit of working another hour. On the flip side, income taxes reduce the benefit of working, because you only get to keep a proportion of each extra dollar you earn. An increase in income tax rates reduces the benefit of working another hour.

Changes in nonwage benefits, subsidies, and income taxes will change the total compensation a worker gets at any given wage, shifting their willingness to work and hence the labour supply curve. At the individual level, whether changes in these factors lead to an increase or decrease in labour supply depends on whether the income or substitution effect dominates. At the aggregate level it's a bit simpler, as the market labour supply tends to be upward-sloping. Consequently, an increase in nonwage benefits or subsidies, or a decrease in income taxes, will lead to an increase in labour supply, shifting the curve to the right. And a decrease in nonwage benefits, a decrease in subsidies or an increase in income taxes will cause a decrease in labour supply, shifting the curve to the left.

11.4 Changing Economic Conditions and Labour Market Equilibrium

Learning Objective *Evaluate how the labour market will respond to changing economic conditions.*

It's time to pull the threads of this chapter together. At this point, you've developed a powerful framework for understanding how the labour market operates. This framework illustrates how the wages in each occupation and the number of people each occupation employs are determined by the intersection of labour demand and labour supply.

A Three-Step Recipe

It follows that anything that causes a shift in labour demand or a shift in labour supply will lead the wages and employment opportunities within your occupation to change. And that's what'll make this framework so useful as you navigate your own career: You can use it to forecast how short- and long-term changes will affect wages, employment, and other conditions in any job that you're considering. Look ahead, and you can adapt your career to take advantage of the positive shifts, and if you're nimble, you can minimise the impact of adverse changes.

To forecast the effects of changing market conditions, use the same three-step recipe that you use to assess the consequences of any shift in supply and demand. Ask yourself:

Step one: *Is the labour supply or labour demand curve shifting? (Or both?)*

Remember that labour demand is all about marginal revenue product—the extra revenue an extra worker generates—so anything that shifts the productivity of workers or the value of their output will also shift labour demand. And labour supply is all about opportunity costs: The opportunity cost of working is not working—staying in education, working outside the market, or retiring; the opportunity cost of working in one occupation is not working in another; and the opportunity cost of working an extra hour is an hour of leisure. So anything that shifts these opportunity costs will shift labour supply.

Step two: *Is that shift an increase or a decrease?*

An increase in labour demand or an increase in labour supply will shift the corresponding curve to the right. A decrease in labour demand or a decrease in labour supply corresponds with a shift to the left.

Step three: *How will wages and the number of jobs change in the new equilibrium?*

Compare the new equilibrium with the old equilibrium.

Let's start practising, by evaluating how changing economic conditions might disrupt your labour market.

Do the Economics

The price of statistical software and powerful computers falls. What happens to the labour market for data analysts?

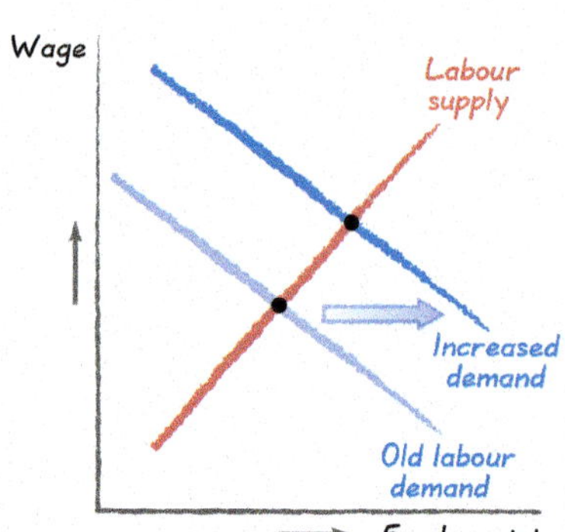

Cheaper price for complementary capital
→ An increase in labour demand

Result: Higher wage, more jobs

McDonald's installs new kiosks at all of its restaurants, but doesn't change the price of its burgers (so there's no scale effect). What happens to the demand for cashiers?

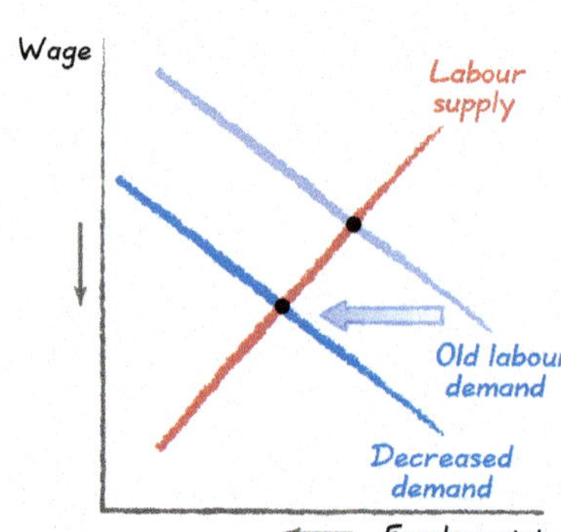

Substituting capital for labour
→ A decrease in labour demand

Result: Lower wage, fewer jobs

Parliament passes an immigration bill reducing the number of foreigners with computer science degrees who can move to Australia. What happens to the labour market for computer programmers?

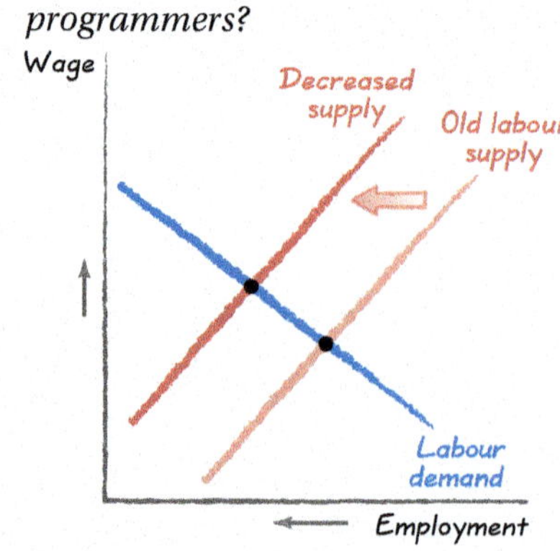

Fewer potential workers
→ A decrease in labour supply

Result: Higher wage, fewer jobs

As the beef industry shrinks, the wages of large-animal vets have declined. What happens to the labour market for small-animal vets?

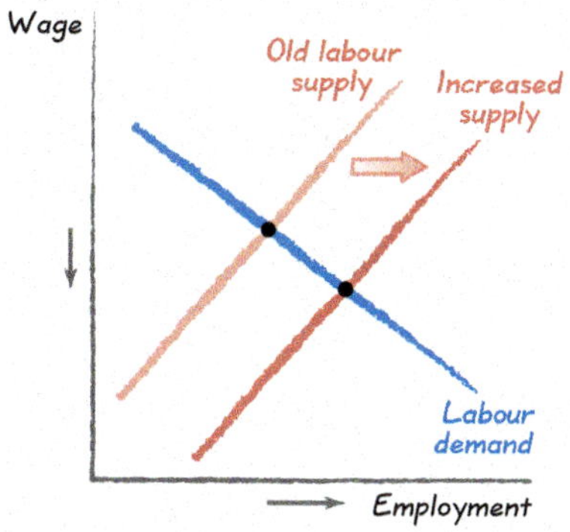

Large-animal vets shift to working on small animals
→ An increase in labour supply

Result: Lower wage, more jobs

Parliament increases the generosity of JobSeeker payments. What happens to the labour market in most occupations?

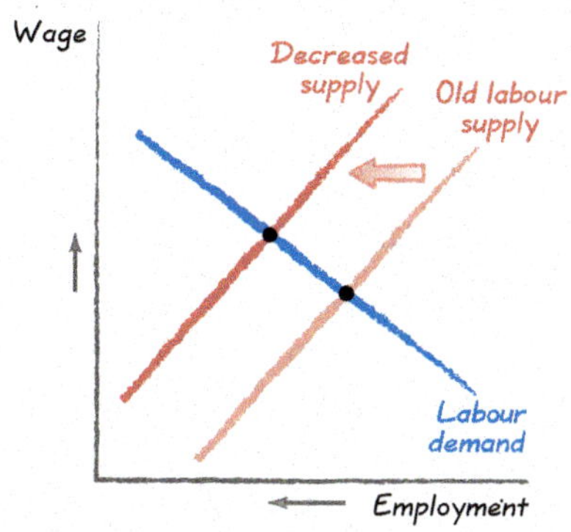

An increase in the opportunity cost of work
→ A decrease in labour supply

Result: Higher wage, fewer jobs

Improvements in voice recognition software mean that court stenographers are no longer needed. What happens to the labour market for stenographers?

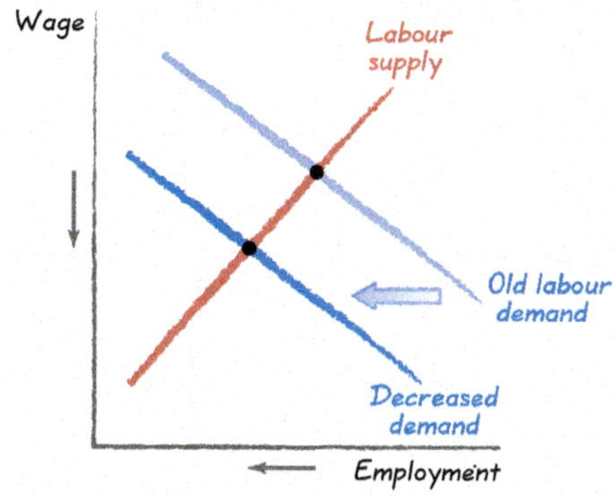

A new technology that's a substitute for stenographers
→ A decrease in labour demand

Result: Lower wage, fewer jobs

As baby boomers age, more people seek in-home elder care for their aging parents. What happens to the labour market for home-health aids?

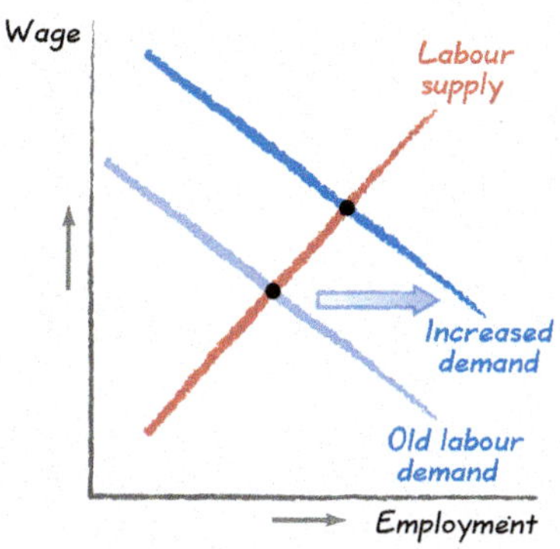

Rising demand for in-home elder care will raise the price, boosting the marginal revenue product
→ An increase in labour demand

Result: Higher wage, more jobs

Some economists believe that new videogames have made leisure time a lot more fun. What might this do to the labour market for young people?

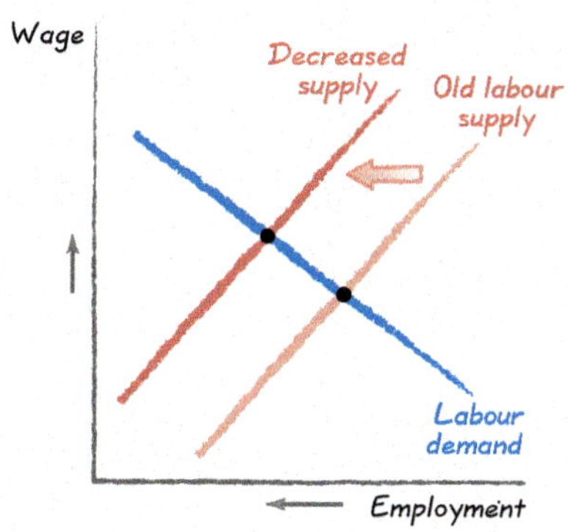

More enjoyable leisure represents a higher opportunity cost of work
→ A decrease in labour supply

Result: Higher wage, fewer jobs

The federal government raises the minimum age to start collecting pension benefits from 66 to 70. What happens to the labour market for older workers?

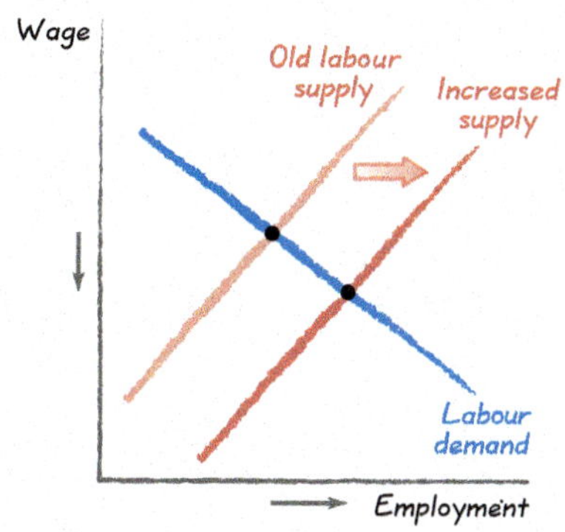

Lower opportunity cost of work (retirement is less tenable without social security)
→ An increase in labour supply

Result: Lower wage, more jobs

Nationwide budget shortfalls force many states to cut public school teacher pay. What happens to the labour market for private school teachers?

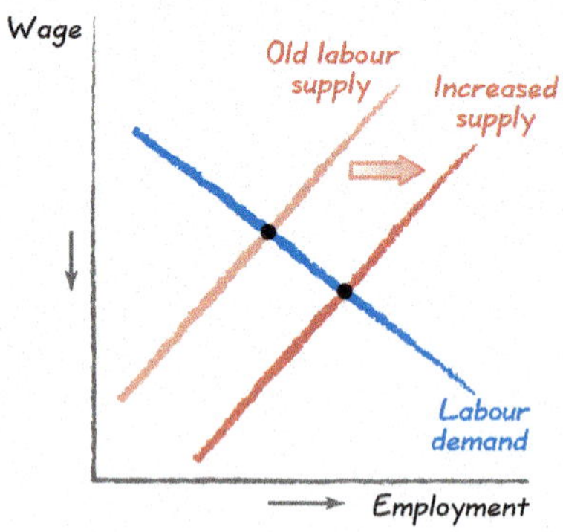

Worse opportunities in alternative occupations
→ An increase in labour supply

Result: Lower wage, more jobs

Competition from Uber has forced limousine companies to cut their prices. What happens to the labour market for limo drivers?

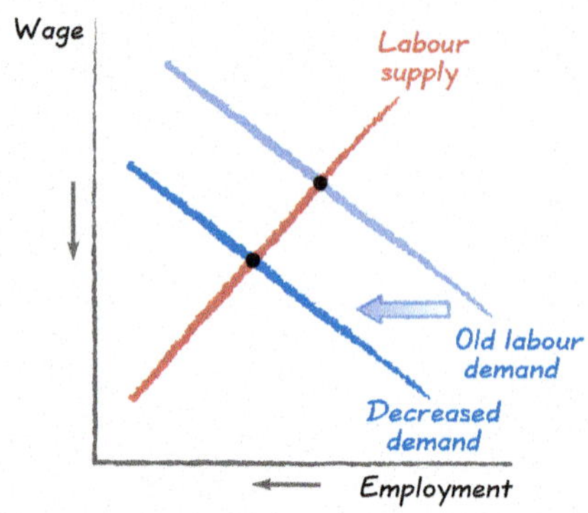

Lower output prices reduces marginal revenue product
→ A decrease in labour demand

Result: Lower wage, fewer jobs

A recession has led many universities to reduce the scholarships they offer some new students. What happens to the labour market for young people?

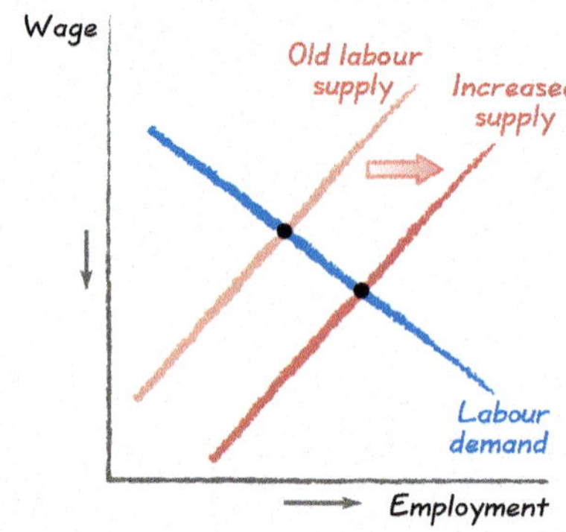

More expensive university will lower the opportunity cost of work
→ An increase in labour supply

Result: Lower wage, more jobs ■

Tying It Together

In this chapter, we constructed a coherent framework for understanding the demand and supply of labour. In fact, we've accomplished a whole lot more.

To see why, realise that what makes the labour market different is that labour is an input into production. Moreover, labour is not the only input into production, and many of the same ideas that we've used to understand the market for labour also apply to the markets for these other inputs. The markets for these inputs—like land, or capital—are often called *factor markets*, because they're markets for the *factors of production*.

Consider the market for capital—the machines, tools, and structures that are also used as inputs in the productive process. A manager will hire an extra person or an extra robot (or indeed, an extra wrench, or another computer) using the same principles. They'll think at the margin, consider costs and benefits, and account for opportunity costs. That process leads them to add another worker, another robot, another wrench, or another computer if doing so will create more additional revenue than their marginal cost. And so just as labour demand depends on whether the marginal revenue product of hiring another worker exceeds the cost of hiring that worker, so too, the demand for capital depends on whether the marginal revenue product from "hiring" another piece of machinery exceeds its cost. You can apply the same idea to land, too: A business will rent another floor of office space if the marginal revenue product of that extra office space exceeds the cost of the annual rent. Businesses will hire any factor of production until its marginal revenue product is equal to the cost of hiring it for a year.

The idea that this framework applies to the market for robots then gives you a hint about why we've got more work to do. People aren't the same as robots. Real people, unlike robots, have feelings; they aren't all the same; they have different desires, different educational experiences, and different skills; they form unions; their working conditions are often tightly regulated; they might slack off when the boss isn't watching; and they're more productive when they're motivated. A complete understanding of the labour market needs to take account of these realities. And that's why our task in the next chapter is to take a closer look at the complexity of the workforce, a place where there can be discrimination, motivation problems, a mismatch between the skills you want and the skills businesses want you to have. None of this is to say that labour demand and supply aren't central to determining wages and employment outcomes, but rather that these factors can help enrich our understanding of what drives labour supply and labour demand.

Chapter at a Glance

The Labour Market

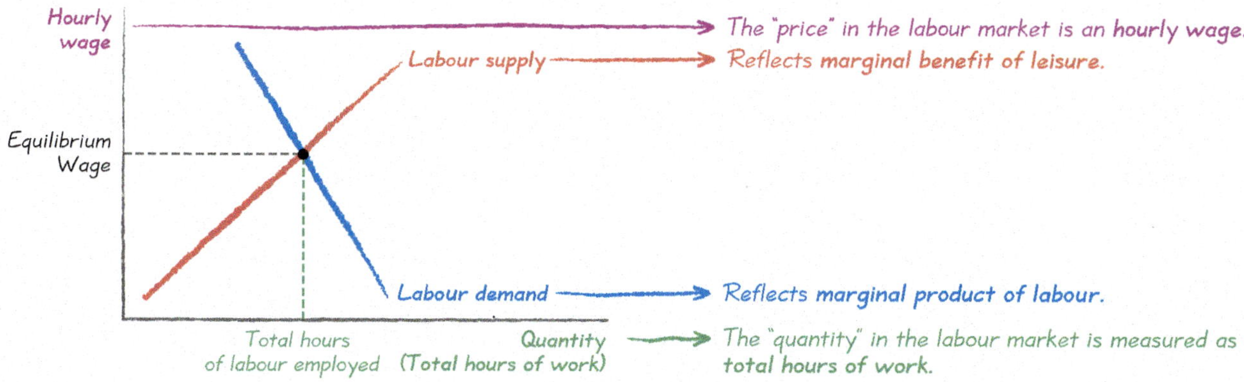

Labour Demand

Marginal product (MP_L): The extra production that occurs from hiring an extra worker.

Marginal revenue product (MRP_L): Measures the marginal revenue from hiring an additional worker.

The **marginal revenue product** = The **marginal product of labour** multiplied by the price of that product.

$$MRP_L = MP_L \times P$$

The Rational Rule for Employers: Hire more workers as long as their **marginal revenue product** is greater than (or equal to) the wage.

The **market labour demand curve** shifts due to:

1. Changes for your product demand
2. Changes in the price of capital
3. Management techniques and productivity gains
4. Nonwage benefits, subsidies, and taxes.

Individual Labour Supply

The Rational Rule for Workers: Work more hours as long as the wage is at least as large as the **marginal benefit** of another hour of leisure.

Substitution effect: Measures how people respond to a change in relative prices. A higher wage increases the returns to work relative to leisure, leading you to work more.

Income effect: Measures how people's choices change when they have more income. A higher wage increases your income, leading you to choose more leisure and hence less work.

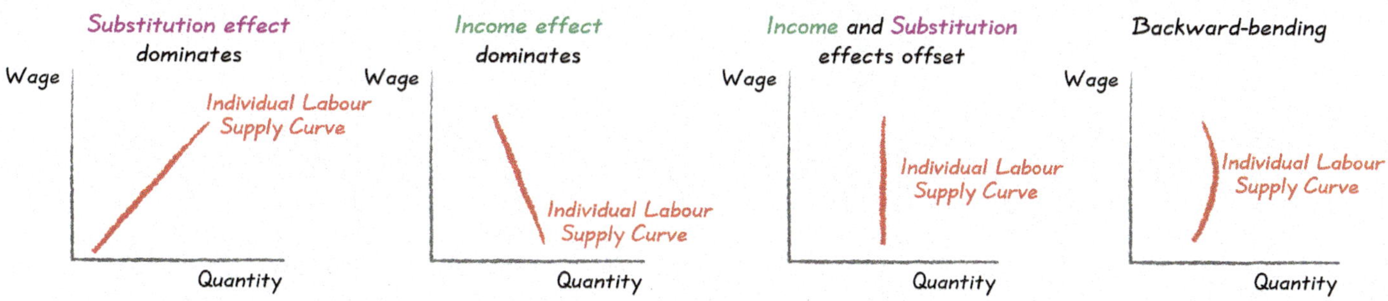

Market Labour Supply

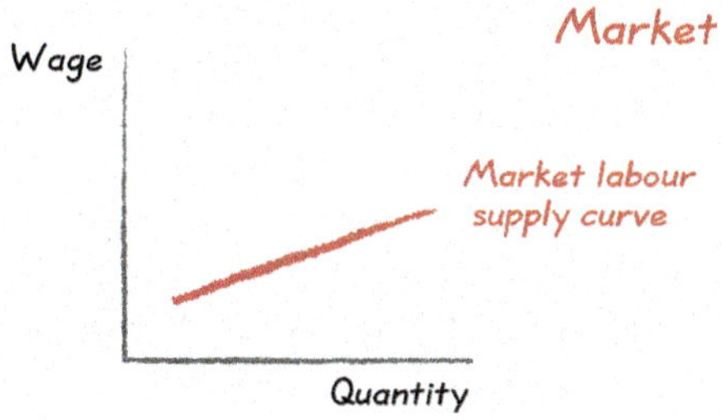

The **market labour supply curve** is upward-sloping and depends on:

1. How many hours existing workers put in
2. How many people decide to work
3. Which occupations people choose

Key Concepts

derived demand, 275
income effect, 280
labour supply, 279
marginal product of labour, 272
marginal revenue product, 272
Rational Rule for Employers, 273
Rational Rule for Workers, 280
substitution effect, 280

Discussion and Review Questions

Learning Objective 11.1 *Understand how wages and employment are determined by the forces of supply and demand.*

1. Explain, using the marginal, opportunity cost, cost-benefit, and interdependence principles, why, in most occupations, the market labour supply curve is upward-sloping.
2. Use the marginal, opportunity cost, cost-benefit, and interdependence principles to explain why labour demand is typically downward-sloping.

Learning Objective 11.2 *Discover how employers decide how many workers to hire.*

3. A local MP is concerned about poverty in their constituency and proposes that the minimum wage be raised from $20.33 per hour to $30.00 per hour. They claim that this would be an effective way to assist lower income families; however, they are worried that a large number of jobs will be lost as a result. Briefly evaluate their arguments using a labour supply and demand graph. Explain how the long-run impact of the minimum wage law may be different than the short-run impact.

Learning Objective 11.3 *Decide how much time to devote to work versus leisure.*

4. Think about the career you hope to have after college. What annual income do you hope to earn and how many hours per week do you plan on working? Use this information to find your future wage. Use the marginal principle to explain how the number of hours you work each week would change if you get an unexpected raise of 50%. Or a pay cut of 50%. Draw your labour supply curve for these values and describe the relationship between the income effect and substitution effect on your various wages.

Learning Objective 11.4 *Evaluate how the labour market will respond to changing economic conditions.*

5. During the period from 2007 to 2009, the number of new vehicles sold in Australia fell from 90,000 to 70,000. How do you expect the decrease in demand for cars affected the price of cars? During that same period, employment in transport equipment manufacturing fell from 106,000 workers to 80,600. Why does a decrease in demand for cars lead to a decrease in demand for transport factory workers?

Study Problems

Learning Objective 11.1 *Understand how wages and employment are determined by the forces of supply and demand.*

1. Consider the labour market for grocery store cashiers. Who are the demanders in the market and who are the suppliers? The average hourly wage for cashiers is $18 per hour. Use a graph to illustrate the market for grocery store cashiers if labour supply is upward-sloping. Be sure to properly label the axes, curves, and equilibrium wage. Use the four core principles to describe why cashiers may have upward-sloping labour supply curves.
2. Judicial law clerks assist judges in court, conduct research for judges, and prepare legal documents. The table shows the quantity of labour supplied and the quantity of labour demanded in a market for judicial law clerks.

Hourly wage ($ per hour)	Quantity of labour **supplied** (thousands of workers)	Quantity of labour **demanded** (thousands of workers)
$24	11	19
$26	13	17
$28	15	15
$30	17	13
$32	19	11

Use the data to graph the demand and supply curves for judicial law clerks. Be sure to properly label the axes, curves, and all values provided in the table. What are the equilibrium quantity of judicial law clerks and equilibrium wage in this market?

Learning Objective 11.2 *Discover how employers decide how many workers to hire.*

3. You have recently opened your own website design business. You charge your clients a price of $1,000 per project and are considering hiring additional workers to assist you in expanding your business.

   The table provides data on your marginal product for each additional website designer you hire. Use the information to calculate the marginal revenue product, total output, and total revenue associated with each number of employees. The market wage for website designers is $5,600 per month. If this is the only cost you incur from hiring an additional worker, calculate the marginal cost and profits for each additional worker. Using the Rational Rule for Employers, how many workers should you hire each month? What's the number of workers that maximises your profits?

Number of website designers	**Marginal product** (completed projects per month)
1	10
2	9
3	8
4	7
5	6
6	5

4. Consider Gabriela's marginal revenue product for each worker hired at Head Area Salon.

Number of hair stylists	**Marginal product** (haircuts per week)	**Marginal revenue product** (marginal product: \$40 per haircut)
1	40	\$1,600
2	35	\$1,400
3	30	\$1,200
4	25	\$1,000
5	20	\$800

How many workers will Gabriela hire if the wage is \$1,400 per worker? How many will Gabriela hire if the wage is \$800 per worker? Complete the following table showing Gabriela's demand for labour at various wages and then graph her labour demand curve.

Wage (\$ per worker per week)	**Quantity of workers demanded**
\$1,800	
\$1,600	
\$1,400	
\$1,200	
\$1,000	
\$800	

5. In 2017, Apple told its suppliers to prepare for the sale of 100 million iPhones; however, in 2018 Apple updated its projections and informed suppliers that it expected iPhone demand to be lower. Given this reduction in demand for iPhones, how will the marginal revenue product of employees in stores selling the iPhone change? Use a graph to illustrate the impact of this change on the labour market for iPhone sales workers.

6. State whether each of the following events will result in a movement along Rio Tinto's demand curve for labour in their Australian mines or whether it will cause its demand curve for labour to shift (and in which direction). Draw a graph that shows the change you predict.

a. New advances in technology reduce the cost to Rio Tinto of machinery used in its mines. Why does it matter whether the substitution or scale effect dominates? What happens if the substitution effect dominates? What happens if the scale effect dominates?

b. Mining companies adopt a new production process that increases the productivity of their workers.

c. The market wage for mining workers increases.

7. The number of bank tellers has declined steadily since the early 1990s, as ATMs replaced human tellers. This meant that the cost of running each branch fell. ATMs shifted employees' work from routine tasks like deposits and withdrawals towards skills machines cannot provide, such as sales and customer service. At the same time, the number of bank branches in Australia fell from just over 7,000 in 1992 to 5,173 in June 2020.

When the use of ATMs became more prevalent and reduced the overall costs to banks, in terms of the impact on labour, did the scale effect or the substitution effect dominate? On net, would labour and capital be considered substitutes or complements in this industry?

Learning Objective 11.3 *Decide how much time to devote to work versus leisure.*

8. Nicole works as a research assistant. When her wage rate was \$50 per hour, she worked 35 hours per week. When her wage rate rose to \$60 per hour, she decided to work 40 hours per week. When her wage rate rose further to \$70, she decided to work 30 hours per week. Draw Nicole's individual labour supply curve. Indicate on your graph the range of wages over which the income effect dominates for Nicole and the range of wages over which the substitution effect dominates.

Learning Objective 11.4 *Evaluate how the labour market will respond to changing economic conditions.*

9. Consider the labour market for workers building boats. For each of the following scenarios draw a graph showing the effect on the labour market for boat builders. How does the equilibrium wage and number of boat builders change?

a. Boat manufacturers begin using more efficient robots on the assembly line and the substitution effect dominates the scale effect.

b. There is an increase in the wage of car manufacturing workers (assume boat builders and car workers have similar skills and can work in both industries).

c. There is a decrease in unemployment benefits.

10. Determine whether each of the following events will result in a movement along the market supply curve for labour in the fast-food industry or whether it will cause the market supply curve for labour to shift. If the supply curve shifts, indicate whether it will shift to the left or to the right.

a. Wages in the retail industry increase (assume that the fast-food industry requires similar skills as the retail industry).

b. New legislation reduces the number of hours that workers under the age of 18 are able to work each week.

c. In order to increase opportunities for lower income families, the government increases the subsidies available for individuals to pursue a university education.

CHAPTER 12

Why Wages Vary: Workers, Jobs, Institutions, and Discrimination

Taylor Swift earned $245 million in 2019. That's $4.7 million per week, or roughly $60,000 per hour even if she is working 80 hours a week! By the time you finish reading this page, Swift will be around $500 richer. But for Peta Milovsky, it's a different story altogether. She is an aged-care worker for which she gets paid an average of $29 an hour (including penalty rates). Even working full time, she earns only $1050 per week, or roughly $50,000 per year. After factoring in the Family Tax Benefit, taxes, her public transportation and child care costs, she has to figure out how to pay her rent and support her two kids with only $500 per week.

Jun Sato/TAS18/Getty Images

Few workers stack money as fast as Taylor Swift.

Many people think that looking after the elderly is more important than pop music. So why does a singer get paid 9,000 times more than an aged-care worker? While these two represent the extremes, there is enormous variation in the distribution of earnings in between. Supply and demand gives you the framework to analyse what drives these differences, but exactly what is it about the supply and demand of singers versus aged-care aids that leads to these differences? What are employers looking for in workers? What are workers looking for in jobs? And how do these factors come together to cause some people to earn more than others?

Beyond supply and demand, government and other institutions also influence labour market outcomes. If you've ever worked a minimum-wage job, you know that it was the government, not the laws of supply and demand, that set your wage. Governments also influence the labour market by setting training and experience requirements to work in some occupations. The government also sets the rules under which employees and employers can bargain over wages and working conditions. The outcome might result in workers forming a union, which is another type of institution that shapes labour market outcomes. Finally, all businesses want to hire productive workers, but it turns out that they can also create more productive workers through better management practices. And so we'll conclude this chapter by examining management practices that work, and some that can backfire.

Chapter Objective

Understand why wages vary.

12.1 Labour Demand: What Employers Want
Learn what skills businesses want from workers.

12.2 Labour Supply: What Workers Want
Discover how wages depend on the characteristics of the job.

12.3 Institutional Factors That Explain Why Wages Vary
Assess how regulations and institutions shape wages.

12.4 How Discrimination Affects Wages
Evaluate how discrimination affects outcomes in the labour market.

12.5 Personnel Economics
Learn how smart employers get their workers to do more with less.

12.1 Labour Demand: What Employers Want

Learning Objective *Learn what skills businesses want from workers.*

Let's start by considering how *labour demand*—that is, what employers want—shapes your wage. The key insight from our study of labour demand is that your productivity plays a central role in determining how much your boss is willing to pay you. Specifically, recall that an employer's demand for workers is determined by the value of what each worker can produce, which is why savvy executives hire workers until the marginal revenue product is equal to the market wage. It follows that if you want to be offered a high wage, you need potential employers to believe that you'll produce a lot of valuable output. And so in this section we'll analyse what makes some workers more productive than others and what employers look for to determine which workers are likely to be most productive.

Human Capital

human capital The accumulated knowledge and skills that make a worker more productive.

You're probably in university because you expect to earn more as a university graduate. In fact, you may even be taking this course because you've heard that economics students earn more than other university graduates. I've got good news for you: Both are true. Over the course of a lifetime, the average worker with a university degree will earn a million dollars more than those who stop their education at high school. And economics majors will earn even more.

Figure 1 | Education and Earnings

Median weekly earnings in 2020

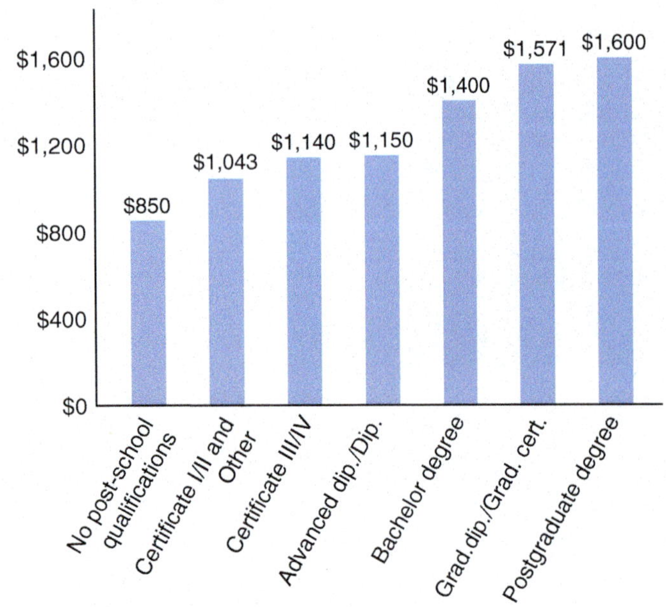

Data from: Australian Bureau of Statistics.

Education makes you more productive. Economists refer to your accumulated productive skills as your stock of **human capital.** Because greater human capital can raise your productivity, workers with more human capital tend to get paid more.

Indeed, Figure 1 shows median annual earnings among people with different levels of education. (The median means that half the people with that level of education earn at least this much.) The median person with a Bachelor's degree, earns roughly 40% more than the median person with only an Advanced Diploma or Diploma. And the median person with only an Advanced Diploma or Diploma earns roughly 40% more than the median person who has no post-school qualifications. These differences should make you feel pretty good about the payoff from your current studies. In fact, the typical person's wages will be higher for each additional year they invest in building their human capital by going to school.

EVERYDAY Economics **Does going to university really matter?**

Some people see these income differences by education and say: "Okay, university graduates earn more than high school graduates. So what? Couldn't this just be because smart people are more likely to go to university? Maybe they would have earned just as much if they didn't go to university." They're asking: Does more education *cause* higher wages, or is some other factor—such as your innate intelligence or family upbringing—responsible for both higher earnings and more education?

Economists have conducted careful studies to try to sort this out. Comparisons of people with similar IQ scores show that people who went to university earned more than similar people who didn't. Comparisons of identical twins—who share the same genes and were brought up in the same home—yield the same conclusion. Also, people who grew up near a university—and hence were more likely to attend university—earn more than otherwise-similar folks who grew up further away from a university and were less likely to attend. All of this suggests: Yes, going to university really does make a difference. A big one. ■

Education can also serve as a signal of your ability. Why does more education lead to a higher salary? So far we've suggested that education makes you more productive, and when you're more productive, you earn more. Most economists agree that education raises people's productivity and that's a big part of why you'll likely earn more than the typical person who gets less education than you. But it turns out that education plays another role as well. Beyond teaching you useful skills, your degree conveys information—that is, it signals—to your employer that you are a good worker.

VGstockstudio/Shutterstock

A degree is a valuable signal.

Here's the idea. Employers value smart and tenacious workers. But in an interview, employers can't easily figure out who actually has these characteristics and who's just saying they do. And so savvy employers look at your past achievements that might convey this information—such as your education. By this view, the fact that your degree requires hard work means that only people with both brains and tenacity will find it worthwhile to complete a university degree. (Applying the *cost-benefit principle*, the cost to those who are less tenacious is just too high.) And so employers looking for smart and tenacious workers realise they should hire university graduates.

But the reason they do this isn't necessarily that they value any specific skills you learned in university. Instead, it's because you did something that many other people would find too challenging, and this conveys otherwise unobservable information about how productive you will be.

The idea is that actions speak louder than words—you can't simply tell a potential employer how hard-working and tenacious you are, because anyone might claim that in an interview. Education serves as a **signal**—a costly action that you take to credibly convey information that would otherwise be hard for someone else, like a potential employer, to verify. A useful signal helps employers figure out which workers are likely to be more productive. However, for education to work as a signal, it must be substantially costlier for less productive workers to earn a university degree than it is for highly productive workers. It's precisely the fact that university is hard—and even harder if you aren't tenacious and hard-working—that makes it serve as a useful signal.

signal An action taken to credibly convey information that is hard for someone else to verify.

EVERYDAY Economics **Which interests should you tell employers about?**

During job interviews, potential employers often ask: What do you like to do in your free time? This isn't just a question to break the ice; your answers can signal otherwise unobservable traits about you. So which interests and hobbies should you mention? Try to focus on the ones that illustrate relevant traits for the job. If you spend a lot of time helping your parents by looking after younger siblings, say so: It signals that you are a team-player and responsible. If you spend time tutoring others, mention it so employers know that you are likely to be helpful to your colleagues. If you've run a marathon, tell employers because it shows that you are persistent and disciplined.

(left) Jaren Jai Wicklund/Shutterstock; (right) Remigiusz Latek/Alamy WAYHOME studio/Shutterstock Aflo Co., Ltd./Alamy

What do your hobbies signal about you?

Enjoy sky diving? Be careful: That might signal that you are fearless, which is a good attribute if you're applying to the military, but a bad one if you're applying to work in child care. ■

Does education raise your productivity or signal your ability? Economists often present the ideas of *signalling* and *human capital* as two competing ideas to explain why more education leads to higher wages. In reality both ideas have some validity. Take signalling: As an employer you'll want to use the information you have about people to try to choose who's likely to be the most productive worker. University is a useful signal, because university graduates have different traits on average than those without university degrees (beyond what they've learned in school). For instance, people who are better able to delay gratification are more likely to go to university. And workers who are able to delay gratification are valuable employees, because they'll endure short-run costs—such as working through dinner—for long-run benefits, such as finalising a big project on time. But human capital is also important. Employers understand that while you're in university you're building your writing, quantitative, and reasoning skills. They value this and will pay you a higher wage because this human capital makes you a better communicator, problem solver, and strategic thinker on the job.

Efficiency Wages

So far we've seen that employers pay more to workers who are more productive. But sometimes employers pay workers more to *make* them more productive. Let me explain. You're a smart, educated person capable of being really productive at your job. But you also get tired, enjoy snacks, and wonder what your friends are doing on social media. Most people find it hard to stay focused on the job all the time. If you follow the *marginal principle*, you'll ask yourself whether it's worth working hard for one more hour. The *opportunity cost principle* reminds you that the alternative is slacking off. And the *cost-benefit principle* says that it's worth slacking off in that hour when the marginal benefit of working hard is less than the marginal cost of that effort. And so if the marginal cost of effort exceeds the marginal benefit, perhaps you'll slack off.

A higher wage provides an incentive to keep working hard. Your boss understands this, which is why in many factory jobs, employers closely monitor what their workers are doing. But if your boss can't monitor your effort closely, they might try a different strategy, tweaking your costs and benefits to keep you working hard. So when no one is watching, how does your employer ensure that you keep your nose to the grindstone? By paying you a wage that's higher than what you could earn elsewhere. They figure that the higher your wage, the more you'll value your job. (As the *opportunity cost principle* highlights, how much you value your job depends on how much you're paid, relative to your next best alternative.) And the more you value your job, the less you'll want to risk losing it by slacking off. Highly paid workers are also more likely to feel valued, inspiring them to give back in the form of greater effort.

efficiency wage A higher wage paid to encourage greater worker productivity.

Indeed, some employers have calculated that a higher wage might inspire you to work so much harder that your higher wage pays for itself. Economists refer to this as an **efficiency wage**—a higher wage paid to encourage greater worker productivity, by increasing worker effort and reducing worker turnover.

Some jobs pay more because effort is costlier to monitor. What this means is that jobs where it's hard for your employer to monitor your effort will tend to pay a bit more. That's one reason that nannies tend to make more than day-care workers. Parents can't monitor nannies as well as managers at day-care centres do. As a result, many parents pay an efficiency wage, while few day-care centres do.

The Market for Superstars

Human capital, signalling, and efficiency wages can't fully explain why Taylor Swift earned $245 million in 2019. That's over 3,000 times more than the median singer or musician. Is she 3,000 times more talented? Swift is good, but maybe not that much better.

When millions of people can enjoy your talents at the same time, small differences in talent can have big effects. Before I explain why, I want you to think of the song you most want to hear right now. Okay, who sings it? Is it a superstar with millions of fans or a local singer in your community? Indie music lovers aside, most people answer that they want to listen to a song by a superstar. After all, there's no point listening to the 100th best musician when you can listen to the best.

Technology expands the reach of superstars. The existence of superstars like Taylor Swift reflects the combination of two facts—that people like to hear the best, and technology makes it easy for the best to reach millions of customers. To see why this matters, look back to the music scene a century ago, when most music was consumed by listening to live concerts. There were hundreds of musicians who would each make a living by filling the biggest concert hall in their town. The reach of the very best musician was limited by the size of the available concert halls. As a result, there wasn't much of a difference in pay between the best musician and the 100th best—both would sell out their local venues. Now fast-forward to the modern era of recorded music and online streaming. Today's top stars have a far greater reach. Swift, for instance, has sold over 200 million albums and her songs have been streamed billions of times. When you can listen to the world's best singer, there's no longer much reason for anyone to listen to the 100th best.

Swift's career illustrates that whenever you can reach millions of customers—each of whom has a slight preference for the very best—the labour market becomes something of a winner-takes-all market. In such a market, the very best performers capture a large share—sometimes all—of the rewards, leaving little for those who are just slightly less skilled. Occupations that demonstrate this winner-takes-all dynamic include actors, authors, and athletes. In these markets, each person competes to be the next global sensation. Pursuing a career in these fields can be very lucrative but very risky, because only a handful of people make it to the very top.

Interpreting the DATA

Why is chief executive pay so high?

If you were on the board of a major corporation, how much would you be willing to pay to get the very best talent to run the company? Before you answer, I'll share with you the results of a recent study, which estimated that getting the very best chief executive will raise the value of your company by 0.016% more than the 250th best alternative. That doesn't sound like much. But if your corporation is Macquarie Group, which is worth roughly $40 billion, then even this very small difference is worth an extra $6.4 million. That's a key reason big firms are willing to pay millions of dollars to get the very best managers.

There's an important idea here: The more broadly you can spread your talent—say, across a big firm or a big market—the more likely it is that being slightly better than the competition will be enough to generate a multimillion-dollar pay deal. ■

Bess Adler/Bloomberg/Getty Images

Shemara Wikramanayake, the CEO of Macquarie Group, earns millions of dollars each year.

12.2 Labour Supply: What Workers Want

Learning Objective *Discover how wages depend on the characteristics of a job.*

So far, we've seen how the demand for workers with different attributes yields different wages. Let's now turn to *labour supply,* which means focusing on the question of what workers want. And so we'll turn our attention from the different attributes of *workers,* to the different attributes of *jobs.*

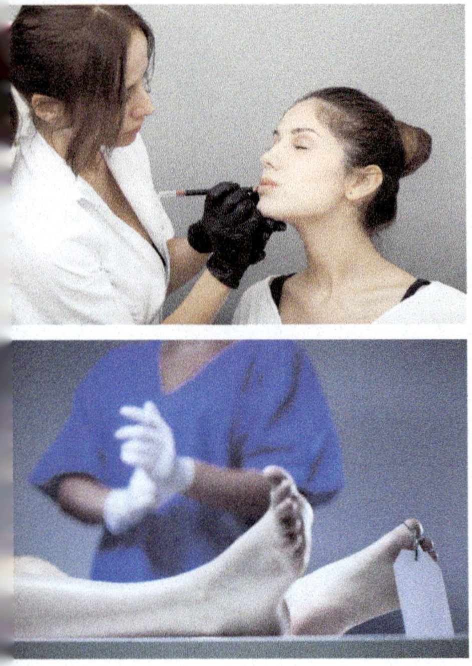

Stocked House Studio/Shutterstock

KatarzynaBialasiewicz/iStock/Getty Images

Which job would you rather have?

Compensating Differentials

Have you ever thought of becoming a cosmetologist? If so, I've got a great deal for you. There's a job that requires a similar amount of training, where you're also paid to make people look good, while also earning a lot more money. And your customers will never be rude to you, nor will they squirm while you work on them. The job? Mortician. Interested? Probably not. I mean, imagine the awkward first dates you'll experience as you describe what you do all day.

Because morticians and cosmetologists require similar training—both require a vocational degree—we can infer that the differences in their pay aren't due to differences in their human capital. Instead, it's because it is unpleasant to spend your days looking after corpses. After all, why would you—or anyone—accept such an unpleasant job unless you were paid a bit more? The extra wage boost that you would earn as a mortician is called a **compensating differential**—a difference in wages required to offset the undesirable (or desirable) aspects of the job. It's *compensating,* because it compensates you for the attributes of the job. And it's a *differential,* because it leads people with similar human capital to earn different wages.

compensating differential The differences in wages required to offset the desirable or undesirable aspects of a job.

Jobs with undesirable attributes pay more. The worse the characteristics of a job, the higher the wage required to induce you—or other workers—into that occupation. There are lots of attributes that may make a job undesirable, and in each case, they lead to higher wages. For instance, construction jobs involve back-breaking work in the sun. Real estate agents face a lot of uncertainty, because they don't know how many homes they'll sell, and hence how much commission they'll earn. Investment bankers and corporate lawyers often work upward of 80 hours per week. Management consultants often travel every week. Chefs typically work nights and most weekends, leaving little time for a social or family life. Miners literally risk their lives every day when they go to work.

These adverse attributes reduce labour supply, and as Figure 2 shows, this leads to higher pay for these jobs. Many people simply wouldn't be willing to supply their labour at lower wages. For example, nurses who work nights earn more than those who work during the day. Why? Because working nights can wreak havoc on your family life and your physical health. If day shifts and night shifts paid the same, lots of workers would be willing to work during the day, while few would volunteer for the night shift. Instead, hospitals pay higher wages for night shifts to induce enough nurses to be willing to work at night.

Figure 2 Compensating Differentials

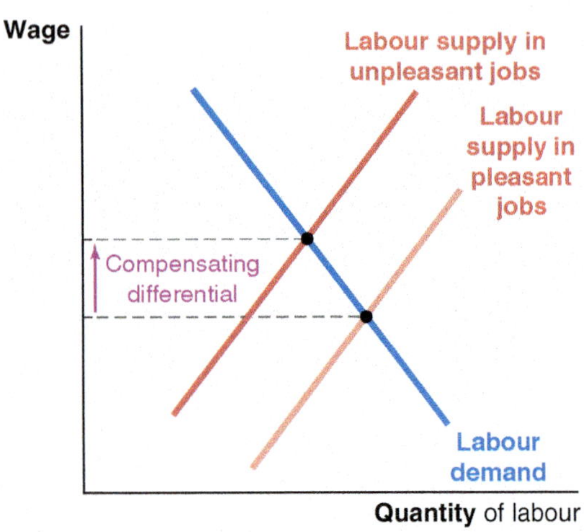

Jobs with desirable attributes pay less. On the flip side, some jobs come with splendid side benefits. Teachers take most of the summer off. Veterinarians play with puppies. Journalists get satisfaction from uncovering the truth. People who work for nonprofits and community organisations often feel like they are making a broader social contribution. And so people are willing to accept these jobs, despite that fact that they're getting paid less than they might earn in another job. As a result, wages in these desirable occupations tend to be somewhat lower to offset these nonfinancial benefits. That is, in some jobs compensating differentials lead to lower wages, as workers essentially "pay" to enjoy the pleasant aspects of their work.

Compensating differentials depend on the preferences of other workers. Whether you're offered a compensating differential or not depends on how the market as a whole—that is, *other people*—view a job attribute, not how *you* view it. That means that if you hate dogs, don't expect to be paid a lot to work as a dog walker, because there are plenty of dog lovers who are thrilled to work with dogs, even if the pay is lousy.

This insight is the *interdependence principle* in action. It also provides useful advice: Think about your tastes compared to those of other workers. You'll find a good match when you've found a job whose positive attributes are even more important to you than they are to others. Or look for a job whose negative attributes don't bug you as much as they bug others, and you'll enjoy the extra pay without being so worried about those negatives.

Interpreting the DATA How much is a life worth?

How much money would I have to pay you to risk your life? You can't say you'll never risk it, because you already take a risk of dying every time you ride in a car. So, how much? It's an important question, because it tells policy makers how much they should spend in trying to reduce these risks. And it's closely related to compensating differentials.

One possible answer comes from analysing how the occupational choices that people make reveal their own willingness to risk their lives. That is, you can compare the compensating differential that workers demand to enter risky industries like mining with that in less risky occupations. Recent research suggests that workers demand somewhere between $8,000 and $13,000 in extra income to compensate for a 0.1 percentage point increase in the probability of a fatal work injury. This means that, taken together, 1,000 workers accept an extra $8 to $13 million, in return for the likelihood that one of them will die. Stated this way, we can say that workers act as if they value one statistical life at $8 to $13 million! ■

Tyler Stableford/Stone/Getty Images

How much would you need to be paid to take these risks?

12.3 Institutional Factors That Explain Why Wages Vary

Learning Objective *Assess how regulations and institutions shape wages.*

The labour market is shaped by laws and institutions that tend to moderate the economic forces of supply and demand. As we turn to exploring these laws and institutions, we'll focus on their implications for wages. But it's worth noting that any force that pushes wages above the equilibrium wage leads the quantity of labour supplied to exceed the quantity of labour demanded. In fact, the idea that unemployment is caused by the market wage getting stuck above its equilibrium level is a key topic we'll return to in macroeconomics.

Government Regulations

The government regulates the labour market in many different ways. It sets a *minimum wage* that employers can pay workers, including requiring that many workers are paid an overtime rate when they work more than 38 hours a week. The government decides *minimum education* or training necessary for many jobs. It sets *safety standards*. And it requires *information* to be disclosed—like how many employees have been injured on the job and differences in the average pay of men and women. These rules shape the labour market and help determine how many workers are hired and the wage they'll be paid.

thierry PRAT/Sygma/Getty Images

S_ _ _ happens. But only if you are licensed.

Licensing laws restrict supply. You probably know that to start working as a doctor, you need to be licensed. The rationale is that this will protect patients from being operated on by quacks. In the case of doctors, such a requirement helps keep you safe. But there's another effect. If it's difficult to get a licence, there will be fewer doctors. And licensing laws don't just apply to doctors, but to nearly one-third of the workforce, including some interior decorators, manure applicators, and security guards. As Figure 3 shows, these licensing requirements decrease labour supply, thereby raising the wages of those who do get licences—perhaps by as much as 15%. So licensing laws increase safety and raise costs. Is it worth it? It probably depends on the job and who you ask.

Figure 3 Occupational Licensing

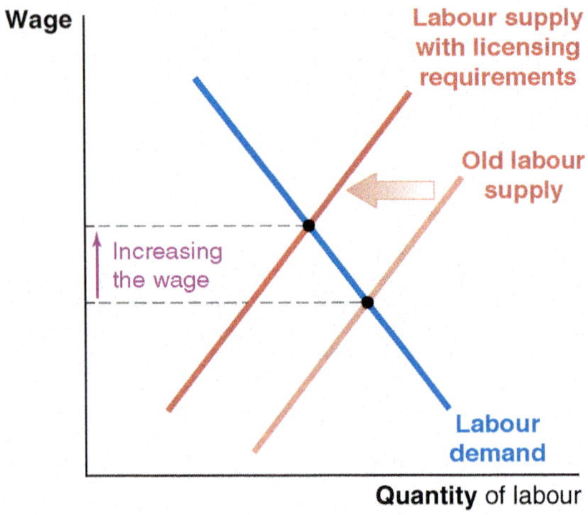

Figure 4 Effect of Minimum Wages

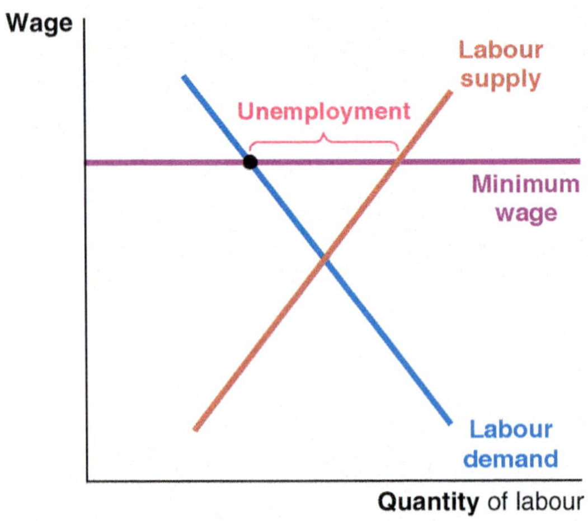

Minimum wage laws raise the wage above equilibrium. The Fair Work Commission says that, as of 2021, your employer can't pay you less than $20.33 per hour. However, there are exceptions for younger ages—those aged under 16 can be paid 40% of the minimum wage, at age 16 it's 50% of the minimum wage, at age 17 it's 60%, and so on up until age 21 or over where employees must receive 100% of the minimum wage. This is why you'll often find that the cashier at your favourite fast-food restaurant is someone who is still at school—it's cheaper for the restaurant that way! A minimum wage is an example of a price floor, which we studied in Chapter 7.

A high enough minimum wage will push wages above the equilibrium wage. As Figure 4 shows, in a competitive labour market this will cause a decrease in the quantity of labour demanded and an increase in the quantity of labour supplied, thereby creating unemployment.

The minimum wage is a hotly contested political issue. Opponents of a higher minimum wage argue that setting the minimum wage too high will lead to unemployment, which is even worse than a low-wage job. Proponents of a higher minimum wage argue that many workers earn low wages because they lack bargaining power. The minimum wage offsets some of this disparity in bargaining power, ensuring that the working poor earn a wage high enough to lift them out of poverty.

Economists have conducted hundreds of studies to try to evaluate the effects of raising the minimum wage, and there's an ongoing debate about the evidence. On average these studies show that a higher minimum wage reduces employment, but quite a few studies show that this effect is quite small, and in some cases it may be barely detectable. However, there are also studies suggesting that the longer-run effects may be larger than what we see in the short run, since it can take a while for businesses to adapt to the higher cost of workers. Whether the minimum wage has small or large effects on employment depends on the elasticity of labour demand. The evidence so far suggests that labour demand is relatively inelastic, but it becomes more elastic over time. Recall that you learned this idea in Chapter 5—in the short run demand tends to be more inelastic than it is in the long run. But even in the long run, it's not clear how elastic labour demand is and the elasticity of labour demand remains an important part of the minimum-wage debate.

Many studies also show that the minimum wage is a poorly targeted antipoverty policy because many minimum-wage workers are either part of a higher-income household or will quickly find a higher-wage job. Thus, another important part of the minimum-wage debate is a value judgement as to whether it's worth trading off somewhat higher wages for some workers for a higher risk of unemployment for others.

Unions and Workers' Bargaining Power

Government regulations give workers the right to jointly negotiate for better pay and conditions. That's where unions come in: They're organisations representing workers who band together to ensure that they are able to jointly negotiate with their employers.

Figure 5 | The Effect of Unions

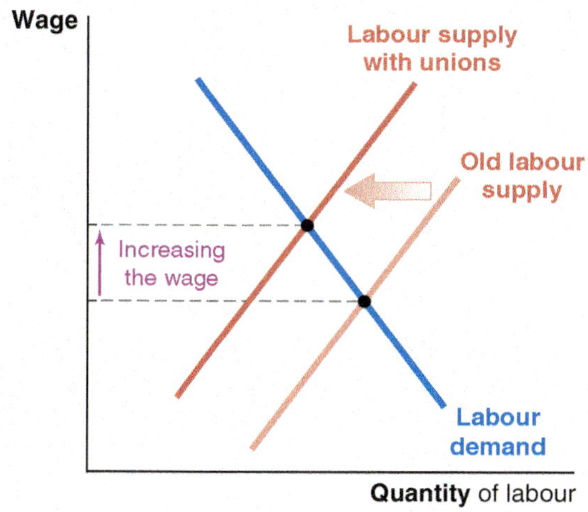

Unions boost the wages of their members. The logic of unions is that when workers band together they have more bargaining power and can push for a better deal. Think about it: If you alone threatened to go on strike unless your boss gave you a pay raise, they would probably just fire you. But if every worker at your company does this together, then your boss is likely to be more responsive. Effectively, the union is working to raise the wage at which their members are willing to supply labour. As Figure 5 shows, by shifting the labour supply curve upward or to the left, unions raise the wages of their members.

On average, unionised workers earn around 30% more than a comparable worker in a comparable non-union job. Union contracts also tend to require smaller wage differences between high-paid and low-paid workers. However, only around 14% of Australian workers are unionised, down from rates that were more than three times as high during the 1970s. Unions remain an important force in some parts of the economy, including the public sector, education, transportation, utilities, construction, and telecommunications. Unions also play a larger role in many European countries, including France, Germany, Italy, and Sweden.

Unions can make businesses more productive. Managers often resist unions because they're worried that the greater bargaining power of workers might reduce their profits. But by providing a voice for their members, unions can improve communication between management and workers. When workers and their bosses communicate well, they can often find more efficient ways to do things; thus improved communication can lead to greater productivity, which can boost profits. So if you're managing a firm with historically hostile labour relations, realise that working toward a more productive relationship might be in your best interest.

Having considered workers' bargaining power, let's turn to evaluating the bargaining power of their employers.

Monopsony and Employers' Bargaining Power

Australia's "seasonal worker program", which began in 2008, has granted entry to more than 20,000 people from the South Pacific for up to nine months at a time to pick fruits and vegetables in Australia.

In one sense this provides an important economic opportunity to workers from relatively poor countries with low wages such as Fiji, Kiribati, Nauru, Timor-Leste, Tonga, and Tuvalu. Workers in the program are guaranteed a minimum of 30 hours a week of work, and are taxed at a flat rate of 15%.

But the program is ripe for exploitation given the relative bargaining power of employers compared to workers in the program.

Workers are subject to losing their visa and being forced to leave the country if their employer is not happy with their performance—an inherently subjective judgement that gives employers a lot of power.

What would an employer's response likely be if one of the workers in the program asked for a higher wage? And what are that worker's alternatives if the employer simply says no?

Perhaps this power imbalance is why there have been reports of worker exploitation. These include workers being forced to pay up to 60% of their wages for lodging and meals, long working hours with unpaid overtime, and little or no access to health care.

Several workers reported being forced to pay $1,000 per week to sleep on a couch.

Monopsony power reduces wages. This means that farmers using migrant workers have a lot of bargaining power. If they decide to offer low wages, the workers' only options are to accept that low wage, get by without a job, or leave the country. So even if a migrant worker's marginal revenue product is $1,000 per week, they might accept a job paying only $600 per week. This is an example of **monopsony power**—a business using its bargaining power as a major buyer to pay lower prices, including lower wages. (And if *monopsony* sounds like an odd word, it might help to realise that just as a *monopoly* is the only seller of a good, a *monopsony* is the only buyer.)

monopsony power A business using its bargaining power as a major buyer of labour to pay lower prices, including lower wages.

While farmers having effective control over the visas of workers is an extreme example, the same ideas apply in many other labour markets. The federal government is the dominant employer in Canberra, for example. Mining companies are the main employers in some regional towns. A few tech behemoths such as Google, Facebook, and Apple play a major role in hiring tech talent in Silicon Valley in the United States. And monopsony power appears to be becoming more important in specific sectors of the economy. For instance, in the supermarket sector, Coles and Woolworths are dominant players that can use their bargaining power to get a better deal for themselves in enterprise bargaining agreements.

There's a vibrant debate about how important monopsony power is in the broader labour market, and there are good arguments on both sides. Consider, for example, the market for teachers. By one view, the department of education in each state or territory in Australia has a lot of monopsony power, because it employs all the public-school teachers in the state or territory. An alternative perspective suggests that teachers still have a lot of bargaining power because if they're unhappy with their pay and conditions, they can threaten to move to independent schools or change occupations.

Monopsony power affects whether minimum wages hurt employment. The importance of monopsony power can change the debate about the minimum wage. If monopsony power is holding down wages, then minimum wages that push companies to pay higher wages won't necessarily lead to less employment. Instead, these laws might simply ensure that workers get a better deal from their bosses. Indeed, monopsony power can lead some businesses to cut back their hiring to keep wages low. A higher minimum wage can even help eliminate this incentive, thereby boosting employment.

EVERYDAY Economics **The importance of asking for a raise**

Many workers—particularly women—are reluctant to bargain for higher wages without a union. But you shouldn't be. Linda Babcock, who is a professor at Carnegie Mellon University in the United States, noticed that the starting salary of her male students was about $4,000 higher than that of her female students. This surprised her, given that the women in her class were typically at least as talented as the men. So she asked them about how they had negotiated their pay. A majority of men—57%, to be precise—had negotiated for a higher salary than they were initially offered, while only 7% of women had done so. Those who had negotiated had succeeded in raising their salary offer by $4,000 on average! These differences in bargaining potentially explain part of the male–female wage gap. This study is the foundation for the advice that Babcock now gives all of her students: If you want a higher wage, ask for it! ■

12.4 How Discrimination Affects Wages

Learning Objective *Evaluate how discrimination affects outcomes in the labour market.*

discrimination Treating people differently based on characteristics such as their gender, race, ethnicity, sexual orientation, religion, disability, social class, or other factors.

Labour market **discrimination** occurs when people are treated differently based on characteristics like their gender, race, ethnicity, sexual orientation, religion, disability, social class, or other factors. Numerous studies show that discrimination affects wages. It shouldn't. But it does. Anti-discrimination law forbids discriminating against people on the basis of race, religion, national origin, age, gender, or disability. Nonetheless, discrimination persists.

There are sizeable differences in outcomes across groups that may be at least partly due to discrimination. Figure 6 shows that women are paid less than men. And only 10 of Australia's 200 largest public companies are led by female CEOs.

However, we should be careful: One group enjoying less success in the labour market than another is not necessarily evidence of discrimination.

Figure 6 | Wages by Sex

Average weekly earnings in 2020

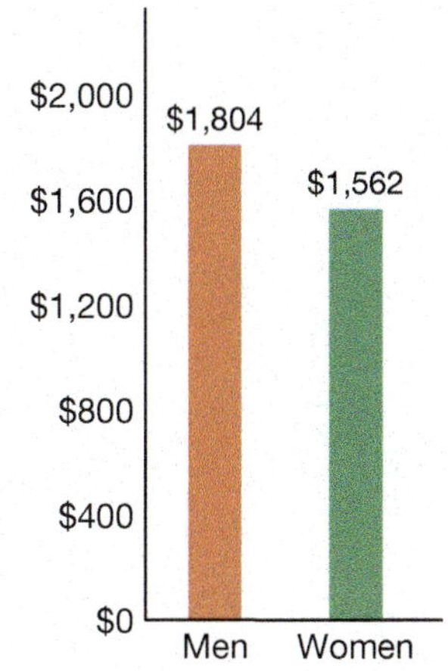

Data from: Australian Bureau of Statistics.

Measuring Discrimination

Remember that wages reflect the characteristics of workers (their human capital) and the characteristics of the job (including compensating differentials), as well as the labour market institutions that shape how wages are bargained. Some of the wage differences between groups reflect the influence of these factors. For instance, there are differences in average educational attainment by race. Accounting for these differences reduces the differences in wages by demographic group somewhat.

Accounting for differences in human capital and jobs explains some of the gaps. This suggests that to truly isolate the differences that are due to discrimination, we need to compare people who have similar human capital, who work in similar jobs, and who are regulated by similar institutions. Thus, more complex analyses compare wages between groups, correcting for the influence of factors that may be related to: human capital differences (such as experience and education), job characteristics (such as industry and occupation), and the influence of institutions (such as union membership). Typically, these comparisons conclude that there remain important wage differences between groups, although these differences are somewhat smaller.

Remaining differences may reflect discrimination, or other unobserved influences. It's tempting to suggest that once these factors have been accounted for, the remaining pay differences must be due to discrimination. But even the most careful studies don't provide definitive proof. Why? That's because no analysis can fully account for differences in ability, effort, human capital, job characteristics, or bargaining power. These unobserved factors might be the reason that wages differ between demographic groups. For instance, while many studies account for whether you have a university degree, they don't account for the quality of your university education, and while they account for your occupation, they lack information about the specific characteristics of your job. It's possible that some of the differences in pay between groups could reflect the influence of these hard-to-measure attributes, rather than discrimination.

Discrimination may lead some occupations to be underpaid. These sorts of comparisons may also underestimate the extent of discrimination if discrimination operates by segregating some groups into low-paying occupations. For instance, male and female nurses receive roughly similar pay, which sounds like evidence against discrimination. But some scholars argue that the real problem is that nursing—and other female-dominated occupations—are underpaid, because hospitals undervalue work that has traditionally been regarded as feminine.

Interpreting the DATA

How large is the gender wage gap?

On average, women who worked full time in 2021 made 14% less than men who worked full time throughout that same year. This difference, which is often called the *gender wage gap*, leads many people to protest that discrimination is the reason that women earn only 86 cents for every dollar a man earns. But it's unlikely that this pay gap is entirely due to discrimination. Some of it likely reflects the different attributes of men and women and the different choices they make, based on the opportunities available to them.

The gender pay gap isn't due to education, as on average women have accrued as much education as men. But in other dimensions, there are important differences. Women tend to work in lower-paid occupations and they tend to work fewer hours and fewer weeks during the year, partly due to family obligations. They're also more likely to have a break in work experience due to taking time away from work for childbirth or to care for a family member.

This points to the fact that providing better, more affordable, and more flexible child care is one important measure to help reduce the gender pay gap. This gender pay gap also translates into less superannuation for women on average—another important public-policy issue to be addressed. And workplace culture also plays an important role. For example, the primary reason women cite for leaving computer science jobs is a hostile work environment. Some of these women go on to take lower-paying jobs so that they can experience less of this hostility. ■

Three sources of discrimination:

1. Prejudice
2. Implicit bias
3. Statistical discrimination

Types of Discrimination

Why then, does discrimination occur? There are three key reasons that people discriminate: They may dislike some groups of people explicitly, they might discriminate against some groups of people without even realising it, or they could be using information about a group to try to infer something about the otherwise hard-to-observe abilities of individuals. Let's explore these types of discrimination in greater detail.

prejudice A preconceived bias against a group that's not based on reason or experience.

Discrimination type one: Prejudice. When most people think about discrimination, they usually conjure up visions of bigots whose hatred of some groups of people causes enormous harm to those people. This is the problem of **prejudice,** which refers to a preconceived bias against a group that's not based on reason or experience. Prejudice remains a problem in some places and among some people, although in much of Australia the degree of prejudice—including the hatred of one group or explicit favouritism of others—appears to be declining.

Economists sometimes call prejudice taste-based discrimination, because it's not based on reason, but rather on people's preference or taste for hiring one group over another. And prejudice is costly, not only to the victims of discrimination, but also to prejudiced employers. Why? A business is most profitable if it hires the most productive people at the lowest wage possible. If you're prejudiced against a group of people, you're limiting the pool of talent available to you. Selecting from a smaller talent pool means both that you've limited the supply of workers competing for a job—which leads to higher wages—and you're less likely to find the most productive workers. It follows that it's costly to be prejudiced.

Indeed, this points to a potentially profitable hiring strategy. If there are a lot of prejudiced employers in your labour market, then there are likely a lot of talented people who—because of their gender, race, ethnicity, religion, or sexuality—are still looking for a job that uses their full set of talents. It follows that a savvy employer can find especially good workers by hiring people that other employers are prejudiced against.

Does this approach work? One owner of a Wall Street firm said that he hired a lot of women, reasoning that he could hire more talent at a lower price, because his competitors were prejudiced against women. If enough employers follow this strategy, they'll offset some of the effects of prejudice. In this way, competitive market pressure can help reduce the role that prejudice plays in the labour market.

This logic also illustrates how prejudice can sometimes lead to *segregation*. For example, a century ago, most car makers in the United States would not hire Black workers, but Ford saw an opportunity to hire talented workers who were overlooked by their rivals. The result was a segregated workforce, with mostly White workers at General Motors and mainly Black workers at Ford.

Discrimination type two: Implicit bias. Psychologists have recently developed a more subtle understanding of discrimination that recognises that people often try very hard not to be biased. While you may strive to be impartial, when you need to make quick judgements, your brain simply doesn't have time to make a complete analysis. And so without your conscious knowledge, your snap judgements may reflect implicit or unconscious associations. For instance, your brain may be more likely to associate masculine with aggression, or feminine with nurturing. It may even make associations between particular groups and honesty, tenacity, or leadership.

The result is a form of discrimination based on **implicit bias,** in which employers' judgements are shaped by their unconscious attribution of particular qualities to members of specific groups. The problem is that these crude attributions can be harder to combat because you may not even be aware you're making them. For instance, even though people may not mean to discriminate when they tip their taxi driver, the quick judgements they form may help explain why Black taxi drivers receive smaller tips than White taxi drivers.

implicit bias Judgements shaped by the unconscious attribution of particular qualities to specific groups.

As an employer, you want to hire the best person for the job, rather than allowing your unconscious attitudes to fool you into overlooking them. You can minimise the impact of your implicit biases by basing your hiring decisions on carefully structured assessments of individual candidates, rather than gut feelings.

Interpreting the DATA — Orchestrating impartiality

One strategy to eliminate discrimination would be for employers to literally hide the gender and race of job applicants. After all, an employer can't discriminate based on characteristics they can't see. In reality, few hiring managers do this, although the experience of America's major orchestras suggests that it might really help. In response to concerns that music directors were overlooking talented women, many of America's leading orchestras adopted a simple but radical new approach to auditions: Musicians trying out for a spot would perform their music from behind a screen. That screen shielded the identity of the aspiring musicians from the judges, ensuring that the judges could not see—and hence couldn't be biased by—the gender or race of each applicant. Researchers Claudia Goldin and Cecilia Rouse, studying these "blind" auditions, found that when the judges could only "see" the quality of the music, they became much more likely to hire women. The researchers described this outcome as "orchestrating impartiality." ■

Nataly Studio/Shutterstock

You shouldn't be treated differently just for looking different.

Discrimination type three: Statistical discrimination. Another type of discrimination occurs when employers don't have a lot of information about job applicants, and rely instead on stereotypes. Why? Often these stereotypes are statistically accurate on average, even if they're inaccurate for specific individuals. Using observations about the average characteristics of a *group* to make inferences about an *individual* is called **statistical discrimination.** It's *statistical* because it's based on the group's average characteristics. And it's *discrimination* because it leads employers to be reluctant to hire people from certain groups.

statistical discrimination Using observations about the average characteristics of a group to make inferences about an individual.

Consider an employer looking to hire a worker who thrives on competition. Employers can't easily observe the competitive spirit of their job applicants. But they do observe the gender of each applicant, and can use that to make inferences about their competitiveness. An employer whose experience suggests that women are typically less competitive will infer—without knowing—that the woman they're currently interviewing is less likely to thrive on competition. This inference will lead them to hire a man rather than an equally well-qualified woman.

It's a strategy that partly succeeds at its objective, and partly fails. It succeeds to the extent that the employer was right that hiring more men will, on average, help them recruit a more competitive workforce. And if they can't find a better way to identify competitive workers, this might be the best they can do. But it fails to the extent that it leads them not to hire those women who are both as qualified as the men and more competitive than them. It fails because this approach effectively discriminates against those women who thrive on competition. The problem is that employers simply assume—based on statistical averages—that these women don't enjoy competition. Stereotypes aren't wrong on average—they're just wrong for those who don't fit the stereotype, which can be a lot of people.

EVERYDAY Economics **Statistical discrimination on campus**

You might see similar problems in on-campus recruiting. Some employers believe that students at the most prestigious universities are more productive than those at other schools. Those employers focus their on-campus recruiting efforts on prestigious universities. Although this may make recruiters' jobs easier, the result is that many qualified students from other schools get overlooked. ■

Different perspectives can lead you to different judgements about statistical discrimination. Employers sometimes defend the practice, arguing that they're just using available information to try to recruit the best workers they can get. That may be true, but it's little solace to those whose career prospects are harmed by employers' use of their gender, race, university, or other attributes. Opponents of statistical discrimination argue that if recruiters put more effort into identifying the best workers, they would no longer need to rely on personal characteristics as a marker for a worker's ability. This suggests a potential solution: Providing more information about the actual capabilities of each applicant might give recruiters less reason to rely on stereotypes to fill in blanks.

The source of discrimination can be employers, customers, or co-workers. It's worth pausing to reflect on the source of discrimination. So far we've described discrimination as reflecting the judgements of *employers,* and in many cases, this is accurate. But similar factors may also affect *customers,* and if they discriminate so that they don't want to be served by people like you, this puts pressure on the boss not to hire you. Or if your *co-workers* discriminate against you, then they'll make life hell for you or pressure the boss not to hire you. All of this means that discrimination will persist as long as employers, co-workers, or customers continue to discriminate.

Wages vary due to differences in:

1. Labour demand and human capital
2. Labour supply and compensating differentials
3. Institutional factors
4. Discrimination

Recap: Differences in wages reflect labour demand, labour supply, institutions, and discrimination. It's time to take stock. So far in this chapter we've analysed four key forces that might lead your wages to differ from your friend's. The first is labour demand, which is all about what employers want. The answer is productive workers, and your productivity is shaped by your human capital. Second, we turned to labour supply, asking what workers want. The answer is enjoyable jobs, and so they'll demand higher wages—that is, compensating differentials—to accept a less pleasant job. Third, your wages are affected by an array of labour market institutions and your bargaining power. And fourth, discrimination continues to be an important factor.

So far we've looked at things mostly from the worker's perspective. And so our next task is to see how you can leverage much of what we've learned to make better personnel decisions as a manager.

12.5 Personnel Economics

Learning Objective *Learn how smart employers get their workers to do more with less.*

Congratulations on your promotion! Now you're the boss. Sure, you've worked for bad bosses in the past. But you'll be different. You've just got to figure out how. As the boss, you'll be in charge of your firm's personnel policies. Your goal will be to get your workers to do more, without costing your company too much. We'll explore five big ideas that real-world managers use:

1. Ensure your workers have the right skills for the job.
2. Motivate your staff with incentives.
3. Shape your corporate culture.
4. Offer the right benefits package.
5. Attract and retain better workers.

As we explore these ideas we'll discover that economic reasoning can lead to some unexpected insights into how to get your workers to be more effective. Let's explore each of these big ideas in turn.

Personnel economics says to:
1. Ensure your workers have the right skills for the job.
2. Motivate your staff with incentives.
3. Shape your corporate culture.
4. Offer the right benefits package.
5. Attract and retain better workers.

Ensure Your Workers Have the Right Skills for the Job

You want to make sure that your workers have the right education and skills for the jobs they do. But how? Should you provide the training yourself, or hire people who already have the necessary skills? The answer might surprise you: It depends on what type of skills you need.

Investing in general skills might help your workers get better jobs elsewhere. Most of what you're learning in university would be categorised as **general skills**, which means they're skills that would be useful to many employers. It's precisely because these skills are portable to other companies that it rarely makes sense for your company to offer general skills training. Why? If you provided your star employees with, say, the skills you learn in an economics class, they could then use those skills to get an even better job at another company. It's a bad investment because your company would pay the cost of the training, but get none of the benefits.

general skills Skills useful to many employers.

Investing in job-specific skills helps your workers do a better job for you. Contrast this with **job-specific skills,** which are those skills that are only useful in a job with one particular employer. Examples include the skills an economist needs to use their firm's forecasting model, the skills a factory worker needs to operate the equipment specific to that factory, or the knowledge a human resources manager needs to learn about their company's employment procedures. Because there's little chance that you'll find workers on the outside market who have these exact skills—after all, why would they know these things?—you'll need to provide this training internally. And because these skills are specific to your company, they're not going to help your workers find a better job elsewhere.

job-specific skills Skills that are only useful in a job with one particular employer.

Motivate Your Workers with Incentives

A key challenge for personnel managers is how to motivate your workers to be on task, rather than spending their day surreptitiously checking social media, gossiping by the water cooler, or slacking off. One way to do this is to provide them with incentives to make the right choices. This is the *cost-benefit principle* at work: Tweak the costs and benefits your staff face so that the best choice for your company also becomes their best choice.

Offer better pay for better performance. If you simply offer your workers a weekly wage—which they get paid no matter how much work they get done—do they really have an incentive to work hard? If they're not self-motivated, probably not. Pretty soon they'll realise they get paid whether or not they work hard. Instead, you can offer a **pay-for-performance** plan, linking each worker's income to their performance on the job.

pay-for-performance Linking the income your workers earn to measures of their performance. Examples include commissions, piece rates, bonuses, or promotions.

Your goal should be to align your workers' incentives with those of your business. There are lots of ways to do this. In sales jobs, it's common to supplement a relatively low base wage with a healthy *commission,* which is a share of the total sales each worker makes.

Want that windshield fixed quicker? Pay him per windshield, rather than per hour.

This gives your workers an incentive to keep making sales, rather than slacking off. Or perhaps you can pay your workers a *piece rate,* which is where you pay workers only for what they actually do—paying them per piece produced—rather than just paying them for turning up. For instance, instead of paying glass installers a fixed hourly wage, the Safelite AutoGlass company shifted to paying them a fixed amount for each window they installed. This increased the incentive for workers to focus on the task at hand, and the number of windows each worker installed rose by 44%!

If a piece rate isn't feasible—perhaps because you can't objectively measure what each employee produces—then you can use *bonuses* to provide incentives. For instance, many financial firms offer their young analysts relatively low base pay, but also the prospect of earning an annual bonus of tens—and sometimes hundreds—of thousands of dollars if they earn strong evaluations. No wonder they work so hard!

There's another more subtle way to provide incentives to your workers: Offer them a clearly defined career path, and combine this with a culture of always promoting your high-performing workers. Then the incentive for working hard isn't a commission, piece rate, or bonus, but rather a *promotion* and a pay raise.

Reward good decisions, not just hard work. Most senior managers already work long hours, but they might slack off in a different sense. Managers can be tempted to make decisions that make them popular (Pay raises for everyone! Free food! Casual Fridays!), rather than making the tough decisions that will increase your company's profits. By offering your senior managers a financial slice of the business—that is, by giving them stock in your company—you give them a personal incentive to make those tough decisions that'll boost your business's bottom line. Some companies also offer stock options, which are financial instruments that provide a big payoff for managers who can raise their firm's stock price.

Incentives can involve both carrots and sticks. You can provide your workers with incentives either by rewarding their good performance (giving "carrots"), or by punishing their poor performance (using the "stick"). So far, we've focused on the carrots. But there's also a very important stick that keeps workers focused: the threat of being *fired.* When Jack Welch was CEO of U.S. company General Electric, he would fire the bottom 10% of his employees each year, which kept them on their toes.

This practice, which has become known as "rank-and-yank," has even gained traction in the Australian public service. In 2015, Public Service Commissioner John Lloyd said "Some companies actively manage out the bottom 10% of performers every year. Why should people and how they perform be any less important in the public sector? Public resources are as important as those allocated by shareholders."

You can motivate your workers with either carrots or sticks.

Short-sighted managers sometimes believe that it's cheaper to use sticks than to use carrots. They argue that sticks don't cost anything, while carrots can be expensive. But this argument forgets that workers also have options. Remember: In order to attract good workers, the whole pay package that you offer—the base pay, plus the benefit of the carrots you offer, less the cost of the sticks—must be at least as attractive as what they could earn in other jobs. If not, your best workers will just go elsewhere. So if you use sticks to motivate workers, you're going to have to make it up to them by either topping up their base pay or offering more carrots. General Electric used more carrots, and the top 20% of their workers each year were rewarded with company shares as a bonus.

But be wary: Incentives can distort effort. Okay, so far so good. What's the drawback with using incentives? The problem is simple: You get what you pay for. Usually, that's a good thing. But it can be a problem if what you *pay for* isn't exactly what you *want.*

Over recent years, governments have increased the incentive for teachers to do a better job. These policies typically threaten to close schools if their students perform poorly on standardised tests. This provides strong incentives for teachers to raise the average grades of their students on standardised tests. But this doesn't necessarily translate into better teaching. Some schools responded by cutting recess, social studies, or any subject that isn't tested. Some teachers focused more on "teaching to the test," rather than true student learning. Other schools tried to raise test scores by expelling bad students, reclassifying some kids as learning-disabled so they're not counted in the school's average, or encouraging weak pupils to stay home on test day. Some teachers have even been caught cheating, erasing their students' wrong answers and filling in the correct bubbles instead.

Similar problems arise in the corporate world, too, a lesson that Wells Fargo discovered the hard way. The bank offered its staff financial incentives for signing up new accounts. Instead of persuading new customers to sign up for new accounts, thousands of staff members got to work creating more than 3 million fake accounts for existing customers. Eventually they were caught, and Wells Fargo was forced to pay millions of dollars in fines.

Bottom line: When "what you pay for" differs a lot from "what you want," strong incentives can be a real problem. The problem is that workers will do *more of what you pay for,* but less of the other stuff you may want.

Shape Your Corporate Culture

Economic thinking about financial incentives is useful for appealing to **extrinsic motivation** of your workers—motivating them to gain external rewards, such as higher pay. But psychologists have also documented the importance of **intrinsic motivation,** which is the desire to do something for internal reasons, such as the enjoyment and pride you get from doing a good job. For instance, millions of people donate blood to local blood banks. They're not doing it for the free biscuit, but because they believe it's the right thing to do. Likewise, your company's corporate culture can be a powerful way to harness intrinsic motivation. A business that lives up to a core set of ideals that workers identify with will be rewarded with a workforce who work hard, help each other out, and try to help the company succeed. When people believe in what they're doing, they do it better.

extrinsic motivation The desire to do something for its external rewards such as higher pay.

intrinsic motivation The desire to do something for the enjoyment of the activity itself.

Thinking about the values your workers hold can be helpful here. Many workers have a sense of *reciprocity,* and when they feel that they're treated well, they're more likely to treat your business well in return by working hard. Thus, paying your staff higher wages can lead them to be more productive as they work hard to return the favour. *Fairness* also really matters, because workers tend to slack off when they feel they're being treated unfairly. To avoid this, your personnel policy should include clear and transparent procedures for promotions and pay raises. And people like to feel *valued.* Remember, praise is free, but it helps boost your workers' morale and hence their productivity.

Your corporate culture also shapes interactions between your workers. One careful study showed that supermarket cashiers are more productive when they're working the same shift as other highly productive cashiers. Why? When you care about what your co-workers think of you, you have a greater incentive to work hard.

EVERYDAY Economics **Why charitable work is unpaid**

Poorly designed incentives can undermine intrinsic motivation. In one famous experiment, high school students were recruited to collect charitable donations. One group was given a speech reminding them of the good they were doing, which activated their intrinsic motivation. The second group was *also* paid an incentive of 1% of the amount collected, which activated their extrinsic motivation. Despite these stronger incentives, this second group actually collected less. The lesson of this experiment is that sometimes intrinsic motivation really is the best incentive, and appealing to financial motives can reduce intrinsic motivation. ■

Offer the Right Benefits

Your ability to attract top-notch staff to your company depends on the *entire* compensation package that you offer—including not only the annual salary but also the *benefits* you offer. That's why it's important to offer the right set of benefits. Generally speaking, workers prefer extra wages to extra benefits—after all, they can always use those extra wages to buy extra benefits. But sometimes there are good reasons to offer benefits rather than more cash. Let's explore.

Some benefits aren't taxed. Many employee benefits are subject to lower taxes than wages are. For instance, there are tax breaks for voluntary superannuation contributions and setting up on-site services such as child care and exercise facilities that are not available if they are not at the worker's physical place of employment. These tax breaks mean that you can provide many benefits for your workers more cheaply than they can provide them for themselves.

Even when there aren't specific tax breaks, it often makes sense to offer fringe benefits. After all, it's cheaper to buy your workers a coffee than it is to pay them more income, let them pay tax on that income, and have them buy their own coffee with what remains. This is part of the reason why technology companies like Google and Facebook provide free snacks to their employees. But the Australian Tax Office (ATO) has figured out that fringe benefits are a popular way to avoid taxes; it has worked to limit the benefits that are tax-exempt and recently raised taxes on free snacks for workers.

Complements can help, substitutes can hurt. You might think that this heading says, "Compliments can help"—that you should be nice to your workers. You should. But economists also think about complements (with an *e*), which are things that go well together. In particular, you should provide complements to hard work as a way of nudging your workers toward being more productive. For instance, my workplace offers free coffee all day, hoping it will keep me alert. Cisco buys its workers laptops rather than cheaper desktop computers, hoping that its staff will take their work home with them over the weekend. Managers of the outdoor store Mountain Designs provide special discounts on gear to their workers. Why? They figure that their staff will come to know the gear, which will make them better salespeople. The software firm SAS offers on-site health care, car cleaning, and a beauty salon, all of which give their employees fewer reasons to be out of the office. And the supermarket chain Coles offers subsidised flu shots to all workers, which reduces the number of sick days. Each of these benefits is a *complement* to hard work.

You should also make sure to minimise the substitutes for hard work. So while free coffee is a good idea, free Sleepy Time tea isn't. A comfortable office chair is a great idea, but avoid couches that can be used for afternoon naps. Have you noticed that hardly any office buildings have a covered, nice outdoor area for smokers? It's because they're trying to discourage unproductive cigarette breaks.

Attract the Best Workers

Whenever you think about your personnel policies, you should also think about how they'll affect the *types* of workers you can attract and retain. For instance, if you offer your workers strong incentives for good performance, then your firm will be more attractive to people who are high performers, and less attractive for those who would prefer to slack off. And this can be a big deal. Recall the 44% gain in productivity at Safelite AutoGlass? Around half of that was due to the fact that the piece rate helped it attract and retain better workers. Likewise, you'll discover an additional benefit of offering training to your employees. It doesn't just make your workers more productive, it also attracts a specific type of worker to your company—those who are motivated to learn new things and who want to advance in their field.

More generally, as you think about what benefits your company should offer, think about how they'll affect which workers you'll attract and retain. For instance, providing a gym will attract fitness fanatics, offering health insurance will attract older workers, and giving workers the flexibility to work from home will help attract parents.

Tying It Together

Your wage will be central to your well-being throughout your career. Indeed, it may be the price that's most important to your personal well-being. Earning a good wage can make all the difference: You'll be able to afford not only the essentials—food, clothes, and shelter—but also a few of life's luxuries. That's why we've just spent a whole chapter exploring the question of what determines wages, and why some people earn more than others. It's time to pan back to see the big picture. Our analysis has identified four key factors that drive wages.

First, there's the question of labour demand, which is really about asking: What do employers want? Businesses get to choose from many different workers, and the key factor driving their hiring decisions is productivity. Education helps build your human capital, making you more productive. And so the effort you're putting into studying this chapter will likely yield a future payoff in the form of higher wages.

Second, there's the question of labour supply, which is about asking: What do workers want? Workers also get to choose—deciding across different occupations that are more or less pleasant, and among different employers who offer different packages of benefits. As a result, unpleasant jobs tend to pay a bit more—that is, they offer compensating differentials—as an offset.

Third, the labour market is not like the market for widgets. It's about real people and their livelihoods. That's why the government regulates some aspects of labour relations, and these institutional factors—such as the minimum wage, unions, occupational licensing, and bargaining power—also shape wages.

Fourth, there's the question of discrimination: Women tend to be paid less than men. Unskilled migrants tend to get paid less than Australian citizens. Hopefully our exploration of how best to evaluate this evidence and what the underlying causes are helps you better understand some ongoing political controversies.

The end result is a framework that suggests wages reflect the characteristics of workers, the characteristics of jobs, the institutional framework that governs how workers and their bosses negotiate, and because of discrimination, other personal characteristics.

Chapter at a Glance

Labour Demand: What Employers Want

Human capital: The accumulated knowledge and skills that make a worker more productive.

Signal: An action taken to credibly convey information that is hard for someone else to verify.

Efficiency wage: A higher wage paid to encourage greater worker productivity, by increasing worker effort and reducing worker turnover.

Labour Supply: What Workers Want

Compensating differential: The differences in wages required to offset the desirable or undesirable aspects of a job. Jobs with undesirable attributes pay more. Jobs with desirable attributes pay less.

Institutional Factors That Explain Why Wages Vary

Licensing Laws	Minimum Wage Laws	Unions and Collective Bargaining Institutions	Monopsony and Employers' Bargaining Power
Set education or training required for a job. By decreasing labour supply, licensing requirements raise the wages of those who do get licenses.	The lowest wage that employers can pay workers. Can mean some people are paid more than the equilibrium wage.	Help workers jointly negotiate for better working conditions and better pay.	When a firm is one of the few key buyers of labour, it will have greater bargaining power, since workers have fewer options.

How Discrimination Affects Wages

Groups who may be responsible for discrimination: employers, co-workers, or customers.

Three Sources of Discrimination:

Prejudice:	Implicit Bias:	Statistical Discrimination:
A preconceived bias against a group that's not based on reason or experience.	Judgements shaped by the unconscious attribution of particular qualities to specific groups.	Using observations about the average characteristics of a group to make inferences about an individual.

Personnel Economics

1. Train your workers to make them more productive.

How should you cultivate human capital? The right decision depends on the type of skills you need:

General skills: Skills useful to many employers.

Job-specific skills: Skills only useful in your current job.

2. Provide incentives for your workers to put in more effort.

Pay-for-performance: Linking the income your workers earn to measures of their performance.

3. Improve your firm's corporate culture.

Extrinsic motivation: The desire to do something for its external rewards such as higher pay.

Intrinsic motivation: The desire to do something for the enjoyment of the activity itself.

4. Reduce costs by offering the right benefits.

Workers will be attracted to your business by the total compensation package that you offer.

5. Attract and retain better workers.

Think about the types of workers your incentives will attract.

Key Concepts

compensating differential, 300
discrimination, 304
efficiency wage, 298
extrinsic motivation, 311
general skills, 309
human capital, 296
implicit bias, 307
intrinsic motivation, 311
job-specific skills, 309
monopsony power, 303
pay-for-performance, 309
prejudice, 306
signal, 297
statistical discrimination, 307

Discussion and Review Questions

Learning Objective 12.1 *Learn what skills businesses want from workers.*

1. On average, university graduates earn more than high school graduates. Briefly describe the two economic explanations for this difference that were discussed in this chapter and how each explains why a university degree increases average earnings.
2. Imagine you're being interviewed for a job you'd like to have after you graduate. What would you tell your potential employer if they ask about what you like to do during your free time? Explain your answer.

Learning Objective 12.2 *Discover how wages depend on the characteristics of the job.*

3. Briefly explain the concept of compensating differentials. Provide *two* examples, one resulting in higher wages and one resulting in lower wages. Briefly explain your reasoning for each.

Learning Objective 12.3 *Assess how regulations and institutions shape wages.*

4. What does it mean for a firm to have monopsony power? Would the concept of monopsony power be relevant in the market for nurses? Why or why not?
5. What benefits do unions provide to workers? It's relatively common for unions to operate in labour markets in which there are a few employers who have some monopsony power. Why do you think this is the case?

Learning Objective 12.4 *Evaluate how discrimination affects outcomes in the labour market.*

6. When researchers estimate gender discrimination in the labour market, they take account of many observable factors that are thought to impact wages. For example, they may adjust wages because of differences between men and women in education, occupation, experience, location, etc. Of course, it is not possible to control for all differences that may affect earnings, but after accounting for many observable differences, the researchers find that men are typically paid more than women. Do you think that this methodology overestimates or underestimates the total effect of discrimination on wages? Briefly explain why, using what you've learned about labour market discrimination.
7. "Companies that engage in workplace discrimination are likely to have lower profits when they compete against other firms that do not discriminate." Evaluate this statement and briefly explain your reasoning. What impact might government policies aimed at increasing competition in the market (such as opening up the market to international trade) have on the ability of businesses to continue to discriminate against certain groups?
8. Briefly explain the concept of statistical discrimination and provide an example that is relevant for labour markets. Why might hiring managers practice statistical discrimination instead of making decisions entirely on the individual abilities of each worker?

Learning Objective 12.5 *Learn how smart employers get their workers to do more with less.*

9. What is the difference between general and specific skills? Why do businesses offer their employees more training that provides job-specific skills than training that provides general skills?

Study Problems

Learning Objective 12.1 *Learn what skills businesses want from workers.*

1. Consider the annual earnings data for 2017 that are provided in Figure 1.

   It shows that the median earnings of a university graduate with a Bachelor's degree is $140,000 per week compared to $85,000 per week for someone with no non-high school qualifications. If a typical university graduate works for 43 years, their lifetime earnings will be $3.1 million. Someone with no non-high school qualifications can be expected to work an additional four years (47 years total), resulting in lifetime earnings of $2.1 million.

   According to Study Australia, an undergraduate student should budget $21,041 per year just for living expenses. What would you tell someone who wonders whether the high cost of a university education is worth the expense?

2. Suppose you own and operate an independent gym. When you opened the business, you worked full time and hired a few trainers to work with you. Business was good so you decided to open a second gym in the next town. Now you have to split your time between two locations, which means that you can't supervise all staff directly. How can an efficiency wage help ensure that employees at both locations continue to work hard, even when you're not around?

3. In 2018, the CEO of General Dynamics (an aerospace and defence company), Phebe Novakovic, received a total compensation of about $20.7 million. This was estimated to be approximately 240 times the median General Dynamics employee's compensation. In 2018, General Dynamics' market value was approximately $47 billion. Given what you know about the effect of a good CEO on a company's value, is Phebe Novakovic worth $20.7 million per year?

Learning Objective 12.2 *Discover how wages depend on the characteristics of the job.*

4. For each of the following scenarios, indicate whether it is an example of a compensating differential.
   a. High-rise construction jobs pay more than other types of construction jobs.
   b. Union workers get paid more than non-union workers in the same industry.
   c. A home health aide who works nights gets paid more than those who work during the daytime.

Learning Objective 12.3 *Assess how regulations and institutions shape wages.*

5. In NSW, interior designers must get a licence in order to do any decorations of over $5,000 in value. This requires a minimum amount of design-related education and training. What would happen to the equilibrium wage and level of employment for interior designers if the proposed licensing legislation were to be removed from law? What would happen to the equilibrium price of interior design services as a result of the removal of this policy?

Learning Objective 12.4 *Evaluate how discrimination affects outcomes in the labour market.*

6. For each of the following, match the definition to the type of discrimination: prejudice, implicit bias, or statistical discrimination.
   a. Employers using a characteristic of a group to make inferences about an individual's skills.
   b. Discrimination that exists as a result of an individual having a dislike towards members of a particular group.
   c. Attitudes or stereotypes that affect our understanding, actions, and decisions in an unconscious manner.

7. You have been hired as an economic consultant to help determine whether employers in a particular industry are discriminating against female employees. You observe that the average man working in the industry is being paid $30 per hour and the average woman is being paid $26 per hour. For each of the following observations identify whether this should lead to higher or lower wages for women and thus whether it provides suggestive evidence for discrimination as being a factor in the differences in wages between men and women in the industry.
   a. Women working in the industry have, on average, more years of education than men in the industry.
   b. Women working in the industry have, on average, the same amount of work experience as men in the industry.
   c. Men in the industry tend to work in jobs that are more stressful than do women.

Learning Objective 12.5 *Learn how smart employers get their workers to do more with less.*

8. You have recently been hired as a manager at an Apple store. One of your first priorities is to increase worker productivity. Briefly explain why each of the following ideas may increase your workers' productivity.
   a. Instead of a fixed hourly wage, pay your workers a commission on each sale.
   b. Offer each employee the opportunity to purchase Apple stock at a reduced price.
   c. Provide free coffee and flu shots for your employees.

Inequality, Poverty, and Social Insurance

CHAPTER

13

Jamil and Alexis are both undergraduates at QUT, where they are each double majoring in economics and psychology. They each dream of running their own company someday, they both love video games, and they are both looking to gain work experience during the summer that will help build their résumés.

Jacob Lund/Shutterstock

They're all studying for the same test, but are they all equal?

In many ways, Jamil and Alexis are similar. But there's an important difference. Jamil's parents are successful doctors. He never experienced financial struggles growing up and, while his parents repeatedly tell him that university is a big investment, they are paying for his education. He hasn't had to take out any student loans and will graduate with no HECS/HELP debt, and when he considers options for a summer job, he is able to focus on the long-term benefits for his career.

Alexis grew up with a single mother who worked two jobs to make ends meet. As soon as she was old enough, Alexis worked part-time. One of her worst childhood memories is being evicted. The HECS/HELP scheme has made it possible for her to go to university, but she's anxious about having to pay back that debt to the government, even though the repayments will depend on her income. When she considers her options for summer employment, how much the job pays is an important factor. An unpaid internship is simply out of the question.

In many respects, Jamil and Alexis have equal educational opportunities, but the economic inequality between the two shapes and constrains their choices. Different views about inequality underpin some of our most contentious public policy debates and the same issues underlie disagreements about choices within our universities, workplaces, and communities.

This chapter will arm you with some important facts about inequality. We'll also develop a framework for thinking about inequality and take a look at the tools the government uses to reduce inequality and poverty. Understanding inequality and poverty is also central to making sound financial decisions. Sure, the average income of university graduates is pretty good. But few people earn the average. Instead, the income distribution of university students is varied—some of you will earn buckets, while others may struggle. It's also likely that your life will involve both periods of plenty and periods of deprivation, so arming yourself with knowledge about inequality and poverty will help you better prepare.

Chapter Objective

Understand inequality, poverty, the tools government uses to address them, and the trade-off between efficiency and equity.

13.1 Measuring Inequality
Measure the extent of economic inequality in Australia.

13.2 Poverty
Assess the prevalence and implications of poverty.

13.3 The Social Safety Net, Social Insurance, and Redistributive Taxation
Discover the ways in which government redistributes.

13.4 The Debate About Income Redistribution
Be prepared to join the debate about income redistribution.

13.1 Measuring Inequality

Learning Objective *Measure the extent of economic inequality in Australia.*

Many political debates boil down to disagreements about how much inequality and poverty there is, and what to do about it. In order to have an informed opinion, you'll need to understand the facts. And so our next task is to survey the data. As we dig into the numbers, we'll discover that there are many different ways to assess the extent of inequality and poverty, each of which yields different insights. Our goal is to present an array of different measures, so that you can see the full picture and form your own judgements.

income The money you receive in a period of time, such as a year.

Figure 1 | **The Australian Income Distribution**

Average weekly family income in the 2017–2018 financial year before tax

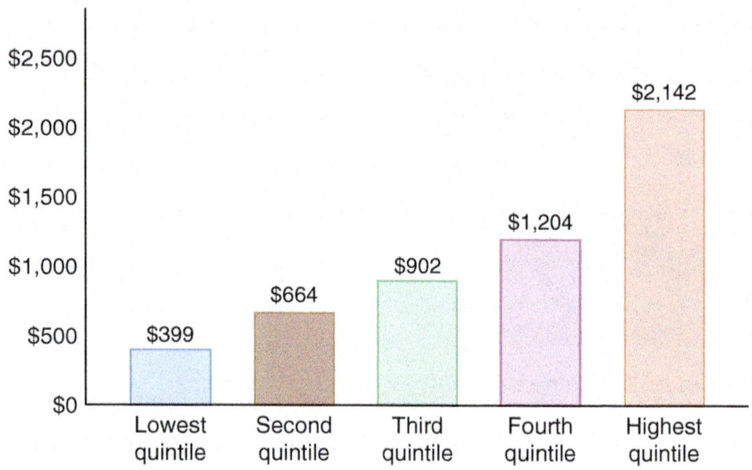

As a share of total income:	7.5%	12.5%	17.0%	22.7%	40.4%

Data from: Australian Bureau of Statistics.

Figure 2 | **Changes in the Distribution of Income Over Time**

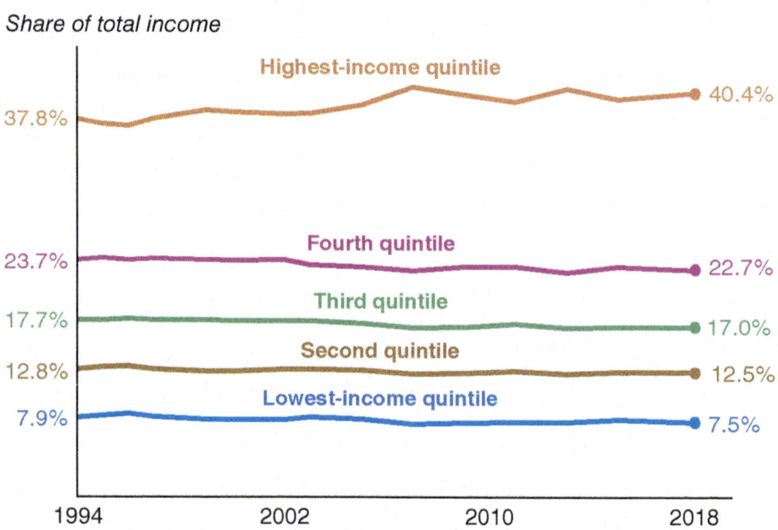

Data from: Australian Bureau of Statistics.

Income Inequality

Let's go to the data to see how much income inequality there is in Australia and how it's been changing. We'll then take a look at inequality around the world.

Income is distributed unequally. Let's be clear on what we mean by **income**—it's the money you receive in a period of time, like a year. To analyse the distribution of income, we sort families from low to high income, and then divide them into five equal-sized groups, called *quintiles*. The left-most bar in Figure 1 shows that the average family income of the lowest-income quintile of families is $399 per week. Taking these folks together, the bottom fifth receives 7.5% of total income. At the other extreme, the right-most bar shows that the highest-income quintile has an average family income of $2,142 per week. Taking all their income together, the highest-income quintile earns 40.4% of all income in Australia.

Income inequality is rising. Figure 2 shows how the income share of each quintile has changed since 1994. The largest shift is at the top: The highest-income quintile has increased their share of income from 37.8% in 1994, to 40.4% in 2018. The share of income accruing to each of the other quintiles has declined.

The income share of the bottom quintile doesn't look like it has changed much—their share has taken a small fall from 7.9%, to 7.5%. It's important to realise, however, that this doesn't mean that their income actually fell, because even though they're getting slightly smaller slices, the size of the pie grew. Incomes grew for many families over this period, but incomes grew fastest for those at the top of the income distribution, which means that their share of all income earned in Australia also grew.

The rich are getting richer. While the rich are a small proportion of the population, they account for a remarkably large share of total income. The top 5% of families receive more than one-fifth of all income (22.9% to be exact). The richest 1% receive just under one-eighth, and the very richest 0.1% of families earn over one-fifteenth of all income.

Figure 3 broadens the historical lens and tracks the income shares of those at the top of the distribution over the last century. Current levels of inequality are high relative to the latter half of the 20th century, however, we saw higher levels of inequality in the 1920s–1950s. Inequality subsequently fell through the 1950s before starting its long recent rise in the 1980s.

Australia is less unequal than many developed countries. Let's compare the income distribution in Australia with that in other developed nations. Each bar in Figure 4 runs from the income held by those at the 10th percentile—meaning that only 10% of people in the country have less income—to the income held by the 90th percentile—meaning that only 10% of the people in the country have more income than them. Among these countries, the gap between the two ends is largest for the United States. The United States stands out because its rich are richer than those in other countries.

The distribution of income around the world is even more unequal. So far we've focused on differences between high- and low-income families within a country. But the differences between high- and low-income countries are much larger. As a result, the level of income inequality across the whole world is much larger than it is in any individual country. Figure 5 shows the global income distribution, plotting the share of the global population at each level of annual income. Be careful as you read this figure to note that the horizontal axis shows a ratio scale. Notice that much of the world's population gets by on an annual income that's less than $1,000 per year. Indeed, many earn an annual income of only a few hundred dollars, or just a dollar or two per day. This global context suggests that even the very poor in Australia are well off compared to the billions of people scraping to get by in India, China, and all the other countries in the developing world.

Alternative Measures of Inequality

So far we've examined inequality in annual income. But annual income is by no means the single best indicator of your living standards, your purchasing power, or your opportunities. Income varies from year to year for many people, and people differ in both the amount of their savings and their ability to

Figure 3 | **A Rising Share of Income Is Going to the Top**

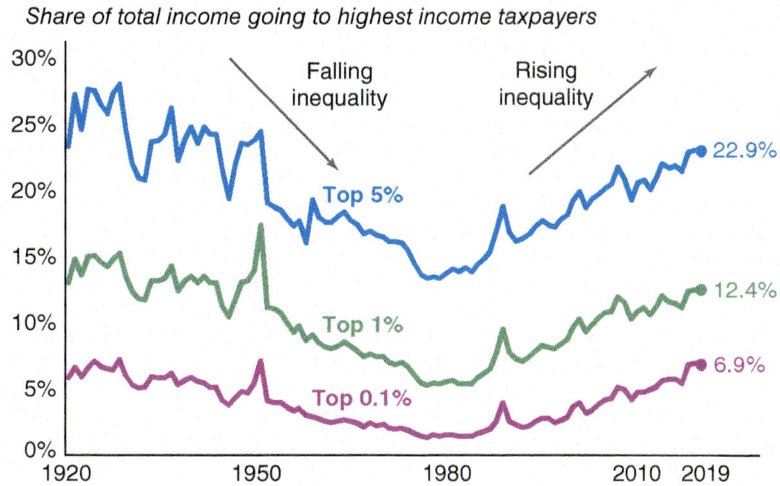

Data from: World Inequality Database.

Figure 4 | **International Comparisons of Income Inequality**

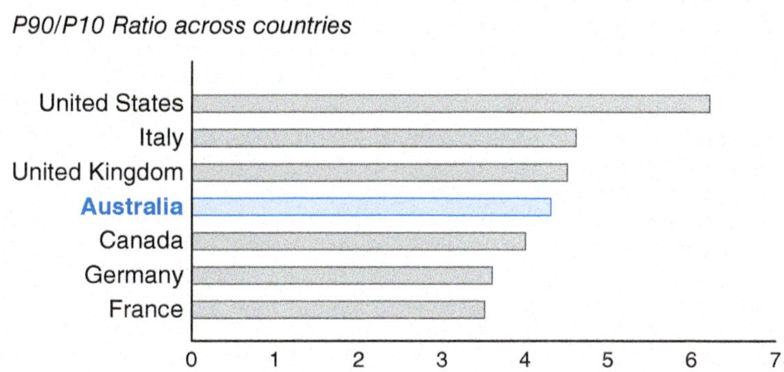

Data from: OECD Database.

Figure 5 | **The World Distribution of Income**

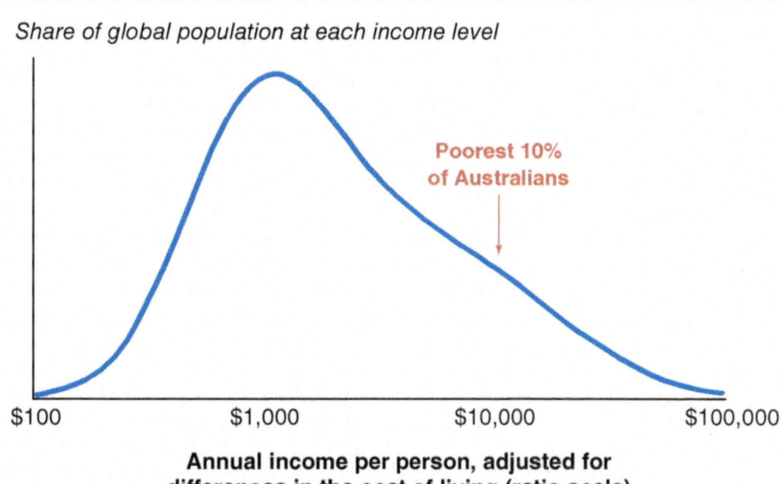

2016 Data from: Branko Milanovic, *Global Inequality: A New Approach for the Age of Globalization*, 2018.

earn more in the future. For instance, if you're like most students you probably have little accumulated savings and a low current income. But five years from now, you'll probably be earning a lot more than you are today. Today, as a student, you're focusing on building your skill set precisely because you expect to earn more down the road. You might also be young, without a lot of work experience. Imagine meeting a 50-year-old who's worked full time since they were 18. If they have the same annual earnings that you have this year, do you think that there is any inequality between the two of you? What if they earn nothing, but have an investment portfolio and savings worth $2 million?

There are no right answers to these questions—they simply represent different ways to think about inequality. Let's explore them.

There is more inequality of wealth than income. Your total purchasing power and your economic resources may be better represented by your wealth than your income. **Wealth** refers to all the assets—including savings, cars, a home—that you currently have. Wealth is considered a stock, which is something that is measured at one specific time and represents the amount of assets you have at that time. In contrast, income is a flow, since the money flows in over time.

wealth All the assets—including savings, cars, a home—that you currently have.

Figure 6 | Distribution of Wealth

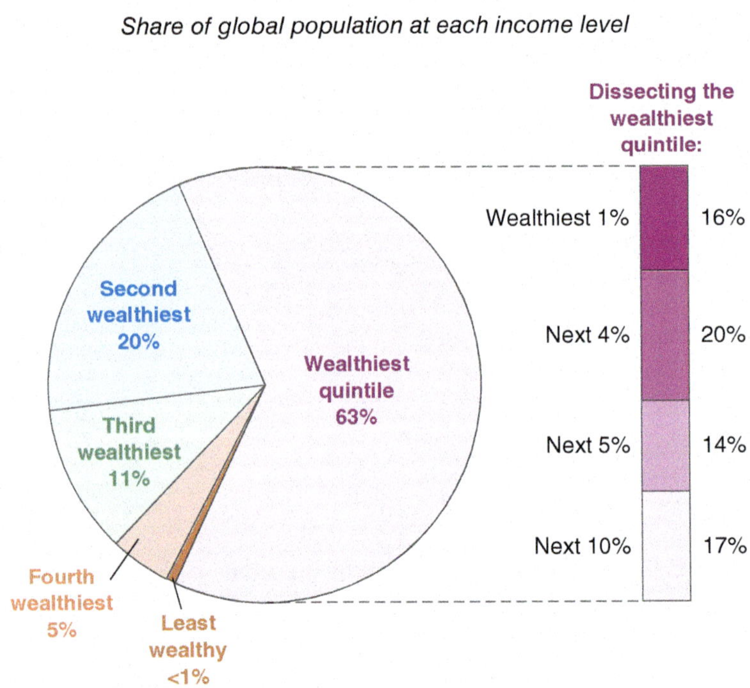

2016 data from: Christopher Sheil and Frank Stilwell, *Wealth inequality in Australia: 2012 to the present, 2019.*

Wealth is much more unequally distributed than income. Figure 6 sorts all households in terms of their wealth. The bottom three quintiles combined hold only 17% of all wealth. At the opposite extreme, 63% of all wealth is held by the wealthiest quintile. And even within this wealthiest quintile, wealth is still extremely unequally distributed. In fact, the wealthiest 1% of all households hold 16% of all wealth. Adding in the next group, the wealthiest 5% hold 36% of all wealth. All told, the people who make up the wealthiest tenth hold about 50% of all wealth. This inequality partly reflects the fact that wealth accumulates and is passed from generation to generation.

Permanent income may be a better measure of living standards. Economists believe that your living standards largely reflect your **permanent income**—which is your average lifetime income—rather than your income in a given year. There is less inequality in permanent income than in measured annual income because some of income inequality reflects temporary ups and downs that don't reflect your long-run economic situation. There are also clear patterns as you age—people earn less when they are young and tend to earn more as they get older and more experienced. So some inequality reflects differences between younger and older people.

Because people can borrow and save, annual income is not as good a predictor of what you can afford to consume compared to your permanent income. For instance, as a university student it makes more sense for you to borrow money than it does for someone in their 50s with the same earnings as you because your highest-earning years are ahead of you. That means that you can consume more today by borrowing from your future, while still having higher future consumption. Similarly, you should always save when you are doing well financially because you'll need your savings when things are not going as well. Savings help people smooth the income bumps in the road that we all face.

permanent income Your average lifetime income.

There is less inequality in spending than in income. An alternative approach suggests that because your living standards are largely determined by the goods and services you actually buy and consume, inequality in living standards may be better measured by focusing on what people spend, rather than what they earn. In Figure 1 we saw that the top quintile of the population receives around 5.4 times as much *income* as the bottom quintile. But differences in *spending* are much less stark. The top quintile spends only around 2.7 times as much as the bottom quintile. You're probably thinking that's because the highest income families save more, and you're right. But people whose incomes are temporarily high or low drive much of the measured inequality in income. Those with temporarily high incomes *are saving* because they know that their good times won't last. Since these folks maintain more moderate spending habits, there is less consumption inequality.

Intergenerational mobility and inequality of opportunity. Inequality in current and permanent income, consumption, and wealth are all examples of inequality in *outcomes*. How might we measure inequality of *opportunity*? Many people believe that regardless of whether you are born into a poor, middle, or upper class family, you should have the same opportunity to succeed. This suggests focusing on **intergenerational mobility**—the extent to which your economic circumstances are independent of those of your parents. Careful studies show that around one-fifth of the economic advantage or disadvantage enjoyed by your parents will be transmitted to you. For instance, if your father earns about 80% more than the typical dad, on average, kids like you will earn about 16% more than the typical child. Economic disadvantage is similarly transmitted from parents to children. So your parents matter, but your own hard work, your investments, and luck also matter.

intergenerational mobility The extent to which the economic status of children is independent of the economic status of their parents.

Australia, along with countries like Canada, France, Germany and Sweden have more intergenerational mobility than the United Kingdom or the United States (the so-called "land of opportunity"). But even across the United States there are large differences in intergenerational mobility. Researchers have shown that the chances that a child raised in a low-income household makes it to the top quintile of the income distribution varies substantially across U.S. cities, even neighbourhoods within cities. This research shows that the neighbourhood that you grow up in can have a big impact on your outcomes as an adult. Researchers have yet to paint a clear picture of within-country intergenerational mobility in Australia. But it is likely to be, like the United States, that the neighbourhood in which one grows up has a meaningful impact on social mobility.

Interpreting the DATA — Why do people disagree about the extent of inequality?

You now have a robust understanding of the degree of economic inequality in Australia. And this understanding is crucial to resolving some of our fiercest political debates.

The top bar in Figure 7 shows the actual distribution of wealth, while the next bar shows the results of a survey asking people what they think the distribution of wealth is. Comparing these bars, we learn that people don't accurately perceive the extent of wealth inequality. They know that the rich have a large share of total wealth, but they underestimate just how lopsided that share is.

The same survey also asked about what they think the ideal distribution would be, and this bottom bar suggests that people would prefer wealth to be more equally distributed. Taken together, we see that while some of the debate about inequality is driven by differences about what people want, some of it is driven by a lack of knowledge of the facts. ■

Figure 7 | Distribution of Wealth

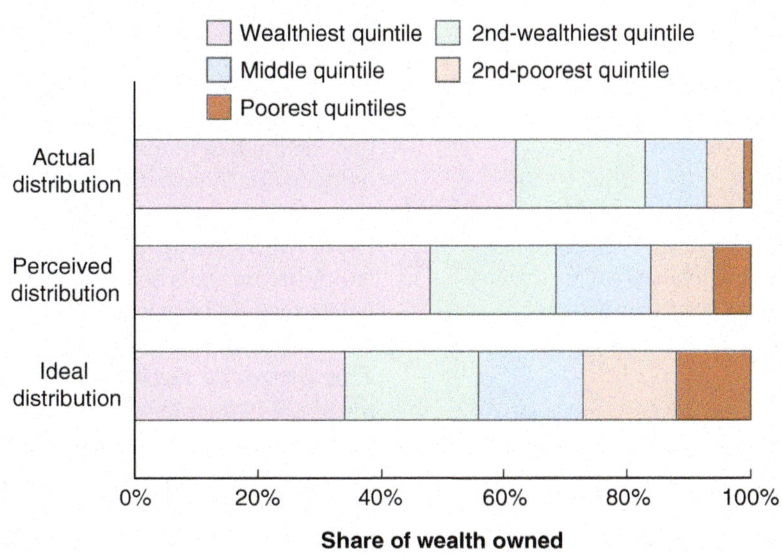

Data from: "The Not-So-Common-Wealth of Australia: Evidence for a Cross-Cultural Desire for a More Equal Distribution of Wealth", by Michael A. Norton et al.

Recapping with a meta observation: How economists collect facts. At this point, it should be clear that measuring inequality is no easy task and that's why people can easily be misled if they hear only one statistic. In fact, if you want to persuade someone of your view, you'll likely find that some statistics are better for your position than others. That's why sometimes people cherry-pick their favorite statistics, which is why you can't always trust what you read or hear.

Notice that you were able to get a useful understanding of inequality by following a recipe that economists often use when trying to learn more about a new area:

- You examined the *current levels* of inequality.
- You dug deeper to see *who* was more or less affected by inequality.
- You analysed how inequality has *changed* over time.
- You compared inequality *across countries*.
- You reexamined the *robustness* of our conclusions to alternative ways of conceptualising, defining, and measuring inequality.

This is a recipe that you'll find tremendously helpful throughout your career. Simply replace the word "inequality" in these bullet points with wages, international trade, taxes, bicycle commuting, vegetarianism, or whatever issue you are trying to learn about, and you'll quickly become an expert.

13.2 Poverty

Learning Objective *Assess the prevalence and implications of poverty.*

Okay, so far we've been analysing inequality. But inequality reflects two phenomena—the abundance of the rich and the poverty of the poor. Many people argue that poverty is the more important phenomenon, and so let's now apply our recipe to understanding the key facts about poverty.

Defining Poverty

If we are going to measure poverty, we have to start by defining it. But defining poverty is not a simple task—in fact, it can be surprisingly controversial. Every country defines poverty somewhat differently, and even within Australia there is more than one definition. But the Organisation for Economic Cooperation and Development (or OECD, of which Australia is a part) has one definition of poverty, so that's a good place to start, though beware that you may come across other measures if you begin looking yourself.

poverty line An income level, below which a family is defined to be in poverty.

The OECD says you are in poverty if your family income is below the **poverty line.** The poverty line is a somewhat arbitrary threshold. In Australia, we define the poverty line as half the median household income of the total population. That is, if the median household income in Australia was $50,000, the poverty line would be $25,000.

poverty rate The percentage of people whose family income is below the poverty line.

How many people are in poverty? The **poverty rate** is the share of people whose family income falls below the poverty line. The poverty rate in 2018 was 8.4% of the population, meaning that roughly one in twelve people were in poverty.

The poverty rate has not changed much over time. Figure 8 shows that the share of people whose income is less than the poverty line has been largely stable at around one in eleven over the past two decades, even though the average income of the population as a whole has increased by 50%. This suggests that those at the bottom of the income distribution have not shared in the rising prosperity of the past two decades.

Notice that the top line in Figure 8 is the poverty rate when housing costs are deducted from income, whereas the bottom line in Figure 8 is the poverty rate before deducting housing costs. The widening gap between the two lines from 2009 suggests that increasing disparities in housing costs prevented the poverty rate from declining after 2009.

Figure 8 | **Official Poverty Rate**

Share of population in poverty before and after housing

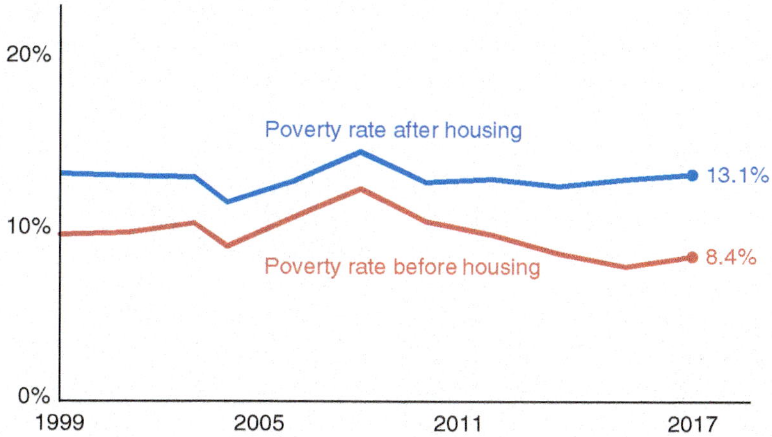

Data from: Australian Council of Social Service and UNSW Sydney.

Absolute versus Relative Poverty

The Australian poverty rate compares people today with a somewhat arbitrary "living standard," namely half the median household income. To understand what this means for making comparisons across time, let's take a look at two different ways of measuring poverty. **Absolute poverty** judges the adequacy of resources relative to an absolute or unchanging standard. By this view, the poverty line measures whether your basic needs are met, assuming a universal, time-invariant standard for basic needs. By this view, the poverty line should be the same in Australia as in Zambia, and the same today as in prehistoric times.

absolute poverty Judges the adequacy of resources relative to an absolute standard of living.

The alternative view is **relative poverty,** which judges poverty relative to the material living standards of your contemporary society. By this view, poverty is not just about physical measures of need, but whether you have the resources necessary to participate in your society. What's considered essential depends on what everyone else in the community has.

relative poverty Judges poverty relative to the material living standards of your contemporary society.

In reality, most people consider something between absolute and relative as a reasonable way to measure poverty, but where to draw the line between the two is the subject of heated debates.

Is the Australian poverty line an absolute or relative standard? The Australian poverty line as we have defined it is an entirely relative standard. This is because it is set at a level that depends on the income of others in society, and we would expect that income is a good measure of material living standards. Of course, there are other countries who take different approaches to defining the poverty line. In the United States, for example, the poverty line is absolute and adjusted for inflation each year. Figure 9 shows the current Australian poverty line of half the median family income, adjusted for inflation. The advantage of the absolute approach is that it tracks through time how many people are below an unchanging standard. The disadvantage is that in most developed countries, living standards have risen over time, and so it has become decreasingly relevant as society has become increasingly prosperous. For instance, in the 1960s, some who weren't in poverty might not have had access to a phone or even running water in their home. These modern conveniences are much more commonplace today.

Which of these alternative poverty lines do you think makes most sense?

Figure 9 | **Alternative Poverty Lines for Households**

Weekly income required to avoid poverty, adjusted for inflation

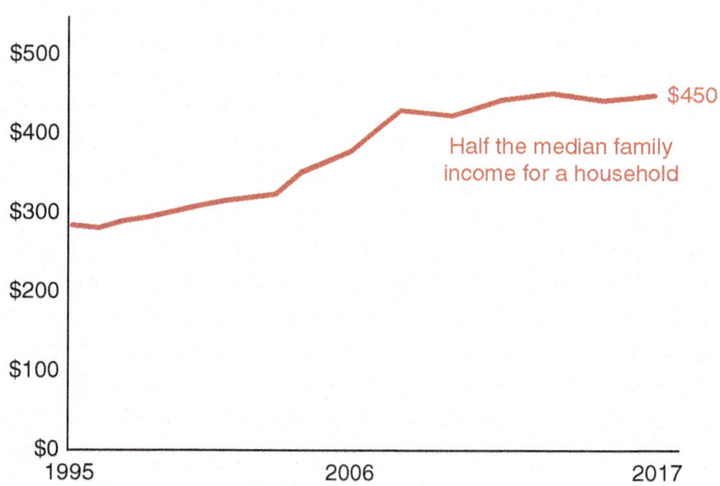

Data from: Australian Bureau of Statistics.

Absolute poverty in a global perspective. The United Nations and the World Bank focus on an absolute poverty line of $2.50 per day. They calculate that this is the minimum needed for human survival in modern times. Globally, 896 million people—including 15% of people in the developing world—are below this poverty line. Under an alternative poverty line of $4.00 per day, the global ranks of the poor rise to 2.1 billion people, or about one-third of all people.

Interpreting the DATA **What is it like to live on $2.50 per day?**

raffaele meucci/AGE Fotostock

She works hard, but has little.

What does it mean to be in poverty? Let's investigate the economic lives of Anuperna and Raja, a couple who are roughly representative of an impoverished family in Udaipur, India. Both Anuperna and Raja work cultivating their land. Raja also works as a labourer; when there's no work nearby he will migrate for a few months and send his meager wages home. Anuperna is also an entrepreneur, making and selling saris. Neither of them are literate. They live with their three kids and Raja's mother in a small two-room house with no electricity, toilets, or tap water. Food accounts for two-thirds of their household spending, leaving little for anything else. They own a bed, but no chairs or tables. While their better-off neighbours have a radio or a bicycle, they do without. Hunger is a key concern, and when income is scarce, they will do without food for an entire day. More often, they make do by eating less in a day than they need to stave off hunger. Of all the deprivations of poverty, this is the hardest, and Anuperna says that she finds it hard to stay in good spirits when she's hungry. Like most of her neighbours, Anuperna is underweight and also anaemic. She, Raja, and the kids are also frequently sick, or weak, but they rarely seek treatment because it is expensive. Instead of complaining, Raja is grateful for the health of her children as around one-eighth of all children in her village die before the age of five. ■

The Australian poor are not members of the global poor. The global poverty line of $2.50 per day is a measure of extreme poverty. This measure is not a very useful benchmark for Australia. This is because Australia has a fairly large social safety net, meaning that an Australian family who found themselves in extreme poverty would be able to access income support payments from Centrelink which would put them above the global poverty line. As such, virtually no-one in Australia is in extreme poverty by the global standard for an extended period of time. For the most part, this is true in other developed countries too, though even in some developed countries (such as the United States) there has been a rise in the rates of extreme poverty in recent decades.

Moreover, throughout most of human history, nearly everyone—even those in rich countries—lived on less than the current Australian poverty line. When considered in either a global or historical context, even those at the bottom of the Australian income distribution have a lot. This is one of the reasons why in Australia, it makes more sense to focus on relative poverty.

Do the Economics

If you believed that the poverty line should be based on public opinion about what is required to "get by," do you think this would lead you to believe that there are more or fewer people in poverty than is measured by the official statistics? ■

Answer: We don't know for sure, but a public opinion poll in the United States found that this alternative poverty line was almost 2.5 times higher (in absolute terms) than the poverty line reported by official statistics. This would lead us to believe that this measure would find more, and not fewer people in poverty.

The Incidence of Poverty in Australia

While there is disagreement about how to measure poverty in Australia, there are a few facts about poverty that turn out to be true regardless of whether one measures poverty using the poverty rate we discussed at the beginning of this section, or alternative measures. First, most people who are in poverty will spend much of their lives in poverty—but most people will spend *some* time in poverty in their lifetime. Second, children and single parents are the most likely to be in poverty. Third, Indigenous people are more likely to experience poverty. Let's take a closer look at each of these facts.

Most poverty spells are short, but most poor people are in long-term poverty. Millions of people both enter and escape poverty each year. Some people spend much of their lives in poverty, while others fall on hard times briefly or even choose to make sacrifices in the short-term, for instance, forgoing income to pursue more education.

There are big differences between experiencing a spell of poverty and a lifetime of poverty. Most *spells* of poverty are temporary, and around half last less than a year. However, at any point in time, long-term poverty is an important problem, and about 700,000 Australians (3% of the population) have been in poverty for 4 years or more. That is, people in long-term poverty are both a small proportion of those who enter poverty, and a large share of the poor at any point in time. The distinction between temporary and long-term poverty is further complicated by the fact that poverty is often recurrent, and over half of all people who escape poverty will return to poverty within five years.

Some groups are more likely to experience poverty than others. Figure 10 shows that while poverty afflicts some more than others, no group is immune to it. The top cluster of bars shows that having an income below the Australian poverty line is much more common among those who are Indigenous. Shockingly, indigenous Australians are almost two and a half times as likely to be in poverty compared to those who are not Indigenous.

Figure 10 | Who Is in Poverty?

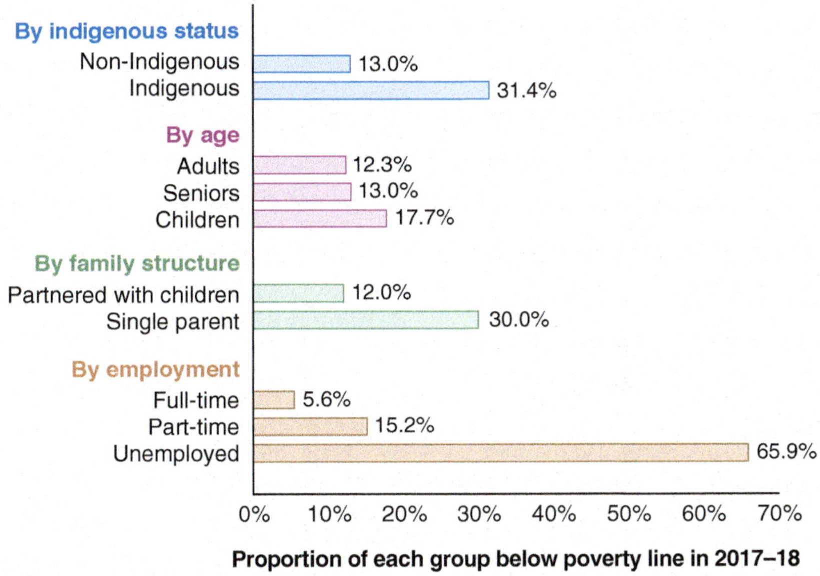

Data from: Australian Council of Social Service.

The next cluster of bars in Figure 10 shows that poverty varies by age. The poverty rate among adults and seniors is comparable to the national poverty rate of 13.6%. Most seniors aged 65 and over have access to the aged pension as well as their life-time retirement savings, so the poverty rate for seniors in Australia, while still lower than the national rate, is relatively high given these considerations. Adults have a lower poverty rate primarily because most of them are working, and if not, they are on some form of welfare. By contrast, child poverty is quite common, and one in six kids are in poverty. That means that you or some of your childhood friends likely grew up in poverty. Even though many people keep it hidden, the fact that a large number of children are in poverty is a reality in most communities.

The third cluster of bars shows another factor that is closely aligned with child poverty. Single parents experience extremely high poverty rates. It's not just a matter of having only one income; single parents also face logistical difficulties juggling work with their child-care responsibilities, and income-based government assistance for single-parent families isn't generous enough to lift them out of poverty. The concentration of poverty among the racial, ethnic, age, and family structures shown in Figure 10 is a long-standing pattern. Moreover, these disadvantages cumulate, families enter into the so-called "cycle of poverty," in which their children, and children's children are more likely to end up in poverty, too.

The deeper cause of poverty is a lack of full-time employment. The bottom cluster of bars in Figure 10 shows that only 5.6% of adults with full-time year-round jobs are in poverty. Those who aren't employed, or could only find part-time or part-year work, are much more likely to be in poverty.

Household and employment changes can trigger a spell of poverty. What precipitates a spell of poverty? The biggest risk is losing a job. Another significant trigger is divorce or separation, which leads family income to be spread across two households. Other changes in the household can also be trigger points for poverty, such as the birth of a child, the death of a breadwinner, or a young adult trying to set up on their own.

All of this reveals a sobering insight: All of us are susceptible to the risks that lead to poverty, including joblessness and changes in family structure. These risks can strike without much warning. Social insurance is designed to help reduce some of the hardship associated with a spell of very little income. Let's turn to exploring what social insurance is and how it works.

13.3 The Social Safety Net, Social Insurance, and Redistributive Taxation

Learning Objective *Discover the ways in which government redistributes.*

The numbers you have seen so far are data on people's incomes before taxes. Once we take taxes and *transfers*—meaning the cash, goods, and services the government provides some people—into account, there is less inequality and less poverty. That's because most governments take actions that help reduce the inequality and poverty that would occur without government.

There are several ways in which government reduces inequality and poverty. Government funds the **social safety net,** which is the cash assistance, goods, and services provided by the government to better the lives of those at the bottom of the income distribution. Part of the safety net are government programs that insure you against bad outcomes such as unemployment, illness, disability, or outliving your savings. These programs are called **social insurance** because it's insurance, but it's provided socially by everyone in society rather than by a private insurance company. Government raises the money for the safety net (and everything else it does!) through taxes—which themselves are an equalising force, since our overall system of taxation is progressive. A **progressive tax** system is one in which those with more income tend to pay a higher share of their income in taxes.

social safety net The cash assistance, goods, and services provided by the government to better the lives of those at the bottom of the income distribution.

social insurance Government-provided insurance against bad outcomes such as unemployment, illness, disability, or outliving your savings.

progressive tax A tax where those with more income tend to pay a higher share of their income in taxes.

Let's explore how the safety net, social insurance, and taxes equalise incomes in Australia.

The Social Safety Net

To help ensure a minimum material standard of living for those at the bottom of the income distribution, the government does more explicit redistribution to those at the bottom through social safety-net programs. The major programs are described in Figure 11.

Let's now analyse the main features of the Australian social safety net.

The safety net is means-tested. In order to ensure that benefits only reach the truly needy, social safety net programs are **means-tested,** which means that your eligibility depends on your income. In addition, some programs also have asset tests to ensure that the idle wealthy don't get benefits.

means-tested programs Programs for which eligibility is based on income and sometimes wealth.

Figure 11 | **Major Australian Government Redistribution Programs**

Program	Provides	Target population	Recipients (millions)	Monthly spending per recipient
Aged pension	Money	Low-income elderly people	2.6	$1627
Family tax benefit Part A & Part B	Money	Low-income families	1.4	$1250
Pharmaceutical Benefits Scheme (PBS)	Health care	All people	25.5	$40
Housing assistance	Subsidised rent	Low-income people, particularly families, elderly, and disabled	1.3	$270

Data on recipients and costs are from 2018. Programs are listed in order of total expenditures.

The elderly are protected by the aged pension; working families are helped by the Family Tax Benefits; individuals and families who need access to medicines receive subsidies through the PBS. Many of those in poverty also qualify for housing assistance. In fact, only those who are already receiving another government benefit (such as the aged pension or Family Tax Benefits) are eligible for housing assistance.

This patchwork of programs means that some people fall through the cracks and don't receive any assistance, while others are eligible for several programs.

The safety net helps support a lot of families. Once we account for the overlap across programs, around 44% of people live in a household currently receiving some form of assistance. An even larger proportion will need this assistance at some point in their lives. Thus, the social safety net provides support for much of the population. This may surprise you if you have never received benefits or you think you don't know anyone who has. But perhaps this is because many people perceive there to be a stigma in relying on the safety net, and so they don't tell friends or family about it.

The safety net provides minimal support. Notice that the typical monthly payments in Figure 11 aren't particularly generous. But these safety net programs often provide enough to raise low-income families with children above the poverty line. Recall that the poverty rate is calculated excluding most of these benefits—direct cash assistance is included, but the other benefits are not.

The safety net includes cash assistance, tax breaks, and in-kind transfers. While some safety net programs provide income or tax breaks, others provide specific goods, which are sometimes called in-kind transfers. For instance, public housing provides about 800,000 Australians in over 400,000 dwellings with subsidised rental accomodation. But this is not a cash payment to recipients—it is effectively a rental discount. Many economists are puzzled by this: Why help people with in-kind benefits, rather than just giving an equivalent benefit as cash? After all, recipients can use cash to buy whatever they most need—food or housing.

There are four key reasons why government provides in-kind benefits rather than cash benefits. First, giving goods rather than cash prevents recipients from making bad choices, such as gambling the money away. Second, taxpayers may care more about reducing homelessness or hunger, rather than about what will make the recipient happiest. Third, providing an in-kind benefit that only the poor will value—such as public housing—makes it more likely that only those who truly need the assistance will get it. And fourth, some in-kind benefits—such as child care—are a complement to work, which helps offset the incentive for recipients to rely on the safety net rather than work.

EVERYDAY Economics **Why parents give gifts rather than cash**

When it comes to birthdays, many parents are a bit like governments, preferring to give gifts rather than cash, despite the fact you could use cash to buy the perfect gift. They do so for similar reasons. Perhaps your parents are worried that you'll make bad choices, spending cash on parties rather than a new warm coat. Or maybe they care more about your success than your happiness. Also, parents understand complements and often give "responsible" gifts to help you succeed—such as an interview suit or a laptop. After all, your success means that you won't need to rely on them for support when you are older. ■

Social Insurance Programs

Don't worry. It's insured.

Rick Friedman/Corbis Historical/Getty Images

Some safety net programs are not means-tested, because they are insurance programs designed to cover everyone—the rich and the poor. You probably know about renters insurance, homeowners insurance, and car insurance: You pay a small amount each month to the insurance company, and if misfortune strikes, your stolen laptop will be replaced, your burnt home will be rebuilt, or your crumpled car will be fixed. Buying insurance is a good way of protecting yourself against these risks. The same logic says that it's also a good idea to insure against the financial risks involved with losing your job, becoming disabled, incurring huge medical bills, or outliving your savings. The problem is that many of the things we want to insure against are difficult for private insurance companies to provide profitably (for more on why see Chapter 19).

Because of failures in the private insurance market, the government steps in to make sure that everyone can get access to certain forms of insurance. It is known as "social" insurance because it is provided "socially"—by your fellow taxpayers—rather than by private insurance firms. Figure 12 outlines the most important social insurance programs in Australia.

Benefits are based on certain bad outcomes. Social insurance—like private insurance—pays you when you experience a bad outcome. JobSeeker exists to provide protection against temporary spells of unemployment. Workers' compensation provides payments and medical benefits if you are injured at work. Disability insurance provides payments if you develop a work-limiting disability. Compulsory superannuation provides income in retirement and therefore insures people against outliving their savings. The "bad" outcome is living longer than you expect or having inadequate savings due to stock market declines or higher than expected inflation (which means your money doesn't buy as many things as you were expecting). Compulsory superannuation, which requires Australian employers to pay an additional 10% on top of their employee's income into the employee's nominated superannuation fund, and which the employee can access after the age of 65, provides a stream of income to the elderly for the rest of their lives to ensure that they don't outlive their savings. Many superannuation funds also provide (at additional cost) life insurance to protect one's dependants against your

Figure 12 | **The Largest Australian Social Insurance Programs**

Program	Insurance against	Paid for by	Beneficiaries (millions)	Average monthly benefit
Medicare	Health Care	All people	25.5	$83
Compulsory Superannuation	Outliving your savings, dying before your kids are grown	Employers are required to pay it	12.9	$527
JobSeeker	Losing your job through no fault of your own	All people	1.5	$1139*
Workers Compensation	Getting injured at work	Employers are required to buy it	0.3	$502
National Disability Insurance Scheme	Developing or caring for someone with a work-limiting disability	All people	0.5	$3113
Private Health Insurance Rebate	Health Care	People with private health insurance	13.6	$36

*Note that the rate for JobSeeker changed substantially during this period (2019-2020) due to the coronavirus pandemic.

Note: The average benefit amount for workers' compensation is the amount spent by employers on total benefits divided by the number of claims in 2018.

early death. Finally, Medicare provides a baseline level of health insurance to all people and therefore covers most, if not all, of the costs of medical care when someone develops health problems. While Australia has what is known as a "universal" health care system—meaning that almost every possible medical procedure under the sun is covered by Medicare—the wait times for certain procedures in the public health system are extremely long (as in, years long), which is why more than half of Australians supplement this baseline level of insurance provided by Medicare with some form of private health insurance.

People pay into social insurance programs. Just like you pay your insurance company a monthly payment to provide you with car insurance, people make regular payments into social insurance programs. Sometimes the money is withheld from workers' wages and sometimes employers pay. For example, the superannuation guarantee levy is 10% of one's income. The Medicare levy is 2% of your income if you earn more than $28,500 a year. Employers pay payroll taxes on workers' wages and are asked to pay a certain amount per worker to ensure that their workers are covered by workers' compensation insurance.

EVERYDAY Economics

Insuring against bad decisions?

Superannuation insures us against outliving our savings; in that way it also insures us against the possibility of making bad decisions about retirement. People who aren't good planners will spend their income having fun today, rather than saving for old age. They only discover what a bad idea this is when they find themselves old, and in poverty. Fortunately, superannuation insures against the risk of making such myopic decisions, ensuring that you'll have enough to get by, and hopefully avoid poverty. But superannuation doesn't guarantee a comfortable retirement, which leads to my advice: When you start your first job, start saving right away. ■

Benefits are based on your past earnings. Superannuation and workers' compensation are a function of your past earnings. Those who have earned more have paid more in, and are eligible to receive more benefits. In Australia, unlike some other countries such as the United States, many social insurance programs are heavily means-tested. This is true of the aged pension, public housing, family tax benefit (parts A and B). Even Medicare involves Australians on high incomes paying an additional surcharge of as much as 1.5% of income if they don't purchase private health insurance. All of these measures reduce costs to the government and allow more generous benefits for those most in need.

kangwan nirach/Shutterstock

You may have a lot in common, but you'll get less insurance marrying someone just like you.

EVERYDAY Economics How marriage provides insurance

Here's an important benefit of marriage: It provides something akin to social insurance. Think about traditional wedding vows: Spouses promise to look after each other "for better, for worse, for richer, for poorer, in sickness and in health." That sounds like a promise to provide unemployment insurance, disability insurance, and health insurance. Just as JobSeeker benefits ensure that you'll still be able to get by when you lose your job, a working spouse effectively provides the same insurance. In both cases, someone—your spouse or the government—will help you pay for groceries if you lose your job. Your spouse can do a better job of insuring you if they don't face the same risks as you do, which is one reason to marry someone who works in a different occupation or at least for a different employer—you're less likely to both experience unemployment if you aren't both working at the same company.

But marriage provides imperfect insurance, because there remains the risk that your spouse will also lose their job. Divorce also provides an escape hatch in which your spouse can fail to provide the promised coverage when a bad event happens. ■

So far, we've examined the redistributive effects of government spending. Let's now turn to analysing the redistributive role played by taxes.

The Tax System

All the goods and services, social insurance, and safety net programs funded by the government are paid for by taxpayers. You've seen so far how spending by the government is used to fight poverty and reduce inequality. Tax dollars fund all of that, but because we don't all pay the same amount in taxes, the tax system itself reduces inequality.

income taxes Taxes collected on all income, regardless of its source.

Federal income taxes are progressive. **Income taxes** are taxes collected on all income, regardless of its source. Income includes earned income from wages and unearned income—such as investment income, pensions, and gifts. The 2021-22 federal income tax bracket for unmarried individuals in Australia is shown in Figure 13. As you can see, the higher your income is, the higher the tax rate that you pay on each additional dollar you earn.

Figure 13 | Federal Tax Rates, 2021–22

For each dollar of income between	Your tax rate is
\$0–\$18,200	Nil
\$18,201–\$45,000	19%
\$45,000–\$120,000	32.5%
\$120,001–\$180,000	37%
\$180,001 and over	45%

While this suggests that the tax system is designed to make sure higher income people pay a higher share of their income in taxes (that is, that it's progressive), it isn't the whole story. Billionaire investor Warren Buffett is often described as the most successful investor in the world. But he's also known for pointing out that he pays a lower tax rate than his secretary. He calculated that he had paid only around 18% of his income in federal income tax, while his receptionist paid around 30%. Is this a widespread problem? Buffett thinks it is. He said:

> I'll bet a million dollars against any member of the Forbes 400 who challenges me that the average federal tax rate including income and payroll taxes for the Forbes 400 will be less than the average of their receptionists.

No one has taken him up on this bet. Let's explore why.

Some investment gains are excluded from income taxes. If you buy an asset for $2,000 and then sell it for $3,000 a year later, the $1,000 gain you make is treated differently from other income. Such gains are taxed in Australia at half one's marginal tax rate. So even the highest-income Australians pay a rate 23.5% on capital gains (half of the 47% marginal rate including the Medicare levy). Because capital gains tax rates are lower than income tax rates, people who earn much of their income from investment gains end up paying a lower average tax rate than people who earn most of their income in wages. Some people think this is unfair, but remember that people have to earn income before they can invest it in the hope of earning a capital gain. And when they earn that income they pay tax at the ordinary rate (as high as 47%). The capital gains discount is really a way of recognising this and avoiding discouraging investment through double taxation.

Higher income people get bigger tax breaks. There's a trick when it comes to the income tax schedule—it only applies to your "taxable income." There are lots of special exemptions that reduce how much of your income counts as taxable income. If you save extra for retirement, the government rewards you by excluding some of what you save from taxable income. If you give to charity this is tax deductible—as are certain business expenses involved in earning income.

Taken together, these exclusions reduce the taxable income of the highest earners the most because they spend more of their money on the types of things for which there are special exemptions. That means that exclusions reduce the progressivity in the tax system.

Many other taxes aren't progressive. Beyond income taxes, there are a raft of other taxes, which taken together are largely regressive. A **regressive tax** is a tax where those with lower incomes pay a higher share of their income on the tax compared to people with higher incomes. Taxes based on the things you buy, rather than the money you earn, tend to be regressive. The reason is that the rich tend to spend a smaller share of their income. The Goods and Services Tax (GST) is an example of this.

regressive tax A tax where those with less income tend to pay a higher share of their income on the tax.

Overall, the tax system is progressive. Let's put the pieces together. The basic income tax scale shown in Figure 13 is progressive, taxing the rich at a higher rate than the poor. But the devil lies in the details, and while these details tend to favour the rich, the tax system still remains progressive. Overall, the poorest fifth of the working-aged population (aged 15 to 64) don't pay any income tax, while the top fifth of such taxpayers pay 71% of all income taxes the Australian government collects. Even regressive taxes such as the GST leave the Australian tax system highly progressive.

13.4 The Debate About Income Redistribution

Learning Objective *Be prepared to join the debate about income redistribution.*

Given everything you've read so far, do you think that the government needs to do more redistribution to combat inequality and poverty, or do you think that it redistributes too much? This question is at the root of many of our fiercest political debates, and it separates left-wing or liberal politicians, who typically advocate for more redistribution, from right-wing or conservative politicians, who usually advocate for less.

utility Your level of well-being.

marginal utility The additional utility you get from one more dollar.

diminishing marginal utility Each additional dollar yields a smaller boost to your utility—that is, less marginal utility—than the previous dollar.

The Economic Logic of Redistribution

Let's begin with the simple logic of redistribution, and explore how it can raise total benefits, or well-being. Money is a means to an end, so when we consider whether redistribution of money is a good idea, it's useful to ask how money affects people's well-being. Economists refer to your level of *well-being* as your **utility.** The *marginal principle* reminds you to think at the margin, and the idea of diminishing marginal benefit also applies to money. That is, your 50,000th dollar—which you might use to pay for entertainment—yields a smaller boost to your utility than your 10,000th dollar—which you will likely spend on food or shelter. To be precise, **marginal utility** is the boost to utility you get from an extra dollar. And because each additional dollar yields a smaller boost to your well-being, you have **diminishing marginal utility.** This means that your marginal utility may be large when you have a low income, but it gets smaller as you get richer.

Tal Cohen/ZUMA Press/Newscom; silentalex88/Shutterstock

Who would benefit the most from an extra $100? Billionaire Clive Palmer? Or this family?

To be concrete, consider Jennifer Walsh, a single mother in South Australia who struggles to pay for her and her son's allergy and asthma medicine. If she had another $100 she could afford to purchase another asthma inhaler. Now imagine instead what billionaire Clive Palmer might do with an extra $100. He likes spending lots of money on questionable political causes, so maybe he'll put it towards the next election campaign. Who do you think has higher marginal utility from the extra $100?

Redistribution can increase total well-being. To find out the role of money in shaping well-being, researchers have asked thousands of Americans to rate their well-being on a 0–10 scale. Figure 14 shows a line of best fit illustrating the average level of

Figure 14 | **Income and Well-Being**

How does income redistribution affect well-being?

Ⓐ The **well-being curve** shows the average level of satisfaction at each level of income. The slope gets flatter as income increases, reflecting diminishing marginal benefits.

Ⓑ If we **redistribute** $25,000 **to the poor**, **from the rich**:

Ⓒ The income of the **poor** person rises from $20,000 to $45,000, and their **well-being rises a lot** (from 5.7 to 6.5).

Ⓓ The income of the **rich** person falls from $200,000 to $175,000, and their **well-being falls a little** (from 7.45 to 7.40).

} Total well-being rises

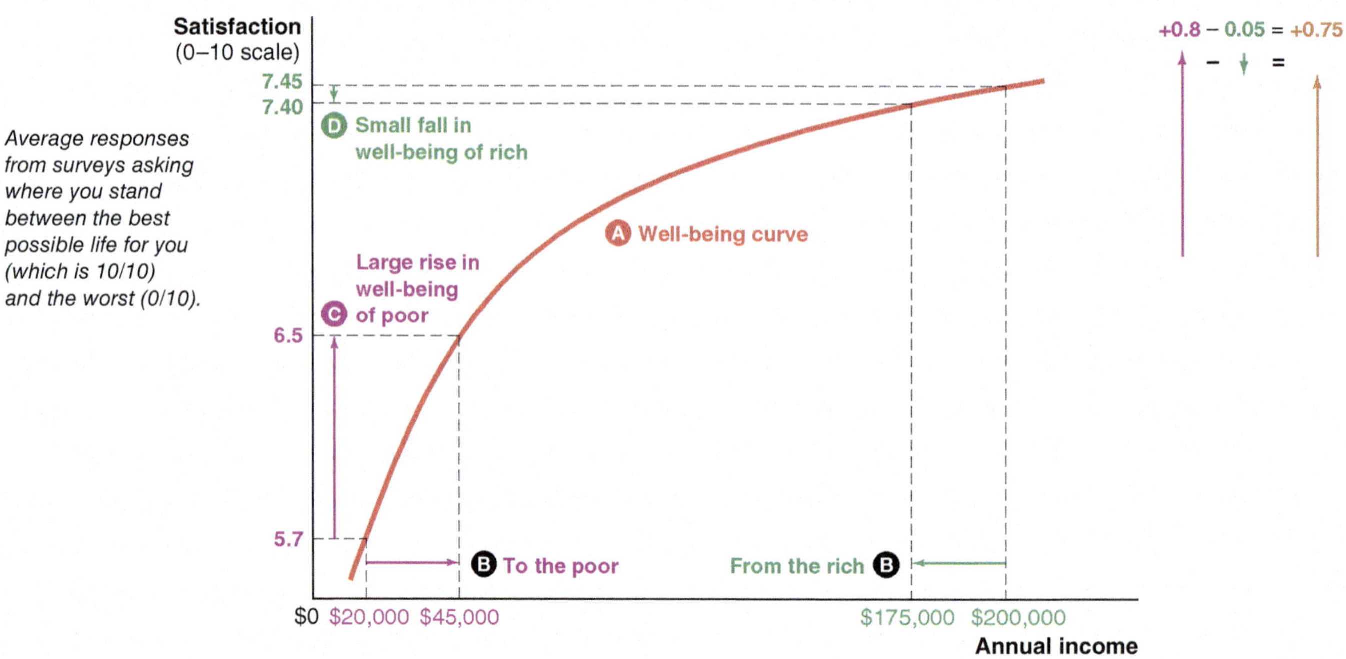

well-being reported (on the vertical axis) at each level of income (on the horizontal axis). The fact that the line is upward-sloping shows that people with more income are happier than those with less income. More importantly, focus on the slope of this curve. The slope illustrates the change in well-being associated with a change in income—the extra benefit from extra income. This curve flattens out as income rises—the slope gets smaller and smaller—which means that the extra benefit of an extra dollar is higher the poorer you are (the slope is larger at low incomes but is smaller at high incomes). That is, these data illustrate a pattern of diminishing marginal benefit from extra dollars.

Now that we've measured the extent of diminishing marginal benefits, we can use Figure 14 to analyse the gains from redistribution. Consider someone in the top fifth of the income distribution earning $200,000, and someone from the bottom fifth, earning $20,000. The well-being curve suggests that we might expect their well-being scores to be 7.45 and 5.7 respectively, which adds up to 13.15. If you redistribute $25,000 from the high-income person to the low-income person, the well-being of the high-income person will fall by 0.05, while the well-being of the low-income person will rise by 0.8. Consequently, this redistribution causes total well-being to rise by 0.75 (from 13.15 to 6.5+7.4=13.9).

The idea of maximising total well-being comes from utilitarianism. The political philosophy that government should try to maximise total utility in society is known as **utilitarianism.** This belief holds that government redistribution is beneficial because transferring $100 from someone with a lot of resources—like Clive Palmer—to someone with fewer resources—like Jennifer—will lead to a society with a higher level of well-being, or utility. That gain arises because taxing $100 of Clive Palmer's income reduces his utility by only a little compared to the utility gain that Jennifer would enjoy from receiving that $100. As such, government can raise total utility by redistributing resources from the rich to the poor.

utilitarianism The political philosophy that government should try to maximise total utility in society.

The Costs of Redistribution: The Leaky Bucket

Even if you consider yourself a utilitarian you face a problem: There's no easy way to redistribute money from the rich to the poor. Redistribution can be like moving money using a leaky bucket—some of the money gets lost along the way. Let's turn to examining the costs of redistribution to see why some of the money gets lost.

Layland Masuda/Moment/Getty Images

A leaky bucket makes redistribution less effective.

Administrative costs subtract from what you can redistribute. The first cost is the bucket itself. There's overhead involved in running social insurance and safety-net programs. New applications for benefits must be processed; auditors make sure that no improper payments are made; policies must be enforced; and payments must be made. All of this is done by government workers, who must be paid. While these administrative costs are the most obvious financial costs of redistribution programs, they're relatively small. As we'll see in a moment, the more important costs arise from how the social safety net distorts work incentives.

Taxes and means-tested programs reduce the incentive to work. Some of the leakage is actually money lost before it is even collected. The problem is that we raise the money to pay for redistribution through income taxes. As you learned in Chapter 11, higher income taxes reduce the rewards from working. When you get a smaller reward for working, you might choose to work less. That's why when the government tries to redistribute money by taxing high earners, those high earners might respond by working less, leaving less money available to be redistributed.

Redistribution is costly, because of:

1. Administrative costs
2. Higher taxes and benefit reductions, both of which can reduce the incentive to work
3. Tax avoidance, evasion, and fraud

. . . which all lead to a leaky bucket.

The presence of a leaky bucket also reduces the incentive to work. The *opportunity cost principle* reminds you that an important cost of working is what you must give up in order to work. Your opportunity cost of work is the benefits you get from whatever you would be doing instead—studying, socialising, taking care of kids or an adult who needs care. The benefit of work is the wage you earn from working. The safety net means that when you work, the relevant opportunity cost is not only your time, but also the potential that you might lose cash or in-kind benefits. If you use the *cost-benefit principle* to decide whether to take a job, the presence of the safety net will make you more likely to turn down a job.

The safety net can also reduce the incentives for people to seek higher paying work. The problem comes from the fact that means-tested benefits are taken away from people as they earn more. That means that recipients not only pay taxes from every extra dollar earned, but they also lose benefits. The sum of higher taxes and reduced benefits accruing from each dollar you earn is called your **effective marginal tax rate.** As the following example shows, those with low incomes can face such high effective marginal tax rates that even though they are earning more through work, their living standards hardly improve at all.

effective marginal tax rate The amount of each extra dollar you earn that you lose to higher taxes and lower government benefits.

EVERYDAY Economics **When earning extra money doesn't pay off**

Phasing out of social assistance programs based on income can lead to very high effective marginal tax rates (EMTRs) that discourage additional work.

> *For instance think about the situation facing Amelia Raen. She's a single mum, living with her two kids, and they each have special needs. Amelia makes $23 per hour so she is eligible for the Parenting Payment from the Australian government. But the income phaseout of the program means that if she works more than 3 days a week she will hardly end up with any more take-home income. This is an example of a very high EMTR.*

This creates what is known as a *poverty trap*. It's a trap because earning a higher income will not improve this single parent's financial situation by much. ■

Higher taxes mean more tax avoidance, tax evasion, and fraud. Because safety net payments are based on your income, there's an incentive to try to make your income appear as low as possible. Likewise, the higher taxes required to fund redistribution provide a strong incentive to engage in complicated accounting tricks to lower your tax bill. These incentives lead to both legal but wasteful *tax avoidance* (doing things explicitly to try to reduce the taxes you owe by taking advantage of loopholes in the tax system), and illegal *tax evasion* (which means not honestly reporting all your income, such as being paid "off the books" and not reporting the income to the Australian Tax Office). When benefits are available only to particular groups, this creates further incentives for wasteful and fraudulent behaviour, such as searching for a doctor willing to classify you as unable to work, or claiming benefits for your kids who actually live with an ex-spouse. To continue the leaky bucket analogy, the problem isn't just that the bucket leaks, it's that some people are actively trying to punch holes in it.

How leaky is the bucket? Okay, so we've surveyed four different ways in which redistribution programs are costly. The first—administrative costs—is fairly small. The remaining three costs are more important. And they are all linked by a common theme—they arise because redistribution distorts incentives. The more that people respond to these incentives, the greater the cost of redistribution. Thus much of the debate about redistribution is between those who believe the costs are high because people are strongly influenced by these financial incentives, and those who believe that the costs are low because people only respond a little to these incentives.

The Trade-Off Between Efficiency and Equality

Let's take stock. Efforts to equalise the distribution of income may help put dollars in the hands of those who value the dollars most, which raises total well-being. But tax and redistribution programs are costly because they distort incentives, thereby reducing work effort. As such, more equal incomes may come at the cost of lower average incomes. Economists refer to this as the *equality-efficiency trade-off.*

To understand the trade-offs, consider the extremes. What would happen if the government redistributed until we all got the same income no matter what? There would be no incentive to work hard, start a new business, or even bother to work since none of your efforts would be rewarded with a higher income. As a result, total production in the economy would plummet. Ultimately we would all be entitled to an equal-sized slice of a pretty small pie.

At the other extreme, imagine a world with no income redistribution. With no safety net programs to finance, taxes would fall, increasing your incentive to work hard, invest, and start new businesses. The size of the pie may grow, but with no redistribution, many of those who are sick, disabled, elderly, or unemployed would be destitute. A larger pie is little solace to those surviving on the crumbs.

So extreme efficiency comes at a cost of terrible inequality, while perfect equality comes at a cost of terrible inefficiency. In reality, no one thinks either extreme makes sense. Instead, our political debates are typically about how much pie to trade off in order to give everyone a fairer share.

canbedone/Shutterstock

canbedone/Shutterstock

Would you choose a bigger pie? Or more equal slices?

Greater equality doesn't always mean less efficiency. But this trade-off isn't a hard and fast rule, and there are cases where there's no efficiency cost to increasing equality. For instance, studies show that societies with greater income inequality typically exhibit less trust, tolerance, and community involvement and more crime. The resulting violence and political unrest can be costly to manage, diverting resources to public safety, prisons, security systems, and other unproductive pursuits.

Income inequality also concentrates political power, which can lead to policies that further increase inequality, such as tax cuts for the rich. These forces may make it difficult for the government to make good policy, by undermining public support for public investment in education, infrastructure, and a clean environment. These adverse outcomes may ultimately lead to weaker economic growth.

There are also instances where social benefits can encourage greater long-term investment among individuals. For instance, paid maternity leave has been shown to increase women's labour force participation. Closing racial gaps in learning may increase long-term economic growth by encouraging further investment in education among a wider group of people. More generally, government investment in both early childhood education and education through university increases worker productivity.

Okay, while it is possible in some cases to make our economy both more equal and more efficient, these cases present the easy choices. But after we exhaust these easy choices, we'll then be stuck with the difficult trade-offs. How do you feel about these trade-offs?

Do the Economics

Let's return to our earlier thought experiment to help you sort out your views about income inequality. Recall that in Figure 14 we evaluated a policy that redistributed $25,000 from each family in the top quintile (earning $200,000) to a family in the bottom quintile (who earned only $20,000). But we didn't account for the leaky bucket. In reality, low-income families will receive less than $25,000, and so greater equality comes at a cost.

- Suppose that 20% leaks out; this would leave a $20,000 grant to the low-income families. Do you think society as a whole would be better off?
- What if 40% leaks out, so each low-income family receives only an extra $15,000?
- What if 60% leaks out, so each low-income family receives only an extra $10,000?

- What if 80% leaks out? Does an extra $5,000 benefit a low-income family more than $25,000 benefits a rich family?
- Where would you draw the line?

It's an interesting thought experiment. If you were to follow the utilitarian logic of maximising total well-being as in Figure 14, even 90% leakage would increase total utility in society. What's your answer? Compare the answer you gave with that of your friends, and it will give you a sense of just how different people's views are about inequality. ■

Fairness and Redistribution

Prasanth Aluri/EyeEm/Getty Images

Are they offering you a fair share?

As much as economists debate things in terms of total costs and benefits, the debate about redistribution is also a debate about fairness. In fact, economists often talk about the trade-off between equity—what's fair or just—and efficiency. But that debate requires settling on a notion of fairness and there are many competing notions of fairness. Your sense of fairness is likely shaped by many different intuitions. It's important to understand these intuitions, because they guide the real-life decisions that you confront every day. As we investigate these different ideas, try to recognise how each of them shapes your own choices. Bear in mind that these different ideas can coexist and each may be important to you, to a greater or lesser degree, or in some settings more than others.

Is fairness about equality of outcomes? One common belief is that *more equal outcomes* are fairer. The following simple experiment demonstrates this. Imagine that I give your friend $10, and I tell them to split it with you in whatever way they see fit. But there's one condition: If you don't agree to the deal they offer, neither of you will get anything. What will you do if they offer you only $1? Go ahead, and think about it before reading the next paragraph. Have you decided how to respond? Okay, read on.

Your accountant would urge you to accept the offer of $1—after all, it's more than the $0 you'll get if you reject the offer. But if you're like most people, you will reject the offer. Experiments repeatedly show that many people reject offers that are below what they regard as a fair share. For most people this idea of fairness is so important that they'll give up what they view as a too small share, rather than accept an an outcome they regard as too unequal. What about you? Would you accept $1? $2? $3? The higher your cut-off, the greater is your willingness-to-pay for fairness. The same reasoning you use in this experiment might lead you to advocate for policies that help create a less unequal distribution of income.

Is fairness about equality of opportunity? An alternative view of fairness emphasises equality of *opportunity,* rather than equality of *outcomes.* The basic idea is that fairness requires a level playing field that ensures that people with the same native talents and ambition can compete on equal terms for higher incomes. Consequently, fairness requires eliminating discrimination on the basis of race, gender, or ethnicity. It also requires ensuring that children from low-income families and disadvantaged communities can compete on equal terms with children whose families provide them with private schools, tutors, and family connections. Typically, this requires redistributing resources—such as through funding of public schools—to ensure that all kids get a fair shot.

Is fairness about the process? Your sense of fairness may also depend on how fair you find the *process* by which inequalities are generated. For instance, think about grading. Most students argue that if the process is fair—the exams are clear, the grading is consistent, and no one cheats—then it's fair that those who did well earn higher grades than those who didn't. These differences are okay when they are the result of a fair process. If you have this sense of fairness, you may think that income differences are okay, unless an unfair process—such as when someone gets rich by stealing—generates them.

Is fairness about what you deserve? Some people think of fairness in terms of what you *deserve*, or what you contribute to society. Unfortunately, the most highly-rewarded people are not always the most deserving. For instance, let's consider the stories of two millionaires. Paris Hilton is a high-school dropout with a criminal record. She's rich, because her great-grandfather founded Hilton hotels, and she inherited some of that wealth.

By contrast, Jo Horgan took a very different path to financial success. After graduating from the University of Western Australia she did a masters degree in mass communication at Boston University. After returning to Australia the London-born Horgan founded Mecca Cosmetica in 1997 at the age of 28. She took a big gamble by selling her own home to open that first small boutique in Melbourne. She launched her own cosmetics brand in 2003 and worked long hours to get the company off the ground. Mecca now has more than 100 stores and in 2020 entered the Chinese market through the e-commerce platform TMall Global.

Michael Tullberg/Getty Images

Is Paris Hilton a deserving millionaire?

Heath Missen/Fairfax Media/Getty Images

What about Jo Horgan?

Do both Paris Hilton and Jo Horgan "deserve" their riches in equal measure? The big difference between them is the role of luck versus hard work in determining their success. If Paris Hilton is representative of those with a lot of money, how much should we redistribute from the rich to the poor? Would you feel differently if Jo Horgan were more representative of those with a lot of money?

Interpreting the DATA **What explains differences in social spending?**

In most developed countries a large share of the population believes that luck plays an important role in determining income. In comparison, in Australia around 40% of the population holds that belief and Australians are more likely to attribute success to hard work. As shown in Figure 15, researchers have found a clear relationship between social spending and the proportion of the population that believes that luck determines income. The more people believe in luck, the more the country tends to redistribute. ■

Figure 15 **Beliefs Determine Social Spending**

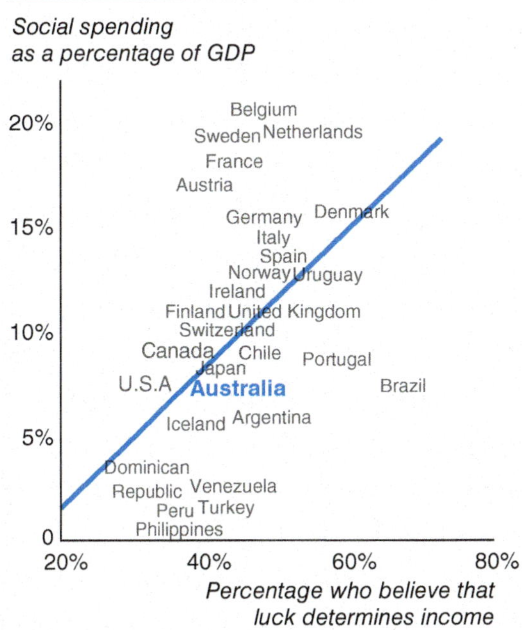

Data from: Alberto Alesina and George-Marios Angeletos (2005), "Fairness and Redistribution."

Is fairness best judged behind the veil of ignorance? As remarkable as Jo Horgan's success is, perhaps it is due to a different kind of luck. She was lucky to be born with intelligence, drive, and entrepreneurial spirit; to be born into a family and community who helped her develop those talents; and in a time and place where her particular skills are highly rewarded. Without this luck, she might be a poor beggar in Mumbai; a struggling single parent in Darwin; or a nomadic tribesman in Africa. The billionaire investor Warren Buffet describes this type of luck as "winning the ovarian lottery." Buffett says his great wealth is due to his luck in being born not just a financial whiz, but also a male, in a supportive family that developed those skills, and in a society that rewards them.

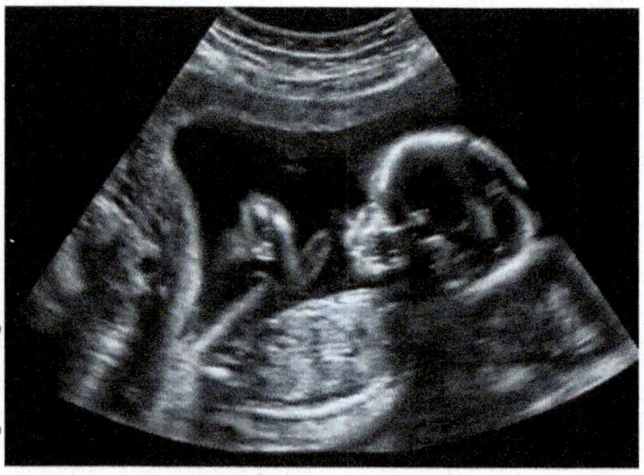

Gagliardiimages/Shutterstock

There's no telling what your circumstances will be.

Before you are born, you haven't done anything to deserve a good or a bad life, and indeed, you don't know what life circumstances you'll be born into. If you could choose, many of you would choose to be born with fortunate circumstances. But you don't get to choose. One way to think about whether society should be more or less equal is to ignore the circumstances you happen to have been born into. Instead, ask yourself what you would want if you didn't know what circumstances you would be born into, what philosophers call behind the "veil of ignorance." It's a powerful way of thinking clearly about what makes for a just society. Behind the "veil of ignorance," what kind of redistribution would you choose?

Is fairness about power and class differences? While economists tend to focus on individuals, sociologists broaden the lens to consider class and group structures. This permits them to analyse how "power" may reside in particular groups, and how inequalities in the distribution of power both cause and result from income inequality. By this view the upper class—the wealthy, the well-connected, those in positions of power—have a lot of control over the political process, and they use this to further their own interests. Even if you don't buy this argument, the deeper point is that your choices and your sense of fairness are likely shaped by your identification with your socioeconomic class, your race, ethnicity, religion, gender, or where you are from.

Okay, so of these different perspectives on fairness, which are "right" or "wrong"? Unfortunately, there's no simple answer, and philosophers and others still debate these issues. So it's up to you to decide how much emphasis to put on different notions of fairness.

Tying It Together

There's an old story about a person who died crossing a stream with an *average* depth of only six inches. Sure, most of the stream was shallow, but parts of it were deep enough to drown them. Just as the depth of the river varies, so do incomes. Just as you can drown crossing a river that is on average shallow, you can fall into poverty even in a country in which average incomes are high. Understanding the economic risks we face requires understanding income inequality and poverty. As we've seen, our high average incomes mask large differences in income, wealth, well-being, and opportunities.

Inequality, poverty, and redistribution are central issues underlying many of our public debates. As a voter, an employer, and a community member, you will be a participant in these debates. This chapter has isolated three key factors that shape your views about redistribution.

First, the logic of redistribution is that it can raise total well-being by redistributing money to the people who can benefit most from it. While nearly everyone agrees on this basic logic, there's a spectrum of views about how important it is. If you think people at the bottom of the income distribution are barely getting by, and so are likely to benefit a lot from an extra dollar, then this provides a powerful argument for redistribution. But perhaps you think this argument isn't so convincing. After all, the bottom of the Australian income distribution still has a high material living standard compared to much of the world. And remember, any dollar we redistribute to a needy family comes out of some other family's budget. The higher the marginal utility of an extra dollar to the families being asked to give up income, the weaker the case for redistribution. You're now an informed player in this debate: You've seen the actual data on the distribution of income. So where are your views along this spectrum?

Second, redistribution occurs via a leaky bucket. The costs of redistribution—the leakage—exist because redistribution also distorts incentives, reducing work effort. Again, there's a spectrum of views about how leaky the bucket is. If people respond strongly to these distorted incentives, then the bucket is extremely leaky. But perhaps people are only vaguely aware of these disincentives, or financial incentives aren't the key factor motivating people to work hard. If so, the bucket may not be that leaky. So far empirical studies haven't fully resolved this debate.

And third, your views about redistribution will depend on your values, not just how much you value fairness, but also which concepts of fairness are most important to you. Some perspectives on fairness lead to a greater emphasis on redistribution, and others suggest less. How much weight would you put on equality of outcomes, versus equality of opportunity? And even if you subscribe to equality of opportunity, there's a spectrum of views about what that means. To what extent are we all born with an opportunity to succeed, or do income disparities create unequal opportunities that need to be redressed? Or consider the role of hard work versus luck. How much do income disparities reflect luck—the inherited privilege of the rich, and the bad luck of the poor—versus hard work? Are the processes that lead to economic disparities fair?

There are differences of opinion in how to answer each of these three questions. But don't let that controversy distract you from a broader truth: Nearly everyone agrees that the right analytic framework for analysing redistribution involves asking: (1) How large are the benefits of redistributing income to those who most benefit from it? (2) How large are the costs due to the leaky bucket? And (3) How fair is this redistribution? Now that you're equipped with this analytic framework, and also a good sense of the data, it's time to draw your own conclusions. Think hard—these issues shape important choices that you'll face in your family, your work life, and your community.

Chapter at a Glance

Income Inequality: The differences in annual income between people.

Alternative measures of inequality:

- **Permanent income:** Your average lifetime income
- **Inequality of opportunity:** Lack of intergenerational mobility
- Wealth
- Consumption

Poverty

Poverty line: An income level, below which a family is defined to be in poverty.

Absolute poverty: Judges the adequacy of resources relative to an absolute standard of living.

Relative poverty: Judges poverty relative to the material living standards of your contemporary society.

Spells vs. People: Even though a large share of people will experience a short spell of poverty, most of those currently in poverty are in a long-term spell of poverty.

The Ways in which Government Redistributes

Social safety net: The cash assistance, goods, and services given to those at the bottom of the income distribution.

- Means-tested → Eligibility is based on income and sometimes wealth.
- Minimal support → lifts about a third of people living in poverty out of poverty.

Social insurance: Government-provided insurance against bad outcomes such as unemployment, illness, disability, or outliving your savings.

- Benefits are based on uncertain outcomes
- Everyone pays into social insurances
- Benefits are based on past earnings

Taxes: Pay for the safety net and social insurance.

Progressive tax: A tax where those with more income tend to pay a higher share of their income in taxes.

Federal income taxes are progressive, however some things reduce overall progressivity in the tax system:

- Investment gains are taxed at a lower rate
- Higher income people get bigger tax breaks
- Many other taxes aren't progressive

Analyzing Redistribution

Question 1: How large are the benefits of redistributing income to those who most benefit from it? → **The Benefits of Redistribution**

A. The slope of the well-being curve gets flatter as income increases, reflecting **diminishing marginal benefits**.

B. If we redistribute **to the poor**, **from the rich**:

C. The well-being of the **rich falls a little**.

D. The well-being of **the poor rises a lot**.

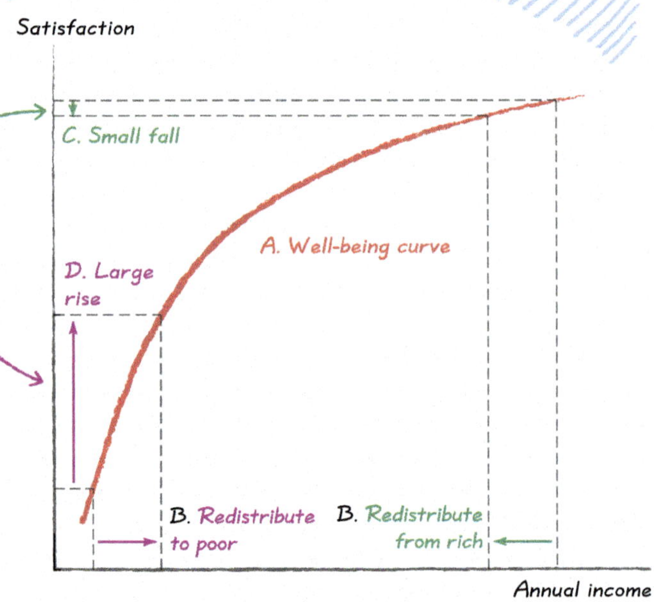

Question 2: How large are the costs due to the leaky bucket? Consider:

- Administrative costs
- Higher taxes ↓ work incentive
- As do benefit reductions
- Tax avoidance, evasion, and fraud

Question 3: How fair is this redistribution? Consider:

- Equality of outcomes
- Equality of opportunity
- Fair processes
- What you deserve
- Veil of ignorance
- Power and class

Key Concepts

absolute poverty, 323
diminishing marginal utility, 332
effective marginal tax rate, 334
income, 318
income taxes, 330
intergenerational mobility, 321
marginal utility, 332
means-tested programs, 326
permanent income, 320
poverty line, 322
poverty rate, 322
progressive tax, 326
regressive tax, 331
relative poverty, 323
social insurance, 326
social safety net, 326
utilitarianism, 333
utility, 332
wealth, 320

Discussion and Review Questions

Learning Objective 13.1 *Measure the extent of economic inequality in Australia.*

1. Discussions of inequality often focus on income inequality. What are two other measures of inequality—and why is it important to consider more than one measure?
2. In Australia, the richest quintile of the population receives 5.4 times as much income as the poorest quintile. However, the richest quintile only spends 2.7 times as much as the poorest quintile. What are some of the reasons that there is such a stark difference between income inequality and consumption inequality?
3. Given your experience and what you've learned from the chapter, what factors lead to a high income? Which are under your control and which are not?

Learning Objective 13.2 *Assess the prevalence and implications of poverty.*

4. Explain whether the Australian poverty line is an absolute or relative measure.
5. If we think about what the poverty line would have been 100 years ago, not everyone who was in poverty had access to a phone or running water in their homes. What are some things you think are necessary to enjoy a reasonable standard of living today? How much do you think it would cost to achieve that reasonable standard of living?

Learning Objective 13.3 *Discover the ways in which government redistributes.*

6. Two of your friends are in a heated debate. Elena says that the rich pay higher taxes, and Warren argues the rich pay lower taxes by cheating the system. Which of them is correct? Are there ways in which both of them are partially correct? Discuss.

Learning Objective 13.4 *Be prepared to join the debate about income redistribution.*

7. Several studies suggest that the availability of free or low-cost child care increases labour force participation, particularly for mothers. In other words, redistributing to low-income mothers by giving them access to low-cost child care leads them to work more hours. What does this insight say about whether greater equality always comes at a cost of lower efficiency?
8. Imagine that you are preparing your will and are trying to decide how to divide your assets between your two grown children. Your daughter Tonya is a chemical engineer who earns a high income. Your son Terry opted out of university and went to work straight out of high school. Now Terry works in construction; he works just as hard as Tonya, but he is less affluent than she is. Elaborate on each of the following concepts about fairness and distribution illustrated in the chapter.
   a. Split your wealth evenly between Terry and Tonya, because you always treat them equally.
   b. Leave Terry your wealth to offset the income gap between him and his sister.
   c. Leave your money to the child who you think deserves more money.
   d. Tell your kids you'll leave your money to whoever does the most to take care of you in your old age.
   e. Leave your money to charity instead.

Study Problems

Learning Objective 13.1 *Measure the extent of economic inequality in Australia.*

1. The accompanying table contains data on the share of income in each of Australia's states/territories. Pick one and sketch out its income distribution similar to Figure 1. How much larger a share of the income does the highest-income quartile earn compared to the lowest? Using what you learned in the text, if current trends continue, how do you expect the share of income going to the highest-income quartile to change in the next 20 years?

Average Annual Family Income

State	Lowest Quartile	Second Quartile	Third Quartile	Highest Quartile
New South Wales	25.0	24.7	24.4	26.0
Victoria	25.1	25.4	25.3	24.1
Queensland	24.9	26.0	25.6	23.4
South Australia	24.8	26.7	27.0	21.5
Western Australia	24.4	23.2	23.5	28.9
Tasmania	26.7	28.0	26.5	18.8
Northern Territory	18.5	21.6	28.2	31.8
Australian Capital Territory	18.2	20.2	26.5	35.2

2. Johanna's parents earn about 30% more than the average household. What does this tell you about Johanna's likely income as an adult given the estimates of Australian intergenerational income mobility discussed in this chapter? What would it tell you about her income if Australia had perfect income mobility?

3. In Australia, we are inundated with statistical claims and information daily—in politics, in media, and in advertising. How do you determine whether a statistic is useful or misleading? Explain your reasoning.

Learning Objective 13.2 *Assess the prevalence and implications of poverty.*

4. Your classmate David tells you that you don't need to worry about people in poverty because most spells of poverty are short. Explain his possible misunderstanding of poverty.

5. Renika has $100,000 dollars in wealth, but the official poverty statistics count her as being in poverty. Explain why this is. If Renika has quit her job in order to go to university, and $100,000 reflects her cash savings, do you agree that she is in poverty? What if Renika is elderly and the $100,000 reflects the value of her rural home?

Learning Objective 13.3 *Discover the ways in which government redistributes.*

6. At Christmas, your uncle complains that he pays taxes for no reason because the government just hands cash out to people who don't truly deserve or need it. He then says, "The system would work if they made sure people who receive help are the ones who really need it." What tools does the government use to help ensure aid goes to those in need? How can you explain the safety net system to him in an objective way?

7. Your friends, knowing you have studied economics, have started asking you for some advice. Briefly explain a government assistance option that may be available to them in each of the following scenarios.

   a. Your friend Carla has been employed by the same company for two years but was recently laid off.

   b. Your cousin Simon always pays his rent on time, but he earns so little that he often doesn't have enough food at the end of the month.

   c. Your roommate Chelsea fell while at work and broke her leg. She won't be able to return to work and do her job properly until the injury fully heals.

   d. Your friends Jaden and Sandy were doing fine, but since the birth of their new child, their income is strained. They worry about providing medical care for their baby.

8. One way to levy a tax on the things people buy is through a sales tax—a tax on purchases that is typically a percentage of the purchase price. For example, in 2000 the Australian Federal Government under John Howard introduced a "Goods and Services Tax" (GST), requiring that all Australians pay a 10% sales tax on their purchases of "non-essential" goods and services (the GST does not apply to items like housing, health care, and certain food). Do you think that this tax is progressive, regressive, or neither? Do you think that it has the same impact on low-income and high-income families? Why or why not?

Learning Objective 13.4 *Be prepared to join the debate about income redistribution.*

9. At a classroom holiday party, there is a slight shortage of lemonade, so that three people will not have any if everyone at the front of the line fills their cups.

   a. One parent tells students to fill their glasses only two-thirds, so that everyone can have some lemonade. Under what notion(s) of fairness is this a fair outcome?

   b. A student at the front of the line says that everyone had the same chance to line up, and therefore, those who were goofing around and ended up at the back of the line should lose out and have tap water instead. Under what notion(s) of fairness is this a fair outcome?

   c. What do you think a utilitarian would do?

10. Using the figure below, calculate the gain from redistributing $25,000 from those earning $100,000 to those earning $50,000. Why do you think that this gain in well-being is smaller than the redistribution in the example in the chapter, which redistributed from someone earning $200,000 to someone earning $20,000? What are some potential problems with this redistribution plan?

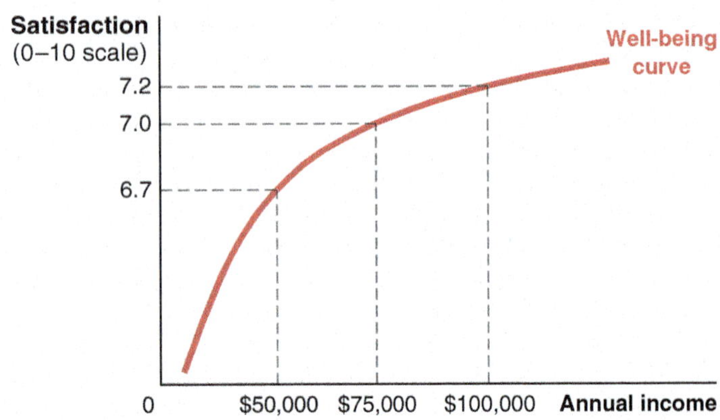

11. Your friend Burrell says that the government should hire fewer social workers in order to reduce the cost of federal assistance programs. He says reducing administrative costs will allow people to pay much lower taxes. Identify the possible flaw in his argument.

PART IV:
Industrial Organisation and Business Strategy

Part IV: Industrial Organisation and Business Strategy

The Big Picture

In this part, we'll explore the messy reality of **imperfect competition**–whether due to monopoly, oligopoly, or monopolistic competition–in which **market power** plays a central role. We'll analyse why businesses value market power, how managers **set prices** when they have market power, and how it creates a conflict between what's most profitable for a business, and what's best for society.

We'll confront some of the most important decisions you'll face as a manager. We'll see how the **entry** of new rivals can shake up an industry, and highlight the strategies that managers pursue to protect their profitability. We'll survey the **sophisticated price strategies** that businesses use to exploit their market power.

We'll then analyse how your **product positioning** affects the type and extent of competition you face. And we'll explore how you can protect your **bargaining power** when negotiating with your suppliers and your customers. All of these ideas are important in creating a successful **business strategy.** We'll examine how these ideas come together in the **five forces** framework, which top executives use to assess their long-run profitability.

Finally, business strategy is like an economic chess match, and so we'll investigate **game theory,** so that you have the toolkit you need to zero in on your best choice in any strategic interaction.

14 Market Structure and Degrees of Market Power

Learn how to set prices when you have market power.

- How does the structure of competition in your market shape your business's market power?
- What pricing strategy will earn you the largest profits?
- How does market power distort market forces?
- How can government policies limit the abuse of market power?

15 Entry, Exit, and Long-Run Profitability

Learn how to remain profitable in the long run.

- What determines your business's long-run profitability?
- How will the entry or exit of competitors affect your business, your profits, and your market?
- What barriers make it hard for start-ups to enter a market, and how can you overcome them?

16 Price Discrimination and Sophisticated Pricing Strategies

Learn to implement sophisticated pricing strategies.

- Why do businesses charge different prices to different people?
- Why is it important to target discounts to the right customers?
- How can you most effectively segment your market?
- Why do businesses sometimes offer a better deal, but make it a hassle to get it?

17 Economics of Strategic Management

Learn to guide strategic decisions that you will make as a manager.

- What are the five forces that shape your business's long-run profitability?
- How can you best position your product relative to your competitors?
- How can you bolster your bargaining power to get a better deal?

18 Game Theory and Strategic Choices

Learn to guide the strategic decisions that you'll make throughout your career and everyday life.

- What are the steps to making sound strategic decisions?
- How can everyone acting in their own best interest lead to a worse outcome for everyone?
- Why can it be difficult to coordinate with your allies to make complementary choices?
- When is there a first-mover advantage, and when are you better off delaying?
- Can repeated interactions lead people to become more cooperative?

Market Structure and Degrees of Market Power

CHAPTER 14

The story begins with a 21-year-old named Steve fooling around with electronics in his parents' garage. Eventually, Steve decided to get serious about building computers, so he and his pals started a company. He was experimenting with a fruitarian diet, so perhaps it's no surprise that he decided to call their company Apple. That garage-built business went on to become the first company to be worth more than $1 trillion. It's more valuable than Samsung, IBM, and HP combined. What makes Apple so profitable?

Bart Pro/Alamy Stock Photo

It all started in Steve Jobs' garage.

Popular accounts focus on Steve Jobs' obsessive perfectionism, his drive for innovation, his vision, and his commitment to designing beautiful objects. Perhaps. But maybe the most important factor was that Jobs really understood economics, and he used that to guide his strategic decisions.

Crucially, Jobs focused his strategy on starting and dominating new markets, rather than trying to compete against existing businesses. Take the iPhone: This innovation essentially started the smartphone market. Today, Samsung, Motorola, and HTC all compete to make Android phones, but only Apple makes the iPhone. Something similar happened with tablets, where the innovation of Apple's iPad led Apple to dominate the tablet market. Even though companies that compete to make Android tablets have gained ground, only Apple sells the iPad. Likewise, Lenovo, Dell, and HP all compete to make Windows computers, while if you want to use macOS, you have to buy an Apple computer.

The result is that Apple faces fewer direct competitors, which allows it to raise prices and enjoy healthy profit margins. By this telling, much of Apple's success comes from developing and exploiting market power.

This chapter is all about understanding the structure of competition in your market, and how it shapes your market power and pricing strategies. Along the way, we'll see how it can become important for the government to intervene, to protect the forces of competition.

Chapter Objective

Learn how to set prices when you have market power.

14.1 Monopoly, Oligopoly, and Monopolistic Competition
Evaluate how market structure shapes the market power your business has.

14.2 Setting Prices When You Have Market Power
Calculate the best price to set when you have market power.

14.3 The Problem with Market Power
Assess how market power distorts market forces.

14.4 Public Policy to Restrain Market Power
Assess policies to limit the problems caused by market power.

14.1 Monopoly, Oligopoly, and Monopolistic Competition

Learning Objective *Evaluate how market structure shapes the market power your business has.*

It's critically important to tailor your business's strategy to the specific competitive environment you face. Do you have a lot of competitors, only a few strategic opponents, or are you the only business selling your good? Do you expect new competitors to enter your industry and try to steal market share? Are your products exactly the same as those of your competitors? Or are you offering different goods, better service, or higher-quality products? Together, these factors describe the structure of your market and they determine the extent and type of competition you'll face.

market power The extent to which a seller can charge a higher price without losing many sales to competing businesses.

Market structure is important, because it shapes your **market power,** which is the ability to raise your price without losing many sales to competing businesses. The more market power you have, the higher the price you can charge.

For instance, if you own the only petrol station in town, then you have some market power, because very few of your customers will drive 20 kilometres for slightly cheaper petrol. But if you own one of four petrol stations at a busy intersection, then you have almost no market power—if you raise your price even pennies above those of your competitors, your customers will buy their petrol elsewhere.

Gerhard Zwerger-Schonermage/iBROKER/Alamy Stock Photo

No bargain hunting here.

Perfect Competition

A petrol station operating at an intersection with other competing petrol stations is likely facing a perfectly competitive market. Recall that much of our analysis so far has focused on perfect competition, including our initial analysis of supply in Chapter 3. **Perfect competition** occurs when your competitors sell an *identical* good and there are *many sellers and many buyers,* each of whom is *small* relative to the size of the market.

If you're doing business in a perfectly competitive market, you have no market power. You could try charging more than the prevailing market price, but you'll lose all your customers to rivals who are offering an identical product at a lower price. And there's no point charging less than the prevailing price, because as a small business you can sell whatever quantity you want at the prevailing market price. Lowering your price will only lower your profit margin. As a result, your best choice is to be a *price-taker,* which means that you simply take the market price as given and follow along, charging the prevailing market price.

perfect competition Markets in which 1) all businesses in an industry sell an identical good; and 2) there are many sellers and many buyers, each of whom is small relative to the size of the market.

In addition to petrol stations operating at intersections with other competing petrol stations, there are a few other examples of perfectly competitive markets: agricultural markets (for example, many small strawberry farmers, each selling the same product); commodities markets like gold, oil, wheat, livestock (there are many sellers, each of whom is selling nearly identical products to a global market); and the stock market (on any given day, there are thousands of people selling identical stock in Apple, BHP, or Telstra).

But in reality, perfect competition is relatively rare. Most goods are not identical, and in many markets there are a handful of dominant players. The dearth of perfect competition is a natural result of managers hustling to accumulate market power by differentiating their products, squeezing out their rivals, and deterring new entrants.

So why did we start by learning about perfectly competitive markets? Partly, because it's simpler. It's easier to generate insight into the production decisions of businesses when we don't need to simultaneously consider their pricing decisions. And our supply-and-demand analysis—which is built on perfect competition—yielded useful intuition about how competition plays out. All markets involve some degree of competition, and so these building blocks will be useful as we turn to formulating business strategy.

Okay, that's it. You've just read the last sentence in this book focusing on perfect competition. As we move on, the key new ingredient we're adding is market power. When you have market power, you don't want to be a price-taker passively following the prevailing market price. Instead, you need to figure out the price that best exploits your market power. And so our task in the rest of this chapter is to figure out how your competitive landscape shapes your market power, and how that market power leads you to make different pricing decisions.

We'll start by analysing monopoly, oligopoly, and then monopolistic competition. But don't focus too much on the distinctions between these types of markets. Most managers focus instead on their market power, which is aligned along a spectrum.

monopoly When there is only one seller in the market.

Monopoly: No Direct Competitors

Look down at your pants. See the zipper? Chances are that it says "YKK." That stands for Yoshida Kogyo Kabushikikaisha, which is the company that makes nearly all of the world's zippers. YKK is an example of a **monopoly,** which means it's the only seller in the market. If you're a monopolist, you have a lot of market power because you can raise your price without losing customers to your competitors. After all, you don't have any direct competitors!

Mark Collinson/Alamy

Is this what a monopoly looks like?

Oligopoly: Only a Few Strategic Competitors

Now, look in your pocket. I bet you found a mobile phone. And that mobile phone probably gets service from Telstra, Optus, or Vodafone. This is an example of an **oligopoly:** a market with only a handful of large sellers.

oligopoly A market with only a handful of large sellers.

Managers of oligopolistic businesses are locked in a strategic battle for market share. When you have only a handful of rivals, their decisions can have a big impact on your bottom line. And this means that it's critically important that you think through how your rivals will respond to your choices. Indeed, your best choices depend on how your rivals will respond, just as their best choices depend on how you'll counter.

Oligopolies have market power, though not as much as a monopolist. That's because when Telstra raises its prices, it loses some customers, but not all of them. Telstra may hang on to many of its customers because its rivals respond by also hiking their own prices. In some areas the competing networks are too patchy to induce Telstra's customers to switch. And some customers remain loyal—either out of a strong preference for Telstra, or simply out of inertia.

Mobile Phone Market

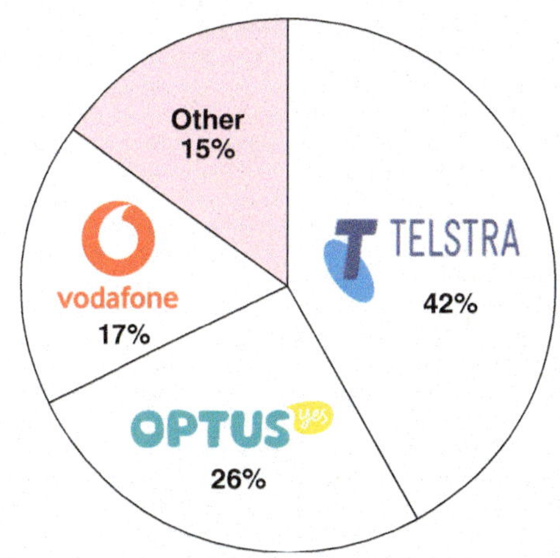

Data from: Statista.

Monopolistic Competition: Many Competitors Selling Differentiated Products

Now look at your pants. Have you ever noticed how there are thousands of different styles? Just think about jeans. They can be bootcut, straight leg, skinny, or flared. They can also be low-rise, classic, or high-rise. They can be raw denim, acid washed, stonewashed, or vintage washed. You can get five pockets, flap pockets, zipped pockets, or side pockets. They can be done up with a button or zip fly. And they can be dark, neutral, light, or faded; blue, green, red, black, or brown.

Different varieties of jeans have proliferated because sellers are seeking market power through a strategy called **product differentiation.** By making each product slightly different from their competitors, sellers hope to make each specific variety especially attractive to a particular group of customers. In turn, they figure that you'll be willing to pay more for a style the more it flatters you. This gives the seller market power, because the most devoted followers of a particular brand or style will stick with it, even if the price is higher. Product differentiation doesn't just involve differences in what you sell. Savvy managers also differentiate their products based on brand image, quality, store location, customer service, return policies, and packaging. Successful product differentiation can create market power even when you face hundreds of competing sellers, because some customers want the precise variety you offer, and they'll pay a little more to get it. In other words, the more distinct you make your product, the less your rivals' products will be a close substitute.

product differentiation Efforts by sellers to make their products different from those of their competitors.

starkovphoto/Deposit Photos

Product differentiation yields market power.

monopolistic competition A market with many small businesses competing, each selling differentiated products.

The jeans market is an example of **monopolistic competition.** This occurs when there are many competing businesses, each selling somewhat differentiated products. It's a useful term, highlighting the fact that such markets are both *monopolistic* and *competitive.* The jeans market is *monopolistic* because there's only one seller making each specific model of jeans. But it's also *competitive* because there are dozens of businesses competing to sell you jeans.

Market Structure Determines Market Power

The structure of your market matters, because it shapes your market power. As Figure 1 shows, the structure with the least market power is perfect competition, where many small businesses sell identical products. At the other extreme, monopolists have the most market power, because they're the only business selling a unique product. Rather than focusing on sharp distinctions between these market structures, Figure 1 emphasises that there's a spectrum along which some businesses have more or less market power.

Figure 1 | **The Spectrum of Market Power**

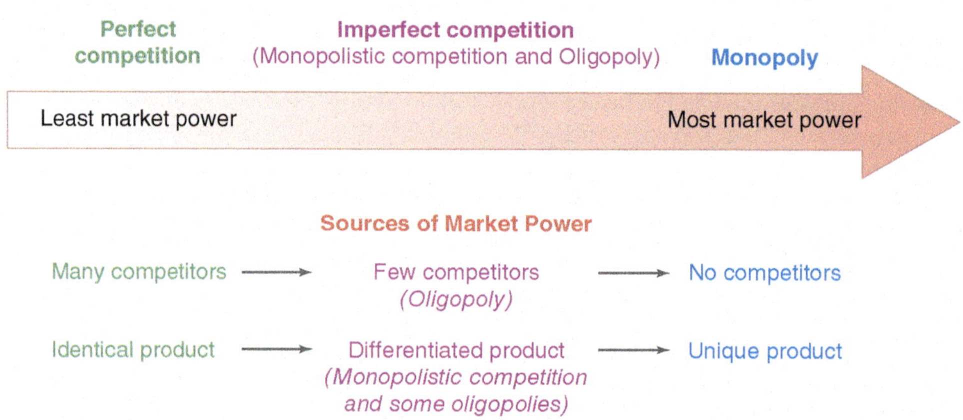

The lower part of Figure 1—the bits below the large arrow—shifts attention from the four specific market structures to the underlying sources of market power. It illustrates that you have *more market power* when you have *fewer competitors,* and when your products are *more unique.*

NearTheCoast.com/Alamy

Even a monopolist in the zipper market faces competition in the broader market for fasteners.

imperfect competition When you face at least some competitors and/or you sell products that differ at least a little from your competitors. Monopolistic competition and oligopoly are examples.

Perfect competition and monopoly are both rare. In reality, few businesses populate the extremes of this spectrum. Perfect competition is rare, because your competitors rarely sell products that are identical to yours. For instance, even though competing petrol stations sell similar products, they differ in convenience (some are closer to your house than others), their petrol includes different chemical additives, and they offer different customer service. Likewise, pure monopoly is rare. Once you broaden your definition of the market sufficiently, you'll find that every business faces at least some competition. For instance, even though YKK dominates the zipper market, its customers could always use button flies instead, which means that YKK has competitors in the broader market for fasteners.

Most businesses operate in imperfectly competitive markets. It's most likely that your business will lie in the intermediate range of **imperfect competition,** which includes monopolistic competition and oligopoly. The term is apt, because you'll face *competition*, but it will be *imperfect*—either because you only have a few competitors or because you sell somewhat different products than your competitors.

An earlier generation of economists focused on drawing sharp distinctions between monopolistic competition, oligopoly, and monopoly. But over time, economists have come to understand that different industries don't neatly fit into one bucket or the other, partly because the structure of markets is constantly evolving.

We'll take that more modern view, focusing on the broader insights that apply to all imperfectly competitive markets. This view emphasises that there's a spectrum of market power, reflecting the number and type of rivals, and how different their products are. It recognises that your business doesn't operate in a static market structure, but rather in a competitive environment that changes in response to the strategies employed by duelling businesses. And it recognises that your best strategies depend on the particulars of your specific market. That's why we'll focus less on market structure, and more on the "deep forces" which both shape your business's market power, and inform the strategies that managers pursue.

Five Key Insights into Imperfect Competition

Our brief tour so far points to five big insights that will set the agenda for the rest of our study of business strategy.

Insight one: Market power allows you to pursue independent pricing strategies. The pricing strategies you'll want to pursue in imperfectly competitive markets are sharply different than those you'd employ under perfect competition, where you're a price-taker who simply charges the prevailing market price. Instead, when you have market power, you can set your own price, but you face a difficult balancing act: Raising your price will boost the profit margin on each item you sell, but it'll also reduce the number of items you sell. Managing this balancing act is crucial to earning a healthy profit. It's so important that we'll spend the rest of *this* chapter exploring how managers in imperfectly competitive markets set their prices.

You can also use your market power to charge different people different prices. Do it right and you'll both expand your market and boost the profit margin you earn on your most devoted customers. We'll explore how to do this in Chapter 16, on Price Discrimination and Sophisticated Pricing Strategies.

Insight two: More competitors leads to less market power. The more competitors selling their wares in your market, the less market power you'll have. The logic is simple: If your customers have many good alternatives to buying from you, they'll be less likely to stick with you if you raise your price. When new rivals enter your industry, they both grab your market share and reduce your market power. If the competition is fierce enough, your competitors may compete away all of your profits.

It follows that your long-run profitability depends on how many rival businesses enter your market. That in turn depends on whether there are barriers preventing the entry of new businesses into your market, and how porous those barriers are. But those barriers to entry aren't simply a naturally occurring defense—to some degree, they're also the result of your strategic choices. These strategic choices are so central to your long-run profitability that we'll devote all of Chapter 15, on Entry, Exit, and Long-Run Profitability to assessing the strategies you can pursue to deter new entrants from competing your profits away.

Insight three: Successful product differentiation gives you more market power. The more different your product is from that sold by your rivals, the less likely it is that your customers will find them to be a useful substitute if you hike your price. As a result, successful product differentiation gives you more market power.

Savvy managers understand that these differences in product attributes are not a fixed attribute of your market. Rather, you get to choose the attributes of your product, and so you face an important strategic choice about how best to position your products. Smart product positioning can boost your market power and hence your profitability. These decisions are a key part of the *marketing* function in most businesses, and they're sufficiently important that we'll spend the first half of Chapter 17, on Economics of Strategic Management, figuring out how best to position your product.

Insight four: Imperfect competition among buyers gives them bargaining power. So far we've mostly focused on the imperfect competition between rival *sellers* in a market. But in many cases, there's also imperfect competition among a limited number of *buyers,* making it important for managers to keep their most valuable clients. This gives buyers a degree of bargaining power which they'll use to demand lower prices.

You'll want to use this insight to negotiate a better deal with your suppliers. After all, you're not just a customer—you're one of their most valuable clients. But realise that your big customers will also try to exploit their bargaining power to extract a better deal from you. Ultimately, your profits depend on managing this conflict well—using your bargaining power as a valued client to extract low prices from your suppliers, while fending off demands from your important clients that you lower the price you charge them. We'll dig more deeply into how to improve your bargaining power in the second half of Chapter 17, on Economics of Strategic Management.

Insight five: Your best choice depends on the actions that other businesses make. The *interdependence principle* is particularly important in imperfectly competitive markets, as your best strategic choices likely depend on the choices that others make. And their best choices also depend on the decisions that you make.

This interdependence arises in all of the strategic decisions described above, including pricing, entry, product positioning, and bargaining with buyers and suppliers. For instance, the best price for your goods depends partly on the prices offered by your rivals, and whether they're trying to steal your customers. This interdependence is fundamental to business strategy—and one of the most fun topics in economics. We'll explore it in detail in Chapter 18, Game Theory and Strategic Choices, so that you develop the tools you'll need to analyse strategic interactions.

Do the Economics

Assess the market power of the following sellers:

Your broadband provider.

rvlsoft/Alamy

Apple, whose iPhone competes with the Android phone.

Gary Glaser/Shutterstock

A scalper selling concert tickets through StubHub, an online marketplace. ■

Answers: 1. In many towns there is only one cable company, meaning that this monopolist has substantial market power. 2. Apple competes with Android, but there are only a handful of mobile phone makers, making this an oligopoly in which each supplier has moderate market power. 3. There are hundreds of tickets available for most concerts, and they're each priced similarly, so no individual seller has much market power.

We've set the agenda for the next few chapters. It's time to focus on our first task. As a manager with market power, you're no longer a price-taker, so you need a pricing strategy.

14.2 Setting Prices When You Have Market Power

Learning Objective *Calculate the best price to set when you have market power.*

Figuring out what price to charge is one of the most important business decisions you'll make. It's a difficult balancing act. If you set your price too low, your profit margin will disappear. But if you set your price too high, then you'll barely sell anything. *You face a trade-off between selling a larger quantity of items versus making more money on each item you sell.*

Figuring out how best to evaluate this trade-off is going to be a lot easier once we've introduced two new analytic tools—your *firm's* demand curve, which summarises your market power, and the marginal revenue curve, which measures your incentive to increase production. Let's master these tools now, and then in a few pages' time, we'll use them to uncover an intuitive approach to pricing.

Your Firm Demand Curve

Your **firm's demand curve** summarises how the quantity that buyers demand from your individual firm varies as you change your price. Notice that your *firm's* demand curve focuses on the quantity demanded from your specific *firm*. In contrast, the *market* demand curve describes the quantity demanded across all firms in the entire market. (It's also different from an *individual* demand curve which describes the quantity demanded by a single *buyer*.)

firm demand curve An individual firm's demand curve, summarises the quantity that buyers demand from an individual firm as it changes its price.

Your market power determines the shape of your firm's demand curve. Consider first the extreme in which you have no market power, as in *perfect competition*. This situation is shown in the far left of Figure 2. With no market power, raising your price by even a penny will lead you to lose all your customers. Likewise, if you lower

Figure 2 | **Your Firm's Demand Curve Depends on the Type of Competition You Face**

Market type	Perfect competition	Imperfect competition: Monopolistic competition	Imperfect competition: Oligopoly	Monopoly
Competitors	Many	Many	Few	None
Products	Same product	Differentiated product	Same or differentiated product	Unique product

Least market power → Some market power → Most market power

With no market power, raising your price a penny above the market price means you'll sell nothing. Lower it a penny, and you'll sell a huge quantity. A basically **flat demand curve**.

You have some market power, and hence a higher price will lose some, but not all, customers. Similarly, a lower price will gain some, but not all, customers. A downward-sloping **firm demand curve**.

As the only seller in the market, you don't need to worry about competitors, and the demand for your goods is equal to the market demand. Firm demand is the **market demand curve**.

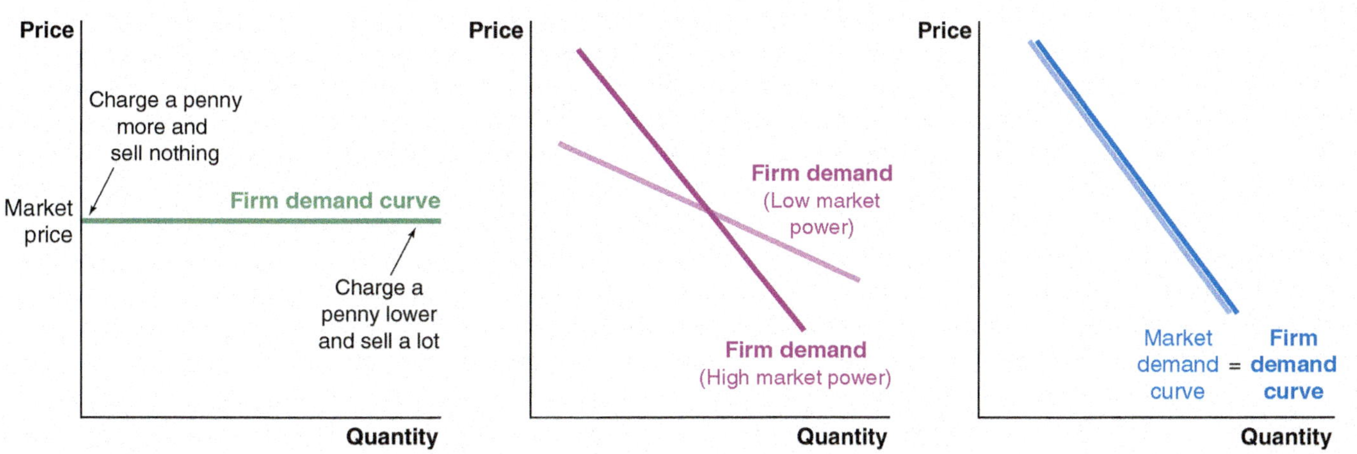

your price by just a penny, your competitors will lose all their customers to you, boosting your sales enormously. As a result, your firm's demand curve is essentially flat because when there are many competitors selling the same product—perfect competition—a minuscule change in price leads to a nearly infinite change in the quantity you sell.

The far right of Figure 2 shows the other extreme. If you are a *monopoly*—the only seller serving the market—then the quantity demanded from your firm is the same as the total quantity demanded by the entire market. As a result, a monopolist's firm demand curve is also the market demand curve. Even though you have no competitors, a higher price will still lower the quantity demanded, because your customers still have the option of not buying your product.

Taken together, Figure 2 summarises the close link between market structure, market power, and the price elasticity of demand along your firm's demand curve. The two extremes bracket the more realistic case of *imperfect competition,* where you have some market power. Unlike perfect competition, you can raise your price without losing all of your customers. And unlike a monopolist, you face some competitors, and so raising your price will lead you to lose market share. Your firm's demand curve can be relatively flat, or steep, depending on how much market power you have. If you don't have much market power, then raising your price will sharply reduce the quantity you sell, and so your firm's demand curve is relatively flat. (Alternatively phrased, it's highly elastic.) By contrast, if you have a lot of market power, a price hike will lead you to lose very few sales, and so your firm's demand curve is relatively steep (which is the same as saying it's quite inelastic).

Experiment with your price to discover your firm's demand curve. Okay, how would you figure out how much market power you have and hence the shape of your firm's demand curve? Here's how businesses actually do it in practice: They experiment with the price they charge, and see how the quantity demanded varies in response. Indeed, research indicates that around 90% of retailers conduct pricing experiments.

Sometimes managers experiment with offering different prices to different *groups of customers.* For instance, when Amazon wanted to figure out its demand curve for popular movies, it programmed its website to show different prices to different customers. By comparing the quantity demanded by customers shown high prices with the quantity demanded by those shown low prices, they could map out their firm demand curve. (The customers who later learned they were offered a higher price were furious.)

Alternatively, some retailers experiment by charging different prices at *different locations.* For instance, the educational toy retailer Zany Brainy experimented with the price of a kids' toy called the "Leapfrog Phonics Traveler," charging $24.99 at some stores, $29.99 at a group of similar stores, and $34.99 in a third set of stores. The first group of stores sold 33 units, the second group sold 26, and the third group sold 15. Figure 3 shows the estimated firm demand curve, plotting the quantity demanded at each price (and then joining the dots).

If you don't have different locations, you can experiment by charging different prices over *time,* assessing how much higher the quantity demanded is when the price is lower.

Experimenting with the price you charge—whether it's to different customers, in different locations, or at different times—can reveal your firm's demand curve. And even though these experiments can be expensive, they're often worth doing, because charging the wrong price can be even more expensive!

Figure 3 | **Estimating Zany Brainy's Firm Demand Curve**

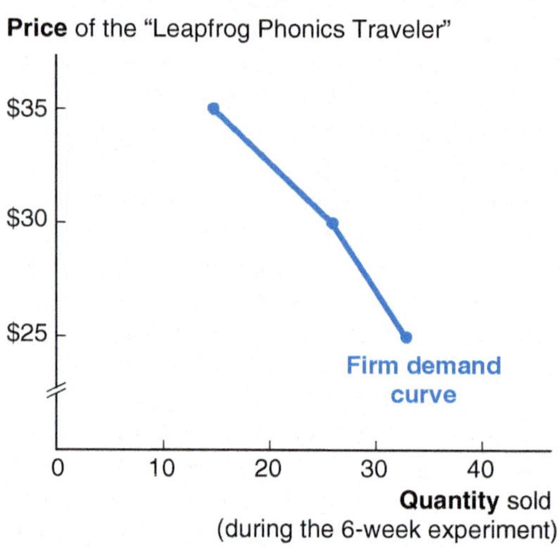

Do the Economics

Sofia runs a Mazda dealership in Perth, Western Australia. When she advertised the new Mazda 2 at $23,000, she sold two cars per week. She then experimented with a discount, cutting the price to $22,000, which led her to sell three cars per week. A further price cut to $21,000 led sales to rise to four cars. And the week she experimented with a price increase, hiking the price to $24,000, she sold only one car.

Plot the results of Sofia's pricing experiments in the graph at right to discover her business's demand curve. ■

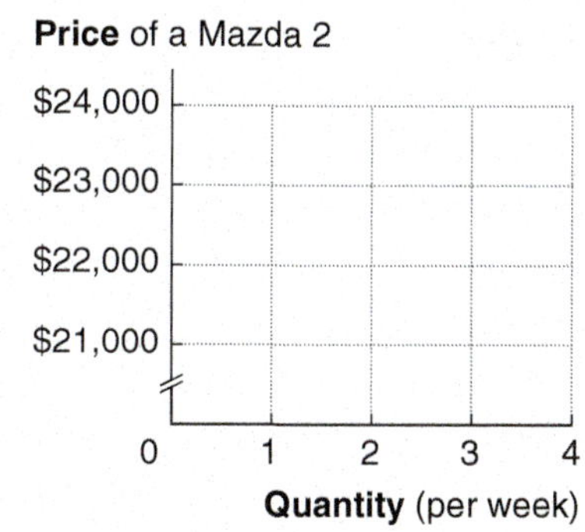

Your Marginal Revenue Curve

Your firm demand curve is a critical input to making smart pricing choices, because it describes the trade-off between selling a larger quantity at a low price versus selling a smaller quantity at a higher price. Let's explore how to use your firm's demand curve to trace out how these alternatives affect your revenue.

Good decisions focus on marginal revenue. Sofia wants to use the data she compiled in her pricing experiment to figure out what quantity of cars she should aim to sell, at what price.

Before proceeding, a reminder: The *marginal principle* tells you to break big decisions into smaller marginal decisions. So instead of asking how many cars she should sell, Sofia should ask whether she should sell one more car. To answer this, she needs to figure out her **marginal revenue**—the addition to total revenue she gets from selling one more car.

marginal revenue The addition to total revenue you get from selling one more unit.

Calculate marginal revenue as the change in total revenue from selling one more unit. You can use the data Sofia collected on her firm's demand curve to calculate and plot her marginal revenue. To do this, she follows three steps. First, calculate total revenue, which is simply the price you charge times the quantity you sell. Second, assess her marginal revenue, which is the change in her total revenue from selling an additional car. Third, plot the results and you'll get the marginal revenue curve, shown in Figure 4.

Figure 4 | **Discover Your Firm's Marginal Revenue Curve**

Use your firm demand curve to calculate your marginal revenue.

Step ❶ *Calculate total revenue*: Your total revenue is simply the price you charge (*P*), multiplied by the quantity you sell (*Q*).

Step ❷ *Calculate marginal revenue*: This is the additional revenue you earn from selling each extra car.

Step ❸ *Plot the marginal revenue curve*. You'll discover that it lies below your firm's demand curve.

Sofia's Pricing Experiments

Sofia's experiments reveal the total quantity of cars that buyers demand from her dealership at each price.

Price (*P*)	**Quantity** (*Q*)	❶ **Total Revenue** (*P* × *Q*)	❷ **Marginal revenue** (Change in total revenue)
$24,000	1	$24,000	$24,000
$23,000	2	$46,000	$22,000
$22,000	3	$66,000	$20,000
$21,000	4	$84,000	$18,000

Your **Firm's Demand Curve** and your **Marginal Revenue Curve**

Demand: How many cars do buyers demand from Sofia at each price?

Marginal revenue: What is the extra revenue from selling one more car?

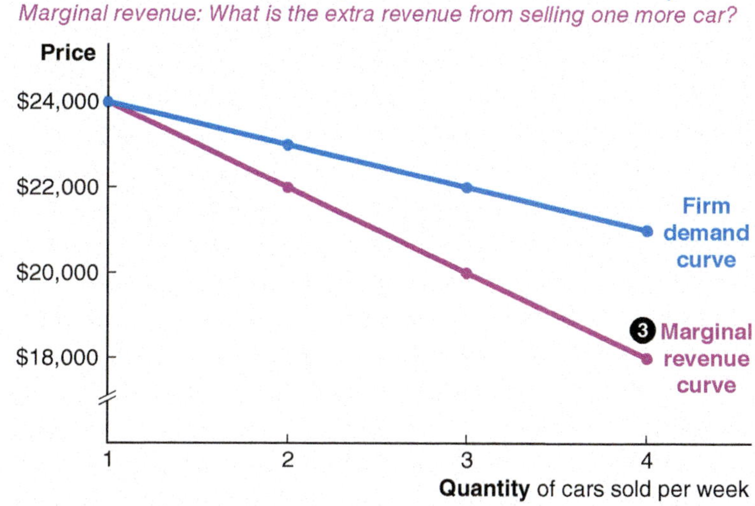

Marginal revenue reflects the output effect, minus the discount effect. Look closely at the table and the graph in Figure 4, and you'll see we've just discovered something important: The marginal revenue Sofia gets from selling one more car is less than the price shown on the demand curve. This is true for all imperfectly competitive businesses. To see why, realise that there are two opposing forces affecting marginal revenue:

- *The output effect:* If Sofia sells one more car, her revenue will rise by the price she gets for it. This is the output effect: An extra unit of output will boost her revenue by an amount equal to the price of the extra item sold, *P*.
- *The discount effect:* To sell that one extra car, Sofia will have to lower her price a bit, which cuts into her revenue. Because this lower price applies to *all* of the cars she sells, even a small price cut might lead to a pretty big decline in revenue. This is the discount effect, and it's equal to the price cut—that is, the discount she needs to give to sell one more car (call it ΔP, where the triangle symbol means "change")—multiplied by the quantity she sells: $\Delta P \times Q$. (If this feels new to you, it is. Under perfect competition you can sell whatever quantity you want without needing to change your price, and so the discount effect is zero.)

Your marginal revenue =

Output effect (*P*)
(which is the price of the extra item you sell)

–

Discount effect ($\Delta P \times Q$)
(the price cut you'll have to offer × the quantity that gets that price cut)

Recall we began this section by noting that: *You face a trade-off between selling a larger quantity of items versus making more money on each item you sell.* Your marginal revenue curve neatly summarises the terms of this trade-off. It tells you how much you'll gain from selling a larger quantity of items (we call this part the output effect), less the revenue you'll lose when you cut your price a bit, so you're not making as much money on each item you sell (this bit's the discount effect). Marginal revenue is the output effect, less the discount effect, and so it reflects the balance of these forces.

Marginal revenue lies below the demand curve, and it declines faster. Let's put together what we've learned about firm demand curves and marginal revenue.

1. If you have market power, you can raise your price without losing all of your customers. This means your firm's demand curve is downward-sloping.
2. Due to the discount effect—that is, the need to cut your price a bit to sell that extra item—your marginal revenue from selling one more item is less than the price you charge for it. This means that your marginal revenue curve lies below your firm's demand curve by an amount equal to the discount effect.
3. The discount effect is bigger when you sell a larger quantity, because a price cut for many customers reduces revenue more than a price cut for just a few customers. As a result, the gap between your firm's demand curve and marginal revenue widens as the quantity you sell increases. That's why your marginal revenue curve declines more sharply than your firm's demand curve.

Figure 5 | Your Marginal Revenue Curve

A Your **firm's demand curve** is downward-sloping.

B **The marginal revenue curve** lies below the price shown on the demand curve, due to the **discount effect**.

C The **marginal revenue curve** declines more sharply than your **firm demand curve**, because the larger the quantity you sell, the bigger the **discount effect** ($\Delta P \times Q$).

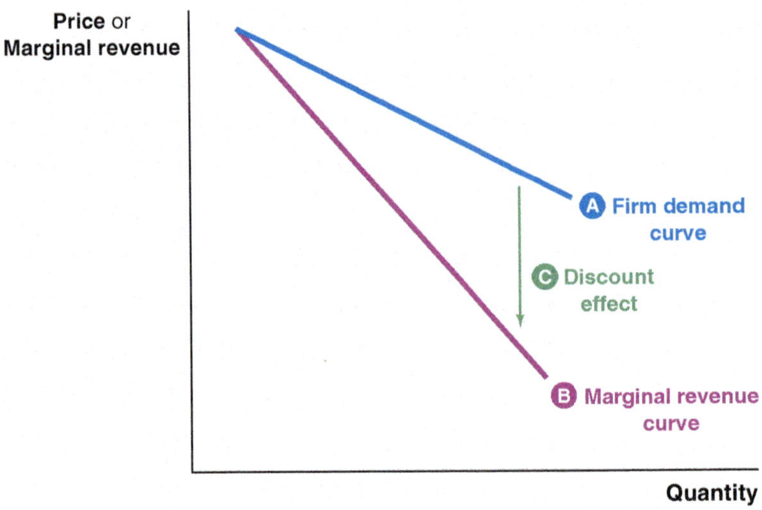

Figure 5 also illustrates a helpful graphing trick: When the demand curve is a straight line, the marginal revenue curve is also a straight line that starts at the same point (when the quantity is one), but it declines twice as sharply.

Finally, and perhaps most importantly: Even though marginal revenue is related to your firm's demand curve, don't make the mistake of saying that they're the same thing.

The Rational Rule for Sellers

Okay, so now it's time to put yourself in Sofia's shoes and make some business decisions. We're going to do this in two steps as illustrated below in Figure 6. In step one, we'll figure out what quantity to produce, and then in step two, we'll figure out what price to charge.

(Study tip: Remember, first calculate the quantity to produce, and then figure out what price to charge. Why do things in this order? It's simpler. While it's possible to analyse the price first, it's *much* more complicated.)

Step one: Keep selling until your marginal revenue equals your marginal cost. So, how many cars should you sell? You should immediately recognise that this is a "how many" question, and simplify it using the *marginal principle*. It's simpler to ask instead: Should I sell one more car? Now apply the *cost-benefit principle*, which suggests that yes, you should, as long as your marginal benefit from selling that car—which is the marginal revenue you'll earn—exceeds (or equals) the marginal cost. That's it! You've just discovered the Rational Rule for Sellers.

Step 1: Set the quantity where *marginal revenue = marginal cost.*

Step 2: Set your price on the demand curve.

The **Rational Rule for Sellers:** *Sell one more item if the marginal revenue is greater than (or equal to) marginal cost.*

The Rational Rule for Sellers Sell one more item if the marginal revenue is greater than (or equal to) marginal cost.

This is a pretty intuitive rule. It says to sell another car if doing so will boost your revenue by at least as much as it boosts your costs. It follows that each car you sell will boost your profits. (When marginal revenue and marginal cost are exactly equal, your profits will neither increase nor decrease. The rule says to still sell that last item, mainly because it'll make the rest of your analysis simpler.)

If you follow this rule and take every opportunity to sell cars when they'll boost your profits, then you'll keep selling until:

$$\text{Marginal revenue} = \text{Marginal cost}$$

Figure 6 | **Setting Prices and Quantities with Market Power**

How many cars should Sofia sell, and what price should she charge?

Step one: What quantity should you produce?

A The Rational Rule for Sellers says to keep producing until marginal cost equals marginal revenue.

B *Look down* to see the quantity, which is 3.

Step two: What price should you charge?

C *Look up* to your firm's demand curve to find the highest price you can set and still sell this quantity.

D This occurs at a price of $22,000.

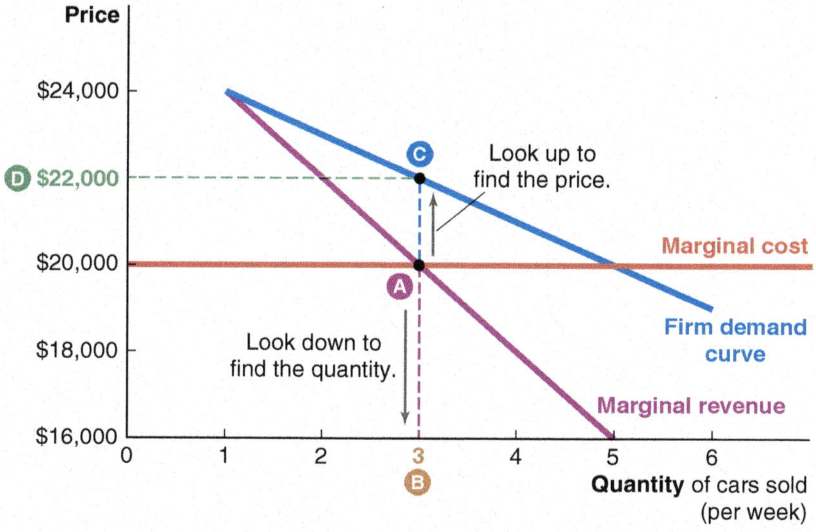

You probably recognise this as a version of the *Rational Rule* that we discovered in Chapter 1, adapted to sellers. That rule said: If something is worth doing, keep doing it until your marginal benefits equal your marginal costs. Applying that idea to a seller, it says: If it's profitable to sell cars, keep selling them until *marginal revenue equals marginal cost.*

In fact, this is the most important advice I can give any seller, so let me repeat it: To figure out what quantity to sell, keep selling until marginal revenue equals marginal cost. This occurs where the marginal revenue and marginal cost curves meet, as shown in Figure 6.

Step two: Set your price on the demand curve (not the marginal revenue curve). OK, so we've figured out what *quantity* to produce. Now it's time for step two, choosing what *price* to charge.

You should always charge the highest price you can, as long as you can sell the quantity you've decided on in step one. You can figure this out by looking at your firm's demand curve: For the specific quantity you've decided to produce, *look up* to the firm demand curve to see what price to charge.

Be careful, because this is a step where students often make the mistake of just looking to see where the curves cross. You look to where marginal revenue and marginal cost cross to figure out the *quantity* to produce. Don't make the mistake of looking at marginal revenue to figure out what price to charge. Rather, realise that the maximum price you can charge is all about what your customers are willing to pay. And so you should look up to the demand curve to see what price you can charge, given this quantity.

Here's a simple memory trick to help you remember the two steps: Once you've found where marginal revenue cuts marginal cost, *look down* to see your quantity, and *look up* to find your best price.

Remember:
1. *Look down* to see your quantity.
2. *Look up* to find the price.

OK, that's it. You now know how you should set prices whenever your business has market power. Want proof that these two steps lead to the largest possible profit? Let's work through Sofia's profit and loss statement.

Do the Economics

Calculate the weekly profit that Sofia will make for each price and quantity combination. Her profit is simply her total revenue (*Price* × *Quantity*), minus total cost, which can be calculated by noting that each car costs her $20,000.

Sofia's Profit and Loss Statement

Quantity (*Q*)	Price (*P*)	Total revenue (*P* × *Q*)	Total cost (*Q* × $20,000)	Marginal revenue (Change in total revenue)	Marginal cost (Change in total cost)	Profit (Total revenue − total cost)
1	$24,000	$24,000	$20,000	$24,000	$20,000	$4,000
2	$23,000	$46,000	$40,000	$22,000	$20,000	$6,000
3	$22,000	$66,000	$60,000	$20,000	$20,000	$6,000
4	$21,000	$84,000	$80,000	$18,000	$20,000	$4,000

Marginal revenue equals marginal cost. Maximum profit

If Sofia follows the *Rational Rule for Sellers,* she will keep selling until her marginal revenue equals marginal cost, which occurs at a quantity of three cars. This decision leads her to earn a profit of $6,000 per week.

To confirm that this was the best decision, look at the final column, which shows the total profit that Sofia earns based on each alternative. Check and you'll see that the *Rational Rule for Sellers* led her to the highest possible profit. ■

There's one more fact worth noticing about Sofia's decisions. If she cut her price even further to $21,000, then she would sell one more car. This implies that there's a buyer out there who would get $21,000 worth of benefits from that car. But each car only costs Sofia $20,000. This suggests that selling one more car could make society better off. But Sofia chooses not to sell that fourth car, because it doesn't make *her* better off. This illustrates a very important point: When businesses have market power, the market outcome does not maximise total economic surplus. To see that even more vividly, we'll have to travel to Africa to see how market power nearly cost millions of people their lives.

14.3 The Problem with Market Power

Learning Objective *Assess how market power distorts market forces.*

RAJESH JANTILAL/Getty Images

AIDS treatments were unaffordable for millions.

When scientists discovered that antiretroviral drugs could dramatically extend the lives of people living with AIDS, the world rejoiced. But those celebrations were premature. The scientific problem had been solved, but soon an even bigger economic problem arose. AIDS drugs were priced at around $10,000 per year to treat a single patient. For the drug companies, this meant large profits selling drugs to people who could pay. But for the millions of AIDS victims in sub-Saharan Africa, this price was so unaffordable as to be effectively a death sentence.

Today, the same drugs are now available in poor countries for only $100 per year, and millions of lives have been saved. And it's all due to the efforts of savvy health activists who used their understanding of economics and market power to save lives. It's an amazing story which also illustrates why it can be a good idea to restrict market power.

Market Power Leads to Worse Outcomes

Fatima knew that she wanted to use what she had learned in university to make a difference. She was deeply concerned about the unfolding AIDS crisis, and so when she graduated, she jumped at the opportunity to work for a nonprofit devoted to helping the millions of sick people who couldn't afford the astronomical price of AIDS drugs.

Her team considered many different strategies. For instance, for every $10,000 Fatima raised, her nonprofit could afford to buy a year's supply of life-saving drugs for one more person. While this makes a difference, millions would still die. Her nonprofit briefly flirted with the idea of trying to develop new and cheaper drugs, but they quickly learned that developing new drugs often requires an investment of billions of dollars. Sex education could help prevent the spread of AIDS, but it would do nothing for those already infected. None of these ideas addressed the AIDS crisis in a compelling way.

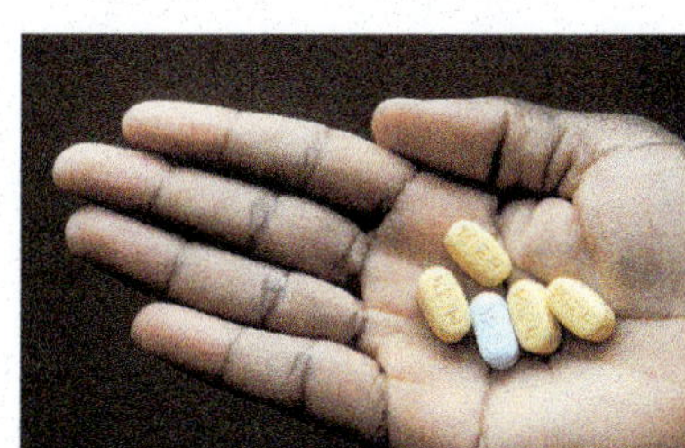

Friedrich Stark/Alamy

If these lifesaving drugs cost so little to make, why was their price so high?

Exasperated, Fatima decided to dig into the economics, investigating why AIDS drugs were so expensive in the first place. The answer startled her: They're not expensive to make. The research required to discover a new drug can cost billions of dollars. But once the formula for an effective drug has been developed—and with AIDS drugs, it has already been developed—it's actually quite cheap to manufacture each dose. In fact, the marginal cost of manufacturing a daily dose of the drugs that one person needs to stay alive is less than a dollar. So why aren't life-saving AIDS drugs widely available at a lower price? The answer turned out to be all about market power.

Sellers exploit their market power. Pharmaceutical companies argue that if their competitors could copy any new drug they invented, there would be no incentive for them to spend the billions of dollars required to invent new drugs. Consequently, governments around the world—including the Australian government—have agreed that if you invent a new product, drug, or business process, you earn a patent. A patent gives you the right to be the only seller of the good you invent for a period of time—usually around 20 years. This right ensures that drug companies make large profits on successful drugs, and the prospect of earning these profits is the incentive that drives them to invest in discovering new drugs.

Fatima quickly understood that the patent meant the inventors of existing AIDS drugs were effectively monopolists, and they used this market power to charge high prices. Indeed, they have even more market power than most monopolists, because very few of their customers—people living with AIDS—will forgo a lifesaving treatment just because of a price increase.

Compare market power and perfect competition. In order to understand how this market power shapes outcomes, Fatima put herself in the shoes of a drug company executive, asking herself: What choices would I make if I were a manager at a pharmaceutical company?

Managers aiming to maximise their profits decide what quantity to supply by following the *Rational Rule for Sellers*—producing until marginal revenue equals marginal cost. They try to sell this quantity at the highest price they can get, which they figure out by looking up to their firm's demand curve. This logic, which should be familiar from Figure 6, is illustrated at point A in Figure 7, as the "market power outcome."

Figure 7 | Comparing Market Power and Perfect Competition

How does a shift from pricing with market power to perfect competition change outcomes?

Ⓐ **Market power**: Set quantity by producing until **marginal revenue** = **marginal cost**, then set price by looking up to the **demand curve**.

Ⓑ **Perfect competition**: Keep producing until **price** = **marginal cost**, which occurs when the demand curve cuts the marginal cost curve.

Comparing these two outcomes:

Lesson 1: The **market power price** exceeds the **competitive price**.

Lesson 2: The **market power quantity** is less than the **competitive quantity**.

Lesson 3: A firm with market power earns a healthy **profit margin** (equal to the **market power price** – **average cost**).

Lesson 4: These profits mean that a business with market power can survive, even if it has inefficiently high costs.

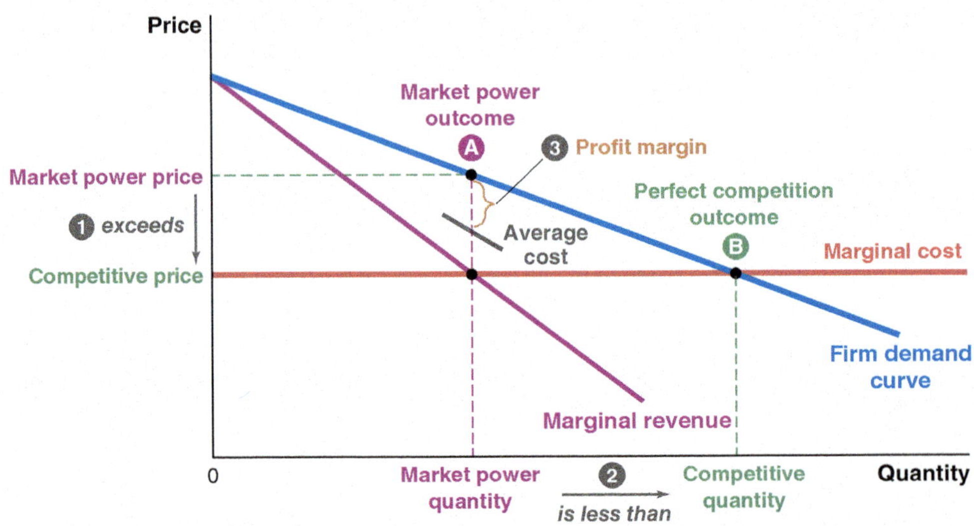

Now, let's compare this to the outcome under perfect competition. As you may recall from Chapter 3 on Supply, under perfect competition, businesses keep producing until price equals marginal cost. This yields the *perfect competition outcome* illustrated by point B in Figure 7.

Four important lessons follow from this analysis.

Lesson one: Market power leads to higher prices. Notice that the market power price is much higher than the marginal cost. By contrast, recall from when we studied supply under perfect competition (in Chapter 3) that price equals marginal cost. Thus, *market power leads to higher prices than perfect competition.*

Companies with market power face a trade-off between enjoying a larger profit margin, and selling a larger quantity. This trade-off means businesses with market power often find it more lucrative to earn a big profit margin on those customers who can pay a high price, even if it means losing those customers unwilling or unable to pay as much.

Lesson two: Market power leads to an inefficiently smaller quantity. This higher price means that fewer buyers will be able to afford AIDS drugs. Thus, the quantity demanded will be smaller. As Figure 7 shows, *the market power quantity is less than the perfect competition quantity.*

Notice that at the market power outcome, the demand curve lies above the marginal cost curve. Recall that the demand curve also measures the buyer's marginal benefits, and you'll see why this is troubling. It means that the marginal benefit of more AIDS drugs is higher than the marginal cost. It follows that society would be better off—that is, total economic surplus would be higher—if a larger quantity were produced. It follows that *businesses with market power supply less than the efficient quantity,* an outcome sometimes called the *underproduction problem.* In contrast, under perfect competition, businesses produce until the marginal benefit to buyers equals the marginal cost, which is the efficient quantity.

Market power leads managers to supply less because of the discount effect—they're reluctant to lower their price because it means they'll get less revenue from their existing customers. But from society's perspective, it would be better if managers ignored the discount effect. After all, the discount effect isn't a net cost to society, because the revenue a drug company loses due to lower prices is exactly offset by the benefit those lower prices confer on its existing customers. By contrast, businesses in perfectly competitive markets don't face a discount effect—because they're only a small part of the market they can sell whatever quantity they want at the market price and so they don't need to offer discounts to boost sales. As a result, they produce the quantity that maximises economic surplus.

Lesson three: Market power yields larger economic profits. On a per unit basis, *your profit margin is the price you charge, less the average cost of production.* In Figure 7, the market power price exceeds average cost, and so the drug company earns a healthy profit.

This profit is larger than it could earn under perfect competition. After all, the managers of businesses with market power could produce at the perfect competition outcome, but they choose not to. They choose the high-price, low-quantity outcome because *the "market power" outcome is more profitable.* Thus, businesses with market power earn more profits than they would if they were forced to compete in a perfectly competitive market. This is why managers work to preserve and enhance their market power.

Lesson four: Businesses with market power can survive even with inefficiently high costs. The profitability conferred by market power leads managers to feel less pressure to adopt cost-saving measures. In the long run, if perfectly competitive businesses are inefficient, they'll make a loss and eventually close. In contrast, a profitable but inefficient monopoly can stay around for years. Your inefficient pay TV company may be an annoying example of this.

Market power leads businesses to:

1. Charge a higher price
2. Sell a smaller quantity
3. Earn larger profits
4. Survive with inefficiently high costs

Recap: The consequences of market power. Putting these lessons together, here's what Fatima learned. First, it's *possible* to sell AIDS drugs cheaply. If the market were perfectly competitive, the price would be equal to the marginal cost, which would push their price down from an exorbitant $10,000 per year to $100 per year. Second, the higher prices associated with market power lead to a smaller quantity demanded. This isn't just an abstract economic insight—it's the reason so many untreated people were dying of AIDS. Third, Fatima realised that because drug companies make larger profits by exploiting their market power, they're unlikely to want to solve this *underproduction problem* by themselves. And fourth, the absence of competition meant that AIDS drugs may also be produced inefficiently.

These four lessons have yielded a powerful diagnosis. The AIDS crisis was not just a medical ailment; it was also an economic malady, reflecting the ills of market power. That realisation set Fatima searching for a solution.

Increasing Competition Can Lead to Better Outcomes

Fatima's diagnosis of the role that market power played in the AIDS crisis immediately suggested a possible solution: Find a way to reduce the market power held by the drug companies. She realised that if there were no patent protection, many generic drug manufacturers would enter the market to compete. That would yield perfect competition, with many competitors selling a chemically identical product. In turn, this would lead to a lower price, which more people could afford, leading more people to receive much-needed treatment.

Kalpak Pathak/Hindustan Times/Getty Images

Campaigning to end patent protection on AIDS drugs, which would allow cheaper generic AIDS drugs.

Competition leads to lower prices, and a higher quantity. Armed with this economic analysis, Fatima recommended that her nonprofit launch an aggressive campaign to end patent protection for AIDS drugs. It was a long and complex struggle involving many other activist organisations. Ultimately, the activist groups were successful, and this campaign led the South African government to trigger a little-known clause in international patent agreements that gave them the right during a humanitarian crisis to allow competitors to also start supplying these drugs.

This change drastically increased competition, which led the price of AIDS drugs to plummet to their marginal cost, which is around $100 for a year's supply. As a consequence, millions more people could afford AIDS drugs. It's no exaggeration to say that an understanding of the problems caused by market power saved millions of lives.

Why market power is bad for society: The underproduction problem. It's important to understand precisely why market power is bad for society. You might think the problem is that *prices* are high, but it's more subtle than that. Yes, high prices pose a real problem to customers who are forced to spend more. But a high price is not only a cost to buyers—it's also a benefit to sellers. When one side pays more and the other side gets more, there's no overall loss to society. It's a wash.

Instead, the problem is that market power creates a *market failure,* because it leads a smaller *quantity* to be produced than is in society's best interest. That is, market power leads to *underproduction*. As Fatima understood, the real tragedy is not that some pay higher prices, but that some people can't afford the higher prices and they go without.

Patents present a trade-off between underproduction and innovation. The AIDS drug market is a particularly vivid example of how businesses with market power can distort market forces. The lesson that market power leads businesses to produce too little at too high a price is a general one that applies to any market.

But the solution that Fatima pursued in this particular case—of ending the patent—is a bit unusual, and it may not be a good solution in other cases. Even though patents create market power—and thus lead to higher prices and lower quantities produced—they still can be good for society. They can be good because they provide a much-needed incentive to engage in research. Think back to your study of externalities. Remember that research is a positive externality, because those who don't invest in the research can typically benefit from it. One way to offset the underproduction of research is to prevent those who didn't pay for research from using it and to find a way to reward those who pay for research. That's what patents do.

Critics of Fatima's approach argue that if the government habitually nullifies patents, then there'll be no incentive for drug companies to innovate and create new lifesaving cures. Activists like Fatima respond that in this particular case, the benefit from preventing a massive humanitarian tragedy was greater than the cost of creating a disincentive for future drug investments. It's a difficult trade-off, and most economists agree that overriding patents isn't a policy that should be used very often if we want to maintain strong incentives for drug companies to fund the research needed to find new cures.

While the government sometimes helps create market power in the form of patents or other protections for businesses, there are also many ways the government can minimise the problems caused by market power. Let's start exploring them, with an eye to understanding how they'll affect the decisions you'll make as a manager.

14.4 Public Policy to Restrain Market Power

Learning Objective *Assess policies to limit the problems caused by market power.*

There's a fundamental tension in how markets operate: More competition yields better outcomes for society as a whole, but less competition and more market power yields larger profits for incumbent businesses. And so businesses often strive to maximise their market power, even though this makes society worse off.

In response, governments regulate markets to ensure that they serve the public interest. Roughly speaking, they do this through two sets of laws:

- Laws that ensure competition thrives; and
- Laws that minimise the harmful ways that businesses might exploit their market power.

It's important that you know how these laws work because they'll affect the types of business strategies you can pursue.

Laws to Ensure Competition Thrives

Competition policy refers to the set of laws that ensure that markets remain competitive. Let's explore the sorts of strategies these laws address.

Anti-collusion laws prevent businesses from agreeing not to compete. When businesses in the same market try to limit competition between them—by agreeing not to offer lower prices or better products—they gain market power. These agreements to limit competition are called **collusion.** It creates market power because colluding businesses can effectively agree to act as if they were a single entity—a monopolist—rather than cut-throat competitors. This raises their profits, at consumers' expense.

collusion An agreement to limit competition.

In an effort to ensure that the forces of competition persist, the government has made many types of collusion illegal. Examples of illegal collusion include agreeing to keep prices high, agreeing to restrict the quantity produced, rigging bids, or divvying up the market so that each area is only served by a limited number of suppliers.

WILLIAM WEST/AFP/Getty Images

Are they merging because it will lead to a more efficient telco, or because they'll gain market power?

Merger laws prevent competing businesses from combining to consolidate market power. The merger of Vodafone and TPG led two former competitors to join together to become Australia's largest telco provider. There are two reasons why managers may find mergers like this to be profitable. From a consumers' perspective, the good reason is that a merger might create cost savings, which will eventually feed through into lower prices. The bad reason is that the merger will yield greater market power for the new super-telco, because Vodafone no longer needs to cut prices to win customers over from TPG. Mergers that yield more cost savings benefit society, while those that increase market power harm society.

In order to ensure that only beneficial mergers proceed, the Australian Competition and Consumer Commission (ACCC) disallows any merger which "would have the effect, or be likely to have the effect, of substantially lessening competition in a market." Indeed, the ACCC initially did not allow Vodafone and TPG to merge due to concerns that the merger would substantially lessen competition by preventing TPG from entering the mobile sector as a separate provider.

Interpreting the DATA Was the Vodafone merger anticompetitive?

How can we figure out whether a merger would be good or bad for consumers? It turns out that the interests of Vodafone and TPG's customers are the exact opposite of their competitors.

If the Vodafone-TPG merger creates a more efficient business, that's good news for customers, but bad news for competing telcos like Optus or Telstra, who'll have to contend with a more fearsome rival.

But if the merger is just about reducing the number of competitors in the industry, then all businesses in the industry will enjoy greater market power, which is bad news for customers, but good news for rivals like Telstra and Optus.

This means that we can figure out if blocking the merger would have been good for consumers, by seeing if it would have been bad for Telstra or Optus. In fact, at one point it was made public that the ACCC would block the merger. Figure 8 shows that in response, the stock prices of both Telstra and Optus—which are a measure of their expected future profitability—fell sharply. That says markets expected Telstra and Optus' profitability to fall if the merger were stopped. The fact that blocking the merger was seen as bad for these companies suggests that letting it go through was good for them, presumably because it boosted their market power. That's bad news for consumers.

And so next time you're frustrated by the high price of your internet, or the cost of your mobile phone plan, this analysis suggests you should blame the government for eventually allowing this merger to proceed (which they did in 2020). ■

Figure 8 | How Competitors Responded to News that the Merger Between Vodafone and TPG Might Be Blocked

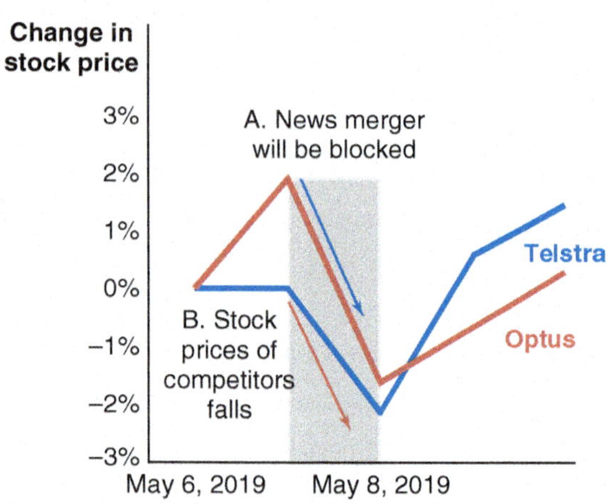

Data from: Yahoo.

Being a monopoly is legal; monopolising a market isn't. It's not illegal for a business to *be a monopoly,* to hold market power, or even to charge high prices. After all, some large companies acquire their dominant position by outcompeting their rivals—providing better service at lower prices. (Perhaps that describes Amazon.) But it's illegal to *attempt to monopolise* your industry by taking actions to exclude competitors or prevent new competitors from entering. The noun, "monopoly," is legal; the verb, to "monopolise" is not. That's why exclusionary or predatory practices are illegal. Examples include pushing your suppliers not to sell to your competitors, or requiring stores that want to sell your product not to sell the products of your competitors. It can also be illegal to use your power in one market to gain market power in another market.

Sometimes, you might feel that your competitors are abusing their market power by charging a price so low that they'll force you out of business. In a few rare cases, this sort of predatory pricing may be illegal, if it's part of an explicit strategy to eliminate competitors with the goal of raising prices later. But a low price is often the result of aggressive price competition, which is good for consumers, and so it's usually judged to be legal.

Encouraging international trade fosters competition. International trade makes it difficult for any business to build up much market power. Consider the market for cars. As Figure 9 shows there are only three large U.S. manufacturers (General Motors, Ford, and Chrysler).

But none of them has much market power. That's because they're forced to keep their prices down in order to compete with Japanese carmakers such as Toyota, Nissan, and Honda; German carmakers like Volkswagen, Mercedes, and BMW; and South Korea's Hyundai.

International competition was so strong that the Australian car industry effectively closed in 2017 with no more cars being produced domestically. For decades before that the industry relied heavily on government subsidies and was inefficient by global standards.

Figure 9 International Trade in Cars Maintains Competition

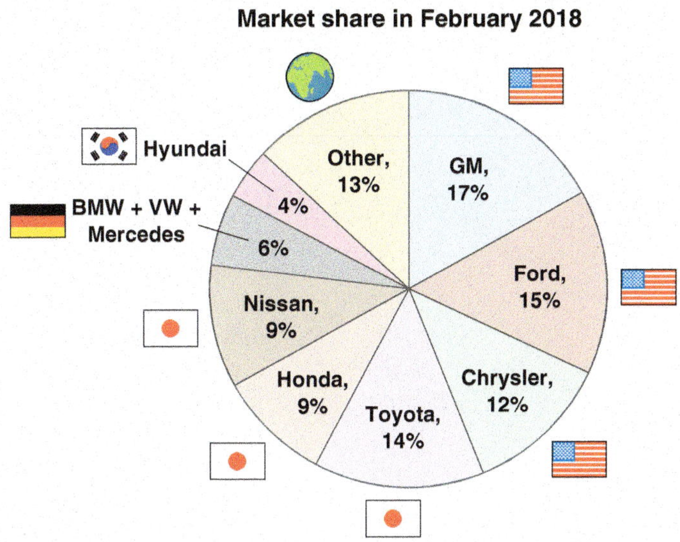

Data from: Motor Intelligence.

Laws to Minimise the Harm from Exercising Market Power

Despite the government's efforts to spur competition, there will always be cases where incumbent businesses have a lot of market power. In some cases, the government might regulate how those businesses act, in order to try to reduce the harm to consumers.

A price ceiling limits abuse of market power. The government can implement *price ceilings* to limit the extent to which monopolies exploit their market power. For instance, if your home is at all like mine, there's only one company providing pay TV service. But in most areas the price for pay TV isn't particularly high because it's limited by government regulations.

This price ceiling effectively makes it illegal to set too high a price, thereby eliminating the incentive to restrict production. If the price ceiling is set at the right level—set equal to the marginal cost—the government can induce businesses with market power to produce the same quantity that they would produce if they were in a perfectly competitive market.

EVERYDAY Economics Phone calls in prison

There are a lot of bad things about being in prison, but there's one you may not have thought of: The price of phone calls. A phone call from a prison or jail used to cost as much as $5 to connect, and then nearly $1 per minute, an astonishingly large markup given that the same call would be included as part of a home- or mobile-phone plan. Add a bewildering array of extra fees, and a 15-minute phone call can yield a punishing financial burden for the prisoner's families who typically end up paying for these collect calls. Many of these families—who are already struggling to get by without a breadwinner—describe the painful trade-off between keeping in touch with an absent family member and buying everyday necessities.

Jim West/imageBROKER/Shutterstock

The price of the call is punishing.

The problem isn't security, it's market power. Each prison system enters into an exclusive contract with one telephone company, effectively making them a monopoly. Prisoners aren't allowed mobile phones, so there really is no competition. Advocates for prisoners have argued that the high price of prison phone calls are an abuse of market power. They have a point. Once some competition was introduced in the provision of phone services for inmates in Australian prisons, call costs came down considerably. It's still relatively expensive, but an unlimited call plan now costs a little over $30 a month. ■

Notice that the argument for these price ceilings is all about eliminating the abuse of market power, and so it only applies to imperfectly competitive markets and monopolies. By contrast, as we saw in Chapter 6, in perfectly competitive markets, price ceilings—such as rent control—are generally thought to be a bad idea, because they decrease the quantity supplied below the economically efficient level and increase the quantity demanded above it—thereby creating shortages.

In practice, price ceilings create their own difficulties. Sometimes, regulators allow businesses to charge a price equal to their costs, plus a small profit margin. But this reduces the incentive for managers to keep their costs down. After all, they can just pass on their inefficiently high costs to their customers in the form of higher prices. A related problem is that if you can't charge a higher price for a better-quality product, there's no incentive to produce high-quality goods.

natural monopoly A market in which it is cheapest for a single business to service the market.

Natural monopolies often lead to government intervention. In a **natural monopoly** a single business can service the whole market at a lower cost than multiple businesses can. This occurs whenever marginal costs continuously decrease as you expand your output. When this happens, competition is never going to work out. The problem is that a new entrant will always be at a cost disadvantage relative to the incumbent. As a result, government intervention can be necessary to reach the socially efficient quantity.

For instance, water, gas, and electricity are all natural monopolies, because it's never going to be cost-effective for a second firm to run pipes and wires to your house. Regulating a natural monopoly involves difficult trade-offs. The government could prevent a natural monopoly from exploiting its market power by insisting that it set its price equal to marginal cost—which would be in society's best interest. But then the natural monopoly might end up making a loss. (While the price covers the marginal cost of the *last* unit produced, if marginal costs of the rest of its output are higher, the price won't cover its costs.) This loss might lead the natural monopolist to quit the industry altogether. To avoid this, the government often ends up providing these services directly, paying for any losses out of its tax revenue.

Recap: Public policy can't eliminate market power, but it can limit abuses. Market power presents a tricky public policy issue. We've seen that companies will exploit this power to set a price that's higher, and produce a quantity that's lower than what's in society's best interest. And so concentrations of market power are bad. But often businesses become the dominant players in their industry through competition. They simply outcompete their rivals, providing better service at lower prices. It would be a bad idea to ban that. So government regulators face a difficult balancing act, trying to limit the worst abuses of market power, while still allowing more productive businesses to outcompete their rivals.

Tying It Together

Let's put all this in a broader context. Economics classes often start by studying perfect competition because it yields simple intuitions. In the first few weeks of the semester, we politely ignored the fact that few businesses are in perfectly competitive markets. Indeed, when we studied supply curves in Chapter 3, we focused on the case of perfect competition, in which businesses have no market power. But in reality, most businesses have some market power. And so in almost any company you start or work for, you'll face the messier reality of making decisions with market power.

In that messier reality, you face a trade-off between selling a larger quantity at a lower price, versus a smaller quantity at a higher price. This chapter has given you the tools to evaluate this trade-off. Importantly, the insights we've developed are useful whether your industry involves many competitors selling somewhat different products (monopolistic competition), just a few strategic competitors (oligopoly), or even no direct competitors (monopoly). In each case, you want to keep producing until marginal cost equals marginal revenue, and then look up to your firm's demand curve to find the highest price you can charge.

Understanding market power is also central to identifying business opportunities. Businesses with more market power face a less stark trade-off between higher prices and higher quantity—they can get away with both—and so they can usually earn bigger profits. As such, as a savvy entrepreneur, you should try to enter a market with few competitors. As a shrewd manager, you can increase your market power by positioning your product so that it differs from your competitors. And as an investor, you want to find those businesses whose market power is likely to endure. We'll dig into these issues over the next few chapters.

The reality of market power also speaks to some of the big debates in economics, challenging our understanding about the efficacy of markets. In Chapter 7 we learned that under perfect competition, markets tend to produce economically efficient outcomes. Much of what we've learned since has illustrated various forms of market failure. This chapter adds another: Businesses with market power typically charge a higher price and produce less than is in the public interest. Market power blunts the forces of competition.

All of this yields an important implication: Markets in themselves do not guarantee good outcomes. Instead, outcomes depend crucially on how markets are organised.

Chapter at a Glance

Market Power: The extent to which a seller can charge a higher price without losing many sales to competing businesses.

Range of market power:

Market type	Perfect competition	Monopolistic competition (Imperfect competition)	Oligopoly (Imperfect competition)	Monopoly
Competitors + Products	Many + Same product	Many + Differentiated product	Few + Same or differentiated product	None + Unique product
	Least market power	Some market power		Most market power

A basically flat demand curve — A downward-sloping firm demand curve — A firm demand curve is the market demand curve

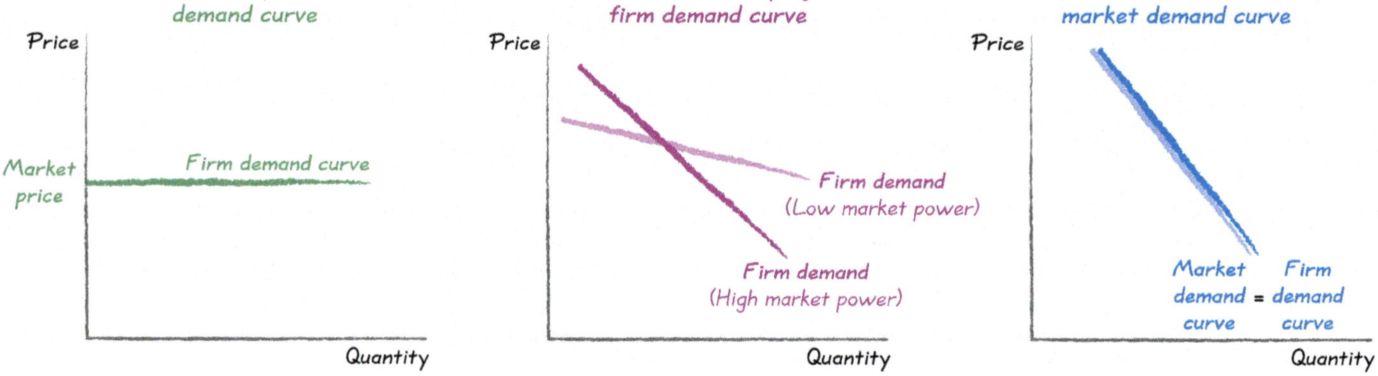

Marginal Revenue with Market Power

Marginal Revenue: The addition to total revenue you get from selling one more unit. = **Output effect (P)** (which is the price of the extra item you sell) − **Discount effect ($\Delta P \times Q$)** (the price cut you'll have to offer × the quantity that gets that price cut)

Setting Price and Quantity with Market Power

Step 1: What quantity should you produce?

A. The Rational Rule for Sellers says to keep producing until marginal cost equals marginal revenue.

B. Look down to see the quantity.

Step 2: What price should you charge?

C. Look up to your firm's demand curve to find the highest price you can set and still sell this quantity.

D. This is the price you should charge.

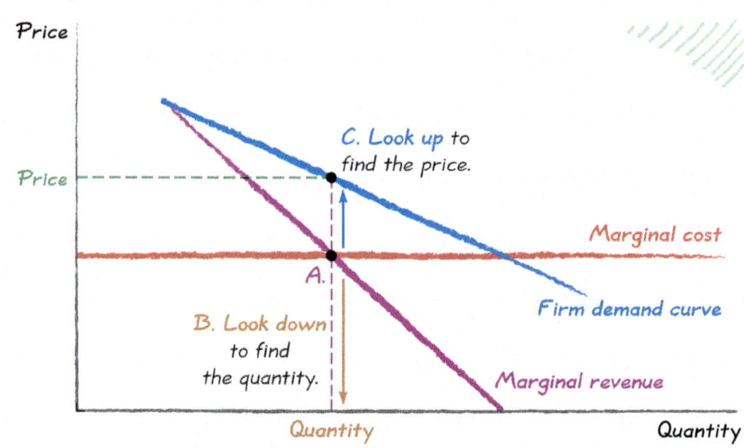

The Problems with Market Power

Market power leads businesses to:

1. Charge a higher price 2. Sell a smaller quantity 3. Earn larger profits 4. Survive with inefficiently high costs

Public policy can't eliminate market power, but it can limit abuses.

Key Concepts

Discussion and Review Questions

Learning Objective 14.1 *Evaluate how market structure shapes the market power your business has.*

1. What is meant by "market power"? What does market power depend on? Briefly explain why a business in a perfectly competitive market does not have market power.
2. Provide an example of each of the following market structures in which you have participated as a buyer or maybe even a seller.
   a. Perfect competition
   b. Monopolistic competition
   c. Oligopoly
   d. Monopoly

Learning Objective 14.2 *Calculate the best price to set when you have market power.*

3. Why is the marginal revenue curve for a business with market power below the firm's demand curve at any given level of output (beyond the first unit)? Is this also true for a firm in a perfectly competitive market?

Learning Objective 14.3 *Assess how market power distorts market forces.*

4. A patent effectively allows a firm to operate as a monopoly for several years. Some people argue that the market power created by patents is harmful to consumers and shouldn't be granted. Others argue that patents are necessary to encourage research and innovation. Briefly explain the arguments for and against patents, and provide an example of a market that supports each argument.

Learning Objective 14.4 *Assess policies to limit the problems caused by market power.*

5. When the ACCC allowed the only two suppliers of the heart medication Amlodipine, Mylan and Upjohn, to merge, it would have been granting a monopoly on this important medication. In order to complete the merger, Mylan and Upjohn agreed to sell Amlodipine, as well as two other pharmaceutical products to an ACCC approved buyer. Why would government regulators require Mylan and Upjohn to divest themselves of these pharmaceutical products before allowing the merger to occur?
6. Describe a situation in which a monopoly might be more efficient than a perfectly competitive market populated by many sellers.

Study Problems

Learning Objective 14.1 *Evaluate how market structure shapes the market power your business has.*

1. For each of the following explain the degree of market power the seller has, and whether the market power is due to limited competitors, product differentiation, or both.
   a. The Toyota Corolla, the bestselling passenger vehicle in the world in 2017
   b. Shuker Farm, a grower of wheat bordering the Darwin River
   c. Archer Daniels Midland (ADM), the largest producer of Lysine, a standardised amino acid used by farmers as a feed additive. ADM competes with a few large corporations in Europe and Japan
   d. McDonald's, the most popular fast food restaurant in Australia
2. For each of the following state whether the market is most accurately described as perfectly competitive, monopoly, oligopoly, or monopolistic competition, and briefly explain your answer.
   a. Endeavour Energy, the sole supplier of electricity to Sydney's Greater West, Blue Mountains, and South Coast areas.
   b. The aircraft manufacturing industry
   c. The dry cleaning industry
   d. The market for smartphones
   e. The hotel industry

3. The figure below illustrates the market shares of the main video-streaming services.

Subscriptions to on-demand video services in Australia in 2019

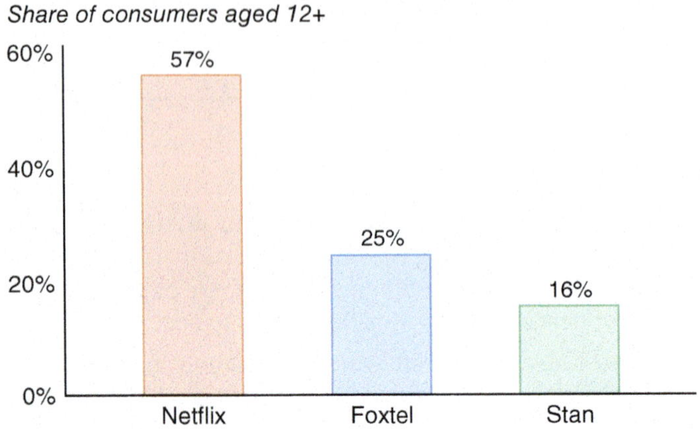

Data from: Roymorgan.com.

Based on this information, answer the following questions:

a. The on-demand video industry is most accurately described as which type of market structure: perfect competition, monopolistic competition, oligopoly, or monopoly?

b. Explain why Netflix and Foxtel have market power in this industry. Do they benefit from limited competition, product differentiation, or both?

Learning Objective 14.2 *Calculate the best price to set when you have market power.*

4. You have just been hired as the assistant manager at the local Rebel Sport store. Your first assignment is to determine the demand curve and the marginal revenue curve for the new NordicTrack elliptical machine. You conduct a price experiment and have accumulated the following data:

Week	Price	Quantity sold
1	$1,000	1
2	$700	4
3	$800	3
4	$500	6
5	$600	5
6	$900	2

a. To start, sort the table by quantity sold, and draw the firm demand curve for elliptical machines at your store.

b. Calculate the total revenue and marginal revenue for each quantity of output, then graph the marginal revenue curve on your demand curve graph.

c. Do you have enough information to determine the price that you should recommend charging? If yes, what price would maximise profits? If no, what additional information do you need?

5. Richela is a successful artist whose works have the following demand curve. Complete the table to represent her demand curve and use the information provided to find Richela's profit-maximising price and level of output.

Price per painting	Quantity	Total revenue	Marginal revenue	Marginal cost
$9,000	1			$2,000
$8,000	2			$1,000
$7,000	3			$2,000
$6,000	4			$3,000
$5,000	5			$4,000

Learning Objective 14.3 *Assess how market power distorts market forces.*

6. In October of 2004, British regulators were forced to suspend the license of a flu vaccine plant in Liverpool operated by the Chiron Corporation due to concerns over bacterial contamination. As a result, the market was less competitive and the remaining suppliers of the flu vaccine experienced an increase in their market power. Suppose that you are the manager of one of the remaining pharmaceutical companies still making this flu vaccine, and that the market for your company is represented by the following graph:

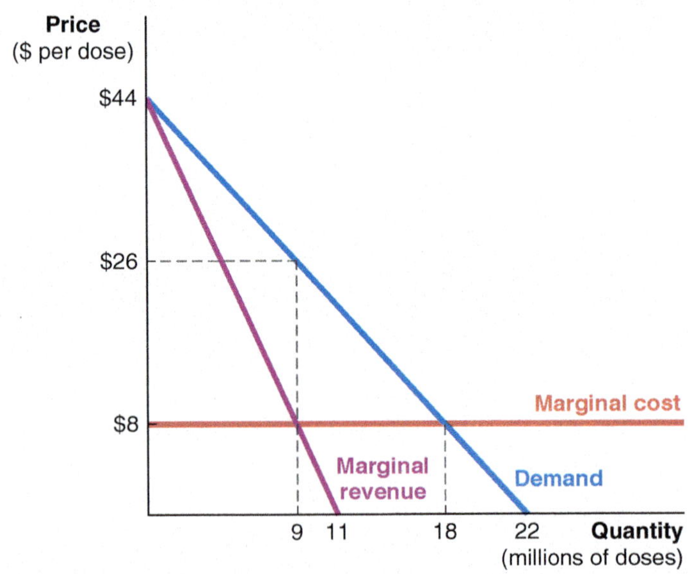

a. What price per dose should your company charge, and how many doses should it produce?

b. Is the profit-maximising price found in part (a) greater than the marginal cost of producing the good (yes or no)?

c. Compare the marginal benefit and marginal cost at your company's profit-maximising level of output (9 million). Are they equal or is one higher than the other?

d. If this was a perfectly competitive market, what price would exist and how many units of the flu vaccine would be produced?

e. Would this market be efficient if it was perfectly competitive?

7. Lynn owns a tutoring centre that supplies NAPLAN and HSC test preparation services for high school students on an hourly basis. Consider the demand, marginal revenue, and marginal cost she faces, shown in the following graph:

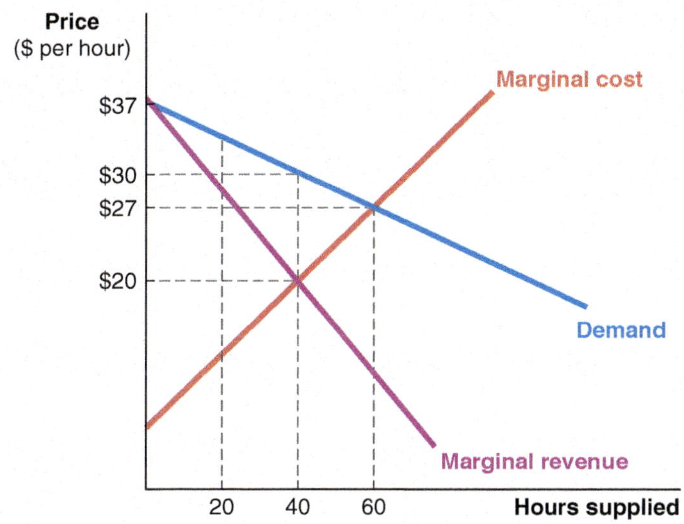

a. Does Lynn's business have market power? Briefly explain your answer.

b. In order to maximise her profits, how many hours of tutoring should Lynn's business supply, and at what price?

c. What would the socially efficient quantity be in this market?

d. Why is the profit-maximising outcome inefficient?

Learning Objective 14.4 *Assess policies to limit the problems caused by market power.*

8. Which of the following types of activities between businesses would be considered illegal in Australia? Select all that apply.

a. Qantas, Virgin, and Regional Express airlines agree to restrict the number of flights they offer each day domestically in Australia.

b. Archer Daniels Midland and the Japanese firm Ajinomoto agree to raise the price on lysine, an additive used in livestock feed.

c. The internet providers Telstra and Optus agree not to compete in certain geographic regions of the country.

d. Qantas and Coke sign a contract to make Coke the exclusive provider of soft drinks on Qantas flights.

9. Suppose that Foxtel is the only provider of pay TV in the city of Devonport, Tasmania. The following graph shows the monthly demand for pay TV services in Devonport and Foxtel's marginal revenue and marginal cost curves. Use the graph to answer the following questions.

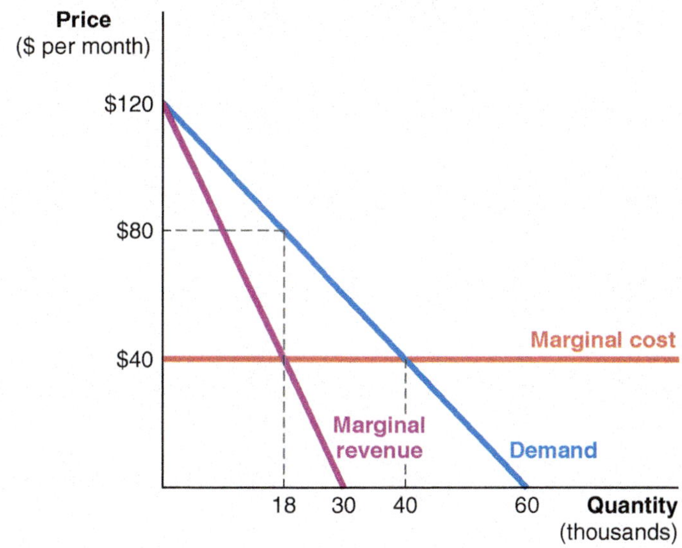

a. Imagine that you are an analyst at Foxtel. What price would you recommend the company charge? At that price, how many customers would they have each month?

b. Does the monopoly outcome result in an efficient outcome in this market?

c. Now, imagine that you are a policy analyst tasked with finding a way to make cable more affordable for Devonport residents. In order to achieve an efficient outcome in this market, what price would the government use as a price ceiling?

CHAPTER

15

Entry, Exit, and Long-Run Profitability

Chapter Objective

Learn how to remain profitable in the long run.

15.1 Revenues, Costs, and Economic Profits
Assess your business's economic profitability.

15.2 Free Entry and Exit in the Long Run
Forecast how new entrants will change long-run prices and profitability in your market.

15.3 Barriers to Entry
Learn strategies to deter new entrants from competing away your profits.

Randy Duchaine/Alamy

Competition makes it hard to stay on top for long.

"Nobody ever got fired for buying IBM." For decades, this catchphrase was something of a meme among office managers, and it sums up the stranglehold that IBM held in the early years of the computer industry. It was simply the largest, most prestigious company in the world. Its computers were faster and more powerful than the alternatives. Its technology was better. Its research and development was so advanced that its scientists won the Nobel Prize in Physics two years in a row. IBM was not only the most valuable company on the U.S. stock exchange; if it split itself in half, it would have been the two most valuable companies.

But that's no longer the case. Profits this big attract attention, and a slew of hungry entrepreneurs—including Steve Jobs, Michael Dell, and Bill Gates—were lured by the scent of opportunity. Their start-ups grew up to become Apple, Dell, and Microsoft, and they took much of IBM's market share. Today, IBM is a shell of its former self, worth hundreds of billions of dollars less than if it had maintained its position as the world's leading computer company.

Apple, Dell, and Microsoft don't find their dominant positions easy to maintain. Like IBM, their success has led a new generation of entrepreneurs to challenge them. Today, some of the hottest tech companies, including Google, Samsung, and Amazon, are rapidly winning market share from this newer old guard. This process of creative destruction is continuing as dozens of ambitious start-ups are working to dethrone today's tech giants.

IBM's decline paints a vivid lesson for all managers: It's hard to stay on top for long in a competitive market. You need to look beyond your current competitors and be aware that new entrants are always looking to disrupt your industry. The last chapter analysed how to adjust your strategy to fit the structure of competition in your market. But when new rivals can easily enter your industry, today's comfortable monopoly can quickly turn into tomorrow's fiercely contested competition. That's why this chapter turns to analysing how the strategic choices that you and your rivals make determine the structure of competition.

As a manager, your task is to focus on your firm's long-run profitability. That's why in this chapter you'll develop tools for assessing competitive threats and making the strategic decisions that will help you outcompete new entrants before they become fearsome competitors.

15.1 Revenues, Costs, and Economic Profits

Learning Objective *Assess your business's economic profitability.*

Let's fast forward a few years: You've been out of university for a while, and you're doing well in your chosen career. Even though you like your job, you're feeling restless, as you think about pursuing your dream of running your own business. You have a great idea for a new start-up—perhaps it's a website connecting organic farmers directly with their customers, so that with a few clicks people can order locally grown organic vegetables—or perhaps you have a different idea.

Economic Profit versus Accounting Profit

Whatever your idea is, how can you be sure it's worth pursuing? Let's run the numbers. Let's say you've made some forecasts as part of your business plan:

- You expect to earn $500,000 per year in revenue.
- You expect to incur $400,000 per year in business-related expenses.

accounting profit The total revenue a business receives, less its explicit financial costs

= Total revenue − Explicit financial costs

Accounting profit is total revenue less out-of-pocket financial costs. Your **accounting profit** is the *total revenue* your business receives minus your total outlays, which we call your *explicit financial costs.* Total revenue is all of the income received from all sources. Likewise, your explicit financial costs include all the money that leaves your business, including rent, wages for your employees, and the cost of your raw materials. You measure your accounting profit by tracking all of the money that goes into and out of a business. This is the number that's typically reported on the bottom line of your profit-and-loss statement and printed in your annual report.

To summarise:

$$\text{Accounting profit} = \text{Total revenue} - \text{Explicit financial costs}$$

Your start-up is expected to earn total revenue of $500,000 per year, and to incur $400,000 in explicit financial costs, providing an expected annual *accounting profit* of $100,000.

Armed with this information, should you launch your start-up?

Don't answer right away. Pause for a moment and think about this.

Really think.

A bit longer.

(Hint: Keep thinking until you've used the *opportunity cost principle*.)

The answer is: *It depends.*

The opportunity cost of running a business includes forgone wages and interest. Here's why it depends: You'll need to quit your current job to start this business. If you're currently earning $150,000 per year, then launching your start-up will mean forgoing your annual income of $150,000 in order to gain an annual profit of $100,000. That's obviously a bad deal—don't start the business! But if you're currently earning $40,000 per year, then giving up your job to start this business is a good idea, because you'll only forgo an annual income of $40,000 to get an annual profit of $100,000.

The point is, whether or not it makes sense to launch this new business depends on your opportunity costs. You need to apply the *opportunity cost principle* and ask, "or what?" You could start this new business, *or what?* As any entrepreneur will tell you, you'll need to pour a lot of time and money into your start-up. And so beyond the explicit financial costs you'll also need to account for the most important implicit opportunity costs of running a business, including:

- *Forgone wages:* If you don't launch this start-up, how much will you earn pursuing your next best career option?
- *Forgone interest:* If you don't invest your funds in this start-up, how much annual interest will you earn by investing it elsewhere?

If there are other opportunity costs you need to think about—perhaps quitting your job will mean forgoing a lot of job satisfaction, or you value the benefits like a company car—then make sure to count them, too. You should think of the sum of all of these opportunity costs as the annual payment you need for it to be worth investing your time and money as an entrepreneur. Don't accept a cent less, or else you'll end up worse off than in your next best alternative.

Economic profits account for both explicit financial costs and implicit opportunity costs. Recognising that these implicit opportunity costs matter just as much as explicit financial costs leads to a new perspective on profitability. Economists focus on **economic profit**—which is total revenue less both the explicit financial costs that accountants focus on *and* the implicit opportunity cost of the entrepreneur's time and money:

Economic profit = Total revenue − Explicit financial costs − Implicit opportunity costs

Entrepreneurs focus on economic profits because they speak directly to the question of whether it's worth starting a new business or not. It says that you should start the new business only if it will earn positive economic profits.

economic profit The total revenue a firm receives, less both explicit financial costs and the entrepreneur's implicit opportunity costs

= Total revenue − Explicit financial costs − Entrepreneur's implicit opportunity costs

Do the Economics

Let's return to that business plan, but this time, we'll make sure to account for your implicit opportunity costs. In order to start your new business, you'll have to:

- Quit your current job, which pays you $60,000 per year, and
- Invest $100,000 in the business, instead of keeping it in a term deposit where it's earning 1% interest per year.

a. *What are the implicit opportunity costs of starting your new business?*

Implicit opportunity cost = $\underbrace{\$60{,}000}_{\text{Forgone wages}} + \underbrace{1\% \times \$100{,}000}_{\text{Forgone interest}} = \$61{,}000$

b. *What are your economic profits?*

Economic profit = $\underbrace{\$500{,}000}_{\text{Total revenue}} - \underbrace{\$400{,}000}_{\text{Financial costs}} - \underbrace{\$61{,}000}_{\text{Implicit opportunity costs}} = \$39{,}000$

c. *Should you start this business?*

Yes. Emphatically yes.

Some students argue that it may not be worth the hassle of starting a business if you'll make only $39,000 in profit. But that's a misreading of economic profit. Remember, economic profit is what's left over after we've accounted for all costs—all explicit financial costs and all implicit opportunity costs—including hassle. And so an economic profit of $39,000 means that you're $39,000 *better off* than in your *next best alternative.* That's a move worth making! ■

Why do accountants and economists disagree? At this point, you might wonder: Why can't accountants and economists agree on what profit is, and which costs to count?

The tension showed in Figure 1 is that each is trying to answer a different question. An accountant answers the question, "Where did my money go last year?" This requires a focus on, well, where your money went. And so accountants focus on explicit financial costs, which are any outlays where money left your business, including rent, the wages you pay your workers, the cost of computers and furniture, and your electricity bill.

Figure 1 Two Perspectives on Profit

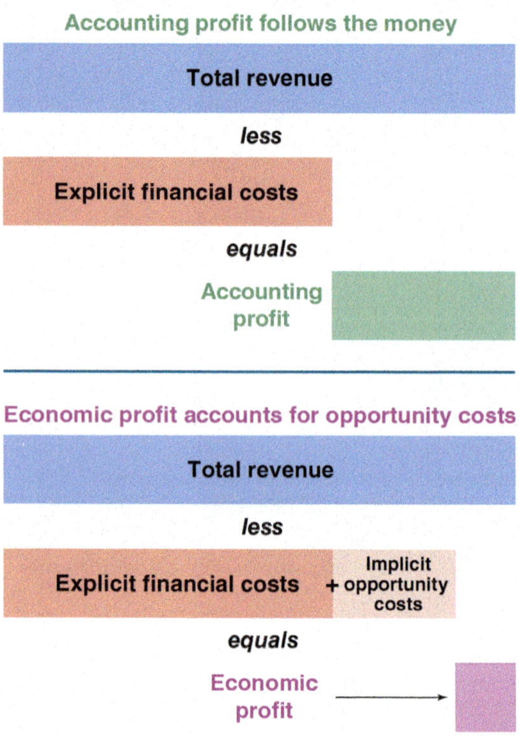

By contrast, the goal of economic analysis is to help you make the best decision. If you're evaluating whether or not to start a new business, then you'll only make a good decision if you account for your other opportunities. Consequently, economic analysis emphasises all of your costs, including both the explicit financial costs your accountants tally up, and the implicit opportunity cost of your forgone opportunities. When we calculate economic profit, it's as if we're insisting your business pay you for your time and money.

Economic profits determine whether it's worth starting a business. As a rule, whenever you see news reports about corporate profits, or when you read a company's profit and loss statement, they're reporting their accounting profits. But *if you're trying to decide whether it's worth starting a business, you want to focus on economic profits*. The same advice applies to managers of existing companies, who should only stay in business if they expect to earn positive *economic* profits.

Because our task in this chapter is to evaluate when entrepreneurs should enter a market or existing businesses should exit, whenever you see the word "profit," I want you to read it as "economic profit." Indeed, whenever you hear an economist talk about profits, you can safely assume they mean economic profits. Likewise when you see the word "costs," continue to think about them as including both explicit financial costs and implicit opportunity costs.

Do the Economics

For each of the following new ventures, calculate accounting profit, implicit opportunity costs, and economic profit, and assess whether you would advise these aspiring entrepreneurs to launch their new businesses:

a. Kiara is thinking of opening an artisanal cheese store. She forecasts revenues of \$200,000 per year, and explicit financial costs of \$120,000 per year. She could only pursue this dream if she quit her current job as a teacher, where she earns \$40,000 per year. She would also need to invest \$100,000 to outfit the store, and she would otherwise use that money to pay down her mortgage, which is at an interest rate of 8% per year.

b. Xavier is considering quitting his job as an editor for a major publisher to become a freelance editor. He currently earns \$85,000 per year, plus an additional \$15,000 worth of benefits. He estimates that as a freelancer, he'll bring in \$140,000 per year in revenue, and he'll have \$40,000 in financial costs. To get started, he'll need to withdraw \$20,000 from his bank where it's earning 5% interest per year.

c. Jasmine currently works as a sports medicine physician at Westmead hospital in Sydney, where she earns \$160,000 per year. She's considering starting her own practice, and expects to bring in revenues of \$500,000 per year, although with all the staff and insurance she'll need, her explicit financial costs will be \$300,000 per year. She'll need to invest \$200,000 to get her office set up, forgoing expected earnings of 6% by investing in the stock market. ■

Answer: a. Kiara: Accounting profit: \$200,000 − \$120,000 = \$80,000; Implicit opportunity cost: \$40,000 + 8% × \$100,000 = \$48,000; Economic profit = \$32,000. Decision: Start the business! b. Xavier: Accounting profit: \$140,000 − \$40,000 = \$100,000. Implicit opportunity cost: \$85,000 + \$15,000 + 5% × \$20,000 = \$101,000; Economic profit = −\$1,000. Decision: Don't start freelancing. c. Jasmine: Accounting profit: \$500,000 − \$300,000 = \$200,000; Implicit opportunity cost = \$160,000 + 4% × \$200,000 = \$168,000; Economic profit = \$32,000. Decision: Start your own practice.

Average Revenue, Average Cost, and Your Profit Margin

In order to measure whether a business is profitable or not (remember: "profitable" means "earns economic profits"), you'll need to focus on a couple of key metrics: Average revenue and average costs.

average revenue Revenue per unit, calculated as total revenue divided by the quantity supplied. Average revenue is equal to the price, if you charge everyone the same price.

Your average revenue is the price. Your **average revenue** is your revenue per unit, and it's calculated as your company's total revenue from selling a product, divided by the quantity supplied. If you charge everyone the same price, your average revenue is simply the price you charge for each unit:

$$\text{Average revenue} = \frac{\text{Total revenue}}{\text{Quantity}} = \text{Price}$$

This means that your firm's demand curve—which shows the price you can charge for any given quantity—is also your average revenue curve.

Average cost is the per unit cost, or total costs divided by quantity. Your **average cost** is the cost per unit, calculated as your business's total costs from making a product, divided by the quantity you produce:

average cost Cost per unit, calculated as your firm's total costs (including fixed and variable costs) divided by the quantity produced.

$$\text{Average cost} = \frac{\text{Total costs}}{\text{Quantity}} = \underbrace{\frac{\text{Fixed costs}}{\text{Quantity}}}_{\text{Fixed costs per unit}} + \underbrace{\frac{\text{Variable costs}}{\text{Quantity}}}_{\text{Variable costs per unit}}$$

Notice that your average cost per unit is based on your total costs, and so includes both your *fixed costs*—such as the cost of land and capital equipment and any other expenses that don't vary with the quantity you produce—as well as your *variable costs*—such as the cost of variable inputs, like raw materials, electricity, and worker time. Your fixed costs include the opportunity cost of the entrepreneur's time and money.

Figure 2 sketches an example of a company's average cost curve, showing how its average costs vary with the quantity produced. While the details may be different for your business, the U-shaped pattern is quite common, and it reflects the influence of two key forces:

Spreading your fixed costs: As you start to increase production from a low level, your average costs typically fall initially. This is because you have to pay for fixed costs just to set up your business. If you only produce a small quantity, these fixed costs constitute a large cost per unit sold. But as you produce a larger quantity, the fixed cost gets "spread" over more and more units, and so it becomes smaller on a per-unit basis. This decline in fixed costs per unit often leads average costs to fall.

Rising variable costs: Eventually, your variable costs become the more important component of average costs. At some point your average costs rise as inefficiencies make it increasingly expensive to increase your production. This is driven by *rising input costs* per unit, which may reflect overtime payments, *diminishing marginal product* reducing the productivity of your workers, coordination problems, or other inefficiencies. And so at some point, your average costs will typically rise as the quantity you produce increases.

Figure 2 | Average Cost Curve

A Increasing production from a low level leads average costs to initially fall as **fixed costs are spread over a larger quantity**.

B At some point average costs rise with quantity, due to **inefficiencies raising your variable costs per unit**.

C The result is a U-shaped **average cost** curve.

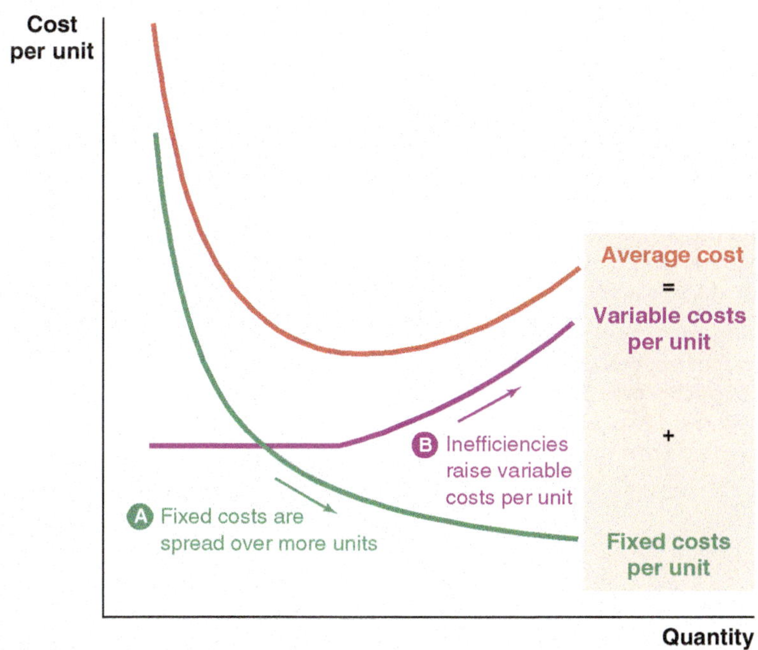

Your profit margin per unit is the price less average cost. Your company's average revenue (which is equal to your price) and average cost are important, because together they determine your **profit margin,** which measures your profit per unit sold:

profit margin Profits per unit sold = Average revenue − Average cost

$$\text{Profit margin} = \underbrace{\text{Price}}_{\text{Average revenue}} - \text{Average cost}$$

As any business leader can tell you, your profit margin is critical to your business's success. If you're earning a positive profit margin, then you're earning an economic profit! Your total profit is your per-unit profit margin, multiplied by the quantity you sell. It follows that if your price exceeds your average cost, you're making an economic profit.

Figure 3 illustrates how you can spot profit opportunities on a graph, showing your firm's demand curve (remember that it's also your average revenue curve) and average costs. Your profit margin per unit is the price you'll charge (shown on the firm demand curve) less your average costs. Graphically, this means that for any given quantity, your profit margin per unit is the gap between your firm's demand curve and its average cost curve.

Figure 3 | **Profit Margins**

Profit margin per unit = Price – Average cost

Ⓐ Your **firm's demand curve** is also the **average revenue curve** because your average revenue per unit is the price.

Ⓑ Your **profit margin per unit** is the difference between **average revenue** and **average cost**.

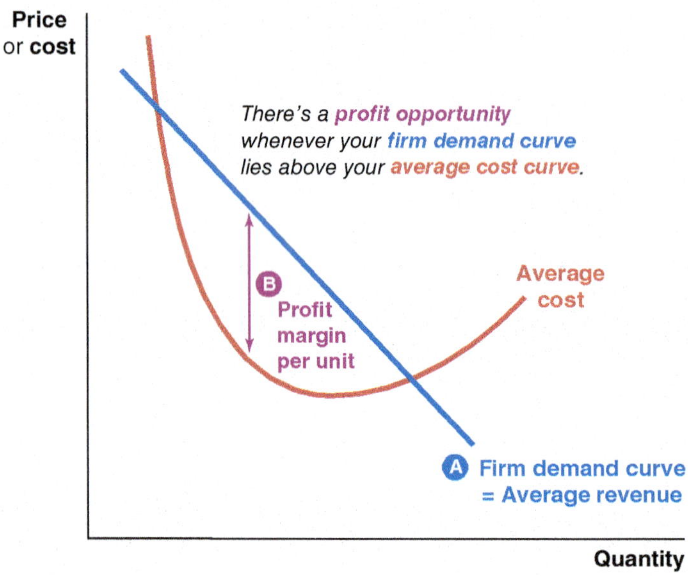

Any time you see a firm's demand curve lying above the average cost curve, there's an opportunity to make economic profits. Go get 'em!

Recap: Economic profit is important for long-run analysis of firm entry and exit. The central insight so far is that when you're thinking about whether to enter or exit a market, you should focus on economic profit.

This focus on profitability is important because this chapter is all about shifting from short-run analysis to focusing on the long run. In the **short run,** you face a fixed set of competitors with given production capacity, and your job is simply to outcompete these existing rivals. These short-run decisions are important, and they've rightly occupied much of our attention throughout this book. But long-run dynamics determine what's sustainable. So for the rest of this chapter we'll analyse what happens in the **long run,** which is the time horizon over which new rivals may *enter* or *expand* into your market, and existing rivals can *contract,* or *exit* the market, and you can adjust your production capacity. As we'll discover, economic profits play a key role in long-run analysis.

Students often ask: How long is the long run? Unfortunately, there's no simple answer. When you're operating a refinery, it may take a decade for companies to enter or exit the market. But if you're running a roadside lemonade stand, a neighbour could set up a table just across the street any minute. IBM discovered that for a tech company, the long run can be a matter of a few years. You'll need to use your judgement to sort out what the long run is in your industry. Generally, short-run analysis is useful for deciding the quantity your company should supply, given today's market price. Long-run analysis is useful for *planning* purposes, such as planning how much to invest in a new plant and equipment for a business expansion, or planning whether to launch your new start-up. And that brings us to our next topic.

short run The horizon over which the production capacity, and the number and type of competitors you face, cannot change.

long run The horizon over which you, or your rivals, may expand or contract production capacity and new rivals may enter the market or existing firms may exit.

15.2 Free Entry and Exit in the Long Run

Learning Objective *Forecast how new entrants will change long-run prices and profitability in your market.*

IBM's failure to see that new rivals would emerge and challenge its dominance in the computer industry stands as one of the great management failures of modern times. Let's take a look at whether it should have forecast the arrival of new entrants into its market, and then assess the consequences of this heightened competition.

Entry Decreases Demand and Your Profits

The simplest way to predict whether new businesses will enter a market is to put yourself in a potential rival's shoes. Imagine yourself as an aspiring entrepreneur looking to start a new business, or perhaps a manager of an existing firm looking to expand your lines of business. What would lead you to enter a specific market?

New competitors will enter profitable markets. The *cost-benefit principle* provides clear guidance: It's worth entering a new market if the benefits exceed the costs. The benefit of entering (or staying in) a market is the revenue you'll earn. The relevant costs, according to the *opportunity cost principle*, include both explicit financial costs, and also implicit opportunity costs, including forgone wages and interest. Economic profit measures the difference between these benefits and these costs. And so this says that it's worth entering a new market if you expect to earn a positive economic profit. This yields a useful guideline for aspiring entrepreneurs:

The **Rational Rule for Entry:** *You should enter a new market if you expect to earn a positive economic profit, which occurs when the price exceeds your average cost.*

Rational Rule for Entry You should enter a market if you expect to earn a positive economic profit, which occurs when the price exceeds your average cost.

This rule simply says that if there's an opportunity to earn an economic profit, you should take it!

As IBM discovered, entrepreneurs actually follow this advice. Profits are a powerful incentive drawing new competitors to your market. And there are many potential new rivals who might respond to this incentive. Your future competitors might include entrepreneurs starting new businesses, existing competitors opening new outlets or factories, or managers in related industries expanding their offerings to include new products that compete with yours. Indeed, there are so many potential entrants that it's hard to keep tabs on them all. If your industry is extra profitable, you should expect some of them to try to compete with you for those profits.

Viewed through this lens, the threat to IBM should have been obvious. Let's now trace out the consequences of new rivals entering a market.

Arco/A. Skonieczny/AGE Fotostock

Just as nectar attracts bees, profits attract new competitors.

New competitors make your market less profitable. When a new supplier enters your market, or an existing rival expands, you'll probably lose some market share as some of your customers will buy from the new entrant instead of you. This *decrease in demand* will lead you to sell a smaller quantity at any given price, shifting your firm's demand curve to the left.

The arrival of new competitors also gives your customers more choices, which means they're less likely to stick with you if you raise your price. (You might recognise this insight from Chapter 5, which suggested that the price elasticity of demand depends on the availability of substitutes.) As a result you have *less market power,* which means that your firm's demand curve is flatter, or relatively more elastic. Businesses with less market power typically charge a lower price, earning a lower profit margin. The left panel of Figure 4 illustrates these consequences.

Figure 4 | **Entry and Exit Shift Your Firm's Demand Curve**

Panel A: Entry Decreases Your Firm's Demand

When a new competitor enters . . .

Ⓐ You'll lose customers, and this **decrease in demand** shifts your **firm's demand curve** left.

Ⓑ You'll **lose market power**, flattening your **firm's demand curve**.

Panel B: Exit Increases Your Firm's Demand

When an existing firm exits . . .

Ⓐ You'll gain customers, and this **increase in demand** shifts your **firm's demand curve** right.

Ⓑ You'll **gain market power**, steepening your **firm's demand curve**.

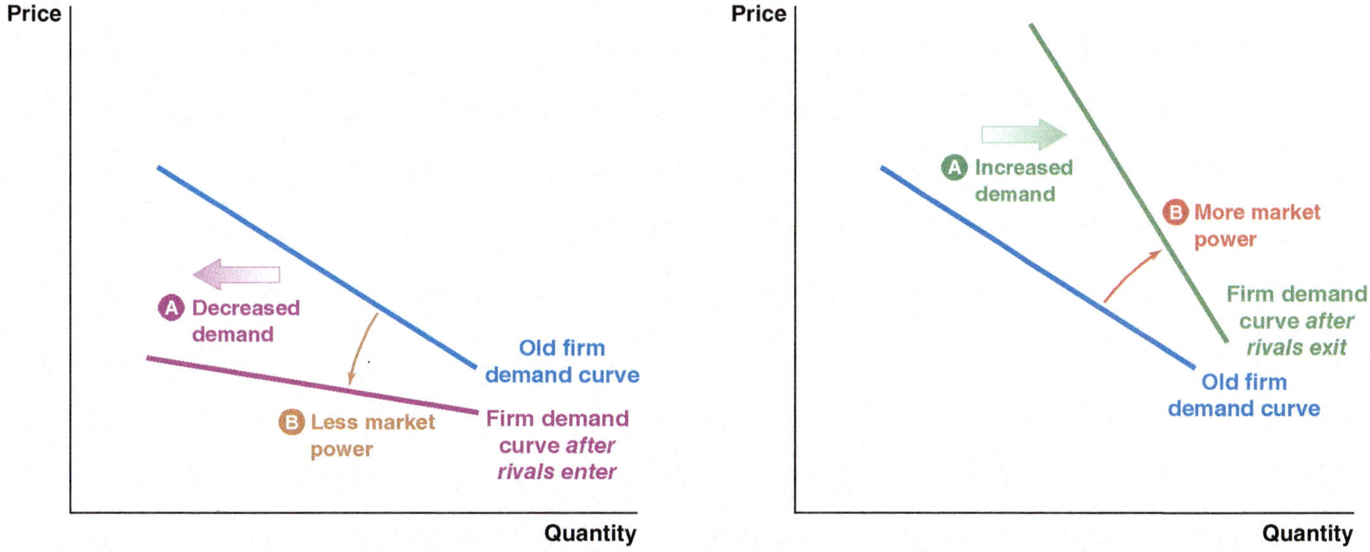

All told, the entry of new rivals into your market will decrease your profits because you'll sell a smaller quantity (due to the decrease in demand) at a lower price with a lower profit margin (because you have less market power). Indeed, as new rivals entered the computer industry, IBM struggled to maintain profitability.

Exit Increases Demand and Your Profits

There's a flip side to all this too. Just as the prospect of earning profits lures new firms to enter a market, the prospect of losses drives existing competitors to exit your market.

Existing competitors exit unprofitable markets, which helps restore profitability. Put yourself in the shoes of the manager of a business trying to decide whether or not to stay in the market. The *cost-benefit principle* says that if the costs of staying in the industry exceed the benefits, then you should exit. Economic profit measures the balance of these costs and benefits, and if it's negative, the costs of staying in the market exceed the benefits. This yields the following advice:

Rational Rule for Exit Exit the market if you expect to earn a negative economic profit, which occurs if the price is less than your average costs.

The **Rational Rule for Exit:** *Exit the market if you expect to earn a negative economic profit, which occurs if the price is less than your average costs.*

This simple rule says that if economic profits are negative, managers should exit the market, either by shutting down or by shifting their focus to another market.

When one of your rivals exits the market, it changes conditions for those businesses that remain. You'll probably win some of their market share as you sell to the customers of your recently departed rival. This *increase in demand* will shift your firm's demand curve to the right. With fewer rivals, you'll *have more market power,* which means that your firm's demand curve will be steeper, or relatively more inelastic. The right panel of Figure 4 illustrates both of these consequences.

The net effect is that as rivals exit the market your profits will recover, because you'll sell a larger quantity (due to the increase in demand) at a higher price (as you exploit your enhanced market power).

Economic Profits Tend to Zero

Okay, we've established four important facts. First, if your industry is currently profitable, new rivals will sniff out this opportunity and enter your market. Second, this extra competition will reduce the market share and market power of existing businesses, leading each of them to sell a smaller quantity at a lower price, which reduces their profitability.

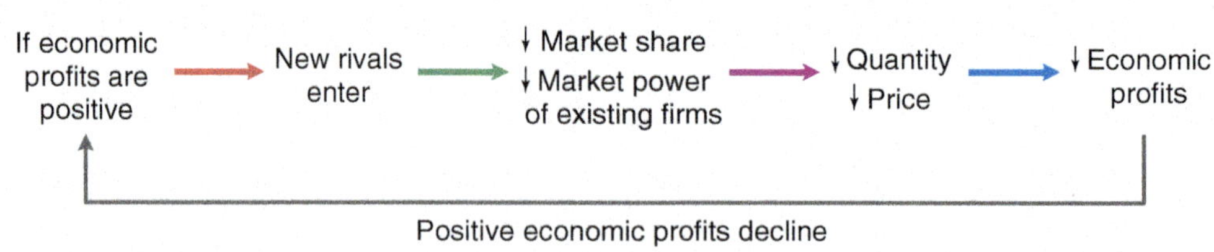

Third, the same dynamics also work in reverse, as negative economic profits lead some producers to exit the market. And fourth, the exit of a rival firm reduces competition, increasing the market share and market power of the remaining businesses, leading each of them to sell a larger quantity at a higher price, which helps restore their profitability.

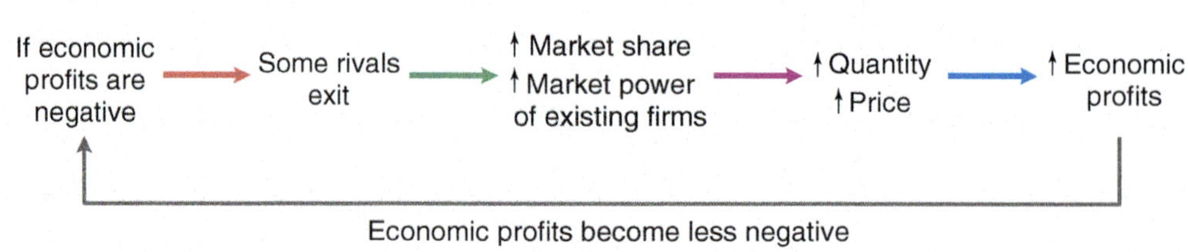

Let's explore how this process plays out in the long run.

Free entry pushes economic profits down to zero, in the long run. Things are going well in your industry, and your business is earning a nice economic profit. If your industry has **free entry,** which means there are no factors making it particularly difficult or costly for a new business to enter (or exit) the market, what do you forecast will happen next?

free entry When there are no factors making it particularly difficult or costly for a business to enter or exit an industry.

Aspiring entrepreneurs who get wind of this profit opportunity will follow the *Rational Rule for Entry* and enter your market. This extra competition will drive everyone's profits down a bit. What next? If your industry is still profitable, expect new entrepreneurs to continue entering your market. New rivals will continue to enter as long as economic profits are positive, with each additional competitor pushing profits down a bit further.

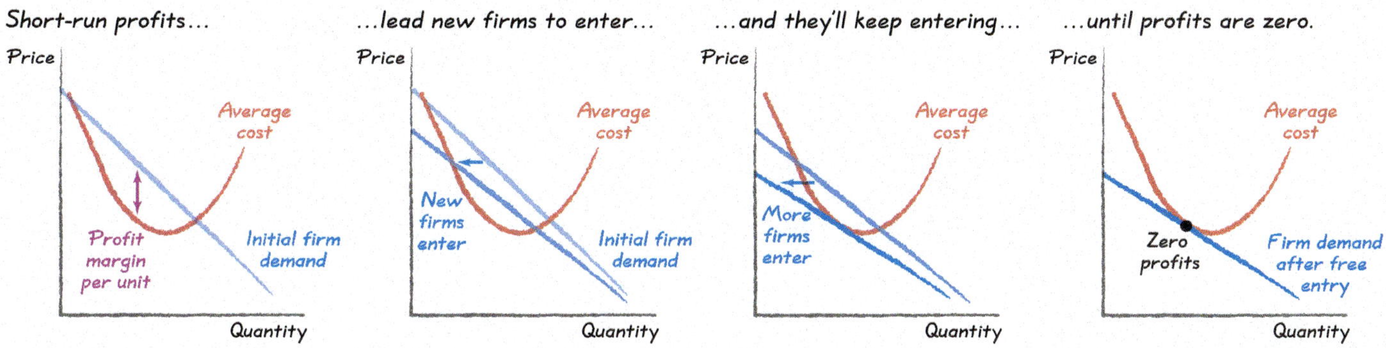

And so the process continues, until there's no longer any incentive for new businesses to enter your market. This occurs when the economic profits available to new entrants fall to zero.

Free exit ensures industries won't remain unprofitable in the long run. On the flip side, the possibility that your rivals may exit means that if your industry is currently unprofitable, it's likely that business conditions will eventually improve. Why? Those rivals facing the prospect of ongoing losses will follow the *Rational Rule for Exit* and leave the market. With fewer competitors, the profitability of the remaining businesses—including yours—will improve. If the market is still unprofitable, more businesses will choose to exit, and their exit will again bolster the profitability of those that remain. Managers will keep leaving as long as economic profits remain negative, with each additional exit improving the profitability of those that remain.

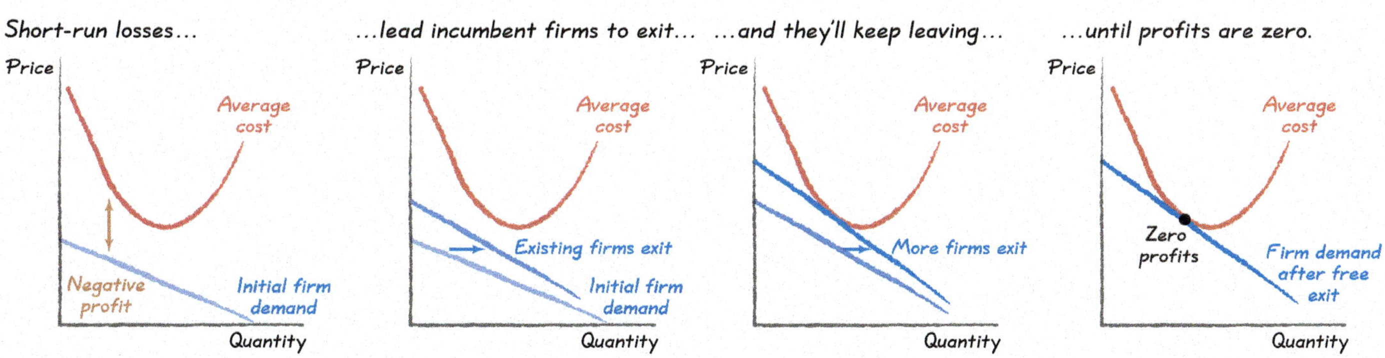

This process of unprofitable businesses leaving the market (or contracting) continues until the market is no longer unprofitable. This occurs when the economic profits enjoyed by incumbent businesses rise to zero.

Economic profits tend toward zero in the long run. Taken together, the dynamics of businesses freely entering and exiting a market—and of existing rivals expanding and contracting—tends to push economic profits to zero in the long run. That sounds like bad news. Perhaps. But don't overreact—it's not that bad. We're talking about *economic profits* of zero here, and economic profits effectively pay the entrepreneur for their time and money. If you earn zero economic profits in the long run, that means that you're doing as well running this business as in your next best alternative.

Desirable opportunities tend to disappear. In fact, there's a much broader idea at play here. Positive economic profits are just one example of a desirable opportunity, and *free entry tends to eliminate especially desirable opportunities*.

You can see this at the supermarket. Next time you're checking out, observe what happens if there's a shorter line for one of the cashiers. Your fellow shoppers understand that they can make a time profit if they join the shorter line. New shoppers will continue to enter the shorter line until this profit opportunity is extinguished. This occurs when that line becomes as long as the others. This dynamic means that in the long run, all the lines are of roughly the same length.

Sadly, the supermarket line is a metaphor for life. As the next case studies illustrate, there are many domains in which long-run entry and exit dynamics lead especially desirable opportunities to disappear.

EVERYDAY Economics

How free entry and exit shapes your chances of getting a table, how crowded your local surfing spot is, which classes are crowded, and where you'll move after college

Free entry is a powerful force that shapes outcomes in many areas of your life. The key insight is that any extraordinary opportunity plays the role that profits do—they're a signal beckoning new competitors to enter your market, and as they enter, those profits will dissipate. Think more broadly about what it means to earn a profit, and you'll find this insight applies elsewhere:

Andrew Shield/redbrickstock.com/Alamy

Your secret spot won't stay secret for long.

- Perhaps you've discovered an amazing restaurant—great meals at very reasonable prices. It's so good that it offers you a culinary "profit opportunity." Here's where free entry comes in: Other people will discover that restaurant, too, and the same thing that attracts you to the restaurant will attract them. As more people discover your hidden gem, it'll get crowded. The wait for a table will become uncomfortably long, and perhaps the restaurant will use its popularity as an excuse to raise its prices. Even so, as long as it remains better than alternative restaurants, even more people will keep flocking to it. They'll keep coming until the restaurant is no longer more enjoyable than other restaurants—the prices are too high, the wait is too long, or the waitstaff become too snooty. The free entry of new diners to your favourite restaurant effectively pushed your culinary profit toward zero.
- The same dynamics spoil all the best surf spots. If you've discovered an unusually good break, enjoy your "surfing profit" now, because it won't last. As other people discover it, your favourite spot will become more crowded, and soon you'll be fighting other surfers for a wave. The free entry of surfers will push your surfing profit back toward zero, and in the long run, no surfing break offers an unusually gnarly day.
- You've probably observed something similar with your classes. Every university has a few fantastic professors, and taking a class with one of them is a great opportunity. But this "educational profit opportunity" won't last. Next year more students will enroll in their class, and if it remains great, even more will enroll the next year. Give it a few years, and that class will be held in a massive lecture hall, with late arrivals watching a video feed in an overflow room. The free entry of new students into the most popular classes continues until the experience is no longer any better than taking an obscure seminar on eighteenth-century underwater basket weaving.
- When you graduate you'll have to decide what city to move to. If jobs are more abundant in Perth than elsewhere in the country, new graduates will flock to Perth to take advantage of those opportunities. As more people move to Perth, it'll become increasingly hard to land one of those jobs. Free entry of job-seekers across city lines will continue until the opportunities in Perth are no longer better than elsewhere in the country. Over time the free entry of job-seekers into different labour markets tends to eliminate the "profit opportunity" of especially abundant high-quality jobs. Indeed, in the long run, the quality of job opportunities tends to be roughly similar around the country. ■

Price Equals Average Cost

So far we've explored how free entry and exit shape your firm's long-term profitability. Let's now explore what this means for where the price will settle in the long run.

Free entry pushes the price down toward average cost. *If the price exceeds your average cost,* then you're making an economic profit. To repeat our earlier analysis: that economic profit is a signal for new entrepreneurs to enter the market. This reduces the profits of the incumbents, because the new entrants steal some of their customers (shifting their firm demand curves to the left), and rob them of some market power. This process of new firms entering and reducing industry profitability will continue until the *Rational Rule for Entry* says that it's no longer worth entering the industry. This occurs when economic profits return to zero, which means that *price is equal to average cost.*

huePhotography/Vetta/Getty Images

Her entry means your days of high profits are ending.

Free exit pushes the price up toward average cost. But, *if the price is less than average cost,* then your market is currently unprofitable. Those economic losses are an incentive for some companies to exit the market. Their exit increases the profitability of the businesses that remain, because they'll each win some customers from the departing company (shifting the firm demand curve of the remaining businesses to the right), and they'll each gain a bit more market power. This process of unprofitable companies exiting the market, thereby increasing the profitability of those that remain, will continue until the *Rational Rule for Exit* says that it's no longer worth leaving the market. This occurs when economic profits return to zero, which means that *price is equal to average cost.*

Carolyn Franks/Shutterstock

Their exit makes it easier for you to charge higher prices.

In the long run, if businesses are free to enter and exit, then price equals average cost.

In the long run with free entry (and exit), price equals average cost. Put the pieces together, and it says that if businesses can freely enter and exit the market they'll do so until new entrants can't earn a positive profit, and incumbent businesses aren't making losses. Thus, in the long run, you should expect:

$$\text{Price} = \text{Average cost}$$

The big idea here is that in the long run, prices are determined by entry and exit dynamics. This is a big deal, because it says that *average costs will be the dominant factor determining prices in the long run.*

This puts our short-run analysis in Chapter 14 in a different light. There, we discovered that businesses with market power can charge high prices—much higher than their costs—and earn high profits. But in a long-run analysis, if there's free entry into your market, then high prices yielding large profit margins are fleeting, because new firms will enter your market, undercut you, and compete your profits away.

Interpreting the DATA **Entry and exit are powerful forces**

Our long-run analysis emphasises how ongoing entry and exit can reshape your competitive landscape. Indeed, most industries are in a state of constant churn as new startups enter and older businesses exit, a process known as creative destruction.

Across the whole economy, there are around 2.4 million business establishments. In a typical year, roughly 13% of existing establishments shut down, to be replaced by a similar number of new entrants entering the market. The rates of entry and exit are roughly similar across different industries. This suggests that you should expect your competitive landscape to be in constant flux, as some rivals die off, and new rivals are born. ■

Your firm's demand curve just touches your average cost curve. Figure 5 illustrates the long-run equilibrium under free entry. Notice that this long-run equilibrium occurs where your firm's demand curve has been pushed left (or right) until it just touches the average cost curve. At the point where the curves touch, the best choice a manager can make—the only one point on the firm's demand curve that avoids a loss—is to set price equal to average cost.

Figure 5 | **Free Entry Continues Until Price Equals Average Cost**

Ⓐ In the short run, firms can earn **profits** when price exceeds **average cost**.
Ⓑ Profits attract new entrants, pushing the **firm's demand curve** to the left and making the curve more elastic.
Ⓒ Entry and exit continues until **profits are zero**.
Ⓓ In this long-run equilibrium, **price equals average cost**.

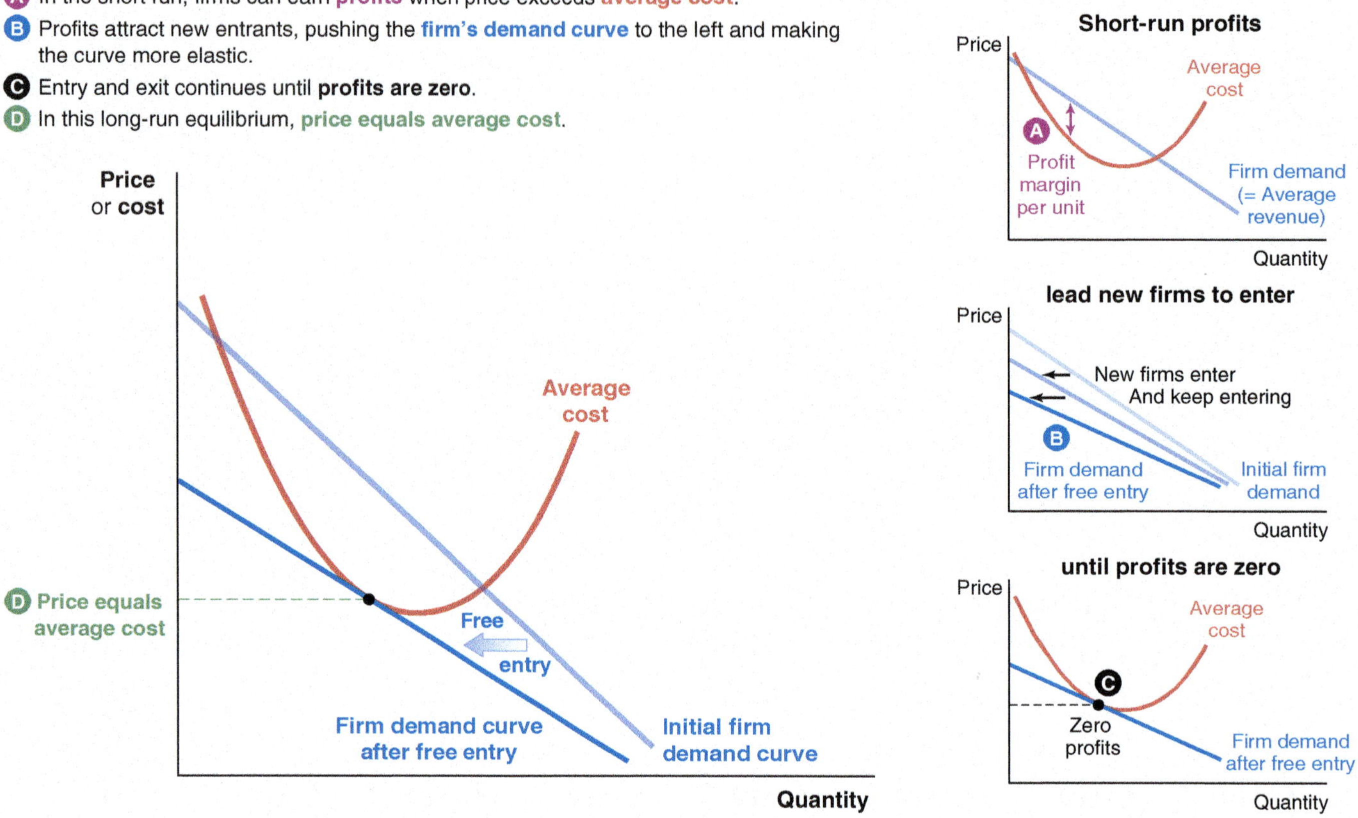

To see why the two curves have to just touch, realise that if any part of the demand curve lies above average costs, there's a profit opportunity—because price exceeds average costs. Free entry will continue until this opportunity is eliminated. And, if the demand curve lies entirely below average costs, then incumbent businesses must be making losses because price is always below average costs. Incumbent businesses will exit until these losses are eliminated. When the two curves touch, the best a company can do is make zero economic profits, which is a long-run equilibrium, because it'll lead the industry to neither expand (through entry) nor contract (through exit).

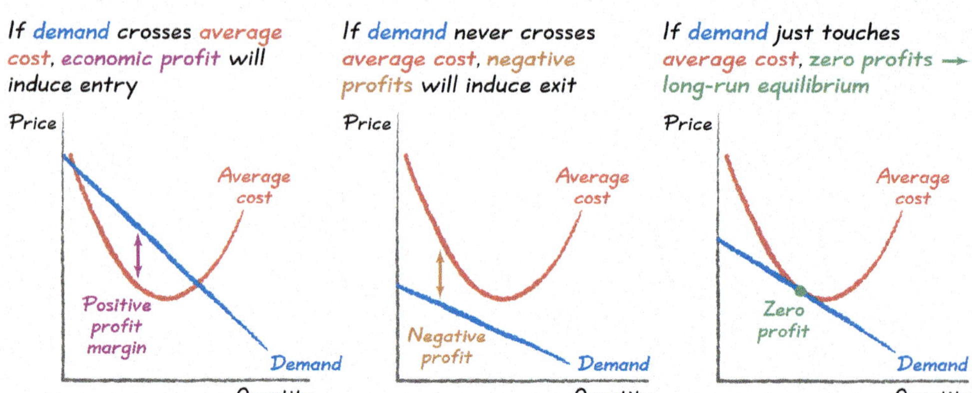

Average costs matter, because they determine the profitability of the marginal firm. The centrality of *average* costs to determining prices in the long run might seem surprising, since the *marginal principle* has typically led us to focus more on *marginal* costs. But in fact, this focus on average costs follows directly from applying the *marginal principle* to a long-run analysis.

To see why, realise that in the short run, the relevant question is whether to produce *one more unit.* So what matters in the short run is the marginal cost and marginal benefit of that extra unit. But in the long run, the relevant question is whether *one more business* will enter or exit. So what matters in the long run is the profitability of that *marginal business*—that's the company right on the cusp of entering or exiting—and that company's profit margin depends on their average costs. So it's actually the *marginal principle* that leads us to focus on average costs.

Interpreting the DATA **Is the mere threat of entry sufficient to lower prices?**

If you got a cheap flight before 2020, you might want to thank Tigerair, even if you flew on a different airline. Tigerair was an aggressive discounter—so aggressive that when it entered a new market, the incumbent airlines like Qantas, Jetstar, and Virgin had to cut their prices to compete. In fact, Jetstar started multiple campaigns in response to Tigerair entering the market, including committing to "doubling the difference" of any competitor fare cheaper than its own.

But sometimes a budget airline can cause prices to be lower even on routes that it doesn't fly. Indeed, economists in the United States analysed the prices of flights between two cities where the budget airline "Southwest" had a base, and found that even if Southwest didn't offer a service between those two airports, its rivals offered large discounts on those routes. The explanation is that the other airlines fear that Southwest will soon start offering service between those two cities. This fear—which is based on the mere *threat* of entry—has been sufficient to cause Southwest's rivals to cut their prices. Indeed, the threat of entry led Southwest's rivals to offer discounts that were nearly two-thirds as big as they would offer if Southwest actually entered the market and started competing with them! ■

Fabrizio Gandolfo/SOPA Images/LightRocket/Getty Images

Even just the threat that Tigerair will fly on a route causes prices to fall.

Recap: Your long-run profitability depends on barriers to entry. We've come a long way, so it's time to catch your breath, and pan back to the big picture. We can summarise it in one sentence: *If* there's free entry and exit, then in the long run, economic profits will be eliminated and price will equal average cost.

The rest of this chapter will be about just one of those words: *If.* That word points to your best chance for maintaining your long-run profitability. It suggests that *if* new rivals *don't* enter, then perhaps your profits won't be competed away.

This insight should change how you think about business strategy. You need to adjust your focus to look beyond outcompeting your existing competitors, so that you also deter new rivals from entering your market. Potential entrants are a threat to your long-run profitability, and your continuing success depends on finding a way to outflank them. Fortunately the business world provides dozens of examples of managers whose savvy strategic choices deterred potential rivals from entering and competing away their profits. And so our next task is to draw out the underlying logic of these strategies, so that you'll be equipped to adapt and apply them in your career.

15.3 Barriers to Entry

Learning Objective *Learn strategies to deter new entrants from competing away your profits.*

Apple, Westpac, and Coles have all been around for decades. Each has substantial market power, and each makes enormous profits. Yet the forces of entry and exit appear not to have pushed their economic profits to zero. Why?

barriers to entry Obstacles that make it difficult for new firms to enter a market.

The ongoing profitability of these businesses reflects **barriers to entry**—obstacles that make it difficult for new businesses to enter the market—and these barriers have prevented new entrants from competing away their profits.

It's not just that these companies got lucky. They got strategic. Each devotes a lot of resources to preventing new rivals from entering their respective markets. The lesson from their success is that you shouldn't think of these barriers to entry as naturally occurring defences. Rather, the barriers to entering your market are also shaped by the strategic choices that you'll make as a manager.

Four strategies to outcompete and deter new entrants:

1. Demand-side: Create customer lock-in.
2. Supply-side: Develop unique cost advantages.
3. Regulatory: Mobilise government to prevent entry.
4. Deterrence: Convince potential entrants you'll crush them.

In order to remain profitable in the long run, you need to focus on the threat posed by potential new entrants and find ways to outcompete and deter them.

Different firms employ different strategies, but they all rely on four big ideas:

1. Find ways to create customer lock-in *(demand-side strategies).*
2. Develop unique cost advantages *(supply-side strategies).*
3. Mobilise the government to prevent entry *(regulatory strategies).*
4. Convince potential entrants you'll crush them *(deterrence strategies).*

Let's explore these strategies in greater detail.

Demand-Side Strategies: Create Customer Lock-In

One way to prevent new entrants from succeeding is to prevent them from winning over your existing customers. That's why you want to create customer lock-in. Because customer-focused strategies shape the demand for your product (and that of your rivals), we refer to these ideas as *demand-side* strategies. Some key strategies include:

switching costs An impediment that makes it costly for customers to switch to buying from another business.

Switching costs lock your customers in. **Switching costs** refer to any impediment that makes it difficult or costly for your customers to buy from another business instead. For instance, around three out of four iPhone owners who upgrade their phones stick with another iPhone. This isn't just brand loyalty, it's partly due to switching costs—if you switch to an Android phone, you'll have to re-buy all of your favourite apps plus go through extra hassle transferring your data.

Savvy managers actively create switching costs to deter competitors. For instance, your bank probably gives you automatic bill-pay services. It's not that your bank is trying to make your life easier, but rather it wants to lock you in. It knows that once you've set all your bills to autopay, you won't want to do all that work again, and so you won't switch to a competing bank. Similarly, when an airline gives you frequent flyer points, it makes it more rewarding to keep flying on that airline, effectively making it more costly to switch to a rival. And if you've ever tried to cancel your Foxtel free trial before your first payment, you've probably experienced how Foxtel tries to make your switch as big of a hassle as they can. (You'll have to return your cable box between 3 P.M. and 3:15 P.M. during a full moon at an office that's miles away.)

In each of these cases, switching costs effectively lock in existing customers, making it harder for new entrants to succeed.

Reputation and goodwill keep your customers loyal. A key reason that doctors, mechanics, plumbers, and electricians work to build a good reputation with their clients is that it helps lock in their customers. This goodwill gives incumbents a robust advantage over potential entrants who have yet to build those relationships.

Here's the basic logic: Think about what you'll do next time you're sick. I bet you're much more likely to visit the doctor who you've built a long-term relationship with, than to shop around to see if a new practice is offering a better deal. That loyalty makes it hard for a recent medical school graduate to successfully set up a rival practice.

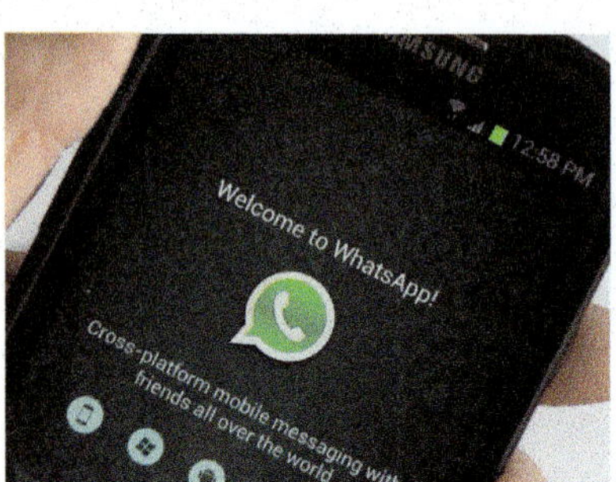

STAN HONDA/AFP/Getty Images

The best reason to use this is because your friends do too.

Network effects mean that your product becomes more useful the more people use it. There are literally dozens of apps that allow you to communicate by text. But most have very few users, while WhatsApp is so popular that Facebook paid $25 billion to buy it (and many analysts think it's worth billions more). Amazingly, it's worth billions even though the technology just isn't that complicated, and programmers could whip up an alternative—let's call it WhatsUp—in just a few weeks. But a new entrant like WhatsUp couldn't really compete, because what makes WhatsApp so useful is that your friends all use it. And so people keep using WhatsApp, because other people use it. The result is that it is virtually impossible for a new entrant like WhatsUp to beat the incumbent WhatsApp.

This is an example of a *network effect,* which occurs whenever a product becomes more useful when others also use it. Savvy managers work to create these network effects, because they make it harder for potential entrants to compete with them. For instance, when more people use Amazon's website, it becomes more useful, because past customers write reviews that are helpful to future customers. As a result, Amazon is great for comparison shopping, and the millions of reviews on its site are an advantage that a new entrant can't easily replicate.

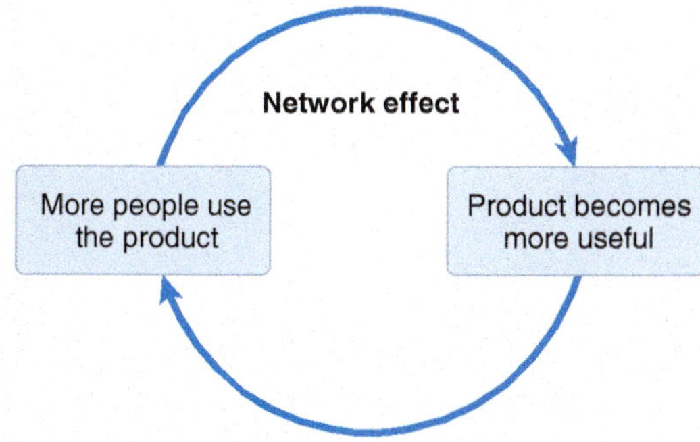

Network effects aren't just about high-tech products either. They're critical to the ongoing success of the major car companies, like Hyundai, Ford, and Toyota. Why? One reason to buy from a popular carmaker is that millions of other people have done so too, and so there are thousands of repair shops with the spare parts in stock, and competent mechanics who can install them. By contrast, a new carmaker that lacks this network of repair shops will struggle to attract customers.

These network effects can be so powerful that they help even bad products succeed. Consider the Windows operating system, which millions of people have a love-hate relationship with. But even the haters keep using it, because there are so many useful programs available for it. Those programs are available because even programmers who despise Windows keep writing software for it, mainly because so many people use it. Despite all the complaints, no major competitor (except Apple) has entered the market, because no one will buy an operating system with few programs, and no one will write programs for an operating system that few people use.

Supply-Side Strategies: Develop Unique Cost Advantages

It's also possible to deter the entry of new rivals by gaining cost advantages that newcomers cannot easily replicate. To see why, remember the key role that the *marginal principle* plays: New competitors will continue to enter a market until the last competitor that enters—the *marginal* supplier, which is the company that's right on the cusp of entering or exiting—expects its economic profit to be zero.

But that doesn't mean *your* economic profits will be zero. Figure 6 illustrates a long-run equilibrium, in which price is equal to the average cost of the marginal supplier, and so no more firms will enter. But if your firm has lower costs than that marginal supplier, then you'll continue to earn economic profits, even if the marginal supplier is earning zero profit.

Even better, if your cost advantages are large enough, they can effectively deter entry. After all, few entrepreneurs want to enter a market where they'll have to compete with an incumbent with lower costs. Your lower costs signal that you're more likely to survive a price war, as you can get by on a somewhat smaller profit margin for much longer than a rival can endure continuing losses.

Your long-run profitability depends on maintaining your cost advantage, and that's only possible if your rivals can't just copy the techniques that you're using to lower your costs. This is why you must develop *unique* cost advantages that others can't simply copy. Let's dig into key strategies for developing unique cost advantages.

Figure 6 | **Cost Advantages Generate Lasting Profits**

Free entry continues until Price = Average cost of the marginal supplier

(A) In a long-run equilibrium, the **marginal supplier** considering entry will earn zero economic profit.

(B) If **your average costs** are lower than the **marginal supplier's average costs**, you can still earn **economic profits**.

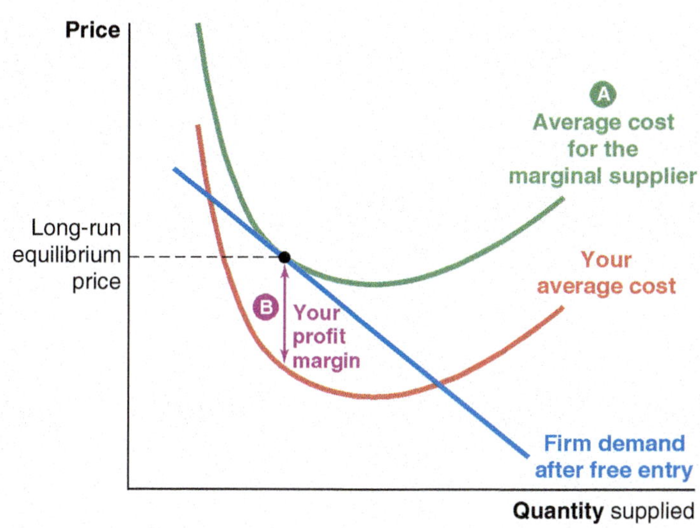

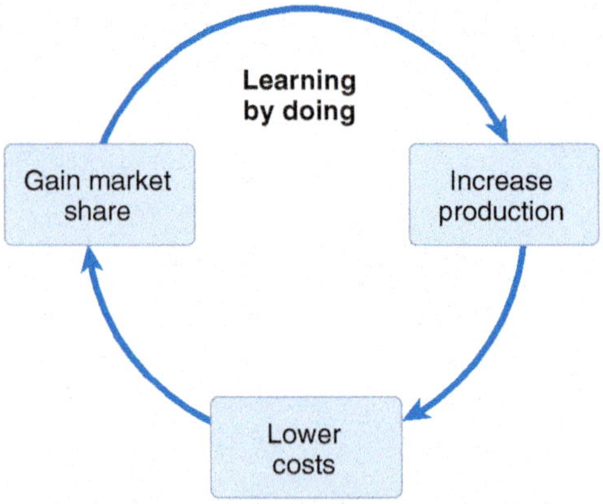

Learning by doing means that experience yields efficiency gains. Many managers report that as they gain experience making a product, they learn how to streamline their operations, making them more efficient. Indeed, some consultants have estimated that every time a business doubles its accumulated production, it'll learn enough to decrease its costs by around 20–30%. If you're the incumbent, this process of *learning by doing* can yield a pretty robust advantage over newcomers whose inexperience means that they're stuck with higher costs.

This insight also has strategic implications. It says to aggressively seek market leadership in order to gain a self-reinforcing advantage: If you're the market leader, you produce the most, which gives you the most opportunities for *learning by doing*, which will lower your costs the most, further reinforcing your position as a market leader. And so it can be worth charging lower prices and forgoing profits in the short run, in order to set in chain this virtuous cycle.

Dobrovizcki/Shutterstock

Mass production can give you a competitive advantage.

The benefits of mass production can keep small firms from being competitive entrants. Mass production is often more efficient than producing in small batches, although it often involves big fixed costs on machinery. These big upfront costs can make it difficult for new entrants to compete. In particular, if small businesses lack the funding to make these investments, they'll operate at a substantial cost disadvantage relative to the large incumbent firms.

Take a quick look on Etsy, and you'll see what I mean. You'll discover an army of woodworkers who would love to devote their careers to making furniture. But building each individual table by hand is much less efficient than the giant production lines that churn out thousands of tables for Freedom. That's why the hand-crafted furniture on Etsy is more costly to produce than the furniture at Freedom. And that cost disadvantage explains why these aspiring furniture makers aren't really a serious threat to major furniture companies.

Research and development can create cost advantages. Too often, executives think about research and development in terms of developing new products. But it can be at least as valuable to develop cheaper ways to make existing products, because it'll give you a lasting cost advantage over potential entrants. In fact, much of the field of management science is about finding new ways of organising the workplace to create cost savings. And there have been some stellar successes. Coles, for instance, is developing an AI-powered logistics system, which will mean that it can maintain stock levels more quickly, cheaply, and with less waste than its rivals. Toyota is famous for its innovative management practices, which mean it can produce cars more cheaply than most of its potential competitors. And Amazon's research into cloud computing means that it can manage its enormous website more effectively than rival e-tailers.

martin berry/Alamy Stock Photo

Coles can afford to sell at Everyday Low Prices because it has negotiated Everyday Even Lower Prices from its suppliers.

Relationships with suppliers can get you cheaper inputs. As you develop close relationships with your suppliers, you'll become a valued business partner. As you grow, your business will become even more important to their success, making them invested in your success. You'll be able to use your buying power to demand discounts on your raw materials, wholesale goods, and other inputs.

It's a lesson that's central to Coles' success, and it has used its relationships and buying power to great effect. Coles is a huge player, and selling to Coles can make or break even large suppliers. Coles uses this leverage to negotiate ferociously. As a result, the wholesale prices that Coles pays its suppliers are much lower than those available to any new entrant. In turn, that cost advantage makes Coles a formidable competitor, and it has driven many rival stores out of business, and deterred countless others from ever entering.

Access to key inputs can freeze your competitors out. Cement Australia purchased "flyash"—a by-product in coal-fired electricity generation—in South East Queensland (SEQ) in the early 2000s. When flyash is processed into a powder it can be used to make concrete.

At the time, there were four power stations in SEQ capable of producing flyash. Cement Australia had existing contracts with two of those power stations allowing them to purchase all the flyash they produced. Cement Australia then entered into contracts with the other two power stations. This led to a court case brought by the Australian Competition and Consumer Commission (ACCC). The court found that Cement Australia had substantial market power but that it did not "take advantage" of that market power.

There was subsequently an amendment to the Competition and Consumer Act 2010 to make it easier to prove that market power had been taken advantage of in such circumstances.

The broader idea is that by tying up key inputs—often through long-term contracts—incumbents can make it difficult for new entrants to succeed. In some cases, these contracts run afoul of regulators. But in others, the effects are less direct. For instance, many Silicon Valley start-ups complain that their biggest problem is hiring software engineers, because most of the best ones are already working for the tech giants like Google or Facebook. By tying up key programming talent, the existing tech companies make it difficult for start-ups to compete.

Jeff Haynes/Invision for Facebook/AP Images

If you're a start-up founder, it's going to be hard to compete with Facebook for top talent.

Regulatory Strategy: Government Policy

The government can be a major force shaping whether new companies can enter your market. Sometimes the government regulates who can enter a market because it's trying to counter some kind of market failure, and sometimes it does so in response to politicians being swayed by corporate lobbyists. Let's explore some of these government-focused strategies.

Patents give you the right to be the only producer. If you invent a new product, the government will grant you a patent, which means that no other company can use your idea without your permission. A patent effectively grants your company a monopoly. The government provides this right in order to provide an incentive for innovation.

This barrier to entry is the reason why Apple doesn't worry about other companies making the iPhone. It's why Alphapharm doesn't worry about other pharmaceutical companies selling their patented antidepressant Coperin. And it's why Toyota is not concerned that anyone else is trying to build a Prius. An alternative approach is to protect your invention by keeping it a secret, which is why Coke ensures that only a few senior executives know the recipe for Coca-Cola. And so even though some rivals make alternative colas, none can enter the market for the precise blend we know as Coca-Cola.

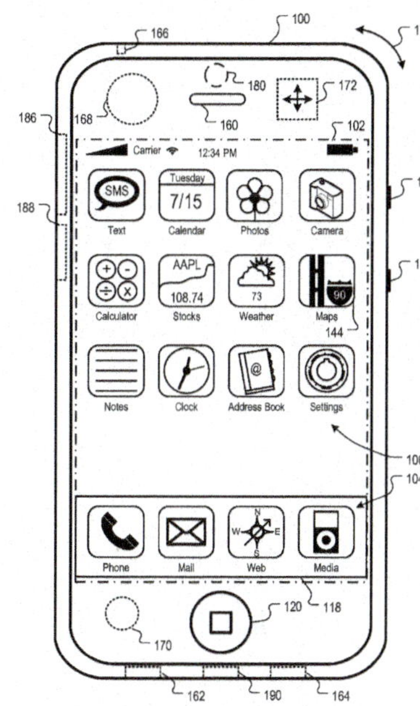
Apple Inc., Patent US20090226091A1

This patent describes Apple's new invention.

Regulations make it difficult for new businesses to enter your market. Government regulations can make it difficult to start a new business. For example, in some countries, it can take more than three months to step through the dozen or so separate procedures required to register a new business, and the associated fees can easily add up to more than a year's income.

That said, there are some sectors of the Australian economy that the government regulates closely—often for good reason. If you're thinking about opening a child care centre, a hospital, or a private school, you'll quickly discover a regulatory burden that's hefty enough to count as a substantial barrier to entry.

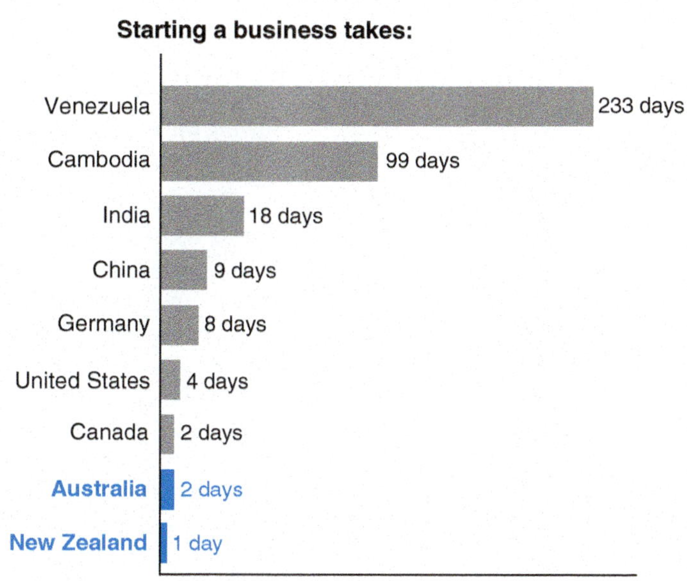

Data from: World Bank.

Compulsory licences can limit competition. The government directly regulates entry in some markets, and you'll need a government-issued licence to be allowed to do business. For instance, you can't operate a radio or TV station without a licence from the Australian Communications and Media Authority. These licences are both scarce and a hassle to obtain, which serves as a barrier to entry. While regulating the airwaves helps minimise static and interference, it also limits competition among radio stations. Sadly these barriers to entry are the reason there are so few stations playing interesting music.

Lobbying can create new regulatory barriers. Many big businesses spend millions of dollars lobbying governments. Sometimes, they do this in ways that serve the common good—perhaps to persuade the government to fix outdated rules. But often it's because they hope to convince the government to implement rules that will interfere with the plans of potential new entrants. You might be surprised to sometimes see incumbent firms arguing for more government regulations in their industry. It's one of the oldest tricks in the lobbyist's book. Look closer, and you'll usually discover that these tighter regulations raise the costs on potential entrants by more than they raise the costs on incumbents. The incumbents are hoping that more intense regulation—while costly—will insulate them from competition.

Of course, business lobbyists never say it this way. They make their case by arguing that restricted entry or tighter regulation is somehow necessary to protect the public. And they'll say this even though it prevents competition that would benefit the public by pushing prices down and providing options. But we know what really worries them: As new rivals enter their market, incumbents fear that their profitability will decline.

Politicians are often quite receptive to these arguments, because of an interesting political asymmetry. When a politician protects an incumbent business from competition, they'll earn the gratitude of both the executives at that company, and the workers whose jobs they helped save. However, this comes at the cost of an unknown potential entrant that won't enter the market and create new jobs. These costs are less politically salient, because no one holds those jobs yet, and so they don't constitute an active lobby group.

Entry Deterrence Strategies: Convince Your Rivals You'll Crush Them

Finally, *entry deterrence strategies* work by convincing potential rivals that if they do enter your market, you'll respond so aggressively that they'll wish they had never entered. Sure, your industry may be profitable now, but you want to convince potential entrants that if they enter, prices will fall by so much that they'll never earn any profits themselves.

The challenge in pulling this off is that top managers will say that they're planning to crush their rivals, whether it's true or not. And because potential entrants understand this, they may not believe you. And so the goal of entry deterrence strategies is to make your threat credible—so that you can convince potential rivals that you really will destroy them if they decide to enter. That's why the key to these effective deterrence strategies is to take concrete steps that commit your firm to compete aggressively. It's the commitment to following through that makes your threats credible.

Let's survey some specific strategies that savvy managers have used.

Build excess capacity so that your rivals expect fierce competition. It's worth considering building more production capacity than you actually need. This does three things. First, it makes it clear that you have the capacity to increase your production and cut prices if new rivals enter the market. Effectively you're showing that you've invested in the infrastructure to start a price war, and win. Second, it's especially useful to invest in excess capacity if it means incurring higher fixed costs today that will enable you to produce at a lower marginal cost in the future. Your lower marginal costs effectively commit your company to charging a low price if a new rival enters. As a result, your potential rivals should expect fierce competition if they do enter. And third, when this excess capacity takes the form of irreversible sunk costs, you're effectively committing your company to stay in the market to fight potential rivals, because you can't deploy those resources elsewhere. You've no choice but to compete, and compete vigorously, and any entrant should expect a bruising fight. For each of these reasons, building excess capacity can convince potential rivals that entering your market is not going to end well for them.

Financial resources signal that you can survive a costly fight. In mid-2018, Apple had an extraordinary $244 billion of cash on hand. That's more cash than Microsoft, Google, and Amazon combined. Many financial analysts remain unsure as to why Apple doesn't return the money to shareholders, invest it in new businesses, or do something more productive with it.

But business strategists see a reason: Apple's mountain of cash is a signal to potential entrants. It's a signal that Apple has the resources to survive a long and costly fight to maintain its market share. I don't know about you, but if I were running a tech company, that mountain of cash would scare me. A well-stocked war chest can be a powerful signal to a potential entrant that perhaps they're better off finding some other company to fight.

Brand proliferation can ensure there are no profitable niches for a rival to exploit. Have you ever noticed that the breakfast cereal aisle at the supermarket is about a mile long, featuring dozens of varieties catering to just about every conceivable whim? It's all about entry deterrence.

In reality, those dozens of different cereals are made by only a handful of companies. Their brand proliferation is a deliberate strategy to ensure that there's almost no way for a new entrant to find a profitable niche. And it works—look closely next time you're there, and you'll see that new entrants haven't really been able to break through.

jason freeman/Alamy Stock Photo

Lots of choice, but few competitors.

Your reputation for fighting can be helpful, too. If you've ever needed to buy a power tool, replace a light bulb, renovate a house, or even just been in the mood for a sausage sizzle, you've probably been to Bunnings Warehouse. Bunnings has been the dominant hardware store in Australia for decades, and no other hardware store has been successful in taking away from Bunnings' national market share. One of the keys to Bunnings' success has been its "Price Guarantee." If you find a lower price on an identically stocked item at one of Bunnings' competitors, Bunnings will beat the price by 10%.

Bunnings has created customer lock-in through its good reputation and substantial goodwill. When Woolworths Limited tried to establish a competing chain of hardware stores called Masters in 2009, things didn't go to plan. Instead of Masters splitting the market with Bunnings, Bunnings' profits continued to increase, while Masters made a loss. Since customers trusted Bunnings more than its newfound competitor, and they knew Bunnings would beat any low price Masters had to offer, people simply continued shopping at Bunnings—and were able to secure even lower prices than before using the price-beat guarantee! Indeed, Masters was closed down by Woolworths in 2016, only 7 years after its establishment. The important lesson here is that price-match policies act as a deterrent for new entrants. The incumbent firm is committing itself to offering a lower price than any entrant could possibly offer, and at that point, it becomes a question of who can last the longest through a price war—and usually it's the incumbent who wins.

Overcoming Barriers to Entry

At this point you've analysed the four key types of barriers to entry summarised in Figure 7. Which tools you should use depends on the structure of your market, and the types of barriers that are easiest to impose. If you get your strategy right, you'll be well placed to defy the odds and make consistently high profits.

So far, most of our analysis has focused on how managers of incumbent businesses *create* these entry barriers. But as an aspiring entrepreneur looking to break into a market, you'll want to *overcome* these barriers to entry. The good news is that the understanding you've developed in this chapter will be just as useful as you develop strategies to break into new markets. Indeed, that's a point that's well illustrated by our final case study—the story of how one savvy entrepreneur overcame what appeared to be insurmountable barriers to entry in the car industry.

Figure 7 | **Barriers to Entry**

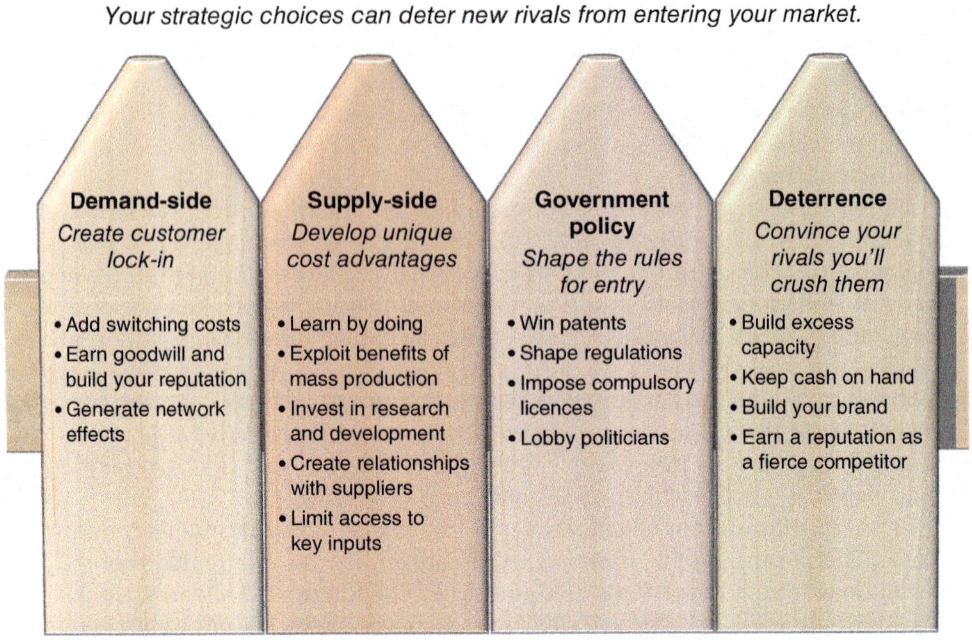

Entrepreneurs need to overcome barriers to entry. In recent years, electric car maker Tesla has become one of America's most iconic brands, so much so that one analyst named the Tesla Model S the "Car of the Decade." Before Tesla could become a household name, however, founder Elon Musk had to figure out how to break into the impenetrable car market. For years, industry analysts had thought that barriers to entry made it impossible for a start-up to compete with established manufacturers like Ford, Toyota, and Volkswagen. And so Elon Musk's task then was not just to develop a new kind of electric car. It was also to combat the barriers to entry that had prevented others from even trying. Let's see how he did it.

Demand-side strategies to combat customer lock-in. One of the biggest hurdles Tesla faced in winning over car buyers was the network effects of traditional petrol-powered vehicles. If you drive a petrol-powered car, you probably take it for granted that there are thousands of petrol stations where you can refuel. For Tesla's potential customers, the absence of a similar network of places to recharge their cars would make owning an electric car a real headache. To overcome this lock-in, Tesla subsidised the installation of thousands of electric car chargers in carparks, hotels, and restaurants.

But developing a nationwide network is a bigger problem than any individual company can solve, and so Musk invited other companies to use Tesla's patented technology. That might sound odd, because this move made it easier for other electric car manufacturers to compete with Tesla. But Musk understood the value of building network effects. He figured that a thriving electric-car industry would lead to a vibrant network of charging stations and repair shops, and without this network, Tesla couldn't succeed.

Supply-side strategies to overcoming cost disadvantages. Previous generations of entrepreneurs had been intimidated by the cost advantages of incumbent car manufacturers—particularly in research and development and manufacturing. But based on his experience in Silicon Valley, Musk realised he could spend a fraction of the research costs of major companies to bring Tesla's cars to market. He did this by partnering with experienced British car manufacturer Lotus to reduce his up-front costs and by getting a low-volume luxury model (called the Roadster) to market quickly. Testing the waters with the roadster provided Tesla with an opportunity for learning by doing, and the company was able to refine its technology and reduce its costs before trying to scale up with a less expensive model for the mass market.

Although Tesla only produced and sold 2,500 Roadsters in the company's first four years, the company demonstrated that it could successfully build desirable electric cars. That early success convinced additional investors that Tesla was worth backing. Tesla used that infusion of funds to invest in research that created unique costs advantages, allowing it to produce lower-cost models that would eventually reach more customers.

Use regulatory strategies to your advantage. The car industry faces heavy safety and environmental regulations, and complying with these complicated rules could impose large up-front costs on new entrants. But Tesla saw the government's concern with the environment as an opportunity. After all, electric cars are far kinder to the environment than gas-guzzlers. Tesla positioned itself to benefit from the U.S. government policies to reduce emissions. It received a US$465 million loan under an Energy Department program to boost fuel-efficient vehicles. Buyers of Teslas and other electric cars received federal subsidies of up to US$7,500, plus some states chipped in further rebates of up to US$5,000 as well as access to carpool lanes and cheaper electricity. Even though Tesla's cars were expensive, these subsidies—and similar ones in other countries—made them more affordable. In recent years, Tesla has joined with other electric car makers to lobby the U.S. government to continue these tax credits.

Ian Shaw/Alamy

Clean enough the government wants to subsidise it.

As a newcomer to the car market, Tesla held one more ace: It could decide where to locate its new factories, and it recognised that state governments would compete vigorously to become its new home. Before deciding where to build its battery factory, Musk negotiated with Texas, Arizona, New Mexico, and California, and finally settled on Nevada—but only after the state government offered US$1.3 billion in tax breaks and other incentives.

Overcoming deterrence strategies to fight the big guys. Ford, Hyundai, and other leading car manufacturers have huge war chests—often holding billions of dollars of cash on hand. Yet Musk did not let this stop him, even when he thought Tesla had a one-in-ten chance of succeeding. Admittedly, Musk had an advantage that not all entrepreneurs do: He had successfully founded and sold the online payment service PayPal, so his deep pockets and strong connections to Silicon Valley investors provided Tesla with its own sizeable war chest to combat the established car companies.

Look closely at Tesla's story, and you can see that Elon Musk's understanding of the economic ideas we've developed in this chapter—he majored in both physics and economics—helped him develop a successful strategy to overcome some pretty fearsome barriers to entry. The final chapter of this case study is yet to be written, as Tesla's long-term success is not yet assured: Electric cars still represent only a tiny sliver of the market. But it has already made an impact. At one point in 2020, Tesla was worth $631 billion, meaning that this brash upstart had risen to be worth more than the combined worth of the next top six car companies. Today, legacy carmakers see themselves as playing catch-up in the electric car market, as they try to replicate the successes of innovative newcomer Tesla.

Tying It Together

The key development in this chapter is that we've shifted our focus from the short run to the long run. This yields a more organic understanding of market structure. In the short run, your competitive landscape consists of a fixed number of rivals. But in the long run, new rivals can enter and disrupt your market. As they do so, they'll change the structure of competition, and shift market power. But incumbent businesses don't passively watch as these changes play out. They're also strategic actors, using the tools at their disposal to impose barriers to entry and stifle competition. Likewise, brash new entrants like Tesla use these same insights to try to overcome barriers to entry. Your competitive landscape evolves as this strategic battle ebbs and flows.

When savvy executives have both the means to deter competitors and the incentive to do so, perhaps it's no surprise that we see most markets are imperfectly competitive, and most businesses manage to retain some degree of market power. This dynamic highlights a central tension in markets. Consumers' best interests are served by vigorous competition in which new businesses enter and compete with incumbents, driving prices lower. Those vibrant newcomers drive inefficient incumbents out of the market, and provide a constant source of renewal. But incumbent businesses want to protect their economic profits, and so they try to deter entry and lessen competition. The tension here is that markets work most effectively when there's vibrant competition, but businesses will do all they can to throttle that competition.

That's why there's often fierce debate about what "free markets" really mean. Does it mean that the government should stay out of the way and let companies create large barriers to entry? Or should the government actively prevent companies from getting too big and powerful, so that more businesses can enter the market? This tension highlights the distinction between *pro-market* policies, which ensure consumers enjoy the benefits of robust competition in the market, and *pro-business* policies, which help existing businesses, often at the cost of destroying opportunities for potential new entrants.

Chapter at a Glance

Accounting profits: The total revenue a firm receives, less its explicit financial costs.

Economic profit: The total revenue a firm receives, less both explicit financial costs and the entrepreneur's implicit opportunity costs.

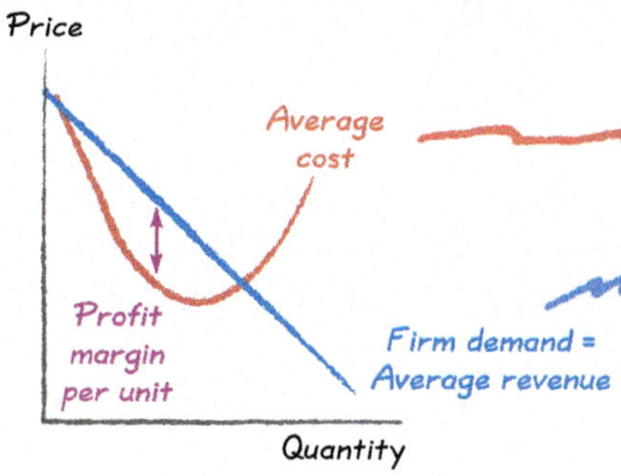

Profit Margin:

Average cost is the cost per unit, calculated as your firm's total costs (including fixed and variable costs) divided by the quantity produced.

Your **firm's demand curve** is also the **average revenue curve** because your average revenue per unit is the price.

Your **profit margin per unit** is **average revenue** less **average cost**.

✳ Free Entry and Exit in the Long Run:

The Rational Rule for Entry: You should enter a new market if you expect to earn a positive **economic profit**, which occurs when the **price** exceeds your **average costs**.

Short run profits . . . . . . lead new firms to enter . . . . . . and they keep entering . . . . . . until profits are zero . . .

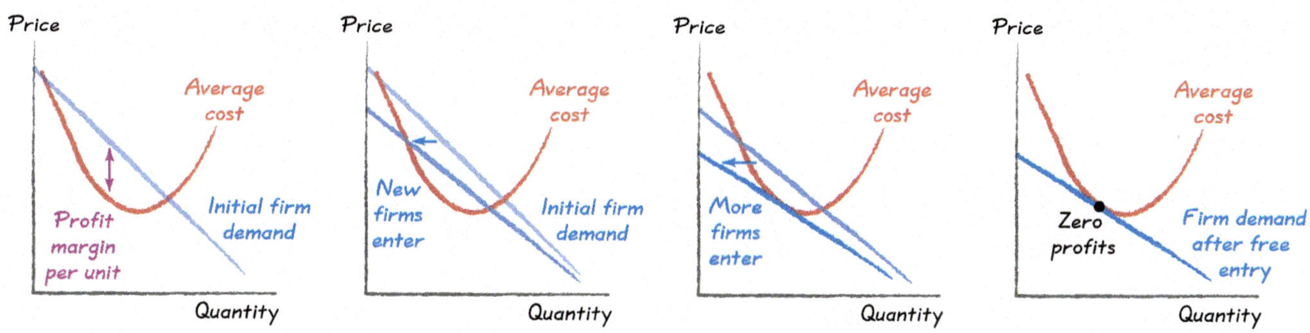

In the Long Run: Price = Average Cost

The Rational Rule for Exit: Exit the market if you expect to earn a negative **economic profit**, which occurs if the **price** is less than your **average costs**.
Short-run losses lead incumbent firms to exit and they'll keep leaving until profits are zero.

Barriers to Entry: Obstacles that make it difficult for new firms to enter a market.

Demand-side
Create customer lock-in

- Add switching costs
- Earn goodwill and build your reputation
- Generate network effects

Supply-side
Develop unique cost advantages

- Learn by doing
- Exploit benefits of mass production
- Invest in research and development
- Create relationships with suppliers
- Limit access to key inputs

Government Policy
Shape the rules for entry

- Win patents
- Shape regulations
- Impose compulsory licences
- Lobby politicians

Deterrence
Convince your rivals you'll crush them

- Build excess capacity
- Keep cash on hand
- Build your brand
- Earn a reputation as a fierce competitor

Key Concepts

Discussion and Review Questions

Learning Objective 15.1 *Assess your business's economic profitability.*

1. What does the decision to start a business have in common with the decision to attend university? Beyond the explicit financial costs, what are the implicit opportunity costs that you need to account for when making each decision?
2. Lukia is thinking of quitting her job as a TV news editor to start her own business as a freelancer, editing video for media organisations from her home studio. Describe how her accounting profit would be different than her economic profit. How should her analysis of her economic profit (or lack thereof) impact her decision to start her business?

Learning Objective 15.2 *Forecast how new entrants will change long-run prices and profitability in your market.*

3. Petra's private equity firm is considering investing in a highly profitable local CrossFit gym. However, after researching the local gym market, she expects rival gyms to easily enter and exit the industry in the long run. How should she explain to her partners why this leads her to expect that in the long run, the gym's economic profits will decline to zero.

Learning Objective 15.3 *Learn strategies to deter new entrants from competing away your profits.*

4. Half a century ago, foreign banks were prohibited from operating in Britain unless they had an office that was within walking distance of the Bank of England, which served as the industry's regulator at the time. How would this requirement serve as a barrier to entry into the banking industry in Britain?
5. For each of the following, briefly explain how it can create a cost advantage for a business.
   - **a.** Learning by doing
   - **b.** Mass production
   - **c.** Research and development

Study Problems

Learning Objective 15.1 *Assess your business's economic profitability.*

1. Joshua owns a small tech start-up that does data analysis for school districts around the country. Which of the following would be included in calculating his business's accounting profit?
   - **a.** He hires several analysts, each of whom is paid an annual salary.
   - **b.** He uses his own time to manage the day-to-day operations of the business.
   - **c.** His business operates out of a loft space in a building that Joshua owns. He could lease the building to another firm for $100,000 per year.
   - **d.** Joshua invested $200,000 to start the business. That money could have generated an additional $20,000 over the past year if Joshua had instead invested the $200,000 in the stock market.
2. You are considering opening a small flower shop. You anticipate that you will earn $100,000 each year in revenue. It will cost you $30,000 each year to rent the space necessary to run your business. Additionally, you will need to spend $10,000 each year buying wholesale flowers, and paying your utilities and other expenses necessary to operate your flower shop. You have just graduated from university with a degree in economics and have received an offer to work for a firm with a yearly salary of $70,000. Should you open the flower shop?
3. A year ago, Shani graduated from university and decided to open her own software company. Over the past year, her start-up has generated $500,000 worth of revenue. She hired two software engineers and paid each of them $150,000 over the past year. She also purchased web-hosting services that cost a total of $30,000. In order to save money, Shani decided to run the business out of the basement of her house. Previously, she had rented this space to a tenant for $6,000 per year. Instead of opening her own business, she could have gone to work for Microsoft and earned $200,000 over the past year.

a. How much were the accounting profits for Shani's business over the past year?

b. How much were her economic profits over the past year?

c. Given this information, should Shani have launched her own business?

4. Lakisha is a professor of economics. She is currently earning $100,000 a year as a professor. She decides to quit her job as a professor and opens a consulting business. In order to do this, she cashes out her savings of $200,000. Her savings has been earning 10% interest each year. At the end of her first year as an economic consultant, she earns $120,000 in accounting profit. What was her economic profit for the year?

5. Determine if each of the following costs would be included when calculating accounting profit, economic profit, or both.

a. Anna, the owner of a local bike repair shop, uses her time to operate her business instead of accepting an annual salary of $100,000 at a Ford Motor dealership.

b. Myer pays $50 per square foot to lease space in a Westfield.

c. In 2018, Qantas paid its key executives nearly $1.2 million in bonuses.

Learning Objective 15.2 *Forecast how new entrants will change long-run prices and profitability in your market.*

6. You run a small but profitable accounting business with many local clients. When you opened your business, there were very few competitors in your area, but you've recently learned that several new businesses providing similar services will be entering the market soon.

a. Use a graph to illustrate the impact on your firm's demand curve when rival businesses enter the market and explain the causes of the change in demand drawn on your graph.

b. Suppose instead you learn that most existing businesses in this market are experiencing negative economic profit. How would your answer to this question change?

c. As a result of rival businesses entering the market, your annual revenue becomes $300,000 and your annual out-of-pocket expenses become $270,000. What is your business's accounting profits? What additional information do you need to determine economic profit?

7. Kylie owns The Doggie Bakery, a small shop that sells gourmet dog treats from a kiosk located in Sydney Markets. Suppose that she is considering expanding her business into Newcastle and Wollongong. The graph below shows the average costs for each kiosk, along with a demand curve for each location.

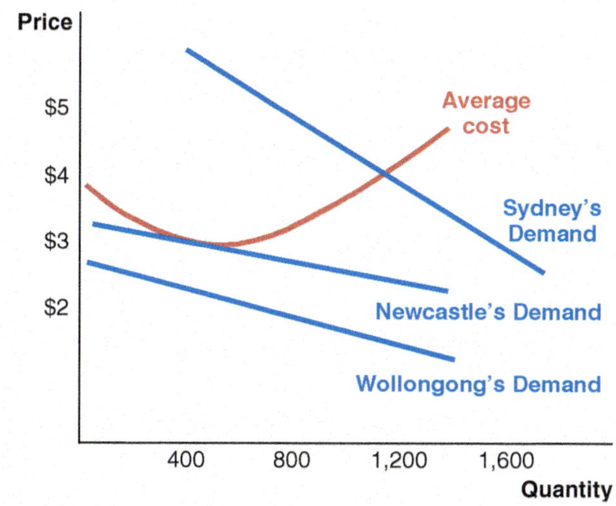

a. Does the demand curve for the Sydney kiosk indicate that Kylie earns positive, negative, or zero economic profits? In the long run would you expect other businesses to enter the Sydney market, exit the market, or neither?

b. Does the demand curve for Newcastle indicate positive, negative, or zero economic profits? In the long run would you expect other businesses to enter the Newcastle market, exit, or neither?

c. Does the demand curve in Wollongong suggest positive, negative, or zero economic profits? In the long run would you expect other businesses to enter the Wollongong market, exit, or neither?

8. The market for lattes in your town is shown below.

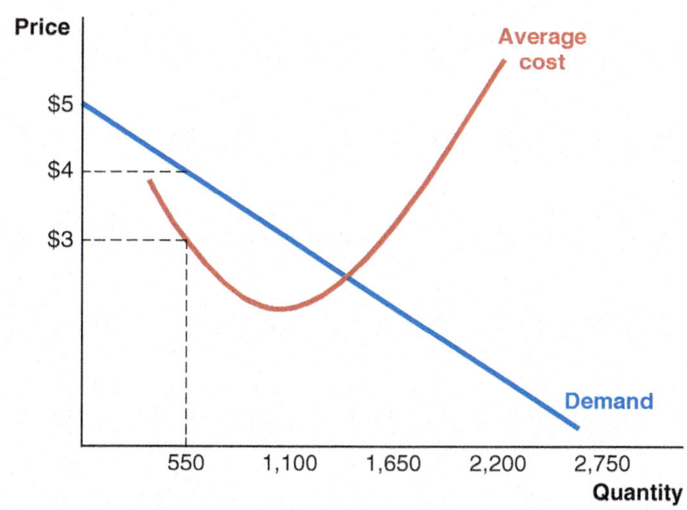

a. If a café charges $4 for a latte, what is its per-unit profit margin on each latte sold? Calculate the profit margin and label it on the graph.

b. Assuming free entry and exit, do you expect more cafés to enter or exit in this market? Why?

Learning Objective 15.3 *Learn strategies to deter new entrants from competing away your profits.*

9. As an investor, you'll want to invest only in businesses that are likely to be profitable in the long run. Assess the barriers to entry in each of these markets, with an eye to forecasting whether they'll yield positive economic profits in the long run.

a. The market for lawn-care services

b. The market for wireless telecommunications, such as mobile phone services

c. The market for SUVs

d. The market for generic paracetamol

10. For each of following scenarios, identify whether it is an example of a demand-side, supply-side, regulatory, or deterrence strategy to limit competition in the market.

a. Qantas provides frequent flyer points to members when they travel. These points can be redeemed for travel and upgrades on Qantas flights.

b. Toyota, Ford, and General Motors have invested in large manufacturing plants that help them efficiently produce millions of cars each year.

c. The top-selling pharmaceutical drug in the world in 2017 was Humira, which is used to treat rheumatoid arthritis. Abbvie has a patent for Humira.

d. Between 2015 and 2018, Facebook had increased the number of active monthly users from 1.4 billion to 2.19 billion.

11. For each of the following strategies used by Microsoft to limit competition, identify whether it is a demand-side strategy, a supply-side strategy, or a deterrence strategy.

a. In 2018, more than 80% of all desktop PCs worldwide used the Microsoft Windows operating system.

b. Microsoft spends a large amount of resources to attract independent software developers to write programs and applications for its operating system.

c. Microsoft was charging an average price of $40 to $60 for its operating system to PC hardware companies such as Dell and HP instead of the monopoly profit-maximising price of $1,800.

CHAPTER 16

Price Discrimination and Sophisticated Pricing Strategies

Chapter Objective

Implement sophisticated pricing strategies.

16.1 Price Discrimination
Boost your profits by charging the highest price each person will pay.

16.2 Group Pricing
Learn to boost your profits by offering group discounts.

16.3 The Hurdle Method
Apply the hurdle method to target your discounts to those who value them.

Sjo/iStock/Getty Images

How far can it go? Depends on the software.

As Hurricane Irma passed through the Caribbean it generated winds as high as 300 kilometres per hour, causing catastrophic damage wherever it made landfall. It destroyed much of the Virgin Islands, killing several people along the way. It then turned northwest, setting its sights on Florida. The governor declared a state of emergency and ordered thousands of people to evacuate.

That's when one technology-lover—the owner of a Tesla electric car—discovered a problem. Their car—a Tesla Model S60—could hold enough charge to drive 320 kilometres, but it would take a trip of 370 kilometres to escape the evacuation zone. A quick phone call to Tesla asking for help yielded a surprising result. Quietly, Tesla sent a fragment of computer code to potentially stranded car owners, temporarily unlocking the car's latent ability to drive further.

You see, Tesla sold two versions of their Model S. The Model S75 came with a 75 kWh battery which gave it a range of 400 kilometres. The Model S60 was $9,000 cheaper, and as you might expect if it had a 60 kWh battery, it had a shorter range of 320 kilometres. But in reality, it had the same 75 kWh battery as its more expensive sibling. The only real difference was that Tesla had added a snippet of code to the cheaper car, and it was that line of code—not any physical battery limitations—that gave it the shorter range.

Why would Tesla purposely cripple some of its cars? The answer is that it's part of a sophisticated pricing strategy. Tesla figured out a way to get different customers to pay different prices for the same good. Price-sensitive customers could pay $90,000 for the S60—as long as they're willing to live with the shorter range. And less price-sensitive customers could pay $99,000 for the S75 and avoid the hassle of charging the car more often.

It's a surprising answer to a question that many managers ask: How can I make as much money as I can from each of my customers? Tesla's answer is to charge some customers more than others. As we're about to discover, there are many sophisticated pricing strategies you can use to do this. Get this pricing strategy right, and you'll drive your profits up.

16.1 Price Discrimination

Learning Objective *Boost your profits by charging the highest price each person will pay.*

If you've ever had to solve a tricky mathematical problem that you didn't want to work out by hand, you may have used WolframAlpha. If you haven't used WolframAlpha before, head on over to wolframalpha.com and take a look. WolframAlpha was built out of the mathematical computing software "Mathematica," which, chances are, your university may provide access to free of charge.

But just how expensive is Mathematica? If you were to ask someone in business, a university student, and a secondary-school educator what it costs them to use Mathematica, you would find that the price each of them pays is quite different. You might think Wolfram (the company that owns Mathematica) charges the same price to everyone, but that's not true. In fact, the price you would pay for Mathematica as a student is several thousand dollars lower than what a business person pays. And so, even though you are both able to perform the same calculations, you end up paying very different prices.

Wolfram is following a sophisticated pricing strategy. They have figured out that they can reap a lot more revenue and attract more customers by charging different people different prices, even though they're purchasing the same product. Our analysis in previous chapters has focused on the case where businesses charge everyone the same price. It's time to explore how businesses increase their customer base and earn higher profits by charging different people different prices for the same good.

Price Discrimination

price discrimination Selling the same good at different prices.

reservation price The maximum price a customer will pay for a product. It is equal to their marginal benefit.

Price discrimination is the strategy of selling the same product at different prices. For instance, once we take into account the various discounts Mathematica offers to different groups, the price is as low as $380 for a typical primary- or secondary-school educator, and as high as $4,220 for people in industry.

Interpreting the DATA How much price discrimination is there for Mathematica?

Price Discrimination for Mathematica

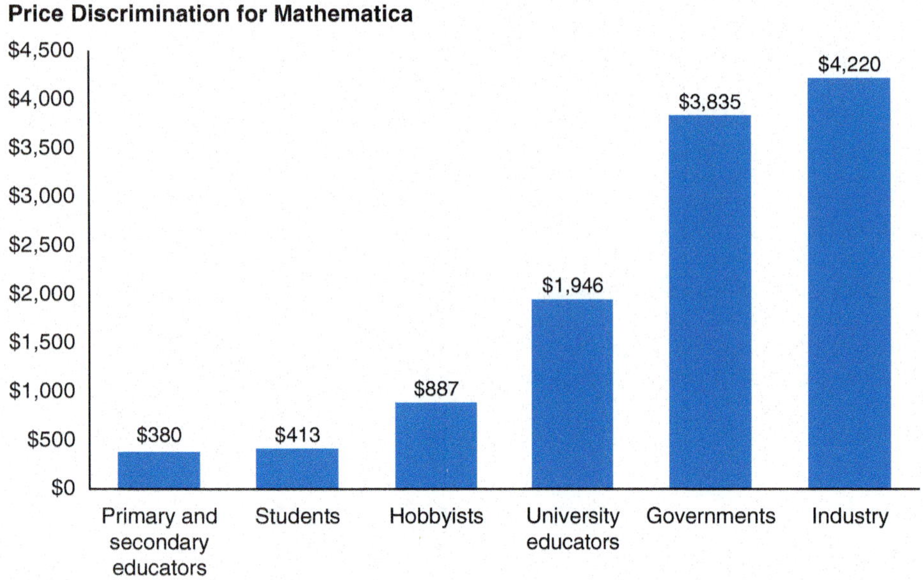

2021 Data from: Wolfram

The price of Mathematica varies enormously. As the figure to the left shows, while university students are charged $413 for Mathematica, "hobbyists" are charged $887, university educators $1,946, and government workers pay a whopping $3,835. Each price level requires authentication of the individual's group (for example, a student ID for university students) to make sure you don't pretend to be a secondary-school educator just to get the lowest price. ■

Set prices close to (and just below) marginal benefit. As a profit-oriented manager, the goal of your price-discrimination strategy is to charge each individual customer the highest price you can get away with. We call the maximum price that a customer will pay their **reservation price.**

What determines your customers' reservation price? If buyers follow the *cost-benefit principle*, the most each is willing to pay for something is their marginal benefit.

And so your goal should be to charge each customer a price that's *just below, but as close as possible to their reservation price, which is also their marginal benefit*. You'll leave your customers willing to purchase your product—but just barely. The case in which you get this targeting exactly right—so that you charge each customer their reservation price—is known as **perfect price discrimination.** Succeed at this, and you'll achieve two profit-boosting objectives:

perfect price discrimination Charging each customer their reservation price.

- Charging the *highest price* you possibly can on each sale; and
- Make *every possible sale* where there's a customer whose marginal benefit exceeds your marginal cost.

The practical challenge in implementing a successful price-discrimination strategy is sorting out which customers need a low price to be induced to buy your product, and which customers will pay more if you charge them a higher price. It's a problem because your customers aren't going to tell you when they have a higher reservation price. We'll set this problem of figuring out each customer's reservation price aside for a few pages, but then we'll return to spend the rest of the chapter solving it.

For now, note that because the demand curve is also the marginal benefit curve, it reveals each customer's marginal benefit, and hence reservation price. Thus, setting the price you charge each customer to be just below their reservation price means setting prices just below the demand curve. The stepped line in Figure 1 illustrates a nearly

Figure 1 | Price Discrimination

Why a business charges different prices to different customers for the same good

A No price discrimination: Everyone pays the same price. Produce where **marginal revenue** = **marginal cost**, and look up to find that price.

Price discrimination:

B Part #1: **Charge higher prices to those who'll pay them.**
- Increases the profit you earn on each of these items sold.
- Reduces consumer surplus (the gap between price and marginal benefit) by an equal amount.

C Part #2: **Offer selective discounts to induce new customers to buy.**
- Increases the quantity you sell, raising profits.
- Benefits those customers who can now afford to buy your goods.

perfect price-discrimination strategy in which the price charged to each customer is just a tiny bit below their marginal benefit.

A successful price discrimination strategy:

1. Charges higher prices to those who'll pay them
2. Offers selective discounts to induce new customers to buy

Price discrimination leads to higher prices for some and lower prices for others. It's worth comparing this sophisticated pricing strategy with the simpler alternative of no price discrimination when you charge all your customers the same price. That's the case we analysed in Chapter 14, and hopefully you recall that a manager with market power first chooses their quantity at the point where marginal revenue equals marginal cost, then chooses their price by looking up to the blue demand curve. Consequently, with no price discrimination, everyone pays the same price, shown as the grey line in Figure 1.

By comparison, the stepped line in Figure 1 reveals that a successful price-discrimination strategy has two parts: Charge higher prices for some customers (the green part of the stepped line), and charge lower prices for others (the purple part). We'll analyse each of these in turn.

Part one: Charge higher prices to those who'll pay them. You can charge a higher price to those customers who have a higher marginal benefit because they're the customers with a higher reservation price. Higher prices for high-marginal-benefit customers are illustrated by the green part of the stepped line in Figure 1. As long as this higher price doesn't exceed your customers' marginal benefit, they'll still buy your product, and you'll enjoy a higher profit margin on each sale.

Your gain from these higher prices comes at your customers' expense—your profits rise because they're paying more. This reduces their consumer surplus, which is the gap between their marginal benefit and the price they pay. They'll be unhappy about this, but their loss is your gain, boosting your producer surplus, which is the gap between the price they pay and your marginal cost. Thus, the "higher prices" part of a price-discrimination strategy *redistributes economic surplus from buyers to sellers,* but it doesn't increase the total amount of economic surplus.

Part two: Offer selective discounts to induce new customers to buy. You should also offer discounts to potential customers who wouldn't otherwise be willing to buy your product. Lower prices for these potential new customers are illustrated by the purple part of the stepped line in Figure 1. As long as you cut the price by enough that it's below the reservation price of these potential customers, you'll increase the quantity you sell. And as long as you don't reduce your price below your marginal cost, these extra sales will increase your profits.

Using selective discounts to induce additional sales *increases the economic surplus enjoyed both by your business and your customers.* You'll enjoy higher producer surplus because you're selling at a price above your marginal cost. And the additional sales will generate some consumer surplus because your customers will only be induced to buy your product if the price is at or below their marginal benefit.

The Efficiency of Price Discrimination

Recall from Chapter 14 that when companies exploit their market power to set higher prices, they sell less than the efficient quantity—an outcome we referred to as the underproduction problem. Price discrimination can help solve this problem.

Price discrimination increases the quantity you sell. That's because price discrimination includes offering selective discounts to *induce additional sales.* And indeed, Figure 1 shows that this type of price discrimination leads your business to sell a larger quantity than if you were forced to charge everyone the same price. It follows that price discrimination partly solves the problem of businesses with market power underproducing.

Selective discounts help solve the underproduction problem. To see why price discrimination helps solve the underproduction problem that otherwise results from market power, it's worth invoking the *marginal principle*, and focusing on your marginal revenue. Evaluate the consequences of selling one more item to a marginal customer who wouldn't otherwise buy your product in these two scenarios:

When You Don't Price Discriminate You charge everyone the same price, and so any discount you give to get this extra sale also applies to *all* of your existing customers. Your marginal revenue is the price you charge that marginal buyer, less the lost revenue from also giving that discount to all your customers. This lost revenue reduces your marginal revenue substantially. In Chapter 14, we called this the "discount effect," and noted that it causes businesses with market power to underproduce relative to society's best interests.

When You Price Discriminate You can be selective about who you offer discounts to. Offer the right discount to the right person—and only that person—and you'll make a sale you wouldn't otherwise have made. Your marginal revenue from this extra sale is the price you charge that marginal buyer, which may involve a small discount offered *only* to that buyer, or perhaps a small number of buyers. The more precisely your price-discriminating strategy targets its discounts, the smaller the discount effect will be, and the less you'll underproduce relative to what's in society's best interest. Indeed, as the example in Figure 1 shows, in the extreme case when you get it exactly right—the case of perfect price discrimination—you'll keep offering discounts and inducing new customers to buy until the point where your marginal cost is equal to your last customer's marginal benefit, which means that you'll produce the efficient quantity. When businesses use selective discounts to increase the quantity they sell, they reduce the underproduction problem.

Interpreting the DATA Is college tuition in the United States really skyrocketing?

There's a lot of concern in the U.S. that the cost of college tuition is skyrocketing. If true, this could lead to less social mobility, an increase in inequality, and a generation of "lost Einsteins" who have the smarts but not the money to get a great education. But is it?

If you focus on the "sticker price" that colleges list on their websites, it looks like it. For instance, the average sticker price at private four-year colleges has nearly doubled from US$18,050 in 1990 to US$35,830 in 2018. (This comparison adjusts for inflation, and so both of these prices are measured in today's dollars.) Prices that high would push a lot of students out of college, leading to underproduction of college graduates.

But if you focus instead on the "net price"—which is the tuition paid, minus the scholarships and grants received—a different picture emerges. The net price that people pay for college is much lower. And on average, the net price has risen by a much smaller amount, from US$12,390 in 1990 to US$14,610 in 2018.

What's really happening is that colleges are now doing a lot more price discrimination. Notably, they are doing more of both parts of a successful price discrimination strategy.

Sticker Price and Net Price of Tuition at Private Four-Year Colleges
Adjusted for inflation

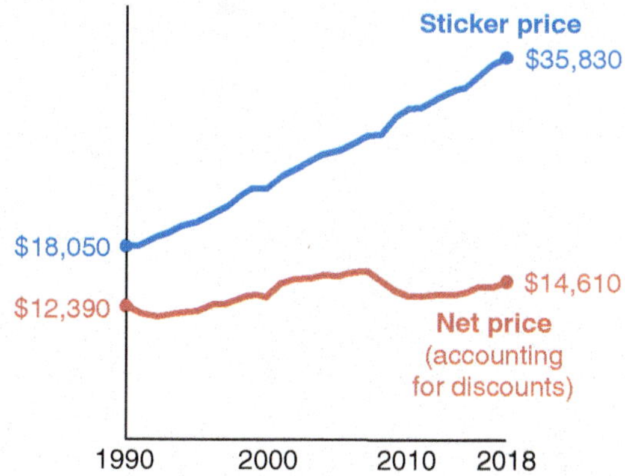

Data from: College Board.

Part one: *Charge higher prices to those who'll pay them.* College administrators understand that wealthy families have high reservation prices, and so they charge them more. To do this, colleges raised the sticker price. In order not to raise prices for other families, they combined these higher sticker prices with offsetting discounts, often known as financial aid, for students from middle-income families, so that their net price has barely risen.

Part two: *Offer selective discounts to induce new customers to buy.* Colleges have come to understand that they can attract students from low-income families if they make the cost of college extremely low or even free. They've actually increased the discounts (or grants) they offer these families by even *more* than enough to offset the rising sticker price. This lower net price for low-income families has led to an increase in the number of low-income students who apply to college.

The result of all this is higher prices for some, lower prices for others, and an increase in the number of applicants, despite little overall change in the average net price actually paid. The student body is probably now stronger because colleges are selecting from a larger pool of applicants. And those selective discounts likely induced people from previously marginalised groups to go to college, creating greater socioeconomic diversity within that student body. ■

Conditions for Price Discrimination

Price discrimination is only feasible if:

1. Your business has market power
2. You can prevent resale
3. You can target the right prices to the right customers

The extra profits that you can earn through price discrimination suggest that it should be part of the strategic arsenal of any sophisticated manager. But it's not for everyone. That's because the whole premise of price discrimination is that you can charge a high price to some people and a low price to others, and this will only work if three specific conditions are met:

Condition one: Your business has market power. If your business has no market power—as in a perfectly competitive market—then trying to charge your customers different prices simply won't work. You could try raising your prices for some customers, but they'll simply buy from someone else instead. And in perfect competition, you can already sell whatever quantity you want at the prevailing price, so there's no reason to offer discounts to get new customers. This is why you don't see price-taking firms like wheat farmers or iron-ore companies trying to price discriminate.

On the flip side, if you do have market power, then price discrimination can help you exploit it, and so it's well worth considering.

Condition two: You can prevent resale. Your price-discrimination strategy can only succeed if you *find a way to prevent resale.* Otherwise, the people who qualify for low prices will buy your product cheaply and then resell it to the people you were hoping to charge a high price to. If you can't prevent resale, you'll end up selling large quantities at the low price—mainly to resellers—and you won't be able to sell much at the high price because the resellers will undercut you with your high-value customers.

As a result, many companies make it a strategic priority to find new ways to prevent their products being resold. It's a priority for Sony, which is a major player in both the movie and videogame industries because physical discs—movie DVDs and videogame discs—are easily resold. The ease of resale prevents Sony from charging higher prices to, say, me, an economics professor. If they did, I would avoid paying that higher price by getting a friend who gets lower prices from Sony to purchase my favourite movies or videogames for me. And it's also the reason Sony won't offer discounts to financially strapped economics students. Sony is worried that you'll resell its products on eBay at a profit, undermining its ability to charge other customers higher prices.

Tony Cordoza/Alamy

Games are cheaper in Asia, but they may not work in your Australian PlayStation.

Sony is using technology to help solve this problem. For example, it price discriminates partly by charging higher prices in Australia than in India, and it prevents Australians from importing cheap discs from India by including a region code on each disc. That code ensures that a low-priced game or movie bought in India won't work on a PlayStation or DVD player purchased in Australia. Sony also hopes to do an even better job at preventing resale by shifting movie and videogame distribution from sales of discs to online streaming, partly because these online streams can't be copied or resold.

Other businesses use simpler strategies to prevent resale. Stores sometimes couple their special offers with fine print restricting each customer to buying only two items. This strategy prevents people from stocking up to later resell items they bought on sale. Airlines prevent resale by requiring you show an ID at the airport that matches the name on your ticket. And in the service sector, it's relatively easy to prevent the resale of services—an hour with your accountant or doctor—because you have to turn up in person for them.

The more aggressively your business price discriminates, the more important it is to prevent resale. This is particularly important for drug companies, which charge around $100 for a year's worth of AIDS treatment in sub-Saharan Africa, but $10,000 in the United States. That's why drug company executives worked with the government to make it illegal to import many pills from Africa into the United States. They're also careful to make the pills they sell overseas a different color or shape, which prevents smugglers from passing them off to U.S. drugstores. These efforts to prevent resale help maintain different prices for different consumers.

Condition three: You can target the right prices to the right customers. There's one more challenge: You need to be able to figure out which customers can withstand a higher price and which customers need a discount to buy your product. You could try asking your customers, but they're usually too smart to admit to a seller that they're willing to pay higher prices.

Solving this problem of how best to target the right prices to the right customers is central to successful price discrimination. That's why we'll spend most of the rest of this chapter developing strategies you can use to target the right prices to the right customers. We'll start with a simple but familiar strategy, which is to offer different prices to people in identifiably different groups.

16.2 Group Pricing

Learning Objective *Learn to boost your profits by offering group discounts.*

Next time you go to the movies, I bet you'll pay a lower price than I do. That's because most students qualify for a student discount. Cinemas also charge less for children and seniors. All of this sounds rather civic-minded—as if they're trying to help those who need it. But it's actually about the cinema boosting its bottom line.

It's practising a form of price discrimination known as **group pricing,** charging different prices to different groups of people. It doesn't know each customer's reservation price, so instead, it uses a proxy—whether you're a student, a child, or a senior—to tailor its prices to different groups of customers.

group pricing Price discrimination by charging different prices to different groups of people.

More generally, group pricing involves offering different prices to groups that differ by their age, location, purchase history, or any other identifiable characteristic. Examples of group pricing include:

- Your campus computer store offers "academic pricing" for Microsoft Office, making it cheaper for students.
- Books are cheaper in India than in Australia.
- Internet companies charge lower prices for residential rather than business service.
- Hairdressers charge more for women's haircuts than for men's (even for a similar cut).
- Microsoft offers lower prices to existing customers by offering upgrades.

Indeed, any time your company offers a higher or lower price to one group than to another, you're engaged in group pricing. But let me offer a hint. Buyers resent being singled out to pay higher prices. So don't say that your cinema is charging professors $5 more. Instead, describe your group pricing strategy in terms of *group discounts*—so that you're charging students $5 less. The result is obviously the same—those who don't get the discount pay a higher price than those who do—but you'll avoid a PR disaster.

EVERYDAY Economics How to be a savvy online shopper

The rise of online shopping has led to some very sophisticated price-discrimination strategies based on group pricing. For instance, some airlines or travel portals offer the same ticket at different prices to different groups of customers, depending on the location of their internet connection. While this tactic is controversial, it's also perfectly legal.

But if you're a savvy shopper, you can work this to your advantage. Before making a major purchase, try logging on from elsewhere. Or, open your browser in private or incognito mode, which prevents the stores from tracking your movements through their online stores. Another trick: Put something in your shopping cart, but don't buy it. Some retailers figure this means that you're in the group of customers with a low enough reservation price that you're unsure about whether to make a purchase. In many cases, they'll email you later that week with a discount in order to close the deal. ■

Setting Group Prices

Group pricing effectively segments what had been one market—say, the market to see movies—into separate markets for each group. It means that your cinema is now a supplier of a number of different products in a number of different markets: It's selling tickets in the market for students to see movies, as well as tickets in the separate markets for children, for seniors, and for other adults. In each of these markets, the cinema faces different demand curves, and so it sets different prices.

Set the price separately for each group. It's time to put yourself in the shoes of the executive team at Hoyts. You've decided to follow a group-pricing strategy, and now you need to figure out what price to charge each of these groups. You can charge different prices to different groups—so students pay less than other adults—but you charge everyone within a group the same price.

Within each market segment—such as the market for student tickets—you now face a familiar question: What price should you charge students to earn the largest possible profit? And then you face a similar question for adults, kids, and seniors. These are all familiar questions because they're simply about figuring out the best price to set when you have market power. In each case you should follow the two-step process we explored in Chapter 14:

Step one: *What quantity should you produce?* Follow the *Rational Rule for Sellers* and keep selling until marginal revenue (in that market segment) equals your marginal cost.

Step two: *What price should you charge?* Look up to your firm's demand curve (for that segment) to find the highest price you can set and still sell this quantity.

The demand curves for each group are different, and so you'll want to follow this two-step process *separately* for *each* market segment.

Set different prices for different groups. Figure 2 illustrates the process for two groups. The left panel shows the market for movie tickets for adults, and the right panel shows the market for movie tickets for students. The demand curve of students is a bit lower because fewer students can afford to pay a lot to see a movie. And it's flatter because students are more responsive to prices. The two markets are otherwise similar. When you're engaged in group pricing and there are no spillovers to consider (so adults don't care how many students are in the cinema, and vice versa), each of these is effectively a separate market, which is why you can analyse them separately. Let's explore how these differences in demand lead cinema executives to choose a lower price for students.

Figure 2 | **Setting Group Prices**

What price should you charge each group?

Step one: *What quantity should you produce?*
Produce the quantity at which **marginal revenue** = **marginal cost**.

Step two: *What price should you charge?*
Look up to the **demand curve** to find the highest price at which you can sell this quantity.

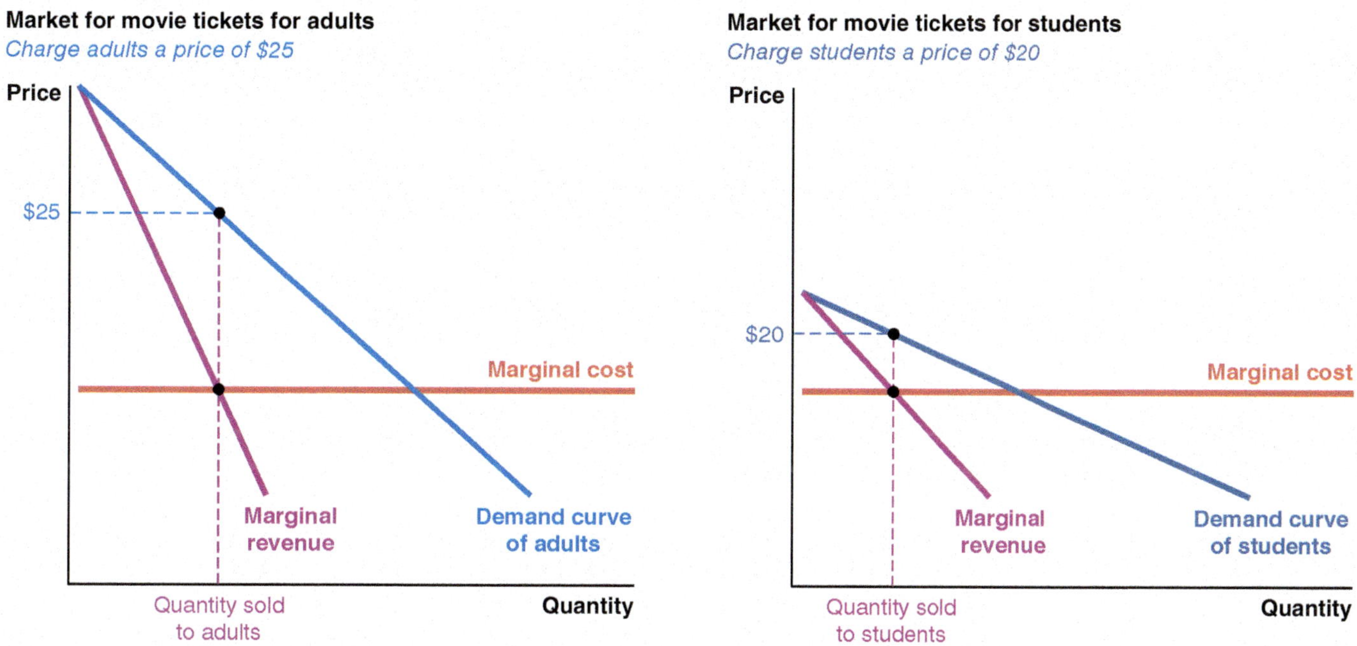

For each group, you should set your quantity at the point where marginal revenue equals marginal cost. In each case, your next step is to look up to the demand curve to find the associated price. In this example, the best choice for Hoyts is to set the price of movie tickets for adults at $25, and the price for students at $20.

Set prices for each group much as you would set different prices in different markets. You can analyse each group separately because each group is effectively a separate market. There are two big ideas to keep in mind:

- *Charge higher prices to groups that value your product more.* This is the idea that the higher the marginal benefit, and hence reservation price, of your customers, the more you'll be able to get away with charging them a higher price.
- *Charge lower prices to groups that are especially price sensitive.* This is the idea that market power matters. You don't have much market power with price-sensitive groups because a small increase in price will lead you to lose a lot of them as customers. And so the more price sensitive a group—that is, the more elastic their demand—the lower the price you'll want to charge them.

These two ideas explain the pattern of group discounts that many companies offer. For instance, businesses often charge higher prices in Australia than they do overseas because the higher disposable income of Australian consumers tends to boost their reservation prices. And businesses charge lower prices to students and other price-sensitive groups because they know that they have a lower reservation price.

How to Segment Your Market

So far we've figured out what price you should charge each group. That's half of your group pricing strategy. The other half lies in figuring out which groups to target. The main

Three criteria for a successful segmentation strategy involve identifying groups:

1. Whose demand differs
2. Based on verifiable characteristics
3. Based on difficult-to-change characteristics

idea is that a successful pricing strategy involves segmenting your market into groups. But how should you do this? There are three criteria that you'll need to follow to successfully segment your market: find groups with different demand curves, whose membership can be easily verified, and whose membership is difficult to change.

Let's dig into each of these ideas, in turn.

Criteria one: Segment your market into groups whose demand differs. The goal of a successful price-discrimination strategy is to set the price you charge each customer as close as possible to their reservation price. And so the idea behind group pricing is to use observable proxies—like being a student—that are related to each customer's reservation price. The better the proxy—that is, the more closely it captures differences in reservation prices—the more successful your strategy will be.

A cinema charges a lower price to students because it believes the demand from students is different than that of other adults. Indeed, students typically have lower reservation prices because they have less money to spend, and they're also likely to be more price sensitive. Because of these demand differences, it's more profitable to charge a lower price to students than other adults.

But notice that no cinema charges different prices for men and women. Partly, that's to avoid stoking public outrage. But it's also partly about economics. Men and women have fairly similar demand for movies, and so a buyer's gender is not a useful proxy for their reservation price. There's no point in segmenting your market into groups whose demand doesn't differ.

How far should you segment your market? It depends on what information you have available to you. Cinemas don't know much about their customers—basically just whether they have a student card or a seniors card in their wallets. As a result, they follow a fairly coarse market segmentation, charging different prices to just a few different groups. By contrast, Amazon knows a lot more about its customers because it can track your browsing history and, if you're an Amazon Prime member, your purchase history, too. This means it uses much more fine-grained segmentation, adjusting the prices of certain products to each individual customer's circumstances, by using their browsing or purchasing history to infer things about their willingness to pay for particular items. Amazon can segment its Prime customers by expenditure, family size and structure (using Prime Video accounts), state and suburb residency, and many other variables. All of this information helps tailor the net price of particular goods much more closely to each household's reservation price.

In deciding which segments to offer group-specific prices to, your goal should be to find the cleavages that best divide your market into segments with distinct patterns of demand.

Interpreting the DATA **Why petrol prices are different across the same city**

There are different types of petrol: unleaded, premium unleaded, diesel, E85, and others. It's not surprising that premium unleaded petrol (PULP)—which is higher octane for better performance, and recommended for higher-end cars—is more expensive than regular unleaded petrol (ULP).

What is more interesting is that within each type of petrol there can be significant price differences across a city at the same time. Economists David Byrne, Jia Sheen Nah and Peng Xue analysed data from the New South Wales state government's FuelCheck website and documented this price dispersion across Sydney (and also Perth from the WA government's FuelWatch website).

Prices in July 2021 for ULP were much higher in the eastern suburbs of Sydney (like Edgecliff) at $172.9/litre than the western suburbs (like Lewisham) at $136.8/litre. With average income higher in the eastern suburbs, it makes sense for petrol stations to charge higher prices there. The markets are also relatively easy to segment, since if you live in the east you have to take time and use petrol to drive west for cheaper fuel. ■

Criteria two: Target your group discounts based on verifiable characteristics. When you offer different groups different prices, you'll quickly discover that buyers will try to come up with cunning ways to avoid paying the higher price. That's why it's important to link your group discounts to *verifiable characteristics,* such as your customer's age, student status, or address. This ensures that people can't just lie about their status to get the discount.

The characteristics that are verifiable vary a bit, depending on your industry. A cinema can verify whether a customer is a student by asking to see their student ID. But an online retailer can't do this. Instead, many websites offer discounts to people with email addresses that end in ".edu." (Your professors love this because it means they also qualify for student discounts!) Companies with a lot of data on you, like Amazon, can get pretty close at inferring your income from your spending habits, so they can tailor their prices to their estimate of your income.

Criteria three: Base group discounts on difficult-to-change characteristics. Finally, you should segment your market based on characteristics that are not only verifiable, but also difficult to change. This is to avoid the possibility that your customers will switch into a different group in order to get a lower price.

Discounts for children pass this test, because people can typically tell whether you are actually a child. Student discounts sort of pass this test, since it's pretty unlikely someone would start attending university just to get $5 off the price of movie tickets. But if too many people start using their old student IDs to get discounts not meant for them, then it would no longer pass this test.

While most people think it's wrong to lie outright to get a discount, economists have also found that any changeable characteristic appears to be on the rise whenever there is a discount to be had. So if the cinema starts offering discounts to people with vision problems, you'll see a lot more people show up wearing glasses.

Recap: Group discounts are a promising price-discrimination strategy. Group pricing can be an effective price-discrimination strategy when verifiable and hard-to-change factors like a customer's home address do a good job in sorting out which buyers have high reservation prices.

But what should you do when observable characteristics aren't a good proxy for your customers' reservation prices? Answering this is our next task, and we'll explore an approach to price discrimination that doesn't require you to know anything at all about your customers' characteristics.

16.3 The Hurdle Method

Learning Objective *Apply the hurdle method to target your discounts to those who value them.*

hurdle method Offer lower prices only to those buyers who are willing to overcome some hurdle, or obstacle.

An alternative strategy induces your customers to sort themselves into groups with higher or lower reservation prices. This strategy is designed to counter the problem that you can't get your customers to tell you their reservation prices. While buyers are unlikely to volunteer that they'd be willing to pay more, sometimes the choices that buyers make reveal their reservation prices. This strategy relies on a very clever trick called the **hurdle method.**

Nathan Stirk/Getty Images

Lower prices await for those who can clear the hurdle.

The idea behind the hurdle method is simple: You only offer lower prices to those buyers who are willing to overcome some hurdle or obstacle. The clever part comes from designing a hurdle so that your customers with high reservation prices find it too costly to bother with the hurdle. If you succeed, your customers will sort themselves, so that those with low reservation prices will leap the hurdle to get the lower price, while those with high reservation prices will not, leading them to pay the higher price.

As we now turn to seeing how companies actually apply the hurdle method in practice, we'll discover that pricing strategies have found some truly ingenious ways to get their customers to sort themselves into high-reservation price and low-reservation price groups. To see the logic, we'll have to take a detour to Hogwarts.

Alternative Versions and Timing

When *Harry Potter and the Deathly Hallows* was released, it was originally sold only in hardcover for $39.99. Several months later, a paperback edition was released for $19.99. Why was it so much cheaper? You might think it's because it's more expensive to print a hardcover book, but the cost difference between the two is actually small. Instead, this is a cunning example of the hurdle method of price discrimination.

(left) Jonny White/Alamy; (right) Mim Friday/Alamy Stock Photo

$39.99 $19.99

Why are the prices so different?

The world contains two types of people: People who love Harry Potter fanatically, and people who merely like him. Fanatics get a high marginal benefit from the book, and so have a high reservation price. They're also unwilling to wait even a couple of days to get the latest installment. Those who merely like Harry Potter have a lower reservation price and are willing to wait to read the book in order to save money. Publishers charge a lot for a book when it's first released in hardcover because they know that the fanatics can't wait to read it and will pay that high price. A few months later, they'll release the paperback at a price that'll also induce those who merely like him to buy it.

In this setting, the hurdle to getting the lower price is waiting a few months for the next Harry Potter book. This hurdle works even though everyone knows a cheaper paperback version is coming. It works because waiting six months to get a better price is a hurdle that a true fanatic won't leap. Less fanatical readers are content to wait a few months to read Harry Potter at half the price.

The hardback and paperback are effectively two alternative versions of the same product, and the key difference is not so much the stiffness of the cover, but when it's available. The same strategy is used in the movie industry. A new release at the cinema costs about $20 to $25 to see, but then it's available a few months later through Apple TV, Google Play, or Amazon Prime for around $4. Still too pricey? Wait a little longer, and it will pop up on one of your subscription services, like Netflix, Stan, or Disney+. If you're really patient, you can eventually watch it on broadcast TV, where it'll cost you $0. Each alternative version appeals to successively less rabid fans with lower reservation prices.

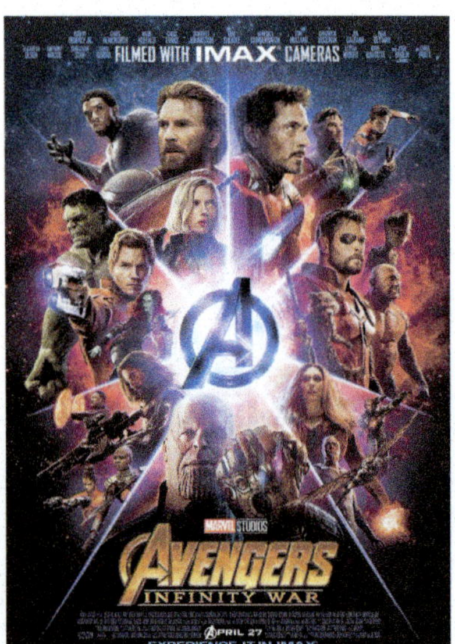

BFA/Alamy stockphoto

The price you pay to see that next Marvel blockbuster depends on how long you're willing to wait.

Alternative versions can create hurdles. Many applications of the hurdle method can be described as sellers creating alternative versions of their products. For instance, Qantas wants to charge high prices to business travellers who typically have high reservation prices (Why not? The boss is paying!), while charging lower prices to price-sensitive leisure travellers. The problem is that business travellers can just say that they're travelling for leisure. And so Qantas sells two versions of an otherwise-identical return airfare to Sydney.

It charges a high price for the version that leaves on a Wednesday and returns that Friday, because this timing is convenient for business travellers who can schedule meetings during the week, and return home in time to spend the weekend with their family. And it charges a low price for the version that leaves on a Friday and returns on Sunday, because this works for leisure travellers who can't skip work. This selective discount works because being willing to stay a Saturday night in another city is a hurdle that many business travellers won't leap over in order to get a cheaper airfare.

Shopping Around

If you're willing to scour the supermarket aisles for bargains—to track discounts and promotions, to figure out whether it's cheaper to buy your soft-drink in twenty-four-packs or in large bottles, to stock up on toilet paper when it's cheap, to visit the store more often to take advantage of each week's sales, and to fill your tank with petrol when it's cheap rather than when it's convenient—then you'll save a lot of money.

You'll save money, but it's hard work. That's partly by design. This extra hassle is a hurdle that many less price-sensitive customers aren't willing to leap over. And so your supermarket effectively price discriminates because the segment that's less price conscious won't get the good deals, while its price-sensitive customers pay lower prices on average.

Fluctuating prices are a hurdle. Why do grocery prices fluctuate so much? For instance, why is Coke on sale this week, while Pepsi was on sale last week? The answer is the hurdle method. If you love Coke, you have a high reservation price for it and will buy it whether or not it's on sale. The result is that Coke buyers get to buy their cola at sale prices only about half the time. By contrast, those who don't really care that much about soft-drink brands—who are likely those with low reservation prices for cola—just buy whatever's on sale, and so they pay less, on average.

In this case, the hurdle to getting the lowest price is being willing to drink Pepsi when it's cheaper.

EVERYDAY Economics Beating Amazon at its own game

You might be surprised by how much prices fluctuate online. For instance, the price of a new Samsung Galaxy Tab A7 on Amazon (list price: $379) changes frequently, fluctuating between $249 and $379. Want to snag the great deal when the price falls again, but without the hassle of checking every day? The price-tracking website au.camelcamelcamel.com will watch the price of any item for you, automatically sending you an e-mail whenever the price falls to your target level. ■

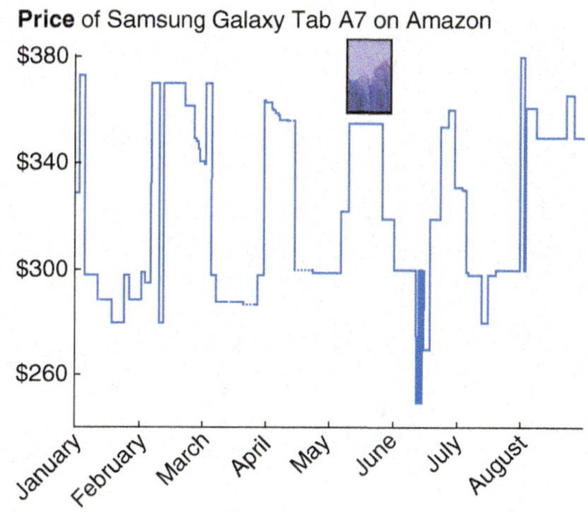

Haggling is a hurdle. You should never pay the actual sticker price for a new car. Instead, you should haggle with the salesperson—they all do it. If you can convince the sales staff that your reservation price is so low that you'll only buy the car if they knock a couple of thousand dollars off the price, you may end up scoring a real bargain.

Sellers haggle because it can be a very powerful form of price discrimination, allowing them to tailor the price they offer to each customer. Car sellers look closely at the clothes you're wearing, the phone you carry, and other cues that might signal your reservation price. They won't budge if they think you're willing to pay the sticker price, but they'll offer a big price cut if they think that's what is required to make the sale.

Consequently, your goal as a savvy buyer should be to convince the seller that you have a low reservation price. Dress in your scruffiest clothes and talk about the problem sets that you have due, so that the seller knows you're a student rather than a wealthy executive. Be prepared to spend a long time negotiating, as if there's nothing more important to you than saving money. And never talk about how much you love the car you're buying. Instead, you want the seller to believe that you would be happy buying just about any car, which means that the marginal benefit you get from *this* car, rather than any other, is small. Make it clear that you'll shop around, as this signals that the marginal benefit you get from buying at this used car lot is tiny. Play your cards right, and you'll get a good deal.

I find haggling to be one of the most annoying parts of buying a car, but that's precisely the point: Haggling is the hurdle you have to leap over to get a low price. Sellers are betting that people with a higher reservation price will prefer to pay a bit more money to avoid spending time and energy haggling for a better deal.

Bruce Laurance/Getty Images

You want to convince this savvy price discriminator that you have a low willingness to pay.

EVERYDAY Economics **You can haggle more often than you might realise**

Haggling is probably more common than you realise. Salespeople in most mattress stores expect to haggle. You should always haggle when you're buying used items off Facebook Marketplace, at a flea market, or at a garage sale. And haggling is even more common in some countries, so learn the norms of the country you plan to visit before you travel.

You can even haggle with large corporations. This can be really important when you face high mortgage rates as many banks offer steep discounts just because you ask. So, if you're unhappy with your mortgage rate, be prepared to haggle. Similarly, you can negotiate with your phone, or internet provider. Simply call customer service and tell them that you're thinking of switching carriers. If you're thinking of joining a gym, ask if they can waive the upfront registration fees. Call your credit card company and tell them you can do better elsewhere. And if missing a payment leads to late fees, try calling to ask them to waive it as a courtesy. More generally, you'll discover that customer service representatives have been empowered to price discriminate, which means they will offer you a break—a cheaper bill, a smaller upfront cost, a cut-price hotel room, or a reduced interest rate—if they think that this is what is necessary to keep you as a customer. ■

Extra Hassle, Bad Service, and Imperfect Goods

Adwo/Alamy Stock Photo

Why is this outlet mall located near the Perth airport?

You might find it surprising how often sellers make it a hassle to buy their goods. But this might just be price discrimination and the hurdle method at work. For instance, you can often buy designer clothes cheaply if you're willing to shop at an outlet store. But designer brands purposely put these outlet stores forty kilometres outside a major city, making them a hassle to get to. The result is that only those who are willing to leap over the hurdle of travelling a long way in order to get a bargain—typically those with lower reservation prices—will get the lower prices. The flip side is that those customers who aren't bargain-motivated will pay the higher price at the flagship stores in the city instead.

Coupons and rebates are hurdles. Similar logic explains why supermarkets give their biggest discounts to people who are willing to clip coupons (or, nowadays, activate their "loyalty rewards"), and electronics stores sometimes offer a lower price if you're willing to claim a rebate. They do this because the hassle of clipping coupons or applying for rebates is a hurdle to getting lower prices. This ensures that many of their less budget-conscious customers—who typically have high reservation prices—will avoid the hassle, choosing to pay the higher price instead. And so coupons and rebates effectively target price cuts to the most budget-conscious shoppers.

Slightly worse service is a hurdle. Similar logic explains why many sellers charge an exorbitant amount to get slightly better service. If you're willing to pay to avoid hassle, then most nightclubs will happily charge you hundreds of dollars for a VIP table, allowing you to skip the line outside. Airlines charge hundreds of dollars more for a business-class seat, and it often seems they're trying to make economy class as miserable as possible. In each case, the hurdle to getting the lower price is being willing to put up with sub-par service. And from the seller's perspective, this makes sense because it leads only the bargain-motivated customers to leap the hurdle required to get the lower prices, while those with higher reservation prices pay more.

Stephen Coburn/Shutterstock

Is it worth the hassle?

Imperfect goods are hurdles. At this point, you might have an inkling as to why Tesla sold two versions of an otherwise identical car. It's the hurdle method at work.

Tesla wanted to sell its car at a high price to those customers with a high reservation price and at a lower price to those with a lower reservation price. So it created two versions—the S75, which it sold for $74,500, and the S60, which it sold for $68,000. But if these versions were literally identical, everyone would buy the cheaper version. So it added a snippet of computer code to the S60 that artificially reduced the range of its battery. The hassle of recharging your car more often is the hurdle that buyers had to leap over to get this lower price. For Tesla's budget-conscious customers, it's a worthwhile leap to make, and so they paid the lower price. But for its wealthier, busier, and more devoted customers, it's a hurdle not worth jumping, and they chose to pay the higher price for the S75 instead.

quantity discount When the per-unit price is lower when you buy a larger quantity.

Quantity Discounts

My local pharmacy offers a second product at half price if you're buying two products. This is an example of a **quantity discount,** which means that the per-unit price is lower when you buy a larger quantity, and it's another form of price discrimination. Discounting the second item effectively targets customers with a lower willingness to pay—those who have already bought their first item. The hurdle to getting the second product cheaply is buying the first.

Sometimes, the rationale for quantity discounts comes from realising that different types of customers buy different quantities. For instance, stores like Costco offer 4L bottles of Fountain tomato sauce at a low price. They figure that this is likely to be a good deal for price-sensitive large families, while apartment-dwellers without the storage space will prefer to buy a more sensible size. The logic, then, is that the lower price per litre in the 4L jug targets the price-sensitive segment of the market, and the hurdles to getting this lower price on tomato sauce are being willing to store it and being able to use it before it turns rancid.

4 L $24.49 | 500 ml $5.35

Which size are you more likely to buy?

Bundling creates a hurdle to getting the second good at a lower price. An alternative form of quantity discount is called **bundling,** and it involves selling different goods together as a package. The bundle is typically sold for a lower price than if you bought the components separately. The price needs to be lower, or no one would ever buy it. And that lower price is actually a form of price discrimination.

bundling Selling different goods together as a package.

To see this, let's dig into the business problem that Microsoft's marketing team faced. Two of their biggest-selling products are Word and Excel, and when they're bought alone, each program is priced at $159. The problem is that at this price, customers whose work mainly involves writing—let's call them "poets"—buy Word, but not Excel. And people who spend most of their time crunching numbers—"quants"—buy Excel, but not Word. To sell more software, Microsoft needs to figure out a way to sell Excel at a lower price to poets, or to sell Word at a lower price to quants. But how can it target price cuts just to poets or quants?

In a clever approach to price discrimination, Microsoft decided to sell a bundle that includes Excel, Word, and a suite of other products that quants and poets wouldn't usually buy, for only $199. Effectively, this bundle delivers a big discount on Excel for poets. Think about it: For a poet who's already going to spend $159 on Word, the bundle means that they can also add Excel for only $41 more, and get the rest of the Microsoft Office suite for free! The hurdle to getting this discount on Excel is that you have to buy Word anyway, and only poets are willing to leap this hurdle. Likewise, from the perspective of quants, the bundle is effectively a big discount on Word: If you were already going to spend $159 on Excel, the bundle now gives you the opportunity to also add on Word for only $41 more, and get the rest of the Microsoft Office suite for free. The hurdle to getting this low price on Word is being willing to buy Excel, and only quants are willing to leap this hurdle.

Notice that the key to this ingenious application of the hurdle method is that the people who get a low marginal benefit from one part of the bundle (and so need a discount) are the same people who get a high marginal benefit from the other (and so are willing to leap over the hurdle required to get this discount). This explains why companies often bundle something you like with something you don't really want or need.

This same logic also explains pay-TV pricing. When you subscribe to Foxtel, for example, you don't just buy the channels you want. Instead, you buy a basic "Foxtel plus" subscription that includes both the handful of channels you really want, and a bunch that you don't really care for. By bundling these, the cable company is engaged in price discrimination, effectively asking you to pay a lot for the channels you love, but giving you the extra channels for just a few dollars more. It works because it induces you to pay a little bit more than if you just bought the channels you love.

Tying It Together

There's a revolution brewing that will eventually transform the nature of commerce and the relationship between buyers and sellers. It reflects the confluence of two forces. The first is the set of ideas that we've analysed in this chapter—that businesses can boost their profits by charging each customer a price that's as close as possible to their reservation price. The second is a technological development: As more of our lives move online, every time you click your mouse you'll add to a trail of digital breadcrumbs that create a detailed map of your life's journey, describing the contours of your social and economic relations.

As businesses mine these massive datasets, they'll learn much more about their customers than has ever been possible before. It'll be as if the same algorithms that somehow figure out which YouTube clip you'll want to watch next were put to work to figure out the highest price a retailer can charge for your next purchase.

This means that the ideas we've explored in this chapter—how to segment markets, set group-specific prices, and apply the hurdle method—will only become more important as big data will lead to more sophisticated pricing strategies. The future likely holds ever more finely personalised prices. Take it to an extreme, and it'll no longer make sense to talk about "the price" of anything. Instead, we'll have to talk about "your price," which likely differs from "my price." Even that may become outdated as "your price" might vary hour by hour, according to the current temperature, whether you're logging in from home or work, or how long your cursor hovered over that cat photo.

In fact, many companies already have the data, the machine-learning tools, and the technical capacity to make some of this happen. Think about how much Netflix already knows about you—whether you like rom-coms, thrillers, or anime, whether you watch bite-sized morsels or binge on whole seasons, and if you're out on the weekend or at home watching. Why doesn't it use this to charge you a higher or lower subscription price?

Part of the answer may reflect concerns about fairness. Anger at perceived unfairness explains why an experiment in which Amazon offered different prices to different people led to a media firestorm. The threat of a consumer backlash led Amazon to backpedal. And so as you consider sophisticated pricing strategies at your business, you need to think carefully about how your customers will react.

There are also delicate ethical issues involved. Even a computer algorithm that's designed not to track the gender, race, ethnicity, sexuality, or religion of buyers might end up raising prices more for one demographic group than another. For instance, if an algorithm discovers that people who buy lipstick have a higher reservation price for shampoo, it's a good bet that it'll eventually lead women to pay more for shampoo than men. It's up to you to decide whether you see this as the benign result of gender-blind market forces or as pernicious computer-generated sexism.

Whatever your view, realise that norms often evolve as the economy changes. Millions of people still do business with Uber even though its pricing algorithm charges you a different price for a five-kilometre trip to an upscale restaurant than for a similar trip to a budget eatery. As you consider these debates, realise that history suggests people can get used to individualised pricing. After all, the price tag—a symbol that represents a uniform price that applies to everyone—is a relatively new innovation. It was popularised by department stores in the United States as recently as the 1870s. But before that—indeed, through most of the history of markets—individual buyers haggled with sellers, and different people paid different prices. And so in this respect, the future may be a lot like the past.

Chapter at a Glance

Price Discrimination: Selling the same good at different prices.

Perfect Price Discrimination: Charging each customer their reservation price. → **Reservation price:** The maximum price a customer will pay for a product. = Marginal benefit

Why a business charges different prices to different consumers for the same good

Price discrimination increases the quantity you sell. => **Selective discounts** help solve the underproduction problem.

Price discrimination is only feasible if: i) your business has **market power**, ii) you can **prevent resale**, and iii) you can **target** the right prices to the right customers.

Group Pricing

How to segment your market:

1. Segment your market into groups whose demands differs
2. Target your group discounts based on verifiable characteristics
3. Base group discounts on difficult-to-change characteristics.

Set different prices for different groups:

Market for first group
Charge a **higher price** to groups that value your product more.

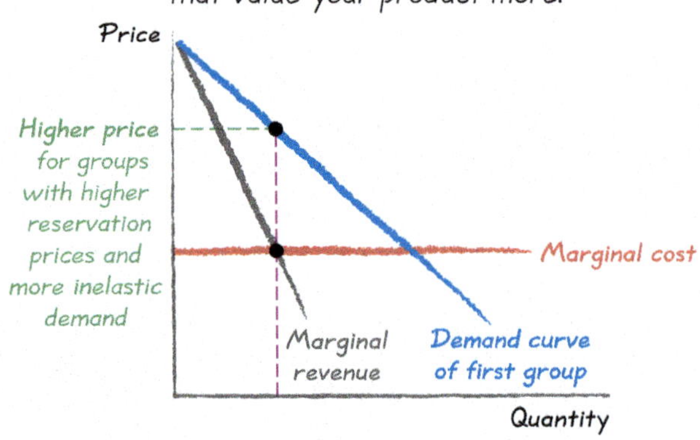

Market for second group
Charge a **lower price** to groups that are especially price sensitive.

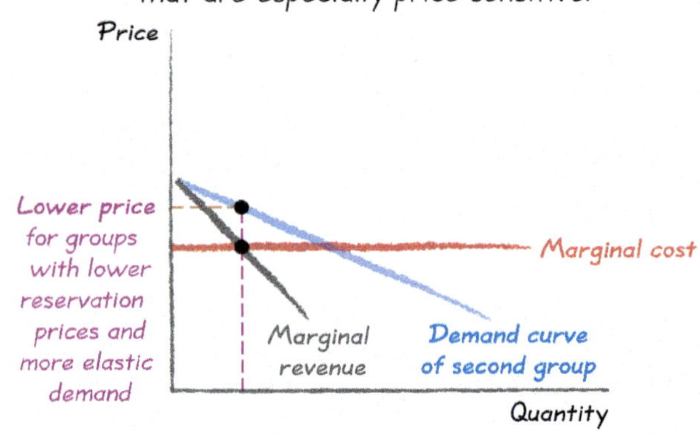

The Hurdle Method:

Offer lower prices only to those buyers who are willing to overcome some hurdle:

- Alternative versions and timing
- Fluctuating prices
- Haggling
- Extra hassle, bad service, and imperfect goods
- Quantity discounts
- Bundling

Key Concepts

bundling, 411
group pricing, 403
hurdle method, 407
perfect price discrimination, 399
price discrimination, 398
quantity discount, 411
reservation price, 398

Discussion and Review Questions

Learning Objective 16.1 *Boost your profits by charging the price each person will pay.*

1. You've been browsing some new styles on Cotton On's website, where you often shop, and have filled your virtual cart with a few nice items. But you leave the site without completing your purchase. A few days later, Cotton On sends you an e-mail with a 10% discount code to apply to your cart, within a limited time frame. Why do companies like Cotton On send specialised offers like this one?

Learning Objective 16.2 *Learn to boost your profits by offering group discounts.*

2. In cities with booming tourism industries, businesses often offer discounts for locals. For example, residents of Far North Queensland can receive discounts to various tours of the Great Barrier Reef. If Queensland brings in so much money from tourism, why offer a local's discount? What type of discount is the local's discount? How can businesses verify those who qualify?
3. In 2018, Spotify was available in many countries around the world. The same year, Spotify offered an attractive deal available only to students: Spotify Premium for one monthly payment of $5.99. The fee was half the amount charged for a standard Spotify Premium account. To qualify for the deal, students had to provide their information, such as name and birthdate, to Spotify and its third-party partner, SheerID. SheerID is a verification service utilised by companies to confirm various personal attributes and qualifications. In other words, your current student status at an Australian university is in a database, which is accessed by SheerID.
   - **a.** Was Spotify utilising group pricing? If so, what are the market segments?
   - **b.** Why would Spotify require third-party verification for the discount, rather than simply requiring an ".edu" e-mail address, as many other retailers do, to verify student eligibility?
   - **c.** How do you feel about the verification process? Do you think this will be the new norm?

Learning Objective 16.3 *Apply the hurdle method to target your discounts to those who value them.*

4. Most stores offer rotating promotions that provide discounts on various products. However, at many of them you must become a rewards member to take advantage of the deals. The price of the membership is free. You are probably familiar with this process at grocery stores, pharmacies, and even pet supply chains. What hurdles are involved in obtaining the promotional deals? How does the rewards membership benefit the store, and how does it benefit you?
5. Duolingo is a widely used foreign language app, with 500 million users in 2020. While there is a free version of the app, a premium Duolingo subscription eliminates advertisements during language practise and offers new quizzes with the ability to save lessons for offline use. Explain how Duolingo uses the hurdle method to allow its users to self-sort into "free" users (from whom Duolingo still earns revenue, through advertising) and "premium" users, who pay to use the enhanced, ad-free app.

Study Problems

Learning Objective 16.1 *Boost your profits by charging the price each person will pay.*

1. Michelle owns an independent bookstore and has observed that university graduates read more than people without degrees. She is considering offering a 10% discount on book purchases to customers who have a university degree. Using the three conditions necessary for price discrimination and the three key ideas for market segmentation, explain how Michelle's pricing strategy may help or hurt her business.
2. You're thinking about buying a Google Home smart speaker and have determined that you would pay a price of $100 but no more. Use the terms you learned in the chapter to discuss your reasoning for each question below.
   - **a.** On Friday you hit JB Hi-Fi and find that the Google Home is priced at $129. Do you buy it? Why or why not?
   - **b.** The following Sunday you go with a friend to JB Hi-Fi. She plans on purchasing a Google Home because she's willing to pay $129. When you get to the store, you see that the Google Home is on sale for $99.99. Do you buy the item now? Does your friend buy it? Why or why not?
   - **c.** Why don't companies just charge everyone their reservation price? How does this example illustrate the challenges companies face in trying to price discriminate?

Learning Objective 16.2 *Learn to boost your profits by offering group discounts.*

3. Currently, perfect price discrimination—in which each person is charged a price a smidge below their reservation price, which is also their marginal benefit—is mostly a hypothetical scenario. However, as data mining becomes more ubiquitous, we may see markets that more closely resemble perfect price discrimination through individual pricing. Use a graph to illustrate what perfect price discrimination would look like. Explain how perfect price discrimination benefits the seller and how it benefits the buyer. Then explain how perfect price discrimination impacts the total market quantity.
4. Your local cinema uses the same group-pricing strategy described in the chapter—charge different prices for adults, children, seniors, and students. However, the cinema uses one additional strategy: On Tuesdays, all tickets cost half the regular adult admission—a lower price than any group discount. You notice that the cinema is always very crowded on Tuesdays. If the Tuesday pricing strategy works so well, why doesn't the cinema cut its prices in half every day?
5. Warner Bros. Movie World charges two different prices for adult and child daily general admission to the park. The price of an adult ticket is \$109. The price of a child ticket (ages 3–13) is \$99. Since the park is already established and operating, suppose the marginal cost of each additional ticket is constant at \$80. Using this information, graph each market segment for Warner Bros. Include the marginal revenue, marginal cost, and demand curves for each segment.

Learning Objective 16.3 *Apply the hurdle method to target your discounts to those who value them.*

6. You're shopping to replace your two front tyres and you've discovered a pattern: Most tyre shops offer promotions that apply to buying four tyres. For example, one place you visited offered free installation and lifetime balance for purchasing four tyres. Another offered \$15 off per tyre for purchasing four tyres. A third place's offer: buy three tyres, get the fourth free. Explain why tyre shops offer quantity discounts.
7. In 2021, Apple released two new iPhone models: the iPhone 13 (priced from \$1,199) and the iPhone 13 Pro (\$1,699). The premium-priced Pro models both feature more cameras, better screens with a faster refresh rate, and faster graphics processors. The more expensive Pro Max also has a larger screen. Apple continued to sell the previous generation iPhone 12 (\$999) and the under-powered iPhone SE (\$679). All the phones use the same operating system, but the higher-end models include new technologies, higher-end parts, and new color choices. Why does Apple release multiple versions of each phone?
8. Suppose that last week you visited Krispy Kreme Doughnuts for an Original Glazed on your way to campus. The cashier explained that if you go to the link printed on your receipt and answer the survey, you can receive a free doughnut. Does everyone who receives a link on their receipt get the free doughnut? Explain why or why not.

CHAPTER 17

Economics of Strategic Management

Bunnings isn't a regular hardware store. From humble origins after being established in Western Australia in 1907 by sawmill owners Arthur and Robert Bunning, it is now the largest retailer of home-improvement and outdoor-living products across Australia and New Zealand. Bunnings is also a large supplier to trades, builders, and the housing industry. They sell everything from light bulbs and garden hoses, to power tools and building materials. Bunnings has a three-pronged strategy captured by their mission statement: "Our ambition is to provide our customers with the widest range of home improvement products in accordance with our lowest prices policy, backed with the best service." To deliver on this strategy Bunnings operates three different formats of stores: "warehouses," smaller format stores, and "trade centres." They also have a significant online presence, selling more than 20,000 items for direct delivery. In 2020 the company brought in $14.9 billion in revenues, had 375 physical stores, and employed 48,000 "team members."

martin berry/Alamy Stock Photo

Bunnings is a one-stop shop for most things involved in building, renovating, and maintaining a home.

The result of all these strategies? Bunnings is the go-to place for most people for home improvement items. You can be pretty sure that Bunnings has what you're looking for because of their large range, and they aim to always have the lowest prices. And for people like me who barely know which end of a saw to hold, but fancy themselves as handy, there are knowledgeable and friendly staff to help point you in the right direction. Why would you go anywhere else for home improvement products?

It may seem mysterious why one big chain would dominate a market as seemingly straightforward as hardware, but Bunnings maintains its dominance because it deals effectively with the competitive forces that it faces. We'll explore Bunnings' competitive situation in detail at the end of the chapter. But first, we've got to develop the tools to analyse the key competitive forces that Bunnings executives spend their days obsessively focused on. Let's get started.

Chapter Objective

Analyse the strategic decisions that you will make as a manager.

17.1 The Five Forces That Determine Business Profitability

Identify business opportunities by analysing the five forces that determine business profitability.

17.2 Non-Price Competition: Product Positioning

Figure out how to position your product relative to your competitors.

17.3 Bargaining Power of Buyers and Sellers

Be ready to use your bargaining power to get a better deal.

17.1 The Five Forces That Determine Business Profitability

Learning Objective *Identify business opportunities by analysing the five forces that determine business profitability.*

If there's one magical power that'll turbocharge your career, it's the ability to figure out which markets are going to be profitable. Think about how useful that will be. As an entrepreneur, you want to identify opportunities that can sustain long-term profits. As a manager, you want to know which parts of your business to expand and which to contract. And as an investor, you want to be able to identify profitable companies before anyone else.

I can't give you this magical power, but I can give you the next best thing—a framework to sharpen your focus on the key factors shaping the long-term profitability of any market. This framework—which brings together many of the key insights of microeconomics—is the tool that business strategists, entrepreneurs, and investors actually use to evaluate new industries. Indeed, it's similar to what you would learn in an MBA course on business strategy.

Five Forces Framework

If someone asked you what determines your company's long-term profitability, how would you respond? You might point to the quality of your products, the talent of your staff, or perhaps the size and prominence of your business. Although those things certainly help, they don't guarantee that you'll be profitable over the long term, when competition can push profits toward zero.

That's where the Five Forces framework comes in. Its core insight is that your long-term profitability is largely determined by the competitive forces in your market, and how you adapt to those forces. It focuses your attention on the five forces that determine the structure of competition in your market, providing a powerful lens for analysing business strategy. It's useful because even though every industry is different, the same economic forces determine profitability across all imperfectly competitive markets.

Five Forces framework The structure of competition in your market can be described in terms of five forces:

1. Competition from *existing competitors*
2. Threat of *potential entrants*
3. Threat of *substitute products*
4. Bargaining power of *suppliers*
5. Bargaining power of *customers*

Thinking about competitors broadly. The **Five Forces framework** systematically describes the competitive forces in your market. It's a counterweight to managers who think about competition too narrowly, focusing only on the direct rivals they currently face. The Five Forces framework helps correct this tendency, reminding you to take a broader view. With this framework, you analyse not only your existing competitors, but also four other economic forces: potential entrants, substitute products, suppliers, and customers. Together, these five forces describe the competitive pressures that determine your long-run profitability.

The five forces are associated with five strategic actors. Each of these five economic forces—which are illustrated in Figure 1—influences your profitability. Your *existing competitors* determine the type and intensity of existing competition. *Potential entrants* shape the nature of your future competition. Producers of *potential substitutes* may become competitors. *Suppliers* use their bargaining power as sellers to charge you higher prices on your inputs. And *customers* leverage their bargaining power as buyers to demand that you charge lower prices.

Wherever there are profits to be made, look out, because each of these five actors is going to try to grab the biggest share they can.

Market structure determines long-term profitability. Our focus is not on the type of good or service you sell, because a truly useful framework will work across all products. Instead, we'll focus on the idea that your long-term profitability is shaped by the

Figure 1 | The Five Forces That Shape Competition and Profitability

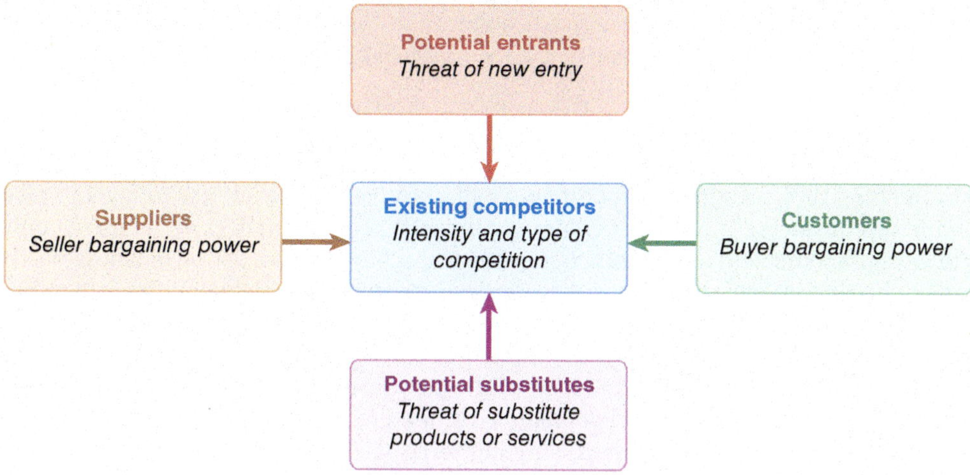

structure of competition in your market, which is summarised by these five forces. This approach reveals both the source of your industry's profitability and potential threats to it. As a result, it gives you a framework for anticipating and addressing how competition—and hence your profitability—will evolve over time.

It's time to dig in a bit deeper. We'll preview the five forces now, and then develop the new ideas they rely on in greater detail later in this chapter.

Force One—Existing Competitors: Intensity and Type of Existing Competition

The first force is one that you should be most familiar with: your existing competitors. The greater the degree of rivalry in your industry, the lower your profits will be. There are two dimensions to consider: the *intensity* of competition and the *type* of competition.

More rivals yields more intense competition. Generally, a rivalry is more *intense* when you face more competitors producing similar goods. This is a theme that should be familiar from our study of market structure and market power in Chapter 14. A monopolist has no direct rivals and hence faces little competitive pressure. Under imperfect competition, the degree of rivalry depends on how many competitors you face and how similar their products are to yours. And in the extreme case of *perfect competition*—when you're just one of many small businesses in the industry selling identical goods—competition is so intense that you have no market power.

You can compete on price and on product. The *type of competition* is also important. **Price competition** occurs when businesses compete to win customers by offering lower prices. The problem with competing on prices is that if your rivals respond with even lower prices, then repeated rounds of price-cutting could destroy your profits. Price competition is most likely when:

price competition Competing to win customers by offering lower prices.

- You and your rivals sell extremely similar products;
- Prices are easily observed; and
- Switching costs are low.

Each of these three factors makes customers less loyal and more likely to focus on price as the biggest differentiating factor.

Managers also try to distinguish their products on factors other than price. With **non-price competition,** businesses compete by differentiating their products—offering different features, service, or brand reputation, and positioning their products to win different

non-price competition Competing to win customers by differentiating your product.

segments of the market. Successful product positioning makes it harder for your rivals to win over your customers with a price cut, and so higher profit margins are more likely to persist. Figuring out the best way to position your product is so central to a successful business strategy that we'll study it in greater detail later in this chapter.

Force Two—Potential Competitors: Threat of Entry

In the long run, you don't just compete with the rivals that you face today, but also with new businesses that might enter your industry. The *threat of entry* refers not only to entrepreneurs who might launch new start-ups, but also to existing businesses that might expand into your market and current competitors that might enter new distribution channels. The threat of entry can intensify competition, which will push down your prices and profits.

The strength of this force varies, depending on the extent to which *barriers to entry* shield existing businesses from competition by new entrants. Strategic management can also help deter entry, thereby weakening this force. We explored strategies to help deter entry from competitors in Chapter 15.

Force Three—Competitors in Other Markets: Threat of Potential Substitutes

Beyond your industry, you also face competition from businesses in other industries whose products are potential substitutes for yours. For instance, many people now get their news online instead of watching television news. Video conferencing is a substitute for air travel. And tax preparation software like Etax is a substitute for hiring an accountant.

Think expansively about potential substitutes. The key to assessing this competitive force is to think expansively—applying the *interdependence principle*—to recognise that potential substitutes can come from unrelated industries. For instance, a florist should understand that roses are a substitute not only for daffodils, but also for chocolate.

Sometimes, substitutes come from innovations that offer better performance, such as the Roomba—a robot vacuum cleaner—which is disrupting the sale of old-fashioned vacuums. But often the disruption comes in the form of a cheaper alternative. For instance, the camera in your mobile phone is not as good as an expensive Canon or Nikon, but given that your phone is always with you, fewer people are bothering to buy separate cameras. The threat posed by substitutes is not just about whether the alternative is better or cheaper, but rather whether it offers more bang for the buck.

Some substitutes are relevant in most markets. Buying from the *secondhand* market is a substitute for buying new. *Making something yourself* is a substitute for buying it. *Buying in the future* is a substitute for buying today. And sometimes the simplest substitute is to just *do without*.

Bulgac/Getty Images

Local coffee shops face competition from savvy home baristas.

Substitutes are a bigger threat when switching costs are low. You should be particularly focused on the threat of substitutes when your customers face a low cost of switching. For instance, it is easy to switch from buying books from Dymocks to buying them on Amazon, but it is far harder to switch from working on a Mac to using Windows, because you'll need to buy new software and relearn where your files live.

Complements can point to new opportunities. Savvy executives monitor other industries, so that they can reposition their offerings when new substitutes emerge. Beyond the threat of new substitutes, you should also keep track of the opportunity offered by *emerging complements*. For instance, Australia Post repositioned itself as the rise of e-mail—which is a *substitute* for regular mail—led to much less demand for sending letters. Today, it's more focused on package delivery, where the parallel rise in online shopping—which is a *complement* to package delivery—has led it to deliver a record number of packages.

Strategies can shape the threat posed by substitutes. A skilled strategist understands that they can shape the availability of substitutes. For instance, Pathology Australia has spent millions of dollars lobbying to halt the government's efforts to cut down their bulk billing incentives. This might seem like a good thing at first, but the reason pathologists don't want their bulk billing incentives removed is because they would probably have to lower their prices—otherwise you will just find a pathologist who doesn't charge a co-payment! Pathology Australia sees bulk billing as a substitute for large co-payments on your medical bill, and by lobbying the government, they have successfully kept these bulk billing incentives in place.

Force Four—Bargaining Power of Suppliers

You might ordinarily think of your suppliers as being your partners because your success contributes to theirs. But they can also threaten your success by charging you higher prices, which will squeeze your profit margins. Many owners of specialty stores are aware of this, as the first signs of their success often lead their commercial landlord to raise the rent on their stores.

It's worth analysing how dependent your success is on your suppliers. If your business is totally dependent on a particular supplier, they could raise the prices they charge you, and you either have to pay up or close your business. A ruthless supplier might exploit this leverage by raising the price it charges you until they've effectively extracted all of your profits. More generally, the ability of your suppliers to charge you high prices depends on the amount of leverage or bargaining power they have.

Force Five—Bargaining Power of Buyers

Just as suppliers can force you to pay high prices, powerful buyers can also force you to offer lower prices. This is an issue that Australian dairy farmers know well. There are many milk suppliers but two very large supermarkets—Coles and Woolworths—that end up selling a lot of the milk in Australia. The supermarkets can play off one supplier against the other to get the best price. They also get milk suppliers to produce their "home brand" milk labels at an even lower price. If a milk supplier alienates one of the supermarkets it is left with just one buyer. Either way, milk suppliers are in a very weak bargaining position. As Australian dairy farmers know too well, customers with a lot of bargaining power can limit your profitability.

Recap: The Five Forces and the Path Ahead

You now know what the Five Forces framework is—a systematic way of summarising the five types of competitive pressures that you'll have to manage. But to assess the strength of each force, forecast how it might change, and formulate a strategically sound response, you'll need a deep understanding of the underlying economics. Fortunately, we've covered a lot of this material over the past few chapters, so you can think of the Five Forces framework as a capstone that helps us bring all that material together in a systematic way. The framework also points to the remaining issues that we'll need to dig into in the rest of this chapter.

The first force is rivalry among *current competitors.* That rivalry has two dimensions: price competition and non-price competition. We've already explored price competition—and how market power shapes the prices that managers set—in Chapter 14. What remains is non-price competition, and so in this chapter we'll explore how best to position your product relative to your rivals. The second force is the threat posed by *potential entrants.* It's so important that we devoted Chapter 15 to it. The third force is *potential substitutes,* and given that we've already explored this issue at quite some length, we won't repeat ourselves any further. The fourth and fifth forces are the *bargaining power of sellers and buyers*. The same factors that determine the bargaining power of buyers also determine the bargaining power of sellers, so we'll deal with these two forces in parallel. By the end of this chapter, you'll have all the tools you need for an insightful Five Forces analysis.

17.2 Non-Price Competition: Product Positioning

Learning Objective *Figure out how to position your product relative to your competitors.*

The product that your business sells is probably quite similar to that sold by some of your competitors, and quite different to that sold by others. Too often, managers think about these similarities and differences as somehow innate to their product (and those of their competitors). But that's a mistake. After all, you get to choose what features to include, the quality of your workmanship, the type of service to offer, your product design, its style, the locations where it's sold, and the way you advertise it. As you make these choices, you effectively choose how to differentiate your product from those of your rivals. And this choice—of how best to position your product—is a key strategic decision that shapes your market power and ultimately your profitability.

The Importance of Product Differentiation

Perhaps the simplest way to appreciate the importance of product differentiation is to see what happens in its absence. And to see that, we'll visit a local highway, so that you can put yourself in the shoes of Hilda, who owns a Shell petrol station. Her petrol station sits right across the street from a BP station, although apart from this one rival, she doesn't face much competition because there are no other petrol stations for miles. But Hilda sells a product—petrol—that's virtually identical whether you buy it from her Shell or from the nearby BP. It's the same chemical compound, sold at the same location, and both petrol stations accept the same credit cards and offer similarly polite service. Let's see how competition plays out in the absence of product differentiation.

Pure price competition can drive your economic profits to zero. Initially, both Hilda's Shell and the rival BP sell petrol for $1.30 per litre, and they each make a tidy profit, because the wholesale price is only $1.15 per litre. Given that they're both charging the same price, they're probably each selling to half the customers. Now, put yourself in Hilda's shoes, and think about what to do next. If you drop your price to $1.29, you'll win over your rival's customers, and with twice the sales, your profits will nearly double. Good idea. But let's see how your rival responds, now that they're selling no petrol. They realise that they can get all of their customers back if they cut their price to $1.29. Better still, they can cut their price to $1.28, and also win over all of your customers, too. So they cut their price to $1.28. Now you discover you're selling no petrol. What's your best response? The smart thing is to cut your price to $1.27, and win all the customers back. And when your rival discovers this, what's their obvious response? They respond by cutting their price to $1.26.

As each price cut is matched by a further cut, eventually BP is charging $1.16, just a cent above its marginal cost. Even then, Hilda's best choice is to cut her price to $1.159. This price war will continue until eventually price equals marginal cost (or perhaps a smidge above it). At that point, neither of them will cut their price any further because that would mean making a loss on every litre. They're not going to raise prices either, because that would lose all their customers. And sadly for Hilda, when prices are this low, neither her Shell nor her rival BP makes an economic profit. The striking thing about this scenario is that Hilda only has one rival, yet her profits were competed away.

Hilda's experience contains a warning for all executives: If you sell identical goods—that is, if you don't differentiate your product—then competition from even just one rival can force the price so low that it eliminates your economic profits.

Non-price competition through product differentiation yields market power. The problem that Hilda faces is that if the rival petrol station cuts its price, she will lose *all* of her customers, and her rival finds this an irresistible incentive. More generally, the problem that any business selling *identical* goods faces is that there is a huge incentive for their rivals to undercut their price. This incentive is particularly strong when competitors sell identical products because gaining even a small price advantage will translate into a large change in the quantity demanded. This suggests that the key to avoiding price competition is to weaken the incentive for your rival to undercut your price.

This is where *non-price competition* comes in. If you differentiate your product so that it better suits some of your customers, then those customers will keep buying from you, even if your price is not the lowest. Through successful product differentiation, you'll gain market power.

To see how important this can be, contrast the very different way that competition plays out between Hilda's Shell and the nearby BP, with the competition between Coke and Pepsi. In both the petrol and cola markets, suppliers sell chemically similar—indeed, nearly identical—products. And both are locked in a fierce contest with their rivals. What's different is the *type* of competition. The prices at many petrol stations are per litre, while ads for Coke or Pepsi almost never mention the price.

Ronald W. Erdrich/The Abilene Reporter-News/AP Images

A price cut on Pepsi means nothing to her.

That's because Coke and Pepsi don't just compete on price. Coke implores you to "Taste the Feeling," (as if you can taste a feeling) and Pepsi boasts that it's the drink for those who want to "Live for Now" (as if there's some other time to live). They've each differentiated their products, so that despite the chemical similarities, each cola has a devoted following. I'm sure you have friends who stick with Coke even when Pepsi is cheaper (just as other friends stick with Pepsi even when Coke is cheaper). As a result, their customers—like their beverages—are somewhat sticky.

This has big implications for how competition plays out. It blunts Pepsi's incentive to undercut Coke's prices since a price cut won't translate into many new customers. By making your rival's product an imperfect substitute for yours, you effectively blunt their incentive to undercut your prices. This makes price competition less fierce, which is why both Pepsi and Coke sell for prices well above their marginal costs.

The contrast between cut-throat price competition in the market for petrol and the larger profit margins in the market for cola highlights the importance of finding ways to differentiate your product.

There are many ways to differentiate your product. Product differentiation is about finding ways other than a lower price to attract and retain customers, and there are many ways to do this. You could offer different *features,* like HP and Dell who compete by offering computers with different combinations of memory, hard drive size, and processor speed. *Quality* is important too, and Gibson handcrafts its guitars to create a sweeter sound than a factory-made alternative. *Customer service* matters, which is why Myer hires more people to help you shop than Kmart does. *Design* counts, which is why Bed Bath N' Table collaborates with leading designers to create more interesting homewares than Target. *Style* is essential, and R.M. Williams competes with Levi's by trying to offer more fashionable jeans. *Reliability* is important, and The North Face backs up its apparel with an impressive money-back guarantee. *Location* and *convenience* are time-savers, and this is a key part of the competition between banks. And even beyond these objective differences, *advertising* can persuade some customers, which explains why Pepsi and Coke spend so much money trying to convince you to prefer one similar-tasting cola over another.

There's fierce competition at each of these margins—in features, quality, service, design, style, reliability, location, and brand image. And that's why you shouldn't think of them as fixed characteristics of your product, but rather as strategic choices you make to best position your product. A successful strategy will give you more customers who are loyal, effectively redrawing your business's demand curve so that it's in a more profitable place. That's why our next task is to develop the tools you'll need to figure out how best to position your product.

Positioning Your Product

The idea of product differentiation is to offer your customers a product that better serves their needs. The payoff is that your customers will still want to buy from you, even if you charge a slightly higher price than your rivals.

So you know differentiation is important, but how should you decide the best ways to differentiate yourself? This is about you choosing the set of attributes—the features, service, brand image, and so on—for your product. The answer depends on how you can best position your product relative to your competitors' products. As we'll see, it involves a delicate trade-off between *demand-side* considerations, positioning your good to be attractive to as many *customers* as possible, versus *supply-side* concerns, positioning it to be as different from your *competitors* as possible. It's a balancing act with big implications. Position your product too close to your rivals—that is, make it too similar—and you risk more intense price competition, leading to lower prices and lower profits, as in the competition between Shell and BP. Position your product too far away—perhaps by including unusual features—and you'll find it hard to win customers from your rivals.

In order to analyse this trade-off strategically, we'll begin with a metaphor. While it might seem a bit contrived, stick with it, because we'll soon see how businesses actually use this framework—sometimes called the Hotelling model (after its founder, Harold Hotelling)—to figure out how to best position their products.

The beach as a metaphor for non-price competition. Here's a very simple story to illustrate non-price competition. It's a hot day out, and so people are spread all along the beach. You're an ice cream seller and have to decide where to position your ice cream cart. This decision is important, because you're not the only ice cream seller, and people will only walk to the nearest cart. For simplicity, we'll assume that people are evenly spaced along the beach, and you have only one rival.

Where are you going to position your ice cream cart? Figure 2 illustrates where your rival is, and two possibilities you might choose.

Figure 2 | **How Should You Position Your Product?**

(A) **Choose your rival's left**, and everyone to your left, and half of those between you and your rival, will buy from you.

(B) **Choose your rival's right**, and everyone to your right, and half of those between you and your rival, will buy from you.

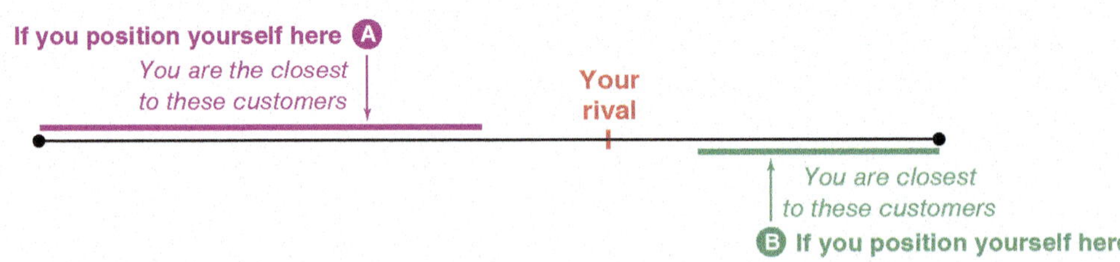

First, take note of where your rival is located, because you want to choose the best position, relative to them. To gain the most sales, you want to position your cart so that your cart is the most convenient one for as many customers as possible. In this case, your rival is on the right end of the beach. You should position your cart so that you can *supply the underserved part of the market*, which in this case is the left end of the beach. Doing this will win you all the customers to your left, as well as half of those between you and your rival. You can see that this is a better outcome, because it yields more customers than if you had taken the position to your rival's right.

Your business's position is a metaphor for the type of product you offer. Okay, that's it: You've now made your first product-positioning decision. And the example can be applied to the many other businesses that regard their location as the most important strategic positioning decision they face.

But it also applies beyond choosing a location. Let's see how we can extend this metaphor to help you think about the positioning of many other products, relative to their competitors. In each case, the trick comes in trying to sort out the important dimensions in which you and your competitors differ.

- A product manager at Kellogg's doesn't choose where to be located on a beach, but rather where to position their new breakfast cereal on a continuum from sweet to nutritious.

- A restaurateur doesn't decide between the left or right end of the beach (or somewhere in-between), but rather between offering convenient fast food or a more elaborate dining experience (or something in-between).

- Automotive engineers design new car models somewhere on the spectrum between compact, fuel-efficient cars at one end, and larger, more powerful gas-guzzlers at the other.

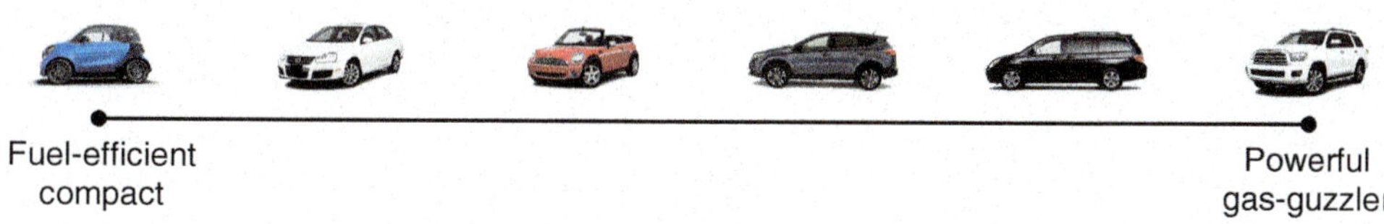

From second car left Alamy Images

- Even in art, product positioning matters. Writers have to place their work somewhere on the spectrum between an enjoyable light read and a challenging intellectual work.

Let's return to the beach, and try to decide exactly where to position your ice cream cart. We'll start with the demand-side considerations figuring out how to position your product to appeal to the most customers, and then turn to the supply side.

Demand side: Position your product next to your rival to get the most customers. We've already decided to place your ice cream cart to the left of your rival so that you cater to the underserved part of the market. But now the question is how close to place it. The answer shown in Figure 3 might surprise you.

Figure 3 | How Close Should You Position Your Product to Your Rival?

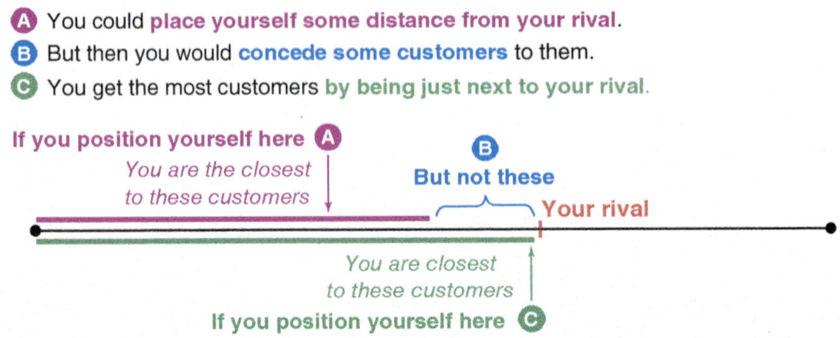

When you only face one rival, you want to *position your offering as close as possible to them.* Why? If you're on your rival's left, then you'll definitely be the preferred choice of every customer to your left, but you'll only be the nearest choice for half of the customers between you and your rival. Those folks are the marginal customers that you could win over by moving just a little closer to them. Every time you shift closer to your rival, you'll start to win more and more marginal customers. Notice that the people to your left don't have a better option, and so they'll still come to your ice cream cart, even if you shift a bit further away. And so you should keep shifting closer to your rival until you're just next to them. At that point, you're selling to as many customers as possible, given where your rival is. Yes, the people all the way at the left end of the beach will be frustrated at having to walk further, but you're going to get their business anyway.

The bottom line here is that demand-side considerations suggest that making your product more attractive to as many customers as possible means positioning yourself just next to your rival.

Interpreting the DATA **Why are political parties so similar?**

It's easy to get disillusioned by politics, and some people say that elections don't offer a real choice. They say that sure, there are two parties, but they're so similar on most issues that it doesn't really matter who wins.

But if you think about policy platforms as an example of product positioning, this is exactly what you should expect. In this case, the left end of the beach represents left-wing ideas (such as more government spending on the social safety net, paid for with higher taxes), and the right end of the beach represents right-wing ideas (such as less government spending and lower taxes). Instead of thinking about beachgoers scattered at different locations along the beach, think about the preferred policies of different voters scattered at different locations along this left-wing/right-wing spectrum.

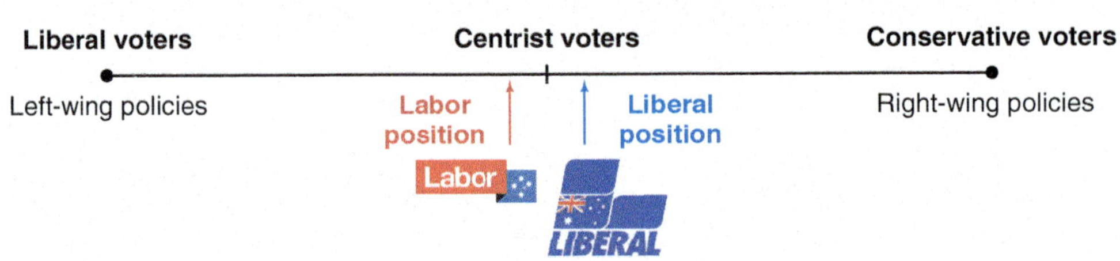

Just as the ice cream vendors want to be close to as many beachgoers as possible, politicians want their policies to be close to the preferences of as many voters as possible because that's what'll help them persuade more people to vote for them. The result is that the Labor and Liberal parties each find it easier to get elected if they set their policy positions quite close to those of their opponents. As each party jockeys to cater to the underserved end of the voter pool, they end up converging in the middle, both trying to win centrist voters—a finding known as the *median voter theorem.*

Of course, the two parties do differ a bit—some people say they differ quite a bit—so perhaps this finding is best viewed as explaining why they don't differ even more. ■

Supply side: Position your product away from your rival to reduce price competition. So far, we have only analysed the demand side of the market and the incentive to be as close as possible to your *customers.* But you also need to consider the supply side, and how your *rivals* might respond. Now it's time to invoke the *interdependence principle* to think through how your product positioning affects the *prices* your competitors set.

As we learned from the neighbouring petrol stations, if you position yourself right next to your opponent so that you're offering essentially identical goods, then intense price competition will push down prices and profits. When your positions are nearly identical, you have no market power.

By contrast, if you position your product far apart from your rival, many of your customers will find your rival's product to be a less useful substitute for yours, giving you some market power. The result will be less downward pressure on your prices. For instance, rather than positioning your petrol station across the street from your rival, you could choose a location in the next suburb. It's likely that you'll win most of the customers in that suburb, and your rival will win most of the customers in their suburb. The advantage of positioning your petrol station some distance away is that a small price cut is unlikely to lead many customers to switch petrol stations, reducing the incentive for either of you to try to undercut the other's prices.

The bottom line here is that you want to position your product to reduce the incentive for your rivals to undercut your price. The more that you position your products so that they're different from those offered by your rival, the more market power you'll have, allowing you to charge higher prices and enjoy larger profit margins. For instance, HP and Dell sell very similar Windows-based computers, and so the fierce competition between them has led to razor-thin profit margins. But Apple has chosen to position itself as offering quite a different type of computer, and its prices and profit margins are much higher.

EVERYDAY Economics

Can you make a dent in the aeroplane market?

Much of the attention paid to aeroplane manufacturing focuses on the two giants, the U.S.-based Boeing and the European-owned Airbus, who both make the large jets that seat hundreds of people. The Canadian company Bombardier makes the Lear jet and other smaller planes used largely as corporate jets. Cessna makes small planes that seat a dozen or fewer people, and Cirrus mainly makes planes for hobbyist pilots. The CEO of the Brazilian company Embraer is trying to decide how to position his company's planes. What's your advice?

PAULO WHITAKER/ REUTERS/Newscom

Smaller, but profitable

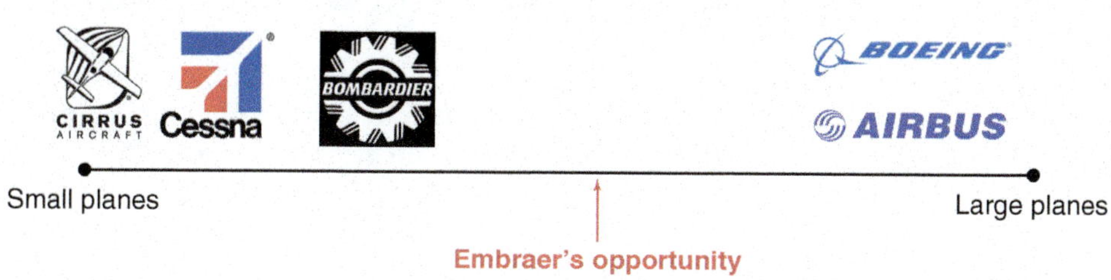

The rough sketch above gives you a sense of how Embraer saw the market. Boeing and Airbus are engaged in a brutal price war for the large plane segment, and it makes no sense to join that fight. Instead, it went looking for an underserved niche in the market. Embraer discovered that neither of these giants bothered making medium-sized planes with 70 to 118 seats, and the traditional small-jet manufacturers didn't have the capacity to build planes that big. Embraer positioned itself to dominate this niche, building jets that have proven to be very popular among regional airlines like American Eagle. And because there is not much price competition—no one really makes a good substitute for its medium-sized planes—this niche has proven to be very profitable for Embraer. ■

Recap: There is a product positioning trade-off. Let's wrap up what we've learned from all of this. The question of how to differentiate your product is really about how best to position your product. There are two competing forces to consider:

1. *Demand side*: Consider your customers. You want to position your product so that you're closer than your rival to the preferences of as many customers as possible, which means positioning your product on the underserved end of the market. But once you're serving this part of the market, the same logic says you should try to locate *closer to your rival*—that is, make it as similar as possible—so as to maximise the number of customers who prefer your product.
2. *Supply side*: Consider your competitors. You want to position your product so as to minimise the incentive for your rivals to undercut your prices. This is a countervailing force to position your product *away from your rivals*—that is, to differentiate your product—so as to soften price competition, which yields market power and larger profit margins.

Putting these together says that positioning your product closer to your rival can help increase the *quantity* you sell, while positioning it further away boosts your market power and hence the *profit margin* on each item you sell. Because both the quantity you sell and your profit margin matter, this is a difficult trade-off to manage. There are no hard and fast rules about how to get it right, but rather some basic rules of thumb:

- If price competition is particularly intense—as it is between neighbouring petrol stations—you want to differentiate your product (as Coke and Pepsi do).
- If price competition is subdued (as in elections, where politicians are not allowed to buy votes), then you want to minimise any differences, so that you can appeal to as many people as possible.

One approach to positioning your product is through advertising, and so our next task is to apply these ideas to putting together a successful advertising campaign.

Figure 4 | Advertising Shifts Firm Demand

Ⓐ You'll gain customers at each price. This **increase in demand** shifts your firm demand curve right.

Ⓑ More loyal customers stick with you when you raise your price. You **gain market power**, steepening your firm's demand curve.

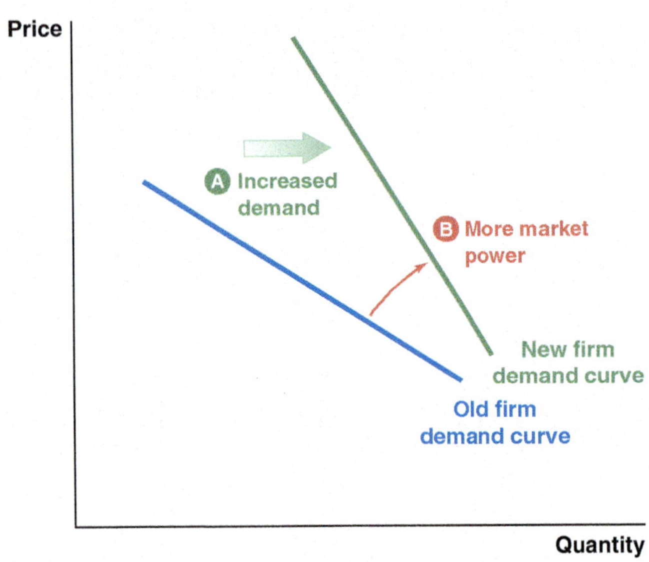

The Role of Advertising

Advertising is an essential part of a successful product positioning strategy. It's so important that businesses spend hundreds of billions of dollars on advertising every year, which is enough to support the TV shows you watch, the newspapers you read, and the web content you enjoy.

Advertising aims to shift and steepen your firm demand curve. A successful advertising strategy will shift your firm demand curve in two important ways, which are illustrated in Figure 4. First, by convincing more people to buy your product at any given price, it increases the demand for your product. This shifts your firm demand curve to the right, allowing you to sell a larger quantity. And second, if your advertising campaign builds brand loyalty, then your customers will stick with you even if you raise your prices. These price-insensitive customers increase your market power, which translates into a steeper or more inelastic firm demand curve and larger profit margins. Both of these changes will boost your profits.

Market structure shapes your advertising strategy. The structure of competition in your market shapes the impact of different types of advertising, and that in turn determines the messages you'll want to emphasise.

In a *perfectly competitive* market it rarely makes sense for an individual business to advertise. After all, when you're only a tiny part of the market, your campaign to convince people to "eat more lamb" will benefit other farmers a lot more than it'll benefit you. The only way advertising makes sense is when it's coordinated and paid for by an industry association, such as Meat and Livestock Australia—which many lamb farmers contribute to—with its message: "We Love Our Lamb."

Monopolies use advertising to shift the market demand curve for their product. DeBeers, which for a long time was a monopolist in the diamond market, used its marketing muscle to help create the modern custom that couples celebrate their engagement with a diamond ring. An increase in demand for diamonds benefited DeBeers exclusively, and so its advertising focused on the *product*, rather than the *brand*, as in its famous tagline, "A diamond is forever."

Under *imperfect competition* it's typically worth advertising even more aggressively because you have an extra incentive beyond increasing demand for your product: Advertising can also help you steal customers from your rivals. To do this effectively, you should emphasise your particular product positioning and the unique value that your product offers. For instance, rather than arguing that chocolate is delicious, M&M's remind you that it's the only chocolate that "melts in your mouth not in your hands." Likewise Visa doesn't describe how useful credit cards are, but rather that it is the world's most widely accepted credit card—"Everywhere you want to be." And Subway's slogan "Eat Fresh," is a subtle dig at the quality of its fast-food rivals.

Search goods lend themselves to informational advertising. The characteristics of your product will also influence the type of advertising you should do. A **search good** is any good that you can easily evaluate before buying it. For instance, a desktop computer is a search good, because once you've read a list of its specifications—such as the type of processor it uses, the size and speed of the hard drive, and the amount of memory—you can figure out whether it provides good value for your money. (In contrast, Pepsi is not a search good because you have to taste it to really evaluate it.)

search good A good that you can easily evaluate before buying it.

Search goods lend themselves to a type of advertising strategy called **informative advertising,** which aims to inform you about a product. The idea is to provide your potential customers with hard data about the specific attributes of your product. Whenever you click on a company's homepage, you'll probably discover informative advertising. Computer companies catalogue the components they use, law firms list the qualifications of their staff, and investment companies describe their recent performance. Generally, economists believe that informative advertising is helpful, as better information leads people to make better choices.

informative advertising Advertising that provides information about a product and its attributes.

When customers are uncertain about quality, branding can help. Branding can be an especially important part of advertising for goods where buyers can't easily discern their quality. It's a lesson you'll recognise from the last time you got hungry on a road trip. As you're scanning the exits far from home, you quickly realise that you don't know whether the local restaurant serves quality burgers or health code violations topped with lettuce and tomato. This uncertainty about the quality of the burger leads millions of people to pull over at the nearest McDonald's, instead.

Versions of this story play out not only at thousands of highway rest stops every day, but also in any market where customers are uncertain about the quality of the goods they're buying. And they illustrate how effective branding provides information to consumers about the quality of your goods. Through careful brand management, McDonald's convinces you its burgers will be safe, Tiffany convinces you its diamonds aren't fake, and Apple convinces you its phones won't be faulty. Even better, it's a self-reinforcing cycle, because the stronger a brand's reputation for quality, the greater the stake it has in maintaining that reputation.

persuasive advertising
Advertising that tries to persuade or manipulate you into believing that you'll enjoy a particular product.

The Advertising Archives

Are you persuaded?

Persuasive advertising aims to persuade. But advertising often contains very little information. Instead, **persuasive advertising** tries to persuade or manipulate you into believing that you'll enjoy a particular product. Persuasive advertising often exploits your emotions, and uses subtext to hint at claims that are not actually true.

When Pepsi tells you to "Live for Now," and Coke says you should "Taste the Feeling," neither provides any information that'll help you choose the tastier or less unhealthy beverage. It's hard to see how this advertising leads buyers to make better decisions, and it might lead them to make worse ones.

A lot of advertising may be wasteful. Indeed, the main effect of Pepsi's advertising might be for it to win business from Coke. This is called a *business-stealing effect.* And it means that while it's privately profitable for Pepsi to advertise, from society's perspective it's wasteful, because Pepsi's gains are offset by Coke's losses. Similarly, if Coke's advertising only helps it steal business from Pepsi, then its advertising campaign is also socially wasteful.

It may even be worse than this. Part of the reason that Pepsi spends so much on advertising is that it can't afford to lose market share when Coke advertises. Likewise, Coke advertises because Pepsi does. The result is an advertising arms race, in which each brand is forced to advertise just to keep up with the amount of advertising by their competitors. This suggests that much of the $180 billion spent each year on advertising may be socially wasteful.

Recap: Product positioning is about non-price competition. OK, now it's time to pan back to the big picture. At this point, you should have a good sense of the first of the five forces—how best to compete with your existing rivals in the market through both price competition and strategic product positioning, including advertising. The second force—the threat of new entrants—was the focus of the last chapter, while the third major force, the threat of substitution was also discussed in detail earlier. So let's now turn to the fourth and fifth forces: The threats posed by the bargaining power of your customers and your suppliers.

17.3 Bargaining Power of Buyers and Sellers

Learning Objective *Be ready to use your bargaining power to get a better deal.*

The week before Apple unveiled the iPad was a tense time, as high-stakes negotiations played out. The iBookstore is a marketplace for iPad-friendly books and was an essential part of the launch. Apple CEO Steve Jobs was determined to persuade all the major publishers to sell their books on his platform. However, Jobs wanted the deal to be on his terms: A price of $16.99 for each e-book, which was higher than on Amazon, with Apple getting a 30% cut of each sale. One publisher, HarperCollins, balked at this proposal, claiming that both the price and the commission were too high. It was the only remaining holdout among the four leading publishers.

D. Ross Cameron/ZUMA Press/Newscom

Negotiations between Steve Jobs and James Murdoch were all about bargaining power.

James Murdoch, an executive at News Corporation, which owns HarperCollins, wrote an e-mail to Jobs arguing that under the proposed terms, "the entire hypothetical benefit" of an e-book "accrues to Apple." Apple's proposed deal offered him barely any profit margin, and so he ended the e-mail saying that if they didn't agree to a deal now, then "maybe in the future." Consider it a polite refusal.

But Jobs pressed on. In a subsequent e-mail, he argued that HarperCollins only had three options, none of them good. It could agree to Apple's terms and potentially reach a mass market. It could stick with Amazon over Apple, but Amazon might eventually offer even worse terms. Or HarperCollins could refuse to sell any e-books and see its books get pirated. He ended the e-mail, saying: "Maybe I'm missing something, but I don't see any other alternatives. Do you?"

Jobs' gambit worked. Murdoch relented, and HarperCollins agreed to Apple's terms the day before the launch. The rest is history.

Perhaps you see a skilled negotiator at work here. But this story is about something a bit deeper—how bargaining power ultimately shapes and constrains negotiations. Notice that Murdoch signalled that he was willing to walk away, which is often the best tactic for getting a good deal. But this threat doesn't help much when you don't have good alternatives. Although there were many publishers, there were only two major e-book sellers: Amazon and Apple. Ultimately, HarperCollins needed Apple more than Apple needed HarperCollins. So Jobs called Murdoch's bluff. Faced with no better option, HarperCollins signed up to a deal that gave Apple what it wanted.

Bargaining Power

Our next task is to help you assess your bargaining power. The outcome of any negotiation will be shaped by the bargaining power of both the buyer and the seller, and so it makes sense to analyse them both at the same time. In this section, we'll explore how to use your bargaining power to get a better deal, and also how your rivals will try to use their bargaining power to extract more favourable prices. Your **bargaining power** is your ability to negotiate a better deal for yourself. When you're a seller, you're trying to negotiate to sell at a higher price, and when you're a buyer, you're trying to negotiate paying a lower price.

bargaining power Your ability to negotiate a better deal.

Your next best alternative determines your bargaining power. The *opportunity cost principle* is central to understanding the source of your bargaining power. Recall that this principle says that you need to always ask, "Or what?" When you're at the bargaining table, you should ask yourself whether you should do a deal or instead pursue your **next best alternative,** which is the value of the best option outside of this deal. As a buyer, your next best alternative might be to buy from someone else, to buy a slightly different good, or to simply do without. Likewise, as a seller, your next best alternative might be to sell to someone else, to make a different product, or to cut back on production.

next best alternative The value of your best option, outside of this deal.

Your next best alternative determines your bargaining power. The better that alternative is, the more bargaining power you have, because you can credibly threaten to walk away from any deal that's not at least as good. That's why James Murdoch ultimately accepted the deal that Steve Jobs offered: Even though the terms weren't good for HarperCollins, his next best alternative was worse, so he couldn't credibly threaten to walk away. Steve Jobs, to his credit, understood this and stayed firm.

Let's apply this idea to your next salary negotiation. Perhaps you're working as a consultant at Deloitte when PricewaterhouseCoopers (which goes by PwC) tries to hire you. In your negotiation with PwC, your next best alternative is staying with Deloitte. The higher your current salary at Deloitte, the greater your bargaining power is when negotiating with PwC.

The other side's next best alternative determines their bargaining power. There's an important symmetry here: The people you're negotiating with have more bargaining power the better *their* next best alternative is. Their next best alternative determines the point at which they'll walk away. For instance, PwC's next best alternative to hiring you might be to hire a recent university graduate instead. The better that university graduate, and the lower their salary, the greater PwC's bargaining power is when negotiating with you.

The range of possible outcomes reflects both sides' next best alternatives. Taken together, the next best alternative of buyers and sellers determines the *range* of possible outcomes: The price must be higher than the seller's next best alternative, and it must be lower than the buyer's next best alternative. Immediately you can see how bargaining power determines outcomes.

For instance, if Deloitte is currently paying you $70,000 per year, you'll only move to PwC if it pays you more than $70,000. And for PwC, if they've interviewed an equally good consultant willing to take the job for $90,000, it'll only be willing to hire you for a salary that is no more than $90,000.

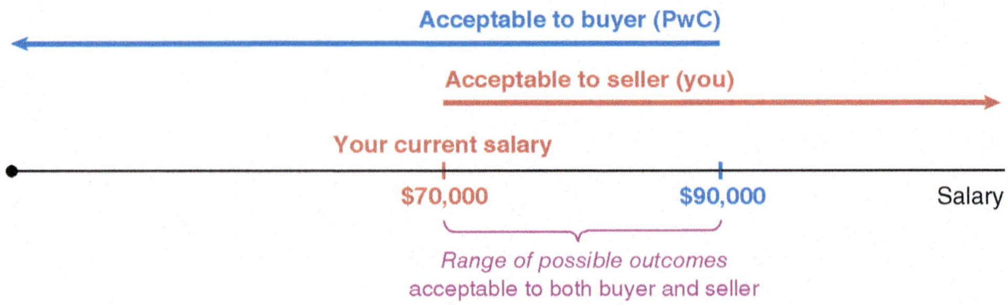

Thus, your bargaining power will push the salary up to at least $70,000, while PwC's will ensure that it doesn't rise above $90,000. The result is your negotiation with PwC will likely yield a salary offer somewhere between $70,000 and $90,000.

You can improve your bargaining power by improving your next best alternative. This analysis yields one clear piece of advice: If you want more bargaining power, then you need to improve your next best alternative. It's up to you to think creatively about how to do that. For instance, a consultant interviewing for a job with PwC would do well by also interviewing for a job with Ernst & Young. If Ernst & Young says it's willing to hire you for $80,000, then this becomes your next best alternative.

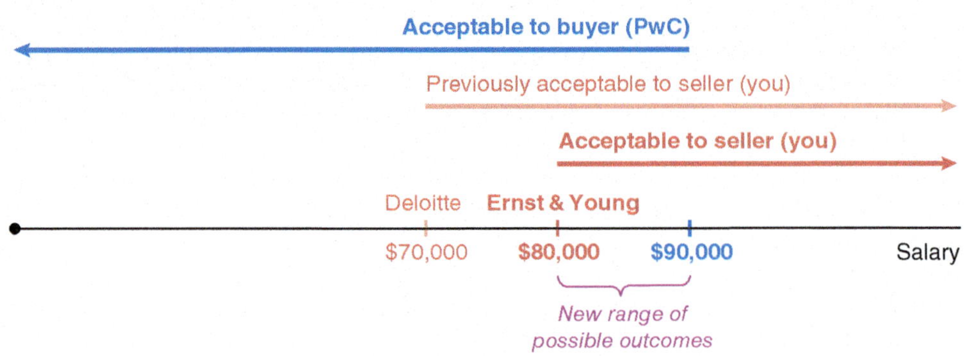

But don't keep this alternative a secret—PwC can only respond to your stronger bargaining position if they're aware of it. And if they're smart, PwC will quickly come to understand that in order to be competitive, they will have to offer you at least $80,000. The result is that the range of possible outcomes becomes even better, and your salary offer from PwC will likely be in the $80,000 to $90,000 range.

Sue Barr/Image Source/Getty Images

Tell him that you're also going to call someone else for a quote.

EVERYDAY Economics How to save money on household repairs

Your roof starts leaking. A pipe bursts. Or perhaps your electrical wiring shorts. Whatever the domestic disaster, you want to make sure to shop around. If you just call one contractor and ask them to make the repair, it's likely they'll charge you a high price. They figure they have a lot of bargaining power, because your next best alternative—living without shelter, water, or electricity—is pretty terrible.

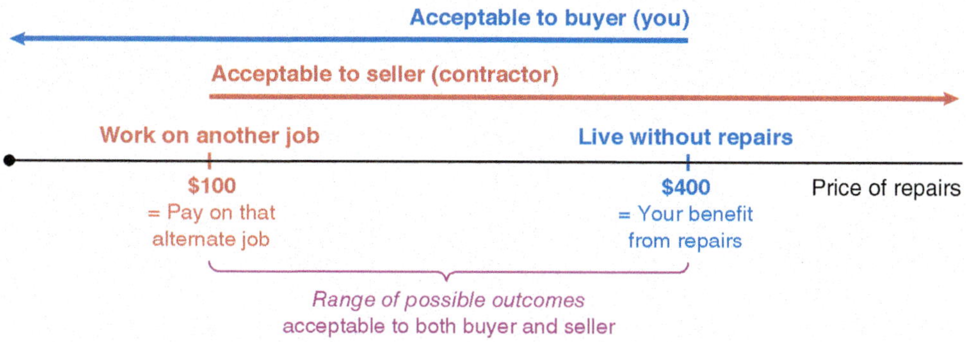

But if you call two other contractors and ask them for a quote so that you can choose the best deal, they'll understand that your next best alternative is to get someone else to do the repair. This improves your bargaining power enormously.

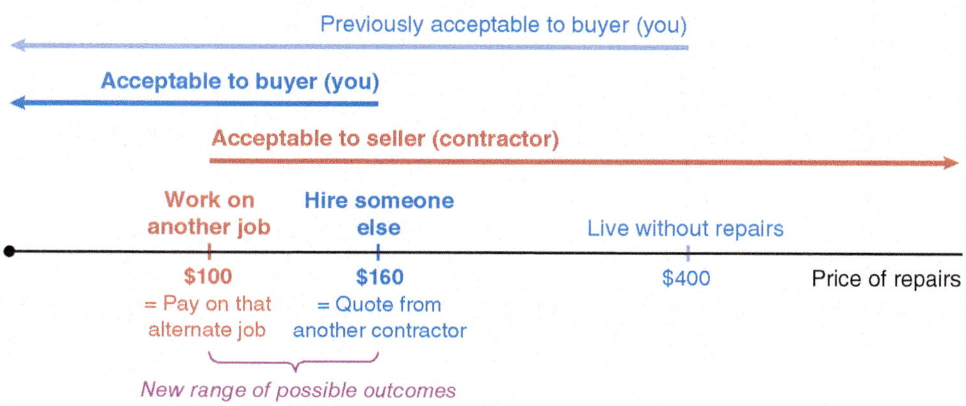

This shift will lead these competing contractors, who each want the job, to offer a much lower price. Even simpler: Just call one tradesperson for a quote, but tell them that you're going to get two more quotes. They won't know if you ever make those calls, but the fact that you are considering it will likely lead them to offer you a more reasonable price. ■

Negotiating can help you get the bigger share of the surplus. Focusing on the next best alternative yields a pretty good sense of each side's bargaining power. You won't accept a wage lower than your next best alternative, and PwC won't pay you any more than their next best alternative. If there's a deal to be made, you'll both have to agree on a salary somewhere between those two extremes.

So focusing on the next best alternative gets us to a *range of possible outcomes.* What next? Often you'll agree to meet halfway, which would suggest a salary of $85,000. Or you might decide to play hardball, saying that you won't sign for a dollar less than $89,000. Perhaps that will work, but be careful because it may not. After all, PwC might also decide to play hardball. It might refuse to pay you more than $81,000. Your demand is no more credible than theirs, and all this posturing might make it hard to reach an agreement despite the fact that you'd each be better off reaching a deal somewhere in the middle, rather than ending with no deal at all.

Ultimately, it comes down to negotiating prowess. Perhaps you can convince PwC that your next best alternative is even better than it actually is—maybe you can convince them that someone else might come along and offer you $86,000. Or maybe you can convince them that their next best alternative is worse—say, that you are much better at your job than anyone else they could possibly hire in that salary range. Perhaps you're willing to stick with an unpleasant negotiation longer, and eventually you'll wear them down. By this view, the next best alternative to signing a deal now is continuing to negotiate tomorrow. And the more you're willing to keep negotiating, the better your next best alternative is, and hence the greater your bargaining power will be.

Let's now explore a particular problem that can arise when your bargaining power shifts over time.

The Hold-Up Problem

You've spent three weeks hunting for the right apartment, and finally you've found the perfect place. It's $500 per week, a bit small, but cute, and you think you'll be happy. You pack your belongings, hire movers, and then take a week off work to unpack your boxes and set up the internet. And you spend your time and money buying just the right furniture for your space. Perhaps you need a small breakfast table that'll just fit into that awkward spot in the kitchen. And you buy a somewhat unusual couch because you think it'll pop next to that exposed brick wall. The first year in your new apartment flies by happily.

asbe/iStock/Getty Images

This cute studio apartment is less wonderful after the landlord raises your rent.

But then the landlord says that they're raising the rent to $550 per week. You're outraged. You would never have moved in a year ago if you knew they would jack up the rent a year later. But that was then, and this is now. Now that you've made this apartment your home, moving out would be expensive: You'd have to spend time searching for another apartment, you'll spend another few thousand dollars hiring movers again, and you'll probably need to buy yet another couch. A year ago, you would never have agreed to pay $550, but now that you're in the apartment, you realise that staying there is your best choice, even at this high price. Your landlord is, in effect, holding you up, demanding a better deal, simply because you no longer have as many good options. When you signed your lease your economic relationship with your landlord went through a "fundamental transformation." You went from being in a pretty competitive market with lots of options, to being in a situation of bi-lateral monopoly with your landlord. And because you needed to make relationship-specific investments but your landlord did not, you have ended up in a worse bargaining position. An economist would say that you should have seen this coming.

relationship-specific investment An investment that is more valuable if the current business relationship continues.

hold-up problem Once you have made a relationship-specific investment, the other side may try to renegotiate so that they get a better deal (and you get a worse one).

The hold-up problem follows from making relationship-specific investments. The investments you made in hiring movers, buying that tiny breakfast table, and purchasing that unusual couch are all **relationship-specific investments**—they're investments that are worth more in the context of a specific business relationship, which in this case is your ongoing lease with your landlord. It's money you spent that will be wasted if you move to another apartment where the couch and table don't work.

The problem you're having with your landlord is an example of the **hold-up problem:** Once you've made relationship-specific investments, staying in the relationship becomes more appealing to you. That puts you in a worse bargaining position, and the other side may try to force you to accept a worse deal. In the case of your apartment, staying became much more valuable to you than your next best alternative after you've moved in and nicely furnished it (that's the relationship-specific investment). You would lose a lot if you were forced to move, and this is what has put you in a worse bargaining position. Your landlord is exploiting the investments you've made in relationship-specific capital.

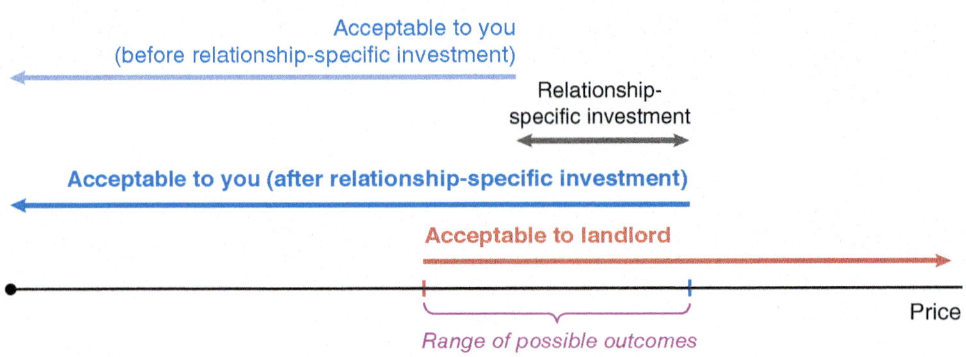

A year ago, your next best alternative was an otherwise similar apartment that was renting for $450 per week. Today, your next best alternative is worse because you would also have to pay for yet another expensive move and sell your furniture. The result is that you are in a much worse bargaining position. So much that you feel you don't really have a better choice than to grudgingly pay the higher rent.

Many businesses need to make relationship-specific investments. The hold-up problem can arise whenever you make relationship-specific investments. And as the following examples illustrate, these investments are incredibly common in the business world:

- You locate your factory close to your biggest customer or important raw-material supplier.
- You integrate your inventory management system so that it can communicate with the computer system used by your key supplier.
- You invest in a specialised machine that you need to meet the particular needs of a key customer.
- You train your salesforce so that they know all the technical details about the products that your company sells.

These are all investments that are necessary for businesses to operate efficiently. But in each case, they're investments whose value would decline if you stop working with that specific customer, supplier, or worker.

The hold-up problem can lead to underinvestment. The mere possibility that a hold-up problem might emerge in the future might lead you not to make relationship-specific investments. After all, even if the investment you're considering is highly productive, you won't reap much benefit if it leads you to get a worse deal in a subsequent renegotiation. And so the mere possibility of hold-up leads people to avoid making what would otherwise be productive investments.

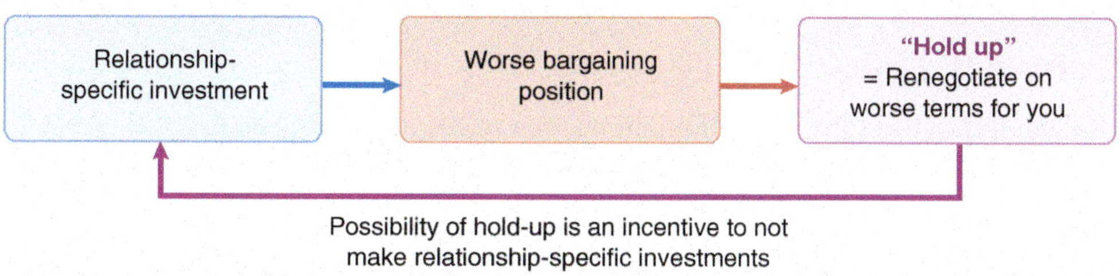

For instance, rather than buying a unique couch that matches your apartment perfectly, you might just buy an old beater. You'd rather invest in the perfect couch for this specific apartment, but you fear that it'll be worthless if you have to move. Moreover, since buying it enhances your landlord's bargaining position, it makes it more likely that they'll end up raising your rent. You buy a cheapo couch instead because it allows you to avoid making a big investment that'll be worthless if you have to switch apartments.

This problem occurs all the time in the business world, too. For instance, Delphi Technologies makes steering and suspension parts for Ford. Delphi could optimise its production process to best fit the needs of Ford, and this relationship-specific investment is worth making as long as Delphi keeps selling to Ford. But it'll make Delphi less efficient at selling to other carmakers. The strategic problem is that this investment will worsen its next best alternative to selling to Ford, thereby weakening its bargaining position. And so Delphi might choose not to make this relationship-specific investment so that it can avoid the possibility of Ford holding it up and renegotiating a lower price for its parts.

The hold-up problem can lead to unproductive investments. The hold-up problem can also lead you to make unproductive investments in order to protect your bargaining power. For instance, rather than buying a bold-coloured couch that looks great against the exposed brick in your new apartment, you might buy something in beige. No one loves beige, but you'll buy it anyway because beige won't clash with the carpet in any apartment. By buying beige, you've made an unproductive investment (beige, sigh), but it's worth it, because it'll retain its value if you have to switch apartments. And this boosts your bargaining power with your landlord, because you've made sure that your next best alternative—moving out—is less costly, and thus a better alternative.

Milkos/Getty Images

Beige goes with everything.

To take it a step further, sometimes companies make wasteful investments in business relationships with others, merely to improve their bargaining position with their current business partners. For instance, Delphi might invest in becoming a more efficient producer of tractor parts—even if it doesn't plan to ever do any business with tractor companies. That might sound wasteful, and it is. But for Delphi it might be profitable because this investment improves its next best alternative to working with carmakers. This increases its bargaining power in future negotiations with Ford, which it can use to demand better terms.

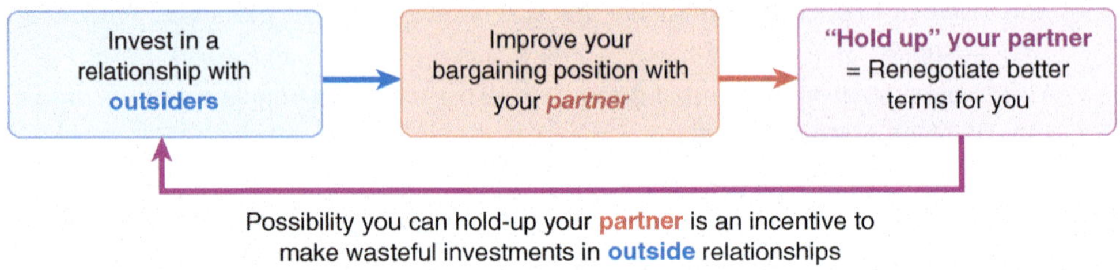

All told, the hold-up problem might lead Delphi to overinvest in technology it never plans to use (such as making tractor parts), and underinvest in the technology it uses in its everyday production. Executives across an array of industries report that similar problems lead their companies to underperform. This has led managers to look for smart solutions to the hold-up problem, which brings us to an emerging area of economics, called contract theory.

Contract Theory

The simplest way to solve the hold-up problem is to write long-term contracts that commit both sides to specific terms for the duration of their relationship. Importantly, if the contract prevents your business partner from behaving opportunistically, they won't be able to hold you up. For instance, you can protect yourself from your landlord raising your rent by negotiating a cap on rent increases in the lease. Likewise, Delphi can write a long-term contract with Ford, specifying the price Ford will pay for its parts, and committing Ford to buy from Delphi rather than other suppliers.

The Asahi Shimbun/Getty Images

Toyota has a reputation for honouring its commitments with its manufacturers.

It's hard to write complete contracts. While solving the hold-up problem with contracts is a great idea in theory, in practice it doesn't always work. For one thing it requires anticipating all relevant future contingencies. If the contract is long-term then that can be very hard—particularly as new technologies emerge that change the contractual relationship. Even with perfect foresight of the future, writing complete contracts is a difficult task, and savvy lawyers can often find ways to break a contract based on a technicality. (What if Delphi delivers its parts 10 minutes late one day? Or what if one batch is claimed to be "imperfect"? What does "imperfect" mean exactly?) Even if the parties to a contract know what they mean at the time the contract is written, they have to rely on a court knowing what they meant and enforcing that meaning. This is often hard. This has led businesses to explore two alternative solutions to the hold-up problem.

Alternative solution one: Reputation and repeated interactions. Ongoing relationships based on trust or reputation can reduce the incentive of your business partners to hold you up. For instance, many auto parts manufacturers have ongoing relationships with Toyota, and in many cases these involve large relationship-specific investments as they set up their production lines to produce exactly the parts Toyota wants. They feel comfortable making these relationship-specific investments because Toyota has built a reputation as a company that won't try to subsequently renegotiate lower prices.

And they're confident that Toyota will continue to treat them well, because the cost to Toyota of losing their reputation as a fair business partner would be greater than the benefit to Toyota from holding up one of its suppliers.

Alternative solution two: Vertical integration. **Vertical integration** occurs when two companies at different stages of a production chain combine to form one company. It's *vertical,* because it involves businesses up and down a production chain, and it's *integration,* because those two businesses now act as one integrated unit. Vertical integration is another way to solve the hold-up problem.

vertical integration When two (or more) companies along a production chain combine to form a single company.

While Toyota relied on reputation with auto parts makers, for many years Ford relied instead on vertical integration. Rather than buy auto parts from a variety of suppliers, in many cases Ford has either bought those suppliers or produced the inputs itself. When both the carmaker and their suppliers join together, there's no longer any incentive for one to try to hold the other up, as it wouldn't benefit the new, larger business as a whole.

As it turns out, this idea is central to figuring out what your business should *make versus buy.* Let's explore this idea further.

What Should You Make, and What Should You Buy?

At this point we've seen several ways in which your profits are vulnerable, to both your suppliers and your customers exerting their bargaining power. The logic of vertical integration is that you can solve these problems by joining forces with your business partners to form a larger integrated company. But how far does this logic go? That is, what should your company make, and what should you buy?

The answer to this question determines the size, scope, and shape of your business. Will you start with the rawest of raw materials, take them through the various stages of production, and sell them? Or will you rely on suppliers, specialise in one part of the production process, and then sell your goods to the next stage of production?

The *cost-benefit principle* tells you that the answer depends on the benefits versus the costs of "make" versus "buy."

The benefits of "make" is that your suppliers won't exploit you. When executives at Ford first decided to make many auto parts within their company, rather than buying them on the market from outside suppliers, they judged that there were substantial benefits from doing so. Those benefits include:

- *Eliminating the hold-up problem:* As we've discussed, vertical integration solves the hold-up problem between Ford and its suppliers. By bringing those suppliers in-house, Ford created strong incentives for them to make valuable Ford-specific investments. It also eliminated the incentive for suppliers to make unproductive investments just to bolster their bargaining power.
- *Reducing transaction costs:* The process of negotiating with suppliers, figuring out what price you'll pay, and writing detailed contracts is expensive. Economists call these *transaction costs,* and you can avoid many of them if the supplier is just another division of your company.
- *Eliminating supplier market power:* If your supplier has market power, they'll charge you a high price, building in a big profit margin. This is in their private interest—higher profits for them!—but not in your joint best interest because their higher profits are offset by lower profits for you. It's inefficient because the high price leads you to buy an inefficiently small quantity of inputs from them. But when you join forces, they'll make decisions that are best from the perspective of the integrated business as a whole.
- *Reduced within-brand competition:* Vertical integration reduces within-brand competition, which can lower advertising and customer service costs. For instance, Apple is vertically integrated—it makes both the computer and the operating

system—and so it only advertises as Apple. But a PC put together by Dell using the Windows operating system, Intel chips, and components from other vendors has all sorts of stickers on it, and each company has large overlapping advertising budgets. This also means that if your Mac crashes, Apple's Genius Bar can service both hardware and software issues, while a broken PC might require a return to Dell, a new chip from Intel, or a call to Microsoft to fix a problem in Windows.

The costs of "make" is that a larger business has weaker incentives. Given all of these benefits to vertical integration, why not vertically integrate and form one huge company? Indeed, follow this logic far enough (too far!), and you'll wonder why the whole economy isn't just one big business.

The problem is that there are costs to vertical integration. After all, vertical integration is the opposite of specialisation, and there are real benefits to specialisation. For instance, Toyota believes that even though it's good at making cars, that doesn't make it good at making auto parts, and so it relies on specialised suppliers instead. Toyota is following the advice of management gurus to focus on its "core competencies."

The key cost of vertical integration is that it can blunt *incentives*. One reason that auto parts companies are so efficient is that many of them are relatively small businesses, and the profit motive leads their owners to work hard to keep costs low and increase revenue. But when you swallow that business up and make it part of a broader business, the ability to provide the same incentives to those managers weakens. This is because it is hard to know the true contribution of individual managers to overall company performance. The bigger the company, the harder it is. Economists have a term for this: "moral hazard in teams." And non-economists have a useful term for it as well: the "free-rider problem." With weaker incentives to excel, efficiency suffers.

Recap: Achieving a balance. Let's step back to recap. If you're worried about the bargaining power of your customers or suppliers, you can consider vertical integration. That is, you can choose to make, rather than buy. This is likely to be a good idea if you're worried about the hold-up problem. By contrast, relying on the market and choosing to buy rather than make is often a good choice when you think it's particularly important for workers to have a strong incentive to work hard. Across the economy, we see managers making different choices, and some supply chains include hundreds of highly specialised small businesses, while others are dominated by huge conglomerates that are involved in every stage of production. The right balance will depend on the specific situation you're in and your business's capabilities.

Tying It Together

We began the chapter with the story of Bunnings—a hardware store whose business strategy led it to become a multibillion-dollar chain. You've now learned the tools—the Five Forces framework—necessary to understand Bunnings' strategy and how it led to its success. So let's tie all this together by evaluating how Bunnings tackled each of the five forces to succeed.

Force one: Competition from existing competitors. Bunnings controls nearly 50% of the do-it-yourself hardware market in Australia and New Zealand. It's main large-scale rival is Mitre 10, and it faces competition from numerous independent retailers. Bunnings has even withstood an attempt by Woolworths to launch a competing chain "Masters"—which failed to gain traction and was closed down in 2016. How does Bunnings maintain its dominant position in the face of so much competition?

In short, by having the biggest range at the lowest prices. It's hard to beat a competitor who can offer customers all the products they want at a low price. How can competitors lure customers away from Bunnings? Maybe they could offer better service, but Bunnings has made that a pillar of their strategy. This strategy is self-reinforcing. By being large, Bunnings can purchase at low prices, pass some of that onto customers, and maintain or grow its high market share.

Force two: Threat of potential entrants. Maybe you think you should start a superior hardware-store chain that will overtake Bunnings. Well, Bunnings has made sure that it won't be easy for you to compete by creating barriers to entry. Woolworths found that out the hard way by pouring a lot of money into the "Masters" chain, but eventually conceding defeat and shutting down the stores.

Bunnings employs demand-side strategies to try to lock in its customers. Its large range and low prices have made it the first stop for many customers looking for home-improvement products of any kind. And it has created brand loyalty so that many of its customers won't easily be won over by a new rival.

David Gee/Alamy Stock Photo

You go to Bunnings because they'll probably have what you need at a low price.

Bunnings has also employed supply-side strategies in a quest to develop unique cost advantages. It has learned by doing, through decades of experience. It knows how to operate on a mass scale efficiently, making sure each store (almost) always has enough of the right items in stock and that employees can point customers in the right direction to find what they need—be it a certain type of screw, a powertool, or building supplies.

Entry deterrence is important to Bunnings, and given its own profitability as well as being part of the larger Wesfarmers group (which includes Coles, Kmart, Target, and Officeworks) it has a huge war chest of cash on hand with which to fight any new rival.

As a result of all these barriers to entry, no new competitor has really been able to challenge Bunnings.

Force three: Threat of substitute products. Bunnings also has to worry about substitute products, but not as much as a company selling its own products. If Makita comes up with a better power drill than Bosch then Bunnings can just stock the Makita drill. Or it can stock both.

In reality, Bunnings own product is its range, price, and service. These are the three things it focuses on relentlessly. And because it has succeeded in the past, its scale means that it can invest some of its profits in improving all of those things.

Force four: Bargaining power of suppliers. Bunnings' suppliers also have options. If you're a lumber supplier, you don't have to sell your lumber to Bunnings; you can sell it to practically any hardware store. Equally, there are many lumber suppliers selling virtually identical products, and so when Bunnings negotiates with any individual supplier, its next best alternative is pretty good: Cutting a deal with other lumber providers instead. Bunnings uses this leverage to negotiate extremely competitive prices on all the goods it purchases.

When it comes to its workforce, Bunnings has quite a lot of bargaining power, since there are millions of potential workers to choose from. As a result, the typical Bunnings employee only makes a little above the award wage. However, there are also many potential employers, so the stronger the labour market is, the higher Bunnings' wages will need to be to attract good workers.

Bunnings faces a tougher situation when it comes to real estate. Many landlords would love to have Bunnings as a tenant. But in any given desirable area, there are only a few suitable locations, and many retailers compete for them. Because the number of total storefronts in an area is relatively fixed, landlords have a lot of bargaining power. They also know that Bunnings has a high willingness to pay, since a highly visible, convenient location is valuable to Bunnings. On the other hand, Bunnings is a destination location for many customers purchasing other homewares. So for a large shopping centre, Bunnings is an attractive tenant who can lead other tenants to want to locate there. This allows the landlord to charge those smaller tenants high rents. This makes Bunnings what retailers call an "anchor tenant"—and they get a good deal on rent because of it.

Force five: Bargaining power of customers. Customers also have bargaining power. If the price isn't right, you can simply stop going to Bunnings and go to another hardware store. However, Bunnings still has a lot of leverage because they probably have what you want and can match or beat the price of their competitors. Your alternative to buying from Bunnings is not that good! Why would you go somewhere else to pay a higher price for the same product—even if you can find it there?

Bunnings also often manages to sell customers more than the products they originally came in for. You might go in for replacement light globe and walk out with some batteries as well. Maybe even some new craft supplies, too. Suddenly you've spent $50 when you planned to go and get $10 worth of light globes.

Let's put the pieces together. Our Five Forces analysis reveals that Bunnings' success is no accident. Like other businesses, it has to worry about existing competitors, potential entrants, substitutes, and the bargaining power of suppliers and customers. But it has managed to deal with all five of these forces successfully, and so it continues to dominate the hardware market.

These are the tools that you'll need to master in order to succeed in any challenging managerial role. We analysed many of these issues in previous chapters, and in this one, we've completed the job, adding a careful analysis of non-price competition, and of bargaining power. Now you can go out and use the Five Forces framework to identify opportunity, and then execute in a similarly strategic way to Bunnings.

Chapter at a Glance

The Five Forces That Shape Competition and Profitability:

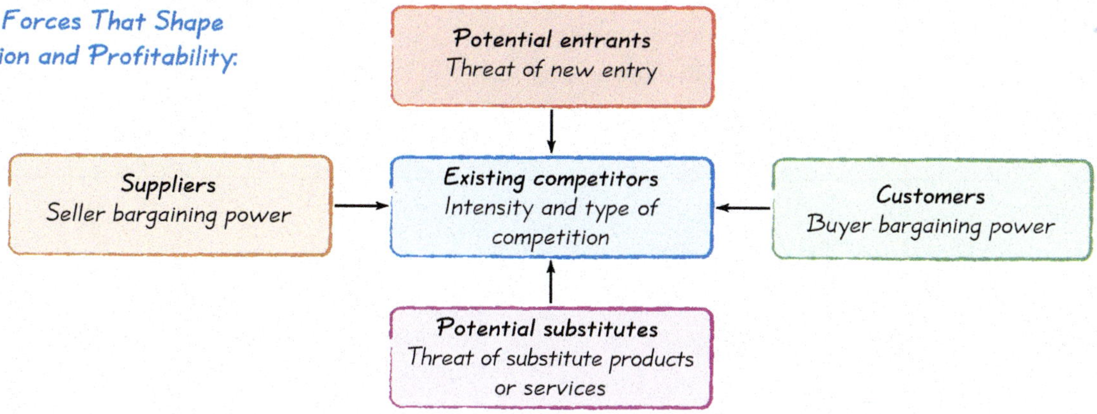

Existing Competitors

Price competition: Competing to win customers by offering lower prices. → Pure price competition can drive your economic profits to zero.

Non-price competition: Competing to win customers by differentiating your product. → Non-price competition through product differentiation yields market power.

The Product Positioning Trade-off

1. **Demand side:** Locate ***closer to your rivals*** to maximise the number of customers who prefer your product.

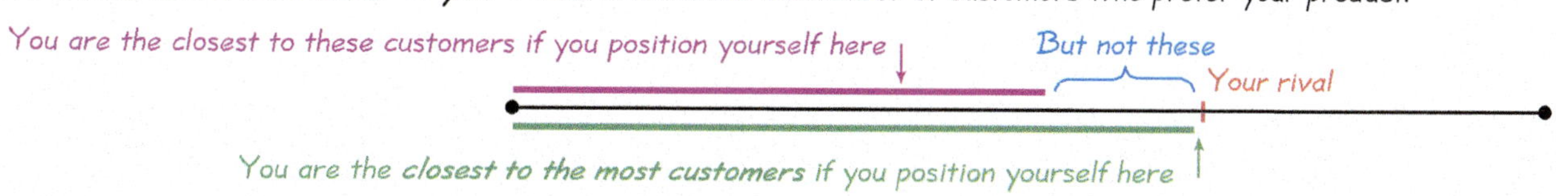

2. **Supply side:** Position your product **away from rivals** (differentiate your product) so as to soften price competition which yields market power and larger profit margins.

Advertising: Advertising aims to increase demand and increase your market power.

Bargaining Power of Suppliers and Customers

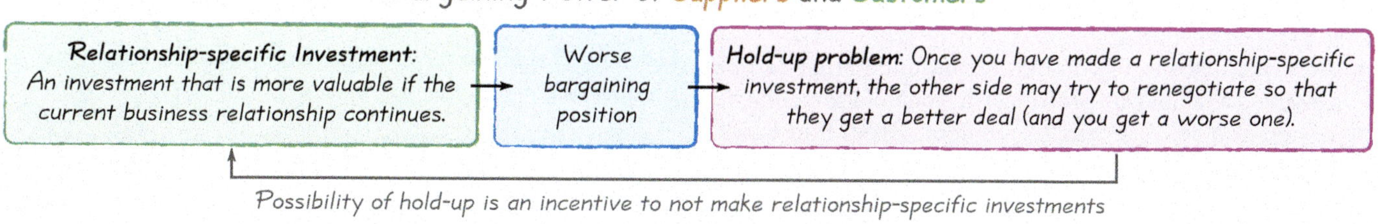

Overcoming the Hold-up Problem

Contract theory: Write long-term contracts that commit both sides to specific terms.

1. ***Long-term contracts*** that **commit** both sides to specific terms
2. ***Reputation and repeated interactions***
3. ***Vertical integration:*** When two (or more) companies along a production chain combine to form a single company.

Benefits:

- Eliminating the **hold-up problem**
- Reducing transaction costs
- Eliminating supplier market power
- Reducing within-brand competition

Costs:

Vertical integration can blunt incentives.

Key Concepts

bargaining power, 431
Five Forces framework, 418
hold-up problem, 434
informative advertising, 429
next best alternative, 431
non-price competition, 419
persuasive advertising, 430
price competition, 419
relationship-specific investment, 434
search good, 429
vertical integration, 437

Discussion and Review Questions

Learning Objective 17.1 *Identify business opportunities by analysing the five forces that determine firm profitability.*

1. Think about a small business you could start that serves a specific community—for example, your campus, your neighbourhood, or even your Instagram followers. Use each of the five forces to conduct a brief analysis of the market you want to enter. Do you think your business could be profitable in the long-run? Why or why not?
2. Toys 'R' Us was one of the largest toy retailers in Australia for decades. In 2018, Toys 'R' Us went into voluntary administration after its stores in the United States and United Kingdom planned to sell or close their stores. Using each of the five forces, analyse the competitive pressures facing the toy store over the past few decades that eroded its long-term profitability.

Learning Objective 17.2 *Figure out how to position your product relative to your competitors.*

3. Describe three examples of advertising you've seen in the last couple of days from any source (apps, online streaming, TV, billboards, etc.). Were the ads examples of informative advertising or persuasive advertising? Could they be examples of both? Briefly explain your reasoning.

Learning Objective 17.3 *Be ready to use your bargaining power to get a better deal.*

4. Describe a scenario you have experienced that can be classified as a hold-up problem. Did you hold someone up or were you held up? Was the problem solved? If so, how?
5. Apple's supply chain—the chain of companies from which Apple purchases parts and manufacturing labour—includes over 200 different companies, including some of their own competitors, such as LG and Samsung. What are the pros and cons of Apple becoming a more vertically integrated company so that it makes these components itself?

Study Problems

Learning Objective 17.1 *Identify business opportunities by analysing the five forces that determine firm profitability.*

1. Trefis, a financial forecasting company, performed a five forces analysis on Under Armour, an internationally active apparel company, and identified each of the following as a threat to Under Armour's future profitability. Determine which of the five forces applies to each threat.
   a. Under Armour products are made by many different manufacturers located in multiple countries.
   b. The sports-apparel market requires a significant investment in capital costs for branding, advertising, and creating product demand.
   c. Under Armour sells much of its product to large retailers such as Rebel Sport or JD Sports, which then sell to end consumers. These large retailers also purchase from Nike and other sports apparel companies.
   d. Brands such as Nike and Adidas also sell athletic footwear and apparel.
2. In the late 1990s, economists at Microsoft estimated that given that the company held a near-monopoly with its Windows operating system—and a computer can't work without an operating system—it could exploit this market power and earn the largest possible profit if it charged about $1,800 per copy of Windows. However, Microsoft priced its operating system at an average price of $40 to $60 per copy. Which of the five forces might Microsoft have been responding to in order to justify this pricing strategy? Briefly explain your reasoning.

Learning Objective 17.2 *Figure out how to position your product relative to your competitors.*

3. Nike has implemented many strategies to compete with other retailers. For each of the following strategies, identify whether the department store is competing on price, customer service, convenience, or design.
   a. Inside many of their department stores, Myer has a "Myer Clearance" section (sometimes an entire floor) dedicated to products which have been discontinued or damaged.
   b. Myer creates a Click & Collect option for their online store where customers can easily search the inventory of their local Myer and reserve items for pick up in as little as an hour to avoid high traffic times.
   c. Myer's in-store and online "New In" sections feature the latest styles from world renowned designers.

4. Cecil wants to open a coffee shop. After doing some market research he concludes that people value one of two things when deciding which coffee shop to go to: (1) convenient with lots of coffee-based drink options or (2) high-quality coffee with room for studying, working, or meetings. In the area where Cecil plans to operate, there is already one coffee shop, Kwik Koffee, which has a drive-thru window, very limited seating, and a large menu of different types of coffee.

   Using the accompanying spectrum, which depicts the difference in consumer preferences for coffee shops and the location of existing cafés in the market, answer the following questions. Assume that consumers are equally distributed along the spectrum so that just as many consumers prefer the convenient option to the high-quality option to anywhere in the middle.

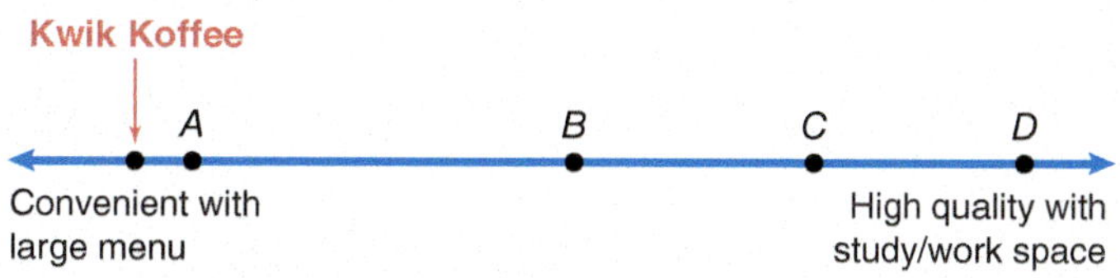

   a. If Cecil is only interested in capturing the largest number of customers in the coffee market, at which point should he position his coffee shop on the spectrum?

   b. If, instead, Cecil is only concerned that Kwik Koffee can undercut his prices when he opens, at which point should he position his coffee shop?

5. A Flight Centre advertisement shows pictures of Flight Centre staff in various exotic locations—with each staff member saying "been there." The accompanying text states: "Experience our experience."

   a. What impact might this advertisement have on the demand curve for Flight Centre flights?

   b. What impact might this advertisement have on the price elasticity of demand for Flight Centre flights?

   c. Use a graph to illustrate the impact of the advertisement on the demand curve for Flight Centre.

6. Which of the following companies are likely to benefit from advertising their own products? How would their demand curves change if their advertising was successful?

   a. Gillette, makers of the Gillette Fusion Razor Blade

   b. Fonterra Farmers, a producer of milk in Tasmania

   c. Cochlear, manufacturer of the Cochlear Nucleus hearing implant

   d. Petty's Orchard, one of the oldest apple growers in Melbourne

7. In Apple's iconic "Get a Mac" advertising campaign, a middle-aged actor in an ill-fitting suit portrayed a Windows PC, and a younger actor, dressed in fashionable yet casual clothes, portrayed a Mac. Is a Mac a search good? Why or why not? What type of advertising is Apple using to differentiate their computer against PCs?

Learning Objective 17.3 *Be ready to use your bargaining power to get a better deal.*

8. Sarah has been a shift manager at McDonald's for several years. Over her time there, the owner has put her in charge of payroll and scheduling for all shifts, not just her own. Sarah feels like she isn't being paid for the extra responsibility, and sits down with her boss to discuss a raise. Her boss has said on several occasions that Sarah is saving him $15,000 a year since he doesn't have to hire a contractor to do payroll and scheduling. Sarah is currently making $35,000 a year and would accept a minimum raise of $5,000 a year.

   a. If Sarah assumes that her boss is being completely honest and he does not have any other alternatives, what is the range of possible outcomes (in terms of her final salary) she should expect?

   b. Suppose that in anticipation of her salary renegotiation, Sarah applied for a manager's position at the competition across the street, where she would be perfectly happy to work, and they offered her a starting salary of $48,000. Has Sarah's or her boss's bargaining power changed? What is the new range of possible salaries Sarah should expect from her salary negotiation?

9. Josephine, the CEO of a microchip manufacturer, is weighing an offer from Huawei, one of the largest smartphone manufacturers in the world. The Huawei purchasing manager says that if Josephine's company would be willing to retool her plant to better serve Huawei, Huawei would buy more chips from her at a higher price. The downside is that Josephine's company couldn't then sell their chips to Samsung because the new chips don't meet Samsung's specifications.

   The manufacturer's revenue from selling to Huawei and Samsung, both with and without retooling the plant, are provided in the table below. For simplicity, assume that all other costs are equal between the two options.

	Revenue (millions of $)	
	From selling to Huawei	**From selling to Samsung**
Without investment in Huawei specific parts production	$59	$33
With investment in Huawei specific parts production	$105	$0

   a. How much revenue would the manufacturer make if Josephine decides not to make the investment to retool the plant? What if she did make the investment?

   b. What is the most Josephine would be willing to spend on the investment? Assume that she would be willing to make the investment as long as it does not make her company worse off.

c. Once the investment is made, will her bargaining power as a supplier to Huawei increase or decrease?

d. Suppose Josephine goes ahead with the investment at a cost of $10 million. Afterward, Huawei tells her they are unwilling to pay the initial price they stated and are only willing to pay a lower price which results in only $100 million in revenue. In hindsight, should the CEO have made the investment?

e. What could Josephine have done to make sure her company did not experience this hold-up problem?

Game Theory and Strategic Choices

CHAPTER 18

Scene one: Judit Polgar surveys the men in front of her. The strongest female chess player of all time, she's now coaching the Hungarian national men's team. Her challenge is to teach these men what she knows instinctively: To beat your opponent you have to know them better than they know themselves.

Yves Forestier/Sygma/Getty Images

Whatever you're thinking, she probably already thought of it.

Scene two: Soviet Leader Nikita Khrushchev has secretly shipped nuclear missiles to Cuba, just 90 miles off the coast of Florida. President Kennedy demands that Khrushchev withdraw his missiles. Khrushchev refuses. The stakes couldn't be higher, as each country possesses enough nuclear weapons to destroy the other. With negotiations at a stalemate, President Kennedy huddles with his advisers, aware that the world is on the brink of a catastrophic nuclear war.

Scene three: Shemara Wikramanayke's agenda is packed. She runs Macquarie Group, and she's arranged separate meetings to evaluate whether to launch a new "green energy" investment fund, to plan her next negotiation with government about removal of the industry-specific "bank tax," and to contemplate investing in a distressed Chinese property developer. As she considers each alternative, she wonders how her rivals at the other major investment banks will respond.

Economics sees the same basic logic at work in all three scenes. Each strategist is trying to outfox their rivals, and each wants to stay a few moves ahead. As each ponders the next move, they all rely on the same set of ideas. These ideas come from game theory, and they provide a framework for making decisions in any strategic interaction.

We'll start with the analytic tools you'll need to analyse strategic interactions. Then we'll highlight two big strategic issues: getting people to cooperate, and getting them to coordinate. For some students, that's as far as they'll dig with game theory. But if you want to dig into some advanced material, we'll then evaluate how to navigate strategic interactions that play out over time.

I bet that you'll find game theory to be incredibly useful as you navigate the strategic issues that arise in your own life. Or maybe I'm just saying this as a strategy to keep you reading. How can you tell?

Chapter Objective

Analyse the strategic decisions that you'll make throughout your career and everyday life.

18.1 How to Think Strategically
Apply the four steps for making good strategic decisions.

18.2 The Prisoner's Dilemma and the Challenge of Cooperation
Understand how the Prisoner's Dilemma highlights the problems of getting people to cooperate.

18.3 Multiple Equilibria and the Problem of Coordination
Figure out how best to coordinate with your allies to make complementary choices.

18.4 Advanced Strategy: First and Second Mover Advantages
Make your move when it's most advantageous.

18.5 Advanced Strategy: Repeated Games and Punishments
Elicit cooperation by threatening punishment in repeated interactions.

Bettmann/Getty Images

One of these involves game theory.

Barratts/PA Images Archive/Getty Images

The other does not.

18.1 How to Think Strategically

Learning Objective *Apply the four steps for making good strategic decisions.*

Think of the difference between a boxing bag and a boxer. To hit a punching bag, you line it up, take your swing—and boom!—you've walloped it. But hitting a boxer is much harder: A boxer will duck and weave, feint one way and move the other, raise their gloves to deflect the blow, or counterpunch. The boxing bag is not strategic; a boxer is strategic—a boxer anticipates, responds, and tries to influence your movements. When two boxers meet, the outcome is determined not only by their skill and strength, but also by the interaction of their competing strategies.

When you're meeting with business partners, political rivals, friends, or romantic partners, you need to figure out whether they're more like a boxing bag or a boxer. If they're more like the boxer, then you're in the realm of game theory. And you're going to need to learn to think like a game theorist in order to avoid getting knocked out.

Introducing Game Theory

Game theory is the science of making good decisions in situations involving **strategic interactions,** which means that your best choice may depend on what other people choose, and likewise, their best choices may depend on what you choose. Your best choice might depend as much on the choices made by your allies as your opponents, and hence this notion of strategic interactions encompasses collaboration as much as competition.

strategic interaction When your best choice may depend on what others choose, and their best choice may depend on what you choose.

Game theory gets its name from the observation that the same notions that inform how you might box or play a strategic game like chess, can also be applied to your business strategies, and indeed, the many strategic interactions that arise in the ordinary business of life. The underlying idea comes from applying the *interdependence principle*, focusing on how your decisions are intertwined with those of others. It might seem a bit unusual to call these interactions "games," but pretty soon you'll see people "playing games"—sometimes high-stakes games—all around you.

Storytelling and metaphors will help you learn game theory. As we explore the science of strategic interactions, we'll work through a series of stories. You shouldn't take each story too seriously, but rather look to see how each highlights a deeper logic that applies much more broadly. Think of each story as a metaphor. Your task is to discover all the different ways that these metaphors apply to your interactions with others. As you get better at this, you'll find yourself applying game theory insights to everything from your business decisions to your dating life.

Games are strategic interactions—and they're all around you. Strategic interactions are central to your economic and social life. For instance, in business you'll have strategic interactions (that is, you'll "play games") with your competitors, particularly in an oligopoly where you have only a few rivals. Business decisions are strategic interactions because the payoff to, say, cutting your prices, depends on whether your competitors respond with a similar price cut. Likewise, your decision on how best to position your product is a strategic interaction because the profitability of targeting a particular market segment depends on how your competitors position their products. And your decision to enter a new market involves a strategic interaction, because your profitability depends on whether the incumbent firms will respond with a price war. Strategic interactions include partners as well as rivals, and the profitability of a new investment might depend on how much your partners invest in the project.

Politics is full of game theory. There are strategic interactions between both political rivals and political allies, because the payoff from voting for a bill depends on whether others vote for it, too. In elections you might choose to vote only if other voters are likely to make it a close election. There are also weighty strategic interactions when countries decide to get involved in an arms race or amass troops off the coast.

Strategic interactions also occur among friends. These interactions highlight that sometimes strategy is more about cooperation and coordination rather than competition. For instance, a party is more fun if your friends are going to it too. So it's natural that your decision about whether to go to a party will depend on what you think your friends will do.

Hopefully this gives you a sense that strategic interactions—games—are a pervasive part of your life. And though they are all different, there's a basic logic that is common to all strategic interactions—making a good choice requires that you anticipate what others will do. This is why our next task is to develop some intuitions that will help you make good decisions in all of the games you play.

The Four Steps for Making Good Strategic Decisions

Making good strategic decisions boils down to following four simple steps. Savvy strategists internalise these ways of thinking so that they become mental habits. That should be your goal too. We'll start by learning the four steps now, and then we'll turn to some specific games to see how these habits will help you uncover deeper strategic insights.

Four steps for making good strategic decisions:

1. Consider all the possible outcomes.
2. Think about the "what ifs" separately.
3. Play your best response.
4. Put yourself in someone else's shoes.

Step one: Consider all the possible outcomes. To make an informed choice, you'll need to consider all the different outcomes that could occur. This means considering every combination of choices that both you and other players might make.

There's a simple trick for listing all the possible outcomes in a two-player game: Construct a table that lists each of your possible actions as a separate row, and each of the other player's possible actions as a separate column. The cells in this table now show all the possible outcomes. Because we usually list the payoffs to both players in each cell, we call this a **payoff table.** For instance, you have two choices right now: Keep reading this chapter, or not. And your instructor has two choices: Put game theory on the exam, or not. We can summarise the possible outcomes as follows:

payoff table A table that lists your choices in each row, the other player's choices in each column, and so shows all possible outcomes, listing the payoffs in each cell.

Figure 1 | **A Payoff Table**

	Instructor puts game theory on the exam	Instructor omits game theory from the exam
You read the rest of this chapter	Ace the exam	You study more than necessary to pass
You don't read the rest of this chapter	Fail the exam	Save time and still get a good grade

Figure 1 describes different payoffs in words. ("You ace the exam.") In most cases though, we'll use numbers such as your grades, your business's profit, or some other measure of your payoff from each outcome.

Step two: Think about the "what ifs" separately. Once you start thinking about strategic interactions, you can easily get overwhelmed by the complexity of it all. For instance, whether you read the rest of this chapter partly depends on whether you think your instructor will put game theory on the exam. And whether they put game theory on the exam depends on whether they expect you to read the rest of this chapter. And so your choice depends on what you expect them to choose, and you know that their choice depends on what they expect you to choose. Keep thinking this way and pretty quickly you will disappear down the rabbit hole of "I think that they think that I think that they think . . ." Let me help you out of that rabbit hole by showing you a simpler way.

Here's the idea: Break the problem into its simpler components, which are the various choices that the other person could make. Think in terms of "what ifs?" and write down each "what if?" separately. In this case, you want to ask: What if they do include game theory on the exam? And what if they don't? When you think about these separately, you get two far simpler problems. You'll then proceed to the next step.

Thinglass/iStock/Getty Images

best response The choice that yields the highest payoff given the other player's choice.

Step three: Play your best response. For each "what if?" your goal should be to play your **best response**—the choice that yields the highest possible payoff for you, given the other player's choice. What is your best response if your instructor does include game theory on the exam? (Probably to keep reading this chapter.) And what is your best response if they don't? (I would say keep reading because game theory is useful, but if all you care about is your exam grade, then you can stop now.)

There's one more thing I want you to do: When you find your best response, put a tick next to it. This tick will help you remember your best response, and it'll be part of a useful trick that we'll get to shortly.

Step four: Put yourself in someone else's shoes. In every strategic interaction your outcomes depend on the choices that other people make. This means that you cannot figure out your best choice without first trying to figure out the choices that others will make. To figure out someone else's choices you need to apply the someone else's shoes technique from Chapter 1. This technique tells you to put yourself in someone else's shoes in order to figure out what decision you would make if you faced their incentives.

SUKJAI PHOTO/Shutterstock

She's thinking strategically.

When you put yourself in your opponent's shoes, you'll often come to see that they are also thinking strategically. Just as you do, they'll consider all the possible outcomes, think through the various "what ifs," and evaluate their best responses. When you work your way through someone else's thought process, you'll find it easier to predict their choices. For instance, put yourself in your instructor's shoes: When they write an exam, they want to make sure that they reward students who read all the material. Understanding this, you realise that it's a good idea to keep reading to the end of this chapter.

Now armed with these four steps for thinking about strategic interactions, let's start applying them to some specific games. We'll begin with the most famous example in game theory, the Prisoner's Dilemma.

18.2 The Prisoner's Dilemma and the Challenge of Cooperation

Learning Objective *Understand how the Prisoner's Dilemma highlights the problems of getting people to cooperate.*

In a typical quarter, Coca-Cola spends nearly a billion dollars on marketing. Pepsi also spends a roughly similar amount. Coca-Cola recently did some market research, and learned that advertising helps it earn market share from Pepsi, but Pepsi then regains that lost market share with its own advertising. The billions of dollars spent on advertising don't do much to convince people to drink more cola overall.

Armed with this insight, the CEO of Coke asks you for strategic advice. You arrive at their office and find them pacing, excited by their new idea. They speak quickly as they explain their radical thought: "Why don't we just abolish our advertising budget altogether?" They explain their thinking: "If Pepsi does the same thing, then both firms will earn higher profits, because both will sell roughly the same amount of cola, with neither of us wasting billions of dollars on useless advertising." Of course, this plan only works if Pepsi's CEO chooses to cooperate. If instead they defect from the plan and keep advertising, then Coke's decision to stop advertising will result in losing customers to Pepsi. It's tricky, because you'll have to make a decision about next quarter's ad buy before you know if Pepsi will play along. What's your advice?

Understanding the Prisoner's Dilemma

As you start to answer, you note that Coke's payoffs from pursuing this plan depend on whether Pepsi will cooperate with it. Likewise, Pepsi's payoffs depend on Coke's choice. Immediately you recognise this as a strategic interaction—the sort of setting where you should apply game theory. Time to work through our four-step recipe.

Step one: Consider all the possible outcomes and construct the payoff table. Let's start with step one of a game theory analysis: Consider all the possible outcomes. You can construct a payoff table that shows all the possible outcomes by listing each of Coke's possible actions as rows, and each of Pepsi's possible actions as columns, as in Figure 2. We'll describe each company's choice as either *cooperating* with the plan to quit advertising, or *defecting* from it. Each of the four cells in this table describes a possible outcome.

For each possible outcome, you need to consider the payoffs to both Coke and Pepsi. You turn to your market research division for some help, and here's what they tell you:

- Currently both Pepsi and Coke advertise, and they each make around $1 billion in profits each quarter. (This is the defect–defect cell at the bottom right.)
- If the CEO of Pepsi cooperates with Coke's plan to stop advertising, then both companies will each save $1 billion per quarter, boosting the quarterly profits of each firm to $2 billion. (This is the cooperate–cooperate cell at the top left.)
- There's a risk: If Coke cooperates and stops advertising, but Pepsi defects from the plan and continues to advertise, then Pepsi will win over a lot of Coke's customers. This will boost Pepsi's quarterly profits to $3 billion, while Coke earns $0 profits. (Top right.)
- Pepsi faces a similar risk: If Pepsi cooperates with the plan but Coke defects, then Coke's quarterly profits will rise to $3 billion, while Pepsi's will fall to $0. (Bottom left.)

Next, translate all of this information into the payoff table shown in Figure 2, which summarises all the possible outcomes and lists the payoffs to each player for each outcome.

The payoff table shows explicitly how your payoffs depend on the choices that others make, and likewise, how their payoffs vary with your choices.

Figure 2 | **The Prisoner's Dilemma**

	Pepsi cooperates (no advertising)	**Pepsi defects** (it advertises)
Coke cooperates (no advertising)	Coke earns $2b Pepsi earns $2b	Coke earns $0 Pepsi earns $3b ✔
Coke defects (it advertises)	Coke earns $3b ✔ Pepsi earns $0	Coke earns $1b ✔ Pepsi earns $1b ✔

Step two: Think in terms of "what ifs" and Step three: Play your best response. Okay, what should you do? Coke's best choice depends on what Pepsi does, while Pepsi's best choice depends on what Coke does. Step two tells you to think separately about the different "what ifs." So Coke needs to separately assess what to do if Pepsi cooperates, and what to do if Pepsi defects. In each of these scenarios, step three says that you want to play your best response.

Applying steps two and three together, you need to think about your best response to any choice that Pepsi might make:

- If Pepsi cooperates: Coke can either cooperate and make $2 billion, or defect and earn $3 billion. *If Pepsi cooperates, Coke's best response is to defect.*
- If Pepsi defects: Coke can cooperate and make $0, or defect and earn $1 billion. *If Pepsi defects, Coke's best response is to defect.*

No matter what Pepsi chooses, you should advise Coke's CEO that his best response is to defect. Notice one more thing: In Figure 2, I put a red tick next to each of these best responses; this is something you should get in the habit of doing, and it will turn out to be helpful in just a moment.

Step four: Put yourself in the other player's shoes and figure out their best response. To figure out what Pepsi will do, move to step four of our analysis and put yourself in the other player's shoes. Pepsi will evaluate its best response to any choice that Coke might make:

- If Coke cooperates: Pepsi can either cooperate and make $2 billion, or defect from the plan and earn $3 billion. *If Coke cooperates, Pepsi's best response is to defect.*
- If Coke defects: Pepsi can cooperate and make $0, or defect and earn $1 billion. *If Coke defects, Pepsi's best response is to defect.*

Putting it together, we see that no matter what Coke chooses, it looks like Pepsi will choose to defect. (And you'll also notice that I put a blue tick next to each of these best responses in Figure 2.)

Nash Equilibrium

Okay, so what's going to happen in this game? In this situation, neither Pepsi nor Coke can benefit by changing its strategy unless it expects the other to change. As a result the likely outcome is simply that each person plays their best response to their opponent's best response.

A Nash equilibrium occurs when you both choose your best response. When everyone is playing their best response to the choices that other players are making, we call the resulting equilibrium outcome a **Nash equilibrium.** In a Nash equilibrium all of the players choose their best responses—they're each making their best choice, given the choices that others are making. It's an equilibrium because no one can do better by changing their choice alone.

Nash equilibrium A profile of choices such that the choice that each player makes is a best response to the choices other players are making.

Use the tick method to find a Nash equilibrium. Remember that whenever we found a player's best response, I suggested that you put a tick next to it? That's because it makes finding a Nash equilibrium really easy: Just look for an outcome with two ticks and you've found a Nash equilibrium. After all, a Nash equilibrium occurs whenever both players choose their best response, and so if you mark each player's best response with a tick, then an outcome with a tick from each player is a Nash equilibrium. This simple trick, called the **tick method,** is so useful that we'll keep using it throughout the rest of this chapter.

tick method If you put a tick next to each player's best response, then an outcome with a tick from each player is a Nash equilibrium.

The Prisoner's Dilemma yields a failure to cooperate. Let's use the tick method to figure out the Nash equilibrium to the Prisoner's Dilemma. Figure 2 shows that there are two ticks in the cell in which both Pepsi and Coke defect, and so this is the Nash equilibrium.

Thus, the predicted outcome of this game is that neither company will cooperate with the plan to quit advertising. Even though both companies are better off if they both quit wasteful advertising, Coke and Pepsi each continue advertising. The logic behind this forecast is this: If Coke expects Pepsi to defect, then its best response is to defect; likewise, if Pepsi expects Coke to defect, then its best response is to defect. And so in equilibrium, each set of executives expects the other to defect, and this in turn leads each of them to choose to defect.

Notice that in a Nash equilibrium two things are true:

- *Best responses:* Each player's choice is their best response to what they expect the other to choose.
- *Correct expectations:* Each player's expectation about what the other player will choose is also correct.

The Prisoner's Dilemma and the Failure of Cooperation

Let's take a step back to put this into a broader context. Both Coke and Pepsi understand that they would be jointly better off if they would cooperate and agree to quit advertising, yet they both continue to spend billions of dollars on wasteful advertising. Even though this isn't the best outcome for either company, it's likely to be the actual outcome because each is making the best choice it can, given the choice the other will make.

Agreements to cooperate are not credible. You might wonder why Pepsi and Coke can't figure out a way to cooperate to both eliminate wasteful advertising. The CEO of Coke could call the CEO of Pepsi, to say "I'll cooperate with this no-advertising plan if you do." The problem is that the CEO of Pepsi understands that if they cooperate, then Coke's best response will be to defect. (Check the payoffs: A $3 billion payoff beats

$2 billion.) Moreover, the Pepsi CEO knows that billions of dollars are more persuasive than mere talk, so they don't find the Coke CEO's promise to be *credible.* Similar logic suggests that the Coke CEO would never believe a promise from Pepsi's CEO to cooperate. The problem is that neither can credibly commit to cooperating, and so neither expects the other to actually cooperate, and this makes defecting the best response. (It's just as well: An agreement to eliminate advertising may be illegal collusion because it limits competition.)

The Prisoner's Dilemma shows how markets can deliver bad outcomes. We've just discovered what may be the most important insight of game theory. It's the juxtaposition of two facts:

- The *best outcome* would be for Pepsi and Coke to both cooperate and quit advertising. They would earn the highest possible joint profit ($4 billion, or $2 billion each) under this outcome.
- But this was not the *equilibrium outcome.* Instead, when both Pepsi and Coke follow their self-interest and play their best responses, they both choose to defect from the plan. The result makes them both worse off, as they each earn a $1 billion profit instead of $2 billion.

That is, the *equilibrium outcome* is not the *best outcome.* Indeed, in the Prisoner's Dilemma, the equilibrium outcome need not even be a good outcome (for the players). The Prisoner's Dilemma is a striking counterpoint to the idea that free markets deliver the best outcomes. Indeed, the Prisoner's Dilemma yields the opposite result, as Coke and Pepsi each pursued their own self-interest but ended up reaching an equilibrium that's worse for both of them.

The temptation to take advantage undermines cooperation. The Prisoner's Dilemma is best read as a parable—an example that applies far more broadly than to just the Coke and Pepsi case. In particular, the big insight is that people often fail to cooperate even when there's a project that could make them all better off. (In this example, that project was to quit advertising.) Even though the benefits of cooperation exceed the benefits of defecting in the Prisoner's Dilemma, defecting to take advantage of a cooperative rival yields an even bigger and more tempting payoff. That temptation can cause cooperation to fail.

The Prisoner's Dilemma

	They cooperate	They defect
You cooperate	Mutual cooperation is the best outcome for both of us	They take advantage of you ✓
You defect	You take advantage of them ✓	Defecting is worse than both of us cooperating ✓✓

How do we reconcile the failure of self-interest to reach the best outcome with our analysis in Chapter 7, which suggested that competitive markets generally yield efficient outcomes? The answer is that our earlier analysis focused on the case of perfect competition, when all buyers and all sellers were so small that the choices made by one business didn't greatly affect the payoffs of others. That is, our earlier analysis didn't involve strategic interactions. But Pepsi and Coke are both big firms, and Pepsi's choices affect Coke's payoffs, and this creates strategic interactions. These interactions can lead people to make strategic choices that lead to inefficient outcomes. And so in a world full of strategic interactions, there's no reason to assume that free markets will yield good outcomes.

Why is it called the Prisoner's Dilemma? Okay, so if the real problem here is getting people to cooperate, why do we call this the Prisoner's Dilemma, rather than the Cooperation Dilemma? It's because the clearest illustration of a cooperation dilemma involves a scenario in which the police are trying to extract a confession from a pair of bank robbers.

Following a bank heist, the police took two suspects—we'll call them Bonnie and Clyde—in for questioning. If the police can't extract a confession, they can only charge Bonnie and Clyde for speeding away from the scene, which will result in jail terms of only one year. And so realising that this minor charge is their best joint outcome, Bonnie and Clyde hatch a plan to both deny the crime.

But the police are savvy game theorists, and so they put Bonnie and Clyde in separate interview rooms and offered each of them a deal that they thought might be tempting: "I can cut you a sweet deal: If your friend persists in denying the crime and you help me make the case against them, you'll avoid jail altogether." But, the police add, "If your friend

GL Archive/Alamy stock photo

The real-life Bonnie and Clyde never got a chance to confess.

confesses and you don't, we'll throw the book at you, and you'll get three years." Finally, the police add that "in the unlikely event that you both confess, you'll each get two years."

What would you do if you were in Bonnie's shoes? And what's likely to happen here? It's time to use your newfound skills as a game theorist.

Do the Economics

It's your turn to solve the Prisoner's Dilemma. Put yourself in Bonnie's shoes and work through the four steps for analysing strategic interactions:

First, *consider all the outcomes* by drawing up the payoff table.

The Prisoner's Dilemma

	Clyde denies	Clyde confesses
Bonnie denies	Bonnie gets 1 year Clyde gets 1 year	Bonnie gets 3 years Clyde gets 0 years ✓
Bonnie confesses	Bonnie gets 0 years ✓ Clyde gets 3 years	Bonnie gets 2 years ✓ Clyde gets 2 years ✓

Second, *think about the "what ifs" separately.* And **third,** *for each of these alternatives, play your best response.*

What if Clyde denies the crime? Bonnie's best response is to confess so that she gets zero years instead of three. Go ahead, put a tick in the bottom-left cell of the table. And what if Clyde confesses? Bonnie's best response is to confess (so she gets two years instead of three), and so you should also put a tick in the bottom-right cell.

Fourth, *apply the other people's shoes technique.*

It's time for Bonnie to think about what Clyde will do. As Clyde considers the possible outcomes, thinking about each "what if" separately, he'll ask: What if Bonnie denies the crime? Then Clyde's best response is to confess and get zero years rather than denying and getting one year. This says that you should put a tick in the top-right cell. And what if Bonnie confesses? Then Clyde's best response is to confess and get two years, rather than denying and getting three years. Add a tick to the bottom-right cell.

Make sure you avoid this mistake: Double check that you're making the relevant comparisons. When you're thinking about the player who has to choose their best row (in this case, Bonnie), you're trying to find your best response to each choice your opponent might make, and so you should compare outcomes within each column. Don't make the mistake of comparing two cells in the same row! And the player who is choosing among columns (Clyde) needs to compare outcomes within each row (and he should not compare two cells in the same column).

The equilibrium: OK, now it's time to look for the Nash equilibrium: Look for a cell with two ticks. It's the bottom-right cell, where both Bonnie and Clyde confess to the crime. ■

This is a rather remarkable use of game theory. The police set a trap that led both Bonnie and Clyde to confess, despite the fact that if they both persisted in denying the crime, they'd get away with it. By offering each criminal a sweet deal for ratting the other out, they elicited two confessions. That sweet deal was so tempting that Bonnie realised she couldn't trust Clyde to cooperate with their plan to deny their crime, just as Clyde realised he couldn't trust Bonnie to cooperate with their plan. This failure to cooperate led to a worse outcome for both of them. The police are the real winners here, and because their strategy got both Bonnie and Clyde to confess, they didn't end up giving either of them the sweet deal. Clearly being a savvy game theorist can confer a strategic advantage.

Examples of the Prisoner's Dilemma

The Prisoner's Dilemma highlights the difficulty of getting people to cooperate. The tension that it highlights extends well beyond the Pepsi versus Coke advertising wars or the story of Bonnie versus Clyde. As you start thinking like a game theorist, you'll come to see the Prisoner's Dilemma everywhere.

The tragedy of commons leads shared resources to be overused. Recall from Chapter 10 that the "tragedy of the commons" is a story that shows how shared resources tend to be overused in a way that makes everyone worse off. It's an insight usually told as a story about two farmers who are both allowed to graze their sheep on the grassy town square, which is called the commons. The best outcome involves both farmers grazing their sheep on the commons only every few days, so that there's plenty of time for the grass to grow back. But there's a temptation to graze your sheep on the commons every day, so that your sheep get more grass, even if this means that there's nothing left for the other farmer's flock. The tragedy is that this temptation yields a Nash equilibrium in which both farmers graze their sheep on the commons every day, and this overgrazing kills the grass, with the unfortunate result that the commons yield little grass for either flock.

Tragedy of the Commons

	They graze every few days	They graze daily
You graze every few days	Both flocks enjoy adequate food	No grass left for your sheep Their sheep eat a lot ✓
You graze daily	Your sheep eat a lot ✓ No grass left for their sheep	Overgrazing yields little grass for both flocks ✓✓

This story is an illustration of the Prisoner's Dilemma, and it's a metaphor for problems that often arise when there are shared resources, as is the case in many environmental problems. Just as farmers are tempted to overgraze the town commons, the oceans are depleted by fishermen who overfish, and the atmosphere is destroyed by factories that emit too much pollution. Beyond the environment, drivers who overuse public roads create traffic jams, politicians who care about special interests overspend, and your friends who overorder when you are splitting the bill are the reason that your group's restaurant bill is so large. In each case, the tragedy of the overuse of common resources is due to a failure to cooperate and only take your fair share.

EVERYDAY Economics **Can game theory help get money out of politics?**

Australia has surprisingly lax campaign finance laws. At the federal level there is effectively no limit on donations, and even disclosure requirements are pretty weak. Why does a country that invented the secret ballot and was a leader in female suffrage have such unreconstructed campaign finance laws? One reason why there's been so little effort to reduce the role of money in politics is that incumbent politicians and political parties get most of the donations, and so few current politicians want to pass a reform bill that would make it harder for them to get elected.

Suppose that an eccentric billionaire wants to see a campaign finance reform bill pass. They could simply promise that if this bill didn't pass then they would donate a billion dollars to fight whichever of the two major parties delivered the fewest votes. The result is that Labor couldn't afford to be the minority responsible for the bill failing, and so they would all vote for the bill. Similarly, the Coalition couldn't afford to be the minority responsible for the bill failing, so they would also vote for it. The result is that the reform bill would pass. And the best part for that billionaire: It costs them nothing. They only promised to make a big donation if the bill failed, and game theory suggests their bill will pass. ■

You may have noticed a similarity across all of these games—the Nash equilibrium involves both players defecting. Don't let that fool you into thinking that you should always defect in all strategic interactions. Rather, each of these examples are variants of exactly the same game, the Prisoner's Dilemma. As we turn to examining other games, you'll see many different outcomes emerge.

18.3 Multiple Equilibria and the Problem of Coordination

Learning Objective *Figure out how best to coordinate with your allies to make complementary choices.*

You're in the middle of an important call with a colleague, and suddenly the line drops out. Annoying! But now you face a simple choice: Should you call back, or should you wait for your colleague to call back? If you both immediately call back, you'll both get bounced to voicemail. If neither of you call back, you'll never connect. You'll only connect if one of you calls and the other waits. But who should call and who should wait?

This situation isn't just annoying, it points to a deeper problem in our economic and social lives, which is that it can be difficult for people to coordinate. The Prisoner's Dilemma was about the problem of *cooperation,* but in this case we both want to cooperate and the problem is that doing so requires *coordinating* who does what.

Coordination Games

The reason that there's a coordination problem in this game of phone tag is that there's more than one equilibrium. In the first equilibrium, your colleague calls you, and this means that your best response is to wait. In the second, if instead they wait for a call back, then your best response is to call. The term **multiple equilibria** describes situations like this with more than one equilibrium.

multiple equilibria When there is more than one equilibrium.

Figure 3 | A Coordination Game: Playing Phone Tag

	They call back	They wait
You call back	Voicemail	Call connects ✓✓
You wait	Call connects ✓✓	You both wait

There's more than one equilibrium when we're playing phone tag. Let's work through this game in a bit more detail. Again, you want to follow our four-step recipe. **First,** consider all the possible outcomes by drawing up the payoff table, as in Figure 3.

Second, think about each of the "what ifs" separately. What if they call back immediately? What if they wait for you to call? **Third:** Play your best response. If they call, your best response is to wait. And if they wait, your best response is to call. Don't forget to put ticks next to your best responses. **Fourth,** put yourself in their shoes. If you call, their best response is to wait, while if you wait, their best response is to call. Add ticks for each of these.

The tick method says that a Nash equilibrium occurs wherever there are two sets of ticks. Notice that this occurs both in the top-right cell where you call and they wait, and in the bottom-left, where you wait, and they call. You've discovered that this game has multiple equilibria!

coordination game When all players have a common interest in coordinating their choices.

Coordination is beneficial, but difficult. Economists call this a **coordination game** because both players will be better off if they can coordinate their choices. The problem is that coordination is difficult because there's more than one equilibrium. The difficulty arises because you really want to make the choice that is complementary to mine, but—because you don't know what choice I'll make (it depends on what choice I think you'll make)—you have no way of knowing what choice will end up being complementary. When we're stuck in a phone tag loop, we might each call back immediately, and so neither call will connect. Or we could each spend forever waiting for the other to call.

Examples of Coordination Games

Phone tag is just one example of a much broader problem, which is that even when we all want the same outcome—in this case to talk on the phone—coordination problems can make it hard to achieve. In fact, coordination games with multiple equilibria recur throughout economic life. As we work through a few important examples, you'll hopefully come to recognise other examples in your own life.

Technology Adoption

	Your friend buys an Xbox	Your friend buys a PlayStation
You buy an Xbox	You can play the same games ✓✓	Systems won't work together
You buy a PlayStation	Systems won't work together	You can play the same games ✓✓

Technology works better with coordination. The adoption of new technologies involves a coordination game. Your business faces a choice between competing technologies, such as coding for iOS or Android, designing websites using Flash or html5, broadcasting on AM or FM, tracking stock prices in dollars or euros, speaking in English or Portuguese, or, for architects, measuring in feet or metres. You could emphasise the pros and cons of each competing choice, but in reality, the most important thing is to ensure that the technology you use works with what your suppliers and customers are using. There are many possible equilibria here, because whatever system your suppliers and customers buy, your best response is to use a compatible system.

In fact, you might recognise this game, because it's the same one you had to play when deciding whether to buy an Xbox or a PlayStation. If you want to be able to play against your friends or share games, then your best response is to choose whatever system they choose. And so some groups of friends hit the equilibrium where they all get an Xbox, while others coordinate on the PlayStation.

Managing a business requires coordination. Much of your work as a manager will involve coordinating your company's activities with those of your customers, workers, and suppliers. Your customers want to shop when your store is open, and you want to open your store when your customers are out shopping. Your suppliers want to provide inputs you need, and you'll want to use inputs that are widely available. Workers want to get the right skills for the sorts of jobs your company offers, and your company wants to create the sorts of jobs that use the skills workers have.

Each of these is a coordination game: There are many different constellations of opening hours, input needs, or skill requirements that could work, but in each case, the most important thing is to make sure that your choices complement the choices your business partners make.

Coordinating Business

	Buyers shop early	Buyers shop late
Stores open early	Buyers and sellers meet ✔✔	Few buyers around / Few stores open
Stores open late	Few buyers around / Few stores open	Buyers and sellers meet ✔✔

Political revolutions require coordination. Millions of people around the world live under oppressive dictatorships that survive even though they are unpopular. And it's all due to a coordination problem. Imagine the dilemma you face when you live in such a society: You would like to protest against the oppressive dictator, but if you're the only protester, you'll be thrown in jail. The result is an oppressive equilibrium in which each citizen figures that if others don't protest, their best response is also to not protest. And when no one protests, the unpopular dictator remains in power.

But there's another equilibrium that leads to a revolution: If all of the oppressed citizens protest at the same time, you'll all be safe, because the police will be severely outnumbered. You're in a strategic game with thousands of other activists, and if many others are protesting, your best response is also to protest. This is a Nash equilibrium between thousands of people. And in this alternative equilibrium the revolution succeeds in overthrowing the government, as the dictator loses control of the country and eventually flees, fearing for their life.

Protest and Revolution

	Others don't protest	Others protest
You don't protest	Oppressive equilibrium: None of us protest ✔✔	You stay home / Others get arrested
You protest	You get arrested / Others stay home	Revolution succeeds: We all protest, so none of us are arrested ✔✔

Coordinating relationships: Is it a friendship or a romance? You get along really well and love spending time together. The question is: Should you remain platonic friends, or do you want to take your relationship up a notch? This may be a coordination game: If your friend wants to remain just friends, then your best response is to also choose friendship. But if they're willing to get romantic, your best response is romance, too. So, what are you going to choose? This example illustrates the problem of coordination games: When you don't know what the other person is going to do, you might end up making the wrong choice for both of you.

Friendship or Romance?

	They're friendly	They're romantic
You're friendly	Best friends ✔✔	Unrequited Love
You're romantic	Unrequited Love	Romance ✔✔

Monkey Business Images/Shutterstock

Anti-Coordination Games

In most of the examples we've considered so far, your best response is to coordinate so that you're making the same choice as others, such as buying the same technology, making similar choices as your customers and suppliers, or protesting on the same day. But there is a type of coordination game—sometimes called an **anti-coordination game**—where the best outcome involves taking a different (but complementary) action. In fact, we've already studied one anti-coordination game—the game of phone tag, in which I want to

anti-coordination game When your best response is to take a different (but complementary) action to the other player.

call you back if you're waiting, but I should wait if you're going to call me back. Let's consider some important examples.

Market Entry

	Rival enters	Rival doesn't enter
You enter	Fierce competition yields losses	You make a profit ✓ Rival makes no profit ✓
You don't enter	You make no profit ✓ Rival makes a profit ✓	Neither of us make a profit

You want to enter new markets that other firms won't enter. In a business context, a new market may expand enough that it can support one more company. The question is: Will you enter this new market, or will I? If we both enter, there'll be too much competition, and we'll both lose money. If neither of us enter, neither of us makes money. Together, we can agree that the best outcome is if one of us enters and earns a healthy profit, and the other does not enter. But given these two equilibria, how will we coordinate which of us enters, and which of us doesn't?

Traffic Game

	Others take highway	Others take back roads
You take highway	Traffic jam on highway	Smooth trip ✓✓
You take back roads	Smooth trip ✓✓	Traffic jam on back roads

Try to avoid traffic by choosing the route that other drivers won't. When you drive home, you probably want to choose the fastest route. That is, your best response if others take the highway is to take back roads. And if other people take back roads, your best response is to take the highway. This means that you and other drivers are engaged in an anti-coordination game, in which you want to choose what others don't. What happens in a traffic jam? It's a coordination failure in which you chose the highway, thinking others would take back roads, and they chose the highway, thinking you'd take the back roads.

Bargaining with the Boss

	Boss is aggressive	Boss is passive
You're aggressive	Fail to strike a deal You get nothing Boss gets nothing	You get a high wage ✓ Boss gets low profits ✓
You're passive	You get a low wage ✓ Boss gets high profits ✓	You get a medium wage Boss gets medium profits

You want to bargain aggressively if the other side is passive. What strategy should you adopt when you bargain with your boss over your wage? You could bargain aggressively or passively, and your boss could also be aggressive or passive. If you're both aggressive, you'll never strike a deal, leaving you with no job, and them with no worker. This creates an incentive for anti-coordination—to ensure that no more than one of you bargains aggressively. In one equilibrium your boss is aggressive and you passively settle for a low wage, which means they get high profits. In another equilibrium you bargain aggressively, and your boss bargains passively, and you agree on a high wage, leaving them with low profits. But here's the coordination problem: When you don't know what your boss is going to do, should you bargain aggressively or not?

Notice that in this situation, even though you and your boss face similar incentives—you're both better off if you can strike a deal to work together—in these equilibria you and your boss have different payoffs, with one enjoying the big share and the other putting up with a smaller share. These different outcomes are good to the extent they avoid a fight. But notice that the jointly best outcome—both agreeing to share the spoils—also won't happen.

Good and Bad Equilibria

The problem posed by multiple equilibria can be even worse than I've made out. In particular, there are situations in which there's a good and a bad equilibrium, and the bad equilibrium is worse for everyone. The problem is that it can be difficult to prevent the bad equilibrium from occurring.

A high-skilled labour market is better than a low-skilled one, but either could happen. Indeed, coordination games might even explain why some countries are rich, and others are poor. Consider the game played between businesses and workers. Workers have to decide whether to invest in training, and businesses have to decide whether to create skilled jobs that require this training or to create unskilled jobs. In the good equilibrium, the best response of workers to businesses creating skilled jobs is to invest in training, and the best response of businesses to workers who get training is to create skilled jobs. Perhaps this equilibrium describes the rich industrialised economies.

But there's also a bad equilibrium, in which the best response of workers to businesses creating unskilled jobs is not to get training, and the best response of businesses to untrained workers is to create unskilled jobs. Perhaps less-developed countries are caught in this alternative equilibrium. Of course, everyone—both businesses and workers—would be better off in the high-income, high-skill equilibrium. The problem is that if workers believe that businesses will create unskilled jobs, or businesses believe that workers won't get training, then we might get stuck in the bad equilibrium, as each plays their best response, given their expectations of the other's choice.

Good Jobs or Bad Jobs?

	Businesses create unskilled jobs	Businesses create skilled jobs
Workers don't get training	Low-skilled labour market ✓✓	Shortage of skilled workers
Workers get training	Shortage of skilled jobs	High-skilled labour market ✓✓

Bank runs can occur when everyone believes a bank run will occur. Bank runs are another example of multiple equilibria. Here's the issue: When you give your savings to the bank, they don't just store it in a vault, instead they lend a lot of it out to generate a return. This means that if too many people want to withdraw their savings at the same time, the vault will quickly empty, and people at the back of the line won't get paid. In the good equilibrium, the banking system works perfectly. All savers are happy keeping their money in the bank earning interest, because that is a best response for each of them when everyone else also keeps their money in the bank.

But there's also a bad equilibrium, which corresponds to a bank run. If you believe that many other people are going to withdraw their money, your best response is to run to the bank to withdraw your savings, before the vault empties. A bank run occurs because everyone tries to withdraw their money before everyone else, and this is a best response for each of them given that everyone else is trying to withdraw their money. This type of bank run leads the bank to collapse and can catalyse a broader economic disaster.

Bank Runs

	Others withdraw	Others keep money in the bank
You withdraw your money	Bank run: We race to see who gets their money out first ✓✓	You don't earn interest Others definitely lose their savings
You keep your money in the bank	You definitely lose your savings Others don't earn interest	Stability: We both earn interest ✓✓

The economy's booms and busts can be a self-fulfilling prophecy. Multiple equilibria can help explain how the economy as a whole alternates between periods of boom and bust. In a booming economy, businesses produce and hire a lot, so the best response of households is to spend a lot because jobs are plentiful. Likewise, when households are spending a lot, the best response of businesses is to produce and hire a lot. The resulting economic boom is the good equilibrium.

But there's also a bad equilibrium, which corresponds to an economic bust. In an economic bust, households believe that businesses will cut back on production and hiring, and because they're worried that jobs will become scarce, their best response is to cut back on spending. Likewise, when businesses believe that households will cut back on spending, their best response is to cut back on production and reduce hiring. During a bust, governments will try to stimulate the economy so as to convince households that businesses will hire, and to convince businesses that households will spend.

Booms and Busts

	Businesses produce and hire a lot	Businesses cut back on production and hiring
Workers spend a lot	Workers spend a lot ✓ Businesses sell a lot ✓	Workers overspend Businesses underproduce
Workers cut back on spending	Workers underspend Businesses overproduce	Workers spend little ✓ Businesses sell little ✓

Solving Coordination Problems

In coordination and anti-coordination games you typically want to make the choice that complements the choices of other players. But when you have multiple equilibria, how can you coordinate with the other players on a specific equilibrium? Let's investigate three possible solutions.

Three solutions to coordination problems:

1. Communication
2. Focal points, culture, and norms
3. Laws and regulations

Coordination solution one: Communication. Here's a simple way to solve the coordination problem in the phone tag game: At the beginning of the call, simply say: "If this call drops out, don't call back . . . I'll call you." We both want the same thing—to be able to complete our call—and so there's no reason for you to doubt my sincerity. And so communication can help us coordinate on the equilibrium where I call back, and you wait for me to call.

The reason that communication works in the phone tag game is that we both want the same thing—to coordinate on the same equilibrium. But in many other strategic games, players have opposing incentives, so communication won't work because you're suspicious that the other player may be trying to fool you, much as we saw in the Prisoner's Dilemma.

Meeting for Lunch

You meet at:	They meet at: 11:30	Noon	12:30
11:30	We meet ✓✓	Miss	Miss
Noon	Miss	We meet ✓✓	Miss
12:30	Miss	Miss	We meet ✓✓

Coordination solution two: Focal points, culture, and norms. Sometimes, we figure out how to coordinate our actions by just thinking about what seems most natural. For instance, think about what you'll do if you've made a plan to meet someone for lunch, but you forgot to specify the time. The meeting-for-lunch game has many equilibria: For both of us, meeting at 11:30 A.M. is a best response if the other person is planning on meeting at 11:30 A.M. Likewise, meeting at noon is a best response if your lunch partner is planning on meeting at noon. And meeting at 12:30 P.M. is a best response to the other person is meeting at 12:30 P.M. The same logic says that there are many other equilibria at any time you might think to eat lunch. So you have many strategies that each could be equilibrium—which will you choose?

When you ask most people this question, they say that they'll meet at noon because that just seems like the most natural time to meet for lunch. This is an example of using a **focal point**—a cue from outside the game—to help coordinate on a particular equilibrium.

focal point A cue from outside a game that helps you coordinate on a specific equilibrium.

Social conventions—like the fact that noon is a common lunch time—provide common focal points. And this yields an economic understanding of culture and norms—that they provide focal points for everyday coordination games. In Australia, the norm of eating at noon serves as a focal point for the lunchtime coordination problem, while in Spain, a 2 P.M. norm does the same job.

Bow or Shake?

	They shake	They bow
You shake	Handshake occurs ✓✓	You're both embarrassed
You bow	You're both embarrassed	Bow occurs ✓✓

Likewise, when you walk into a business meeting, should you bow, or shake hands? Truth is, neither matters, but your business meeting will get off to a smoother start if you do the same thing as the person you're meeting. In this coordination game, there's both a hand-shaking equilibrium and a bowing equilibrium. But how do you know whether to bow or shake? Culture helps solve this coordination game, and in Australia, we usually shake hands, while in Japan meetings often begin with a bow.

lkpro/Shutterstock.com

The law helps decide which direction is the equilibrium.

Coordination solution three: Laws and regulations. When focal points and social conventions don't naturally arise, then there's a natural role for government laws and regulations to help enforce coordination. To take a simple example, if other people drive on the left-hand side of the road, then your best response is also to drive on the left. But if they drive on the right-hand side, then your best response is also to drive on the right. So should you drive on the left- or the right-hand side of the road?

Either works, it's just important that we all choose the same one. And so this is why we have traffic laws. Remember, there really are multiple equilibria here: In Australia and New Zealand the law says to drive on the left, while in most other countries, the law says to drive on the right.

Recap: Coordination games can lead markets to yield bad outcomes. The Prisoner's Dilemma and coordination games are two of the most important ideas in game theory, and their implications fundamentally shape how economists think about efficiency. Together, they spell bad news for the idea that markets lead to efficient outcomes—as they show that self-interest can make both cooperation and coordination difficult to achieve. And that in turn suggests an important role for government policies in sustaining cooperation and helping people to coordinate on good outcomes.

For many people, these big ideas are as far as they'll delve into game theory. But if you want to further build your toolkit for analysing strategic interactions, keep reading, and we'll explore how to analyse interactions that play out over time. But be warned, the final two sections of this chapter cover more advanced material.

18.4 Advanced Strategy: First and Second Mover Advantages

Learning Objective *Make your move when it's most advantageous.*

In the games that we've analysed so far, you make your choice without knowing what the other players have chosen, and so it's *as if* you're choosing at the same time. We'll now turn to analysing strategic interactions that play out over time, so that either you can see your rival's action before choosing yours, or they can see your action before choosing theirs. As we'll see, the order in which you make choices can really matter.

Games That Play Out over Time

You might not have given much thought to airline timetables, but they're the result of complicated strategic games. For example, put yourself in the shoes of a manager of the scheduling group within Qantas. You have to decide how many flights per day to schedule between Melbourne and the Gold Coast. This is not just a logistical question, but also a strategic one, because your profitability depends both on your choice, and also on how your rival, Virgin Australia, responds.

In a simultaneous game you choose without knowing the other player's choice. If both Qantas and Virgin make their choices without knowing the other's choice, what's the likely outcome? Let's step through our analysis. **First**, consider all the possibilities: The payoff table in Figure 4 shows that each airline might choose to schedule one, two, or three flights per day. The payoffs reflect a tension common in business: If both airlines cut their quantity—say, by restricting the number of flights they run—they can charge higher prices, which increases the industry's profits. But each airline also wants to run more flights so that it gets a larger share of the total industry profits.

Figure 4 | **The Scheduling Game**

	Virgin runs one flight per day	Virgin runs two flights per day	Virgin runs three flights per day
Qantas runs one flight per day	Qantas earns $40m Virgin earns $40m	Qantas earns $25m Virgin earns $50m ✔	Qantas earns $15m ✔ Virgin earns $45m
Qantas runs two flights per day	Qantas earns $50m ✔ Virgin earns $25m	Qantas earns $30m ✔ Virgin earns $30m ✔	Qantas earns $12m Virgin earns $18m
Qantas runs three flights per day	Qantas earns $45m Virgin earns $15m ✔	Qantas earns $18m Virgin earns $12m	Qantas earns $0m Virgin earns $0m

Given these payoffs, what's the equilibrium? In the **second** step, consider each "what if," and in the **third**, play your best response, making sure to mark each best response with a tick. **Fourth**, put yourself in Virgin's shoes, and evaluate each "what if," noting their best responses with a tick.

The Nash equilibrium—where there are two sets of ticks—involves both airlines running two flights per day, and they each earn a $30 million profit. So far, so good.

Qantas Moves First

	Virgin schedules: 1 flight	2 flights	3 flights
Qantas chose 3 flights	\$45m \$15m ✓	\$18m \$12m	\$0m \$0m

A first mover advantage occurs when you commit to being aggressive. Let's now consider what happens if Qantas can move first. In particular, the CEO of Qantas is considering announcing their schedule for the next year. Say Qantas chooses to run three flights per day. How will Virgin respond? Virgin's best response is to run only one flight per day. By moving first, Qantas will increase its profit from \$30 million to \$45 million. In this game, there's a **first-mover advantage**—a strategic gain from an anticipatory action—and it arises here because Qantas' aggressive choice forces Virgin to adapt and respond less aggressively.

first-mover advantage The strategic gain from an anticipatory action that can force a rival to respond less aggressively.

However, it's not enough for Qantas to just announce its new choice, because Virgin might not believe it'll follow through. To gain this first-mover advantage, it'll have to *credibly commit* to running three flights per day. It needs to take concrete actions that'll make any other choice costly. In order to be convincing, Qantas needs to invest in new jets, rent extra gates, and presell tickets with hefty penalties if it cancels. Once Qantas credibly commits to following through on its aggressive choice of running three flights, Virgin will understand that its best response is to schedule fewer flights.

Using Tree Logic

Let's now try an alternative way of looking at this game—one more suited to games that play out over more than one period.

game tree Shows how a game plays out over time, with the first move forming the trunk, and then each subsequent choice branching out, so the final leaves show all possible outcomes.

A game tree shows all possible outcomes. A **game tree** shows how all possible outcomes can play out over time. It begins with the trunk, where the first person makes a decision, and from this trunk, each possible action they could take forms another branch. At each branch, we then allow a new set of branches for each possible choice the second person can make. And the tree continues to branch each time someone makes another decision. The leaves at the end show all of the possible outcomes, and the payoff for each.

Figure 5 shows the same payoffs from the airline scheduling game in Figure 4, but this time it's shown as a game tree. To make this game tree readable, we'll show the tree on its side:

Figure 5 | A Game Tree

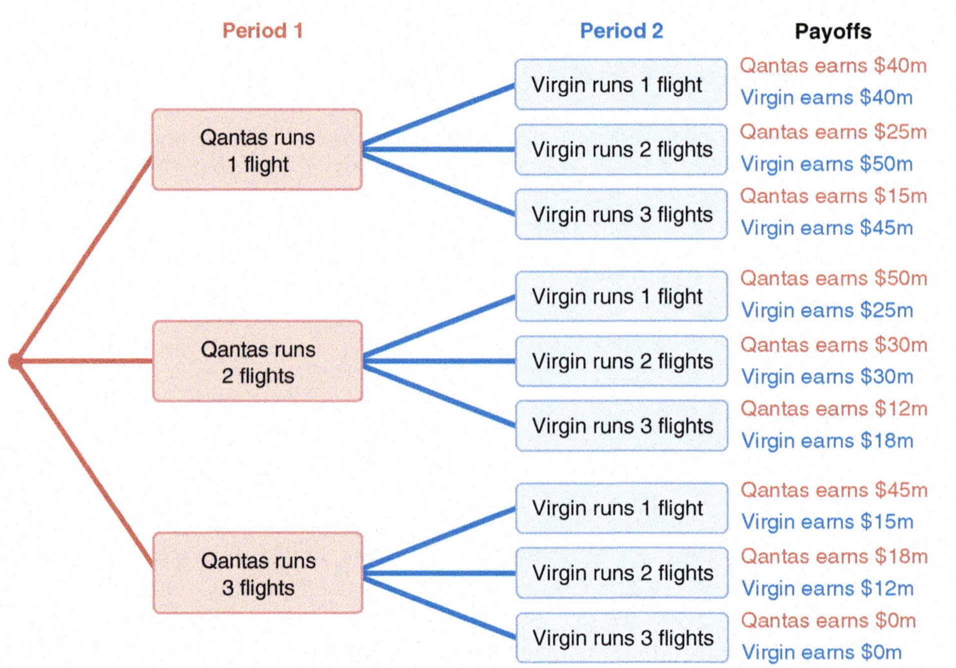

Look forward and reason backward. The game tree is helpful in games that play out over time because figuring out your best response requires that you **look forward** and **reason backward.** The *look forward* part means that you need to anticipate the likely consequences of your decisions. The *reason backward* part means that once you've figured out all the potential ways the game could play out, you should start from the end—the right side of the tree—and reason backward. Let's explore these two ideas further.

look forward In games that play out over time, you should look forward to anticipate the likely consequences of your choices.

reason backward Start by analysing the last period of the game. Use this to figure out what will happen in the second-to-last period, and keep reasoning backward until you can see all the consequences that follow from today's decision.

It's not sufficient just to think about your best choice today—you also need to consider how your choice will change the decisions that the other players will make tomorrow. But then you must consider how you would then react to their response, and how that would change their subsequent choices, and so on. Indeed, to ensure that you account for all the ways in which today's choices will ripple through shaping future choices, you need to look forward all the way through to the consequences in the final period.

The easiest way to do this is to follow the advice of master detective Sherlock Holmes, who said, "In solving a problem of this sort, the grand thing is to be able to reason backward." Start by envisioning the last move in the game. Once you've figured out what will happen in the final period, you can use this knowledge to forecast what choices people will make in the period before that. In turn, your assessment of the likely consequences in the final two periods of the game will be helpful when forecasting the likely decisions that'll be made in the third-from-final period. And so the process continues in which your analysis rolls back from the final period, to the previous period, to the period before that, and so on, until eventually you've rolled all the way back to the first period. When you roll your analysis all the way back, you'll be able to make the best choice in the first period, because you will do so armed with an understanding of the full set of consequences of that choice. This process of rolling your assessment back from the last period to the first is sometimes also called *backward induction*.

"In solving a problem of this sort, the grand thing is to be able to reason backward."—Sherlock Holmes

Do the Economics

The first step of our analysis—consider all the possibilities—led us to draw the game tree in Figure 5. Now, we're on to step two, which requires you to do some "what if" thinking. Because this is a game that plays out over time, your "what if" thinking should *look forward and reason backward.* Remember, this means that you should start by analysing the final period of the game, and then roll your analysis back from there. What if Qantas chooses one flight? Look forward to the final period, and realise that Virgin's best response will be to schedule two flights, so Qantas' profit will be $25 million. What if Qantas chooses two flights? Look forward to the final period, and you'll see that Virgin's best response is to also schedule two flights, and Qantas' profit will be $30 million. What if Qantas schedules three flights? Again, look forward to the final period, and you'll see that Virgin's best response is to schedule one flight, and so Qantas will make a profit of $45 million.

Now, it's time for step three, which is to evaluate your best response. You should do this by reasoning backward. Given the likely responses of Virgin in the final period, your highest profits occur when you schedule three flights in the first period. This yields some clear advice for Qantas. It should quickly commit to running three flights on the Melbourne–Gold Coast route, and Virgin will respond by scheduling only one flight. This yields Qantas a profit of $45 million. ■

As you get used to the logic of looking forward and reasoning backward, you'll discover that "tree logic" can be incredibly helpful in your everyday life, even if you don't need to explicitly draw the trees.

prune the tree method A method for solving game trees: Start by looking forward to the final period and highlighting out your rival's best responses, then prune the options the rival would never choose—the "dead leaves"—off your game tree.

Prune the tree to see what's likely to happen. Here's a simple method for solving game trees, we'll call it the **prune the tree method** because it involves pruning the dead leaves off a game tree. Again, you need to start by looking forward to the final period—in this case, period two—and figuring out your rival's best response. Highlight that best response. You can now prune the other leaves: You've figured out that Virgin will never choose them, and so they're effectively irrelevant. Figure 6 shows the "pruning" by crossing out the leaves you know Virgin will never choose.

Figure 6 | Pruning the Tree

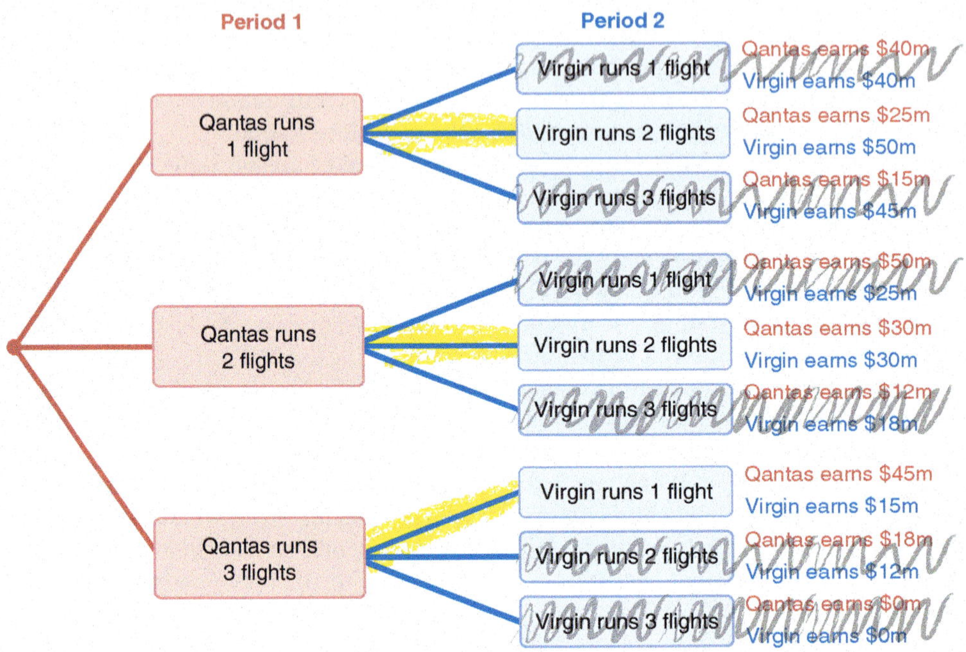

Next, reason backward, by going one step closer to the base of the tree. Given the remaining branches and the leaves that they lead to, what choice will you make? Highlight that choice, then as shown in Figure 7 prune the other options, and keep going until you've reasoned back to today's decision.

Figure 7 | Keep Pruning the Tree

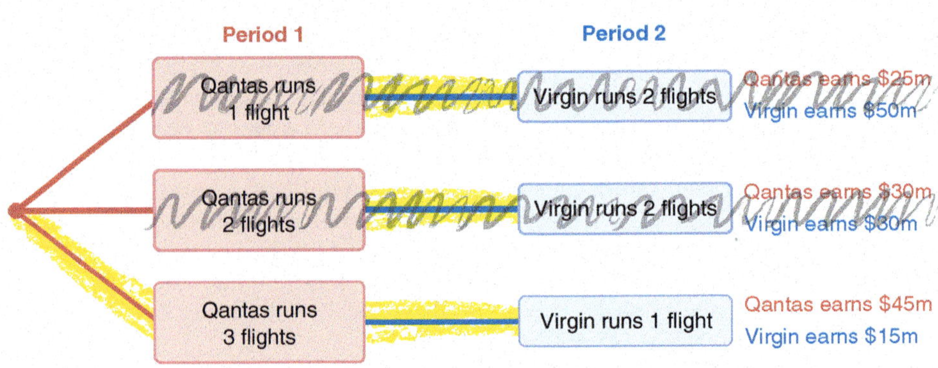

As you can see, all this pruning can get pretty messy. So you might also notice that once you've highlighted the parts of the game tree that are a best response, you can simply look for the highlighted path. If you've found a highlighted route all the way from the leaves in the last period to the trunk at the first period, then that's the equilibrium, as it involves each player making a best response at each stage of the game.

First-Mover Advantage versus Second-Mover Advantage

Perhaps you find the first-mover advantage to be fairly intuitive. But there's a sense in which it is a bit unusual. Think about it: The second mover, Virgin, knows more when it decides than the first mover (Qantas) did. That is, Virgin knows what its rival did, whereas Qantas didn't. We usually think that people make better decisions when they know more. But the first-mover advantage shows that this intuition is incomplete in strategic interactions.

The first-mover advantage is about the benefits of commitment. The first-mover advantage arises when you preemptively commit to an aggressive position, and your rival's best response is to be less aggressive. By scheduling three flights, Qantas effectively commits to taking "the big half" of the market, making it in Virgin's best interest to schedule only one flight. By contrast, if Qantas couldn't commit to this aggressive posture, then this would be a simultaneous-move game and it would schedule only two flights, because it would anticipate that Virgin would also offer two flights.

The second-mover advantage is about the benefits of flexibility. There isn't a first-mover advantage in all situations. Indeed, in some cases, there may be a **second-mover advantage.** For instance, if Bunnings is first to print a flyer detailing its Christmas specials, Masters will enjoy a second-mover advantage, because it can respond by offering the same products at slightly lower prices, helping it win customers from Bunnings.

second-mover advantage The strategic advantage that can follow from taking an action that adapts to your rival's choice.

In politics, a candidate who takes a firm stand on an issue is particularly vulnerable, because they have given their rival the choice of whether to attack them from the left or from the right. Likewise, in a product-positioning game, the second mover gets to figure out which part of the market remains underserved, and then position their product to get the largest customer base.

In each case, the second-mover advantage arises because it gives you the *flexibility* to adapt your strategy in light of the choices made by the first mover.

Interpreting the DATA — How Bunnings Warehouse's price-beat guarantee leads to higher prices

Bunnings is famous for its price-beat policy (well, that and its sausage sizzles). It's a promise that if you find a lower price on any good, it'll beat that lower price by 10%. It's a savvy business strategy, designed to regain the second-mover advantage. Here's the logic: Bunnings' competitors—like Masters—try to gain the second-mover advantage by offering lower prices than those listed in the latest Bunnings flyer. But Bunnings' price-beat guarantee nullifies Masters' advantage, because Bunnings automatically offers the same low price to any customers who may have been drawn to Masters by the promise of lower prices. And so Bunnings' price-beat guarantee effectively ensures that it gets to be the last mover in the hardware store pricing game.

Now, think through the implications of this. Executives at Masters realise that offering great discounts will no longer win them new customers, and so they'll stop offering discounts. This in turn reduces the pressure on Bunnings to offer lower prices. This strategy worked so well for Bunnings that Masters went out of business in 2016! The end result is less fierce price competition, and higher prices for shoppers like you. ■

Recap: Moving early or late depends on the value of commitment versus flexibility. Where does this leave us? Is there a first- or second-mover advantage? There are no hard and fast rules. You'll need to use your judgement to figure out the specifics of your situation. Moving first can be useful if you want to *commit* to a particularly aggressive strategy. But moving second can be an advantage when *flexibility* is important, and you can adapt your strategy to improve upon the choices made by your rival. The value of moving first versus second depends on the value of commitment versus flexibility.

18.5 Advanced Strategy: Repeated Games and Punishments

Learning Objective *Elicit cooperation by threatening punishment in repeated interactions.*

So far we've focused on situations in which you interact with the other players only once. When you're never going to see someone again, you have every reason to be as aggressive as possible. But if you interact with them repeatedly, then the decisions you make today will colour your future interactions. As we'll see, this sets the stage for even richer strategies. We'll discover that the threat of punishment can actually lead to more cooperation.

Collusion and the Prisoner's Dilemma

collusion An agreement by rivals to not compete with each other, but to all charge high prices instead.

Let's return to the Prisoner's Dilemma and explore whether it's possible to induce other players to cooperate. We'll focus on an extreme example of cooperation, called **collusion,** which refers to agreements by rivals to stop competing with each other. Instead of each offering lower prices in an attempt to gain market share, when firms collude, they all agree to charge a higher price in the hope that they'll all earn larger profits. We'll analyse collusion because it presents an interesting example of the Prisoner's Dilemma.

When rivals collude to raise prices, they increase their profits. In 2009, executives at several major book publishers organised a series of private lunches in various New York restaurants. Their goal was to figure out how to remain profitable in the emerging e-book marketplace. Spurred on by Apple—who wanted to counter Amazon's dominant role selling e-books—they came up with a plan. Rather than each competing to offer the lowest prices, they would all agree to charge the same high price for their e-books.

That is, they agreed to collude, with each effectively promising to raise the price of their bestsellers from US$9.99 to US$12.99. Colluding like this to fix prices is illegal because it hurts consumers. But the publishers were interested in something more direct. Would this agreement work?

Figure 8 Will Rivals Collude?

	HarperCollins cooperates (Charges $12.99)	HarperCollins defects (Charges $9.99)
Penguin cooperates (Charges $12.99)	Penguin earns medium profit; HarperCollins earns medium profit	Penguin makes a loss; HarperCollins earns large profit
Penguin defects (Charges $9.99)	Penguin earns large profit; HarperCollins makes a loss	Penguin earns zero profit; HarperCollins earns zero profit

Collusion is a Prisoner's Dilemma. To evaluate the likely outcome, put yourself in the shoes of David Shanks, CEO of Penguin Books. Should he go along with the plan to raise his prices to $12.99?

Game theory is particularly useful in the sort of high-stakes strategic interactions that often arise in oligopolies. Following our four-step recipe, begin by considering all the possible outcomes. Penguin can cooperate with this plan to raise prices, or defect, and keep charging $9.99. The other publishers face similar alternatives. To simplify things, the payoff table in Figure 8 sets this up as a game involving only two publishers—Penguin and HarperCollins—though in reality there were five publishers involved. But this simpler game is sufficient to highlight the key forces involved.

Initially each publisher was charging $9.99 per book, and they each earned zero economic profit. Their hope was that if they all cooperated with the plan to raise their prices to $12.99, then they could all be better off, and earn a medium profit.

But collusion is an example of the Prisoner's Dilemma, which means that we should expect the publishers to fail to cooperate. To see this, move to step two and consider the "what ifs." If your rivals charge $12.99, then (step three!) your best response is to defect and charge only $9.99, because you'll gain enough market share to earn a large profit. If your rivals defect, you don't want to be the only company selling at $12.99, because then you'll lose so much market share that you'll make a loss. Now, in step four, put yourself in the shoes of your rivals. You'll discover that even if Penguin cooperates with the plan to collude, HarperCollins will defect, leading Penguin to make a loss. The Nash equilibrium is that each firm chooses to defect from the agreement to collusively charge high prices.

Based on this analysis, you might predict that collusion won't work. It says that Penguin will defect from the collusive agreement, and if it doesn't, its rivals will. This is an example where the failure to cooperate in the Prisoner's Dilemma is good for society, because it prevents collusion from occurring.

It's a comforting thought. But in reality, all of the major publishers ended up colluding and charging $12.99 for their e-books. Why?

Lukia Kliossis

It only takes a few clicks to change the price on an e-book.

Finitely Repeated Games

We've treated Penguin's choices as if it were playing a **one-shot game,** which means that this strategic interaction occurs only once. In a one-shot game you don't need to worry about how today's decision might change how other others will treat you in the future. But in reality, Penguin effectively plays the game shown in Figure 8 every day. That is, Penguin faces the same rivals and the same payoffs in successive periods—a situation we call a **repeated game.**

one-shot game A strategic interaction that occurs only once.

repeated game When you face the same strategic interaction with the same rivals and the same payoffs in successive periods.

Solve finitely repeated games by looking forward and reasoning backward. In a **finitely repeated game,** the players interact a *fixed* number of times. For instance, if Penguin and HarperCollins thought they would interact exactly three times, that would be an example of a finitely repeated game. Even though that's not the situation they actually faced, we can do a quick analysis on that premise to see how it would play out over three periods.

finitely repeated game When you face the same strategic interaction a *fixed* number of times.

Remember that in games that play out over time you should *look forward* and *reason backward.* So let's look forward to the last interaction. In the final period, both players know they'll never interact again, and so they effectively face a one-shot Prisoner's Dilemma. In a one-shot Prisoner's Dilemma, both will choose to defect. Now let's reason back to the second-to-last period. Both players understand that no matter what they do, their rival will defect in the next period. Given this, the second-to-last round is also effectively a one-shot game, and so again, both players will likely defect. And so as you continue to roll back your analysis to earlier periods, you'll conclude that neither publisher will cooperate in any period.

That is, the Prisoner's Dilemma continues to yield uncooperative outcomes when it's repeated a *fixed* or finite number of times. This is because when there's a known final period, both players know that they'll cheat in that final period. The incentive to defect in the final period then rolls back to the next-to-final period, and so on all the way back to the first period, undermining the incentive to cooperate in every stage.

Indefinitely Repeated Games

The CEO of Penguin realises that he isn't going to interact with his rivals a *fixed* number of times. There's no known end date, and so the logic of a finitely repeated game is of little help to him. And, with no known end date, there's no reason to expect that cooperation will necessarily unravel.

In fact, he faces an **indefinitely repeated game,** which arises when you expect to keep interacting with the other players for quite some time—perhaps until one of you goes out of business—but you don't know precisely for how long. The result is that the game is repeated an *indefinite* number of times. This is important because, if you don't know when your interactions will end, there's no last period in which you or your rival will definitely be tempted to defect. And this undermines the logic that leads you to want to defect in earlier periods. Perhaps this points to a reason to be more optimistic that you can sustain cooperation.

indefinitely repeated game When you face the same strategic interaction with no definitive endpoint.

strategic plan A list of instructions that describes exactly how to respond in any possible situation.

A strategy is a list of instructions. In this sort of repeated interaction, you'll need a **strategic plan** that describes or lists how you'll respond to any possible situation that might arise. This is a "complete contingent plan," and you can think of it as a list of instructions that you could leave with your lawyer, telling them exactly how to respond in any situation that may arise. In a game that plays out over time the list of instructions might be quite complex, describing how to respond to different contingencies. Importantly, your strategic plan may depend on past choices made by other players. This means that your strategic plan might include a threat to your rivals that if they defect from a collusive agreement, you'll follow up with a punishment. If that threat is credible, it might be sufficient to elicit cooperation in an indefinitely repeated Prisoner's Dilemma.

The Grim Trigger strategy punishes your rival for not cooperating. One difficulty with analysing indefinitely repeated games is that there are millions of possible strategic plans to consider. Rather than evaluating them all, we're going to focus on a specific plan that's particularly likely to elicit cooperation.

Grim Trigger strategy If the other players have cooperated in all previous rounds, you will cooperate. But if any player has defected in the past, you will defect.

The **Grim Trigger strategy** is relatively simple, and involves only two instructions:

1. If the other players have cooperated in all previous rounds, then you'll cooperate.
2. If any player has defected in any previous round, you'll defect.

Effectively this strategy says: I'm willing to cooperate, but if you fail to play along, I'll punish you by defecting forever. You can see how this might provide a strong incentive for your rivals to cooperate!

Cooperation can be an equilibrium. If you and your rivals play the Grim Trigger strategy, what will the equilibrium be? We can analyse this using our four-step recipe.

Start with step one: Consider all of the different possibilities. We'll start by considering what happens if neither player has defected yet. You have two choices: continue to follow your strategic plan, which means cooperating given that no one has defected, or deviate from your strategic plan by unilaterally defecting. Likewise, your rival has the same two choices. We can see these alternatives in Figure 9.

Figure 9 | **Payoff Table if Both Firms Have Cooperated in the Past**

	HarperCollins follows Grim Trigger strategy (Continue to cooperate)	**HarperCollins deviates from strategy** (Defect today)
Penguin follows Grim Trigger strategy (Continue to cooperate)	Penguin earns: - Medium profit today, and - Chance to cooperate in the future, earning medium profit ✔ HarperCollins earns: - Medium profit today, and - Chance to cooperate in the future, earning medium profit ✔	Penguin earns: - A loss today, and - Zero profit in the future HarperCollins earns: - A large profit today, and - Zero profit in the future
Penguin deviates from strategy (Defect today)	Penguin earns: - A large profit today, and - Zero profit in the future HarperCollins earns: - A loss today, and - Zero profit in the future	Penguin earns: - Zero profit today, and - Zero profit in the future ✔ HarperCollins earns: - Zero profit today, and - Zero profit in the future ✔

Notice something different about the payoff table. The two choices are whether to continue following your strategic plan or whether to deviate. And the payoffs consider both what will happen today, and also how this changes the future.

Okay, step two—consider the "what ifs"—and step three—play your best response.

What if your rival follows their strategic plan and continues cooperating?

- You can cooperate: You'll earn a medium profit today. You also need to consider the future. If you both cooperate today, you'll also be in a position to keep cooperating tomorrow, which ensures you can continue to earn a medium profit in the future.
- Or you can defect: You'll earn a large profit today. But the downside is that your rival will never cooperate with you again, and so you'll earn zero profits in all future periods.

How do these compare? As long as you value those future profits enough, you're better off cooperating, so we put a red tick in the upper-left corner.

What if your rival deviates from their strategic plan and defects?

You can continue to cooperate and make a loss today (and zero in the future), or defect and make zero today (and zero in the future). Comparing these, your best response is also to defect. So put a red tick in the lower-right box.

Time for step four: Put yourself in your rival's shoes. Your rival needs to consider two "what ifs."

If you follow your strategic plan and cooperate, your rival has to decide whether to:

- Continue following its strategic plan of cooperating with you: This earns your rival a medium profit today and also keeps alive the possibility of cooperating and earning a medium profit in the future.
- Deviate from its strategic plan by defecting today: This earns your rival a large profit today, but destroys the possibility of future cooperation, leading to zero profits in all future periods.

If your rival values the future benefits enough, it'll choose to cooperate, so we put a blue tick in the top-left box.

What if you deviate from your strategic plan and defect?

Your rival can continue to cooperate and make a loss today (and zero in the future), or defect and make zero today (and zero in the future). Comparing these, its best response is also to defect, and so we put a blue tick in the bottom-right corner.

Now, look for a Nash equilibrium, and you'll discover two ticks in the top-left corner. For both you and your rival, continuing to follow the Grim Trigger strategy—and continuing to cooperate—is a Nash equilibrium! (It's not the only equilibrium, though.) Even though the whole point of the Prisoner's Dilemma is to illustrate that often cooperation won't be an equilibrium in the one-shot game—or indeed in a finitely repeated game—it can be an equilibrium now that the game is indefinitely repeated.

This is a big deal! It should restore your faith that cooperation is possible—as long as people continue to interact for an unknown period of time. It won't always occur, but it can.

And indeed, cooperation is exactly what occurred, as the publishers cooperated with their joint plan to collude, continuing to charge $12.99 for e-books. Eventually, they faced a different problem; collusion like this is illegal, and when it was discovered, each company ended up paying the government millions in fines.

Punishment drives cooperation. The logic of the Prisoner's Dilemma—at least the one-shot version—is that defecting rather than cooperating is an attractive short-run option because you'll immediately earn a large profit. But in the indefinitely repeated version, defecting is not a good long-run choice because it triggers a large punishment. Your rival could refuse to cooperate with you again in the future. And it's the loss of these future profits that makes cooperating a better choice.

Threats of punishment only work if they are credible. Of course, your threat to punish your rival for not cooperating will only work if your rival believes you'll follow through with it—that is, if it is a *credible threat*. For a threat to be credible, it must be in your best interest to take the actions you threatened to take. If your rival is playing a Grim Trigger strategy, then the threat to defect forever after your rival has defected is your best choice. It's credible, because after either player defects, your rival will continue to defect forever, and so your best response is also to defect. The Grim Trigger strategy ensures that any defection destroys any possibility of future cooperation, and so you can resume playing as if this were a one-shot game, in which case your best response is to defect.

There's also some good news worth emphasising. If the punishment is strong enough to deter cheating, it need never actually be inflicted. We might simply both cooperate forever!

Repeated play helps solve the Prisoner's Dilemma. Where does this leave us? The key insight of the Prisoner's Dilemma is that it can be difficult to sustain cooperation in strategic interactions. But it's not necessarily a deal-breaker. If you're repeating your interactions—and repeating them an indefinite number of times—then you have another tool to help you solve it: the threat of future punishments. And this threat can be sufficient to sustain cooperation.

Tying It Together

Two friends are visiting Kakadu National Park in the Northern Territory, and they come across a crocodile. They both freeze. One of them starts to dig through their pack, looking for pepper spray. The other puts on running shoes. Their friend screams: "What are you doing? You can't outrun a croc!" The friend replies: "I don't have to outrun the croc; I only have to outrun you."

Dave Watts/Alamy Stock Photo

Game theory reminds you that you don't need to outrun the croc.

It's a joke, but it points to a deeper truth. Strategic interactions—where your best choice depends on what I choose—play out from the hiking trail to the boardroom, and everywhere in between. Game theory reveals sometimes unexpected insights—that you have to outrun your friend, and not the croc—that will guide you to better strategic decisions. The *interdependence principle* reminds you that economic decisions are linked to each other, and game theory provides the road map to making better decisions that take account of those interactions.

That road map consists of four simple steps: consider all the possible outcomes; think about the "what ifs" separately; play your best response to each; and apply the someone else's shoes technique.

The idea of putting yourself in someone else's shoes is critical to understanding how any interaction will play out. Throughout this chapter we've suggested that your rival will follow the same four-step process that you do. That is, we've characterised other players as being sophisticated strategists, just like you. Is this realistic? Sure, it's a lot of work to be perfectly strategic all the time, but even people who've never been formally trained in game theory are pretty good at figuring out what's in their best interest. That means that your best response usually is to think of your rivals as strategic. Ultimately, it's up to you to figure out how smart your rival is, but in my experience, it's far more common to see managers make bad decisions by underestimating their rivals than by overestimating them.

Our approach in this chapter has been to provide a unified view of game theory, showing how a set of simple ideas inform many strategic situations. We've seen that the results of any strategic interaction depend crucially on the rules of the game. Outcomes can change depending on details such as whether the players move simultaneously, who moves first, whether the game is repeated, and how often. And this is good news for strategists, because it suggests that if you're savvy, you can use what we've learned to shape the rules of the game to your advantage.

Chapter at a Glance

Four Steps for Making Strategic Decisions

1. Consider all possible outcomes → 2. Think about the "what ifs" separately → 3. Play your best response → 4. Put yourself in someone else's shoes

Nash Equilibrium: An equilibrium in which the choice that each player makes is a best response to the choices other players are making.

Apply the Four Steps to:

1. The Prisoner's Dilemma

- The Prisoner's Dilemma yields a failure to cooperate
- The temptation to take advantage undermines cooperation
- The best outcome would be to cooperate, but this is not the equilibrium outcome

2. Coordination Games

- In coordination and anti-coordination games you typically want to make the choice that complements the choice of the other players
- Coordination is difficult because there's more than one equilibrium
- Communication, focal points, culture and norms, and laws and regulations can help solve the coordination problem

3. Games That Play Out Over Time (Finitely-Repeated Games)

A **game tree** 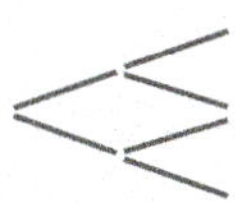 shows how all possible outcomes can play out over time.

In games that play out over time, your "what if" thinking should:

Look forward and **Reason backward**

Look forward: To anticipate the likely consequences of your choices . . .

Reason backward: . . . Start by analysing the last period of the game. Use this to figure out what will happen in the second-to-last period, and keep reasoning backward until you can see all the consequences that follow from today's decision.

First-mover advantage: The strategic gain from an anticipatory action which can force a rival to respond less aggressively.

Second-mover advantage: The strategic advantage that can follow from taking an action that adapts to your rival's choice.

4. Indefinitely Repeated Interactions

Indefinitely repeated games: When you face the same strategic interaction with no definitive endpoint. → The Grim Trigger strategy punishes your rivals for not cooperating. → Punishment drives cooperation. Indefinitely repeated play helps solve the Prisoner's Dilemma.

Key Concepts

anti-coordination game, 455
best response, 448
collusion, 464
coordination game, 454
finitely repeated game, 465
first-mover advantage, 460
focal point, 458
game tree, 460
Grim Trigger strategy, 466
indefinitely repeated game, 465
look forward, 461
multiple equilibria, 454
Nash equilibrium, 450
one-shot game, 465
payoff table, 447
prune the tree method, 461
reason backward, 461
repeated game, 465
second-mover advantage, 463
strategic interaction, 446
strategic plan, 466
tick method, 450

Discussion and Review Questions

Learning Objective 18.1 *Apply the four steps to making good strategic decisions.*

1. Think about a situation you've experienced lately where you've made a decision based both on your best interest and on the decisions of others. Use the interdependence principle to explain how your best choice was dependent on what others chose.

Learning Objective 18.2 *Understand how the Prisoner's Dilemma highlights the problem of getting people to cooperate.*

2. In 2020 Australia and China engaged in a trade war where each country was imposing trade tariffs on goods imported from the other country. China announced that it would be imposing tariffs of 80.5% on barley imports, bringing close to $1 billion worth of trade to a halt. Australia quickly responded by issuing a formal dispute with China to the World Trade Organisation (WTO). China then countered by imposing additional tariffs of over 200% on wine imports. Australia responded with another dispute claim to the WTO.

   Briefly explain how this is an example of a Prisoner's Dilemma.

Learning Objective 18.3 *Figure out how best to coordinate with your allies to make complementary choices.*

3. Your instructor challenges you to solve this classic economics thought experiment called *the stag hunt*: Suppose you and a hunting partner are hunting for food to feed your families in a post-apocalyptic world with no stores, farms, or trade. You lay a trap for a deer that will provide a large number of calories for your two families to continue to survive. While waiting, you both spot a hare running through the trap. If you chase after the hare, you'll catch it but you will scare any wildlife in the area and you won't catch the deer you were waiting for. The hare only provides a small amount of calories for your own family and none for your partner's family. Would you chase after the hare or keep waiting for the stag?

   Create a payoff matrix that illustrates this example. You can use whatever values you want as long as they align with the outcomes described above. Use the four steps and the tick method to determine the best possible responses for you and your partner. Which would you choose and why?

Learning Objective 18.4 *Make your move when it's most advantageous.*

4. The Village Roadshow Theme Parks and Ardent Leisure are both considering building a new theme park in Queensland. They each have two viable options for the new location: Cairns and the Gold Coast (GC). The expected profits are provided in the following payoff table:

	Ardent Leisure builds in Cairns	Ardent Leisure builds on the GC
Village Roadshow builds in Cairns	Village Roadshow receives $60 million profit Ardent Leisure receives $30 million profit	Village Roadshow receives $90 million profit Ardent Leisure receives $80 million profit
Village Roadshow builds on the GC	Village Roadshow receives $120 million profit Ardent Leisure receives $50 million profit	Village Roadshow receives $60 million profit Ardent Leisure receives $60 million profit

   a. If Village Roadshow and Ardent Leisure make this decision simultaneously, what would the Nash equilibrium be for this game?

   b. Explain, using game trees, why it is in Village Roadshow's best interest to build first.

Learning Objective 18.5 *Elicit cooperation by threatening punishment in repeated interactions.*

5. Visy and Amcor are corrugated fibre packaging producers who, in the early 2000s, controlled around 90% of the $2 billion/year market. The two companies colluded in order to charge higher prices. In 2007, Visy admitted

its role in the cartel and was fined $36 million by the Federal Court, as well as being ordered to pay tens of millions in damages to customers. Consider the following payoff table:

	Visy charges high prices (conspire)	Visy charges low prices (defect)
Amcor charges high prices (conspire)	Amcor receives $0.9 billion profit Visy receives $0.9 billion profit	Amcor receives $0.6 billion profit Visy receives $1.1 billion profit
Amcor charges low prices (defect)	Amcor receives $0.6 billion profit Visy receives $1.1 billion profit	Amcor receives $0.7 billion profit Visy receives $0.7 billion profit

a. If Visy and Amcor are setting prices for one period only, what will the Nash equilibrium be? Briefly explain your reasoning.

b. If, instead, Visy and Amcor play this game over and over, how could they find a way to cooperate with each other? Use a payoff table to help illustrate your answer.

c. The reason Amcor was not fined was that they were granted immunity from prosecution by the ACCC in exchange for divulging their role in the cartel. Explain how the ACCC used the Prisoner's Dilemma to uncover the collusion. Did Amcor have a first-mover, or second-mover advantage here?

Study Problems

Learning Objective 18.1 *Apply the four steps to making good strategic decisions.*

1. For each of the following scenarios, identify whether or not it involves strategic interactions.

a. It is dinner time and you are sitting at the dinner table with your five-year-old daughter. She is refusing to eat her vegetables and you explain to her that failure to eat her vegetables will result in no dessert.

b. You have been elected to the Australian Senate from the state of South Australia. One of your colleagues has proposed a bill that will increase the tax on alcohol to help pay for additional health care for lower-income families. You are in favour of the bill, but are concerned that a negative response by wineries in your state will hurt your reelection chances.

c. You buy a monthly subscription to Spotify.

d. Economics is your favourite course and you are trying to determine how early you need to arrive for class in order to secure a front row seat.

2. Netflix and Stan are both considering producing a new television show. They could produce either a romantic comedy or a historical drama. The profits are illustrated in the following payoff matrix:

	Stan produces romantic comedy	Stan produces historical drama
Netflix produces romantic comedy	Netflix receives $19 million profit Stan receives $13 million profit	Netflix receives $22 million profit Stan receives $10 million profit
Netflix produces historical drama	Netflix receives $30 million profit Stan receives $14 million profit	Netflix receives $25 million profit Stan receives $8 million profit

Use the information provided to identify whether each of the following statements is True or False.

a. If Netflix chooses to produce a romantic comedy, then Stan's best response is to produce a historical drama.

b. Netflix's best response is to always produce a historical drama.

c. Stan's best response is to always produce a romantic comedy.

Learning Objective 18.2 *Understand how the Prisoner's Dilemma highlights the problems of getting people to cooperate.*

3. Founded in 1960, the Organization of Petroleum Exporting Countries (OPEC) is an intergovernmental organisation of 13 nations that meets periodically in order to establish oil production quotas for each individual nation, resulting in greater profits overall. However, OPEC has a history of failing to enforce its own quota limits. Consider a simplified example with just two countries: Venezuela and Kuwait. Currently, both countries are producing 2.5 million barrels per day. If both countries agree to cooperate with each other, they will each restrict output to 2 million barrels per day, causing the price of oil to rise. If one of the countries defects from the agreement, they will produce 2.5 million barrels and total output will rise from 4 million barrels to 4.5 million barrels. As a result, the price will fall slightly. If both nations defect from the agreement, each nation will again produce 2.5 million barrels and the price will fall to the original level. The payoffs for each possible outcome are illustrated in the following payoff table:

	Venezuela cooperates	Venezuela defects
Kuwait cooperates	Kuwait receives $60 million Venezuela receives $60 million	Kuwait receives $40 million Venezuela receives $70 million
Kuwait defects	Kuwait receives $70 million Venezuela receives $40 million	Kuwait receives $50 million Venezuela receives $50 million

a. In terms of their collective profits, what is the best outcome for Kuwait and Venezuela?

b. What is the Nash equilibrium outcome? Use the tick method to help illustrate your answer.

c. In terms of their collective profits, of the possible outcomes illustrated in the payoff table, is the Nash equilibrium the worst outcome for Kuwait and Venezuela?

Learning Objective 18.3 *Figure out how best to coordinate with your allies to make complementary choices.*

4. The Old Familiar and The Beehive are the only two pubs in town. Each one is trying to decide whether or not it should advertise in the local newspaper. The following payoff matrix gives their weekly profits under each possible outcome:

	The Beehive advertises	The Beehive doesn't advertise
The Old Familiar advertises	The Old Familiar earns $*X* profit. The Beehive earns $*Y* profit.	The Old Familiar earns $3,500 profit. The Beehive earns $2,250 profit.
The Old Familiar doesn't advertise	The Old Familiar earns $2,000 profit. The Beehive earns $4,000 profit.	The Old Familiar earns $2,500 profit. The Beehive earns $3,500 profit.

Here are four combinations of X and Y.

i. $X = \$1{,}500$; $Y = \$2{,}500$

ii. $X = \$2{,}500$; $Y = \$2{,}000$

iii. $X = \$1{,}200$; $Y = \$1{,}500$

iv. $X = \$3{,}300$; $Y = \$1{,}250$

a. Which of the combinations of X and Y would make The Old Familiar not advertising and The Beehive advertising a Nash equilibrium?

b. Which of the combinations of X and Y would cause this game to have multiple Nash equilibria?

Learning Objective 18.4 *Make your move when it's most advantageous.*

5. Pfizer is one of the largest pharmaceutical companies in the world and has a patent on one of the Covid-19 vaccines. If the patent were about to expire, then Pfizer would have two options: continue to charge a high price for its product or charge a low price. In response, a drug company that produces generic drugs must decide whether to enter the market or not enter the market. The associated payoff table is as follows:

	Generic manufacturer enters market	Generic manufacturer stays out of market
Pfizer charges a high price	Pfizer receives $15 billion profit. Generic receives $10 billion profit	Pfizer receives $50 billion profit. Generic receives $0 profit
Pfizer charges a low price	Pfizer receives $10 billion profit. Generic receives $2 billion loss	Pfizer receives $25 billion profit. Generic receives $0 profit

a. If Pfizer and the generic manufacturer were making these decisions simultaneously, what would the Nash equilibrium be? Briefly explain how you found your answer.

b. If Pfizer is able to allow the generic manufacturer to make a decision first and then responds to that decision with its pricing strategy, relative to the simultaneous play game, would Pfizer gain a second-mover advantage by waiting? Briefly explain your reasoning.

c. If Pfizer is able to select its pricing strategy first and allows the generic manufacturer to respond to its decision, relative to the simultaneous-play game, would Pfizer gain a first-mover advantage by moving aggressively? Briefly explain your reasoning.

d. In a sequential-play game, would Pfizer be willing to pay the generic manufacturer to guarantee that it would not enter the market? If so, what is the most that Pfizer would be willing to pay?

6. The NSW state government has decided to build a new off-ramp for the M1 in Sydney. 7-Eleven and Shell are both interested in building a petrol station near the new off-ramp. They could build the petrol station near the off-ramp for northbound traffic or they could build the petrol station near the off-ramp for southbound traffic. The profits, in thousands of dollars, for each outcome are illustrated in the following payoff table:

	Shell builds near northbound ramp	Shell builds near southbound ramp
7-Eleven builds near northbound ramp	7-Eleven receives $60 thousand profit. Shell receives $50 thousand profit	7-Eleven receives $110 thousand profit. Shell receives $100 thousand profit
7-Eleven builds near southbound ramp	7-Eleven receives $80 thousand profit. Shell receives $120 thousand profit	7-Eleven receives $50 thousand profit. Shell receives $50 thousand profit

a. If 7-Eleven and Shell make these decisions simultaneously, what is the Nash equilibrium (or equilibria)? Use the tick method to help illustrate your answer.

b. What happens if 7-Eleven moves first and builds a petrol station before Shell? Draw a game tree for this sequential-move game. Your diagram must be clearly labelled and contain all relevant information.

c. Use the prune the tree method to illustrate the Nash equilibrium for the sequential-move game. What is the Nash equilibrium in this case?

d. What happens if Shell moves first and builds a petrol station before 7-Eleven? Draw a game tree for this sequential-move game. Your diagram must be clearly labelled and contain all relevant information.

e. Use the prune the tree method to illustrate the Nash equilibrium for the sequential-move game. What is the Nash equilibrium in this case?

7. You have developed a new computer operating system and are considering whether you should enter the market and compete with Microsoft. Microsoft has the option of offering their operating system for a high price or a low price. Once Microsoft selects a price, you will decide whether you want to enter the market or not enter the market. If Microsoft charges a high price and you enter, Microsoft will earn $30 million and you will earn $10 million. If Microsoft charges a high price and you do not enter, Microsoft will earn $60 million and you will earn $0. If Microsoft charges a low price and you enter, Microsoft will earn $20 million and you will *lose* $5 million. If Microsoft charges a low price and you do not enter, Microsoft will earn $50 million and you will earn $0.

a. Use the information provided to make a payoff table for your and Microsoft's decisions.

b. If both you and Microsoft are making your decisions simultaneously, what is the Nash equilibrium (or equilibria)?

c. What if Microsoft selects a price first, and then you decide whether you will enter the market? Draw a game tree for this sequential-move game. Your diagram must be clearly labelled and contain all relevant information.

d. Use the prune the tree method to illustrate the Nash equilibrium for the sequential-move game. What is the Nash equilibrium in this case?

Learning Objective 18.5 *Elicit cooperation by threatening punishment in repeated interactions.*

8. Consider a market dominated by just two airlines, Qantas and Virgin. Each can choose to restrict capacity and charge a high price or expand capacity and charge a low price. If one of the two airlines expands capacity and reduces the price and the other does not, the airline that reduces its price will be able to capture customers from the other airline. The economic profits for each outcome are illustrated in the following payoff table:

	Virgin charges a high price	Virgin charges a low price
Qantas charges a high price	Qantas receives $2 billion profit Virgin receives $1.5 billion profit	Qantas receives $0.5 billion loss Virgin receives $2 billion profit
Qantas charges a low price	Qantas receives $2.5 billion profit Virgin receives $0.5 billion loss	Qantas receives $0 profit Virgin receives $0 profit

a. If Qantas and Virgin are playing a simultaneous game, what is the Nash equilibrium (or equilibria)? Use the tick method to help illustrate your answer.

b. Is this game an example of the Prisoner's Dilemma?

c. If Virgin and Qantas were to play this game as a repeated game for two periods, what outcome would occur in the second period?

d. What outcome would occur in the first period?

e. If Virgin and Qantas play this game for an indeterminate number of periods so that neither Qantas nor Virgin knows when the game will effectively end, then each will play a Grim Trigger strategy. In this case the payoff table will become:

	Virgin charges a high price (continues to cooperate)	Virgin charges a low price (deviates from cooperation)
Qantas charges a high price (continues to cooperate)	Qantas receives $2 billion profit today and in every period in future. Virgin receives $1.5 billion profit today and in every period in future.	Qantas receives $0.5 billion loss today and $0 profit in every future period. Virgin receives $2 billion profit today and $0 profit in every future period.
Qantas charges a low price (deviates from cooperation)	Qantas receives $2.5 billion loss today and $0 profit in every future period. Virgin receives $0.5 billion loss today and $0 profit in every future period.	Qantas receives $0 profit today and in every period in future. Virgin receives $0 profit today and in every period in future.

What is the Nash equilibrium (or equilibria)? Use the tick method to help illustrate your answer.

PART V: Advanced Decisions

Part V: Advanced Decisions

The Big Picture

It's time to expand your decision-making toolkit to account for a complication you run into every day: You won't always have all the information you need to make a perfect decision.

We'll introduce a framework you can use to make decisions when you know something that others don't or when they know something you don't. We'll see that these information asymmetries create a fog of mistrust. Is that used car listed on Carsales because the owner needs to sell it, or because they know it's a lemon? Your insurer will wonder whether you're buying insurance because you're expecting to make a costly claim. And your manager will wonder whether you're working hard, or hardly working. These problems can lead markets to misfire or even collapse entirely. You know a lot more about your health than anyone else does, which is why we'll see that these issues are a particularly big deal in the healthcare market.

Then we'll move on to a related problem: How do you make decisions when you're **uncertain about the consequences** of your choices? We'll discover the critical role the financial sector plays in reducing and redistributing risk. And we'll explore the psychological biases that can distort people's choices, and show you how to reduce their effects.

19 Decisions Involving Private Information and Hidden Actions

Learn how to make decisions when you don't have all the facts.

- Why is it hard to buy a good-quality used car?
- If everyone wants health insurance, why is it so hard for companies to deliver it?
- Why do your staff slack off when you're not watching, and what can you do about it?
- Why does insurance lead people to take more risks?

20 Decisions Involving Uncertainty

Learn how to make good decisions when you don't know what will happen.

- Why do people dislike risk?
- How can you make good decisions when you're uncertain about the consequences of your choices?
- How can you reduce the various risks you face in your life?
- How do mental shortcuts lead people to incorrectly assess risk and its consequences, and how can you avoid these psychological traps?

CHAPTER 19

Decisions Involving Private Information and Hidden Actions

Pcess609/Shutterstock

Do you know the whole truth?

What happens when you know something that others don't? Or they know something you don't? For instance, you know better than your manager how you make use of your time at work—whether you stay on task or spend it checking Facebook. When you buy a used car, the owner knows things you don't—whether the car has been well cared for, if it sputters rather than starts on cold mornings, or if it's been in an accident. And you know better than your health insurer whether you're healthy and how likely you are to need medical care.

Trouble arises when differences in information collide with conflicting incentives. Your manager wants you to work hard; you want to take it easy. You want a good car; the seller just wants to close the deal. Your insurer hopes you're healthy; you know that you're not. You can't know for sure when someone is telling you the whole truth, and others can't know for sure when you are. This creates a fog of misinformation that has far-reaching effects. It distorts supply and demand and leads to inefficient outcomes. You may be a desirable buyer, or you may be selling desirable goods—but how would I know? I don't. Information problems can cause a market to break down, making it hard for you to buy what you want and for sellers to connect with the right buyers.

Our task in this chapter is figuring out how best to do business when buyers or sellers have information that the other side can't easily get. We'll assess how to make the best choices possible in the face of this information imbalance. And we will develop some strategies to restore the transparency and trust needed to help you do business. You'll be better able to negotiate an employment relationship that works well for you and your manager, become a savvier shopper, and get the best possible price on insurance. We'll proceed in three parts. First, we'll assess what happens when sellers know something about their goods that buyers don't. Next, we'll evaluate what happens when buyers know something about themselves that sellers don't. Finally, we'll analyse what happens when actions can't be observed. By the end of this chapter you'll have all the information you need to make good choices even when you don't have all the information you want.

Chapter Objective

Learn how to make decisions when you don't have all the facts.

19.1 Adverse Selection When Sellers Know More Than Buyers

Discover how sellers' private information can reduce the quality of goods offered for sale and distort market outcomes.

19.2 Adverse Selection When Buyers Know More Than Sellers

Discover how buyers' private information can drive up sellers' costs and distort market outcomes.

19.3 Moral Hazard: The Problem of Hidden Actions

Understand how incentives, monitoring, and task design can help improve outcomes when actions are hidden.

19.1 Adverse Selection When Sellers Know More Than Buyers

Learning Objective *Discover how sellers' private information can reduce the quality of goods offered for sale and distort market outcomes.*

How do you know who's telling the truth? You might ask your car mechanic if they're honest, and if they are, they'll say, "Yes." But if they're not, they're still probably going to say, "Yes." When the person you're buying a good or service from has information that you don't have, it can be hard to figure out whether to do business with them. **Private information** arises when one party to a transaction knows something the other doesn't. (It's sometimes called *asymmetric information,* because your private information creates an asymmetry between you and them.) In this section, we'll focus on problems that arise when sellers have private information about the quality of their goods. As a buyer in these situations, you'll need to be careful not to get ripped off.

private information When one party to a transaction knows something the other doesn't.

Photo 12/Alamy

Of course I'm a prince!

Hidden Quality and the Risk of Getting a Lemon

If you've ever bought a used car, you've probably wondered what the seller knows about the car—its defects, history, and reliability—that you don't. Buying a used car is risky because you don't know if you're being sold a lemon—a hunk of junk that'll end up having one problem after another. Unfortunately, it's hard to learn about these problems without spending a lot of time with the car.

The problem with buying a used car is that sellers have private information. They've learned from experience whether they have a lemon. They know whether their car breaks down regularly and whether they drove it in ways that can lead to costly maintenance down the line—like braking or accelerating too rapidly.

Konstantinos Moraitis/Alamy

Is it a lemon?

As a buyer, you don't have this information. You can't tell whether the car you're looking at is a lemon or not. But you do know there's a risk it's a lemon. That's why the amount that buyers are willing to pay for a used car is lower than it would be if they could be sure that it's of high quality. When buyers can't tell the difference between lemons and high-quality cars, both lemons and high-quality cars will sell for the same price. After all, if buyers can't tell the difference, how can sellers charge different prices? In turn, this means that lemons will sell for more than they would if buyers could tell them apart, and high-quality cars will sell for less than they would if their buyers could discern their quality.

The amount that buyers are willing to pay for cars of unknown quality also affects what kinds of cars sellers will offer for sale. To see how, let's fast forward a couple of years to explore the types of decisions you might make as a potential seller in the used-car market.

Sellers of high-quality goods may choose to not sell. Perhaps, after you graduate, you get a job in an urban area in another part of the country with good public transportation. You don't need a car to get to work and moving your car across the country will be costly. You wonder if you should sell your car. Importantly, you know that it's in excellent condition and that you've taken great care of it. But when you go to sell it, buyers can't tell that it's not a lemon. As a result, they'll offer you a low price for your car. You compare the price you can get for it, with its alternative value to you. A road trip to your new city sounds fun, and while you don't need a car, it would be convenient. When you compare the benefit to you of having a high-quality car with the small amount you could get by selling it, you decide to keep the car. When potential sellers like you—people looking to offload a high-quality car—decide not to sell because they can't get a price high enough to offset what the car is worth to them, there are fewer high-quality cars offered in the used-car market.

Sellers of lemons are more likely to sell. Now consider the same scenario, except this time consider the choice you'll make if you know that your car is a lemon. It burns through oil and you can feel the transmission slipping from time to time. This car's not worth much to you—you don't trust it to drive across the country to your new location and you figure that you'll spend more time keeping it running than using it to do errands. When you go to sell it, buyers can't tell that it's a lemon. When they ask you why you're selling, you'll probably tell them that you're moving for a new job and don't need a car anymore. After all, these things are true! And while you know that you should, you don't mention that it's a lemon, perhaps convincing yourself that maybe it'll be ok for the next buyer.

Buyers aren't sure whether your car is high-quality or a lemon, but it could be high quality, so they'll offer more than they would pay if they knew it was a lemon for sure. You think these offers are great—after all, you're offloading a lemon! That means that the price they are willing to pay is above what the car is worth to you, so you accept the offer. When sellers like you—people looking to offload an unreliable car—decide to sell because the price is higher than the value of a lemon, there will be more lemons available in the used-car market.

Adverse selection of sellers can cause the market to collapse. Putting these two insights together—that owners of lemons get a high price compared to what the car is actually worth, and owners of high-quality cars get a low price compared to what the car is actually worth—means that lemons are more likely to be offered for sale in the used-car market than otherwise would be there if everyone had the same information. As a result, you're more likely to encounter a lemon at a used-car dealership than in an ordinary car park. This is known as **adverse selection of sellers**—the tendency for the mix of goods offered for sale to be skewed toward more low-quality goods when buyers can't observe quality. It's *selection* because the sellers get to choose what's offered for sale, and it's *adverse* because they're more likely to offer low-quality goods.

Figure 1 | Adverse Selection of Sellers

The tendency for the mix of goods to be skewed toward more low-quality goods when buyers can't observe quality.

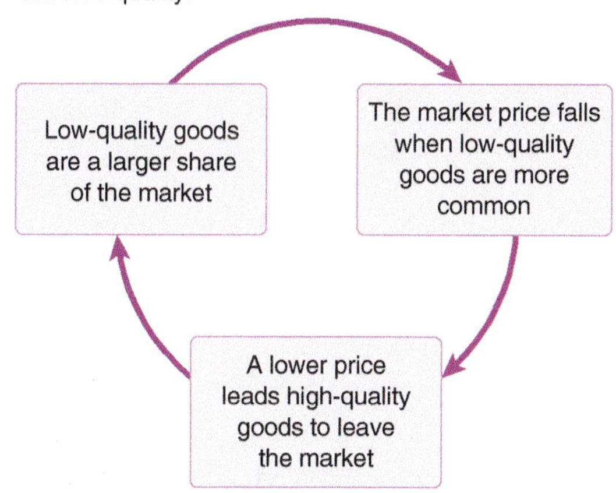

Key example: Lemons in the used-car market.

Figure 1 highlights the problem with adverse selection of sellers. The risk of buying low-quality goods reduces the price that buyers will pay, this lower market price leads sellers to offer fewer high-quality goods, which means that the mix of goods sold includes more low-quality goods. And these effects are self-reinforcing, as the fact that low-quality goods are a higher share of the market drives the price down even further, which causes more high-quality goods to exit.

This is sometimes called the *adverse selection death spiral,* because this cycle can continue until there's nothing left in the market but low-quality goods. When that happens the market price will be the price for lemons, and only lemons will be sold. For example, how many real Rolexes or Coach bags do you think are sold on Facebook Marketplace? Knockoffs are so prevalent that buyers are only willing to pay prices so low that no seller would supply authentic merchandise. It's a market for fakes only.

adverse selection of sellers The tendency for the mix of goods to be skewed toward more low-quality goods when buyers can't observe quality.

Do the Economics

To see how all this works, let's analyse the used-car market in a bit more detail. We'll see how the prices buyers are willing to pay help determine which cars get sold, and how that then feeds back into the prices that buyers are willing to pay.

Let's start with the buyers. In this example, let's say that buyers value lemons at \$2,000, they value good cars at \$12,000, and buyers are risk-neutral (which means they're indifferent to risk).

What price will buyers be willing to pay if 20% of the cars offered for sale are lemons?

Start by figuring out the value of a used car on average. Since 20% are lemons, and those cars are worth \$2,000 to buyers, while 80% are high-quality cars they value at \$12,000:

$$\text{Value to buyer of used car on average} = 20\% \times \$2{,}000 + 80\% \times \$12{,}000 = \$10{,}000$$

Now let's consider the sellers. 100 people are considering selling their cars. 20 have lemons, which they would sell for as little as \$2,000. 30 have a high-quality car that they need to sell, so they'd sell it if offered at least $5,000. (At lower prices, they'll decide to give it to a relative instead.) And 50 have a high-quality car but they don't really need to sell their car, so they'll sell it only if they're offered a price of at least $11,000.

What share of all used cars are lemons?

20 lemons out of 100 cars = 20% of cars are lemons

If buyers are willing to pay $10,000 for a used car, as we found above, what fraction of cars offered for sale will be lemons?

There will be 20 sellers of lemons, and 30 sellers who have a high-quality car that they need to sell. (The other 50 people with high-quality cars will choose not to sell since the price is less than the $11,000 needed to induce them to sell.)

Share which are lemons = 20/(20 + 30) = 20/50 = 40%

Let's see how buyers will respond.

If 40% of cars offered for sale are lemons, what price will risk-neutral buyers be willing to pay for a used car?

Value of used car on average = 40% × $2,000 + 60% × $12,000 = $8,000

At this price the used-car market stabilises with buyers willing to pay up to $8,000 and 40% of the cars offered for sale are lemons.

Extension: What if 75% of all used cars are lemons, what will happen?

Buyers: Value of used car on average = 75% × $2,000 + 25% × $12,000 = $4,500

Sellers: Only sellers of lemons will offer their car for sale.

Buyer response: If 100% of cars are lemons, price = $2,000

In the first example, the market stabilises at a price of $8,000 which is lower than the value of the average used car. Lemons are overrepresented among the used cars offered for sale, but some high-quality cars are still sold. However, in the extension the large number of lemons ends up driving all the high-quality cars out of the market. Since buyers can't distinguish between lemons and high-quality cars, the used-car market collapses, and the only cars sold are lemons. ■

EVERYDAY Economics **Why you should consider buying a used car from a relative or friend**

Holly Bickerton/Alamy Stock Photo

It may not be cool, but at least you know it's not a lemon.

The problem with the used-car market is that you can't sell a high-quality used car for what it's actually worth. That means that if a family member or close friend—indeed, anyone you can trust—is thinking of selling their car, you can get a great deal. Even if you pay your sister more than the prevailing price in the used-car market, you benefit from knowing that she would likely tell you the truth if the car was a lemon. This is why good-quality used cars are often kept in the family or sold to friends. These sales benefit both sides: If you buy from your sister, she can charge you a fair price given the condition of the car; and you get the comfort of knowing you're driving a reliable car. Buying from people you trust helps solve the lemons problem. ■

Adverse Selection and Your Ability to Buy High-Quality Products

So far we've seen that when quality is hard to observe, sellers are more likely to supply goods they know to be of lower quality. This in turn reduces the price that buyers are willing to pay, which leads more sellers of high-quality goods to leave the market.

The result is a market failure in which the forces of supply and demand lead to an inefficient outcome. The failure is that many people will be unable to buy or sell some products—particularly high-quality products—even when the marginal benefit to buyers of purchasing a high-quality product exceeds the marginal cost to sellers of supplying it. There are buyers who would benefit if they could find a reliable seller of high-quality products, and they're willing to pay a good price for one. Sellers of high-quality products would also benefit if they could find a buyer willing to pay a good price for their product. But they won't be able to sell them at a price that reflects their products' high-quality, because buyers can't tell that they're not getting a lemon. That makes buyers reluctant to pay the high price needed to get a high-quality product. Buyers are right to be worried because suppliers can trick them into buying a lemon. The problem is that buyers can't be sure they'll get the right product. When sellers know more than buyers about quality, mistrust makes the market function poorly, leading it to fail to work for many buyers and sellers.

Adverse selection problems can arise whenever sellers have private information. The lemons problem is not just about used cars. Far from it! It can occur whenever there's an information gap in which sellers know more than buyers. As a buyer, you'll need to watch out for adverse selection problems so that you know what you're getting. Here are a few real-world examples:

- You want to buy a Tiffany bracelet online, but how do you know if it's a fake? eBay shoppers demand a discount because they suspect some bracelets are fakes, but this discounted price makes those with authentic Tiffany bracelets reluctant to sell. As a result fakes become relatively more prevalent, which explains why Tiffany discovered 70% of products labelled Tiffany for sale on eBay were fake.
- You want to buy health supplements, but how do you know what's really in the capsules? Suppliers who use cheap fillers instead of promised ingredients will be more profitable at lower prices, shifting the mix of sellers toward those with fake products. In recent years Chinese authorities have cracked down on counterfeit products and raked in large hauls of popular Australian-branded vitamins, as well as wines and cosmetics, that were fakes.
- You want to buy wild salmon, but how do you know if the fish is wild or if it's even salmon? Since consumers can't tell when cheaper fish are masquerading as more expensive fish, imposters are offered for sale, but that drives down prices. Low prices then make it harder for fishing vessels to profitably supply genuine wild salmon. Oceana, an advocacy group, tested the DNA of over 1,000 seafood samples from hundreds of retail outlets in America and found that a third weren't what they said they were.
- You may want to invest your money by buying shares in a company. But be careful: Corporate executives are more willing to issue new shares when they believe their company's share price is overvalued. Since buyers tend to know less than the company's executives, they have a hard time telling if this stock is overvalued. This drives down the price buyers are willing to pay. These low prices discourage undervalued or correctly valued companies from issuing shares. As a result, new stock issues are disproportionately made up of overvalued companies.

James Baigrie/Getty Images

Can you tell which one is wild salmon?

The problem in each of these situations isn't simply that some products are higher quality than others—it's that buyers can't accurately evaluate quality when they make their purchase, but sellers can. This reduces how much buyers are willing to pay, which drives out some high-quality sellers, leaving a larger share of low-quality sellers. If the adverse selection problem is bad enough, the market will consist of only suppliers of low-quality products.

James D. Morgan/Getty Images

But the website said this was a nice hotel.

Be sceptical, especially when the price seems too good to be true. As a buyer, you won't always know how many low-quality sellers there are. Many people use

Solutions:

1. Buyers can learn from third-party verifiers.
2. Sellers can signal their product's quality.
3. Government can increase information or weed out low-quality goods.

price as an indicator of the likely quality. When a price seems too good to be true, it probably is! Low prices are often an indicator that there are a lot of low-quality goods and services in the market. But be careful: A high price doesn't mean something is high quality. If choosing a high price made you think that something was high quality, then sellers of low-quality goods would simply set a high price to try to fool you. You can't trust a price to tell you about quality when it's otherwise unobservable.

Solutions to Adverse Selection of Sellers

Thankfully, there are ways to address the adverse selection problems that can arise when sellers have private information. When you're a seller, these solutions can help you provide better information that can make buyers more comfortable buying your product. And when you're a buyer, these solutions can help you tell high- and low-quality products apart.

Third-party verifiers can help you spot a lemon.

Solution one: Buyers can learn from third-party verifiers. As we've seen, an information gap can be costly to both buyers and sellers. This points to a business opportunity for savvy entrepreneurs to try to bridge that gap. For example, CarHistory is a web-based company that checks tens of thousands of sources to learn a car's ownership history, maintenance records, and whether a car has ever been in an accident. While it would be difficult for an individual buyer to do this on their own, a trusted independent third party like CarHistory can help solve adverse selection problems by reliably and efficiently gathering and sharing that information. This is an example of a business operating as a third-party verifier, reducing the amount of private information held only by sellers. Third-party verifiers gather credible information and make it available to potential buyers, thereby making it easier for them to identify high-quality products.

Third-party verifiers can help shoppers learn about the quality of products. Your mechanic is another resource—a third-party verifier—who can give you expert information about the current state of a car you're thinking of buying. When you're buying a used car, it's a good idea to do both—check a third-party report like CarHistory and get it inspected by your mechanic.

Third-party verifiers exist for many goods. Choice collects customer reviews and reports on their quality, giving information about the reliability of everything from dishwashers to solar panels. The Shanghai ARWU ranks universities using data that would be difficult for prospective students to gather on their own. Moody's rates the creditworthiness of companies looking to borrow money, so you know which corporate bonds are safest.

Other organisations provide certifications that reveal useful information about workers in professional services. For instance, if you want to find a financial advisor who's knowledgeable and has your best interests at heart, then you can look to the Financial Planning Association of Australia, who certify only qualified financial advisers who commit to not taking any kickbacks for recommending specific investments.

Ann Kirby-Payne

Don't say you weren't warned.

Third-party verifiers can help shoppers learn about the experiences of past customers. Some third-party verifiers aggregate the experiences of past customers. The internet has made it easier for you to share your experiences, and many companies are using it to help buyers figure out which sellers offer high-quality goods and services. Companies like Yelp, TripAdvisor, and Amazon provide customer ratings and reviews of products and services. When potential buyers have easy access to the experiences of past customers, there's a stronger incentive to treat your customers well, because a reputation for providing shoddy products will quickly catch up with you.

Solution two: Sellers can signal their product's quality. Actions speak louder than words, particularly when there's private information. Sellers can't simply tell you about how great their products are, because why should you believe them? But sometimes they can reveal their private information by taking a costly action. A **signal** is an action taken to credibly convey private information. In Chapter 12 we analysed how education can be a useful way for workers to credibly signal to employers that they are capable and tenacious workers. Private information is a problem in the labour market because workers (who are sellers of labour) know how capable and tenacious they are, but buyers (that is, employers) don't. An employer can't figure this out just by asking, because no one in a job interview ever responds by saying "thanks for asking, because really, I'm neither capable nor tenacious." So employers rely instead on actions—like earning a degree—which signal that information.

signal A costly action taken to credibly convey private information.

There are all sorts of signals that sellers can use to convey their true quality. A useful signal helps you differentiate good products from bad ones. However, in order for a signal to work, it must be meaningfully costlier for sellers of low-quality products to send the signal than for sellers of high-quality goods to do so. That way, only the high-quality sellers will choose to send the signal.

For example, a car dealer who wants to signal that they're selling high-quality used cars, will offer a warranty—paying for any needed repairs for the first few years after the purchase. Such a warranty is costlier for people selling lemons. If offering a warranty is too costly for those with lemons to offer, then high-quality used cars might come with warranties, while lemons won't. For similar reasons, a person trying to sell you their high-quality used car might show you maintenance records, offer to pay for a mechanic's inspection, and give you a CarHistory report.

Signals like this help buyers discern whether they're being offered lemons or high-quality products. They're reliable only when sellers of high-quality products are much more likely to find it worthwhile to send the signal. This will lead to a price difference between those products in which the seller credibly signals high-quality and those in which the seller doesn't. For example, cars with warranties sell for more than cars without. Importantly, this price difference reflects not just the value of the warranty, but also the fact that the warranty signals to buyers that this is a high-quality car. As long as it's too expensive for an owner of a lemon to offer the warranty, then the presence or absence of a warranty effectively tells you whether you're considering a high-quality used car or a lemon.

Solution three: Government can increase information or weed out low-quality goods. Government policy can help in three ways. The first is by providing information directly to buyers; the second is by giving sellers an incentive to reveal truthful information; and the third is by regulating quality, and therefore keeping sellers of the lowest-quality products out of the market.

Government reveals information. Have you ever wondered if it was worthwhile to buy organic produce? Before you answer, think about whether you can tell whether the "organic" produce you're being sold is actually grown organically. For many years it was virtually impossible. But then private bodies acting as "certification clubs" sprang up. There are also "truth in labelling" requirements enforced by the Australian Department of Agriculture.

Government creates incentives for sellers to reveal private information. The government can also help close the information gap between buyers and sellers by giving sellers an incentive to reveal what they know. For instance, when you sell your house, the law requires you to reveal any problems that you're aware of—such as a roof that needs to be replaced or asbestos that needs to be removed. There are also consumer protection laws and requirements for real estate agents to disclose all "material facts" that might be relevant to a purchaser. In one legal case, the purchasers got the contract rescinded and the real estate agent was fined $10,000 for failing to disclose a triple murder on the premises.

Byron Hirsch/EyeEm/Getty Images

Would you want to buy a house with a chilling past?

Government can outlaw the lowest-quality product. There may be situations where it's best to simply eliminate low-quality sellers. For instance, you probably don't want a doctor who doesn't know anything about medicine. That's why many types of jobs—including medicine—require an occupational licence in order to ensure a minimum quality of service. Similarly, various state and federal laws—and government authorities—set minimum quality levels for some products, with the aim of effectively eliminating low-quality products from the market. If suppliers aren't allowed to sell low-quality products, then their private information, and hence the problem of adverse selection, disappears.

19.2 Adverse Selection When Buyers Know More Than Sellers

Learning Objective *Discover how buyers' private information can drive up sellers' costs and distort market outcomes.*

You've now seen what happens when sellers know something that buyers don't. Now it's time to turn the tables and explore what happens when buyers know something sellers don't. It turns out that this information gap creates similar problems, but in this case, it's buyers who are adversely selected. Instead of too few high-quality goods, the problem in this case is the quality of the customers.

How does customer "quality" vary? Some customers cost the seller less than others. For example, customers who borrow money differ in their likelihood of paying it back. Loaning money to someone who pays it back on time is less costly than loaning money to someone who must be hounded to make a payment. People looking to rent on Airbnb differ in how neat and tidy they will be as well as in their likelihood of doing damage to the property. Thus, some renters are lower cost than others. And in the health insurance market, healthy people are lower cost compared to unhealthy people who are going to require a lot of medical care. The problem for suppliers is that the customers have private information—they know whether they're likely to be high cost or low cost—while the seller can't tell. Let's investigate how this shapes the market.

Hidden Quality and the Risk of Getting High-Cost Customers

Justin James is the CEO of HIF—a not-for-profit Australian health insurer. Because HIF is a nonprofit, his goal is simply to take in enough in payments to cover the medical costs of the people he insures. He could have his team of researchers find out average annual medical expenditures in his area so that he can sell insurance at a price a smidge above average spending on medical care. For instance, if average annual medical expenses not covered by Medicare in Australia are $2,000 per person, he hopes to sell health insurance for a smidge above $2,000, so that he can also cover his overheads.

Justin Wolfers

Giving birth in a private hospital costs about $8,500 and that's if everything goes as planned.

People expecting a lot of health care costs will pay more for insurance. While James only knows the average medical expenditures in Australia, it turns out that his potential customers know some things that he doesn't. Some of his customers know they're genetically predisposed to cancer, some suspect that they are developing diabetes, and others are planning on getting pregnant. These potential customers have private information that they're each likely to have higher-than-average medical expenses. If James sells HIF insurance policies at the cost of average medical care expenses, those policies will be a great deal for these customers! Anyone expecting higher-than-average costs will be excited to sign up for health care coverage from HIF.

People expecting few health care costs will pay less for insurance. There are other people who know that their health is good. They're young, they're fit, and they drive safely. Sure, anyone can get cancer, and accidents happen, but these people don't expect to be costly clients. Healthy people value insurance, but if their expected health care costs are only $500 per year, they question whether private insurance priced at the community average cost of $2,000 per year is really worth it. They'd be willing to pay something for health insurance, but they're willing to buy insurance only if it's relatively cheap—something closer to the average medical expenses for healthy people like them. That means that for some of these healthier people, when insurance is priced at the community average medical expense, it's too expensive to be worthwhile for them. As a result, they won't buy private health insurance. As we will see later, the government can affect this calculus. One way is by providing the Australian Private Health Insurance Rebate, which covers nearly 25% of the cost of insurance for singles under the age of 65 earning less than $90,000 a year.

Adverse selection of buyers can cause the market to collapse. If James can't figure out who is likely to have high or low medical expenses, he'll charge everyone the same price for health insurance: a smidge above $2,000, the community average cost. But then some healthy people won't want to buy health insurance, while those who are most likely to need expensive medical procedures will see it as a good deal. This leads to a larger share of customers having high health insurance costs compared to the community average. This is known as **adverse selection of buyers**—the tendency for the mix of buyers to be skewed toward more high-cost buyers when buyers have private information about their likely costs. This problem arises because of private information—people buying insurance know things about their health that sellers do not. And in this case, James's customers are *adversely* selected—the folks who are going to cost him the most in medical bills are the ones who are most likely to buy health insurance from him.

adverse selection of buyers The tendency for the mix of buyers to be skewed toward more high-cost buyers when sellers don't know buyers' type.

If James could differentiate among people's likely health care costs, he would just offer a low-price insurance contract to people who are healthy—because they're likely to have lower medical-care costs on average—and a high-price contract to those who will likely have high medical expenses. But because he doesn't know, he has to charge everyone the same price. Adverse selection of buyers is a problem for sellers, because it means you won't get the (low-cost) customers you want.

Figure 2 shows how the problem occurs. The problem is that buyers know something sellers don't, and they use that information to their advantage. Because some low-cost people choose not to buy health insurance, the average amount James ends up paying out in health care costs is above the community average. So he needs to charge higher prices to break even. But higher prices lead more people to opt out—particularly those who expect to have moderately low health care costs. This once again means he pays out more than he has charged people on average. And this cycle can be self-reinforcing.

In fact, insurance companies can face an *adverse selection death spiral,* where they charge more in an effort to break even, but that causes even more people who are likely to be relatively low-cost to stop buying health insurance, and that in turn raises their average payouts. Sometimes the spiral doesn't end until only the very highest-cost buyers are left.

Figure 2 | Adverse Selection of Buyers

The tendency for the mix of buyers to be skewed toward more high-cost customers when sellers don't know buyers' type.

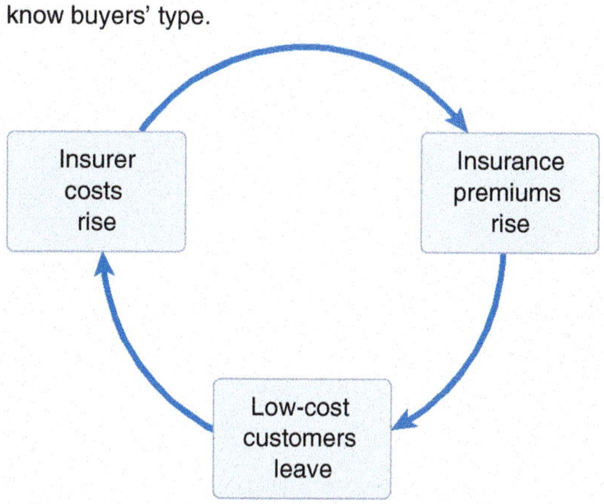

Key example: Private health insurance death spiral.

Adverse selection makes it hard for some people to buy the products they want. As a buyer, if you have private information that you're likely to be a low-cost customer—you're healthy and unlikely to need expensive medical care—you may not be able to find insurance that is fairly priced for you. The problem is that insurance companies can't tell the difference between you and unhealthy higher-cost customers, and therefore must charge you a higher price because they're worried that you're a high-cost customer. This higher price may lead you to decide not to buy insurance.

The result is a market failure. The fact that some people don't buy insurance doesn't mean that they wouldn't benefit from insurance. Even relatively healthy people want to be insured. And insurance companies would love to sell more insurance policies, especially to low-cost customers. The problem is that the insurance company can't offer low-cost customers a policy that would be attractive to them without also attracting so many high-cost customers as to render those policies unprofitable. Adverse selection in insurance markets pushes prices up, which causes many low-cost buyers to be unable to find insurance that makes sense for them.

Shared ignorance is bliss in insurance markets. The problems of adverse selection depend on how large the information gap is between buyers and sellers. For instance, you don't have much private information about the likelihood of a robbery or an electrical fire at your house. The likelihood that you will file a claim is largely determined by factors such as how dangerous your neighbourhood is, how old your house is, and what materials were used in the construction. Since insurers are able to learn this information, they can tailor the price of your homeowners insurance to your specific circumstances. You don't have much private information, so your best guess as to the how likely you are to have an electrical fire is similar to the insurance company's best guess. As a result, adverse selection isn't as much of a problem in the market for homeowners' insurance. But note that insurance works best when neither side knows how likely it is that the insured event will happen.

Letting people opt back into insurance when they need it worsens adverse selection. This insight that insurance markets work best when there is very little private information explains why there are often limits on when you can opt into or out of insurance. For instance, if you could purchase fire insurance as soon as you smelled smoke, then only people whose houses were already on fire would buy insurance. That's the sort of risk no insurer will take on, leading the market to collapse. To prevent people from exploiting their informational advantage, there are often rules that limit the ability of buyers to opt into insurance once they have more information.

This is a big issue in the health insurance market. If customers could opt out of health insurance when they're healthy, and then opt back in as soon as they got sick, insurance companies would end up with only customers who are sick and require expensive treatment. This worsens adverse selection problems. And it explains why we have a system in Australia called "lifetime community rating." This effectively makes it more and more expensive to buy private health insurance for the first time after the age of 31. This reduces the incentive to opt in only after your risk increases, and so it limits adverse selection. This logic also explains why BUPA, one of Australia's largest private health insurers, has a 12 month waiting period for preexisting conditions and pregnancy and birth related services—and three years for laser eye surgery. If everyone must buy insurance, then insurers no longer need to worry about buyers opting in to insurance only when they're sick.

Risk aversion may help undo some of the problems of adverse selection. Most people don't like to take gambles, particularly with their health. They're risk averse, which means that they dislike uncertainty and will often pay to avoid it. Risk-averse people will pay more than the actuarially fair price for insurance, meaning that they will pay more than they expect to get back on average. They help insurance markets function because, by being willing to pay more, insurance companies can sell policies to some risk-averse, healthy customers even though they have private information that they'll likely be lower cost on average. This helps limit adverse selection.

Adverse selection problems can arise in any market where buyers have private information. The adverse selection problem extends well beyond insurance markets. Indeed, the central insight here is that whenever buyers have private information about their likely costs, your business will find it hard to get the customers you want. Low-cost customers are more likely to decide what you're selling is too expensive, while high-cost customers are more likely to see it as a great deal. Here are a few real-world examples:

- Life insurance companies—which offer your loved ones a payout if you were to die—may find that people who don't take good care of their health are more likely to purchase life insurance.
- Car insurance companies may find that people who drive the most recklessly are the most interested in buying a lot of collision protection.
- An entrepreneur trying to offer divorce insurance may discover that only people whose marriages are on the rocks are interested in purchasing it.
- Landlords may find that people who are financially irresponsible and not interested in taking good care of their living space are the most interested in renting rather than buying a place to live.
- Restaurant managers may find that people with really large appetites are the most interested in the all-you-can-eat buffet.

These are all situations in which you might not get the customers that you want. As a buyer, these are also instances where you might not be able to buy what you want. You may prefer the variety of a buffet, but if the enormous appetite of your university's football team has pushed the price up, paying that much might not make sense given your small appetite.

So what can you do about it? Let's now turn to considering solutions to adverse selection among buyers.

Solutions to Adverse Selection of Buyers

Thankfully, there are ways to address the adverse selection problems that arise when buyers have private information. These solutions can help you get more information about your customers—helping you tell high- and low-cost customers apart.

> Solutions:
> 1. Sellers can use information that is related to buyers' likely costs.
> 2. Sellers can offer different contracts so that buyers separate themselves.
> 3. Government can increase information, offer subsidies, enforce mandates, or provide insurance.

Solution one: Sellers can use information that is related to buyers' likely costs. Insurance companies are always on the lookout for buyers exploiting their private information. That's why they ask you so many questions before telling you how much your policy will cost or whether they will even offer you one at all. Car insurers use your age, your gender, your marital status, your credit rating, your car's safety rating, where you live, and of course, your driving record. Similarly, health insurance companies will ask whether you smoke or exercise. But the law limits the characteristics they can use. For instance, it is illegal to charge men and women different prices for health insurance even though they can have very different medical expenses.

This explains why car rental agencies won't rent to you if you're under a certain age—they're worried you'll be a high-cost customer, perhaps more likely to crash the car. Holiday rentals may specify "families only," effectively rejecting unrelated groups of people—that is, groups of friends—because they figure that friends are more likely to throw a party that trashes the place. And health insurance companies charge a lot more to smokers, figuring that they're the customers most likely to face high medical costs.

Solution two: Sellers can offer different contracts so that buyers separate themselves. One way to get the customers you want is to offer a product that only low-cost customers will want. For instance, insurers are sometimes able to differentiate between high- and low-risk customers by varying the size of the deductible. A *deductible* is the amount you pay out of pocket before insurance kicks in. For example, your travel insurance might require you pay for the first $200 of lost-luggage expenses—that's the deductible—and it will pay any expenses beyond that.

An insurance policy with a large deductible will only be attractive to people who think it's unlikely they'll need to file a claim. As a result, these policies attract low-cost customers.

And that in turn means that insurance companies can offer these high-deductible plans at particularly low prices. By contrast, the high-cost people who believe they're likely to file a lot of claims will want a low deductible. Thus, when people choose the low-deductible plan, they're effectively revealing their private information—their choice to opt for a low deductible reveals to the insurance company that they expect to be high-cost customers. In turn, this lets the insurance company know that they'll need to charge a lot more for those plans. This explains why you typically pay a lot more for insurance plans with low deductibles.

This leads to some advice: If you think you're a low-cost customer who is unlikely to need to file a claim, you'll often get a much better deal if you choose the insurance plan with a high deductible. But realise that this doesn't completely solve the problem of adverse selection. In order to get the good deal, you have to risk some of your own money—if something goes wrong, you'll have to pay a high deductible—which means that you're only partly insured.

Some managers use a related approach, bundling their products with something that only low-cost customers will want. For instance, if you think that parents eat less at a buffet than university students, then it might be worth providing Lego sets for kids to play with. Those Lego sets will attract more families to your restaurant, which is profitable because they're your low-cost customers.

EVERYDAY Economics **Will you soon pay more if you are a bad driver?**

For decades, insurers have charged young people much higher rates for car insurance. Their logic is that some young people take more risks behind the wheel and get in more accidents. But not all young people are bad drivers, and if you're a good driver you might feel that you deserve a better deal. The problem is private information. Insurers don't know if you're a good or bad driver, so they have to charge you a price that accounts for the risk you're a bad driver. But what if your car insurer could use technology to close this information gap?

Some car insurers now have programs where you can allow them to track your driving—in many cases, using a simple phone app. Why would you want an insurance company tracking your movements? It's simple: If the data they collect show that you're a safe driver, they'll offer you cheaper insurance. This also helps insurance companies figure out who the bad drivers are—they're the people who won't sign up to use the app.

It's worth thinking about where this will lead. As fewer good drivers buy unmonitored car insurance, insurers will need to raise prices on unmonitored insurance to cover the higher average costs of covering mainly bad drivers. Those higher prices will push more good drivers into using the monitoring app. Eventually only bad drivers will be left buying unmonitored car insurance. At that point, insurance companies have app-related data to identify the good drivers, and they can also identify the bad drivers, because they're the ones refusing to use the app. The insurance company can use this information to offer prices tailored to each person's driving skill. As a result, technology that reduces the adverse selection of buyers will lead to lower prices for good drivers and higher prices for bad drivers. ■

Solution three: Government can increase information or directly reduce adverse selection. The government can help solve adverse selection problems in insurance markets in four ways: By providing incentives for buyers to reveal their private information, by subsidising insurance, by mandating that everyone buys insurance, and by providing insurance directly.

Government creates incentives for buyers to reveal private information. The government can give people an incentive to tell the truth, thereby revealing private information.

If you lie to an insurance company, that's called insurance fraud, and it's a crime. The government helps the insurance market work by ensuring that the insurance company can count on buyers to tell the truth. You won't be asked if you expect to die soon, since it would be hard for anyone to ever prove if you're lying. But insurers often ask if you're a smoker, if you use drugs, or if you have dangerous hobbies like skydiving. The threat of punishment for lying helps ensure that you tell the truth. And your truthful answers to these questions reduce the extent of private information, thereby limiting adverse selection.

Government can subsidise insurance. The government can also subsidise insurance so that it's a good deal for more people. The idea is that if you're only paying part of the cost of health insurance, you're more likely to buy it. That inducement might lead more healthy or low-cost customers to buy health insurance, reducing adverse selection. To reduce the burden on Medicare, the Australian government provides a bunch of carrots and sticks to get you to purchase private health insurance. If you earn above $180,000 and don't buy private health insurance you pay an extra 1% in taxes (scaling up to 1.5% for family incomes above $280,000). But there is also a tax rebate for buying private health insurance.

Government can require everyone to buy insurance. The government can eliminate adverse selection by requiring everyone to buy insurance. When the government forces everyone to buy insurance, sellers no longer have to worry that only the high-cost customers will buy it, and so there's no pressure to set higher prices. The information gap between buyers and sellers still exists, but buyers can't exploit it to their advantage because they don't get to choose whether to buy insurance. This is why most states require that all drivers have compulsory third-party (CTP) insurance "greenslips," and it helps keep the price down.

Government can provide insurance. Finally, the government can ensure that everyone has insurance by providing the insurance itself, making sure to provide it to everyone who qualifies. When the government offers insurance, your taxes usually cover the cost. As long as everyone in a specific group is covered by the government-provided insurance, there's no adverse selection problem because no one can opt out. The government directly provides health insurance to Australians through Medicare. Beyond health insurance, the government also provides unemployment benefits to protect you against job loss, the NDIS that insures you against a disabling injury or disease, and the aged pension that insures you against outliving your savings.

So far, we've analysed two types of private information, exploring what happens when sellers know something that buyers don't (that was the lemons problem), and in this section, what happens when buyers know something sellers don't. Our final task is to explore what happens when your actions can't be observed, meaning they can't be contracted on.

19.3 Moral Hazard: The Problem of Hidden Actions

Learning Objective *Understand how incentives, monitoring, and task design can help improve outcomes when actions are hidden.*

A famous economist once said "nobody in the history of the world ever washed a rental car." He was joking, but only kind of. This aphorism highlights the concept of **moral hazard**. When people's actions are not observable (i.e., "hidden") then they will act in their own self-interest. And that might not be good for the people they are interacting with. This idea goes well beyond dirty rental cars. The 2008 Financial Crisis was caused in part by Wall Street creating "mortgage-backed securities" where the people lending

moral hazard The actions you take because they are not fully observable and you are partially insulated from their consequences.

money to homeowners didn't have a big stake in whether the loans got repaid. This led to lots of bad loans being written to people who couldn't pay their mortgages.

The basic insight that when people don't bear all the consequences of their actions they tend to be less careful is familiar to anyone who has ever bought insurance. But the concept of moral hazard is much broader than that. Moral hazard occurs any time somebody is insulated from the full consequences of their actions.

principal–agent problem The problems that arise when a principal hires an agent to do something on their behalf, but the principal cannot perfectly observe the agent's actions.

The basic framework economists have developed for thinking about the trade-offs involved in this is known as the **principal–agent problem**. It is sometimes also referred to as the moral hazard or *hidden-action* problem. This arises whenever a *principal* (perhaps the owners of a business, or a delegate such as the chief executive) hires an *agent* (perhaps a middle manager, or "shop-floor" worker) to perform a task. These principal–agent problems are everywhere, such as when you hire a lawyer, visit your doctor, or even whenever citizens expect their elected officials to make good decisions that serve the public interest.

The Principal–Agent Problem

If you've ever worked in retail—like a department store—then you've been an agent involved in a principal-agent problem. Your supervisor—either the owner of the store, or more likely your manager if it was a big department store—was the principal. You took some *actions*, like how hard you tried to help customers or how polite you were. At least some (maybe most?) of the time your supervisor wasn't watching every interaction you had with customers. That wouldn't have been a very efficient use of their time. So they didn't know exactly how hard you were working.

Moral hazard can cause you to slack off on the job. Since you're taking this course, I'm betting you were a hard worker who took pride in doing a good job. You had some degree of intrinsic motivation. But let's face it, being really nice to sometimes demanding and annoying customers isn't easy. One way to think of that is that you bore a private cost—a kind of psychic tax—of working hard. The harder you worked the more likely it was that customers would spend more in the store. If your job was anything like mine then you probably got paid a base wage and a commission based on sales.

Why didn't you get paid based on effort? For one thing it's really hard to measure. But on top of that, it's pretty hard to write down in an employment contract. If you disagree about your commission based on sales, you could sue your employer and force them to turn over sales receipts. What would you do if your manager just said at the end of every week: "I don't think you put in much effort, so no bonus for you." There's a reason that "sales commissions" are common but I've never heard of an "effort commission".

Incentives can help make agents work harder. Now put yourself in the shoes of your employer. You're the principal. How should you design the sales commission for your employees? It's helpful to think about the extremes. One extreme is to pay a fixed wage and no commission. How hard would you expect your employees to work? Probably not very hard, right? You will get whatever effort comes from intrinsic motivation, and for some employees that could be quite a lot. But they will probably give up on that difficult customer who wants to try on 11 pairs of shoes and keeps changing their mind back and forth. At the other extreme you could give them all of the profit from sales as a commission. But that would be very expensive for you. And you'd be paying commissions for sales that would have happened anyway. A good salesperson helps, but some sales just happen because customers know what they want to buy already.

The right level of incentives balances risk and reward for the agent. If you're like me you probably think that some "middle-ground" commission is the best way to go. But how big should it be? 5%, 10%, 25%, or more? To figure this out we also need to think about the base wage. Overall—taking account of the base and commissions—you obviously need to pay at least the award wage. But you may want to pay more than that in order to attract better employees. Once you figure out how much you think you need to pay on average, the question is then how much should be in the basic wage and how much in commissions.

Now, the base wage the employee gets for sure. Even if they make no sales. They can count on that amount. The commission offers some upside, but it's risky. The economy might be doing badly, so retail sales could be down all year. In a given week there could be bad weather or a disease outbreak that drives down sales. The employee can't do anything about this.

As we will discuss in Chapter 20, people who are risk averse prefer a sure thing to an uncertain outcome that gives the same amount on average. It's a safe bet that your employee is risk averse. They need to pay rent and buy food. And their landlord doesn't care about how the shoe business in Melbourne is going, they just demand your employee pays the rent.

This points to an important trade-off for your employee. You can give them a perfect safe outcome with a base wage and no commission. This means they bear no risk, but they don't have an extrinsic incentive to work hard. Or you can give them a low base wage and a high rate of commission which gives them big incentives, but imposes lots of risk on them. This trade-off between insurance and incentives is the fundamental driver of how best to structure your employee's pay. In fact, this trade-off is not just true in retail sales with base wages and commissions, it's a general feature of the principal-agent problem and all types of *incentive schemes.* In general incentives aren't limited to commissions. They could include promotions, better working conditions, stock options, or even just not being fired! A way to talk about incentives including all these factors is to say that incentives can be more or less *intense.* In the case of a commission, a higher rate of commission is more intense than a lower rate.

Lesson 1: Incentives should be weaker when agents are more risk averse. The more that your agent dislikes risk, the less closely you should link their pay to volatile outcomes. The same logic implies that when output is a less accurate measure of the agent's action, incentives should be less intense.

This comes from the fundamental trade-off between insurance and incentives. When the agent is more risk averse, or faces a more uncertain environment, it is best for them to bear less risk and have the principal absorb the risk. That's the most cost-effective way for the principal to pay the agent.

Lesson 2: Incentives should be weaker if the agent finds effort more costly. When the agent's cost of effort gets higher and higher it becomes more and more expensive for the principal to motivate the agent to work hard. The principal should give up on trying to get the agent to work very hard to save on the overall wage bill.

Lesson 2 comes from the *marginal principle* and the *opportunity-cost principle.* There are only 24 hours in a day, so as incentives increase, the agent's effort will increase. But the marginal principle tells us that the 9th hour of work is more costly than the 8th hour of work, and the 10th hour more costly than the 9th. If I'm asking the agent to work 20 hours a day they're giving up most of their sleep and all of their leisure time. And that has a really high opportunity cost. So I'm going to have to pay them a huge amount. If the agent has a high marginal cost of effort it's more effective for me to cut back on the incentives and just accept that they won't work very hard, but not overpay.

Lesson 3: Incentives should be more intense when the outcome matters more to the principal. Lesson 3 might seem pretty obvious. When the principal cares more about the outcome, they are willing to pay more to the agent in terms of a performance bonus to get the agent to work harder and increase the likelihood of better outcomes.

Incentive Design with Multiple Tasks

So far, we have focused on situations where the agent performs a single task for the principal. In reality, of course, there are many settings where the agent performs *multiple tasks*. For instance, a principal may want a worker on a manufacturing line to work fast, but also work carefully. In other words, the two tasks are: speed and quality. Companies like Google or Apple might want employees to have lots of ideas, but also to have *good* ideas.

When agents perform two tasks the interactions between them matter. Let's go back to your job as an employee at a retailer. Suppose one day your manager says that there's been lots of shoplifting and that they want you to keep an eye out for suspicious activity while serving other customers. And because they know that incentives are important, they're going to increase your sales commission from 10% to 15% (nice!) but they are also going to deduct losses from shoplifting that show up in the inventory management system (not so nice).

One reaction you might have to this is that it's just like having two versions of the one task you had before—helping customers. But that might not be right. The first issue is whether doing one task has an effect on the difficulty of doing the other task. As a salesperson that is probably the case. Even just keeping an occasional eye out for shoplifters is going to make you less effective at serving your (paying) customers. They probably want your full attention and don't like you looking over their shoulder for shoplifters.

The second issue is that the principal might care about the combination of efforts you put into the tasks. For instance, great customer service is part of what's expected at a high-end retail store. But high-end stores also sell expensive clothes, which makes shoplifting very costly and deterring it very valuable.

Some tasks are easier to measure than others. Another issue with multitasking is that one aspect of the agent's performance might be easier to measure than others. For instance, there's some randomness in what customers buy, but sales are not a bad measure of how good you are at customer service. What about the amount of goods shoplifted? That tells us something about how hard you are working to deter shoplifting. But petty crime waves—like shoplifting—tend to come and go in neighbourhoods. And plenty depends on how well the store security guards and the police are doing at their jobs. It's probably harder to measure how well a salesperson is doing at deterring shoplifting than it is to measure how good their customer service is.

These issues lead us to some additional lessons about multi-task incentive design.

Lesson 4: When one task is hard to measure incentives should be low on both tasks. In fact, it can be optimal to have *no incentives at all*.

Sometimes people think it's a mistake that schoolteachers don't typically get performance bonuses based on their students' test scores. But it actually makes sense not to give teachers performance pay or they might "teach to the test"—focus on standardised test scores to the exclusion of teaching students how to think clearly. In fact, in some school districts in the United States, when high-powered incentives were offered to standardised test scores, that's exactly what happened. Worse, still, in one city a handful of unscrupulous teachers held pizza parties to illegally alter their students' answers on tests from the wrong ones to the right ones!

This bring us to one of the most important lessons of this chapter—people respond to incentives, so be careful what incentives you provide.

This is what economists refer to as the *effort substitution problem*. Providing incentives on one task *crowds out* incentives on the other task. Why? Because the agent shifts (or "substitutes") their effort from the less incentivised task to the more incentivised task.

Lesson 5: The principal should assign complementary tasks to the same agent. One thing the principal can sometimes control is how severe the effort substitution problem is. An important aspect of *job design* is to reduce effort substitution. For example, why is it that most university instructors do both teaching and research? Might it not make more sense for people to specialise in one or the other? Part of the answer lies in the fact that teaching and research are complementary activities. Doing more of one makes an instructor better and more effective at the other. At least up to a point!

Lesson 6: Transparent incentives can sometimes be gamed. If the agent knows more than the principal about which task they find less costly to perform, then very clear incentives will lead the agent to shift effort to their preferred task. If the principal cares about balanced efforts on the tasks then this is bad news. A way to combat gaming is with *opaque* incentive schemes.

There are plenty of situations where we want balanced effort from agents. We would like hospitals to treat patients quickly, but also make sure patients get all the care they need. What good is really fast but ineffective care? In the early 2000s, highly transparent incentive schemes in British hospitals were criticised for being *gamed*—hospitals focused on what they were rewarded for, not necessarily what was best for patients or what the government intended. In fact, more opacity was introduced into incentive schemes for hospitals in the U.K. in response to this.

If you think about it, lots of incentive schemes are opaque. Instructors don't tell you exactly what will be on the exam so you study all the material in the course. Google smudges over the criteria of their search algorithm to deter gaming. And judges often articulate broad *standards* that can be applied to a range of circumstances rather than *bright-line rules* that are susceptible to being gamed. As one famous jurist said of pornography: "I know it when I see it."

Lessons:

1. Incentives should be weaker when agents are more risk averse.
2. Incentives should be weaker if the agent finds effort more costly.
3. Incentives should be more intense when the outcome matters more to the principal.
4. When one task is hard to measure incentives should be low on both tasks.
5. The principal should assign complementary tasks to the same agent.
6. Transparent incentives can sometimes be gamed.

Real World Contracts

Relationships between employers and employees, between a construction company and a homeowner, or between one business and another are typically governed by legally binding contracts. These specify what each side will do and what they will get paid. Importantly, contracts also spell out *how* they get paid. What you've learnt about the principal–agent problem can help you understand why contracts look as they do, and how to bargain for a better contract yourself.

The optimal amount of incentives might be no incentive at all. We have already seen one striking implication of multi-tasking: that incentives may be very low-powered. But there are others. It also speaks to the puzzle of *missing incentive clauses*—the lack of explicit incentive provisions in actual contracts. For instance, when doing home renovations or construction it is not typical for there to be a bonus for timely completion (or penalty for non-timely completion), even though this is clearly an important issue to the homeowner. They may have to live in costly or unsatisfactory rental accommodation, disrupt their and their family's routines, and simply want to live in their own house! Moreover, these clauses *are* typical in commercial construction contracts, so it seems that they can be described to a court.

One reason for this might be that there is greater standardisation in commercial construction, and that important aspects of performance in a non-commercial setting are things like courtesy and advice to the homeowner. But these things are hard to measure. The multi-tasking framework implies that putting high-powered incentives on timely completion would crowd out effort on the more intangible components of performance. A similar argument applies to the absence of piece-rate incentives in manufacturing, when quality is an important but hard-to-measure attribute.

Incentives for employees are often weaker than for contractors. A similar line of argument can help explain why incentives for employees are often quite weak, whereas they tend to be strong for independent contractors. Multi-tasking almost helps explain the very different incentives in franchised versus company-operated stores—such as fast food restaurants. One way to look at this is that there are two basic activities: cost containment and reputation building—with the latter being hard to measure. So, incentives for employees must be muted on the former so as not to crowd out effort on the latter.

Limiting what workers can do is about incentives. A final implication is the presence of *limits on outside activities*. When tasks interact in the agent's cost of effort, the full suite of tasks an agent performs matters for incentive design. It is often the case that some employees have a fair amount of freedom about how they go about their job, whereas others are quite constrained. There are often bans on certain activities for certain employees—such as using the internet for personal purposes at work, or making personal telephone calls. The multi-task framework leads to the idea that *authority* and *responsibility* are complements—and hence are likely to be observed together.

Tying It Together

The magic of supply and demand is that buyers and sellers are both made better off by trading with each other, and market forces ensure that all beneficial trades happen. But a key ingredient in our supply-and-demand framework is good information. Without it, things start to fall apart.

When someone knows things that others don't, the forces of supply and demand are disrupted. If buyers can't tell who is selling high-quality goods, sellers of high-quality goods have less of an incentive to sell them, and buyers may have less interest in the lower-quality goods that end up being available. The result is lower prices and fewer sales. When you can't tell how much each customer will cost you, you will end up with more high-cost customers, driving up your costs. This then causes you to raise your prices, which drives away lower-cost customers. The result is higher prices and fewer sales. And when you want to hire someone, but can't tell how hard they are going to work, you can expect them to do less of what you want. This reduces your willingness to hire people to do things on your behalf. The result is less hiring.

In each of these cases, private information leads to lower quantities bought and sold. Opportunities for mutually beneficial trade or cooperation are lost. In the worst cases, markets can collapse completely. Most of the time though markets don't quite collapse. Instead, they operate less efficiently than if all people were similarly informed.

People holding an informational advantage are not necessarily trying to take advantage of others. Instead, they're simply responding to incentives. Imagine if you woke up this morning and found out that your car insurance had expired. Would you drive more carefully? And if you started spending more time in a high-crime neighbourhood would you tell your car insurer about the increased risk of car theft? If you're selling your car will you 'fess up about all of its problems?

Markets would yield better outcomes if everyone always told the truth and trusted each other. Since information problems pervade so many of our interactions, societies with higher levels of trust often have better-functioning economies. This is also part of why people rely so much on personal networks for everything from jobs to housing to shopping. Inside our personal networks, we face greater pressure to be honest about what we know and to be true to our promises—pressures that reduce the problems of private information.

Beyond trust, improving information or better aligning incentives can help markets function more smoothly—allowing more people to buy and sell what they want. When there is private information, both the private sector and the government can help markets function better by encouraging truth-telling, providing information directly, or creating incentives for the right mix of participants in the market.

To be a savvy shopper in a world full of private information, you need to be on the lookout for what you don't know, understand how it shapes incentives faced by sellers, and take action to fill in your information gaps. And when you're the one with private information, you can make better deals if you find credible ways to signal your qualities or otherwise credibly reveal your private information. Any time you do something that somebody of a worse "type" wouldn't find it in their interests to do, you implicitly reveal yourself to be a better type. That's why going to university not only gives you knowledge and skills, it credibly signals that you like to work hard.

We began this chapter with big differences in information. I knew about moral hazard and adverse selection, and you didn't. We've solved that information problem, and now you have the tools to tackle other information problems you encounter.

Chapter at a Glance

Adverse selection of sellers	Adverse selection of buyers	Moral hazard
The tendency for the mix of goods to be skewed toward more low-quality goods when buyers can't observe quality.	The tendency for the mix of buyers to be skewed toward more high-cost customers when sellers don't know buyers' type.	The actions you take because they are not fully observable and you are partially insulated from their consequences.

When you have private information—you know something others don't—it distorts what's bought and sold.

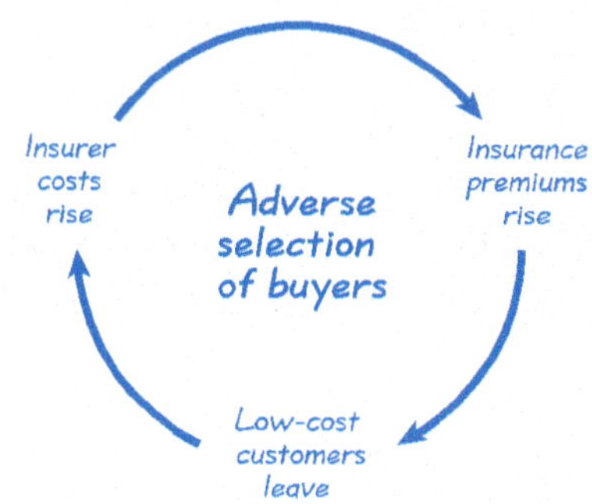

Hidden Information and Action Problems

	Adverse selection of sellers	Adverse selection of buyers	Moral hazard
Source of problem	Buyers don't know the quality of goods.	Sellers don't know how much their buyers will cost them.	Principal doesn't know whether the agent will make unhelpful choices.
Occurs when . . .	Sellers have private information.	Buyers have private information.	The agent's actions are hidden from the principal.
Result	The mix of goods will be skewed toward lower-quality goods.	The mix of buyers will be skewed toward high-cost buyers.	Actions taken by the agent are not in the principal's best interest.
Example	Used-car market	Health insurance	Employee effort at work
Solutions • Improve information • Align incentives • Regulation	1. Buyers can learn from ***third-party verifiers***. 2. Sellers can **signal** their quality. 3. Government can ***increase information*** or ***weed out*** low-quality goods.	1. Sellers can use ***information*** that is related to buyers' likely costs. 2. Sellers can offer different contracts so that buyers ***separate*** themselves. 3. Government can ***increase information*** or directly reduce adverse selection.	1. ***Monitoring*** that provides more information about the actions taken. 2. Provide financial or other ***incentives***. 3. Design an agent's job so that tasks are more ***complementary***. 4. Make incentives ***opaque*** to deter gaming.

Key Concepts

Discussion and Review Questions

Learning Objective 19.1 *Discover how sellers' private information can reduce the quality of goods offered for sale and distort market outcomes.*

1. Go online to eBay, Gumtree, Amazon, or any other site where you can buy used products and find something you may be interested in purchasing. Does the seller have private information about the quality of the good? How much are you willing to pay for the product? Explain how the seller's private information influences your willingness to pay. What are some strategies that you can use to determine the quality of the used product before you make a purchase?
2. For each of the following, explain how it may serve as a possible solution to the private information problem in the used-home market.
   - **a.** A home warranty contract.
   - **b.** Hiring a home inspector who takes a careful look at the house's structural integrity, plumbing, and electric circuits.
   - **c.** Laws requiring sellers to disclose known defects.

Learning Objective 19.2 *Discover how buyers' private information can drive sellers' costs and distort market outcomes.*

3. Consider the market for private health insurance.
   - **a.** Describe the concept of adverse selection as it relates to this market and explain why it may result in a "death spiral" in private markets.
   - **b.** What are some possible steps the government might take to mitigate the market failure that could result from adverse selection?
   - **c.** What steps could private insurance companies take in order to reduce the problems resulting from adverse selection?

Learning Objective 19.3 *Understand how incentives, monitoring, and task design can help improve outcomes when actions are hidden.*

4. Veronica manages a team of medical transcribers, who all work from home and are paid hourly. What potential problems might she have getting her remote team members to work as productively as she needs them to? What are some possible solutions?
5. When you rent an apartment or house, most landlords will require that you pay a refundable security deposit. Why do you think landlords do this? Relate their actions to possible problems caused by moral hazard.

Study Problems

Learning Objective 19.1 *Discover how sellers' private information can reduce the quality of goods offered for sale and distort market outcomes.*

1. Jack is considering selling his elliptical machine, which he never really used, is of high quality, and has been taking up space in his spare bedroom. He lists it on Facebook Marketplace for "$1,200 or best offer" but in reality won't sell it for less than $1,000. Lina is looking to purchase a used elliptical machine. For a high-quality elliptical, she is willing to pay up to $1,300, and for a low-quality elliptical, she is willing to pay $600.

   Lina is risk neutral but she cannot tell if the elliptical machine is high quality or low quality. If she believes that 60% of used elliptical machines are high quality and 40% are low quality, what is the maximum price that Lina would be willing to pay? Would Jack agree to this price?
2. CarHistory is a service that supplies vehicle history reports on used cars, including their ownership history, mileage, and past accidents. The existence of CarHistory as a third-party verifier in the used-car industry can result in which of the following? Choose any that apply.
   - **a.** An increase in buyers' willingness to pay for used cars.
   - **b.** An increase in the number of cars available in the used-car market.
   - **c.** A more efficient outcome in the used-car market.
3. Sophia operates her own accounting practice and is looking to hire two entry-level accountants. A high-productivity worker will generate $90,000 in revenue per year and a low-productivity worker will generate $60,000. Tasia is a high-productivity worker and wants a salary of at least $80,000. Rick is a low-productivity worker and wants at least a $55,000 salary.
   - **a.** If Sophia can identify Tasia's and Rick's productivity, who should she hire and what would her profits be?
   - **b.** It's more likely that Sophia can't tell who will be a high- or low-productivity worker from an interview. But based on her experience, she believes that 65% of workers are low productivity and 35% of workers are high productivity. Find the maximum salary that she would be willing to pay and determine who will accept her job offer. Does this change the maximum she is willing to pay for an accountant of unknown quality?
   - **c.** How do employers try to determine a job candidate's productivity before hiring them?

Learning Objective 19.2 *Discover how buyers' private information can drive sellers' costs and distort market outcomes.*

4. For each of the following scenarios, identify how it will likely reduce or increase the problems associated with adverse selection of buyers.
   a. Advances in technology make it less expensive for people to take a DNA test that provides them—but not their health insurer—with information about their risk of developing various diseases.
   b. The government mandates that all drivers must purchase car insurance.
   c. Qantas decides to offer multiple travel insurance plans to its customers. One plan offers a high deductible, but a low premium. The other plan offers a low deductible, but a high premium.

5. Dalia owns a small public relations firm and wants to contract with her insurance provider to offer her employees the option to purchase short-term disability insurance. The insurance will pay out $5,000 to any worker who has to miss at least three consecutive weeks of work due to an illness or accident that occurred outside the workplace. Her employees' probabilities of using the insurance in any year are in the accompanying table.

Employee	Probability of using the insurance
Carol	20%
Jose	50%
Fan	15%
Andre	85%
Birat	40%

   a. If the insurance company can easily figure out the probabilities of each employee using the short-term disability insurance, and it can tailor its price to each customer, what is the lowest price it's willing to charge each person?
   b. Now suppose that each of Dalia's employees knows their own probability of using the insurance, but the insurance company only knows that, on average, the probability of a worker suffering a qualifying injury or illness is about 40%. Based on this, how much on average does the insurance company expect to pay out per policy if everyone buys it?
   c. Who will purchase the insurance at the price you calculated in part (b) and how much expected profit will the insurance company earn?
   d. How much will the insurance company need to increase the premium it charges to each person in order to avoid making a loss? Who will continue to buy the insurance and how much profit will the insurance company now earn?
   e. How much will the insurance company need to increase the premium charged to each person in order to earn zero profits? Who will continue to buy the insurance?
   f. What is happening to the size of the insured population? What is this called?

Learning Objective 19.3 *Understand how incentives, monitoring, and task design can help improve outcomes when actions are hidden.*

6. You are working at a marketing firm in ad sales. Your manager announces that the company is starting a new incentive program to increase the number of potential customers, or leads, for salespeople to contact. For every lead submitted by an employee, the employee will receive $10 in their next pay cheque.

   After a week, the sales manager realises that staff are simply submitting lists of names of everyone they know for $10 a name, resulting in a net loss to the company because the vast majority of the leads are useless. For each of the following changes, explain to your manager whether or not it will fix the problem.
   a. Instead of offering $10 for each lead, offer $25 instead.
   b. Instead of offering $10 for each lead, offer $5 instead.
   c. Instead of paying $10 for each lead, offer to pay employees a percentage of revenue actually earned from a lead they submit.
   d. Hire a consultant to sift through the leads and only pass along useful leads to the sales team.

7. For each of the following scenarios, identify whether it is an example of adverse selection of sellers, adverse selection of buyers, or moral hazard. Come up with a possible solution to each problem.
   a. You hire your neighbour to check on your cat every day while you are travelling. The neighbour checks on your cat every other day instead.
   b. Your local seafood shop advertises fresh seafood, but you are not certain if the seafood is actually fresh or if it has been frozen.
   c. People with asthma are more likely to buy health insurance.

Decisions Involving Uncertainty

CHAPTER 20

Chapter Objective

Learn how to make good decisions when you don't know what will happen.

20.1 Risk Aversion
Learn how to make good decisions when the outcome is uncertain.

20.2 Reducing Risk
Be ready to apply five strategies for reducing the risk in your life.

20.3 Behavioural Economics: How People Make Mistakes Around Uncertainty
Prepare to overcome common pitfalls when faced with uncertainty.

bernie_photo/Getty Images

Every day, you roll the dice on countless decisions.

Uncertainty pervades every part of your life. You set your alarm at night, expecting it to wake you up in time to get to your first class, but there's a chance you might sleep through it. You wake up and get dressed, picking attire appropriate for normal weather, but there's always the risk that it turns out to be colder or hotter or wetter. You jump in the car expecting to make it to class on time, but a car accident along the way could make you late. You arrive at class expecting to be able to eat breakfast while listening to a lecture, but your instructor could surprise you with a pop quiz. Then you head out to meet your friends for lunch. There's risk there, too. You might catch a cold from one of them. Or today might be the day that you discover your friend is actually the love of your life. Risks, everywhere!

Now turn to thinking about some of the big decisions. You have to decide on your future occupation, but who knows if they'll still be hiring app designers when you graduate? If you start your own business you'll have to take a leap of faith, not knowing for sure how popular your products will be or whether other businesses will start competing with you. You have to decide where to live, but you don't really know what it would be like to live in Brisbane. So, if you're offered a great job there, you'll face a risk that you won't really like living there. When you contemplate marriage, you'll wonder whether your current love will still be a good match in 40 years. Eventually you'll think about kids, but you don't know if you'll like being a parent or what your kids will be like. You need to save for retirement. But you don't know what your income will be over the next several decades before you retire, how well your investments will perform, how many years you'll live after you retire, or what the tax policy will be in the future. All that uncertainty makes it hard to know how much to save.

Every day, you're going to have to make decisions in partial ignorance of their consequences. And so our task in this chapter is to give you the tools to assess how best to make risky choices and show you strategies you can use to reduce risk.

20.1 Risk Aversion

Learning Objective *Learn how to make good decisions when the outcome is uncertain.*

When you finish university, should you work for a large, stable company that will pay you a reliable salary? Or launch a start-up, which could either succeed wildly or fail dismally? It's a tough choice. But it's just one of the many risky decisions that you're going to have to make.

Life is risky, and whether you're skiing, investing, or just trying to cross the street without getting run over, you never really know what's going to happen. You're going to need to make good decisions even when the consequences of each choice are uncertain. And so our next task is to figure out how to extend the *cost-benefit principle* so that it can provide useful guidance even when you don't know the exact consequences of each choice.

Understanding Risk

There's risk whenever you don't know what the outcome will be with certainty. And you can't eliminate risk from your life. Rather, the smart thing to do is to make the best decisions you can, taking account of those risks.

Risk is a set of probabilities and payoffs. While every risk is different, you can always strip it down to two essential elements: *probabilities* and *payoffs*. You should look at the probability of each outcome occurring, and the payoff you'll get from each of these outcomes if they do occur.

For instance, perhaps you have the opportunity to invest in a new, promising tech company—SharkField. However, it's still in its early stages, so success isn't guaranteed. If you invest in this company, your wealth could be $20,000 higher. But, it's a risky business and there's uncertainty involved. If SharkField fails, your wealth would be $20,000 lower. You do some analysis and you decide that SharkField has a 50% chance of success. Should you invest?

If your winnings offset your losses on average, it's a fair bet. Whether you should invest in SharkField depends on how you feel about uncertainty. Making this investment is like making a bet: Heads, your wealth is $20,000 higher; tails, your wealth is $20,000 lower. In fact, this is an example of a **fair bet**—a gamble that, on average, will leave you with the same amount of money. In any particular instance, your wealth will change. Half the time, it'll be $20,000 higher; the other half, it'll be $20,000 lower. But *on average*, these gains and losses will cancel out, leaving your wealth unchanged.

fair bet A gamble that, on average, will leave you with the same amount of money.

Risk-averse people reject fair bets. Here's the thing about risk: You're better off avoiding it. Most people are **risk averse,** which means that they dislike uncertainty. A risk-averse person will never take a fair bet, because the fair bet simply takes your current level of wealth and adds further uncertainty. In fact, risk-averse people will often pay good money to avoid risk—that's what insurance markets are all about.

risk averse Disliking uncertainty.

Let's look at their risk aversion through the lens of the *cost-benefit principle*. You should refuse a fair bet if the costs exceed the benefits. What's the cost of taking this bet? It's a 50% chance that your wealth will be $20,000 lower. And the benefit? It's a 50% chance that your wealth will be $20,000 higher. The probabilities are the same in both cases, and so are the sums of money. Yet risk-averse people find that the cost—the decline in their well-being when their wealth level is $20,000 lower—exceeds the benefit, which is the gain in their well-being when their wealth level is $20,000 higher. Why is that?

What's happening here is that you're not just looking at financial costs and benefits; you're thinking about the costs and benefits for your well-being. Let's turn to figuring out how and why the marginal decrease in your well-being from your wealth level being

$20,000 lower outweighs the marginal increase in your well-being from your wealth level being $20,000 higher.

Diminishing Marginal Utility

To evaluate a risky choice, you need to be able to think in terms of the marginal benefits, and not just focus on the dollar amounts involved. After all, money is just a means to an end—a way to enjoy a better life. The marginal benefit of a dollar is how much that dollar helps you enjoy a better life or, put another way, how much it improves your well-being. Economists use the word **utility** to describe your level of well-being. If your ultimate objective is to live the best possible life, you should make utility—rather than money—central to how you evaluate your choices.

utility Your level of well-being.

Marginal utility is highest when you are poor and declines as your wealth grows. Your utility is closely related to your wealth. After all, greater wealth enables you to make choices that will make you happier and enjoy more utility, whether it's due to buying more stuff, working less, helping those you love, or donating to charity. As a result, more wealth leads to more utility. But your utility probably doesn't rise one-for-one with your wealth. After all, when you're poor, an extra $20,000 would make a big difference in your quality of life and hence utility. But when you're doing well, an extra $20,000 doesn't help as much. Figure 1 shows a typical utility function, which embodies this idea. The utility function starts off steep—each extra dollar raises utility by a lot—and then flattens out, because at high levels of wealth, more money doesn't make as much of a difference as it does at lower levels of wealth.

Figure 1 | **Your Utility Function**

Your utility function describes how your well-being varies with your level of wealth.
As wealth rises, diminishing marginal utility means that further boosts to your wealth yield smaller boosts in utility, causing the utility function to flatten. As a result:

Ⓐ **The utility gain from winning $20,000** is smaller than
Ⓑ **The utility loss from losing $20,000.**

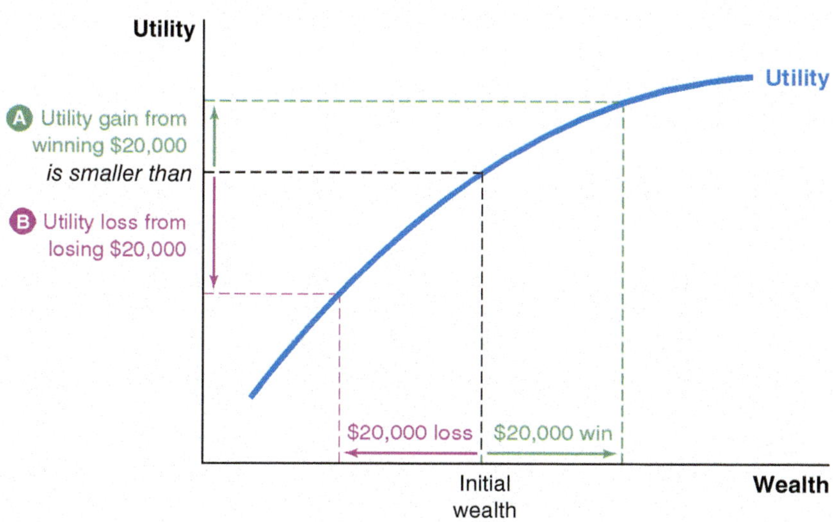

The *marginal principle* reminds you to think at the margin, and there's diminishing marginal benefit from each extra dollar. Just as your third pair of jeans yields a smaller marginal benefit to you than your second pair, your 30,000th dollar is less useful than your 20,000th. To be precise, **marginal utility** is the boost to utility you get from one more dollar. And because each additional dollar yields a smaller boost to your well-being, you have **diminishing marginal utility.** This means that your marginal utility may be large

marginal utility The additional utility you get from one more dollar.

diminishing marginal utility Each additional dollar yields a smaller boost to your utility—that is, less marginal utility—than the previous dollar.

when you are poor, but it gets smaller as you get richer. Diminishing marginal utility is the reason that the utility function gets flatter at each higher level of wealth.

Diminishing marginal utility makes you risk averse. Diminishing marginal utility explains why you're risk averse. Again, consider your opportunity to invest in SharkField. But now focus on the payoffs in terms of what they mean for your utility, rather than your level of wealth.

Figure 1 illustrates that the gain in utility from a $20,000 higher level of wealth is smaller than the loss in utility from a $20,000 lower level of wealth. And so if you apply the *cost-benefit principle* and evaluate the costs and benefits in terms of utility, the costs of a fair bet exceed the benefits. When you look at utility rather than money, the potential upside isn't large enough to compensate for the potential downside.

Notice the central role of diminishing marginal utility in making you risk averse. You dislike risk because you stand to gain money that has a low marginal utility, while you stand to lose money that is more valuable to you because it has a higher marginal utility.

The Risk-Reward Trade-off

Risk aversion should not lead you to avoid all risks. Rather, you should take risks when the benefits exceed the costs—again, making sure to measure benefits and costs in terms of utility. That's more likely to happen when greater risk is also coupled with greater reward.

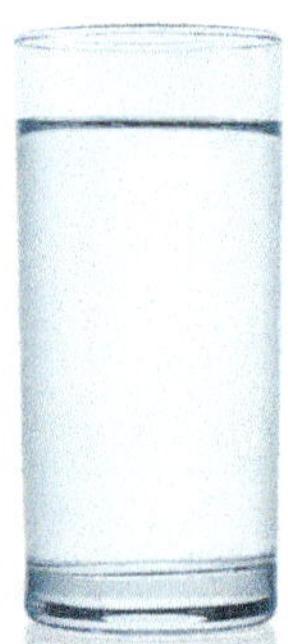

Classen Rafael/EyeEm/Getty Images

You don't want to eliminate all risk. Let me tell you a story about I.M. Scared, who went on a mission to eliminate risk from their life. They never gambled in a casino or at the races, never invested in risky stocks, and never went skydiving. Beyond that, they never ate eggs for breakfast because of the risk that the eggs were contaminated with Salmonella. Come to think of it, they never ate because they didn't want to risk choking on their food. They didn't drink water because they were worried about the risk of contaminants. They didn't get a job because they didn't want to risk getting fired. In fact, they never left the house because they didn't want to risk getting exposed to cancer-causing sunrays or getting run over by a car. And they never fell in love because they wanted to avoid the risk of heartbreak.

You know how this story ends. When you've eliminated all risk from your life, you're only left with certainty: the certainty of a quick and lonely death.

ZUMA Press, Inc./Alamy Stock Photo

It all involves risk.

There's a trade-off between risk and reward. While you want to avoid some risks, you shouldn't try to eliminate all risk. Indeed, it's often worth taking calculated risks. The question is simply whether the rewards outweigh the risk. That is, you should think in terms of a risk-reward trade-off, where you're better off taking a risky choice if it comes with a sufficiently high reward.

We've already seen that risk aversion will lead you not to make an investment in SharkField if its upside potential is equal to its downside potential. That lesson, which we first saw in Figure 1, is now illustrated in the left panel of Figure 2. Now let's reevaluate the investment when SharkField has better prospects than you originally thought. If it succeeds, your wealth will increase by $30,000; if it fails your wealth will only decrease by $10,000. It still has only a 50% chance of succeeding. But now you are comparing the utility gain from your wealth level being $30,000 higher to the utility loss of your wealth level being $10,000 lower.

This investment is just as risky as before—the difference in your wealth between the good and bad outcomes is still $40,000—but the reward is now $10,000 higher. Now that it's a more rewarding investment, you might just find it a bet worth making. Indeed, the right panel of Figure 2 illustrates an example of someone whose utility gain from their wealth being $30,000 higher exceeds their utility loss from their wealth being $10,000 lower. The *cost-benefit principle* says they should make this risky investment.

The big idea here is that the greater the potential reward, the more willing you should be to make a risky investment.

Figure 2 | **The Risk-Reward Trade-off**

The greater the potential reward, the more willing you are to take the risk.

High Risk, Low Reward

Risk aversion leads you to refuse a fair bet.

This fair bet fails the cost-benefit test, because:

(A) **The utility gain from winning $20,000** is smaller than

(B) **The utility loss from losing $20,000.**

Same Risk, Higher Reward

Bigger payoffs make the bet worthwhile.

This higher-reward bet passes the cost-benefit test, because:

(C) **The utility gain from winning $30,000** is larger than

(D) **The utility loss from losing $10,000.**

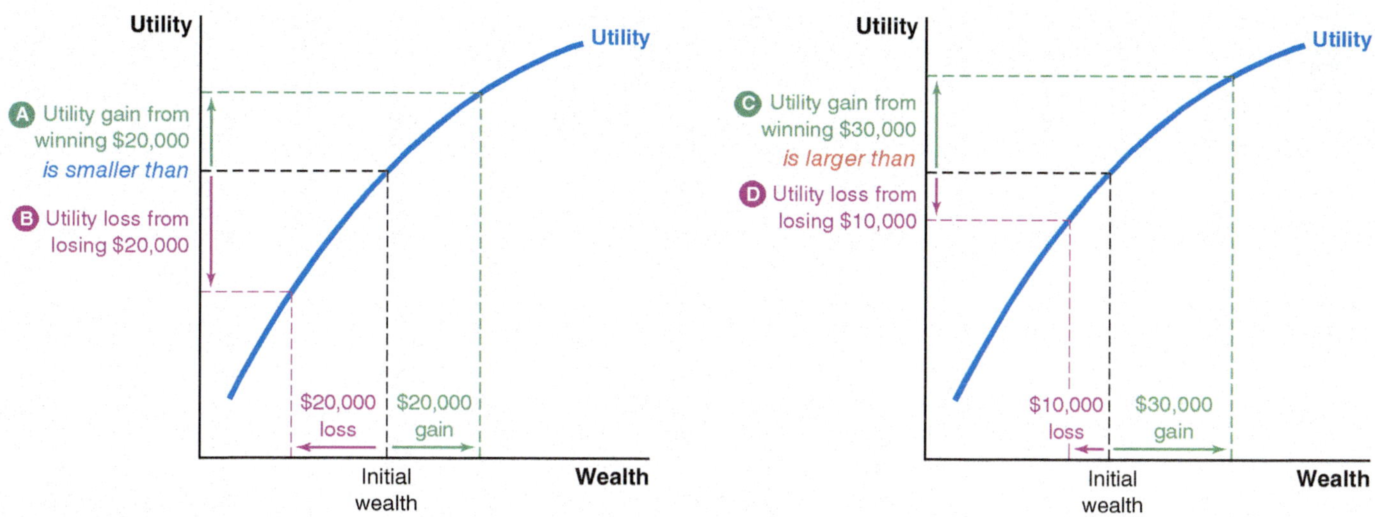

Interpreting the DATA The risk-reward trade-off

The risk-reward trade-off has an obvious implication: People will only be willing to make risky investments if the potential returns are high enough. And sure enough, the history of investment returns bears this out.

Figure 3 shows the average historical risk and reward associated with several major types of investments. The vertical axis shows the reward, which is the average annual return—the yearly increase in your wealth—from a $100 investment. The horizontal axis shows how risky each investment is. (The standard deviation is a measure of how much the value of an investment typically rises or falls each year.) The least risky investment is to buy 90-day bank bills, which are effectively a loan to the Australian government for a few weeks. There's virtually no chance of the government going bust and not paying back the loan. So when you invest in 90-day bills, you have little chance of losing your investment. That's why people are willing to invest in 90-day bills despite the low average annual return. By contrast, buying stocks in newly emerging economies, or stocks in small companies, is very risky. So while lots of people lose their investment, when it works out there's a high return. That's because investors will only take on this much risk if they expect a high return on average.

Figure 3 | **The Risk-Reward Trade-off for Investments**

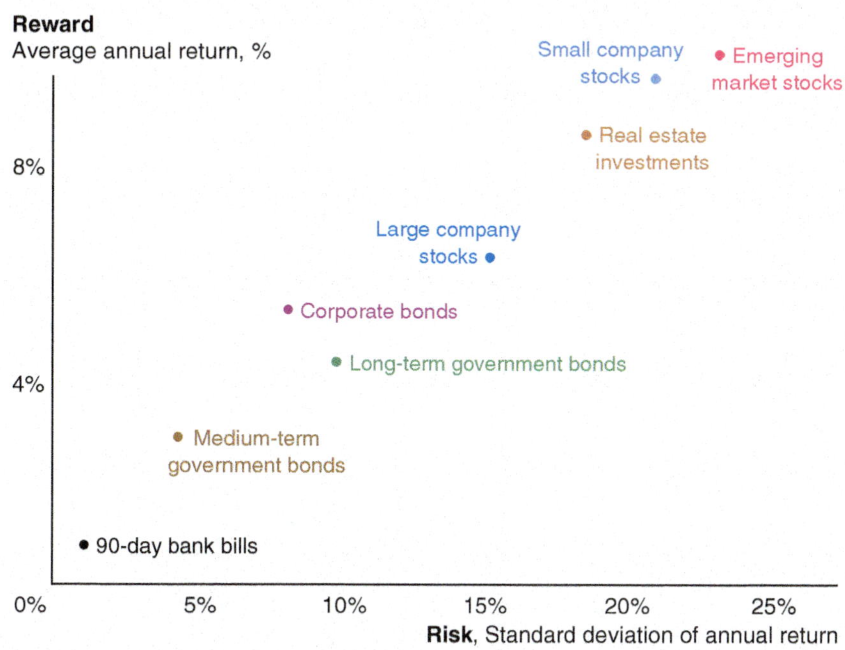

Realise that each of us has different degrees of risk aversion. And so as you think about your own investment strategy, you'll need to think about whether the reward associated with riskier investments is high enough to make it a good deal for you. ■

AF archive/Alamy Stock Photo

Who is more likely to make a risky investment?

More risk-averse people will accept fewer risks. Your willingness to accept a given risk-reward combination reflects your level of risk aversion, which in turn depends on your temperament and your life situation. Let's return to SharkField with its more favourable assessment—a fifty-fifty chance of a \$30,000 increase in your wealth or a \$10,000 decrease in your wealth. This time, however, we'll look at the choice through the eyes of two people in different circumstances and see why they might make different decisions.

Imani works as a nonprofit executive, has no debt, and rents an affordable one-bedroom apartment. She's been diligent about saving and has a \$20,000 nest egg built up. She's a happy-go-lucky type who says she has a bit of a Tigger-like personality. She's excited about the idea of investing in a new tech company, and she doesn't feel that she has a lot to lose. If she loses \$10,000, she would have to cut back on some expenses like eating out, but she won't have to make any big changes in her spending habits. If the business succeeds, she'll probably move to a nicer apartment and take an international vacation. All of this means that while she has diminishing marginal utility, it's not diminishing very rapidly—her marginal utility at low levels of wealth is only a little bit higher than at high levels of wealth. This means that she's not very risk averse, and the left panel of Figure 4 shows that her utility function doesn't flatten out much. As a result, Imani's utility gain from winning \$30,000 exceeds the utility loss from losing \$10,000. The *cost-benefit principle* tells her that investing in this new business is a risk worth taking.

Now, meet Lucas. He's a regional manager for a large corporation, and as a single dad, he's responsible for providing for his two kids. He has worked hard to save despite the expenses associated with raising kids, and he's succeeded in building up a \$20,000 nest egg. Lucas knows how important the nest egg is in case he ever loses his job. He's a bit of an Eeyore, perpetually worried that the worst will happen. His job pays as well as Imani's,

Figure 4 | Your Willingness to Take on Risk Depends on Your Level of Risk Aversion

If you are more risk averse, you will take on fewer risks.

Imani Is Slightly Risk Averse

Weakly diminishing marginal utility.

In this case, the gamble passes the cost-benefit test because:

A The utility gain from winning \$30,000 is larger than

B The utility loss from losing \$10,000.

Lucas Is Very Risk Averse

Strongly diminishing marginal utility.

The same gamble does not pass the cost-benefit test because:

C The utility gain from winning \$30,000 is smaller than

D The utility loss from losing \$10,000.

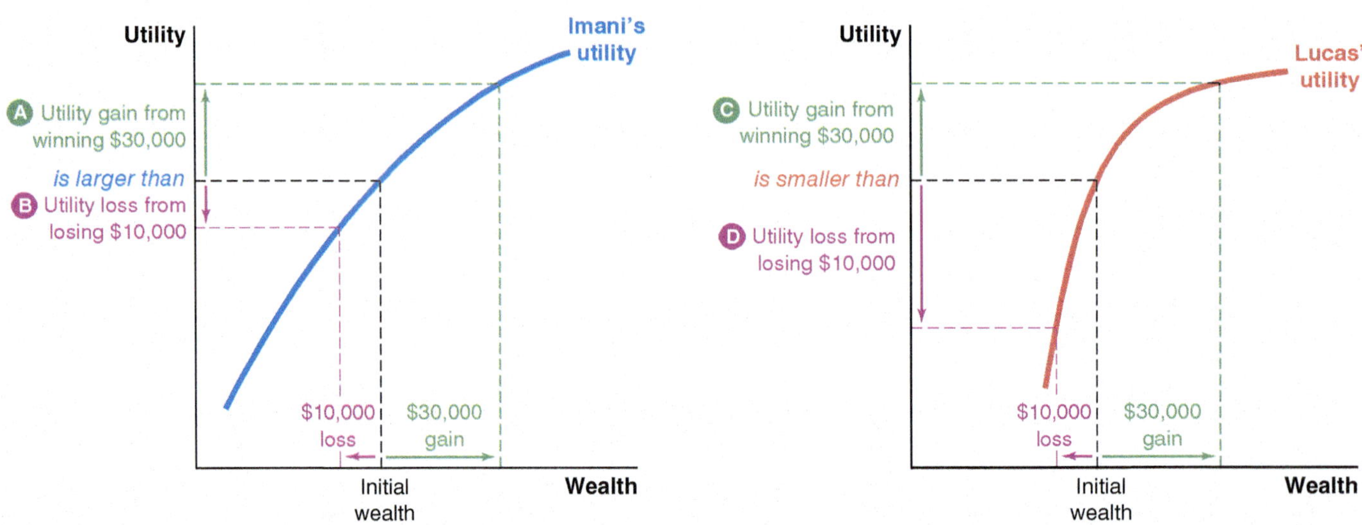

but his family has a lot of expenses. His kids go to the public school, but as a single parent he has a babysitter who picks them up in the afternoon and takes care of them until he gets home from work. He has a larger apartment than Imani so that his kids can have their own room. Even though he's doing as well financially as Imani, he spends more on necessities like food, housing, and work-related expenses like commuting and child care. That means that his family could experience real hardship if he faces a decrease in his wealth. All of this means that he's very risk averse. His utility function, shown in the right panel of Figure 4, is initially very steep. This indicates how hard it would be to absorb a $10,000 loss. Then his utility function flattens out quickly because he has rapidly declining marginal utility. For Lucas, the utility gained from a $30,000 increase in his wealth just isn't big enough to offset the utility sacrificed from a $10,000 decrease in his wealth. The *cost-benefit principle* tells him not to make this risky investment.

Are you more like Imani or Lucas—more of a Dory or a Marlin? The more risk averse you are, the less willing you are to take on risk. As you evaluate risky choices, it's important to do so with an awareness of your level of risk aversion, which reflects both your temperament and your circumstances.

EVERYDAY Economics How risk averse are you?

Here's a simple quiz to assess how risk averse you are, compared to other people:

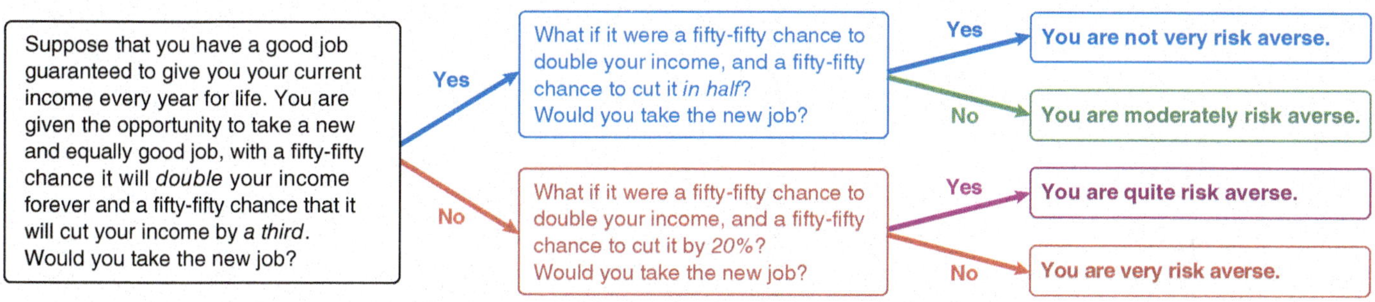

Risk aversion motivates many choices you make. Risk aversion doesn't just guide your financial choices; it should also guide the many risky decisions you face across different domains of your life. Indeed, studies have found that the more risk averse someone is, the less likely they are to take risks with their health by smoking, binge drinking, being overweight, or failing to wear a seatbelt. Risk averse people are less likely to start their own businesses and less likely to invest in stocks. They're less likely to change jobs, move to another city, or emigrate. They're more likely to buy insurance and they're more likely to own their own home. They are more likely to work in steady public-sector jobs that offer a reliable wage and little risk of being fired. The logic in each case is the same: If you're sufficiently risk averse, the lower utility associated with the downside outweighs the potentially higher utility from the upside.

Expected Utility

Let's summarise what we've learned so far. Whenever you're deciding whether to take a risk, your decision should depend on three factors: the size of the risk relative to the reward, whether the stakes are high or low, and your degree of risk aversion. A choice that's good for me might be bad for you since your level of risk aversion likely differs from mine.

This means that you can't rely on someone else to tell you how to invest, what career to pursue, or whether to start a new business. No outside expert can judge whether you should take a particular risk without knowing your utility function. And if you can't rely on experts, you'll need a systematic approach so that you can evaluate risky choices for yourself. That's our next task.

Expected utility is just your average utility. When you're comparing choices that involve no risk—do you want a Pepsi or a Coke?—you'll choose whichever makes you happiest. That is, you'll make the choice that yields the most utility.

But when you're choosing among risky alternatives, you don't know what the outcome will be. For instance, if you start your own business, your utility might be quite high (if your business succeeds), or it might be low (if it fails). Even though you don't know what your utility will be in any specific instance, you can calculate what it will be on average.

expected utility What your utility will be, on average, if you make a particular choice.

Your **expected utility** measures what your utility will be, on average, if you make a particular choice. You calculate your expected utility as a weighted average of the different utility levels associated with each possible outcome, weighted by the probability that outcome occurs. For instance, if there are two possible outcomes from starting a new business, your expected utility is:

$$\text{Expected utility} = \text{Probability business succeeds} \times \text{Utility if business succeeds} + \text{Probability business fails} \times \text{Utility if business fails}$$

Do the Economics

You currently have a wealth of \$50,000 and are offered a chance to invest in a risky company. If you invest, there's a 50% chance that you'll gain \$30,000 next year, raising your wealth to \$80,000, and a 50% chance the company fails and you'll lose \$10,000, bringing your wealth down to \$40,000.

Your expected utility is:

$$\text{Expected utility} = 50\% \times U(\$80{,}000) + 50\% \times U(\$40{,}000)$$

Note: U(\$80,000) means "Your utility when your wealth is \$80,000."

The answer will depend on your utility function. There isn't a natural unit for measuring utility, so we'll measure it in terms of how you feel about your life, on a 0 to 10 scale. Let's say that with \$80,000 in wealth, you'd rate your utility as being 8 out of 10. And if you only had \$40,000, you'd rate your utility as being 6 out of 10. Therefore:

$$\text{Expected utility} = 50\% \times 8 + 50\% \times 6 = 7$$

By comparison, with your current wealth of \$50,000, you rate your utility at 6½ out of 10. As a result, your expected utility if you invest in this company is higher than your current utility, so you should make the investment.

What should you do if there's only a 20% chance your investment will pan out?

$$\text{Expected utility} = 20\% \times 8 + 80\% \times 6 = 6.4$$

Since your current wealth yields a utility level of 6½, you'll be happier if you don't invest in that company.

As an exercise, show that you'll be better off investing in this company as long as the probability of success is at least 25%. ■

In other words, you should choose the options with the largest expected utility. If you follow this rule, your decisions will, on average, yield a higher level of well-being.

Why do people gamble? Risk aversion is a powerful concept that explains why it's a good idea to try to avoid unnecessary risk. But some people seem to seek out risk through gambling or buying lottery tickets. Why do people do this? Some people speculate that gamblers are **risk loving,** which means that they actually prefer uncertainty. Someone who is risk loving is not only comfortable with uncertainty; they like it so much

risk loving Liking uncertainty.

that they're willing to lose money in order to experience it. (And people lose money on average when gambling.)

But I don't find this to be a convincing explanation for gambling. Most people who spend a few dollars on lottery tickets also spend money insuring their houses against burning down, or insuring their cars against theft—both ways in which they pay to reduce risk. So most people who gamble don't seem to like risk in their daily lives. A better answer for why people gamble is that it is a form of entertainment. A night at the casino can be fun, just as you might enjoy a night at a concert. A few bets at the racetrack is part of how some people cheer on some extraordinary athletes, just as you cheer on your favourite players at a soccer game or cricket match. A lottery ticket offers you the fantasy that you might one day be rich, just as a sci-fi novel can offer you the fantasy of a better future. By this view, it's fun, not love of risk, that drives many people to gamble.

Quinn Rooney/Getty Images

Part of the fun is that if they win, you win.

20.2 Reducing Risk

Learning Objective *Be ready to apply five strategies for reducing the risk in your life.*

We now have a better understanding of why people are risk averse. But if you want to reduce the role risk plays in your life, then you need to figure out how. We're going to explore five effective risk-reduction strategies: risk spreading, diversification, insurance, hedging, and gathering information. As you learn about each strategy, you should think about how you can apply it to your own life. These strategies can be applied to almost any risky decision you'll confront.

You can reduce risk by:

1. Risk spreading
2. Diversification
3. Insurance
4. Hedging
5. Gathering information

Strategy One: Risk Spreading—Transforming Big Risks into Small Risks

You have an exciting idea for an app. But hiring programmers is expensive, and there's no guarantee that your app will succeed. There's a 50% chance it will become popular, and you'll earn $200,000. But there's also a 50% chance that it will fail and you'll lose the $100,000 you spend to develop it. Would you make this risky investment? Even though it's better than a fair bet, most students would say no. The consequences of a $100,000 decrease in wealth, in terms of lost utility, are just too great.

But consider a different approach. You could start the business, but take on co-owners—shareholders—who would also take a share of your financial risk. If you issue 1,000 shares, then each shareholder now faces the smaller gamble of either increasing their wealth by $200 or having their wealth decline by $100. What's your choice now? More students are willing to make this investment.

By simply breaking a big bet into many smaller bets, you can transform an investment that's too risky for any one individual to make into a sound investment for many people to share. This is the idea behind **risk spreading**—taking a large risk and spreading it out over more people. By spreading the risk thinly, you ensure that the stakes for each person are low, and that makes them willing to take a share of it. It follows that risk won't prevent a profitable investment from being made—as long as you're willing to spread the risk thinly enough.

risk spreading Breaking a big risk into many smaller risks so that it can be spread over many people.

Make risk-averse choices when the stakes are large. When the stakes are large, most people don't want to make a risky investment. But when they're offered a small enough slice of a risky investment such that the stakes are small, more people are willing to do so. Let's consider why.

When the stakes are large, the difference in your wealth between winning and losing is big. It could mean the difference between wealth and poverty. This means that, on average, the marginal utility of each dollar you stand to lose is *a lot* larger than the marginal utility of each dollar you stand to gain. Since it's such a big gamble, you feel much more pain from each dollar lost than satisfaction from each dollar gained. A decline of $100,000 could wipe out your entire wealth and leave you with debt. You might be barely able to pay your rent even though you eat two-minute noodles every day. Sure, an increase in your wealth of $200,000 would let you buy a house, but struggling to eat and keep a roof over your head is so bad that risking that scenario isn't worth a chance to own your own home. So even though the financial upside is larger than the financial downside, your utility gain from the increase of $200,000 is likely to be less than the decrease in utility that happens when your wealth falls by $100,000. And that's why most people make the risk-averse decision to refuse this high-stakes gamble.

Make nearly risk-neutral choices when the stakes are small. Here's why it's different when the stakes are small: Your wealth won't be much higher or lower whether the investment works out or not, so your marginal utility will be pretty similar in either case. Imagine that you have a wealth of $40,000 and you're asked whether you want to make an investment that could raise your wealth to $40,002 with 50% probability or lower it to $39,999 with 50% probability. Your life won't much change in either circumstance! That's why the marginal utility of your 40,001st and 40,002nd dollar—even if they aren't *exactly* the same as the marginal utility of your 39,999th dollar—are still *very similar*. As a result, the marginal utility of each dollar is pretty much the same whether you gain or lose a few dollars. This means that you gain nearly twice as much utility from winning $2 as you sacrifice from losing $1. (If marginal utility didn't change at all, it would be exactly twice as large.) As such, even when measured in terms of utility, the benefit of winning this small-stakes bet is nearly double the cost of losing, and so of course you should take it. Even though you're risk averse, it makes sense to accept this low-stakes gamble.

Following this logic suggests that when the stakes are small enough that your marginal utility is roughly the same whether you win or lose, you should act as if you're nearly **risk neutral**—that is, as if you neither like nor dislike uncertainty. When you're risk neutral, you're indifferent to risk—you only care about whether a choice offers positive financial returns on average. So when the stakes are small enough, it's a good idea to take any risk that's better than a fair bet.

risk neutral Indifferent to uncertainty.

EVERYDAY Economics — Why you should never take the extended warranty

Whenever you buy a TV, laptop, or printer—or virtually any electronic device—the salesperson will try to pressure you to buy an extended warranty that extends the length of time in which you can bring in your product for repairs, cost-free. The salesperson will wax lyrical about the extra security and peace of mind they're offering you.

Don't fall for it. These extended warranties are a rip-off. Many of the businesses offering them take in twice as much money from the warranties as they ever pay out. The salespeople try to scare you not out of concern, but because they stand to gain larger commissions for pushing the warranty. In fact, extended warranties are so profitable that in some years, they account for roughly half of all profits at some large big-box retailers.

Remember: When the stakes are high, it makes sense to be risk averse. But the small chance that you'll need to replace your printer is not a high-stakes risk. When the stakes are small, you shouldn't worry too much about risk. Instead of buying the extended warranty, put the cost of the warranty in your own, separate, "rainy day" account. If you follow this advice every time you're offered an extended warranty on low-to-moderate cost consumer goods, it's likely that you'll end up saving enough that you can replace any of those malfunctioning devices out of your rainy day account and still have money left over. ■

Risk spreading explains why big investments require a lot of shareholders. The idea of risk spreading is central to how we fund modern corporations. Consider the risks facing the young Sandy Lerner and her husband Leonard Bosack, the founders of Cisco, when they had to figure out how to fund an aggressive expansion of their computer networking business. They could have borrowed the money Cisco needed, leaving them as the sole owners. But that would have meant bearing all the risk of the expansion not working out. That's such a big risk that they probably wouldn't have taken it.

Instead, Lerner (who has a degree in economics) and Bosack funded their expansion plans by selling shares of Cisco on the stock market. This allowed thousands of people around the world to buy a slice of the action. Each share effectively takes some of that very large risk and breaks it into a much smaller risk. Even though investing in Cisco's expansion was too risky for two people to bear, it's a risk worth taking when that risk is spread across thousands of owners. And so the stock market makes many risky investments possible by allowing the risk to be spread across many shareholders. In fact, millions of Australians own small slices of major companies through their super funds.

Strategy Two: Diversification

I'm going to offer you a choice for your final exam in economics. You can either take an exam that has five multiple-choice questions, or one that has 50. Either choice is risky, because you don't know exactly which questions will be on the exam. But most students prefer the final exam with 50 questions because it involves less risk. Figure 5 shows that they're right.

Figure 5 | Distribution of Test Scores

Grade	5 questions	50 questions	500 questions
High Distinction	66%	79%	95%
Distinction	29%	21%	5%
Pass	0%	0%*	0%*
Fail	5%	0%*	0%*

*<1 in 500 chance

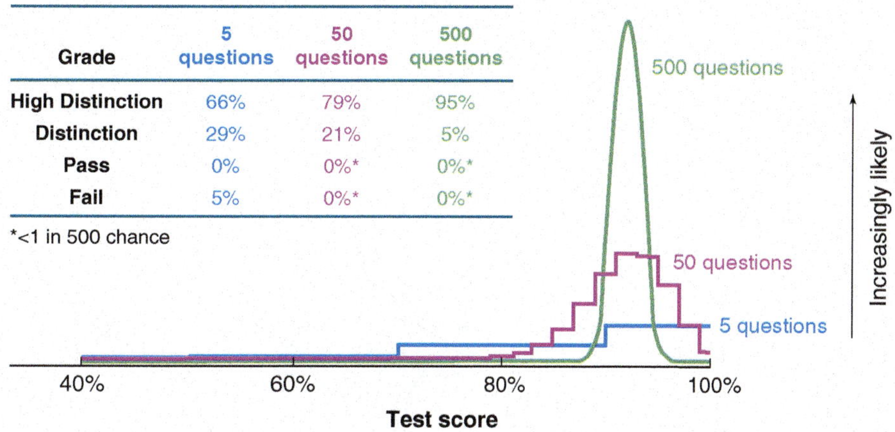

Let's say you've studied enough that, on average, you know the right answer to 92% of all exam questions. That *should* be enough to earn you a High Distinction. But there's a risk, because it's possible that the exam has more of the questions you struggle with. If the exam is five questions long, there's a 5% chance that you'll get two or more questions wrong, which means that you'll get a Pass or even a Fail. If it's 50 questions long, the risk of earning a Pass or a Fail falls to less than a one-in-a-million chance. With a 50-question exam, there's a 79% chance you'll get the High Distinction that you deserve, but if the exam is 500 questions long, your chance of an HD rises to 95%. The longer the test, the smaller the risk that you'll get a lower grade than you deserve. And so just by choosing to make your exam longer, your instructor made it less risky!

Diversification reduces risk. This is an example of the benefits of **diversification,** which means reducing risk by combining a large number of small risks whose outcomes are not closely related. Since you're reducing your reliance on any one bet working out, your overall outcome will be less risky.

diversification Reducing risk by combining a large number of small risks whose outcomes are not closely related.

An exam with one question is like betting your entire fortune on one company. It's incredibly risky. The exam with five questions is like betting a fifth of your fortune on each of five companies. That's less risky, because it's unlikely that you'll get unlucky on all five. And the exam with 50 questions is like a diversified portfolio, in which you've invested a 50th of your wealth in each of 50 companies. The more you diversify your wealth across independent risks, the less risky it will be.

Investors use diversification to make stock investments less risky. Diversification is pretty amazing. You can take many different risks, and if you put small amounts of each of them together, you can create something that's less risky!

For investors, this is fantastic. It's like you can make risk disappear. Diversification offers the promise you rarely hear in economics: something for nothing. You get less

Figure 6 | Diversification Reduces Risk

The more stocks you include in your portfolio, the less risky it is.

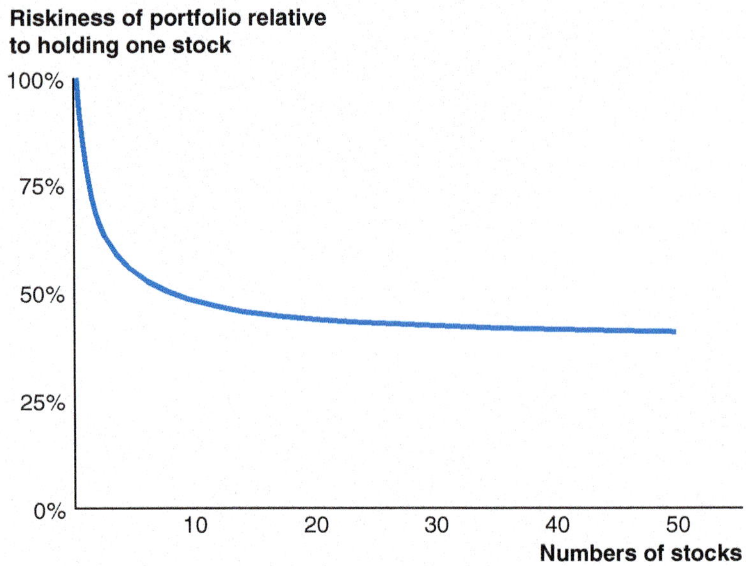

risk, and you don't have to pay anything to reduce it. All you need to do is hold many different stocks. In fact, Figure 6 shows from research findings that if you include about 30 or 40 different stocks in your portfolio, that's probably enough to get most of the benefits of diversification.

Make sure the risks are not closely related. Diversification works best when you combine many different risks together. If you combine investments that are governed by a common risk, diversification can't eliminate that common risk. For instance, Newcrest Mining, Northern Star Resources, and Evolution Mining are all gold-mining companies. A portfolio of these three companies remains very risky, because a decline in the price of gold would cause the stock prices of all three companies to fall sharply. If you're buying stock in Newcrest Mining, a better strategy is to also invest in companies like Macquarie Bank and Woolworths Group. This way, if the price of gold falls, it only affects a small part of your portfolio, and you've effectively diversified away this risk. Overall, diversification will yield larger benefits when you're combining investments that are exposed to different risks.

EVERYDAY Economics **Put your money in index funds to easily diversify your savings**

index fund An investment that automatically invests in a predefined portfolio of stocks.

An **index fund** invests your money—along with that of thousands of other investors—in a wide portfolio of stocks. For instance, many index funds buy stock in all 200 companies in the ASX 200, which gives you a diversified portfolio that includes most major Australian companies. Most economists I know invest in index funds. They do so because an index fund gives you a well-diversified portfolio that reduces risk, and it charges low fees to do this.

Index funds charge low fees partly because they follow a mechanical investment strategy. They simply buy whatever stocks happen to be in a particular market index. You might think that you could do better by only buying stock in those companies that are doing well. But in fact, picking stocks that will outperform the market is much harder than it looks. Many investment advisers will tell you that they can do this. But research shows that it's virtually impossible to find an adviser who consistently earns higher returns than an index fund. In fact, researchers have found that the investment advisers who did well this year are no more likely to do well next year than those who did poorly. The law requires that investment advisors warn you that past success is no guarantee of future performance, but the reality is far worse. Past success is virtually unrelated to future performance. ■

Diversification is not just about investment. The idea of diversification applies to all risks in your life, and not just to investments. When you applied to university, you probably applied to a diversified portfolio of programs—maybe your dream program, but also some that were realistic, and one or two that were a fallback. This reduced the risk of not getting into a good program. Now you're at university, and you're probably taking a diversified portfolio of classes, which reduces the risk that you'll hate all your classes. More importantly, your diversified portfolio of classes helps you develop a diversified portfolio of skills, which means that you'll be employable even as the labour market changes.

Many university programs require that you do this through things like "general education" requirements. You probably have a lot of friends, and this diversified portfolio ensures that you'll still have people to hang out with, even if your best friend is busy. If you're wearing a T-shirt underneath your jumper, your diversified clothing portfolio ensures you'll be comfortable if it's warm or cool. And you probably have a diversified portfolio of music, so that whatever mood you're in, you'll have something to listen to.

These ideas are also important in the business world. Farmers plant several crops to diversify the risk of disease wiping them all out. Stores carry a diversified portfolio of products to insulate their profits against temporary fads. Accountants, architects, and lawyers work with a diversified portfolio of clients so that they don't go out of business if any individual client leaves. And businesses hire a diversified portfolio of people with different talents so that they can respond to any challenge that may come along.

Mehrdad Pazhouhandeh/Shutterstock

Diversification is just the idea that you should not put all your eggs in one basket.

Diversification reduces risk, but doesn't eliminate it. As much as diversification can reduce risk, it won't eliminate risk altogether. This is because all investments are exposed to **systematic risk**—that is, common risks across the economy. For instance, a recession will reduce the value of nearly every investment. Since people have less money during recessions, they buy less stuff, reducing the value of companies in almost every industry. Other systematic risks include wars, natural disasters, financial crises, and pandemics—all of which disrupt the economy. Diversification doesn't help you with such systematic risk, which is why we're now going to explore a strategy that can also help you reduce systematic risk.

systematic risk Risks that are common across the whole economy.

Strategy Three: Insurance

There's a risk that a natural disaster like a bushfire might destroy your home, but if you have insurance, you'll be okay because your insurer will send you a payout to rebuild. When you buy **insurance,** you're buying a promise of compensation if a specified bad thing happens. The price of insurance is called the **premium.** In return for buying insurance, if the specified bad thing happens, your insurance company will foot the bill. Insurance softens the risks you face because it promises that you'll get a payout to help counter the worst outcomes.

insurance A promise of compensation if a specified bad thing happens.

premium The price of insurance.

Risk-averse people should buy actuarially fair insurance. An insurance policy that, on average, is expected to pay out as much in compensation as it receives in premiums is said to be **actuarially fair.** Think of it as the insurance equivalent of a *fair bet.* Like a fair bet, on average, actuarially fair insurance won't change your wealth. But a fair bet increases your risk, while actuarially fair insurance decreases it.

The same risk-aversion logic that leads you to reject a fair bet—you don't want extra risk if you don't get an extra return—says that you should buy actuarially fair insurance because it reduces your risk, and on average, you don't have to pay any extra for it.

actuarially fair An insurance policy that, on average, is expected to pay out as much in compensation as it receives in premiums.

Insurance presents a risk-reward trade-off. In reality, most insurance is not actuarially fair—an insurance company typically takes in more in premiums than it pays out in compensation—partly to pay for the insurer's administrative costs and also because the insurer may build in a profit margin. It follows that buying insurance typically involves a risk-reward trade-off. Insurance reduces your risk, but if it's not actuarially fair, this lower risk is coupled with a negative reward because, on average, you'll pay more than you get back. And so you'll have to decide whether this decreased risk is worth this decreased reward. This means that insurance is more likely to be a good idea:

- the closer the insurance is to being actuarially fair;
- the more risk averse you are; and
- the larger the stakes involved.

Insurance opportunities come in many different guises. In Chapter 19 we explored how market failure can prevent the private sector from offering specific forms of insurance. When the private sector won't offer insurance, the government often steps in to provide it instead. This is one of the reasons why the government offers unemployment benefits, which insure you against job loss. When you're older, you'll be eligible for the age pension, which is government-provided retirement-income insurance.

A key risk you face is that you don't know how successful you'll be in your career. So redistribution through a progressive tax-and-benefit system is like a form of insurance. If your earnings are low, government benefits like the Family Tax Benefit boost your income. And if your earnings are high, your higher tax payments are like insurance premiums that you pay each year for this protection.

Beyond the government, your family is a key insurance mechanism. If you fall on hard times, it's likely that your parents or siblings will help you out. And the premium that you pay is that you'll help them out in hard times. Once you start to think broadly about insurance, you'll start to see insurance-like systems everywhere. But sometimes you have to design your own form of insurance, which leads us to our next risk-reducing strategy.

Strategy Four: Hedging—Offsetting Risks

Getting a big metal tube to fly through the air takes a lot of fuel. In fact, jet fuel is typically an airline's largest operating expense, and it accounts for up to a third of their spending. A major risk for any airline is the possibility that the price of fuel will increase. For many years, higher fuel costs made most of the major airlines in the United States unprofitable. But an airline called Southwest was an exception. Let's find out why.

hedge Acquire an offsetting risk.

Hedging reduces risk by acquiring offsetting risks. Southwest's innovation was to **hedge** their risk—that is, its managers acquired an offsetting risk. Through a series of sophisticated financial trades, they bet hundreds of millions of dollars that fuel prices would be high. When fuel prices rose a few years back, Southwest's fuel bill rose, but its hedge also paid off, giving it extra money to pay for that fuel. A hedge reduces both upside and downside risk, and so when fuel prices fell a few years later, Southwest's profits didn't jump as much as those of its competitors because it had to pay off its losing bets. But this hedging strategy was still a success because it kept Southwest consistently profitable, even as changing fuel prices led the fortunes of rival airlines to fluctuate wildly. And when profits are more consistent, it's easier to plan for the future.

Justin Sullivan/Getty Images

It's like he's pumping money.

There's something a bit cheeky about hedging. After all, if you're worried about risk, the last thing you might think of is making another bet. But Southwest's hedge worked because the gamble it took *offset* an existing risk.

Hedging in action. Hedging can be an effective and cheap way to reduce risk. To use it effectively, you need to be creative in identifying offsetting risks. Here are some examples of hedging in action:

- Whenever my favourite sports team is playing for the championship, I hedge the risk of disappointment by betting on the other side. This bet offsets the risk of my team disappointing me, ensuring that after the game I'm either celebrating a great win or enjoying a financial windfall.
- If you have a mortgage and are worried that interest rates might rise, you can fix part or all of your repayments for a number of years. You may miss out on the benefits of lower interest rates if rates go down, but you will be protected against higher monthly payments if rates go up.

- If you're worried that increasing automation will take your job, you can hedge that risk by taking a few computer science classes. It's a hedge because if computers start to take over more jobs, your computer-related skills will become more valuable, which offsets the risk that your other skills have become obsolete.
- People who are worried about inflation—that is, higher prices—can hedge their risk by stocking up on nonperishable goods. Buying nonperishable goods is a hedge because if prices rise, your jars of vegemite are now worth more, which offsets the risk that your pay cheque now buys less.
- If you're worried that a recession will make it hard to find a job when you finish university, you should think about applying for a postgraduate degree as a hedge. That application is a hedge because it offsets the risk that work will be hard to find, ensuring that you'll spend next year doing something productive—either working or pursuing further education.

EVERYDAY Economics **Why you shouldn't hold stock in your employer**

American coffee chain Starbucks offers many of its workers the opportunity to purchase stock in their company at a discount. It's a common practice in the business world, often provided as an incentive so that workers care more about their company's performance. If the discount is large enough, buying the stock might be a good idea. But you should sell it as soon as you can, because holding stock in your company is a bad idea.

Here's why. It's the opposite of hedging. If your company goes bust, you're going to lose your job AND your stock will become worthless. Far better to invest your money in something that will be worth *more* if you lose your job. It's a lesson that thousands of workers at energy giant Enron wish they had learned. The company had engaged in deceptive accounting and financial fraud to hide its losses. When the shareholders found out, the stock plummeted. Eventually, Enron declared bankruptcy, leading thousands of workers to lose not just their jobs, but also most of their retirement savings, which had been held in Enron stock. This double-whammy left them jobless and poor. So remember, while stock options are nice, a better option is to hedge by investing in companies that will do well if your employer does poorly. This hedging perspective suggests that Enron's staff would have been better off holding stock in Enron's rivals, who gained market share when their employer collapsed. ■

Strategy Five: Gathering Information to Reduce Risk

You wake up, put on jeans and a jumper, and head to your 9 A.M. class. That outfit is the first risky investment you'll make today. It's risky, because if it turns out to be unseasonably cold, you'll spend the day shivering. And if it's unseasonably hot, you'll be sweating. Not to mention that if it's raining, you'll be wet. There's a simple way to virtually eliminate that risk: Check a weather app, and you'll have a pretty good sense of whether it will be a colder or warmer day than usual. You'll also find out whether it might rain. Dress accordingly, bring an umbrella if you need to, and it's much less likely that you'll be caught ill-prepared. Simply by gathering more information, you've reduced the risk of shivering, sweating, or being soaking wet.

Many risks simply reflect insufficient information. Choosing a career is risky, but it's a much smaller risk that you'll make a bad choice if you do a lot of research first. That's why high schools have guidance and career counsellors. Choosing a spouse is also risky, but it's less risky if you invest a lot in finding out if they really are "the one." That's why many couples spend a long time engaged or living together before marrying. Starting a business is risky, but it's less risky if you research the market first, learning about demand for your product, costs, and likely competitors. In each case, gathering more information reduces the risks you face.

Information is valuable to risk-averse people because it reduces risk. Information is key to reducing uncertainty. As you gather more information, you can become more certain about the likely outcomes. In turn, this decreases the risk you face and makes it easier to make better choices.

But gathering information is costly, and often the market won't produce enough information because it can be hard to get people to pay for it even though it's valuable (in the language of Chapter 10, information is often a public good). That's why the government will often fund valuable information. For instance, the government funds the Bureau of Meteorology (BOM), a scientific agency, to gather and publish information about the weather. The BOM spends nearly $300 million a year, part of which helps to provide information that your favourite weather app uses to give you a daily forecast. That part of the BOM's budget is about $4 per Australian per year.

Now that you know what learning about the weather costs, let's see if this information is worth it. Consulting a simple weather app may reduce the chance that you're inappropriately attired for the day from 30% to 10%. Over the course of the year, this will reduce the number of days you're improperly attired from 109.5 days (that's 30% × 365 days) to 36.5 days (10% × 365 days), meaning that you'll spend 73 fewer days sweating, shivering, or soaking wet. If your willingness to pay to avoid the discomfort of wearing the wrong clothes is $1 per day, then the information in your weather app generates $73 in benefits per year. That's a pretty good deal for the $4 per person annually that it costs the BOM to collect that data.

Notice that the value of information is greater:

- the more it reduces uncertainty, and
- the higher the stakes involved in the decision.

If a weather app can generate $73 per year in benefits for you, just imagine the value of the information that generates better economic forecasts for companies on the cusp of making multibillion-dollar investments. Information has real value. As a result, good economists, particularly those with good data skills, are in high demand. By providing more accurate forecasts, they reduce risk. This helps explain why economics majors are in such demand, and why they're better paid than most other university graduates.

Do the Economics

A group of computer scientists and meteorologists have been working together, and they reckon they can generate even more accurate weather forecasts. Their new algorithm reduces the risk of an inaccurate weather forecast from the 10% rate of your current app, down to 9%. What's the annual value of this information for you?

Change in days inappropriately attired = 10% × 365 days − 9% × 365 days = 3.65 days per year

If the cost of being inappropriately attired is $1, then the value of this information is $3.65 per year for you. ■

EVERYDAY Economics Reducing the risk of university

University life is full of risks, but gathering more information can help reduce many of them. High school students can reduce the risk of choosing the wrong program by gathering information from university websites, from students and alumni willing to tell you about their experiences, and from campus visits. If you're worried about your employability when you graduate from university, you can reduce that risk by gathering information about the types of jobs that each major typically leads to. If you're worried about choosing subjects that are a poor fit for your abilities and interests, you can reduce that risk by gathering information from an academic adviser before choosing your classes. If you're worried that your instructor will speak in a relentless monotone that bores you to tears, you can reduce that risk by sitting in on a few classes during the first week of the term. And if you're worried that you'll make bad decisions when faced with risky choices, you can reduce that risk by rereading this chapter. ■

20.3 Behavioural Economics: How People Make Mistakes Around Uncertainty

Learning Objective *Prepare to overcome common pitfalls when faced with uncertainty.*

You've now developed a robust understanding of how to make good decisions in the face of uncertainty and learned some strategies you can pursue to reduce risk. But risk is a difficult concept, and people often struggle with it. In 2018, the Nobel Prize in economics was given to the brilliant and famously witty Richard Thaler, who in his acceptance speech said that he was receiving the prize because he "discovered the presence of human life in a place . . . my fellow economists thought it did not exist: the economy." He and many economists in the last few decades have studied how human beings process information to understand what it means for economic decision making. This type of research has been called **behavioural economics** because it includes psychological factors in assessing how people make economic decisions. All of economics is concerned with human behaviour; in recent decades economists have developed a better understanding of the behaviour of actual humans.

behavioural economics Economic analysis that includes psychological factors in assessing how people make economic decisions.

This is a big deal when it comes to uncertainty because people often make fairly predictable mistakes when assessing probabilities and payoffs. These mistakes stem from relying on snap judgements, rather than more reasoned consideration. Psychologists distinguish between two styles of thinking. System 1 refers to your intuitive thoughts. They are fast, effortless, and almost automatic. These intuitions rely on rough, but often accurate, rules of thumb. The first psychologist to win the Nobel Prize in economics, Daniel Kahneman, calls System 1 "thinking fast." By contrast, System 2 is your slower, deliberative, logical self, and it uses a methodical style of thinking that requires cognitive effort. Not surprisingly, he calls that "thinking slow." When you're thinking through expected utility calculations, you're thinking slow. But most of the time, you're using System 1 and thinking fast. Life is too short to think slow all the time. Even so, thinking fast leads us astray a lot, particularly when it comes to uncertainty.

David Plunkert

System 1 and System 2

Good decision makers know when it's time to overrule their snap judgements and revert to thinking slow. And so you can think of what follows as an operating manual for your mind. This operating manual will help you figure out when thinking fast will yield bad answers, so that you pause your intuition and apply the more deliberate approach of thinking slow instead.

Overconfidence

Let's begin with a quiz. For each of the following 10 questions, you should come up with your best guess, without looking for answers online. Don't worry if these are questions you know nothing about—the point is to explore how you react when you're uncertain. The most important real task is to put a lower and upper bound around your estimate, so that you're 95% sure that the true number lies in this range. If you really don't know, be sure to make the range a bit wider to reflect your uncertainty.

	Estimate	95% confidence interval: Lower bound	95% confidence interval: Upper bound
Q1. What is the value of shares that are sold each day on the ASX?	______	______	______
Q2. What is the world's population?	______	______	______
Q3. How many people live in the Northern Territory?	______	______	______
Q4. How many Woolworths supermarkets are there in Australia?	______	______	______
Q5. What is the total revenue of Apple?	______	______	______
Q6. How many Woolworths employees are in Australia?	______	______	______
Q7. How many sheep does New Zealand have?	______	______	______
Q8. How many different books have ever been written?	______	______	______
Q9. What is the ratio of prices today to prices in 1913?	______	______	______
Q10. How many Australian mammals have gone extinct since 1788?	______	______	______

Answers: 1. $6.6 billion; 2. 7.4 billion people on Earth; 3. 246,000; 4. 995 Woolworths stores; 5. $274.5 billion Apple revenue; 6. 216,000 Woolworths employees; 7. 30 million sheep; 8. 130 million books; 9. 24:1 price ratio; 10. 28 species extinct.

You are probably overconfident. Now take a look at the answers in the margin. How many times did the actual answer lie between your lower and upper bound? If you constructed your range to contain the true answer 95% of the time, then across these 10 questions, the truth should have fallen between your lower and upper bounds 9 or 10 times. How did you do?

Most people find that the true number fell within their estimated ranges only 3–7 times. If you got less than 9 or 10 correct, then you've just learned that you're **overconfident.** You assessed the likelihood that your range contained the truth as being 95%, but in reality, the probability that you were wrong was far greater than this.

overconfidence The tendency to overrate the accuracy of your forecasts.

Don't worry, it's not just you. Researchers have analysed forecasts made by thousands of people, and they found similar problems. Indeed, when top executives were asked to make stock market forecasts that they were 80% sure of, their intervals contained the eventual outcome only 36% of the time.

Overconfidence can lead you to underestimate risks and make bad decisions. For instance, entrepreneurs often start new businesses with specific estimates of revenues and costs, but they don't sufficiently account for the risk that those estimates will turn out to be wrong. As a result, too many entrepreneurs lose their life savings to businesses that ultimately fail. Stock traders buy and sell shares based on the conviction that they can predict where the market is going. But investors who trade the most typically perform the worst. Overconfidence that things would run according to plan was a factor leading to the explosion of the Space Shuttle Challenger, and the Chernobyl nuclear meltdown. Even the slow Covid-19 vaccine rollout in Australia was bred by the overconfidence that came from Australia suppressing the virus so well in 2020. Prime Minister Scott Morrison came to regret saying of the vaccine rollout: "It's not a race."

Being too confident about your own success—whether you're deciding how hard to study, how easy it will be to find a job, or how likely it is a new venture will succeed—is a recipe for failure. Being too confident in your own judgement can delude you into thinking your assessment is better than that of others. This can lead you to not pay sufficient attention to the good advice that others offer.

The lesson is clear: Your first instincts about the accuracy of your assessment almost surely understate uncertainty. You're better off using the more deliberate approach of thinking slow to remind you that better and worse outcomes are also possible. As Gandhi once said, "It is unwise to be too sure of one's own wisdom."

Problems Assessing Probability

If you want to make good choices in the face of uncertainty, you'll need to accurately assess the likelihood of each outcome. Unfortunately, your mind isn't wired to be a perfect probability calculator. Instead, it relies on an array of mental shortcuts. These shortcuts generally point you toward an adequate answer without too much mental effort, but sometimes they'll send you off course. For many decisions, it makes sense to rely on these shortcuts. After all, the *cost-benefit principle* says that you should only think harder if the extra mental exertion will yield a sufficiently better estimate. If you learn to recognise when these shortcuts are most likely to lead you astray, you'll know when it's worth the extra effort of thinking slow to overrule them.

Availability bias leads you to overestimate vivid and easily recalled outcomes. Quick question: Are there more words that start with the letter *r*, or more that have *r* as their third letter? Most people find it easier to think of words that begin with *r* (running, racing, riding), even though there are more than twice as many words with *r* as their third letter. It's easier to conjure up words that begin with *r* because they're more *available* in your memory—they're easier to access—and this is what probably led you to mistakenly judge that they're more common.

Your mind often assesses the frequency or probability of an event not through a careful, well-informed process—but instead by how readily instances come to mind. **Availability bias** refers to the tendency to overestimate the frequency of events that are easily recalled, and to underestimate the frequency of less memorable events. For instance, vivid stories in the media might lead you to advise the World Health Organization that it's more important to prevent starvation than respiratory infections. But that would be a disastrous recommendation because respiratory infections kill around seven times more people worldwide.

availability bias The tendency to overestimate the frequency of events that are easily recalled, and to underestimate the frequency of less memorable events.

Availability bias can also lead you astray in the business world. If you ever think about dropping out of university to seek fame or fortune, you might find it easy to remember Mark Zuckerberg, Janine Allis, Oprah Winfrey, or Bill Gates—university dropouts who famously went on to brilliant careers. Less readily available are the thousands of university dropouts whose careers fizzled and who now wish they had stayed on until graduation. Availability bias will lead you to dramatically overestimate your chances of success.

More generally, availability bias can lead you to spend far too much time worrying about risks that are often in the news, but are actually very rare. Take sharks. There's virtually no chance of being killed by a shark. On average, they kill only six people worldwide each year. But the movie *Jaws* and the incessant Australian news coverage focusing on the few shark attacks that occur have convinced many that they're an ever-present threat. Likewise, the precautions that governments take to avoid terrorism dwarf their efforts to prevent more lethal threats, like influenza. Dramatic plane crashes lead some people to be scared of flying, even though you're much more likely to die if you drive to a faraway city rather than fly. Availability bias can also lead your decisions to overweight recent history, as you can more easily recall recent events. For instance, people are more likely to buy bushfire insurance immediately after a big summer bushfire season. Far better to buy it before the blaze, instead!

Mogens Trolle/Shutterstock

Statistically, they're not that scary.

When you recognise attention-grabbing events distorting your probability assessments, realise that you're better off thinking slow so that your deliberate and logical self can look up reliable statistics rather than being misled by a snap judgement.

Anchoring bias leads to excessive focus on an initial estimate. A survey asked auditors working for major accounting firms whether they thought that there was significant management-level fraud in more than 10 out of 1,000 businesses. They were then asked for their precise estimate of the rate of management fraud. A separate group of auditors were asked similar questions, except this time the first question asked whether fraud affected more than 200 out of the 1,000 firms, rather than 10 in 1,000.

You might expect these groups to give similar estimates of the rate of fraud given that the actual underlying likelihood of fraud was the same in both groups. But the first group estimated a fraud incidence of 17 per 1,000 on average, while the second group estimated an incidence of 43 per 1,000 firms. This is an example of **anchoring bias,** which is the tendency people have when thinking fast to grab onto an anchor—some kind of starting point—and adjust from there. The problem is that people insufficiently adjust. So the auditors were given two different "anchors": 10 and 200. The bigger anchor led to a bigger assessment because they started with the anchor and insufficiently adjusted.

anchoring bias The tendency to begin with an anchor, or starting point, and insufficiently adjust from there.

It's a bias that matters a lot. It tells us that first impressions matter, because once someone decides you're a jerk, or not good at your job, it's hard to get them to adjust their views. Anchoring can also lead to big mistakes. For instance, when a group of experienced real estate agents were all shown the same house, some were told that the seller was asking a high price, while others were told the seller was asking a lower price. Those who were told the seller was asking the higher price said that they thought the house was worth 11% more. Despite their expertise in assessing price per square metre, they allowed their judgement to be swayed by the first number the seller suggested.

Anchoring bias will lead you to systematically overestimate some probabilities. Anchoring can mess with your ability to estimate probabilities. Let's say your boss asks you to assess the likelihood that your project gets done in time, and for that to happen, there are eight independent steps that must each be done in a timely fashion. Any one step has an 80% chance of being done on time. What's the chance that your team delivers by the due date? Without picking up a calculator, write down your guess, here: ______ %.

The rules of probability say that the right answer is 80% × 80% × 80% × 80% × 80% × 80% × 80% × 80%, which equals 16.8%. I bet your estimate was higher than this. And the reason is anchoring: You were anchored on the original 80% and adjusted insufficiently. It's not just you. It's a pervasive problem, and it explains why new product launches nearly always get delayed, why infrastructure projects are never finished on time, and why renovating your home takes longer than planned. When each step of your plan must succeed, anchoring bias is likely to lead you to overestimate the chances your overall project succeeds.

Anchoring bias will lead you to systematically underestimate some probabilities. By contrast, when you're evaluating system failure—when any one event could cause a disaster—you're likely to underestimate the likelihood. For instance, a nuclear reactor will break down, a space mission will go awry, or a computer will malfunction if any individual component fails. Fortunately, the chance of any individual component failing is very low. If there are eight components, each with only a 1% chance of failing, what are the odds of disaster? Without picking up a calculator, write down your estimate here: ______ %.

In this case, I'm betting you underestimated the probability. Here, the rules of probability say that the true answer is 1 − 99% × 99% × 99% × 99% × 99% × 99% × 99% × 99%, which equals a 7.7% chance of failure. I'm guessing you underestimated this, because you were anchored on the 1% failure rate. When any one event can cause failure—as in complex systems—anchoring bias will lead you to underestimate the probability of failure.

Next time you're making calculations like this, realise that your mind tends to get stuck on the initial anchor and you need to start thinking slow, so that your logical self can make a more realistic assessment.

Representativeness bias leads you to overemphasise similarity. In a famous psychology experiment, someone describes their neighbour—let's call her Sarah—as "very shy and withdrawn, invariably helpful, but with little interest in people, or in the world of reality." Further, Sarah "has a need for order and structure, and a passion for detail." They're then asked whether Sarah is more likely to be a librarian or a teacher.

Most people guess that Sarah is a librarian. Here, they're judging this probability by how representative they believe Sarah is of librarians. It's an example of

representativeness bias, which arises when you assess the likelihood that something or someone (Sarah) belongs in a category (librarians) by judging how similar they are to your perceptions of that category.

representativeness bias The tendency to assess the likelihood that something belongs in a category by judging how similar they are to that category.

The problem with this thinking is that there are very few librarians, and shy and reserved people like Sarah work in a huge variety of occupations. In fact, there are about 300,000 teachers in Australia and only 2,000 librarians. It is much more likely that Sarah is a teacher than a librarian. Even if people fitting Sarah's description are ten times more likely to choose a library job than other people and half as likely to choose a teaching job, Sarah is still more than twice as likely to be a teacher than a librarian. Most people make the mistake of ignoring the base rate of teachers and librarians in the broader population. This phenomenon is so systematic it is referred to as "base-rate neglect."

More generally, people often assess how likely it is that someone is a member of some group by how similar they are to the group. For instance, venture capitalists often evaluate new ideas by thinking about how similar they are to past successes. If you're trying to get them to fund a new app that allows customers to order a pizza for delivery with a single touch of a button on a smartphone, try pitching it as being "like Uber, but for Pizza." In this case, you're hoping that representativeness bias might lead them to think you're more likely to become a billion-dollar multinational than really seems reasonable for a pizza delivery business. Just as people judging Sarah ignored base rates, you're hoping the venture capitalist forgets how many pizza delivery companies go bust, and that instead they think about how similar your company is to success stories like Uber.

Representativeness bias might also lead you to unconsciously discriminate when you're hiring. If your mental image of a great manager is an older white man wearing a pinstripe suit, then when you interview a younger Asian woman, she might not fit your mental representation of a great executive. If you judge the probability that she'll be successful based on how representative she is of other successful executives, you might end up underestimating her abilities. You might not mean to discriminate, but representativeness bias leads you to do so unconsciously.

When you find yourself judging probability by thinking about how similar things are, it's time to realise you're better off thinking slow, so that your deliberate and logical self can make a better estimate.

Problems Evaluating Payoffs

So far, we've seen how people make mistakes when estimating how likely it is for different scenarios to occur. Now, we'll turn to errors they make in forecasting their own well-being in each of these scenarios.

The focusing illusion can lead you to mis-predict your happiness. One of the biggest decisions you'll face is choosing where to live. How happy do you think you'll be if you move to Queensland? What about if you move to Tasmania? To answer, you'll have to imagine how good life is in each location. What do you think?

Surveys have asked participants to imagine what life would be like for people like them living in Queensland and Tasmania. Overwhelmingly, they expect to be happier in Queensland. After all, in many parts of the state, it's sunny and warm year-round, while winters in Tasmania can be pretty cold. Yet in reality, people in Tasmania evaluate their lives as favourably as those in Queensland. The common prediction that life is better in Queensland turns out to be wrong. This mistake is due to the **focusing illusion,** which leads people to mis-predict their utility when they focus on a few salient factors at the expense of others.

focusing illusion The tendency to mis-predict your utility by focusing on a few factors at the expense of others.

It's a common mistake. University students overestimate how happy they'll be if they're assigned to a desirable dorm. Football fans overestimate how happy they'll be the day after their team wins. People overestimate the misery they'll feel a couple of months after a breakup. And university professors overestimate how unhappy they'll be a few years after being denied an important promotion. None of these things matter for utility as much as people think, and it's likely that you make similar mistakes.

Mark Kolbe/Getty Images

Jodie Griggs/The Image Bank/ Getty Images

Don't just focus on the salient differences.

loss aversion Being more sensitive to losses than to gains.

If you can diagnose this problem, you can do a better job. When you compared Queensland and Tasmania, you probably zeroed in on the most salient difference—the weather!—and concluded that life would be better in Queensland. But the reality is that the weather is just part of the background music of your life. Your utility depends on dozens of other things—your friends, your work, your finances, your safety, your family, and so on. When you overly focus on a salient difference—the Queensland sun versus the nippy mornings in Tasmania—you end up underweighting the many other determinants of your well-being.

The solution to the focusing illusion is thinking slow, and in your more deliberate approach to remember to think about what you're not thinking about. Even better, rather than trying to predict your feelings—which is hard!—ask people living in Queensland about their feelings.

Loss aversion can make you sensitive to how a situation is framed. People tend to think differently about losses than about gains. In fact, psychologists have found that people are about twice as sensitive to losses as to gains. This phenomenon is known as **loss aversion,** and it can distort your decision making. It's not the same thing as risk aversion—which comes from the fact that most people have diminishing marginal utility of each additional dollar of wealth they get. Instead, loss aversion refers to the fact that if I give you $10 right now, the pain you'll feel from losing it is greater than the joy you felt when I gave it to you.

Let's take a look at how loss aversion changed the behaviour of teachers in Chicago Heights, U.S.A. As part of a field experiment conducted by economists, in conjunction with the school district, all teachers were offered an incentive of $8,000 for helping their students reach specific learning targets. But one group of teachers was told they'd get the bonus only after their students reached specific learning targets. A second group was given a big chunk of the bonus upfront and were told that they would have to give it back if they didn't reach the targets. Both groups got the same net payoffs. But in the first group if the teachers underperformed, they would see a smaller *gain* in their bank balance. For the second group, underperformance meant giving back some of the money they had already been given, which was perceived as a *loss*. The prospect of a loss served as a more effective motivator, leading the second group of teachers to be much more effective.

Feverpitch/Deposit Photos

Who cares what price you paid for it ten years ago?

Loss aversion can also motivate you to make poor choices. Recall back in Chapter 1 you learned that good decision makers ignore sunk costs. Car owners should ignore what they paid for their car when they go to sell it. After all, that's a sunk cost and irrelevant to the current decision. Loss aversion leads many people to forget the lesson of sunk costs, and so they refuse to sell their car for less than they paid for it even if they get a different job which is easily accessible by public transport and so have much less need for a car, or if ridesharing services like Uber make car ownership less attractive.

Evaluating your payoffs as gains or losses relative to an arbitrary baseline distorts your decisions. When you find yourself obsessing about losses, it's time to start thinking slow, so that you can focus on the underlying payoffs instead.

Recap: Just because people sometimes make mistakes doesn't mean they always do. At this point you might feel a bit depressed about people's ability to make good decisions in the face of uncertainty. It's true that people do systematically make mistakes about probabilities and payoffs. But perhaps it's more remarkable just how accurate that 1.5 kg mass of grey matter between your ears is most of the time. I've highlighted the mistakes people make, but it's just as important to note just how often they make accurate evaluations in very complex situations. That grey matter isn't perfect, but it's still the most powerful computer the world has ever invented. And hopefully we've figured out some hacks to make it work a little bit better.

Tying It Together

Risk is everywhere. You're uncertain about your career, your relationships, the economy, and your future. You can't avoid risk. Instead, the challenge is to make good decisions in spite of it. Uncertainty doesn't just create risk, it also causes confusion. Your first instinct is typically to use mental shortcuts to guess the probabilities of different outcomes, or the utility from those outcomes. But your intuition is often wrong. Your task is to learn to overrule snap judgements that lead you astray, and instead replace casual intuition with careful reason. This is why we've developed tools to help you reason more carefully about risk.

The central problem posed by risk is that the pain of a bad outcome outweighs the pleasure of an equally good outcome. This stems from the fact that most people have diminishing marginal utility. And that explains why you prefer certainty over risk—why you're risk averse. Purely financial evaluations miss this. This is why you need to shift your focus to thinking about utility rather than money. After all, you're trying to get the most out of life, not get the most dollar bills out of it. Reducing risk will raise your average, or expected, utility. But while you should avoid unnecessary risk, you can't eliminate it altogether.

So when should you take risks? Ultimately, you should be willing to take a risk if it's coupled with a large enough potential reward. It's a trade-off: More risk raises the potential costs, but it still can be worth it if the offsetting benefit is large enough. However, you should be less willing to take on risk when the stakes are large. That's because higher stakes yield a lot more potential pain, but only a little more potential gain in utility terms. The flip side is that you should be largely indifferent to risk when the stakes are small, since the pain of a loss won't be very different from the pleasure of a gain.

Markets—and especially financial markets—provide you with opportunities to reduce risk. You can reduce risk by risk spreading—that is, by dicing it up into lower-stakes risks that other investors are happy to take. You can reduce risk by diversifying your portfolio, since a large number of independent investments is less likely to yield really bad outcomes. You can also reduce risk by buying insurance. You can counter risk with offsetting risks by hedging. And more information can help you tackle the many uncertainties you face.

Now that we're at the end of this chapter, I hope we've largely eliminated one major uncertainty in your life: how best to deal with uncertainty.

Chapter at a Glance

Every choice involves risk. You face risk whenever the outcome is uncertain.

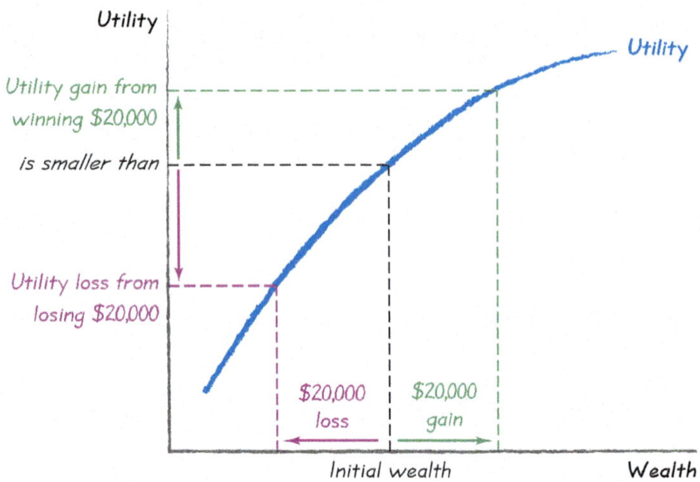

Diminishing marginal utility
(less additional utility from each additional dollar)

↓

Reject a fair bet
($won = $lost, but utility won < utility lost)

↓

Risk averse

↓

Focus on expected utility
$= p_a \times U_a + p_b \times U_b + \ldots$

↓

Risk is more likely to be worth taking if:
a) Reward is large
b) Stakes are low
c) Not very risk averse

Five strategies to reduce risk include:

- **Risk spreading** → Break up big risks into smaller-stakes risks
- **Diversification** → Instead of one big risk, take many unrelated risks
- **Insurance** → Buy compensation if something bad happens
- **Hedging** → Find a risk to offset an existing risk
- **Gathering information** → Will reduce uncertainty

Evaluate payoffs and probabilities carefully, by avoiding these biases:

Assessing probabilities
- **Overconfidence** → Your forecasts are less accurate than you think
- **Availability** → Don't be swayed by easily recalled events
- **Anchoring** → Don't get hung up on an initial estimate or starting point
- **Representativeness** → Look beyond how similar things are

Assessing payoffs
- **Focusing illusion** → Think about what you're not thinking about
- **Loss aversion** → Don't be more sensitive to payoffs appearing as losses

Key Concepts

actuarially fair, 511
anchoring bias, 518
availability bias, 517
behavioural economics, 515
diminishing marginal utility, 501
diversification, 509
expected utility, 506
fair bet, 500
focusing illusion, 519
hedge, 512
index fund, 510
insurance, 511
loss aversion, 520
marginal utility, 501
overconfidence, 516
premium, 511
representativeness bias, 519
risk averse, 500
risk loving, 506
risk neutral, 508
risk spreading, 507
systematic risk, 511
utility, 501

Discussion and Review Questions

Learning Objective 20.1 *Learn how to make good decisions when the outcome is uncertain.*

1. You are thinking about funding a Kickstarter campaign for a hybrid mechanical/digital calendar for which you're willing to pay $125. To receive a calendar, the company required that you pledge $100. You think there's about an 80% chance of the company succeeding, but if the product fails, you will not receive a refund. Is this a fair bet? Would you pledge the $100? Hint: Use your consumer surplus if the company succeeds to evaluate the bet.
2. You are considering investing $2,000 in the stock market. If you invest, there is a 30% probability that in one year's time, your investment will be worth $3,000 and a 70% probability that your investment will be worth $1,600. Alternatively, if you do not invest, you simply keep the $2,000. Would you invest? What does your decision indicate about how you view risk?

Learning Objective 20.2 *Be ready to apply five strategies for reducing the risk in your life.*

3. You are preparing to choose your major. (If you already have, this will still be a good reflection exercise to make sure you're making a good decision!) Apply the five strategies for reducing risk in your life to this decision. Which strategies can you use to help you reduce the risk of choosing the wrong major for you? How would you apply them?
4. There were about 8 million households and 29,377 residential fires in Australia in 2014. Therefore, on average, households faced a 0.37% chance of a fire in a year. You are looking at purchasing renters insurance that costs $100 a year and provides you with $20,000 a year in coverage in the event of a fire. Is this policy actuarially fair? Would you buy the policy? Why or why not?

Learning Objective 20.3 *Prepare to overcome common pitfalls when faced with uncertainty.*

5. You're a project manager overseeing five teams that are developing a new app. Each team must complete their work by 1 July in order to release the app by the end of the year. Based on your work managing the project, you know that each team has about a 75% chance of meeting that deadline.
   - **a.** At your weekly status meeting, the CEO turns to you and says, "Give me your gut reaction: What are the chances we actually get this done by the end of the year?" How do you answer?
   - **b.** Now work out the answer with a calculator. You can either multiply 0.75 five times or raise 0.75 to the power of five. Was your estimate correct, too high, or too low? What aspect of behavioural economics could explain your gut reaction?

Study Problems

Learning Objective 20.1 *Learn how to make good decisions when the outcome is uncertain.*

1. You are analysing two possible stock market investment strategies. For each of the following, identify whether or not it would be classified as a fair bet. Would a risk-averse person make either of these investments? Why or why not?
   - **a.** One strategy is to invest in a blue-chip stock like Microsoft that has a proven track record. There is a 25% chance that the company continues its steady growth and your wealth increases by $30,000. There is a 75% chance that the company becomes unprofitable and your wealth decreases by $10,000.

b. Another strategy is to invest in a startup. There is a 10% chance that the company is a success and your wealth increases by \$100,000. However, there is a 90% chance that the company fails and your wealth decreases by \$20,000.

2. When Devon experiences an increase in wealth, her total utility increases as depicted in the accompanying table.

Wealth level	Utility
\$20,000	2.0
\$40,000	3.8
\$60,000	5.4
\$80,000	6.8
\$100,000	8.0

a. Graph Devon's utility function. Does it exhibit diminishing marginal utility?

b. Her wealth is currently \$60,000. How much would her total utility change if her wealth increased by \$20,000? What if, instead, it fell by \$20,000?

c. Is she risk averse, risk neutral, or risk loving? Explain your reasoning.

3. The following graph illustrates the utility functions for both Rashawn and Juliana, who both have the same amount of wealth:

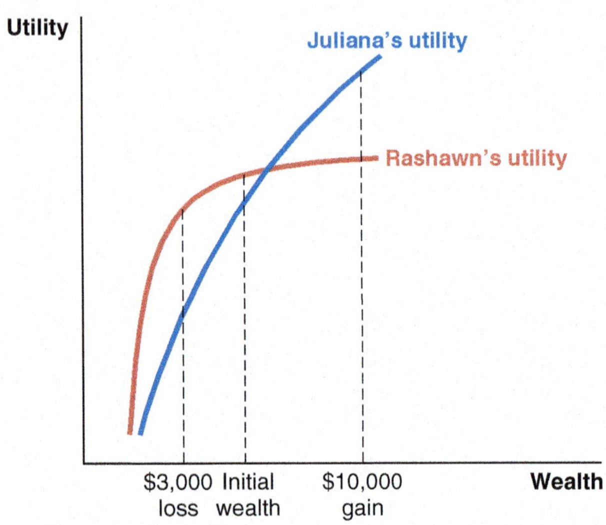

a. Based on the graph, who is more risk averse, Rashawn or Juliana?

b. Both Juliana and Rashawn work for the same company, which announces a new investment option for their super fund. This new option has a 50% chance of increasing their wealth by \$10,000 and a 50% chance that it will cause them to lose \$3,000 in wealth. Based on their utility functions, would either of them choose to transfer the value of their superannuation into the new investment option?

4. You currently have \$10,000 in total wealth and rate your current utility at 4.25. You are deciding if you should invest your money in your friend's automotive restoration business. There is a 50% probability that you will double your money, in which case your total utility will be 6. There is a 50% probability that your friend's business will fail and you will lose the entire \$10,000 and your total utility will be 2.5.

a. What is the expected utility of investing in your friend's company?

b. If you are risk averse, should you take the gamble and invest in your friend's company?

c. Would your answer to part (b) be different if there was a 75% chance that you would double your money by investing in your friend's business?

Learning Objective 20.2 *Be ready to apply five strategies for reducing the risk in your life.*

5. You are considering opening your own photography studio specialising in weddings and other events. You think that there is a 40% probability of your business being successful, at which point you will have \$60,000 in wealth, and a 60% probability that your business will fail, and you will lose everything. The relationship between your financial situation and your utility is as provided in the following table.

Wealth	Utility
\$0	0
\$15,000	4.1
\$20,000	5.8
\$30,000	7.3
\$35,000	8.5
\$60,000	9.6

You're planning to finance the new business with all of your current wealth of \$20,000.

a. If your goal is to maximise your utility, should you open the business?

Another option is to bring aboard three investors. Instead of financing the business on your own, the four of you will evenly split the start-up costs so that now you will contribute \$5,000 of your \$20,000 in wealth to start up the company. If the company is successful, you will *add an additional* \$15,000 to your wealth. If the company fails, you are left with a total of \$15,000 in wealth.

b. If your goal is to maximise your utility, should you open the business with three partners?

c. Does the ability to spread the risk impact your decision about opening the business?

6. Alexandria currently has $80,000 in wealth saved up from her private speech therapy practice. Alexandria plans on working for 15 more years and is afraid there's a 5% chance that she will face a malpractice lawsuit during that time, which would cause her wealth to fall to $20,000 as she would have to pay for legal fees and her practice would suffer. If she doesn't face a malpractice lawsuit, then she expects her wealth to grow to $120,000. She decides to buy malpractice insurance even though the annual premium of $3,200 is more expensive than the actuarially fair annual premium of $2,800. What are some reasons that she would purchase insurance that costs her more than actuarially fair insurance?

7. You have $500 to invest in the stock market and are considering buying shares in Westpac and ANZ, both of which are trading at $30 per share. Analysts believe there's a 50% chance of the economy growing or a 50% chance of the economy falling into a recession. If the economy grows, then the price of the Westpac stock will fall to $20 per share and the price of the ANZ stock will rise to $50 per share. If, however, the economy goes into a recession then the price of the Westpac stock will rise to $50 per share and the price of the ANZ stock will fall to $20 per share. For each of the following, determine the expected value of your portfolio.

   a. Buy $500 of Westpac stock.

   b. Buy $500 of ANZ stock.

   c. Buy $250 of Westpac stock and $250 of ANZ stock assuming the economy goes into recession. Does the answer change if the economy grows instead?

   d. Do all three possible investments result in the same expected value for your portfolio?

   e. Do all three possible investments result in the same level of risk?

Learning Objective 20.3 *Prepare to overcome common pitfalls when faced with uncertainty.*

8. For each of the following scenarios, identify whether it is best explained as an example of overconfidence, availability bias, anchoring bias, representative bias, focusing illusion, or loss aversion.

   a. Dorothy watched news reports about a devastating bushfire in a neighbouring state and in response she decides to quadruple the amount of home insurance that she currently has.

   b. David is the risk manager at a mortgage company. In 2007, he was asked by his boss to estimate the probability that 20% of the company's borrowers would default on their loans at the same time. David stated that this was extraordinarily unlikely, so the firm should not worry about loaning to too many risky borrowers. A year later, mortgage default rates were at an all-time high.

   c. Mandy was working at a Fortune 500 company earning $200,000 per year before she lost her job during a recession. The economy has largely recovered and she has received several job offers, but Mandy is still unemployed because she refuses to accept any job that pays her less than $200,000 per year.

PART VI:

Macroeconomic Foundations and the Long Run

Part VI: Macroeconomic Foundations and the Long Run

The Big Picture

It's time to shift focus from *your economy* (microeconomics) to see what all those decisions mean for *the economy* (macroeconomics). As we'll discover, there's a close link, because macroeconomic outcomes reflect millions of individual microeconomic decisions. So macro builds on micro, while adding a sharper focus on the interdependence between all of these decisions.

In the chapters ahead, we'll examine the key measures that are used to assess an economy's health. Macroeconomics is all about enabling people to live better lives, and so these chapters will focus on the long-run factors that determine whether an economy performs well, or poorly. We'll start by exploring what **gross domestic product** is, and why it's a closely-watched measure of economic health. We'll then ask what drives **economic growth,** analysing why some countries have become rich, while others remain poor. It matters, because insights that raise the growth rate can potentially raise billions of people from poverty. We'll then turn to **unemployment,** analysing what causes joblessness, who it effects, and how costly it can be for society. Finally, we'll examine **inflation** and how **changes in the overall price level** are measured, and what they mean for individuals, businesses, and for the economy overall.

21 Sizing Up the Economy Using GDP

Measure and analyse total economic activity.

- What is macroeconomics all about?
- What is gross domestic product, and how is it measured?
- How effectively can economists measure living standards?
- How can you measure output and income over time when prices are always changing?
- Are there tricks you can use to help make sense of unimaginably big numbers?

22 Economic Growth

Understand what determines the rate of economic growth.

- How has economic growth shaped modern life?
- What are the ingredients that determine total output?
- Can the economy continue to grow forever?
- Where do new ideas come from, and how do they shape economic growth?
- What role do government institutions play in economic growth?

23 Unemployment

Assess the causes and costs of unemployment.

- Who is unemployed, and who isn't?
- Why are there always some people who are unemployed?
- What causes unemployment?
- What are the social and economic consequences of unemployment?
- How can you protect yourself from the harmful effects of unemployment?

24 Inflation and Money

Evaluate the rate of inflation and its consequences.

- What is inflation and how is it measured?
- How can you adjust dollar amounts to account for the effect of inflation?
- What is money, what does it do, and how is it affected by inflation?
- What are the consequences of inflation?
- How does inflation trick people into making bad decisions? (And how can you avoid this?)

CHAPTER 21

Sizing Up the Economy Using GDP

Inga Koster was a business student enjoying a semester abroad in Scotland when she discovered a university shop selling a simple pleasure that she had never encountered in her native Germany: a smoothie. It was a delicious blend of fresh fruit and vegetable juices. Even better, the extra vitamins provided a welcome boost in the face of the bleak Scottish weather.

Katja Kuhl

GDP data can help Inga Koster figure out which markets are ripe for smoothies.

Six months later she was back in Germany, trying to figure out what to do with the rest of her life. Her attention soon returned to that smoothie. She couldn't find a similar product in nearby supermarkets, and soon, the idea for her business was born. She teamed up with two friends to write a business plan, and they founded True Fruits, which today is a successful smoothie company with over $55 million in annual sales.

True Fruits has now grown to the point that Inga and her team are looking to expand internationally. But where? True Fruits smoothies are a small everyday luxury, so they're most likely to sell well in countries with high incomes. That sets Inga's team searching for data that can tell them which countries have high incomes. This is where GDP comes in.

Our task in this chapter is to figure out how to measure the size of the entire economy. We'll focus on a measure called *gross domestic product*—or *GDP* for short—which measures a country's total income. It's the most closely tracked measure of macroeconomic performance. People track GDP because it provides valuable insight into how much is being produced, spent, and earned. That information can help policy makers, investors, and entrepreneurs like Inga Koster make good decisions. We'll also see how GDP is used to track how the size of an economy is changing over time. In the next chapter we'll dig into the determinants of those changes. Our first step is learning how to measure the size of an economy.

You'll also need to know how to interpret what these numbers are telling you. We'll evaluate what GDP counts, what it misses, and how useful it is as a measure of what really matters, which is our living standards. Finally, because this chapter is about how best to size up an economy, we'll develop a few tricks that will help you make better sense of economic numbers.

Chapter Objective

Measure and analyse total economic activity.

21.1 GDP and the Macroeconomy
Learn how to measure the size of an economy using gross domestic product.

21.2 GDP Measures Total Spending, Output, and Income
Analyse GDP as a measure of total spending, output, and income.

21.3 What GDP Captures and What It Misses
Assess GDP as a measure of living standards.

21.4 Real and Nominal GDP
Distinguish between real changes in quantities and the effects of changing prices.

21.5 Millions, Billions, and Trillions
Scale large numbers into something more manageable.

21.1 GDP and the Macroeconomy

Learning Objective *Learn how to measure the size of an economy using gross domestic product.*

macroeconomics The study of the economy as a whole.

You've reached the point at which we'll shift our attention from *microeconomics*—studying individual decisions in specific markets—towards **macroeconomics,** which is the study of the economy as a whole.

From Microeconomics to Macroeconomics

While this marks an important turning point, don't draw too sharp of a distinction. The macroeconomy—that is, the economy as a whole—is simply the result of a whole bunch of individual decisions and interactions. Don't think about micro- and macroeconomics as distinct halves of economics. Rather, think about macroeconomics as being built upon your understanding of microeconomics. This means that the tools you've developed so far—the core principles of economics, a framework for analysing supply, demand, and equilibrium, and an awareness of market failure—will continue to be useful as you study macroeconomics.

What really shifts is our focus, from *individual* income, output, or spending decisions and the implications for individual markets, to the *total* amount of income, output, or spending across all the households, businesses, and levels of government that collectively make up the economy, as shown in Figure 1. Thus, rather than focusing on your individual income, we'll analyse total income in the whole country. And rather than focusing on the output your business produces, we'll analyse total output across all businesses in the country. Lastly, instead of focusing on an individuals' spending, we'll analyse total spending across all consumers, businesses, and the government.

Figure 1 | **Shifting from a Microeconomic to a Macroeconomic Perspective**

	Microeconomics	Macroeconomics
Income	Your individual income.	Total income in the whole country.
Output	The output your business produces.	Total output produced by all businesses in a country.
Spending	Your spending, or the spending of your family or your company.	Total spending across all people, businesses, and the government in a country.

skynesher/E+/Getty Images

A microeconomic decision . . .

Nick Rains/Corbis/Getty Images

. . . with macroeconomic consequences.

Our task in this chapter is to figure out how to *measure* total income, total output, and total spending within a country. Each of these paths of inquiry lead to the same destination: gross domestic product, or GDP. I'll tell you more about what GDP is in just a moment. But first, we're going to need to dig a bit deeper to see how this one key statistic can answer three different questions.

The Circular Flow

The *interdependence principle* is central to macroeconomics because across an entire economy, there are many important connections linking individual decisions, people, markets, and time periods. In this sense, macroeconomics is a lot like traffic. A driver who slows down to gawk at something interesting might think they've merely slowed their journey by a few seconds, but they'll also cause the car behind them to brake, causing the car behind that one to slow as well, and so on. The effects of that one brief slowdown ripple backward because effects can cascade in an interdependent system.

The circular flow illustrates interdependence in the macroeconomy. In macroeconomics, as in traffic, your choices depend on what others do, and what others do depends on what people like you do—you should recognise the *interdependence principle* at work. Your household income depends on how many people businesses hire, which depends on how much output they want to produce, which depends on how much households want to spend, which depends, in turn, on how much income households earn. While your income might seem like an output of the system, it's also an input in an interdependent cycle, both impacting and impacted by macroeconomic conditions.

The *circular flow diagram* provides a conceptual framework for analysing macroeconomic interdependence. This diagram, shown in Figure 2, illustrates the flow of money and resources through the economy, highlighting the linkages between households—like yours!—and businesses. (To keep things manageable, for now we'll omit the government, the financial sector, and the rest of the world.)

Figure 2 | **The Circular Flow of Income and Resources**

The circular flow shows that the **market value of output** = **spending on output** = **income received** = **wages** + **profits**. **GDP** is defined as the value of these flows.

The **green arrows** show that each **flow of goods or services in one direction** is matched by **a flow of money in the other direction**, shown by the **purple arrows**.

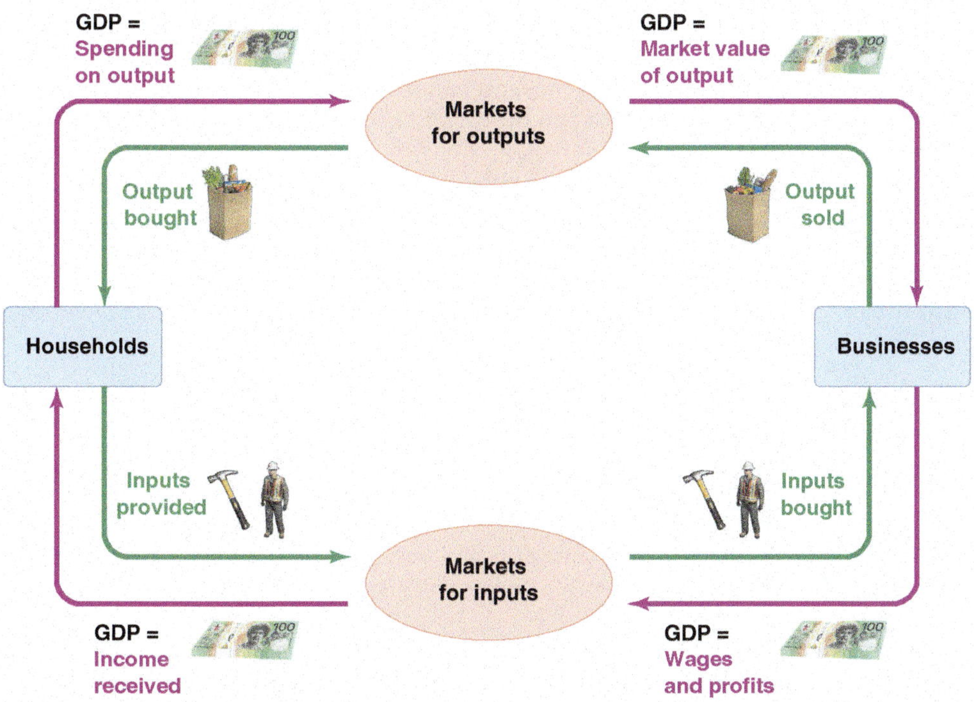

Businesses and households interact in the markets for both inputs and outputs. The circular flow diagram highlights two types of interactions. The top of the diagram shows the market for outputs, where consumers like you demand food, cars, haircuts, and other finished products, and businesses supply them. Your spending pays for this output. The bottom of the diagram shows the market for inputs, where businesses demand labour and capital, and households provide them in return for wages and profits.

All flows of resources are matched by a flow of money. The circular flow shows that there are two ways to track what's going on in the economy. First, the green arrows show the flow of *real resources*—the flow of actual inputs like the labour that households sell to businesses, and the flow of actual outputs like the goods and services that businesses sell to households. Second, the purple arrows represent the flow of *money* exchanged for resources, and so show us the market value of these resource flows. Each flow of real resources is matched by an equal and opposite flow of money.

Total income, total output, and total spending are all equal. The flow of money is a measure of the market value of the resources that are bought, sold, produced, and earned. This reveals that:

- All output that's produced gets sold at some market price, and so the *market value of total output must be equal to total spending.*
- Every dollar that someone spends is a dollar of income for someone else, and so *total spending must be equal to total income.*

It follows that total output, total spending, and total income in an economy all have the same value. That value is an economy's GDP.

Digging into the Definition of GDP

gross domestic product (GDP) The market value of all final goods and services produced within a country in a year.

GDP, which stands for **gross domestic product (GDP),** is a key measure of economic activity. Specifically, it's the *market value of all final goods and services produced within a country in a year.* Conceptually, you can think about all the things that people get paid to do in a year in Australia. If you tally up the value of all the goods and services they produce, you'll know what our collective output is. Add up all the apples, oranges, haircuts, meat pies, precious metals, education, housing, cars, shoes, and everything else that was produced, and in 2019, it came to a grand total of $2 trillion.

GDP per person Total GDP divided by the population.

A number this big can be hard to wrap your mind around, so it's often more intuitive to analyse GDP on a per-person basis. Per-person numbers are also more useful when comparing GDP over time or across countries. That's why we'll focus on **GDP per person** (sometimes called GDP per capita), which is total GDP divided by the population. Dividing $2 trillion per year by 25.7 million people reveals that GDP per person was $77,800 in 2021. This means that:

- average income per person was $77,800;
- average output per person was $77,800; and
- average spending per person was $77,800.

Okay, that's the big picture. It's time to get a bit more precise. The definition of GDP is: **The market value of all final goods and services produced within a country in a year.** That's a bit of a mouthful, so let's unpack it, piece by coloured piece.

"The market value . . ." The grand total of $2 trillion is the *market value* of everything that was produced in 2019. Getting to this grand total requires adding up the value of everything that was produced, from thousands of armchairs to millions of Tim Tams.

If this sounds a bit like comparing apples and oranges, realise that the old expression is wrong: In fact you can compare apples and oranges—and armchairs and Tim Tams, too—as long as you find a common unit. And for GDP—as with many measures in economics—that common unit is the dollar. GDP adds the total dollars spent on armchairs to the total dollars spent on Tim Tams, and everything in between. This means that GDP values each good according to its market price—valuing each $300 armchair as if it's one hundred times as valuable as a $3 pack of Tim Tams. In a competitive market, the price of a product is equal to its marginal benefit, so valuing goods at their market prices effectively values them the same way consumers do.

". . . of all . . ." GDP aims to be as comprehensive a measure as possible, and thus attempts to include everything that's produced and sold in markets. This includes both goods, such as armchairs, and services, such as zoo visits. It's not just the stuff that you buy for yourself, but also the things that the government purchases for you, such as public education and national defence.

As much as GDP tries to be comprehensive, it doesn't include economic activity that occurs outside of markets. This means that the vacuum that you purchased at Big W is part of GDP, but the cleaning services you provide your household when you use it are not. Paradoxically, when you hire someone to use your vacuum to clean your floors, their work is counted as GDP, but when you do it yourself, your work isn't.

". . . final goods and services . . ." GDP only counts **final goods and services,** which are *finished* goods or services.

When you buy a bedhead from Adairs, it's considered a final product because you're the final user, so the $1,500 price of the bedhead gets added to GDP. That $1,500 price includes the value of all the contributions that created your bedhead, from the tree that's now your bedhead frame, the lumberjack who felled that tree, the manufacturer who assembled the bedhead, the driver who trucked it to the store, and the salesperson who sold it to you. Because the price of a final good incorporates all the contributions of the prior stages of production, it's sufficient to just count the final goods produced.

Vasily Gamayunov/Shutterstock

Intermediate Good: Wood waiting to be used to build a bedhead.

Importantly, this means that GDP doesn't separately include **intermediate goods and services,** which are those goods and services used as *inputs* in the production of other products. If you were to count both the value of the bedhead and the value of the wood that went into it, you'd be effectively counting the cost of the wood twice. That's why when you're trying to figure out how much is produced in the economy, you should focus on *final* goods and services, such as the bedhead you might buy at Adairs.

Final Good: The bedhead on the showroom floor, waiting for you to buy it.

". . . produced . . ." Because GDP measures production, it doesn't count *resale* of existing finished goods. If you buy a new bedhead from Adairs, that sale adds to GDP, because that bedhead was just produced. But when you buy a second-hand bedhead from Facebook Marketplace or eBay, your purchase won't add to GDP, because it doesn't involve any new production. Second-hand sales merely change the ownership of goods that have already been produced and were previously counted in GDP.

". . . within a country . . ." GDP measures what we're collectively *producing* domestically, meaning *within Australia.* It includes everything produced in workplaces in Australia—even if they're made by a foreign-owned business, and even if the goods are sold to people outside Australia. It also excludes anything produced in other countries, so doesn't count goods produced in Australian-owned factories in other countries, or goods produced overseas that'll be shipped to Australian consumers.

final goods and services Finished goods or services.

intermediate goods and services Goods or services used as inputs in the production of other products.

". . . in a year." When you measure GDP, you add up all the activity that's occurred during a given time period. Most countries add up all the activity that occurs within a year. In order to stay up-to-date, we typically take four measurements a year—one every three months, called a quarter. We add up the production over the four quarters to find out what was produced during the full year. (And when the government reports GDP for just one quarter, it usually multiplies it by four, so that it's reporting GDP at an annual rate.)

Notice that GDP is a *flow,* measuring the new output that's produced within a year. Alternatively phrased, it's the new spending you do this year, or the new income you earn this year. Make sure not to confuse the flow of income with wealth, which is the *stock* of assets—everything you own—measured at a specific point in time.

Recap: GDP is the market value of the final goods and services that are produced within a country in a year. GDP simultaneously measures total spending, total output, and total income. That's why economists often use these terms interchangeably. So when you hear folks discuss total spending, output, or income, realise that they're all referring to GDP. Okay, it's time to put the pieces back together. Remember:

GDP is . . .

the market value →	*Value each product at its market price*
of all →	*Include all goods and services*
final goods and services →	*Count only final goods and services, omitting intermediate goods*
produced →	*Omit resale of already-produced goods*
within a country →	*Include all goods produced within Australia (even by foreign-owned businesses), but exclude goods produced overseas (even by Australian-owned businesses)*
in a year. →	*Add up the flow of output over a year*

21.2 GDP Measures Total Spending, Output, and Income

Learning Objective *Analyse GDP as a measure of total spending, output, and income.*

The fact that GDP is three things at once—total spending, total output, and total income—is not just a surprising insight; it's also useful. It means that there are three different ways to measure GDP:

> GDP measures:
> 1. Total spending
> 2. Total output
> 3. Total income

- by adding up every dollar of *spending*;
- by adding up every dollar's worth of *output* produced; or
- by adding up every dollar of *income* earned.

In order to get a good estimate of the state of the economy, the government does all three. That's why our next task is to explore how each of these measures is compiled and to investigate the useful business intelligence that each reveals. The simplest way to do this is to follow a single item on its path through the economy, which is why I want to begin by telling you about a bedhead.

The story begins with Britton Timbers, a family-owned lumber company in Tasmania. Britton Timbers chops down and transforms trees into lumber that can be used to make furniture. The company might sell $200 worth of lumber to Mark Tuckey, a furniture manufacturer in Melbourne. Mark Tuckey turns that lumber into a bedhead that it will sell to a retailer, such as Adairs, for $500. Adairs markets the bedhead and sells it to a happy customer for $750.

As we're about to discover, there are three different ways of figuring out how much GDP this little story just created, and they all lead to the same answer.

Perspective One: GDP Measures Total Spending

The first perspective on GDP comes from viewing it as the sum of total spending in the economy. Tracking spending is useful, because you can figure out who's doing all that spending—whether it's businesses, households, governments, or foreigners—and what they're buying.

GDP is total spending on final goods. This method of measuring GDP simply adds up total spending in the economy. But remember: GDP only includes spending on final goods, so the key transaction occurs when the *final user* buys the bedhead at Adairs. We focus on the final good—the Adairs bedhead—because its price embodies the productive efforts of the earlier stages of production at Britton Timbers and Mark Tuckey. Consequently, total spending on final goods—and hence the GDP created by this chain of production—is $750.

(forest) Alalal/Shutterstock; (lumber) Vasily Gamayunov/Shutterstock

GDP includes new inventories. Because GDP is a measure of production (that's the "P" in "GDP"), it counts goods in the year they're *made*, regardless of the year in which they're *sold*. This means that it's important to also count new inventories—goods that have been produced but not yet sold—as part of GDP. And so when more unsold bedheads sit in Adairs' showrooms or warehouses, they're included in GDP, because they've been produced. You can think of this as a form of spending—if you're willing to imagine that Adairs' inventory division bought those bedheads from its bedroom division. Because everything that's produced will either be bought this year or stored as inventories, the inclusion of inventories in GDP ensures that total spending equals total output.

GDP is the sum of consumption, investment, government purchases, and net exports. Now here's the big payoff to measuring GDP by tracking spending: You can track who's doing all that spending, and what they're buying. Indeed, total GDP is calculated by adding up the value of different types of spending.

Economists often use abbreviations to describe each type of spending: Consumption is denoted *C*; Investment is *I*, Government purchases are *G*, and Net eXports is *NX*. Finally, GDP is denoted *Y*. (Why *Y*? Y not!)

Because GDP is the sum of each type of spending, it's calculated as follows:

$$\underbrace{Y}_{\text{GDP}} = \underbrace{C}_{\text{Consumption}} + \underbrace{I}_{\text{Investment}} + \underbrace{G}_{\substack{\text{Government}\\ \text{purchases}}} + \underbrace{NX}_{\text{Net exports}}$$

This equation is an identity, which means that it's always true because it describes the definition of GDP. That's because consumption, investment (including investment in inventories), government purchases, and net exports collectively define all the goods and services produced in the economy.

Figure 3 | **GDP Is the Sum of All Spending on Final Goods and Services . . .**

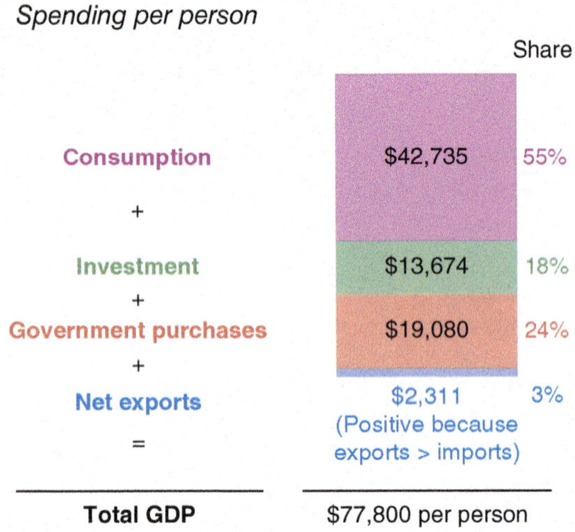

2021 Data from: Australian Bureau of Statistics.

As a result, we measure GDP by adding total spending on consumption, investment, government purchases, and net exports. Figure 3 illustrates these calculations.

Okay, that's the big picture. Now, let's take a look at the details of each of these types of spending.

Household purchases are typically called consumption. When your household buys goods and services, it's counted in GDP as **consumption.** Your consumption includes goods such as food, clothes, and petrol, as well as services such as doctor visits, bus fares, and your mobile phone bill. It also includes *durable goods,* which are long-lasting goods such as cars, bedheads, and washing machines. Even though durable goods take many years to fully use, they're counted as consumption in the year that they're purchased.

The money you spend on rent is also counted in GDP as a form of consumption. This raises a tricky issue, because homeowners enjoy a similar stream of benefits in terms of shelter and comfort, but don't pay any rent. In order to treat all housing services equally, GDP also counts an *imputed rent*—an estimate of the rental value of your home—that you (the consumer of housing services) effectively pay to yourself (the homeowner). We'll dig deeper into consumption in Chapter 25.

consumption Household spending on final goods and services.

investment Spending on new capital assets that increase the economy's productive capacity.

Business purchases are typically called investment. Economists use the word **investment** to refer to spending on new capital assets that increase the economy's productive capacity. It includes both the *purchase* and the *production* of long-lived assets that contribute to future production. Building a factory is an investment because you'll use it to produce goods for many years. Office furniture, computers, and aeroplanes are all investments in equipment that you'll use to produce more goods and services. Business investment also includes spending on research and development. New inventories are counted as a form of investment because they'll lead to future sales.

But be careful, because this macroeconomic definition of the word *investment* is very different from its everyday usage. Remember, GDP is about production, so a macroeconomist says that investment occurs only when something new—such as a newly constructed office building—is *produced.* By contrast, casual conversations about "investing," are often about depositing your money in the bank, buying stocks, or purchasing a block of land. But when you put your money in the bank, you're not actually buying anything—you're saving it to spend later. When you buy stocks, you're usually buying a share of an *existing* business from someone else. And when you buy a block of land, you're buying an existing asset. Because GDP measures what's produced, it doesn't count the storage of your savings, the resale of stock in existing companies, or the resale of real estate as investment.

While most investment is done by businesses, when your household buys a newly built home, it counts as investment, because it increases the economy's capacity to provide housing services. And so newly built houses are added to GDP as residential investment. But if you buy an existing house, you're simply changing who owns an existing asset, so your purchase isn't included in GDP. We'll take a deep dive into investment in Chapter 26.

government purchases Government purchases of goods and services.

transfer payments Payments that transfer income from one person to another.

Matt King/Getty Images

JobSeeker payments transfer income and so they don't count towards GDP.

Government purchases are called . . . government purchases. Whenever the government buys stuff—goods and services—it's counted as **government purchases.** This includes local government spending on schools, state government expenditure on highways, and federal government outlays on the military.

When the government pays the salary of a teacher or a lieutenant in the Royal Australian Navy, it's paying them to produce educational or defence services, so their salaries are counted in GDP as government purchases. But a lot of government spending doesn't count as government purchases. For instance, the government sends out billions of dollars in welfare payments, such as JobSeeker and the Age Pension. These are examples of **transfer payments,** which transfer income from one entity (the government) to another (an individual). Because transfer payments involve no new production of goods or services, they're not counted in GDP. The term *government purchases* might sound a bit clunky, but the word *purchases* is there to remind you that it's all about the stuff the government buys (and so excludes transfers). We'll take a closer look at government spending in Chapter 35.

Foreign purchases of our goods less our purchases of foreign goods is called net exports. Finally, we need to account for linkages with the global economy, while remembering that GDP measures *domestic production.* **Exports** are goods and services that we produce domestically in Australia and sell to people and businesses in other countries. Because exports are *produced* domestically, this spending is included in GDP.

exports Goods or services produced domestically and purchased by foreign buyers.

Imports are goods and services that are produced in other countries and purchased by domestic Australian buyers. Because imports aren't produced domestically, they're *excluded* from GDP. This means that your spending on New Zealand lamb isn't included in Australian GDP. This gets a bit tricky because that lamb was purchased by a household and so was already counted as consumption. Indeed, all imports of final goods and services are already counted as either consumption, investment, or government purchases (depending on who bought them). So to exclude any influence of foreign-produced goods and services from GDP, we need to subtract spending on imports from total spending.

imports Goods or services produced overseas and purchased by domestic buyers.

As a result, GDP adds in exports and subtracts imports. This is why it counts **net exports,** which is spending on exports minus spending on imports. But don't let this confuse you into thinking that imports subtract from GDP. They don't. They're simply *excluded* from GDP—they're neither a positive nor a negative. But in *calculating* GDP, we need to subtract spending on imports to offset the fact that spending on imports has already been counted in the other categories.

net exports Spending on exports minus spending on imports.

We'll explore imports and exports further in Chapter 28.

Perspective Two: GDP Is Total Output

An alternative perspective views GDP as the sum of total output. It's a useful perspective, because it highlights what's being made and by whom. It provides an economy-wide benchmark against which you can compare your company's size and productivity. And by tracking goods through the production process, this perspective maps the structure of production, so that you can assess which sectors are large (*Hint:* the services sector), which are growing, and how interdependent they are.

GDP is the sum of value added at each stage of production. So far, we've seen that GDP is equal to total *spending.* Because every dollar that is spent buys someone else's output, it's also a measure of the market value of total *output.* And this in turn implies that we can measure GDP by adding up total output across all businesses.

Economists have devised a clever way to measure the output of each business involved in a complicated production process. It's based on the idea that at each step of the production process, a company uses materials prepared by others, and then transforms them into something more valuable. The amount by which your company increases the value of an item is called its **value added,** and it's a measure of your contribution towards producing that item. This means that your company's value added is your total sales minus the cost of the intermediate goods and services you bought from other firms.

value added The amount by which the value of an item is increased at each stage of production.

= Total sales – Cost of intermediate inputs

Each stage of the production process before the final sale adds value. Let's return to the bedhead to really explore these issues. The production process began when Britton Timbers took raw material—a tree—and turned it into lumber that it sold to Mark Tuckey for $200. That tree cost Britton Timbers nothing (we'll come back later to the problems with valuing natural resources as if they're free). And so the work it did felling the tree, sawing it into planks, and drying and finishing it into commercial grade lumber that sold for $200, created $200 of value. Next, Mark Tuckey used that $200 worth of lumber and turned it into a bedhead that it sold to a retailer for $500, which means that transforming raw lumber into a bedhead added $300 of value. The bedhead then went to Adairs, which advertised it and helped get it in the hands of a customer who loves it.

Adairs bought the bedhead for $500 and sold it for $750, which means that its efforts—online ads, the sales staff, and its retail location—added $250 of value.

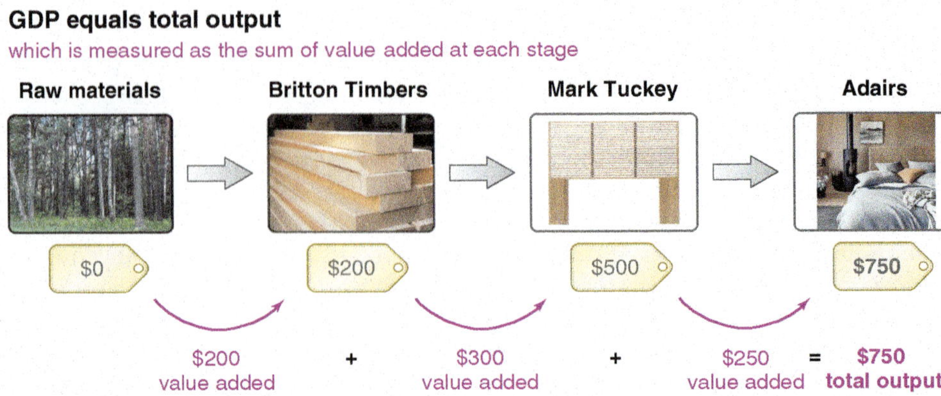

(forest) Alalal/Shutterstock; (lumber) Vasily Gamayunov/Shutterstock

Add the output of each firm in this production chain—$200 of value added by Britton Timbers plus $300 from Mark Tuckey plus $250 by Adairs—and you'll discover that this production process added $750 to GDP. More generally, total GDP is the sum of the value added across all businesses in the economy.

Total output and total spending are equal (and they both equal GDP). This calculation of total output yields the exact same answer as calculating GDP based on spending on final goods. Both suggest the bedhead adds $750 to GDP.

I didn't "fix" the numbers to work this way. Rather, it always works out this way, because of a deeper truth. The spending-based measure of GDP focuses on the value of the bedhead once it emerges from the final stage of production. The output-based measure takes a different perspective, adding up the value created at each stage along the way. But these are just two different perspectives on the same bedhead, and they must yield the same answer because whatever value that bedhead has at the end of the process (that's the spending-based measure) must have accrued somewhere along the way (which is what the sum of value-added measures).

Do the Economics

Let's work through the value added of one particular business. In 2020, Bega reported revenue of $1.5 billion from sales of cheese, vegemite, and related products. It used $1.2 billion in intermediate inputs to make this output. What was its value added?

Value added = $1.5 billion − $1.2 billion = $0.3 billion

As a result, Bega's cheese, vegemite, and other products added $0.3 billion to GDP in Australia.

You can use the idea of value added to calculate the total GDP created by your favourite business. Many companies release data on their sales and costs and a quick Google search will turn up annual reports that provide you with the data you need. ■

Output of Bega	
Total sales	$1.5 billion
less intermediate inputs	− $1.2 billion
equals value added	*= $03 billion added to GDP*

2020 Data from: Bega Annual Report 2020, www.begacheese.com.au

Production of services dominates goods. Once you've measured the value added by businesses in different sectors of the economy, measuring total output simply requires adding up the output across each of these sectors, as shown in Figure 4. These data are particularly valuable because they reveal the structure of production. They show that the modern Australian economy is dominated by the service sector, which accounts for 75% of output. By contrast, goods account for only 25% of the economy. Make sure that your image of a modern economy matches this service-based reality. If you're thinking about a factory, you've got the wrong image. It's far more realistic to picture banks, hospitals, schools, restaurants, wholesalers and retailers, as well as consulting, legal, and accounting firms.

While Figure 4 shows total output broken down into a handful of broad industries, you can dive into the numbers at https://www.abs.gov.au/statistics/economy/national-accounts, and drill down into dozens of sub-sectors, comparing output of, say, coal mining to air & space transport.

Figure 4 GDP Is the Sum of Output across All Sectors . . .

Output by industry

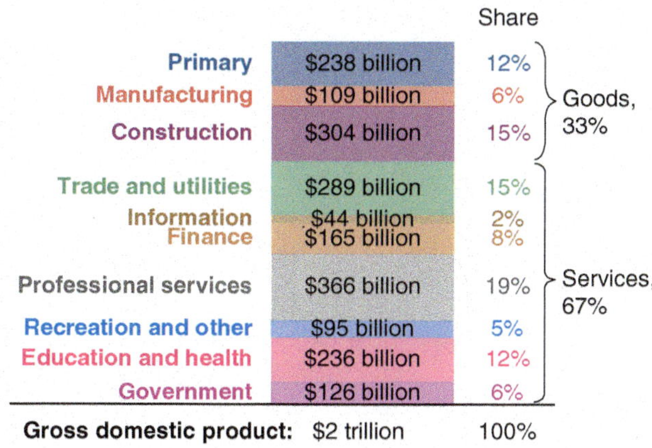

2021 Data from: Australian Bureau of Statistics.

Perspective Three: GDP Measures Total Income

Our final perspective views GDP as the sum of all incomes. It's a particularly useful perspective, because GDP per person measures average income, which you can use to assess the material living standards in a country, and whether they're improving. And by tracking whether this income is going to workers as wages or to business owners as profits, this perspective tells you who is enjoying the fruits of all this economic activity.

GDP is total income, which is the sum of total wages and total profits. There are two sides to every transaction—a buyer and a seller—and so every dollar that a buyer spends also registers as a dollar of income to a seller. This means that we can also measure GDP by adding up the *total income* earned in productive activities. That means adding up all of the wages earned by workers, as well as the profits that shareholders and business owners earn.

Let's return to the bedhead to see how this plays out. In our example, Britton Timbers started with raw materials that cost it nothing, and ended up with $200 of revenue. In terms of income flows, it paid $150 in wages to its workers, leaving it with a $50 profit. Mark Tuckey got $500 revenue from selling its bedhead, paid $200 to Britton Timbers, and spent an additional $250 on wages, so the company was left with $50 in profit. Finally, Adairs got $750 from selling a bedhead it bought for $500. It paid $100 in wages and salaries, which left it with a $150 in profit. Across all three firms, total wages add up to $500 and total profits add up to $250.

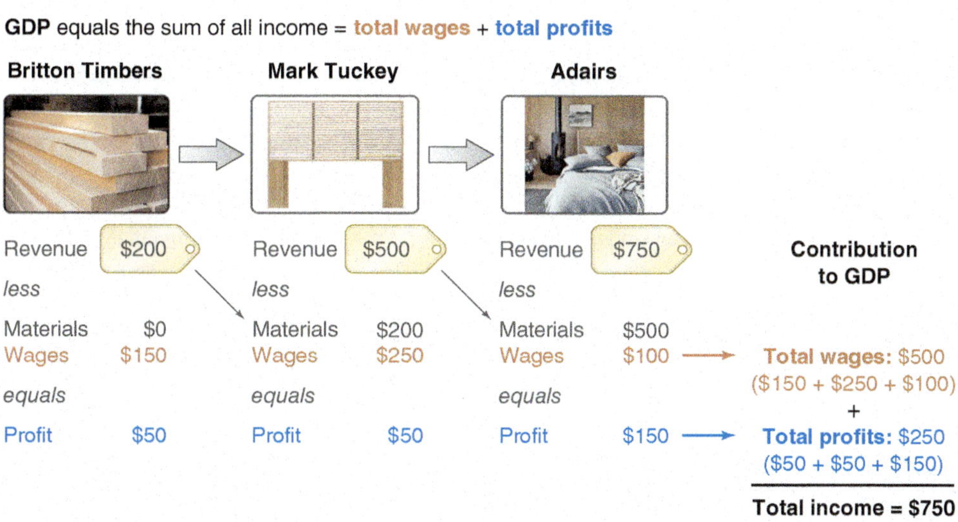

(lumber) Vasily Gamayunov/Shutterstock

Total income is the sum of wages and profits, so measuring GDP as total income suggests that this bedhead added $500 + $250 = $750 to GDP. More generally, GDP can be calculated as the sum of all wages earned by workers plus profits earned by the owners of capital.

Capital gains and losses aren't counted as new income. Just as your purchase of an existing asset isn't counted as new investment, your earnings from selling an existing asset (such as shares, land, or other financial assets) doesn't count as new income. Capital gains don't count as GDP even when you sell assets at a higher price than you paid

Figure 5 | **Labour's Share of GDP Has Declined over Recent Decades**

Data from: Austalian Bureau of Statistics.

for them, because they're simply the resale of existing assets, rather than income earned from productive activity. Nothing is gained from speculative transactions, because a seller's gain from getting a higher price is offset by the buyer's loss at having to pay that higher price.

Labour's share of total income is declining. These income-based data are useful, because they describe how we divide the economic pie between workers and the owners of capital. As such, they reveal the extent to which GDP boosts the purchasing power of households, versus the financial status of businesses.

The *labour share* describes the share of total income that goes to workers as wages, salaries, and benefits. Historically workers received nearly two-thirds of all income, but as Figure 5 illustrates, the labour share has declined over recent decades. In turn, the *capital share*—the share of income that goes to the owners of capital—has risen. Because capital is owned by a smaller and richer group of Australians, this rising capital share has led to rising income inequality.

Recap: Three Perspectives on GDP

Okay, it's time to take a breath and look at the big picture to see how far we've come. We started by *defining* GDP as "the market value of all final goods and services produced within a country in a year." Next came the *conceptual insight* that you can think of GDP as total spending, as total output, and as total income. Finally, we've dug into the practical implication that we can *measure* GDP by adding total spending, total output, or total income.

Even though these each measure the same thing—GDP—Australian government statisticians give them different names, which are listed in Figure 6. While total production, total spending, and total income are the same in *theory,* they get different names because real-world *measurements* can differ because each relies on different sources of imperfect data.

Figure 6 | **Alternative Measures of GDP**

GDP is . . .	. . . it can be measured as a . . .	. . . that measurement is called
Total spending	$Y = C + I + G + NX$	"Gross Domestic Product"
Total output	Sum of value added	"Gross Value Added"
Total income	Total wages + Total profits	"Income from GDP"

You're now equipped to make sense of all these data. If you want to dig in deeper, point your browser to https://www.abs.gov.au/statistics/economy/national-accounts.

21.3 What GDP Captures and What It Misses

Learning Objective *Assess GDP as a measure of living standards.*

There's an old saying in business that "what gets measured gets managed." It captures the idea that measuring an activity helps you understand it and provides insight into how to improve it. Managers focus on the stuff that's measured, because they're the outcomes for which they're held accountable. This idea has implications for macroeconomics, too, because it suggests that policy makers tend to focus on outcomes that are well measured.

And that in turn raises important questions: Is GDP an adequate gauge of economic conditions? Does it provide a reliable measure of living standards or, more ambitiously, the quality of life?

Limitations of GDP

Former U.S. Senator Robert F. Kennedy famously argued that GDP misses much of what's important to a good society. He said:

> [GDP] does not allow for the health of our children, the quality of their education, or the joy of their play. It does not include the beauty of our poetry or the strength of our marriages, the intelligence of our public debate or the integrity of our public officials. It measures neither our courage, nor our wisdom, nor our devotion to our country. It measures everything, in short, except that which makes life worthwhile.

Kennedy was right that GDP misses a lot of what's important. Let's explore some of the most important limitations of GDP.

Harry Benson/Hulton Archive/Getty Images

Robert F. Kennedy said GDP misses a lot of what's important.

Limitation one: Prices are not values. Oscar Wilde once wrote that the definition of a cynic is one who "knows the price of everything but the value of nothing." He might have said the same about GDP. That's because GDP is the *market value* of all goods and services, so it effectively assigns each item a *value* equal to its *market price.*

But our values are not the same as market prices. The collected poems of Banjo Paterson, one of Australia's greatest writers, sell for $26.96. That's about half the price of *This Book Loves You*, by popular YouTuber PewDiePie, which is priced at $51.45 and includes such profound advice as "Don't be yourself. Be a pizza. Everyone loves pizza." Most people would say that Paterson's work is more valuable, but at these prices, each copy of PewDiePie's book adds more to GDP.

The argument for valuing goods at their market prices is that in a perfectly competitive market, the price is equal to the marginal benefit of a good. But this still misses a lot. Consider the value of clean water. When the price of water is low, you keep buying it until the last litre has a pretty low marginal benefit, perhaps using it to wash your car. But the earlier litres—the litres that prevent you dying from dehydration—are much more valuable. The problem is that GDP only counts your spending on a good, but your benefit is often much larger if you enjoy *consumer surplus.* This is a particularly pressing problem when it comes to analysing the value of internet services such as Google, Snapchat, or Wikipedia, each of which is sold at a price of zero, and so counts very little towards GDP. Additionally, the price of a good is not equal to a consumer's marginal benefit when firms have market power or other market failures exist.

Limitations of GDP:

1. Prices are not values.
2. Nonmarket activities—including household production—are excluded.
3. The shadow economy is missing.
4. Environmental degradation isn't counted.
5. Leisure doesn't count.
6. GDP ignores distribution.

Limitation two: Nonmarket activities—including household production—are excluded. GDP only measures goods and services that are sold in markets, which misses a lot of productive activity. You probably do your own laundry, clean your own apartment, wash your own car, and mow your own lawn. If you have kids or pets, you likely spend a lot of time playing with them, feeding them, and bathing them. All of this activity is productive—you're creating valuable goods and services—but none of it is counted in GDP. One recent estimate suggests that the value of all the uncounted housework, cooking, odd jobs, gardening, shopping, and child care that we do for ourselves over the course of a year adds up to roughly $21,000 per person. And that's a conservative estimate!

The omission of nonmarket activities can lead to some weird results. If instead of doing these tasks for ourselves, we paid others to do them, they would suddenly be considered market activities that are counted towards GDP. As a result, measured GDP per person would suddenly be $21,000 higher, even though the total amount of productive activity hadn't changed.

jirawat phueksriphan/Shutterstock

Pargovski Jove/Shutterstock

Taking care of your babies won't count towards GDP.

Sean Locke Photography/Shutterstock

When you pay cash, you may be participating in the shadow economy.

Limitation three: The shadow economy is missing. A large amount of economic activity occurs "in the shadows," purposely conducted out of view of the government, because it involves illegal products such as drugs, banned services such as gambling, businesses operating without necessary licences, workplaces that flout labour standards, or the use of cash to avoid paying taxes. Together, these activities are called the *shadow economy.* Many of these activities occur deep enough in the shadows that they're unmeasured, and thus they're effectively excluded from GDP. The shadow economy includes organised crime, the guitarist busking on a street corner, and the plumber who repaired your sink and asked for cash payment. It may even include the $60 you were paid to babysit last weekend, if neither you nor the family plan to report that payment in government surveys.

Figure 7 | **How Much Larger Would GDP Be if It Counted the Shadow Economy?**

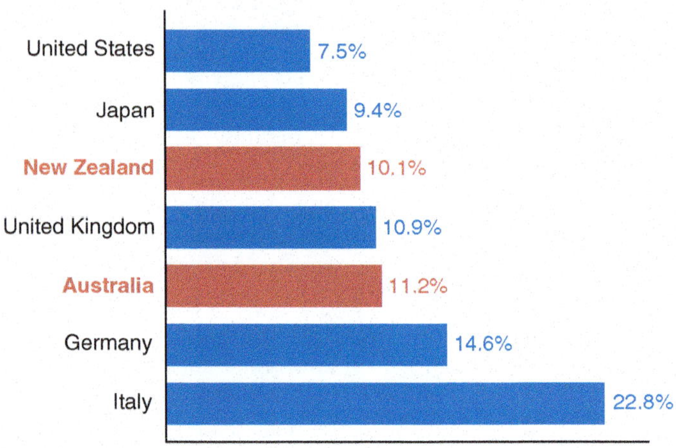

Data from: Engle, Dominik H., "The Shadow Economy in Industrial Countries."

Interpreting the DATA

Measuring the shadow economy

Most (but not all) transactions in the shadow economy occur in cash, and so excessively strong demand for currency for transactions is an indicator of a thriving shadow economy. Indeed, recent estimates suggest that the shadow economy could use up to $6 billion in Australian banknotes every year—that's 8% of all banknotes in circulation!

Economists have used insights like this to guesstimate the size of the shadow economy. The results, shown in Figure 7, suggest that it's quite large. Counting the shadow economy would boost GDP in Australia by about 11% and in New Zealand by about 10%. It's even bigger in many other countries, partly because their higher taxes and more restrictive regulations provide a greater incentive to push economic activity into the shadows. ■

Panther Media GmbH/Alamy

Destruction or production?

Limitation four: Environmental degradation isn't counted. When Britton Timbers cuts down trees and sells the lumber for $200, this is counted as adding $200 to GDP. Effectively GDP treats natural resources as if they have no value until they're transformed into something else. What you might see as *destruction*—the clear-cutting of an old growth forest—GDP counts as *production,* because it only sees new lumber being produced. Because GDP treats nature as if it's free, it ignores the costs of environmental degradation, fails to account for biodiversity, and takes no account of global warming, even as it counts the output of polluting factories as positive contributions.

Hudzilla/fStop/Getty Images

Boosting happiness, but not GDP.

Limitation five: Leisure doesn't count. One way to produce more is to work more. If your boss pays out your annual vacation, so that you clock more hours at work, you'll earn more income even if your quality of life suffers. Similarly, if everyone worked more, GDP would get a boost. But that extra output comes with a cost that GDP ignores. To understand the cost of working, you can apply the *opportunity cost principle* which reminds you to ask, "or what?" If you weren't working, what would you be doing? Would you be spending time with your friends or family? Enjoying a day at the park? Going to the movies? Whatever you choose, a day of work means a day less of leisure. The problem is that GDP counts the benefit of work—more income!—but omits the cost, which is less leisure.

EVERYDAY Economics **Would you rather live in the United States or in Australia?**

Australia has instituted a 38-hour workweek, requiring employers to pay overtime to compensate for any extra hours worked. By contrast, in the United States the typical workweek is 40 hours. Australia also requires that employees have access to substantial paid vacation time, paid sick leave, and paid parental leave. None of these are required in the United States. Add it all up, and over the course of a year, a typical Australian employee works 100 fewer hours than their American counterpart. That's the equivalent of two and a half fewer workweeks! But this comes at a cost. The average income in Australia—that is, GDP per person—is 9% lower than it is in the United States. Which would you prefer: more money, or more time off? ■

Michele Jackson/Alamy Stock Photo

Australians have more time to sit in cafés than Americans do, but less money to spend in them.

Limitation six: GDP ignores distribution. You can think of GDP as measuring the size of our economic pie, with GDP per person measuring the size of the average slice. But what really matters to people is their *actual* slice, not the average slice. And so the distribution of income matters, too. This point has become particularly salient over recent decades, because much of the income growth since the 1980s has accrued to the very richest households. Figure 8 shows that the living standards of the *average* Australian have risen rapidly, while the living standards of the average Australian with an income in the lowest quintile have risen by about 10% less.

Figure 8 | **Average Income Has Risen, but Not as Much for the Lowest Income Households**

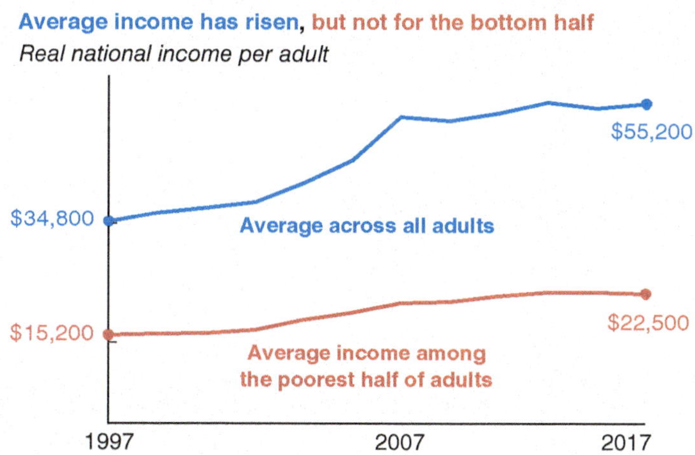

Data from: Australian Bureau of Statistics.

GDP as a Measure of Living Standards

While there's a lot that GDP leaves out, there remains a compelling underlying logic to it. GDP per person measures average income in a country, and higher income makes it easier to invest in children's health, in education, in creating beautiful art and poetry, and in taking the time to invest in your personal relationships. By this argument, it's not that GDP measures what matters, but rather that it measures the *resources* that a society has available to pursue what matters. If we use those resources well, then people who live in countries with high GDP per person will live happier, more fulfilling lives.

Indeed, Figure 9 illustrates that people who live in countries with higher GDP per person tend to enjoy better life outcomes. The top left panel shows the results of surveys asking people to rate how satisfied they are with their lives on a 0–10 scale. The average score is much higher in countries with high GDP. Other surveys reveal that people in countries with high GDP are more likely to rate themselves as being happy, they're more likely to smile or laugh a lot, and they're more likely to feel that they're treated with respect. They're also less likely to experience pain and less likely to feel depressed.

The other three panels turn to more objective indicators and show that in countries with higher GDP per person, people get more education, live to older ages on average, and have fewer babies die before their first birthday. This is partly because higher GDP is associated with better access to a variety of necessities—including water, sanitation, food, shelter, medical care, and education. People in countries with high GDP also tend to enjoy more rights and personal freedoms and to live in more inclusive societies. For all of its shortcomings, GDP appears to be quite closely related to many other indicators of quality of life.

Figure 9 | Higher GDP Is Correlated with Better Life Outcomes

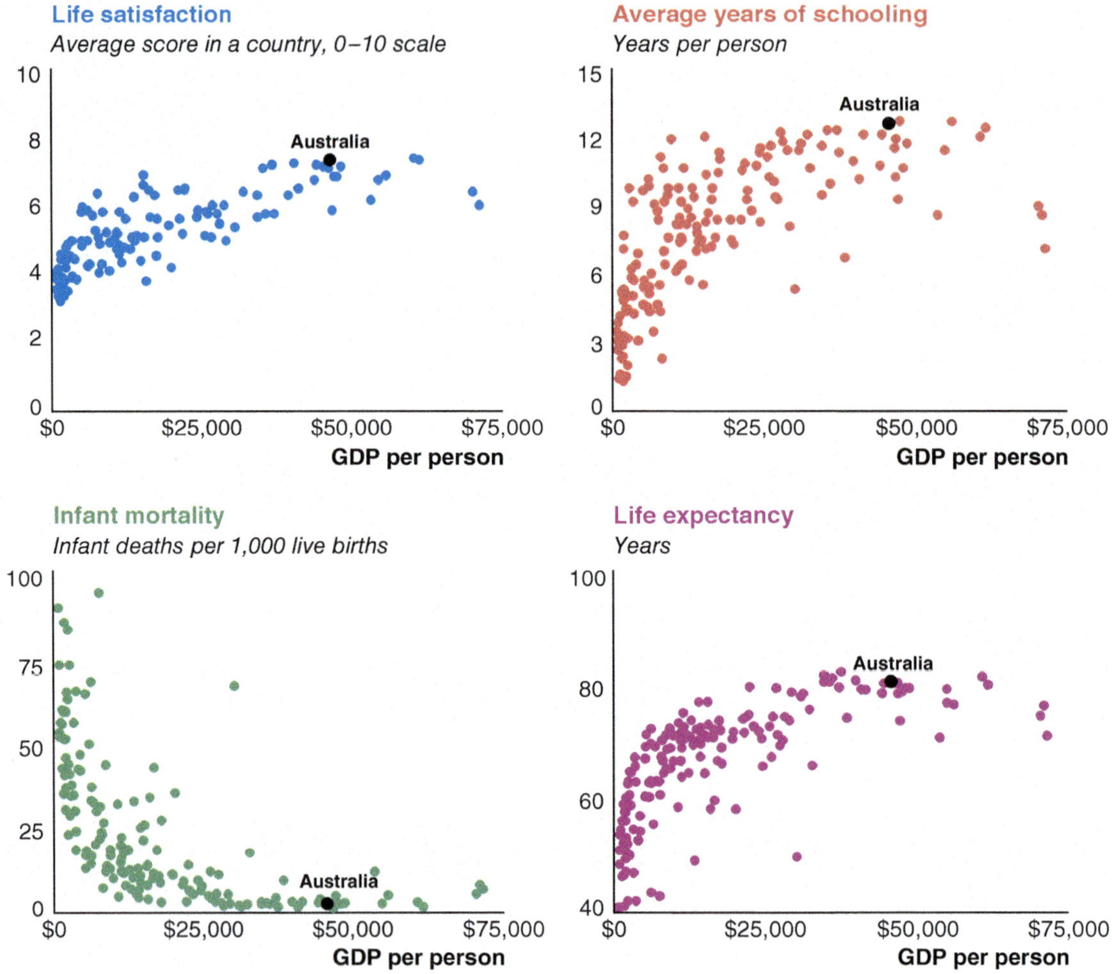

Data from: Gallup; World Bank.

EVERYDAY Economics **Visualising differences across countries**

Ann Rosling Rönnlung started the website Dollar Street to help people visualise everyday life in countries at different levels of economic development. You can see differences in the houses people live in, what they're about to purchase, and the things they aspire to one day buy. Let's take a look at three typical families in countries with very different levels of GDP per person:

The Pingol family lives in the Philippines, where GDP per person is US$8,900.

The Zhao family lives in China, where GDP per person is US$18,200.

The Howard family lives in United States, where GDP per person is US$62,600.

Abraham works as a truck driver. His wife, Evelyn, works as an accountant.

They have four children and live in this two-bedroom house.

Their next big purchase will be food, but they dream of one day buying a car.

Tiecai works as a taxi driver. His wife, Yanqing, works in a grocery store.

They have one child and their home is in the same area where they grew up.

Their next big purchase will be a TV, but they dream of buying a car.

Bryan works as a sales director for a wine company. His wife, Christina, is a stay-at-home mum.

They have two children and live in this four-bedroom house.

Their next big purchase will be a car for their daughter. They dream of purchasing a vacation home. ■

Pingol family: Luc Forsyth for Dollar Street; Zhao family: Benikhlef Abdelhak for Dollar Street; Howard family: Zoriah Miller for Dollar Street

21.4 Real and Nominal GDP

Learning Objective *Distinguish between real changes in quantities, and the effects of changing prices.*

Australian GDP has increased by over 70% since the end of the last century. In 2019, it was \$2 trillion, compared to 2000 when it was \$1.2 trillion. But total economic activity didn't increase by 70% over this period. The problem is that the *market value* of total production can double because we're making twice the *quantity* of stuff, or because we're making the same quantity of stuff but *market prices* are 70% higher. Or, as in this case, it can reflect some combination of rising prices and rising quantities. It's a distinction that matters, because an increase in the quantity of stuff we produce raises living standards, while a change in the price tags attached to that stuff doesn't change anyone's quality of life.

Real and Nominal GDP

nominal GDP GDP measured in today's prices.

Nominal GDP is GDP measured in today's prices. To calculate nominal GDP you add up the market value of total production in a year using the *current prices* prevailing in that year. Nominal GDP is useful if you want to know what GDP is right now, based on the prices that you face right now. However, nominal GDP is not very useful for making comparisons over time. The problem is that when prices rise over time—a process known as inflation (which we'll explore in Chapter 24)—nominal GDP will rise even when actual production is unchanged. For instance, nominal GDP values last year's apple crop at last year's price (say, \$3 per kilo), while this year's nominal GDP will value apples at this year's price of \$5 per kilo. If we produce the same number of apples but count this year's apples as if they're 70% more valuable, it appears that apples' contribution to GDP has increased by 70% even though actual apple production is unchanged.

real GDP GDP measured in constant prices.

When you're trying to evaluate changes over time in economic activity, you should analyse real GDP instead. **Real GDP** is GDP measured in constant prices, so that it excludes the effects of price changes. By focusing only on changes in GDP due to changes in the *quantity* of output produced, real GDP isolates economic growth. It's calculated by adding up GDP as if no prices changed between last year and this year. It's called *real* GDP to remind you that it measures the *real* change in production, rather than changes in the price tags attached to each product.

When economists talk about GDP growth they nearly always mean "growth in real GDP." In fact, most people who talk about changes in GDP are referring to changes in real GDP. So when you see an ABC report that the "Australian economy grew 2.3% last year," you can safely assume it's describing real GDP.

How to Calculate Real GDP

You'll better understand the distinction between real and nominal GDP by seeing how they're calculated. In order to make the numbers as simple as possible, we'll calculate GDP growth as if Adairs were the only business in the whole economy. (Expanding this example to include the rest of the economy won't change anything beyond making the calculations more complicated.)

Figure 10 gives the key inputs to our calculations, for both "last year" when 100 bedheads were sold at a price of \$750 each, and "this year," when 103 bedheads were sold at a price of \$780 each. Over these two years, the average price, $\overline{P}$, is \$765.

Figure 10 Calculating Real and Nominal GDP

		Calculating Nominal GDP		Calculating Real GDP	
	Quantity sold (Q)	Actual price (P)	Nominal GDP $= P \times Q$	Average price $\overline{P} = \frac{P_t + P_{t-1}}{2}$	Real GDP $= \overline{P} \times Q$
Last year	100 bedheads	\$750	\$750 × 100 = \$75,000	\$765	\$765 × 100 = \$76,500
This year	103 bedheads	\$780	\$780 × 103 = \$80,340	\$765	\$765 × 103 = \$78,795
Growth rate	+3%	+4%	+7%	+0%	+3%

Calculate nominal GDP using current prices. Nominal GDP is calculated as the market value of total output in each year, where each year's output is valued based on the market price in the year it was produced. So in this example, nominal GDP grew from \$75,000 (=100 bedheads × \$750) last year, to \$80,340 (=103 bedheads × \$780) this year. This is an increase of 7%, and this rise reflects an increase in both the price of bedheads and the quantity produced. Because nominal GDP in each year is calculated using the current price for that year, it's sometimes referred to as *GDP at current prices.*

Calculate real GDP using constant prices. Real GDP is calculated by computing growth in the value of output between this year and last year, where that output is valued using an unchanging, or constant, set of prices. As a result, it's sometimes referred to as *GDP at constant prices.* To be precise, GDP growth between any pair of adjacent years is calculated using the *average* price level over those two years. (This is part of a procedure known as *chain-weighting,* which calculates the growth in real GDP over time by first calculating growth between pairs of adjoining years using the average price in that specific pair of years, and then chaining together or accumulating these year-to-year growth rates to estimate growth over longer periods.)

So in our example, we calculate real GDP as if the price were constant at its average level over these two years of $765. As a result, we compute that real GDP grew from $76,500 (=100 bedheads × $765) to $78,795 (=103 bedheads × $765). This is an increase of 3%, which is the same growth rate as the quantity of bedheads sold.

Do the Economics

Last year, Dell sold 100 laptops at $1,000 each, and this year, it sold 104 laptops at $1,060 each. Calculate (a) the growth rate of prices; (b) the growth rate of Dell's contribution to nominal GDP; and (c) the growth rate of Dell's contribution to real GDP. ■

Answers: a. Prices grew by 6%. b. Nominal GDP rose from 100 × $1,000 = $100,000 to 104 × $1,060 = $110,240. This is a growth rate of (110,240 − 100,000)/100,000 × 100 = 10%. c. The average price is ($1,000 + $1,060)/2 = $1,030. Thus, real GDP rose from 100 × $1,030 = $103,000 to 104 × $1,030 = $107,120, a growth rate of (107,120 − 103,000)/103,000 × 100 = 4%.

There's a trick that will let you move quickly between real and nominal GDP growth. If you had to do calculations like this all the time, it would quickly become tiresome. But there's a simple math trick that makes it a lot simpler. For changes over short periods of time (perhaps a few years):

$$\%\text{ Change in nominal GDP} \approx \%\text{ Change in real GDP} + \%\text{ Change in prices}$$

In Figure 10, real GDP rose by 3%, and the price of bedheads rose by 4%, and so this formula correctly predicts that nominal GDP rose by 7%.

If you rearrange a bit, this also gives you a way to calculate growth in real GDP:

$$\%\text{ Change in real GDP} \approx \%\text{ Change in nominal GDP} - \%\text{ Change in prices}$$

Thus, the growth rate of real GDP is simply the growth rate of nominal GDP, less the average growth rate of prices. In Chapter 24, we'll describe a general rise in prices as *inflation* and the specific measure of inflation used to estimate real GDP is called the *GDP deflator.*

Do the Economics

a. In 2019, nominal GDP grew 4.4%, and prices rose by 1.8%. Calculate the growth rate of real GDP.
b. Head to https://www.abs.gov.au/statistics/economy/national-accounts/australian-national-accounts-national-income-expenditure-and-product/latest-release and find the growth rate of nominal GDP last year, as well as the growth rate of the GDP deflator. (Hint: Check out the first few Tables in the "data downloads" section.) Calculate growth in real GDP. ■

Answers: a. % change in real GDP ≈ 4.4% − 1.8% = 2.6%. b. You can find nominal GDP growth for each quarter last year in the "Economic Overview" section of the national accounts report, and then add the quarterly numbers up to get the yearly growth. The GDP deflator is in a downloadable table labelled "implicit price deflators". You can check your estimate of real GDP growth by looking at the Economic Overview section which reports quarterly real GDP growth for the last few years.

Finally, I bet you've noticed that macroeconomics often involves unimaginably large numbers—such as the $2 trillion worth of Australian GDP. Our last task is to develop some strategies you can use to make sense of these huge sums.

21.5 Millions, Billions, and Trillions

Learning Objective *Scale large numbers into something more manageable.*

If you've seen the movie *Austin Powers: International Man of Mystery,* you'll know one of my favourite lines. Austin Powers' nemesis, Dr. Evil, wakes up from a 30-year sleep with a dastardly plan—he wants to steal a nuclear warhead and "hold the world to ransom for. . . . ONE MILLION DOLLARS." The joke is that what sounds like a lot to Dr. Evil is a pittance in the grand scheme of things. It's less than the Australian Government spends *per minute.*

New Line/Everett Collection

Holding the world for ransom . . . for one million dollars.

The Problem of Big Numbers

It turns out that Dr. Evil is in good company. I have worked with many policy makers, and it's amazing how often they confuse millions, billions, and trillions, even though they're tasked with considering or implementing legislation costing millions and billions of dollars! The problem is that everyday life gives our brains plenty of practice at making sense of small numbers. But we have very little experience with much larger numbers, so it can be hard to wrap your mind around them. It's no surprise, then, that psychologists have found that people often have faulty intuitions about large numbers, noting that once numbers get beyond a certain point, they start to lose meaning to people. That's why people sometimes just give up and say, "a gazillion." So we'll spend some time now making sure that you think clearly about these differences, since they're critically important for understanding the macroeconomy.

Start by visualising the difference. One simple trick is to visualise amounts you're analysing. Start by closing your eyes and picturing a single $100 note. It is thin, small, and can easily fit in your pocket. $10,000 is a tidy bundle of notes. Figure 11 shows that 100 of those stacks—which adds up to a million dollars—fills a briefcase. Next, realise $1 billion is 1,000 of these briefcases of cash. You can probably jam 1,000 briefcases of cash into a school bus (but only just), and so a billion dollars is roughly a busload of $100 notes. In order to get to a trillion dollars, you'll need to get 1,000 busloads of cash together, and you can probably fit this into a football field if you double-stack them. So a trillion dollars is a football field stacked with $100 notes to a bit above your head.

Figure 11 | **Millions, Billions, and Trillions**

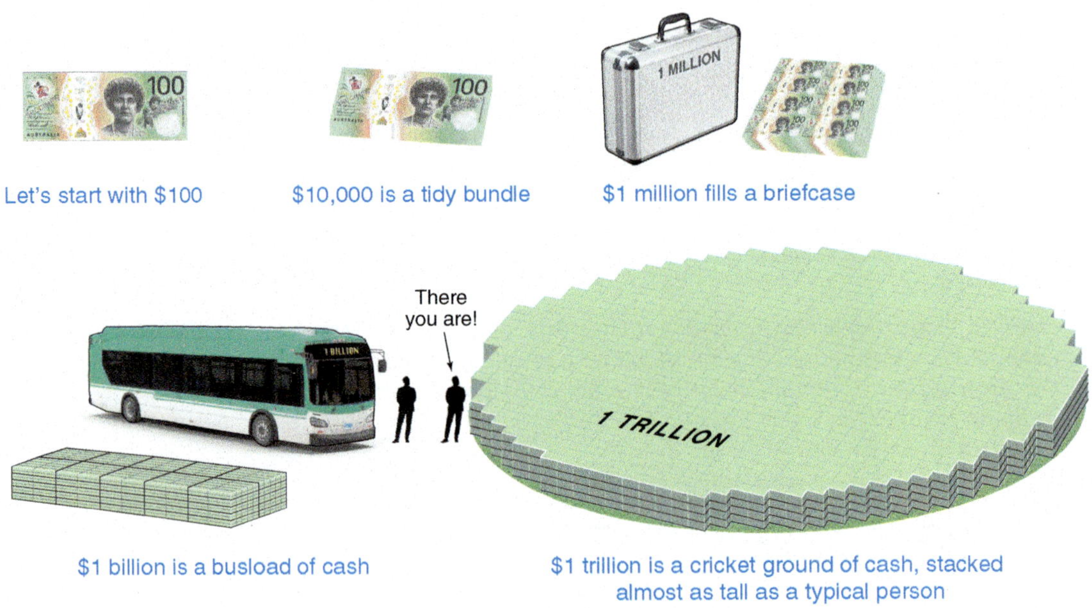

Want to picture the total amount of annual GDP for Australia? It's about $2 trillion. This time, imagine your favourite cricket ground, and fill it with $100 notes nearly as high as a typical cricket player. That's roughly annual Australian GDP.

Four Strategies for Scaling Big Numbers

I've got a confession, big numbers sound big to me, too. So how do I make sure that I don't get confused? I scale big numbers so that they're easier to manage. Here are a few strategies you can use to make sure that you don't get confused.

Strategy one: Evaluate what it means per person. The size of the Australian economy is almost unimaginably large. What does it even mean to produce a football stadium full of $100 notes each year? Instead of trying to imagine this, try reducing this number to more human terms by thinking about it in terms of what it means per person. Total GDP in 2019 was $2 trillion, but it's far more intuitive to think of this as $77,800 per person.

Keeping a few baseline numbers in the back of your mind will help you apply this strategy as you encounter more macroeconomic data:

- The world population is nearly 8 billion.
- The Australian population is about 26 million.
- There are around 10 million households in Australia.

When you encounter other large numbers, you'll better comprehend their scale if you convert them to per person or per household measures. This means that if I tell you that Australia spends $200 million dollars per year on research to develop clean energy or that the travel and accommodation sector spends $800 million per year on advertising, you can translate these numbers to $20 and $80 per household. These are easier numbers to evaluate.

Strategy two: Compare big numbers to the size of the economy. An alternative approach scales big numbers by comparing them to the size of the total economy. This is why macroeconomists often compare big numbers to total GDP. For example, in the 2019–2020 financial year, the federal government's budget deficit—its outlays less its revenue from taxes and other sources—was $85.3 billion. Without further context, it can be hard to make sense of a number this big. But compare it to total GDP, and you'll discover that the budget deficit was equal to 4.3% of GDP, which gives you a better sense of the scale of the problem.

Strategy three: Compare big numbers to their own history. Another way to scale big numbers is to evaluate their size relative to their previous values. This is what percentage changes do. For instance, 640,000 Australians were unemployed in July 2021, which sounds like a lot. But when you scale it relative to past numbers, you discover that it's about 40% less than the number of people who were unemployed in July 2020 during the height of the coronavirus pandemic, which is a useful context for understanding the scope of the problem.

Strategy four: Use the Rule of 70 to evaluate long-run growth rates. Sometimes small differences in percentage changes can have bigger implications than you might think, and you can help sort these out by using a simple rule of thumb. The **Rule of 70** says that you can figure out approximately how many years it will take something to double if you divide 70 by its annual growth rate:

Rule of 70 Divide 70 by the annual growth rate to get the number of years until the original amount doubles.

$$\text{Years it takes something to double} \approx \frac{70}{\text{Annual growth rate}}$$

For instance, between 1980 and 2020, real GDP per person in Australia grew at an average rate of 1.56% per year. At that rate, it would take $\approx 70/1.56 = 45$ years for average income to double. (Note that you divide by 1.56, not 0.0156.) Indeed, by the end of these 40 years, it was about 85% larger, on track to double relative to 1980 levels by 2025. By comparison, in Singapore, real GDP per person grew at an average annual rate of 5.3%, which means that it doubled every $\approx 70/5.3 = 13$ years. And indeed, over these 40 years, Singapore's average income doubled, then doubled again, and then almost tripled by 2020!

You can use this approximation to figure out how long it will take you to double your savings, how long it will take a country to double its average income, and how long it will take your business to double your number of customers. As you'll discover—and as Figure 12 shows—relatively small

Figure 12 | Years Until Something Doubles

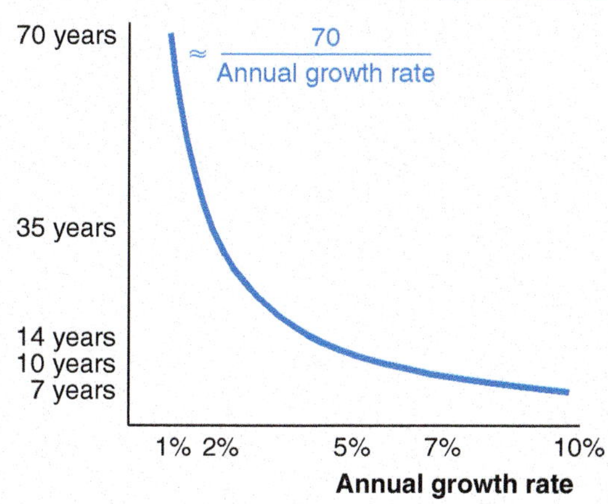

differences in annual growth rates lead to big differences over many years because growth tends to compound over time.

Do the Economics

The ability to convert big numbers into more manageable terms is a valuable skill beyond macroeconomics. Indeed, if you ever interview for a job in consulting, it's likely they'll test you on these abilities. So it's worth practicing:

a. Does Woolworths employ roughly 200 thousand, 200 million, or a 200 billion Australians?

b. Is the total amount paid in wages and salaries in Australia each year several millions, billions or trillions of dollars?

c. McDonald's boasts that it sells "billions and billions of burgers" each year. Is this really plausible?

d. Does Amazon Prime have 100 thousand members, 100 million, or 100 billion?

e. In 100 years do you expect the price of a cup of coffee to be $3, $30, or $300? ■

Answers: a. Woolworths employs over 200 thousand people in Australia, which sounds large until you realise it's about 1-in-130 Australians. b. In 2019, total wages and salaries were a little under a trillion. c. Yes, it's plausible. If McDonald's only sold 4 burgers per Australian per year, that would already be 100 million burgers, and McDonald's operates in countries with much bigger populations than Australia. d. Amazon Prime has 100 million members around the world. e. If prices rise on average by 2% per year, then they would double every 35 years. So over 100 years, the price of a cup of coffee would double, then double again, and nearly have time to double again. A cup of coffee currently costs around $4, so if prices will be nearly 8 times higher, then a cup of coffee will cost close to $30.

It's worth building your skill in working with big numbers like this, because it will prove to be a valuable asset that you'll use every time you confront new economic data. So keep practicing!

Tying It Together

You now know quite precisely what GDP is, how it's measured, and how to interpret it. This is a vital skill, because GDP will be a consistent theme through the rest of your study of macroeconomics. That's because GDP is a useful measure of material living standards, and a key goal of macroeconomics is to find ways for people to live better lives.

You can use GDP per person to assess differences in average income across countries. Figure 13 reveals some striking disparities. GDP per person is $77,800 in Australia compared to only $810 per person in the Democratic Republic of the Congo. Much of the world's population lives in India, where GDP per person is $2,900, or in China, where it's $16,900. These differences in GDP per person have enormous implications for child mortality, life expectancy, and happiness. Finding a way to raise these countries' GDP per capita to the level of Australia would have astounding consequences for human welfare. That's why the next chapter analyses the long-run determinants of economic growth, providing a framework that you can use to assess why GDP per person is so much lower in the Congo than in Australia, and the types of institutions and policies that can spur greater economic development.

Figure 13 | Australia Is One of the World's Richest Countries

GDP per person (2015 $USD) in the world's 18 most populous countries plus Australia and New Zealand, adjusted for differences in the cost of living

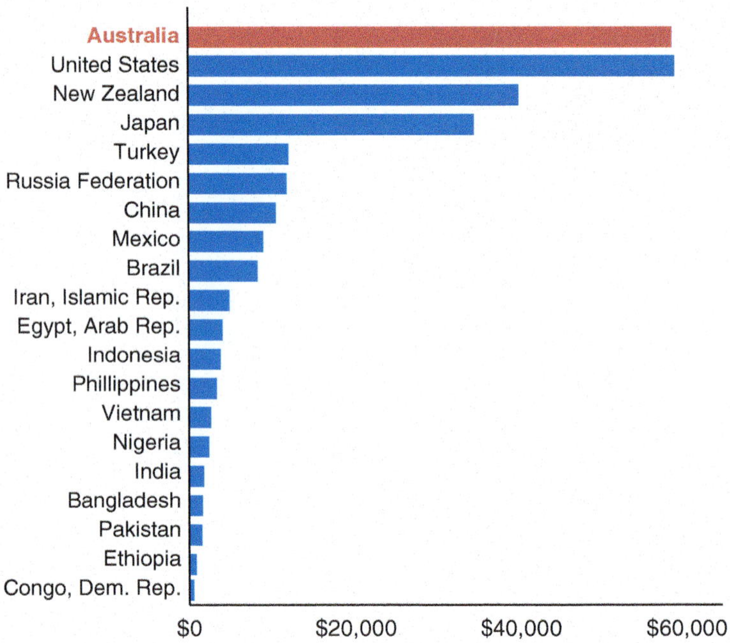

2020 Data from: World Bank.

The following two chapters continue our tour of important macroeconomic indicators, focusing on unemployment and inflation. Unemployment and GDP are intricately linked because when people aren't working they're not producing, earning income, or spending much. Unemployment not only robs people of their purpose, it also leads the economy to produce less GDP than it potentially could. The next chapter focuses on inflation, building upon what you've already learned about the distinction between real and nominal GDP. We'll assess the extent to which higher rates of inflation can disrupt the economy, reducing GDP.

The subsequent set of chapters dig into the "microfoundations" of macroeconomics, analysing the individual choices that add up to GDP. If you remember that $Y = C + I + G + NX$, you'll have a roadmap for the path ahead. We'll devote a chapter to study each of these components of GDP, beginning with consumption, then investment, and the chapter on international finance explores how imports and exports affect and are affected by exchange rates. We'll come back to studying G—that is, government purchases—in a later chapter on fiscal policy.

The next group of chapters focus on the year-to-year fluctuations in GDP and other economic indicators. These short-term fluctuations are called the business cycle, and they can be incredibly disruptive as output, unemployment, and inflation rise and fall. Over a series of several chapters, we'll explore the role of spending, financial, and supply shocks in creating these fluctuations.

The last two chapters will turn to the macroeconomic policies that governments pursue both to boost GDP and to reduce its year-to-year fluctuations. The chapter on monetary policy explores how the Reserve Bank of Australia adjusts interest rates in order to influence economic activity, while the chapter on fiscal policy assesses how the government shapes the economy through its tax and spending decisions.

At the end of all this, you might think that economists are obsessed with GDP. We're not. Economists and policy makers focus on GDP because it is a useful measure of material living standards. When you boost GDP, you boost the resources that a society has to pursue what's important to its citizens and often that means that they are able to live richer, fuller, and happier lives. That's what really matters.

Chapter at a Glance

Gross Domestic Product (GDP): The market value of all final goods and services produced within a country in a year.

The market value →	Value each product at its market price
of all →	Include all goods and services
final goods and services →	Count only final goods and services, omitting intermediate goods
produced →	Omit resale of already-produced goods
within a country →	Include all goods produced within Australia (even by foreign-owned businesses), but exclude goods produced overseas (even by Australian-owned businesses).
in a year. →	Add up the flow of output over a year

$$\underbrace{Y}_{\text{GDP}} = \underbrace{C}_{\text{Consumption}} + \underbrace{I}_{\text{Investment}} + \underbrace{G}_{\text{Government purchases}} + \underbrace{NX}_{\text{Net exports}}$$

GDP is . . .	. . . It can be measured as...	. . . That measurement is called
Total spending	$Y = C + I + G + NX$	"Gross Domestic Product"
Total output	Sum of value added = Total sales − cost of intermediate inputs	"Gross Value Added"
Total income	Total wages + Total profits	"Income from GDP"

These measurements of GDP get different names because even though they are the same in theory, real-world measurements of each can differ because each relies on different sources of imperfect data.

Limitations of GDP

1. Prices are not values
2. Nonmarket activities are excluded
3. The shadow economy is missing
4. Environmental degradation isn't counted
5. Leisure doesn't count
6. GDP ignores distribution

Real and Nominal Variables

Nominal GDP: Adds up the market value of total production in a year using the current prices prevailing in that year.

Real GDP: Excludes the effects of price changes, so it isolates economic growth that's due to changes in the quantity of output produced.

% Change in real GDP ≈ % Change in nominal GDP − % Change in prices

Four Strategies for Scaling Big Numbers

1. Evaluate what it means per person
2. Compare big numbers to the size of the economy
3. Compare big numbers to their own history
4. Use the **Rule of 70** to evaluate long-run growth rates

✳ The Rule of 70: Years it takes something to double $\approx \dfrac{70}{\text{Annual growth rate}}$

Key Concepts

Discussion and Review Questions

Learning Objective 21.1 *Learn how to measure the size of an economy using gross domestic product.*

1. You and your friend Karen decide to open a salad shop. Use the interdependence principle to describe how this impacts the economy by drawing a circular flow diagram. Make sure you draw and explain the flows of resources and money between your salad shop, your employees, the output market, and the input market. How does your salad shop impact total spending, total output, and total income in the economy?
2. You bought an old car a couple of years ago for $1,000 and put about $5,000 of parts and labour into improving it. You sold it yesterday for $3,000. How does this sale affect GDP? Explain.

Learning Objective 21.2 *Analyse GDP as a measure of total spending, output, and income.*

3. After reading a report that says that around 55% of Australia's GDP is consumption, your friend Alex states, "Spending 55% of GDP on consumption is a lot. All people care about is buying stuff, consuming stuff, and accumulating stuff. We would be much better off if we spent our money on services or experiences." Identify Alex's misunderstanding of GDP.
4. Think of a good or service you've purchased in the last month. Explain how your purchase changed GDP by using each of the three ways to measure GDP: adding up every dollar spent, adding up every dollar's worth of output produced by detailing the value added at every stage of production, and adding up every dollar of income earned. How should GDP differ based on the way it is measured?
5. Explain how total spending and total income for an economy must be equal.
6. From your own experiences, provide an example of each: consumption, investment, government purchases, and net exports.

Learning Objective 21.3 *Assess GDP as a measure of living standards.*

7. Jeremiah expressed his disdain for the economic reports he heard on the news. "All economists care about is increasing GDP," he said. "I wish economists cared about living conditions and well-being instead of just some economic indicator." How could you acknowledge the shortcomings of GDP to Jeremiah, while also showing him how GDP functions as both an economic indicator and a measure of well-being?
8. In 2009, it's estimated that up to 150,000 barrels of oil spilled into the Timor Sea during a 75-day-long oil leak at the Monterra oil field. Describe both the negative and positive impact this disaster had on GDP. Explain how this example highlights the limitations of GDP.
9. Between 2000 and 2020, real GDP per person grew, on average, 1.16% per year in Australia. Did this GDP growth benefit all Australians? What does this tell us about the limitations of GDP as a measure of living standards?

Learning Objective 21.4 *Distinguish between real changes in quantities, and the effects of changing prices.*

10. You read two articles online. The first says GDP grew by 5% last quarter, but the second states that the economy grew by 3.4% over the same time period. What do you think explains the difference in the two measures?

Learning Objective 21.5 *Scale large numbers into something more manageable.*

11. In 2021, the Australian Government delivered personal income tax cuts worth $7.8 billion to working Australians. The total expenditure in the 2020–21 financial year for the Australian Government was $640 billion. How could you explain the magnitude of the tax cuts by developing a sense of scale?

Study Problems

Learning Objective 21.1 *Learn how to measure the size of an economy using gross domestic product.*

1. For each of the following transactions, determine if it takes place in the market for outputs or the market for inputs. Then, determine the direction of the flow of goods and services and the flow of money between households and businesses. Finally, determine how GDP as measured by the market value of output, spending on output, income received, or wages and profits changes.

a. Labanya purchases a vacuum cleaner on Kogan for $399.

b. Matt gets paid $3,000 to teach a creative writing class at his local TAFE.

c. The Reject Shop hires 10 new workers at the minimum wage to staff a new store.

d. 6 million people purchased a monthly Spotify premium subscription for $12 last month.

2. In 2017, GDP in Switzerland was $883 billion (measured in Australian dollars) and GDP in Australia was $1.88 trillion. Does this indicate that the standard of living in Switzerland must be well below that of Australia? Switzerland has a population of 8 million people, while Australia has a population of (roughly) 26 million people. How could you better scale the numbers to compare their standards of living?

Learning Objective 21.2 *Analyse GDP as a measure of total spending, output, and income.*

3. Determine whether each of the following transactions contributes to the calculation of GDP as total spending, then, identify the relevant component of GDP (*C, I, G,* or *NX*).

a. A Chinese company sells packaging materials to Cochlear to use for their latest hearing implants that are produced and sold in Australia.

b. Optima Cleaners provide house cleaning services across Australia.

c. Australian consumers import $1 billion of woven apparel from Bangladesh.

d. The Australian government spent $44.6 billion on national defence.

e. Entrepreneurs and *Shark Tank* investors Naomi Simson and Steve Baxter purchase a total of 8.4% of the student payment platform QPay for $190,000 each.

4. Use the data to calculate nominal Australian GDP using the spending approach in 2017 and 2018.

	2017 (billions of dollars)	2018 (billions of dollars)
Consumption	$1,046	$1072
Investment	$355	$362
Exports	$440	$463
Imports	$408	$424
Government spending	$443	$460

5. Consider an economy which produces and sells, among a host of other things, 100 million T-shirts a year. The average T-shirt begins life when a farmer plants seeds she put away last year, waters them, harvests the cotton, then sells the cotton to a mill for $0.75, which sells the fabric to a T-shirt factory for $1.50, which sells the T-shirt to a wholesaler for $5, who sell it to Cotton On for $10, which finally sells it to you for $17. Determine the impact of T-shirts on annual GDP by calculating the total output of the entire production process. Then, compare it to total spending on final T-shirts. What do you notice about the two?

6. Explain why total spending on T-shirts in the previous problem is also equal to the total incomes earned in the economy. Hint: there are two sides to every transaction.

Learning Objective 21.3 *Assess GDP as a measure of living standards.*

7. Vinny and Sandra have just had their first baby, and need to make a decision about how to handle work and child-care responsibilities. Explain how each of the options below will affect measured GDP, relative to when they both worked full time and had no child-care responsibilities.

a. Both Vinny and Sandra will return to work, and pay a child-care provider $600 per week to care for their child.

b. Both Vinny and Sandra will return to work, while Sandra's mother (who is not in the labour force) takes care of their child without financial compensation.

c. Both Vinny and Sandra will return to work, while Vinny's brother, who was previously unemployed, takes care of their baby. They'll pay him $600 a week to care for their child, but neither they nor Vinny's brother will report those payments to the ATO or on any government surveys.

d. Vinny and Sandra will each return to work part time, and split child-care responsibilities.

e. Vinny will stay home to care for the baby, while Sandra returns to work full time.

8. The following graph plots GDP per person and life expectancy of countries around the world. Identify possible reasons for the relationship shown by the graph.

9. Identify the limitation of GDP relevant to each scenario.

a. The Great Barrier Reef Marine Park Authority reports that "coral bleaching"—a stress response of coral to warmer (or cooler) than usual temperatures for an extended period—has caused severe damage in substantial regions of the reef. It is attributed to climate change.

b. The World Bank reports that in 2014 the income share held by the lowest 10% of the Australian population was 2.8%. The income share held by highest 10% of the population was 27%.

c. Data from the Australian Institute of Family Studies shows that one-in-three Australian parents in two-parent families are stay-at-home mums or dads.

d. Australia's GDP per person is around 5% higher than the Netherlands' GDP per person. However, in Australia, people work about 19% more hours than people in the Netherlands.

e. Most internet searches (86.5%) occur via Google, Google Maps, or Google Images, all of which provide search results for free.

Learning Objective 21.4 *Distinguish between real changes in quantities, and the effects of changing prices.*

10. If nominal GDP rose, does that mean that production has increased as well? Why or why not? What about if real GDP increased? Why is it important to use real GDP when comparing changes over time?

11. The table contains price and quantity information for the hearing implants produced by Cochlear in the years 2018 and 2019.

	2018		2019	
	Price	**Quantity**	**Price**	**Quantity**
Cochlear Implants	$23,568	35,260	$24,795	34,083

a. Calculate the amount contributed by Cochlear to Australian GDP (real and nominal) from the sales of the two models in 2018 and 2019.

b. Determine the growth rate of nominal GDP (if Cochlear were the entire economy).

c. Determine the growth rate of real GDP (if Cochlear were the entire economy).

d. Use the shortcut you learned to convert between real and nominal growth rates to determine the growth rate of prices.

e. Is the increase in nominal GDP due to a change in quantity, a change in prices, or both?

12. The growth rate of nominal GDP was 9.4%, and the growth rate of real GDP was 7.4% for Iceland in 2016. Approximately what was the percentage change in prices?

Learning Objective 21.5 *Scale large numbers into something more manageable.*

13. In 2018, India was the world's seventh largest economy, with a $2.69 trillion GDP (as measured in U.S. dollars). India was also one of the world's fastest-growing economies, with an annual growth rate of real GDP of 7.3%.

a. If the country maintains the same growth rate, how many years will it take for India's GDP to double?

b. Bangladesh's GDP was $286.27 billion, but its growth rate was equal to India's. How many years will it take for Bangladesh's economy to double?

c. Although Bangladesh and India have the same annual growth rate, their economies are very different in size. How can you explain the size difference to someone who is unfamiliar with scaling large numbers? Which strategies would you use?

CHAPTER 22

Economic Growth

You live a life that is extraordinarily luxurious compared to most of human history. It's not just that you have the modern conveniences of computers, mobile phones, and the internet. A hundred years ago only one-third of households had electricity, few houses had air conditioning, and many lacked indoor plumbing. Many people didn't have enough to eat.

Since it was harder to keep things sanitary, people got sick a lot more. Much of modern medicine hadn't been invented yet, including antibiotics and most major vaccines. A bad case of the flu, a stomach bug, or a bout of diphtheria could kill you. Without antibiotics, surgery was unsafe. Famines and outbreaks of communicable diseases killed millions of people. The average Australian could expect to live only to age 60.

Mark Wallinger's The World Turned Upside Down, at LSE/Photo by Betsey Stevenson and Justin Wolfers

Perspective matters.

In 1920 real GDP per person was the equivalent of about $4,500. This means that you'll likely earn more in the first decade of your career than your great-grandparents did in their entire lifetimes. By 2021, GDP per person was more than six times higher, having risen to $78,700. This higher income means that most Australians have enough to eat, a comfortable place to live, good health care, instant communication, reliable transportation, and almost unlimited information at our fingertips. Today, the average Australian can expect to live to age 83. Economic growth has improved both the quantity and the quality of our lives.

While life was hard in Australia a century ago, it remains hard in much of the rest of the world. Today, the average income of Australians is more than five times that of people in China, ten times that of Fijians, and twenty-five times the average in sub-Saharan Africa. Many aspects of daily life in Australia are the result of more than a century of robust economic growth. Not all countries have experienced as much growth. In places like Sierra Leone and the Democratic Republic of the Congo, life isn't much different from 100 years ago, and a large share of the population remain focused on survival—struggling to get enough to eat, to find adequate shelter, and to get treatment when they're sick. In this chapter, we'll explore how economic growth got Australia to where it is today, why some countries are still so far behind, and what countries can do to grow faster.

Chapter Objective

Understand what determines the rate of economic growth.

22.1 Economic Growth Facts
Learn how economies have grown over time.

22.2 The Ingredients of Economic Growth
Uncover the ingredients for economic growth.

22.3 The Analytics of Economic Growth
Understand how workers, capital accumulation, and technological progress work together to create economic growth.

22.4 Public Policy: Why Institutions Matter for Growth
Find out why government institutions matter for economic growth.

22.1 Economic Growth Facts

Learning Objective *Learn how economies have grown over time.*

To understand economic growth today, it's useful to start by understanding how much people struggled and how little progress there was for most of human history. So let's step way back in time to more than a million years ago.

World Economic Growth Since 1 Million B.C.

There aren't a lot of records back to 1 million B.C., but we now have a few clues, and they all paint a bleak picture. People lived hand-to-mouth, first as hunters and gatherers. And then, sometime around 12,000 years ago, our ancestors began to farm. The invention of agriculture allowed people to settle down into communities and form societies. While they no longer had to roam to find food, most people toiled daily in agriculture. Even so, they did not produce enough food to feed everyone adequately. People were so poor that starvation and malnutrition were common. Skeletal remains show severe deficiencies in vitamins and minerals, and widespread disease. Men were 15 centimetres shorter, on average, compared to today, reflecting the malnutrition they faced as children. While there were some bright spots, such as ancient Greece, and there were rulers who amassed riches, most people from 1 million B.C. through to 1200 A.D. lived in grinding poverty. And each successive generation was as poor as the previous.

Economists have tried to measure what was produced back in 1 million B.C. and the years that followed. They estimate that from around 1 million B.C. until around 1200 A.D., GDP per person was only around $200 per year in today's dollars. While it's hard to know the exact amount for sure, it was roughly the minimum of what was needed to sustain life. What is clear is that GDP per person didn't change much until around 1200 A.D., when it started to rise, albeit very gradually. In fact, growth was so slow that it took roughly 600 years for GDP per person to double. At the start of the 1800s, world GDP per person was roughly $400. Remember that's adjusted for inflation, so that means $400 worth of goods and services at prices similar to those you face today. Imagine trying to get by for a whole year on only $400!

Agricultural advances meant more food and less hunger. For much of human history, most people's primary job was securing enough food to avoid starvation. But as agricultural techniques improved over the centuries, people could produce more food with less work. The benefits of these changes became most apparent in the 1800s, with advances in farming such as better crop rotation, the use of farm enclosures, switching to higher-yielding crops, and new farm equipment. Markets to distribute food became more sophisticated, thanks to better transportation infrastructure. The expansion of inland waterways and roads reduced the cost of selling what farmers produced. Taken together, these developments meant less hunger and fewer people needed to work on farms. By 1850, less than a quarter of the British workforce worked in agriculture; these benefits were also seen in much of Europe and North America.

PHAS/Universal Images Group/ Getty Images

Technological advances transformed agriculture.

The Dark Emu Debate sheds light on the precolonial Australian economy. There is an active debate in Australia about the nature of the precolonial economy in Australia. In a highly acclaimed 2014 book *Dark Emu*, Bruce Pascoe claims that indigenous Australians in the precolonial era were not "hapless wanderers across the soil, mere hunter-gatherers." According to Pascoe, they were "in the early stages of an agricultural society...[not] simply wandering from plant to plant, kangaroo to kangaroo in a hapless opportunism." By his account, indigenous Australians were in many ways farmers who tilled the soil, sowed and irrigated crops before harvesting and storing them. Several other scholars have disputed this depiction of precolonial Australian society. Wherever one stands on these issues, the bulk of the rest of this chapter builds on technological advances that happened, worldwide, from the 1800s.

The Industrial Revolution created an engine of economic growth. Because fewer resources were needed to grow food, increased agricultural production also sowed the seeds for the Industrial Revolution—a revolution that brought machine power to our efforts to make and transport food and goods. Now that people had more time to pursue other activities, intellectual life thrived. Inventors pioneered revolutionary new products such as the steam engine, sewing machine, telephone, and light bulb. Prior to these inventions, most things were powered by humans or animals. It can be hard to comprehend the magnitude of this change, but take a minute to imagine what your life would be like if you had nothing but your own energy and that of animals to help you get through your day.

Chronicle/Leonid Andronov/Alamy Stock Photo

A century of growth transformed Sydney.

The invention of machines that could substitute for human or animal labour, and the subsequent investment in making these machines available, brought enormous growth in what people could produce. Workers moved from farms to factories, and their ability to produce output increased at a rapid pace. This was the real beginning of an increase in income and living standards. After taking nearly 600 years for global GDP per person to double, it more than doubled between the early 1800s and the early 1900s. Economic growth then exploded: Worldwide GDP per person doubled again by the 1950s, and then again by 1975, and again by the early 2000s.

Economic growth means rising living standards and longer lives. Economic growth means that people produce more, and when they produce more, they can consume more. That means fewer people go hungry, and more people have a comfortable place to live, sanitary conditions, and more resources to invest in their health and education. Growth doesn't just mean you consume more stuff; it's what enables you to live and thrive. That's why economic growth led the world population to grow and life expectancy—the average number of years that a person may expect to live—to rise. In 1800, there were a billion people in the world; today, there are 8 billion. In 1800, average life expectancy in every country was below age 50. Today, the average person in many of the richest countries in the world can expect to live well into their 80s. (And Australia has one of the highest average life expectancies in the world.)

And yet even today, average life expectancy in many of the world's poorest countries is not much above age 50. The problem is that the agricultural and industrial revolutions didn't lead to economic growth everywhere. Some countries thrived, while others stagnated. And some countries started down the right path, but got lost along the way. Let's zoom in on the past 200 years to see how these big differences between rich and poor countries emerged.

Economic Growth Over the Past Two Centuries

When economic growth was proceeding at a glacial pace, there wasn't much of a difference in GDP per person between countries. Figure 1 shows GDP per person in various parts of the world, first in 1820 and then in 2018. In 1820, annual GDP per person averaged around $830 in Australia, $800 in Africa, $930 in Asia, and roughly $950 in Latin America and Eastern Europe. In the wealthiest parts of the world—Western Europe and the United States—GDP per person was more than $2,000. While that was double much of the rest of the world, hunger was still never too far from people's minds.

Figure 1 | **Small Differences in Growth Rates Have Big Consequences**

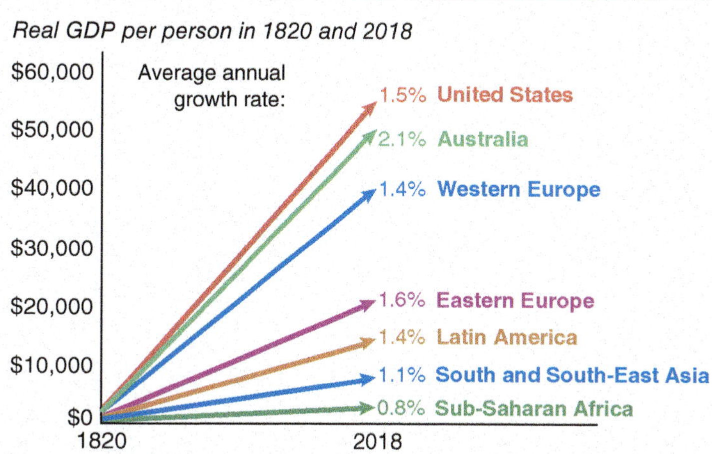

Small differences in growth rates can have big effects. The Industrial Revolution led to a rapid rise in GDP, but it fuelled more economic growth in some parts of the world than others. As Figure 1 illustrates, what may seem like small differences in growth rates lead to enormous differences over time. In fact, only a few tenths of a percentage point in annual growth rates differentiates today's economically developed countries from less-developed countries—but those small differences in growth rates were compounded over hundreds of years. The countries with fast-growing GDP were disproportionately concentrated in Europe and North America. In fact, Australia's GDP per capita grew at 2.1% a year from 1820 to 2018. That means that, per person, GDP in Australia was a staggering 60 times higher than it was 200 years earlier. By 2018 there was a clear distinction between the "rich" West and the rest of the world, where GDP per person grew, but at much slower rates. In Africa output per person grew at roughly half the rate as in the West, which meant that by the time it doubled in Africa, it would have quadrupled in the West.

There have been growth successes and disasters. Spain was once a great power, sending explorers around the world, fostering international trade, and establishing an enormous empire. But between 1600 and 1850, its economy barely grew, while income per person in Great Britain more than doubled. Spanish GDP per person grew so slowly that by 1900, it was only roughly double what it had been back in the 1600s! Even in 1950, when some of today's older Spaniards were born, their incomes were only about two and half times what their ancestors would have had four hundred years earlier. The second half of the twentieth century was more successful for Spain; income per person in 2018 was roughly eight times what it was in 1950.

Argentina provides another example of what happens when growth stalls. Just before the turn of the twentieth century, Argentina was one of the richest countries in the world, and its economy was growing rapidly. Figure 2 shows that in around 1900 its GDP per person was comparable to that in Australia and Britain. But growth sputtered in the early 1900s, and it made little progress for decades. A country that had once been richer than Spain, Japan, and South Korea fell behind those countries' economies. In 2019, its average income was about one-fifth of that in Australia.

Figure 2 also shows the success stories of Japan and South Korea. Both countries had little growth through the mid-1900s. The second half of the twentieth century, however, was a time of robust GDP growth. Both countries now have GDP per person on par with many affluent Western nations.

Countries like India and China stagnated for centuries, before taking off during the past few decades. In 2017, India's average income was nearly four times higher than in 1990, and China's average income had grown tenfold. In comparison, the average income in Australia only rose by a bit over half during that same time period. Recent rapid growth in poorer countries has helped decrease inequality between nations around the world.

Figure 2 | **Growth Disasters and Miracles**

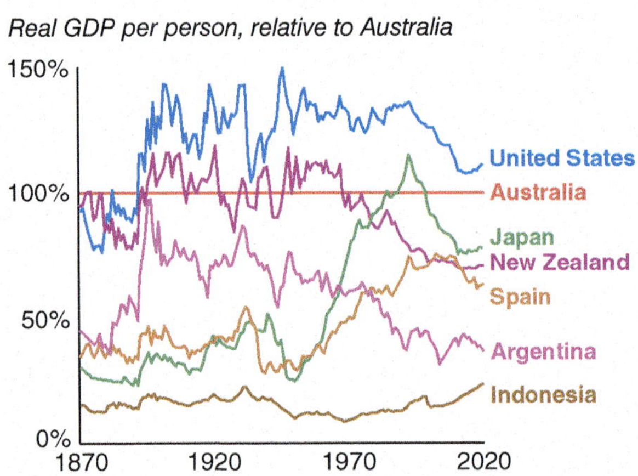

The facts about economic growth are astonishing. Over the past 200 years the global economy has grown enormously, transforming our quality of life. But this development has been uneven, creating remarkable disparities with average income in some countries many times larger than in others. Now let's turn to figuring out why.

22.2 The Ingredients of Economic Growth

Learning Objective *Uncover the ingredients for economic growth.*

Why are some countries rich, while others are so poor that they barely produce enough for people to survive? And what makes some countries grow richer over time, while others stagnate? Perhaps no other question in economics—indeed, in all of the social sciences—has such far-reaching implications for human well-being. An answer might provide a roadmap that poor countries could use to become rich, helping billions of people escape poverty and hunger. And so we turn to asking: What determines how much output each country produces?

The Production Function

Whether you're analysing how much your household, your business, or a whole country produces, you'll find it useful to organise your thoughts around the idea of a production function. A **production function** describes the methods by which inputs are transformed into outputs, and so it determines the total production that's possible with a given set of ingredients.

production function The methods by which inputs are transformed into output which determines the total production that's possible with a given set of ingredients.

A production function is like a cookbook. If you've ever baked a cake, then you've got some experience with a production function. You probably looked in a cookbook, and when you found a recipe that relied on ingredients that you had, you followed the instructions on how to combine flour, sugar, milk, and eggs in order to produce your cake. That cookbook told you how much cake you'd produce, given the quantity of ingredients you used.

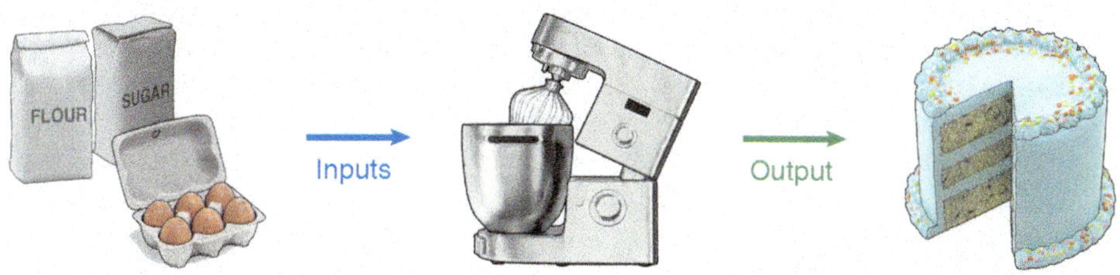

Production function
Methods for transforming inputs into output

In this example, think of the production function as the whole cookbook, rather than an individual recipe. A recipe describes a particular production technique that relies on a specific quantity of milk, flour, and eggs. A cookbook is a collection of the most important recipes and each page lists a different production technique you might choose, depending on the ingredients you have available. A cookbook and a production function both describe how different mixtures of inputs can be combined to produce valuable output.

A production function describes how a business transforms inputs into outputs. The same ideas apply to any productive activity. Your company's production function describes the cookbook of management techniques you can use to transform your inputs into output. By this view, running a business is a lot like baking a cake, and your job as a manager is to acquire the right ingredients—the right people, skills, and

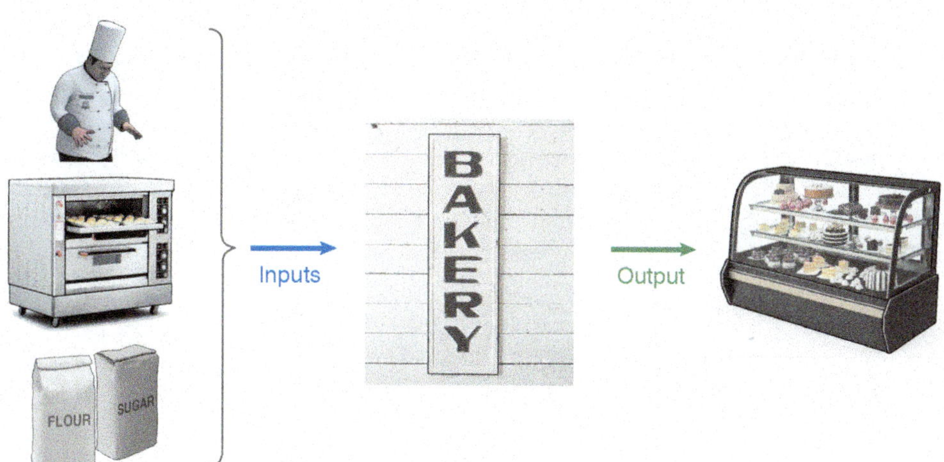

Production function
Methods for transforming inputs into output

machinery—and mix them in the appropriate proportions to produce valuable output. For instance, if you're running a cake shop, you'll mix together the hard work and skills of pastry chefs, cake decorators, and cashiers with retail space, display cases, commercial mixers, and ovens, along with raw ingredients like flour, butter, and sugar. Your bakery's production function describes how the quantity of cake you'll produce varies according to the amount of each ingredient you add to the mixture.

Just as a cake shop has a production function so too does a consulting firm, a hotel, a law firm, a hospital, or a high school. In each case, managers play the role of chef, mixing together workers, specialised skills, and equipment, to bake consulting services, a restful night, legal victories, healthy patients, or educated students. Your company's production function describes the total quantity of output your business can produce depending on the quantities of each input you employ.

human capital The skills that workers bring to the job.

physical capital Tools, machinery, and structures.

The aggregate production function links GDP to labour, human capital, and physical capital. The same idea can be applied at the level of the whole economy where the *aggregate production function* relates total output—that is, GDP—to the quantity of inputs employed. As with individual businesses, the key ingredients are Labour (denoted L), **human capital,** which describes the skills that workers bring to the job (denoted H), and **physical capital,** which describes the tools, machinery, and structures we work with (the letter C is usually reserved for "Consumption," so economists follow the German spelling of Kapital and label physical capital as K). The aggregate production function doesn't include a separate role for intermediate inputs such as the flour used by a pastry chef, because intermediate inputs are typically produced by other businesses within the economy. Flour, for instance, is produced by mills that process the wheat grown by farmers, and so it's already the result of combining labour, skills, and capital.

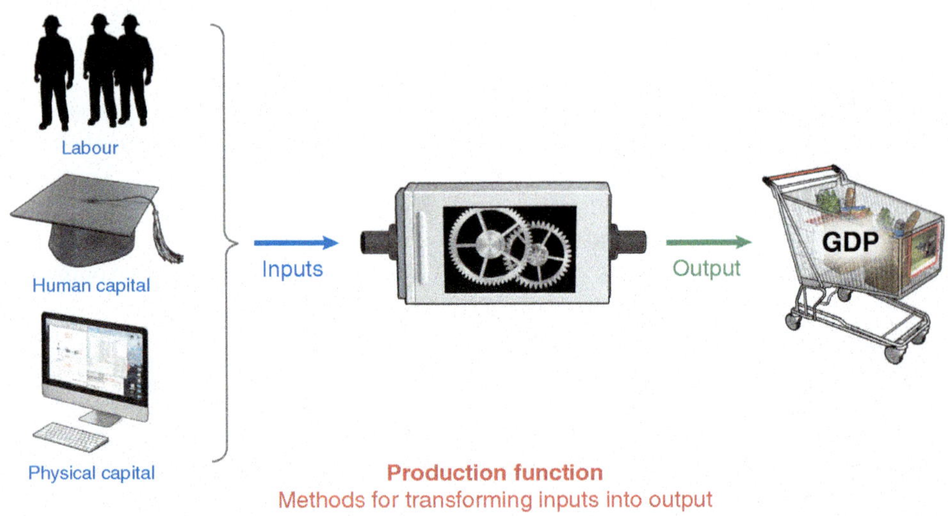

A production function describes how output varies with inputs. The aggregate production function captures the idea that when you use more ingredients—more labour, more human capital, and more physical capital—you'll get more output. It quantifies this relationship, telling you how much extra output businesses will produce as they add more labour, human capital, or physical capital. It can be useful to represent this idea mathematically, and the following equation simply says that the quantity of output a country will produce depends on the quantity of each of these inputs:

Output is a function of inputs

$$Y = f(L, H, K)$$

Labour Human capital Physical capital

The aggregate production function illustrates that a country will produce more output if:

- It employs more labour
- Its workers become more highly skilled, accumulating human capital
- It accumulates more physical capital

Finally, a production function reflects the production techniques or recipes that are known at a specific point in time. Finding new and more efficient recipes will shift the production function, creating an additional engine of growth:

- Discovering new and more efficient recipes makes it possible to transform a given quantity of ingredients into a greater quantity of output.

Let's dig into each of these factors in turn.

A country's output depends on . . .
Available inputs:
1. Labour input
2. Human capital
3. Physical capital

And also:
4. Recipes for transforming inputs into output

Ingredient One: Labour and Total Hours Worked

As you know from personal experience, the more hours you work, the more you get done. The same thing applies to the whole economy: The more labour that workers do, the more output gets produced. The total quantity of labour input is measured as the sum of all hours worked across the whole economy. It reflects four factors: the size of the population, the fraction who are of working age, the share of those working-age people who choose to work, and how many hours each worker puts in. Let's consider each of these, in turn.

sirtravelalot/Shutterstock

More babies means more workers, eventually.

Population boosts total GDP, but not GDP per person. The total population of a country provides the upper limit to how much labour it can supply, which explains why the countries with the largest populations tend to produce the most GDP. Countries that experience more rapid population growth—more births, fewer deaths, and more immigration—also tend to experience faster economic growth. But that doesn't mean that a larger population will yield higher living standards, because that larger GDP gets shared over more people. Population is a key determinant of GDP, but not GDP per person.

As we analyse material living standards, we'll focus on the determinants of GDP per person. And that in turn will lead us to focus on other per person variables: hours worked per person, human capital per person, and physical capital per person.

Unfavourable demographics are likely to slow economic growth. The demographic structure of the population matters, because children and the elderly rarely work. The *dependency ratio* measures the number of people either too young (under 15) or too old (65 or older) to work, per 100 people of working age. Figure 3 shows that the dependency ratio rose sharply in Australia due to the baby boom that followed World War II. The dependency ratio then fell, and by 2016, for every 100 people of working age, there were 46 people either too young or too old to work. This dependency ratio is projected to rise sharply over the next few decades, as those born in the postwar baby boom retire, and it will remain high due to increased life expectancy. The rising share of dependents is likely to slow economic growth over coming decades.

Figure 3 The Dependency Ratio Is Projected to Rise

Number of people too old or too young to work, per 100 people of working age

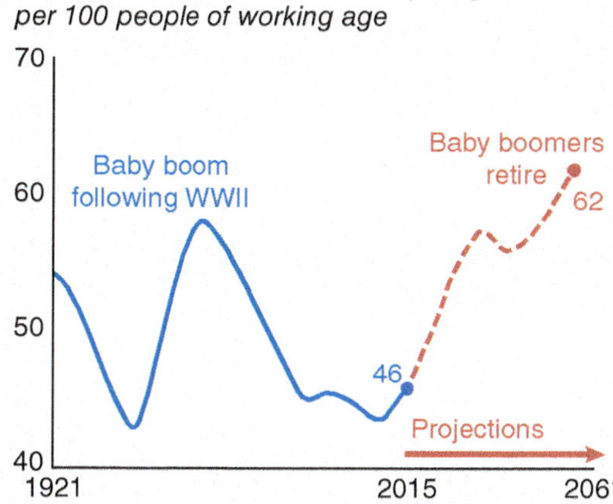

Data from: Australian Bureau of Statistics; Australian Historical Population Statistics.

Women's increased employment created economic growth. The labour pool grows when a larger share of the working-age population chooses to work. The main driver of the rising participation over the past century, shown in Figure 4, has been an extraordinary transformation in attitudes towards women in the workplace. In the early 1900s few women worked outside the home, particularly once they married. By the early 2000s more than half of all working-age women were participating in the labour force. Much of this change occurred in the 1960s, 70s, and

Figure 4 | Share of Working-Age Women Who Are Employed

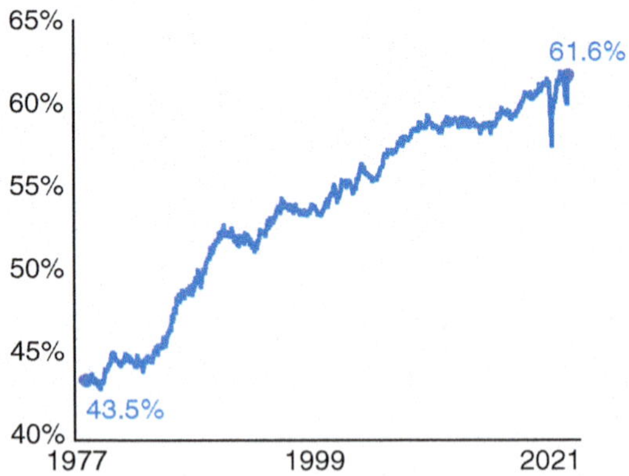

Data from: Australian Bureau of Statistics

80s. This shift of women from the home into the market was responsible for a substantial share of the rise in Australian GDP per person through this period. But although progress has continued, it has slowed down since the 1990s.

Shorter workweeks will reduce GDP, but may raise well-being. Total labour input reflects not only the number of workers, but also how many hours each person works, on average. The more hours that people work, the more GDP they'll produce.

But that doesn't mean we should work all the time! Recall that one limitation of GDP as a measure of well-being is that it doesn't capture the benefit of the leisure you enjoy when you're not working. As countries get richer, people tend to choose more leisure over work time. The reduction in the average work week has slowed GDP growth, but probably improved well-being.

Ingredient Two: Human Capital

labour productivity The quantity of goods and services that each person produces per hour of work.

While hours of work reflect the quantity of labour used, output also reflects how productive people are while at work. The more each worker produces per hour, the higher GDP will be. Economists refer to output per hour of work as **labour productivity.**

Your labour productivity depends critically on your human capital, which describes the skills and knowledge that you develop through education, training, and practice. As you learn economics you are building your human capital: You're acquiring new analytic tools that'll help you make better decisions, developing frameworks you'll use to transform data into insight, and building the intellectual muscles that you'll apply to better understand, analyse, and predict human behaviour. This human capital is a key reason that economics graduates are more productive and highly paid than most other university graduates. Your ability to learn economics builds on a foundation you laid many years ago.

Figure 5 | Adult Literacy Rates Vary Across Regions

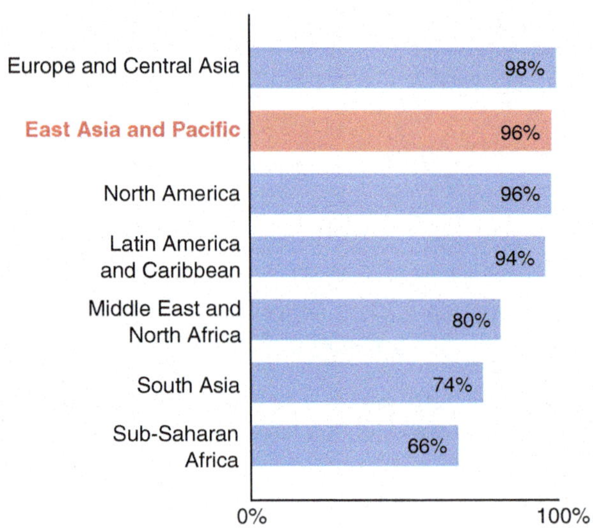

Data from: World Bank.

Primary education develops literacy, which is a key tool for further learning. You probably spent your first few years of elementary school learning to read and write. Literacy is such a foundational skill that you probably take it for granted. Yet it's essential for economic life: You need to be able to read to follow written instructions, communicate asynchronously with co-workers, execute written contracts, send e-mail, look things up online, read a newspaper, or evaluate political candidates.

Figure 5 shows that while literacy is nearly universal among industrialised countries, it remains a substantial barrier in many poorer countries. This is important because literacy is the foundation of all later learning, empowering people to acquire further specialised knowledge. Indeed, right now it's empowering you to learn about the economic impact of literacy!

Secondary education promotes greater productivity in a range of jobs. One of the key reasons Australia was one of the fastest-growing economies in the twentieth century is that it invested more in the education of its citizens than other countries did. A century ago, many mocked the idea of making high school free and available to everyone, arguing that there remained a great need for physical labour and that labourers wouldn't benefit from having a high school degree. Despite these arguments, support for high school education grew rapidly in Australia. That's why Figure 6 shows that only 11.7% of Australians attain an education lower than high school. The claim that this education wouldn't be useful turned out to be wrong, as it enabled blue-collar workers to work with increasingly sophisticated machinery, boosting their productivity.

capital stock The total quantity of physical capital used in the production of goods and services.

Further gains in human capital will come from improving and expanding education. Most Australians complete high school, or close to it. There are still important gaps—particularly among lower socio-economic status and indigenous communities. But compared to a century ago, improving human capital in Australia will not come from large increases in the amount of secondary schooling.

That said, education is a key driver of individual incomes. The median Australian with a university degree earns about $700,000 a year more in lifetime earnings compared to the median school leaver.

So it's not just the quantity of education that matters, so does quality. So far we've measured human capital mainly in terms of the quantity of education you get, but it also depends on the quality of that education. Figure 7 shows that when common international exams are given across countries, Australia is in the middle of the pack of high-income countries. This explains why education policy debates are focused on improving the quality of education. In fact, Figures 8 and 9 show that Australia's international test scores have been declining over time. This is true in absolute terms, but also relative to high-performing education systems like Singapore.

Figure 6 | High School and College Graduation Rates Have Risen

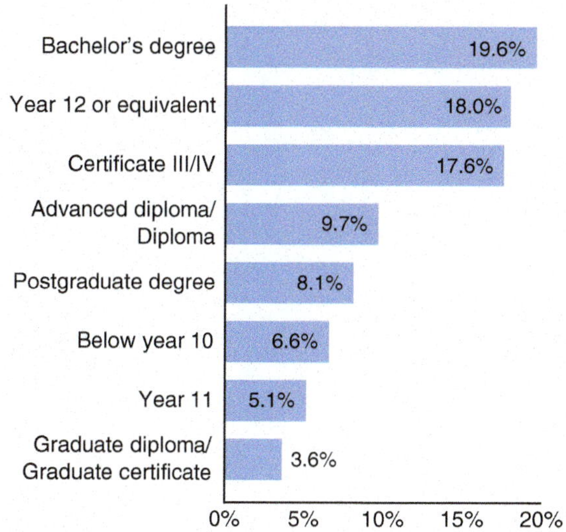

Data from: Australian Bureau of Statistics.

Ingredient Three: Capital Accumulation

The third factor that determines how much you can produce per hour is the equipment you'll work with. For instance, a pastry chef is more productive when they're working with commercial-grade mixers, large ovens, and other kitchen equipment. The **capital stock** is the total quantity of physical capital, and it includes all equipment and structures used in the production of goods and services. It includes both privately owned tools, machines, and factories, and government-provided infrastructure, such as roads, electricity networks, and telecommunications.

Physical capital is a complement to labour. Workers produce more when they have the right tools available to them, so physical capital is best viewed as a *complement* to labour. As such, the quantity of capital per worker is an important determinant of labour productivity. While some people worry that machines are a *substitute* for labour, the reality is that they help you get more done. After all, a pastry chef equipped with a commercial mixer doesn't

Figure 7 | Average Exam Scores in 2018 Around the World

Each dot shows the average test score for each country on a common international exam.

Data from: OECD Programme for International Student Assessment.

Figure 8 | Average Reading Scores in Australia and Singapore since 2000

Each dot marks the average reading test score for each country on a common international exam.

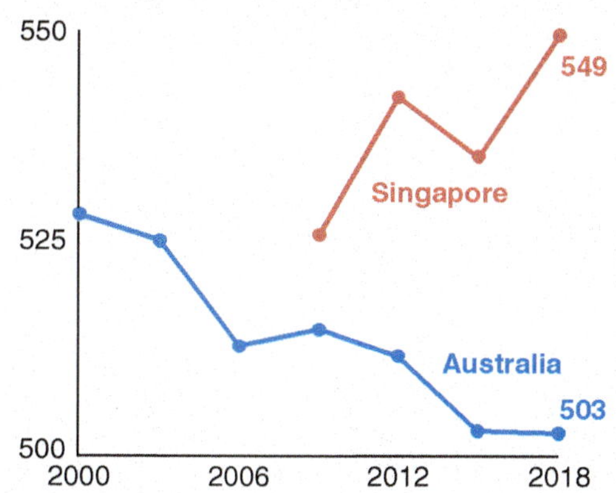

Data from: OECD Programme for International Student Assessment.

Figure 9 | Average Mathematics Scores in Australia and Singapore since 2003

Each dot marks the average mathematics test score for each country on a common international exam.

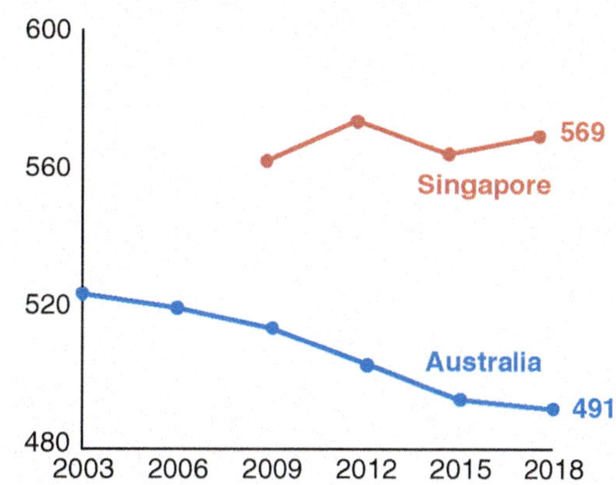

Data from: OECD Programme for International Student Assessment.

have to mix their recipes by hand, so they can use the time they save to bake even more cakes. Indeed, the Industrial Revolution—in which workers went from working with hand tools to harnessing machine power—marked a turning point in history as it sparked a productivity boom that led economic growth to take off. Even the person who monitors the self-serve checkouts at the supermarket can now "serve" eight people at a time instead of one.

Investment depends on the saving rate. Companies grow their capital stock by investing in new equipment and structures. This process is so important that we'll spend all of Chapter 26 on investment and all of Chapter 27 exploring the role that financial markets play in this process. For now, the key point is that investment occurs out of resources that are saved rather than consumed. As a result, the savings rate is a critical determinant of investment, which ultimately determines the amount of capital each worker has to work with.

Foreign investment builds the capital stock. The other way to grow the Australian capital stock is through *foreign investment*. For instance, in 1996, the Japanese noodle company Hakubaku decided to build a noodle production plant in Ballarat, Victoria, that added $13 million to the Australian capital stock. While the plant is owned by Japanese companies, it employs Australian workers who work with that capital, and the noodles that roll off that production line will be made in Australia, and so will count towards Australia's GDP. The wages that are paid will accrue to the Australian workers employed at this plant, while the profits will go to the Japanese owners of the plant.

New Recipes for Combining Ingredients: Technological Progress

Recall that a production function is like a cookbook, listing the most important recipes for mixing labour, human capital, and physical capital together to produce output. This points to the final source of economic growth: New ideas, recipes, or production techniques. Economists refer to new methods for using existing resources as **technological progress.** It is important because these new methods create ways to produce more valuable output from your existing inputs.

technological progress New methods for using existing resources.

New recipes make it possible to produce more from given physical inputs. Technological progress can involve new production techniques that build on scientific discoveries. For instance, the discovery of how to rotate crops to replenish the soil led to a massive boost in crop yields. It's effectively a new recipe for farmers, telling them how to combine their land, labour, and capital in a way that produces more output from their existing inputs. Technological progress can also involve new and better ways of doing things. For instance, the Japanese auto industry is famously efficient due to ingenious management techniques its automakers use to run streamlined production lines. Their recipe for combining workers and capital has since spread around the world.

Sometimes technological progress literally is a new recipe—a new way to combine existing ingredients that yields more valuable output. Oral rehydration therapy might be the most important medical advance in a generation. It's a blend of sugar, salt, and water, which if mixed in just the right proportions, will revive a child dying from cholera-induced diarrhea. Since this recipe was discovered in the 1960s it has saved tens of millions of lives.

Computers embody technological progress. The technological progress that sparked the computer revolution is also a new recipe. The key ingredient of computers is sand (or silicone dioxide), and it has existed for thousands of years, but we typically used it in other recipes: Kids at the beach built castles out of it, builders used it as an ingredient in their cement mixes, and artisans in Venice melted it to create glass. What's new is the understanding that silica can both conduct and block electricity, which means that it's a semi-conductor. That understanding created new recipes in which sand can be combined with other ingredients to create the sophisticated chips that power modern computers.

This highlights an important distinction. Technological progress doesn't refer to computers, or even the silicone chips that power them. Those are items of physical capital that *embody* technological progress. But the underlying technological change is the idea or recipe for combining these ingredients to create a computer.

Interpreting the DATA **The falling cost of light**

Technological progress is responsible for one of the most transformative changes you've probably never thought about: The increased production of light. The bulb that's shining above your head right now is providing what was once an extraordinary luxury. New recipes for producing light have made it plentiful and cheap today.

Go back far enough in human history, and the only recipe to create light involved gathering wood, rubbing two rocks or sticks together, and using the resulting spark to light a fire. It would take a solid 60-hour week of work to gather enough firewood to produce 1,000 lumen-hours of light, which is probably less than your overhead light will give off over the next hour. Thousands of years later, a new recipe was developed, in which wicks were dipped into molten animal fat to create candles. George Washington calculated that burning one candle for five hours each night would cost him £8 per year, more than most American families could afford. Many families lived in darkness, instead.

All that changed when Thomas Edison created an extraordinary new method for producing light by inventing the electric light bulb. Your great-great-grandparents could work a 60-hour week to get five months of continuous light. Today, we have LED lights, and that same amount of labour will buy you all the light you'll need for the rest of your life, plus some. Figure 10 shows just how much the price of light has fallen due to these new recipes for producing light. The declining cost has transformed modern life, so that we can spend our evenings reading, studying, or socialising. It's a story that illuminates just how important technological progress can be. ■

Figure 10 | The Declining Price of Light

Hours of work to produce 1,000 lumen-hours; ratio scale

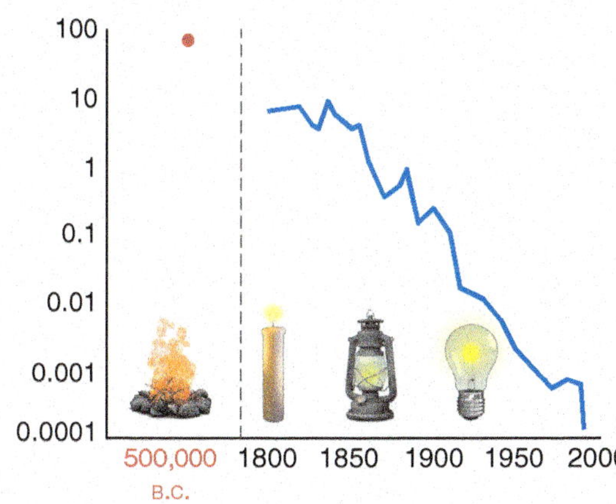

22.3 The Analytics of Economic Growth

Learning Objective *Understand how workers, capital accumulation, and technological progress work together to create economic growth.*

So far we've explored the ingredients that determine how much a country produces at a given point in time. Now it's time to see what happens when we put these ingredients together to answer the question: Where does economic growth come from, and will it continue?

Analysing the Production Function

We'll return to the production function, because it determines the roles that new ideas, labour, human capital, and physical capital play in determining output. This framework generates a number of important insights into the process of economic growth.

Insight one: Constant returns to scale means doubling inputs will double output. Most economists believe that doubling all of the physical inputs to the aggregate production function—doubling the labour, physical capital, and human capital used—will lead to twice the output. This implies that the production function has **constant returns to scale,** which means that increasing all inputs by some proportion will cause output to rise by the same proportion. The *replication argument* explains why. If you want to double the output of your factory, you can simply replicate everything you're already doing—opening a second, identical factory that will produce just as much as your first, using just as much labour, human capital, and physical capital. In total then, you'll be using twice the inputs—twice the labour, human capital, and physical capital—to produce

constant returns to scale Increasing all inputs by some proportion will cause output to rise by the same proportion.

twice the output. You can also apply this argument at the level of the whole economy, so that replicating each individual business would yield an economy that is twice as big and that uses twice the inputs to produce twice the output.

This means that if the Australian population (and therefore the Australian workforce) grows, and the capital stock grows enough that capital per person stays the same, and investment in education also rises in proportion so that human capital per person is unchanged, then GDP per person will stay the same.

Insight two: There are diminishing returns to capital. If you double all your inputs, then you'll double all your outputs. But what happens if you just double your physical capital and don't change the number of workers? You'll produce more, but you won't produce twice as much. Increasing only physical capital will produce a less than proportionate increase in output. Precisely how much extra it produces depends on how much capital you have to begin with.

law of diminishing returns When one input is held constant, increases in the other inputs will, at some point, begin to yield smaller and smaller increases in output.

The **law of diminishing returns** says that when one input is held constant, increases in the other inputs will, at some point, yield smaller and smaller increases in output. In this case, if there's a fixed number of workers and technology isn't changing, successive increments of physical capital will yield smaller and smaller boosts to what each worker produces. Similarly, with a fixed capital stock, adding more workers will yield smaller boosts to production. This doesn't mean that more capital or more workers aren't helpful, but just that each additional investment is less helpful than the previous one when at least one factor of production is held constant.

Figure 11 shows the relationship between the amount of physical capital per worker and the output they produce—in other words, GDP per worker. When workers don't have many tools to work with, the marginal benefit of adding one more unit of capital per

Figure 11 | Diminishing Returns to Capital

A given increase in physical capital per person raises GDP per worker, but at a diminishing rate.

(A) A given **change in the capital stock** will increase GDP per worker, but by how much depends on how much capital you start with.

(B) When capital per worker is low to begin with, GDP per worker **increases by a lot**.

(C) When capital per worker is high to begin with, GDP per worker **increases by less**.

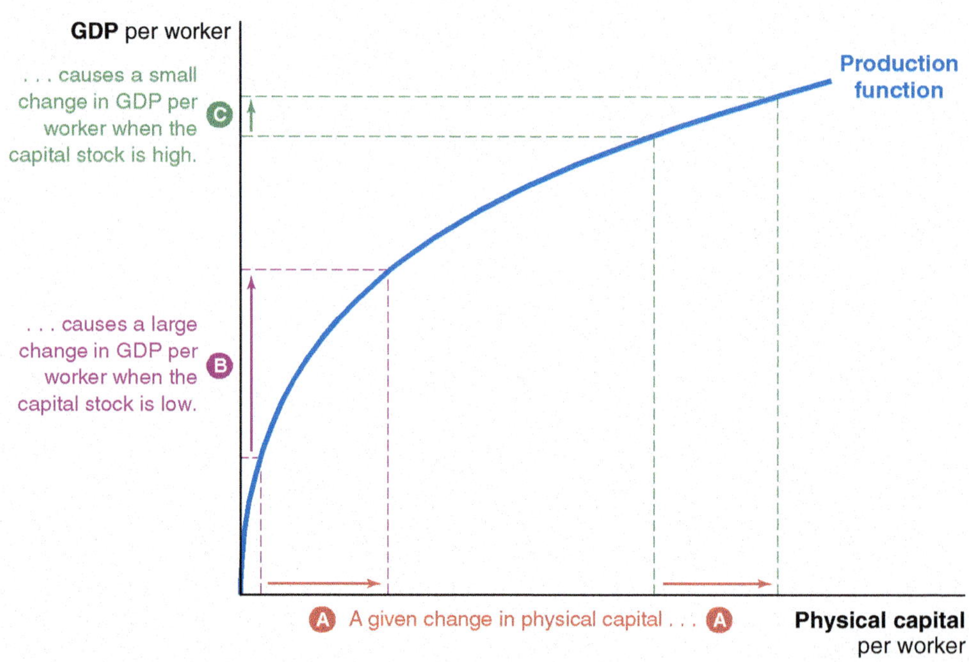

person will lead to large gains in output. But once each worker has a lot of capital, adding more capital has a smaller effect. This is just the idea that more tools are helpful, but at some point, extra tools won't make that much of a difference.

PKphotograph/Shutterstock

South Korea is no longer a poor country, thanks to catch-up growth.

Insight three: Poor countries can enjoy catch-up growth. Diminishing returns means that additional investments in physical capital don't significantly boost output in rich countries which already have a lot of capital. But it can lead to a much bigger gain in output for poor countries which have very little capital to start with. So if a relatively poor country starts investing in machines, factories, and other equipment, it will experience relatively rapid output growth.

Indeed, this is the story of South Korea's extraordinary growth that rocketed it from a poor country to a rich one. In 1970, South Korea had very low levels of capital per person. Over the next thirty years, GDP grew by a factor of 12, fuelled by a 27-fold increase in the quantity of capital. A comparison with Australia makes the point clearly. Capital per person increased by roughly $65,000 in both South Korea and Australia, but because Australia already had abundant capital, it didn't generate growth anywhere near as impressive.

The rapid growth that occurs when a relatively poor country invests in capital is known as **catch-up growth.** It raises the possibility that if poor countries make similar investments to rich countries, the gap between poor and rich countries will narrow.

catch-up growth The rapid growth that occurs when a relatively poor country invests in its physical capital.

Capital Accumulation and the Solow Model

Our analysis so far suggests that capital accumulation can play an important role in boosting output. But can capital accumulation, by itself, serve as an engine for *ongoing* growth in output per person? To answer this question, we'll need to *jointly* consider both the production function (which describes how more capital creates more output) and the process of capital accumulation (in which more output leads to more investment in physical capital). The set of insights that we'll gain from simultaneously analysing the production function, investment, capital accumulation, and economic growth is sometimes called the *Solow model*.

Insight four: The capital stock will grow as long as investment outpaces depreciation. A country's capital stock evolves over time as a result of investment and depreciation. Investments in new equipment and structures boost the capital stock and, therefore, the economy's capacity to produce output. But machines break down, factories crumble, and roads get potholes, so each year some proportion of the existing capital stock is destroyed by depreciation.

This means that the capital stock will grow—that is, capital will continue to accumulate—as long as investment exceeds depreciation. And the production function tells you that as long as capital per person is growing, then so is output per person, and so living standards are rising. Put these pieces together, and it says that the economy will keep growing as long as investment exceeds depreciation.

Insight five: Capital per worker will eventually stop growing. Sadly, this won't continue forever. First, there's the problem of rising depreciation: As the capital stock grows, there are more machines, and if a fixed fraction of them fail each year, total depreciation will grow. That means the economy will need to generate larger and larger amounts of investment merely to replace the capital lost to depreciation. Second, there's the problem of diminishing returns: Each increment of capital creates a smaller and smaller increment to output. If businesses devote some share of their output to investment, then these smaller boosts to output will yield successively smaller boosts to investment.

Wavebreak Media/AGE Fotostock

This machine makes her more productive, but how many can she use at once?

This combination of diminishing returns and depreciation means that at some point the amount of new investment the economy generates will no longer exceed the amount of capital lost to depreciation. When investment and depreciation are equal, the capital stock stops growing.

Insight six: Capital accumulation can't sustain long-term economic growth. The key question the Solow model asks is whether capital accumulation can generate sustained economic growth. Will a burst of investment set in motion a virtuous cycle, in which the increase in capital leads to more output, and that output is used to fund more investment which will further increase the capital stock, which in turn will further boost output, and so on?

That virtuous cycle exists, but we've discovered that eventually this process peters out. Each successive cycle of increased capital yields successively smaller boosts in output, and so smaller boosts in investment. But on each successive cycle the economy's depreciation bill keeps rising. Eventually the process stalls because the economy grows to the point where new investment in capital merely offsets depreciation. The capital stock remains at a rest point that we call the *steady state.* And when the capital stock stops growing, then—in the absence of technological progress or other factors changing the number of workers or their skills—output will stop growing too. Economic growth has petered out, and the economy has come to rest.

We've discovered that while capital accumulation alone can't support *sustained* economic growth, it can explain why poor countries will experience rapid growth as they catch up or converge to the rich countries. But capital accumulation can't explain why rich countries such as Australia and much of Europe have enjoyed sustained economic growth. That means we're going to need to look elsewhere to figure out what's driving the ongoing rise in output per person in the advanced economies.

Technological Progress

The key to sustained economic growth is technological progress. The development of new production methods creates new ways to combine existing resources to produce more valuable output. Businesses can use these new and improved recipes to produce more output from any given set of inputs.

Technological progress shifts the production function. That means that technological progress shifts the production function, increasing the output that's produced from any given level of inputs. As Figure 12 illustrates, this shifts the production function upward, boosting the amount of output each person produces, for a given level of capital per person.

Technological progress can make investing in capital more productive and more valuable. Specifically, notice that the new production function in Figure 12 is steeper, which means that the extra output you get from investing in one more machine has risen. As a result, a burst of technological progress will also spur a burst of new investment, and the economy will grow towards a new and higher steady-state level of capital. So technological progress both leads to more output from existing inputs, and also spurs capital accumulation, raising the level of inputs.

Figure 12 illustrates that one burst of technological progress can push the production function up, which will raise the level of GDP. And so it follows that sustained and continual bursts of technological progress will lead to sustained growth in GDP. By this view, the key to sustained economic growth is sustained technological progress, continually pushing the production function up.

Figure 12 | Technological Progress Shifts the Production Function

(A) Technological progress leads to an **increase in the output produced with a given set of inputs.**

(B) An economy with a given amount of capital per worker can now **produce more output** per person than before.

(C) Technological progress also boosts the **extra output** that each extra machine produces, making investment more productive and valuable.

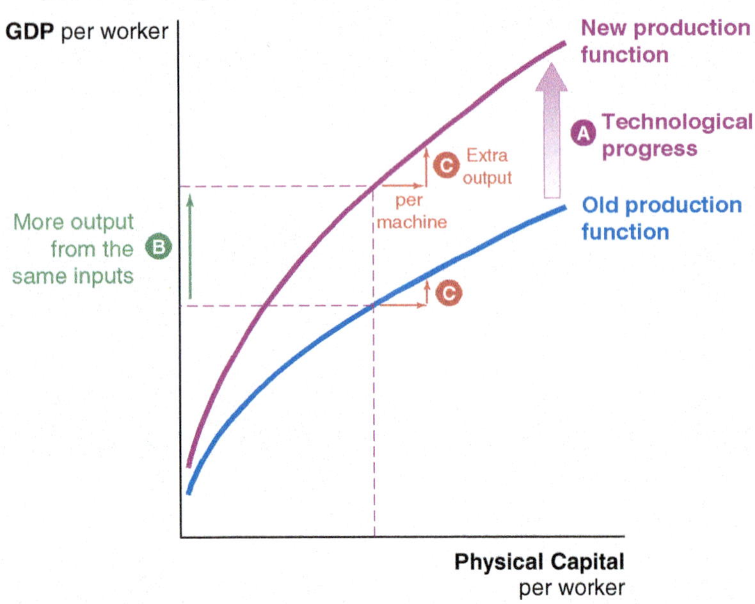

Technological progress relies on new ideas. Now that you know how important technological progress is to economic growth, a natural question is: How do we get it? New technology is fundamentally about new ideas. It is new ideas that create new ways to transform existing physical inputs into more valuable outputs. But where do new ideas come from, and how do they power economic growth?

Two things drive technological progress: how quickly new ideas are created, and how many resources are devoted to generating new ideas. Workers can produce either goods and services or new ideas. So the number of workers focused on new ideas can rise both from a rising population, and also by allocating resources away from producing goods and services towards producing new ideas. There's a trade-off here: In the short run, if everyone produced goods and services, our economy would produce more goods and services. But in the long run, with no one investing in technological progress, there would be no economic growth. But if enough resources are devoted to ongoing research and development, that will yield a steady stream of new ideas, powering ongoing economic growth.

Pictorial Press Ltd/Alamy

Marie Curie's ideas about radiation led to discoveries, and eventually treatments, that could cure cancer.

The absence of technological progress explains why growth took so long to occur. The insight that technological progress requires resources can help explain why the world went millennia without generating economic growth: When people were in a battle to survive, there were no spare resources to devote to generating new ideas. And so subsistence living begat subsistence living.

This insight also explains why the agricultural revolution was the catalyst that sparked the modern era of sustained economic growth. Improvements in agriculture allowed societies to produce enough food so that it freed people to pursue other tasks, including generating new ideas. And those ideas spurred the Industrial Revolution, which led to the modern era of sustained economic growth. It's a process that builds on itself, as the more an economy is already producing, the easier it is to sacrifice production today in order to invest in generating the ideas that will power future economic growth. You can think about all this through the lens of the *opportunity cost principle*—the true cost of something is the most valuable alternative you must give up. Back when humans weren't producing enough food to prevent starvation, the opportunity cost of producing new ideas instead of farming was producing less food, which translated to starvation, and death. Today, the opportunity cost of having people work on innovation is lower, and so we do more of it.

Technological progress allowed us to break the cycle of poverty. Some wonder if there are any limits to how fast the economy can grow. They worry that if the economy grows too quickly, we may run out of the things we need, such as oil, land, and other natural resources. Thomas Malthus, an eighteenth-century economist, feared that living standards could never truly improve because as more food was produced, the population would grow, which would require more food production. He believed that food production would never successfully outpace population growth, so the world was forever doomed to subsistence living. Malthus was wrong about the future, but he was right about the past. Remember that for more than a million years, there was so little economic growth that GDP per person remained near the minimum necessary to sustain life. The reason for this is that for most of history, there was little technological progress.

Malthus was wrong about the future because technological progress in agriculture vastly outpaced population growth. The earth's ability "to produce subsistence for humanity" was much greater than he ever thought possible, and that change occurred because of new ideas about how to produce more with less. We now grow food using a small fraction of the resources that were required in Malthus's time.

If there are no limits to technological progress, there are no limits to economic growth. Modern-day concerns about the limits of economic growth have often focused on energy consumption. Not only might greenhouse gases warm the planet, but energy use gives off waste heat, and so the more energy we use, the hotter the planet will become. But it turns out that even as countries like Australia have continued to grow, we haven't increased our energy consumption much. Indeed, the consumption of fossil fuels in Australia declined over the last decade. On a per person basis, Australian energy consumption peaked in the 2000s. This doesn't mean that you shouldn't worry about pollution; it just means that you can't conclude that it means economic growth is limited.

If new ideas are the engine of economic growth, then our ability to combine existing resources in ever more productive and valuable ways is only limited by our imagination. As long as we keep coming up with new ways to do more with less, the economy can keep growing. As a result, most economists expect that we will enjoy ongoing economic growth and continually rising living standards for the foreseeable future.

Remember:
- Ideas can be freely shared
- Ideas do not depreciate with use
- Ideas may promote other ideas

Ideas can generate unlimited growth. Society's ability to continually produce new ideas is the key to unlocking long-run growth. And idea-driven, rather than capital-driven, economic growth can be sustained because ideas are different from physical capital in three ways:

- *Ideas can be freely shared.* My use of a new idea doesn't make it harder for you to use that idea. Economists refer to this as *nonrival,* which means that one person's use of an idea doesn't subtract from another's.
- *Ideas do not depreciate with use.* An idea doesn't wear out the way a factory does.
- *Ideas may promote other ideas.* Ideas can beget new ideas through spillover effects. For example, Apple's invention of the iPhone spurred app creators to invent new applications for smartphones. Ideas can also beget new ideas by lowering the opportunity cost of producing new ideas. This means that ideas can create a virtuous cycle of more ideas, more growth, and then even more ideas.

The fact that ideas can be *freely shared* means that any new idea can be deployed across thousands or even millions of producers, making the entire economy more productive. Because ideas *don't depreciate* with use, we don't need ongoing annual investments to be able to keep using an idea. This means that unlike investment in physical capital, all new investment in ideas will boost the stock of ideas, which generates higher levels of output. As long as we continue investing in the research and development that generates the ideas that fuel technological progress, the economy will continue to grow. And the insight that ideas may *promote other ideas* means that the process of discovering new ideas can be self-sustaining, leading economic growth *to be self-reinforcing.*

EVERYDAY Economics

Innovative companies make time for new ideas

Sean Gallup/Getty Images

You may think it's just a washing machine, but it started with an idea.

Successful managers know that new ideas are the key not just to economic growth, but to the growth of their own business. Google founders Larry Page and Sergey Brin recognised the trade-off workers face between producing goods and services and producing new ideas—and they wanted to ensure that their employees spent time working on new ideas. That's why Google embraces the "20% rule," which empowers all employees to spend up to 20% of their workweek dreaming up and developing their own ideas for new products. Google argues that this option helps keep their highly creative employees engaged in generating new ideas. It also ensures that workers maintain control over their creative energy and some of their work time. Does it work? It sure seems to: Gmail, Google Maps, and Google News all started as projects that employees pursued in their 20% time.

Lots of companies implement similar tactics to ensure that their employees devote some time to developing new ideas. For example, the CEO of Bosch Group asked its entire workforce to form into teams that were tasked with trying to come up with ways to compete against Bosch. They took the best ideas these teams came up with and gave a selected group of people eight weeks' leave from their regular duties to see if they could turn the idea into a new or improved product for Bosch.

The bottom line is that it takes time to come up with new ideas, and smart managers make sure that their workers have time to innovate. ■

The problem with ideas is that they are often *nonexcludable,* which means that it's hard for you to prevent others from using—and profiting off—your idea. It's a problem that can lead people to underinvest in coming up with new ideas, creating innovations, and bringing them to the market. Here's why: If you invent a safe self-driving car, you can sell those cars and potentially make a nice profit. But the faster others can copy your idea and get their competing cars ready to sell, the smaller your profits will be. You might be better off copying someone else's idea, rather than spending a lot of your time and resources coming up with a new idea. And so the nonexcludability of ideas creates an incentive to imitate rather than innovate.

As a result, businesses will devote fewer resources to innovation than is in society's best interests. To see this, let's apply the core principles of good decision making to the question of how much your business will invest in research and development. Apply the *marginal principle,* which says to break the question of how much to invest down to: Should I invest one more dollar? Next, apply the *cost-benefit principle* and conclude that you should if the marginal benefits *to your business* of the additional dollar invested exceed the marginal costs *you pay.* This leads to the right decision for you, but the wrong decision for society if others benefit from your research and development. Because ideas can be copied and innovations have spillover effects, others benefit from your investments in generating new ideas. Yet those benefits are not included in your personal cost-benefit calculation. That's why market forces tend to lead businesses to invest too little in generating new ideas.

But well-designed intellectual property laws can help ensure that more innovation occurs. Indeed, institutions—the "rules of the game"—play an important role in fostering economic growth, and so our next task is to explore their effects.

22.4 Public Policy: Why Institutions Matter for Growth

Learning Objective *Find out why government institutions matter for economic growth.*

So far we've focused on the proximate causes of economic growth: It's the result of new ideas, as well as investing in human capital and accumulating physical capital. But that just pushes the question one level deeper: What factors determine whether people will invent new ideas and invest in human or physical capital? That's our next task. To preview, the key is *incentives,* which depend on *institutions.*

The *cost-benefit principle* provides a useful reminder of the importance of incentives. What's the benefit of investing in research and development if your competitors can steal your ideas? Why work hard if the government can seize your output? Why work to develop new products if there aren't roads and networks that will allow you to distribute them? The government, and institutions more generally, provides the framework that creates the right incentives for people to come up with new ideas and bring them to the marketplace. The institutional environment created by the government determines the rules that people follow, and the incentives for their work. That environment is a crucial determinant of people's willingness to invest in education, capital, and ideas.

> Institutions that promote economic growth:
> 1. Property rights
> 2. Government stability
> 3. Efficient regulation
> 4. Government policy encouraging innovation

The most common reasons that countries fail to grow are related to their institutions and government. Two countries may have the same amount of physical and human capital, but what they produce depends on how efficiently workers, workers' skills, and physical capital are allocated across the economy. And that allocation has a lot to do with the "rules of the game," or the institutional structure in a country. Do property rights protect people's investments? Can you count on the government to enforce the laws so everyone is playing by the same, agreed-upon rules? Can you trust the government? Is it stable? The answers to these questions should guide your choices, and they determine how fast your country's economy will grow. The government also plays an important role in encouraging investment in physical and human capital and funding research into new ideas. Let's explore some of the important ways a country's institutions and government determine its outcomes.

Property Rights

property rights Control over a tangible or intangible resource.

Jose Luis Pelaez Inc/DigitalVision/Getty Images

Property rights matter.

Property rights determine who controls a tangible or intangible resource. When property rights are well defined, the rules are clear, and people can spend less time fighting over a particular resource. This is also what provides the incentives for you to work hard to be able to get a resource like money, land, or an ownership stake in a company—since you know that once you have it, that right will be respected.

If you grew up with siblings, you probably have a good sense of the importance of property rights. If so, perhaps a parent ("the government" in your household) helped enforce whose turn it was to use a shared household resource like a computer. Without clear rules and enforcement, you might have wasted a lot of time fighting with a sibling to claim your right to a resource instead of actually spending time with that resource. Or perhaps you got a part-time job to be able to afford your own iPad. Would you have worked as hard if your sibling could simply take it from you without asking?

To have well-defined property rights requires having a clear set of laws that establish your rights, and a stable, trusted system of enforcing those rights. If you decide to invest in a friend's new designer clothing rental business, you have to trust that you'll receive and be able to keep your share of the business and profits. Without property rights and a trusted enforcement system, no one creates wealth because they fear that they will simply lose it. That means that trusted and efficient enforcement institutions play an important role in creating the right environment for economic growth.

People are reluctant to make investments when they worry that their business partners or others will successfully take off with their money, or when they fear that contracts are unlikely to be enforced. Sometimes the government does too little to enforce property rights and the rule of law, and sometimes the government itself becomes part of the problem. In corrupt countries and political systems, people fear that government will strip them of their wealth.

Government Stability

Federico Rotter/NurPhoto/Getty Images

If you don't trust the government, you probably won't start a new business.

Corruption and political instability can discourage investment and innovation. Turmoil at home creates the incentives for political leaders to extract resources for their personal gain, and it discourages investment since political uncertainty means people can't count on receiving the returns on their investment.

Think back to the tragedy of Argentina. After several decades as the world's fastest-growing economy, Argentina suffered military coups in 1930, 1943, 1955, 1962, 1966, and 1976! Needless to say, generations of Argentinians lived with political instability throughout their lives, and it shaped the choices they made. The problem wasn't only political instability, but also a periodic overhauling of the Supreme Court, a perception that property rights were insecure, and a lack of confidence in the central bank to control inflation. These were all important reasons why Argentina failed to thrive over the past century.

Efficiency of Regulation

How quickly can you start your own business? In Australia, the typical business is up and running in just a handful of days. And if you want to start selling your uniquely designed jewellery on Etsy, you can start your business in just a few minutes. In some cases, it's essential to have regulators to ensure that your new business is going to do good, rather than harm. For instance, it's better for society if a new restaurant is following health standards, or a new manufacturing plant isn't dumping harmful chemicals into the local water supply. Sometimes it even helps get your business going when potential customers know that they can trust that your product won't hurt them, since government regulations provide some basic assurances.

In general, regulatory oversight in Australia is lighter than in most of the rest of the world. The World Bank estimates that it takes 2 days to start a business in Australia. By contrast, it takes 12 days to open a business in Argentina, and even this reflects a substantial improvement from the 66 days it took in 2003. Political instability often goes hand in hand with excessive bureaucratic obstacles. For example, in Venezuela, it took 230 days to open a business in 2019! In the time it takes you to get through the red tape in Venezuela to open a business, you could have opened more than 100 businesses in Australia.

chris24/Alamy Stock Photo

It isn't hard to set up your own business in Australia.

You may find it surprising that, on average, it's harder to open a business in poorer countries than in richer countries. After all, the poorer the country, the more they could benefit from entrepreneurship. Yet this is the trap a lot of countries are in—it's hard to invest or innovate because of excessive red tape. But even though there are too many bureaucratic obstacles, there's also often government corruption and insufficient enforcement of property rights. Together, this creates few incentives to invest and innovate, which is an important reason why some countries are poor.

Government Policy to Encourage Innovation

A trusted government, with clear property rights, a well-functioning legal framework, and regulations that effectively balance protecting the public with encouraging entrepreneurship, are all part of the institutional structure that economists have shown is crucial for economic success. Regulation and rules are essential to a well-functioning market economy, but they can also be inefficient or excessive and create more problems than they solve.

Government policy plays a particularly important role when it comes to innovation. Recall that when ideas can be easily borrowed or imitated there's not much of an incentive to innovate. Government policy can create incentives and support the development of new ideas in two ways: The government can create property rights around ideas, and it can subsidise the creation of ideas. Let's explore these two approaches.

How the government encourages innovation:

1. Intellectual property laws
2. Research and development subsidies

Innovation strategy one: Create incentives through intellectual property laws. Discovering new ideas, coming up with new inventions, or designing innovative business processes can be an expensive endeavour, costing you millions of dollars in research and development. The *cost-benefit principle* suggests that entrepreneurs will only make this investment if the benefits to them exceed the costs. But if other businesses can simply copy your ideas, then some of the benefits that your idea creates will end up benefiting them rather than you. And if enough rivals copy your invention, competitive forces will push the price down, meaning that customers benefit at the expense of your bottom line. This undermines the incentive for businesses to invest in innovation. The government uses intellectual property laws to protect the value of your innovation. These laws typically give you an exclusive right to use your idea, ensuring that other businesses that want to use it will have to pay you for the right to do so. One form of intellectual property right is copyright, which gives authors and artists exclusive rights to their work. Trademarks protect firms from competitors who want to use their brand names. And patents grant people and companies exclusive rights to inventions, whether it's the design for the iPhone or how to make a new pharmaceutical drug.

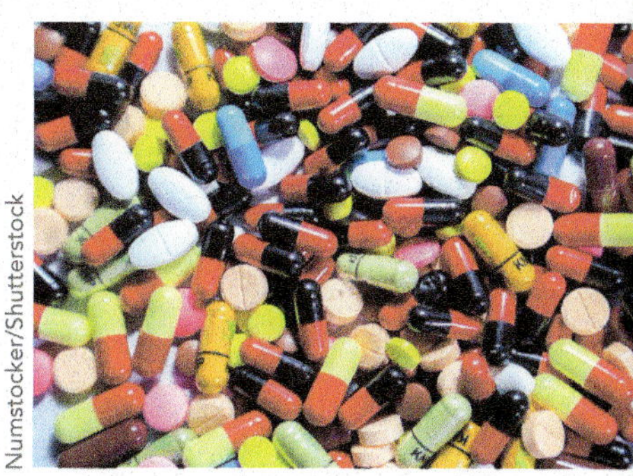

Numstocker/Shutterstock

Patents encourage innovation in areas ranging from iPhones to pharmaceutical drugs.

If you invent something new, patents give you the right to be the only seller, typically for a period of several decades, giving you an effective monopoly. This gives you the power to charge a high price and hence to enjoy large profits. The prospect of these large profits represents a large benefit to innovating, leading businesses to do more of it. The difficult

LiliumBosniacum/Shutterstock.com

The government subsidises important research.

policy question is to figure out how long of a period an inventor should be given the right to be a monopolist. Since the government is trying to balance the benefit of providing a strong incentive for innovation against the cost to consumers of allowing a monopolist to charge high prices, protections make sense, but only up to a point. For instance, a country might want to let a drug company be the only seller of a new drug for a few decades, but it wouldn't want to protect that drug from competition forever.

Innovation strategy two: Subsidise research and development. While intellectual property laws aim to boost the benefit of innovation, an alternative approach focuses on reducing the cost of innovating. In particular, governments can directly subsidise research into new ideas. When the government helps lower the cost of innovation, businesses do more of it. In Australia, research and development subsidies go to companies, the government, research centres, not-for-profit organisations, and universities.

Interpreting the DATA **How did Australia get so rich?**

Economists credit the success of Australia to a combination of factors. Australia has strong institutions like the rule of law, competitive markets, and a democratic system of government. It also has a strong base of both physical capital and human capital, as well as highly developed technology, norms, and institutions that transform capital and labour into products and services that people want to buy. Australia industrialised before many other countries, and it was a centre of innovation, manufacturing, and trade. It grew enormously, from a GDP per person of roughly \$800 in 1800 to over \$78,700 in 2021.

In contrast, many other countries are not so lucky. They suffer from political instability or from governments that seize property or run on bribes. This can lead to inadequate investment in physical and human capital, little technological development, and a lack of institutions promoting growth. Poor countries tend to stay poor until their institutions improve. ■

Tying It Together

If you compressed the last million years of human history into 24 hours, then it's only in the last one minute that humanity has moved beyond grinding poverty and subsistence. This makes that last minute seem rather miraculous: Something unleashed the forces of economic growth, and as a result, today you live in one of the richest countries in the world, at the richest moment in the history of humanity.

Perhaps that inspires a feeling of gratitude. For me, it also inspires a sense of wonder: What caused this growth, and will it continue? While some countries have enjoyed the good fortune that economic growth brings, others have experienced slower growth, and as a result, billions of people remain poor. What explains this? A Nobel Prize–winning economist who pondered these questions was moved to write that:

> *The consequences for human welfare involved in questions like these are simply staggering: Once one starts to think about them, it is hard to think about anything else.*

I agree. As we've seen, small differences in economic growth rates, once they've compounded for hundreds of years, can have massive effects. This means that the insights that might yield even a small change in the rate of economic growth have staggering consequences for human well-being.

This chapter has drawn together the key insights from several generations of economists trying to uncover the drivers of economic growth. The result is a basic framework that sees the key ingredients of output as being labour, human capital, and physical capital, together with the recipes or technology we use to combine them. More inputs lead to more output. An earlier generation of economists had hoped that the process of capital accumulation—boosting the quantity of machinery available to workers—would be enough to sustain ongoing growth. But the insights of the Solow model dashed that hope. It delivered the good news that boosting the rate at which we invest in capital will boost output, which in turn will generate more investment in capital, and hence a further boost in output. As a result, greater investment can lead the rate of economic growth to rise for a few decades as the economy transitions towards a new high-output steady state. But the Solow model also delivers bad news, explaining why capital accumulation is not a strong enough force to generate sustained economic growth. The problem is that eventually diminishing returns kick in, and extra machines won't generate enough extra output to pay for the extra maintenance they require. When the economy hits its new steady state, this force no longer propels the economy forward.

RichVintage/Getty Images

Economic growth can continue as long as we keep coming up with new ideas.

What, then, drives economic growth? New ideas—in the form of ingenious inventions, advanced business processes, and innovative management techniques—provide new recipes for combining labour, physical capital, and human capital. These new recipes allow us to create more output with the same resources. Ideas don't depreciate, and hence if we keep generating new ideas, the economy can keep growing. As long as ideas help us use our existing resources more effectively, there are no limits to growth.

All of this identifies the proximate causes of growth: It's due to labour, physical capital, human capital, and—perhaps most importantly—new ideas. But what are the deeper causes of economic growth? What economic settings will lead to more investment in new ideas, supplemented by investments in capital that embodies these new ideas, and in the human capital needed to take advantage of new technologies? Focusing on the deeper causes of economic growth suggests that what really matters are the incentives and institutions that spur more of these investments. Careful studies of the varied growth paths of different countries over many periods of history reveal that property rights, government stability, effective regulation, and research and development policies all encourage the investments that will cause growth. Together, these insights provide a roadmap that poor countries might be able to use to ignite economic growth.

As important as these findings are, economists have yet to discover the perfect recipe for generating new ideas. This is why economics is engaged in a search for new ideas about how to generate . . . new ideas. Yes, that sounds a bit meta. But it also explains just why economics is so important: If ideas are important drivers of growth, then the ideas of economists about how to motivate businesses to invest in creating more ideas are the most important ideas of all. If economists can figure out which rules and incentives will generate the most new ideas, we may catalyse an era of even faster economic growth. The possibilities here are extraordinary. This suggests that creating new ideas about ideas could turn out to be the most transformative idea in the history of humanity.

Chapter at a Glance

Economic Growth: Increased production of goods and services, leading to rising living standards.

Ingredients of Economic Growth

Labour input: Number of workers to transform raw materials into products and services that people want to buy.

Human capital: The accumulated knowledge and skills that make a worker more productive.

Physical capital: The total amount of tools, machinery. and structures that can be used in the production of goods and services.

Technological progress: New methods for using existing resources to produce more valuable output.

How the Components Work Together

Production function: The methods for transforming labour input, human capital, and physical capital into goods and services (outputs).

Constant returns to scale: Doubling *all* inputs (labour input, human capital, and physical capital) leads to a doubling of all the outputs.

Diminishing returns: When *one* input (labour input, human capital, or physical capital) is held constant, increases in the other inputs will, at some point, begin to yield smaller and smaller increases in output.

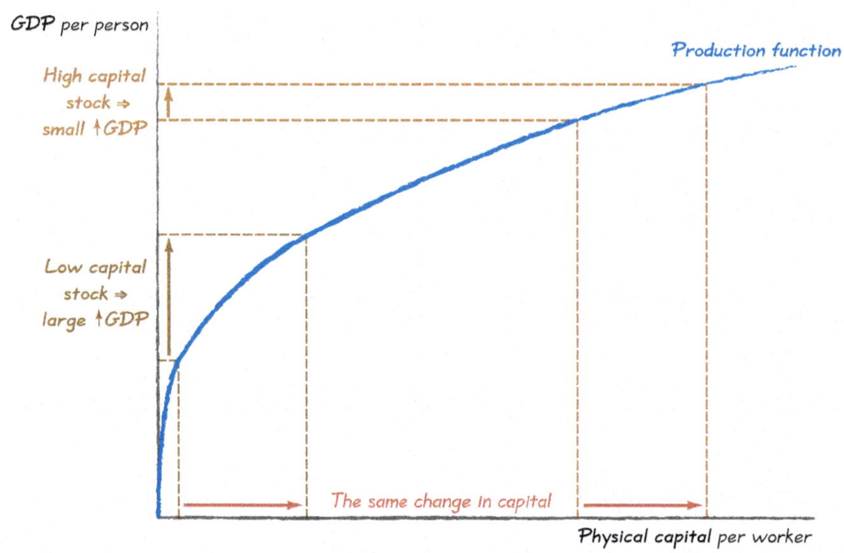

Diminishing returns and **depreciation** mean that investment in physical capital is a **limited source of growth**.

Technological change increases GDP per person for any level of capital per person.

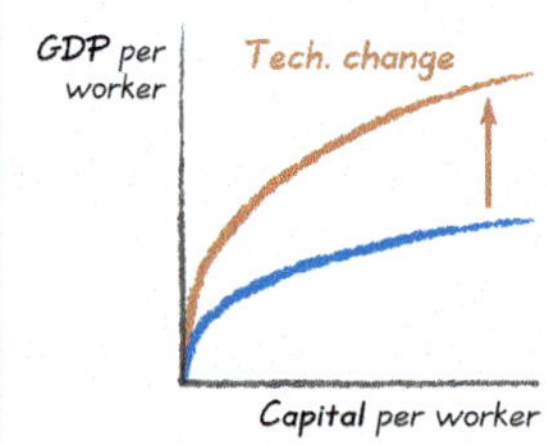

Technological progress relies on **new ideas**.

Ideas can generate **unlimited growth** because they:

1. **Can be freely shared**
2. **Don't depreciate with use**
3. **May promote other ideas**

Catch-up growth: The rapid growth that occurs when a relatively poor country (with low capital stock) invests in its physical capital.

Why institutions matter for economic growth: They provide the framework that creates the right incentives for people to invest in physical and human capital and generate **new ideas and products**.

Property rights	Without property rights and a trusted enforcement system, no one creates wealth.
Government stability	Corruption and political instability discourage investment and innovation by reducing the potential benefits from such investments.
Efficiency of regulation	Excessive red tape can make it hard to invest or innovate.
Government policy to encourage innovation	Government policy can support development of new ideas by: 1. Increasing the marginal benefit through intellectual property laws 2. Decreasing the marginal cost by subsidising research and development

Key Concepts

Discussion and Review Questions

Learning Objective 22.1 *Learn about how economies have grown over time.*

1. Since the Industrial Revolution, economic growth has increased tremendously. Discuss some of the outcomes of that economic growth.

Learning Objective 22.2 *Uncover the ingredients for economic growth.*

2. All Australian states and territories require children to attend school. Mandatory school attendance ends at Year 10, at which point students have the option of pursuing vocational training or, in some cases, full time employment. The adult literacy rate in Australia was 96.3% in 2013. Discuss how compulsory education impacts labour productivity, the aggregate production function, and overall economic growth.
3. An example of U.S. foreign investment was the state-of-the-art aircraft factory that was opened in Port Melbourne, VIC, but owned by the U.S.-owned Boeing. Describe how this investment affects the three inputs into the aggregate production function and GDP growth. (Hint: You may want to look up what intent-based networking is.)
4. Discuss an example of technological progress not mentioned in the chapter and how it impacted economic growth.

Learning Objective 22.3 *Understand how workers, capital accumulation, and technological progress work together to create economic growth.*

5. Your friend Owen is a bit of a pessimist. "The world already has 8 billion people," he says. "The population is growing too fast. Soon, there will be a food shortage—especially for people in undeveloped countries. They are too far behind modern times." Using what you've learned about economic growth, why might Owen be wrong?
6. One analyst predicts that self-driving trucks will ultimately reduce the number of trucks that are produced. She argues that because self-driving trucks can drive other people rather than sitting in people's driveways or commercial sites, Australia will need to produce fewer trucks. She argues that growth will slow because we are producing a decreasing number of trucks each year. Do you agree? Why or why not?

Learning Objective 22.4 *Find out why government institutions matter for economic growth.*

7. In early 2019, *The Economist* reported that Venezuela's GDP had fallen by 50% over just five years. During the same time period, charges of bribery and corruption were piling up upon members of the Venezuelan government, including President Nicolás Maduro, whose reelection that year was widely perceived as illegitimate. Using what you learned in the chapter, discuss how bribery and corruption in the Venezuelan government could lead to declines in GDP. What are some of the crucial elements that governments must provide to encourage innovation and growth?
8. You've started developing an app that examines students' personalities and other characteristics, and sorts them into highly effective study groups. Using the cost-benefit principle, compare your incentives to innovate and develop the software if (1) anyone could just copy your code and sell it or (2) the government allowed you to patent your code. How do your marginal benefits differ with and without intellectual property laws?
9. For each of the following institutions, provide a real-world example and explain how it promotes economic growth.
   a. Enforceable property rights
   b. Predictable and stable government
   c. Efficient regulation

Study Problems

Learning Objective 22.1 *Learn about how economies have grown over time.*

1. Consider the history of the world from 1 million B.C. until now. Although limited data exists from early history, we still have some information about how people lived and how much they consumed.
   a. Has the global rate of economic growth remained constant throughout history?

b. Which of the following time periods experienced the highest *average annual growth rate*?

- 1 million B.C. to 1200 A.D.
- 1200 to 1800 A.D.
- 1800 to 1950 A.D.
- 1950 to 1975 A.D.

Learning Objective 22.2 *Uncover the ingredients for economic growth.*

2. For each of the following, identify which inputs into the production function changed and their effects on economic growth.

a. The government passes a new program that encourages more employers to provide on-the-job training.

b. Improvements to health care cause an increasing share of older people to work instead of retiring.

c. The federal government increases annual spending on national infrastructure.

d. A large baby boom occurred two decades ago.

3. The Australian savings rate has fallen from an annual rate of around 18% in the mid-1970s to 4% at the end of 2019. What are the consequences of a declining savings rate for economic growth?

Learning Objective 22.3 *Understand how workers, capital accumulation, and technological progress work together to create economic growth.*

4. What can you tell about an aggregate production function if real GDP per worker increases by 10% in response to all of the inputs increasing by 10%? What would you expect to happen if you doubled all the inputs? Explain your answer.

5. In the movie *Avengers: Infinity War,* antagonist Thanos believes that he can limit suffering and starvation by erasing half the population from existence. You've just watched the film with your pessimistic pal Owen. "Thanos did the right thing," Owen tells you, again claiming that humanity would be better off if the population were smaller. Use the aggregate production function presented in the chapter to show Owen how an economist would analyse Thanos's decision.

6. Technological advancements in the restaurant industry are increasing the output that can be produced by chefs and their equipment. For example, Robo is a restaurant that opened in 2020 with robotic chefs that allow each human worker to produce and serve more meals. How will this technological progress impact the Australian economy? Use a graph of the production function to explain the impact and clearly label the effect.

7. In Uganda GDP per person is $1,110 per year, and in Japan it is $54,260. What do you think is likely to happen to each country's GDP per person if they both increase their physical capital per person by 20%? Which country do you expect to have a larger relative change in its output per person? Explain your answer.

8. In the debate over the Small business tax cuts of 2020, The Liberal Party argued that businesses needed an incentive to invest more in physical capital in order for Australia to recover from the economic effects of the pandemic. In a rich country like Australia, why is investing in physical capital both important and yet unlikely to lead to a large increase in economic growth?

9. The International Monetary Fund (IMF) publishes World Economic Outlook Updates biannually. According to the July 2018 Update, the expected annual growth rate of advanced countries was 2.2% for 2019. On the other hand, expected annual growth for developing countries was 5.1%. Explain why developing countries might be growing so much faster than developed countries.

Learning Objective 22.4 *Find out why government institutions matter for economic growth.*

10. For years, Invisalign faced no direct competitors and was an industry leader within its niche in the orthodontics appliances market, earning a $300 million profit in 2017. Invisalign pioneered the creation of clear dental trays that straighten teeth without the use of metal braces. What type of government policy fostered Invisalign's innovation and provided protection from competition? Why does the government provide protection to companies like Invisalign who can dominate a market? What do you expect to happen when the government protection expires?

CHAPTER 23

Unemployment

Chapter Objective

Learn to assess the causes and costs of unemployment.

23.1 Employment and Unemployment
Understand what unemployment is and how it's measured.

23.2 The Dynamics of the Labour Market
Learn how people move in and out of jobs and in and out of the labour market.

23.3 Understanding Unemployment
Analyse the causes of unemployment.

23.4 The Costs of Unemployment
Learn about the economic and social costs of unemployment.

Mary left a lucrative job at Google to work as a product manager at a tech start-up. But her new company has not been as successful as expected, and she—along with half the staff—just got made redundant. Two weeks into unemployment, she runs into a former colleague who is gushing about a new promotion. Mary would rather avoid telling her that things at the start-up did not go well, but she summons her courage and admits that she's been made redundant because she knows that any conversation can be a job lead.

Image Source RF/Cadalpe/Getty Images

Unemployment can happen to anyone.

Mary is a diligent job-seeker. She works hard each day to find and follow up on leads. After two months, she lands a position at a technology company where a friend works. She's thrilled to have a paycheque, but she also knows that she'll have to live on a tight budget for a while: She went a few months without her usual salary and had to dip into savings to cover expenses. She wants to build her savings back up quickly, as she now knows just how important it is to have savings when facing unemployment.

Searching for a job is time-consuming and hard, both financially and emotionally. Yet jobs end as businesses fail, work becomes automated or outsourced, and factories close. And people leave jobs to pursue other opportunities, to meet personal obligations, and sometimes to take a break from a job they hate. It might sound a little terrifying to you, but most people transition jobs at least ten times before they turn 50. Some job transitions may involve a period of unemployment—a time when you're ready to work, but don't have a job. No matter what the reason, when you're unemployed, you'll spend your days looking for work instead of doing work.

Some unemployment is inevitable, but that doesn't make it any less miserable when it happens. Thankfully, unemployment doesn't always last long, and understanding it will help you better manage those transitions for yourself. In this chapter, we'll learn more about unemployment and its causes. First, we'll delve into the different ways unemployment is measured to get a better understanding of the labour market. Then, we'll investigate the causes of unemployment. Finally, we'll examine the costs of unemployment, which go far beyond lost wages. The job market is a critical institution for millions of Australians, and it will be for you too when you graduate. So let's get started.

23.1 Employment and Unemployment

Learning Objective *Understand what unemployment is and how it's measured.*

The unemployment rate is one of the most followed economic statistics. Why? It's a good indicator of the state of the economy. But it also matters for you. Your job prospects will depend on the unemployment rate when you graduate. You or someone you love will probably be unemployed at some point. The desire to understand unemployment drives many people's interest in macroeconomics. You probably already have a sense that the unemployment rate measures the percentage of people who can't find work, but it has a formal definition and measurement approach. When the Australian Bureau of Statistics (ABS) collects data on unemployment, it works with governments and other statistics bodies around the world to agree on the use of a common definition of unemployment over time and across countries. Let's start by digging into what is meant when you hear people discussing the unemployed.

The Employed and the Unemployed

Before we can begin to count who among us doesn't have a job, we need to figure out who to include in the group of people we are considering. After all, we don't expect toddlers to have a job, so we can't consider them unemployed! Let's begin with what we'll call the **working-age population,** those age 15 or older who are not in the military or institutionalised (meaning that they live in something like a nursing home, a mental health residential facility, or a prison).

working-age population Those age 15 or older who are not in the military or institutionalised.

The Australian Bureau of Statistics—which has been charged by the Australian government to measure the employed and the unemployed—assesses the employment status of working-age adults by surveying them. They start at 15 because that's the age at which you get to decide whether to go to school or undertake a full-time apprenticeship or traineeship with the permission of your parents and school principal (perhaps you didn't know this was an option!). Other countries follow a similar definition—often starting the measure at their legal school-leaving age. Notice that there isn't an upper age cutoff: If you're still kicking around your own home at age 100, you'll be counted among the working-age population.

Now that you know who's in the working-age population, it's easy to define the **employed:** They are simply people in the working-age population who are working. "Employed" doesn't necessarily mean that you have an employer; working age adults who are self-employed are also counted as employed. For example, Uber drivers are self-employed, rather than employees of Uber. Many people work in all sorts of jobs in which they aren't considered employees—but as long as they work at least one hour during the week for pay of some kind then they are considered employed. Additionally, people who have jobs but are temporarily absent from them are considered employed whether or not they are paid for the time they are taking off.

employed Working-age people who are working.

The **unemployed** are people in the working-age population without jobs who are trying to get jobs. To be counted among the unemployed, you must be

unemployed Working-age people without jobs who are trying to get jobs.

- part of the working-age population;
- not currently working;
- actively searching for work; and
- able to accept a job if it were offered.

Notice that to be unemployed you have to do more than want a job: You must be actually trying to get a job and available to work if you find one. This is a standard definition that has been consistently used all over the world for decades, which allows us to compare unemployment rates over time and across countries.

The employed plus the unemployed are the labour force. The **labour force** is the part of the working-age population that is employed or unemployed—they're the people who are available to produce goods and services.

labour force The employed plus the unemployed.

Everyone in the working-age population falls into one of three categories: employed, unemployed, or a third category called **not in the labour force.** Those who are not in the labour force are working-age people who are neither employed nor unemployed. There are nearly 7 million working-age adults who are not in the labour force. Some are retired, in school, taking care of a child or other family member, or too unwell to work. Others may have decided that it's too hard to find a job and have given up on trying to find one.

To get a sense of the magnitudes, Figure 1 shows the entire working-age population divided into the employed, the unemployed, and those not in the labour force. Most working-age adults are employed, and only a small sliver are unemployed. The unemployed and the employed form the labour force, and together they are just under two-thirds of the working-age population. The remaining third are those not in the labour force.

Figure 1 Australian Working-Age Population

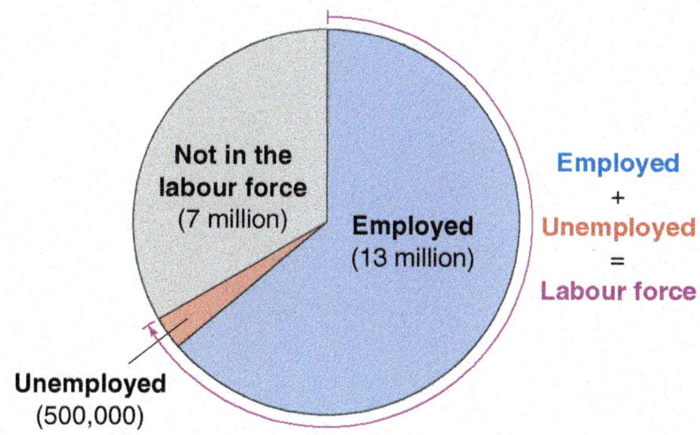

2021 Data from: Australian Bureau of Statistics.

The ABS collects monthly data on who's employed, unemployed, and not in the labour force. You can see the latest data yourself by looking up the ABS's monthly Labour Force report (available at www.abs.gov.au/ausstats/abs@.nsf/mf/6202.0).

not in the labour force Those in the working-age population who are neither employed nor unemployed.

Do the Economics

Identify whether each of these people are employed, unemployed, or not in the labour force.

a. Aidan recently graduated from university without a job. He hasn't started looking for one yet, but he plans to start searching for a job next month after he's moved back to his family's house and had time to catch up with his friends.

b. Mariko is working 40 hours a week in a salaried position as an administrative assistant but is searching for a new job where she can better use her skills and earn more money.

c. Stephanie just finished a degree in primary education and is hoping to find a teaching job. In the meantime, she works 10 hours a week as an after-school nanny for one family. She also works one day a week as a housekeeper for another family.

d. Gita is a current full-time student. She's excited to graduate, but she has another semester to go. She scours online job listings at night to get a sense of the jobs that are available and to see if she can secure a job offer before she graduates.

e. Wei was a manager at a Target store that closed. When he heard he was being made redundant, he immediately applied to drive for Uber. He's now driving for Uber part-time while he searches for a new position as a retail manger.

f. Malik was recently made redundant. He is actively looking for a job and has several promising interviews lined up. ■

Answers: a. Aidan is not in the labour force because he isn't actively looking for work. b. Mariko is employed—the fact that she is currently searching for a new job doesn't change her employment status. c. Stephanie is employed because she is getting a few hours of paid work each week. d. Gita is not in the labour force because she is a full-time student and therefore not currently available to start a job. e. Wei is employed because he is earning money driving. f. Malik is unemployed.

labour force participation rate The percentage of the working-age population that is either employed or unemployed.

Labour Force Participation

The **labour force participation rate** is the percentage of the working age population that is either employed or unemployed:

$$\text{Labour force participation rate} = \frac{\text{Employed} + \text{Unemployed}}{\text{Working-age population}} \times 100$$

Figure 2 shows that the labour force participation rate grew throughout the roughly three decades beginning around 1980 as an increasing share of adults worked outside the home. This growth in the labour force was an important source of GDP growth. In contrast, the labour force participation rate has stagnated at around it's pre-"Global Financial Crisis" (GFC) high of 65.6% in mid 2008, and began to fall sharply in 2020 due to the coronavirus pandemic.

Figure 2 Australian Labour Force Participation Rate over Time

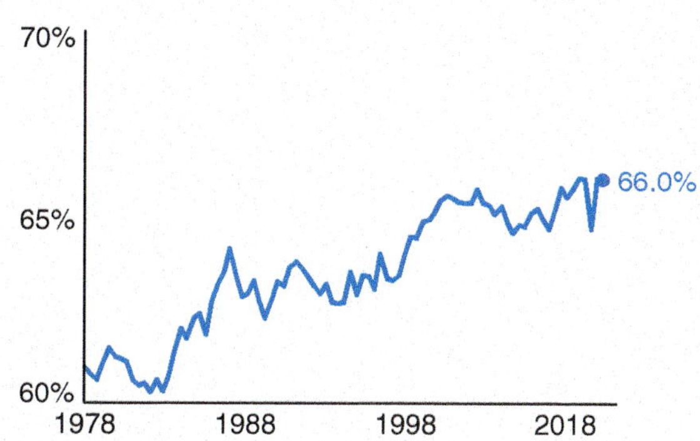

Data from: Australian Bureau of Statistics.

Figure 3 | Labour Force Participation Rate for Men and Women

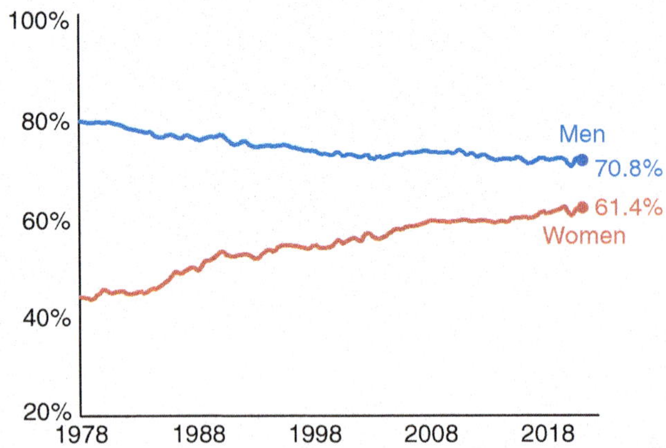

Data from: Australian Bureau of Statistics.

The labour force participation rate patterns differ for men and women. There were two strong trends in the labour force participation rate during the twentieth century: growth in women's participation and decline in men's. Figure 3 shows labour force participation rates separately for men and women. In the late 1970s, men were almost twice as likely as women to be in the labour force. Women's labour force participation grew throughout the twentieth century with rapid growth right up to the GFC. In contrast, male participation in the labour force has fallen over much of the past 40 years. The growth in women's labour force participation more than offset the decline in male participation for most of the period leading up to the GFC in 2008. Since that time the modest increase in female participation has more-or-less matched the small decrease in male participation.

Interpreting the DATA: Why has women's labour force participation risen while men's has declined?

An invention that helped spur the rise in women's labour force participation.

In the 1960s, only about a third of women worked outside the home. Back then, it was legal to refuse to hire women, or to fire them once they married or had children. Women could be paid less than men for doing the exact same work. As their husbands' incomes from paid work grew, middle- and upper-class married women often chose to focus on household tasks like cooking, cleaning, and taking care of children.

However, a combination of cultural, technological, and legal changes in the 1960s, 1970s, and 1980s encouraged women to leave the kitchen and enter the labour force. New technology like automatic washing machines, prepackaged foods, and dishwashers made home production more efficient, lessening the need for a full-time "homemaker". New access to control over fertility enabled women to invest in their education and career more reliably, which fuelled an increase in women's educational attainment and work experience. Laws forbidding gender discrimination opened new doors for women, and beginning with the NSW *Female Rates Act* in 1958, various laws required equal pay for equal work (although this has proven difficult to enforce). Finally, cultural attitudes against working mothers have changed, although even in 2005, 41% of men and 36% of women surveyed by the Australian Institute of Family Studies agreed with the statement "it is better for the family if the husband is the principal breadwinner outside the home and the wife has primary responsibility for the home and children."

All of these changes helped lead women's labour force participation rate to grow to 62% before the coronavirus pandemic.

In contrast, male labour force participation has declined in every decade for the past 40 years. This long-standing decline in male labour force participation reflects many social changes and remains an area of concern among policy makers and researchers. There are two easy explanations: Rising university enrollments mean that more young men stay out of the labour force in order to focus on their education, and there are a lot more working age men who have retired. But these explanations don't resolve the problem. They do, however, suggest that we focus our attention on the labour force participation rates of people ages 25–54 so that we can ignore students and retirees. In 1978, 79% of men in this age range worked. That rate has now declined to 65%. That's around 700,000 men who are in what many consider to be the prime working years that are neither working nor looking for work. The truth is that economists don't fully understand why.

The factors that are likely to be important drivers of recent declines like automation replacing workers or jobs moving to other countries don't explain early decades of decline. But they do point to the fact that the labour force participation rate is an important indicator of whether the labour market is working for everyone. Other factors, such as men staying home to care for their children or aging parents, or going back to school at older ages, explain only a very small amount of the decline.

Recent research has pointed to a decrease in the share of men with family responsibilities: Fewer men are marrying and having children than in the past, and without a family to help support, some men choose to work less. Other research has argued that some men are choosing not to work because an increase in the quality of video games has increased the opportunity cost of work! In sum, many social and labour market changes have led fewer men to seek and find employment. This is an ongoing problem with consequences that go well beyond the labour market. ■

The Unemployment Rate

The **unemployment rate** is the percentage of the labour force that's unemployed:

unemployment rate The percentage of the labour force that is unemployed.

$$\text{Unemployment rate} = \frac{\text{Unemployed}}{\text{Labour force}} \times 100$$

Because the unemployment rate is designed to tell us what percentage of people who are trying to find work have failed to do so, it's measured as a percentage of the labour force, not as a percentage of the working-age population. If it were measured as a share of the working-age population, a country's unemployment rate would differ based on how big a share of the population is retired, in school, or staying home to take care of kids. By measuring the unemployed as a share of the labour force we can compare unemployment rates across states and countries with different labour force participation rates. We'll discuss later in the chapter how the unemployment rate might differ if we considered more of the people who are out of the labour force as unemployed.

Unemployment rates vary for different groups. Figure 4 shows that some groups experience higher unemployment rates than others. The top group of bars shows that the unemployment rate is lower for those with more education. Only 2.3% of university graduates are unemployed, compared to 5.5% of those who didn't finish year 12 and 8% of those who didn't finish year 10. Now you see why people have been telling you your whole life to stay in school!

The unemployment rate also differs by place of birth. Australians born in Southern and Central Asia or North Africa and the Middle East have higher unemployment rates than those born in Europe, the Americas, sub-Saharan Africa, or Australia.

Figure 4 also shows that unemployment is much more common when you're young.

Finally, the lowest panel shows that unemployment rates don't really differ much between men and women.

Figure 4 | **Unemployment Rates in Australia by Group**

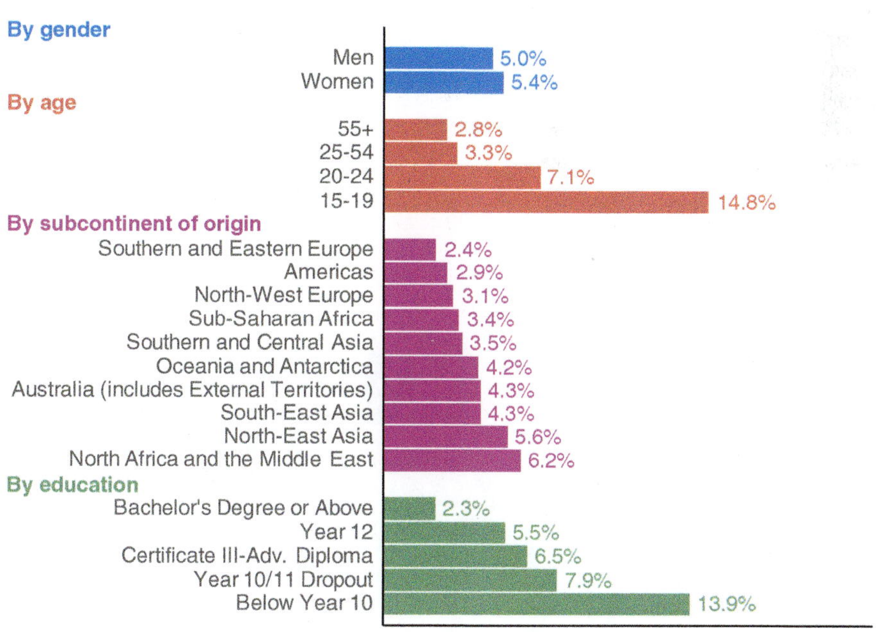

2021 Data from: Australian Bureau of Statistics.

Do the Economics

Let's now figure out the unemployment rate in Australia. In 2020, there were 20.8 million adults in Australia. Of these people, 1.0 million were unemployed, 12.5 million were employed, and 7.4 million were not in the labour force.

What was the unemployment rate?

$$\text{Unemployment rate} = \frac{\text{Unemployed}}{\text{Labour force}} \times 100 = \frac{1.0 \text{ million}}{12.5 \text{ million} + 1.0 \text{ million}} \times 100 = 7.5\%$$

So, the unemployment rate was 7.5%. ■

Figure 5 | Unemployment Rates Around the World

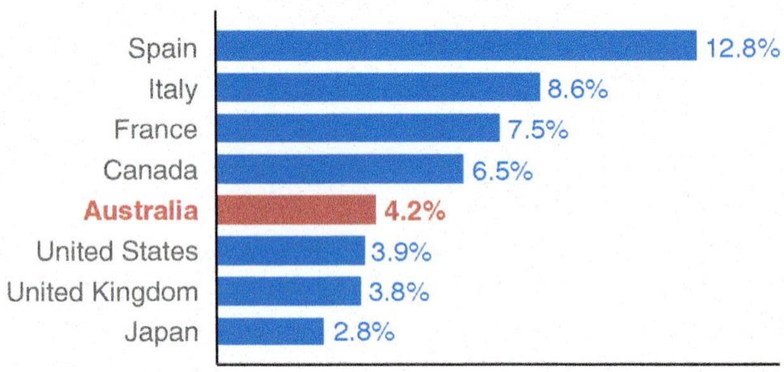

2022 Data from: OECD.

Figure 6 | Australian Unemployment Rate over Time

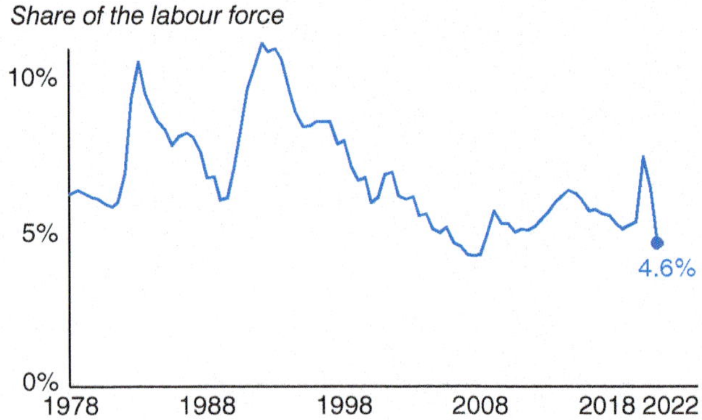

Data from: Australian Bureau of Statistics.

Unemployment rates differ around the world. Australia has a lower unemployment rate than many other countries. Figure 5 shows that among these countries, the United Kingdom and Japan have lower unemployment rates than Australia. The United States has an unemployment rate of just 3.9% and Australia's was 5.1% before the pandemic hit, falling to 4.2% (and even touching 3.9% on the very latest data). Spain has a high unemployment rate (12.8%) and other European countries, like France and Italy, have unemployment rates roughly double that of Australia.

The unemployment rate fluctuates over time, but it's never zero. The unemployment rate also varies over time as the economy strengthens and weakens. When the economy is growing fast, the unemployment rate tends to fall, and when the economy is slowing down, it tends to rise. Figure 6 shows that the Australian unemployment rate moves up and down, but it typically returns to a rate of around 5% to 6%. The **equilibrium unemployment rate** is the long-run unemployment rate to which the economy tends to return. The unemployment rate tends to fluctuate around this level as you see in Figure 6. Some economists call this the "natural rate of unemployment," but there isn't anything natural about it. Instead, you should think of it as the unemployment rate that can persist in equilibrium.

So why does the unemployment rate stay above zero in equilibrium? After all, no one really wants to be unemployed. The causes of unemployment are varied, but before we turn to the causes of unemployment, let's explore the mechanics of how people flow into and out of jobs. The speed of that process is part of what determines unemployment.

equilibrium unemployment rate The long-run unemployment rate to which the economy tends to return.

23.2 The Dynamics of the Labour Market

Learning Objective *Learn how people move in and out of jobs and in and out of the labour market.*

Takatoshi Kurikawa/Alamy Stock Photo

As some customers leave, others take their place.

To better understand the labour market, it's helpful to start with an analogy. Picture a busy restaurant: As customers leave, new customers are seated. Tables are always turning over, so while most tables are full, new customers arriving are able to find a table without much of a wait. Sometimes, though, things clog up and there are more customers than tables or it takes a lot of time to get tables ready for new customers.

The labour market is in many ways like a crowded restaurant, where jobs are like tables and workers are like hungry diners. Every day, thousands of people leave and start jobs. People leave jobs for all sorts of reasons—they may get made redundant or fired, they may quit for a better job, or they may quit to exit the labour force. Just like a dynamic restaurant, where a large number of tables turning over regularly makes it easy for new people to arrive and find a table quickly, a dynamic labour market makes it easy for new people to enter the labour market and find a job quickly.

But, like a restaurant, the labour market can also get backed up. Potential workers may not be well matched to the jobs available. If many people become unemployed at once, there may not be enough job openings for everyone, and it may take longer to find a job. There may be barriers to employers eliminating inefficient jobs or workers, which slows down the process of creating new jobs or hiring new workers. Let's take a closer look at the dynamics of the Australian labour market.

Labour Market Flows

The dynamics of the Australian labour market are pretty amazing. In any given month, around 400,000 people in Australia start a new job and about the same number of people leave jobs. Entrepreneurs hire people for their new businesses, and existing businesses fill positions as people leave and create new jobs as they expand. Businesses eliminate jobs, sack workers, and even close their doors completely when the market no longer wants their products. Entire sectors of the economy shrink or expand.

Chris Ratcliffe/Bloomberg/Getty Images

Jobs come and go.

Sectoral shifts often capture a lot of our attention, particularly shrinking sectors. Manufacturing and agriculture are examples of sectors that have shrunk in recent decades in Australia. These sectors have lost jobs, partially due to labour-saving technological change. But there are also expanding sectors that are adding even more jobs. For example, Australia has seen rapid growth in health care, education, construction, and information technology. But these sectoral shifts are just a tiny slice of what happens every day.

A dynamic labour market makes it easier for people to find new jobs. Open up an online jobs board and look at the postings today. You'll see jobs in expanding sectors, like new media managers, but you'll also see plenty of manufacturing jobs and retail jobs despite the fact that those sectors are shrinking or leveling off. The largest source of job openings comes from people leaving existing jobs, and even when sectors are in decline they continue to have a lot of transitions, with people leaving jobs and new people being hired. While many people who leave jobs move on to other jobs, thereby increasing the number of people searching, the fact that there's a lot of movement makes it easier for workers and jobs to find each other.

Most job-seekers are employed. One aspect of a dynamic labour market is that most people seeking new jobs are already employed. This makes finding a job harder for the unemployed because they are competing not just against other people without jobs, but also people with current jobs. Research shows that employers tend to prefer people with jobs, so it's easier to find work when you already have a job.

Most unemployment spells are short. Nearly half of people who become unemployed in Australia are back in work within 13 weeks, and about one in five find a new job in less than 4 weeks. But not everyone is so lucky. Some find themselves unemployed for a long time. This is more likely to happen when there are fewer job openings, such as during and in the aftermath of the recession of the early 1990s, when one in three unemployed people had been unemployed for more than 6 months. By contrast, between 2010 and 2019 that figure was around 20%.

Even when there are many openings, a few people will be unlucky, and none of the jobs they apply for will work out. Anyone who spends more than twelve consecutive months unemployed is **long-term unemployed.**

long-term unemployed People who have been unemployed for twelve consecutive months or longer.

Discrimination and skill loss make it hard for the long-term unemployed to find work. Studies show that those who experience long-term unemployment are discriminated against by potential employers. Workers who have similar skills but have a long spell of unemployment on their resume are less likely to be given an interview and less likely to be hired. In addition to discrimination, the long-term unemployed may lose skills and connections the longer they are out of work. For both of these reasons, the number of opportunities the long-term unemployed get dwindles over time, and some lose hope and stop searching altogether.

Alternative Measures of Unemployment

When people lose hope and stop searching, should we count those people as unemployed? There are also lots of people who have jobs, but want more hours, or would prefer a job that used more of their skills. Are these people a bit unemployed? Let's consider broader measures of unemployment, looking beyond those who are actively seeking and available for work and are yet without any work. There are two groups of people we need to consider: those who are not in the labour force because they have become discouraged from looking for work, and those who do work but want to work more.

marginally attached Someone who wants a job, and who has looked for a job within the past year, but who isn't counted as unemployed because they aren't currently searching for work.

discouraged worker Someone who wants a job, but isn't looking for work because they don't think there are jobs available for them.

underemployed Someone who has some work but wants more hours, or whose job isn't adequately using their skills.

involuntarily part time Someone who wants full-time work and is working part time because they haven't found a full-time job.

Some people not in the labour force would work under the right conditions. Some people are not classified as unemployed but would like to work. For instance, people who aren't currently searching for a job, but have searched in the past year are called **marginally attached** to the labour force. An important subcategory of marginally attached workers are **discouraged workers**, shown in the third column of Figure 7. They are called "discouraged" because the reason they are not looking for work is that they don't think there are jobs available for them.

Some people who are employed would prefer to work more. A broader measure of unemployment considers people who are **underemployed.** There are three ways to be underemployed. The first is that you want a full-time job, but aren't getting full-time hours. The second is that your job isn't adequately using your skills. The third is that you are working part-time (say three days a week) and would like to work more, but not full time (say four days a week). All three versions of underemployment are important for thinking about how people's skills are being utilised. But for measuring that underutilisation, it's easier to count the people who want more hours. Let's see why.

Figure 7 | Australian Unemployment Including Alternative Measures

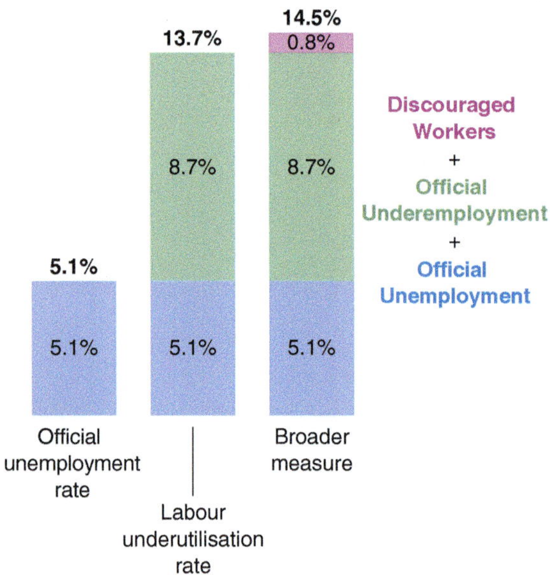

February 2020 data from Australian Bureau of Statistics.

Imagine that you are working part time as a server at a restaurant while you are looking for a full-time job in market research. You will be counted among the employed. But you didn't spend all of that time working hard at university to wait tables 12 hours a week. Because you have a part-time job and you want a full-time job, you would be considered **involuntarily part time.**

Okay, but what if the restaurant offers you full-time work? You'll probably still consider yourself underemployed even if you take the hours to help pay the bills. It might seem obvious that a university graduate waiting tables is underemployed, but what if you've decided to be a fiction writer and are working full-time waiting tables to pay the bills while you write your first novel? Or what if you are considering opening your own restaurant and are waiting tables to become better informed about the market you are considering entering? The problem with full-time employment is that, while it's easy to measure whether you're getting enough hours, it's hard to develop a set of criteria that successfully measures whether your skills are being used as effectively as possible.

Now imagine you have young children. When they were in the early years of primary school you worked two days a week from 10am to 3pm. Now they're a little older and you'd like to work 9:30am to 4:30pm, 4 days a week. You don't want to work full time, but you do want more hours. If you can't get those hours you would be classified as underemployed. Figure 7 shows this in the second column.

Alternative measures of unemployment tend to follow movements in unemployment. Figure 8 shows the broader measures of unemployment seen in Figure 7 over many years. You can see that the difference in the share of the labour force is roughly stable over time as these measures tend to move together. Typically, when the unemployment rate goes down, so does the share of people who are underemployed or discouraged.

Alternative measures of unemployment are important if you want to know how many people are potentially available to work as businesses create more jobs. But since the relationship between alternative measures and the unemployment rate is fairly stable over time, a good guess is that the broadest measure of unemployment is roughly 2 to 2.5 times the unemployment rate.

Notice that the underemployment category doesn't tell us anything about how underemployed people in it are. Somebody who works three days a week and would like to work four is 25% underutilised. Somebody who works one day but wants to work four is 75% underutilised. The broader measure of unemployment that includes underemployment doesn't capture this fact.

Figure 8 | Alternative Measures of Unemployment over Time

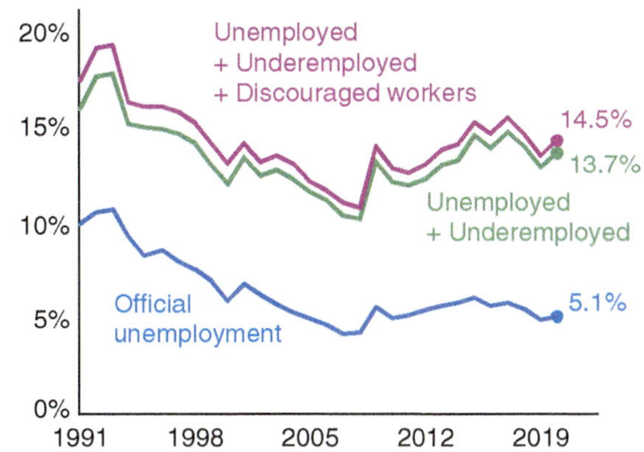

Data from: Australian Bureau of Statistics.

23.3 Understanding Unemployment

Learning Objective *Analyse the causes of unemployment.*

Now that we've explored the labour market and discovered how to measure unemployment, it's time to dig into what causes unemployment. The starting point is supply and demand in the market for labour. Workers supply their labour, selling it for a price (their wage). Like other markets, supply is upward-sloping, meaning that workers supply more labour when wages are high. Employers—buyers of labour—demand less when the price of labour is high, so they hire fewer people when wages are high.

If market forces worked perfectly, wages would adjust to the point where the quantity of labour demanded is equal to the quantity of labour supplied as shown in Figure 9. The forces of supply and demand would ensure that everyone who wanted to work at wages that employers were willing to pay would find jobs. That's because workers who wanted a job but couldn't find one would be willing to work for a bit less, pushing wages down so that employers would hire more people, and fewer people would want jobs. This process means no one is left unemployed—willing to work at market wages, but unable to find a job.

Figure 9 | Labour Demand Equals Labour Supply

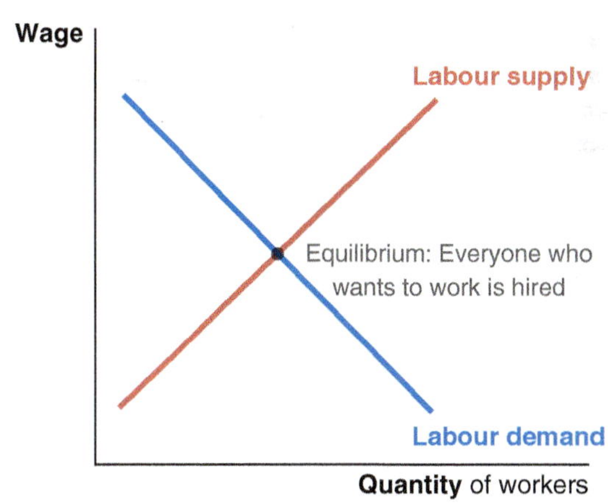

Types of Unemployment

Unemployment reflects the failure of the market to bring the demand for labour in balance with its supply. Why does this happen? There are three categories of reasons that people experience unemployment. Let's start by learning what the three categories are.

Unemployment type one: Frictional unemployment. Frictional unemployment occurs because it takes time for employers to search for workers and for workers to search for jobs. Labour demand and labour supply might be in balance—in other words, there might be enough jobs for all the people who want them—but the process of matching workers and jobs isn't instantaneous. When you graduate from university with an economics degree there is a good job out there for you, but you'll still

frictional unemployment Unemployment due to the time it takes for employers to search for workers and for workers to search for jobs.

Three types of unemployment:
1. Frictional
2. Structural
3. Cyclical

spend time talking to employers, going on interviews, and trying to figure out which job has the right mix of tasks, co-workers, location, and perks that will make it the best fit for you. You may even need to relocate to where your skills are most in demand by employers.

Unemployment type two: Structural unemployment. **Structural unemployment** occurs when there are structural barriers that prevent wages from falling to the point where labour demand and labour supply are in equilibrium. Because wages remain higher than the equilibrium level, more workers want to work, but employers offer fewer jobs. There are many reasons that this happens: Employers sometimes want to pay higher wages to get more effort out of workers; unions may push for higher wages; and governments may enact policies that make it hard for the labour market to clear. These features of the labour market can lead to unemployment, and we'll explore why in this section.

structural unemployment Unemployment that occurs because wages don't fall to bring labour demand and supply into equilibrium.

Unemployment type three: Cyclical unemployment. **Cyclical unemployment** occurs when there is a temporary downturn in the economy. It explains why the unemployment rate was so high during the 2007–2009 Global Financial Crisis and why it came down as the economy recovered. Cyclical unemployment reflects the fact that during a downturn there are lots of unused resources in the economy—unfortunately that includes workers.

cyclical unemployment Unemployment that is due to a temporary downturn in the economy.

Frictional and structural unemployment explain why the equilibrium unemployment rate is above zero, while cyclical unemployment explains why unemployment rises and falls around the equilibrium unemployment rate. In later chapters, we'll explore why there are temporary ups and downs in the economy and how they lead to unemployment. In this chapter, we'll examine the unemployment that can persist even when the economy is doing well. So we'll focus on better understanding what causes frictional and structural unemployment and how these types of unemployment can be reduced.

Frictional Unemployment: It Takes Time to Find a Job

Frances Roberts/Alamy

Frictional unemployment includes time spent looking for the right job.

Frictional unemployment occurs when there are enough jobs for everyone, but the process of matching workers to jobs isn't instantaneous. Searching for a job reflects an information problem—there's a good job out there for you, but you don't know where it is. You have particular training, interests, and experiences for a job that would be a great fit for you, but a terrible fit for someone else, and vice versa. The longer it takes for workers and employers to find each other, the higher frictional unemployment will be.

Three major factors determine how much time it takes for workers and jobs to find each other and thus how much frictional unemployment there is. The first is the efficiency of all the technology, networks, and other resources that help workers and employers find each other. The second is the distribution of skills among workers, compared to the distribution of skills needed by employers. And finally, there's workers' access to financial support when they're looking for work. Let's go through each of these.

The efficiency of the resources employers and workers use to find each other. Employers and workers have to find each other. They may rely on word of mouth, online job postings, recruiting firms, or career centres on university campuses. Since frictional unemployment reflects an information problem, anything that affects the information that's available can affect the amount of frictional unemployment. The better workers are at identifying jobs that are a good fit for them, the less time they need to spend searching. Similarly, when managers can use technologies to screen applications effectively, it typically takes less time for them to identify a worker that will be a good fit for them.

Sources of frictional unemployment:
1. Job-search resources
2. Skills mismatch
3. Unemployment benefits and other income support

The more efficient the resources available for workers and managers to find each other are, the lower frictional unemployment is likely to be. Many of these tools are provided by the private sector—job postings, informational interviews, online jobs boards, headhunter agencies, and job placement services. But there's also a role for public policy, since improving job matching can lead to less frictional unemployment. That's why governments often run job-search centres in which they work with businesses to identify unemployed workers with the right skills for their open positions. Similarly, governments try to help job-seekers target their search to the jobs that are the best possible fit for them. Research shows that when workers get access to job-search assistance, they are reemployed faster.

The alignment of the skills workers have and the skills employers desire. If all workers had the same skills and all jobs used the same skills, then it wouldn't take very long for workers and jobs to match. Imagine a 500-piece jigsaw puzzle in which all the pieces are identical. It's a snap to put it together!

But when each piece is unique, you have to find the one piece out of 500 that fits to put it together. Similarly, when workers all differ in their skills and personalities, and jobs differ in their attributes and the skills that they need, it becomes harder for workers and businesses to find each other. So the more diverse workers and jobs are, the more difficult it is for workers and employers to find the right match.

There can also be *skills mismatch,* meaning that the skills workers have are not the skills that employers want. Technological change and international trade lead to changes in the mix of industries and occupations in which jobs are available, and this can lead to skills mismatch. In fact, the labour market is constantly adapting, with some sectors growing more slowly or disappearing altogether, while other sectors grow rapidly. The Australian economy has become increasingly service-oriented—consulting, other professional services, and health services have grown by hundreds of thousands of jobs since 2000. Meanwhile, goods-producing sectors such as manufacturing have been in decline as technological change has led many workers to be replaced by machines and globalisation has led to a lot of manufacturing moving offshore.

When sectors are in decline, it can be hard for workers to find a new job in the industry in which they previously worked. While there are still typically millions of jobs available, they are increasingly more competitive as there are more workers than jobs. Hundreds of thousands of workers change occupations each month, but it can take time for people to realise that their skills are not in as much demand and to seek retraining. As a result, shifts in the skills needed by employers can lead to increases in frictional unemployment as workers take longer to find jobs.

Some people call the changing mix of occupations and industries *structural unemployment*, but they mean the term differently than we use it. They are referring to structural changes in the labour market that reduce the number of jobs that are a match for the skills and experiences of some workers. But the reality is that throughout your lifetime you'll likely need to adapt your skills to the changing needs of the labour market—you'll probably change occupation (most people do!) and you'll need to learn to use new technology. Perhaps the most important set of skills you are developing right now is the ability to take in new information and adapt based on what you are learning.

Public policy can respond by helping workers learn what jobs do fit their skills, helping them identify regions where job growth is occurring, and offering job-retraining programs. Retraining programs can reduce frictional unemployment by helping workers develop the skills that are in demand by employers.

Unemployment benefits and other income support during unemployment. When the government supports people financially during unemployment, unemployment is likely to last longer. In Australia, JobSeeker (formerly called "Newstart") is a program through which the government provides financial assistance to workers who've lost their job through no fault of their own. The program pays a fairly modest amount ($567.50 per fortnight, although this was increased by as much as $550 per fortnight during the coronavirus pandemic). It also comes with "mutual obligation requirements" that involve searching for work. The program's goal is to reduce the hardships people face as they struggle to pay for housing, food, and other necessities while unemployed.

To understand why unemployment benefits can lead to longer unemployment durations, apply the *opportunity cost principle*. When you are unemployed you can choose to focus on the jobs that are a best fit for your skills; if you do that, you'll be more likely to land a higher-paying job that you'll want to stay in. Alternatively, if you are desperate for cash you might walk into the local convenience store that has a "help wanted" sign up and take their minimum wage job. The opportunity cost of staying unemployed to focus on searching for a better job is the wage you could earn by taking that convenience store job, or whatever would be the easiest job for you to get.

Unemployment benefits reduce the opportunity cost of another day spent searching because if you took the job, you'd get the wage but lose the JobSeeker payment. So if you could have earned $100 working, but would lose $40 in unemployment benefits, your opportunity cost is only $60. Not surprisingly, when people have access to unemployment benefits they tend to spend more days searching and focus their search more on the jobs that are the best fit for them.

Studies show that countries offering more financial support to people when they're unemployed tend to have higher unemployment rates. But studies also show that people without access to JobSeeker suffer from bigger declines in consumption and more hardship. Moreover, without sufficient savings or unemployment benefits, some people end up settling for worse jobs because continuing to search means not having enough to eat or losing their housing. In these situations, income support during job search can lead workers to better long-term outcomes.

EVERYDAY Economics **Why you should ask your friends to help you find work**

Shutterstock

Personal referrals help.

Studies show that if you have a personal referral when you apply for a job, you're more likely to get a job interview—and if you get an interview, you're more likely to get a job offer, which is also likely to come with a bigger pay package. No wonder people who get job offers through referrals are more likely to accept the offer.

Why is it so great to have a referral? Referrals contain information that's hard to get elsewhere. It can be hard for employers to credibly learn whether you're likely to fit in with your co-workers, and whether you're a hard worker with the right skills for the job. If someone who works at the company vouches for you, they are providing valuable information that the hiring manager can't easily see in a resume or learn in an interview. And they're likely to tell the truth—after all, if you get hired, they have to work with you. Similarly, your friend has information about the job you want. They can tell you if workers are happy, if the company is well managed, and whether hard work is likely to lead to a promotion. While you can ask about those things in an interview, it might be hard for a manager to credibly tell you the answers. After all, who's going to admit to unhappy workers, poor management, and no career path?

Roughly half of available jobs are filled using a personal referral to help make the connection, and many companies have a program to encourage referrals. You may even find that your company offers to pay you a bonus if you refer someone. Sometimes people think that referrals are unfair. But employers use them because referred workers tend to be better matches. Referred truck drivers have fewer accidents than those hired without a referral. Referred high-tech workers generate more patents. And referred workers overall are much less likely to quit. All this means that referred workers are more profitable. Referrals are a win-win situation for job-seekers and employers, but they do mean that people who know more people get a leg up. It's a good idea to try to get to know—and stay in touch with—people who are in the line of work you want to be in so that you can build your network of potential referrers. ■

Structural Unemployment: When Wages Are Stuck Above the Equilibrium Wage

Structural unemployment occurs because there simply aren't enough jobs for everyone who wants to work at the prevailing market wage. In other words, there are structural impediments preventing wages from falling to the point where the quantity of labour supplied is equal to the quantity of labour demanded.

Figure 10 shows that in a well-functioning labour market, equilibrium occurs at the intersection of the labour supply and labour demand curves. At that point, there is no structural unemployment—there are just as many jobs as there are workers. However, sometimes wages are prevented from falling to the equilibrium point. Employers demand fewer workers when the prevailing wage is above the supply-equals-demand equilibrium wage. Yet, the quantity of labour supplied is higher because more people want to work at higher wages. Putting these two together reveals that when the prevailing market wage is above the equilibrium wage, there's a gap between the number of jobs available and the number of available workers. This gap is structural unemployment. The number of people unemployed is equal to the difference between the quantity of labour supplied at the market wage and the quantity of labour demanded.

Figure 10 | Structural Unemployment

Structural unemployment occurs when wages are unable to fall to the market-clearing wage.

A When wages can easily adjust to market conditions, equilibrium occurs at the **market-clearing wage**, where the **labour supply curve** meets the **labour demand curve** and there is no unemployment.

B Sometimes, the **bargained wage** gets stuck above the **market-clearing wage**.

C As a result, there's a persistent gap between the **supply** of labour and the **demand** for it. This causes **structural unemployment**.

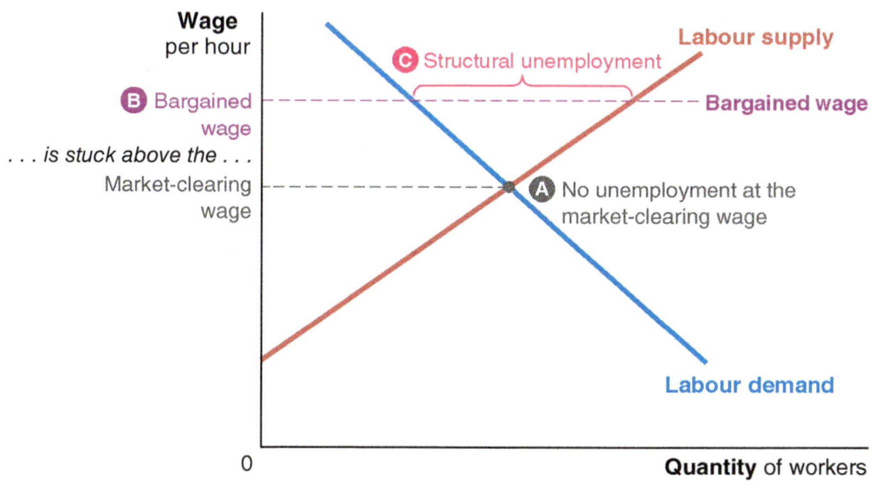

The prevailing wage can persist above the equilibrium wage for several reasons. Employers might choose to pay higher wages in order to get employees to work harder, employees might use their bargaining power to demand higher wages, and there might be institutional barriers to lowering wages. Let's start by considering why employers might choose to pay higher wages, and then we'll turn to other factors.

Efficiency wages: One cause of structural unemployment. In 1913, Henry Ford made history with the introduction of the moving assembly line in auto production. Workers would stand in place and focus on a single simple task—such as screwing in a particular nut over and over again. This innovation allowed Ford to more than double his production. But he quickly ran into a problem. The work was painfully, mind-numbingly dull. Similar low-skill factory jobs were plentiful in Detroit, Michigan, so when workers couldn't take the monotony any longer, they quit. The average worker stayed only a few months, meaning that Ford was constantly hiring and training new workers.

So in 1914, Henry Ford made history again—this time by more than doubling wages to what has famously become known as the US$5 day. That doesn't sound like much today, but back when the prevailing market wage was US$2.25, it was a big deal. Applicants flooded his factory gates looking for work. To get a job with Ford in 1914, you had to be two things: a good worker and lucky. If you slacked off on the job, came in drunk, or failed to show up, you were fired. But even if you were a hard worker, there were more workers hoping to land a $5-a-day job than there were positions at Ford. That's why you also had to be lucky. Persistence also helped, and people would line up day after day, hoping to get hired.

Hulton Archive/Getty Images

Happy workers building Fords.

Efficiency wages make it unprofitable for employers to lower wages. Not only did Henry Ford pioneer the assembly line, but he helped pioneer a new cause of unemployment. Paying higher than the equilibrium wage meant that not everyone who wanted to work at that wage was able to get a job. Those who queued hopefully at the factory gate could have been working elsewhere at the prevailing market wage; instead, they were unemployed, taking their chances at getting a higher-paying Ford job.

efficiency wage A higher wage paid to encourage greater worker productivity.

Economists refer to Ford's higher-than-market wage as an **efficiency wage**—a wage above the prevailing market wage, paid to encourage greater worker productivity. When you're paid a wage that's higher than what you can get elsewhere, you're more careful not to lose it, meaning you don't slack off, skip work, or antagonise co-workers or managers. Highly paid workers are also more likely to feel valued, inspiring them to give back to their employer in the form of greater effort.

Many parents pay efficiency wages to nannies or babysitters. The market wage for nannies or babysitters is not very high—maybe $20 an hour—but paying $30 an hour generates loyalty and goodwill. Having a babysitter take extra care with your children because they really like working for you compared to their next best alternative is really valuable! And for some parents it's definitely worth the extra $10 per hour.

Efficiency wages can lower total labour costs. Henry Ford's problem of rapid turnover ended with the $5 wage. And his workers became even more productive. Any worker who was feeling frustrated simply had to glance out the window at the queue of hopeful workers ready to take their job to be reminded of how good they had it. Workers who quit knew that their next job would probably only pay $2.25. Since the marginal benefit of a new job offer was low compared to what they currently had, Ford's workers stayed focused on their tasks to avoid being fired. Ford later referred to the $5 wage as one of his greatest cost-saving moves.

from the Collections of The Henry Ford

Unemployed workers who want to build Fords.

Efficiency wages create unemployment. Ford was able to hire all the workers he wanted at $5 a day because he was paying more than other employers. His higher wage increased labour supply to the Ford plant by encouraging people to try to get a job at his plant. To understand why labour supply increases apply the *marginal benefit principle*: the marginal benefit of applying rises due to the higher efficiency wage. But not everyone can get hired at the higher wage. Some accept jobs at a lower wage at another car manufacturing plant—for them, the marginal benefit of standing outside the Ford factory (the chance at getting the Ford wage premium) isn't as big as the marginal cost of the forgone wage they would earn working at another plant. But for some workers, that marginal benefit will be big enough that they'll give up working elsewhere or they'll enter the labour market in order to stand in line and hope to get their lucky break at the Ford plant.

Institutional causes of structural unemployment:

1. Unions
2. Job protection regulations
3. Minimum wage laws

Institutions: Additional Causes of Structural Unemployment

Efficiency wages are not the only reason why wages don't fall to bring labour supply and labour demand into balance. The labour market has many unique institutional features that can keep the wage above its supply-equals-demand equilibrium wage. These causes of structural unemployment result in workers with jobs being better off, but their higher wages and compensation and greater job security make jobs scarce for others.

There are three institutional factors that tend to be primary causes of structural unemployment around the world: unions, job protection regulations, and minimum wage laws. Let's find out more about how each of these can contribute to structural unemployment.

Lynn Grieveson/Getty Images

A union strike.

Unions can keep wages high for some workers. Unions are organisations representing workers who band together to negotiate jointly with their employers.

There are lots of reasons why unions are effective. Unions give more bargaining power to workers, allowing them to extract some of the profits that might otherwise go to management or investors. They might have different information than management, allowing businesses to make better decisions because they have an effective way to gather input from workers. Regardless of the reason, union wages mean that more workers want union jobs than there are union jobs available, and employers might demand fewer workers at the higher wage. The result is structural unemployment.

Unions aren't a big deal in most industries in Australia. Only around 10% of private-sector workers are unionised. However, unions play a much larger role in education and other public-sector jobs, like nursing. In other countries like Belgium, Norway, and Germany, unions play a large role in the labour market.

Job protection regulations make it hard to fire workers. If you want to reduce the number of people unemployed, why not just make it harder for businesses to fire people? In Australia these are called "unfair dismissal" laws. This is a strategy that many countries have tried. But let's think through what you'd do as a manager. When you consider whether to hire someone, you know that if it doesn't work out, you'll either have to keep paying that person anyway or pay a large price to let them go. That price could be a redundancy or termination payment, and it could also involve time-consuming "performance management" where employers have to give workers a chance to improve over many months and document the feedback they give. Not surprisingly, that ends up causing you to think twice before making someone a job offer. You'll want to be confident that they'll generate enough additional revenue to justify their wage; after all, if they don't, you can't fire them.

Let's also think back to the reasons employers pay efficiency wages—workers are more productive when they don't want to lose their jobs. So what do you think happens to worker productivity if employers can't fire workers? Some workers may decide to slack off, knowing that it's hard for them to be fired. Because workers are less productive, employers want to hire fewer of them.

Taken together, while job protection policies succeed in reducing the number of people who lose their job, they also reduce the number of workers businesses want to hire at any given wage. These policies reduce labour demand and thus employment is lower than what would occur without these policies. These policies could result in lower wages or they can exacerbate structural unemployment if there are other factors making it hard for wages to fall. Such policies can also increase frictional unemployment by encouraging employers to search longer to find a good match. This leads to a dynamic where fewer workers are willing to leave jobs because they know it will be hard to find another job. Job protection regulations make for a less dynamic and less flexible labour market.

The challenges of high firing costs are apparent in Western Europe, where some countries make it hard to fire workers. In France and Italy, employers need to have a government-approved reason to fire a worker, and there are obstacles to laying off many workers at once. Such policies are good for people who are already employed and want to stay in their current jobs, but they're not good for the unemployed or workers who want to change jobs or employers.

The minimum wage keeps wages from falling below the set minimum wage. The federal minimum wage law says that your employer can't pay you less than $21.38 per hour. Casual workers, who have fewer employment protections and don't receive annual leave and other benefits, receive a 25% casual loading.

Effect of Minimum Wage

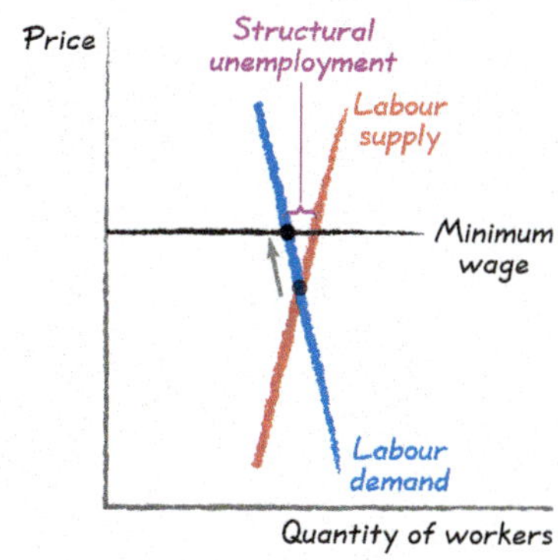

But this is just the overall minimum. Australia also has a system of "Awards" which specify the minimum wage for a whole range of different jobs and type or level of work within those jobs. Awards also specify hours of work, rosters, breaks, allowances, penalty rates, and overtime. In 2021 there were more than 100 different Awards.

For instance, a "Food and beverage attendant grade 4" under the Restaurant Industry Award in 2021, aged 20 years or over, receives a minimum of $899.46 per week for a 38-hour week, before overtime and penalty rates. Awards are a way of having separate minimum wages for workers doing different jobs and with different skills. In some other countries, like the United States, there is just one overall minimum wage. The Australian system is more complex, but in some ways fairer.

On top of this sits the Enterprise Bargaining System. This allows employees in a business to negotiate with management on different conditions than those specified in the Award. This negotiation often happens through a union. These Enterprise Bargaining Agreements, or EBAs, have to make workers better off overall, but can allow for conditions better suited to a particular workplace that benefit both workers and the firm.

The minimum wage is a hotly contested issue. Opponents focus on the unemployment that's created by the minimum wage. Setting the minimum wage too high will lead to fewer jobs. For many, unemployment is even worse than a low-wage job. Proponents argue that the poor earn low wages because they lack bargaining power relative to employers, and a slightly higher wage won't lead to much of a change in the labour market. Essentially, they argue that neither supply nor demand for labour changes very much with the wage.

Economists who've studied the effects of raising the minimum wage suggest that raising the minimum wage by a small amount leads to a negligible change in overall unemployment. Most workers earn wages well above the minimum wage, and thus the minimum wage applies only to a small subgroup of workers. Among minimum wage workers, many studies find only small changes in the number of workers hired, although economists disagree about just how big or small the effect is. The change in unemployment also depends on just how high the minimum wage is relative to the supply-equals-demand wage: the higher it is the more structural unemployment there'll be.

The biggest impact of minimum wage laws is on the unemployment rate of teenagers—more of whom want to work when the minimum wage is high, but fewer of whom are desired by employers. Instead, slightly more experienced or older workers get the jobs.

Recap: Frictional and Structural Unemployment

Frictional and structural unemployment explain why the equilibrium unemployment rate is above zero. Frictional unemployment occurs because looking for a good job takes time. Structural unemployment occurs when more people want to work at the prevailing wage than there are employers desiring workers. You've also seen that there are things government can do to reduce frictional and structural unemployment, but there are other things government does that can increase these types of unemployment. Sometimes these choices involve trade-offs—like helping people get through unemployment with less hardship versus encouraging them to take a job right away. To better understand these trade-offs, we'll next turn to the costs of unemployment for individuals and society.

23.4 The Costs of Unemployment

Learning Objective *Learn about the economic and social costs of unemployment.*

When workers are unemployed, everyone loses: workers, their families, and the communities in which they live. When more people are unemployed, more people suffer.

The Economic Costs of Unemployment

Instead of earning an income, the unemployed have to spend their time looking for work. The process can take weeks and often months, and some may give up and drop out of the labour force entirely. This has serious economic costs—both for the unemployed and for society more generally.

The unemployed often end up with lower wages and worse career opportunities. The unemployed don't just have to worry about lost wages while they're looking for work—they also have to worry about lower pay in the future. Even when someone finds work again, they often receive lower pay for decades. This earnings loss is especially acute if they lost their job during a recession.

Permanent unemployment can arise from periods of high unemployment. When unemployment rates are high, it becomes even harder to find work. It can take years, so some workers lose hope and stop trying to find work. They may also lose skills or important contacts, or be unable to keep up with new developments. The loss of skills and hope, as well as discrimination against the long-term unemployed, all contribute to lower lifetime earnings for those who experience long-term unemployment.

If long durations of joblessness shake workers' desire to search for work, then labour force participation rates may fall in response. When long durations of unemployment make it harder for the unemployed to find work, a phenomenon known as **hysteresis** may occur. You might have heard of this term in other contexts—it refers to any system that depends on its past. In the context of unemployment, hysteresis occurs when a period of high unemployment leads to a higher equilibrium unemployment rate. In other words, the temporarily bad economy makes it harder for people to find jobs, so even when the economy recovers to the point that enough jobs are available, it takes people longer to find them. As a result, a temporary period of high unemployment permanently creates more frictional unemployment, since it takes everyone longer to find work. Research shows that the large rise in long-term unemployment in Europe in the early 1980s was to blame for the chronically high unemployment rates that occurred in the decades afterward.

hysteresis When a period of high unemployment leads to a higher equilibrium unemployment rate.

High unemployment means that the government receives lower tax revenues but spends more. When fewer people have jobs, the government takes in less tax revenue. When fewer people are working and paying income and payroll taxes, they're not only unable to provide for themselves, but they're also contributing less to public goods such as infrastructure, the military, and scientific research. Meanwhile, higher unemployment can strain government budgets, as more people need to use the social safety net. This can divert government spending from other priorities and, if it goes on for long enough, can cause tax rates to rise.

The Social Costs of Unemployment

The cost of unemployment is more than lost wages and output. There are also costs in terms of health, well-being, crime, and children's outcomes—all of which affect more than just those who are unemployed. Work is one of society's most important institutions, and it's a key source of identity and community as well as income. When people lose their jobs, they often lose much more than just income.

Unemployment is isolating and painful. Unemployment is very disruptive. Your day may be less structured and seem endless. You may find yourself more isolated, more stressed, and unable to spend money on the things that used to be part of the everyday rhythm of your life.

Surveys reveal that the unemployed are sadder, more stressed, and more dissatisfied with their lives than the employed. They're more likely to experience depression, anxiety, poverty, and divorce. All of these negative outcomes also come with a higher risk of death, including suicide. Unemployment can lead to social isolation and a loss of self-confidence and sense of purpose.

Unemployment can be miserable.

Long-term unemployment is associated with worse outcomes. You've seen that those who are long-term unemployed lose skills and face discrimination when looking for work. Studies also show that long-term unemployment leads to greater permanent earnings losses, as the wages that long-term unemployed workers get when they do find work are much lower than what they were previously earning. The long-term unemployed also are more likely to have health problems. A job loss nearly doubles their chances of dying a year later, and their death rates are higher for decades later.

Children whose parents experience unemployment suffer. It's probably no surprise that the families of the unemployed also suffer. Redundancies lead to higher divorce rates. The children of workers who have been made redundant suffer from the lost household income and from the stress that the family goes through.

These children end up with worse academic outcomes, worse mental health outcomes, and worse employment outcomes, making less money as adults. When a parent loses a job while a child is in high school, that child is less likely to go to university.

Protecting Yourself from the Harmful Effects of Unemployment

Unemployment can be terrible. But there are some things you can do to help protect yourself from the harmful effects of unemployment.

Do more job searching than you really want to do. Job searching when you're unemployed is not a fun experience. People have a tendency to procrastinate in looking for a job, which is part of the reason why unemployment benefits in Australia are tied to searching for work. But remember the core principles of economics and apply for any job for which the marginal benefit of applying (the probability of getting a job offer times the wage) exceeds the marginal cost of applying (and remember that the emotional pain of applying is short-lived!).

Rob Hyrons/Shutterstock

It's always a good idea to save for a rainy day.

Build up a nest egg. Now that you know half of those who lose their job end up unemployed for more than 13 weeks, and it's not unusual for it to take six months to find work, you probably understand why financial advisers tell you to have three to six months of expenses saved up. You should understand how much you get paid on the JobSeeker unemployment benefit, and what obligations you have to look for work when receiving it. Remember that anyone can end up finding themselves unemployed. But the experience is not as bad if you have enough in savings that you don't have to worry about paying the rent.

Build new skills. The economy is constantly adapting, and you must too. Continuing to learn and build your skills is necessary to advance your career, but it'll also help you land on your feet if you find yourself unemployed.

Keep an eye out for better opportunities when you're employed. Many employed people keep searching for other opportunities. Keeping an eye out for better opportunities when you're employed can help you advance in your career by identifying jobs that use recent skills you've built, but it can also help if things start to get rocky in your current position. Many people who think their job is likely to come to an end begin searching long before a "Notice of Termination" arrives. Such searching increases the chance that you'll avoid unemployment by being able to start a new job right away.

Tap into all your networks if you become unemployed. You're more likely to get hired if you have a referral. So if you find yourself unemployed, it's time to call on everyone you know to tell them that you're looking. It takes courage to tell your friends you're looking for work, or to broadcast your job search through social media, but letting people know that you're looking for a new opportunity can pay off.

Avoid long-term unemployment. Sometimes you're offered a job that's not quite as good as you think you could get. If it's your first week searching, you might want to turn it down, but don't keep turning jobs down forever. You've learned about the scarring effects of long-term unemployment—that means you might have to settle—in the short term—for a job that doesn't use all your skills and isn't something you want to be doing forever! Remember, the good news is that you can keep searching for a better job while you're employed. In fact, the security of having a job can make it easier to search for a better one.

Tying It Together

The labour market is a vital part of most people's lives, and during your lifetime you'll be both a seller and a buyer in the labour market. You'll be a buyer as a manager hiring employees or in your personal life hiring people to do home or car repairs, or look after your children. You'll be a seller any time you work to generate income, either working for yourself or for an employer.

As both a buyer and seller of labour, unemployment will be an important factor in your life, and not just when you yourself are unemployed. As a worker, the opportunity cost of quitting your current job or spending time out of the labour market will depend on how easy it is to find work when you want it. That in turn affects how easy it is to get a promotion, how much you earn, and sometimes even how hard you work. Likewise, the ease with which employers can find the right people to fill positions and their ability to retain good workers can have a profound effect on their bottom line.

It's easier to find or fill a job in a labour market in which workers and jobs match easily—that is, when frictional unemployment is low. But high frictional unemployment means that as an employer it's hard to find the right workers for your needs. You're spending resources—time, energy, and money—looking for employees instead of concentrating on your business. If a job opening takes two months to fill, that's two months that you don't have someone in the job helping you to increase revenue. As a worker, high frictional unemployment means spending your time and energy searching for work instead of bringing home a paycheque. Thus, both workers and employers benefit from technologies and policies that help match workers with employers.

But sometimes the problem is not that workers and employers can't find each other—it's that there simply aren't enough jobs to go around. Labour market institutions, such as unions and the National Employment Standards, can offer protections and improve conditions for workers on the job. But because they affect employers' ability to hire, fire, and determine the pay of their workers, they have an impact on businesses' hiring decisions and can contribute to structural unemployment. As a policy maker or a voter you'll have to decide how you feel about the trade-off of better working conditions and more unemployment.

This chapter focused on frictional and structural unemployment, the two types of unemployment that can persist even when the economy is doing well. We also touched briefly on cyclical unemployment, which is the result of economic shocks that reduce the use of resources in the economy. During periods of cyclical unemployment, factories sit idle, machines go unused, and unfortunately workers get pushed to the sidelines. We'll focus on why that happens when we turn to business cycles in Chapter 29.

But whatever the cause, unemployment is never fun and it can have devastating consequences for workers, their families, and their communities. We all work and hire people in the shadow of the unemployment rate. That's why unemployment is the macroeconomic issue you've probably heard the most about, and it's why we'll continue to examine unemployment throughout our study of macroeconomics.

Chapter at a Glance

Working-age population
Noninstitutionalised civilians age 15 and over

Not in the labour force	Labour force
Neither employed nor unemployed	Working-age population that either **has a job or would like a job**

Employed	Unemployed
People with jobs	People without jobs who are trying to get a job

Labour force participation rate:	Unemployment rate:	Equilibrium unemployment rate:
the share of the working-age population that is either employed or unemployed $= \frac{\text{Labour force}}{\text{Working-age population}} \times 100$	the share of the labour force that's unemployed $= \frac{\text{Unemployed}}{\text{Labour force}} \times 100$	the unemployment rate to which the economy tends to return in the long run

Alternative Measures of Unemployment Might Also Include

Underemployed: Someone who has some work but wants more hours or whose job isn't adequately using their skills.

Marginally attached: Someone who wants a job, and who has looked for a job within the past year, but who isn't counted as unemployed because they aren't currently searching for work.

Involuntarily part time: Someone who wants full-time work and is working part-time because they haven't found a full-time job.

Causes of Unemployment

	Frictional unemployment	Structural unemployment	Cyclical unemployment
Definition	Unemployment due to the time it takes for employers to search for workers and for workers to search for jobs.	Unemployment that occurs because wages don't fall to bring labour demand and supply into equilibrium.	Unemployment that is due to a temporary downturn in the economy.
Sources	1. Job search resources 2. Skills mismatch 3. Unemployment benefits and other income support	1. Efficiency wages: Higher wages paid to encourage greater worker productivity 2. Institutional causes: • Unions • Job protection regulations • Minimum wage laws	You'll learn more about how unemployment rises and falls later, in the chapter on Business Cycles.

Costs of Unemployment

- Lower wages and worse career opportunities
- Permanent joblessness can arise from periods of high unemployment
- Lower tax revenue and higher government spending
- Unemployment is isolating and painful
- Long-term unemployment is associated with worse outcomes
- Children whose parents experience unemployment suffer

Key Concepts

cyclical unemployment, 590
discouraged workers, 588
efficiency wage, 594
employed, 582
equilibrium unemployment rate, 586
frictional unemployment, 589
hysteresis, 597
involuntarily part time, 588
labour force, 582
labour force participation rate, 583
long-term unemployed, 587
marginally attached, 588
not in the labour force, 583
structural unemployment, 590
underemployed, 588
unemployed, 582
unemployment rate, 585
working-age population, 582

Discussion and Review Questions

Learning Objective 23.1 *Understand what unemployment is and how it's measured.*

1. Think of three people from your own life (or even from popular TV shows and movies) who are or were unemployed, employed, and not in the labour force. What events and choices led to their employment situation?
2. Describe three economic or social changes that have contributed to the trends in labour force participation rates for men and women since the 1970s. How have these changes impacted the trade-offs people face between home production and the labour market?

Learning Objective 23.2 *Learn how people move in and out of jobs and in and out of the labour market.*

3. From the perspective of workers and employers, discuss the benefits and the costs of a dynamic labour market.
4. Explain why it is possible to find many job openings online in shrinking industries such as newspaper publishing or bricks-and-mortar retail.
5. Should the official unemployment rate include people who may want to work but have given up searching? Would such a measure be better or worse than the official measure of the unemployment rate?

Learning Objective 23.3 *Analyse the causes of unemployment.*

6. What is the equilibrium unemployment rate and why isn't it equal to zero? Explain.
7. Why would a company want to pay its workers more than the prevailing market wage? What is the impact on employers, workers, and the overall labour market?

Learning Objective 23.4 *Learn about the economic and social costs of unemployment.*

8. Kevin has two children and is a steel worker who became unemployed, along with most of his coworkers, when the plant that he worked at closed. Describe and discuss the economic costs of unemployment to Kevin, to his family, and to his community.
9. Your friend talks to you about how the company she works for is having a terrible year. She's terrified of being made redundant and the impact it would have on her family. What advice would you give her to prepare for the possibility of unemployment?

Study Problems

Learning Objective 23.1 *Understand what unemployment is and how it's measured.*

1. Sarah, Alicia, and Philip all lost their jobs when the technology start-up they worked for was acquired by another company. After a few weeks of searching for another full-time job, Sarah decided to go back to university to get a graduate diploma in business. In order to finish as fast as possible, Sarah chose not to work while finishing her GradDip. Alicia took a part-time job in retail shortly after losing her job, but she continues to search diligently for full-time work. Philip searched for a job for the first five weeks after being made redundant, but as bills began piling up, he found himself moving into his parents' house. He recently gave up looking for work because he figures that there just aren't jobs available right now so there is no point looking. Are Sarah, Alicia, and Philip unemployed, employed, or not in the labour force? Would any of the three be considered a discouraged worker? How would each contribute to the unemployment rate?
2. Using the following data from the ABS calculate the size of the labour force, unemployment rate, and labour force participation rate for 2009 and 2018.

Type of worker	Number of individuals in 2009	Number of individuals in 2018
Working-age population	17.2 million	19.9 million
Unemployed	654,000	722,000
Employed	10.8 million	12.5 million

Learning Objective 23.2 *Learn how people move in and out of jobs and in and out of the labour market.*

3. Determine the labour market status of each of the following people. If they are unemployed, can they be considered long-term unemployed?
   - a. Demetrius is a voice-over actor. He has a gig this week, but next week he'll have to start auditioning for new roles.
   - b. Megan is made redundant and has to take a part-time retail job because she can't find a full-time job. She is spending her extra time learning how to code.
   - c. Kathryn quit her job when it was relocated too far away from her family. She has been looking for work for eight months, but so far hasn't been called in for an interview.
4. Use the table below from the Australian Bureau of Statistics to answer the following questions.

Category	Feb 2020
Labour force	13.7 million
Employed	12.9 million
Unemployed	696,000
Underemployed	1.2 million
Discouraged workers	104,000

   - a. What was the unemployment rate in Feb 2020?
   - b. If we were to count discouraged workers as unemployed, what would the unemployment rate have been in Feb 2020?
   - c. If we were to count all of those who are underemployed as unemployed, what would the unemployment rate have been in Feb 2020?
   - d. If you repeated this calculation over all time periods for Australia and graphed the data, do you think the changes in the unemployment rates would all look similar or different? Why?
5. Consider the following scenarios and explain for each what the effect is on the official unemployment rate.
   - a. Unemployed people become discouraged and stop searching for work.
   - b. Previously unemployed people find part-time jobs, even though they need full-time work.
   - c. Formerly discouraged workers find work.
   - d. People who were previously discouraged workers begin looking for work again.

Learning Objective 23.3 *Analyse the causes of unemployment.*

6. Classify the following scenarios as examples of frictional, structural, or cyclical unemployment, and explain your answer.
   - a. Amanda just finished a computer science degree and wants to live in Sydney. There are lots of openings for people with her skills, but she wants to be sure to find a job that's a good fit for her. She moves to Sydney without a job and crashes on a friend's couch while she interviews for jobs.
   - b. A food-processing factory decides to increase its wages by 50% above what their competitors are paying. They find that fewer workers quit or call in sick, and that they have lower spoilage rates as a result of the more consistent, productive workforce. Their competitors respond by raising wages as well. The quantity of labour supplied to the industry increases to try to take advantage of the higher wages and is higher than the quantity demanded by employers at the new wage.
   - c. Li Wei owns a homebuilding company. During a severe downturn in the housing market, he has to fire many of his subcontractors.
   - d. Which of the three types of unemployment (frictional, structural, or cyclical) will persist even if the wage is at the equilibrium wage? Explain your answer.
7. Consider whether each of the following would increase or decrease frictional unemployment.
   - a. LinkedIn improves its algorithms, enabling it to more efficiently connect employers with workers who have the experience and skills they need.
   - b. Rapid innovation in the tech sector means that tech companies are constantly changing the skills they require to develop, manage, and service new products.
   - c. JobSeeker becomes less generous.
8. Jane is the general manager at a new café and wants to hire a few baristas. The going rate for baristas in the area is $26.50 per hour. Jane has heard that many of the local coffee shops have high turnover with baristas ghosting them—simply not showing up for their shift and never coming back. Jane starts to put together an advertisement to hire baristas for $26.50 per hour, but changes her mind and lists the wage she'll pay at $29 per hour. Why would Jane pay $26.50 per hour? What's the rationale for paying $29 (or any wage higher than $26.50)?

9. Suppose the graph depicts the labour market for retail workers in Adelaide classified as "Retail employee level 5" under the federal Award.

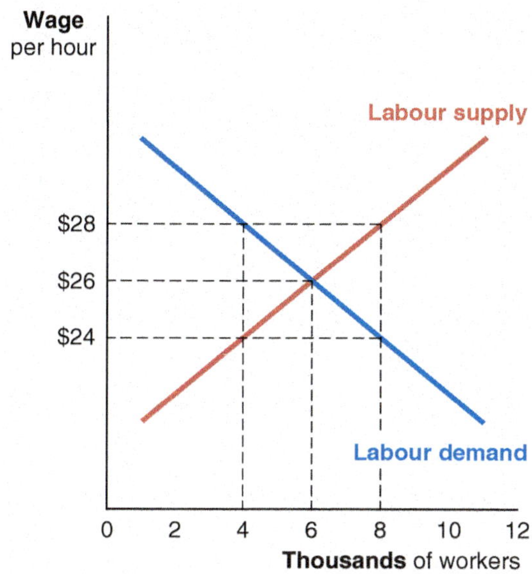

a. What is the equilibrium wage for retail associates? How many associates are employed at the equilibrium wage and what is the unemployment rate?

b. Suppose the Fair Work Commission raises the Award wage for Retail employee level 5 to $24.00 an hour. How many workers are employed at $24.00 an hour? Is there any unemployment?

c. Unions make a submission to the Fair Work Commission and the Award wage is raised to $26.00 per hour. How many workers are employed at $26.00 per hour? Is there any unemployment? If so, are these workers frictionally, structurally, or cyclically unemployed?

Learning Objective 23.4 *Learn about the economic and social costs of unemployment.*

10. An economic downturn leads to hundreds of thousands of people losing their jobs. In some industries, workers who remain employed, or "insiders," continue to develop their skills, enabling them to push wages above the level at which less-skilled "outsiders" could be employed. What do you expect to happen to the equilibrium unemployment rate due to hysteresis? Explain your reasoning.

Inflation and Money

CHAPTER

24

Australia was the first country to introduce mandatory helmet laws for bicyclists; now, instead of paying for negligence with their lives, bicyclists who don't wear helmets pay with a hefty fine. But thanks to inflation, forgetting your helmet has become a lot more expensive in some states than in others. The helmet laws were introduced in every state between 1990 and 1992, allowing police to issue on-the-spot fines to cyclists who did not adhere to the rules. These fines varied from state-to-state, from $15 in Victoria, to $35 in Queensland. Let's look at how these fines have changed over time in New South Wales (NSW) and the Northern Territory (NT).

Elke Meitzel/Image Source/Getty Images

Don't forget your helmet!

NSW started with a fine of $32 in 1991. The fine steadily increased over the years, reaching $73 in 2016 – that's about $39 in 1991 dollars. The NT on the other hand introduced a fine of $25 in 1992. In 2016, the fine was still $25, in fact, it's probably still $25 today! Over time, prices tend to rise on average, a process known as inflation. And over time the price of police labour, administration, transportation, and all the other stuff that goes into issuing a fine rose. That means that it's a lot more costly for police to issue a helmet fine in the NT than it was in 1992, in fact, once you factor in all the costs, it might not even be worth issuing the fine at all.

NSW have kept their fine up to date with inflation, which means that in 2016 the helmet fine was about as severe as it was when it was first introduced (although since 2016, NSW have increased the fine to a whopping $349, but this is probably more for revenue raising than for inflation). Indeed, many states now express their fines in terms of something called "penalty units," whose value automatically increases each year with inflation. This avoids the need to constantly revise fines, something which is long overdue for the NT.

The NT have misjudged the effects of inflation and it's leading to millions of dollars of lost revenue – a costly mistake. This is a mistake you should learn from, which is why the rest of this chapter will analyse inflation. We'll explore how inflation is measured, how it affects you, and why it's costly. And hopefully along the way, you'll gain some insights that will help you make better choices than NT officials did.

Chapter Objective

Evaluate the rate of inflation and its consequences.

24.1 Measuring Inflation
Understand what inflation is and how to measure it.

24.2 Different Measures of Inflation
Pick the right inflation measure for the task at hand.

24.3 Adjusting for the Effects of Inflation
Learn to account for the influence of inflation before making big decisions.

24.4 The Role of Money and the Costs of Inflation
Analyse the role of money so that you can assess the costs of inflation.

24.1 Measuring Inflation

Learning Objective *Understand what inflation is and how to measure it.*

I bet you've heard people, particularly older people, complain about rising prices. It seems like every time they turn around, nearly everything is more expensive than it used to be. They worry that prices will keep rising, making it hard for them to save, send their kids to a good school, or prepare for retirement.

They'll tell stories about how cheap things used to be. Like how in 1990, the average price of a movie ticket was only \$6.61, a litre of U91 petrol was \$0.67, and bananas were a mere \$1.39 a kilo. Ah, the good old days. Today you'll pay more for those things. In mid-2019, a movie ticket cost \$16, a litre of U91 petrol was \$1.54, and bananas were \$3.00 a kilo.

inflation A generalised rise in the overall level of prices.

They're describing **inflation,** which is *a generalised rise in the overall level of prices.* Inflation can also be described as *a rise in the cost of living.* As a result, inflation is also *a decline in the purchasing power of money,* because it means that a \$20 note buys fewer movie tickets, less petrol, and fewer bananas than it did in 1990. When there's been inflation, it means that you'll be spending more to buy the same stuff you bought the year before. The good news is that wages rise on average too. But that means you have to pay attention to inflation in order to know whether your wages are rising enough for you to be able to continue to afford all the things you buy. Let's take a deeper look at inflation and how to measure it.

The Price of a Basket of Goods and Services

consumer price index (CPI) An index that tracks the average price consumers pay over time for a representative "basket" of goods and services.

There is more than one measure of inflation, but the inflation measure that's most relevant to your life as a consumer is calculated using the **consumer price index** (or **CPI** for short). The CPI is a measure of the average prices people pay over time for the goods and services they buy in their everyday lives. More formally, it is an index that tracks the average price consumers pay over time for a representative basket of goods and services. Statisticians refer to the lists they compile of the goods and services people typically buy as a basket. It's a metaphor—after all, a haircut can't go into a basket!

The CPI is a closely watched indicator, and headlines in the business press like "Inflation ticks up" or "Inflation falling" are typically about the CPI.

Romariolen/Shutterstock

Track the price of a basket of goods and services over time.

The inflation rate is the percentage change in the price of a fixed basket of goods. The CPI measures how much prices change on average, but not all prices rise by the same amount. Some prices will rise more than others, and some prices will even fall. To know how much inflation is occurring, we need to figure out how to tally up all these price changes. Government statisticians effectively create a shopping list of the things that a typical consumer would buy, and then send people to grocery stores and other retailers to track the price of each of those items.

inflation rate The annual percentage increase in the average price level.

The price of that basket of goods is a measure of the average *price level* in the economy. The **inflation rate** is the annual percentage increase in the average price level, and it's calculated as the percentage change in the price of this basket of goods and services:

$$\text{Inflation rate} = \frac{\text{Price level this year} - \text{Price level last year}}{\text{Price level last year}} \times 100$$

And so if the price of that basket rose from \$100 last year to \$102 this year, this calculation says that inflation was 2%. That means that:

- On average, prices are 2% higher this year than last year;
- The cost of living is 2% higher than it was last year; and
- A dollar buys 2% less than it did last year.

Not every price change is a sign of inflation. You should distinguish the macroeconomic phenomena of inflation, which is a *generalised rise in prices,* from the microeconomic phenomena of *relative price adjustment,* in which the price of individual goods rises or falls relative to other prices as their specific supply and demand ebbs and flows.

Constructing the Consumer Price Index and Measuring Inflation

To measure inflation:
1. Find out what people buy
2. Collect prices
3. Tally up the cost of the basket
4. Calculate inflation as the percentage change in the price of the basket

Now that you know what the CPI is, let's dig into understanding how it's constructed and used to measure inflation. The government agency in charge of measuring consumer prices is the Australian Bureau of Statistics (the ABS for short). In order to construct the CPI, it needs to know what people buy, how much they pay for it, and how those prices are changing over time. Let's take a closer look at each of these four steps.

Step one: Find out what people typically buy. The first thing the government needs to do is to figure out what to put into the basket—and how much of each item to put into it—to represent the goods and services that the average consumer buys. To do that, the ABS surveys thousands of people, asking them how much they spend on bread, coffee, rent, haircuts, medical expenses, bus fares, and so on. Government statisticians use these surveys to construct a basket of goods and services that represents the average household's purchases.

Figure 1 shows what's in the basket and it reveals that people spend most of their money on housing, food, and transport. While your spending patterns may differ a bit, this basket matches the average Australian's purchases pretty closely.

Each of these categories contains many different goods and services. Housing includes spending on rent, as well as all the associated costs like electricity, fuel, water, and household goods like furniture. Food includes groceries, prepackaged foods, and restaurant meals. Transport includes new and used cars, petrol, train rides, and bus fares. The basket includes just about everything that you spend money on, so it includes not only physical stuff you buy (and could put in an actual basket) but also services.

Figure 1 | **The CPI Basket**

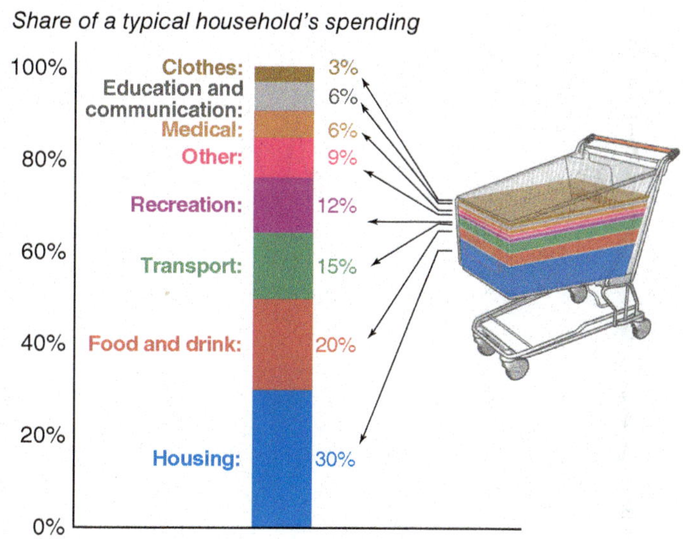

Data from: Australian Bureau of Statistics.

Step two: Collect prices from the stores where people do their shopping. Once you've assembled a representative basket of goods and services, you need to track how much it costs to buy everything in it. And that means tracking the price of thousands of goods and services. Government surveyors visit thousands of retailers around the country from massive Kmart stores to local cafés. They click through to online stores, call doctors' offices, and collect rental prices on real estate. Altogether, the government keeps track of the prices of thousands of goods and services.

Step three: Tally up the price of the basket of goods and services. The next step is to tally up the price of the representative basket of goods and services, accounting for the fact that this basket includes more of some items than others. The totals, shown in Figure 2, aren't a simple average of every price. Rather, the CPI puts more weight on products you buy more of, so that if on average people buy five times as much coffee as tea, then the basket includes five times as much coffee as tea.

Figure 2 | **Consumer Price Index**

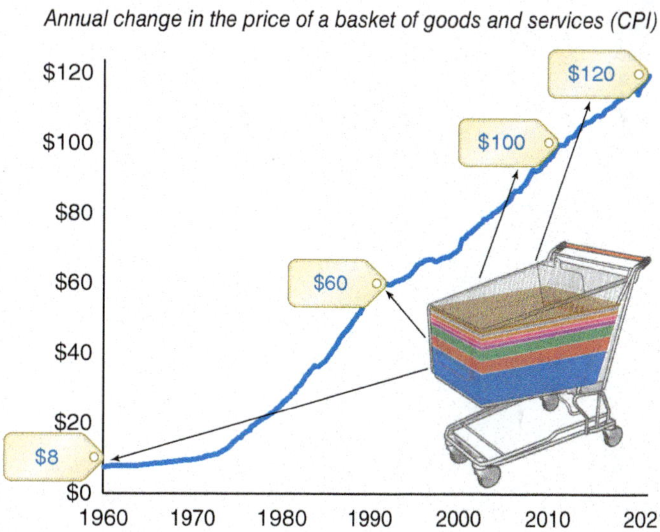

Data from: Australian Bureau of Statistics.

The total cost in dollars of this representative basket of stuff is somewhat arbitrary. Sure, we could tell you how much the average person spent in a particular year. But you aren't the average person and the CPI is focused on how much the prices are changing, not how big the average person's basket is. As a result, the government statisticians create an *index* in which the basket is set just big enough that it'll cost $100 in some arbitrary year (called the *base year*), and they then track changes in the cost of that exact basket of goods and services through time. Figure 2 shows how the cost of this basket has changed over time and therefore how much prices have risen on average.

Figure 3 | **Inflation Rate**

Annual change in the price of a basket of goods and services (CPI)

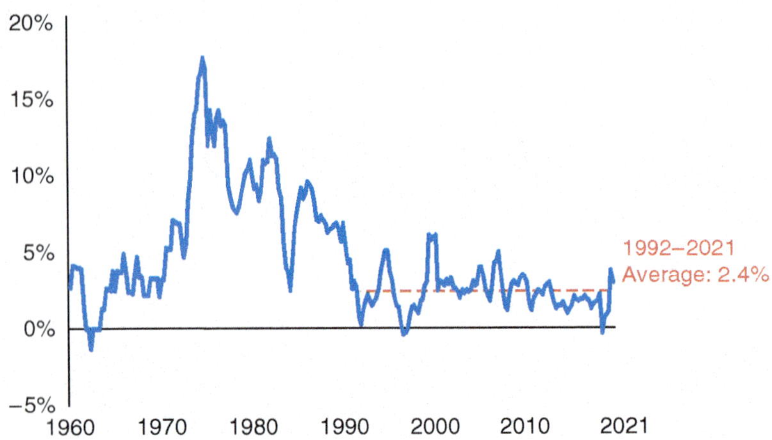

Data from: Reserve Bank of Australia.

Step four: Calculate the inflation rate. You've already done all the hard work. The last step is to calculate the inflation rate, remembering that it's the percentage change in the price of that fixed basket of goods over a year.

Figure 3 shows the inflation rate for each year since 1970. It shows that over recent decades the inflation rate has been relatively low at around 2% per year. But in the late 1970s inflation was much higher, sometimes above 10%. And in 2020, when the economy was in a deep downturn, average prices actually fell. A generalised decrease in the overall price level is known as **deflation.** Deflation may sound good, but it actually can cause big problems in the economy because some people stop buying goods and services in order to wait for them to get cheaper. We'll discuss the problems of deflation and the tools the government uses to fight it in Chapter 34.

deflation A generalised decrease in the overall level of prices.

Do the Economics

You now know how to calculate the inflation rate for the average Australian consumer. Let's put your new skills to the test and calculate an inflation rate. To do this for the average Australian consumer requires enormous amounts of data because people buy a lot of different goods and services. To keep it simple, let's calculate the inflation rate experienced by one really simple consumer: my dog Bailey. He's pretty much the average Australian dog—as a mutt, he's an average of many breeds—and he has average tastes.

Step one: Find out what Bailey typically buys.

Bailey eats a small can of dog food each morning and another in the evening, which means that he goes through 730 cans per year. He also gets a few scoops of kibble each day, which adds up to seven 12-kilo bags per year. He visits the vet twice per year on average, and he gets a couple of new chew toys on his birthday. This list describes Bailey's basket of goods and services, and it's recorded in the first column of Figure 4.

Step two: Collect prices.

You need to find the prices of dog food, vet visits, and dog toys. I've listed what I paid for each of these throughout the year in 2018 (shown in the second column) and 2019 (in the third column) of Figure 4.

Step three: Tally up the cost of a fixed basket of goods.

Next, add up the total cost of Bailey's basket of goods and services each year. That's the total spending on canned food plus spending on kibble, vet visits, and chew toys. Because he eats a lot more cans of canned food than bags of kibble, the price of canned food gets a much higher weight in this total cost. As the bottom row of Figure 4 shows, the cost of this basket of goods rose from $1,944 in 2018 (yes, dogs are expensive!), to $2,007 in 2019.

Richard Holden

Meet Bailey the wonder dog.

Figure 4 | Calculating Inflation

Step 1: What do dogs buy?	Step 2: Collect prices		Step 3: Tally up the costs	
Bailey's basket of goods and services	Price in 2018	Price in 2019	Cost in 2018 (= Price in 2018 × Quantity)	Cost in 2019 (= Price in 2019 × Quantity)
730 cans of dog food	\$1.80 per can	\$1.85 per can	\$1.80 × 730 = \$1,314	\$1.85 × 730 = \$1,351
7 bags of kibble	\$70 per bag	\$72 per bag	\$70 × 7 = \$490	\$72 × 7 = \$504
2 vet visits	\$60 per visit	\$65 per visit	\$60 × 2 = \$120	\$65 × 2 = \$130
2 chew toys	\$10 per toy	\$11 per toy	\$10 × 2 = \$20	\$11 × 2 = \$22
Cost of Bailey's basket			\$1,944	\$2,007

Step 4: Calculate the inflation rate $= \frac{\$2{,}007 - \$1{,}944}{\$1{,}944} \times 100 = 3.2\%$

Step four: Calculate the inflation rate.

A representative and fixed basket of dog consumption cost \$1,944 in 2018, and \$2,007 in 2019, so the inflation rate for dogs was $\frac{\$2{,}007 - \$1{,}944}{\$1{,}944} \times 100 = 3.2\%$ Woof!

Dogs had a slightly higher inflation rate than humans because the prices of the stuff dogs consume went up by more than the stuff people consume. If you want to see how much inflation there is in the things you buy, keep a record of what you buy and track the corresponding prices over time. ■

The Challenges of Measuring the True Cost of Living

One goal of the CPI is to measure changes in the cost of living—how much your spending has to rise to maintain a given quality of life. However the CPI is an imperfect measure of the cost of living. The problem is that it tracks the changing price of a *fixed* basket of goods, while in reality, people often change the basket of stuff that they buy. People change what they buy so that they can achieve a given quality of life at a lower cost as new products are developed and as the availability and price of goods and services change relative to other options. As such, failing to account for these changing buying patterns tends to overstate changes in the cost of living. There are three related biases to the way the CPI is measured and they all suggest that the CPI overstates changes in the cost of living.

Quality improvements can hide price decreases. Businesses are constantly working to improve their products, but how should we think about price changes that come with quality changes? A 64 GB iPhone XS cost \$1,629 in 2019, a price increase of 99% over the first iPhone. But the first iPhone had a maximum of 8 GB of storage. Storage isn't the only difference: The processor speed is much faster on the iPhone XS, the screen is bigger, and the battery life is longer. The original iPhone did have a camera, but it was pretty bad: low resolution, no low-light capabilities, and no front-facing "selfie" features. If you're getting something better, then how should you think about the price change?

This is an issue that the people who measure inflation confront on a daily basis. To truly measure inflation, we need to compare price changes on a quality-adjusted basis. In many cases, this is what the government statisticians try to do. But it's not possible to account for every possible quality improvement, and so some part of the measured rise in prices is likely due to unmeasured quality improvements, rather than a true rise in the cost of living.

Since it's only ever possible to partially control for quality, the CPI overstates inflation because of quality improvements that are not accounted for in adjustments.

giedre vaitekune/Shutterstock

It used to cost a lot more to take a picture.

New products can make you better off, thereby reducing your cost of living. The CPI ignores the fact that the price of an iPhone fell from infinity in 2006 (you couldn't buy one at any price!), to $820 when it was released in 2007. It's an invention that reduced the cost of living, because it replaced many goods and services that people previously spent a lot of money on: landline phone service and answering machines; watches and calculators; cameras, film, and photo processing; GPS devices and iPods; and newspapers and magazines. Because the CPI only tracks the changing prices of existing goods, it doesn't account for the reduction in the cost of living due to the introduction of new products.

Even if you didn't buy these things before, people who buy a smartphone today are better off because they now have access to this technology. When the iPhone was introduced, people shifted their budget from other things towards the iPhone. Why? Because their marginal benefit from spending $820 on an iPhone was higher than whatever else they could have spent that $820 on (or else the *cost-benefit principle* tells us they wouldn't have bought the iPhone).

The ABS doesn't attempt to compare new products to the products being replaced in the basket. Over time, the ABS adds new products to the basket and removes others, but they don't compare the price of new products (like an iPhone) to the products being replaced (like iPods). Once they become part of the typical person's basket of goods and services, changes in the prices of the new goods and services will be included as part of changes in the overall price level. But the fact that you were made better off by the invention of the new good or service is never accounted for by the CPI. Because the CPI only tracks the changing prices of *existing* goods and services, it doesn't account for gains we get from the invention of new ones.

Ian Waldie/Getty Images

What will you do when their price goes up?

You can save yourself money without sacrificing much. Whenever prices rise, people adapt and change the products in their actual shopping baskets. For instance, when the price of bananas rises, you might buy oranges or avocados instead. You *substitute* what's in your shopping basket to find cheaper ways to achieve the same quality of life.

substitution bias The overstating of inflation that occurs because people substitute toward goods whose prices rise by less.

Substituting low-inflation goods and services for high-inflation ones is a good strategy for you, but it also means that the CPI overstates inflation on average. The CPI measures the prices of a fixed basket of goods, so it effectively assumes that people keep buying the same number of bananas no matter how expensive they get. It doesn't capture substitution across items. This leads measured inflation to outpace changes in people's actual cost of living. This is called **substitution bias**—the overstating of inflation that occurs because people substitute toward goods and services whose prices rise by less.

It's hard to know for sure how much substitution bias there is. Even though you substituted an orange for a banana to minimise the negative effect of more expensive bananas on your well-being, there's still a negative effect. How big is it? That depends on how much worse off you are from the switch. And that's going to depend on your personal preferences.

How much does the CPI overstate the inflation people experience? Economists continue to debate how big these measurement problems are. Careful studies suggest that these three biases together lead the CPI to overstate the rising cost of living by nearly 1% per year. Most of this is due to new products and unmeasured quality improvements. The *chained CPI* is an inflation measure that is designed to update the basket of goods each month to correct for substitution bias. The chained CPI is a measure of inflation that's about 0.25 percentage points lower on average than the CPI and many economists argue that it's a truer measure of changes in the cost of living.

24.2 Different Measures of Inflation

Learning Objective *Pick the right inflation measure for the task at hand.*

Inflation data are used for many different tasks: They're a guideline for cost-of-living adjustments, an input to adjusting financial and economic indicators, a guidepost for Reserve Bank of Australia (RBA) policy makers, and an indicator that forecasters use to project where the economy is going. Each role is best served by slightly different measures of inflation. While the CPI remains the most popular measure of inflation, it is in fact just one of several price indices that can be employed to meet the needs of specific decision makers. Different measures of inflation consider different baskets of goods and services, and are therefore useful for different tasks.

Consumer Prices

So far we've been focusing on the prices that consumers pay when they buy goods and services. Let's take a look at how various measures of inflation in consumer prices differ, and what each is useful for.

The CPI is used for cost of living adjustments. The CPI is the most widely accepted measure of the change in cost of living. That's why workers who want to protect themselves from the effects of the rising cost of living insist that their employment contracts include **indexation** clauses which automatically adjust their wages in line with the CPI. The government also indexes the Aged Pension and other welfare payments so that they're automatically adjusted to keep pace with the rising cost of living. And the income cutoffs to qualify for many government programs are automatically adjusted each year to account for inflation.

indexation Automatically adjusting wages, benefits, tax brackets, and the like to compensate for inflation.

Monetary policy focuses on the flexible inflation targets. One of the key goals of the RBA is to achieve low and stable inflation. Indeed, as we'll discuss in Chapter 34, it tries to manage the economy to hit a target rate of inflation of 2–3%. But rather than trying to get inflation within this target band every quarter, the RBA uses a "flexible" inflation target. According to the RBA, "This means that inflation does not need to be in the target range at all times, but rather, on average, over time." Indeed, since the flexible inflation target was introduced by the RBA in 1992, the long term average inflation rate (measured quarterly) is 2.4%. Yet inflation has been outside the 2–3% target bound during more than half of all quarterly measurements since then!

Forecasters focus on core inflation. When forecasters look for the underlying trend in inflation, called "core inflation", they consult alternative measures to the CPI. We have lots of measures of core inflation, but the most common one is just like the CPI, except that it excludes items like food and fuel. Sometimes people think this is odd because food and fuel are two of the most critical purchases people make. They are excluded not because they aren't important, but because their prices are often volatile and they don't track broader inflation trends. Food prices rise and fall with agricultural harvests, and oil prices fluctuate with geopolitical tensions. Excluding these volatile prices often provides a clearer reading of underlying inflation trends. As Figure 5 illustrates, core inflation tends to be similar to the headline measure, but it bounces around a bit less.

Figure 5 | **Alternative Measures of Inflation Move Together**

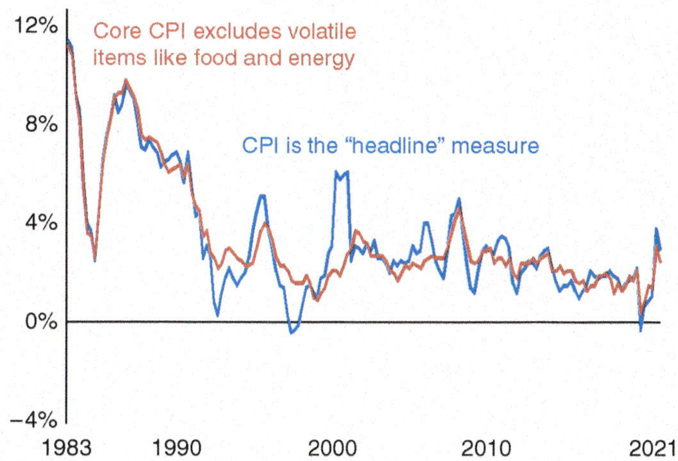

Data from: Reserve Bank of Australia.

Business Prices

The CPI is designed to measure inflation as experienced by people in their day-to-day lives. But what if you're running a business? Then you might care about the prices of inputs into your production process or the price at which you can sell your output. Similarly, if you want to know if a country is producing more output or just charging higher prices, you need to account for inflation in the prices of all the goods and services that are produced.

producer price index (PPI) A price index that tracks the prices of inputs into the production process.

Inflation experienced by businesses is measured by the producer price index. The **producer price index** (or **PPI** for short) measures the price of inputs into the production process. It's useful because it helps businesses see how the prices that matter to them are changing. It's also useful because it can help you keep tabs on what's likely happening to your competitors' costs. From a macroeconomic perspective, it's worth tracking the inflation that businesses are facing because rising input prices eventually cause businesses to raise their prices.

GDP deflator A price index that tracks the price of all goods and services produced domestically.

The GDP deflator tells us about the rising prices of all goods and services produced. When you're adjusting dollar amounts describing what the economy produces, you should focus on the **GDP deflator,** which is an alternative price index that's calculated based on a basket of goods and services that represents everything the Australian economy *produces.* That means it accounts for the prices of everything we make from sandwiches to submarines, and unlike the CPI, it includes capital goods but excludes imported goods. The GDP deflator is particularly important because it can be used to convert nominal GDP into real GDP. Recall from Chapter 21 that real GDP is measured using a fixed price level so that it isolates changes in the amount of stuff being produced from changes in the price level. That means we can compare real and nominal GDP to compute the GDP deflator:

$$\text{GDP deflator} = \frac{\text{Nominal GDP}}{\text{Real GDP}} \times 100$$

Now that you know many different measures of inflation, let's turn to adjusting for the effects of inflation.

24.3 Adjusting for the Effects of Inflation

Learning Objective *Learn to account for the influence of inflation before making big decisions.*

The force of inflation made this appear to be the most popular Star Wars movie.

When *Variety* magazine held a poll asking readers which was the best Star Wars film of all time, almost no one voted for episode seven, *Star Wars: The Force Awakens.* Yet in dollar terms it appears—at least at first glance—to be the most successful Star Wars film ever. When it was released in the United States in 2015, its box office revenues added up to \$937 million, more money than any film had ever made before at the time. By this measure, *The Force Awakens* was more than three times as successful as the original Star Wars, which took in only \$307 million when it was first released in 1977.

But fans, critics, and economists agree that the original Star Wars (that's *Episode IV: A New Hope* to you youngsters) was a much better film. The problem is that the dark side has distorted these numbers.

Comparing Dollars over Time

The dark side here is inflation. Rising prices effectively mean that the value of a dollar has declined over time. And that makes it difficult to compare dollar amounts from different time periods, because past amounts are measured in dollars that were more valuable than today's dollars.

Use the inflation adjustment formula to adjust for changing prices. You'll make better judgements if you compare dollar amounts from different eras using a common metric. This is where you'll find the CPI to be useful. The CPI tracks the average price level over time, so you can use it to convert dollar amounts from the past (or the future) into their equivalent purchasing power in today's dollars.

To do this, multiply the dollar amount from another time by the ratio of today's price level to the price level at that time:

$$\text{Today's dollars} = \text{Another time's dollars} \times \frac{\text{Price level today}}{\text{Price level in another time}}$$

Do the Economics

You can see how this formula works by converting the box office take from different eras into today's dollars (and to help you, Figure 6 shows you the price level for each year). *Titanic* ranks as the eighth-highest-grossing film of all time in Australia, bringing in \$57.7 million, but it was released in 1997 when the CPI was 66.9. In 2021, the CPI was 119.7. Therefore:

$$\text{Revenue in 2021 dollars} = \$57.7 \text{ million} \times \frac{119.7}{66.9} = \$103.3 \text{ million}$$

Rank	Movie	Release year	Aus CPI in release year	Box office total	
				In release year dollars	In 2021 dollars
1	*Avatar*	2009	93.4	115.8	
2	*Star Wars: The Force Awakens*	2015	107.7	94.0	
3	*Avengers: Endgame*	2019	115.1	84.2	
4	*Spider-Man: No Way Home*	2021	119.7	80.5	
5	*The Lion King*	2019	115.1	64.1	
6	*Avengers: Infinity War*	2018	113.3	62.0	
7	*Star Wars: The Last Jedi*	2017	111.2	58.1	
8	*Titanic*	1997	66.9	57.7	
9	*Bohemian Rhapsody*	2018	113.3	55.3	
10	*The Avengers*	2012	101	53.5	

Data from: Box Office Mojo.

Figure 6 | The Consumer Price Index

Year	CPI
1980	26.4
1981	28.9
1982	32.1
1983	35.4
1984	36.8
1985	39.2
1986	42.8
1987	46.4
1988	49.8
1989	53.5
1990	57.5
1991	59.3
1992	59.9
1993	60.9
1994	62.1
1995	65.0
1996	66.7
1997	66.9
1998	67.4
1999	68.4
2000	71.5
2001	74.6
2002	76.9
2003	79.0
2004	80.8
2005	83.0
2006	85.9
2007	87.9
2008	91.8
2009	93.4
2010	96.1
2011	99.3
2012	101.0
2013	103.5
2014	106.1
2015	107.7
2016	109.1
2017	111.2
2018	113.3
2019	115.1
2020	116.1
2021	119.7

Data from: Australian Bureau of Statistics.

Answers: \$148.4m, \$104.5m, \$87.5m, \$807m, \$66.7m, \$65.5m, \$62.5m, \$103.3m, \$58.4m, \$63.4m.

Once you account for the influence of inflation, the truth emerges: *Titanic* was a very high-grossing film—third on the all-time list adjusted for inflation. That makes sense because it was very popular and was released a long time ago. Alright, now try some on your own: Convert the box office take for the original release of all ten top-grossing movies into 2021 dollars. ■

Real and Nominal Variables

The broader idea here is that when you're comparing dollar amounts from different time periods, inflation can distort your comparisons. It's an insight that applies well beyond box office receipts, to GDP, wages, your income, revenues, costs, or indeed any variable measured in dollars.

nominal variable A variable measured in dollars (whose value may fluctuate over time).

real variable A variable that has been adjusted to account for inflation.

Real variables adjust for inflation. This is why economists distinguish between two types of measures. A **nominal variable** is measured in dollars (or some other currency) whose values may fluctuate over time. As a result, nominal variables can rise or fall due to either changing quantities (the number of people seeing a movie) or inflation (which changes the price of movie tickets).

By contrast, a **real variable** has been adjusted to account for the influence of inflation. You can convert nominal variables into real variables by converting dollar amounts from different time periods into the equivalent number of today's dollars.

In fact, macroeconomists often adjust variables into dollars from a specific year called the *base year*. For instance, real GDP data are published in 2012 dollars, which means that 2012 is the base year, and so it's adjusted as follows:

$$\text{Real value in 2012 dollars} = \text{Nominal value in year } t \text{ dollars} \times \frac{\text{Price level in 2012}}{\text{Price level in year } t}$$

By analysing dollar amounts once they've been converted into dollars from some fixed year—whether it's this year or some other base year—you're effectively holding the average price level constant, which means that you've stripped out the effects of inflation. Because real variables aren't affected by changing prices, they change only in response to changes in physical quantities.

You should focus on real variables. Real variables are important because they give you a better sense of the underlying trade-offs, particularly when you're making comparisons over time. To give a few examples:

- To analyse whether you are becoming better paid, you should analyse your *real wage,* which adjusts for the effects of inflation, rather than your nominal wage in dollars.
- To assess whether your stocks have become more valuable, focus on the *real wealth* in your portfolio, rather than its nominal value.
- To evaluate whether your sales staff are performing better, focus on your company's *real revenues,* rather than nominal revenues, which rise with inflation. Let's see how this works in the next case study.

Do the Economics

In 2016 (when the CPI was 108.6) Coles's annual revenue was \$39,242 million. By 2018, Coles's annual report boasted that revenue had grown to \$39,388 million (and the CPI rose to 113.0). Calculate the growth in Coles' real revenue, using 2014 as the base year (when the CPI was 105.9).

- Revenue from 2016 in 2014 dollars = \$39,242 million × 105.9 / 108.6 = \$38,266 million.
- Revenue from 2018 in 2014 dollars = \$39,388 million × 105.9 / 113.0 = \$36,913 million.

Therefore real revenue fell from \$38,266m to \$36,913m, a decline of −3.5%. ■

You can calculate real growth as nominal growth minus inflation. This calculation took a fair bit of work. Fortunately, you can use a shortcut that you learned in Chapter 21 that will make it easier to calculate real growth rates. Recall that for relatively small percentage changes (say, changes of less than 10%):

$$\text{Percent change in real value} \approx \text{Percent change in nominal value} - \text{Percent change in prices}$$

For instance, between 2016 and 2018, Coles' nominal revenue rose by 0.4%, and over the same period, the CPI grew 4%. Thus Coles' real revenue fell by approximately 0.4% − 4% = −3.6%. You may notice that this isn't exact, but it's pretty close, and that's the point—it's a useful approximation.

Do the Economics

The average nominal wage grew 2.4% in 2019, and the CPI grew 1.3%. How much did real wages grow? ■

Answers: Percent change in real wage = Percent change nominal wage − Percent change in prices = 2.4% − 1.3% = 1.1%.

Real and Nominal Interest Rates

Let's now see how all this applies to the benefits and costs of saving or borrowing money. Typically, you receive interest payments when you save, and you pay interest when you borrow. If you put \$100 in the bank at the start of the year and your bank adds \$5 in interest you'll have \$105 at the end of the year. But does this really measure the benefit to you?

The nominal interest rate measures the return in dollars. That extra 5% you receive is the **nominal interest rate,** which is the stated interest rate without a correction for the effects of inflation. It reflects the return *measured in dollars,* for the use of \$100 for a year. How much better off you are depends on *what you can buy* with that \$105. If inflation has led prices to rise by 3% so that it now takes \$103 to buy what would have cost \$100 last year, then you're only \$2 better off.

nominal interest rate The stated interest rate without a correction for the effects of inflation.

The real interest rate focuses on what you can buy with those dollars. If you want to accurately measure the benefit you'll get from saving \$100 for a year—or the cost of borrowing \$100 for a year—you'll need to account for the influence of inflation. That's what the **real interest rate** does: It measures the interest rate in terms of changes in your *purchasing power*. It's useful because it shifts your focus from how many extra dollar bills you'll receive, to what you can buy with those dollar bills. It's called the real interest rate because it focuses on the real benefit you'll get from saving. For low rates of inflation, there's a simple short cut you can use to calculate the real interest rate:

real interest rate The interest rate in terms of changes in your purchasing power; ≈ Nominal interest rate − Inflation rate

$$\text{Real interest rate} \approx \text{Nominal interest rate} - \text{Inflation rate}$$

And so in this example where the nominal interest rate was 5%, and the inflation rate was 3%, the real interest rate is 5% − 3% = 2%. That's why we said that saving \$100 for a year makes you \$2 better off.

Overcoming Money Illusion

money illusion The (mistaken) tendency to focus on nominal dollar amounts instead of inflation-adjusted amounts.

When *The Force Awakens* smashed box office records, the press trumpeted it as the most successful movie ever made. This is an example of **money illusion**—the (mistaken) tendency to focus on nominal dollar amounts—and it can lead you to be fooled by inflation. People make some pretty costly mistakes when they focus on nominal rather than real variables. Reading this chapter will be more than worth it if you can use what you learn to avoid being suckered by money illusion into making bad decisions.

Money illusion can distort decisions. A survey asked people to consider what choices they would make if all prices throughout the economy—including their income—were to rise by 25%. In particular, it asked them to think about a leather chair that they had planned to buy for $400, and asked what choice they'd make now that it cost $500. Apply the *opportunity cost principle,* and you'll see that the opportunity cost of buying the chair remains unchanged because anything else you could spend that money on has also become 25% more expensive. But money illusion led people to focus instead on the higher dollar cost of that chair, so nearly two-fifths of respondents said they would be less likely to buy the chair. Don't let money illusion fool you into focusing on the price in dollar terms; pay attention to the real opportunity cost instead.

Money illusion can lead to mis-pricing. When you sell your house, you'll need to decide your asking price. Many homeowners start by thinking about the price that they paid, but money illusion leads them to think about the price they paid in nominal dollars, without adjusting for inflation. That can be a disastrously bad guide if you bought your home a long time ago when average prices were a lot lower. Failing to account for how much inflation has pushed up prices has led some homeowners to sell their houses at prices that are tens of thousands of dollars too low. Don't make the same mistake. The best guide to the value of your home isn't the price you paid years ago—focus instead on the price that similar houses in your neighborhood sold for recently.

nominal wage rigidity Reluctance to cut nominal wages.

Figure 7 Distribution of Nominal Wage Changes

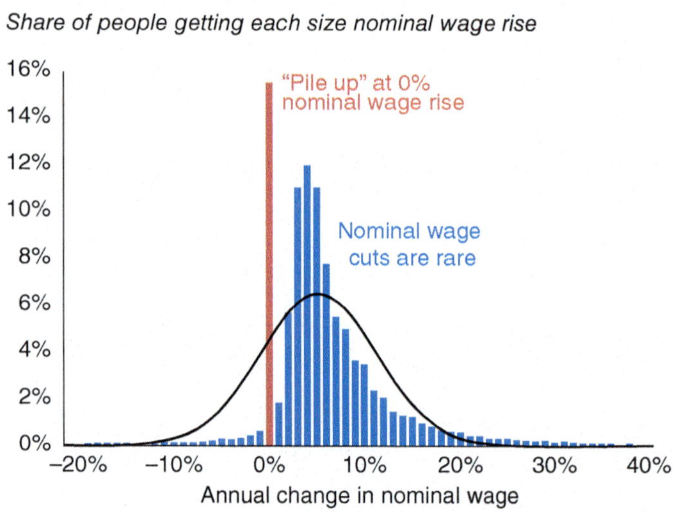

Data from: Australian Bureau of Statistics.

Money illusion creates nominal wage rigidity. People hate it when their employer cuts their wage. It feels unfair, and they resent it. Smart managers understand this, so even when their business is struggling, they'll try to get by without ever cutting nominal wages, a pattern known as **nominal wage rigidity.** You can see this in Figure 7, which shows the distribution of pay raises for Australian workers. There's a big pile-up at 0%, which shows that the boss often chooses to stick with last year's wage rather than to cut anyone's pay. But notice, this pile-up occurs at a zero percent *nominal* wage rise. Money illusion led workers to feel okay because their wage—*measured in dollars*—wasn't being cut. But the reality is that with inflation of 2%, their real wages fell by 2%.

EVERYDAY Economics How to beat money illusion by negotiating for a real raise

A few years back a friend of mine was negotiating a raise with his boss and reached out to me for advice. He was earning $100,000 per year and his boss offered him a contract that would see his wage rise by 5% over the five-year term of the contract. My friend wanted more, but he understood his boss had limited funds, and he was pleased to see his hard work rewarded with a pay increase.

But he wasn't getting a real pay raise. Inflation was running at about 2% per year, so over five years, the average price level would rise by about 10% while his wages would only grow at half that rate. If your nominal wage rises by 5% over a period when prices rise by 10%, then your boss is actually cutting your real wage by about 5%.

My friend's mistake was to think about his current nominal wage as the baseline in his wage negotiations. Relative to that reference point, any boost to his nominal wage was framed as good news. Instead, you want to make your current *real* wage the starting point.

So when you next negotiate over your pay, begin the conversation with your boss by pointing out that inflation has reduced the value of your wage. Lay out the latest numbers and suggest that you expect an inflation-based adjustment to offset the rising cost of living. There's not really a good counterargument, so it's likely they'll agree. Now that you've set your real wage as the baseline, turn the conversation to what sort of *real* wage boost you deserve for your hard work over the past year. If you've performed well, this conversation should also go well. How well? When I advised my friend to follow this script in his negotiation, he ended up with a much bigger raise than his boss originally offered—more than enough to offset inflation. If his experience is any guide, it will work for you, too. ■

PictureLux/The Hollywood Archive/Alamy Stock Photo

He doesn't want to give you a raise.

24.4 The Role of Money and the Costs of Inflation

Learning Objective *Analyse the role of money so that you can assess the costs of inflation.*

People really dislike inflation. Surveys of economists reveal that they think inflation is costly, but they're a bit less concerned. We're going to explore both why the general public is so concerned by inflation, and what economists believe are the true costs of inflation. But first, we need to turn to the topic of money.

The Functions of Money

You've probably spent much of your life thinking about money, worrying about money, or dreaming about money. But have you ever just sat down and thought hard about what money *is?* It's not just the pieces of paper in your wallet; it's also the deposit in your everyday banking account and the bits and bytes in your Paypal account. **Money** is any asset that's regularly used in transactions.

money Any asset regularly used in transactions.

More importantly, think about what money *does*. It's an essential component of our modern economy because it serves three key functions: It's a medium of exchange, a unit of account, and a store of value. Let's explore each of these in turn.

> The three functions of money:
> 1. Medium of exchange
> 2. Unit of account
> 3. Store of value

Function one: Money is a medium of exchange. You're using money as a *medium of exchange* whenever you hand it over to buy stuff, or alternatively, when you accept it from your employer in exchange for your hard work. If there were no such thing as money, you would either have to make everything you need for yourself, or barter for it. But barter constrains you to only do business when there's a *double coincidence of wants:* You can only trade your extra milk for bread if you can find someone who wants milk and coincidentally has extra bread.

Money eliminates this constraint, creating opportunities for you to *specialise.* You can focus on the narrow set of tasks where your skills are most valuable, knowing that you can spend the money you earn to buy fresh bread from a professional baker, a smartphone manufactured in Chinese factories, and shares in Westpac. Without a widely used medium of exchange, bartering small slices of your workday for some bread, a smartphone made on the other side of the world, and part ownership of an online company would be a logistical nightmare. With money, it's an everyday convenience.

But money can only be an effective medium of exchange if it's widely accepted. And that depends on sellers maintaining faith that when they accept money, they'll subsequently be able to use it to buy stuff at reasonable prices.

Function two: Money is a unit of account. Money is also a *unit of account,* which means that it's a common unit that people use to measure economic value. Indeed, just as nearly all architects use metres to measure distance, nearly everyone uses

Aedka Studio/Shutterstock

A common unit of account makes these comparisons easier.

dollars as the common unit to describe prices, record debts, and write financial contracts. Putting everything in the same unit is useful because it makes it easier to apply the *opportunity cost principle* and ask, "Or what?" If apples cost $1 a pound and oranges cost $1.25 a pound, then you know you have to give up more apples to get a pound of oranges.

It's important to have a stable unit of account for measuring economic value for the same reason that it's useful to have a stable unit of account to measure distance—it simplifies comparisons and eases communication. If your architect's measuring tape were to shrink or expand each day, it would no longer be very useful. The same is true for money—the value of a dollar needs to be relatively stable for it to be a reliable unit of account.

gary corbett/Alamy Stock Photo

You could store your wealth this way, but do you really want to?

Function three: Money is a store of value. When you save money for a rainy day, you're using money as a *store of value,* storing your purchasing power for another day. Want to ensure that you have goods and services to consume in retirement? You can do that by earning money today, saving or storing that money, and then using it in the future to buy stuff. While there are other ways of shifting wealth to the future—you could try storing gold bricks, fine art, or canned food instead—none of these is a good store of value: the price of gold fluctuates a lot, fine art is hard to store, and canned food loses its value as it reaches its expiration date.

Money will successfully function as a store of value when it's easy to store and it can reliably hold its value over time.

Inflation undermines the productive benefit of money. Money plays a productive role in the economy similar to a lubricant that keeps the economic engine operating efficiently. When inflation is low and stable, money serves its three functions well, and the economic engine hums along.

But when inflation is high or unpredictable, problems emerge. You'll be less willing to use money as a *store of value* if rising prices mean that the $100 you put in your wallet today will only buy half as much next week. Money is also a less effective *unit of account* when its value is uncertain, because a price denominated in dollars is less informative when you aren't sure what a dollar is worth. You'll be less willing to sign an employment contract spelling out your future wages in dollar terms if you can't be sure those dollars will buy you a reasonable quality of life. Skyrocketing inflation can undermine the role of money as a *medium of exchange* when it becomes too much of a hassle to get your hands on enough cash, push it around in wheelbarrows, and spend it before it loses its value. Likewise, sellers will stop accepting money if they fear that they won't be able to spend it.

As we're about to see, when inflation makes money a less effective economic lubricant, it can cause the whole economic engine to seize up.

The Costs of Hyperinflation

hyperinflation Extremely high rates of inflation.

The costs imposed by inflation become most obvious in the worst-case scenario of an extremely high rate of inflation, also called a **hyperinflation.** There's no precise cutoff between a high inflation rate and hyperinflation, but think of prices at least doubling every few months. Fortunately, hyperinflation is rare. One of the most famous examples is the chaotic German hyperinflation of 1922–23, when prices doubled every few days!

Unfortunately hyperinflation continues to be a modern reality. Recently Venezuela has struggled with hyperinflation. An annual inflation rate measured in thousands of percent per year has pushed the price of a café con leche—a delicious local coffee drink—from 450 Venezuelan bolivars in mid-2016 to 800,000 bolivars less than two years later, as you can see in Figure 8.

Hyperinflation makes most aspects of life harder. Within a few years, a crate of bolivars that would have bought a house could no longer buy a carton of eggs. The currency became so worthless that when thieves looted a store, they left behind dozens of 20 bolivar bills because they didn't think it was worth the effort to pick them up.

Venezuela's experience illustrates how the logistical challenges of dealing with hyperinflation come to dominate everyday life. In late 2016, the highest denomination note, 100 bolivars, had become worth less than 5 cents. The government responded by printing even higher value notes. But inflation raced ahead even faster, and soon the new 100,000 bolivar notes also came to be worth less than 5 cents. As a result, it takes heaping fistfuls of cash to buy anything. Wallets can't fit enough cash, so people have taken to stuffing bundles of notes into backpacks. One shopkeeper said that instead of counting banknotes he weighs them using the same scales he uses to weigh cheese. Bank branches regularly run out of money. All of this wreaks havoc with ATMs, some of which needed to be refilled every three hours. For some people, the only way to get cash is to wait in a long ATM line in which the withdrawal limit is so low they can only get enough bolivars to pay for a few bus rides. Some stores have responded to the shortage by selling cash to customers, who buy it with a credit card. But the markups are steep, and you might pay a 180,000 bolivar credit card charge to get a 100,000 bolivar note.

Figure 8 | **Price of Café con Leche in Venezuela**

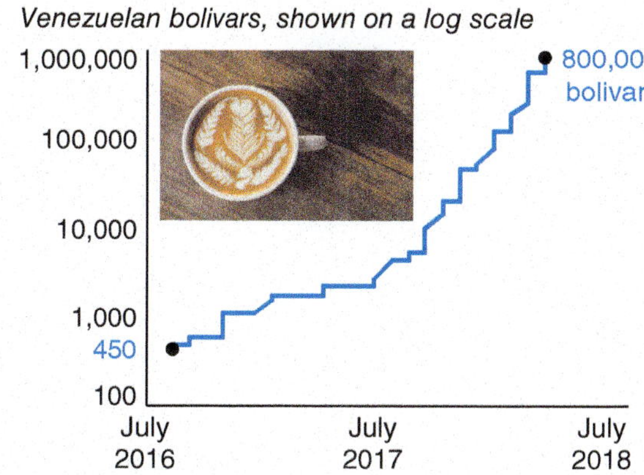

Mutita Narkmuang/Shutterstock

Data from: Bloomberg.

Hyperinflation erodes all the functions of money. Hyperinflation destroyed the bolivar as a *store of value*. Indeed, the bolivar lost its value so quickly that Venezuelans would race to spend their cash before it became worthless. The hassle required to get cash also made the bolivar an unattractive *medium of exchange*. Instead, people figured out workarounds. Barter became more common—taxi drivers took cigarettes in lieu of cash, a haircut could be bought for five bananas and two eggs, and Facebook pages sprang up so that people could swap toothpaste, baby formula, and other essentials. The well-connected used U.S. dollars instead of Venezuelan bolivars. American Airlines refused to accept bolivars for flights out of Venezuela, insisting their customers use foreign credit cards to buy their tickets online. Amid all this chaos, there was no reliable *unit of account* in Venezuela. Even in real estate, where the law requires contracts to be written in bolivars, a group of real estate agents established a password-protected website that lists the prices of houses in U.S. dollars.

Georg Ismar/picture alliance/Getty Images

A huge stack of Venezuelan bolivars that's now worth less than AUD$2.

The Venezuelan hyperinflation aptly illustrates the problem that arises in every episode of hyperinflation—when money no longer works as it should, every facet of economic life becomes more difficult. As one Venezuelan said, "Something so simple as taking money out of a bank machine or buying a coffee or taking a taxi has become a race for survival." While hyperinflation is not the only problem in Venezuela—add in a big dose of corruption and mismanagement and stir—the result was an economic depression, widespread poverty, and a humanitarian disaster in which millions of people starved despite living in a country blessed with extraordinarily valuable oil reserves.

The Costs of Expected Inflation

While hyperinflation illustrates the costs of high rates of inflation, it's worth remembering that this is an extreme outcome. More moderate rates of inflation have more moderate costs. At the other extreme, some economists argue that the 2% to 3% inflation target that Australia aims for is close enough to price stability that it imposes few costs. But when inflation creeps a bit higher—as it did in the 1970s when it averaged more than 10% and rose almost as high as 16%—it becomes more disruptive. We'll explore this by first analysing why expected inflation is costly, and then turn to the extra costs that arise when inflation is unexpected.

Cost one: Inflation creates menu costs for sellers. Put yourself in the shoes of a manager who has to decide how many times to change their prices each year. The *marginal principle* reminds you that it's simpler to ask whether to raise your price one more time. The *cost-benefit principle* says: Yes, adjust your price today if the marginal benefit of doing so exceeds the marginal cost. The cost to a restaurant of raising prices is printing new menus, which is why economists describe the marginal cost of adjusting your price as **menu costs.** The marginal benefit of adjusting your price is that you'll shift to a price that covers the rising cost of your inputs. The higher inflation is—and the faster your costs rise—the larger this marginal benefit is. As a result, higher inflation leads to more frequent price adjustment.

menu costs The marginal cost of adjusting prices.

Inflation is costly because it leads businesses to devote valuable resources to reprinting menus, adjusting price tags, and reprogramming vending machines more often. These costs arise because inflation renders money an *unstable unit of account*—prices are marked in dollars, but those dollars are worth less—and so last year's price is no longer suitable this year.

Marco Bello/Reuters/Newscom

People waiting to get cash in Venezuela.

Cost two: Inflation creates shoe-leather costs for buyers. Next, think about how inflation will affect your relationship with money. Every time you go to the ATM, you have to decide how many dollars to withdraw and how much to leave in your account earning interest. This is a "how many" question, so the *marginal principle* says to focus on the simpler question of whether to withdraw one extra dollar. The *cost-benefit principle* says yes, withdraw that extra dollar if the marginal benefit exceeds the marginal cost. The marginal benefit of withdrawing an extra dollar is the convenience of having more cash in your wallet that you can use to buy stuff. The marginal cost comes from the *opportunity cost principle,* which reminds you that every dollar you withdraw would otherwise stay in your savings account earning a real interest rate. Inflation adds another cost: As prices rise, the cash in your wallet comes to be worth less. This cost is a big deal in Venezuela, because the 100,000 bolivar note you have in your wallet this week might only buy half as much next week. It follows that when inflation is high, the marginal cost of holding money is high, leading people to hold less of it.

Just as inflation erodes the value of banknotes, it also eats into the value of the balance in your PayPal or everyday banking accounts. So inflation will also lead you to hold less of these other forms of money. As many Venezuelans have discovered, that means you'll need to visit your bank more often, withdrawing money only as you need it, and rushing to spend it quickly. The time and effort this takes are called **shoe-leather costs,** because they arise from running around town (which wears down the leather on your shoes). Shoe-leather costs arise because inflation undermines money's function as a *store of value,* forcing people to take costly measures to keep their wealth in assets that better maintain their value.

shoe-leather costs The costs incurred trying to avoid holding cash.

The Costs of Unexpected Inflation

So far we've considered the costs that arise when everyone expects inflation to occur. There are additional costs that occur when inflation is unexpectedly higher or lower than anticipated.

Cost three: Inflation confuses the signals that prices send. Microeconomics teaches us that prices play a key role in coordinating economic activity. An increase in the price of an individual good like quinoa is a signal from buyers that they really want quinoa; the price transmits this information to quinoa producers, who see it as an incentive to expand production. By contrast, macroeconomics teaches us that when inflation causes all prices to rise, there's no reason to expand production because the higher price of your output is matched by an equal rise in the price of your inputs.

Ildi Papp/Shutterstock

Did the price rise because demand for quinoa increased, or is it just inflation?

The problem is that if the price of quinoa rises, it can be hard for producers to figure out whether that higher price is due to increased demand for quinoa or to a burst of unexpected inflation. In the resulting confusion, some managers will respond to unexpected inflation by expanding production, although they'll later discover that was a mistake because their costs have risen. At other times they'll fail to expand production when demand for their product has risen because they mistakenly guessed that the higher price reflected an unexpected burst of inflation. These mistakes occur because inflation undermines the stability of dollars as a *unit of account,* and this instability confounds the signals that price sends.

Cost four: Inflation redistributes. Unexpected inflation also redistributes from savers and lenders toward borrowers. This occurs because most loans specify repayment schedules in nominal terms—they use dollars as the *unit of account*—and so unexpected inflation changes the real value of your repayments. For instance, if you borrow $15,000 to buy a car at a 5% nominal interest rate, the repayment schedule commits you to pay $283 per month for the next five years. Perhaps that 5% nominal interest rate reflects expectations of 2% inflation and a 3% real interest rate. But if inflation ends up being higher—say if it's 4%—then the real interest rate you'll pay will be 1%, instead. You'll gain, and your bank will lose, because even though you'll keep sending in that $283 each month, the dollars you send your bank aren't worth as much.

Shutterstock

Dean Drobot/Shutterstock

Inflation that's higher than expected is good for borrowers and bad for lenders.

When this happens, lenders can go broke, as several did during the 1974 "Liquidity Squeeze". The seeds of the crisis were sown in the 1960s, when expectations of 2% inflation led some lenders to make long-term loans at nominal interest rates as low as 5%. Then inflation unexpectedly rocketed above 10% in the 1970s and it stayed high through to the early 1980s. This unexpected inflation was good news for borrowers, because their monthly loan repayments remained fixed in dollar terms even as their nominal income rose. But for lenders, it was disastrous. They had loaned money at what turned out to be a negative real interest rate, so in inflation-adjusted terms, borrowers repaid *less* than they borrowed. Many financial institutions went belly-up as a result.

On the flip side, when inflation is lower than anticipated, the opposite happens: The real value of your repayments rises, so lenders gain at the expense of borrowers. This happened in Australia in the early 1980s, when the RBA brought inflation down faster than anyone expected. Borrowers who had expected inflation to continue at 10% had signed up for 30-year mortgages charging nominal interest rates of 15%. When inflation nosedived—it fell as low as 2%—they ended up paying extremely high real interest rates. Banks made huge profits at the expense of homeowners, many of whom struggled to meet these higher-than-anticipated real mortgage payments.

The Inflation Fallacy

Ok, now you know the costs of inflation. Inflation has very real costs, and economists worry about inflation. But you might have noticed that it's not for the reasons that most people worry about inflation. People worry about inflation because they go to the store and see higher prices. That sounds bad. If you have to pay more for what you're buying, then you can't buy as much as before, right? Surveys show that more than three-quarters of people agree that inflation erodes their purchasing power. But that's only true if your income stays the same, which it rarely does. Inflation means that on average *all* prices are rising, and that usually means that wages and salaries are also rising.

The **inflation fallacy** is the (mistaken) belief that inflation destroys purchasing power. It's a fallacy because it tells only half the story. While a $1 price rise makes a buyer $1 poorer, it also makes the seller $1 richer. It follows that higher prices don't destroy purchasing power.

inflation fallacy The (mistaken) belief that inflation destroys purchasing power.

Moreover, inflation is a *generalised* rise in all prices, and so it raises the price of what you sell just as much as it raises the price of what you buy. You sell your labor, and inflation typically boosts the price of labor—meaning your wages—in lockstep with the price of the stuff you buy, as shown in Figure 9. Likewise, the price of the stocks in your portfolio and the interest you earn on your savings rise with inflation, leaving your purchasing power roughly unchanged.

Figure 9 | **Nominal Wages Grow in Lockstep with Inflation**

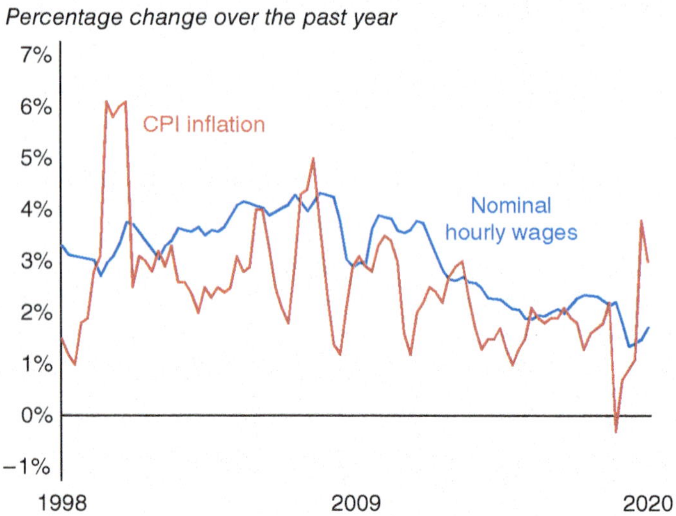

Data from: Australian Bureau of Inflation.

The inflation fallacy reflects a psychological bias in which people are quick to blame inflation for the higher prices they pay, but take personal credit for the parallel rise in their nominal wages, interpreting it as a well-deserved reward for their hard work unrelated to inflation. While their logic is wrong, their unhappiness is real, making inflation a potent political issue.

It's the real stuff that matters, not how it's measured. To see the error that drives the inflation fallacy, consider the following thought experiment. Imagine that you wake up on New Year's Day, and every price tag in the economy has an extra zero on the end of it. Gumballs sell for $5.00 instead of 50c. Trinkets at the two dollar shop sell for $20. And a pair of jeans sells for $1000 instead of $100. It's not just the price of stuff that changes, but the price of everything. Your wage will rise from $25 per hour to $250. That $10 note in your wallet now says "$100." And your bank statement says that your $4,000 in savings is now $40,000. Everything involving a dollar sign gets multiplied by ten. It's like the dollar has shrunk and its value is one-tenth of what it was before. But in another sense, nothing has changed, because everyone has 10 times as many of these shrunken dollars.

Now think about how this new economy will work. Apart from all those extra zeros floating around, nothing will change. Your purchasing power won't change, because your paycheque is 10 times higher to compensate for prices being 10 times higher. You won't change how many gumballs, trinkets, or jeans you buy, because the opportunity cost of buying each of these items remains unchanged. More generally, you won't change what stuff you buy, what you'll produce, or how many hours you work. Indeed, no one will change the *quantities* of the stuff they buy, sell, produce, or do. So that means that across the whole economy, this purely nominal change—a change in the number of zeros on each price tag—will have no effect on *real variables*: There'll be no change in the total amount of each good purchased, the quantity of production, or the purchasing power of your income.

This thought experiment highlights the idea that the costs of inflation aren't due to the price level being higher. Rather, it's the *process* of changing all these prices that's costly. The process of changing prices leads sellers to incur menu costs, buyers to incur shoe-leather costs, and unexpected price changes also create costly confusion and arbitrary redistribution.

Tying It Together

Congratulations on completing what's been a pretty thorough introduction to inflation. We've analysed what inflation is, how it's measured, and why it really matters. It's time to pull these threads together to see how what you've learned can guide you to make better decisions. When inflation strikes, there can be a big payoff from pursuing some of the following strategies:

Strategy one: Don't think in nominal terms. Recall the problem of money illusion: When people focus on dollar amounts rather than the underlying trade-offs, they make costly mistakes. Don't make that mistake. Whenever you're analysing dollar amounts—whether its pay raises, rosy revenue numbers, or investment returns—ask yourself whether inflation-adjusted numbers would better represent the underlying trade-offs. In most cases, they will.

Strategy two: Take opportunities to index for inflation. Savvy negotiators insist that their contract include *indexation* clauses, which means the wages or prices listed automatically rise with inflation. You'll worry less about a surprise burst of 5% inflation if you know that your contract ensures you'll automatically get a compensating 5% nominal wage rise. An added bonus is that you won't need to negotiate with your boss as often.

Strategy three: When inflation is high, spend more time looking for cheaper alternatives. Even though inflation describes a rise in the general price level, it typically reflects staggered rounds of individual price rises, as one store changes its prices this week, another changes next week, and so on. As a result higher inflation leads to greater dispersion across outlets in the price of individual goods and services. And that means it's worth shopping around a bit more, hoping to stumble upon a store that hasn't updated its prices in a while. When you do, you're likely to find a few bargains.

Strategy four: When inflation is high, avoid holding cash. Inflation eats away at the value of money, and so when inflation starts running above a few percent a year, you should limit your holding of cash. This advice also applies to other forms of money: Keep the balance in your PayPal account down, and limit your use of everyday banking accounts that don't pay interest. You'll be better off stashing your funds in a savings account, where the nominal interest rate tends to rise with inflation, thereby protecting the real value of your savings.

Strategy five: Hedge against inflation risk. There are now some kinds of investment that allow you to hedge against the risk of inflation. In particular, the government issues inflation-indexed bonds, whose nominal interest payments automatically rise with inflation rate. These are arguably among the safest investments you can make, because there's no risk that inflation can undermine the real interest rate you earn.

Chapter at a Glance

Inflation: ***A generalised rise in the overall level of prices.***
Inflation can also be described as ***a rise in the cost of living.***
As a result, inflation is also ***a decline in the purchasing power of money.***

Measuring Inflation

The inflation measure that's most relevant to your life as a consumer is calculated using the **consumer price index (CPI)**, an index that tracks the average price consumers pay over time for a representative "basket" of goods and services.

To measure inflation:

1. Find out what people buy and construct a representative basket of goods and services.
2. Collect prices from the stores where people do their shopping.
3. Tally up the cost of the basket of goods and services.
4. Calculate the **inflation rate**: The annual percentage increase in the average price level.

$$\text{Inflation rate} = \frac{\text{Price level this year} - \text{Price level last year}}{\text{Price level last year}} \times 100$$

Adjusting for the Effects of Inflation

Real variable: A variable that has been adjusted to account for inflation.

Nominal variable: A variable measured in dollars (whose values may fluctuate over time).

You can convert **nominal variables** into **real variables** by applying the inflation adjustment formula:

$$\text{Today's dollars} = \text{Another time's dollars} \times \frac{\text{Price level today}}{\text{Price level in another time}}$$

For relatively small percentage changes:

$$\text{Percent change in real value} \approx \text{Percent change in nominal value} - \text{Percent change in prices}$$

$$\text{Real interest rate} \approx \text{Nominal interest rate} - \text{Inflation rate}$$

Money illusion: The (mistaken) tendency to focus on nominal dollar amounts instead of inflation-adjusted amounts.
Money illusion creates **nominal wage rigidity** (reluctance to cut nominal wages).

Different Measures of Inflation

Consumer Prices

1. **Cost of living adjustments** → consumer price index (CPI)
2. **A flexible target for monetary policy** → 2%-3%
3. **Forecasting underlying inflation trends** → Core inflation (excluding volatile items)

Business Prices

1. **Cost of inputs** → producer price index (PPI)
2. **Estimating the price of all output and hence real GDP** → GDP deflator

Inflation Overstates the Cost of Living Because of . . .

- Unmeasured quality improvements
- New products
- Substitution bias

Money: ***Any asset regularly used in transactions.***

- Medium of exchange
- Unit of account
- Store of value

The Costs of Inflation

Expected inflation

1. Menu costs for sellers
2. Shoe-leather costs for buyers

Unexpected inflation

3. Confuses the signals that prices send
4. Redistribution

The inflation fallacy: The mistaken belief that inflation destroys purchasing power.

Key Concepts

consumer price index (CPI), 606
deflation, 608
GDP deflator, 612
hyperinflation, 618
indexation, 611
inflation, 606
inflation fallacy, 621
inflation rate, 606
menu costs, 620
money, 617
money illusion, 615
nominal interest rate, 615
nominal variable, 614
nominal wage rigidity, 616
producer price index (PPI), 612
real interest rate, 615
real variable, 614
shoe-leather costs, 620
substitution bias, 610

Discussion and Review Questions

Learning Objective 24.1 *Understand what inflation is and how to measure it.*

1. You go to the petrol station and see that the price of petrol is unchanged. Can you use this observation to determine that the economy is not experiencing inflation? Explain your reasoning.
2. Does a change in the average price of water or a change in the average rent for housing have a bigger impact on CPI?
3. Think about constructing a CPI for students. What do you think belongs in the basket of goods and services for the average student? Do you think that the value of the basket over time has likely changed more or less than the CPI? Why?
4. Besides smartphones, come up with an example of a good that has increased or even decreased in quality over time while the price has remained relatively constant. Explain how the change in quality could bias CPI.

Learning Objective 24.2 *Pick the right inflation measure for the task at hand.*

5. Both CPI and the GDP deflator measure the change in the price of goods and services and tend to change in similar ways over time. In the third quarter of 2019, CPI rose by 1.7% from the previous quarter while the GDP deflator rose by 2.1% over the same time period. Explain what might lead them to rise at different rates using what you know about the differences between CPI and the GDP deflator.

Learning Objective 24.3 *Learn to account for the influence of inflation before making big decisions.*

6. You tell your grandmother about a car you're thinking of buying and, as expected, she tells you a story about buying her first brand new car for $1,500. You feel envious of older generations and wish you could buy a new car for $1,500. Explain how you are falling victim to money illusion.
7. During the 2020 coronavirus pandemic, a slight majority of economists came out in favour of freezing the minimum wage to support economic recovery. What would this do to the real incomes of workers on the minimum wage and why?

Learning Objective 24.4 *Analyse the role of money so that you can assess the costs of inflation.*

8. Explain how you would trade your efforts for goods or services you need if the economy did not use money of any kind? How does money make trade easier?
9. Is inflation more costly if it is expected or unexpected?

Study Problems

Learning Objective 24.1 *Understand what inflation is and how to measure it.*

1. Which of the following are signs of inflation?
   a. The price of a house in a high-demand market increased by 6% last year.
   b. CPI in the European Union was 101 in 2017 and 104 in 2018.
   c. The price of lithium-ion batteries falls as new production technologies make manufacturing cheaper.
2. CPI in Australia was 116.2 in 2019 and 117.2 in 2020. What was the inflation rate in 2020?
3. Suppose the typical university student spends money primarily on the products in the following table.

Product	Quantity	2020 price	2021 price
Soft Drink	365	$2.25	$2.30
Pizzas	200	$10.00	$11.00
Chicken wings	165	$7.00	$7.50
Rent	1	$10,000	$10,800
Textbooks	4	$150	$165

   a. What is the cost of the basket in 2020?
   b. What is the cost of the basket in 2021?

c. What is the 2021 inflation rate for a university student?

d. Has the cost of living for university students risen or fallen?

4. For each scenario below, determine which challenge of measuring the true cost of living—quality improvements, new products, or substitution bias—a price index constructed 15 years ago would experience.

a. A typical family owns more mobile phones and fewer landline telephones than it did a decade ago. The average price of a mobile phone plan is lower than that of a residential line.

b. Very few households had high-speed internet connections 15 years ago. Now most households do and the average price has fallen each year.

c. Over the last 10 years, personal computers have gotten faster and acquired many new features that enable users to perform many more tasks.

Learning Objective 24.2 *Pick the right inflation measure for the task at hand.*

5. Which measure or measures of inflation should be used in the following scenarios and why?

a. You're a buyer at an oil refinery that is facing rising input costs. Your manager asks you to determine if your competitors are also experiencing rising input prices.

b. A teacher's union wants to include annual cost-of-living adjustments in their next contract.

Learning Objective 24.3 *Learn to account for the influence of inflation before making big decisions.*

6. The average weekly household income in Australia in 1994 was $640 and CPI was 62.8. Convert the average income in 1994 to 2021 dollars if CPI was 117.2 in 2020.

7. In 2003, Julia Roberts was paid a then record-shattering US$25 million for her role in the film *Mona Lisa Smile*. In 2013, Sandra Bullock earned US$70 million for the film *Gravity*. Given that the CPI in the U.S. was 184.0 in 2003, and 233.0 in 2013, determine which of the two had higher real earnings.

8. In 2016, BHP's revenue was $31 billion, and it grew to $61 billion in 2021.

a. What is the nominal growth rate of BHP's revenue from 2016 to 2021?

b. What is the value of BHP's 2021 revenue in 2017 dollars? (In 2017, the CPI was 112.1 and in 2021, it was 118.8.)

c. What is the real growth rate of BHP's revenue from 2017 to 2021?

9. You open a savings account with a 0.5% per year nominal interest rate, and the economy experiences 3% per year inflation. What is your nominal and real annual interest rate on the account? What will happen to the purchasing power of money you place in the account over time?

10. Behavioural economists have discovered that people view a 2% decrease in their income without inflation as unfair, but a 3% increase in their income in the presence of 5% inflation as fair. What are the nominal and real rates of change in their incomes? What tendency is leading people to feel like the pay decrease is unfair?

Learning Objective 24.4 *Analyse the role of money so that you can assess the costs of inflation.*

11. For each scenario, determine which function of money is being described.

a. Robert pays $4.00 to cross the Harbour Bridge.

b. Liza considers which is the better deal: a desk lamp priced at $24.99 or a hanging lamp priced at $29.99.

c. Gilberto deposits $1,000 in his savings account.

d. Carmela examines a menu posted outside a restaurant, trying to determine whether a meal there would fit within her budget.

12. Identify which cost of inflation—menu costs or shoe-leather costs—is illustrated in each of the following scenarios.

a. During the German hyperinflation of 1922–1923, some workers reportedly were paid two to three times per day. They would then rush out to spend their earnings before they became nearly worthless.

b. A hyperinflation in Zimbabwe was so severe that, according to one observer of supermarket employees, they were "running around that store with label makers, changing the prices three, four times a day."

13. You take out a home loan to help pay for your first house at a 3% annual interest rate. Assume the bank expected inflation to average 2% per year. What real interest rate did they expect to earn from your loan? What happens if inflation is actually 3% per year? Who is better off if inflation is higher than expected? What if it is lower than expected? Why?

14. The cost of the average consumer's basket of goods and services in 2020 is roughly 25 times what it was in 1950. In other words, what the average consumer bought for $100 in 1950 would cost a consumer $2,500 in 2020. Does this mean that the purchasing power of the average consumer is one-twenty-fifth what it was in 1950? Explain your reasoning.

PART VII:

Micro Foundations of Macroeconomics

Part VII: Micro Foundations of Macroeconomics

The Big Picture

The chapters ahead are all based on the same idea: The behaviour of the macroeconomic whole reflects millions of individual microeconomic decisions. And so if you want to understand the big picture, you'll need to understand decisions that you—and countless people just like you—make every day.

We'll start by analysing how people make **consumption and saving** decisions. We'll see that deciding whether to spend your money today or save it for the future is all about making trade-offs over time. Next, we'll examine how managers make **investment** decisions that involve trading off a big upfront cost for an ongoing stream of future benefits. Along the way, we'll share economic insights into how you can make better consumption, saving, and investment decisions in your own life.

We'll then apply these ideas to the **financial sector,** where we'll evaluate the different opportunities offered by stocks, bonds, and banks. We'll assess whether to trust financial experts, whether you can beat the market, and whether your money is safe. Finally, we'll turn to the **international sector,** where we'll explore the opportunities offered by globalisation, as we analyse the decisions you make about whether to invest abroad, whether to buy or sell Australian dollars, and whether to import or export goods.

25 Consumption and Saving

Learn to make smart spending and saving decisions.

- Why do Australians spend so much money?
- How much should you spend and how much should you save?
- Does consumption respond differently to changes in income that are temporary or permanent? Does it respond differently to changes in income that are anticipated versus unanticipated?
- How do consumers respond to changing economic conditions?
- Why do people save, and should they save more?

26 Investment

Analyse how managers can make good investment decisions.

- Why are investment decisions so important in determining macroeconomic outcomes?
- How can investors compare the values of money they receive at different points in time?
- When is an investment worth pursuing?
- How do changing economic conditions affect whether an investment is worthwhile?
- What determines the long-run real interest rate?

27 The Financial Sector

Understand the role played by the financial sector.

- What are banks, what do they do, and is your bank really safe?
- What are bonds, and what does the bond market do?
- What are stocks, and what does the stock market do?
- How can you value stocks, and can you predict where stock prices are going?
- Are expert stock pickers any good?
- How can you make better decisions with your own investments?

28 International Finance and the Exchange Rate

Understand the linkages between the exchange rate, imports, and exports.

- How closely is the Australian economy linked to the global economy?
- What's a dollar really worth?
- Why does the Australian dollar rise and fall?
- How does the value of the Australian dollar affect your company's international competitiveness?
- How can you track how money flows around the world?

CHAPTER 25

Consumption and Saving

Carla Gottgens/Bloomberg/Getty Images

What will you do with your money?

Chapter Objective

Learn to make smart spending and saving decisions.

25.1 Consumption, Saving, and Income
Understand how consumption and saving vary with income.

25.2 The Micro Foundations of Consumption
Apply the core principles of economics to make good consumption decisions.

25.3 The Macroeconomics of Consumption
Predict the behaviour of aggregate measures of consumption.

25.4 What Shifts Consumption?
Assess how changing macroeconomic conditions shift consumption.

25.5 Saving
Learn how to form a smart saving plan.

Turn on a TV, skim through your news feed, or talk to an older relative, and you'll be bombarded with advice about how you should spend, save, or borrow. Spend more, says one; avoid debt, says another. A talking head on TV warns of the perils of debt only hours before you use Afterpay to buy that new shirt you've been wanting. As you read a newspaper bemoaning a housing debt crisis, a low-balance text alert reminds you that you could really use a bit more money to help you through university. One budget guru advises you to avoid the perils of credit cards, while another urges you to take out a credit card to improve your credit score. Your parents tell you to get a part-time job, but your academic advisor suggests that you borrow money so you can focus on your studies.

The reason for all the conflicting advice is because your best spending and saving choices depend on your personal situation, including your personal goals, life trajectory, and the risks you face along the way. This means that you're the one who's going to have to steer the ship. But there are some general principles that tend to guide people's spending and saving decisions. We'll carefully lay out the economic logic that will give you the tools you need to figure out the best spending, borrowing, and saving decisions for you. Along the way, we'll also consider some common mistakes people make.

As you think through your own spending and saving decisions, you'll gain insight into how other people think about theirs. The macroeconomy is simply the sum of the decisions of many individuals, and so this approach (known among economists as building from the micro foundations of macroeconomics) will give you an understanding of the broad drivers of consumption and saving across the whole economy.

We'll begin the chapter by analysing total consumer spending, or *consumption*, across the whole economy. Then we'll zoom in on individual consumers—like you!—to assess how people tend to make consumption choices. We'll then pan back, and assess what that means for the macroeconomy. Consumption and saving are linked, since what you don't spend, you save. So we'll conclude by exploring what all this means for saving—both your saving and national saving.

25.1 Consumption, Saving, and Income

Learning Objective *Understand how consumption and saving vary with income.*

Figure 1 | Gross Domestic Product

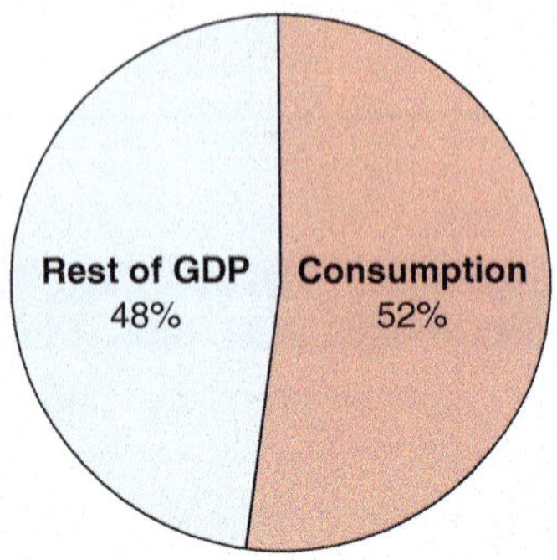

2021 Data from: Australian Bureau of Statistics.

consumption Household spending on final goods and services.

consumption function A curve plotting the level of consumption associated with each level of income.

Consumption refers to household spending on final goods and services. It's a big deal, because it's by far the single largest component of GDP, and as Figure 1 shows, it accounts for more than half of total spending. Consumption includes spending on things like food, rent, clothes, electricity, medical bills, mobile phones, cars, computers, and internet service. Just about the only thing that people buy in their personal lives that is excluded from consumption is the purchase of a new home, which is counted as investment.

Consumption and Income

Income is one of the key factors determining consumption, and we use the **consumption function** to show the relationship between consumption and income.

The consumption function plots the level of consumption associated with each level of income. It's a summary of household spending plans, showing how total consumption spending varies with the level of total income. Figure 2 shows the consumption function, illustrating how different levels of income (shown on the horizontal axis) lead to different levels of consumption spending (shown on the vertical axis). The consumption function is upward-sloping: It starts low on the left, and as you move to the right, it rises, illustrating that higher income leads to higher consumption. In this example, it's shown as a straight line, but it need not be—its shape depends on the actual choices that people make. The consumption function is upward-sloping because when people have more income, they tend to spend more.

Figure 2 | The Consumption Function

A The consumption function shows how consumption varies depending on the level of income.

B It is upward sloping because more income leads to more consumption.

C The slope of the consumption function, called the **marginal propensity to consume,** describes the extra consumption that arises from each dollar of extra income.

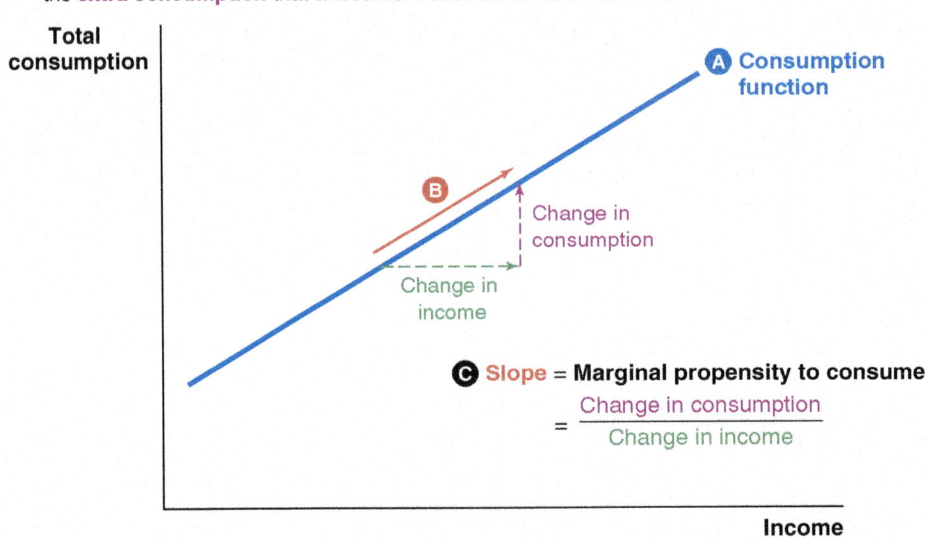

marginal propensity to consume The fraction of each extra dollar of income that households spend on consumption.

The marginal propensity to consume tells you how much consumption rises when income rises. The fraction of each extra dollar of income that households spend on consumption is called the **marginal propensity to consume.** You can measure the marginal propensity to consume by observing how consumption responds to a change in income. It's the ratio of the change in consumption to the change in income. Your individual marginal propensity to consume is one if you immediately spend all of any extra income you receive, and it's zero if you save all of any extra income (spending none of it right away). Most people will spend some of their extra income right away, but will also typically save some of it (to spend later). And so the marginal propensity to consume, which is the proportion of each extra dollar consumed, is typically greater than zero, but less than one.

The marginal propensity to consume is an important concept in macroeconomics because it tells you how much consumption will increase when total income or GDP increases. If the average marginal propensity to consume is 0.6, then a $100 billion increase in total income will lead to a $60 billion rise in consumption.

The marginal propensity to consume determines the slope of the consumption function. To see this, remember the slope of a line is "rise over run," and so the slope of the consumption function is the ratio of the change in consumption to the change in income (which is the marginal propensity to consume!).

Interpreting the DATA Why consumption is so high in Australia

Casper Hedberg/Bloomberg/Getty Images

Consumption per person in Australia is higher now than at any time in our history, and is higher than in many other countries.

You're living in extraordinary times. Average consumption per person in Australia is higher than at any time in our history, and it's also higher than in many other countries. We're consuming more, per person, than we ever have been. The consumption function helps explain why. Consumption is higher than it was in the past because incomes are higher. Each dot in the scatterplot shown in the left panel of Figure 3 shows average consumption and average income—that is, GDP per person—in Australia in an individual year. (In this graph, as throughout the whole chapter, all data are adjusted for inflation and thus are real GDP per person.) The dots lie along an upward-sloping line, illustrating that average consumption per person has risen as GDP per person has risen over time—just as the consumption function predicts. The most recent data are at the top right, and they show that current record levels of consumption per person are exactly what you'd expect given recent levels of GDP per person.

Each dot in the right panel of Figure 3 plots average consumption and GDP per person for an individual country in 2019, which is the latest comparable data. This figure

Figure 3 | **Consumption and GDP**

Consumption Rises with Income over Time

Each dot shows average income and consumption in Australia in one year

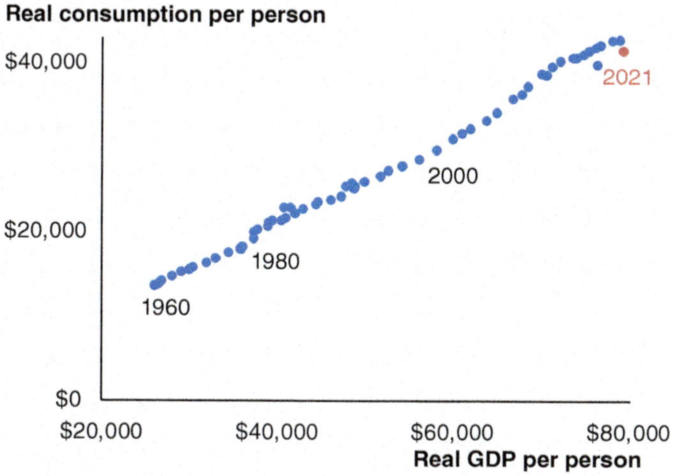

Consumption is Higher in High-Income Countries

Each dot shows income and consumption for a country in 2019, adjusted for differences in the cost of living

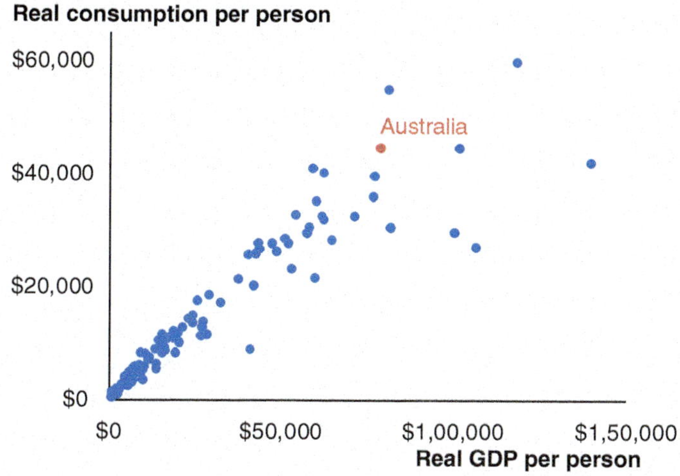

Data from: Australian Bureau of Statistics; World Bank.

shows that average consumption is higher in Australia than in lots of other countries because Australians enjoy a higher average income than nearly any other country. Again, the dots are clustered along an upward-sloping line, illustrating that people in countries with higher GDP per person tend to spend more on consumption. These two charts show the consumption function in real life! ■

Saving and Income

saving The portion of income that you set aside, rather than spending on consumption.

Consumption rises with income, but most people don't tend to spend all of the additional income they get right away. What do they do with the rest? They save it. **Saving** is the portion of income that you set aside rather than spending on consumption. Because every dollar you don't spend is saved, your consumption decisions determine your saving. Equally, every dollar you don't save you must spend, and so your saving decisions determine your consumption. Consumption and saving are simply two sides of the same coin:

$$\text{Saving} = \text{Income} - \text{Consumption}$$

dissaving The excess amount you consume above your income in a given period that you therefore must pay for by either withdrawing money from your savings or borrowing money.

If you consume less than your income, then you'll save the remainder. Whether you sock that unspent income away in the bank or use it to pay down existing debts such as your credit card, car loan, or HECS-HELP loan, it counts as saving. Alternatively, if your consumption exceeds your income—as it does for many students—you are **dissaving** (sometimes referred to as negative saving). Whether you fund this gap between your spending and your income by borrowing money—say, by taking on credit card debt—or by withdrawing money from your savings, it counts as dissaving.

From a microeconomic perspective, saving is important because it adds to your wealth, allowing you to boost your consumption in the future. From a macroeconomic perspective, saving is important because it provides the flow of resources the financial sector uses to fund investment projects.

net wealth The amount by which your assets exceed your debts.

In all of this, we're focusing on the *flow* of new saving—the extra money you save during a specific period of time, such as a year. Over many years of saving, you'll build up a *stock* of wealth, and the amount by which your assets exceed your debts is called your **net wealth.** Saving increases your net wealth, but dissaving decreases it.

Do the Economics

Let's apply these new ideas—of the consumption function and the relationship between income and savings—to your personal situation. Your financial life in college is often a bit tricky, so let's fast-forward and imagine your economic future a few years after graduation. How much will you spend each year if your annual income is $20,000? What if your income is $40,000? Or $60,000? How much of an $80,000 income will you spend? As you answer these questions, fill in the blanks in the middle column of the table in Figure 4. Make sure your choices are responsible, because if you can't pay your bills, you'll find yourself in debt. Since saving and consumption are two sides of the same coin, once you've decided how much to spend at each level of income, you've also made your saving plans. Calculate your saving in the final column of the table in Figure 4.

Finally, plot your consumption choices in the chart on the right of Figure 4. Connect the dots, and that's it! You've discovered your consumption function. If you're like most people, you'll discover that:

- Your consumption function is upward-sloping because more income leads you to increase your consumption.
- But for each extra dollar of income that you receive, your consumption rises by less than a dollar.

Figure 4 | Discover Your Consumption Function

Panel A: Your Consumption Function

Income includes income from all sources, but not loans. Consumption counts all spending on goods and services.

Your income	Your consumption	Your saving (= Income − Consumption)
$20,000		
$40,000		
$60,000		
$80,000		

Panel B: Your Consumption Function

How much higher will your consumption spending be at each different income level?

To graph your consumption function, plot the results from the table on the left, and connect the dots.

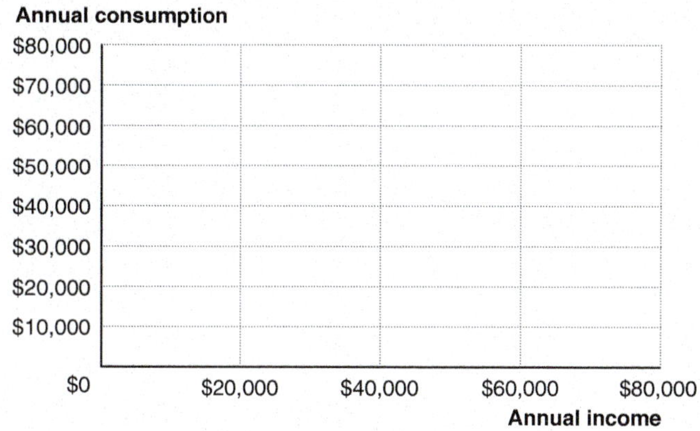

At this point, we've used the consumption function to describe the spending (and hence saving) decisions that people make. Now it's time to analyse how people figure out how much to spend, save, and borrow. This window into consumers' thinking will help us evaluate how changing macroeconomic conditions affect total consumption across the whole economy.

25.2 The Micro Foundations of Consumption

Learning Objective *Apply the core principles of economics to make good consumption decisions.*

It's the start of the university year. You've saved wisely from your full-time job over the summer. And although you work one day a week during semester, you need to make your summer-job money stretch throughout the year. You realise that you need to figure out how to allocate your scarce funds over the next several months, deciding how much to spend this month, versus saving for next month and the months after. It's a consequential decision. Get it wrong, and you won't have enough money for entertainment, or even good food in a few months time.

How should you decide how much to spend now, versus save for later? This question motivates our next task, which is to develop a framework that you can use to make smart spending, saving, and borrowing choices throughout your life. This framework also yields insight into how other people make spending and saving decisions. Total consumption is the sum of consumption decisions made by millions of Americans, and so these same insights will help you understand the macroeconomics of consumption. By understanding how individual people make their consumption decisions, we'll build up an understanding of the whole.

UpperCut Images/Getty Images

How much should you spend?

Choosing How Much to Spend and How Much to Save

The *interdependence principle* says that the choices available to you in the future depend on the decisions you make today. This insight is particularly relevant to your consumption decisions because the spending and saving decisions you make today determine your future options. Spend too much today and your credit card debt will create future repayment challenges. Alternatively, saving instead of spending provides a buffer you might find helpful next month. It's critical that your consumption decisions account for these future consequences.

Apply the core principles to decide how much to consume. The key consumption decision you face is: *How many* dollars should you spend this month given your income? Your answer will determine not only how much you'll consume, but also how much you'll need to borrow or be able to save for next month.

This is a "how many" question, and the *marginal principle* reminds you that it's simpler to break it into a series of smaller marginal choices, asking: Should I increase my current consumption by one more dollar? If the answer is yes, then you need to ask whether to spend one more dollar, and then another dollar, and so on.

At each iteration, the *cost-benefit principle* says yes, you should increase your consumption by a dollar if the benefit of an extra dollar of consumption exceeds the cost. *The benefit of an extra dollar of consumption is called the marginal benefit of consumption.*

What about the cost of that extra consumption? Turn to the *opportunity cost principle*, which reminds you to ask, "Or what?" You could consume an extra dollar this month, *or what?* Or you could save that dollar, earn interest, and then spend that dollar-plus-interest in the future. As such, the cost of an extra dollar of consumption this year is the forgone opportunity to consume a dollar-plus-interest in the future. (When in the future? Opportunity cost is all about the next best alternative, so you should think about whenever in the future you'll get the largest marginal benefit.) Thus, *the opportunity cost of an extra dollar of consumption today is the marginal benefit of consuming a dollar-plus-interest in the future.*

The Rational Rule for Consumers

At this point, we've figured out that you should weigh the marginal benefit of increasing your consumption in the present against the marginal benefit of increasing your consumption by a bit more in the future. Put the pieces together, and you'll discover that we've uncovered a powerful rule that you can apply to your consumption decisions:

Rational Rule for Consumers Consume more today if the marginal benefit of a dollar of consumption today is greater than (or equal to) the marginal benefit of spending a dollar plus interest in the future.

The **Rational Rule for Consumers:** *Consume more today if the marginal benefit of a dollar of consumption today is greater than (or equal to) the marginal benefit of spending a dollar-plus-interest in the future.*

This rule brings together three of our four core principles, in one sentence: You should think at the margin and evaluate whether to spend one more dollar (the *marginal principle*); compare the marginal benefit of raising consumption today with the marginal cost (the *cost-benefit principle*); and in evaluating that marginal cost, account for the forgone opportunity to increase consumption in the future by a dollar-plus-interest (the *opportunity cost principle*).

Compare the marginal benefit of spending a dollar today to the marginal benefit of spending a dollar-plus-interest in the future. Notice that the *Rational Rule for Consumers* effectively turns your attention from the original question of *how much* to spend today to the more helpful question of *when* to consume. It says to be *forward-looking*, so that you should spend another dollar today only if it yields a larger marginal benefit than spending a dollar-plus-interest in the future. By following this rule, you'll spend each dollar at the moment in which it yields the largest possible benefit to you. As such, it ensures that you'll get the largest possible benefit from your limited income.

You should keep spending until the marginal benefit is the same over time. The trade-off underlying the *Rational Rule for Consumers* is that the benefit of delaying consumption is the interest you can earn, while the cost is that you'll have to wait to enjoy that consumption. For most people, the benefit of earning interest roughly cancels out the cost of waiting, and so we can simplify the rational rule by putting these two factors aside for now (though we'll return to interest rates later). That simplification allows the rational rule to speak more directly: It says that you should keep increasing today's consumption and decreasing future consumption until the marginal benefit of a dollar of consumption is *the same* today as it will be tomorrow. If you apply this rule again tomorrow, you'll make adjustments until the marginal benefit of consumption is the same tomorrow as the day after. Follow the logic further, and you'll end up making consumption plans so that *the marginal benefit of the last dollar of consumption is the same in the present as in every future period.*

Consumption Smoothing

consumption smoothing Maintaining a steady or smooth path for your consumption spending over time.

Consumption smoothing describes the idea that you should maintain a steady or smooth path for your consumption spending over time. Indeed, it says that you should try to maintain a stable level of consumption over time, even if your income fluctuates. As we're about to see, it's one of the most important implications of the *Rational Rule for Consumers*.

Consumption smoothing helps you avoid diminishing marginal benefits. Diminishing marginal benefit is the idea that each additional dollar of consumption yields a successively smaller marginal benefit. It says that the marginal benefit of the first few dollars of spending are high and then decline as you spend more. It's relevant because the *Rational Rule for Consumers* says to reallocate your spending so that the marginal benefit of the last dollar of consumption is the same in the present as in the future. And so following this rule means reallocating your spending from times when the marginal benefit is low (which is when consumption is high) to times when the marginal benefit is high (which is when consumption is low). As such, it suggests reallocating your spending from times when your consumption is high to times when it's low, leading your consumption to be relatively smooth or stable over time.

This logic says that instead of spending your summer-job earnings early in the year, you'll be better off distributing your spending evenly, or smoothly, throughout the year. Figure 5 illustrates this point, showing that redistributing a dollar of consumption from a time when your spending is high (a time of plenty) to a time when it's low (a time of poverty) leads to an increase in your total benefits. Indeed, each move you make towards more equal consumption over time raises your well-being because you're moving your spending from times when the marginal benefit is low to times when the marginal benefit is high. Follow this logic far enough, and you'll conclude that—as long as your needs aren't changing—it's best to spend the same today as tomorrow. That is, you're best off smoothing your consumption.

Figure 5 | Smooth Your Consumption

(A) **Diminishing marginal benefit** leads to a declining **marginal benefit curve**.

(B) **Consumption smoothing** requires redistributing spending from times of **plenty (high consumption with a low marginal benefit)**, to times of **poverty (low consumption with a high marginal benefit)**.

(C) This is beneficial because the **marginal benefit of an extra dollar during times of poverty** exceeds the **marginal benefit of an extra dollar during times of plenty**.

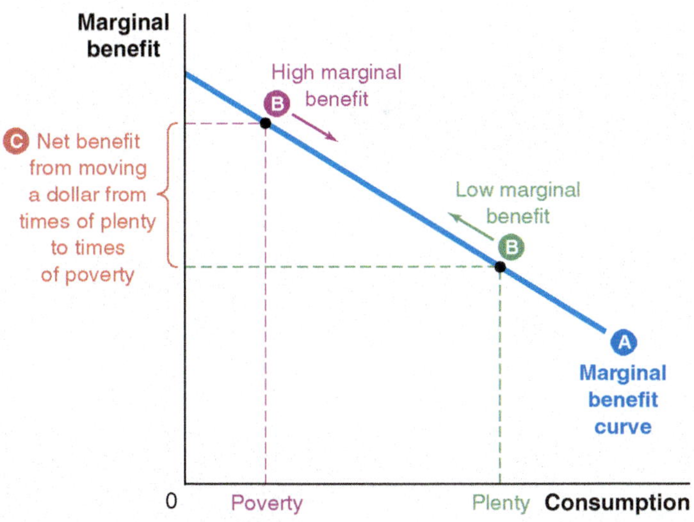

Make a deal with your future self.

It's like making a deal with your future self. Thinking about how much to spend today versus in the future can seem like a hard problem. There's another way to think about this that you might find more intuitive. It's just about making sure your decision takes account of both your current self, who enjoys this month's consumption, and your future self, who'll enjoy next month's. Put too much weight on your future self and you'll spend too little today. Put too much weight on your current self and you'll spend too much. Your current and future selves have to figure out how to split your resources over time in a way that makes these two versions of you as happy as possible. If you decide that they each should consume as much as the other, then you've decided that you should smooth your consumption across time.

TeamDAF/Shutterstock

Pace yourself.

EVERYDAY Economics **How to run a marathon, enjoy a bag of cookies, and survive the weekend**

In fact, the idea of consumption smoothing is so intuitive that you probably already apply it to many areas of your life. It's relevant whenever you have to distribute scarce resources over time in the presence of diminishing marginal benefit.

When you toe the starting line of a marathon, you have limited energy to distribute over the next 42.2 kilometres. Most runners aim to smooth their energy consumption, running the first half at exactly the same speed as the second half. Spend too much energy in the first half, and the second half will be painful and slow. (Justin swears that this is true!) Save too much energy in the first half, and you'll fall so far behind your target pace that even the extra energy you've stored up won't be enough to make up those lost minutes. It's far better to smooth your energy consumption.

Marathon strategy is surprisingly similar to cookie strategy. If you've ever bought a bag of delicious cookies, you'll know the temptation to eat the whole bag today, leaving none for tomorrow. That would match your cookie consumption with your cookie income. Don't do it. You'll be even happier if you smooth your cookie consumption, enjoying a delicious cookie every day until the bag runs out.

And that's the same challenge you face over the weekend. Stay up all night on Friday night, and you won't have enough energy left to enjoy Saturday's party. Pace yourself by smoothing your socialising over the weekend, and you'll enjoy it more. ■

The same advice applies: Pace yourself.

The timing of your income is irrelevant. There's an interesting implication of all of this: The *timing* of your income—whether you receive it today or in the future—should not be relevant to your consumption choices. After all, the *Rational Rule for Consumers* says to allocate your consumption to whenever it'll yield the largest marginal benefit. It doesn't say anything about whether you received that income today, next month, or next year. But even if the *timing* of your income isn't relevant, the *level* of your income does matter. To see precisely how, we'll need to introduce one more big idea.

Permanent Income Hypothesis

Ultimately, your income does constrain your consumption, although when you can save or borrow money, it isn't just today's income that matters. Rather, your forward-looking spending plans are constrained by the total resources you have available to allocate to consumption over the long term. That's why instead of your *current* income, you should focus on your **permanent income,** which is your best estimate of your long-term average income. It measures the resources that are available for you to consume, on average, over the course of your lifetime.

permanent income Your best estimate of your long-term average income.

The higher your permanent income, the more you can afford to consume both today and in the future. And so before deciding whether you want to take on that HECS-HELP loan, you should think about what you expect to earn after you graduate. If you're earning good grades in a highly paid field—say, computer science—then your expectation of a high income after you graduate means that your permanent income is high, even if your current income is low. That higher permanent income means that you can afford to take on more loans and spend more in your student years, knowing that you'll find it easy to repay those loans out of the big bucks you expect to earn after graduation. But if you dream of being a social worker—earning good vibes, but not big bucks—your permanent income is lower, and so you'll want to be more cautious with your consumption (and hence borrowing) while you're in university.

The idea that people choose how much to consume based on their *permanent income* (rather than their *current income*) is called the **permanent income hypothesis.** It has important macroeconomic implications because it says that economic fluctuations only matter to the extent that they affect permanent income. (We'll return to this idea shortly.)

permanent income hypothesis The idea that consumption is driven by permanent income rather than current income.

You'll need to borrow and save to smooth your consumption. If you set your consumption level based on your permanent income, then you'll need to borrow or save whenever your current income and permanent income differ. For instance, whenever your current income is below your permanent income—that is, when your income is less than you expect its long-term average to be—you'll spend more than you earn, and so you'll need to borrow or run down your savings. You'll fund this by saving when your current income is higher than your permanent income. This suggests that you can gauge whether you should be saving or dissaving by comparing your current income with your permanent income.

Saving will vary over your life course. This logic explains why saving varies over your life course. Figure 6 illustrates with a stylised example. The red line shows how income typically varies over the course of your life—it rises sharply as you accumulate experience and seniority and then peaks in mid-career, before slowly declining as you get older. The blue line shows a constant (that is, smooth) level of consumption, set equal to the permanent or average income associated with the red line. Borrowing, saving, or dissaving make up the difference between current consumption and current income. This figure shows that the combination of a hump-shaped life cycle in income, and relatively constant consumption explains why people tend to borrow while they're young, save during their working years, and spend down their savings during retirement.

Figure 6 | Income and Saving over the Life Cycle

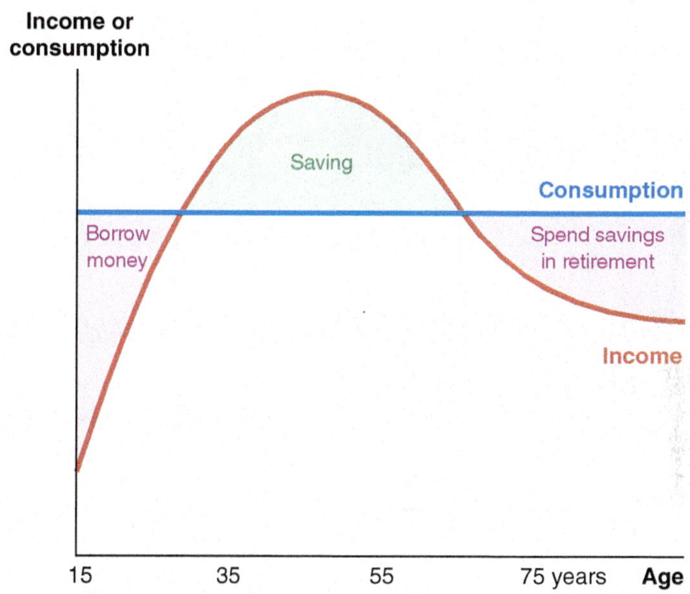

Of course, your reality will be somewhat messier than this stylised example, as your consumption needs will change over your lifetime. That means your spending patterns may not be as stable as in this example. You'll also learn new information over time about your permanent income, and you'll adjust your consumption to fit your new expectations about your earnings. Even after adjusting for these issues, the basic idea of the life-cycle pattern holds. It describes the reality that the typical young person accumulates debt, while the typical retiree lives off their savings. In the middle, people have to pay their debt and build their retirement savings, and so they spend less than they earn.

25.3 The Macroeconomics of Consumption

Learning Objective *Predict the behaviour of aggregate measures of consumption.*

We've now uncovered the two big ideas that are the building blocks of the macroeconomics of consumption. People make decisions about how much to consume—and thus how much to save—considering their *permanent income,* and they prefer to *smooth consumption* over time. Because these forces drive individual people's consumption choices, they also drive total consumption in the economy. And so these two big ideas have important implications for the macroeconomic link between total income and total consumption. They'll help you see where the economy is going and

Five insights about the relationship between consumption and income:

1. A temporary change in income leads to a small change in consumption.
2. A permanent change in income leads to a large change in consumption.
3. An anticipated change in income leads to no change in consumption.
4. Learning about a future income change leads to a change in consumption.
5. It's hard to forecast changes in consumption.

Carla Gottgens/Bloomberg/Getty Images

Don't spend it all at once.

better understand how total consumption will change in response to changing macroeconomic conditions.

The Relationship Between Consumption and Income

Income is an important determinant of consumption and when income changes, consumption changes. But there are different kinds of changes in income and these different kinds of changes in income have different implications for consumption. We'll now dig into five important insights that will help you identify different types of income changes and how those changes will likely impact consumption.

Insight one: A temporary change in income leads to a small change in consumption. What would you do if you won a $1 million lottery (after tax)? A lottery win is a *temporary* boost in income because you don't expect to win it again. So how would you adjust your consumption in response? I hope you won't go out and blow the whole million bucks tomorrow. I hope that you don't even spend half of it right away. A financial planner might advise you to spend $50,000 of it each year, so that you can enjoy higher consumption for the rest of your life.

The desire to spread a *temporary* spike in income out over your lifetime is why a temporary increase yields only a relatively small increase in consumption. In this example, a temporary increase in income leads this year's consumption to rise by only $50,000. This yields a marginal propensity to consume (or *MPC*) out of a transitory rise in income of 0.05:

$$MPC_{Temporary} = \frac{\text{Change in consumption}}{\text{Temporary change in income}} = \frac{\$50{,}000}{\$1{,}000{,}000} = 0.05$$

Insight two: A permanent change in income leads to a large increase in consumption. A new job that'll boost your income by $50,000 per year forever is a much bigger deal than a one-off signing bonus of $50,000 that only temporarily raises your income. It's a bigger deal because a permanent change in income leads to a much larger change in your lifetime income. As a result, a permanent change in income leads to a larger change in consumption. This means that the marginal propensity to consume out of permanent income is much higher than it is out of temporary income.

For example, perhaps when you graduate you'll land a job as a first-year analyst at Macquarie with a starting pay of $110,000—which is much more than you ever expected. Even better, that initial job puts you on a career path in which you can expect to go on to earn even higher wages throughout your career. So it's not just a one-year boost, your future income is now a lot higher than you had previously anticipated. How should you respond? If your job at Macquarie Bank means that your income will be $50,000 per year higher than you anticipated, and you'll get that unexpected boost every year for the rest of your life, then that means that your permanent income has risen by $50,000 per year. Unlike a one-time gain, which you allocate over your remaining years of life, a permanent increase in your annual income means that you can enjoy increased consumption and income every year for the rest of your life.

The marginal propensity to consume out of a rise in permanent income is typically fairly high. In fact it could be as high as 1:

$$MPC_{Permanent} = \frac{\text{Change in consumption}}{\text{Permanent change in income}} = \frac{\$50{,}000}{\$50{,}000} = 1$$

To summarise: an unanticipated change in income that's likely to continue every year for the rest of your life yields an equally large change in permanent income, and so there is a correspondingly large increase in consumption.

Interpreting the DATA — What is your permanent income?

We've seen that your level of consumption should reflect your permanent income. But what is your permanent income? I don't know you personally, but a useful starting point is to analyse the typical earnings of people in different industries who work full time. By looking at the average salary in a particular industry, we can estimate what your total earnings are likely to be throughout your career.

Figure 7 illustrates the typical lifetime earnings of people working in different industries. We focus on the mean earnings, though this tends to be a little higher than the median because some people earn substantially more money than others in the same industry. At present, those who work in the mining industry seem to make the most (on average)—around $5 million over a full lifetime of work. This probably won't be the case forever, but Australia has had a large demand for mine workers for a long time. If you're reading this, the industry you're probably the most interested in is "Financial Services" or "Professional, Scientific, and Technical Services." These industries have an expected lifetime earnings of around $4 million, or $110,000 per year.

Figure 7 | Average Annual Earnings of Full-Time Workers over the Course of a Career

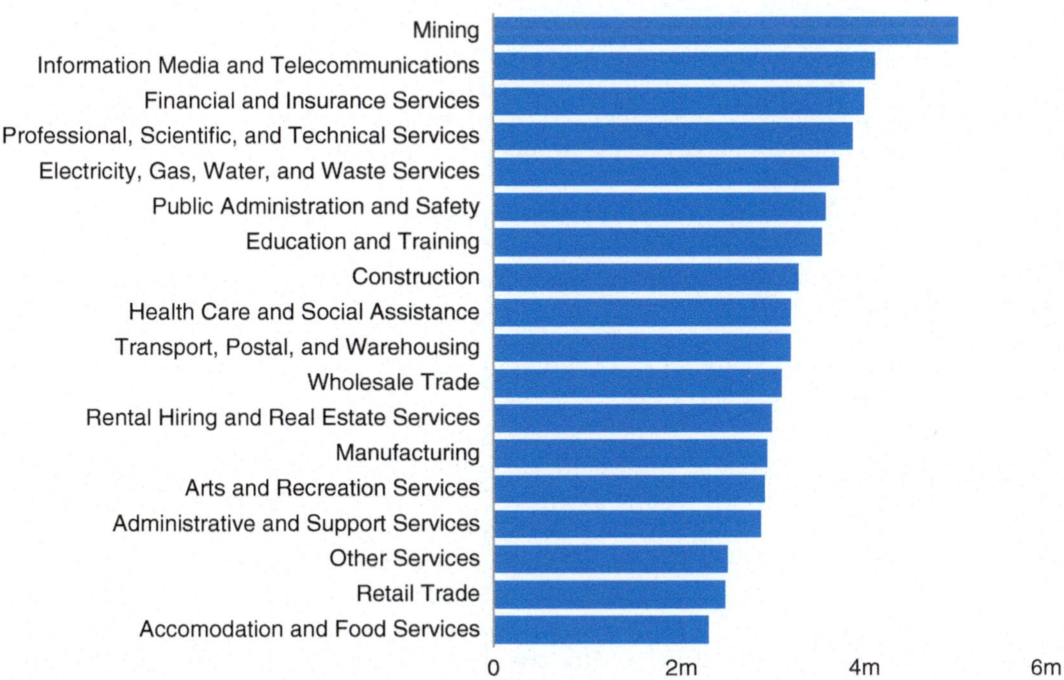

Data from: Australian Bureau of Statistics.

You might also notice that the industries with lower lifetime pay tend to be those that require less education (with the exception perhaps of mining). With more education, you not only start your career with higher earnings, but your earnings will tend to grow more sharply as you gain experience. In other words, choosing to go to university is even better than winning a million-dollar lottery because, relative to not attending university, the industries you can work in will earn you more than $1 million more than working in retail your whole life!

But don't expect to be making money like this straight away. Studies show that starting salaries are about half what they are at midcareer. So your earnings right out of the gate don't represent your permanent income, and it's likely your income will keep growing for another decade or more. ■

Insight three: An anticipated change in income leads to no change in consumption. Your permanent income is your best estimate of your long-term average income, and so it reflects your expectations about how your income will evolve over time. As such, it already factors in anticipated future changes to your income. And so if you set your consumption in line with your permanent income, then anticipated changes in income won't affect your consumption. As a result, the marginal propensity to consume out of anticipated changes in income is zero.

To see this concretely, put yourself in the shoes of a polling expert expecting to earn $60,000 in every third year (when there is a federal election), but $45,000 in other years (when you have fewer clients). Instead of cutting your consumption spending every second year only to raise it the next, you'll be better off spending $50,000 each year, which is in line with your permanent income. And so the anticipated rise in income in an election year has no effect on your consumption, just as the anticipated cut in income in off-election years has no effect.

Insight four: Learning about a future income change leads to a change in consumption. When does consumption respond to changes in future income? If you're basing your consumption on your permanent income, then you'll respond as soon as you get the news about a change in your future permanent income, rather than when the money actually arrives. (By that time, it has been fully anticipated and already factored in to your spending decisions.)

For instance, if your employer *unexpectedly* announces that in a year's time everyone will get a 4% higher-than-normal raise, then a consumption smoother will use that information to boost their consumption right away. This also works the other way—if your company unexpectedly announces a pay freeze such that next year's expected pay raise disappears, the permanent income hypothesis suggests that you should cut your consumption right away.

The broader point is that today's consumption can be quite sensitive to expectations about future income. This also suggests that changes in macroeconomic policy might have their largest effect on consumption when they're announced, rather than when they actually go into effect.

Insight five: It's hard to forecast changes in consumption. The final implication of all this is that changes in consumption are very difficult to forecast. After all, we've seen that consumption does not change much in response to *anticipated* changes in income. It only responds to *unanticipated* changes in income. But unanticipated changes are, by their nature, very difficult to forecast. After all, if they were easy to forecast, you would have anticipated them!

If changes in individual consumption are difficult to forecast, then it follows that changes in total consumption—the sum of the consumption decisions of millions of individual Australians who follow a similar logic—should also be difficult to forecast.

It's worth being careful about this implication. It doesn't say that the *level* of consumption is difficult to forecast. In fact, it's not: The level of consumption is usually a bit over half of GDP. Instead, it says that future *changes* in consumption are hard to predict. Take a look at the annual changes in aggregate consumption shown in Figure 8, and I think you'll agree that changes in consumption are hard to forecast. The change in consumption in each year appears roughly unrelated to what happened in previous years. And because consumption is about half of GDP, this also means that it's awfully difficult to predict changes in GDP.

Figure 8 | **Changes in Consumption Are Difficult to Forecast**

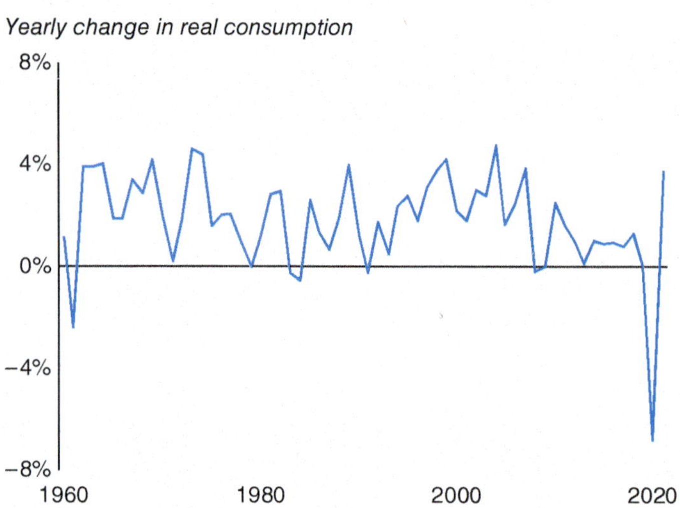

Data from: Australian Bureau of Statistics.

Adding Behavioural Economics and Credit Constraints to Our Analysis

We're exploring these ideas to give you a window into the thinking that underlies the consumption choices of the millions of Australians who make up the macroeconomy. Along the way you might have wondered: Do people actually make their consumption choices like this? As you might have guessed, there are limitations to how much people can smooth their consumption. It relies on people knowing a lot about their future income and being able to both borrow and save when required. Unfortunately, borrowing and saving isn't always easy or even possible.

These practical limitations don't undermine our previous insights, but they do require us to modify them slightly. Let's start by looking at the problems people can run into, and then we'll see what this means for the insights we've developed about the relationship between income and consumption.

People can't always borrow. Some people don't follow the *Rational Rule for Consumers* simply because they are unable to borrow. **Credit constraints** limit the amount that some people can borrow. If you don't have savings or credit, you're constrained to only spending no more than what's in your latest paycheck, and therefore you can't smooth your consumption. This is an important constraint for many Australians.

credit constraints Limits on how much you can borrow.

Credit constraints arise because banks are often reluctant to lend money to fund consumption when the loan isn't backed by *collateral*—an asset they can take over if you fall behind on your repayments. This means that you'll find it easier to borrow for certain kinds of spending, like buying a house or a new car, because the bank retains the right to foreclose on your house or repossess your car. But it's much more difficult to find a bank willing to lend you money to buy groceries or pay the rent if you don't have sufficient current income. And yet you're most likely to want to borrow money to fund consumption when your income is temporarily low, such as when you're unemployed. Banks are also reluctant to loan money to people who have yet to build up a solid credit history, and this makes it difficult for students to borrow all that they need to consumption smooth.

It's hard to make deliberate forward-looking plans and stick to them. Even if banks were willing to lend to you, it's really hard to perfectly forecast your permanent income and make consumption plans that you stick to. Our insights into consumption come from applying a framework that's deliberate, forward-looking, and requires thinking hard about difficult trade-offs. Following the *Rational Rule for Consumers* requires you to constantly compare the present to the future, to make plans about when to spend and when to save, and to follow through on those plans.

Shutterstock

Planning is hard work, but worth it.

The reality is that not all consumers are this deliberate about their choices all the time. I bet you've occasionally made spending decisions without a careful evaluation of marginal benefits. Too many students fail to draw up a budget when their paycheque arrives. And even among those who do, temptation or unexpected needs can get in the way, disrupting even the best-laid plans. The bottom line is that cognitive or behavioural limitations—from being poorly informed, tired, or impulse-driven—mean that some people don't smooth their consumption. They don't save enough; they run up debt without a plan to pay it back; and they make impulse purchases.

Incorporating insights from psychology into our understanding of how people make economic decisions refines our understanding of the relationship between income and consumption. The ideas that people are impulsive, that they procrastinate, and that when it comes to making trade-offs between today and tomorrow they can be impatient, all mean that some people won't follow the *Rational Rule for Consumers*. Instead, some people will simply spend what they have in the moment.

Hand-to-mouth consumers spend their current income; consumption smoothers spend permanent income. Together, these two factors—psychological limitations and credit constraints—mean that some people don't smooth their consumption or they don't smooth it fully. Instead, they live paycheque to paycheque. As a result, their consumption reflects their current income rather than their permanent income. Economists call these people "hand-to-mouth consumers." For many people, hand-to-mouth consumption is not so much a choice, as a reality—they find it hard to borrow, and rather than save, they spend all their income on necessities. Calling people *hand-to-mouth consumers* is not a judgement on their lifestyle, but rather it's intended to describe the different relationship between their consumption and income. Because these people spend their income as they receive it, their marginal propensity to consume is 1, and it's the same in response to a change in income that's temporary or permanent, anticipated or unanticipated.

Total consumption is a mix of hand-to-mouth consumers and consumption smoothers. The macroeconomy includes both people who smooth their consumption *and* people who live hand to mouth. The earlier insights that we developed to understand how different kinds of income changes impact consumption were based on the behaviour of consumption smoothers. We've just seen that hand-to-mouth consumers tend to spend what they have, so their consumption reflects their current income. Let's take a look at how aggregate consumption across the economy will respond to a change in income, modifying our earlier insights to account for the responses of *both* consumption smoothers and hand-to-mouth consumers.

Modified insight one: *A temporary change in income* will lead to a small change in consumption for consumption smoothers and a large change in consumption for hand-to-mouth consumers. For example, what would you do if you got a $500 tax refund this year? Most people say that they would put most of it in savings or use it to pay off debt, implying that they are consumption smoothers. But others say that they would use the money right away, on any number of things ranging from healthcare needs to car repairs or vacations. Total consumption reflects the spending decisions of both groups, and so the aggregate marginal propensity to consume out of a temporary income change will be larger the more hand-to-mouth consumers there are in a society.

Modified insight two: *A permanent change in income* will lead to a large change in consumption from both consumption smoothers and hand-to-mouth consumers, leading to a large change in total consumption. Indeed, consumption will rise by about as much as permanent income. The marginal propensity to consume out of permanent changes in income remains close to 1, regardless of the mix of hand-to-mouth and consumption smoothers.

Modified insight three: *An anticipated change in income* will lead to no change in the consumption of consumption smoothers, but a large change for hand-to-mouth consumers who consume their income as it arrives. The marginal propensity to consume out of anticipated income changes will depend on the share of hand-to-mouth consumers: The larger the share of hand-to-mouth consumers, the higher the marginal propensity to consume out of an anticipated change in income.

Modified insight four: *Learning about a future income change* will lead to a large change in consumption from consumption smoothers, who respond to news about future income straight away, but no change from hand-to-mouth consumers, who won't respond until the extra income arrives. Once again the marginal propensity to consume out of anticipated income changes will depend on the share of hand-to-mouth consumers. However, in this case, the larger the share of hand-to-mouth consumers, the *smaller* the marginal propensity to consume, since hand-to-mouth consumers do not increase consumption when learning about a future income change.

Modified insight five: *Forecasting changes in consumption depends on the share of hand-to-mouth consumers.* Hand-to-mouth consumers spend what they have, so you can forecast changes in their consumption if you know how their income will change. For example, if you know that a tax cut is coming, you can reasonably predict that hand-to-mouth consumers will spend it. Consumption smoothers, however, don't change their consumption in response to anticipated income changes, so you can't forecast changes in their consumption. Therefore, your ability to forecast changes in consumption depends on the mix of consumption smoothers and hand-to-mouth consumers.

Putting it all together, *on average* the economy shows some influence of permanent income driving consumption and some influence of current income driving consumption. Figure 9 summarises the effect of a rise in income on consumption (labelled *C*) for consumption smoothers in the first column and for hand-to-mouth consumers in the second column. To forecast how aggregate consumption across the economy will respond to the rise in income, you need to account for the responses of *both* consumption smoothers and hand-to-mouth consumers, and this is shown in the final column of Figure 9.

Figure 9 | **Implications of Income Changes for Consumption**

Effect of . . .	Consumption smoothers	+	Hand-to-mouth consumers	=	Total consumption
A temporary rise in income	Small ↑*C*		Large ↑*C*		Intermediate ↑*C*
A permanent rise in income	Large ↑*C*		Large ↑*C*		Large ↑*C*
An anticipated rise in income	No change		Large ↑*C*		Intermediate ↑*C*
News of a future rise in income	Large ↑*C*		No change		Intermediate ↑*C*
Forecasting consumption changes	Hard to forecast		Forecast by looking at income changes		Difficult, but not impossible to forecast

25.4 What Shifts Consumption?

Learning Objective *Assess how changing macroeconomic conditions shift consumption.*

So far our analysis of the link between income and consumption has held other factors constant. It's time to see what happens when those other factors change. This is where the *interdependence principle* comes to the fore, highlighting how consumption depends on other factors, including the real interest rate, expectations, taxes, and wealth.

First, let's focus on the distinction between a shift in the consumption function and a movement along the curve. The consumption function shows how consumption depends on income. So a change in income doesn't shift the consumption function; instead, it leads to a *movement along* the consumption function, as shown in Panel A of Figure 10. But other factors—including the real interest rate, expectations, taxes, and wealth—will change consumption at any given level of income. As a result, they shift the consumption function. Panel B of Figure 10 shows that an increase in consumption at any level of income shifts the consumption function up, while a decrease in consumption shifts it down. Our next task is to analyse the four factors that shift the consumption function.

Four consumption shifters:
1. Real interest rates
2. Expectations
3. Taxes
4. Wealth

Figure 10 | **Movement Along the Consumption Function versus Shifts in the Consumption Function**

Panel A—Changes in Income: Lead to a Movement Along the Consumption Function

(A) An increase in **income**
(B) Leads to a **movement along the consumption function**
(C) Leading to **higher consumption**

Panel B—Changes in Other Factors: Shift the Consumption Function

(A) Other factors that cause an **increase in consumption** at a given income level lead the consumption function to **shift up**.
(B) Other factors that cause a **decrease in consumption** at a given income level cause the consumption function to **shift down**.

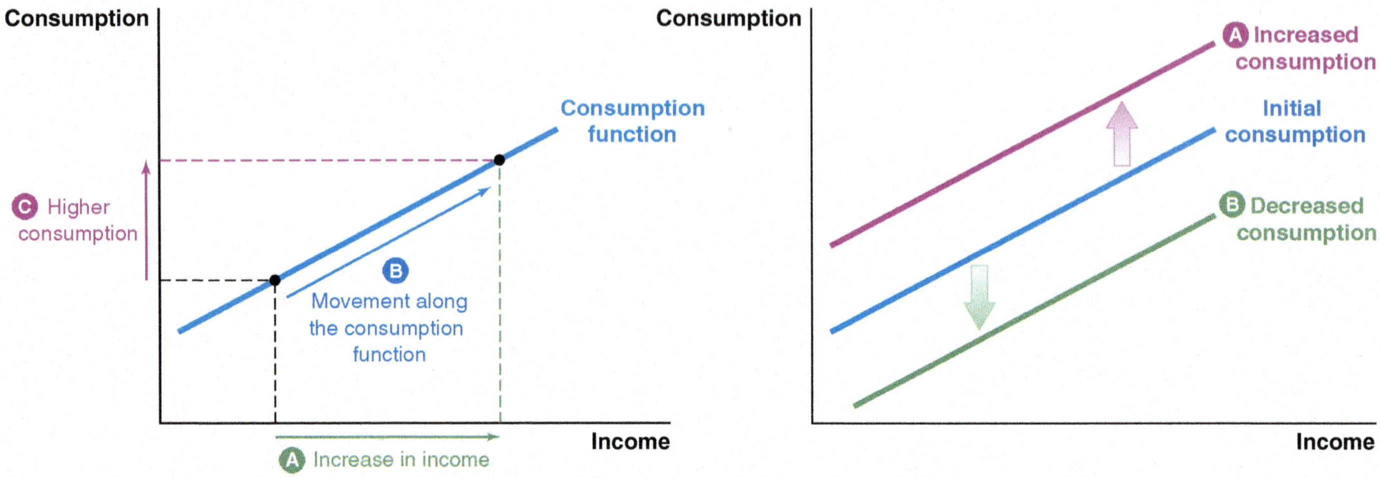

Consumption Shifter One: Real Interest Rates

It's time to add the real interest rate back into our analysis. We'll analyse its effects on saving and consumption separately.

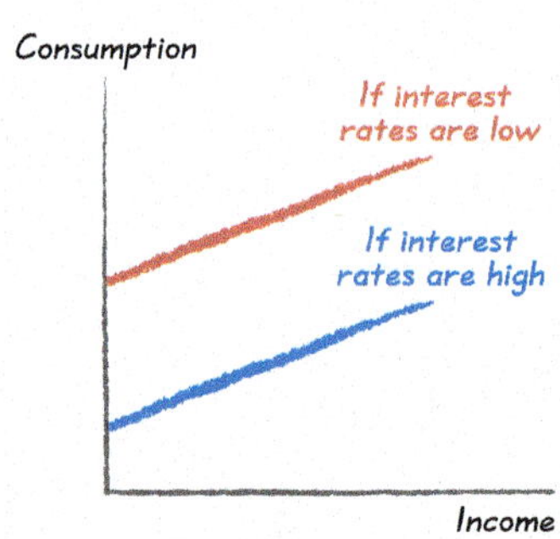

Let's start with saving because it's most straightforward. The benefit of saving is that you'll earn interest. Consequently, a higher real interest rate raises the benefit of saving, and the *cost-benefit principle* tells you that people will respond by doing more of it. That is, a higher real interest rate leads to an increase in saving.

The effects of a higher interest rate on current consumption are a bit more complicated because there are two forces that sometimes work in opposition to each other. First, a higher real interest rate is an incentive to substitute towards more consumption tomorrow and less today. This *substitution effect* arises because the opportunity cost of spending a dollar on consumption today is saving that dollar and spending it plus the interest earned on it in the future. The higher the real interest rate, the higher this opportunity cost, leading consumers to reduce their current consumption.

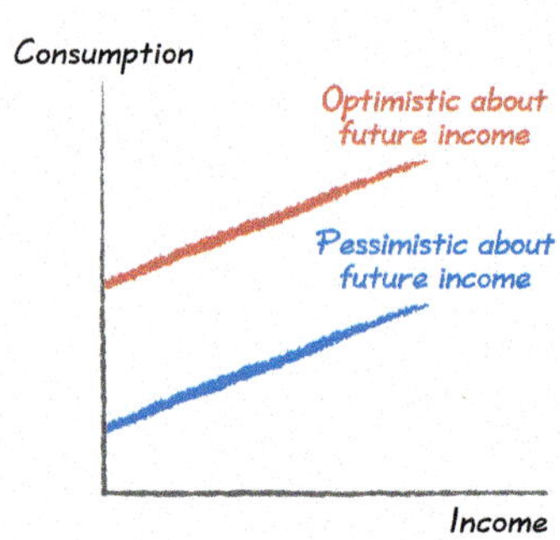

Second, a higher real interest rate boosts your income if you're a lender and decreases it if you're a borrower. That's because lenders get paid interest, and borrowers have to pay it. So if you're a lender, higher interest rates boost your income, and this *income effect* leads to higher consumption. But if you're a borrower, higher interest rates effectively reduce the income you have left after making interest payments, and this income effect reduces your consumption.

The net effect of these two sometimes-conflicting forces could go either way. But most evidence suggests that an increase in the real interest rate leads to a decrease in consumption.

Consumption Shifter Two: Expectations

Consumers' expectations about the future state of the economy can play a big role in driving consumption. Optimism about future economic growth means that people expect their future incomes will be higher. And to the extent that consumption is driven by permanent income—what consumers expect to earn in the future—optimistic expectations translate into higher consumption.

You can track consumer optimism by following the Westpac-Melbourne Institute's consumer sentiment index shown in Figure 11. This index summarises the results of hundreds of monthly interviews asking consumers a battery of questions about their confidence in the economy. As Figure 11 illustrates, high levels of consumer sentiment tend to predict rapid growth in total consumption.

Figure 11 | Consumer Sentiment Predicts Consumption Growth

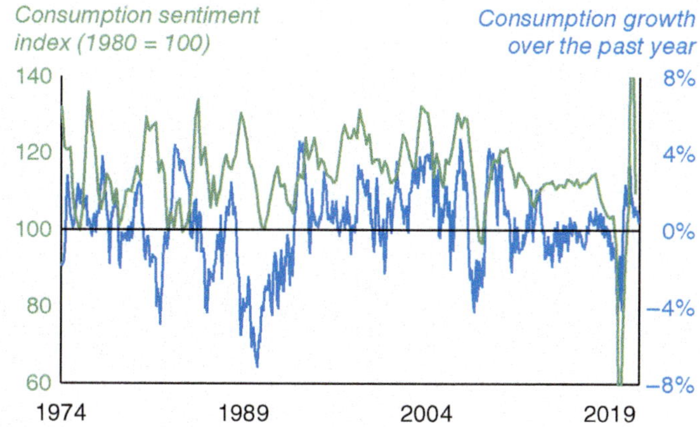

Data from: Reserve Bank of Australia; Westpac-Melbourne Institute.

Consumption Shifter Three: Taxes

The federal government taxes a chunk of your income before you even get a chance to think about whether to spend or save it. Because you can't spend that money, taxes are an important factor shaping consumption. Higher taxes reduce your **disposable income**—that is, your after-tax income—which leads to lower consumption at any given level of pre-tax income. Total pre-tax income is the same thing as GDP, so that means that high taxes lead to lower consumption for any level of GDP. That is, a tax increase will shift the consumption function downward.

disposable income Your after-tax income.

On the flip side, tax cuts increase disposable income, shifting the consumption function upward, leading to higher consumption at any level of GDP. This is why governments sometimes use tax cuts to help stimulate more spending when the economy slows. Economists debate how effective tax cuts are as a stimulus. If consumers spend most of their tax cut—as hand-to-mouth consumers will—then it'll be an effective stimulus. But consumption smoothers will recognise that a temporary tax cut doesn't boost their permanent income by much, and so they'll save rather than spend most of their tax cuts. When this happens, the tax cut doesn't yield much of an effective stimulus and the government might be better off spending the money itself. We'll assess some of the evidence on this in Chapter 35 on fiscal policy.

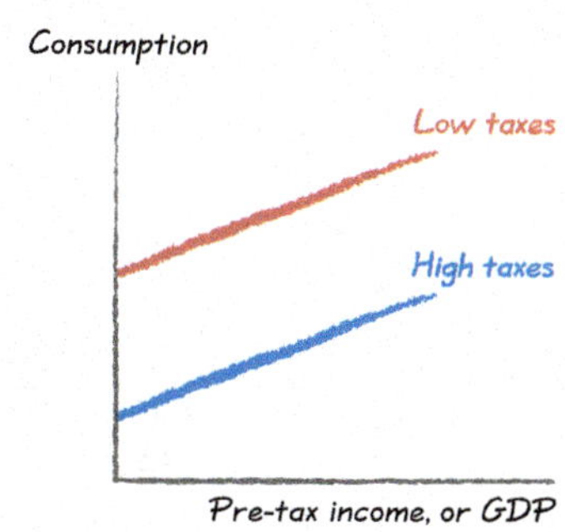

Consumption Shifter Four: Wealth

Your total resources include not just your income, but also your accumulated stock of wealth (which can be negative, if you're in debt). Greater wealth leads to an increase in consumption at any given level of income, shifting the consumption function upward.

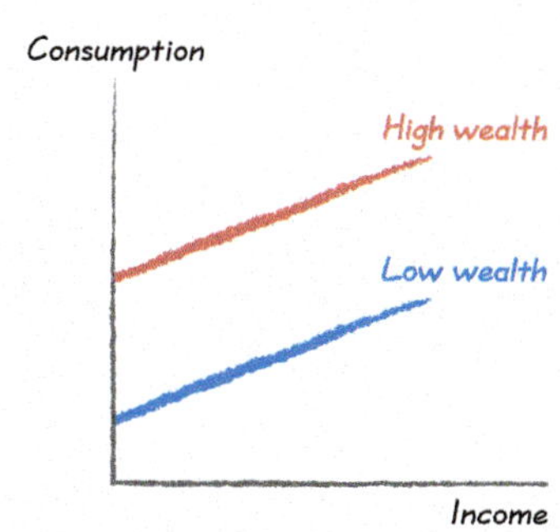

This gives financial markets an important role in shifting consumption. For instance, rising stock prices lead the wealth of shareholders to rise, and they may choose to spend some of this extra wealth on consumption, shifting the consumption function up.

Likewise, many Australians hold most of their wealth in housing, and so an increase in house prices can also make people feel wealthier, leading them to consume more. Before spending your newfound housing wealth, realise that a broad-based rise in house prices is a two-edged sword. Higher house prices are good news because they boost your wealth. But they're also bad news because if you sell your house to realise that gain in wealth, you'll have to find somewhere else to live, and the increase in house prices will make buying another house more expensive.

Okay, that's it. At this point we've worked out how changing macroeconomic conditions shift consumption. Figure 12 summarises what we've learned.

Figure 12 | **The Macroeconomics of Consumption**

Consumption Function Shifters	
The consumption function *shifts up in response to:*	↓Real interest rates Optimistic expectations of future income ↓Taxes ↑Wealth
The consumption function *shifts down in response to:*	↑Real interest rates Pessimistic expectations of future income ↑Taxes ↓Wealth
The consumption function *doesn't shift in response to:*	Changing income. That's a movement along the curve.

Do the Economics

For each of the following examples, figure out how the consumption function responds to changing macroeconomic conditions:

The Reserve Bank raises interest rates.

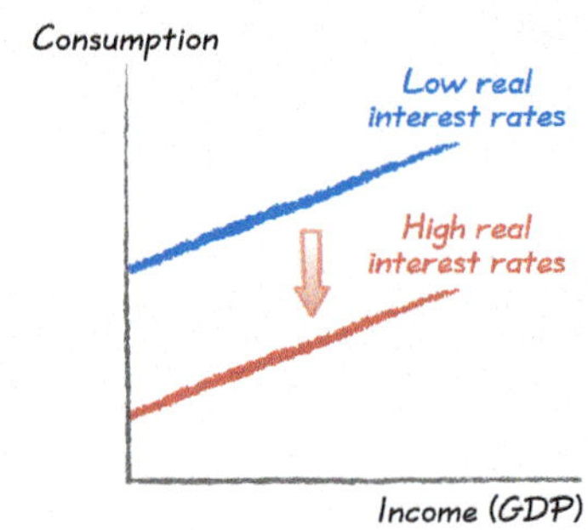

Increase in real interest rates
→ Consumption function shifts down

The stock market rises to a record high.

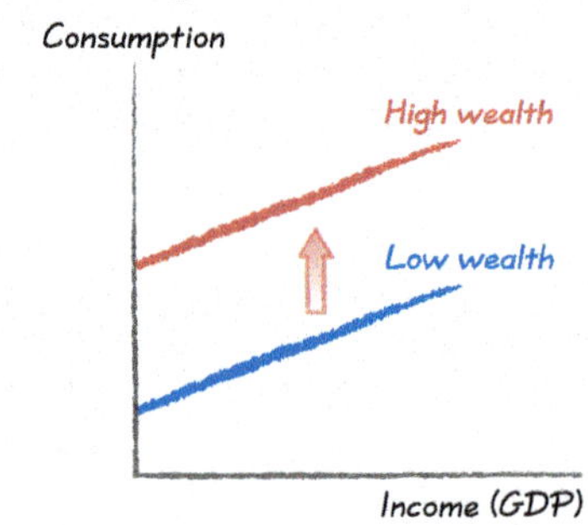

Increase in wealth
→ Consumption function shifts up

The government gives a one-time tax rebate.

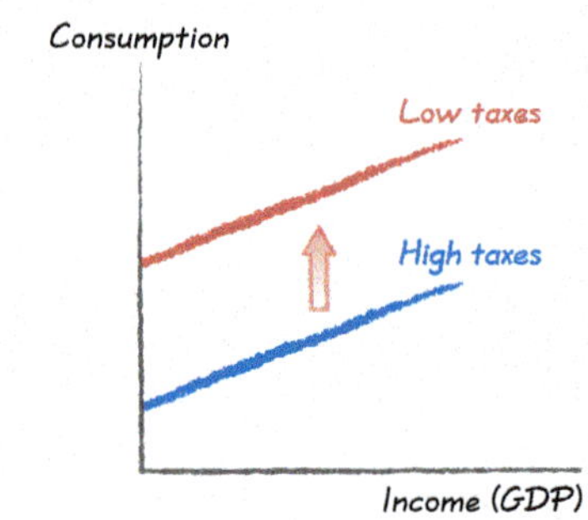

Lower taxes
→ Consumption function shifts up

People start to feel better about their financial prospects.

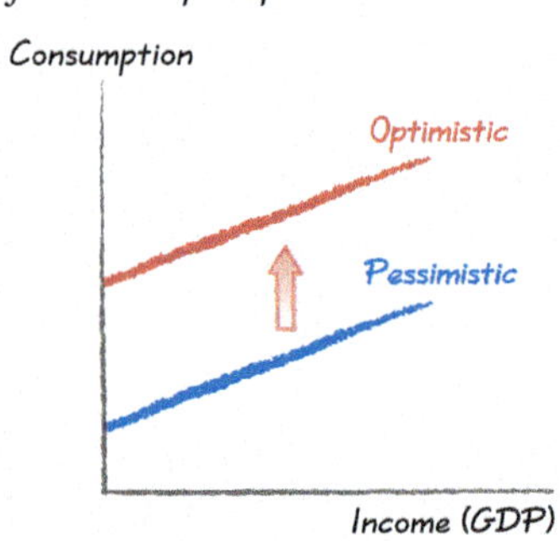

Optimistic expectations
→ Consumption function shifts up

The government raises taxes to pay off some of its debt.

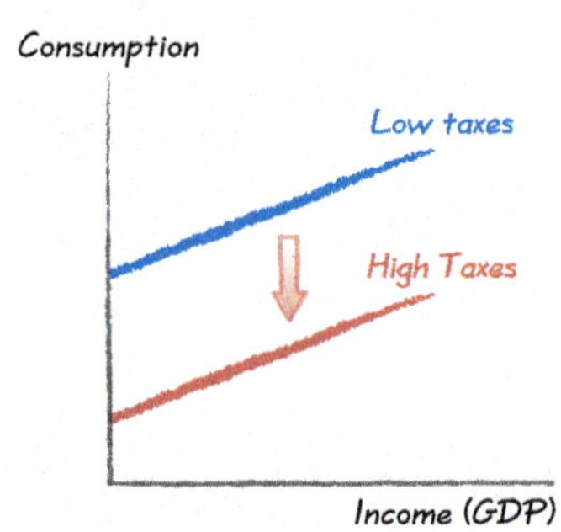

Increase in taxes
→ Consumption function shifts down

House prices plunge.

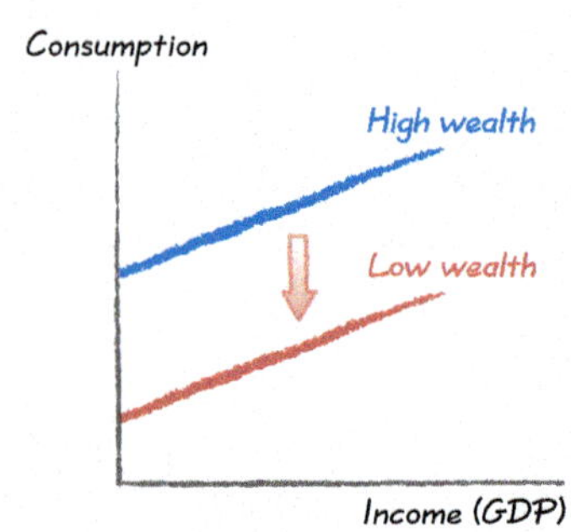

Decline in wealth
→ Consumption function shifts down

25.5 Saving

Learning Objective *Learn how to form a smart saving plan.*

It's time to turn our attention from consumption to saving. Of course, this isn't a change of focus at all—how much you save depends on how much you consume, and vice versa.

Don't think of this as a separate analysis of saving, but rather as a continuation of our analysis that will lead to a more complete understanding of both consumption and saving.

There are four key motives that drive saving, and it's time to explore their implications for saving, consumption, and macroeconomic outcomes.

Savings motives:

1. Changing income over the life cycle
2. Changing needs over the life cycle
3. Bequests
4. Precautionary saving

Saving Motive One: Changing Income over the Life Cycle

You've already seen that most people borrow when young, save in midlife, and spend down their savings in retirement. This pattern is driven by how income typically changes over the life course. Your income will probably start low and then rise over your 20s and 30s; you'll enjoy your peak earning years in your 40s, 50s, and maybe 60s; and then your income will drop off sharply when you retire. That is, your income will probably follow a hump-shaped pattern. As Figure 13 shows, it looks like this . But your consumption shouldn't follow the same pattern. The logic of consumption smoothing is that you should save money in those phases of your life when your income will be predictably higher, so that you can spend more than your income when it's lower.

As a result, people tend to spend more than their meager incomes in their 20s and thus accumulate debt. Then as their earnings grow, they pay down their debt and accumulate savings in their 30s, 40s, and 50s. People tend to spend down their accumulated assets starting around the mid-60s, as they head into retirement.

These patterns mean that demographics have macroeconomic implications for national savings. If a large share of the population is very young or very old, then national savings will be lower than it would be if more people were middle-aged. The share of the Australian population aged over 65—the age at which many people retire and move from saving to dissaving—has more than doubled over the past several decades. This demographic shift has helped push the national savings rate down from over 14% in the 1950s to 6.5% at the end of 2019. Note that although the savings rate did go all the way back up to 18% in 2020, this was not primarily due to a sudden influx of retirees, but rather due to Saving Motive Four, precautionary saving, in response to the coronavirus pandemic.

Figure 13 Income over the Life Cycle

2021 Data from: Australian Bureau of Statistics.

Saving Motive Two: Changing Needs over the Life Cycle

So far, we've analysed how your *income* varies over your life. Your *needs* also vary over your life course. You should save more (and spend less) in periods when you have fewer needs, so that you'll have more to spend when there's a greater need.

So look ahead now and forecast how your needs will vary over your life course. For most university students, their most important needs are accommodation, and living expenses. Although the HECS-HELP system might take care of your student loans (if you're a domestic student), you'll have to start paying these down when you graduate. Different people follow different life paths, but for many, the next big expense comes when they get married, which might involve a costly wedding, a honeymoon, and setting up a new household. But a wedding is cheap, relative to the cost of feeding, clothing, and raising kids. If you're planning a family, be aware that those first few years with young kids involve some big expenses. It's not just nappies and toys; you'll need to budget for child care if you plan to keep working, and that often costs a LOT, though the Australian government offers hefty subsidies for child care, to encourage parents

Cavan Images/Getty Images

They're little, but they're expensive. Believe me.

to go to work. All of this means that for many people it's a good idea to spend modestly in your early 20s—even though your permanent income might allow higher consumption—because your needs are likely to rise as you enter your 30s.

This may sound like the opposite of consumption smoothing, since it says that you should *spend more when your needs are greater,* but it's not. The *Rational Rule for Consumers* says that if your needs are *similar* over time, then you should smooth your consumption. But if your needs are *changing,* then your consumption should also change over time. The *Rational Rule for Consumers* tells you to spend more when the marginal benefit of spending today is more than the marginal benefit of spending a dollar-plus-interest in the future. At certain times in your life the marginal benefit of each dollar of consumption will be higher, so you'll want to consume more. In turn, that means that you'll need to save more in those phases of your life when your needs aren't so great. The main idea here remains the same—you want to shift your spending to the times in your life when it'll yield the largest marginal benefit.

Saving Motive Three: Bequests

The third motive for saving is that you might want to build up a stock of wealth that you'll pass on when you die. For some people, that means leaving an inheritance for their children. For others, it's about leaving money to a cause they care about. It's important to draw up a detailed will in order to ensure your bequest goes to help the people you care about most.

The bequest motive helps explain why many elderly people don't spend down all their wealth—they're hoping their money will outlive them, and that it'll make a difference even if they aren't around to see it.

Saving Motive Four: Precautionary Saving

The final motive for saving comes from the old saying that you should hope for the best, but prepare for the worst. This suggests that you should build up a buffer stock of saving to protect you in case financial misfortune strikes. That misfortune could be a layoff that leaves you unemployed, a medical emergency, or any other unexpected cost. Saving to be prepared for a financial emergency is called **precautionary saving** because you're building up that buffer as a precaution. It's the idea that you should save for a rainy day.

precautionary saving Saving to be prepared for a financial emergency.

Save enough to weather the financial risks you face. Let's take a measure of your financial health: How would you cope if you needed to replace your fridge if it suddenly packed up? Such a shock might set you back around $1,000. Could you come up with the money? Figure 14 shows that most Australians would not be able to do so, without going into (more) debt. In fact, one-fifth of Australians couldn't cover an unexpected $500 expense out of their savings. That could be something like a dental bill, or replacing school uniforms and shoes for one's kids.

Figure 14 | **Many Australians Are Financially Unprepared**

Proportion of Australians who would need to borrow to cover an unexpected...

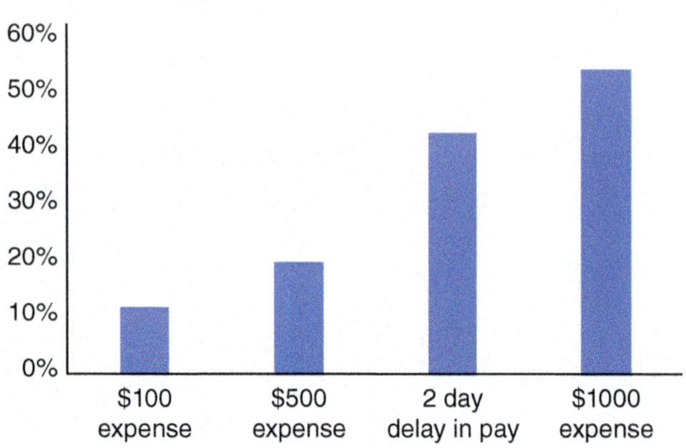

Data from: finder.com.au and Budget Direct.

If you're in a similar situation, my advice is to start saving to build up your rainy-day fund. It's an urgent task because once you get into financial trouble, your problems can quickly cascade. If you can't fix your car, then you can't get to work, and if you can't get to work, you'll lose your job, and then you'll never be able to afford to fix your car.

While many people can't come up with $1,000 to replace their fridge, people often face even more critical risks. To evaluate how much you'll need to save, think through the sorts of financial risks you face and how much money you'll need to have on hand to weather them. One of the biggest risks you'll face is unemployment. The good news is that most people who lose their jobs find a new job within a few months; the bad news is that this still means going a few months without a paycheque, and being forced to rely on JobSeeker and its very modest payment. That's why financial planners typically advise that you build up a buffer stock that's equivalent to three-to-six months of your typical consumption.

Precautionary saving is why national savings goes up when economic uncertainty rises. The more uncertain your economic future looks, the larger your rainy-day fund should be. So when economic uncertainty rises, millions of people increase their precautionary saving. But remember that saving and consumption are two-sides of the same coin—to save more, they have to consume less. As a result, growing uncertainty can lead to a decline in total consumption.

Precautionary saving also shapes how the economy recovers following a recession, as shown in Figure 15. A recession puts hundreds of thousands of people out of work, leading them to deplete their rainy-day funds or go into debt. And so even after the economy has returned to normal, people will save more (and thus consume less) in order to rebuild their financial buffers. The result is that saving rates remained high after the 2020 coronavirus pandemic.

Figure 15 | Saving Stayed High After the Recession

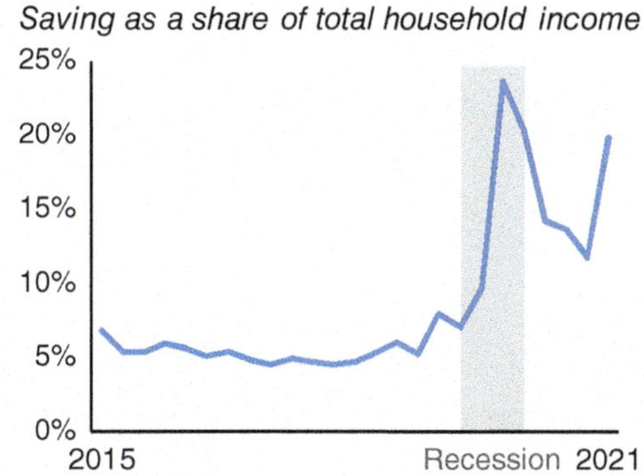

EVERYDAY Economics — Preparing for the unexpected

If a financial emergency strikes before you've built up your rainy-day fund, you'll quickly discover there are no great options for borrowing money—but some options are less bad than others. The first thing to consider is whether you have a friend or family member who can loan you the money. This is often the cheapest option in dollar terms, but in personal terms it can be pretty costly, so be careful.

The rest of your options involve borrowing money through the financial sector, and it's worth evaluating the costs and benefits of each of your alternatives.

- *Credit cards:* One quick option is to use your credit card to cover expenses. But note that credit cards typically charge high interest rates. It's better to use your card to make purchases than to get a cash advance because you get a a 30-day grace period to repay purchases before interest starts accruing. Borrowing cash on your credit card is worse because it typically involves fees in addition to the interest charges.

  Pay off your balance as quickly as you can (and always make minimum payments on time). If you must carry a balance, it's worth calling your credit card company to ask for a lower rate—you'll be surprised how often it works. Try asking if they have any balance transfer offers. Be careful: Sometimes they'll offer a low introductory rate for a few months, so they can jack up their rates later. But if you read the terms carefully and plan accordingly, you can work a balance transfer offer to your advantage.
- *Loans:* Some banks offer personal loans, precisely to help their customers handle a financial emergency or to pay off a high-interest credit card. You can call a few banks and ask what you need to qualify for one and what interest rate they'll charge. If you own your car or your house, you can take out a car loan or a home equity loan. These loans tend to charge lower interest rates since they have the car or house to back them—but if you don't pay them back, you risk losing your car or house.
- *Retirement accounts:* If you have a retirement plan, you might have the option of borrowing from it, and paying yourself back with interest. But ask a lot of questions first, because if you don't follow the rules precisely, this can lead to a significant increase in your tax obligations.
- *Payday loans:* Be very wary about payday loans. These lenders lend you small amounts of money at very high interest rates if you agree to pay the money back when you get your next paycheque. Unless you're absolutely sure you can repay the loan with your next paycheque, you should avoid these loans because they quickly get out of hand once they start to compound: The annual interest rate is often over 100%, and sometimes over 1,000%!

Andrew Winning/Reuters/Newscom

Be prepared.

Jerome Wilson/Alamy Stock Photo

Notice that they're not advertising their interest rate.

It's easier to get a loan at a reasonable interest rate when you've established a reputation as a responsible borrower, so it's a good idea to build up good credit before you need it. This means making all your payments on time, even when it's somewhat difficult. A credit card can be a great way to start building a good credit history. You can use it to make routine purchases for things you know you can afford, and then pay it off immediately. Good credit can help you out during times of financial stress—so don't let bad decisions ruin your credit! ■

Smart Saving Strategies

As economists have studied people's financial lives, they've come up with some smart strategies to help you manage your financial life successfully. Here are a few such strategies:

(left) Maks Narodenko/Shutterstock; (right) Valentina Proskurina/Shutterstock

Plan ahead to avoid temptation.

Set a budget and stick to it. The smart way to save is to make your spending and saving plans in advance by setting a budget. It's valuable, because people find it easier to make good decisions in advance. In one famous experiment, when people were asked to choose a snack to eat in a week's time, many chose a piece of fruit over a chocolate bar, but when offered a snack to eat right away, they chose the chocolate. The same problem makes it hard to save unless you've planned—that is, budgeted—your spending in advance. If you're constantly deciding in the moment how much to spend, you'll easily find yourself giving in to temptation. Instead, assess your financial situation and make a plan for how much to consume—and therefore how much to save or borrow—when you're best able to be analytic and forward-looking. Once you've made that plan, stick to it. If your plan isn't working, then go back and reassess it.

Make sure you can handle an unexpected cost. Once you graduate, you may find yourself in a predicament in which you think you should start saving, but you have a mountain of student debt to pay. Your employer will automatically deduct minimum repayments for your HECS-HELP loan if you earn more than the repayment threshold, but you can choose to make extra contributions to pay off your loan faster. What should you do? Remember that paying off debt is a form of saving, so choosing to pay off your debt is moving your net wealth in the right direction. But unless you can borrow money easily, you also want to accumulate a rainy-day fund to protect yourself in case you lose your job, your car breaks down, or you have an unexpected health cost. So build up your rainy-day fund before you start making extra payments on your student loans.

Increase your superannuation contributions. In Australia we have compulsory superannuation. This means your employer is required by law to put aside a certain percentage of your income into an individual account that you won't be able to access until you turn 65. As of the 2021–2022 financial year, that percentage is 10%, but the government plans to increase it to 12% by 2025. You probably already knew this, but did you know that you can make extra contributions to your superannuation through something called "voluntary contributions"? This is an agreement you make with your employer to put aside a larger percentage of your income into your chosen superannuation fund. The best part? This sacrificed income is (for most people) taxed at only 15%, which is probably a lot lower than your marginal tax rate. The bad part is you can't access those funds until you retire. But if you want to be really prepared for retirement, you may want to boost your superannuation contributions this way.

Plan to save more tomorrow. One of the reasons people struggle to pay their loans or to save adequately for retirement is that they get used to their current consumption spending and don't want to give anything up. Financial advisers often tell people to give up some small habit like a daily coffee and to save that money instead. But giving up an already established habit is hard.

What's easier is planning to save out of future income. One plan for building your retirement savings is to plan to keep making your student loan payments forever. Once you earn enough money, your employer will be making regular payments to the government out of your paycheques. Once you've paid off your loans, you can keep making those payments—but make them to your retirement account. You'll never miss the money because you've never had a chance to spend it. You can do the same thing with every increase in your pay: If you get a raise of 10% with a promotion, put half of it straight into your retirement account—you'll still feel the increase in your take home pay, while saving even more.

Keep as much of your money as you can. This sounds obvious, right? But it turns out that there are some important things you need to do to follow this advice. The first is to avoid high fees. When you put your money in a retirement or investment account, you'll be charged fees. You need to look for the smallest fees you can to keep as much of your money as possible. Minimising fees also means trying to avoid carrying a balance on your credit card or holding on to other high-interest-rate debt for long.

You can also hang on to more of your money if you take advantage of government programs designed to increase saving. There are many different programs—mostly geared towards saving for retirement or a house—for example, in NSW the government will give you $10,000 to put towards your first house, making your savings go that little bit further.

Tying It Together

Our focus in this chapter on individual consumption decisions might feel like microeconomics, which is about individual decisions, rather than macroeconomics, which is about understanding how things work at an aggregate level. In fact any useful understanding of the macroeconomy must have micro foundations. This is the idea that the behaviour of the whole is determined by the choices made by each individual. It says that the only reliable way to understand the economy-wide aggregates that are the focus of macroeconomics is to understand what drives each of the individual decisions that make up those aggregates.

This is why many leading macroeconomists describe their field as being about applying the tools of microeconomics—from the core principles on up—to build a reliable understanding of the big-picture questions that macroeconomics focuses on. This chapter has demonstrated that understanding the choices made by individual consumers can help you figure out how the economy as a whole will respond to changing conditions. The terms *microeconomics* and *macroeconomics* may not be that useful; we're just doing *economics*. Our approach has been to ignore these distinctions, in favour of using all the tools at your disposal to figure out what drives consumption.

It's an approach that we'll continue to follow throughout the rest of this book. In the next chapter, we'll focus on investment. We'll zoom in on the individual decisions that executives make about whether or not to invest in a new project. Just as we did in this chapter, we'll discover that understanding the drivers of individual choices will be incredibly helpful when it's time to work out the macroeconomic implications.

Chapter at a Glance

Consumption: Household spending on final goods and services.

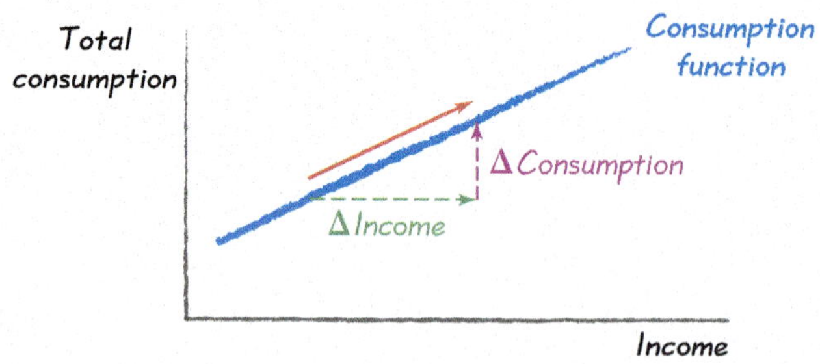

A curve plotting the level of consumption associated with each level of income.

Marginal propensity to consume: The fraction of each extra dollar of income that households spend on consumption.

$$= \text{Slope} = \frac{\Delta \text{Consumption}}{\Delta \text{Income}}$$

Saving: The portion of income that you set aside, rather than spending on consumption.

$$\text{Saving} = \text{Income} - \text{Consumption}$$

Consumption Choices

The Rational Rule for Consumers: Consume more today if the marginal benefit of a dollar of consumption today is greater than (or equal to) the marginal benefit of spending a dollar-plus-interest in the future.

Permanent Income Hypothesis: The idea that you choose how much to consume based on your permanent income (your best estimate of your long-term average income) rather than current income.

Consumption smoothing: The idea that you should maintain a steady or smooth path for your consumption spending over time.

Real world modifications:

- Some consumers won't follow sophisticated consumption plans.
- Credit constraints limit the amount that some people can borrow.

⇒ Hand-to-mouth consumers spend their current income.

Implications

Effect of . . .	On consumption smoothers	+	On hand-to-mouth consumers	=	Total consumption
A temporary rise in income	Small ↑C		Large ↑C		Intermediate ↑C
A permanent rise in income	Large ↑C		Large ↑C		Large ↑C
An anticipated rise in income	No change		Large ↑C		Intermediate ↑C
News of a future rise in income	Large ↑C		No change		Intermediate ↑C
Forecasting consumption changes	Hard to forecast		Forecast using income changes		Difficult to forecast

How Changing Economic Conditions Shift Consumption

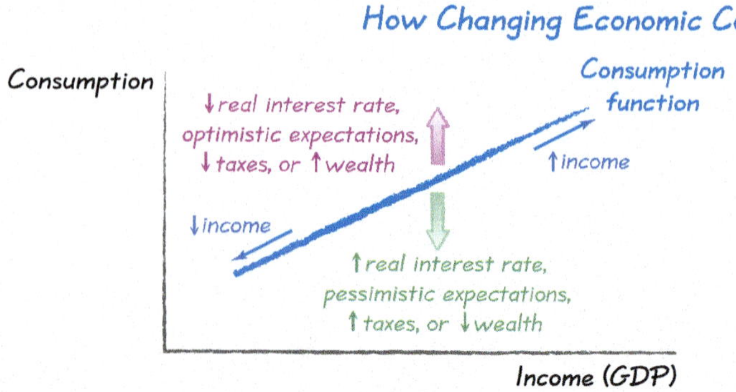

Is there:

- **Changing Income:** Leads to a *movement along* the consumption function.
- **Changes in Other Factors:** *Shifts* the consumption function.

  Four consumption shifters:
  1. Real interest rates
  2. Expectations of future income
  3. Taxes
  4. Wealth

Key Concepts

Discussion and Review Questions

Learning Objective 25.1 *Understand how consumption and saving vary with income.*

1. At your future job, you get an unexpected raise from \$50,000 a year to \$75,000 a year. How do your consumption and savings change? Provide a rough estimate of your marginal propensity to consume.
2. Real GDP per person falls during a devastating recession, which in turn causes consumption to fall by 5%. Would giving everyone 5% more income during the recession lead consumption to go up 5%? Why or why not?

Learning Objective 25.2 *Apply the core principles of economics to make good consumption decisions.*

3. Nicolas Cage, an award winning and prolific actor, once had a net worth of about \$150 million dollars (he earned \$40 million in 2009 alone!). By 2011, he had to sell off much of his collection of homes, cars, and novelties to pay off debts and had a net worth of about \$25 million. Describe how Cage could have better applied the four core principles to get the largest benefit from his once-large income.
4. In university, most students receive a HECS-HELP loan in order to finance their education. At the same time, they still spend money on consumer goods and services: food, clothes, books, haircuts, and so on. Use the ideas of consumption smoothing and the permanent income hypothesis to explain whether this is a smart decision or not.

Learning Objective 25.3 *Predict the behaviour of aggregate measures of consumption.*

5. Over long periods of time, the percentage of households' income spent on consumption does not change much even as income rises. Use the five insights into the relationship between income and consumption to explain this observation.
6. Describe some cognitive or behavioural limitations you have experienced when making consumption decisions and how these limitations can lead to hand-to-mouth consumption. Why is it easier to forecast the impact of an income change on consumption for hand-to-mouth consumers than for consumption smoothers?
7. What factors lead people to be credit constrained? What are the consequences? What would you expect to happen to total consumption if many people and businesses in the economy became credit constrained?

Learning Objective 25.4 *Assess how changing macroeconomic conditions shift consumption.*

8. The 2020–21 Low and Middle Income Tax Offset (LMITO) was a temporary tax cut designed to help pull the Australian economy out of the coronavirus pandemic-induced recession by increasing consumer spending.
   a. Show graphically how a tax cut changes the consumption function.
   b. Some economists argued that the tax cuts would increase consumption more if they were permanent rather than temporary. Explain why a permanent tax cut might increase consumption more than a temporary tax cut.

Learning Objective 25.5 *Learn how to form a smart saving plan.*

9. Explain why people tend to save more in times of economic uncertainty.
10. Paige is a supervisor at Australia Post. She just got a big promotion and went from working part time for \$30,000 a year to full time for \$65,000 a year. Her new manager tells her, "You should live like you're still making the part-time income for two years and save everything else. You'll thank me when you're my age." Should Paige follow her manager's advice?

Study Problems

Learning Objective 25.1 *Understand how consumption and saving vary with income.*

1. Your friend just got an unexpected \$1,000 tax refund. She plans to put \$800 towards paying off credit card debt, put \$100 towards her HECS-HELP loan and use the remaining \$100 to purchase a new barbecue for her deck. What is your friend's marginal propensity to consume? By how much has she increased her net wealth?

2. The table below contains data on per person income and per person consumption in Australia for several years.

Year	Real income per person	Real consumption per person
2015	$75,300	$41,100
2016	$76,100	$41,500
2017	$76,700	$41,800
2018	$77,900	$42,700
2019	$78,800	$42,800

a. Draw the consumption function for Australia for these years.

b. What is savings at each level of income?

c. Between 2015 and 2019, how much did income rise? What about consumption? What was the marginal propensity to consume out of the increase?

Learning Objective 25.2 *Apply the core principles of economics to make good consumption decisions.*

3. Use the graph below, which illustrates the marginal benefit of consumption, to answer the following questions.

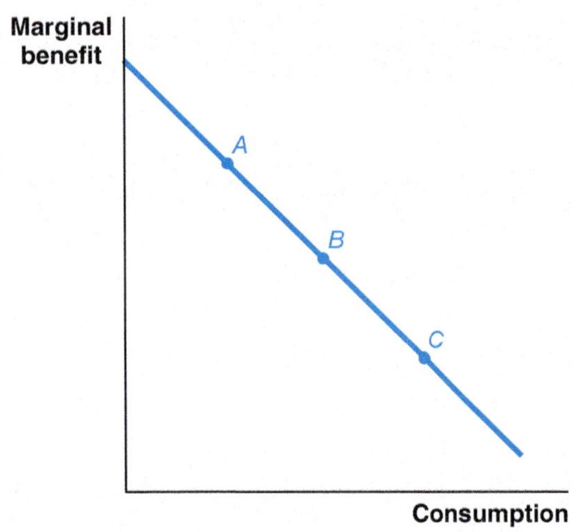

a. You became a licensed electrician last year, and have been enjoying a higher income than ever before. You choose to spend the majority of your income on amenities you couldn't previously afford. Which point on the graph most likely represents your current level of consumption?

b. After many years of work as an electrician, a major economic downturn leaves you unemployed. You're finding that you must pinch pennies just to afford basic necessities. You decide to go back to university, so you can pursue a career in computer programming. Which point on the graph most likely represents this level of consumption?

c. Given the two previous events, which point on the graph would help you best smooth your consumption over the long run?

4. Which of the following people are consumption smoothing and which are not? Explain your reasoning using the opportunity cost and marginal principles.

a. Sharon Tirabassi won $10 million in the Ontario lottery in 2004. By 2015, she had burnt through almost all the winnings, was riding the bus to part-time jobs, and was living in a rental property.

b. Karyn takes out a modest student and personal loan to pay for living expenses while she finishes her degree. She plans to get an accounting degree and enter the workforce making about $60,000 a year, and will eventually earn close to six figures.

Learning Objective 25.3 *Predict the behaviour of aggregate measures of consumption.*

5. For each of the following scenarios, predict how consumption changes for both consumption smoothers and hand-to-mouth consumers. How does total consumption change?

a. Household incomes rise 6% this year, but income growth is expected to return to its normal growth rate of 2% next year.

b. A country with an economy based heavily on agricultural production experiences a natural disaster so severe that it will take decades for farmers to recover.

c. People expect the economy to experience a recession over the next six months.

Learning Objective 25.4 *Assess how changing macroeconomic conditions shift consumption.*

6. Graph the effect of an increase in the real interest rate on the consumption function for both savers and borrowers.

7. Consider the following situations. What is the effect on consumption for each scenario? Demonstrate each answer with a graph.

a. The federal government raises taxes.

b. Housing prices increase.

c. Consumer incomes rise.

d. Consumers' expectations of their future incomes plummet.

Learning Objective 25.5 *Learn how to form a smart saving plan.*

8. The increasing cost of university has reduced how much millennials have saved for retirement. How does a higher cost of university change the life-cycle pattern of saving?

9. If parents increasingly worry about the costs their adult children and grandchildren will face because of climate change, how might that change their savings behaviour?

10. Policy makers are increasingly worried that Australians are not saving enough, so one policy maker proposes increasing the amount of government support available when people experience tough times like unemployment. How would this impact savings rates?

Investment

CHAPTER 26

There's a wind farm in regional Queensland and other wind farms are springing up in Victoria, Tasmania, and New South Wales—there are wind farms all across Australia. These sleek, modern wind turbines look nothing at all like the windmills of old. The biggest is twice the height of the Sydney Harbour Bridge and its massive blades sweep out over an area as large as two football fields. When the wind blows, the blades spin, and a single turbine can generate enough electricity for hundreds of thousands of households. They're at the cutting edge of a renewable energy revolution that could power a new economy, freeing it of dependence on foreign oil. It could be the start of a greener economy that saves the environment by reducing the need to burn fossil fuels.

sal2apao/Shutterstock

Spinning wind into energy.

A wind farm is a massive investment. Each turbine costs millions of dollars. The owners aren't spending these sums for the environment; they're making hard-nosed investment decisions and will only invest in wind if it's profitable.

The entrepreneurs running wind farms face the same decision that confronts all managers considering whether to invest in a new piece of equipment: Is the large up-front cost worth it in order to generate a stream of future revenues?

The tools that managers use to make multimillion-dollar investment decisions are the same tools that you'll want to apply in your own life whenever you're making decisions whose consequences play out over time.

Your task in this chapter is to explore the framework that executives use to evaluate investment decisions. We'll develop some basic tools and then apply them to real-world investment decisions. We'll use the insights we gain from studying individual investment decisions to explore what determines broader macroeconomic patterns in investment. But first, we'll start by evaluating the important role that investment plays in driving macroeconomic conditions. Let's make like a turbine and get going!

Chapter Objective

Analyse how managers can make good investment decisions.

26.1 Macroeconomic Investment
Learn what macroeconomists mean by investment and assess the role that it plays in the economy.

26.2 Tools to Analyse Investments
Master two tools for comparing sums of money at different points in time: compounding and discounting.

26.3 Making Investment Decisions
Evaluate whether an investment opportunity is worth pursuing.

26.4 The Macroeconomics of Investment
Assess how macroeconomic conditions drive investment.

26.5 The Market for Loanable Funds
Forecast the long-run real interest rate.

26.1 Macroeconomic Investment

Learning Objective *Learn what macroeconomists mean by investment and assess the role that it plays in the economy.*

Investment is going to be a big part of your life. As an entrepreneur, you'll invest in starting a new business; as a manager, you'll invest in new technology; in operations, you'll invest in more efficient logistics; in accounting, you'll invest in collecting valuable information. People in advertising tell you to invest in your brand, while those in human resources tell you to invest in your workers. In your personal life, you'll invest in your community, in your friends, and in your romantic relationships. Right now you're investing in your education by reading about investment. And if that education lands you a job interview, you might invest in a good suit.

Defining Investment

All of these investments involve the following proposition: You incur some *up-front cost* today in the hope of receiving *future benefits.* As such, your investment decisions link the choices you make today to your future well-being. In casual conversation people use the word "invest" any time the costs you incur today determine your outcomes in the future. For example, you've probably heard people talk about investing in the stock market. When you buy stocks, you are incurring an up-front cost today—giving up your money—in the hope of receiving a future benefit—more money at a later date. But this isn't what macroeconomists mean when they talk about investment.

investment Spending on new capital assets that increase the economy's productive capacity.

Macroeconomists use the word **investment** to refer to spending on new capital assets that increase the economy's productive capacity. Because saving money to purchase existing stocks doesn't add to the productive capacity of the economy, it isn't part of investment. While we'll focus on the narrower set of choices that macroeconomists mean when they talk about investment, you can use the analytic framework that we're about to develop to analyse any decision you face that involves up-front costs and future benefits. Let's start by exploring what macroeconomists mean when they talk about investment.

Figure 1 | Gross Domestic Product

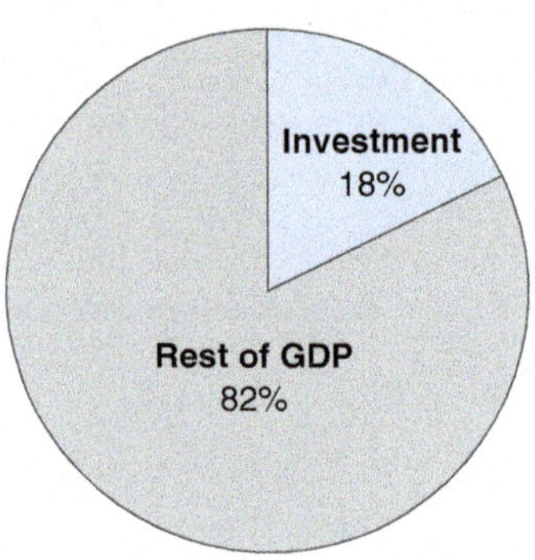

Data from: Australian Bureau of Statistics.

Macroeconomic investment refers to spending on capital. When macroeconomists talk about investment, they mean spending by businesses on new software, equipment, and structures, the accumulation of inventories, and spending on new housing. They include not just physical capital, but also intellectual property.

Macroeconomists focus on this specific definition because macroeconomic investment in capital is a key driver of macroeconomic performance. It's an important component of spending and a critical ingredient into future production. Figure 1 shows that investment comprises around 18% of total Australian GDP, which means that investment spending adds up to around $13,000 per person each year.

Don't confuse investment and saving. As you've seen, the macroeconomist's definition of investment excludes a lot of stuff that most people refer to as investments. That's because people often fail to draw a distinction between *saving*—which is the money you have left over after paying for your spending—and *investment* which is spending on new capital that'll increase the productive capacity of the economy. Putting money in the bank is a form of saving. It isn't an investment because it doesn't involve any actual spending on new capital. (As we'll discuss later in this chapter, saving and investment are related because if your bank lends the money you save to a business which uses it to fund a factory, then that spending will count as investment.) Buying shares in the Commonwealth Bank, bars of gold, or a block of land doesn't count as macroeconomic investment because you're simply buying an *existing* asset from someone else, without creating any new productive capacity.

Investment adds to the capital stock; depreciation subtracts from it. The total quantity of capital at a point in time is called the **capital stock.** Investment is the *flow* of new purchases of capital that add to this stock. But capital also declines over time due to **depreciation,** which includes wear and tear, obsolescence, accidental damage, and aging. As a result, this year's capital stock is equal to last year's capital stock, less depreciation, plus new investment over the past year. This means that the capital stock rises when new investment exceeds depreciation, but declines when depreciation exceeds investment.

capital stock The total quantity of capital at a point in time.

depreciation The decline in capital due to wear and tear, obsolescence, accidental damage, and aging.

business investment Spending by businesses on new capital assets.

housing investment Spending on building or improving houses or apartments.

Types of Investment

Macroeconomists break investment into four primary categories. The biggest category is business investment and Figure 2 shows you some of its subcomponents as well. Let's take a closer look at three of these types of investments.

Figure 2 | Investment

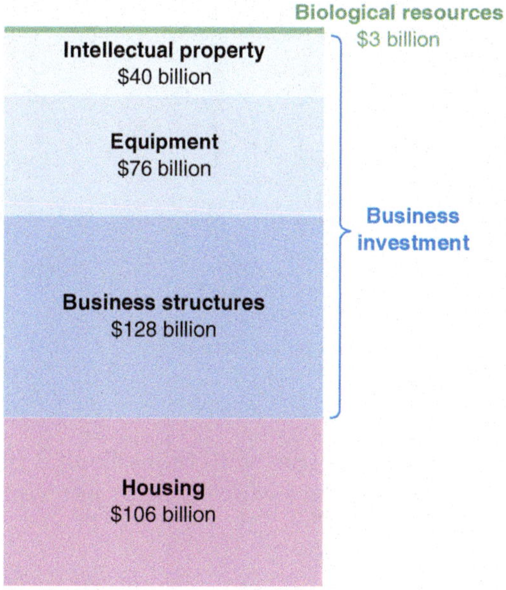

Data from: Australian Bureau of Statistics.

Investment type one: Business investment. **Business investment** refers to spending by businesses on new capital assets. This includes spending on equipment (new computers, machinery, and company cars), structures (new offices, stores, factories, and remodelling of existing facilities), and intellectual property (spending on software; on literary, television, movie, and music production; and research and development). These three types of business investment all have one thing in common—they are purchases by businesses that increase the productive capacity of the economy.

Investment type two: Housing investment. **Housing investment** refers to spending on building new houses or apartments, as well as improvements to existing housing. It includes both homes that you buy to live in and housing that you plan to rent out.

Housing investment is a bit different from business investment, because when you live in a house, it doesn't generate revenue. But the *opportunity cost principle* reminds you that your family home *could* be used to generate rental income. Thus, building a new family home counts as investment because it's an increase in the stock of capital that increases the economy's productive capacity—increasing the economy's *capacity* to generate rent. For similar reasons, remodelling a home is an investment. But sales of existing homes simply transfer ownership from one person to another, and hence don't count as investment because they don't increase the economy's productive capacity.

CapturePB/Shutterstock

Buying an old home doesn't count as investment—but spending on renovations does.

Investment type three: Inventories. Businesses also invest by maintaining inventories of raw materials, work-in-progress, and unsold goods. For instance, the cars you can test-drive at your local car dealership are counted as inventories. Because it's necessary to keep at least some level of inventories on hand as part of the production process, they're counted as part of the capital stock. And so an increase in inventories is counted as investment.

The change in inventories is only a tiny share of total investment. But it's also volatile, because unsold goods build up quickly when sales are weak. Changes in inventories swing from being positive to negative—often from one year to the next. Because of this fluctuation, it is not shown in Figure 2.

Investment Is a Key Economic Variable

While investment only accounts for around one-sixth of all spending, it's a category that economists pay close attention to because it has an extraordinarily important impact on the economy.

Figure 3 | **Investment Drives the Business Cycle**

Percent change in GDP and Investment over the past year

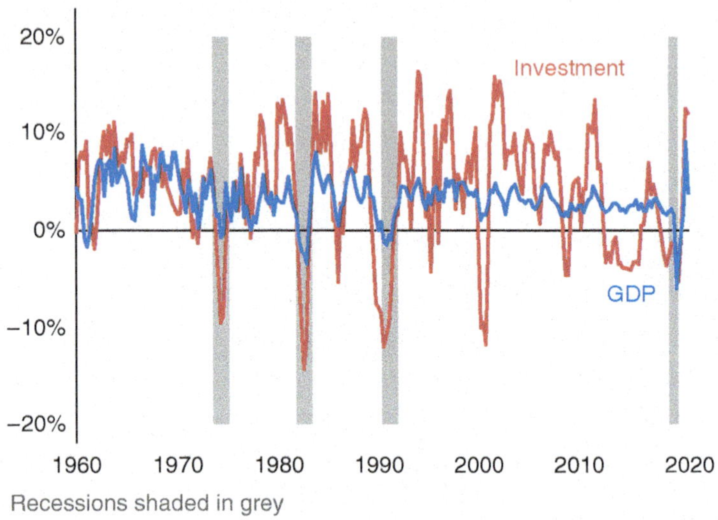

Data from: Australian Bureau of Statistics.

Investment drives the business cycle. Investment fluctuates dramatically as business conditions change, so it plays an outsized role in driving the ups and downs of the business cycle. Figure 3 shows the relationship between the annual percent change in GDP and investment. A recession might lead GDP to decline by 1% from the previous year. In contrast, investment might decline by more than 10% from the previous year, as it did in 1982. Likewise, a strong economy might lead GDP to grow by 2%, but it could cause investment to grow by 10 times as much. In short, investment changes more from year to year than GDP does.

Investment is very sensitive to business conditions partly because managers can easily delay or cancel expansion plans. Moreover, because investment decisions are forward-looking, they're extremely sensitive to expectations about the future state of the economy. Investment is also sensitive to financial sector conditions because businesses often have to get a loan to fund their investments. It's often said that once you figure out what drives investment, you've figured out much of what drives the business cycle.

Figure 4 | **Countries with More Capital per Worker Produce More Output per Worker**

Output per worker

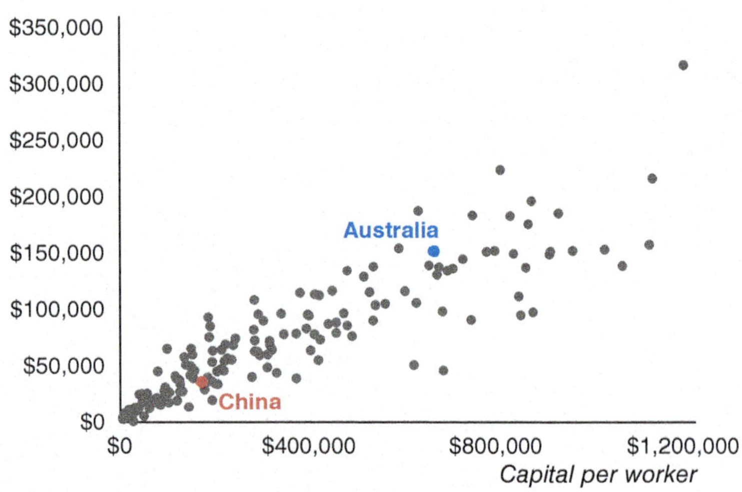

Data from: Penn World Tables 10.0.

Investment changes quickly, but the capital stock changes slowly. Today's capital stock is the accumulation of investments made over many previous years. As a result, even though investment—the *flow* of new spending on physical capital—often fluctuates quite dramatically, the capital stock—which is the *stock* typically of physical capital—only moves slowly. Indeed, the capital stock typically rises gradually over time, and it doesn't change much from year to year. As such, the capital stock provides a relatively stable link between last year's economy and today's economy.

Investment is a key driver of long-term prosperity. Investments in capital are an important source of differences across countries in productivity and hence prosperity. The more capital—tools, machines, and computers—your workers have to work with, the more output they'll be able to produce. Indeed, Figure 4 shows that countries with more capital per worker typically have more productive workers, producing more output per worker.

Education is another big driver of worker productivity, but investments in human capital—that is, going to school and university—aren't counted in macroeconomic investment. If they were to be included, then the role of investment in making some countries more productive, and therefore more prosperous, would become even more dramatic.

26.2 Tools to Analyse Investments

Learning Objective *Master two tools for comparing sums of money at different points in time: compounding and discounting.*

Our task for the rest of this chapter is to develop a framework that you can use to evaluate investment decisions. This means developing tools you can use to compare costs and benefits that accrue *at different points in time.* While our focus will be on business investments, you can use these tools to assess any decision in which you face *an up-front cost to gain a stream of future benefits.*

To see how these issues play out in the business world, put yourself in the shoes of Valentina Garcia, an economics graduate now working as an energy analyst for a renewable energy company in Queensland. The company already operates eight wind turbines, which harness enough energy to power nearly 15,000 homes. As wind energy is becoming more popular, her CEO is trying to decide whether to invest in one more turbine. The CEO asked Valentina to crunch the numbers to see if this would be a worthwhile investment. Valentina's inner environmentalist is thrilled that wind is becoming a more mainstream energy source, but she also knows that her company can only play a role in this transformation if it makes good investment decisions.

As a former economics student, Valentina knows that the *cost-benefit principle* says it's worth investing in a new wind turbine if the benefits are at least as large as the costs. But the cost of the turbine is incurred up front, while the benefits will be spread out over many years, as the company will sell the electricity that turbine generates for decades to come. How can she compare costs and benefits that accrue at different points in time?

There are two tools you can use to analyse how value changes over time: compounding and discounting. Compounding helps you calculate how money grows over time when you leave it to accumulate interest in a bank. Discounting is the flip side of the same coin. You use it to figure out how much money in the future is worth today, by calculating how much you would need to put in the bank today, in order to grow into that sum in the future. We'll first develop these two tools and then we'll apply them to illustrate how they'll help Valentina evaluate whether to purchase that extra wind turbine.

Investment Tool One: Compounding

A new turbine requires an up-front investment of \$4 million. The *opportunity cost principle* reminds Valentina to account for the next best option for her company's money. One way to do this is to consider what would happen if her company instead put the money in the bank and allowed it to accumulate interest.

To see how money grows with interest, let's start with a simpler example: What happens when you put \$100 in the bank? If the interest rate is 6%, then a year later, you'll get your \$100 back, plus \$6 in interest. More generally, for each dollar that you put in the bank today, a year later you will get your dollar back, plus interest of r cents per dollar (for example, when the interest rate is 6%, r is 0.06):

$$\text{Future value in one year} = \underbrace{\text{Present value}}_{\text{You get your money back}} + \underbrace{r \times \text{Present value}}_{\text{plus } r\% \text{ interest}}$$
$$= \text{Present value} \times (1+r)$$

Each year you leave your money in the bank, it is multiplied by $1+r$. What happens if you leave your money in the bank for more than a year? Short answer: It will continue to grow. By how much? In the second year, you won't just get interest on your original deposit; you'll also get interest on the interest you've earned. In the third year, you'll also get interest-on-interest-on-interest and so on. So when you put \$100 in the bank earning 6% annual interest, in the first year you earn interest on \$100. In the second year, you earn interest on \$106 (your original \$100 plus the \$6 in interest you earned the first year). In the third year, you earn interest on \$112.36 (\$100+\$6+\$6.36). Because you're earning interest on ever-increasing amounts, the interest you earn each year grows.

This is the magic of *compound interest:* You earn interest not only on your initial deposit but also on previously earned interest, so your wealth compounds. As we'll see, the numbers can really add up. How much? We'll need a formula to calculate how much your money will grow into by a specific future date, and we'll call this amount the **future value** of your money.

future value The amount that your money will grow into by a future date, as a result of earning interest.

The key to calculating the *future value* of a sum of money is to note that each year your total balance grows by r percent, the interest rate. This means that each year your balance is simply whatever it was the previous year, multiplied by $(1+r)$. Figure 5 illustrates how your balance will grow:

Figure 5 | The Compounding Formula

Your money grows over time, earning interest and interest-on-interest and so on.

(A) Begin with an initial deposit of \$*P*, called the **present value.**

(B) Each year your money will earn **interest** and grow to be **$(1+r)$** times larger.

(C) After *t* years, your money has grown to be worth: **Future value** = **Present value** × **$(1+r)^t$**.

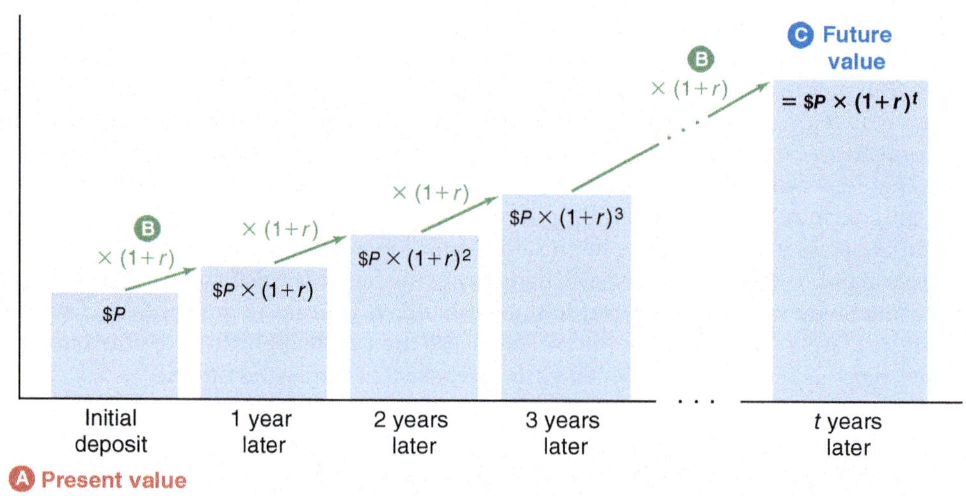

If you invest \$$P$ today, it becomes \$$P\times(1+r)$ next year. The next year that balance also grows by $(1+r)$, so after two years your balance is \$$P\times(1+r)\times(1+r)$, which can also be expressed as \$$P\times(1+r)^2$. The third year it's multiplied by $(1+r)$ again. Keep doing this for t years and the end result is the **compounding formula:**

compounding formula Future value in t years = Present value × $(1+r)^t$

$$\text{Future value in } t \text{ years} = \text{Present value} \times (1+r)^t$$

Figure 6 | Calculating Future Value

Punch in the present value, the annual interest rate, and the number of years, and the spreadsheet will calculate the future value your funds will grow into.

	A	B
1	**Inputs**	
2	Present (or initial) value	\$4,000,000
3	Annual interest rate, *r*	6%
4	Years of compounding, *t*	30
5		
6	**Future value**	**\$22,973,965**
7	= Present value × $(1+r)^t$	=B2*(1+B3)^B4

Use a spreadsheet to apply the compounding formula. You can use the compounding formula to figure out the future value of your money. It's even easier to let a spreadsheet do the calculations for you. Let's return to Valentina's project and use a spreadsheet to figure out how much \$4 million would grow into if, instead of buying a turbine, she put that money in the bank where it earned 6% interest per year for 30 years.

Figure 6 shows how to implement the compounding formula in a spreadsheet such as Microsoft Excel, Google Sheets, or Apple's Numbers. You need to punch the inputs into separate cells—the initial balance, which we'll call the present value since it's money you have right now in the present; the annual interest rate; and the number of years it compounds or grows. In another cell you can then apply the compounding formula:

$$\text{Future value in } t \text{ years} = \underbrace{\$4{,}000{,}000}_{\text{Present value}} \times \underbrace{(1+0.06)^{30}}_{(1+r)^t} = \$22{,}973{,}965$$

The only real trick is to know that spreadsheets interpret the hat or caret character "^"—the one above the number 6 on your keyboard—as "to the power of," while they interpret the asterisk or star ("*" above number 8) as "multiplied by." Putting it all together, the spreadsheet shows you that over 30 years at a 6% annual interest rate, $4 million grows to roughly $23 million. (To be precise, it's $22,973,965.) If that sounds like a lot, perhaps you now understand why it's called the magic of compound interest.

EVERYDAY Economics **The extraordinary power of compound interest**

Compound interest is an example of an *exponential process*. In each time period, the original amount invested grows by a certain rate, but the previous amounts of growth also grow themselves. They "compound". Perhaps this is why when Albert Einstein—the most famous scientist of all time—was asked what humankind's greatest invention was he cheekily suggested compound interest. He described it as the "eighth wonder of the world," saying, "he who understands it, earns it; he who doesn't, pays for it."

We saw exponential processes at work during the coronavirus pandemic. As billionaire philanthropist Bill Gates observed in early 2020: "Exponential growth is not intuitive. If you say that 2 percent of the population is infected and this will double every eight days, most people won't immediately figure out that in 40 days, the majority of the population will be infected."

This property of exponential growth also explains the power of compound interest in building wealth. A rich and quirky New York lawyer Jonathan Holdeen wanted to harness this power. Holdeen was a bit of an oddball—he was a tightwad who cut his own hair, lived on a diet of prunes, milk, and shredded wheat, and cut the worn sleeves off his sweaters so he could use the remainder as a vest. He was also obsessed with compound interest. He did some maths, figuring that if he invested a penny at a 4% interest rate and allowed it to compound for a thousand years, it would grow into a thousand trillion dollars. Go ahead, check his math: $\$0.01 \times (1+0.04)^{1{,}000} \approx \$1{,}000{,}000{,}000{,}000{,}000$. Every penny saved, to Mr. Holdeen, was a thousand trillion dollars gained.

Keystone Press/Alamy Stock Photo

Albert Einstein joked that compound interest is the "eighth wonder of the world."

Mr. Holdeen wanted to use the power of compound interest to change the world. He put millions of dollars in charitable trusts and ordered that they were to compound for up to 1,000 years. He hoped that his trust would grow into quadrillions or maybe quintillions of dollars—enough that he could abolish all taxes in Pennsylvania.

Instead, he set off a 50-year legal battle as lawyers debated whether his big idea was a good idea. The problem, according to one economist, was that the trust would grow so big that "everyone in the world would work for the Holdeens." The courts agreed that this was a bad idea, ruling that the trust had to donate each year's interest payments to charity. This ruling robbed the trust of the ability to earn interest that could compound, and so it simply stopped growing, which is why Pennsylvanians will have to keep paying taxes. ■

Investment Tool Two: Discounting

You need to understand the power of compound interest to make investment decisions because it shows why revenue received in the future is worth less than revenue that you get today. It's all about the *opportunity cost principle:* Money that you're paid in the future rather than in the present comes with a large opportunity cost—the forgone opportunity to benefit from the power of compound interest.

Discounting reflects the opportunity cost of revenues you receive in the future. To measure this opportunity cost, you can reverse the compounding formula to figure out how to compare money received in the future with money that you get

present value The amount of money that you would need to invest today in order to produce an equivalent benefit in the future.

discounting Converting *future values* into their equivalent *present values*.

discounting formula Present value = Future value in t years $\times \frac{1}{(1+r)^t}$

in the present. The **present value** is the amount of money that you'd need to invest *today* in order to produce an equivalent benefit in the future. The process to calculate present value is called **discounting,** which means converting future values into their equivalent present values. Discounting is the opposite of compounding—you're converting large future values into the smaller present values from which they could have grown.

To take a simple example, when the interest rate is 6%, the present value of receiving \$106 in a year's time is \$100, because you could get \$106 next year just by putting \$100 into the bank today and waiting. More generally, you can take the compounding formula—Future value in t years = Present value $\times (1+r)^t$—and rearrange it to get the **discounting formula:**

$$\text{Present value} = \text{Future value in } t \text{ years} \times \frac{1}{(1+r)^t}$$

The discounting formula shows how much money you'd need today to create a specific future value in t years' time.

Discounting converts future values into present values. Figure 7 illustrates that just as the compounding formula converts money you have in the present into its potential future values, the discounting formula converts potential future values into their equivalent present values.

Figure 7 | **Compounding and Discounting**

Compounding and Discounting

As money moves through time, its value changes

A Put \$4 million in the bank for 30 years at a 6% interest rate and it'll grow from a \$4 million present value to a \$23 million future value.

B To calculate the future value of money you put in the bank today, use the compounding formula: Future value in t years = Present value $\times (1+r)^t$.

C To calculate how much money you would need to put in the bank today to get a specific payoff in the future, use the discounting formula: Present value = Future value $\times \frac{1}{(1+r)^t}$.

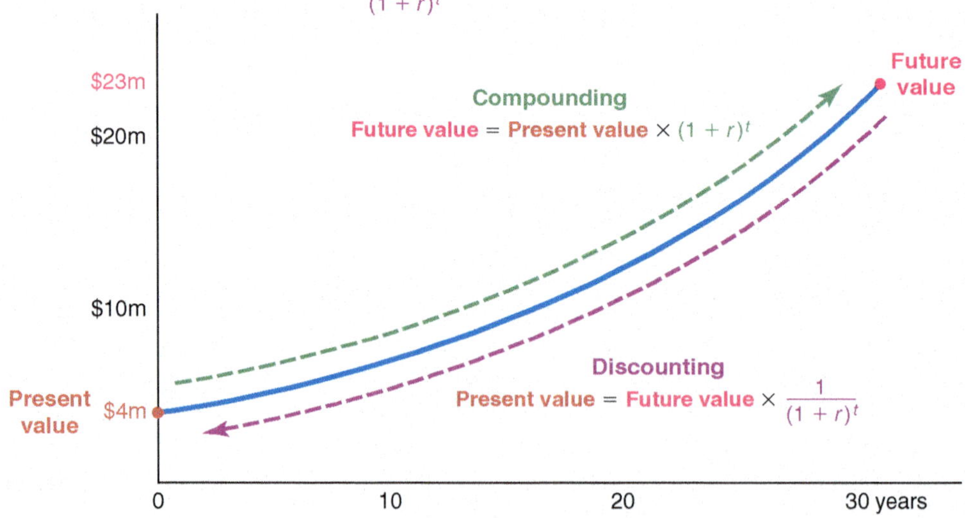

Let's apply this logic: Remember that Valentina discovered that \$4 million dollars invested for 30 years at 6% interest will grow to be \$22,973,965. We can turn that around and ask: What's the present value of receiving a payment of \$22,973,965 in 30 years, if the interest rate is 6% per year? I bet you know the answer, but let's work it out using the discounting formula:

$$\text{Present value} = \underbrace{\$22{,}973{,}965}_{\text{Future value}} \times \underbrace{\frac{1}{(1+0.06)^{30}}}_{1/(1+r)^t} = \$4{,}000{,}000$$

And so just as $4 million would grow into a future value of $22,973,965 over 30 years (at a 6% interest rate), the present value of $22,973,965 in 30 years (when the interest rate is 6%) is $4 million.

Use a spreadsheet to apply the discounting formula. No one expects you to do these calculations in your head! Figure 8 shows how you can use a spreadsheet to work it out. This time, you enter the future value and let the spreadsheet calculate the present value by applying the *discounting formula*.

This calculation suggests that Valentina should value $23 million that her company receives in 30 years' time as much as receiving $4 million today. The logic of discounting is just the inverse of compounding—Valentina could use $4 million today to create $23 million in 30 years, simply by putting it in the bank.

Figure 8 | Calculating Present Value

Punch in the future sum of money, the number of years until you receive it, and the annual interest rate, and the spreadsheet will calculate the present value, which is how much you need to invest today to get to that sum in the future.

	A	B
1	**Inputs**	
2	Future value	$22,973,965
3	Annual interest rate, r	6%
4	Years of compounding, t	30
5		
6	**Present value**	**$4,000,000**
7	= Future value × $1/(1+r)^t$	=*B2**1/(1+*B3*)^*B4*

Present values tell you how much you should pay for a future payoff. To see how present value calculations can be useful, let's return to Mr. Holdeen, the oddball New York lawyer. During the Great Depression, rich heirs and heiresses who fell on hard times found themselves in the awkward position of being poor today, but expecting a big inheritance in the future. Mr. Holdeen offered them a way out of this fix. He offered to buy up the right to their inheritance, usually at a steep discount. If they accepted, the heirs got Mr. Holdeen's cash today, and he got their inheritance when the rich relative died. Mr. Holdeen used discounting to figure out how much he'd be willing to pay for an inheritance in the future.

Bettmann/Getty Images

How much will you pay for her inheritance?

Do the Economics

A down-on-her-luck heiress stands to inherit $1 million from a rich aunt who's likely to die in 14 years. She offers to sell Mr. Holdeen her inheritance rights. If you were in his shoes, what's the most you'd pay for this if the interest rate is 6%?

$$\text{Present value} = \frac{\$1,000,000}{(1+0.06)^{14}} = \$442,301$$

To see why Mr. Holdeen wouldn't want to pay more than this, realise that he could create $1 million in 14 years simply by putting $442,301 in the bank today and allowing it to compound for 14 years. ■

Real versus Nominal Interest Rates

You can use the compounding and discounting formulas to figure out how much either the *nominal* or *real* value of your money changes through time. The trick to figuring out how the nominal or real value of your money changes through time is picking the right interest rate:

- If you're evaluating the *nominal value* of your funds—that is, how many dollar bills you'll have in a few years' time—make sure that you plug the *nominal interest rate* into the compounding or discounting formula.
- To evaluate the *real value* of your funds—that is, your changing purchasing power, after adjusting for inflation—plug the *real interest rate* into the compounding or discounting formula.

Let's see how much this matters.

Do the Economics

Value of Buying $1,000 Worth of Stocks In 1920

Real value of stock portfolio

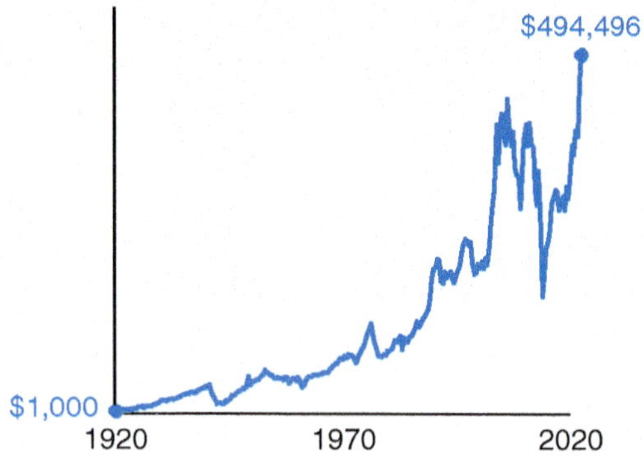

Between 1920 and 2020, money in the stock market grew at an average rate of 10% per year. If you had put $1,000 in the stock market in 1920, how much would it have compounded into by 2020?

$$\text{(Nominal) future value in 100 years} = \$1{,}000 \times (1+0.10)^{100} = \$13{,}780{,}612!$$

Your $1,000 would have grown over 13,780 times larger! But part of this reflects the influence of inflation, which averaged 3.6% per year. To evaluate what your change in purchasing power would have been, you must focus on the real interest rate. Recall that the real interest rate is (approximately) equal to the nominal interest rate (here, 10%) minus the inflation rate of 3.6% a year. Thus, funds in the stock market grew by 6.4% per year in real terms. That 6.4% represents how much more stuff you could buy each year as a result of your interest earnings.

Calculate the real growth rate of your $1,000:

$$\text{(Real) future value in 100 years} = \$1{,}000 \times (1+0.064)^{100} = \$494{,}496!$$

That 3.6% inflation makes a big difference. While you'd have had 13,780 times as many dollars, you wouldn't have been able to buy 13,780 times as much stuff. Instead, in real terms your purchasing power would have grown 494 times larger, meaning that you would have been able to buy 494 times as much stuff after 100 years in the stock market. While that's a lot smaller, it is still pretty awesome. The magic of compound interest is why financial advisors tell you to start saving early! ■

26.3 Making Investment Decisions

Learning Objective *Evaluate whether an investment opportunity is worth pursuing.*

Now that you've got these tools in your analytic toolkit, it's time to put them to work. They'll be essential for our next task, which is to develop the framework that top managers use to evaluate investment opportunities.

How to Evaluate an Investment Opportunity

There's no better way to illustrate this framework than to work through a real-world problem, so put yourself in Valentina's shoes as we work through her assignment. She has gathered all the relevant information and now needs to put it together to figure out whether to invest in another wind turbine.

Compare the present value of costs and benefits. An investment is like any other choice—the *cost-benefit principle* says it's worth doing if the benefits exceed the costs. The wrinkle is that the costs and benefits accrue at different points in time. The *opportunity cost principle* reminds you that revenues you receive in the future are less valuable because you'll forgo the opportunity to earn interest on those funds. That's why you should focus on the *present value* of the costs and benefits associated with an investment, which account for this opportunity cost. Computing the present value of both your costs and benefits puts them in similar units—today's dollars—which makes them comparable. The difference between the present value of your revenues and the present value of your costs tells you how much an investment opportunity will boost your profits relative to investing those funds in your next best alternative.

All of this yields clear advice that should guide your analysis: *Invest in new capital if the present value of the benefits exceeds the present value of the costs.*

The present value of an up-front cost is simply the up-front cost. Valentina sets to work, making a few calculations. The cost of this investment is the easy part: Buying a wind turbine costs $4 million. Because this cost is incurred in the present, it has a present value of $4 million. (If the costs accrued over many years, then you would evaluate the total of the present value of each of those future costs.) As we're about to see, the real work of evaluating most investment projects comes in valuing the stream of future benefits.

Carol Heesen/Alamy Stock Photo

Turbines depreciate.

Take account of depreciation when projecting future revenue. To figure out the benefits, Valentina needs to forecast the future annual revenues one extra turbine will generate, and then calculate their corresponding present values. Her company's engineers have provided Valentina with data summarising their expectations for the extra energy the new turbine will generate each year; and she has translated those gains into revenue forecasts.

This year: Installing the turbine will take all year, so it will generate no revenue.

First year revenue: The turbine will generate revenue of $600,000.

Revenue in following years: As the turbine ages, it won't be as productive due to *depreciation*. It'll break down more often and spend more days out of service being repaired. The engineers report that, on average, a wind turbine will produce 4% less output each year than it did in the previous year. They're describing the **depreciation rate,** which is the proportion of an investment's remaining productive capacity you lose each year due to depreciation. We'll use the letter d to denote the depreciation rate.

depreciation rate The proportion of an investment's remaining productive capacity you lose each year due to depreciation.

Valentina makes sure her revenue forecasts account for this depreciation rate. She expects the price she'll get for the electricity the turbine generates will keep up with inflation, and so depreciation is the only reason her real revenues will change over time. That's why she forecasts that the real revenue the turbine generates will decline from $600,000 in the first year, to be 4% lower at $576,000 in the second year, and then another 4% lower at $552,960 in the third year. As you read down each row of Figure 9, you'll see that in each subsequent year, she forecasts that the turbine will generate 4% less revenue than it did the previous year.

Figure 9 | Calculating the Stream of Revenues in Present Value

Using a depreciation rate of d = 4% and interest rate of r = 6%

Year	Future revenue = Last year's revenue × $(1-d)$		Present value of future revenue = Future revenue × $\frac{1}{(1+r)^t}$	
			Discounting	
0		$0		$0
1	Depreciation	$600,000	$\times \frac{1}{(1+r)^1}$	$566,038
2	$\times (1-d)$	$576,000	$\times \frac{1}{(1+r)^2}$	$512,638
3	$\times (1-d)$	$552,960	$\times \frac{1}{(1+r)^3}$	$464,276
4	$\times (1-d)$	$530,842	$\times \frac{1}{(1+r)^4}$	$420,476
. . .		. . .		. . .

Convert future revenues into their present values. Having forecast the turbine's future revenues, Valentina needs to account for the fact that the value of this money depends on when she receives it. She does this by calculating the *present value* of each year's revenue forecast. She applies a 6% real interest rate to the discounting formula, because that's what the people in her company's treasury department say they could earn if they invested the $4 million elsewhere.

The final column of Figure 9 shows the present value of each year's revenue forecast. The turbine generates no revenue while it's being installed. After one year, it creates $600,000 in revenue. But it'll take a year to get that revenue, so Valentina needs to discount it, multiplying $600,000 by $1/(1+0.06)$, to calculate the present value of $566,038. As the discounting formula dictates, revenue earned in two years' time is discounted by multiplying it by $1/(1+0.06)^2$ and so on.

A good wind turbine can last a long time, so Valentina's actual spreadsheet goes on for dozens more rows showing the present value of the revenue she forecasts it'll generate each year over many future decades. I can't show you the whole thing here, but Figure 10 shows the column that matters most to Valentina—the present value of the additional revenue she forecasts the turbine will generate in each year. Add it all up, and you get

Figure 10 | **Present Value of Each Year's Future Revenue**

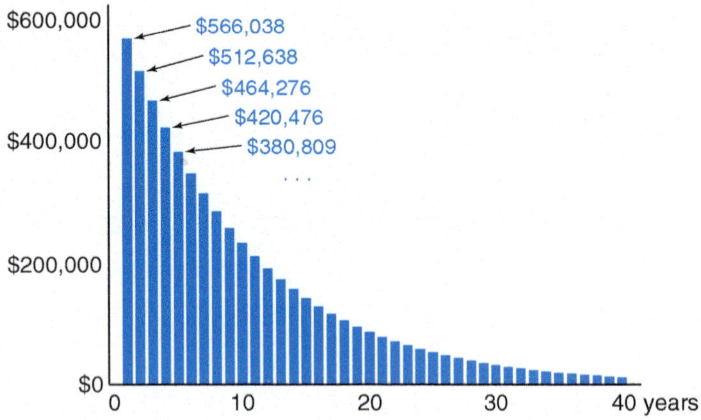

$566,038 + $512,638 + $464,276 + $420,476 + $380,809 + . . . and so on. In her actual spreadsheet, Valentina keeps adding the revenue from all future years, arriving at a total of $6 million. (You can punch the numbers into a spreadsheet to check this for yourself.)

A shortcut: Use the valuation formula to calculate the present value of a stream of future revenues. It might appear that calculating the present value of a stream of future revenues takes a lot of spreadsheet work. But there's a shortcut that makes it a lot easier. The **valuation formula** says that the *present value* of a stream of payments that starts with *next year's revenue* and where the subsequent payments decline or *depreciate* each year by d percent is:

valuation formula Present value of an ongoing stream of payments $= \frac{\text{Next year's revenue}}{r+d}$

$$\text{Present value of a stream of payments} = \frac{\text{Next year's revenue}}{r+d}$$

It's called the *valuation formula* because it tells you how much you would value this future stream of revenue in today's dollars. (This bit is in parentheses, so you can skip it. If you want some intuition for where this formula comes from, notice in the last column of Figure 9 that the present value of each year's revenue is $(1-d)/(1+r)$ times as large as the previous year, which makes it a *geometric series*. The valuation formula follows from evaluating the infinite sum of this geometric series.)

Top executives know how to use this formula, even if they've forgotten the maths that leads to it. Most importantly, they know when it applies, which is anytime you're evaluating the expected value of a long-lasting stream of future revenues that start next year and then decline at a constant proportional rate over time.

Do the Economics

Let's apply the valuation formula to Valentina's investment decision. Her turbine will generate $600,000 revenue in its first year, the real interest rate is 6%, the depreciation rate is 4%, and it'll keep generating revenues for many decades:

$$\text{Present value of a stream of payments} = \frac{\text{Next year's revenue}}{r+d} = \frac{\$600{,}000}{0.06+0.04} = \$6 \text{ million}$$

This shortcut worked perfectly, producing exactly the same answer as when we calculated each year's revenues and calculated their present values. ■

Invest if the present value of benefits exceeds the present value of costs. At this point, Valentina has all the information she needs. Having assessed both the costs and benefits in present value terms, she can return to the *cost-benefit principle*. The total benefits of purchasing the turbine—many years of future revenue that add up to a present value of $6 million—exceed the up-front cost of $4 million. This looks like an extremely profitable investment, so she advises her company's CEO to purchase that extra wind turbine. It's a smart decision that will add $2 million to her company's value.

The Rational Rule for Investors

You'll boost your company's long-run profitability any time you invest in an opportunity where the present value of your future revenues exceeds the up-front cost. It's profitable because the benefits exceed the costs. We focus on present values to put these costs and benefits in comparable terms, accounting for the opportunity cost of having to wait to receive those future revenues.

At this point, you've uncovered a powerful rule you can apply to your company's investment decisions:

The **Rational Rule for Investors:** *Pursue an investment opportunity if the present value of future revenues exceeds the up-front cost, C.* This means you should invest when:

$$\underbrace{\frac{\text{Next year's revenue}}{r+d}}_{\substack{\text{Present value}\\\text{of future revenues}}} > \underbrace{C}_{\substack{\text{Up-front}\\\text{cost}}}$$

Rational Rule for Investors Pursue an investment opportunity if the present value of future revenues exceeds the up-front cost.

Follow this rule, and every investment will boost your long-run profits. The *Rational Rule for Investors* puts together the advice from three of the four core principles in one sentence. It takes the big question facing managers about how much to invest, and applies the *marginal principle*, focusing on the simpler question of whether you should invest in one more turbine. The *cost-benefit principle* suggests that yes, you should, if the benefits—which are the future revenues you'll receive—exceed the up-front cost. To compare these, you should focus on present values that embed the *opportunity cost principle*, evaluating future revenues in terms of what you would have to give up to get them.

The *Rational Rule for Investors* provides good advice because it'll lead you to invest only when it'll boost your long-run profitability. Let's apply it to the most important investment decision you may ever make.

EVERYDAY Economics Your decision to invest in education

Your education is a lot like a wind turbine: It involves a big up-front cost (which you're incurring now), and it'll yield a stream of benefits that will accrue over the rest of your life. Indeed, you can evaluate the benefits of investing in your intellectual machinery using the same ideas that managers use to evaluate investments in any other kind of machinery.

One of the biggest benefits of education is the higher salary you'll earn as a result of having more education. Let's take a stab at valuing these higher earnings using the *valuation formula*. We'll need three inputs: the extra revenue you get from your university degree, the depreciation rate of your degree, and the real interest rate you could earn investing in your next best alternative.

CulturalEyes-AusGS2/Alamy Stock Photo

An incredibly important investment.

Measuring the extra revenue: The median earnings of someone with a bachelor's degree (but no graduate degree) in 2020 was $74,300, while those with only a high school degree earned $46,800. The difference is $27,500 dollars per year. (A certificate III/IV or diploma boosts your earnings by about half this amount.)

Measuring the depreciation rate: University graduates continue to outearn high school graduates throughout their lives, suggesting that whatever you learn in university sticks with you throughout your career. But your degree still depreciates because as you age you're less likely to work, and economists estimate the depreciation rate to be around 2% a year.

The real interest rate: We'll plug in a value for the real interest rate of 3%, which is roughly the rate at which university graduates can borrow and lend. (You can experiment with other values.)

Put it all together, and we get:

$$\text{Present value of a college education} = \frac{\text{Next year's revenue}}{r+d}$$

$$= \frac{\$27{,}500}{0.03+0.02} = \$550{,}000$$

Let that sink in. A four-year university degree is so valuable that it's worth more than half a million dollars in present value. (And it follows that a certificate III/IV or diploma provides around half this boost and is worth over a quarter of a million dollars.) To evaluate the relevant costs, apply the *opportunity cost principle* and ask "or what?" Don't just count the costs of tuition; you also need to factor in the opportunity cost of the income you could otherwise have earned if you were in the workforce instead of university. It's a good bet that the present discounted value of your degree will be much higher than the present value of tuition plus the wages you're giving up to study.

In short, it's unlikely that the up-front cost of university is as large as the present value of the benefit, suggesting that university is a very profitable investment. Given how profitable it is, I would urge you to invest in reading the rest of this chapter about investment! ■

An Alternative Perspective: The User Cost of Capital

So far, we've analysed Valentina's investment decision as if she's deciding whether to buy a wind turbine that her company will keep forever—or at least until it breaks down. That required assessing the full set of costs and benefits that accrue over the turbine's entire lifetime. You can gain an alternative perspective on the *Rational Rule for Investors* by pushing the *marginal principle* even further. Instead of asking whether to buy a machine you'll keep for many decades, you might ask: Should I buy one more machine *for one more year?* That is, should you buy a machine even if you plan on selling it in a year's time?

The *cost-benefit principle* says your answer should be yes, if the marginal benefits exceed the marginal costs. And so this alternative perspective focuses on the marginal benefit and marginal cost of using that extra machine *for one more year.* (And at the end of that year, you can evaluate what to do the following year.)

The marginal benefit is fairly straightforward: That extra machine will generate extra revenue, and we'll describe this extra revenue you'll earn next year as being *next year's revenue.*

The user cost of capital is forgone interest plus depreciation. What is the marginal cost of buying one more wind turbine at the start of the year, and then selling it at the end? There are two costs to consider:

Depreciation: The turbine will be worth less at the end of the year because of depreciation. If the depreciation rate is 4%, then a \$4 million turbine will sell for 4%×\$4 million = \$160,000 less at the end of the year because it's 4% less productive. More generally, when you buy capital equipment and sell it a year later, you can expect to lose an amount equal to the depreciation rate times the cost of the investment: $d \times C$.

Forgone interest: The *opportunity cost principle* reminds you that there's another cost to consider, because you're tying up your funds for a year. To assess this cost, ask yourself: I could invest in this machine, or what? The opportunity cost for Valentina of investing \$4 million in the wind turbine for a year is that her company could earn a 6% return on those funds, which means that she's forgoing 6%×\$4 million = \$240,000 in interest. More generally, this opportunity cost is equal to forgone rate of return times the cost of purchasing the machine: $r \times C$.

Putting these two pieces together yields the **user cost of capital,** which is the extra cost associated with using one more machine next year. It's called the *user cost*—or sometimes the *rental cost*—because it's what you're effectively paying to "use" or "rent" the turbine for a year. The user cost of employing one more machine for a year is equal to the depreciation cost ($d \times C$) plus the forgone interest ($r \times C$), which adds up to:

user cost of capital The extra cost associated with using one more machine next year $= (r + d) \times C$

$$\text{User cost of capital} = (r+d) \times C$$

Do the Economics

The engineers tell Valentina that if she spends $4 million buying a new wind turbine to use next year, at the end of the year it'll be worth 4% less. The real interest rate is 6% per year. Calculate the user cost of owning this turbine for one year.

$$\text{User cost} = (0.06 + 0.04) \times \$4{,}000{,}000 = \$400{,}000$$ ■

Compare the user cost of capital with next year's additional revenue. The user cost of capital represents the marginal cost of adding one more machine for a year. You should compare it to the corresponding marginal benefit of adding that extra turbine, which is the extra revenue you'll earn next year. Comparing these suggests that it'll be profitable to invest in an additional turbine for next year if:

$$\underbrace{\text{Next year's revenue}}_{\text{Marginal benefit}} > \underbrace{(r+d) \times C}_{\text{Marginal cost}}$$

Let's apply this logic to Valentina's company. The marginal benefit of investing in a turbine for a year is the extra revenue it'll generate next year. If she's looking at a new turbine, that'll be the first-year revenue, which you may recall is $600,000. That marginal benefit exceeds the user cost of capital we just calculated to be $400,000, so this alternative perspective also concludes that she should invest in buying the turbine.

Both perspectives yield the same advice. You can rearrange this formula by dividing both sides by $(r + d)$. Now it says you should invest if:

$$\underbrace{\frac{\text{Next year's revenue}}{r+d}}_{\substack{\text{Present value} \\ \text{of future revenues}}} > \underbrace{C}_{\substack{\text{Up-front} \\ \text{cost}}}$$

This is exactly the same as the *Rational Rule for Investors*! That means you'll come to the same decision by evaluating:

- Whether the present value of all future revenues over the life of the machine exceeds the up-front cost (as we did a few pages back); or
- Whether next year's marginal revenue exceeds the user cost of buying a machine for just one year (as we just did).

This equivalence is useful because it means you can apply whichever approach you find most intuitive in the context of the investment opportunity you're evaluating. In some settings, it'll be easiest to evaluate the present value of future revenues, while in others it'll be more natural to analyse the user cost of capital.

EVERYDAY Economics **The true cost of car ownership**

moisseyev/iStock/Getty Images

Depreciation is costly.

Most people who buy a car do so because it's convenient. But before you invest in a car, it's worth evaluating how much you're paying each year for that convenience. Try asking your friends what they think the annual cost of car ownership is. Chances are they'll focus on the out-of-pocket costs, like gas, insurance, repairs, and registration.

But too often, people miss the most important expense: The user cost of capital. Cars depreciate rapidly: If you buy a new car you'll lose 20% almost right away, and beyond the first year, cars typically lose around 15% of their remaining value each year after that. That means that if you buy a used car, it will lose 15% of its value each year that you own it. If you buy a used car worth about $10,000, a year later, it'll only be worth $8,500. And you won't earn any interest on the money tied up in that car, so if the real interest rate is 3%, you'll forgo $300 in interest. Add it up, and the user cost of capital is $(r+d)\times C = (0.03+0.15)\times \$10{,}000 = \$1{,}800$ in the first year. While this isn't an out-of-pocket cost, it's a real cost nonetheless because if you didn't own the car, you would be $1,800 wealthier at the end of the year. ■

26.4 The Macroeconomics of Investment

Learning Objective *Assess how macroeconomic conditions drive investment.*

Let's now explore the macroeconomic implications of all this. Macroeconomic investment is the sum of millions of individual investment decisions, as managers across the country evaluate whether to buy more wind turbines, buildings, machinery, or software. In each case, savvy managers try to make decisions in accordance with the *Rational Rule for Investors*, which means they'll invest only in those projects where the present value of future revenues exceeds the up-front costs. And so the framework that you use to make individual investment decisions will also prove to be useful as we turn to assessing how changing macroeconomic conditions will affect total investment across the economy.

To see the link between individual (or microeconomic) investment decisions and the macroeconomic whole, it can be useful to think about a list of the millions of potential investment projects out there, each with its own costs and benefits. When individual managers analyse each of these projects, they'll only invest in the fraction of them that they perceive to be profitable. But if business conditions change, so will the perceived profitability of many of these projects, and that'll affect how many of these investment projects businesses will undertake.

EThamPhoto/Alamy Stock Photo

The real interest rate determines whether this investment project is worthwhile.

The Real Interest Rate and Investment

The real interest rate plays a central role in investment decisions. It matters because of the *opportunity cost principle:* When managers evaluate whether to invest in new equipment, they ask "or what?" For many, the alternative to investing in new machinery is leaving their money in the bank to earn interest. The higher the interest rate, the more attractive this alternative is. This opportunity cost is the reason that a higher real interest rate leads to a higher user cost of capital. And it's the reason that the *Rational Rule for Investors* directs you to focus on present values, which account for the forgone opportunity to earn bank interest.

Consequently, higher real interest rates lead managers to invest less in buying new capital.

Do the Economics

Let's explore how the real interest rate shapes Valentina's decision. She asks you whether she should still invest in this turbine if the real interest rate rises to 8%. What's your advice?

$$\text{Present value of revenues} = \frac{\$600{,}000}{0.08 + 0.04} = \$5 \text{ million}$$

The present value of future revenues ($5 million) still exceeds the up-front costs ($4 million), so yes, she should still invest in the turbine.

Next, she asks: Should she still invest if the real interest rate rises to 12%?

$$\text{Present value of revenues} = \frac{\$600{,}000}{0.12 + 0.04} = \$3.75 \text{ million}$$

Now the present value of future revenues ($3.75 million) is less than the present value of the costs ($4 million), so no, she should not invest. ■

Investment declines as the real interest rate rises. As Valentina's example illustrates, whether or not an investment project will go forward depends critically on the real interest rate. More generally, the higher the real interest rate, the lower the present value of future revenues, and hence the *Rational Rule for Investors* will judge fewer investments as worthwhile.

In turn, this means that high real interest rates lead to lower levels of investment across the whole economy. Or to say it the other way, lower real interest rates lead to higher levels of investment. The **investment line** shown in Figure 11 illustrates how the quantity of investment rises as the real interest rate falls.

investment line The line that shows how the quantity of investment increases as the real interest rate falls.

Figure 11 | The Investment Line

The real interest rate determines investment.

Ⓐ A **higher real interest rate** leads to **low investment**.

Ⓑ A **lower real interest rate** leads to **high investment**.

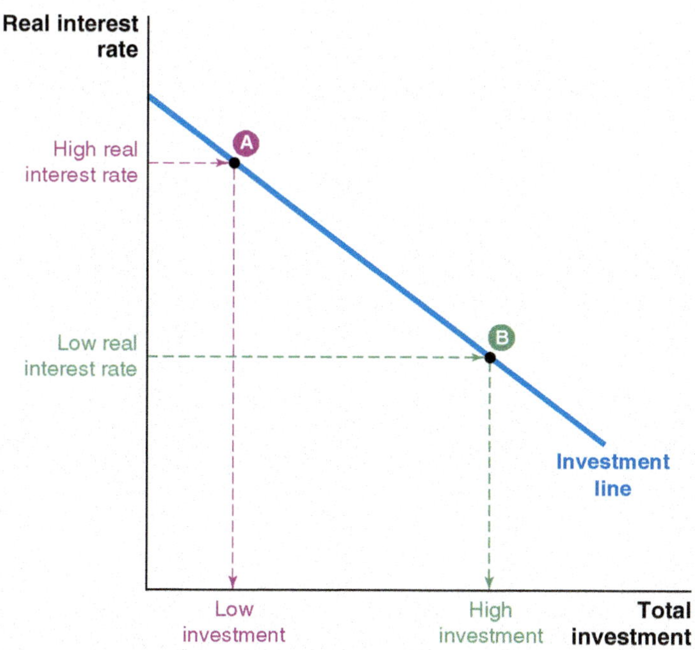

Figure 12 | Other Factors Shift the Investment Line

Investment depends on the present value of expected future revenues and the upfront cost of capital.

Ⓐ An **increase in the expected future revenues** from an investment, or a **decrease in the upfront cost** will make more investments profitable, shifting the **investment line to the right**.

Ⓑ A **decrease in the expected future revenues** from an investment or an **increase in the up-front cost** will make fewer investments profitable, shifting the **investment line to the left**.

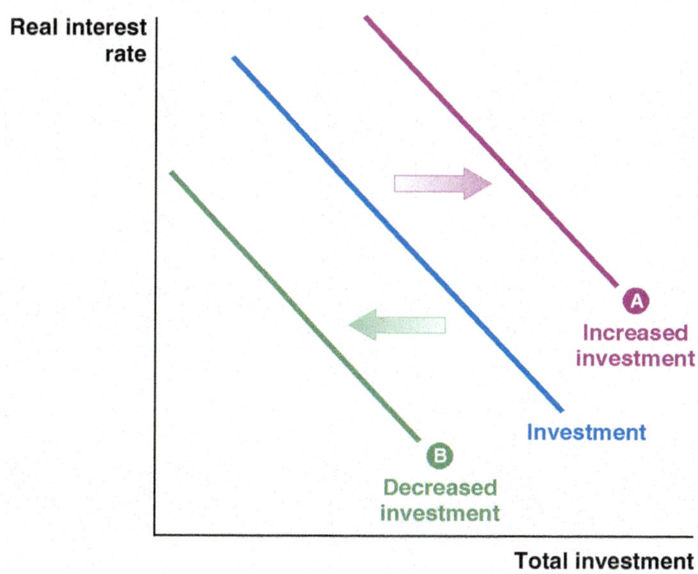

Factors That Shift the Investment Line

While the real interest rate is a key determinant of investment, it's not the only factor. The *Rational Rule for Investors* highlights that any favourable change in business conditions will lead to an increase in investment if it either increases the anticipated present value of future revenues or decreases the up-front cost of an investment. Such a change will shift the investment line to the right as seen in Figure 12 on the previous page. Conversely, a change that leads the anticipated present value of future revenues to fall, or the up-front cost of investing to rise, will cause the investment line to shift to the left also seen in Figure 12. Let's dig into four of the key factors that can cause the investment line to shift.

Investment shifter one: Technological advances. Technological advances that make capital equipment more productive will boost the revenue that you'll generate from buying that equipment, providing an incentive to invest more. For example, advances in wind engineering have increased the amount of electricity that an individual wind turbine generates. For a renewable energy company, that extra output translates directly into more revenues. The prospect of earning more revenue makes more turbine investments more profitable at any given interest rate. That's why technological advances shift the investment line to the right.

The development of electronic turbine monitoring technology is also expected to prevent damage to turbines due to high winds. By reducing the depreciation rate, this technology will boost future revenues, thus making more investment projects profitable. Thus, advances that reduce the depreciation rate also shift the investment line to the right.

Figure 13 | Expectation of Higher Earnings Drive Investment

Average expectations among chief financial officers

2018 Data from: Duke Fuqua CFO Survey.

Investment shifter two: Expectations. Investment is motivated by *expectations* about the reward of future revenues. As a result, optimism and pessimism play an important role. If managers are optimistic about future economic conditions, they'll forecast that new investments are likely to yield robust revenues. These optimistic expectations will lead them to invest more at a given real interest rate, shifting the investment line to the right. By contrast, pessimism about future economic conditions will lead managers to revise downward their revenue forecasts. These pessimistic expectations will lead them to conclude that fewer investment projects will be profitable, shifting the investment line to the left.

The key insight is that investment isn't driven by last year's revenues, but rather *expectations* about future revenues. As such, the "animal spirits" of managers can drive investment to rise or fall. Indeed, Figure 13 shows that, in practice, greater optimism about future earnings translates into more investment.

Investment shifter three: Corporate taxes. The higher the corporate tax rate, the smaller the share of future profits that your company gets to keep. As such, higher corporate tax rates effectively reduce the revenue that you'll get (or get to keep) from your investment. This leads to less investment at any given interest rate, shifting the investment line to the left.

On the flip side, the wind industry has benefited from tax breaks that apply specifically to wind farms. These tax breaks increase the revenue that renewable energy companies get from each turbine, and they've made investing in turbines in some lower-wind areas profitable. As such, lower taxes can shift the investment line to the right.

Four investment shifters:
1. Technological advances
2. Expectations
3. Corporate taxes
4. Lending standards and cash reserves

Investment shifter four: Lending standards and cash reserves. The difficulty investment poses is that you need to pay for your new machines upfront, but you'll only get the offsetting revenues in the future. This creates a financing problem: How will you finance—that is, get the up-front cash to pay for—your new investments?

For many companies, the answer is that they'll borrow the funds from a bank. But even if you're willing to pay the prevailing interest rate, it can be hard to get financing for risky projects. The problem is that banks sometimes don't want to lend for very risky projects because it's difficult for them to assess the true risk and therefore set appropriately high interest rates. When you can't get financing, you'll only be able to invest if you can pay the up-front cost out of your cash reserves. Thus, less restrictive lending standards or more abundant cash reserves lead to more investment at any given interest rate, shifting the investment line to the right.

26.5 The Market for Loanable Funds

Learning Objective *Forecast the long-run real interest rate.*

Our analysis so far has taken the real interest rate as given. That's about to change, as we dig into the factors that shape interest rates, and hence investment.

To figure out what determines the real interest rate, we need to distinguish between two time horizons because they point to two distinct sets of forces. In the *short run,* the interest rate rises and falls from month to month as the Reserve Bank tweaks interest rates in an effort to dampen the economy's short-run ups and downs. We'll devote Chapter 34 on monetary policy to explore how the RBA lowers interest rates when the economy is operating with excess capacity and inflation is low, and it raises rates when the economy is operating above full capacity and inflation is high. But the RBA's adjustments only nudge the interest rate a bit above or below its long-run level. In the *long run*—which is our focus here—the real interest rate evolves slowly over many years in response to the balance of saving and investment.

Supply and Demand of Loanable Funds

To assess the long-run drivers of the real interest rate, we'll analyse the **market for loanable funds,** which is the market for the *funds* used to buy, rent, or build capital. It brings together savers who want to lend their funds and investors who want to borrow those funds. This market determines the long-run real interest rate, and therefore the quantity of investment.

market for loanable funds The market for the funds used to buy, rent, or build capital.

Savers supply funds, and investors demand them. In this market, *savers are the suppliers,* supplying their funds to businesses who want to borrow them. *Investors are the demanders,* demanding funds to help fund their investments in new capital like wind turbines. The financial sector—banks, the bond market, and the stock market—is the *marketplace* where suppliers of funding (savers) meet demanders (investors).

The *price* of a loan is the real interest rate. It represents the real resources that a borrower must pay a lender to borrow $100 for a year. The long-run interest rate is determined by the forces of supply and demand for loanable funds, as shown in Figure 14.

The *supply curve* is upward-sloping because a higher real interest rate raises the benefits of saving (as discussed in Chapter 25), leading a larger quantity of loanable funds to be supplied. The *demand curve* is downward-sloping, because a higher real interest rate makes fewer investment projects profitable, leading a smaller quantity of loanable funds to be demanded.

The real interest rate is determined by supply and demand. *Equilibrium* in the market for loanable funds occurs at the point where the supply and demand curves cross, and it determines the equilibrium real interest rate.

In order to abstract from short-run business-cycle influences, we're focusing on the supply and demand curves that apply when the economy is operating at its potential. It follows that this is the equilibrium real interest rate that applies on average over the long run. This is called the **neutral real interest rate** because it's the interest rate that operates when the economy is in neutral—producing neither above nor below its potential.

neutral real interest rate The interest rate that operates when the economy is in neutral—producing neither above nor below its potential.

Figure 14 | **The Market for Loanable Funds**

The long-run real interest rate is determined by supply and demand.

(A) The **price** in the market for loanable funds is the long-term real interest rate.

(B) The **supply** of loanable funds is upward-sloping because higher real interest rates lead to more saving.

(C) The **demand** of loanable funds is downward-sloping because higher real interest rates lead to less investment.

(D) **Equilibrium** occurs where supply and demand curves cross.

(E) The **neutral real interest rate** is the equilibrium real interest rate when the economy operates at potential output.

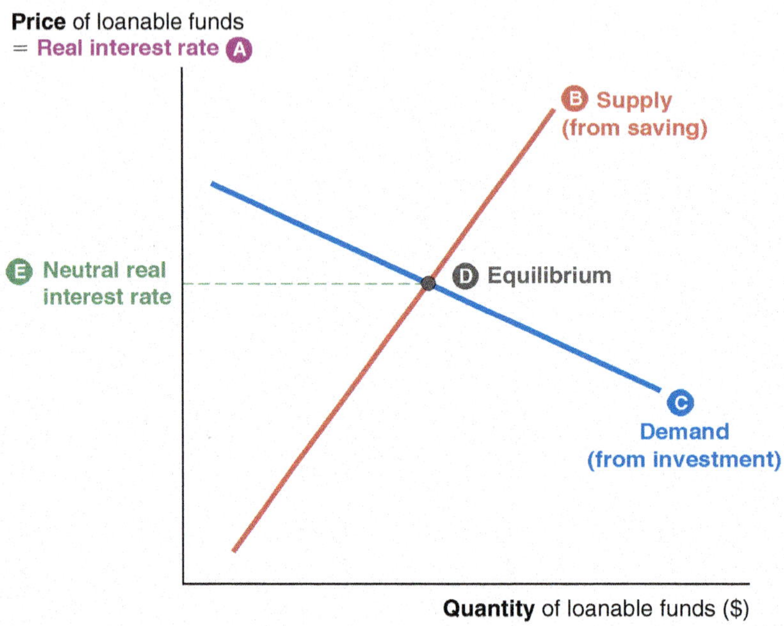

Our next step is to forecast how changing economic conditions change the neutral real interest rate. We'll start by analysing factors that might shift saving and the supply of loanable funds, and then we'll turn to factors that shift investment and the demand for loanable funds.

Three factors that shift the supply of loanable funds:

1. Changes in personal saving rates
2. The budget surplus (or deficit) shifts government saving
3. Global shocks shift foreign saving

Shifts in the Supply of Loanable Funds

A shift in saving at any given real interest rate will shift the supply of loanable funds causing the neutral real interest rate to change.

Figure 15 illustrates that a decrease in saving, which shifts the supply curve to the left (shown in green), will lead to a higher real interest rate. It also illustrates (in purple) the opposite case, in which an increase in saving shifts the supply curve to the right, which leads to a lower real interest rate.

The supply of loanable funds will shift only if there's a change in savings by one or more of the three types of economic actors who supply loanable funds: private savers, the government, and foreigners.

personal saving Saving by households of whatever money they don't either spend or pay as taxes.

Supply shifter one: Changes in personal saving rates. **Personal saving** refers to saving by households of whatever income they don't spend or pay as taxes. Just as putting money in the bank counts as saving, so does paying down your debt, because it frees up loanable funds for others to use. Any factor that shifts people's willingness to save will shift the supply of loanable funds.

For instance, the government offers big tax breaks to save for your retirement. These tax breaks increase the incentive to save, thus shifting the supply of loanable funds to the right, which lowers the neutral interest rate. If these incentives were removed, saving would decrease at each interest rate, leading the supply curve to shift to the left, which would raise the neutral interest rate.

Figure 15 | Shifts in the Supply of Loanable Funds

A A decrease in saving shifts the supply of loanable funds to the left, leading to a higher real interest rate.

B An increase in saving shifts the supply of loanable funds to the right, leading to a lower real interest rate.

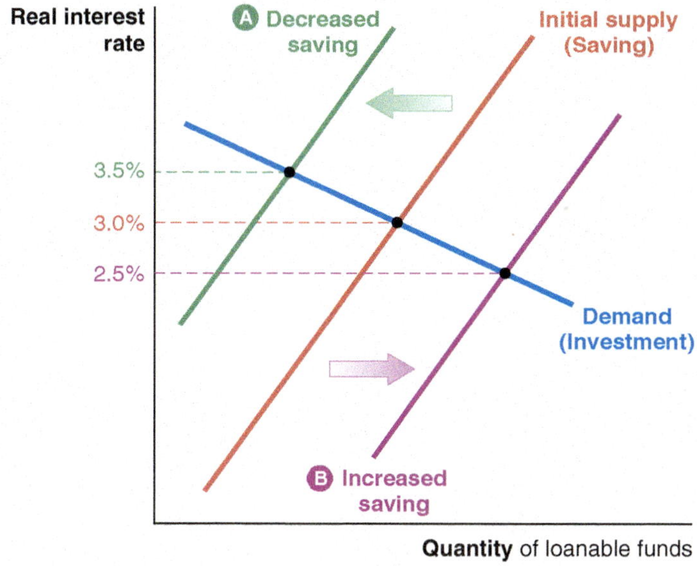

Supply shifter two: The budget surplus (or deficit) shifts government saving. **Government saving** refers to saving by the government. When the government's revenues exceed its outlays, the government's budget is in surplus, and so it accumulates extra funds. This budget surplus adds to the supply of loanable funds. By contrast, a budget deficit means that the government is *dissaving*—that is, spending more than it takes in—thereby reducing the supply of loanable funds available to businesses, because the government must borrow to fund its deficit.

As a result, an increase in the budget deficit will make government saving even more negative, which shifts the supply of loanable funds to the left. As Figure 15 illustrates, the new equilibrium following a decrease in saving involves both a higher real interest rate and lower investment. The decline in private investment due to a larger budget deficit is called **crowding out** because, when the government borrows, it leads to higher real interest rates, which effectively crowds out some of the firms looking for loans to fund their own investments.

government saving Saving by the government.

crowding out The decline in private spending—and particularly investment—that follows from a rise in government spending.

On the flip side, shifting from a budget deficit to a surplus will increase public saving, which shifts the supply of loanable funds to the right. The new equilibrium will involve a lower real interest rate and higher investment, effectively "crowding in" extra private investment. This insight motivated President Bill Clinton's macroeconomic strategy in the 1990s, as he pushed the federal budget from a large deficit into a modest surplus. As our analysis would predict, this led to a decline in long-run real interest rates, which spurred more private investment.

Supply shifter three: Global shocks shift foreign saving. **Foreign saving** refers to funding that comes from foreigners lending money to Australians. These funding flows are often called *net financial inflows.* (The term *net* means that we're focusing on the financial inflows coming to Australia from foreigners, less the financial outflows going to foreigners from Australia.)

foreign saving Funding that comes from foreigners lending to Australians.

These international financial flows are an important channel through which the global economy affects the Australian economy. For example, in the early 2000s, an increase in saving in the rapidly growing Asian countries and the oil-producing Middle East caused a global glut of saving. Australia is a relatively attractive destination for these funds, and the resulting increase in foreign saving shifted the supply of loanable funds to the right. As Figure 15 suggests, this pushed down the neutral real interest rate.

Shifts in the Demand for Loanable Funds

The demand for loanable funds reflects businesses borrowing to fund their investments. This means that any factor that shifts the investment line—which describes how much investment businesses will undertake at each real interest rate—will also shift the demand for loanable funds. And so based upon our earlier analysis, it follows that the demand for loanable funds will increase, shifting to the right in response to:

Four factors that shift the demand for loanable funds:

1. Technological advances
2. Expectations
3. Corporate taxes
4. Lending standards and cash reserves

Figure 16 | **Shifts in the Demand for Loanable Funds**

Ⓐ An **increase in investment** shifts the demand for loanable funds to the right, leading to a **higher real interest rate**.

Ⓑ A **decrease in investment** shifts the demand for loanable funds to the left, leading to a **lower real interest rate**.

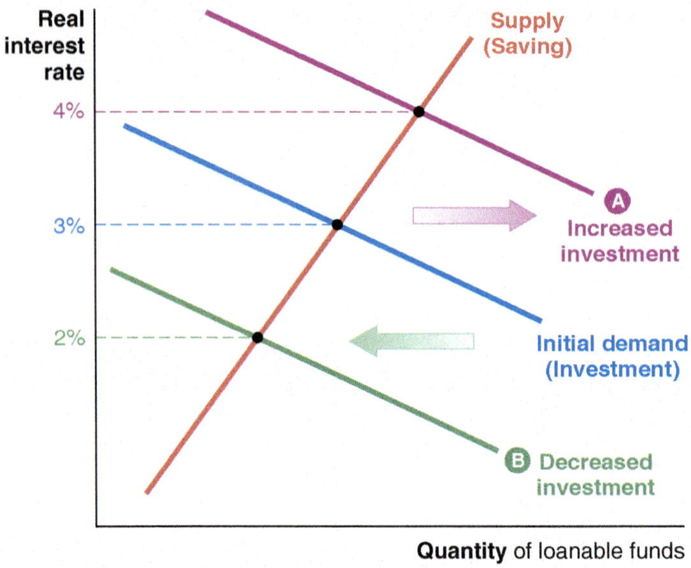

- *Technological advances* that make capital equipment more productive
- *Expectations* of stronger future revenues
- *Corporate tax* cuts that mean businesses keep more of their revenues
- *Easier lending standards* that allow more businesses to qualify for a loan, or if businesses have larger *cash reserves* many won't need a loan to fund their investments.

Figure 16 illustrates (in purple) an increase in investment, which shifts the demand for loanable funds to the right, will lead to a higher real interest rate. If any of these factors shifts in the opposite direction, it will lead to a decrease in investment, which shifts the demand for loanable funds to the left (shown in green), leading to a lower real interest rate.

Figure 17 | **Estimates of the Neutral Real Interest Rate**

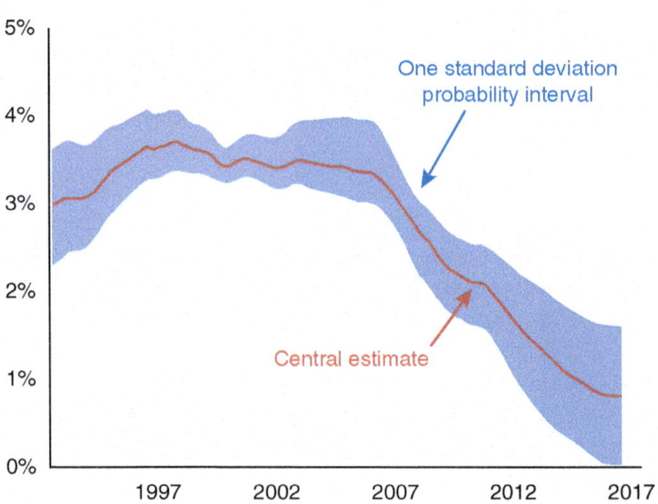

Data from: Reserve Bank of Australia.

Interpreting the DATA: Secular stagnation and the declining real interest rate

Several long-term trends have also led to a decrease in the demand for loanable funds. First, population growth is slowing, and fewer new workers mean less investment is required to equip them. Second, the modern economy is increasingly powered by technology firms, which don't use much physical capital. For instance, Afterpay grew to be worth about as much as Coles Group without building a single warehouse. And third, as capital equipment—particularly computers—becomes cheaper, businesses need fewer funds to meet their equipment needs.

Each of these factors shifts the demand for loanable funds to the left. And together, they help explain why Figure 17 shows that the neutral real interest rate has declined to very low levels since the turn of the century, a trend sometimes called "secular stagnation." ■

Do the Economics

Think you've got this stuff all figured out? Okay, let's practice by predicting how the neutral real interest rate will respond to changing economic conditions. To do this, apply the same three-step recipe that you can use to predict the results of any supply-and-demand analysis:

Step one: Will this shift saving and hence the supply of loanable funds, or will it shift investment and the demand for loanable funds?

Step two: Is that shift an increase, shifting the curve to the right? Or is it a decrease, shifting the curve to the left?

Step three: How will the price—that is, the neutral real interest rate—change in equilibrium? And what about the quantity of saving and investment?

Now let's apply this three-step recipe to the follow scenarios:

The government cuts corporate taxes, so businesses get to keep a larger share of their revenues.

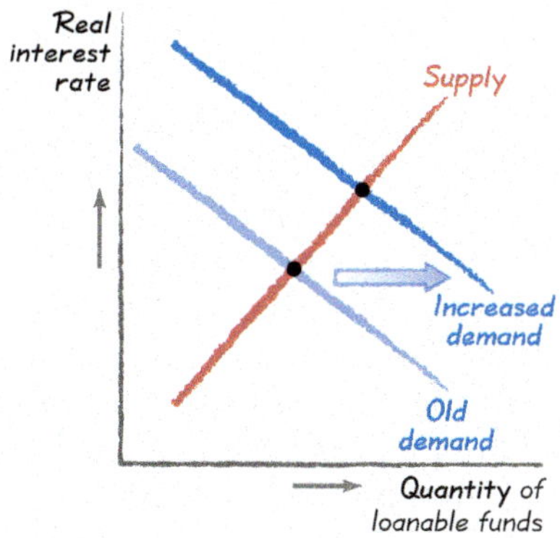

A tax cut makes investment more profitable so investment will rise.
→ Increased demand for funds

Result: Higher real interest rate, with more saving and investment.

Political strife overseas makes foreign savers look for a "safe haven" to park their money.

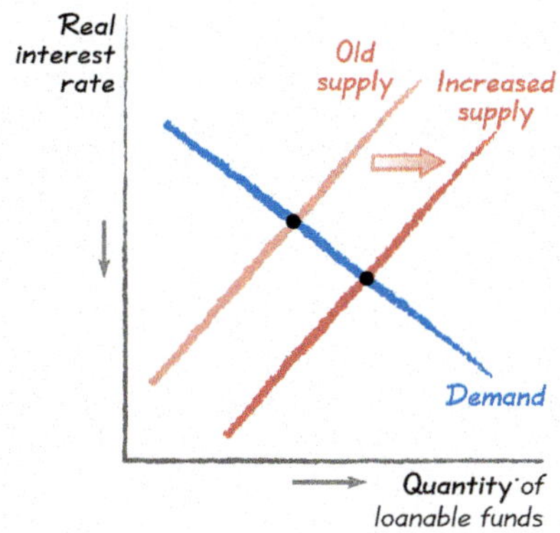

Australia is a safe haven, so foreign saving will rise.
→ Increased supply of funds

Result: Lower real interest rate with more saving and investment.

The federal government embarks on a major spending program that puts the budget into deficit.

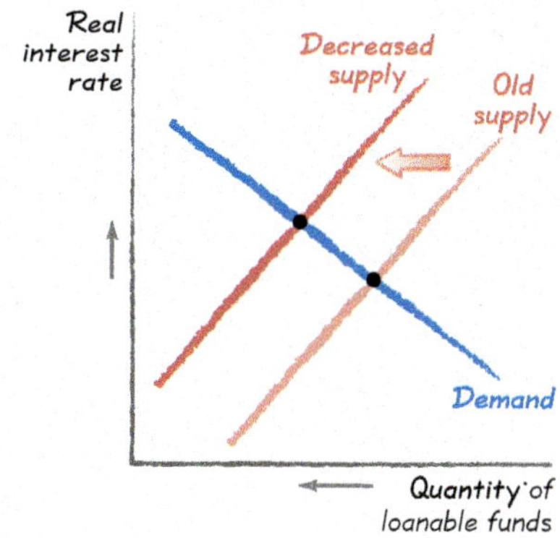

A budget deficit will decrease public saving.
→ Decrease in supply of funds

Result: Higher real interest rate with less saving and investment.

As good education becomes more important, an increasing share of parents open private school savings accounts.

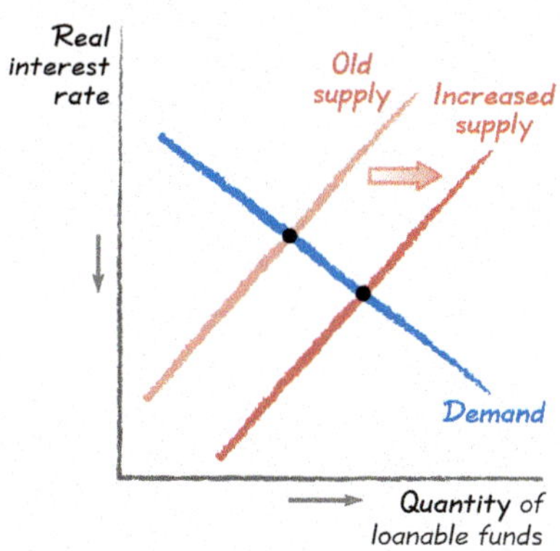

More people putting away money means private saving will rise.
→ Increased supply of funds

Result: Lower real interest rate with more saving and investment.

Business executives expect their profit margins to decline over the next decade.

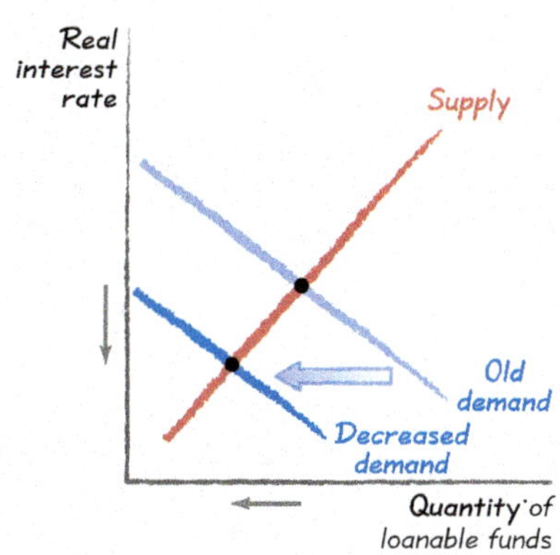

Lower future profits will reduce investment.
→ Decrease in demand for funds

Result: Lower real interest rate with less saving and investment.

The nominal interest rate rises by 2% in response to inflation rising by 2%.

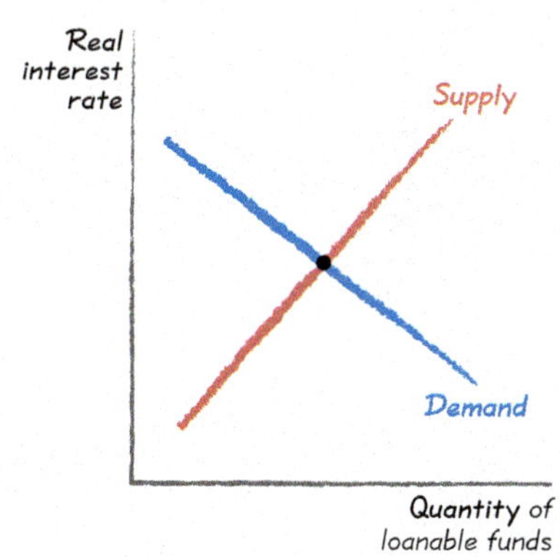

Trick question: Saving and investment respond to the real interest rate, not the nominal rate. An unchanged real interest rate has no effect on the supply or demand for loanable funds. ■

Tying It Together

The central issue we've addressed in this chapter is how to make good choices when you face an up-front cost and future benefits. We've developed a powerful framework that you can use to evaluate whether an investment is worthwhile. While we've focused on the macroeconomic implications of this—analysing whether a business will invest in productive capital—the same framework applies to a much broader notion of investment. Indeed, it applies anytime you have to decide whether to incur some up-front cost in return for a benefit you'll enjoy in the future.

Wavebreak Media ltd./Alamy Stock Photo

They are making an investment in their health capital.

This means that you'll find these ideas to be useful in broad swathes of your life. While you're in university, you're investing in your *human capital,* incurring the up-front costs of studying hard, getting a loan for tuition, and getting by without an income, so that you'll enjoy the future benefit of a more rewarding career. When you exercise, you're investing in your *health capital,* incurring the up-front costs of working out (lifting weights is hard!), so that you'll benefit from better health in the future. Or perhaps you've just started life at a new university, and you're going to more parties than you really want to. You're investing in your *network capital,* incurring the up-front cost of feeling awkward at social events where you don't know many people, so that you'll enjoy the future benefit of building a network of friends.

In each case, the *Rational Rule for Investors* gives useful advice: It's worth investing if the present value of the benefits exceeds the present value of the costs. But in reality, people often have trouble following this advice. I'm sure that you've been in a situation like this: You've got a big test coming up and need to study. Studying is an investment—an up-front cost, with even larger future benefits. Yet instead of following the *Rational Rule for Investors*, you procrastinate. You say you'll study tomorrow, but then tomorrow comes, and you put it off again. As a result, you underinvest in studying.

It's a pattern that people repeat in many aspects of their lives. You know you should work out to keep healthy, but going to the gym involves an up-front cost and future benefits. So you put it off. Your pile of dirty clothes is practically begging you to invest in the up-front cost of doing a load of laundry, so that you get the benefit of clean clothes next week. But you tell yourself you'll do it tomorrow. You know you should start applying for summer internships, but the up-front cost of working on your résumé sounds daunting. So you procrastinate.

This tendency to procrastinate can also play havoc in your financial life. You know you should invest in a car, in furniture for your apartment, or eventually, in making a down payment on a house. But it's more fun to spend your money on other things today and think about the future tomorrow. If you keep putting it off until tomorrow, one day you'll wake up to discover that you've been working for years but have nothing to show for it. This is an extraordinarily common mistake that I've seen hundreds of people make.

Psychologists tell us that the problem is that delayed gratification is hard. We're too quick to enjoy today's benefit, rather than investing in something with even larger long-run payoffs. All of the advice in this chapter comes to naught if you won't follow through. So how can you do better?

Reward yourself: The *cost-benefit principle* says that if you want to do more of something, you should increase the benefits, or decrease the costs. So reward yourself for studying with a bowl of ice cream. Or make it costly not to study: Make a plan with a friend to study together, and make sure it's a friend you wouldn't want to let down.

Break it up: A large task can be daunting, leading you to procrastinate. But the *marginal principle* reminds you that any big task can be broken up into a series of smaller, simpler steps. Don't try to write that 3,000-word essay tonight; plan on writing the introduction today, each of the three main arguments on each of the three next nights, and the conclusion at the end of the week. On any given night, there'll be less reason to procrastinate.

Constrain yourself: The *opportunity cost principle* reminds you that the real cost of something is your next best alternative. So constrain your future choices by making that next best alternative less appealing. Cancel Netflix during exams, lend your Xbox to a friend, or head to the library to study and leave your phone at home so you won't have any distractions.

Plan ahead: Temptation often bites you hardest "in the moment," and if your friends ask you to go out when you should be studying, too often you'll make the wrong choice. Add a little distance, and you'll probably make a better choice. It's the *interdependence principle* in action: Your choices depend upon the temptations that surround you, so make those choices in the best possible circumstances. Plan ahead which nights are for socialising or studying, so that you're making decisions when temptation exerts less of an influence.

Now that you've paid the up-front cost of reading this chapter, it's time to enjoy the future benefits of making better investment decisions for the rest of your life!

Chapter at a Glance

Investment: Spending on new capital assets that increase the economy's productive capacity.
Types of investment: Business investment, change in inventories, and housing investment.

Capital Stock: The total quantity of capital at a point in time. **Investment** is the flow of new purchases of capital that add to this stock. But capital also declines over time due to **depreciation**, which includes wear and tear, obsolescence, accidental damage, and aging.

Tools to Analyse Investments

Compounding

Helps you calculate how money grows over time when you leave it to accumulate interest in the bank.

$$\text{Future value in } t \text{ years} = \text{Present value} \times (1 + r)^t$$

Discounting

You use it to figure out how much money in the future is worth today.

$$\text{Present value} = \text{Future value in } t \text{ years} \times \frac{1}{(1 + r)^t}$$

Interest rate (r): The rate of r cents per dollar (use the real r for real values and nominal r for nominal values). The interest rate you use in the discounting or compounding formula should be the rate of return you could get from investing your funds in your next best alternative.

Evaluating an Investment

Rational Rule for Investors:
Pursue an investment opportunity if:

$$\underbrace{\frac{\text{Next year's revenue}}{r + d}}_{\text{Present value of future revenues}} > \underbrace{C}_{\text{Up-front cost}}$$

is the same as

Compare the **user cost of capital** (the extra cost associated with using one more machine next year) with next year's additional revenue and invest if:

$$\underbrace{\text{Next year's revenue}}_{\text{Marginal benefit}} > \underbrace{(r + d) \times C}_{\text{Marginal cost}}$$

Depreciation rate (d): The proportion of an investment's remaining productive capacity you lose each year due to depreciation.

Market for Loanable Funds: The market for the funds used to buy, rent, or build capital.

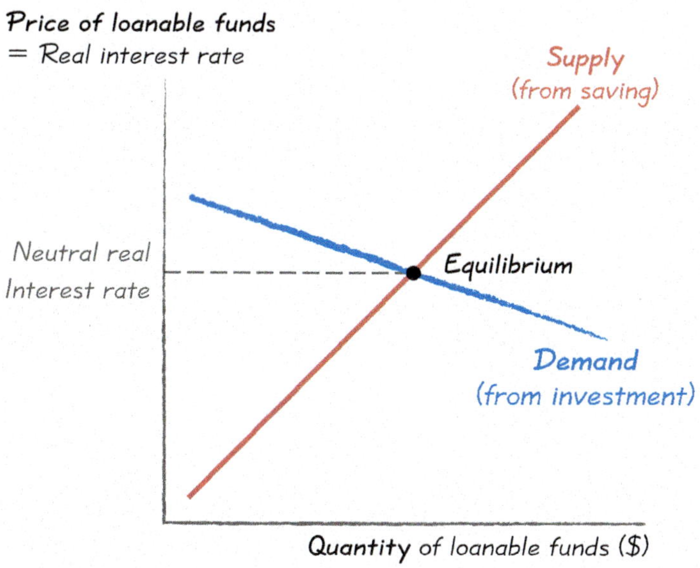

Predicting changes in the neutral real interest rate:

1. Will this shift **saving** and hence the **supply** of loanable funds, or will it shift **investment** and the **demand** for loanable funds?

   Supply shifters: changes in personal saving rates, government saving, or foreign saving.

   Demand shifters: Technological advances, expectations, corporate taxes, or lending standards and cash reserves.

2. Is that shift an increase, shifting the curve to the right? Or is it a decrease, shifting the curve to the left?
3. How will the price—the neutral real interest rate—change in equilibrium? What about the quantity of saving and investment?

Key Concepts

business investment, 657
capital stock, 657
compounding formula, 660
crowding out, 675
depreciation, 657
depreciation rate, 665
discounting, 662
discounting formula, 662
foreign saving, 675
future value, 660
government saving, 675
housing investment, 657
investment, 656
investment line, 671
market for loanable funds, 673
neutral real interest rate, 673
personal saving, 674
present value, 662
Rational Rule for Investors, 667
user cost of capital, 669
valuation formula, 666

Discussion and Review Questions

Learning Objective 26.1 *Learn what macroeconomists mean by investment and assess the role that it plays in the economy.*

1. You buy $1,000 worth of Atlassian stock. Why wouldn't a macroeconomist call this investment?
2. Describe how something you purchased depreciated over time and how its value changed.
3. Describe, using flows, stocks, and depreciation, why big changes in investment have relatively small impacts on the amount of capital in the economy.
4. Explain, using the opportunity cost principle, why building a new house for personal use counts as investment.

Learning Objective 26.2 *Master two tools for comparing sums of money at different points in time: compounding and discounting.*

5. Would you prefer $1 million when you retire in 40 years, or $70,000 today that's put in a bank account to compound for the next 40 years?
6. Would you be better off saving for retirement early in your career or later when you're earning more? Explain.

Learning Objective 26.3 *Evaluate whether an investment opportunity is worth pursuing.*

7. Explain how you applied the Rational Rule for Investors to your own choice to invest in a university education, using the marginal principle, the cost-benefit principle, and the opportunity cost principle.
8. Do you think that people always follow the Rational Rule for Investors? Why or why not? Explain.
9. Think about how much you paid for your smartphone and how much it's worth today. What's the depreciation rate of your phone? Why has it lost value?

Learning Objective 26.4 *Assess how macroeconomic conditions drive investment.*

10. Do you think that companies should engage in investment during recessions? Explain.
11. Use the opportunity cost principle to explain the relationship between the real interest rate and investment spending. What does this tell you about the slope of the investment line?
12. Use the cost-benefit principle to describe how expectations change manager's decisions to make new investments.

Learning Objective 26.5 *Forecast the long-run real interest rate.*

13. Are you currently a participant in the market for loanable funds? If so, which side? What effect does your current participation (or lack thereof) have on the market? Explain.
14. Come up with a real-world example of how an increase in the budget deficit would crowd out private investment.

Study Problems

Learning Objective 26.1 *Learn what macroeconomists mean by investment and assess the role that it plays in the economy.*

1. Determine whether the following scenarios are describing savings or investment. If they describe investment, which type of investment? Explain.
   a. Kmart purchases $100 million worth of products from a Chinese manufacturer to add to its warehouse inventory.
   b. The Royal Australian Air Force spends $5 million on writing and testing new code to improve its rocket stability.
   c. The stock market experiences a major increase after the Reserve Bank announces that it won't raise the interest rate.
   d. 230,000 new homes were built in 2018 in Australia.
2. How do the following impact the capital stock? Be sure to identify depreciation and investment flows. Explain.
   a. A consultant drops their laptop on the way to a big meeting and their IT department buys a replacement the next day.
   b. The *Sydney Morning Herald* decommissions an older printing press instead of repairing it due to a decrease in print subscriptions.
3. If GDP is confidently expected to grow at a rapid 4% rate this year, how do you predict investment spending to change? Is it likely to grow at a larger, smaller, or the same rate as GDP? Why?

4. Capital per worker in China almost doubled between 1990 and 2010. How do you expect China's output per worker to have changed over the same period? Why?

Learning Objective 26.2 *Master two tools for comparing sums of money at different points in time: compounding and discounting.*

5. Use the compounding or discounting formula to answer the following questions.
   - **a.** Your small business has a cash reserve of about $200,000, earning 2% annual interest. How much will that be worth in 3 years?
   - **b.** You want $1 million in your retirement account in 50 years. If your account grows at an annual rate of 4%, how much would you have to deposit today to reach $1 million in 50 years?
6. If you deposit $1,200 in your retirement account in your first year of work, how much will that $1,200 be worth after 5, 10, 20, 30, 40, and 50 years at an 8% interest rate? Graph your results. What do you notice? It may be easiest to use a spreadsheet to make the calculations.
7. Nigeria's real GDP is expected to grow by about 5% per year for the next 5 years and inflation is expected to be about 8% per year. If its GDP is $300 billion, what will its nominal and real GDP be in 5 years?

Learning Objective 26.3 *Evaluate whether an investment opportunity is worth pursuing.*

8. Management at TK Maxx is deciding whether to build a new goods distribution centre that will cost $12 million to build; the estimated additional first-year revenue will be $1 million. Future real revenues will decline due to a depreciation rate of 5% per year. The opportunity cost of this investment is the 7% real interest rate it could otherwise earn on its funds. Should TK Maxx build the new distribution centre? Explain. What level of first-year revenue would make this building profitable?
9. Consider the owner of a local boutique. They are deciding if they should upgrade the storage and display containers. The total cost would be $2,000, and the depreciation rate is 8% per year. The expected increase in next year's revenue as a result of the investment is $400. Assuming an interest rate of 5%, use the marginal principle to determine whether the owner should make this investment.
10. Martha is considering acquiring another piano for her piano academy. The cost of a new Steinway grand is around $148,000. Pianos depreciate at a rate of about 5% per year, and the academy's investment fund typically earns a return of about 10% per year. Additional revenues obtained through the increased teaching capacity enabled by the piano and renting the piano out for performances are expected to be about $30,000 per year. Should Martha acquire the piano?

Learning Objective 26.4 *Assess how macroeconomic conditions drive investment.*

11. The manager of a T-shirt company is considering investing in a new embroidery machine that would cost $8,500, and the depreciation rate is 6.5% per year. The expected increase in next year's revenue as a result of the investment would be $1,500. For what values of the interest rate should the company make this investment?
12. You are working for a major bank, forecasting investment. Consider what happens to investment in each of the following scenarios. Show the change graphically, using the investment line.
    - **a.** The economy is in a recession, and firms' cash reserves are declining.
    - **b.** Parliament passes a bill lowering the taxes paid by Small to Medium businesses in response to the coronavirus pandemic.
    - **c.** The Reserve Bank decides to raise interest rates.
    - **d.** A new technology is discovered that increases the productive capacity of factories.

Learning Objective 26.5 *Forecast the long-run real interest rate.*

13. Determine if the following people are demanders, suppliers, or not involved in the market for loanable funds.
    - **a.** Latisha wants to save up for a new laptop to use in her business, so she puts aside $100 a month until she can afford it.
    - **b.** Gerardo borrows $30,000 from his local bank for a new addition to his warehouse.
    - **c.** Dana buys $1,200 of stocks every year in her retirement account.
14. Evaluate the effect of each of the following events on the market for loanable funds. Explain the effects on savings, investment, and the neutral real interest rate.
    - **a.** The government runs a government budget surplus instead of a deficit.
    - **b.** The government decides to forgive some of the $66 billion in student loan debt.
    - **c.** Chinese investors stop sending their funds to Australia, reducing net capital inflows.
    - **d.** The nominal interest rate rises 1% in response to a 1% rise in the inflation rate.
15. Which of the following factors could cause the neutral real interest rate to fall?
    - **a.** Massive government budget deficits in Australia
    - **b.** Slowing population growth
    - **c.** A global savings glut
    - **d.** The falling costs of capital equipment

CHAPTER 27

The Financial Sector

Wang Ying/Xinhua/Alamy Stock Photo

It's no place for the timid.

In one sense, Wall Street is just a street that runs through New York's financial district and is home to banks, the stock market, and the bond market. In a larger sense, "Wall Street" is an avatar for the financial industry around the world—from Sydney to London to Shanghai. For some people "Wall Street" is synonymous with greed. For others, it is the purest distillation of market forces. Either way, it's the central nervous system for the whole financial system.

The financial sector touches every aspect of your life. Perhaps you're funding your education with a HECS-HELP loan or you're driving a car financed by a car loan. If you fly home for the holidays, you might buy your ticket with a credit card. Even if you haven't yet touched the financial sector, you likely use public goods that depend on the financial sector. For example, the roads you drive on were probably funded by the government issuing bonds.

When you finish university and start working, you might put aside a portion of your income to regularly invest in the stock market. Or perhaps you'll be an entrepreneur whose success hinges on getting your big idea funded. At some point, you'll buy your first home, funded with a home loan that might get bought and sold dozens of times in the debt market. And your quality of life when you retire will depend on how well your investments performed.

There are three key pillars of the financial sector: banks, the bond market, and the stock market. We'll explore each of these in turn. Along the way, you'll learn how to get the best deal you can in your financial dealings.

Chapter Objective

Understand the role played by the financial sector.

27.1 Banks
Assess the role that banks play in funnelling money from savers to investors.

27.2 The Bond Market
Understand how companies and governments raise money by issuing bonds.

27.3 The Stock Market
Learn how companies raise money by issuing stock.

27.4 What Drives Financial Prices?
Discover what drives financial prices.

27.5 Personal Finance
Make better decisions in financial markets.

27.1 Banks

Learning Objective *Assess the role that banks play in funnelling money from savers to investors.*

The original Nike logo design.

Phil Knight was a track enthusiast who ran for the legendary University of Oregon Ducks. He was also a business student with a paper to write for an entrepreneurship course. So he wrote about what he knew: running shoes. At the time, Japanese cameras were starting to take market share from the once-dominant German camera companies. In his paper, he argued that the time was ripe for Japanese-made shoes to challenge the German athletic giants such as Adidas and Puma. When he presented the paper in class, his fellow students were bored. No one asked any questions, but at least he got an A.

Phil couldn't stop thinking about his big idea. After graduation, he decided to give it a try. He visited a Japanese shoe factory, presenting himself as an American tycoon. His ruse worked, and he landed a deal to sell Japanese athletic shoes in the United States. When his old track coach saw the shoes, he was so impressed that he asked to become Phil's business partner. Initially they called the company Blue Ribbon Sports. Later on, they changed it to Nike.

Phil bought his first shipment of shoes with a loan from his father. He quickly sold his first shipment, so for his next shipment he did what many other small businesses do: He turned to his bank for a loan. The First National Bank of Oregon lent him enough money to buy nine hundred pairs of shoes.

Banks are an important funding source for many of life's major investments. Banks provide car loans to fund your car purchase, home loans to help you buy a home, and small business loans to help you start or expand your business. And so our first task in this chapter is to explore just what it is that banks do.

What Do Banks Do?

When you put your money in a bank, your bank takes your money and puts it to work by lending it out, perhaps to provide a loan to a student, a home loan to a young couple, or short-term funding for Nike. Putting your money to work is how the bank earns itself a profit.

Banks make money by charging higher interest rates than they pay. When you deposit your money in the bank, it is not storing your money for you. Instead, it's borrowing money from you. This changes how you think about your relationship with your bank: As a saver, you're the lender, and it's the borrower. Your bank borrows from you so that it can then lend that money to others, and in the process both you and the bank make money.

The price your bank pays to borrow your money is the interest you receive. If you earn 2% per year interest, then depositing $100 in the bank now means that a year from now, you'll have $102 in your account. Your bank makes money by lending that money out to someone else at a higher interest rate. If it charges 6% per year interest on its loans, then someone who borrows $100 will owe them $106 a year later. At that point, the bank owes you $102, but borrowers owe it $106, meaning that the bank made $4.

Your bank is just a middleman; it's buying and then selling a somewhat unusual product: the right to use $100 for the next year. Just like the middleman in any other business, it buys its products at a low price (the 2% interest rate), and then sells it at a higher price (the 6% interest rate).

People willingly pay for this because banks provide valuable services. There are five important functions that banks provide. Let's look at them one by one.

What banks do:
1. Pool savings from many savers
2. Spread the risk of lending money across many borrowers
3. Solve information problems
4. Provide payment services
5. Create long-term loans from short-term deposits

Function one: Banks pool savings from many savers. Your bank pools the savings of many savers and lends that pool of savings to a specific borrower. For savers, this is a valuable service because it means that even if you only have $100 in savings you can earn interest on the money, even if that amount is too small for you to efficiently find someone who needs to borrow it. The flip side is that it's also easier for borrowers to go to one bank than it is for them to try to borrow from dozens of individual lenders. Imagine trying to directly approach dozens of people, asking to borrow their savings, when you need a car loan.

Function two: Banks spread the risk of lending money across many borrowers. Banks also make lending your money much less risky because they lend to a diverse array of borrowers. Your bank doesn't lend all your savings to Nike or any one borrower. Instead, your bank pools money from thousands of savers and lends that money to thousands of borrowers. Effectively, you're lending a dollar of your money to Nike, five cents to a local small business, ten cents to your neighbour's home loan, and so on. The more diverse this portfolio of loans is, the less risky it is.

Function three: Banks solve information problems. Your bank is also an important information intermediary. It doesn't lend your money out to just anyone. Before a borrower can get a loan, your bank will delve into their credit history, check on their assets, and examine their debts. Banks are particularly effective at figuring out who to lend to because they're privy to the financial histories of their customers, and they use this to identify which borrowers will be able to repay their loans.

EVERYDAY Economics

Build a good credit score

One way that banks decide who to lend money to, and what interest rate to charge, is by checking a borrower's *credit score*. Whether you know it or not, you probably have one. It summarises everything that credit bureaus have learned by tracking your financial life. Your credit score (sometimes called your FICO score) is like a Weighted Average Mark (WAM) or GPA for your financial life, and it has far-reaching consequences. So it's a wise idea to take care of your credit score by following these good practices:

- Pay your bills on time. A missed payment will stay on your credit report for seven years.
- If you miss a payment, catch up as soon as possible.
- Develop a history of using credit responsibly. Ironically, not having a credit card doesn't help—you need to show that you can be responsible when you have credit.
- Once you have a credit card, pay off the full balance every month.
- If it looks like you might be getting into trouble, call the lender. Often, they will be willing to work with you to negotiate an arrangement.
- You have the right to see the data that goes into your credit report and to demand corrections. You can check it for free at www.getcreditscore.com.au. ■

Function four: Banks provide payment services. The other reason that you want a bank account—beyond earning interest—is that it makes your economic life a lot simpler. You'll likely find it easier and safer to have your pay deposited directly into a bank account than to go and collect cash. Similarly, you might find it easier to pay your rent electronically, pay your bills online, send money overseas with a bank transfer, and shop online using your credit card. In each case, your bank is providing you with payment services that are often more convenient than using cash.

Function five: Banks create long-term loans from short-term deposits. There's an interesting tension at the heart of banking: Your bank borrows money from savers like you who want to be able to withdraw their funds whenever they want. But your bank then lends this money to borrowers who don't have to repay their loan on demand.

Instead, borrowers tend to repay over a fixed (and long) period of time. For example, homeowners might take out a loan in which they agree to a 30-year repayment plan.

The fact that you want to be able to wake up any day and take your money out of the bank means that effectively you loan the bank money overnight. If you don't withdraw it on any given day, then you are loaning it for another night (and thus giving yourself the option of withdrawing the money the next day). In other words, by making your funds available to you on demand, your bank effectively gets its money from taking short-term (overnight) loans from people like you. But it needs to use those funds to make longer-term loans. What it's doing is called **maturity transformation**—using short-term loans to make long-term loans. Maturity transformation ensures that investors can fund long-term projects, even when no individual savers are willing to make a long-term loan.

maturity transformation Using short-term loans to make long-term loans.

While banks typically successfully engage in maturity transformation, it can cause problems. In fact, it creates a risk that can lead the whole system to come crashing down. Let's see how.

Bank Runs

If your bank doesn't just store your money in its vault and leave it waiting for you, how do you know that your money will be there when you want it? The answer: You don't.

Your bank makes money by lending money. That means that it doesn't keep your money in a bank vault waiting for you. Of course, your bank knows that some people will withdraw their cash, so it keeps enough cash on hand to meet a typical level of withdrawals, plus a bit extra just in case. But it can't keep it all, because if it did, it wouldn't be able to pay you interest or pay its employees.

A **bank run** occurs when many customers try to withdraw their savings at the same time. If a much larger number of customers than usual try to withdraw their savings at the same time, your bank might not be able to pony up your money. When this happens, it can cause a bank to collapse.

bank run When many bank customers try to withdraw their savings at the same time.

Jeff Cameron Collingwood/Shutterstock

When there's a bank run, run.

Bank runs can cause a bank to collapse. On a typical day, few savers will make a withdrawal and banks have plenty of money on hand to give them when they request it. But what makes a day typical? Well, it turns out that a day is typical if most people believe that it is a typical day.

If you believe that tomorrow will be a typical day, then you can go to bed confident that if you need your money, your bank will be able to pay you since your bank can pay everyone who withdraws their money on a typical day. Given this, you're happy keeping your savings in the bank if you don't need the cash.

If you believe that tomorrow will not be a typical day—meaning you expect more people than normal will try to withdraw their money—then you shouldn't feel so reassured. Perhaps you've heard that some people are so worried about your bank's financial health that they're planning to withdraw their savings tomorrow. You realise that an abnormally large number of withdrawals might clean your bank out of cash, and so you can't afford to wait to withdraw your money. Your best response is to run—don't walk!—to the bank and withdraw your savings before other customers beat you there. If other customers follow similar logic—and I believe they will—then they'll also run to the bank.

In fact, this was the story of the Government Savings Bank of NSW (GSB), a bank that was otherwise completely healthy during the roaring 1920s. In November 1929 customers got wind of an impending recession in Australia and many ran to the bank to take their money out. The bank managed to stay afloat, but when the Labor party won the NSW state election in 1930, people worried about the future of the economy, and many raced to the bank simply to beat those where were making panicked withdrawals. It wasn't long before GSB was unable to conduct day-to-day business, and the bank closed down.

A bank run is likely whenever people believe that a bank run is likely. While some banks fail from poor financial health, the challenge for banks is that a bank run can happen even when they are financially healthy, as in the case of GSB. In fact, almost anything can trigger a bank run. For example, more than 10,000 Latvians rushed to the bank to withdraw their money after a false rumour spread on Twitter that the bank was planning on shutting down operations in Latvia. In this sort of panic, it can be rational for you to pull your money out of the bank even if you know the rumour is untrue.

If you believe that others are going to run to withdraw their savings, then your best response is to try to get there first—before the bank runs out of money. And this is your best response whether they're doing this for good reasons (the bank is in financial trouble) or crazy reasons (it's a lunar eclipse) or for a Twitter-based rumour of bank closure that you know is false. And if other people believe that you're going to run to the bank, their best response is to try to get there first, no matter the reason.

This is the *interdependence principle* at work—your best choice depends on what others will do, and their best choice depends on what you will do. In normal times, this interdependence means that you're happy keeping your money in the bank, as long as others are happy keeping their money in the bank. But it also means that there's the possibility of a self-fulfilling panic: You'll panic because you're worried that others will panic, and they'll panic because they're worried you'll panic.

Bank runs can be contagious. Because you panic if someone else panics, it's also easy to see how bank runs can be contagious. For example, after GSB officially closed down in 1931, many people were concerned about another bank run. The Primary Producers Bank, which had low cash reserves, approached larger banks for the possibility of a merger, hoping to avoid the same fate as GSB. It was turned down by both the National Bank of Australia and the Commonwealth Bank, and once consumers got wind of their financial trouble, it faced a run on deposits and went under. The Federal Deposit Bank also failed in 1931 with a similar story. This sentiment continued in the months that followed, and when the Commonwealth Bank acquired GSB in December 1931, there was a significant run on deposits at the Commonwealth Bank. Thankfully the Chairman of the bank was able to stop the runs by dispelling fears that the bank was facing financial difficulties. After this, things began to stabilise, but as the CEO of a bank who faced a run during the 2008-2009 Financial Crisis put it "You could go from being OK . . . to in trouble in a matter of days. I don't think people understand how quickly events unfolded."

Deposit insurance makes bank runs much less likely. While Australia experienced a few bank runs in the 1930s, they have been quite rare throughout your lifetime. During 2008, the U.S. experienced several bank runs, causing a global cascade in financial markets. The Australian Government took proactive policy measures to mitigate the effects of the crisis on Australians. In 2008, the Government established the Financial Claims Scheme (FCS), a form of **deposit insurance**, which effectively guarantees that you'll always get your savings back, even if your bank collapses. This ensures that you won't lose the money you deposit in the bank. But this insurance only covers up to $250,000 in an account.

deposit insurance A guarantee that you won't lose the money you deposit in the bank.

Deposit insurance is designed to break the interdependence that leads to self-fulfilling panics. When you have deposit insurance, you know that your savings are safe, no matter what other people do. Even if others withdraw their money from the bank, you don't need to try to beat them to the bank, since you know that you'll ultimately get your money back. Deposit insurance is a simple idea, but it really works. Since the government implemented deposit insurance in 2008, Australia has not experienced a single bank failure.

Shadow Banks and the Financial Crisis

At this stage, you might be wondering: If deposit insurance works so well, why did the world suffer a major financial crisis in 2008? One answer is that not all financial firms are banks and only banks are covered by deposit insurance.

shadow banks Financial firms that are similar to banks, but are not regulated like banks.

Shadow banks perform banking functions, but aren't regulated as banks. **Shadow banks** are pretty similar to banks—they get their funds from depositors who can withdraw their money at any time, and they use those funds to make long-term loans to investors. But because they're not officially called banks, they're not regulated like banks, which frees them up to rely on innovative and risky funding. It also means that there's no deposit insurance, and that makes them vulnerable to bank runs. That's the short-story version of what happened in 2008. The crash originated in the U.S., where large financial firms such as Bear Stearns were shadow banks, and when their depositors lost faith in them, they withdrew their money, causing a (shadow) bank run.

Fire sales can cause shadow bank runs to spread. The problem quickly spread. A shadow bank facing a bank run has to sell its assets quickly in order to repay its depositors. Putting billions of dollars of financial assets up for sale at once floods the market, pushing the price of those assets down. Then the *interdependence principle* kicks in: Because other shadow banks hold similar assets, a fire sale of assets by one shadow bank in trouble reduces the market value of other shadow banks' assets. And that reduction in market value makes the customers of other shadow banks more nervous, leading to further bank runs. As more shadow banks go belly up, there are more fire sales, and the problem spreads like a virus.

Clive Gee/PA Images/Getty Images

The insurance company AIG is a shadow bank that got in trouble and needed a bailout in 2008.

Shadow banks are opaque. There's another problem in all of this: The shadow banking system is incredibly opaque, and so when one financial institution can't pay its debts, it's hard to know who will be hurt. Unknown interdependencies can make small problems balloon into big ones. It's a bit like knowing that a small share of the meat supply is infected with illness-inducing bacteria, but not knowing which particular shipments or suppliers are affected. When this happens, millions of people stop eating meat rather than risking illness.

Bad loans are the financial equivalent of bacteria. Depositing money with a shadow bank infected with bad loans may put you in financial distress. If you don't know which shadow banks are infected and there is no deposit insurance, you won't want to lend money to any of them. That's how a relatively small number of bad loans in 2008 caused lending to decline sharply, which then sparked a major recession.

Okay, that completes our tour of banks and shadow banks. Let's now turn our attention to another way to borrow money: the bond market.

27.2 The Bond Market

Learning Objective *Understand how companies and governments raise money by issuing bonds.*

Fast-forward from Nike's humble beginnings to 2016, and you'll find that it's grown to become one of the world's largest companies. Every investment it made seemed to make the company more valuable. Buoyed by this success, senior management decided they had to invest more, particularly in improving Nike's computing infrastructure and global distribution network. It's worth doing, but it's also expensive. Nike's financial team crunched the numbers and figured they needed another $1 billion to fund this new investment.

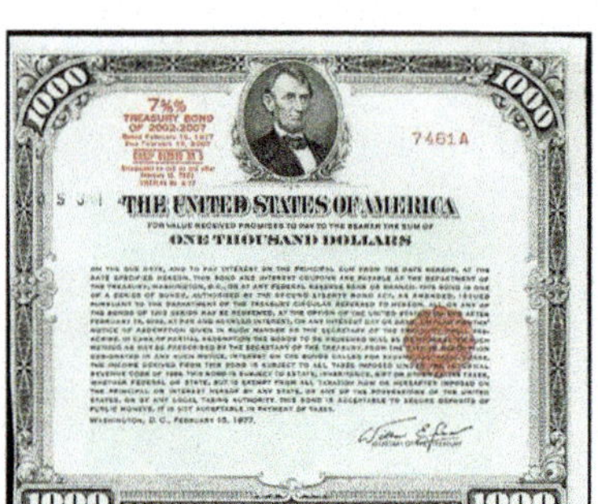

A bond certificate.

What Does the Bond Market Do?

When you want to borrow money, you probably go to the bank. But what if you're Nike, looking for a cool billion? I'm afraid your local bank manager just isn't prepared to deal with a loan that big. Instead, Nike did what many other corporations do—and also what the government does when looking for a loan. It turned to the bond market. The simplest way to think of the bond market is that it's where the big dogs go to borrow the big bucks.

A **bond** is just an IOU. When Nike issued its bonds, it borrowed a billion dollars and promised to pay it back in the future, with interest. The bond is just the piece of paper recording the terms of the IOU. When you buy a bond, you give Nike cash, and it gives you a piece of paper, promising to pay you back.

bond An IOU. Specifically, a promise to pay back a loan with interest.

That piece of paper is important, though, because it spells out the terms of the loan. It records the borrower (called the *issuer,* which is Nike), how much Nike has to repay at the end (the *principal,* which is $1 billion), when the loan must be repaid (the *maturity date,* which is November 1, 2026), and the interest it has promised to pay along the way (these are called *coupons,* and Nike promised to pay 2.375% interest per year).

The bond market is a big deal. As of 2016, the total quantity of outstanding bonds issued in the United States was close to $39 trillion, or a bit more than $100,000 per American. Many students believe that they don't own any bonds. Perhaps that's true, at least while you're a student. But you'll probably go on to a career that includes a retirement plan, and your retirement plan will likely invest some of your money in bonds. This means that in a few years, you're going to be a big player in the bond market, albeit somewhat indirectly.

What the bond market does:

1. Channels funds from savers to borrowers
2. Funds government debt
3. Spreads risk
4. Creates liquidity

So what purpose does the bond market serve? The bond market performs four key functions.

Function one: The bond market channels funds from savers to borrowers. The bond market provides an alternative to banks; it's an alternative market where companies can borrow the large sums of money they need to fund their investments, and savers can lend the funds they aren't using. As such, it channels unused resources from savers (like you) to borrowers (like Nike).

While the stock market tends to hog the headlines, in fact bonds are a much bigger source of corporate financing. In 2016, companies raised around $250 billion by issuing new stock, but they raised nearly $1.5 trillion from issuing bonds. This equates to a bit less than $1,000 per American each year in new stock issues, and about $5,000 per American in new bond issues.

Function two: The bond market funds government debt. It's not just companies that borrow by issuing bonds—so do governments. In fact, the U.S. federal government is the biggest player in the bond market: It has borrowed over $15 trillion by issuing bonds. Whenever you hear about government debt, realise that it borrowed all that money by issuing bonds. Beyond the federal government, state and local governments borrow money by issuing bonds. Foreign governments also borrow money by issuing bonds.

Function three: The bond market spreads risk. Instead of issuing just one $1 billion bond to one person, Nike issues thousands of bonds in denominations as small as $1,000. This way, even if no one individual has a spare billion to lend to Nike, thousands of investors may be willing to each make a smaller loan. By making it easy to spread borrowing across many lenders, bonds spread the risk that Nike won't repay its loan across many lenders.

As an investor, even if you had a billion dollars to invest, you probably wouldn't want to lend it all to Nike. Instead, you should diversify your portfolio, investing small amounts in bonds issued by many different companies. By not holding all your eggs in one basket, you'll make sure that if Nike collapses, you won't lose all your savings.

liquidity The ability to quickly and easily convert your investments into cash, with little or no loss in value.

Function four: The bond market creates liquidity. The problem with lending someone money for 10 years is that you might suddenly discover you need the cash before the loan is due. Fortunately, you can sell your bond to other investors in the bond market. Because there are many buyers, you'll usually get something close to a fair price. That is, the bond market creates **liquidity,** which is the ability to quickly and easily convert your investments into cash, with little or no loss in value.

Gorodenkoff/Shutterstock

Trading bonds creates liquidity.

In this way, the bond market—like banks—creates long-term loans from short-term loans. This *maturity transformation* is done through the ability to resell bonds in the bond market. When you sell your bond to someone else, you get your money back—the cash value of your bond—and they take over the loan, getting the future interest payments and the principle repayment on the maturity date.

Evaluating Risks

Bonds have the advantage of clear terms: You know the interest rate you'll be paid, the date at which you'll be paid back in full, and these promises will be honoured as long as the company hasn't gone bust. But there are some specific risks that you face. The first is the chance that the company goes bust: *default risk*. The second is *term risk* and the third is *liquidity risk*. Let's explore each in turn.

default risk The risk that your loan won't be repaid.

Figure 1 | **Interest Rates Rise with Default Risk**

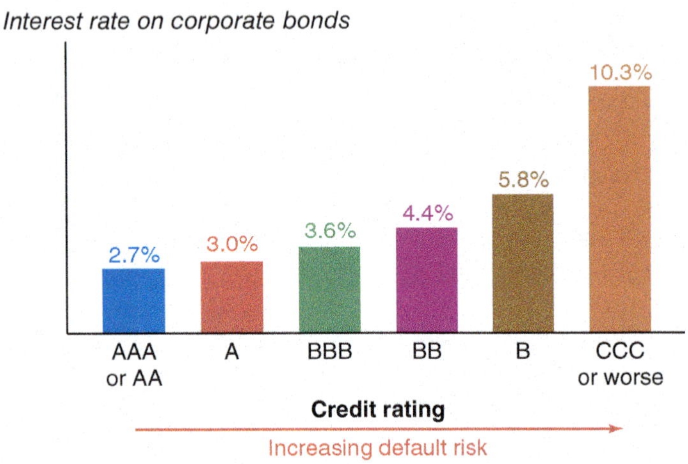

Data from: Bloomberg.

Risk one: Default risk is the risk of not getting paid. One risk of lending people money is that they won't repay their loans, and this risk also exists for bonds. If Nike goes bust, it may not have enough money to repay people who bought Nike bonds. The risk that you won't be repaid (or won't be repaid in a timely fashion) is called **default risk.** Domestic companies like Australia Ratings, and U.S. companies like Fitch, Standard & Poor's and Moody's evaluate companies and assign *credit ratings,* which are like credit scores for businesses. Because it's difficult for each investor to assess Nike's chances of default, investors rely on these credit ratings to assess default risk.

A rating of "AAA" is the highest possible rating, meaning the company has an *extremely* strong capacity to repay its debt. Nike's $1 billion bond issue earned a rating of "AA-," which is not quite perfect but still good enough to suggest it has a very strong capacity to repay its debt. Figure 1 shows that the worse the rating, the higher the interest rate: As the default risk rises, lenders demand a higher return in order to take on the additional risk that the loan won't be paid back.

Bond risks:
1. Default risk
2. Term risk
3. Liquidity risk

Risk two: Term risk arises when there's uncertainty about future interest rates. The *opportunity cost principle* reminds you that tying up your money comes with an opportunity cost—you could invest that money in the bank and earn interest on it. The problem is that when you buy a bond, you don't know what future interest rates will be, so you are taking a risk as to what the opportunity cost will be over the term of the bond. The investors who agreed to loan Nike money for a term of 10 years at 2.375% per year were hoping that the opportunity cost over the next 10 years would be less than 2.375%. If interest rates shoot up to 4%, they are stuck earning only 2.375%, and the forgone opportunity to earn a bigger return can be an expensive opportunity cost.

term risk The risk that arises from uncertainty about future interest rates.

The risk that arises from uncertainty about future interest rates is called **term risk** because the risk is connected to the length, or term, of the loan. The more uncertain you are about future interest rates, the greater this risk is. The longer the term, the more interest rates might change, and so the higher the term risk. Nike borrowed $500 million over 30 years and faced a higher interest rate (3.375%) than it had when it borrowed $1 billion over 10 years (2.375%). Term risk explains why it had to pay this higher rate.

Risk three: Liquidity risk arises when your bond will be hard to sell. Another risk in lending out your money is that you might end up needing those funds yourself. If your money is in the bank, you solve this by just making a withdrawal. But to "withdraw" your money from a bond, you have to sell it. While the bond market creates liquidity, there is a risk that you won't be able to quickly find a buyer for your bonds. **Liquidity risk** refers to the risk that if you need to sell an asset quickly, you may not be able to get a good price for it.

liquidity risk The risk that if you need to sell an asset quickly, you may not be able to get a good price for it.

Billions of dollars of federal government bonds are traded each day, and so these involve very little liquidity risk. But it can be harder to quickly find a buyer for a bond issued by small company, making liquidity risk a much bigger deal.

U.S. government bonds are the safest investment. Putting all of this together, you'll discover that the safest investment you can make is to buy bonds issued by the U.S. government, which are often called *Treasuries*. They're considered safe because the U.S. government can always pay its debts simply by printing more money. (However, there remains a political risk that Congress might choose not to make debt payments in a timely fashion.) U.S. government bonds are also the most heavily traded bonds in the world—around $500 billion in Treasuries are traded each day!—and so they carry basically no liquidity risk. And a short-term loan carries almost no term risk, which is why the interest rate on short-term loans to the federal government is often described as a risk-free interest rate.

The cost of all of this safety is that lower risk comes with a lower reward, and so the interest rate on U.S. government bonds is lower than the interest rate on other bonds. That's why the U.S. government can borrow money at a lower interest rate than any other organisation. Of course, it doesn't have to be this way: When investors became concerned about whether Greece could repay its debts in 2012, the interest rate on Greek government bonds rose to over 25%.

Australian government bonds aren't quite as safe as U.S. Treasuries, but they're close. The risk that the Australian government doesn't pay back its debts is really low. Because Australia has never defaulted on its government debt, is a stable democracy, and has low government debt as a share of the economy, the Australian government can borrow at close to the same rate as the U.S. government can.

If you're a company looking to raise money, you don't have to turn to banks or the bond market—you also have the option of issuing stock instead. So let's turn our attention to the stock market.

27.3 The Stock Market

Learning Objective *Learn how companies raise money by issuing stock.*

While Nike's early years were bumpy, it grew quickly into a major force. In a bit more than 15 years, Phil Knight had grown from selling shoes out of the back of a van to being the CEO of a company selling nearly half of all running shoes in the United States. But Nike's impact beyond the United States was more limited, and that bugged Phil, who had global ambitions for his company. It would take a lot of money to aggressively expand into Europe and elsewhere—more money than Nike had. So Phil decided to sell Nike stock to the public, using the money raised to fund his ambitious global expansion plans. Let's see what this entails.

This stock certificate represents partial ownership in Nike.

What Do Stocks Do?

In most countries they're called "stocks" and in Australia they're sometimes called "shares," but they're the same thing. A stock represents partial ownership in a firm. When you own stock in a company, you own a share of the company, which is why a stock is also sometimes called a share. In 2019, there were roughly 1,600,000,000 shares in Nike, each worth roughly $65 each. That means for $65 you can own 1/1,600,000,000 of Nike. As a partial owner of Nike, you'll make money if it makes money, and you'll lose money if it loses money. Think of your Nike stock as a claim to a (very small!) share of Nike's assets and its future profits.

What stocks do:

1. Channel funds from savers to investors
2. Spread risk
3. Reallocate control

A stock entitles you to a share of future profits. You stand to benefit from your ownership in two ways.

First, there are **dividends.** At the end of each year, Nike's management tallies up its profits and may pay some of it out to shareholders as a dividend. Nike usually pays a dividend every three months, and over the course of the year, the dividend adds up to an annual return equal to the value of about 1% or 2% of the value of the stock. The profits that Nike elects not to send out as dividends are called **retained earnings,** and Nike reinvests these remaining profits into the company.

dividends A share of profits that a company pays to its shareholders.

retained earnings The profits that a company chooses not to give as dividends to shareholders.

Figure 2 | **Nike's Stock Goes** 

Value of $1,000 invested in 1980

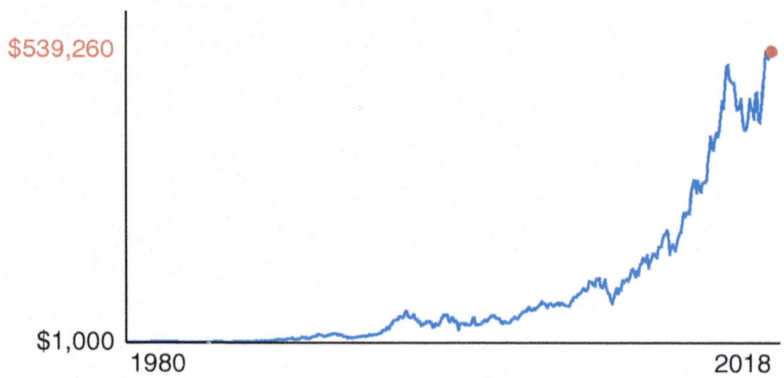

Data from: Bloomberg.

This brings us to the second way you can profit from owning stock: The value of your shares can rise. As the outlook for Nike's future profitability grows, so will the value of the company, and hence so will the price of your stock. Figure 2 shows that Nike's stock price has gone "swoosh": If you had been smart enough to buy $1,000 in Nike stock in 1980, your investment would be worth over $500,000 today!!!

Stocks perform three key functions, which we'll review here.

Function one: Stocks channel funds from savers to investors. The primary reason that businesses issue stock is to raise money to fund their investments. When a business issues stock, it is essentially expanding by taking on new partners who will each own part of the company. When Nike decided to issue stock, it offered 2.7 million shares for sale to the general public at $11 per share, which raised $30 million, and it used this money to fund its expansion plans. Thus, stocks provide a similar function to banks and bonds, channelling unused funds from savers to investors.

When companies raise money by issuing new stock, they usually sell those shares directly to the public through what's known as an **initial public offering** (or "IPO," for short). IPOs aren't sold through the stock market. Typically IPO shares are handled by an investment bank or broker dealer, who sells the shares, typically to big institutional investors.

initial public offering When a company first sells stock directly to the public.

Function two: Stocks spread risk. Issuing stock is like taking on new business partners. The new stockholder provides additional cash that will allow the business to grow. What shareholders get in return is a share of whatever the company produces. If the company has a great year, shareholders have a great year. They may receive more in dividend payments or they may see the value of the stock go up. In short, they gain when the company gains. But when the company has a bad year, shareholders have a bad year. Poor performance might mean that smaller dividends are paid and the value of the stock might decline. Stocks therefore spread the risk of business performance across many shareholders, reducing the risk that any one person faces.

stock market The market where people buy and sell existing stocks.

Function three: Stocks reallocate control. As a shareholder who owns part of Nike, you also get a chance to have a say in how it's run. Not directly—being a shareholder doesn't make you a manager. But shareholders get to vote in shareholder meetings. Nike's management reports to a board of directors that's elected by the shareholders. You'll also get to vote on major issues like whether to merge with another company, and what to pay senior management. Each share buys you one vote, although all shareholders—no matter how small—are entitled to turn up to the annual meeting to ask questions.

The stock market creates liquidity and makes it easier to own stocks. The **stock market** is a market for second-hand stock, where people buy and sell existing stocks. This means that when you go to the stock market to buy Nike stock, your funds aren't going to Nike to help it open a new factory; you're simply buying from an existing shareholder who owns some Nike stock they want to sell. Just as Toyota gets nothing when you buy a pre-owned car, Nike gets nothing when you buy pre-owned stock.

The stock market still plays an important role, but it's different than you might have guessed. Around $500 million worth of stock in Nike is bought and sold *each day*. All of this trading creates liquidity, meaning that if you need access to your cash, it will be easy to sell your Nike stock at something close to a fair price. Part of the reason that people were willing to buy Nike stock in their initial public offering is that they knew that if they wanted their cash back, they could easily sell their stock on the stock market. Liquidity makes investing in Nike a less risky bet.

Tim Boyle/Bloomberg/Getty Images

She's buying used goods.

Comparing Stocks and Bonds

Let's step back to compare bonds and stocks more completely, so that you can choose which works best for you. It's a decision that you'll face both as an investor choosing where to invest your money, and as an entrepreneur deciding how to fund your next big expansion.

Bonds pay certain annual interest payments, while stocks pay uncertain dividends. Both when a company borrows money by issuing bonds and when it issues new stock, it gets money to fund its investments, and is committed to make future payments to whoever provides that funding. But borrowing commits you to a known set of future payments: A bond specifies exactly what interest payments (the coupon payments) will be made each year. In contrast, a stock pays a dividend that depends on how the company is doing. If Nike has a bad year, it might not pay a dividend to its stockholders, but it'll still have to make the specified interest payments to its bondholders. And if Nike has a good year, it may issue a really big dividend to stockholders, but it'll give bondholders nothing more than the promised interest payment. For an investor, this makes bonds a safer bet than stocks. But for a company looking to fund a big expansion, getting funding from stocks instead of bonds is less risky because it means offloading some of your risk onto your shareholders.

Bondholders get paid before stockholders if a company declares bankruptcy. Second, there's the question of who gets what if the company goes bust. When a company declares bankruptcy, its assets are sold and used to pay off its debts. Because a bond is a debt, bondholders get paid out of the proceeds of this sell-off. If there's not enough money to fully repay the bondholders, they'll get partial payment. But the stockholders get nothing unless there's money left over after the company pays all its debts. This makes bankruptcy a much greater financial risk for stockholders than it is for bondholders.

Stockholders help control how a company is run. Third, a bondholder has no say in how a company is managed, while a stockholder is a partial owner, and hence has some say in how it's run. Corporate raiders will often use this power to try to force a company to make changes that they believe will enhance their profits. And this can make many entrepreneurs—particularly those who value total control over their company—nervous about issuing stock. In some cases, shareholders have voted in a corporate board that then fired the founder of a company from his or her own firm!

Figure 3 summarises the major differences between bonds and stocks. As you'll see, it's all about the difference between lending money to a company and owning part of that company.

Figure 3 | **Bonds versus Stocks**

Bonds	Stocks
• Specified future interest payments	• Uncertain future dividends; depending on how well the company is doing
• First in line to get paid if the company goes bankrupt	• Last in line to get paid if the company goes bust
• No rights to help control the company	• Shareholders have a vote in how the company is run

Understanding Stock Market Data

Okay, let's dig into a bit of the jargon surrounding stocks and the stock market. Figure 4 shows you a snapshot of the stock market downloaded from Google Finance. I'm going to make it easy to interpret.

Figure 4 | **What Do All Those Numbers on Google Finance Mean?**

Interpreting Nike's stock market numbers

- The current *stock price* tells you how much your stock is worth.
- The *opening price, high price,* and *low price* summarise what has happened to the stock price during today's trading session: what it traded for at the start of the day, the highest price it sold for today, and the lowest price it sold for today.
- You can get a better sense of how risky a stock is by evaluating its ups and downs over a period of several months or years. This is what a *stock price chart* can show you.
- *Market capitalisation* tells you the value of the entire company. It's the number of stocks, multiplied by the stock price.
- Figure 4 also shows some important ratios like the *price-earnings ratio,* which we'll turn to in the next section.

27.4 What Drives Financial Prices?

Learning Objective *Discover what drives financial prices.*

Our next task is to ask: What drives financial prices? We'll focus most of our discussion on what drives stock prices, but as you read, you'll find this material even more useful if you think about how similar ideas apply to the price of other investments. After all, many of the same motivations that lead people to buy and sell stocks lead them to buy and sell other assets such as real estate, fine art, and even truly unusual assets such as alpacas. In each case, you're buying an asset with a limited intrinsic value—perhaps the possibility of a stream of payments if your stock pays a dividend or someone rents your house—and also the potential for big profits or losses if their prices shift sharply.

Valuing Stocks

What determines the price of a stock—or indeed, any other financial asset? As with just about everything else, it's all about supply and demand. Figure 5 shows that the price of a stock reflects the same forces as in any other market. There's a demand curve for Nike stocks describing how many shares investors will buy at each price, just as there's a supply curve describing how many shares investors will sell at each price. As in other markets, the price moves to the equilibrium point where supply equals demand.

The only real difference is that as a savvy investor, you're on both the demand and supply side of the market. If the price of Nike stock is low enough, you'll conclude that it's such a good deal that you'll want to buy it, while if the price is high enough, you'll want to sell it, making you a supplier.

This pushes the question one level deeper: What determines the price at which investors are willing to buy or sell stock? Let's explore some of the different approaches that investors use to value financial assets, including stocks.

Figure 5 | The Market for Nike Stock

Ⓐ The **demand curve** shows how many stocks investors will buy at each price.

Ⓑ The **supply curve** describes how many stocks investors will sell at each price.

Ⓒ The **equilibrium price** is determined where supply equals demand.

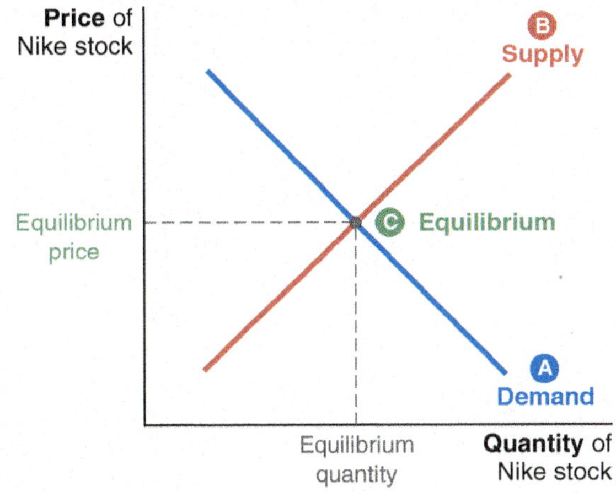

Fundamental value is the present value of future profits. The goal of **fundamental analysis** is to assess an asset's fundamental value. The starting point comes from recognising that the benefit of owning stock is that it entitles you to a share of a company's future profits. As such, the **fundamental value** of a business is the present value of the future profits it will earn. The fundamental value of a firm determines the fundamental value of stock in that firm. A stock is a good deal when its price is below its fundamental value.

fundamental analysis A framework for assessing an asset's fundamental value.

fundamental value The present value of the future profits that a company will earn.

Assessing a business's fundamental value is a four-step process.

Step one: *Forecast future profits.* Analysts typically build sophisticated spreadsheet models that project the business's revenues and costs in each of the next 5–10 years. The difference between revenues and costs is the business's expected profits for that year. Beyond that time horizon, analysts usually make their projections by assuming that profits will continue to grow at some constant rate, perhaps reflecting the broader growth rate of the industry.

Step two: *Discount these profits.* The *opportunity cost principle* reminds you that tying up your money comes with an opportunity cost—you could invest that money in something else. Consequently, you should convert each year's profits into their *present values* to account for this opportunity cost using the discounting formula we introduced in the last chapter. When you're evaluating a risky stock, make sure to use a higher discount rate because the opportunity cost is investing in another risky stock, and riskier stocks typically earn a higher return.

Step three: *Add up the sum of those discounted future profits.* The sum of the present value of all of Nike's future profits is your estimate of Nike's fundamental value.

Step four: *Divide the company's fundamental value by the total number of shares.* There are 1,600,000,000 Nike shares and each has a claim on Nike's future profits. So the fundamental value of a single Nike stock is 1/1,600,000,000 of the company's fundament value.

How to assess a business's fundamental value:

1. Forecast future profits
2. Discount these profits
3. Add up the sum of those discounted future profits
4. Divide the company's fundamental value by the total number of shares

If you find Nike stock cheaper than this, then the *cost-benefit principle* says you should buy the stock. If you're right, and the stock price heads toward its fundamental value, you'll be able to sell the stock for a profit. But even if the market never corrects itself, you can hold that Nike stock, and your calculations suggest that over the long term you'll enjoy a stream of dividends that's more valuable than the price you paid for it.

Here's the big caveat: This investment strategy will only succeed if your estimate of Nike's fundamental value is more accurate than the stock price. If it's not, you may think you're buying an underpriced stock, but actually end up buying an overpriced one.

relative valuation An assessment of the value of an asset by comparing it to similar assets.

Relative valuation relies on comparable businesses. An alternative approach, called **relative valuation,** assesses the value of an asset by comparing it to similar assets. In the simplest form of relative valuation, you assess the price of something by comparing it with an almost identical "twin." For example, relative valuation says that if a two-bedroom fourth-floor apartment sold for $120,000, then the value of the almost identical apartment across the hallway is also $120,000. Of course, this only makes sense if the first apartment was sold at an appropriate price.

Relative valuation gets a bit more difficult when you can't find an identical twin. For instance, no company is anywhere near being Nike's twin—Nike is more than twice the size of its nearest competitor, Adidas (and is 10 times larger than Under Armour). To get around the problem of comparable size, you can look at *financial ratios* that abstract from each firm's size. Two of the relative-valuation ratios used by Wall Street analysts are:

- *Price-to-book ratio,* which measures a firm's stock price relative to the *book value* per share, which is a measure of the business's net assets per share (calculated as total assets less liabilities). If Nike uses its assets to generate profits at a similar rate to Adidas, then both Nike and Adidas should have a similar price-to-book ratio.
- *Price-to-earnings ratio,* which measures a firm's stock price, relative to last year's profits, measured as *earnings per share.* The idea is that a company with twice the earnings of Adidas should be worth twice as much. If this is true then Nike and Adidas should have a similar price-to-earnings ratio.

Do the Economics

Figure 6 | **Adidas Financial Data**

adidas Financial Data	
Stock price per share	$157.91
Earnings per share	$5.34
Book value per share	$33.97

2016 Data from: Bloomberg.

Use relative valuation to price Nike's stock.

Figure 6 contains some key 2016 financial data for Adidas, which is one of Nike's key competitors. We're going to use these numbers to estimate Nike's value.

a. Calculate the price-to-book ratio for Adidas stock.

$$\text{Adidas' price-to-book ratio is } \frac{\text{Price per share}}{\text{Book value per share}} = \frac{\$157.91}{\$33.97} = 4.65$$

b. Calculate the price-to-earnings ratio for Adidas stock.

$$\text{Adidas' price-to-earnings ratio is } \frac{\text{Price per share}}{\text{Earnings per share}} = \frac{\$157.91}{\$5.34} = 29.6$$

Okay, let's use your calculations to value Nike's stock.

c. Nike's book value per share was $7.31. If Nike can produce the same price-to-book ratio as Adidas, what's the value of Nike stock?

$$\frac{\text{Price per share}_{\text{Nike}}}{\text{Book value per share}_{\text{Nike}}} = 4.65$$

$$\text{Rearranging: Price per share}_{\text{Nike}} = 4.65 \times \text{Book value per share}_{\text{Nike}} = 4.65 \times \$7.31 = \$34$$

d. Nike's earnings per share was $2.16. If Nike had the same price-to-earnings ratio as Adidas, what is the value of Nike stock?

$$\frac{\text{Price per share}_{\text{Nike}}}{\text{Earnings per share}_{\text{Nike}}} = 29.6$$

$$\text{Re-arranging: Price per share}_{\text{Nike}} = 29.6 \times \text{Earnings per share}_{\text{Nike}} = 29.6 \times \$2.16 = \$64$$

Okay, we've used two relative-valuation techniques, and they give different values. One says that Nike stock was worth $64, while the other says it was worth $34. In fact, during 2016, Nike's stock price fluctuated between $49 and $64, suggesting that these valuations gave a pretty good indicator of the price at which investors were willing to buy and sell Nike stock. ■

The key to getting a relative valuation right is to make sure that you're comparing companies that are otherwise quite similar. This means that you should only compare Nike to companies with similar risk, growth prospects, and funding needs. But this doesn't mean just comparing Nike to other sporting goods companies. Some analysts have argued that Nike should also be compared with other shoe companies, such as Crocs, fashion companies, such as Ralph Lauren, and luxury brands, such as Coach.

EVERYDAY Economics **How much should you pay for that house?**

You can apply the same principles you use to value stocks to figure out how much you're willing to pay for a house.

Just as the *fundamental value* of a business derives from the profits it delivers each year, the fundamental value of a house derives from the "profit" you make from not having to pay rent each year. And just as you can figure out how much a stock is worth by adding up the present value of these future profits, you can figure out how much a house is worth by adding up the future value of the rent that you'd otherwise have to pay to enjoy equally nice housing.

You can also use *relative valuation* to value a house. If you can't find a twin for the house that you're buying, focus instead on a relative-valuation ratio. The most common ratio investors use when valuing houses is the price-to-size ratio. As with all relative-valuation techniques, it's important to compare like with like, and in this case, it means comparing houses of a similar quality in a similar neighbourhood. If similar-quality houses in your neighbourhood typically sell at a price-to-size ratio of around $1,000 per square metre, then this approach says that a 200-square-metre house will sell for around $200,000. It also says that a 40-square-metre tiny house will sell for $40,000. ■

Ariel Celeste Photography/Shutterstock

What's a good price for this tiny house?

The Efficient Markets Hypothesis

Nike's stock price is determined by supply and demand. Demand to buy Nike stock comes from investors who believe that its fundamental value is higher than the price. Supply of Nike stock comes from investors who want to sell it because they believe its fundamental value is lower than the price. In equilibrium, demand equals supply, which means that Nike's stock price moves to the exact point where there are as many bets placed that it is overpriced as there are that it is underpriced. This perspective suggests that a stock price represents the market's collective judgement about a company's fundamental value.

Stock prices reflect all publicly available information about a company's fundamental value. When an analyst discovers some good news for Nike—perhaps the cost of rubber used to make runners will be a little lower—it leads her to upgrade her assessment of Nike's value. As a result, the fund she manages will buy more stock in Nike, and this extra demand will nudge the price up. Another analyst discovers some bad news—sales are slow in Malaysia!—leading his fund to sell the stock, which nudges the price down.

As thousands of analysts dig into the details, Nike's stock price will come to reflect all of this information. That's the idea behind the **efficient markets hypothesis,** which holds that at any point in time, financial prices reflect all publicly available information.

efficient markets hypothesis The theory that at any point in time, stock prices reflect all publicly available information.

It's tough to beat the market. The efficient markets hypothesis doesn't mean that a stock's price is always exactly equal to its fundamental value. Rather, it says that it's impossible to predict whether it is under- or overpriced based on publicly available information.

This explains why it's so hard to make money buying and selling stocks. As a savvy investor, you're looking to buy a stock whose fundamental value is higher than its price. But the efficient markets hypothesis says that it's impossible to tell whether a stock is under- or overpriced—or at least it's impossible unless you have inside information, and

Peter Ptschelinzew/Lonely Planet Images/Getty Images

Everyone at the flea market is hoping they'll find an underpriced treasure.

it's illegal to trade on inside information. (That's called insider trading.) The market includes many traders, each of them diligently looking for an edge. If any information indicated that Nike were underpriced, all these traders would have already snapped up the Nike stock, thereby bidding the price back up to its fundamental value.

The same idea applies to other financial markets, too. Billions of dollars' worth of bonds and foreign currencies are traded every day, with thousands of analysts and traders looking for every little edge. As such, it's nearly impossible to identify a bond or foreign currency that is undervalued.

Some markets are less competitive. For example, the market for houses, Picassos, and baseball cards may not be perfectly efficient. But even so, there are enough smart cookies trading these assets that even sophisticated professional investors find it very difficult to identify undervalued assets. That's why people digging through flea markets for undervalued antiques typically end up with little to show for their efforts.

Financial prices move unpredictably. The logic of the efficient markets hypothesis also suggests that it will be impossible to predict whether stock prices will rise or fall over the next minute, hour, day, week, or year. After all, if there's information suggesting that the stock price should rise next Friday, then some trader will figure out they can make money by buying the stock on Thursday to sell on Friday afternoon. You could beat them to it by buying the stock on Wednesday instead, but some smarty might jump ahead of you and buy stock on Tuesday. Follow the logic far enough, and you'll see that people buy and sell stock today based on news about the future, and they'll do this to the point that they eliminate any predictable future stock price changes.

If forward-looking traders eliminate all predictable stock price changes, all that's left will be unpredictable changes. This logic suggests that stock price *changes* are unpredictable. This is really just an application of the idea that stock prices already reflect all publicly available information—in this case, it says that the stock price already reflects the information that would otherwise cause the stock price to rise or fall in the future. When a price moves in an unpredictable way, we say it follows a **random walk,** which means that it follows an unpredictable path.

random walk When a price follows an unpredictable path.

Technical analysis looks for patterns—even where none exist. All this means that *technical analysis*—studying graphs of financial prices over time, finding patterns, and trying to use those patterns to predict the future—doesn't really work. You can't make money predicting the unpredictable. This can be hard for people to believe. Humans have an instinctive need to try to find order among chaos, and that instinct can easily lead you to believe that you can spot patterns even where none exist.

A random walk doesn't mean that stock prices move in any crazy old way. Good news still means that a stock price will rise, but the stock price will rise as soon as traders get wind of it, which may even be before the positive outcome occurs. For example, the stock of a pharmaceutical company will rise as soon as investors learn that the company has a new allergy drug. And it will rise again when they learn that the new drug has been approved by the FDA. By the time the company actually shows a profit from selling you the drug to treat your allergies, all those profits are already expected by stockholders and thus are reflected in the stock price.

Do the Economics

Can you predict stock price movements?

Let's test out this random walk idea. Can you predict whether stock market prices will rise or fall? Figure 7 shows stock price data for a random month for each of 99 leading stocks. If you think the stock rose the next day, mark it with a ✓, but if you think it fell, mark it with a ✗.

Answer: Hey, make sure you've finished making your predictions before you look up the answer! Seriously. Finish it first.

Figure 7 | **Can You Predict Whether These Stocks Will Rise or Fall Next?**

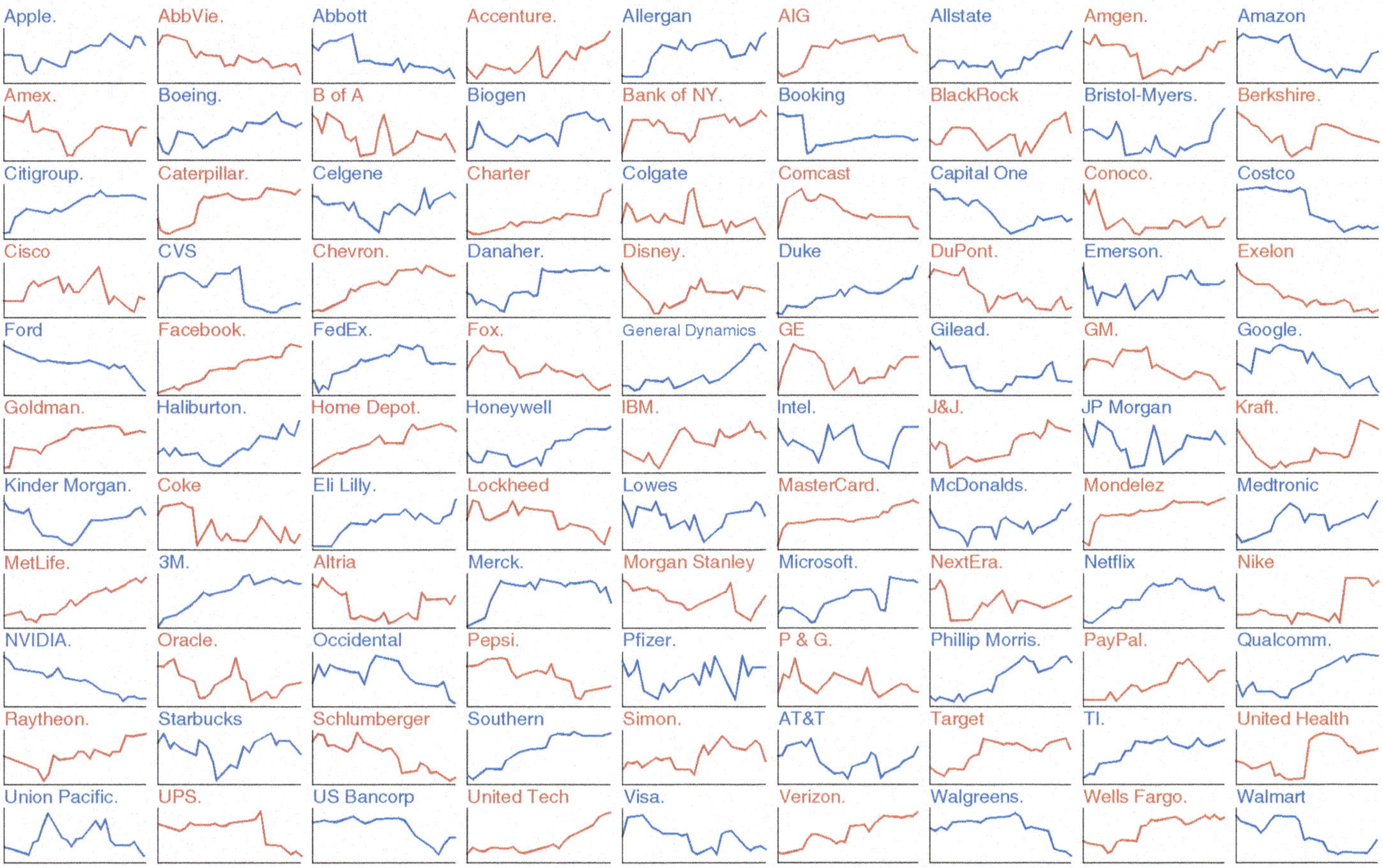

Data from: Bloomberg.

Okay, so now you're really done? If there's a full stop at the end of a stock's name, that means the stock rose the next day.

How did you do? Most students get roughly as many right as they get wrong—somewhere between 44 and 55 out of 99—which is just what the random walk theory suggests. Occasionally there's a student who gets a few more right than wrong, but the margin is still small enough that it could be luck. ■

The Value of Expert Advice

A few years back, an English newspaper ran a stock-picking contest pitting a leading wealth manager, a stockbroker, and a fund manager against a ginger cat called Orlando. The investment pros did what investment pros normally do, crunching reams of data to find what they considered the best stocks to buy. By contrast, Orlando threw his favourite toy mouse onto a grid representing different stocks. At the end of the year, Orlando had beaten the pros.

That's nuts, right? Wouldn't you figure that knowing nothing about stocks—or being a cat—would be a severe handicap in a stock-picking contest?

Not so fast, says the efficient markets hypothesis. If it's impossible—or at least really difficult—to beat the market, then it must also be really hard to do worse than the market. After all, if Orlando really were a worse stock picker on average, then you could make money just by doing the opposite of whatever he did. It follows that if the efficient markets hypothesis is right, Orlando is as good at picking stocks as any investment professional. (And in this case, he got a bit lucky and beat them.) This is the logic that once led an economist to claim that "a blindfolded monkey throwing darts at a newspaper's financial pages could select a portfolio that would do just as well as one carefully selected by the experts."

Courtesy of Jill Insley

Orlando wasn't quite purrfect, but he beat three pros.

Thousands of researchers—including both university professors and Wall Street quants—have conducted careful studies trying to assess whether they can predict where stocks are going. The conclusion tends to be that it's incredibly hard to predict stock prices, although it may not be impossible. You've probably heard of Warren Buffett—he's made billions by seeking out businesses that he thinks are undervalued. But while everyone wants to be like Buffett, few have been able to mimic his success.

Not even experts can beat the market consistently. In fact, here's the surprising truth about financial analysts: While some make money, even more lose money, relative to a strategy of just buying a small chunk of each company. So what keeps these analysts going? The short answer is that the money they're losing belongs to investors like you, and people like you keep hoping that they've found the right financial expert that will allow them to beat the market. But hope isn't reality, and you probably haven't found one of the handful of financial whizzes who can beat the market.

To see this, let's consider how the typical person invests in the stock market. Most people invest through **mutual funds,** which buy a portfolio of stocks (and sometimes bonds) on their behalf. Your employer's retirement plan will probably allow you to choose from a list of different mutual funds to invest in. There are two types of mutual funds:

mutual fund A fund that buys a portfolio of stocks (and sometimes bonds) on your behalf.

actively managed When a fund is managed by stock pickers.

index fund A mutual fund that consists of a broad market index.

- **Actively managed** mutual funds pay handsome salaries to expert stock pickers who invest your money in the stocks that they think are likely to do particularly well.
- **Index funds** don't pay for any fancy stock pickers; instead, they just program a computer to automatically buy every stock that is in the ASX 200 or some other broad market index.

Figure 8 | It's Hard to Beat the Stock Market

Average annual investment returns from 2012–2022

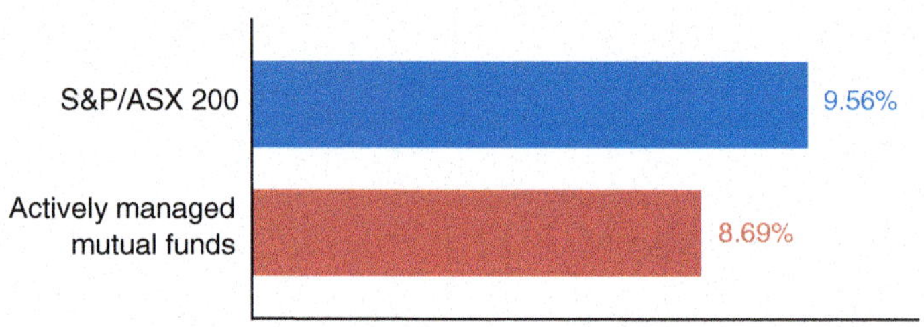

Data from: S&P Dow Jones Indices.

A careful analysis of major mutual funds between 2012 and 2022 found that simply investing in the S&P/ASX 200—which is what index funds do and involves no expertise at all—earned an annual average return of 9.56%. By contrast, Figure 8 shows that the average of all comparable actively managed mutual funds run by expert stock pickers earned an annual return of 8.69%. That difference might sound small, but it adds up. A $100,000 investment in the S&P/ASX 200 would have grown to $249,000 over this period, while the actively managed funds would have yielded $230,000. You would have netted an extra $19,000 by *not* hiring an expert stock picker.

What explains this? It's not that professional stock pickers are particularly bad at picking stocks. Rather, they're not particularly good. The stocks they pick rise roughly in line with the ASX 200, but they charge you a lot of money for their "expertise." These high fees make investing with them a bad bet.

Past performance is no guarantee of future performance. Even so, if you think there are stock pickers who can beat the market, good luck finding them. In my experience, nearly every stock picker will tell you that they're going to do well in the next few years. Many of them will tout their track records, telling you that they've beaten the market in the past. But these same claims always have an asterisk* next to them directing you to the fine print:

*past performance is no guarantee of future performance.

Did you see the fine print? It actually understates the case. It should say this instead:

Past performance is almost completely unrelated to future performance.

Let's focus on the best-performing actively managed mutual funds over the period 2006–2011. Of the top quarter of these funds, only 20% were in the top quarter again for the 2011–2016 period, which was roughly the same chance that the worst-performing actively managed mutual funds had of being in the top quarter. In other words, past performance didn't predict future performance.

Whatever made a stock picker do well in the past didn't much help them in the future. It's the sort of pattern that suggests that none of them are better than the market all the time, but some of them get lucky some of the time.

Remember Warren Buffett? A few years ago he offered to bet that the S&P 500 stock index would outperform the most actively managed funds—known as hedge funds—over 10 years. Buffet said that he waited expectantly for "a parade of fund managers . . . to come forth and defend their occupation." After all he said, if they were so confident in their ability why wouldn't they put a little of their own money on the line? Well, there was a good reason that only one person took the bet: That person lost. The loser conceded, stating, "Passive investing is all the rage today." Why? Because the difficulty of beating the market means that your portfolio will grow faster if you put your money in well-diversified index funds.

EVERYDAY Economics **How to invest like an economist**

What do economists do with their own money? Given the evidence so far, you won't be surprised to hear that most of them invest in well-diversified index funds. Figure 9 shows the results of a survey that asked economists how they handle their money. Buying all 200 stocks in the ASX 200 ensures that you have a well-diversified portfolio. An index fund doesn't pay for any fancy stock pickers, which helps them keep their fees really low. The best of these funds are so lean that they have very few expenses—about 0.2% of the money they're handling for you, compared to a number closer to 1% or sometimes as much as 2% for an actively managed mutual fund. Economists ignore past stock-picking performance because it doesn't predict future performance. The only indicator they focus on is the fees that are charged, which are sometimes called expense ratios. They focus on fees because they're the best predictor of a fund's returns. After all, even if it's hard to predict good stocks, it's easy to predict that paying high fees will make you poorer. While saving a fraction of a percentage point on fees each year doesn't sound like a big deal, it is. If you put $100,000 in an index fund for 30 years and let it compound, you'll end up saving around $120,000 in fees if you choose the lowest-cost option. ■

Figure 9 | How Economists Handle Their Money

"In general, absent any inside information, an equity investor can expect to do better by choosing a well-diversified, low-cost index fund than by picking a few stocks."

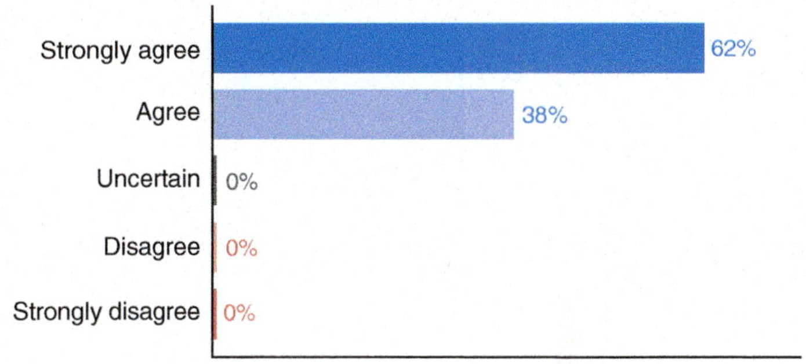

2019 Data from: University of Chicago's Booth School of Business.

The efficient markets hypothesis teaches you the value of modesty. There's so much money to be made by whoever can figure out how to predict which stocks will rise, and when, that it remains a hot area of research. For now, it's probably best to say the debate is between those who think that the efficient markets hypothesis is right most of the time, versus those who think it's right nearly all of the time. If you can be first to bring new information to the market, you can probably profit from it, but realise that new information gets incorporated so quickly that you might only have milliseconds to react.

More importantly, even if you don't believe the efficient markets hypothesis is exactly right, it sounds an important warning that you should always bear in mind: Be modest about your ability to pick stocks, or indeed any financial asset. Before you trade, you should ask yourself: Is it likely that the market has overlooked the information you're relying on? Is it likely that your analysis is smarter than the collective wisdom of thousands of traders who spend their lives studying that stock? Always remember that if a stock's price doesn't align with your valuation, there's a good chance that it's your valuation that's wrong, rather than the stock price.

Figure 10 | **Stock Prices Predict GDP**

Percent change in GDP (left scale) and stock prices ASX 200 shown on the right scale) over the past year

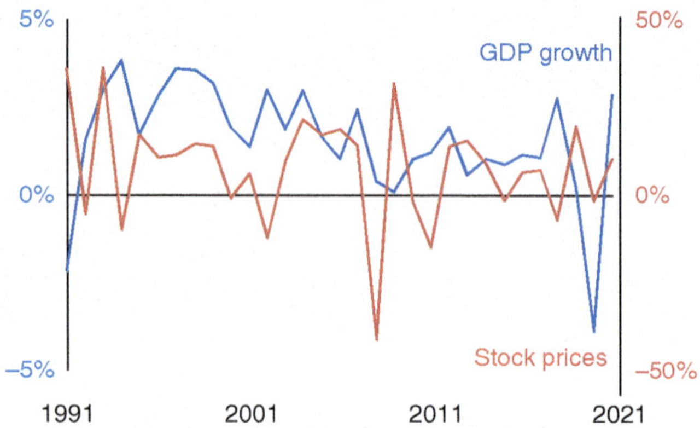

Data from: Australian Bureau of Statistics, RBA, CEIC.

The stock market can help predict economic changes. Experts find it hard to beat the stock market because market prices already embed so much expertise and information. But this also means that stock prices reflect what people think will happen to individual companies and the economy overall. If stocks in many companies are rising, that's a signal that traders are expecting good times ahead, and if stocks are falling, that's a signal that perhaps there's bad news ahead. As Figure 10 shows, the ASX 200—which is a broad indicator of stock prices—tends to rise in anticipation of a strong economy, and fall in anticipation of an economic downturn.

As a result, stock prices are a closely watched macroeconomic indicator. That said, stock prices are extremely volatile, and not every blip translates into changing economic conditions. In fact, sometimes stock prices do some pretty puzzling things, which brings us to our next topic: stock market bubbles.

Financial Bubbles

In the wake of the 2008 financial crisis, many people felt disenfranchised by the existing financial system, as well as its rules and its regulators. The poor management of the financial system in the lead-up to the crisis created a general distaste for centralised authority over finance. A new solution was born in 2008, when the anonymous Satoshi Nakomoto released a plan (white paper) for a digital currency, one that didn't require trust in any centralised party for ownership or transaction-its name: Bitcoin.

For many years, Bitcoin holders were only those interested in cryptocurrencies, but as knowledge of the currency spread, many people began buying Bitcoin. Some individuals bought Bitcoin because they believed in the underlying ethos of decentralisation, but as Bitcoin's price continued to rise and rise, investors became excited for a piece of the action, paying increasingly higher and higher prices for the digital currency. By December 2017, Bitcoin hit a then all time high price of almost $26,000 ($20,000 USD), as shown in Figure 11. A digital currency, whose value had been only a few hundred dollars a coin for years, was now totally disconnected from its value.

Figure 11 | **The Bitcoin Bubble**

Bitcoin Price in $US

Data from: NASDAQ QMX Group.

At least that's what legendary investor Warren Buffet thought, saying "Stay away from it. It's a mirage basically." He hasn't changed his mind. In May 2022, Buffet said he "wouldn't buy all the Bitcoin in the world for $25."

When the price of an asset—like a stock or, in this case, a cryptocurrency—rises above what appears to be its fundamental value, we call it a **speculative bubble** because prices are highly inflated. And just like a bubble, it can keep inflating for a while, until POP!, it bursts. In December 2017, the Bitcoin bubble burst, and the value of Bitcoin, and other cryptocurrencies, plummeted. Bitcoin's price fell from $26,000 to $16,800 by the end of December, and by the same time a year later, it cost only $5000 per Bitcoin. If you had invested $1,000 in Bitcoin in December 2017, it was worth only $190 a year later.

speculative bubble When the price of an asset rises above what appears to be its fundamental value.

What could possibly lead to a bubble like this? To answer that, we'll have to talk about cute puppies.

The stock market is like a puppy beauty contest. One view of the stock market is that it's like a puppy beauty contest. Here's how: In a puppy beauty contest, there are photos of a bunch of puppies, and if you correctly guess which is most popular—that is, the one that most people guess to be cutest—then you're eligible for a prize.

It's your choice now:

Which puppy would you pick?

(Hint: If you're thinking, "Which puppy is cutest?" think again.)

Michael Pettigrew/Shutterstock

The best strategy isn't to pick the cutest puppy. It's to pick the puppy that you think others are most likely to think is cutest. Or go a step further: You want to pick the puppy that you think others are most likely to think that others will pick. And so it goes on. Keep thinking this way, and soon enough, you won't be thinking about which puppy is cute at all, but rather you'll focus on other people's expectations about other people's expectations.

How does this relate to stocks or other assets like cryptocurrency? Stock buying behaviour can resemble a puppy beauty contest because what a stock is worth is what someone else will pay for it. So, instead of picking the stock that is the soundest investment, you might pick the stock that you think others will soon bid up. This idea, that people buy an investment because they expect other people to buy it from them at a higher price, is called the **"greater fool" theory** because it means that you'll buy a stock at five times what it is really worth, as long as you think there's some greater fool out there who will be willing to pay 10 times what it is worth next week. If everyone believes that everyone else believes that cryptocurrencies will keep rising, then everyone will keep buying cryptocurrencies in the hope of selling them later at an even higher price. And that's how a bubble keeps getting inflated.

"greater fool" theory The idea that people buy an investment because they expect other people to buy it from them at a higher price.

This is not an investment strategy that I recommend. While it'll work for a while—as long as the bubble keeps inflating—all bubbles eventually burst, and one day you'll wake up to discover that you can't find a "greater fool" willing to overpay for your overpriced stock. This happened to Bitcoin in 2017 and then again in 2022, and when the market crashed, it wiped out many people's savings.

Even if it's a bubble, it might not be about to burst. Our analysis of stock market bubbles is not quite complete. There's one remaining mystery: Why aren't speculative bubbles stopped by other investors taking the opposite position? There are three key reasons why bubbles persist.

Reason one: *It can be hard to spot a speculative bubble.* Cryptocurrency was new and exciting, and no one really knew how much it would transform the global economy. You might suspect that Bitcoin is overvalued, but in the excitement over crypto, you convince yourself that maybe it'll be truly transformative.

Reason two: *Even if you spot a speculative bubble, it can be hard to bet against it.* Okay, you think Bitcoin is overpriced. Now what? You won't buy it, but beyond that, if there's no easy way to bet that a stock will go down, the price won't reflect your opinion.

Reason three: *You don't know when the bubble will burst.* Financial history is littered with examples of people who correctly predicted that a bubble would burst, but lost a lot of money or even their reputation as investors along the way. The problem is that even if you're right that the bubble will eventually burst and bet against it (what is known as "short selling"), you can lose money along the way. If prices keep rising you have to make "margin calls" where you are required to put more and more money into the trade. Eventually you might run out of money, or lose your nerve. Or, if you run an investment fund, your investors might pull their money out. This happened to many short-sellers during the internet bubble of the late 1990s.

EVERYDAY Economics — What do houses, tulips, and alpacas have in common with the stock market?

Speculative bubbles don't just drive occasional bouts of cryptocurrency or stock market exuberance—they're also important in many other markets, too.

Perhaps the most consequential bubble this century occurred in the early 2000s in the United States. Home loans were easy to get, and house prices always seemed to rise.

Catherine Hood/EyeEm/Getty Images

What is this alpaca worth?

Together, these trends made home ownership seem both accessible and profitable. Some people bought houses to live in, while others bought them with an eye to making a few quick improvements, and then selling (or "flipping") them at a higher price. For a while, it worked, and house prices more than doubled in some U.S. cities. Then the housing market bubble burst, and house prices fell by half or more. The decline in house prices left many people with debts they could not repay. This was the first domino that caused the financial sector to freeze up in 2008, causing a global recession.

Perhaps the strangest ever bubble occurred in 17th-century Holland, when investors became enamoured with tulips. They saw tulips as valuable because a single tulip could be used to breed more tulips, which could be sold to investors who saw tulips as valuable. At the peak of the bubble, the price of a single tulip bulb rose to the value of a luxury house. You can guess what happened next: The bubble burst, and tulip prices fell by over 95%.

A similar story happened with alpacas, the cute South American animals with llama-like long necks, and long eyelashes. In the 1990s and 2000s, American farmers became gripped by an alpaca craze, paying top dollar for alpacas, in the hope of breeding more alpacas that other farmers might pay top dollar for. For a while, it worked, and prices spiralled as high as half a million dollars for a top breeder. But then the bubble burst, and prices plummeted, forcing many investors into bankruptcy. Some were forced to sell their herd for $100 per head or less. ■

27.5 Personal Finance

Learning Objective *Make better decisions in financial markets.*

Our final task to conclude our tour of the financial sector is to bring together the major lessons for how you can do a better job managing your personal finances. There are six important lessons I want you to apply to your financial life.

Lesson one: Harness the power of compound interest. In Chapter 26 on investment, you learned about the magic of compound interest. The power of compound interest depends a lot on the interest rate you get. Between 1992 and 2022, the average real annual return from investing in short-term Australian government bonds was only 1.8%. Over the last century, 10-year Australian government bonds have returned 2.5% per annum, while stocks have returned 7.5%. While past performance is no guarantee of the future, let's take a look at how different investments would have fared over that 100-year period. Recall that the compounding formula is

$$\text{Future value in } t \text{ years} = \text{Present value} \times (1+r)^t$$

Calculate the real future value of $1,000 invested in each of these alternatives:

	Average annual real return	Real future value of $1,000 investment in 100 years
Short-term government debt	1.8%	$\$1{,}000 \times (1+0.018)^{100} = \$5{,}954$
10-year government bonds	2.5%	$\$1{,}000 \times (1+0.025)^{100} = \$11{,}814$
Stocks	7.5%	$\$1{,}000 \times (1+0.075)^{100} = \$1.38$ million

If you're surprised by how much a small investment can grow over time, you're not alone. There's a (most likely apocryphal) story that Albert Einstein once declared "the power of compound interest is the most powerful force in the universe."

While compounding happens automatically with bank deposits—the interest you earn is deposited into your savings account where it too earns interest—the same principle applies to long-term investments in bonds or stocks. If you reinvest what you earn, your little nest egg will grow into a secure retirement fund. That's why you should start saving early and keep investing your gains. You might also want to consider saving some of your money in the stock market because over the past century, stocks have had a much larger average annual return.

> Financial lessons:
> 1. Harness the power of compound interest.
> 2. Don't pick individual stocks.
> 3. Diversify your portfolio to reduce risk.
> 4. Past performance is no guarantee of future performance.
> 5. Minimise paying fees.
> 6. Follow all five rules with low-cost index funds.

Lesson two: Don't pick individual stocks. If you do want to put your money in stocks, it's best not to try to pick winners and losers in the stock market. Even if the efficient markets hypothesis is not perfectly right—meaning that it may not be completely impossible to beat the market, it's still really, really, hard. Here's a sad truth. Research shows that many investors are overconfident, believing that they have the ability to beat the collective wisdom of the market, even though most of them actually can't. Give up on trying to pick individual stocks that will outperform the market. Remember, Orlando the cat might do a better job.

Lesson three: Diversify your portfolio to reduce risk. If you invest in just a few big things, you run the risk of losing your life savings. It's far better to invest small amounts of money in lots of different investments. This diversification will reduce how much your wealth will move up and down each year, making it less risky. The easiest way to diversify your stock holdings is to buy index funds, which do all the work for you of buying a basket of many different stocks.

Lesson four: Past performance is no guarantee of future performance. Instead of picking stocks, some people pick stock pickers, investing in actively managed mutual funds. Some of these stock pickers have done well in the past. Not only is past performance no guarantee of future performance; they're almost unrelated. So there's no reason to believe professional stock pickers who promise you that they'll beat the market.

Lesson five: Minimise paying fees. While it's hard to find a way to pick better stocks than others, the easy way to ensure you still get a better return is to minimise the fees you pay. The most predictable parts of investment returns are fees. Don't buy and sell stock a lot—that'll cost you brokerage fees, and the stock you're buying probably won't be any better than the stock you're selling. Avoid actively managed mutual funds that charge hefty fees for their useless "expertise." And if you're looking at passively managed indexed funds, shop around to find the fund that charges the lowest fees.

Lesson six: Follow all five rules with low-cost index funds. The easiest way to follow all of these lessons is to invest in low-cost index funds. It's what most economists do with their money!

Tying It Together

The financial system performs several important functions in modern economies, without which existing businesses would find it difficult to expand and new businesses would find it hard to get started. That means that economies would struggle to grow, which means lower living standards for people. In short, we all benefit when the financial system works.

The financial sector facilitates the growth of businesses by moving resources to where they can best be used. You can think of it as a *bridge*, connecting savers who have spare resources, with borrowers who need more resources than they currently have. When savers put their money in the bank, when they buy bonds, or when they buy stock, the financial sector trucks that money across the bridge so that investors can fund their investments. This funding enables people to invest—in a university education, a family home, or launching or expanding their business—when they wouldn't otherwise be able to pay for those investments up front.

What the financial sector does:

1. It reallocates resources from savers to borrowers.
2. It shifts resources through time.
3. It reallocates, spreads, and reduces risk.
4. It creates liquidity.
5. One big risk: It creates interdependence.

Another way to think about this is that the financial sector is a *time machine* that can move your money through time. This is particularly important for investments that involve a big up-front cost today that'll generate ample returns in the future. The financial sector makes it possible to spend money today that you'll only earn in the future. It effectively gives you the means to zap money from the future to the present—by borrowing from a bank, issuing stock, or issuing bonds. Alternatively, if you want to zap money from the present into the future, you just need to deposit that money in the bank, or alternatively put it in stocks or bonds. Then, in the future, when you need that money, you can make a bank withdrawal or sell those stocks or bonds. Voila! Your money just travelled through time to meet Future You. And hopefully it grew a bit along the way.

The financial sector does more than move money around, it also plays a protective role, *reallocating, spreading, and diversifying risks*. Putting your money in one big investment or loan is risky because if that investment fails, you'll lose your life savings. The financial sector helps people avoid this by slicing risk into smaller pieces that can then be bought and sold. It means that you can buy a small amount of many different stocks and a small amount of bonds issued by many different companies, and your bank will lend your savings to many different borrowers. The result is that you'll hold a diversified portfolio, which is a lot less risky than one big bet. As people buy and sell these risks, they will be reallocated to those best positioned to bear them. The result of all this diversification and reallocation is that each of us faces less risk, which means you can sleep easier, knowing your savings will still be there tomorrow.

The financial sector also creates *liquidity*, which means that you can quickly and easily convert your investments into cash, with little or no loss in value. As a partial owner of Nike, you'll always have easy access to your money because you can easily sell your stock on the stock market. Likewise, buying a 10-year bond doesn't commit your money for 10 years because you can sell that bond on the bond market. And it's easy to turn your bank balance into cash, simply by going to the ATM to make a withdrawal. All of this liquidity is a good thing: It means that you can make long-term investments, but if something comes up and you end up needing your money, you'll still be able to access it.

Yet the usefulness of financial markets comes with a warning. The financial sector illustrates the *interdependence principle*, and all this interdependence can make the economy more *vulnerable to financial shocks*. The value of a stock or a bond depends on what other people are willing to pay for it, which depends on what they think others are willing to pay for it. This raises the possibility of speculative bubbles, which can burst savagely, destabilising the economy. When your money is used to fund other financial investments that can be used to fund other financial investments, a chain of interdependence is created, which can cause one bad investment to have ripple effects. If no one knows which other financial institutions are exposed to those losses, then these ripple effects can create a wave of fear as no one knows whose money is safe.

The point is that even though the financial sector does a lot to make the economy work better—reallocating resources from savers to investors, shifting money through time, spreading and reducing risk, and creating liquidity—it also makes the economy more vulnerable to manias, panics, and crashes.

Chapter at a Glance

Banks	The Bond Market	The Stock Market
	What they are:	
A **bank** borrows money from savers and lends it out in an effort to earn itself a profit.	A **bond** is an IOU. Specifically, a promise to pay back a loan with interest.	A **stock** represents partial ownership in a firm that may pay uncertain future dividends.
Shadow banks are financial firms that are similar to banks, but are not regulated like banks.	The **bond market** is where companies and governments can borrow large sums of money.	The **stock market** is the market where people buy and sell existing stocks.
	What they do:	
	1. Reallocate resources from savers to borrowers	
A saver deposits money in the bank which the bank lends to others, helping fund their investments.	A saver buys bonds, funding company or government investments.	A saver buys shares in a company, funding company investment.
	2. Shift resources through time	
Money deposited today can be withdrawn in the future. Money borrowed today is repaid in the future.	Bonds bought today can be sold in the future. Bonds sold by companies or governments today must be repaid in the future.	Stocks bought today can be sold in the future. A company selling shares today gives up a share of its profits in the future.
	3. Reallocate, spread, and reduce risk	
Savings are lent out to multiple borrowers.	Bonds can be bought in multiple companies or governments.	Stock can be bought in multiple companies.
	4. Create liquidity	
Savers can always withdraw their savings. Borrowers get long-term loans.	Bondholders can sell their bonds. The issuer repays whoever owns the bond on maturity.	Shareholders can sell their stock. The investment remains with the company forever.
	5. One big risk: They create interdependencies	
Bank runs	Default risk, term risk, and liquidity risk	Speculative bubbles
	Other functions	
Solve information problems Provide payment services	Fund government debt	Reallocate control

What is:

Liquidity:	The ability to quickly and easily convert your investments into cash, with little or no loss in value.
Speculative bubble:	When the price of an asset rises above what appears to be its fundamental value.
Bank run:	When many bank customers try to withdraw their savings at the same time.
Efficient market hypothesis:	The theory that at any point in time, stock prices reflect all publicly available information.

Key Concepts

Discussion and Review Questions

Learning Objective 27.1 *Assess the role that banks play in funnelling money from savers to investors.*

1. You deposit money into a bank account. Explain what happens to that money and how the bank makes a profit.
2. Do you have an everyday or savings account? Why or why not? Would you still have an account if you earned no interest on your deposits? What if you had to pay fees?
3. How does maturity transformation impact long-term investment spending? What are some risks a bank can face trying to balance the tension that maturity transformation creates?
4. Bank runs are often called manias, or panics, but are individual people acting irrationally when they participate in a bank run? Explain your reasoning.

Learning Objective 27.2 *Understand how companies and governments raise money by issuing bonds.*

5. Explain the differences between a company issuing a bond versus taking a loan from a bank. How are they similar and how are they different?

Learning Objective 27.3 *Learn how companies raise money by issuing stock.*

6. You get a large bonus at the end of the year that you don't plan on spending anytime soon. Should you put your money in stocks, in bonds, or in the bank as savings? What factors inform your decision? Explain.
7. You are discussing buying stocks with a friend and mention that you want to buy a few shares of the a2 Milk Company stock. Your friend says that's a terrible idea because the a2 Milk Company has never paid dividends to its shareholders so you would never receive any of their profits or make any money off the stock. Is your friend right or wrong? Explain your answer.

Learning Objective 27.4 *Discover what drives financial prices.*

8. Search online to find a company that issues stock on the Australian Stock Exchange. Describe how you can assess the company's fundamental value and how you could use that information to decide whether to purchase the stock or not.
9. Do changes in stock prices precede economic downturns and expansions, or do they follow changes in economic activity? Are stock market prices a cause or an effect of changes in the macroeconomy?
10. The following graph shows the price of Bitcoin—an online cryptocurrency—over time.

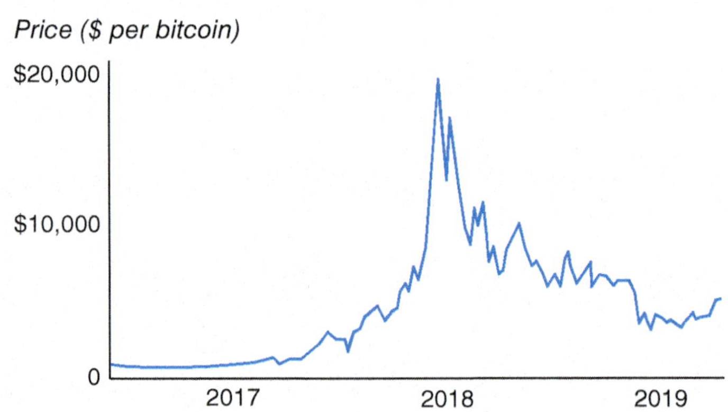

Do you think Bitcoin experienced a speculative bubble? Explain why someone acting rationally would purchase bitcoin even at a price so much higher than its historical level.

Learning Objective 27.5 *Make better decisions in financial markets.*

11. You are just beginning to invest in the stock market. A friend that you trust advises you to invest all your money in the stock of one certain company. "It's done really well in the past," she states. "The stock price is only

going to go up. If you go all in now, you'll make a tonne of money later." Which lessons did you learn from the chapter that will help you analyse your friend's advice?

12. Why do people value liquidity? What are the different ways that banks, the bond market, and the stock market create liquidity?

Study Problems

Learning Objective 27.1 *Assess the role that banks play in funnelling money from savers to investors.*

1. For each situation, explain why seeking out an individual saver to borrow money from is not ideal. Then, identify which function of banks eliminates the problem.
   Hint: Banks serve five functions. Read all the scenarios, then determine which function best addresses each situation. A function will only be used once.
   a. As a first-year student, you need to borrow $20,000 for living expenses. You intend to repay this loan over time after you graduate.
   b. You are starting a business in a new industry and need $300 million for your initial investment.
   c. You need to take out a $15,000 loan to purchase a new car. No one who knows you personally has the money to lend.
   d. You want to be able to pay your bills online instead of paying for everything using cash.
2. When the Federal government introduced deposit insurance during the Global Financial Crisis, what effect did this have on the occurrence of bank runs? Did the introduction of deposit insurance have the same effect on other financial markets, such as the stock or bond market? Explain.

Learning Objective 27.2 *Understand how companies and governments raise money by issuing bonds.*

3. Your parents are thinking about purchasing bonds with a 25-year term, but they are a little worried that they might need the money before the 25-year term is up. How would they go about accessing the money if they needed it before the end of the term?
4. Around $500 billion in U.S. Treasuries are traded each day and many countries hold U.S. Treasuries, as they are considered a very safe investment. For example, as of October 2018, Japan held $1,018.5 billion in U.S. Treasuries, and Ireland held $287.3 billion. Use the three types of bond risks to explain why U.S. government bonds are considered such a safe investment. What is the trade-off that accompanies this low risk?

Learning Objective 27.3 *Learn how companies raise money by issuing stock.*

5. For each part, determine whether you should invest in stocks or bonds. Explain your reasoning.
   a. You want a high return and are not concerned about risk.
   b. You would like to participate in how the companies you invest in are managed.
   c. You are worried about losing money if a company declares bankruptcy.
   d. You want a guaranteed, regular payment from your investment.
6. My Foodie Box Ltd is a newly-publicly-traded company. My Foodie Box offers a subscription that provides users with a personalised box of fresh produce and meal instructions, with which the subscriber can cook their meals. Use the stock market snapshot from Google Finance to interpret the questions about My Foodie Box.

a. How much was a share of My Foodie Box worth at the time of the snapshot?

b. What is the market capitalisation? What does that mean?

c. Assess the level of risk associated with investing in My Foodie Box Ltd.

Learning Objective 27.4 *Discover what drives financial prices.*

7. Use the following data for Temple & Webster to estimate the values for a comparable homewares and furniture store, Adairs.

Temple & Webster:

Stock price per share (March 2022)	$7.15
Earnings per share (in the previous 12 months)	$0.07
Book value per share (quarter ending March 2022)	$0.76

a. Adairs' book value per share was $1.04. If Adairs produces the same price-to-book ratio as Temple & Webster, what is the value of Adairs' stock?

b. Adairs' earnings per share was $0.21. If Adairs has the same price-to-earnings ratio as Temple & Webster, what is the value of Adairs' stock?

c. The actual price of Adairs' stock as of March 2022 was $2.93. What does this tell us about our valuation technique? What issues (if any) may be leading to any differences?

8. Your friend just received a promotion and wants to invest the extra annual income from their raise. They tell you that they're thinking of hiring a fund manager, saying: "The fee is only 1.1%, and this stock picker has a great track record!" What advice would you give your friend?

9. On March 13, 2020, the stock market fell more than 7%. How can we reconcile these kinds of huge losses in the stock market with the efficient market hypothesis?

Learning Objective 27.5 *Make better decisions in financial markets.*

10. The 1980s was a period of rapid economic growth that yielded an average annual return of 13.1%!

a. If you invested $1,000 at the beginning of the decade, and you reinvested the returns you earned every year, calculate the value of your investment at the end of the decade.

b. Did this high rate of return continue into the 1990s and beyond? Look online at stock charts for the S&P/ASX 200 to figure out what happened. Use what you learned in the chapter to explain why.

CHAPTER 28

International Finance and the Exchange Rate

In 1947, the Warmoll family began a small farm near Gunnedah, New South Wales, growing soybeans, cotton, corn, and raising livestock. Over time, the farm grew, and they began selling their yields at local markets. By the 1970s they were able to use their profits to buy a cattle ranch in Willow Tree (NSW) called Big Jack's Creek, and they began to specialise in cattle production.

Searsie/iStock/Getty Images

Family farm, global market.

The Warmolls' success didn't really take off until 1991. As live cattle imports became more accessible, the Warmoll family was able to cross their Black Angus herd with Tajima Wagyu Sires from the Hyogo region of Japan, becoming one of the first Australian companies to breed, grow, feed, process, and market Wagyu beef. This innovation laid the foundation for exporting their beef around the world. Today, the Warmolls' company, Jack's Creek exports beef to over 20 countries.

All of this has required the Warmolls to become conversant in exchange rates and international finance. We'll follow the Warmolls' decisions in this chapter, analysing what determines how competitive they'll be in the global market, and whether it makes sense to sell their produce abroad. International transactions often involve foreign currencies, and so we'll dive into how exchange rates are determined, how they respond to changing economic conditions, and how they'll affect the Warmolls' business. Along the way we'll see how developments in the global economy affect the prices you'll pay as you seek goods, services, customers, investments, and investors from around the world. As you read this chapter, keep your eye on the broader theme, which is that increasingly all business is international business, and so the fates of businesses, communities, and countries around the world are becoming increasingly interdependent.

Chapter Objective

Understand the linkages between the exchange rate, imports, exports, and international financial flows.

28.1 International Trade and Global Financial Flows
See the connections between the domestic economy and the global economy.

28.2 Exchange Rates
Analyse prices that are quoted in different currencies.

28.3 Supply and Demand of Currencies
Analyse the market for currencies and forecast the nominal exchange rate.

28.4 The Real Exchange Rate and Net Exports
Assess how exchange rates and relative prices affect exports and imports.

28.5 The Balance of Payments
Track how money flows around the world using the current account and the financial account.

28.1 International Trade and Global Financial Flows

Learning Objective *See the connections between the domestic economy and the global economy.*

Carrying more—and carrying it further.

The story of the Warmolls is the story of millions of businesses that are becoming more tightly integrated into the global economy. We explored the logic of international trade in Chapter 21, where we noted that trade is driven by the idea of comparative advantage—by focusing on those tasks that we can do at the lowest opportunity cost, we can all get more done. This logic explains why a family in Gunnedah might focus on growing livestock, and their customers might include a couple in Tochigi, Japan who spend their workdays applying advanced Japanese management techniques to make air conditioner production lines run more efficiently. Their choices explain why Australia exports beef and imports air conditioners.

Our goal in this chapter is to explore the macroeconomic implications of all this. It puts the *interdependence principle* front and centre as we'll see how Australia has become more tightly linked with the global economy. We'll begin by exploring how international trade links the Australian economy to the rest of the world, and then turn to analysing the linkages that occur through global financial flows.

International Trade

exports Goods or services produced domestically and purchased by foreign buyers.

imports Goods or services produced in a foreign country and purchased by domestic buyers.

Let's start with international trade, which occurs when people buy or sell goods and services across national borders. **Exports** are goods and services produced domestically and purchased by foreign buyers. **Imports** are goods and services produced in a foreign country and purchased by domestic buyers.

Global trade is growing. *Globalisation* describes the increasing global integration of economies, cultures, political institutions, and ideas, and it may be the most important economic trend of your lifetime. But it's not an entirely modern idea: International trade has been an important driver of economic growth for centuries. In fact, the first modern corporation—the "East India Company"—was formed in 1600 to engage in trade between Britain and the Indian Ocean region. International trade grew strongly in the wake of the Industrial Revolution.

Sharp reductions in the cost of international transport and communication have led to explosive growth in trade over recent decades. The largest cargo ships carry 100 times more cargo than half a century ago. Air transport has become cheaper, enabling more trade in perishable items. Modern computer networks allow vast amounts of data to be zapped around the world nearly instantly, which has boosted trade in services. And governments in nearly every country have tried to help their citizens take advantage of these new opportunities by negotiating trade deals that give them better access to foreign markets.

As Figure 1 shows, these changes led global exports to rise from around 13% of global output in 1970, to 26% in 2020. It's a good bet that globalisation will continue its relentless march throughout your life, and so the global economy will play an even larger role throughout your career.

Figure 1 Globalisation Is Leading to Rising World Trade

Total world exports (which equals total world imports) as a share of world GDP

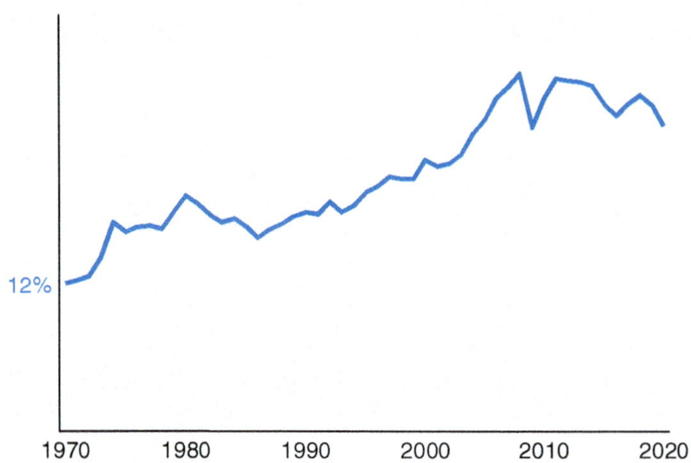

Data from: World Bank.

Imports and exports have grown rapidly in Australia. Australia has followed the world trend of rising trade. Both imports and exports are almost 20 times as large a share of the economy as they were a half century ago. Major Australian exports include natural resources, such as iron ore and coal, and agricultural products such as beef and wine. But we don't just export goods. Around one fifth of our exports are services including business and financial services, personal travel services, the licensing fees that companies pay to use Australian technology, and the money that tourists and foreign students spend when visiting Australia.

You probably recognise many imported goods when you're shopping for clothes, household appliances, or cars. But it's important to think beyond consumer goods, as some of our largest imports are intermediate goods or raw materials that are used as inputs by Australian businesses. Indeed, our imports and exports are closely linked due to global supply chains that connect businesses around the world. For instance, we import crude oil, and then Australian businesses refine it and ship some of it out as exports of refined petroleum.

Figure 2 | Imports to and Exports from Australia

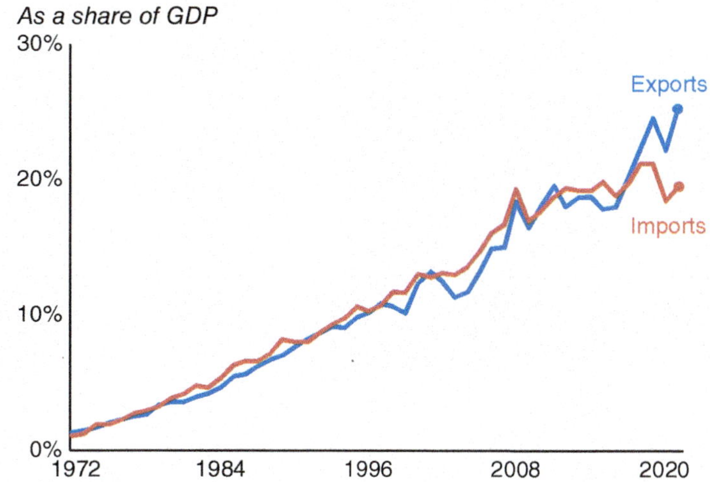

Data from: Australian Bureau of Statistics.

Figure 2 shows that imports slightly exceeded exports from the mid-1970s until about the 2010s, which means that **net exports**—the difference between spending on exports and spending on imports—were negative during this time, and are now positive. The *trade balance* is another name for net exports, and so negative net exports are sometimes called a *trade deficit*.

net exports Spending on exports minus spending on imports; also referred to as the trade balance.

Australia trades with nearly every country. Australia trades with nearly every country in the world. Figure 3 shows our top seven trading partners, who together account for 63% of our total trade. Our top three trading partners are China, the United States, and Japan. We trade a lot with Southeast Asia or the ASEAN region, and when you add up all of our imports and exports with ASEAN countries (excluding Singapore), it ends up being as important a trading partner as Japan.

The remaining 37% of our trade is spread across dozens of countries, and just as Australia doesn't rely on these smaller trading partners, these smaller trading partners also don't tend to rely on Australia, which has only a moderately large-sized economy on the global stage.

Figure 3 | Australia's Major Trading Partners

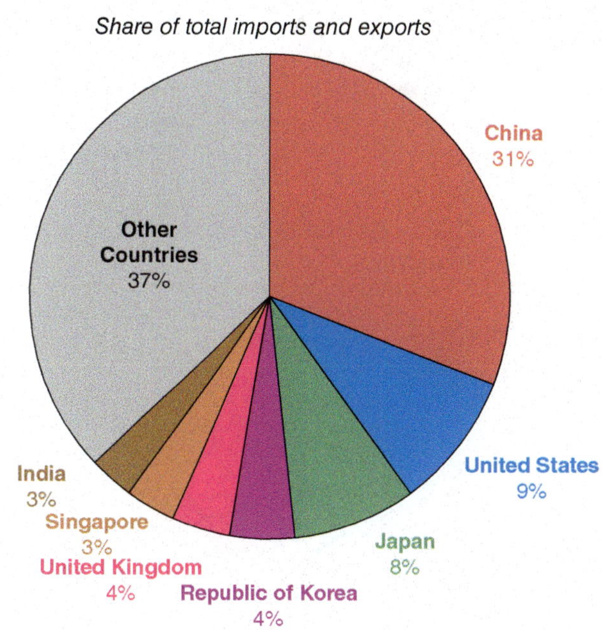

2020 Data from: The Department of Foreign Affairs and Trade.

Many countries import and export less than Australia. This is partly because the Australian economy is relatively small and so a lot of commerce has to occur across national boundaries.

Even though international trade is a big part of the Australian economy, it plays a bigger role in some other countries, such as South Korea and the United Kingdom. In comparison to most of our major trading partners, Australia both exports a larger share of its output and relies on imports for a larger share of its spending, as shown in Figure 4.

Global Financial Flows

It's not just goods and services that are flying around the world. So too are investment dollars, looking for the most profitable investments. These financial flows reflect investors buying and selling assets in a global capital market. **Financial inflows** refer to foreigners investing in Australia. They're called *in*flows, because their funds flow *in* to

financial inflows Investments by foreigners in Australia.

Figure 4 | **Imports and Exports as a Share of GDP**

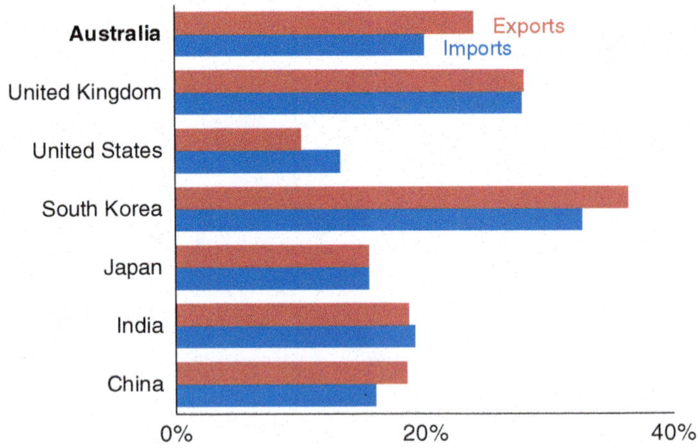

2020 Data from: World Bank.

financial outflows Investments by Australians in foreign countries.

Australia. **Financial outflows** describe Australians investing their money in other countries. They're *out*flows, because these funds flow *out* of Australia.

Financial flows are large and include investment in foreign physical assets, financial assets, and loans. These financial flows take three main forms. When foreigners invest in physical assets—such as when Hitachi purchased a Sydney-based advanced engineering manufacturer—it's called *foreign direct investment*. This manufacturing plant hires Australian workers, but its profits will return to its Japanese owners. When foreigners buy Australian stocks or bonds, it's called *portfolio investment*, and while Australian businesses might use these funds to invest in new equipment, foreign investors will receive future payments in return. And when foreigners lend money to Australians, it falls in a final category of *deposits and loans*. This includes both loans made directly to Australians, as well as foreign deposits in Australian banks, which are then used to fund domestic loans. In each case, these financial inflows help fund investment in new capital assets within Australia. In return, foreigners enjoy the profits, dividends, or interest that their investments generate.

All told, financial inflows added up to an eye-popping $171 billion in 2021, which is roughly $6,000 per Australian. But that's not the whole story, as Australians also invest their funds abroad, creating financial outflows. These financial outflows are also large, and they collectively added up to $246 billion in 2021, or roughly $9,000 per Australian. Just as financial inflows can be categorised into foreign direct investment, portfolio investment, and deposits and loans, so too can financial outflows.

Financial linkages are becoming more important over time. Financial flows between Australia and the rest of the world have risen sharply over the past 50 years, a trend sometimes called *financial globalisation*. As Figure 5 shows, both financial inflows and outflows grew up until the global financial crisis that began in 2008, which reversed their momentum until after the coronavirus pandemic. Financial flows started rising in the 1970s and 1980s as many countries removed *capital controls*, which were rules designed to limit the flow of money across borders. *Deregulation* of the financial sector, both in Australia and elsewhere, also led to new opportunities for money to roam the world looking for better returns. Large *institutional investors* such as pension funds and mutual funds have become more important over time, and they're more likely to look abroad to diversify their portfolios. And *technology* has led to more rapid transmission of information, making investors more comfortable sending their money overseas. *Financial innovation* has created sophisticated new ways for investors to take advantage of new opportunities to diversify and hedge their risks in foreign markets.

Figure 5 | **Financial Outflows from and Financial Inflows to Australia**

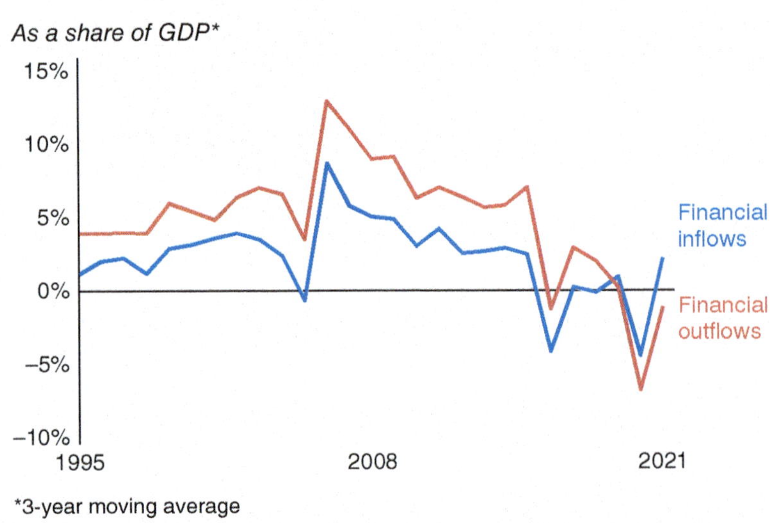

Data from: Australian Bureau of Statistics.

Foreign ownership is becoming more common. As a result of these financial inflows, foreigners have acquired a rising stock of assets in Australia, as shown by the blue line in Figure 6. Some of these are physical assets like Hakubaku's new noodle factory in Victoria, some are ownership shares like BHP stock owned by the U.S. financial firm Goldman Sachs, and some are financial assets like Australian government bonds held by foreign investors. Likewise, the red line shows that the stock of foreign assets owned by Australians has also risen dramatically. This reflects Australian businesses like BHP setting up mines and refineries in other countries, Australians buying stock in companies like Hitachi, or your bank lending money to foreigners. Whether you're aware of it or not, it's likely that some of your money is invested overseas. Indeed, the average Australian held more than $98,000 in foreign assets in 2016.

Figure 6 | **Ownership of Foreign Assets Is Growing**

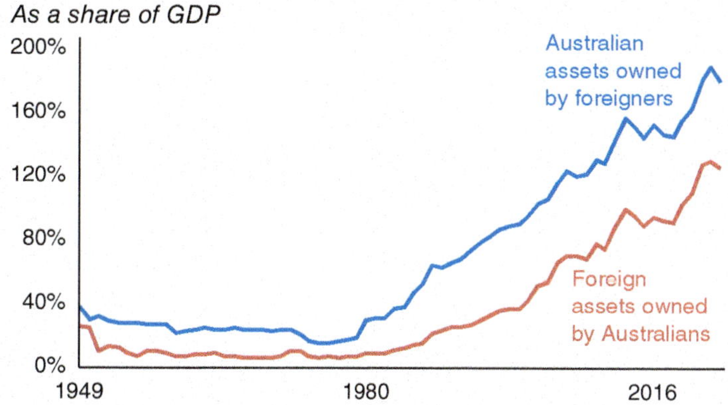

Data from: The Department of Foreign Affairs and Trade.

Financial linkages help diversify risk across the world. This rise in cross-border ownership has led the Australian economy to become more tightly linked to developments in the global economy. From a *macroeconomic perspective*, it means that disruptions in foreign markets—such as a sudden fall in the Japanese stock market—have an immediate effect reducing the wealth of Australians. Similarly, when the Australian economy falters, some (though not much) of the effect is felt overseas.

From a *risk management* perspective, this rising cross-border ownership is a good thing for everyone. Greater diversification reduces the total risk that both Australians and foreigners face. For example, when your retirement account is partly invested in foreign assets, you don't need to worry as much that a domestic downturn will wipe you out.

Recap: International business is increasingly important. The linkages between the Australian economy and the global economy—through both international trade and global financial flows—have become more important over time, and they'll likely become even more important over the course of your career. This makes it a good bet that you'll engage in at least some international transactions, in which you'll need to compare prices measured in dollars with prices measured in other currencies. To do that, you'll need to learn about exchange rates.

28.2 Exchange Rates

Learning Objective *Analyze prices that are quoted in different currencies.*

When the Warmolls sell their Wagyu beef for $100 a kilo to a butcher in Darwin, they get paid $100. (To be extra clear, we'll write this as "A$100," which should be read as "one hundred Australian dollars.") But if a Japanese customer offers to pay them ¥9,000 per kilo, they have to decide whether that's a better deal. (¥ is the symbol for yen, which is the currency used in Japan, just as A$ is the symbol for Australian dollars.) When the Warmolls are comparing prices in different currencies they're going to need to find a way to make an apples-to-apples (or in this case, a beef-to-beef) comparison. So they're going to need to figure out the value of a dollar relative to the yen.

Javier Larrea/AGE Fotostock

How expensive is beef in Japan compared to in Darwin?

Exchanging Australian Dollars for Foreign Currencies

The price of a country's currency (in terms of another country's currency) is called the **nominal exchange rate.** The word "nominal" often gets dropped, so when you hear someone talk about the "exchange rate," they typically mean the nominal exchange rate.

nominal exchange rate The price of a country's currency (in terms of another country's currency).

The nominal exchange rate formula describes the price of a country's currency. We'll focus on the price of an Australian dollar, since that's the currency that matters most to you. If the price of an Australian dollar is 90 yen, then the nominal exchange

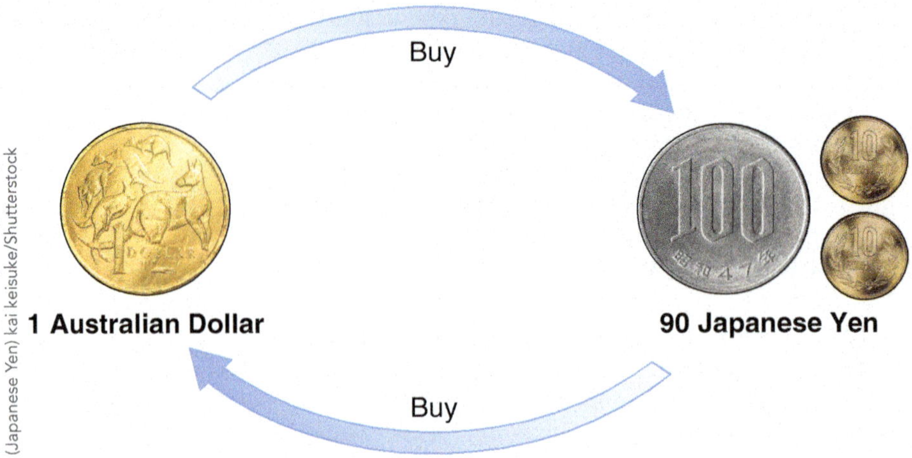

(Australian dollar) Benny Marty/Alamy Stock Photo; (Japanese Yen) kai keisuke/Shutterstock

rate is 90 yen per Australian dollar. This means that you can buy one Australian dollar for ¥90. You can exchange yen for dollars, or dollars for yen, so this also means that with one Australian dollar you can buy ¥90.

Just as you can exchange ¥90 for A$1, you can also exchange ¥180 for A$2, ¥270 for A$3, and so on. The nominal exchange rate defines the ratio at which you exchange units of a foreign currency like yen for Australian dollars. This gives us the **nominal exchange rate formula:**

nominal exchange rate formula
Nominal exchange rate = $\frac{\text{Number of units of a foreign currency}}{\text{Number of dollars}}$

$$\underbrace{\text{Nominal exchange rate}}_{\text{Price of a dollar (in yen)}} = \frac{\text{Number of yen}}{\text{Number of dollars}}$$

Rearrange the nominal exchange rate formula to convert dollars into yen. If the Warmolls are selling a kilo of Wagyu beef for A$100, a Japanese butcher owner needs to figure out how many yen it'll cost them. You can rearrange the nominal exchange rate formula to tell them how many yen they'll pay:

$$\text{Number of yen} = \text{Number of dollars} \times \text{Nominal exchange rate}$$

Let's try this out. If the exchange rate is ¥90 per U.S. dollar, then the price of a A$100 kilo of Wagyu beef in yen is:

$$\text{Number of yen} = \underbrace{\text{A\$100}}_{\text{Number of dollars}} \times \underbrace{\text{90 yen per dollar}}_{\text{Nominal exchange rate}} = ¥9{,}000$$

Rearrange the nominal exchange rate formula to convert yen into dollars. A potential Japanese client might suggest to the Warmolls that she'll buy their Wagyu beef if they beat her current supplier's price, which is ¥6,300 per kilo. To figure out whether they can beat this price, the Warmolls need to convert this sum back into Australian dollars. This time, they rearrange the nominal exchange rate formula to tell them how many dollars this is worth:

$$\text{Number of dollars} = \frac{\text{Number of yen}}{\text{Nominal exchange rate}}$$

Skyimages/iStock/Getty Images

Beef for sale in Japan.

So if the Warmolls have been offered a price of ¥6,300, and the exchange rate is ¥90 per dollar, then the number of dollars per kilo they've been offered is:

$$\text{Number of dollars} = \frac{\overbrace{¥6{,}300}^{\text{Number of yen}}}{\underbrace{\text{90 yen per dollar}}_{\text{Nominal exchange rate}}} = \text{A\$70}$$

Don't accidentally get the exchange rate backwards. So far, we've focused on the *price of a dollar*, which is the number of units of foreign currency you can buy with a dollar. You can also think about the *price of a yen*, which describes how many dollars it costs to buy one yen. Instead of saying that one dollar costs 90 yen, you can say that one yen costs 1/90 of a dollar, or A$0.0111. Both are correct; they're just different perspectives.

When you look up an exchange rate, make sure to pay attention to whether you're learning the price of a dollar (which is measured in yen), or the price of a yen (measured in fractions of a dollar). Getting this wrong could lead to some costly mistakes!

EVERYDAY Economics What's that currency called?

Australia calls its currency the dollar. But it's not the only dollar. A bunch of other former British colonies—including Canada and New Zealand—also call their currencies "dollar", as does the U.S.! These dollars all have different values, and so it's common to put the country's initials before the dollar symbol to keep them straight. (So the Aussie dollar is called the A$, and the U.S. dollar is the US$.) Pay attention when you visit a country that uses "dollars," because some countries—Ecuador and El Salvador, for example—gave up on their own currencies and use actual U.S. dollars.

Peso is also a common name for a currency. Mexico, Argentina, Chile, Colombia, and Cuba all also have pesos (which have different values). Eight countries have rupees including India, Pakistan, and Indonesia. Japan has the yen. China has the renminbi, which is the official name of the currency and means "the people's currency." But renminbi are measured in yuan. The British call their currency the "pound sterling," or "pound" for short. While most countries have their own currency, many European nations gave up their individual currencies in 2002 and adopted a new European currency called the euro whose symbol, €, looks like the first letter of "€urope." As of 2019, 19 countries that are part of the European Union use the euro, although some European Union members don't use it. Several other (mostly small) countries also use the euro. This new super-currency is now the second-most traded currency in the world, behind the U.S. dollar. ■

Country	Currency	Symbol
Australia	Dollar	A$
19 European Union countries (inc.: Germany, France, Italy, Spain)	Euro	€
Brazil	Real	R$
Canada	Dollar	C$
China	Yuan	元
Mexico	Peso	Mex$
India	Rupee	₹
Japan	Yen	¥
Russia	Ruble	₽
South Korea	Won	₩
United Kingdom	Pound sterling	£
United States	Dollar	US$

Recap: The three uses of the nominal exchange rate formula. Let's recap. The nominal exchange rate formula is incredibly versatile, because it serves three purposes:

It defines the nominal exchange rate:

$$\underbrace{\text{Nominal exchange rate}}_{\text{Price of a dollar (in yen)}} = \frac{\text{Number of yen}}{\text{Number of dollars}}$$

You can rearrange it to convert dollars into yen:

$$\text{Number of yen} = \text{Number of dollars} \times \text{Nominal exchange rate}$$

You can rearrange it to convert yen into dollars:

$$\text{Number of dollars} = \frac{\text{Number of yen}}{\text{Nominal exchange rate}}$$

Of course, you can apply this formula to any other country. Just replace the word "yen" with "peso," "yuan," "euro," or whatever currency you're using to measure the price of an Australian dollar. Let's try it out.

Do the Economics

a. The Warmolls are trying to make a deal to sell Wagyu beef in Germany. If they charge A$100 a kilo how many euros will a kilo of beef cost a German butcher if the nominal exchange rate is 0.66 euros per Australian dollar?

Chris Hill/Getty Images

How expensive is Wagyu beef in Germany?

Answers: a. Number of euros = Number of dollars × Nominal exchange rate = A$100 × €0.66 per dollar = €66. b. Number of dollars = Number of euros/Nominal exchange rate = €924/€0.66 per dollar = A$1,400. c. Number of dollars = Number of pounds/Nominal exchange rate = £630/£0.56 per dollar = A$1,125, which is a better deal.

b. The Warmolls have to pay a local logistics company €924 to help them with some customs paperwork. How much is this in Australian dollars?

c. A British logistics company has offered to do this paperwork for £630 instead. If the nominal exchange rate is £0.56 per Australian dollar, which is a better deal? ■

Exchange Rates and the Price of Foreign Goods

Exchange rates are among the most important prices in the economy because when an exchange rate changes it will automatically affect how much it costs to buy millions of imported or exported goods.

Figure 7 | **Japan/Australia Nominal Exchange Rate**

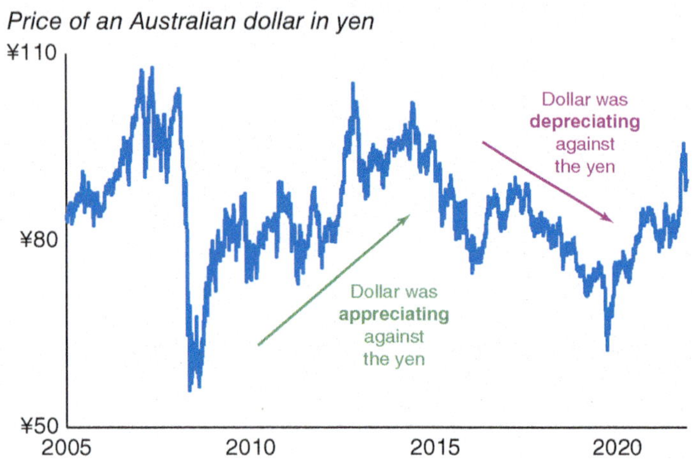

Data from: Refinitiv.

Currencies appreciate when they become more expensive and depreciate when they become cheaper. Be careful, it's easy to get confused when you're describing exchange rate movements. For instance, when the rate at which you exchange yen for dollars *rises* from ¥80 per dollar to ¥90, then the rate at which you exchange dollars for yen *falls* from A$0.013 per yen, to A$0.011: Rather than argue about whether to describe this as a rise or a fall, economists use different words altogether.

When the number of yen you're charged to buy one dollar goes up—that is, the price of a dollar rises—we describe this as an **appreciation** of the dollar. We say it appreciates because a dollar is now worth more yen (and anyone holding dollars would appreciate that!). Figure 7 shows that the dollar appreciated against the yen for much of 2009 through to 2013.

Conversely, when the number of yen that are needed to buy a dollar goes down—that is, the price of the dollar falls—we describe this as a **depreciation** of the dollar. The dollar is like a used car, because when it depreciates, it's worth less. Figure 7 shows that the dollar depreciated against the yen for much of 2015 through to 2020.

appreciation When the price of a currency rises.

depreciation When the price of a currency falls.

An appreciating dollar makes imports cheaper and exports more expensive. When the dollar appreciates, the goods we import from other countries become cheaper in Australian dollars. For instance, importing a ¥72,000,000 Nikon camera costs A$900 when the exchange rate is 80 yen per dollar, but that falls to A$800 when the price of a dollar appreciates to 90 yen. Some people describe an appreciation as leading to a *stronger* dollar; it's stronger because it buys more foreign goods and services.

While an appreciation in the dollar is good news for importers, it's bad news for exporters. For instance, the Warmolls sell their Wagyu beef at A$100 per kilo, which translates to ¥8,000 per kilo for their Japanese customers when the exchange rate is 80 yen per dollar, but that price rises to ¥9,000 per kilo when the price of a dollar rises to 90 yen. As a result, an appreciation of the dollar causes Australian exports—like the Warmolls' Wagyu beef—to become more expensive for foreign buyers. The problem is that while Japanese customers pay more in Japanese yen, the Warmolls don't get any more dollars per kilo.

Figure 8 | **Different Ways to Describe a . . .**

Higher price of a dollar	Lower price of a dollar
• An appreciation of the dollar	• A depreciation of the dollar
• A depreciation of the other currency	• An appreciation of the other currency
• Stronger dollar	• Weaker dollar
• Higher exchange rate	• Lower exchange rate
• Imports are cheaper	• Imports are more expensive
• Exports are more expensive for foreign buyers	• Exports are cheaper for foreign buyers

A depreciating dollar makes imports more expensive and exports cheaper. When the dollar depreciates, the goods we import from other countries become more expensive in terms of Australian dollars. Some people refer to a depreciation as leading to a *weaker* dollar because it buys fewer foreign goods. While a depreciation is bad news for importers, it's good news for Australian exporters. Even if they don't adjust the price they charge in Australian dollars, foreign buyers will find that they now pay less in their currency, leading them to buy more of our exports. Figure 8 summarises these different ways of describing changes in the exchange rate, and what they mean.

Interpreting the DATA — Tracking the value of the Australian dollar

On any given day, the dollar trades against many different currencies. It might appreciate against the yen, depreciate against the euro, not change against the yuan, and also rise or fall relative to each of dozens of other currencies.

In order to keep track of the overall strength of the dollar, economists have compiled a summary measure of the value of the Australian dollar called the *trade-weighted index*. Think of this as being the price of Australian dollars in terms of a basket of currencies, with each country's weight in that basket reflecting their importance as a trading partner. It effectively averages many different exchange rates into a single index that describes the international value of Australian dollars. Figure 9 shows this index which describes whether, on average, the Australian dollar has appreciated or depreciated over time. You can check out the latest value by looking it up here: https://www.rba.gov.au/statistics/frequency/exchange-rates.html ■

Figure 9 | **Australian Nominal Exchange Rate: Trade-Weighted Index**

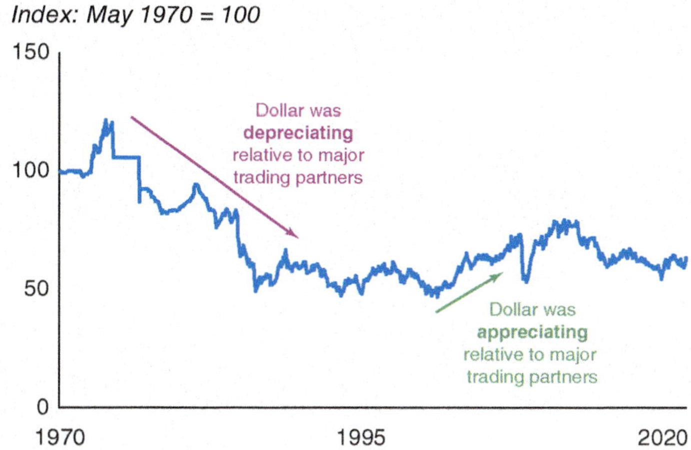

Data from: Reserve Bank of Australia.

28.3 Supply and Demand of Currencies

Learning Objective *Analyse the market for currencies and forecast the nominal exchange rate.*

When the Warmolls sell Wagyu beef to a butcher in Tokyo, they need to get paid in dollars. But a Japanese butchery does business in yen. Thus international trade is only possible if there's a market where they can exchange one currency for another. That market is the **foreign exchange market.** It's the market in which currencies like the Australian dollar and the Japanese yen are bought and sold.

foreign exchange market The market in which currencies are bought and sold.

The Market for Australian Dollars

The market for currencies is like any other competitive market, where the forces of supply and demand determine the equilibrium price and quantity. In the foreign exchange market, the *products* are currencies like the Australian dollar. *Demanders* are those, like a Japanese butcher, looking to buy Australian dollars in order to purchase Australian Wagyu beef. The Japanese butcher buys Australian dollars with Japanese yen. *Suppliers* are those who are looking to sell their Australian dollars in return for Japanese yen. For instance, an Australian camera shop that imports Nikon cameras will supply Australian dollars in exchange for yen so that it can pay its Japanese wholesaler. The *price* in this market is the price of a Australian dollar, which the nominal exchange rate measures as the number of yen you have to pay to buy one Australian dollar.

There are two main types of international transactions that lead people to demand or supply dollars. First, there are *trade flows,* such as exports of Wagyu beef and imports of Nikon cameras. Second, there are *financial flows,* such as when Hitachi invests in building a new factory in Australia, or Australian investors buy stock in Japanese companies.

The demand for Australian dollars reflects foreigners buying Australian exports and investing in Australia. When Japanese consumers want to buy Australian products—that is, exports from Australia—they need to pay

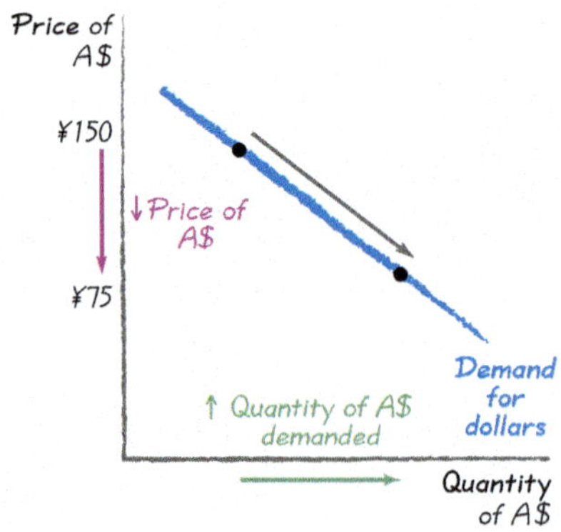

with Australian dollars. This means that every dollar of exports from Australia creates a demand in the foreign exchange market for one Australian dollar. Similarly, when Japanese investors want to buy Australian assets they need Australian dollars. For example, when Hitachi buys or builds a factory in Australia, it needs to buy Australian dollars to pay for it. Thus, every dollar of financial inflows creates a demand for an Australian dollar.

The demand curve for Australian dollars illustrates how the quantity of Australian dollars demanded varies with the price of Australian dollars (which is the exchange rate). This downward-sloping demand curve shows that a lower price for Australian dollars leads to a larger quantity of dollars demanded. It's downward sloping because when the price of the Australian dollar is low, Australian dollars cost fewer yen. It follows that it costs fewer yen to buy Australian products. From the perspective of Japanese buyers, it's as if goods exported from Australia are on sale, so they buy more of them. They'll need more Australian dollars to pay for these Australian exports, and so a lower price for the Australian dollar leads them to demand a larger quantity of dollars.

↓ Price of A$ → ↓ Price in yen of Australian exports to Japan → ↑ Australian exports to Japan → ↑ Quantity of A$ demanded

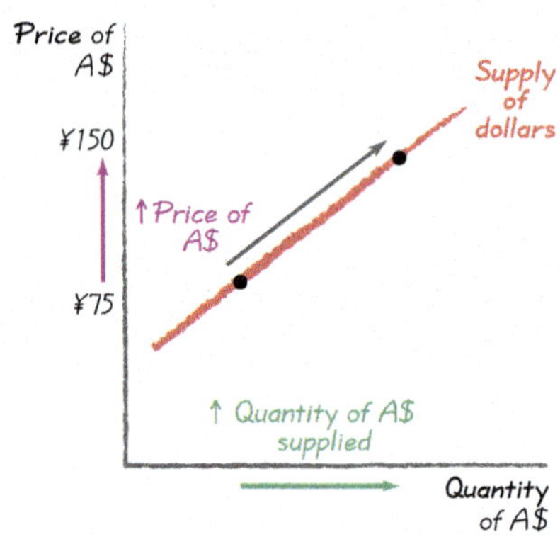

The supply of dollars reflects Australians buying imports and investing abroad. When Australian buyers pay for Japanese goods—that is, imports into Australia—they need to pay with Japanese yen. They'll supply Australian dollars to obtain yen in return. This means that every dollar of imports creates a supply in foreign exchange markets of one Australian dollar. Likewise, when Australian investors want to invest abroad, perhaps buying stock in Hitachi, they'll need Japanese yen to do so. Thus each dollar of financial outflows creates a supply of one Australian dollar.

The supply curve for Australian dollars illustrates how the quantity of Australian dollars supplied varies with the price of Australian dollars (which is the exchange rate). This upward-sloping supply curve shows that a higher price of Australian dollars leads a larger quantity of dollars to be supplied. It's upward sloping because when the price of Australian dollars is high, you'll get a lot of yen in exchange for your dollars. This means that Japanese stuff is cheaper in terms of Australian dollars, and so from the perspective of Australian buyers, it's like Japanese imports are on sale, and so they'll buy more of them. If the value of Australian imports from Japan rises, then Australians will need to exchange more dollars into yen to pay for them. As a result, the higher the price of the Australian dollar, the higher the quantity of dollars supplied.

↑ Price of A$ → ↓ Price in A$ of imports from Japan → ↑ Australian imports from Japan → ↑ Quantity of A$ supplied

(There's a subtle issue here: A higher price for the Australian dollar causes Australians to buy a larger *quantity* of imports, but the number of dollars required to buy each imported item falls. As a result, the total number of Australian dollars spent on imports—and hence the supply of dollars—will rise only if the quantity of imports increases enough to offset the decline in price. In reality, that's what typically occurs, which is why the supply curve is upward-sloping.)

The exchange rate is determined by supply and demand. The foreign exchange market operates much like any other competitive market, with the forces of supply and demand determining the equilibrium price and quantity. The vertical axis in Figure 10 shows the price of an Australian dollar, and the horizontal axis shows the quantity of dollars exchanged for yen. The price of an Australian dollar describes how many yen a buyer has to pay to get one Australian dollar. The higher the exchange rate, the more expensive the dollar is in terms of yen.

Figure 10 | The Market for Australian Dollars

The price of the Australian dollar is determined by the supply and demand of dollars.

Ⓐ The **supply of Australian dollars** is upward-sloping because as the dollar appreciates, it buys more yen, and so imports of Japanese goods become cheaper for Australians. This leads them to spend more on imports, which they can only pay for by supplying more dollars to exchange for yen.

Ⓑ The **demand for Australian dollars** is downward-sloping because as the dollar depreciates, exports of Australian goods become cheaper for Japanese people. This leads them to buy more exports, which they can only pay for by demanding more dollars in exchange for yen.

Ⓒ The **equilibrium exchange rate** occurs at the point where **demand is equal to supply**, setting the price of an Australian dollar at 90 yen.

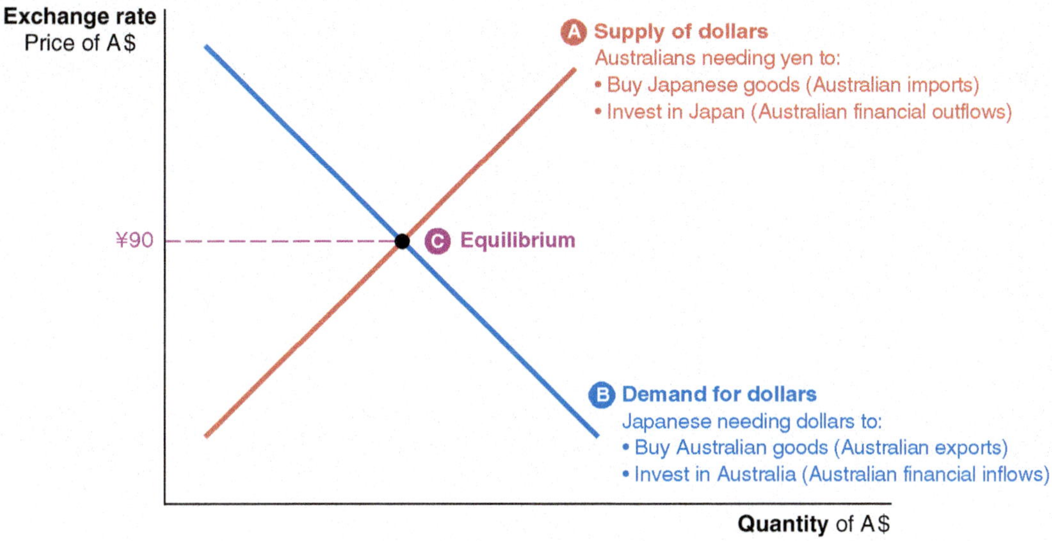

Equilibrium occurs at the point where the supply and demand curves cross, and this determines the price of Australian dollars. Consequently, the equilibrium exchange rate reflects the balance between the forces of supply and demand, which means that it reflects the influence of Australian imports and financial outflows on one side, and Australian exports and financial inflows on the other.

EVERYDAY Economics — How to keep exchange rates straight

You've learned that the supply of Australian dollars comes from Australians looking to exchange their dollars for yen. But if you were studying economics in Japan, you'd learn that Australians looking to exchange their dollars for yen create the demand for yen. Similarly, you've learned the demand for Australian dollars comes from Japanese folks who are looking to exchange their yen for dollars. But in Japan, you'd learn that this creates the supply of yen. These dual identities arise because the market for Australian dollars (paid for with yen) is also the market for yen (paid for in Australian dollars). These are just two sides of the same, umm... coin. So to keep straight which side is up, always:

- ***Clarify which market you're analysing.*** Don't just say that you're analysing the foreign exchange rate market; describe it as the market for Australian dollars, paid for with Japanese yen.
- ***Specify what price you're evaluating.*** If you're assessing the market for Australian dollars, be clear that you're analysing the price of an Australian dollar, which we describe as the number of yen needed to buy one dollar. If you're forecasting the price of the yen, the relevant price is the number of Australian dollars needed to buy one yen.
- ***State the origins and destinations.*** Don't just say "exports"; say "exports from Australia to Japan."

Follow these three pieces of advice, and you'll avoid *a lot of* confusion. ■

The exchange rate will change when macroeconomic conditions change. You'll find this framework to be particularly useful for forecasting how the exchange rate will change in response to changing macroeconomic conditions. Our next task is to analyse shifts in the demand for dollars, and we'll then turn to shifts in supply. But before we dive in, remember that in any supply-and-demand analysis, a change in the price—which in this case is a change in the exchange rate—will not shift either the demand or supply curve.

Shifts in Currency Demand

Demand for Australian dollars shifts due to:

1. Shifts in exports from Australia
2. Shifts in financial inflows into Australia

. . . but not the exchange rate.

An increase in demand for Australian dollars shifts the demand curve to the *right*. As the left panel of Figure 11 shows, an increase in demand causes the price of the Australian dollar to *rise*, which is an exchange rate *appreciation*. The demand curve for Australian dollars shifts right whenever people want to buy more dollars at any given exchange rate. By contrast, the right panel shows that a decrease in demand for Australian dollars shifts the demand curve to the *left*. A decrease in demand causes the price of the Australian dollar to *fall*, which is an exchange rate *depreciation*. The demand curve shifts left whenever people want to buy fewer dollars at any given exchange rate.

Figure 11 | The Demand for Dollars

An Increase in the Demand for Dollars

(A) An increase in exports or financial inflows causes an increase in demand for Australian dollars, shifting the demand curve to the right.

(B) This leads the price of the Australian dollar to rise, an exchange rate appreciation.

A Decrease in the Demand for Dollars

(C) A decrease in exports or financial inflows causes a decrease in demand for Australian dollars, shifting the demand curve to the left.

(D) This leads the price of the Australian dollar to fall, an exchange rate depreciation.

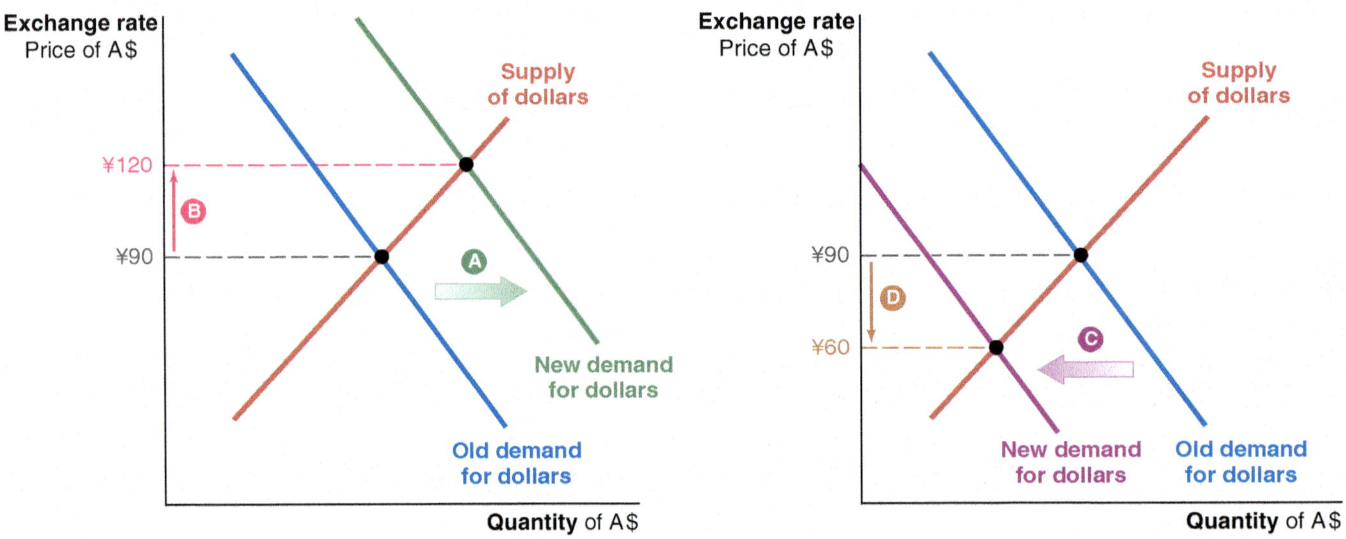

Recall that demand for Australian dollars comes from foreigners who either need dollars in order to buy Australian exports or to invest in Australia. The *interdependence principle* reminds us that their decisions depend on developments in other markets and in other countries. As a result, anything—besides the exchange rate—that shifts either how much foreigners spend on exports, or how much they invest in Australia (that is, financial inflows), will shift the demand for dollars. Let's evaluate each of these shifters in turn.

Demand shifter one: Exports from Australia. Any factor that shifts the dollar value of exports at a given exchange rate will shift the demand for dollars. As a result, exports from Australia—and hence the demand for dollars—shift in response to the following factors:

- *Strength of the global economy:* An increase in the GDP of our major trading partners usually causes an increase in Australian exports, shifting the demand for Australian dollars to the right. For instance, an economic recovery in Japan will increase the income of Japanese consumers, and they'll spend some of this extra income on the Warmolls' Wagyu beef and other Australian goods and services.
- *Barriers to trade in foreign markets:* When foreign governments provide easier access to their markets, exports will increase, shifting the demand for Australian dollars to the right. For instance, Japanese officials require Australian beef to be quarantined before it can be sold, which can cause spoilage. If this trade barrier were scrapped, the Warmolls might start exporting more beef to Japan.
- *Domestic innovation and marketing:* Successful innovation and marketing of Australian goods and services to foreign customers will increase exports, shifting the demand curve for Australian dollars to the right. For example, the Warmolls have developed meat processing and marketing technologies that make their beef more attractive to foreign customers.
- *Foreign prices:* When foreign prices are higher than their Australian counterparts, foreign customers switch to buying the Australian-made goods instead. This increased demand for Australian exports will shift the demand curve for Australian dollars to the right. For example, if Japanese beef producers raise their prices, then some Japanese consumers will switch to Australian-produced beef, increasing the demand for Australian dollars. Or if the price of beef from a third country—say, New Zealand—were to rise, some Japanese consumers will switch from New Zealand to Australian-grown beef.
- *Domestic prices:* When Australian sellers cut their prices it leads to a large increase in exports, thereby increasing the demand for dollars. For example, if the Warmolls cut the price of their Wagyu beef, foreigners will buy more of it. This is where it gets a bit tricky: While this means that the Warmolls will export more Wagyu beef, each kilo costs fewer dollars. Therefore, the total number of dollars that foreigners spend on Wagyu beef could either rise or fall. In practice, lower domestic prices tend to lead to such a large increase in exports that the demand for dollars will increase.

An increase in exports will increase the demand for dollars due to:
↑ World GDP
↓ Barriers to foreign markets
↑ Domestic innovation and marketing
↑ Foreign prices
↓ Domestic prices

In each of these cases, you've seen what happens if exports were to increase at a given exchange rate. These same influences also operate in reverse: A *decrease* in exports would lead to a *decrease* in the demand for dollars, which causes the exchange rate to *depreciate*.

Demand shifter two: Financial inflows into Australia. Foreign investors are usually seeking a combination of a healthy return on their investment, and relatively low risk. This means that financial inflows—and hence demand for dollars—change in response to the following factors:

- *Interest rate differentials:* Foreign investors are sensitive to the *opportunity cost principle*, and the opportunity cost of investing in Australia is investing in either their home country or some other country. As a result, financial inflows are driven by the difference between Australian interest rates and foreign interest rates. A higher interest rate differential—due to either higher interest rates in Australia or lower interest rates in a foreign country—will increase financial inflows, shifting the demand curve for dollars to the right.
- *Business profitability:* The more opportunities there are for profitable investments in Australia relative to such opportunities in other countries, the larger will be financial inflows. As a result, financial inflows are sensitive to factors that affect business profitability, like taxes, wage rates, and demand. Any change that creates a more profitable business climate in Australia will lead to more financial inflows, shifting the demand curve for dollars to the right.
- *Political risk:* Australia is a "safe haven" for investing, making it an attractive destination for foreign investors worried about political risks in their own country.

Financial inflows will increase, and thereby increase the demand for dollars due to:
↑ Australian interest rates relative to foreign interest rates
↑ Australian business profitability relative to foreign businesses
↑ Foreign political risk relative to Australian political risk
↑ Expected future value of the dollar

Whenever foreign risks rise relative to political risk in Australia—such as the risk of a foreign government coup or seizure of assets—financial inflows into Australia increase, and thus so does the demand for Australian dollars, shifting the demand curve to the right.

- *Expected exchange rate movements:* Right now, thousands of foreign exchange speculators are evaluating how changing economic conditions are likely to shift the price of the Australian dollar. Any news that might cause the dollar to rise in the future has an immediate impact, as speculators rush to buy dollars in anticipation of them later rising in value. Increased demand for Australian dollars by speculators shifts the demand curve for Australian dollars to the right.

In each of these cases, you've seen what happens if these factors lead financial inflows to increase at a given exchange rate. These same influences also operate in reverse: A *decrease* in financial inflows would lead to a *decrease* in the demand for dollars, which causes the exchange rate to *depreciate*.

Okay, these are the factors that shift the demand for Australian dollars. Let's now turn our attention to shifts in the supply of dollars.

Shifts in Currency Supply

Supply of Australian dollars shifts due to:

1. Shifts in imports into Australia
2. Shifts in financial outflows from Australia

. . . and not the exchange rate.

An increase in the supply of Australian dollars at any given exchange rate shifts the supply curve to the right. As the left panel of Figure 12 shows, an increase in supply will cause the price of the Australian dollar to decline, which is an exchange rate *depreciation*. By contrast, the right panel of Figure 12 shows that a decrease in supply at any given exchange rate shifts the supply curve to the left, leading to a new equilibrium in which the price of the Australian dollar rises, an exchange rate *appreciation*.

As with the demand for dollars, the supply of dollars reflects the *interdependence principle* at work. The supply of Australian dollars comes from Australians who need to exchange their dollars for foreign currency, so that they can buy imports or invest their savings abroad and those decisions depend on developments in other markets. As a result, anything—besides the exchange rate—that shifts either how much people spend on

Figure 12 | **The Supply of Dollars**

An Increase in the Supply of Dollars

A An increase in imports or financial outflows causes an **increase in supply** of Australian dollars, shifting the supply curve to the **right**.

B This leads the **price of the Australian dollar to fall**, an exchange rate **depreciation**.

A Decrease in the Supply of Dollars

C A decrease in imports or financial outflows causes a **decrease in supply** of Australian dollars, shifting the supply curve to the **left**.

D This leads the **price of the Australian dollar to rise**, an exchange rate **appreciation**.

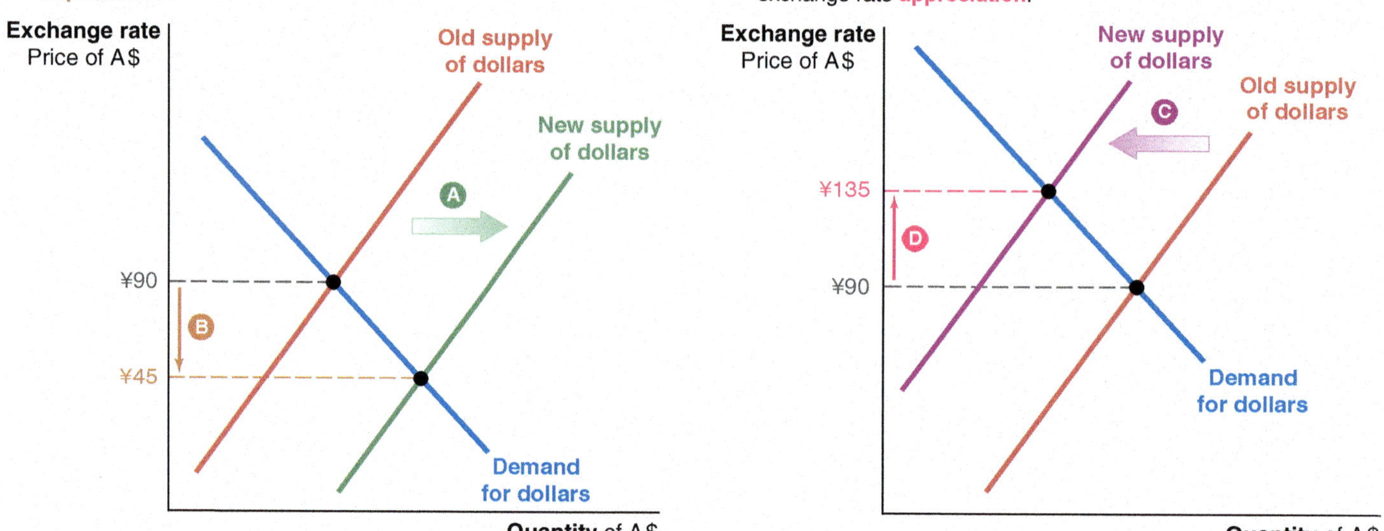

imports, or how much they invest abroad (that is, financial outflows), will shift the supply of dollars. Let's evaluate each of these shifters in turn.

Supply shifter one: Imports into Australia. Any factor that shifts how much Australians spend on imports will shift the supply of dollars. As a result, imports—and hence the supply of dollars—shift in response to the following factors:

- *Strength of the domestic economy:* An increase in Australian GDP means that Australians have more income to spend, including on imported goods like Japanese electronics. Thus, an increase in Australian incomes means more imports, shifting the supply of Australian dollars to the right.
- *Trade barriers protecting domestic producers:* When Australia reduces tariffs and other barriers that make it difficult for foreign companies to sell their goods to Australians, demand for imports will increase and thus so will the supply of Australian dollars. For example, when China joined the World Trade Organization, some countries purchased more Chinese imports, which shifted the supply of their currencies to the right.
- *Foreign innovation and marketing:* Innovation in foreign products and better marketing of foreign products to Australians will lead to an increase in Australian demand for imports. For example, Japanese innovation disrupted the camera industry, shifting demand from Australian companies to Japanese companies such as Nikon. The result was an increase in imports, which shifted the supply of dollars to the right.
- *Domestic prices:* If Australian producers raise their prices relative to foreign alternatives, Australian buyers will switch from buying domestically-produced goods and services to buying more imported ones. The result is an increase in imports, which shifts the supply of Australian dollars to the right.
- *Foreign prices:* Similarly, if foreign producers cut their prices, Australian buyers will buy more imported goods. Typically, demand for imports is very price sensitive, and so lower foreign prices usually lead to an increase in the quantity of dollars supplied, shifting the supply of Australian dollars to the right.

Imports increase thereby increasing the supply of dollars due to:
↑ Australian GDP
↓ Barriers protecting domestic producers
↑ Foreign innovation and marketing
↑ Domestic prices
↓ Foreign prices

In each of these cases, you've seen what happens if the quantity of imports were to increase at a given exchange rate. These same influences also operate in reverse: A *decrease* in imports leads to a *decrease* in the supply of dollars, shifting the supply of dollars to the left, which causes the exchange rate to *appreciate.*

Supply shifter two: Financial outflows from Australia. Remember that when Australians invest abroad, they'll need foreign currency to do so. And so any factor that shifts financial outflows at a given exchange rate will also shift the supply of dollars. The decisions that Australian investors make about whether to invest their funds abroad or at home lead financial outflows—and hence the supply of dollars—to respond to:

- *Interest rate differentials:* A lower interest rate differential—due to either lower interest rates in Australia or higher interest rates in a foreign country—will increase financial outflows as Australians seek better investment opportunities outside of Australia, shifting the supply curve for dollars to the right.
- *Business profitability:* The fewer the opportunities available for profitable investments in Australia, the larger will be the resulting financial outflow. Any change that creates a less investment-friendly business climate in Australia will lead to more financial outflows, shifting the supply curve for dollars to the right.
- *Political risk:* Whenever foreign political risks decline, Australian investors are more interested in investing abroad, increasing the supply of Australian dollars, shifting the supply curve to the right.
- *Expected exchange rate movements:* Any news that might cause the dollar to fall in the future has an immediate impact, as speculators rush to sell dollars in

Financial outflows increase thereby increasing the supply of dollars due to:
↓ Australian interest rates relative to foreign interest rates
↓ Australian business profitability relative to foreign businesses
↓ Foreign political risk relative to Australian political risk
↓ Expected future value of the dollar

anticipation of them later falling in value. Increased supply of Australian dollars by speculators shifts the supply curve for Australian dollars to the right.

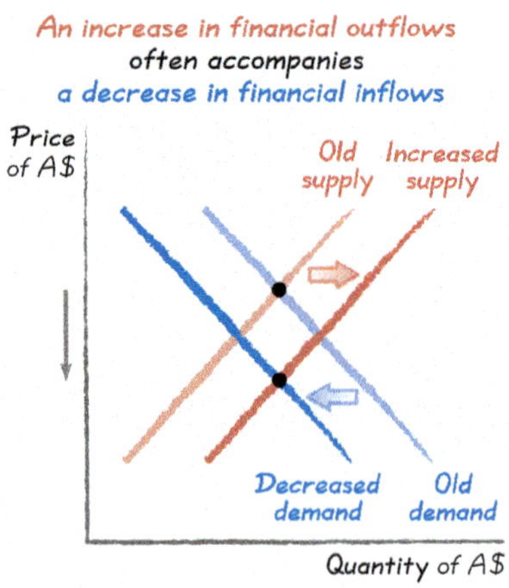

Look closely, and you'll notice that this list of factors that shift financial outflows is the mirror image of the list of factors that shift financial inflows, and hence the demand for dollars. This symmetry arises because Australian and foreign investors are in the same business of scouring the world looking for good investment opportunities, and so they'll respond to similar factors. When investing abroad becomes a better bet, Australian investors invest less here and more abroad, *increasing* financial *outflows*. When foreigners follow suit and also invest less here and more abroad, the result is a *decrease* in financial *inflows*.

This can make it tricky to analyse financial flows, as nearly any factor that shifts financial outflows, and hence the supply of dollars, in one direction will shift financial inflows and the demand of dollars in the opposite direction. Ultimately these effects will reinforce each other, as an increase in the supply of dollars will cause a depreciation that's reinforced by a decrease in demand. Likewise, a decrease in the supply of dollars will cause an appreciation that's reinforced by an increase in demand.

Okay, that's it—we've analysed the set of factors that might cause the demand or supply of dollars to shift, and I've summarised them for you in Figure 13. But remember: There's one factor that won't shift either the demand or supply curves, and that's the exchange rate.

Figure 13 | Factors That Shift the Demand and Supply of Australian Dollars

Shifter	Graphically	Examples
↑**Exports** increase the **demand** for dollars	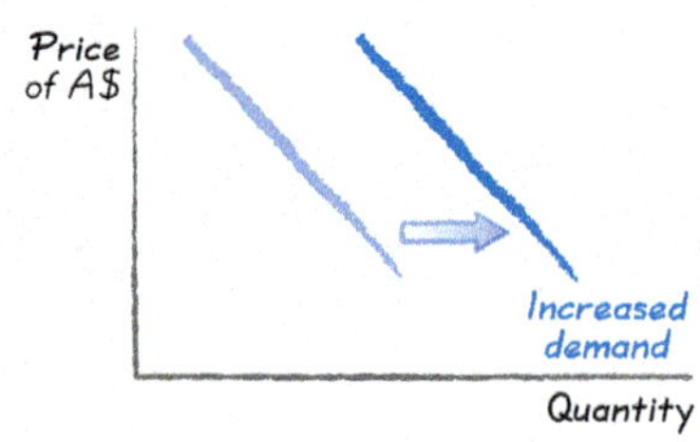	• ↑ World GDP • ↓ Barriers to foreign markets • ↑ Domestic innovation and marketing • ↑ Foreign prices • ↓ Domestic price
↑**Financial inflows** increase the **demand** for dollars	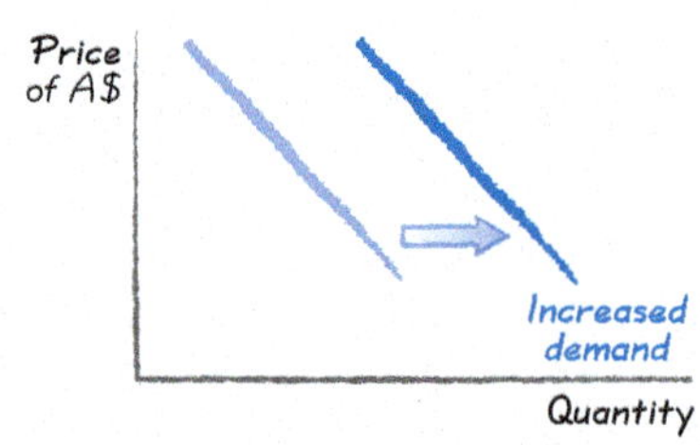	• ↑ Australian interest rates • ↓ Foreign interest rates • ↑ Business profitability in Australia • ↓ Business profitability in foreign countries • ↑ Foreign political risk • ↓ Australian political risk • ↑ Expected future value of the dollar
↑**Imports** increase the **supply** of dollars	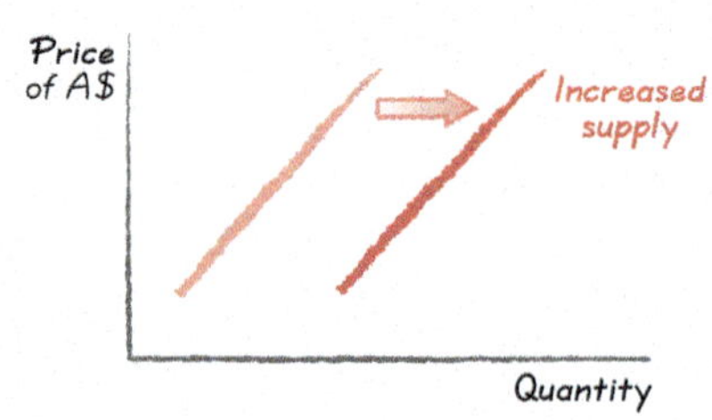	• ↑ Australian GDP • ↓ Barriers protecting domestic producers • ↑ Foreign innovation and marketing • ↑ Domestic prices • ↓ Foreign prices
↑**Financial outflows** increase the **supply** of dollars	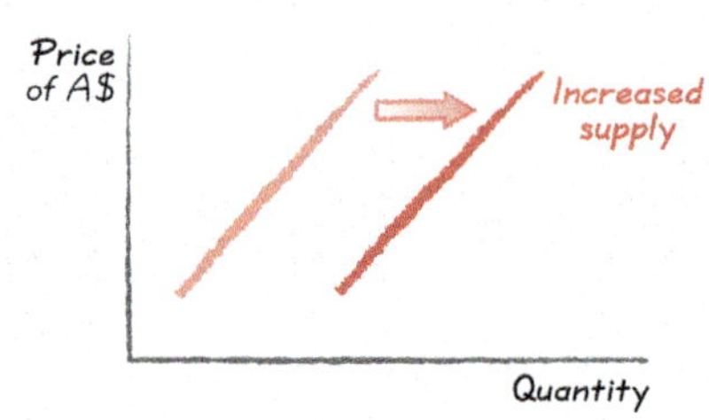	• ↓ Australian interest rates • ↑ Foreign interest rates • ↓ Business profitability in Australia • ↑ Business profitability in foreign countries • ↑ Australian political risk • ↓ Foreign political risk • ↓ Expected future value of the dollar

Forecasting Exchange Rate Movements

You're now ready to apply these tools to forecast how the exchange rate will respond to changing economic conditions. Simply apply the same three-step recipe you use to predict the results of any supply-and-demand analysis:

Step one: *Is the supply or demand curve shifting (or both)?*

Will this shift exports or financial inflows into Australia—in which case it shifts the demand curve? Or will it shift imports or financial outflows abroad—which will shift the supply curve?

Step two: *Is this an increase that will shift the curve to the right, or a decrease that will shift the curve to the left?*

Increases in any international transactions—in imports, exports, financial inflows, or financial outflows—will shift the relevant curve to the right. And decreases in these transactions will shift it to the left.

Step three: *How will the price—that is, the exchange rate—change in equilibrium?*

Remember, the new equilibrium occurs where the new demand and supply curves cross.

Do the Economics

Think you're ready to try your hand at this? Try working through the following examples.

A "Buy Australian" campaign leads millions to buy Australian-made goods instead of imports.

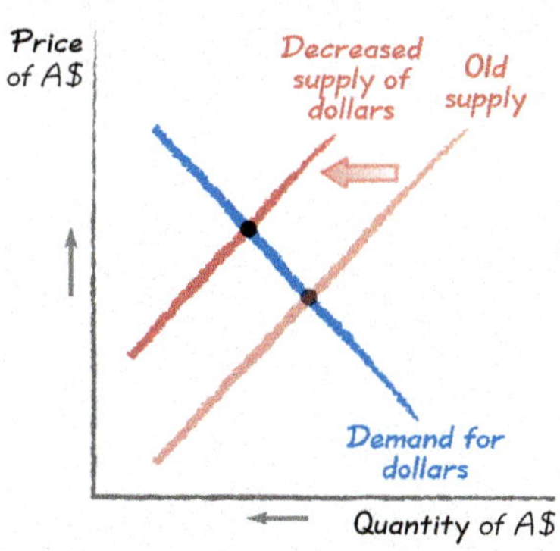

Decreased imports to Australia → Decreased supply of A$.

Result: A$ appreciates

Germany imposes a 30% tariff on Australian medical equipment.

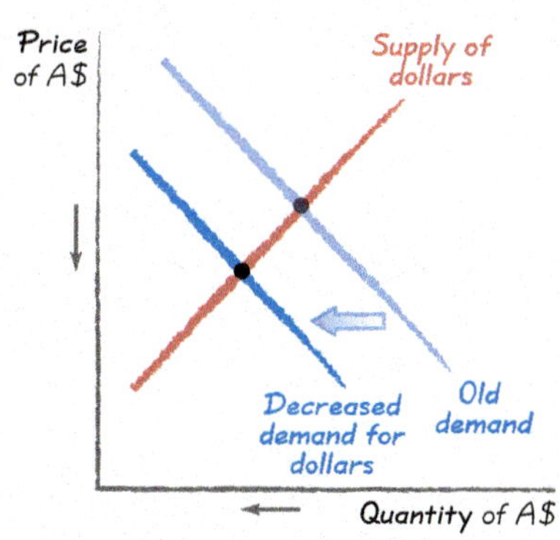

Decreased exports from Australia → Decreased demand for A$.

Result: A$ depreciates

People in China are travelling more to Australia, so they're purchasing more Australian travel services.

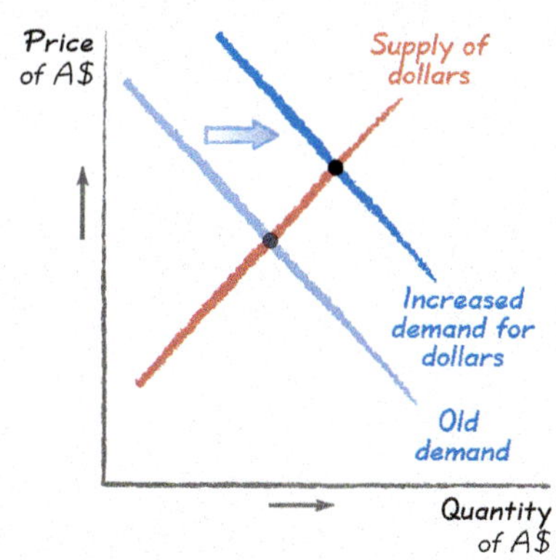

Increased exports from Australia → Increased demand for A$.

Result: A$ appreciates

A strong Australian economy leads Australians to buy more imports.

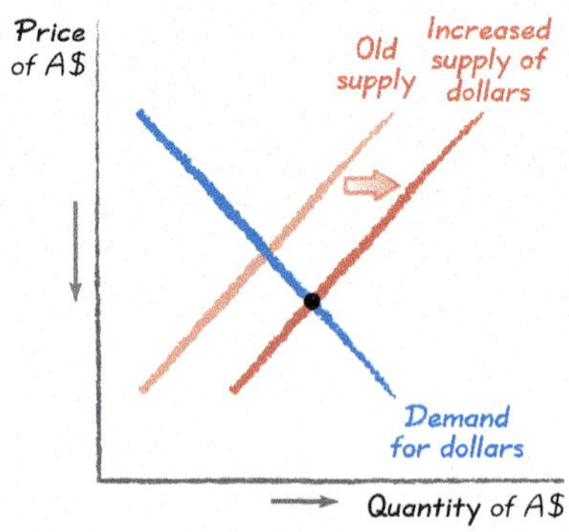

Increased imports to Australia
→ Increased supply of A$.

Result: A$ depreciates

The Reserve Bank of Australia unexpectedly raises Australian interest rates.

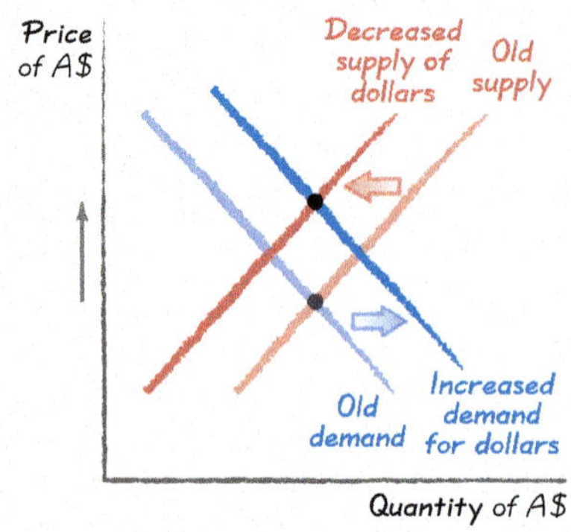

Increased financial inflows and decreased financial outflows
→ Decreased supply of A$ and increased demand for A$.

Result: A$ appreciates

Political turmoil in Australia leads investors to question whether it really is a safe haven.

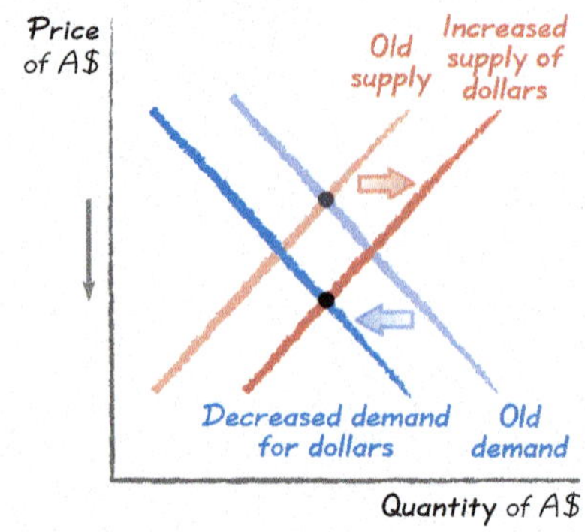

Increased financial outflows and decreased financial inflows
→ Increased supply of A$ and decreased demand for A$.

Result: A$ depreciates ■

Australian/Euro Exchange Rate
Price of a euro

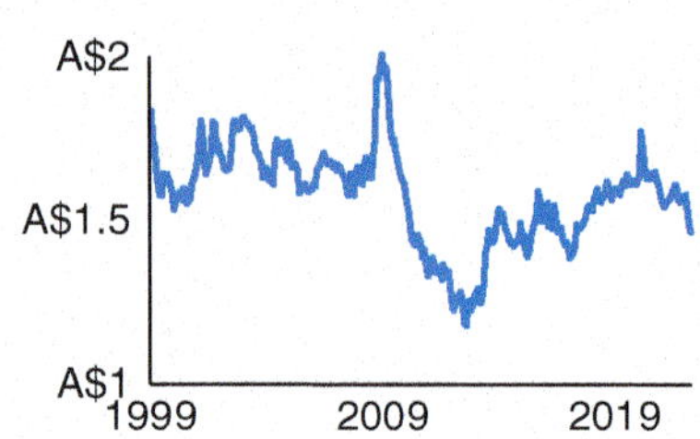

Hong Kong/U.S. Exchange Rate
Price of a Hong Kong Dollar

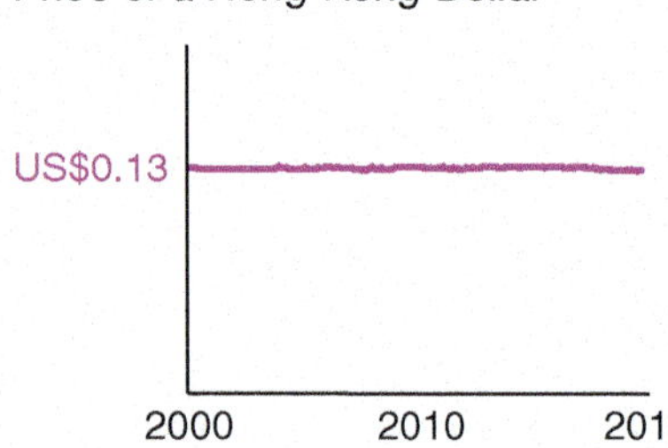

Australian/China Exchange Rate
Price of a Chinese Yuan

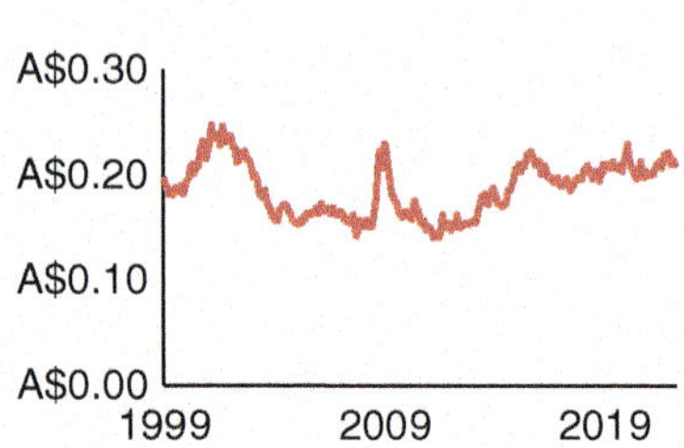

Data from: Refinitiv, and Investing.com.

Government Intervention in Foreign Exchange Markets

So far we've described the foreign exchange market as determined purely by the forces of supply and demand, and this system is called a *floating exchange rate*. We've done this because today most countries have a floating exchange rate. The Australian dollar and the euro are both examples of floating exchange rates and, as a result, the Australian dollar/euro exchange rate rises and falls as macroeconomic conditions change.

Some countries actually fix their exchange rate. A *fixed exchange rate* is one where the government effectively sets the price of the currency. For instance, Hong Kong maintains a fixed exchange rate with the United States, and for several decades the price of a Hong Kong dollar has not budged from US$0.13. Hong Kong's central bank achieves this by buying or selling as much currency as needed to prevent the price from moving. When the demand for its currency exceeds supply, it sells Hong Kong dollars, and when there's more supply than demand, it buys Hong Kong dollars. Fixed exchange rates were more common in the decades following World War II.

Some countries operate between these extremes, in what's called a *managed exchange rate* (or a "dirty" float). China is an important example of a country that manages its exchange rate. It officially abandoned its fixed exchange rate (to the U.S. dollar) in 2005. But in an effort to boost the competitiveness of China's exporters, China held the value of its currency artificially low for much of the next decade, by selling trillions of yuan (and buying trillions of U.S. dollars). This also kept the yuan artificially low against the Australian dollar. This cheap yuan policy led to frictions. It meant low-prices for Australian consumers, but that also meant that it helped Chinese exporters win business from Australian companies. China appears to have abandoned this policy sometime around 2015. It still continues to somewhat manage its exchange rate, but to a lesser degree.

28.4 The Real Exchange Rate and Net Exports

Learning Objective *Assess how exchange rates and relative prices affect exports and imports.*

The Warmolls, like all Australian businesses, are engaged in a fierce battle to win over price-sensitive customers in a global marketplace. The more internationally competitive they are, the more Wagyu beef they can export. Greater international competitiveness will also help the Warmolls persuade Australian consumers to buy their local Wagyu beef rather than importing Wagyu beef from Japan. In short, a company's international competitiveness determines its foreign and domestic sales. And for a country, the international competitiveness of its businesses is a major factor determining how much it imports and exports.

Real Exchange Rate and Competitiveness

To assess the relative competitiveness of Australia's Wagyu beef farmers, put yourself in the shoes of a buyer trying to choose whether to buy Australian Wagyu or those of a foreign rival. You'll compare how much it'll cost you to buy Australian Wagyu beef to how much it'll cost you to buy foreign Wagyu beef. The lower this ratio, the more likely you are to buy Australian.

The real exchange rate is the ratio of domestic to foreign prices, measured in the same currency. That's the idea behind the **real exchange rate**, which is the domestic price of a product divided by the foreign price (after converting that price into domestic currency):

real exchange rate The domestic price divided by the foreign price, expressed in the domestic currency. Calculated as: $\frac{\text{Domestic price}}{\text{Foreign price / Nominal exchange rate}}$

$$\text{Real exchange rate} = \frac{\text{Domestic price in dollars}}{\text{Foreign price converted into dollars}}$$

In practice, the price charged by foreign producers is typically quoted in foreign currency—the price of a kilo of Japanese Wagyu beef is ¥11,250—and so we'll need to convert it into dollars to make it comparable. The nominal exchange rate formula is helpful here: It says that you can convert a foreign price into dollars simply by dividing by the nominal exchange rate (and so a foreign price of ¥11,250 when the nominal exchange rate is ¥90 per Australian dollar converts into 11,250/90 = A$125 per kilo). As such we calculate the real exchange rate as:

$$\text{Real exchange rate} = \frac{\text{Domestic price in dollars}}{\underbrace{\text{Foreign price in foreign currency/Nominal exchange rate}}_{\text{Foreign price converted into dollars}}}$$

Do the Economics

If the domestic price of Australian Wagyu beef is A$100 per kilo, the nominal exchange rate is 90 yen per dollar, and the foreign price of Wagyu beef is ¥11,250 per kilo, what's the real exchange rate?

The real exchange rate is:

$$\frac{\text{Domestic price}}{\text{Foreign price/Nominal exchange rate}} = \frac{\text{A\$100}}{\text{¥11,250/¥90 per dollar}} = \frac{\text{A\$100}}{\text{A\$125}} = \frac{4}{5}$$

This says that after converting both prices into the same currency, the price of Australian Wagyu beef is four-fifths that of Japanese Wagyu beef. Given this lower price, the Warmolls can expect to export a lot of Wagyu beef. (As an exercise, confirm that if you converted both prices into yen instead of dollars you would get the same answer.) ■

The real exchange rate measures the (un)competitiveness of Australian products. A low real exchange rate means that Australian goods are cheap relative to their foreign rivals—which means that they're internationally competitive. This is why the real exchange rate is often described as a measure of *international competitiveness*. Be careful, though: You might be better off thinking about it as a measure of international *uncompetivenness*, because a *higher* real exchange rate means that you're *less* competitive.

A real exchange rate depreciation leads Australians to import less and export more. Economists find the real exchange rate to be particularly useful because it summarises the key prices—the domestic price, the foreign price, and the nominal exchange rate—that jointly determine both imports and exports. For instance, a lower real exchange rate means that Australian Wagyu beef has become cheaper relative to its foreign counterparts, and this will:

- *Decrease imports*: As Australian buyers switch towards buying the relatively cheaper local goods rather than imported foreign goods.
- *Increase exports*: As foreign buyers will switch to buying the relatively cheaper goods exported from Australia, rather than their foreign alternative.

The same logic also operates in reverse, implying that a higher real exchange rate will lead to an increase in imports and a decrease in exports.

The real exchange rate is the exchange rate for output. So far we've described the real exchange rate as measuring the price of domestic goods relative to their foreign competitors. By this interpretation, a real exchange rate of $^4/_5$ tells you that domestic producers charge a price that's four-fifths that of foreign producers. There's an alternative interpretation: The real exchange rate is the rate at which you can exchange Australian goods for foreign goods. Think of it as an apples-to-apples (or beef-to-beef) exchange rate: A real exchange rate of $^4/_5$ tells you that each kilo of Australian Wagyu beef effectively buys you four-fifths of a kilo of Japanese Wagyu beef. By this view, the *real exchange rate* is the rate at which you can exchange one country's output for another country's output. It's the exchange rate for real stuff, while the *nominal exchange rate* is the rate at which you can exchange one country's currency for another's.

The Real Exchange Rate Determines Net Exports

All of these ideas scale up from thinking just about Wagyu beef to thinking about the whole economy. If the price of Australian products, on average, were to become cheaper relative to the Australian dollar price of goods produced overseas, then it follows that Australian businesses, on average, have become more internationally competitive. Consequently, an economy-wide *real depreciation* will lead total exports to increase, and total imports to decrease. (And a *real appreciation* will decrease total exports and increase total imports.)

An economy-wide real exchange rate reflects broad changes in competitiveness. The economy-wide version of the real exchange rate compares the price of a typical basket of goods and services in each country by comparing movements in the consumer price index in each country after adjusting for changes due to the nominal exchange rate:

$$\text{Real exchange rate} = \frac{\text{Domestic price index}}{\text{Foreign price index/Nominal exchange rate}}$$

The trade-weighted real exchange rate that's shown in Figure 14—the *real trade-weighted index*—broadens this idea so that it evaluates Australia's competitiveness relative to a weighted average of dozens of our most important trading partners. You can track the value of this index here: https://fred.stlouisfed.org/series/RBAUBIS

The real exchange rate drives imports and exports. This broad measure of the real exchange rate is useful because it summarises changes in the average competitiveness of Australian businesses, whether they're caused by changes in the prices charged by domestic or foreign producers or by changes in the exchange rates of dozens of our trading partners.

The real exchange rate is a key factor driving net exports. After all, if Australian businesses have become more competitive, they'll be able to outcompete foreign firms in foreign markets, and so they'll export more. They'll also do a better job competing with the foreign businesses that Australians import from, leading to fewer imports into Australia. Figure 14 illustrates that this insight is borne out by real-world data, as movements in the real exchange rate do a good job of predicting changes in net exports.

Figure 14 | After the Real Exchange Rate Falls, Net Exports Rise

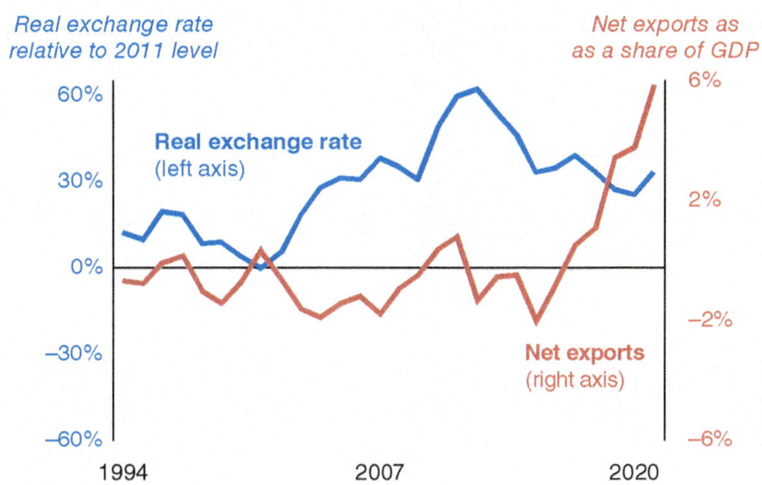

Data from: Reserve Bank of Australia; Federal Reserve Board.

28.5 The Balance of Payments

Learning Objective *Track how money flows around the world using the current account and the financial account.*

It's time to draw together the threads of this chapter. We began by noting that the Australian economy is linked to the global economy through international trade and global financial flows. We then explored the role that these play in shaping the supply and demand for Australian dollars, and analysed how the real exchange rate also affects imports and exports. Our final task is to describe how to keep track of all of this using the *balance of payments*, which summarise a country's transactions with the rest of world.

The Current Account and The Financial Account

The balance of payments tracks two important sets of transactions. The *current account* tracks how much *income* crosses national borders each year, while the *financial account* tallies up *financial flows* across borders.

The current account tallies up income flows into and out of a country. The **current account balance** measures the difference between the income that Australians receive from abroad, and the income that Australians pay to people abroad. The current account tracks *all* income flows with the rest of the world, and so it's a broader measure than net exports, which only tracks the income earned from exports less the income paid for imports.

current account balance Measures the difference between the income that Australians receive from abroad and the income that Australians pay to people abroad.

Figure 15 | **The Current Account**

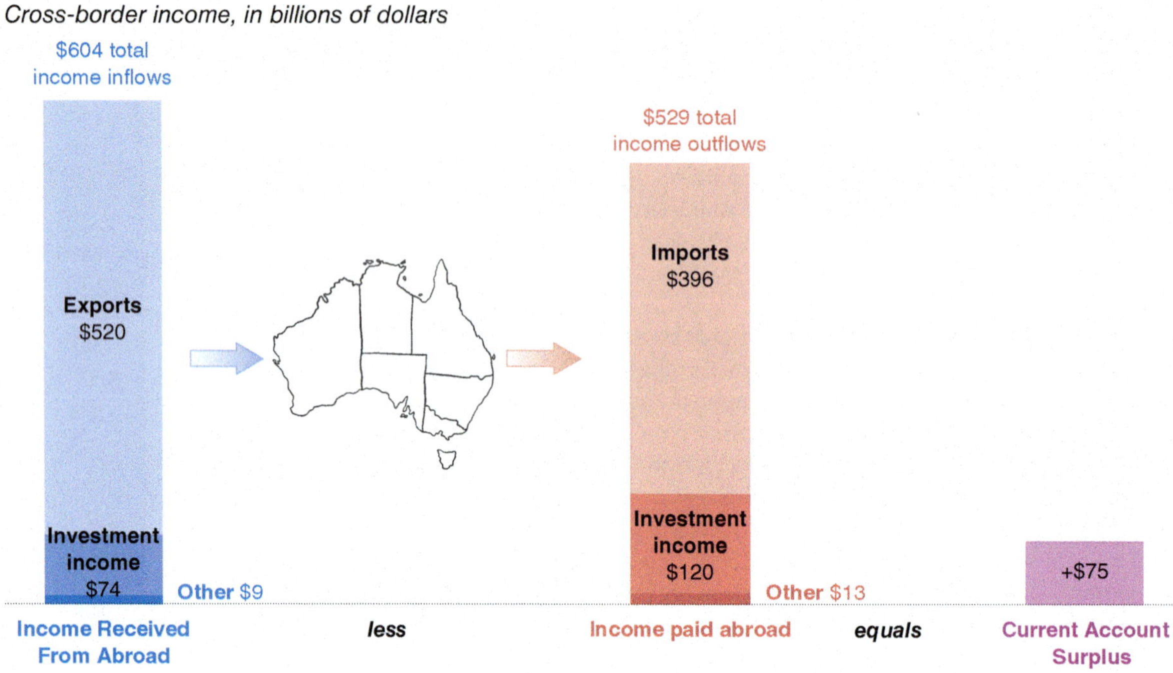

Data from: Australian Bureau of Statistics.

The blue bar in Figure 15 shows the income that Australians receive from abroad. The largest source of income from abroad comes from selling *exports*, such as the income the Warmolls earn from selling their Wagyu beef to Japanese buyers. The next most important source of income is the investment income that Australians earn on their foreign assets.

The red bar in Figure 15 shows the income that Australians pay to people abroad. The largest source of this income is the money that Australians spend buying imports from abroad. Investment income that foreigners earn on the assets they own in Australia is the next largest source. This includes the profit that Hitachi's Australian factories generate for their Japanese owners, the annual interest that Australian borrowers pay to foreign banks that have loaned them money, and the dividends that Australian companies pay to their foreign shareholders. In addition, there are some other smaller income flows.

All told, in 2021, Australians received $604 billion in income from abroad, and made $529 billion in income payments to foreigners. As a result, Australia ran a current account deficit of –$75 billion. Put differently, this is a current account surplus of 75 billion. To put this in more human terms, on average, each Australian received roughly $2,900 more income from abroad than they paid to foreigners.

Notice that the current account doesn't count the sale of assets as income. That's because when you sell $10,000 of your stock in the Commonwealth Bank to a foreigner, you're not really generating any income: You're sending someone a financial asset worth $10,000 (your stock certificate), and in return, they're sending you a financial asset worth $10,000 (the cash they hand over). A transfer of existing assets doesn't generate any new income, which is why it's not part of the current account. However, these financial flows are important because they reflect the changing international ownership of assets, and so our next task is to see how we keep track of them.

financial account balance The difference between financial inflows and financial outflows.

The financial account tallies up changes in the ownership of assets. The financial account tracks incoming and outgoing foreign investments. The **financial**

Figure 16 | **The Financial Account**

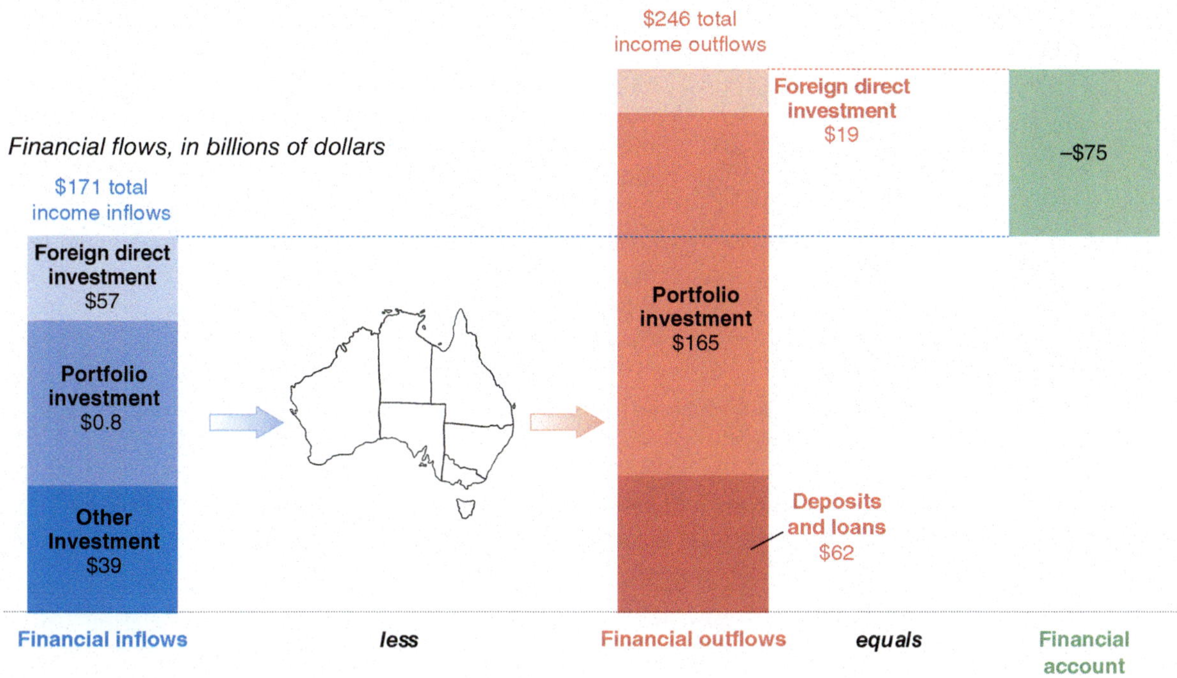

Data from: Australian Bureau of Statistics.

account balance measures the difference between financial inflows and financial outflows. Figure 16 shows that in 2021, financial inflows totaled $171 billion, while financial outflows were $246 billion. This yields a financial account balance of a –$75 billion surplus (or $75 billion deficit), which means that foreigners invested $75 billion less in Australia than Australians invested abroad. In other words, foreigners bought $75 billion less Australian assets than Australians bought foreign assets.

Australia has run a current account deficit and financial account surplus for decades. The purple line in Figure 17 shows that Australia has run a persistent current account deficit since the early 1990s until very recently. It was only in 2019 that we crossed into running a surplus. This deficit means that the income that Australians have paid foreigners has exceeded the income that Australians have earned from abroad, until now. The green line shows that through this same period, Australia has also consistently run a financial account surplus (and now, a deficit), meaning that historically, more funds have been invested each year in Australia from abroad than Australians have invested overseas.

Put these two pieces together, and the current account deficit describes a net outflow of funds that is exactly offset by the net inflow of funds from the financial account surplus. This connection is not a coincidence: You can think about the current account deficit as the gap between the income and the expenditure of Australians. The financial account is how we pay for it.

Figure 17 | **Financial Account and Current Account Balances**

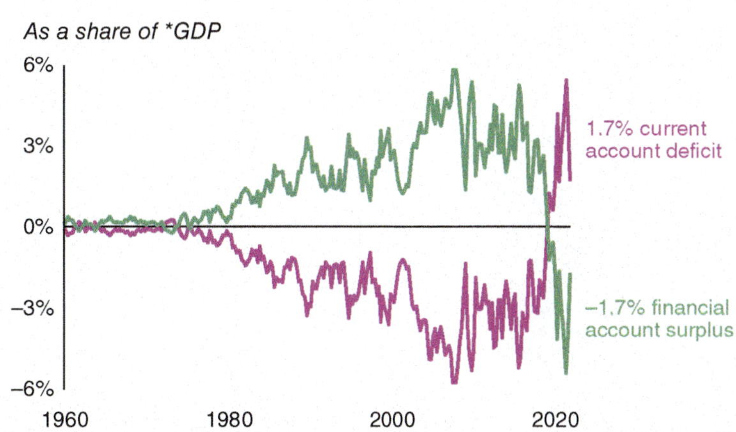

Data from: Australian Bureau of Statistics.

Figure 18 | **Inflows Equal Outflows**

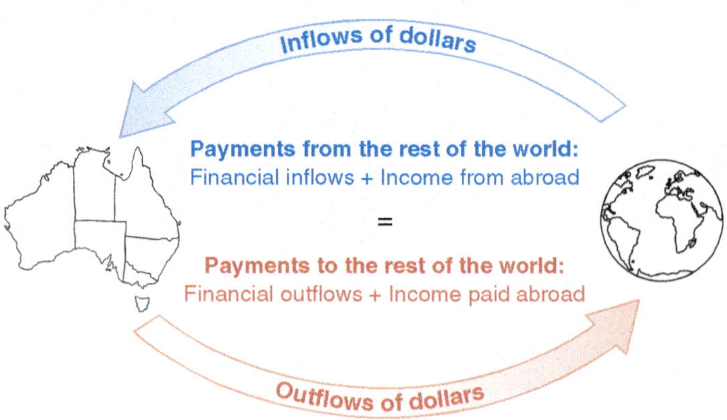

Inflows of dollars must equal outflows of dollars. This close connection between the current account and the financial account balance reflects a deeper truth: You can only buy a dollar if someone sells it to you, just as you can only sell a dollar if someone buys it from you. And so inflows of dollars from abroad (which requires buying dollars) must be equal to the outflow of dollars (which requires selling them).

Figure 18 shows that the total inflow of dollars (which reflects both financial inflows and income received from abroad) must be equal to the total outflow of dollars (which reflects both financial outflows and income paid abroad). And so it follows that:

$$\underbrace{\text{Financial inflows} + \text{Income from abroad}}_{\text{Total inflow of dollars}} = \underbrace{\text{Financial outflows} + \text{Income paid abroad}}_{\text{Total outflow of dollars}}$$

Equality between inflows and outflows implies equality between the current and financial accounts. If we take this inflows-equals-outflows equation and do a quick bit of rearranging, we get the following insight:

$$\underbrace{\text{Income from abroad} - \text{Income paid abroad}}_{\text{Current account deficit}} = \underbrace{\text{Financial outflows} - \text{Financial inflows}}_{\text{Financial account surplus}}$$

The left-hand side of this equation is the current account deficit, while the right-hand side is the financial account surplus. It says that the current account deficit must *always* be matched by an equal financial account surplus. It follows from a simple idea: The uses of cash must be equal to the sources of cash—and the current account describes the uses of cash, while the financial account describes its sources.

EVERYDAY Economics The global consequences of buying a kimono

Ray Evans/Alamy Stock Photo

The A$100 you send to pay for this kimono will eventually return to Australia.

For every international action, there's an equal and opposite reaction which ensures the current account deficit and financial account surplus remain equal. To see this, let's track your $100 after you spent it buying imports. Perhaps you logged on to Etsy and paid a Japanese artisan A$100 to make you a kimono. Because your new kimono is an import, it added $100 to the current account deficit (or equivalently, removed $100 off the current account surplus). What's the equal and opposite reaction?

It depends on what the Japanese artisan does with your $100. They really only have three possibilities:

- They might invest it, buying $100 worth of Australian assets, which would boost Australian financial inflows by $100. In this scenario your initial purchase, which added $100 to the Australian current account deficit, is exactly offset by a foreign investment which adds $100 to the Australian financial account surplus, maintaining their equality.
- They might buy $100 of Australian goods and services. In this case, your initial purchase boosted Australian imports by $100, and their purchase boosted Australian exports by $100, and in total, the Australian current account deficit is unchanged.
- They might trade that A$100 on the foreign exchange market to a third person. This just transfers the question of what to do with that A$100 to that third person, who faces the same choices about whether to invest it in Australia or spend it on

goods exported from Australia. Whichever choice that third person makes, it'll ensure that the current account deficit and financial account surplus continue to be equal.

The travels of this $100 highlight a deeper truth: every dollar that's spent overseas eventually returns to be spent in Australia, and this truth ensures that the current account deficit is equal to the financial account surplus. ■

Saving, Investment, and the Current Account

There's another perspective on all this that's worth considering. Recall that the total output of the Australian economy is measured as:

$$Y = C + I + G + NX$$

A current account deficit arises when we spend more than we earn. In order to simplify things, let's abstract away from investment income, so that the current account deficit is determined purely by net exports. We can rearrange the expression above to make the current account deficit the focus (remembering that the *Current account deficit* $= -NX$):

$$\text{Current account deficit} = \underbrace{C + I + G}_{\substack{\text{Total}\\\text{spending}}} - \underbrace{Y}_{\substack{\text{Total}\\\text{income}}}$$

This says Australia has a current account surplus because total income exceeds total spending. Just as with your own finances, if you're spending less than you're earning, then you're effectively saving. In the balance of payments, the excess saving is called the current account surplus, and the cash outflow is called the financial account deficit.

The current account deficit reflects the imbalance between saving and investment. Another important perspective on the current account focuses on the role of saving. If we add and subtract tax revenues (abbreviated as T) on the right-hand side of the previous equation:

$$\text{Current account deficit} = C + I + G + (T - T) - Y$$

And then rearrange this expression, we get:

$$\text{Current account deficit} = I - \underbrace{(Y - C - T)}_{\substack{\text{Private}\\\text{saving}}} - \underbrace{(T - G)}_{\substack{\text{Government}\\\text{saving}}} = I - \underbrace{S}_{\substack{\text{National}\\\text{saving}}}$$

The first expression in parentheses is *personal saving*, which comes from households who save whatever income they don't either spend or pay in taxes. The second expression in parentheses is *government saving*, which is the tax revenues less government spending. (When it runs a budget deficit, government saving is negative.) All told, this says that the current account deficit arises because investment exceeds total national saving (which is the sum of private and government saving, and we denote as S).

When you observe the current account deficit (or alternatively, the trade deficit), you might be tempted to focus on the tradeable sector of the economy to see if there's a problem. This alternative perspective suggests that it's worth focusing on what's driving saving and investment decisions, instead.

Investment is funded by a combination of domestic saving and savings from abroad. Another way to see the link between domestic investment and saving decisions and the balance of payments is to focus on the financial account balance. Recall that a country's current account deficit must be equal to its financial account surplus (so current account deficit = financial account surplus), and rearrange the previous expression to make investment the focus:

$$I = S + \text{Financial account surplus}$$

All investment spending needs to be funded somehow. The right-hand side of this equation illustrates that investment must be funded either out of national savings, or from the savings of foreigners. By this view, financial inflows from abroad are useful because they help fund investment.

Current Account Controversies

The current account deficit—and its mirror-image twin, the financial account surplus—are both politically polarising and poorly understood. And so it's worth asking: Should Australia be worried about a current account deficit? Right now Australia has a current account surplus, but for many years there was a (sometimes large) deficit.

A current account deficit can reflect people living beyond their means. Some people bemoan the "international imbalances" that lead to current account deficits. They note that as Australians spend more than they earn, they fund the gap by selling assets and borrowing from overseas. As a result foreigners are increasingly taking ownership of Australian factories and equipment, and Australians are going into debt to foreigners. This *might* be a signal of a country living beyond its means, especially if the spending is wasteful, and if people borrowing money have no idea how they'll ever pay it back. Even the possibility that the borrowing is unsustainable can cause trouble, as it might lead to a *sudden stop* in which foreign investors lose confidence that they'll be repaid and suddenly stop making loans. While sudden stops are more common in developing countries, the consequences can be severe, as a rapid decline in financial inflows requires difficult adjustments that in many cases lead the economy to tank.

A current account deficit can reflect valuable investments in the future. Others argue that Australia's current account deficit might best be thought of as a sign of economic health. The flipside of Australia's current account deficit is a financial account surplus, and this inflow of funding from foreign investors has increased the supply of loanable funds, and spurred more investment. In an economy that's ripe with opportunity, spending more than your current income can be a really good idea, particularly if that spending is directed to high-quality investments that will boost your future income. Under these conditions, reducing the current account deficit (and hence the financial account surplus) would do more harm than good, preventing businesses from making valuable investments that could be the foundation of future economic growth.

And so we're left with the difficult conclusion that a current account deficit might be a symptom of future economic trouble, or it might be a signal of future economic strength. It really depends on how sound the millions of decisions that make up that deficit are.

bilateral trade balance How much we buy from a specific country compared to how much they buy from us.

Don't worry about bilateral trade balances. One thing nearly all economists agree on is that you shouldn't worry about **bilateral trade balances**—how much we buy from one specific country compared to how much they buy from us. For instance, Australia is one of the few countries that exports more to China than they import from China, and so Australia has a bilateral trade surplus with China. But from a macroeconomic perspective, this is largely irrelevant. What matters is whether the totality of Australia's international transactions are sustainable, not just the part related to China.

The question you should ask when you're trading is whether you're getting a good deal, not whether the other side is buying as much from you as you are from them. As one economist memorably put it, "I have a chronic deficit with my barber, who doesn't buy a darned thing from me."

Tying It Together

We might be able to make better sense of some of the themes in this chapter by studying the most interesting economy in the world: That's the nation of Youville, population one. It was formed when you—and only you—seceded from Australia. Not much changed—you still live at your current address and go about your regular life—but now anything that enters or exits your home counts as an international transaction. The economy of Youville will help illustrate what we can learn from a country's balance of payments.

Let's start by considering Youville's imports, the most obvious of which are the food and clothes you import from stores beyond your national borders. Youville, also imports services, the most important of which is the big tuition bill you pay each year for imported educational services. As for Youville's exports, if you hold a part-time job—say, tutoring local high school students—then you're exporting tutoring services. If you're at all like most students, the money you send "abroad" to pay for food, clothing, and tuition exceeds the income you're receiving, and so Youville is running a current account deficit.

If you're spending more than you're earning, how do you pay the bills? Most people in university rely on a student loan from the Government in the form of HECS-HELP. These count as financial inflows into Youville, and so Youville runs a financial account surplus. Your current account deficit must be equal to your financial account surplus, because you can only spend more than your income if you have financing coming in to pay those bills.

Should Youville be worried about its current account deficit? It depends. If you're cutting class and loading up on debt so that you can party now without worrying about the money you'll have to pay back later, you're making a mistake. In this case, the current account deficit is a signal that Youville will eventually face economic trouble when those bills come due.

But if you're studying hard, and improving your skills, you'll be well-placed to get a higher-paying job later. Remember, over their lifetime a typical university graduate will outearn a typical high school graduate by more than a million dollars. In this case, there's no reason to worry about Youville's current account deficit, as repaying those debts won't be too difficult. Indeed, the current account deficit is simply a side effect of using "foreign" financing to help fund productive investments that will underpin Youville's future economic growth.

Finally, Youville illustrates a much broader trend. It's a nation that's fully integrated into the world's economy. The population in Youville specialised in a few tasks and it relies on the global economy beyond its borders for most things. It's like globalisation on steroids. Now I'm not suggesting that the Australian economy is ever going to become this integrated into the global economy. But you can bet that through your lifetime, Australia is going to become more like Youville, and international trade and global financial flows will become even more important. And that in turn, means that the material you've learned in this chapter is only going to become even more valuable.

Chapter at a Glance

Trade balance = Net export = Exports sold to foreign buyers − Imports bought from foreign sellers

Exchange Rates

Nominal exchange rate: The price of a country's currency (in terms of another country's currency).

Convert Australian dollars to yen:

Number of yen = Number of dollars × Nominal exchange rate

$$\text{Nominal exchange rate} = \frac{\text{Number of yen}}{\text{Number of dollars}}$$

Australian Dollar → Yen

Yen → Australian Dollar

↑ Appreciation: Become more expensive

↓ Depreciation: Become cheaper

Convert yen to Australian dollars:

$$\text{Number of dollars} = \frac{\text{Number of yen}}{\text{Nominal exchange rate}}$$

Foreign Exchange Market

A market where you can exchange one currency for another.

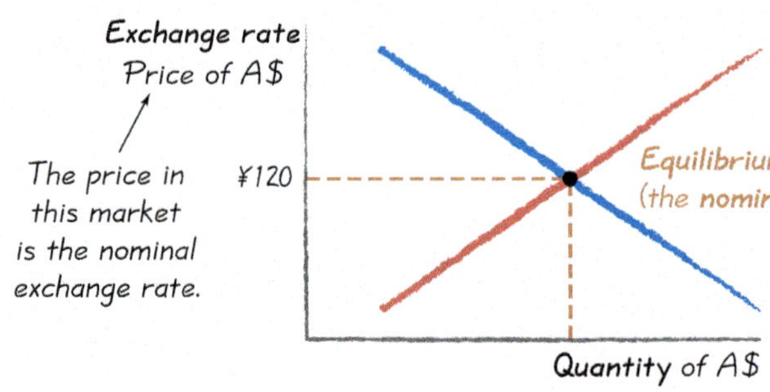

Supply of dollars: Increases when Australians buy foreign products and assets (imports and capital outflows).

Equilibrium: Determines the price of Australian dollars (the **nominal exchange rate**).

Demand for dollars: Increases when foreigners buy Australian products and assets (exports and capital inflows).

Real Exchange Rates and Net Exports

Low	High
Internationally competitive Australian prices (in A$) are low relative to foreign prices (also in A$)	**Internationally uncompetitive** Australian prices (in A$) are high relative to foreign prices (also in A$)
Australians import few foreign goods; Foreigners buy a lot of Australian exports	Australians import a lot of foreign goods; Foreigners buy few Australian exports

$$\textbf{Real exchange rate} = \frac{\text{Domestic price in dollars}}{\text{Foreign price converted to dollars}} = \frac{\text{Domestic price in dollars}}{\text{Foreign price in foreign currency/Nominal exchange rate}}$$

The Balance of Payments

Current account balance = Income from abroad − Income paid abroad

Financial account balance = Financial inflows − Financial outflows

Inflows = Income from abroad + Financial inflows (World → Australia)

Outflows = Income paid abroad + Financial outflows (Australia → World)

Inflows = Outflows

Income from abroad + Financial inflows = Income paid abroad + Financial outflows

Financial inflows − Financial outflows = Income paid abroad − Income from abroad

(Financial account surplus) = (Current account deficit)

Key Concepts

Discussion and Review Questions

Learning Objective 28.1 *See the connections between the domestic economy and the global economy.*

1. What are the factors that led international trade and global financial flows to rise over recent decades? Do you expect international trade and global financial flows to continue to grow? Why or why not?
2. Australians own almost seven times as many foreign assets as they did four decades ago. Some people worry that this makes Australians more vulnerable to the ups and downs in the economies of other countries, while others argue that Australians are more protected against risks. Assess which of these arguments you find more persuasive. (*Hint:* Consider the macroeconomic perspective and the risk management perspective.)

Learning Objective 28.2 *Analyse prices that are quoted in different currencies.*

3. Think about your favourite country, and search online for its exchange rate. What is its nominal exchange rate—that is, the price of its currency in terms of Australian dollars? Has the currency appreciated or depreciated relative to the Australian dollar over the course of the past year? Are imports to this country more or less expensive than a year ago? Explain your reasoning.

Learning Objective 28.3 *Analyse the market for currencies and forecast the nominal exchange rate.*

4. In 2020, China enacted trade barriers to restrict imports from Australia. Use the three-step recipe for forecasting exchange rate movements to explain how you expect the price of the Australian dollar in yuan to respond to these trade barriers. Australian policy makers responded by lodging a complaint against China with the WTO. How do you think this response affected the price of the Australian dollar in yuan?

Learning Objective 28.4 *Assess how exchange rates and relative prices affect exports and imports.*

5. Technology-driven improvements in farm productivity led the cost of growing wheat in Australia to fall, leading Australian farmers to cut their prices. If the nominal exchange rate is unchanged, what will this mean for the Australian real exchange rate?
6. You and your friend decide to backpack around Europe. You've been debating whether Europe or Australia is more expensive. She spies a McDonald's and says that she can prove that Europe is more expensive by comparing the price of a Big Mac in Paris with what it costs in your university town of Adelaide, South Australia. How would you go about comparing these two prices? Why would this information help inform your debate?

Learning Objective 28.5 *Track how money flows around the world using the current account and the financial account.*

7. At a family gathering, one of your cousins says, "We spend so much more on imports than other countries spend on our exports. It isn't fair and we should raise tariffs on imports to reduce how much we buy from other countries." How would you explain to your cousin that current account deficits aren't necessarily a sign of economic troubles to come? Think of the best way to describe this intuitively to someone who may not have taken an economics course before. What effect would her policy suggestion—raising tariffs on imports—have on the current account and the financial account? What would happen if our trading partners retaliated by then raising tariffs on goods exported from Australia?

Imports to and exports from Japan

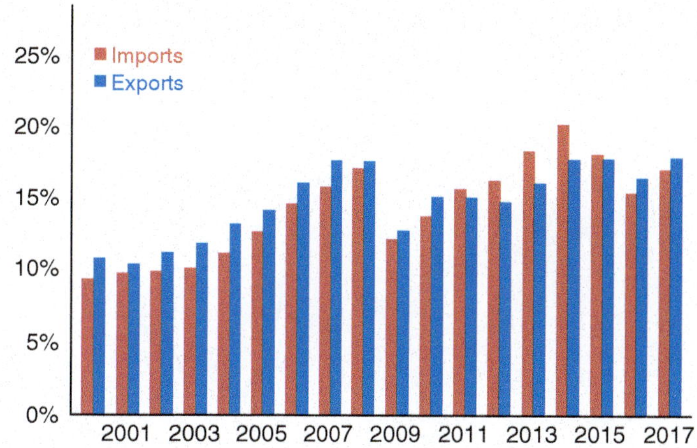

Data from: World Bank.

Study Problems

Learning Objective 28.1 *See the connections between the domestic economy and the global economy.*

1. The preceding graph depicts Japanese imports and exports.
   a. Describe the general trend in imports and exports for Japan since 2000.
   b. In which years did Japan run a trade surplus? A trade deficit?
2. Determine whether each of the following is an example of an import, export, financial inflow, or financial outflow. If it is a financial flow, is it an example of foreign direct investment or portfolio investment?
   a. An Australian Wool company began building a factory dedicated to large-scale carbonisation of wool in Suzhuo.
   b. A German business pays an Australian consultant for financial advice.
   c. An Australian family spends $2,000 on hotels and meals while taking a holiday in London.
   d. Australian oil refineries purchased A$2 billion of crude petroleum from Middle-Eastern oil companies.
   e. You sell a hand-knitted scarf on Etsy to a woman who lives in France.
   f. A saver in New Zealand purchases $100 in Australian government bonds.

Learning Objective 28.2 *Analyse prices that are quoted in different currencies.*

3. Theresa, who lives in Australia, finds a jacket she really wants to buy, but it is only available from Amazon UK, where it is selling for £65. Luckily the seller is willing to ship internationally for an additional £10. If the exchange rate is A$1 for £0.56, how much does the jacket cost in Australian dollars?
4. You just spent two weeks in Fiji on holiday. Your trip is over, and you realise that you overestimated how much local cash you would need while in Fiji. Now you want to convert your remaining 1,500 Fijian dollars (FJD) back to Australian dollars. The exchange rate is A$1 for 2 FJD. How many Australian dollars will you receive?
5. Consider the following graph of the Australian/euro nominal exchange rate.

Australian/Euro Exchange Rate
Price of a euro

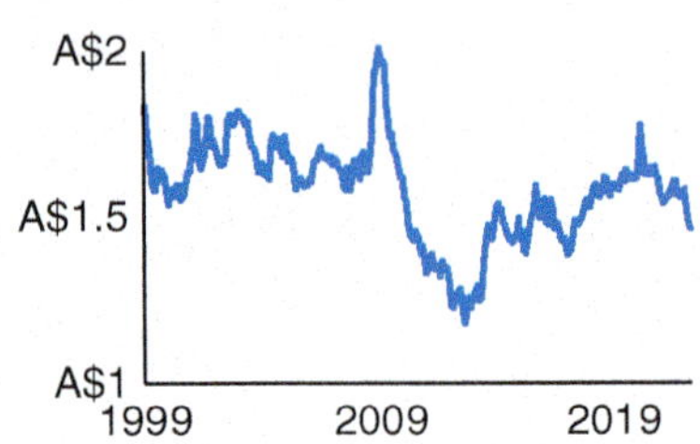

Data from: Refinitiv, and Investing.com.

   a. If you travelled to Europe in 2013 and converted A$1,000 to euros, how many euros would you get? What if you were traveling in 2016?
   b. Did the Australian dollar appreciate or depreciate relative to the euro between 2013 and 2016?

Learning Objective 28.3 *Analyse the market for currencies and forecast the nominal exchange rate.*

6. What happens to the amount Australians pay for imported goods if the price of the Australian dollar depreciates? Will Australians import more or fewer goods if the Australian dollar depreciates?
7. How does a recession in Japan affect the market for Australian dollars? What do you expect will happen to the price of an Australian dollar in yen? Illustrate your answer with a graph.
8. If the Reserve Bank of Australia unexpectedly cuts the interest rate, what effect do you expect this will have on the Australian dollar?

Learning Objective 28.4 *Assess how exchange rates and relative prices affect exports and imports.*

9. You are a purchasing manager for Transurban Group and need to decide whether you should buy stainless steel from a supplier in China or source it from a foundry in Queensland, to construct a new bridge. If you buy it from the Queensland company, you'll pay $3,000 per tonne. If you buy from China, you'll pay 10,000 yuan per tonne. Both prices include transportation costs. The nominal exchange rate is A$1 for 5 yuan.
   a. Calculate the real exchange rate—the price of domestic steel in dollars, relative to the price of imported steel converted into dollars—and use this to decide whether you should buy the domestic or imported steel.
   b. A rise in the cost of Chinese labour leads to a rise in the price of Chinese steel to 20,000 yuan per tonne. The nominal exchange rate is still A$1 for 5 yuan. What has happened to the real exchange rate? Does this make it more or less likely that Transurban Group purchases steel from the foundry in Queensland?

Learning Objective 28.5 *Track how money flows around the world using the current account and the financial account.*

10. In 2018, Germany had the world's largest current account surplus of A$392 billion. Using this one piece of information, answer the following questions.
    a. Which was greater, the income Germans earned from abroad or incomes paid abroad from Germany?
    b. What is Germany's financial account balance? Is it a surplus or deficit?
    c. Were financial inflows or financial outflows greater for Germany?
    d. Was total spending or total income greater in Germany in 2018?

PART VIII: The Business Cycle

Think of the macroeconomy as if it were a concert with an array of musicians on stage playing different roles. Instead of a singer, guitarist, drummer, keyboard player, and bassist, the players are consumers, investors, importers, exporters, and government policy makers. The interactions of all these players create harmony and melody, generating the broader movements that form the music of macroeconomics.

But we can watch the concert from different vantage points. A seat that's up high and to the west of the stage gives a different perspective on how the music is made than one that's over on the east side of the stage. Both seats provide a good view of the show—it's largely a matter of opinion about which perspective reveals more about the music you're hearing. So it is with macroeconomics: The facts of the economy don't change, but you can examine them from different angles.

This brings us to a decision: Where will you sit for this concert? The next set of chapters offers the opportunity to examine business cycles from one of two different vantage points; your instructor will choose the perspective they judge best suited to your needs. Each perspective gives you a good view of the stage—and if you choose to continue your study of economics beyond this course, you will explore them both in time.

The first option is what we call **The RBA View.** Think of this as the view from backstage. Just as government policy makers do, we use an *IS* curve to track the real economy, an *MP* curve to illustrate the Reserve Bank's interest rate decisions, and a Phillips curve to analyse inflation.

The second option is **The *AD-AS* View**, short for aggregate demand and aggregate supply. It's a perspective that instructors often find useful when teaching first-time economics students. Think of this as a centre seat in the mezzanine, from which you can clearly see the interplay between output and the price level.

The roadmaps ahead present an overview of each path through this material. Either path will get you to the same place, which is a clear understanding of business cycles. And they both prepare you for the final part of our journey in Part IX, on economic policy, where we'll use what we've learned about business cycles to see how policy makers can help counter the ups and downs of the business cycle. We'll explore how the RBA adjusts interest rates as part of its monetary policy. And then we'll turn to how the government adjusts its spending and taxation as part of its fiscal policy.

Part VIII: The Business Cycle (Option 1)

The Fed View

In this pathway, we'll start with a broad overview of **business cycles.** You'll learn to distinguish between short-term fluctuations and longer-term trends, to recognise some common characteristics of business cycles, and to use some key macroeconomic indicators to assess where the economy is and where it might be going.

From there, we'll take our seats at the concert and learn to find the **macroeconomic equilibrium** using the ***IS-MP*** **framework.** If the economy were a concert, you might think of this as the view from the Reserve Bank because it's the perspective from which government policy makers view the economy. We'll start with a brief introduction to **aggregate expenditure** and how it responds to changes in the interest rate, before learning how to use the ***IS*** **curve** and the ***MP*** **curve** to build a framework for forecasting macroeconomic outcomes.

Continuing down this path, you'll learn to use the Phillips curve to forecast inflation, taking account of the role of inflation expectations, the output gap, and supply shocks.

In order to bring all the pieces together–to truly see the show the same way the RBA does–then we bring together real interest rates, the output gap, and inflation in a brief capstone chapter on the **RBA model.**

29 Tracking the Business Cycle

Learn how to track the ups and downs of the economy.

- What are business cycles? What happens during recessions and expansions?
- How do the ups and downs of the business cycle affect you?
- What economic indicators should you follow?
- How can you use these indicators to track the economy?

30 Linking Interest Rates and Output through *IS-MP* Analysis

Analyse the links between spending, interest rates, financial markets, and output that shape the business cycle.

- What causes business cycles?
- Why does the real interest rate shape spending?
- How do financial markets and the RBA affect interest rates?
- What can policy makers do to counter the ups and downs of business cycles?
- How can you forecast where the economy is going?

31 The Phillips Curve and Inflation

Assess the causes of inflation.

- What causes inflation?
- How can expectations of inflation actually cause inflation?
- How do economy-wide changes in demand affect inflation?
- How do changes in suppliers' production costs affect inflation?
- Can you forecast where inflation's going next?

32 The RBA Model: Putting the Pieces Together

Put the pieces together into a complete model of business cycles.

- How do real-world policy makers view the economy?
- What are the links between the demand and supply sides of the macroeconomy?
- What types of shocks can hit the economy, and what effects will they have?
- How do real-world economists diagnose the causes of economic fluctuations?

Part VIII: The Business Cycle (Option 2)

Tracking the Business Cycle 29

Learn how to track the ups and downs of the economy.

- What are business cycles? What happens during recessions and expansions?
- How do the ups and downs of the business cycle affect you?
- What economic indicators should you follow?
- How can you use these indicators to track the economy?

Aggregate Demand and Aggregate Supply 33

Analyse how aggregate demand and aggregate supply determine macroeconomic outcomes.

- How are the tools that microeconomists use to analyse individual markets similar to those that macroeconomists use to analyse the whole economy?
- What determines the total quantity of output that purchasers want to buy?
- What determines the total quantity of output that businesses want to supply?
- How can you forecast the economy's total level of output and average price level?
- How will the economy respond to changing business conditions?
- How does this response vary as the economy has more time to adjust?

The *AD-AS* View

This alternative option for examing business cycles provides you with a different but equally useful view of the economy. We begin once again with a broad overview of **business cycles.** You'll learn to distinguish between short-term fluctuations and longer-term trends, to recognise some common characteristics of business cycles, and to use some key macroeconomic indicators to assess where the economy is and where it might be going.

From there, you'll skip ahead to Chapter 33, to explore the **aggregate demand and aggregate supply framework.** This perspective provides a familiar view of the economy. Think of it as the view from the centre mezzanine. You'll see how the tools of supply and demand can be effectively scaled up to demonstrate how **aggregate demand and aggregate supply** determine **macroeconomic equilibrium.** You'll learn to use this framework to forecast how the economy will respond to a variety of economic shocks.

A Closer Look at Aggregate Expenditure and the Multiplier A

Explore the influence of aggregate expenditure and the multiplier on the business cycle.

- Why does spending rise and fall and why does it matter?
- What happens when spending and production get out of sync?
- How can an economy get stuck in a depression?
- Why do changes in government spending have a multiplied effect on the broader economy?

Appendix

Depending on the path you take, Chapter 30 or Chapter 33 provided a brief introduction to two key concepts in economics: **aggregate expenditure** and **the multiplier.** For a deeper dive into these topics, dig into the more thorough treatment in this fully developed appendix (located at the back of this book).

CHAPTER 29

Tracking the Business Cycle

Before Mirvac decides to build a new apartment complex, it looks at the forecasts of people like Nerida Conisbee—chief economist at Ray White real estate. She's in charge of making sure that property investors are well informed about the economy. To prepare projections, Conisbee's team pores over spreadsheets containing thousands of pieces of economic data. When the government releases a new data point, like the most recent jobs numbers, Conisbee gets a new piece of the puzzle and quickly incorporates it into her analysis.

Her assessment of the strength of the economy and how long she expects it to stay strong is actionable information that will help her colleagues adjust their property development, sales, and financing plans. Mirvac's development team needs to know how many new apartments to build and that depends on the state of the economy. In a boom, lots of people will be in the market for a new apartment. If Mirvac needs to ramp up construction, then it will need to purchase new land, file development applications, and engage subcontractors. In a recession, however, people tend to postpone big purchases like housing. If Conisbee is worried that the economy is about to slow down, she might advise Mirvac to hold off on new projects until it can be more confident about its sales in the coming years.

https://heroshotphotography.com

She keeps her eye on the economy so that property investors are informed.

You might notice that Conisbee's not talking about trends from decade to decade, but rather, she's trying to figure out how the economy will perform over the next year or two. This brings us to our next topic. So far, we've been taking a long-term view of the economy. Now we're going to turn to short-run analysis and take a look at the economy's year-to-year fluctuations. Sometimes the economy is doing well; sometimes it's not. And that has a major impact on businesses and people's lives. First, we'll examine what business cycles are and their common qualities. Then, we'll dig into how you can track how well the economy is doing. Your goal is to develop the tools to track economic conditions so that, just like Nerida Conisbee, you've got the info you need to make better decisions.

Chapter Objective

Learn how to track the ups and downs of the economy.

29.1 Macroeconomic Trends and Cycles
Distinguish between economic trends and short-run fluctuations.

29.2 Common Characteristics of Business Cycles
Describe the common features of business cycles.

29.3 Analysing Macroeconomic Data
Learn to analyse macroeconomic data.

Nicolaus Czarnecki/ZUMAPRESS.com/ Alamy Stock Photo

The economy affects university graduates' job prospects.

29.1 Macroeconomic Trends and Cycles

Learning Objective *Distinguish between economic trends and short-run fluctuations.*

I remember looking forward to graduation, excited to join a world that seemed to be teeming with opportunity. The economy was strong, the stock market was booming, and jobs were plentiful. But by the time I started my job, all that had changed. The economy stalled, the stock market tanked, and unemployment rose: The economy was in a recession. I had secured a job before all this happened, but I was lucky to hold onto it. Friends had their offers rescinded, employers were firing recent hires, and nerves were fraying.

The economy eventually recovered, but the recession I graduated into wasn't the last recession. In fact, it's a pretty typical story. Hopefully you won't face tough economic times when you graduate, but at some point you will experience both dramatic downturns and periods of calm prosperity. The sharp reversal of fortune that my classmates and I experienced is an example of the brutal short-term economic fluctuations in economic activity—called the **business cycle**—that can occur. The business cycle knocks the economy off course from its longer-run trend.

business cycle Short-term fluctuations in economic activity.

potential output The level of output that occurs when all resources are fully employed.

Trend Growth and the Output Gap

Annual growth in GDP per person has averaged 1.5% in Australia for more than a century, as shown in Figure 1. Long-run economic growth reflects growth in an economy's **potential output**—which is the level of output that occurs when all resources are fully employed. As in ordinary usage, the word "potential" reflects what is possible: Potential output is what we can feasibly produce given our current resources. It reflects the quantity and quality of our inputs to production—how skilled our workers are, how many of them we have, and how much capital they have to work with, as well as all the ideas we have about how to combine those inputs. You learned about the long-run determinants of potential output in Chapter 22.

But in the short run, the economy may fail to meet its potential. Sometimes GDP is higher than potential output, and sometimes it's lower. These short-term wiggles around potential output make up the business cycle.

Figure 1 | **Real GDP per Person over the Long Run**

Shown on a log or ratio scale

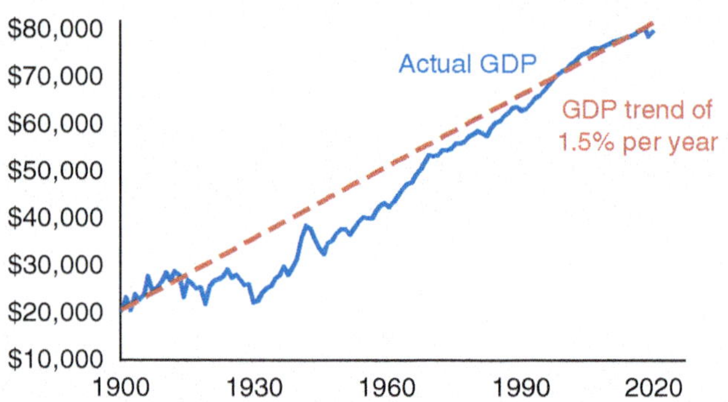

Data from: Australian Bureau of Statistics.

The ups and downs of the business cycle are very disruptive.

When viewed over the long run, the movements of the business cycle look small. In a typical recession, GDP may decline by a few percentage points. This may seem small, and indeed, the business cycles in Figure 1 look small compared to the overall trend. But when you're in the midst of a downturn, it can feel ferocious as businesses fail, workers lose their jobs, and the lives of your friends and family are uprooted.

The unemployment rate rises substantially in a recession. Figure 2 shows that the unemployment rate begins to rise in a recession—marked by gray bars—and often continues rising for a few years after the recession officially ends before it slowly declines. One of the striking things about Australia is that, until the coronavirus pandemic, we had a "world record" of nearly 30 years without a recession. Those who lose their jobs may struggle to find new jobs, and often it can take years for the unemployment rate to fall back to where it was prior to

Figure 2 | **The Unemployment Rate Fluctuates over the Business Cycle**

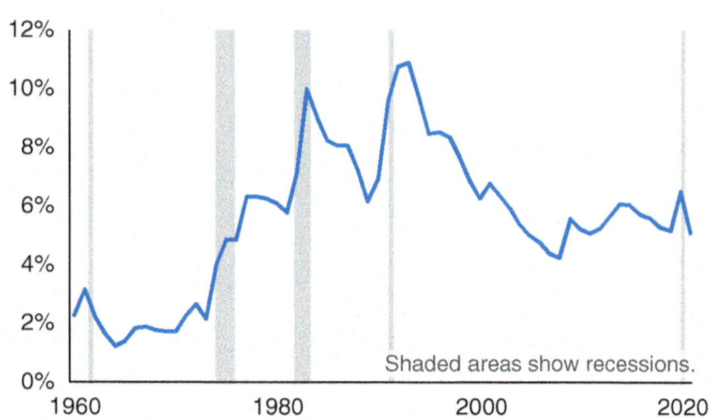

Data from: Australian Bureau of Statistics.

the recession. Many people are forced to take lower-paying jobs that don't make full use of their skills. Businesses that otherwise might have succeeded may not be able to weather the storm of a recession and will permanently shut their doors.

Recessions usually don't last long, but they have a lasting impact on people's earnings and careers. Researchers have found that even decades later, people who graduated in a recession tend to earn less than those who graduated in better economic times.

trekandshoot/Shutterstock

Producing above potential will eventually catch up with you.

The output gap measures fluctuations in GDP around its trend growth. The business cycle reflects the tendency for economies to deviate—sometimes for years at a time—from potential output. We measure this deviation using the **output gap,** which is the difference between actual and potential output, measured as a percentage of potential output:

$$\text{Outgap gap} = \frac{\text{Actual output} - \text{Potential output}}{\text{Potential output}} \times 100$$

When actual output is below its potential, the output gap is negative. A negative output gap means there are idle resources: Workers can't find jobs, equipment lies unused, and storefronts are shuttered. A negative output gap typically corresponds with high unemployment.

output gap The difference between actual and potential output, measured as a percentage of potential output.

A positive output gap means that actual output is above potential output. When the output gap is positive, the economy is using its resources with an unsustainable intensity: People work extra shifts, factories put off repairs, and prices start to rise. This can only continue for a limited time because eventually the repairs need to be made and people want to reduce their hours. One way to think about a positive output gap is to consider how hard you work in the few days leading up to an exam. You might get too little sleep, postpone doing your laundry, and ignore your friends and family. Your actual output is higher than your sustainable output, and eventually, you'll need a good night's rest, clean clothes, and a social life. No one can stay above potential forever, but sometimes we can push ourselves hard for a short period. The same thing is true for an economy.

The top half of Figure 3 shows the evolution of potential output over time as a dashed red line, contrasting it with actual output shown on the blue line. The difference between them is a measure of how the economy is performing relative to its potential at each point in time.

The bottom half of the figure shows these deviations as measured by the output gap. Purple shading indicates periods in which actual output was below potential output; green areas show periods in which actual output was above potential. A positive output gap of +2% means that actual GDP is running 2% above potential GDP. A negative output gap of −5% means that actual GDP is running 5% below potential GDP. An output gap of zero means that actual output equals potential output, so the economy is producing at its maximum sustainable level. This is great news: It's the highest sustainable rate of production.

Figure 3 | **The Output Gap**

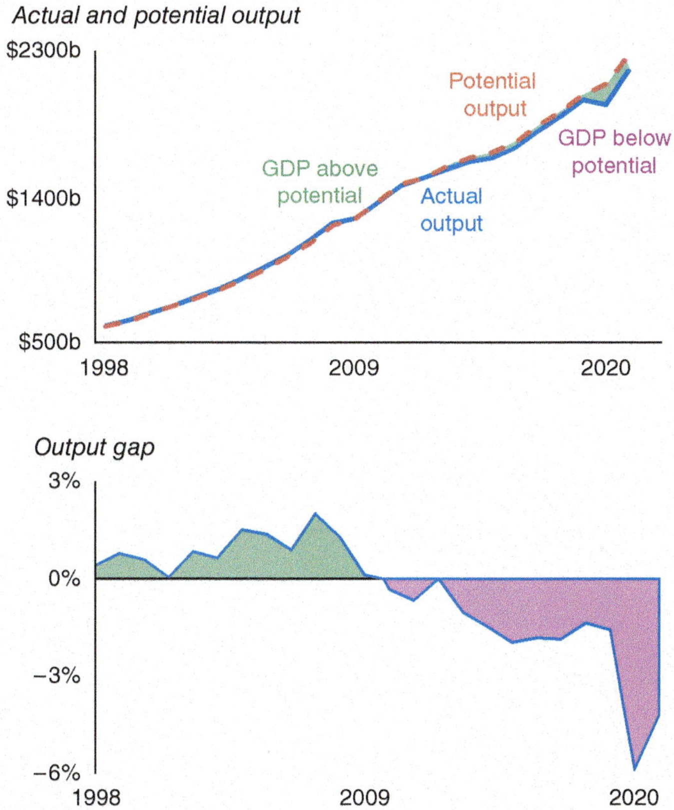

Data from: OECD Database, CEIC.

The figure shows that producing exactly at potential isn't something that happens for many years in a row. However, often there is only a small output gap, meaning that the economy is producing near its potential. Figure 3 also shows how long and deep the 2020 recession was compared to the negative output gap that occurred in 1991, Australia's next most recent recession.

A business cycle runs from a peak, through a recession, to a trough, then into an expansion. Let's take a closer look at the typical stages of a business

peak A high point in economic activity.

trough A low point in economic activity.

recession A period of declining economic activity.

expansion A period of increasing economic activity.

cycle. A **peak** is a high point in economic activity, which is followed by a fall in output. Eventually output hits a **trough**—a low point in economic activity. Economic activity declines between a peak and a trough, a period we call a **recession.** The gray bar in Figure 4 shows the period of the 2020 recession. Recessions are sometimes called "contractions" because the economy shrinks or contracts. If it's a particularly bad recession, we might call it a depression.

Figure 4 shows the economy was growing in the mid-2010s, but GDP hit a peak in 2020. When economic activity is increasing, it's called an **expansion.** It will keep going until some shock—for example, a global pandemic, a collapse in consumer confidence, a sudden crash in financial markets, or a spike in oil prices—halts further growth, and the economy hits another peak. Sometimes people think that a recession might be coming because an expansion has been going on for so long. But the truth is that expansions don't die of old age after a certain period of time. Instead they keep going until they're killed by an adverse shock. An expansion encompasses all of the years between a trough and a peak.

Figure 4 | Stages of the Business Cycle

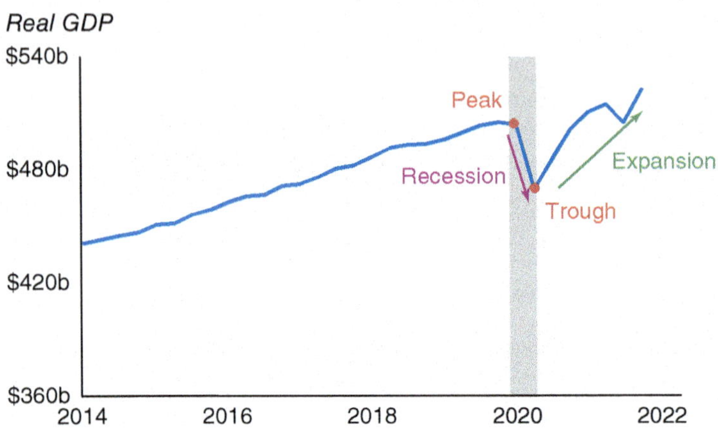

Data from: Australian Bureau of Statistics.

Levels tell you where the economy is; changes tell you where it is going. GDP measures the *level* of output, and thus potential GDP is the highest sustainable level of output. The output gap presents this level another way by scaling GDP relative to the level of potential output. The output gap therefore tells you how well the economy is doing relative to its potential. GDP growth rates are about *changes,* describing the rate at which the size of the economy is expanding or contracting.

As you work through this chapter, keep the difference between *levels* and *changes* in mind. Business cycle peaks and troughs describe *levels*—the recent high and low in the level of GDP. But whether an economy is in an expansion or a recession is not about levels; it's about *change*—whether GDP is growing or shrinking. So when the economy begins expanding, there is positive change, and the recession ends. However, the output gap doesn't close until actual output has grown fast enough and long enough to catch up to potential output. It can take many years of an expansion to eliminate a negative output gap.

Figure 5 | Duration of Economic Expansions

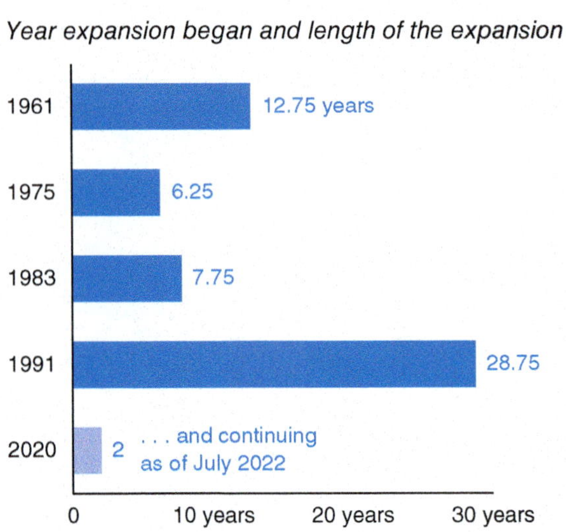

Data from: Australian Bureau of Statistics.

Business Cycles Are Not Cycles

Business cycle is an important term, but it's a somewhat misleading choice of words. The word *cycle* makes it sound like the economy rises and falls at regular intervals, like a seagull bobbing up and down on a wave, or like a mathematical sine curve. But the economy's fluctuations are anything but rhythmic, reliable, or predictable. Figure 5 shows that some expansions have lasted for only a year, while others have lasted for decades.

Recall that an economic expansion ends because of some adverse shock. And there is no rule of thumb about how long that will take. Recessions aren't an inevitable law of nature—the economy can keep growing as long as nothing goes wrong. Unfortunately, things often do go wrong. That's what makes it likely that you'll experience a number of recessions during your lifetime. But just because an expansion has gone on for a while doesn't mean that a recession is just around the corner. In fact, in recent decades, expansions have lasted longer than they did in the past. The expansion that began following the 1991 recession is the longest expansion on record in Australia.

Interpreting the DATA Has there been a Great Moderation?

Since the mid-1980s, the U.S. economy has become less volatile—a phenomenon sometimes dubbed "the Great Moderation." Australia's economy went through a similar change. You just saw that the last few economic expansions have lasted longer, which means that recessions have become less frequent. Figure 6 shows that GDP growth now fluctuates less than in previous decades.

Economists have offered several hypotheses to explain why economic growth may have become less volatile. One hypothesis is that the Reserve Bank has got better at managing the economy, meaning it has more effectively offset bad shocks.

Another hypothesis is that it's the economy that has changed: Globalisation ensures that there will be demand abroad for Australian products even if there's a recession at home. It may be that companies have got better at managing inventories, and the financial system better weathers shocks. Or maybe we've just been lucky, and the economy has been hit by fewer bad shocks. Indeed, the 2007–2009 Global Financial Crisis (GFC) led many to wonder whether the Great Moderation was over or whether it had just been a statistical fluke. But the expansion that followed the 2007–2009 GFC has been extremely strong—in fact, Australia didn't even go through a recession during the crisis, perhaps suggesting that there is something to the idea of a Great Moderation. ■

Figure 6 | **Real GDP Growth Has Become Less Volatile**

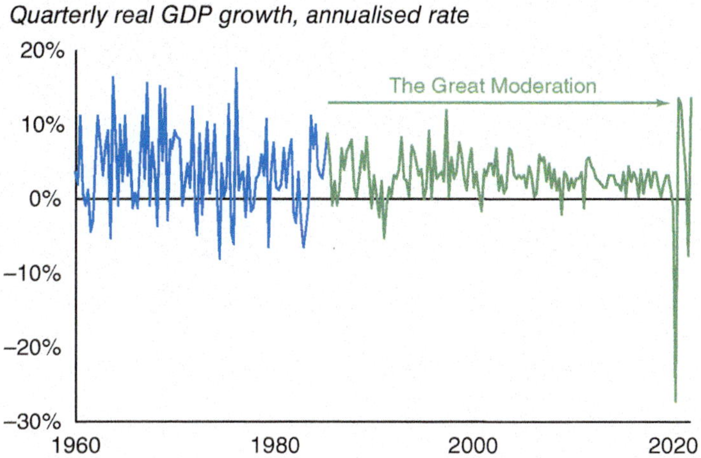

Data from: Australian Bureau of Statistics.

29.2 Common Characteristics of Business Cycles

Learning Objective *Describe the common features of business cycles.*

The novel *Anna Karenina* opens with the observation that "every unhappy family is unhappy in its own way." The observation applies to unhappy economies too, as each recession is unique. Recessions vary in their causes, their duration, and their depth. The same thing is true of expansions, meaning that no two business cycles are ever the same.

While each business cycle is unique, they also tend to have some common features. Let's take a look at what they are.

Figure 7 | **Short, Sharp Recessions and Long, Gradual Expansions**

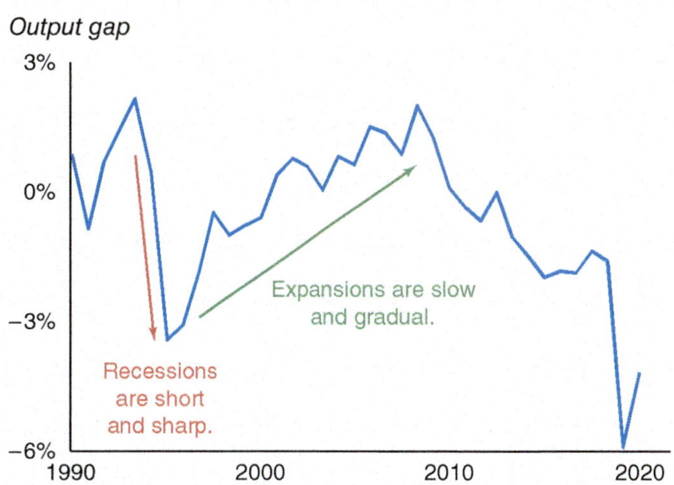

Data from: Reserve Bank of Australia.

Recessions Are Short and Sharp; Expansions Are Long and Gradual

As you can see in Figure 7, a typical business cycle involves a *short and sharp recession*, followed by a *long and gradual expansion*. Since World War II, the average recession has lasted less than one year, while the average economic expansion has lasted 11 years, reflecting the fact that an economic expansion could go on forever with the economy operating at potential. Recessions happen quickly and tend to involve steep declines in output and a sharp rise in unemployment. Expansions tend to be more gradual as the economy slowly recovers and grows. It can take years for the economy to heal and return to normal after a recession.

The disruptions that cause an economy to go into recession are varied and have included slowing productivity, oil price hikes, high interest rates, banking crises, and a pandemic.

The Business Cycle Is Persistent

Business cycle conditions are *persistent*, which means that it's a reasonable bet that current conditions will continue in the near future. To illustrate this, Figure 8 plots the output gap in a given year against the output gap in the following year. If this year's conditions were to always repeat themselves the next year, each dot would lie on the 45-degree line and the output gap would never change. The fact that most of the dots are clustered around the 45-degree line illustrates the fact that the output gap in any one year is typically similar to the output gap the next year. While the output gap does in fact change over time, these changes are both slow enough and unpredictable enough that your best prediction of next year's output gap is simply this year's gap. That's why economists describe business cycles as persistent.

This tendency for current conditions to persist makes predicting the short term a lot easier! Many forecasters begin with an assumption that whatever happened this year is the best starting point for figuring out what will happen next year. So however the economy is performing this year is how it will probably perform next year.

Figure 8 | **Business Cycles Are Persistent**

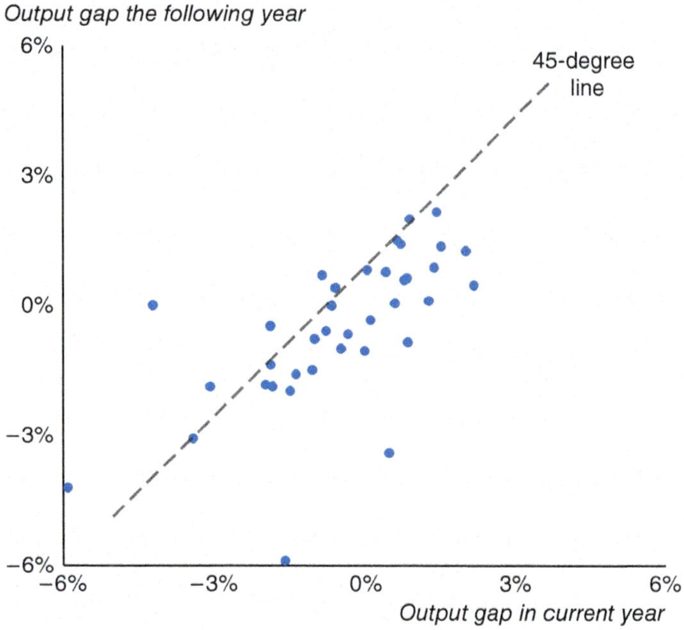

Data from: OECD Database, CEIC.

The Business Cycle Impacts Many Parts of the Economy

The *interdependence principle* reminds us that the many different parts of the economy are interconnected. As a result, many economic variables move up and down together over the business cycle. This *co-movement* means that if one part of the economy is doing well, then other parts of the economy are probably also doing well. Likewise, if one part of the economy is doing badly, it's likely that the same is true for other parts of the economy. Let's see how.

Figure 9 | **State Unemployment Rates Rise and Fall Together**

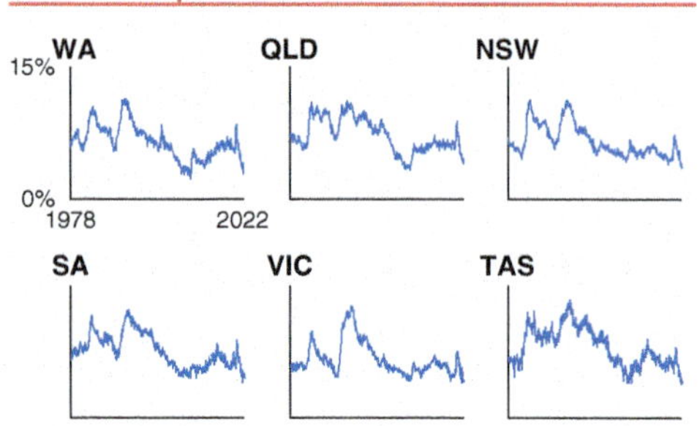

Data from: Australian Bureau of Statistics.

Different states rise and fall together. The business cycle also affects economic conditions in just about every state in the country, as shown in Figure 9.

When a recession hits, the effects ripple across the country, as Volvo produces fewer trucks in Queensland, banks in New South Wales make fewer loans, and families in Western Australia reduce their spending. And when there's an economic expansion, it also affects every state. Find your state or territory in Figure 9 and compare its unemployment rate with that in nearby states and territories and the rest of the country. While there are some differences across states and territories in how high unemployment goes, no state is immune from a recession.

Different economic indicators rise and fall together. There are many different indicators that track economic activity, and they tend to move together. Figure 10 shows that if GDP is rising, then it's also likely that industrial production is rising, retail sales are rising, and employment is rising. And it's not just these indicators—the creation of new businesses, housing construction, car sales, imports from overseas, new investment projects, business profits and workers' real wages, stock prices, inflation and interest rates—all tend to rise and fall with the business cycle. When we turn to analysing macroeconomic data, you'll learn the top 10 indicators that economy watchers track.

Figure 10 Many Economic Indicators Rise and Fall Together

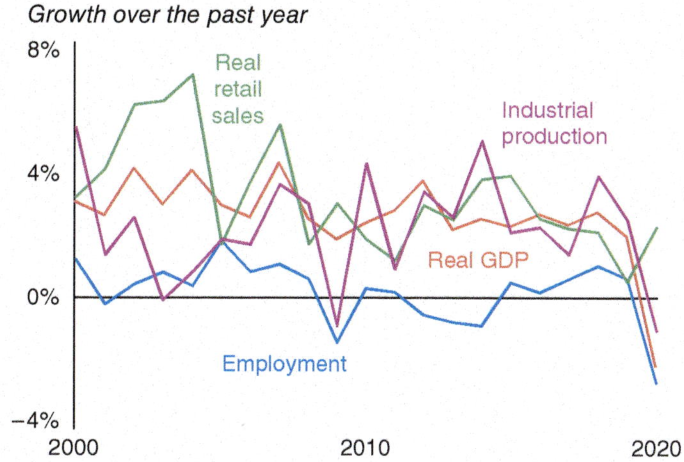

Data from: Australian Bureau of Statistics, CEIC.

Different industries rise and fall together. The business cycle affects just about every sector of the economy. Figure 11 illustrates that whatever industry you're in, a recession is usually bad for business, while an expansion is usually good for business. There's an exception, and it's not shown on the chart: The business cycle is really about the private sector, and so the public sector often follows a different pattern. That's because the output of the public sector is determined by the political process rather than by market conditions. In addition, the demand for some government services tends to rise when the rest of the economy falls.

You'll also notice that some sectors are more sensitive to business cycles than others. In particular, spending that's easy to put off—like building a new house or buying a car—tends to rise and fall more strongly with business cycle swings.

Figure 11 Most Private-Sector Industries Rise and Fall Together

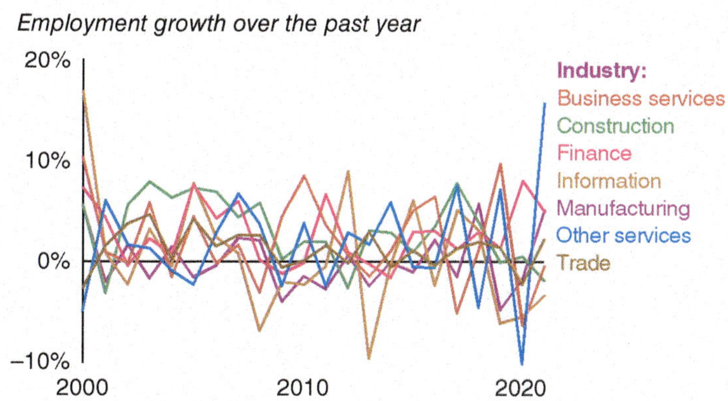

Data from: Australian Bureau of Statistics.

Some variables lead the cycle, while others lag. **Leading indicators** are variables that tend to predict the future path of the economy. Important leading indicators include business confidence, consumer confidence, and the stock market. Leading indicators help you get a better sense of where the economy is headed because they tend to change first. For example, consumers lose confidence in the economy before they start to substantially cut back their consumption.

leading indicators Variables that tend to predict the future path of the economy.

Lagging indicators are variables that tend to follow business cycle movements with a bit of a delay. Unemployment tends to be a lagging indicator because managers who have invested in developing their staff are reluctant to make cutbacks until they're convinced they're really necessary.

lagging indicators Variables that follow the business cycle with a delay.

Okun's Rule of Thumb Links the Output Gap and the Unemployment Rate

Economic activity starts to increase at the end of a recession, but the economy will continue to have unused resources until the output gap is closed. One of those

Figure 12 | **Okun's Rule of Thumb Links Unemployment and GDP**

Each dot shows a year's unemployment rate and output gap

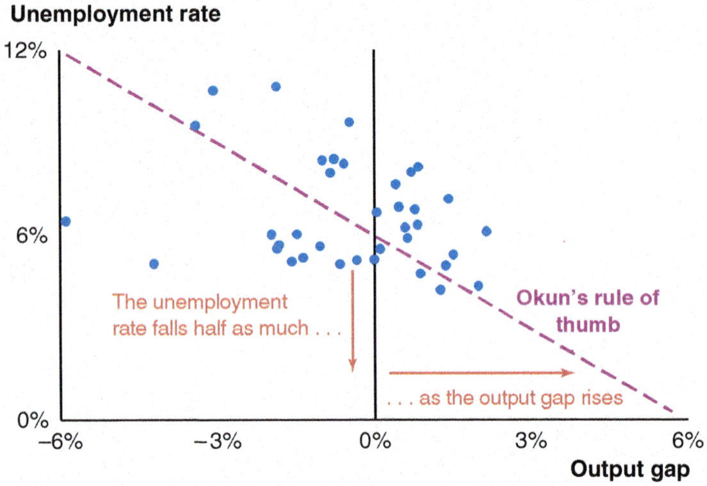

Data from: Australian Bureau of Statistics, OECD Database, CEIC.

resources is workers, and so the unemployment rate moves in sync with the output gap. Figure 12 illustrates this relationship, showing that when output is below potential, unemployment tends to be high, and when output is above potential, unemployment tends to be low.

When output is at potential, the unemployment rate is equal to the *equilibrium unemployment rate*. You learned in Chapter 23 that the equilibrium unemployment rate is the unemployment rate that the economy tends to return to over time, and it occurs when the economy is operating at potential. The equilibrium unemployment rate isn't zero because of both frictional and structural causes of unemployment. Indeed, over the past century the equilibrium unemployment rate in Australia has averaged around 5.5%.

Okun's rule of thumb quantifies the relationship between output and the unemployment rate. It says that for every percentage point that actual output is less than potential output, the unemployment rate will be around half a percentage point higher. For instance, if you project the output gap will decline from zero to −2%, the unemployment rate will likely rise by about 1 percentage point, from, say, 5% to 6%.

Okun's rule of thumb For every percentage point that actual output falls below potential output, the unemployment rate is around half a percentage point higher.

29.3 Analysing Macroeconomic Data

Learning Objective *Learn to analyse macroeconomic data.*

The business cycle influences just about every aspect of your life. It's something you'll need to factor in when figuring out whether to spend big because you expect smooth economic sailing, or whether to tighten your belt so you can withstand a coming economic storm. It influences whether you're likely to succeed in finding a better job or whether you need to worry about unemployment. It'll shape whether it's a good time to start a business, whether you'll be able to find qualified workers, and whether your input costs are likely to rise.

And so our next task is to figure out how best to analyse macroeconomic data and learn how to read the top indicators that most economists follow. You can look the numbers up for yourself by getting familiar with the Australian Bureau of Statistics database, which is available at: https://www.abs.gov.au/statistics/. We'll then pull all these ideas together to give you a toolkit for tracking the economy.

The Basics of Macroeconomic Data

If you log onto the ABS database to look up the latest economic statistics, one of the first things you might notice is that there are a lot of choices. Real or nominal? Seasonally adjusted or not? Quarterly or annual? Let's start with a guide to the most commonly used terms.

Seasonally adjusted data take out seasonal patterns. For lots of data series you need to choose between "seasonally adjusted" and "not seasonally adjusted." The reason some data are seasonally adjusted stems from a fact about economic life: There are strong seasonal patterns in some of the things that we do. For instance, Figure 13 shows that retail sales spike in December (Christmas time) and plummet in the new year. It's not just retail, though. Seasonal patterns are evident in many data series, such as teen employment, which spikes when school ends, and ice cream sales, which rise in the summer. In each case, **seasonally adjusted** data remove these predictable seasonal influences. The reason to do this is so that you can spot the changes in the underlying trends. Figure 13 shows that retail sales have been on a pretty stable upward trend once you take out the seasonal pattern.

If you're trying to assess the underlying strength of the economy, you're usually better off focusing on the seasonally adjusted numbers.

Figure 13 | Retail Sales

Quarterly Retail Sales (Chain Volume, 2019-20 dollers)

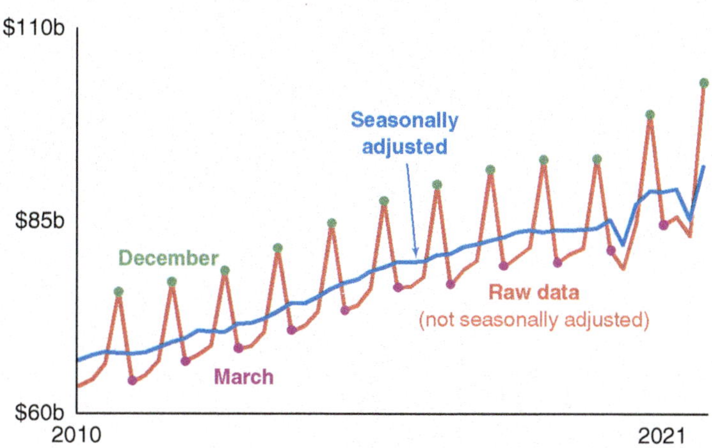

Data from: Australian Bureau of Statistics, CEIC.

The frequency of different data series varies, but you can compare annualised rates. Most data that you'll want to follow won't be collected annually—they will be weekly, monthly, or quarterly (every three months). But you'll sometimes see an option to choose what's called "annualised" data. These data are from a time period of less than a year converted into an **annualised rate**—that is, as if the same growth rate occurred throughout the year. This makes it easier to compare growth rates measured across different time periods.

seasonally adjusted Data stripped of predictable seasonal patterns.

annualised rate Data converted to the rate that would occur if the same growth rate had occurred throughout the year.

You typically want to focus on real data. You'll also run into the words "real" and "nominal" quite a bit. As you learned in Chapter 24, real variables adjust for inflation so that you're comparing quantities, holding prices constant. Nominal variables are expressed in the prices of the year of the data—so nominal GDP in 2010 reflects GDP measured in 2010 prices and nominal GDP in 2020 reflects GDP measured in 2020 prices. The problem with nominal data is that it's hard to tell whether an increase reflects rising prices or rising quantities, which is why you'll typically use real data, such as real GDP, to track the economy's performance over time. Real data series will typically be described as being measured in something like "chained 2019 dollars."

Pay attention to data revisions. Some data are frequently revised, so when you look up data, realise that it might be different from the last time you looked at it. Updates to earlier estimates are called **revisions,** and they can be quite substantial because initial estimates can be based on incomplete data.

revisions Updates to earlier estimates.

Top 10 Economic Indicators

Okay, now that you know something about how to analyse macroeconomic data, let's take a look at some key macroeconomic indicators. I often get asked what's the one indicator that I follow to know how the economy is doing. My response? You shouldn't only look at one indicator if you really want to know what's happening. That's because different types of data tell you different things. Let's take a look at the top 10 economic indicators that those who track the economy follow.

Top 10 Economic Indicators

1. Real GDP
2. Real GDI
3. Employment growth
4. Unemployment rate
5. Real retail sales
6. Business confidence
7. Consumer confidence
8. Inflation
9. Wage price index
10. The stock market

Indicator one: Real GDP is the broadest measure of economic activity. First, there's real GDP, which measures the total size of the economy. Real GDP is the broadest measure of economic activity since it measures total production, total spending, and total income across the whole economy. It's typically calculated by adding up all spending in the economy—you know, $Y = C + I + G + NX$. (See Chapter 21 for a refresher.) You should focus on GDP growth to see how fast the economy is growing. But keep in mind that GDP data can be very incomplete when they're first released.

Indicator two: Real GDI provides a useful cross-check on GDP. There's another closely related measure of the economy's total output. An alternative measure called Gross Domestic Income (or GDI, for short) is calculated by adding up total income. Because every dollar of spending is also a dollar of income for whomever received it, GDP and GDI should be equal. In practice, these measurements can differ because they're each constructed using different data sources with different shortcomings. Early reports of the income data are often more reliable than the spending data, and so GDI often flashes warning signs for the economy sooner than GDP does. In fact, many countries combine income and expenditure measurements to create their primary GDP statistic. Australia doesn't, so it's worth tracking both measures.

Bryan Esler/Moment Open/Getty Images

Is the labour market improving?

Indicator three: Employment tells you if the labour market is improving. Employment, or "total persons employed," tracks how many jobs are created each month. Employment is one of the most important indicators because it's released soon after the end of each month, so it provides an early and quite reliable look at how quickly the economy is creating jobs.

Indicator four: The unemployment rate is an indicator of excess capacity. The unemployment rate tells you the share of the labour force that wants a job and hasn't been able to find one. It's a snapshot of how strong the labour market is and how easy it is to find a job. It's important both as an economic indicator—a measure of excess capacity—and also because unemployment is a major source of misery for many people.

Indicator five: Real retail sales provide a timely indicator. Real retail sales tell you how much money people are spending, including on discretionary items. People got to Zara a lot less when they feel the economy isn't doing well. These numbers often bounce around a lot, but they're valuable because they're available quickly and offer timely insight into what was happening as recently as last week.

Evan Vucci/AP Photo

Business confidence tells you what managers are planning.

Indicator six: Business confidence tells you what managers are planning. Business confidence surveys ask managers about their plans over the next few months or years. Business confidence is a leading indicator, and when it starts to fall, a recession might be on the horizon. The most closely watched data series is called the Purchasing Managers' Index. In the U.S. the PMI contains the results of a survey of business executives in which they are asked about their plans to increase or decrease production, hiring, prices, and more. This survey isn't conducted in Australia, so an estimate of the PMI is usually calcuated using the Performance of Manufacturing Index. While you can download the Performance of Manufacturing Index from the ABS, you can't download the Purchasing Manager's Index. They are also asked whether the pace of change will slow down or quicken.

Indicator seven: Consumer confidence tells you what consumers are thinking. Consumer confidence surveys ask regular people how optimistic they are about the economy, which provides useful information about how much they're likely to spend in coming months. The consumer confidence index rises when consumers become more upbeat about the economy, signalling that they're likely to spend more, particularly on big-ticket items like cars or consumer durables. Like business confidence, consumer confidence is a leading indicator. There are a few surveys of consumer confidence, but one of the most frequently cited is the Westpac/Melbourne Institute Consumer Sentiment Index.

Indicator eight: The rate of inflation tells you what's happening with prices. Economists pay close attention to the consumer price index because it provides a sense of how much economy-wide prices are growing. For example, if businesses find that sales are booming so much that they're hitting capacity constraints, they may raise their prices faster or more often than they usually do, boosting inflation. As such, rising inflation may indicate that the economy is producing above potential, while falling inflation suggests there remain unused resources.

CHARLIE VARLEY/Sipa Press/Newscom

Inflation tells you about price changes.

Indicator nine: The wage price index tells you what's happening with wages. The wage price index tells you how fast wages and benefits are rising. Rising compensation is a sign of a healthy economy, and higher wages often translate into more spending. While there are other measures of wages, this is the only index that accounts for changes in the composition of the workforce. Importantly, it accounts for both wages and benefits, and so it measures the rise in labour costs experienced by businesses. Because higher costs often lead to higher prices, this index is a leading indicator of inflationary pressure.

Indicator 10: The stock market tells you about the future expected profits of businesses. Traders bid up or down individual stocks based on their estimate of each business' future profits. Through this process, stock prices come to reflect investors' expectations about the future strength of corporate profits. A strong overall stock market suggests that traders are optimistic about the future of business profitability, and so it often signals a vote of confidence in the economy more generally. If the stock market is falling, there's reason to be worried.

The ASX 200—the stock market index that tracks the value of 200 large publicly traded firms—provides a useful summary of the state of the stock market. Stock prices are often the first sign of either a strengthening or weakening economy, although it's also been known to send false signals. It's worth following, but don't obsess over every blip. As one economist cheekily said, "The stock market has predicted nine out of the last five recessions."

Interpreting the DATA **Why do financial markets sometimes rise after a good employment report, and other times fall?**

Sometimes when new data come out showing strong jobs growth, stock prices fall in response. That sounds crazy, right? Aren't strong job numbers good for the economy, and hence the stock market? Of course they are.

But the stock market is forward-looking, and today's stock prices already incorporate investors' expectations about the future path of the economy. Thus, what matters to investors is whether the latest numbers show the economy is strong or weak *relative to their expectations*. For instance, if stock prices already reflect expectations that the economy is growing very strongly, and the latest numbers show that it's only growing somewhat strongly, then investors will be disappointed by this news. They'll revise their expectations about economic conditions downward, leading the stock market to fall.

To predict how financial markets respond to new economic data, focus on the difference between outcomes and expectations. ■

TORSTEN BLACKWOOD/ AFP/Getty Images

Sometimes stock prices fall after a good jobs report.

Put the 10 indicators together in a dashboard. Figure 14 puts the 10 indicators together to form a "dashboard" that will help you track the economy. It shows how the economy has evolved since the turn of the century.

Figure 14 | A Dashboard for Tracking the Economy

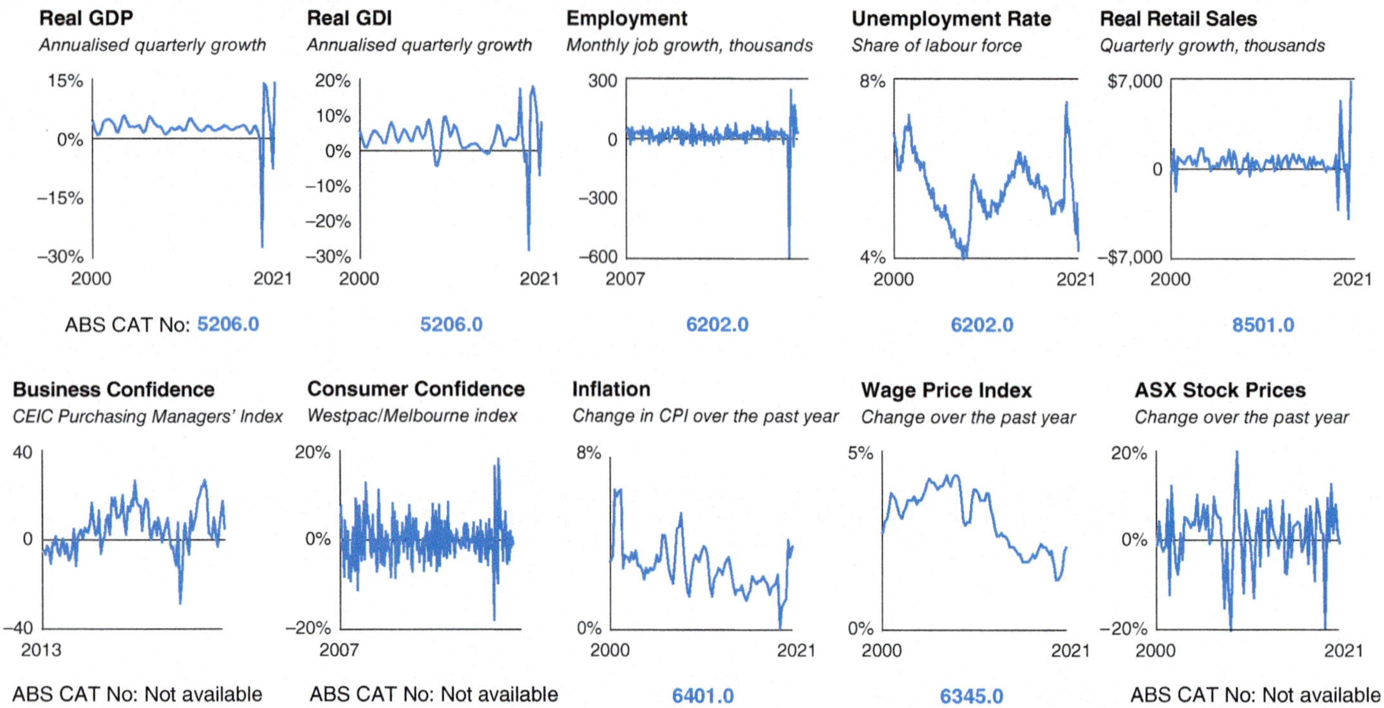

Data from: Australian Bureau of Statistics, CEIC, Refinitiv.

Do the Economics

Head over to the Australian Bureau of Statistics database and look up the latest numbers for our top 10 economic indicators, and use these to come to your own judgement about the current state of the economy. In Figure 14, I've included some of the category numbers (CAT No.) you'll need in order to look up the ABS report which contains each indicator. In Figure 15, you can get a sense of a "typical" outcome by looking at the first column, which shows the median for each indicator since the year 2000. The next column shows the range that the data points are typically in half the time (economists call this the interquartile

Figure 15 | Economic Indicators' Typical Outcomes

Indicator	Median	Interquartile range	Latest data
Real GDP growth *(quarterly growth at an annualised rate)*	2.75%	1.2%–3.8%	
Real GDI growth *(quarterly growth at an annualised rate)*	3.53%	0.6%–4.5%	
Change in nonfarm payrolls *(monthly change)*	17,600	1,300–36,000	
Unemployment rate *(percent of the labour force)*	5.5%	5.1%–6%	
Change in real retail sales *(quarterly change)*	595,400	82,000–895,000	
Business confidence *(Purchasing Managers' Index)*	2.344	–5.82628–7.037008	
Consumer confidence *(Westpac/Melbourne Institute index)*	0.3%	–3%–3.3%	
Inflation *(annual percent change in consumer price index)*	2.5%	1.8%–3.0%	
Wage price index *(annual percent change)*	3.2%	2.3%–3.8%	
Annual growth in ASX 200 *(percent change over the quarter)*	2.0%	–2.0%–6.0%	

range), so you can get a sense of which numbers are roughly normal. Numbers outside that range bear watching because they might suggest the economy is either particularly weak or strong.

Your task is to look up the latest data and fill in the final column. What's your assessment? Is the economy doing well or poorly? ■

Tracking the Economy: An Economy Watcher's Guide

Five tips for tracking the economy:

1. Track many indicators
2. Look at broader indicators
3. Seek just-in-time data and leading indicators
4. Find the signal in the noise
5. Change your outlook when data differ from expectations

Now that you know how to understand macroeconomic data and the main economic indicators to look out for, let's put all of it together. Here are five tips for tracking the economy.

Tip one: Track many indicators. I've given you a list of 10 top economic indicators for a reason: It's best to track many economic indicators, not just one. Our measures of the economy are still imperfect, and the Australian economy is large and complex, so it's best to keep track of many different indicators to get a full view of the economy.

As you grow more sophisticated, you may want to add other data series to your dashboard, particularly given how fast new data is becoming available. We're in the middle of a data revolution that could transform our understanding of the economy. Just about everything you buy is tracked by credit cards, supermarket scanners, and customer loyalty cards. Your feelings about the day are reflected in your Google searches and social media posts. And your weekly pay is tracked by your employer, their payroll company, and the tax authorities. This enormous stream of data—sometimes called "big data" (there's a lot of it!)—is becoming an increasingly important source of new economic indicators. Already, economists are collecting data on online prices to help track inflation, data on credit card purchases to track spending, data on Google searches for "new car" to track car sales, and data on tweets mentioning "lost my job" to track unemployment.

Tip two: Broad indicators beat narrow indicators. Some indicators are a better reflection of the economy than others, and you should give greater weight to indicators that account for a greater share of the economy. For instance, we have lots of data about the industrial sector because it's easy to measure what rolls off a factory production line. But only about a quarter of the economy is in the industrial sector, and so you might be learning about sector-specific factors (such as what's going on with the mining industry) rather than broader trends. For example, in 2014, industrial production grew even as the rest of the economy stayed relatively stagnant. Focusing too much on the narrow measures of industrial production would have led you to overestimate the economy's broader strength, as indicated in Figure 16.

Figure 16 | A Narrow Sector May Conceal Broader Trends

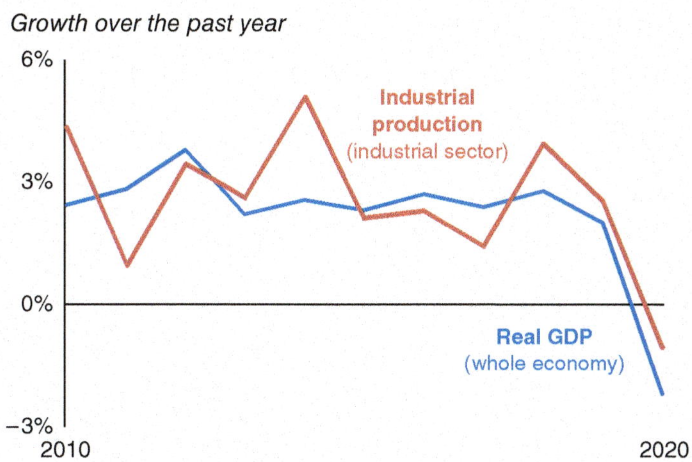

Data from: Australian Bureau of Statistics.

Tip three: Seek just-in-time data and distinguish between leading and lagging indicators. Some indicators are published months and months after the fact, while others are published only a few days later. To stay up to date, it's best to give more weight to indicators that are published quickly. Employment numbers come out only a few weeks after they are collected, as does the Westpac/Melbourne Institute consumer sentiment index. And the stock market incorporates information in real time. These are timely indicators, telling you about current trends.

In contrast, reliable GDP data are not released until two months after the end of each quarter, which means that on 1 June you're reading about how the economy performed in January to March. To keep on top of the latest trends, you'll need to be more up to date than that!

But while you want to pay attention to just-in-time data, also remember that some indicators lead the business cycle, while others lag it.

Tip four: Find the signal amid the noise. Macroeconomic data are often rough estimates based on incomplete samples. This means they contain a lot of *noise,* jumping up and down for reasons unrelated to the underlying trends. That noise makes it harder to discern the *signal* about where the economy is going.

Averaging over the past few data points can help you minimise the influence of this noise, allowing a clearer picture to emerge. The left side of Figure 17 shows that month-to-month changes in employment bounce around a lot, but if you focus on the average over the last 12 months, the signal emerges from the noise. To calculate the 12-month moving average, simply add up every monthly data point from the past 12 months and then divide by 12.

Figure 17 | **Finding the Signal by Ignoring the Volatile Noise**

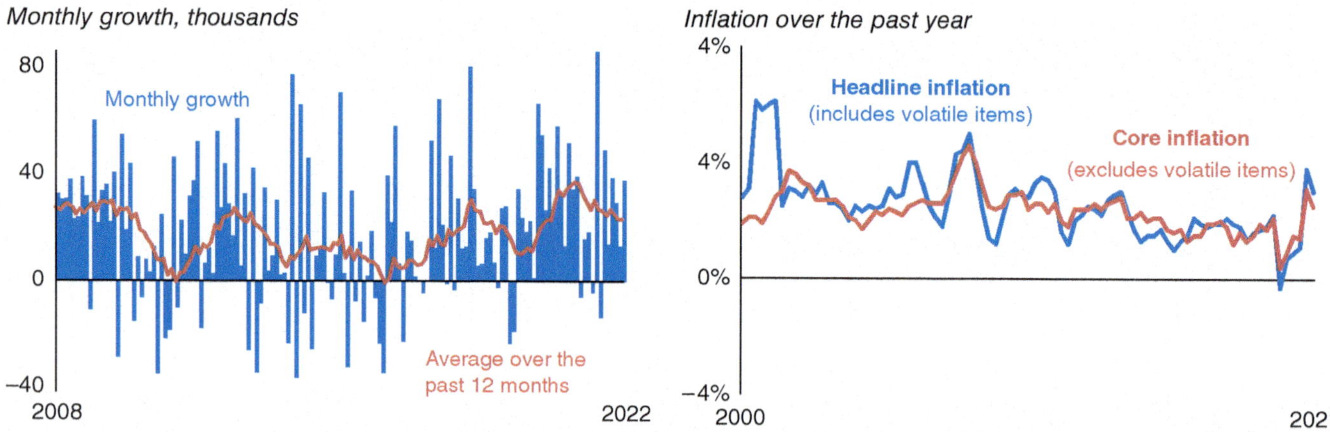

Data from: Australian Bureau of Statistics, Reserve Bank of Australia.

Another strategy for finding the signal in the noise is to *look past volatile components* of the data so the trend can shine through. For instance, food prices often rise and fall due to the weather, while oil prices reflect geopolitical developments in the Middle East. Neither gives a useful signal of the underlying inflation rate. The right side of Figure 17 shows core inflation, which excludes the influence of fruit, vegetables, and petrol prices, along with a measure of inflation that includes those volatile components. The two measures follow the same long-run patterns, but in the short run core inflation is less volatile and hence is more predictive of long-run inflation trends.

Tip five: Adjust your outlook when data differ from expectations. An indicator that suggests strong economic growth when you already expected strong economic growth shouldn't change your outlook. What really matters is whether that indicator came in stronger or weaker than expected. When the data matches your expectations, there isn't much news there. But if the data show that the economy is stronger or weaker than you expected, then that's news, and you'll need to adjust your outlook.

EVERYDAY Economics **How to better understand your favourite company, your WAM, and your health**

These five tips aren't just about how to better track the economy. They apply to tracking just about anything: the performance of your favourite company, your performance in university, and even your health. In each case, you'll do better if you:

Track many indicators: An analyst tracking Apple follows its revenues, costs, prices, inputs, and so on. A good student tracks their study time, their performance on homework, and their grades on quizzes and exams. And if you want to track your health, you might track your sleep, your diet, and your exercise. Your doctor will also tend to follow a "dashboard" of data like your blood pressure, heart rate, and lab tests.

Look at broader indicators that are more representative of Apple's performance, your learning, or your health. For example, while you might own a scale and therefore can easily track your weight, it's not a very broad indicator of overall health. Your resting heart rate or blood pressure is a broader indicator.

Seek just-in-time data, and in particular, the latest news about your company, your academic performance, and your health. Pay particular attention to news that might be a leading indicator of change. Have there been leaks about the next iPhone? Are you keeping up with your class reading? Have you started eating more junk food?

Look through the noise: Don't let an unusual result shape your views too much. Look beyond one particularly good earnings report, an in-class quiz that you took after not getting much sleep, or your latest cold, to form a better understanding of the true state of your company, your WAM, and your health.

Adjust your outlook when outcomes differ from what you expect: When Apple's sales are up 5%, whether it's good news or bad news depends on what you were expecting. If you thought that the latest iPhone was going to lead to a 10% increase in sales, then the paltry 5% might be bad news. Similarly, if you go into an exam fully prepared and expecting to ace it, a B might be a negative surprise; that same grade might be good news for a student who was struggling. Finally, your doctor telling you that you have moderately high blood pressure is good news if you expected it to be very high, but it's bad news if you expected it to be normal. ■

Tying It Together

Economists tend to keep short-run and long-run analyses separate. In the long run—as in Chapter 22—we focus on how to increase potential output, which is determined by supply-side factors like the number of available workers and the quantity of physical and human capital, as well as the technology for combining them. Generally, long-run analysis is useful for predicting economic changes over decades.

In contrast, when we look at business cycles, we're turning to short-run analysis, which focuses on fluctuations around potential output that typically only last for a few years. In the next few chapters, we'll dig more into the drivers of these short-term fluctuations. You'll see that this typically involves paying greater attention to demand-side factors, meaning that we'll focus more on how much people want to spend rather than how much can be produced.

This division of macroeconomic analysis into long-run versus short-run analysis is based on the implicit assumption that the ups and downs of the business cycle have no long-term repercussions. It's an assumption that's helpful because it allows us to separate our analyses of supply-side factors and demand-side factors. It's also an assumption that's probably not quite right.

It's not quite right because "short-run" changes can have long-lasting effects. A recession that throws millions of people out of work is temporary in the sense that the recession will eventually end, and most of the newly unemployed people will find work again when the economy recovers. But it won't undo the damage that people incur from having spent months or sometimes even years without work. The experience they could have gained during that jobless spell is forever lost. Their knowledge of the specifics of working for their former employer will never be useful again. Their next job may not use their skills as effectively. Many people lose skills and valuable work habits, and in some cases, they lose hope. People who are pushed to retire early never return, and a long jobless spell can make it hard for some people to ever fully reconnect with the world of work.

There are other lasting losses. Managers typically cut back on investment during a recession, and it can take years before they've fully caught up. The investment in new ideas that drives long-term growth may be put on hold, and it's hard to know if those missing ideas will be generated during the subsequent economic expansion. Valuable relationships are destroyed when businesses stop working together.

The possibility that business cycle fluctuations have longer-run implications makes the task of understanding the business cycle all the more important. We've taken a first step in this chapter by showing how you can track the business cycle. The next few chapters dig deeper, providing you with a framework for understanding what drives business cycles, so that you can better forecast how market conditions are likely to evolve and assess possible policy responses.

Organisational note: *As discussed on page 741, different economists like to examine business cycles from slightly different perspectives. Much like viewing a concert, you can see things differently depending on where you sit. Now that you've been introduced to business cycles, it's time for you—or more likely, your instructor—to choose your seat for the show. If your instructor wants you to see the economy from the same perspective as the RBA does, they'll direct you to read Chapters 30 and 31 (perhaps with Chapter 32 as a capstone). If your instructor recommends a more traditional view, then read Chapter 33. And if they want you to really appreciate the role of aggregate expenditure, they might recommend you start with the appendix. Remember that you'll still be able to see the whole show, no matter where you sit.*

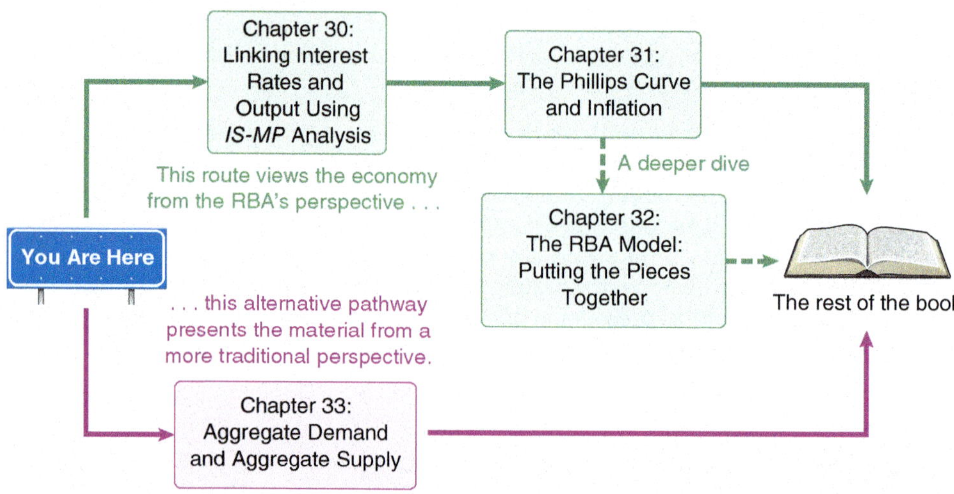

Chapter at a Glance

Business cycle: Short-term fluctuations in economic activity. The business cycle reflects the tendency for **actual output** to deviate from **potential output**. This deviation is measured using the **output gap**.

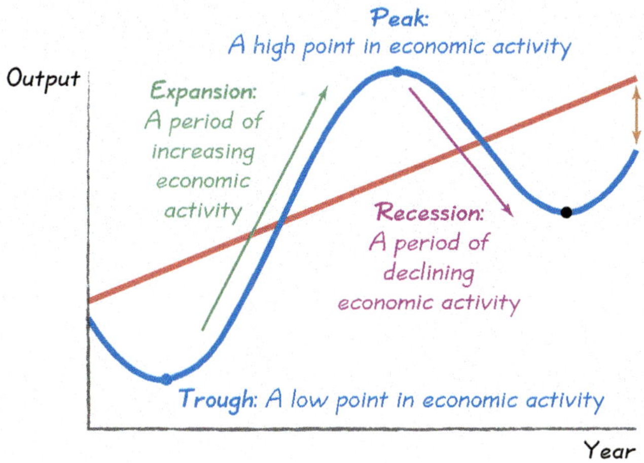

Potential output

Actual output

Output gap: The difference between actual and potential output, measured as a percentage of potential output.

$$= \frac{\text{Actual output} - \text{Potential output}}{\text{Potential output}} \times 100$$

Distinguish between **levels** (GDP measures the level of output) and **changes** (GDP growth is about changes).

Features of Business Cycles

1. Business cycles are **not cycles.**
2. Recessions **vary** in their causes, their duration, and their depth.
3. Some variables **lead** recessions, while others **lag.**
4. The business cycle is **persistent.**
5. A typical business cycle involves a **short, sharp recession,** followed by a **long and gradual expansion.**
6. Many economic variables **co-move** up and down together over the business cycle.

Okun's rule of thumb: For every percentage point that actual output falls below potential output, the unemployment rate is around half a percentage point higher.

Using Macroeconomic Data

Seasonally adjusted: Data stripped of predictable seasonal patterns.
Annualised rate: Data converted to the rate that would occur if the same growth rate had occurred throughout the year.
Nominal variables: Variables expressed in dollars, using the prices of that year's data.
Real variables: Variables adjusted for inflation so you're comparing quantities, holding prices constant.
Leading indicators: Variables that tend to predict the future path of the economy.
Lagging indicators: Variables that follow the business cycle with a delay.
Revisions: Updates to earlier estimates.

Top 10 Economic Indicators

- Real GDP growth
- Real GDI growth
- Employment rate
- Unemployment rate
- Real retail sales
- Business confidence
- Consumer confidence
- Inflation rate
- Wage price index
- Stock market

Five Rules to Track the Economy

1. Track many indicators
2. Broad indicators beat narrow indicators
3. Seek just-in-time data
4. Find the signal amid the noise
5. Adjust your outlook when data differ from expectations

Key Concepts

annualised rate, 753
business cycle, 746
expansion, 748
lagging indicators, 751
leading indicators, 751
Okun's rule of thumb, 752
output gap, 747
peak, 748
potential output, 746
recession, 748
revisions, 753
seasonally adjusted, 753
trough, 748

Discussion and Review Questions

Learning Objective 29.1 *Distinguish between economic trends and short-run fluctuations.*

1. A politician makes the following comment: "The fundamentals of our economy are very strong. According to market economists, we are producing more than anyone expected and even beyond what they call our potential output. My goal is to guarantee that we continue to produce more than our potential output throughout the next few decades." In the long run, do you think the politician could achieve this goal? Explain your reasoning.
2. What do economists mean when they say that business cycles are not cycles?

Learning Objective 29.2 *Describe the common features of business cycles.*

3. In 2019 the output gap in Australia was –1.6%. Make a prediction about what you think the output gap will be in 2020. Explain your reasoning.
4. Explain how you can use consumer and business confidence indices to make predictions about the future state of the economy. For example, how would you expect consumer spending to change over the next year if consumer confidence indices have been falling for several months?
5. Describe some of the historical similarities and differences between recessions. For example, do they always have the same duration and severity? What about expansions?

Learning Objective 29.3 *Learn to analyse macroeconomic data.*

6. Explain how you would use the five tips to track the economy to form an outlook of the economy and job market you are hoping to enter after finishing your education. Go online to find data that will help inform your outlook. Hint: labourmarketinsights.gov.au has excellent information on the outlook of various jobs and the ABS has lots of data on economy-wide indicators.

Study Problems

Learning Objective 29.1 *Distinguish between economic trends and short-run fluctuations.*

1. Use the graph of Turkey's real GDP to answer the following questions.

Real GDP in Turkey
Annual percent change in output

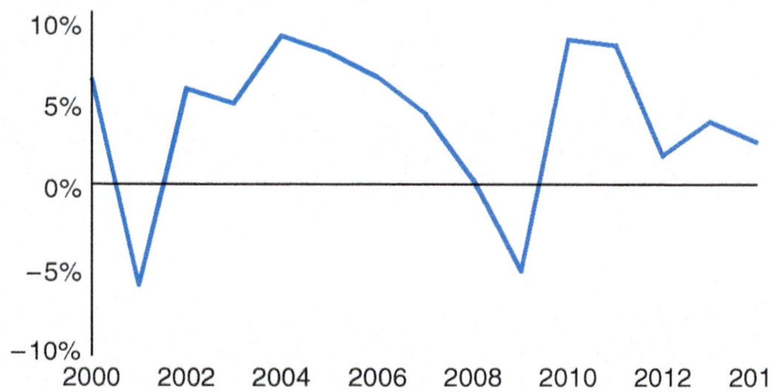

   a. In what year(s) did Turkey experience a recession? Explain your reasoning.
   b. What likely happened to unemployment during the recessions?

2. Use the accompanying table to answer the following questions.

Year	Real GDP (trillions of $)	Potential Output (trillions of $)
2014	$17.11	$17.38
2015	$17.46	$17.69
2016	$17.78	$17.99
2017	$18.22	$18.29
2018	$18.77	$18.65

   a. Calculate the output gap for each year.
   b. What does it mean when the output gap is negative? What does it mean when it is positive?
   c. For each year, calculate how much the output gap changed. Compare this to the growth rate of actual output that year, less the growth rate of potential output.

Learning Objective 29.2 *Describe the common features of business cycles.*

3. What does it mean if a macroeconomic variable is a leading indicator? A lagging indicator? Give some examples of both leading and lagging indicators.
4. Assuming the equilibrium unemployment rate is 5%, if actual output falls to 5 percentage points below potential output, how would you expect the unemployment rate to change? (Hint: Use Okun's rule of thumb.)

Learning Objective 29.3 *Learn to analyse macroeconomic data.*

5. For each of the following, should you use seasonally adjusted data? Why or why not?
   - **a.** You are trying to look at economic growth over the past few quarters and you want to figure out the trend so that you can predict growth over the next year.
   - **b.** You are starting a retail business and want to know how consumer spending changes over the course of the year so that you can hire the appropriate number of staff.
6. What indicators should you use to track each of the following, and why?
   - **a.** The overall size of the economy
   - **b.** Labour market performance
   - **c.** The future trajectory of economic activity
   - **d.** Wages and benefits
7. The ASX 200 has been increasing steadily over the last few months. What does this signal about how investors view future profits? Explain your reasoning.
8. What do you expect to happen to the ASX 200 if it is announced that GDP grew at an annual rate of 2% last quarter but economists were expecting it to grow at an annual rate of 3%?

CHAPTER 30

Linking Interest Rates and Output through *IS-MP* Analysis

A trader sits in front of a Bloomberg terminal watching the clock. The Reserve Bank of Australia (RBA) is about to release news of its latest decision, and it could change the economy's trajectory. The clock ticks over to 2:30 pm. The announcement is out: The RBA has lowered interest rates, and it's committed to reducing them as much as is needed to kickstart the flagging economy. The trader immediately buys stocks and watches the stock market soar.

Ingo Schulz/imageBROKER/Alamy Stock Photo

At 2:30 pm, things may change.

Later that afternoon, the Commonwealth Bank passes on the rate cut by lowering their mortgage rates. Within half an hour the other three big banks follow suit. A week later, a lawyer in Adelaide gets an email from Westpac, offering a mortgage at a low interest rate. The lawyer calls their spouse because they've been considering buying a house; with interest rates down, they decide now is the right time. A few months later, they're homeowners. Meanwhile, a financial executive at Woolworths has secured a business loan at a low interest rate from National Australia Bank. Woolworths uses the loan to install new self-service checkout technology at stores across the country.

The interest rate might be the most important price in the economy. It tells you how expensive it is to borrow, shows you the opportunity cost of spending, and plays a key role in economic decisions. In this chapter, we'll see why. We'll start by examining how spending responds to changes in the interest rate. Next, we'll delve into how interest rates help determine the economy's total output. After that, we'll look into how interest rates are determined. Finally, we'll use what we've learned to forecast how changing market conditions affect output.

By the end, you'll have a useful framework to analyse changing economic conditions. This framework, called *IS-MP* analysis, is the real deal: It's the approach that people in industry, government, and the RBA use to analyse the business cycle. Let's get started.

Chapter Objective

Analyse the links between spending, interest rates, financial markets, and output that shape the business cycle.

30.1 Aggregate Expenditure
Assess the role of aggregate expenditure in driving short-run fluctuations in output.

30.2 The *IS* Curve: Output and the Real Interest Rate
Use the *IS* curve to analyse the relationship between the real interest rate and equilibrium GDP.

30.3 The *MP* Curve: What Determines the Interest Rate
Use the *MP* curve to summarise how the real interest rate is determined.

30.4 The *IS-MP* Framework
Forecast economic conditions and how they'll respond to monetary and fiscal policy.

30.5 Macroeconomic Shocks
Use the *IS-MP* framework to forecast the effects of macroeconomic shocks.

30.1 Aggregate Expenditure

Learning Objective *Assess the role of aggregate expenditure in driving short-run fluctuations in output.*

Dinendra Haria/Alamy Stock Photo

A costly mistake.

In 2017, fast fashion retailer H&M was facing increased competition and changing consumer tastes for clothes. The Australian operation was no exception. H&M's sales dropped but its purchasing continued as if market conditions hadn't changed. By 2018 this had led to more than $6 billion worldwide in unsold clothes. This bloated inventory tied up valuable capital that could have been put to a more productive use. As a savvy retail industry analyst, you could have predicted that H&M would cut back on it's purchases while it tried to sell down the excess apparel.

Aggregate Expenditure and Short Run Fluctuations

The same dynamics play out across the whole economy as executives in every market adjust their production plans to keep pace with the ebb and flow of demand. This suggests that—at least in the short run—changes in demand drive changes in output. In turn, that implies that you'll do a good job forecasting short-run fluctuations in output if you can predict what's happening to demand.

Aggregate expenditure describes everyone's spending plans. That's why our analysis of business cycles will start by focusing on the demand side of the economy. In particular, we'll focus on **aggregate expenditure,** which refers to the total amount of goods and services that people want to buy across the whole economy—the sum of consumption, planned investment, government purchases, and net exports.

aggregate expenditure The total amount of goods and services that people want to buy across the whole economy

= *Consumption*

+ *Planned investment*

+ *Government purchases*

+ *Net exports*

Aggregate expenditure is the sum of four components:

= *Consumption*: When households buy goods and services

\+ *Planned investment*: When businesses purchase new capital

\+ *Government purchases*: When the government buys goods and services

\+ *Net exports*: Spending by foreigners on Australian-made exports, less spending by Australians on foreign-made imports.

Economists often use abbreviations to simplify things, and so you might find it easier to write it this way:

$$\underbrace{AE}_{\text{Aggregate expenditure}} = \underbrace{C}_{\text{Consumption}} + \underbrace{I}_{\text{Planned investment}} + \underbrace{G}_{\text{Government purchases}} + \underbrace{NX}_{\text{Net exports}}$$

Some abbreviations:
AE: Aggregate Expenditure
C: Consumption
I: Planned Investment
G: Government purchases
NX: Net exports
Y: Output, as measured by GDP

When you're trying to assess economy-wide demand, you want to focus on how much people (including businesses) buy, not the unsold inventories that companies accumulate. That's why the measure of investment that's counted in aggregate expenditure is *planned investment,* which includes all the spending on new capital that businesses do, but excludes unplanned changes in inventories.

Output adjusts to meet aggregate expenditure. The key idea here is that when the total quantity of output exceeds aggregate expenditure, businesses will cut back their production. And when output is less than aggregate expenditure, businesses will ramp up production, so as not to miss out on making profitable sales. An equilibrium describes a stable situation with no tendency to change, and so a **macroeconomic equilibrium** occurs when the quantity of output that buyers collectively want to purchase is equal to the quantity of output that suppliers collectively produce. As such, macroeconomic equilibrium occurs when aggregate expenditure (which measures the total demand for output) equals GDP (which measures the total production of output):

macroeconomic equilibrium Occurs when the quantity of output that buyers collectively want to purchase is equal to the quantity of output that suppliers collectively produce.

$$\underbrace{Y}_{\text{Output}} = \underbrace{C + I + G + NX}_{\text{Aggregate expenditure}}$$

This equation simply states that across the whole economy businesses will adjust their production so that total output matches total spending. And this implies that—at least in the short run—demand conditions determine output. In this context, *short run* refers to the year-to-year ups and downs of the business cycle.

Can aggregate expenditure differ from output? For a brief period, yes. If people purchase less than businesses produce, the extra output will be stored as inventories. But that's not an equilibrium because managers will respond by cutting back production. Likewise, aggregate expenditure might be greater than production for a short while, as businesses make sales with delayed delivery dates or sell their existing inventories. But managers will quickly ramp up production so they don't lose profitable sales. These adjustments will push the economy towards the macroeconomic equilibrium where total output is equal to aggregate expenditure.

If you want to dig into how businesses adjust production so that total output equals aggregate expenditure, then you should turn to the appendix, "A Closer Look at Aggregate Expenditure and the Multiplier." Spoiler alert: It all boils down to one big idea, which is that output adjusts to meet aggregate expenditure. And that in turn means that forecasting GDP is all about forecasting what will happen to each component of aggregate expenditure.

The Demand-Driven Short Run and the Supply-Driven Long Run

Our focus in this chapter on the *demand* side of the economy—on aggregate expenditure and its components—sounds quite different from our analysis in Chapter 22 of long-run economic growth. In long-run analysis—relevant to a period of say, a decade or more—economists focus on the *supply* side of the economy, analysing the available *supply* of labour, capital, and human capital, plus the production function that summarises the state of technological progress. That supply-driven long-run analysis explains the economy's *potential output.* Potential output is the level at which all resources are *fully employed.* It's the economy's maximum *sustainable* level of output.

In the short run, actual GDP may fail to meet potential. Our focus in this chapter is on the short run and explaining year-to-year fluctuations in actual output. And that's where the demand side really matters. If people don't want to buy all that businesses are capable of producing, then companies like H&M decide they're better off producing less than their potential. And so weak aggregate expenditure can lead the economy to adjust to an equilibrium in which *actual output* falls short of *potential output*, as shown in Figure 1. Even though companies like H&M could produce more, there's no point in doing so if there's no demand for more output. This can lead to an equilibrium in which output is less than potential—an unhappy outcome in which production lines sit empty and workers are left unemployed. An economic slump can be an equilibrium because businesses don't want to produce output that people won't buy, and people don't want to spend more because the economy is weak.

Figure 1 | Potential Output and Actual Output

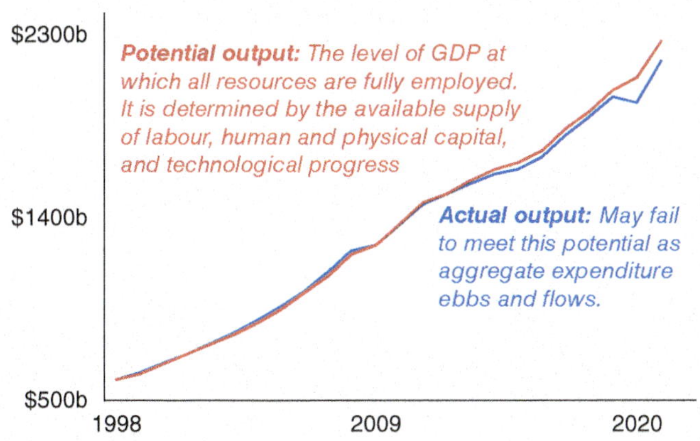

Data from: CEIC, OECD.

When actual GDP exceeds potential GDP, the economy will overheat. There's also the possibility that output will exceed the economy's potential. This describes the situation where available resources are *more* than fully employed, and so GDP exceeds the economy's maximum sustainable output. Producers will do what they can to keep up, deferring maintenance, running extra overnight shifts, and paying their workers overtime. But this isn't sustainable. Eventually the economy will overheat, and—as we'll discuss in the next chapter—these pressures can spark inflation.

The output gap focuses on the balance between demand- and supply-side factors. This suggests we take a "Goldilocks" approach to evaluating the state of the economy. Potential output describes the economy's maximum sustainable rate of output. When output is below potential, the economy is running too cold. When output exceeds potential, it risks overheating. Only when output is equal to potential output will Goldilocks declare that business cycle conditions are "just right."

This chapter is about understanding these short-run fluctuations, so we'll focus our analysis on the *output gap,* which measures the gap between actual and potential output, as a percentage of potential output:

$$\text{Output gap} = \frac{\text{Actual output} - \text{Potential output}}{\text{Potential output}} \times 100$$

When actual output is greater than potential, the output gap is a positive number. And when the economy is producing less than potential, the output gap is a negative number. Be careful when you're describing changes in the output gap. For instance, when output falls from being 2% below potential to being 3% below potential, some people say the output gap has gotten smaller (because it's now −3% which is less than −2%), while others say it has gotten bigger (because the size of the gap is now 3% rather than 2%). You'll be better off avoiding words like bigger and smaller altogether. Instead, when output fails to rise as much as potential (pushing the output gap from −2% to −3%, or from +4% to +3%), you should say the result is a *more negative* output gap. And when output rises more than potential (pushing the output gap up from +3% to +4%, or from −3% to −2%), you should say the result is a *more positive* output gap.

Figure 2 | **The Output Gap Fluctuates Widely**

Difference between actual and potential output, as a percentage of potential output

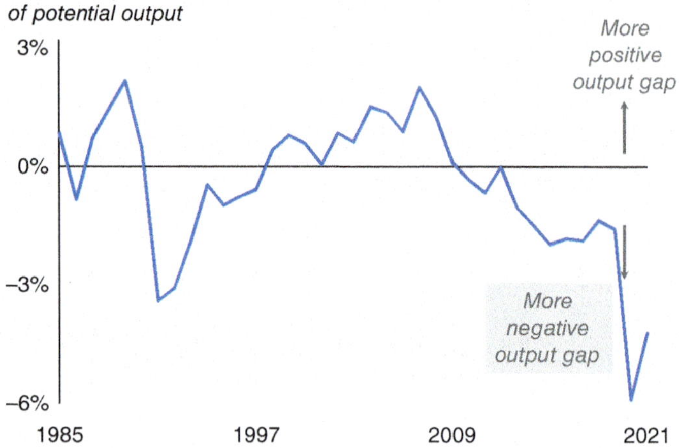

Data from: CEIC, OECD.

Focusing on the output gap is helpful because it provides a way to disentangle the roles of the demand- and supply-side determinants of GDP. The supply side of the economy—the supply of labour, human and physical capital, and the state of technological progress—determines potential output. The supply of these inputs grows smoothly over time, which is why Figure 1 shows that potential GDP typically grows smoothly over time. But actual GDP moves in fits and starts, suggesting that demand-side factors can drive actual GDP to deviate quite substantially from potential GDP, which is why Figure 2 shows that the output gap fluctuates widely. Our task in this chapter is to explain these fluctuations.

Be careful not to confuse equilibrium GDP with potential GDP. *Equilibrium GDP* describes the level of GDP at the point of macroeconomic equilibrium—the point at which the economy will come to rest. This occurs at whatever level of output is equal to aggregate expenditure. In contrast, *potential GDP* is the economy's highest sustainable level of production, and it's determined by available inputs. It's important to remember that they're different: Equilibrium GDP describes the economy's resting point; potential GDP is where Goldilocks wishes it would rest. Bear that in mind as we explore the drivers of aggregate expenditure.

30.2 The *IS* Curve: Output and the Real Interest Rate

Learning Objective *Use the IS curve to analyse the relationship between the real interest rate and equilibrium GDP.*

The real interest rate may be the most important price in the economy because it represents the opportunity cost of spending. The *opportunity cost principle* tells you that before spending money, you should ask, "Or what?" You can spend money now, *or* you can save it, earn interest, and buy even more in the future. The real interest rate, denoted by *r,* tells you how large this opportunity cost is—how much more stuff you'll be able to buy if you wait until next year. So, the real interest rate—which is the nominal interest rate adjusted for inflation—is the price that determines this year's aggregate expenditure.

The real interest rate is also critical because it's one of the levers policy makers use to influence the economy. The Reserve Bank raises the interest rate—which increases the opportunity cost of spending—when it wants to induce people to spend less. And when the RBA wants to stimulate more spending, it reduces the interest rate, which reduces the opportunity cost of spending money today. As such, careful adjustments to the real interest rate can help offset booms and busts.

These insights inform the roadmap ahead. Our goal is to develop a comprehensive framework for understanding how interest rates affect the economy and why rates rise and fall. We're going to proceed in two steps. First, we'll figure out how the real interest rate affects GDP—a relationship that we'll call the *IS* curve. Second, we'll assess how changing financial conditions determine the real interest rate, summarising our findings in a line we'll call the *MP* curve. Putting them together will yield a framework you can use to analyse changes in economic conditions. And if you're puzzled about how these two curves got their names, don't worry, we'll also get to that.

Aggregate Expenditure and Interest Rates

Before we can get there, we need to lay the foundation, analysing how the real interest rate affects aggregate expenditure. We'll do this by separately exploring how the real interest rate shapes each of the components of aggregate expenditure: consumption, planned investment, government purchases, and finally, net exports. (We explored some of these themes in greater detail in Chapters 25–28 so we'll just hit the key ideas here.)

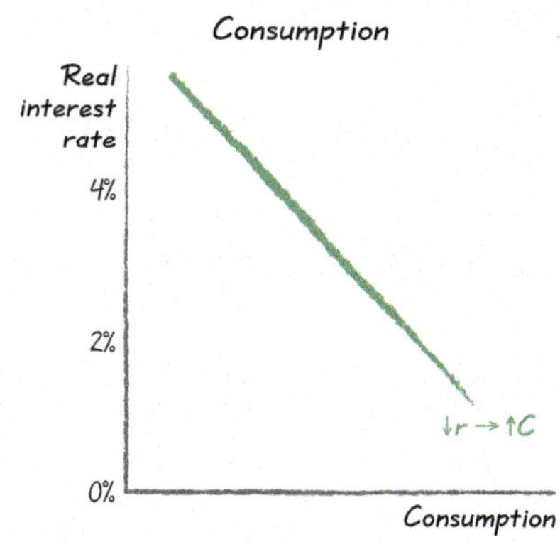

Lower interest rates boost consumption. The real interest rate is central to your spending decisions as a consumer because of the *opportunity cost principle*: You can save and earn interest on any income you don't spend. As a result, the real interest rate represents the opportunity cost of boosting this year's consumption spending. The lower the real interest rate is, the lower this opportunity cost. That's why a low real interest rate leads to more consumption.

The real interest rate is also the cost of borrowing. If you need a loan in order to buy a car, a house, or some other big-ticket item, your bank will charge you interest. The lower the real interest rate is, the less you'll have to repay your bank, which is another reason that low interest rates lead people to increase their spending on big-ticket items.

Note, however, that there's one group for whom a low real interest rate will reduce consumption, and that's people who rely on interest payments for their income. In their case, lower interest rates translate into less income, which can lead them to cut back on their consumption spending. While this describes some people (particularly retirees), across the whole economy this effect is relatively small. And so, on average, lower interest rates lead to more consumption.

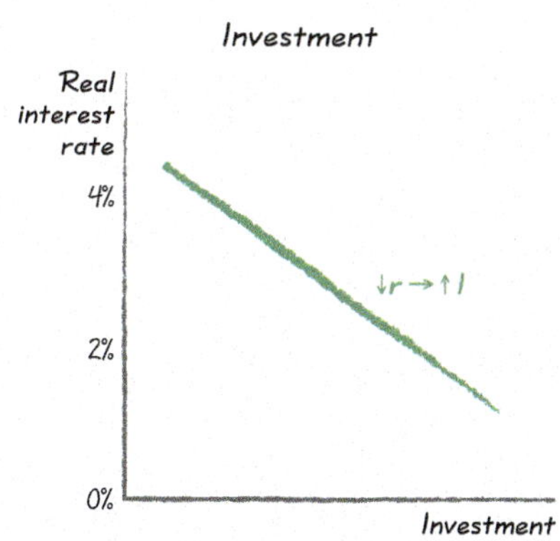

Lower interest rates boost investment. For businesses considering capital investments, the real interest rate is important, again because of the *opportunity cost principle*: If you spend your money buying new equipment or structures, you can't put that money in the bank to earn interest. And so the opportunity cost of investing in new capital is lower when real interest rates are lower. As a result, low real interest rates lead to more investment spending. Indeed, a low enough interest rate can be the difference that makes billions of dollars of investment projects worth pursuing, which is why investment is particularly sensitive to the real interest rate.

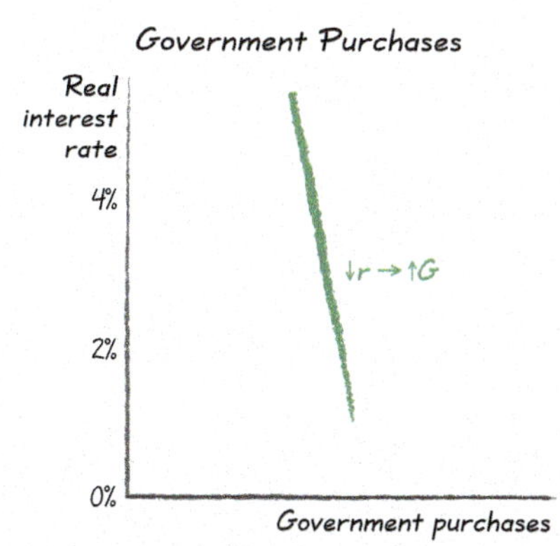

Lower interest rates boost government purchases. Low interest rates reduce the cost of interest payments on government debt. These interest payments—which are a transfer from the government to those it borrows from—don't directly affect aggregate expenditure. But low interest payments mean that there's more money left in the government budget for spending on roads, bridges, and other forms of aggregate expenditure. As a result, lower interest rates can lead to an increase in government purchases, particularly for state governments. Low interest rates don't always spur more government purchases though, because governments might use their extra funds to pay down their debt instead.

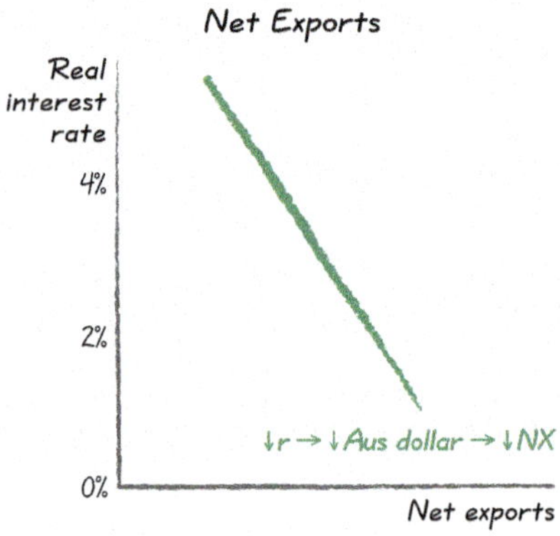

Lower interest rates boost net exports. Net exports also depend on the real interest rate, but through an indirect mechanism: Low interest rates make the Australian dollar cheaper, and this increases net exports (which is exports less imports). Let's take each of these steps in turn.

A low real interest rate in Australia leads international money managers to send their funds to other countries that offer better returns. This means they'll demand fewer Australian dollars, leading the dollar to become cheaper. So the initial effect of a lower interest rate is that it takes fewer U.S. dollars, yen, euros, or yuan (the currencies of the United States, Japan, Europe, and China) to buy an Australian dollar.

This cheaper dollar increases exports and reduces imports. Start by considering exports: An Australian-rock lobster that costs AU$200 ("AU$" means "in Australian dollars") now sells for fewer U.S. dollars yen, euros, or yuan than it did before. This effective price cut leads foreigners to buy more of our exports. As a result, spending on our exports rises. Next, consider imports: A cheaper dollar means that it now takes more Australian dollars to buy a US$100 Maine lobster (the "US$" sign means "U.S. dollars"). This effective price rise leads Australians to buy fewer imports. If the quantity of imports declines by enough to offset the higher prices, then total spending by Australians on imported goods will also fall. Put these effects together, and lower real interest rates lead to a cheaper Australian dollar, causing exports to rise and imports to fall, and hence higher net exports.

The *IS* Curve Describes the Link Between the Real Interest Rate and the Output Gap

Let's summarise what we've found so far. We discovered that a decrease in the real interest rate leads to an increase in every component of aggregate expenditure, boosting consumption, investment, possibly government purchases, and net exports.

The real interest rate is the opportunity cost of spending money this year (rather than next).

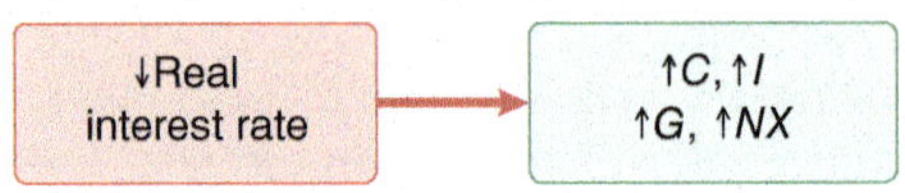

Of these effects, the boost to investment is usually the most important because investment—both in machinery and housing—is particularly sensitive to the interest rate.

Lower interest rates boost aggregate expenditure. The top row of Figure 3 shows that consumption, investment, government purchases, and net exports are each

Figure 3 The Real Interest Rate and Aggregate Expenditure

Lower real interest rates yield more consumption, investment, government purchases, and net exports,

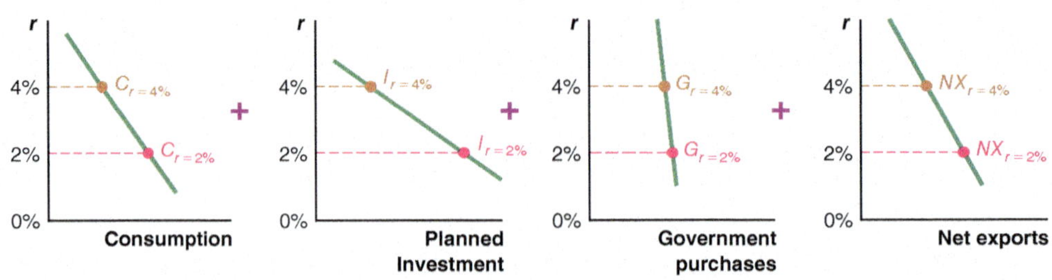

which implies that lower real interest rates yield higher ***aggregate expenditure****.*

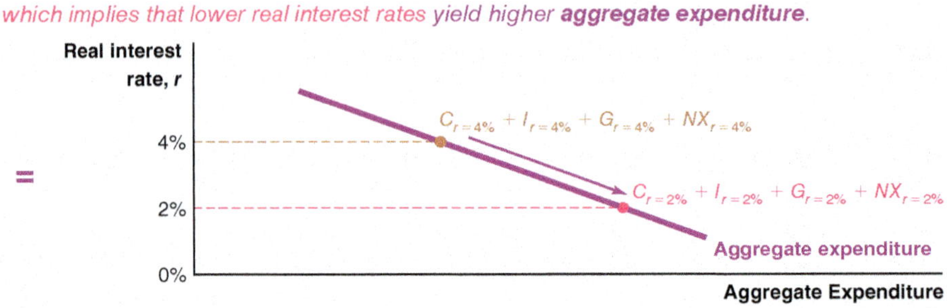

higher when the real interest rate is lower. The bottom row simply adds these up to illustrate that aggregate expenditure—which is the sum of each of these forms of spending—is higher when the real interest rate is lower.

This insight—that a lower real interest rate will boost aggregate expenditure—is central to the framework we're developing. We summarise this finding as:

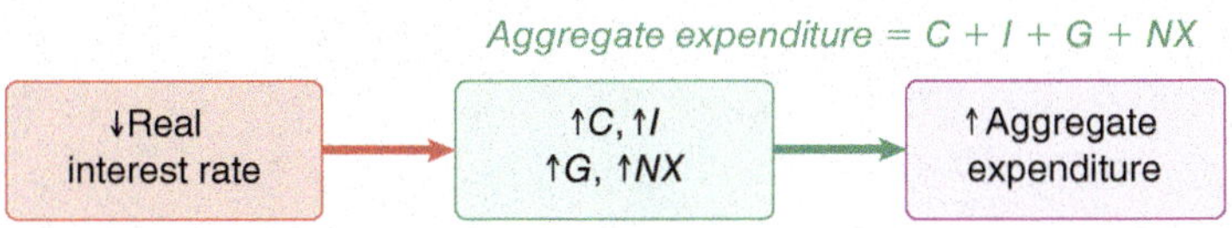

A rise in aggregate expenditure is matched by a rise in production and hence GDP. Recall our previous finding that businesses adjust their output to meet demand, so that output adjusts until it's equal to aggregate expenditure. As a result, a lower real interest rate which boosts aggregate expenditure will increase the level of GDP:

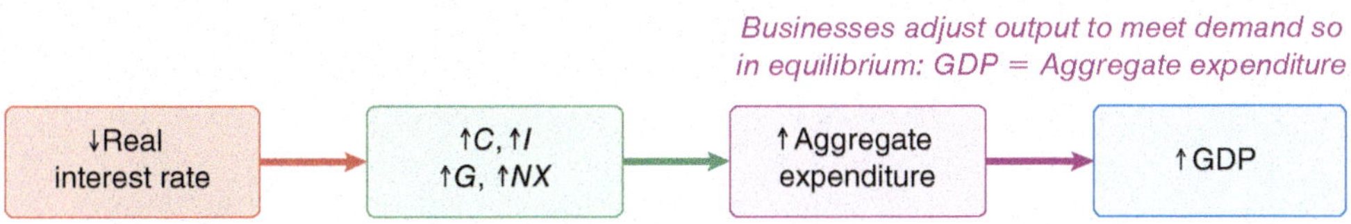

Finally, potential output is determined by long-run factors that are unaffected by these business cycle changes. Since potential output is unchanged, the interest-rate-induced increase in output also increases output relative to potential output, leading to a more positive output gap.

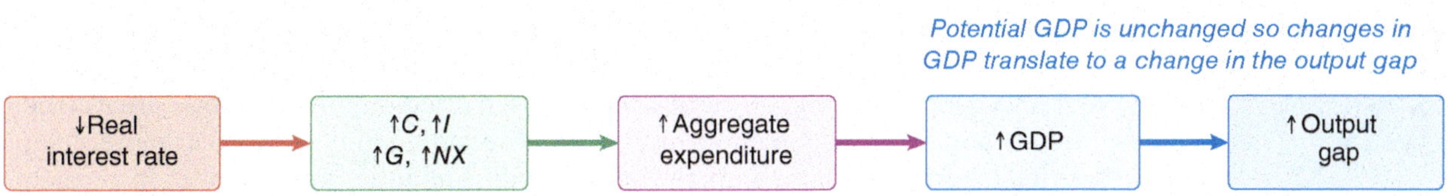

The *IS* Curve illustrates the link between interest rates, GDP, and the output gap. That's it! We've uncovered the link by which lower real interest rates lead to higher real GDP and a more positive output gap.

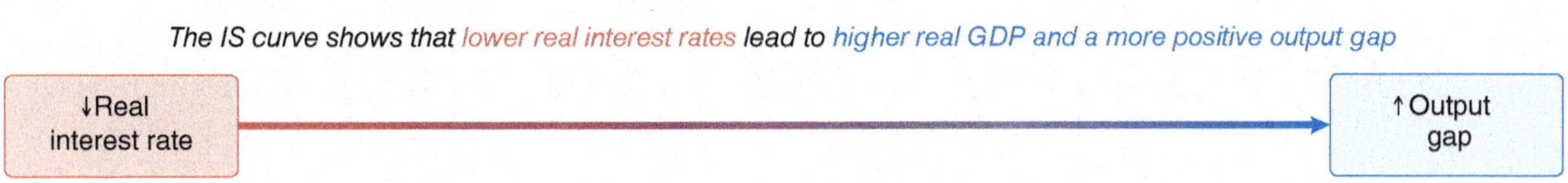

Figure 4 shows this relationship by graphing the ***IS* curve,** which illustrates how lower real interest rates lead to more spending and hence more output and a more positive output gap. It's called the *IS* curve because it describes Investment and Spending decisions. And it illustrates the Interest Sensitivity of output. (Historically, it was called the *IS* curve because Investment is the key form of interest-sensitive spending, and Saving is used to fund investment.)

***IS* curve** Illustrates how lower real interest rates raise spending and hence GDP, leading to a more positive output gap.

You construct the economy's *IS* curve by adding up the level of aggregate expenditure at each real interest rate. Because output adjusts to the level of aggregate expenditure, this also reveals the level of GDP, and then it's just a matter of comparing GDP to potential GDP to calculate the corresponding output gap. Calculate this output gap when the real interest rate is 1%, 2%, 3%, and so on, then connect these dots, and you've estimated the *IS* curve.

Figure 4 | The *IS* Curve

The IS curve illustrates that a lower real interest rate leads output to be larger, relative to potential output.

Ⓐ The **real interest rate** is on the vertical axis

Ⓑ The **output gap**, which goes on the horizontal axis, measures output relative to potential GDP.

Ⓒ The ***IS* curve** is downward-sloping because **lower real interest rates** boost aggregate expenditure, which leads to a higher level of GDP, and hence a **more positive output gap**.

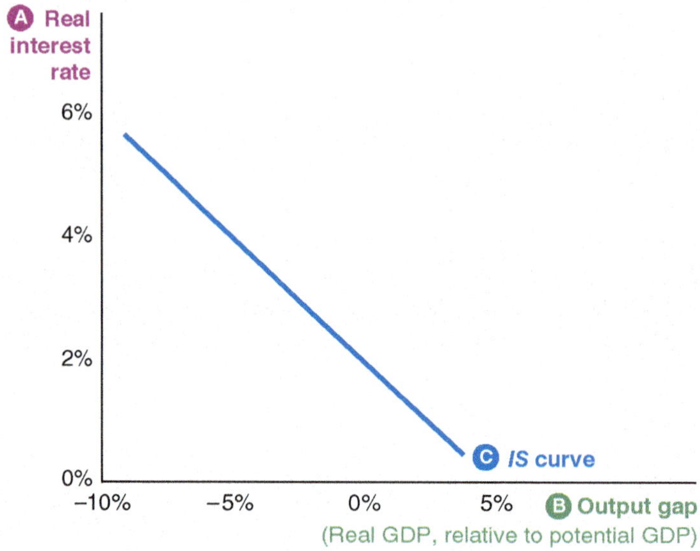

The IS Curve: Graphing Conventions

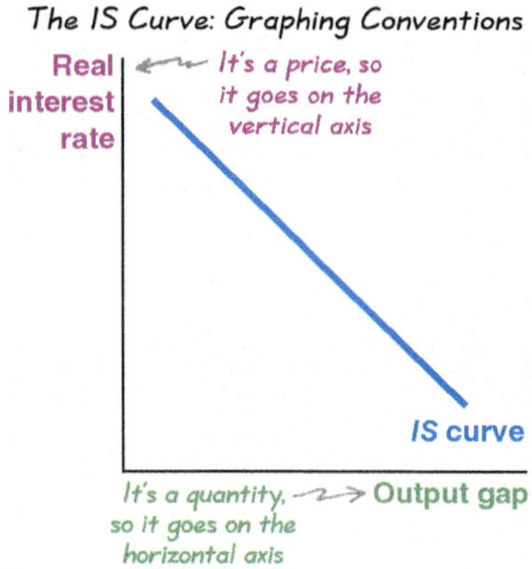

The IS Curve Is Downward-Sloping

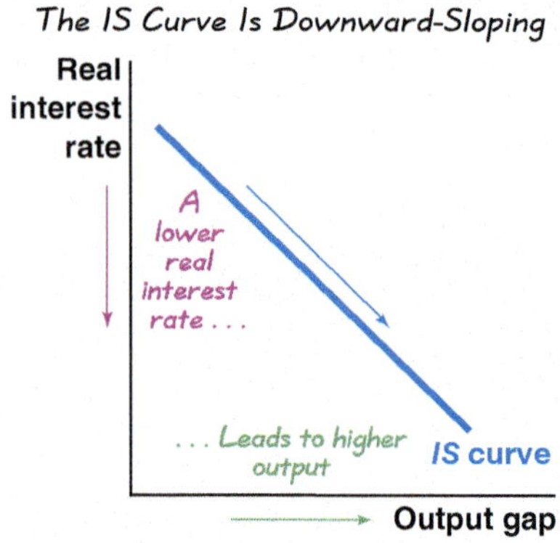

The *IS* curve is like a macroeconomic demand curve. You are probably used to thinking about a demand curve as showing this year's demand for a specific product, like petrol. In many ways, the *IS* curve is similar—it shows this year's demand for *all* types of output and so you can think of it as showing the macroeconomic demand for output.

As with a demand curve, the vertical axis shows a price—in this case, that price is the real interest rate, which is the opportunity cost of spending money this year rather than next. And the horizontal axis shows the corresponding quantity—the output gap—which is the total quantity of goods and services purchased across the whole economy, relative to potential output.

The *IS* curve is downward-sloping, like a typical demand curve. That's because a lower real interest rate decreases the opportunity cost of making purchases this year, leading people across the whole economy to respond by buying more goods and services. Or you can say this the other way: The higher the real interest rate is, the greater the opportunity cost of buying stuff this year (rather than next), and so the smaller the quantity of stuff people demand this year. And while we call the *IS* curve a curve, as Figure 4 illustrates, it could also be a straight line.

How to Use the *IS* Curve

The *IS* curve is a valuable tool for forecasting economic conditions. For instance, can you forecast what the output gap will be if the real interest is 4%?

Figure 5 illustrates how to figure this out. First, locate the 4% real interest rate on the vertical axis. Then look across until you find the *IS* curve. Now look down to discover that the corresponding level of GDP is 5% *below* its potential level. That's it, you've now got your forecast.

If other things change, so should your forecast. Of course, this is your forecast, holding other things constant. If other factors change, then so should your forecast.

This points to another way the *IS* curve can be helpful: You can use it to forecast the consequences of changing economic conditions.

A change in the real interest rate leads to a movement along the *IS* curve. In Figure 5, you started by looking at point A, where the real interest rate is 4%. Now consider what happens if policy makers cut the real interest rate to 1%. Locate the new 1% real interest rate on the vertical axis and look across until you hit the *IS* curve. Look down, and you'll see that it corresponds to an output gap of +2.5%, which means that GDP will be 2.5% *above* potential GDP. And so you can conclude that reducing the real interest rate from 4% to 1% will cause the output gap to change from −5% to +2.5%.

Notice that this change in the real interest rate led the economy to move from one point on the *IS* curve to another point on the same curve. This makes sense: The point of the *IS* curve is to illustrate how the output gap responds to changes in the real interest rate, and so changes in the real interest rate lead to *a movement along* the IS curve.

This is where it's important that you distinguish between:

- *Changes in the real interest rate:* which cause a *movement along* the *IS* curve
- *Changes in other factors* that change aggregate expenditure at a given interest rate: which cause the *IS* curve to *shift*

Later in the chapter, we'll look at the changes in other factors that can shift the *IS* curve.

Figure 5 | Changing Interest Rates Leads to a Movement Along the *IS* Curve

Ⓐ When the real interest rate is 4%, the output gap is −5%
Ⓑ When the real interest rate is 1%, the output gap is +2.5%
Ⓒ Changes in the real interest rate lead to a movement along a fixed *IS* curve.

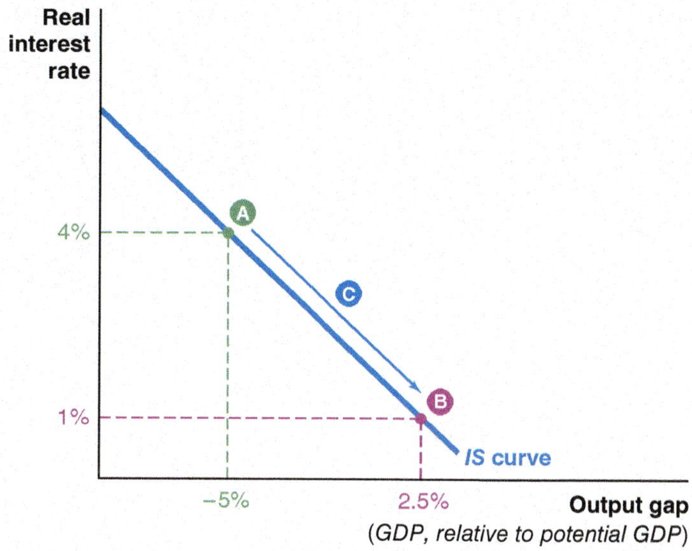

Interpreting the DATA **What caused the early 1990s recession?**

After being elected in 1983, the Hawke–Keating Labor Government embarked upon a series of economic reforms that opened up the Australian economy to the world. Tariffs were cut, the banking system was opened up to foreign competition, an "Accord" with the trade union movement was reached to reform industrial relations, and the Australian dollar was "floated"—letting market forces determine its value. The economy boomed, with GDP growth as high as 5.3% in 1985 and 5.7% in 1988.

Concerned that the economy was "overheating" and with inflation running at over 7.5%, the Reserve Bank began ratcheting up interest rates. Official rates rose fairly rapidly from 10.7% to 18.7%. This put the real interest rate at over 10%.

Just as our analysis suggests, a high real interest led businesses to sharply curtail investment and households to cut back on consumption, and it caused the Australian dollar to rise, leading net exports to fall. Aggregate expenditure fell, causing GDP to drop. In the September quarter of 1990, GDP fell by a stunning 1.6%.

Households with mortgages faced interest rates of over 20%, causing a public outcry. Treasurer Paul Keating made an infamous remark in a November 1990 press conference: "The first thing to say is, the accounts do show that Australia is in a recession. The most important thing about that is that this is a recession that Australia had to have."

High real interest rates ended up being too successful at slowing the economy. GDP fell to far below potential output, which created a very negative output gap. The unemployment rate rose from 6.1% in 1989 to 10.7% in 1992. This episode settled any remaining debate in Australia about the importance of the real interest rate in shaping the business cycle. It vividly demonstrated the relevance of the *IS* curve, as this bout of high interest rates led to lower levels of aggregate expenditure, lower GDP, and a sharply negative output gap. ■

At this point, you've got a good handle on the *IS* curve: It tells you what the output gap will be at each real interest rate. But what determines the real interest rate, and what could cause it to change? Figuring that out is our next task.

30.3 The *MP* Curve: What Determines the Interest Rate

Learning Objective *Use the MP curve to summarise how the real interest rate is determined.*

Our next stop is the financial markets, where interest rates are determined. We'll start by analysing the role of the Reserve Bank. We'll then incorporate the rest of the financial system to see how other market factors—including the price of risk—shape the interest rate. We're digging into the factors determining interest rates because the *IS* curve tells us that they have major economic consequences. Our goal is to bring these insights together in a few pages into a compact and useful framework.

The Reserve Bank

Lisa Maree Williams/Getty Images

RBA governor Philip Lowe pondering the *IS* curve.

On the first Tuesday of each month (except for January, but including Melbourne Cup Day in November), the board of the Reserve Bank of Australia meet at their head office in Martin Place, Sydney, to set the interest rate. They consider all kinds of data about how the economy is doing, discuss what trends they're seeing in different parts of the economy, debate the implications, and think through a variety of scenarios. As policy makers discuss where to set the interest rate, they, at least implicitly, consult their estimates of the *IS* curve in order to assess the implications of each possible choice.

At the end of this meeting, the Reserve Bank issues a statement (typically at 2:30 pm) to let everyone know how it plans to change the interest rate. When the RBA sets interest rates in an effort to influence economic conditions, this process is called **monetary policy.** It's so important that we'll devote all of Chapter 34 to studying it. For now, we'll focus on the big picture, leaving the details for later.

monetary policy The process of setting interest rates in an effort to influence economic conditions.

The RBA sets the nominal interest rate to influence the real interest rate. When the Reserve Bank announces that it's setting the interest rate at 5%, it's actually setting the *nominal* interest rate. But just as we have focused on the real interest rate because that's the rate that people respond to, so does the RBA. If inflation is 2%, then it's just as accurate to say that the RBA set the nominal interest rate at 5% as it is to say that it set the real interest rate at 3%. And so we'll describe the Reserve Bank as setting the *real* interest rate because in practical terms that's what it is doing.

The RBA's decisions percolate throughout the whole economy. The RBA doesn't set every interest rate in the economy. Rather, its policy tool is a specific interest rate called the *cash rate,* which is the interest rate on a set of overnight loans between banks that are almost certain to be repaid the next day. There's no such thing as a loan with zero risk, but these overnight loans come pretty close—so close, in fact, that for our purposes you can think of the Reserve Bank as effectively setting the **risk-free interest rate.**

risk-free interest rate The interest rate on a loan that involves no risk.

Changes in the risk-free interest rate then percolate through the rest of the economy, affecting the interest rate you're paid on your savings, the interest rate at which you can borrow money for a house or car, the interest rate on your credit card, and the interest rate at which businesses can borrow to fund their investments. But the RBA is not the only force affecting interest rates.

The Risk Premium

There's another critical factor that affects interest rates: risk. Whenever you lend someone money, there are risks involved. You might not get paid back, you might set the interest rate too low, or you might end up needing those funds yourself.

The interest rate on any loan reflects the risk-free rate plus a risk premium. Banks and other lenders demand to be paid extra for taking on risk. The extra interest that they charge to account for risk is called the **risk premium.** It's the reason that the interest rate you pay on your credit card, car loan, housing mortgage, or a business loan is typically higher than the risk-free interest rate set by the Reserve Bank. While riskier borrowers and riskier types of loans might get charged a higher risk premium, for now we'll simply focus on the risk premium that's charged for a typical loan.

risk premium The extra interest that lenders charge to account for the risk of loaning money.

As a result, the real interest rate that's relevant to the typical borrower—and hence is relevant for our analysis—reflects two influences: It's the risk-free rate (set by the RBA), plus the risk premium, which is determined by financial markets.

$$\text{Real interest rate} = \text{Risk-free real interest rate} + \text{Risk premium}$$

The risk premium is determined in financial markets. This is where financial markets come in. That's where the buyers and sellers of risk—mainly big banks and other financial institutions—meet to trade risk. They do this by buying and selling complicated financial contracts that allow them to reallocate the risks in their portfolios—including the risks associated with the money they have loaned you. You can think of the market for risk as being like other markets: There are many buyers and sellers, and just as a buyer of T-shirts has to pay $10 to induce a supplier to produce one, a borrower has to pay a financial institution a risk premium to induce it to make a risky loan. Seen this way, the risk premium is a price—the price at which financial institutions are willing to bear the risk associated with lending you money. This price is determined by the forces of supply and demand, and so it reflects changing financial conditions and sentiments in financial markets.

Ruffer/Agencja Fotograficzna Caro/Alamy Stock Photo

This is where risk is traded.

EVERYDAY Economics **Why you pay different interest rates on different loans**

Macroeconomic analysis focuses on the typical risk premium faced by the typical borrower. But in your own life, you'll confront different risk premiums on different types of loans, leading you to pay different interest rates.

The riskier the loan, the higher the interest rate you'll end up paying. For instance, a family member might be willing to lend you money at a lower rate than a bank because they'll trust that you'll repay them. (And unlike a bank, they might have other ways of making you pay, like making you feel guilty or withholding something important to you.) When you take out a car loan, the lender (usually a bank) has the right to repossess your car if you fall behind on your repayments. That makes a car loan less risky than a personal loan, which is why banks offer lower interest rates on car loans than they do on personal loans. Try to borrow money at a payday lending shop (actually, don't ever do that unless you are under acute financial stress and have exhausted all other possibilities), and you'll discover outrageously high interest rates. That's partly because these are risky loans. And it's partly because the only people who aren't driven away by those high rates are usually in some kind of financial pickle, making them riskier still. ■

The *MP* Curve

MP curve Illustrates the current real interest rate, which is shaped by monetary policy and the risk premium.

It's time to integrate our analysis of the RBA and financial markets into the broader framework we're developing. We do this by adding a new curve, the ***MP* curve,** which stands for "Monetary Policy," because we use it to illustrate the current real interest rate, which is largely shaped by monetary policy. The name is a bit misleading, because we also use the *MP* curve to illustrate how changes in the risk premium affect the real interest rate.

Figure 6 The *MP* Curve

The MP curve describes the real interest rate, which reflects both the risk-free interest rate set by the Reserve Bank, and the risk premium.

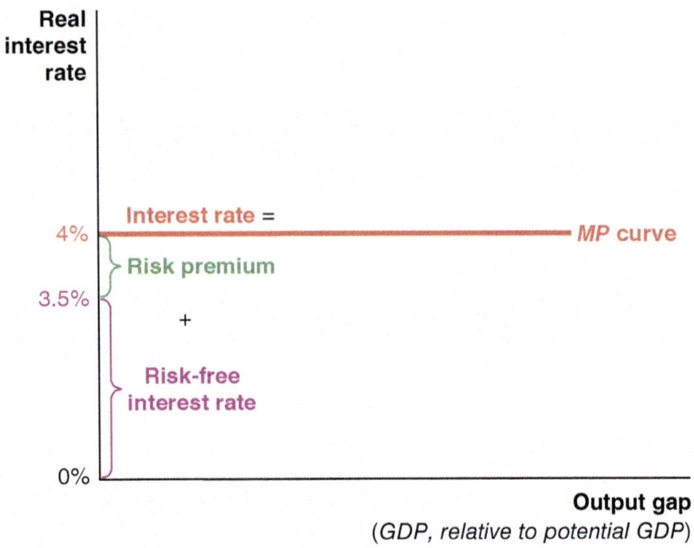

The *MP* curve illustrates the real interest rate. As Figure 6 shows, if the Reserve Bank sets the real interest rate at 3.5%, and the risk premium is 0.5%, then the *MP* curve is a horizontal line at 4%. We draw the *MP* curve as a horizontal line to illustrate that 4% is the real interest rate, no matter what the output gap is.

The *MP* curve illustrates the current real interest rate. If the interest rate changes—either because the RBA changes monetary policy, or changes in financial markets shift the risk premium—the *MP* curve will shift to illustrate this.

You can measure the risk premium using interest rate spreads. Here's a simple trick you can use to track the risk premium: Calculate the difference between the interest rate at which you can borrow and the risk-free interest rate (and make sure you're comparing loans of the same duration). This difference, which is called an *interest rate spread,* is an estimate of the risk premium.

A useful proxy for the risk-free interest rate is the interest rate on loans to the Australian government, because the Australian government is almost certainly going to pay its debts. And so you can calculate the risk premium as the difference between the interest rate at which you can borrow and the interest rate on a similar duration loan to the Australian government.

Figure 7 TED Spread

Interest rate on three-month loans to banks, less interest rate on three-month loans to the Australian government

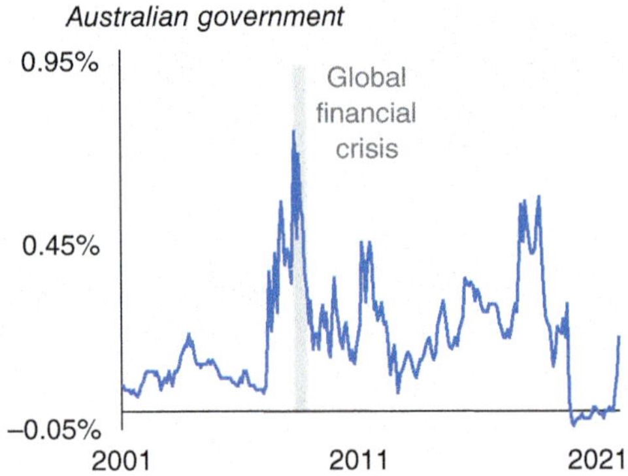

Interpreting the DATA **Measuring financial risk**

The TED spread is an important interest rate spread that economists watch closely to monitor the health of the banking system. Ignore the name—it's an obscure financial acronym used in the U.S.—and focus instead on what it is: the difference between the interest rate at which banks lend to each other for a three-month period, and the interest rate at which the Australian government can borrow for three months. As such, it's a measure of the perceived riskiness of the banking system. As you can see in Figure 7, the TED spread is usually low and stable. However, during a major financial crisis, it will spike, pointing to increased risk in the financial system. Each spike corresponds to a rise in the risk premium. As the global financial crisis emerged in 2008, the TED spread rose sharply, indicating a higher risk premium, which shifted the *MP* curve upward. If anything, this understated the problem: The TED spread tells you about the risk premium *if* you can get a loan. During the worst days of the crisis, many borrowers couldn't find anyone willing to lend to them. Interestingly, the TED spread was much higher in the U.S. during the financial crisis—it shot over 3%. That reflected the shaky state of U.S. bank balance sheets compared to the relatively prudent Australian banks. ■

The *MP* curve is simple because monetary policy is simple. Before we continue, a historical note. You'll notice that the *MP* curve is pretty simple—you just draw a horizontal line to show whatever the current real interest rate is. That's because the Reserve Bank simply announces where it wants to set the interest rate, and the *MP* curve reflects that (plus the risk premium). But it wasn't always so easy. Several decades ago, the Reserve Bank implemented monetary policy by announcing changes in the money supply instead. Figuring out how this affected the economy required a careful analysis of Liquidity and Money, which is why some economics textbooks describe a more complicated *LM* curve, instead of the

MP curve. So if you come across a reference to *IS-LM* analysis, you should know that they're describing similar ideas, but analysing an older approach to monetary policy.

You've now developed two powerful tools for understanding the business cycle—the *IS* curve and the *MP* curve. Our next task is to bring them together, into an integrated *IS-MP* framework. Just as businesses, investors, and policy makers do, you'll be able to use this framework to organise your thoughts about the implications of changing economic conditions.

30.4 The *IS-MP* Framework

Learning Objective *Forecast economic conditions and how they'll respond to monetary and fiscal policy.*

Okay, let's put it all together. The *IS* curve illustrates how the output gap depends on the real interest rate. And the *MP* curve tells you what the real interest rate will be. Put them together, and you'll have a complete story of what determines the state of the economy. As a manager and as an investor, you'll be able to use this framework to interpret economic news and figure out what it means for your future.

IS-MP Equilibrium

We bring the *IS* and *MP* curves together in Figure 8. As you know, the *IS* curve shows you the level of the output gap that corresponds with each possible value of the real interest rate. The *MP* curve tells you what the real interest rate is. Their intersection determines the macroeconomic equilibrium, revealing the level of the output gap that's consistent with the real interest rate. In this example, the risk-free interest rate plus the risk premium sets the real interest rate at 4%, which yields an equilibrium GDP that is 5% below its potential level, for an output gap of –5%.

Figure 8 | **The *IS-MP* Framework**

The state of the economy is determined by the intersection of the IS curve and the MP curve.

- A The *IS* curve describes the level of aggregate expenditure and hence the output gap associated with each real interest rate.
- B The *MP* curve describes the real interest rate set by monetary policy and financial markets.
- C The economy moves to the point of macroeconomic equilibrium where the two curves intersect.
- D This occurs when the real interest rate is 4% and the equilibrium output gap is –5% (which means that GDP is 5% below potential GDP).

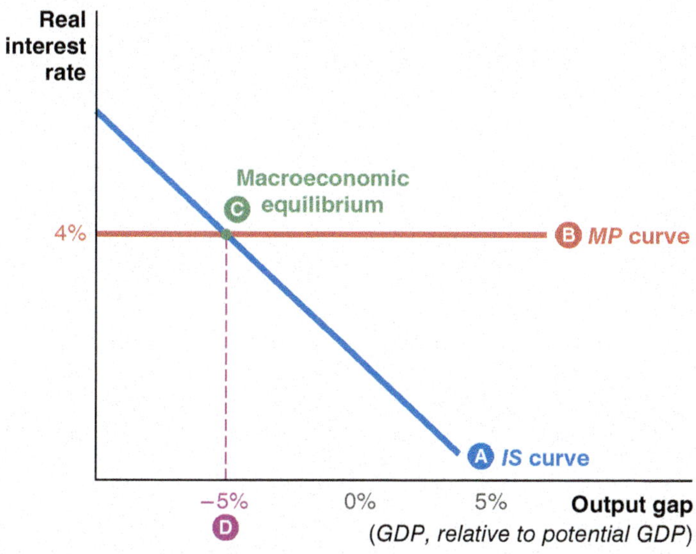

That's it—you've got your forecast for economic conditions. More than that, you've now put together a comprehensive framework for understanding business cycles. This isn't just a textbook exercise—this is the framework that guides the macroeconomic forecasts produced by many government policy makers, professional investors, and business analysts.

Fluctuating Demand and Business Cycles

So far, we've seen that aggregate expenditure plays a central role in determining the macroeconomic equilibrium. This suggests that perhaps we can understand recessions and depressions as periods of weak or declining aggregate expenditure. By this view, the booms and busts of the business cycle reflect the economy shifting between periods of strong and weak demand. We explore this idea in Figure 9, which illustrates two alternative macroeconomic equilibria.

Strong aggregate expenditure leads to a booming economy and full employment. One possibility is that people are optimistic about the future. Students who are optimistic that they'll get a good job after graduation will spend more money at any given interest rate, as will workers who are optimistic about promotions and pay raises, and entrepreneurs who are confident about their business success. These optimistic spending plans are illustrated by the blue *IS* curve in Figure 9, which shows high levels of aggregate expenditure at each level of the real interest rate. This leads to a macroeconomic equilibrium with an output gap of zero, which means that GDP is at its highest sustainable level. In this booming economy, output is high, unemployment is low, and the economic outlook is sunny enough that continued economic optimism is warranted. Think of this as the macroeconomic equilibrium in good times.

Figure 9 | Booms and Busts

Bouts of optimism and pessimism can drive the economy into booms and busts.

A. The **optimistic *IS* curve** describes spending plans in good times when people are optimistic about their economic future.

B. It leads to a **boom equilibrium** where output is at potential, validating people's optimism.

C. But if people become **pessimistic** about the future, they'll cut back on how much they plan to spend at any given interest rate, and businesses will respond by cutting production. This decrease in output at any given real interest rate **shifts the *IS* curve to the left**.

D. The economy shifts to a **bust equilibrium,** where output declines to be less than potential output. Because this economic slump is an equilibrium, it will persist if nothing changes.

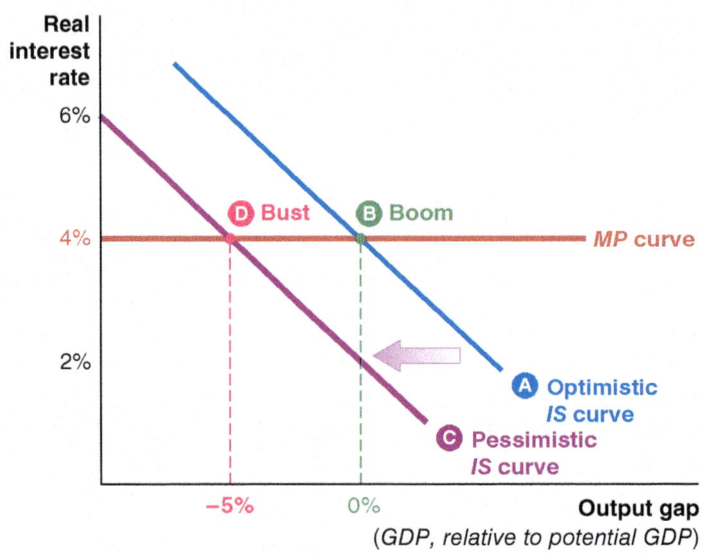

Insufficient spending can lead to an economic slump and unemployment. There's also the possibility that a wave of pessimism hits. Pessimism about future economic conditions might lead consumers to cut back on their spending, or businesses to cut back on their investment plans. In each case, the result is a decrease in aggregate expenditure at any given real interest rate and level of income, which causes the *IS* curve to shift left to the purple line.

This lower level of aggregate expenditure yields a new macroeconomic equilibrium at a much lower level of GDP. The output gap is now negative, which means that the economy is producing below its potential. Because businesses are producing less, they need fewer workers. As a result, in this recessionary equilibrium, people have lower incomes, and there's widespread unemployment. In this new equilibrium, the pessimism that caused the downturn now appears to be warranted. Pessimism about an economic slump has caused an economic slump. Think of this as the equilibrium during the Great Depression, or in any of the downturns since.

Changes in aggregate expenditures create macroeconomic fluctuations. In this analysis, the economy fluctuates between periods of boom and bust—and points in between—due to changes in aggregate expenditure shifting the *IS* curve. While we've focused on what happens when spending changes due to bouts of optimism or pessimism, similar booms and busts will follow in response to any factor that causes aggregate expenditure to shift at a given interest rate. The broader lesson is that many of the ups and downs of the business cycle reflect shifts in aggregate expenditure.

Interpreting the DATA **Tracking waves of optimism and pessimism**

By this view, the key to understanding changing business conditions is to keep track of changing spending patterns. If your business sells mainly to consumers, then surveys of consumer confidence can help you keep track of changing consumption plans. If your business sells machinery and investment goods to other companies, then surveys of business confidence can help you keep track of their spending plans. As Figure 10 shows, the economy does indeed appear to experience periods of optimism and pessimism. ■

Figure 10 | **Consumer Confidence and Business Confidence**

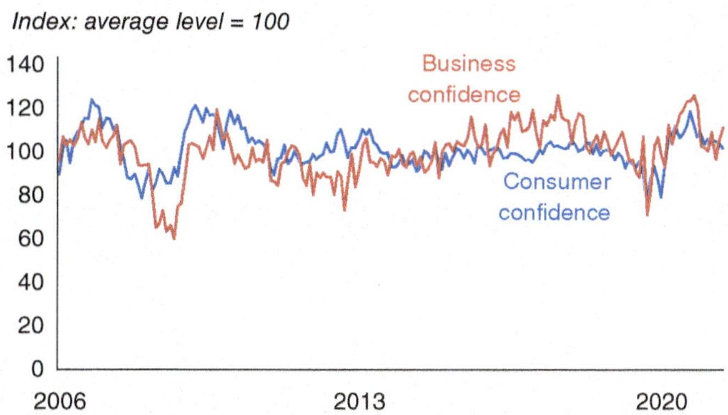

Data from: Refinitiv, CEIC Purchasing Managers Index.

Recessions can be individually rational and collectively terrible. Many of these ideas about the possibility of deficient demand causing recessions were first put forward (in somewhat different terms) by economist John Maynard Keynes in the wake of the Great Depression, the worst economic slump in modern memory. The Depression shook the faith of many economists, leaving them wondering how it's possible for the economy to perform so poorly as to leave millions of people unemployed. Amid this deep and prolonged downturn, Keynes argued that the economy can be in macroeconomic equilibrium even when output is far below its potential and unemployment is widespread. In doing so, he argued that unless the government intervened, an economic slump could persist for years.

The economic slump we outlined in Figure 9 illustrates the modern form of his argument. It illustrates a macroeconomic equilibrium in which the economy produces less than its potential. If nothing changes, a prolonged recession will follow. That's because once we're in this bad equilibrium, there's no reason for either buyers or sellers to change their plans. After all, businesses cut back on production because people spend less, and people spend less because they're worried about a prolonged recession.

This highlights the paradox of recessions: Each person is individually making the best decision they can, but those decisions add up to a collectively terrible outcome in which the economy is stuck in a bad equilibrium. The depressing lesson is that there's no guarantee that businesses will produce enough to keep everyone employed.

EVERYDAY Economics **How the economy is just like a concert**

Ivica Drusany/Shutterstock

It's just like widespread unemployment.

If you want to better understand how recessions happen, think of the Australian economy as being like a concert. In a concert economy, your backside is an employer, and your seat is a worker. If you sit down, your seat is fully employed, but if you stand up, your seat is unemployed. How do you decide what to do? The *interdependence principle* dictates that your best choice depends on what others do. At the concert, you'll stay seated if all your neighbors are sitting down. In this equilibrium every seat is fully employed. But if your neighbors stand up, you're better off standing too, because that's the only way you'll be able to see. When you stand, then others might also have to stand. The result is an equilibrium in which many seats are unemployed. I bet you've been at a concert that switches between the equilibrium in which all seats are employed, to one in which thousands are unemployed.

The same thing happens in the economy: You'll employ plenty of workers at your business if there are plenty of customers willing to buy your products. But the number of customers willing to buy your products depends on how many workers other companies employ. Just as you'll be forced to stand at a concert if others stand, you might be forced to fire some workers if your customers lose their jobs as other companies cut their payrolls. The concert economy can quickly shift from an equilibrium in which every seat is employed by someone to a different equilibrium in which many seats are unemployed, and so too the macroeconomy can shift from the good equilibrium in which every worker has a job, to a bad equilibrium in which millions of workers are unemployed.

Importantly, neither unemployed seats nor unemployed workers are inevitable. At the concert, if everyone else can be persuaded to sit down, you'll also sit down, and the seats will be fully employed again. Likewise, in the economy, if people can be persuaded to spend money again, then businesses will increase their production to keep up, and they'll hire the unemployed workers. In fact, as we'll explore shortly, this is precisely how policy makers try to kickstart the economy out of recession. ■

Let's now see how you can use this framework to understand the effects of macroeconomic policy.

Analysing Monetary Policy

Late 2008 was the apex of one of the most tumultuous periods in Australia's economic history. The stock market plummeted, house prices fell for the first time in many people's memory, U.S. financial institutions like Bear Sterns and Lehman Brothers collapsed, and there were genuine fears of a run on Australian banks. Businesses stopped investing, consumers cut their spending, and nearly 200,000 people lost their jobs. Overseas, the news was even worse: The global economy was in free fall, and no one knew how bad things could get. Was the next Great Depression just a few months away?

Policy makers in Treasury and the Reserve Bank met late, and continued into the early hours of the morning for days on end. The pressure to make sure that Australia didn't suffer a repeat of the Great Depression was intense. And thanks to the lessons of the past, and some quick thinking from the policy makers involved, Australia was one of the few countries to actually avoid a recession—let alone a calamity like the 1930s.

By the end of the year, GDP was well below potential GDP. These aren't abstract statistics; they summarise a landscape littered with dormant factories, hundreds of thousands of jobless workers, and families doing without. If you were a member of the Reserve Bank or the Treasury, what would you do?

Monetary policy shifts the *MP* curve. Policy makers at the Reserve Bank responded quickly and decisively, cutting its benchmark interest rate four times over the course of 2008. It's rare to see the RBA act this boldly. What did this mean for the economy, and for businesses? Fortunately, you can use the *IS-MP* framework to figure this out.

When the RBA changes the real interest rate, it shifts the *MP* curve. In this case, the RBA cut the interest rate, which shifted the *MP* curve down. As Figure 11 illustrates, this shift in the *MP* curve leads to a new equilibrium, which involves higher GDP at a lower real interest rate. Armed with this analysis, savvy managers realised they no longer needed to keep cutting back. Indeed, consistent with the forecast from our *IS-MP* analysis, the RBA's dramatic actions halted the economy's nosedive, and eventually there were signs that the worst days were behind us.

But it also became increasingly clear that monetary policy alone could not cure all of the economy's ills. The Reserve Bank cut official interest rates from 7.25% to 3% between September 2008 and April 2009. The RBA normally leaves the rate unchanged at their monthly meeting, and when they do change the rate it is in 0.25% increments. But three different times during this period they cut rates by a full percentage point.

Yet right from the start of the financial crisis, Treasury Secretary Ken Henry and Prime Minister Kevin Rudd knew that monetary policy alone would not be enough to save the Australian economy.

Figure 11 | Changes in Monetary Policy Shift the *MP* Curve

When the Reserve Bank cuts real interest rates, it stimulates an increase in equilibrium GDP.

A In the **recessionary equilibrium**, GDP is less than potential GDP.

B Cutting the real interest rate causes the ***MP* curve to shift down**.

C This leads the economy to shift to a **new equilibrium, with higher GDP**, eliminating the negative output gap.

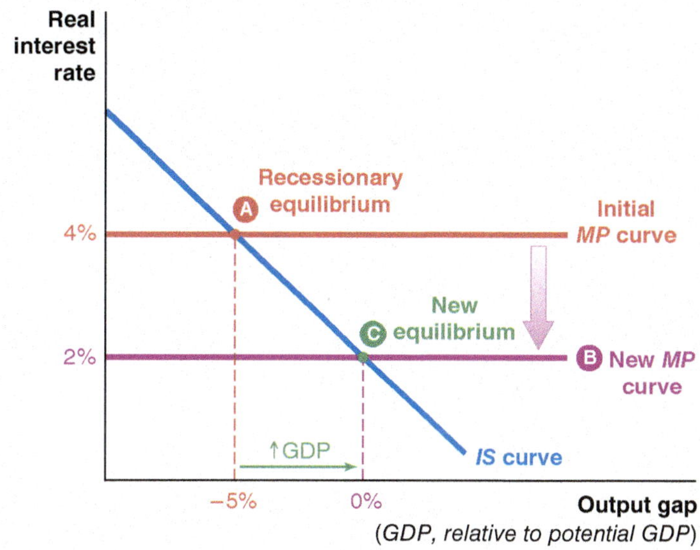

fiscal policy The government's use of spending and tax policies to influence economic conditions.

Analysing Fiscal Policy and the Multiplier

The government can also influence the economy through **fiscal policy**—that is, by adjusting its own spending and tax policies. And so in mid-October 2008, the Rudd Government announced a \$10.4 billion stimulus package involving \$1000 to \$2000 direct payments to pensioners and low- and middle-income households. Treasury Secretary Ken Henry famously described the strategy to quickly get cash into the pockets of those most likely to spend it as "go hard, go early, go households."

In early February 2009, the Government followed up with a (then) massive \$42 billion additional stimulus package known as the "Nation Building and Jobs Plan" which consisted largely of infrastructure spending.

When the federal government adjusts fiscal policy, it shifts the *IS* curve. In this case, an expansionary fiscal policy boosts aggregate expenditure, which shifts the *IS* curve to the right. Figure 12 shows that this expansionary fiscal policy leads to a rise in output and hence a more positive output gap. But to see how big this effect is, we need to explore an idea called the multiplier.

Figure 12 | Changes in Fiscal Policy Shift the *IS* Curve

When the government increases spending, it stimulates an increase in equilibrium GDP.

A Increased government spending causes the ***IS* curve to shift right**. It has a multiplied effect, and so shifts by **ΔG × Multiplier**.

B This leads the economy to shift to a **new equilibrium**.

C This new equilibrium involves **higher GDP** and an unchanged interest rate.

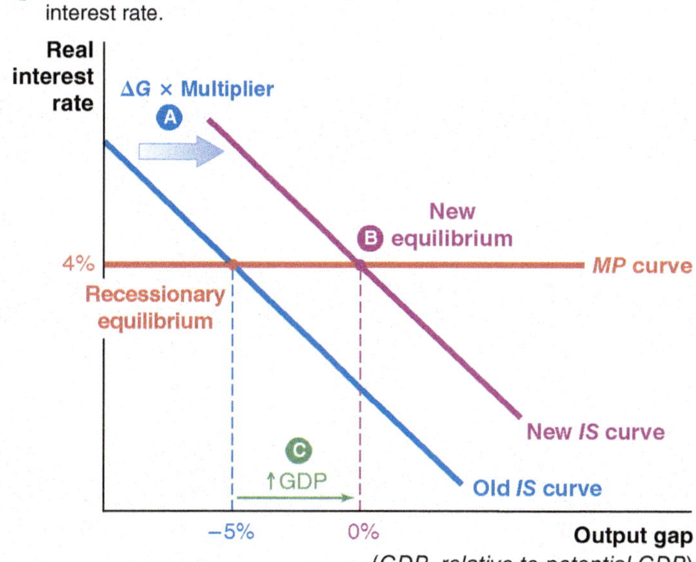

An increase in spending has a multiplied effect on aggregate expenditure. An initial burst of government spending will have repercussions throughout the economy. Consider the money spent building new roads. The direct effect is that unemployed transportation engineers, construction workers, and road maintenance crews will be hired and put

Ufuk ZIVANA/Shutterstock

An initial boost in spending reverberates through the economy.

to work. There will also be important ripple effects. For instance, a worker who decides to spend some of their earnings on home improvement gear at Bunnings boosts the incomes of Bunnings workers and Wesfarmers (the parent company of Bunnings) shareholders. There are also second-round ripple effects. As Bunnings sells more gear, it'll hire more workers, who might buy lunch at a local Subway, leading the franchise owner to hire more staff. There are third-round effects, too. If the new Subway staff buy clothes, the owner of the nearby clothing store also receives a boost to their income. And so it continues.

As this initial boost in spending reverberates through the economy, it illustrates the importance of the *interdependence principle* for understanding macroeconomic developments. This interdependence arises because one person's spending is another person's income. It means that extra spending by the government stimulates extra spending by construction workers, which stimulates extra spending in home-improvement, food, and clothing industries. As the initial burst of government purchases ripples through the economy, it has a multiplied effect, leading to an even larger boost to aggregate expenditure.

The multiplier summarises the effect of an initial burst of spending on output. You can summarise the consequences of a rise in spending—including both the direct impact and the many rounds of subsequent ripple effects—with a single number called the multiplier. The **multiplier** measures how much GDP changes as a result of both the direct and indirect effects flowing from each extra dollar of spending. For instance, if the multiplier is 2, then an initial $1 boost to spending will generate a total of $2 in additional spending and hence output. When people have a greater propensity to spend any additional income they receive, the ripple effects of an initial burst of spending will be larger, leading the multiplier to be larger.

multiplier A measure of how much GDP changes as a result of both the direct and indirect effects flowing from each extra dollar of spending.

The multiplier is useful, because you can use it to forecast the effects of changes in spending as follows:

$$\Delta \text{GDP} = \Delta \text{Spending} \times \text{Multiplier}$$

You can use the multiplier to figure out the likely consequences of the 2008–09 stimulus bills. (To simplify, we'll treat the entire $52 billion cost of the stimulus bill as if it were a rise in government purchases, which is not strictly accurate.)

Do the Economics

How much will GDP rise after a $52 billion increase in government purchases, if the multiplier is 2?

$$\Delta \text{GDP} = \underbrace{\$52 \text{ billion}}_{\Delta \text{Spending}} \times \underbrace{2}_{\text{Multiplier}} = \$104 \text{ billion} \ \blacksquare$$

If you want to dig more deeply into the logic (and maths) of the multiplier, turn to the appendix titled "A Closer Look at Aggregate Expenditure and the Multiplier."

The multiplier determines how far the *IS* curve shifts. The multiplier is relevant to our *IS-MP* analysis because it determines how far the *IS* curve shifts following an initial burst of spending. The new *IS* curve shifts to reflect the new level of aggregate expenditure, and so it needs to account for both the direct effect of new spending and its ripple effects stimulating yet more spending. As a result, Figure 12 illustrates the *IS* curve shifting by an amount equal to the initial change in spending times the multiplier. This shift in the *IS* curve leads to a new equilibrium, which involves higher GDP, but no change in the real interest rate.

This analysis tells you that fiscal stimulus will help the economy grow, and so managers should get ready to increase production. In fact, the economy largely followed this forecast, as the 2008–09 stimulus was an important factor leading to a stronger economy in 2010 and 2011.

30.5 Macroeconomic Shocks

Learning Objective *Use the IS-MP framework to forecast the effects of macroeconomic shocks.*

So far, we've used the *IS-MP* framework to analyse how fiscal and monetary policy affects the economy. We can also use it to assess the likely consequences of other changes in economic conditions like changes in consumer spending or investment. We'll start by identifying the shocks that shift the *IS* curve, and then turn to the shocks that shift the *MP* curve.

spending shocks Any change in aggregate expenditure at a given real interest rate and level of income. Spending shocks shift the *IS* curve.

Spending Shocks Shift the *IS* Curve

Recall that the *IS* curve reflects aggregate expenditure at each real interest rate. This means that at a given real interest rate and level of income, *any change in spending will shift the IS curve*. As Figure 13 illustrates, this has a multiplied effect, and the resulting increase in aggregate expenditure will shift the economy to a new equilibrium with a higher level of GDP and hence a more positive output gap.

The same dynamic operates in reverse, too, and a decrease in spending shifts the *IS* curve to the left. The multiplier also applies to spending cuts, because less spending by one person means less income for another, which leads them to cut their spending. As these cutbacks ripple through the economy, the net result is a multiplied decrease in aggregate expenditure shifting the *IS* curve further to the left. This shifts the economy to a new equilibrium with a lower level of GDP and hence a more negative output gap.

Shifts in the *IS* curve are driven by **spending shocks,** which change the level of aggregate expenditure associated with a given real interest rate and level of income. As you think through the possible sources of spending shocks, simply think about each component of aggregate expenditure: consumption, investment, government purchases, and net exports.

Figure 13 | **Changes in Spending Shift the *IS* Curve**

When spending rises, it stimulates an increase in equilibrium GDP.

(A) Increased spending causes the ***IS* curve to shift right**. It has a multiplied effect, and so shifts by **Δ Spending × Multiplier**.

(B) This leads the economy to shift to a **new equilibrium**.

(C) This new equilibrium involves **higher GDP**, and an unchanged real interest rate.

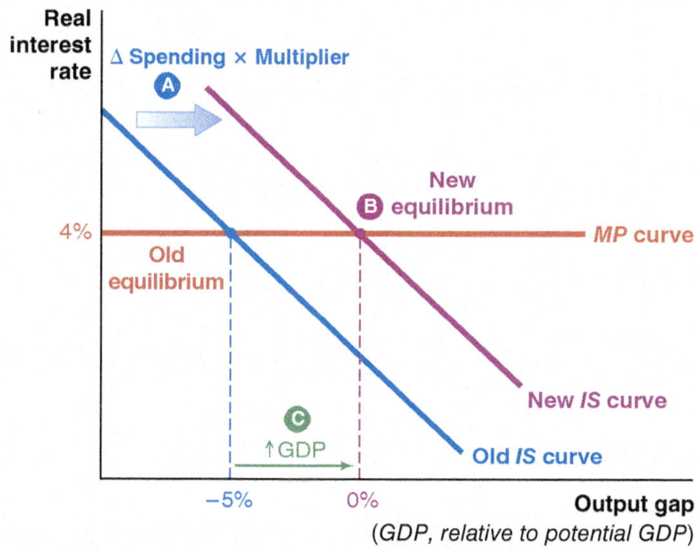

Spending shock one: Consumption increases when people feel more prosperous. People typically increase their spending when they have more money to spend, or are confident that they soon will. Thus, any development that makes people feel more prosperous—or more confident that they will soon be prosperous—leads to an increase in consumption. This means that consumption will shift in response to:

Consumption increases if people feel more prosperous:
↑ Wealth
↑ Consumer confidence
↑ Government assistance
↓ Taxes
↓ Inequality

Wealth: When the stock market booms, or house prices rise, stockholders and homeowners feel more prosperous because their wealth has increased. As those lucky stockholders and homeowners spend some of their newfound wealth, consumption will increase.

Consumer confidence: The *interdependence principle* reminds you that the decisions you make today depend on your expectations about what's going to happen in the future. And when you feel confident that your income will grow in the future, you might ramp up your spending in advance. As a result, consumption increases when an improved economic outlook boosts consumer confidence.

Taxes and government assistance: When the government cuts taxes, or when it increases government assistance payments like rent assistance or JobSeeker, people have more disposable income that they can use to buy stuff. And so consumption increases when government policy puts more money in people's pockets.

Inequality: People with low incomes tend to spend a larger share of their income than do those with higher incomes. It follows that redistributing income from those with higher incomes to those with lower incomes—including through government transfer payments and changes in the tax system—tends to increase consumption.

Investment increases if it's profitable to expand production:
↑ GDP growth
↑ Business confidence
↑ Investment tax credits
↓ Corporate taxes
↑ Easier lending standards and more cash reserves
↓ Uncertainty

Spending shock two: Investment increases when it's profitable for businesses to expand. As a manager, you'll invest in new machinery when you believe that it will be profitable to expand your production. The *cost-benefit principle* reminds you to consider both the benefits of the extra revenue you'll earn from enhancing your production capacity, and the cost of making that investment. As a result, investment will shift in response to:

An expanding economy: When the economy is expanding, so is the demand for your products. In order to produce more, managers need to expand their production capacity. As a result, investment in new equipment increases when the economy is expanding more rapidly.

Business confidence: Because capital investments tend to last for years, or even decades, your assessments about whether to buy new equipment should depend not only on today's profits, but also on your expectations about future profitability. That's why investment increases when managers are more confident about their long-term profitability.

Corporate taxes: Lower corporate taxes increase the after-tax profits that entrepreneurs earn from investing in new equipment. As a result, investment falls in response to higher corporate taxes. Conversely, investment rises in response to targeted investment tax credits that reduce the after-tax cost of buying new equipment.

Lending standards and cash reserves: If your business finds it hard to borrow money at a reasonable interest rate, your best alternative is to invest in new equipment only when your company has the cash on hand to do so. It follows that investment tends to increase when loans are easier to get, or businesses have large cash reserves. Cash reserves are particularly important when the financial system is not working well.

Uncertainty: If you're uncertain about the economic outlook—it could be great, it could be terrible—remember that you usually have the option to postpone breaking ground on major investment projects until the outlook is a bit clearer. Lower uncertainty leads managers to restart these shelved projects, leading to an increase in investment.

Government purchases increase in response to fiscal policy:

- Spending bills
- Automatic stabilisers

. . . but not transfer payments (at least not directly)

Spending shock three: Government purchases increase when fiscal policy seeks to expand the economy. Government purchases rise when the government uses fiscal policy to stimulate the economy—for instance, by building highways or buying new military equipment. In addition, some government programs—known as *automatic stabilisers*—automatically increase spending when the economy is weak.

Remember that government outlays only directly increase aggregate expenditure—and hence shift the *IS* curve—when the government purchases goods and services. By contrast, many government programs—such as rent assistance, or JobSeeker—simply transfer money from one bank account (the government's) to another (the recipient's), and so they don't *directly* increase aggregate expenditure. If there's an effect, it's indirect, as redistributing money to people who are more likely to spend it might increase consumption.

Net exports increase in response to global factors:
↑ Global GDP growth
↓ Australian dollar
↓ Trade barriers in foreign markets
↑ Trade barriers to Australian market

Spending shock four: Net exports increase due to global factors. Net exports rise when people in other countries want to buy a lot of Australian-made goods and services. It's the *interdependence principle* at work, as net exports link the Australian economy with economies around the world. Net exports shift in response to:

Global economic growth: When the economies of Europe, Japan, the United States, and China do well, their consumers and businesses have more money to spend, and so they buy more goods, including more Australian-made goods, leading net exports to rise.

The exchange rate: Net exports also shift in response to changes in the exchange rate. When the Australian dollar becomes cheaper, our goods become cheaper to foreign buyers, leading exports to rise. A cheaper Australian dollar also means that foreign goods become more expensive (in dollars) for Australian buyers, leading imports to fall. Both forces—rising exports and falling imports—cause net exports to increase.

Trade barriers: Exports increase when there are fewer barriers preventing Australian businesses from selling their goods in foreign markets, while imports increase when there are fewer barriers preventing foreign businesses from selling to buyers in Australia. Because trade agreements typically reduce barriers preventing both imports and exports, their effect on net exports (which is exports less imports) is unclear. Likewise trade wars—in which higher trade barriers preventing imports lead other countries to retaliate by raising barriers that prevent foreigners from buying Australian exports—will reduce both imports and exports yielding an unclear effect on net exports.

Recap: Anything that shifts any component of aggregate expenditure shifts the *IS* curve. At this point, this list of spending shocks that can shift the *IS* curve might seem a bit exhausting. I've put it all together for you in Figure 14.

Figure 14 | Spending Shocks Shift the *IS* Curve

IS Curve Shifters	Examples*
Consumption *rises if people feel more prosperous*	↑Wealth, ↑Consumer confidence, ↑Government assistance, ↓Taxes, ↓Inequality
Investment *rises if it's profitable to expand production*	↑GDP growth, ↑Business confidence, ↑Investment tax credits, ↓Corporate taxes, ↑Easier lending standards and more cash reserves, ↓Uncertainty
Government purchases *rise in response to expansionary fiscal policy*	Spending bills, Automatic stabilisers . . . but not transfer payments (at least not directly)
Net exports *rise in response to global factors*	↑Global GDP growth, ↓Australian dollar, ↓Trade barriers in foreign markets, ↑Trade barriers to Australian market

* These examples all cause an increase in aggregate expenditure which shifts the *IS* curve to the right. Reverse the sign of any arrow and you'll get a change that decreases aggregate expenditure, shifting the *IS* curve to the left.

financial shocks Any change in borrowing conditions that change the real interest rate at which people can borrow. Financial shocks shift the *MP* curve.

But this whole analysis is really just about one idea: The *IS* curve shifts in response to an increase in any component of aggregate expenditure. That's the easy way to remember this list: It's just *C, I, G,* and *NX.*

Okay, with the *IS* curve behind us, what causes the *MP* curve to shift?

Financial Shocks Shift the *MP* Curve

Let's start with the mechanics of shifts in the *MP* curve. As Figure 15 illustrates, these are pretty straightforward. An increase in the real interest rate shifts the *MP* curve up. This leads to a new equilibrium with lower GDP and hence a more negative output gap. Conversely, a decrease in the real interest rate shifts the *MP* curve down, which leads to a new equilibrium with higher GDP and a more positive output gap.

When the Reserve Bank adjusts the risk-free real interest rate, or shifts in financial markets change the risk premium, the real interest rate will change, leading the *MP* curve to shift. We call these changes in borrowing conditions that shift the *MP* curve **financial shocks.**

Figure 15 | Shifting the *MP* Curve

The MP curve shifts due to changes in monetary policy or the risk premium.

Ⓐ At the initial equilibrium, GDP is equal to potential GDP.

Ⓑ An increase in the real interest rate causes the *MP* curve to shift up, leading to a new equilibrium with lower GDP and a higher interest rate.

Ⓒ A decrease in the real interest rate causes the *MP* curve to shift down, leading to a new equilibrium with higher GDP and a lower interest rate.

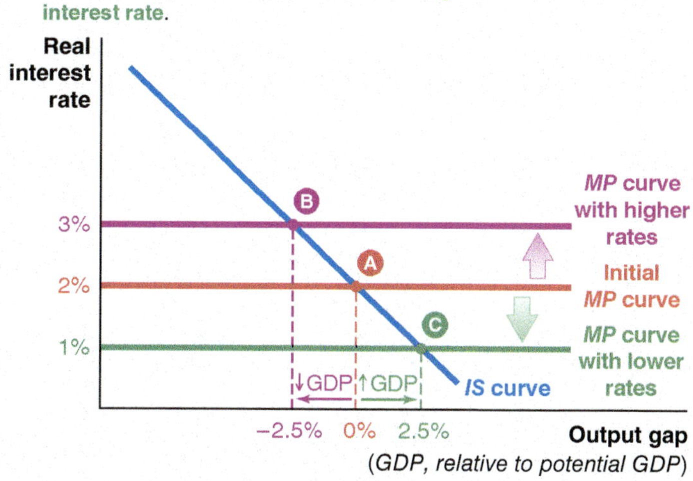

Monetary policy can raise interest rates either by:
↑ Risk-free rate
↑ Expected future interest rates

Financial shock one: Changes in monetary policy. When the Reserve Bank decides to raise its benchmark interest rate, its decision percolates through financial markets, eventually raising interest rates through the rest of the economy. This higher real interest rate shifts the *MP* curve up. Likewise, when the RBA cuts the real interest rate, it shifts the *MP* curve down.

But that's not the only way the RBA can shift the *MP* curve. Longer-term interest rates are based partly on the current short-term interest rate, and partly on *expectations* about how that interest rate will evolve over the coming months and years. The RBA will often try to influence these expectations. A signal that it expects to raise interest rates in the future is often enough to increase the long-term interest rate, thereby shifting the *MP* curve up.

It's also worth remembering that not every interest rate change that the RBA announces will change the real interest rate. The interest rate the Reserve Bank directly sets is a nominal interest rate, and so if inflation rises by 1%, the RBA will need to raise the nominal interest rate by 1% simply to keep the real interest rate unchanged.

Simon Belcher/Alamy Stock Photo

Those rising risks will shift the risk premium.

Financial shock two: Financial market risks shift the risk premium. The *MP* curve also shifts when the risk premium changes. The mechanics here are the same as those following a change caused by the Reserve Bank: A rise in the risk premium raises the real interest rate, which shifts the *MP* curve up. And a decline in the risk premium lowers the real interest rate, which shifts the *MP* curve down.

Recall that the risk premium reflects various financial risks, and so it will shift in response to:

Default risk: When there's an increased risk that borrowers will *default*—that they won't repay their debts or won't repay in a timely fashion—lenders demand a larger risk premium, which leads the *MP* curve to shift upward.

Liquidity risk: When banks need cash—that is, *liquidity*—they can usually get it by selling some of their loans to other lenders. Liquidity risk arises when disruptions in financial markets mean that there aren't any buyers, or there aren't any willing to pay a reasonable price. A rise in liquidity risk increases the risk premium, which shifts the *MP* curve upward.

A higher risk premium will raise interest rates due to:
↑ Default risk
↑ Liquidity risk
↑ Interest rate risk
↑ Risk aversion

Interest rate risk: Lending someone money at a fixed interest rate for a long time, as in a 30-year mortgage, raises another risk: The long-term interest rate you offer today might turn out to be a bad deal if future interest rates or inflation are unexpectedly higher. And so increasing uncertainty about future interest rates or inflation raises interest rate risk, which increases the risk premium, shifting the *MP* curve up.

Risk aversion: When lenders become more reluctant to take on risk—that is, when they become more *risk averse*—they'll only be willing to make a loan if they can charge a higher risk premium. Thus, swings in market sentiment that make lenders more risk averse will shift the *MP* curve up.

Recap: Any change in the real interest rate shifts the *MP* curve. To sum up, the *MP* curve shifts whenever the real interest rate shifts, and as Figure 16 shows, that in turn reflects the influence of the RBA on the risk-free rate, and changes that lead financial markets to adjust the risk premium.

Figure 16 | **Financial Shocks Shift the *MP* Curve**

***MP* Curve Shifters**	**Examples**
The risk-free rate *rises in response to monetary policy*	↑Risk-free rate, ↑Expected future interest rates
The risk premium *rises if lending becomes riskier*	↑Default risk, ↑Liquidity risk, ↑Interest rate risk, ↑Risk aversion

Predicting Economic Changes

Okay, let's put all of this together into a simple recipe so that you can forecast how changing economic conditions will shape your market. To assess the likely effects of any change in economic conditions, ask yourself:

Step one: Is there a *spending shock* (which shifts the *IS* curve), or a *financial shock* (which shifts the *MP* curve)?

Step two: In which direction, and how far does this shift the *IS* or *MP* curve?

Step three: What happens to GDP (and hence the output gap), as well as the real interest rate in the new equilibrium?

It's time to try this out.

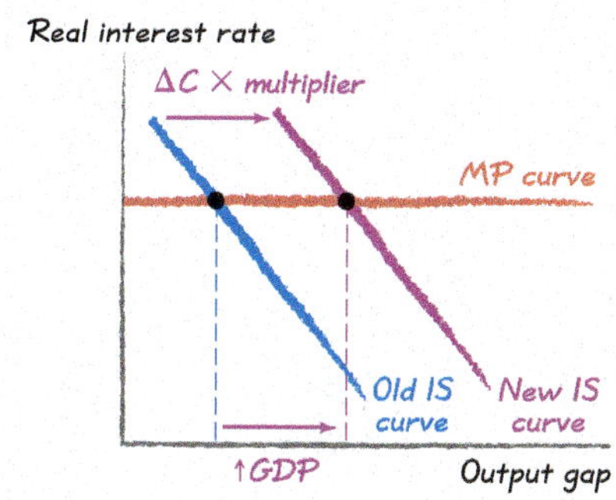

Example one: *In early 2008, the government was worried that the economy was underperforming. In an effort to prevent a recession, the federal government sent stimulus cheques of more than $1000 to pensioners and low-and-middle-income households. How did this affect the economy?*

Step one: The stimulus payments meant that people had a larger after-tax income. In response, consumption rose, leading to an increase in aggregate expenditure, which is a positive spending shock.

Step two: As a result, the *IS* curve shifted to the right.

Step three: This shift led to higher GDP and hence a more positive output gap, and an unchanged real interest rate.

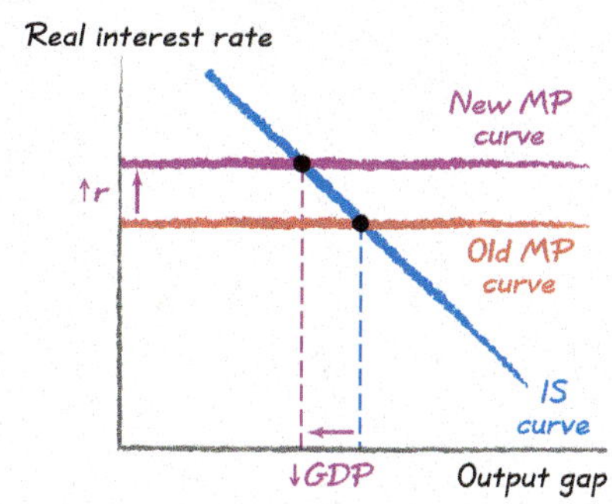

Example two: *In September 2008, the world's financial system froze. Even though the Reserve Bank cut interest rates on 2 September from 7.25% to 7.0%, the grim reality was that if businesses needed to borrow, they had to pay much higher interest rates. How did this affect the economy?*

Step one: Even though the RBA slightly reduced its interest rate, it was now much riskier to lend. In response, the risk premium rose, leading to higher real interest rates, which is a financial shock.

Step two: As a result, the *MP* curve shifted up.

Step three: This shift led to a higher real interest rate and lower GDP, and hence a more negative output gap.

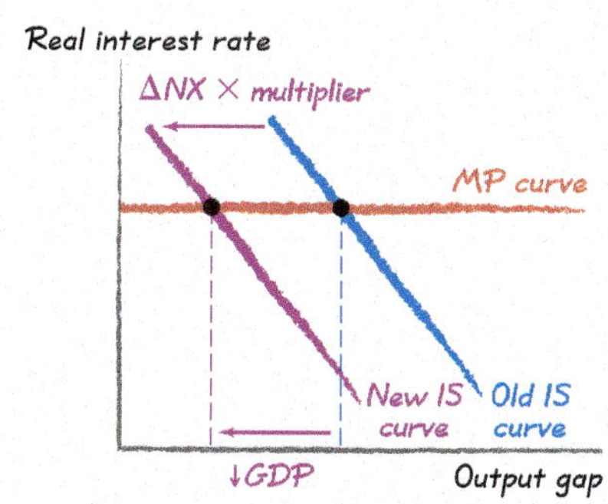

Example three: *When China's economy slowed in 2018, how did this affect the Australian economy?*

Step one: When China's economy slowed, the demand for goods exported by Australian businesses fell. In response, net exports fell. From an Australian perspective, this decline in net exports is a decline in aggregate expenditure, which is a negative spending shock.

Step two: As a result, the *IS* curve shifted to the left.

Step three: This shift led to lower GDP and hence a more negative output gap, and an unchanged real interest rate.

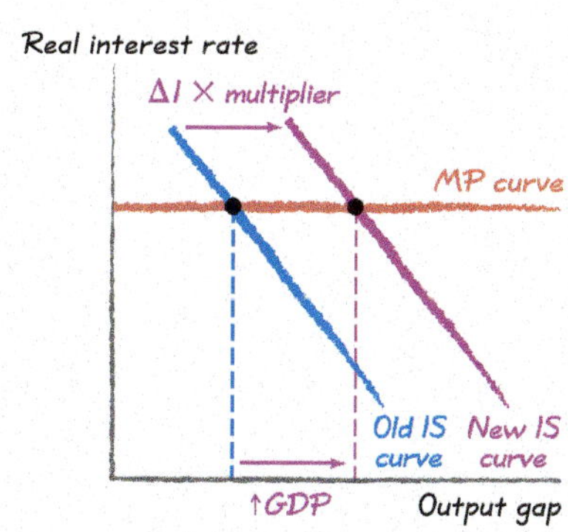

Example four: *In 2011, the government launch the Small-scale Renewable Energy Scheme, which provided households with rebates of between $2700 and $3700 for installing residential solar panels. How did this affect the economy?*

Step one: This rebate reduced the cost of investing in solar power projects. In response, investment in solar power rose, leading to an increase in aggregate expenditure, which is a positive spending shock.

Step two: As a result, the *IS* curve shifted to the right.

Step three: This shift led to higher GDP and hence a more positive output gap at an unchanged real interest rate.

Do the Economics

Think you've got the economy all figured out? Here's your chance to practice, as you work through a dozen more examples. In each case, your job is to assess what happens, if the economy starts from that comfortable place where equilibrium GDP is equal to potential GDP.

In an effort to balance the budget, the federal government reduced its spending on the military.

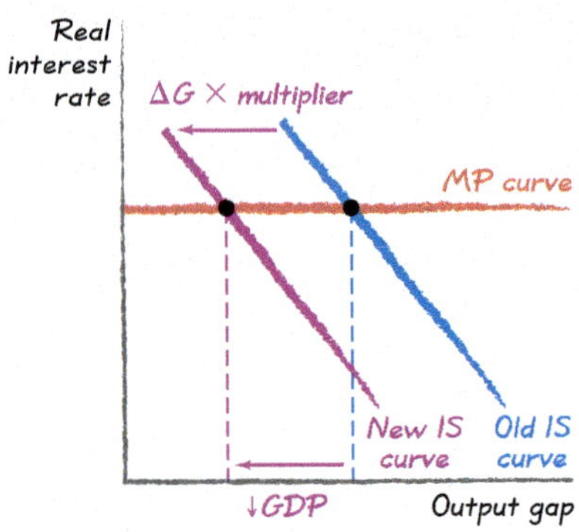

Fewer government purchases
→ Shift *IS* curve to the left

Result: Decrease in GDP and an unchanged real interest rate.

As consumer confidence boomed, people became more willing to buy cars, appliances, and furniture.

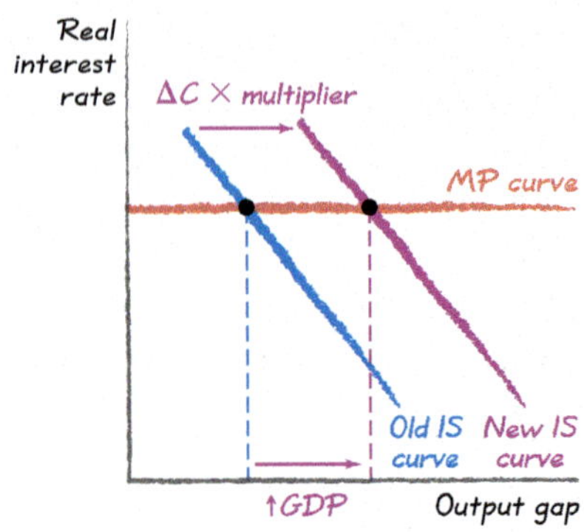

More consumer spending
→ Shift *IS* curve to the right

Result: Increase in GDP and an unchanged real interest rate.

Uncertainty about the future path of interest rates led lenders to increase the risk premium on their loans.

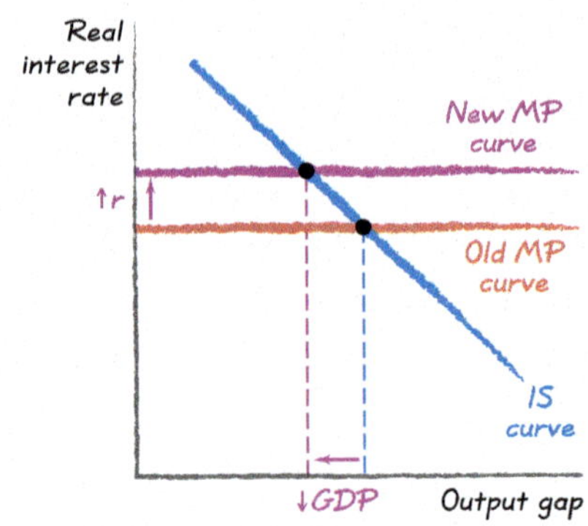

A rise in the risk premium
→ Shift *MP* curve up

Result: Decrease in GDP and a higher real interest rate.

After an escalation in tensions, China imposed a tariff on Australian exports.

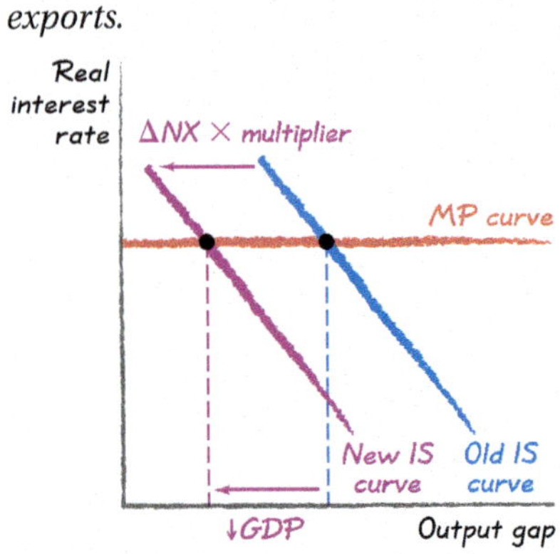

Decrease in net exports
→ Shift *IS* curve to the left

Result: Decrease in GDP and an unchanged real interest rate.

In an effort to boost the economy, the Reserve Bank lowered the cash rate.

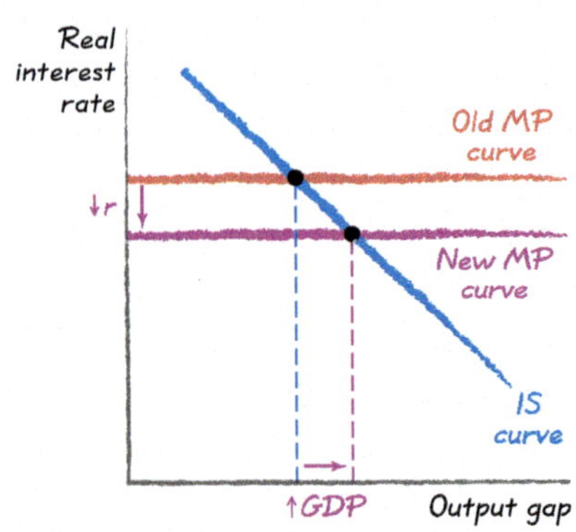

RBA cuts its interest rate
→ Shift *MP* curve down

Result: Increase in GDP and a lower real interest rate.

Growing business confidence led Harvey Norman, Officeworks, and other retailers to expand operations in Australia.

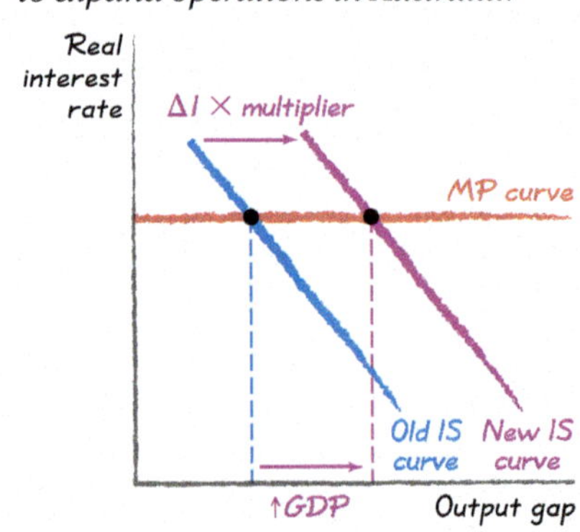

Increase in investment
→ Shift *IS* curve to the right

Result: Increase in GDP and an unchanged real interest rate.

As economic growth in Japan picked up, Australian exporters enjoyed stronger demand for their products.

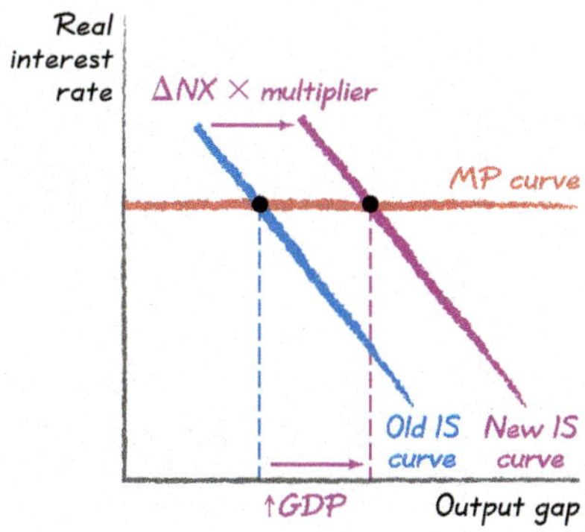

Increase in net exports
→ Shift *IS* curve to the right

Result: Increase in GDP and an unchanged real interest rate.

Rising political uncertainty led many executives to put their investment plans on hold.

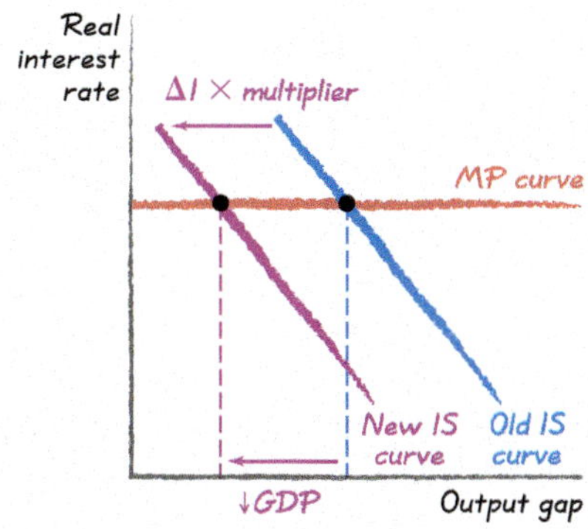

Decrease in investment
→ Shift *IS* curve to the left

Result: Decrease in GDP and an unchanged real interest rate.

The Reserve Bank intervened in financial markets in an effort to reduce the risk premium for lenders.

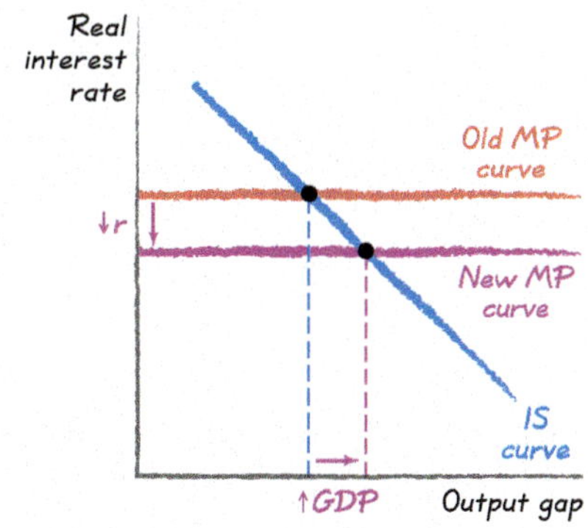

A decline in the risk premium
→ Shift *MP* curve down

Result: Increase in GDP and a lower real interest rate.

The stock market fell sharply, leading people who had lost some of their wealth to cut back on their spending.

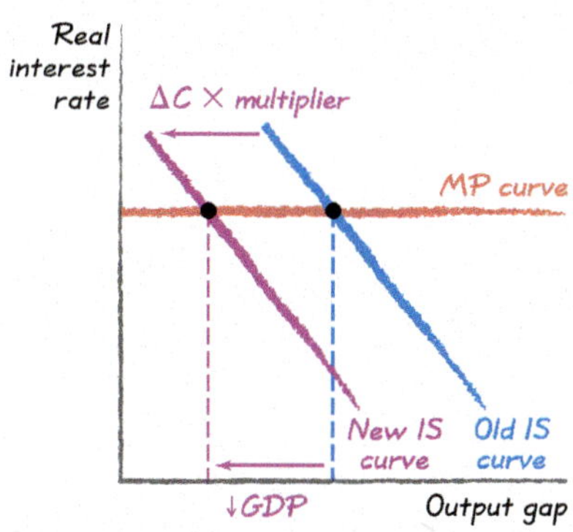

Decrease in consumption
→ Shift *IS* curve to the left

Result: Decrease in GDP and an unchanged real interest rate.

After a long period of low interest rates, the Reserve Bank raised the cash rate.

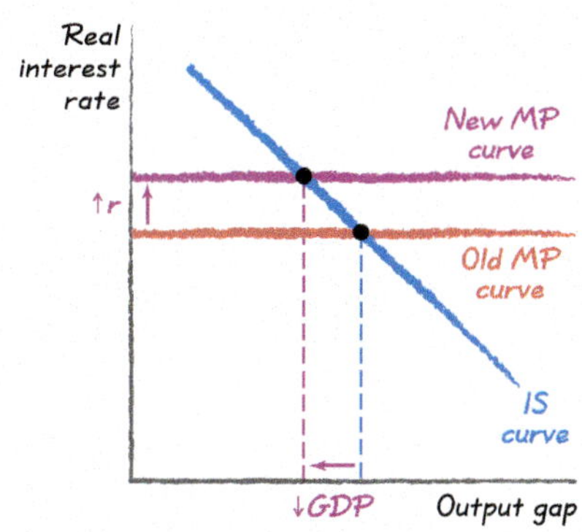

Increase in interest rates
→ Shift *MP* curve up

Result: Decrease in GDP and a higher real interest rate.

Disruptions in global markets led investors to bid up the price of the Australian dollar which made Australian exports more expensive for foreigners.

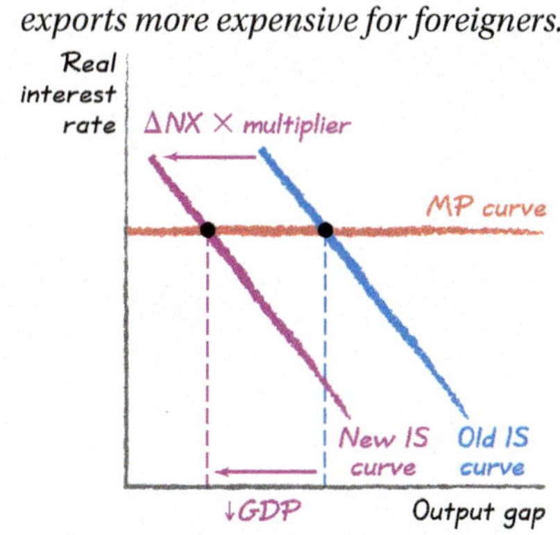

Decrease in net exports
→ Shift *IS* curve to the left

Result: Decrease in GDP and an unchanged real interest rate. ■

Tying It Together

The *IS-MP* framework is the real deal: It's the same tool that governments, the RBA, and private-sector forecasters use to organise their thoughts about the economy. It's a framework for understanding how the interplay of aggregate expenditure and interest rate changes drives the ups and downs of the business cycle, and how fiscal and monetary policy can be used to counter these fluctuations. It's essential for business because it tells you how broader macroeconomic changes will buffet your industry.

The *IS* curve reflects the influence of real interest rates on aggregate expenditure. The *MP* curve brings in the financial system, and it illustrates how monetary policy and changes in financial conditions are important influences.

The result is a flexible framework that you can use to make sense of the constant flow of economic news—on fiscal policy and monetary policy; consumer confidence and business sentiment; developments in the United States, Japan, Europe, and China; movements in the exchange rate; and shocks to the financial system.

My only fear is that if you take this framework a bit too literally, it might make managing the economy look too simple. It seems to say that you can achieve any level of the output gap just by finding the corresponding real interest rate on the *IS* curve.

Reality is messier. The actual *IS* curve isn't a fixed chart in a textbook that real-world economists just look up. The truth is, the *IS* curve is constantly shifting, which means that the policy that was appropriate yesterday might not be appropriate today. And we don't know the slope of the *IS* curve. Instead, we have to rely on statistical estimates based on how the economy has responded to different interest rates in the past. Who knows if it will respond the same way in the future?

Moreover, the *MP* curve seems to suggest that there's only one interest rate, and it's controlled by the RBA. That's a useful simplification, but in reality, there are many different interest rates for different types of loans, and while the RBA has some influence on each of them, it doesn't control them with any precision. And while our analysis tells you what will happen if the *IS* or *MP* curve shifts—which is useful!—it doesn't say much about how quickly those effects will play out.

But as messy as reality is, the point of macroeconomics is to focus on the big picture. The *IS-MP* framework is useful because it focuses your attention on the most important economic forces at play. And it's useful because it's the language that economists, politicians, traders, and business executives use when debating how to make sense of economic developments. Now that you've learned that language, let me say: Welcome to the conversation!

Chapter at a Glance

IS Curve: Illustrates how lower real interest rates raise spending and hence GDP, leading to a positive output gap.

↓r ⇒ ↑C, ↑I, ↑G or ↑NX ⇒ ↑GDP ⇒ ↑Output gap

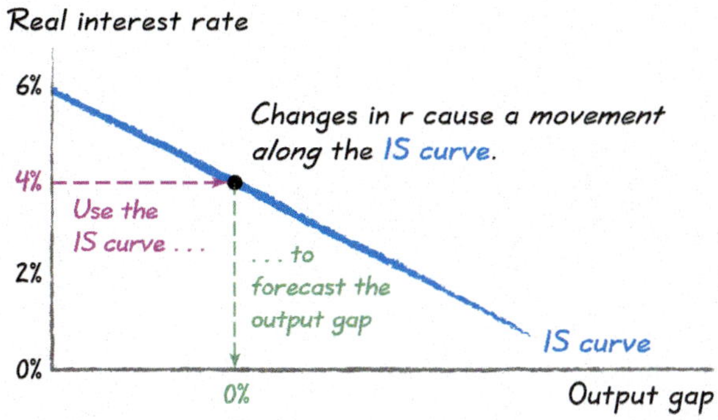

MP Curve: Illustrates the current real interest rate, which is shaped by monetary policy and the risk premium.

Interest rate = Risk-free interest rate + Risk premium

Risk-free interest rate ↑ Monetary policy; Risk premium ↑ Financial markets

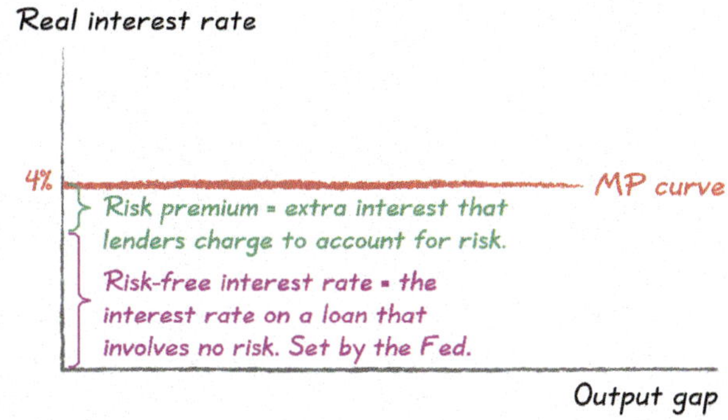

IS-MP Framework

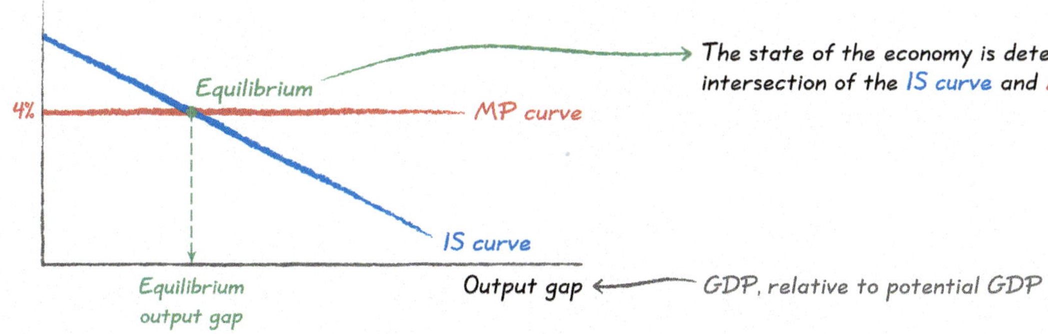

Effects of Macroeconomic Shocks

1. Is there a spending shock (which shifts the IS curve), or a financial shock (which shifts the MP curve)?
2. In which direction, and how far does this shift the IS curve or MP curve?
3. What happens to GDP in the new equilibrium?

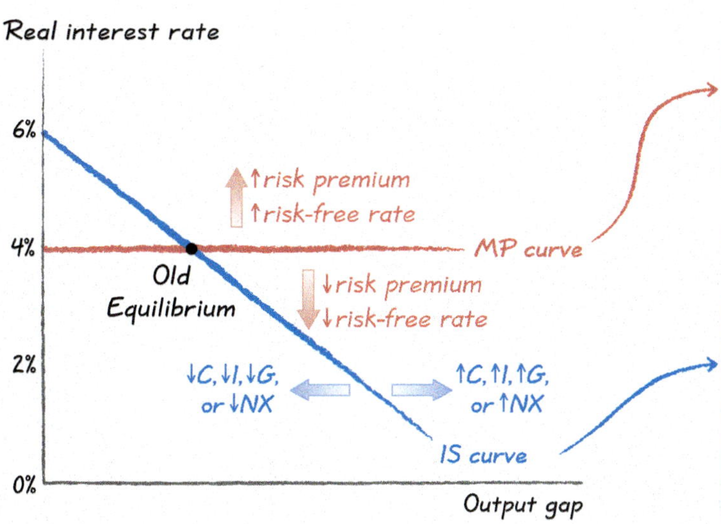

Shifts MP Curve

The risk-free rate rises in response to monetary policy

The risk premium rises if lending becomes riskier

Shifts IS Curve (by ΔSpending × Multiplier)

Consumption (C) rises if people feel more prosperous

Planned investment (I) rises if it's profitable to expand production

Government spending (G) rises in response to expansionary fiscal policy

Net exports (NX) rise in response to global factors.

Key Concepts

Discussion and Review Questions

Learning Objective 30.1 *Assess the role of aggregate expenditure in driving short-run fluctuations in output.*

1. Javier is a department manager at a supercentre. Over the last month sales have slumped and he has lots of inventory going unsold. Now it's time to put in his orders to restock for next month. How should he adjust his order for new products and why? How will this decision impact his suppliers?

   Most other businesses are experiencing a similar decline in sales, which has lasted for several months. What does this tell you about aggregate expenditure and output in the economy?

2. How is macroeconomic equilibrium related to equilibrium GDP? How does equilibrium GDP differ from potential GDP?

Learning Objective 30.2 *Use the* IS *curve to analyse the relationship between the real interest rate and equilibrium GDP.*

3. Provide an example of how your own consumption would change as the real interest rate changes. Specifically, describe how your opportunity costs change. If other consumers made similar changes to their consumption, how would that affect aggregate expenditure?

4. Pick a product that you typically buy and draw the demand curve for it. Then draw the *IS* curve for the economy. Compare and contrast the two. What are the prices and quantities for each?

Learning Objective 30.3 *Use the* MP *curve to summarise how the real interest rate is determined.*

5. What determines the risk premium and how does it affect the real interest rate and *MP* curve?

Learning Objective 30.4 *Forecast economic conditions and how they'll respond to monetary and fiscal policy.*

6. The economy is experiencing an output gap of –3%. Discuss how monetary policy or fiscal policy could be used to raise actual output towards potential output. Could monetary policy and fiscal policy be used together? If so, how?

7. Explain how prolonged recessions can occur and how an economy can become stuck in a bad equilibrium even if both buyers and sellers are making the best decisions they can. How can the economy become unstuck?

Learning Objective 30.5 *Use the* IS-MP *framework to forecast the effects of macroeconomic shocks.*

8. Recent releases of leading economic indicators have been a mixed bag: Some of them indicate stable economic growth, while others indicate a looming recession. Explain how businesses will adjust their investment spending as a result of the increased uncertainty. Predict how the economy will change.

9. How can the Reserve Bank influence long-term interest rates, and shift the *MP* curve, without changing the current risk-free interest rate?

10. In 2020, China enacted tariffs on imports from Australia. Many people expected Australia to enact a tariff on Chinese imports in retaliation. How would the output gap change in response to this trade war? Explain your reasoning.

Study Problems

Learning Objective 30.1 *Assess the role of aggregate expenditure in driving short-run fluctuations in output.*

1. If the economy is currently in macroeconomic equilibrium, how will businesses adjust their production in response to each of the following changes to aggregate expenditure?
   a. Consumers become more confident in the economic outlook and increase their consumption spending.
   b. Parliament passes a new budget that decreases overall government purchases by 0.5% of GDP.

2. In 2020, potential GDP was $2.09 trillion and real GDP was $1.97 trillion. In 2021, potential GDP was $2.27 trillion and real GDP was $2.17 trillion. Calculate the output gap for each year. How did the output gap change between 2020 and 2021? Did it become more positive or more negative?

Learning Objective 30.2 *Use the* IS *curve to analyse the relationship between the real interest rate and equilibrium GDP.*

3. The following graph depicts an *IS* curve for the economy.

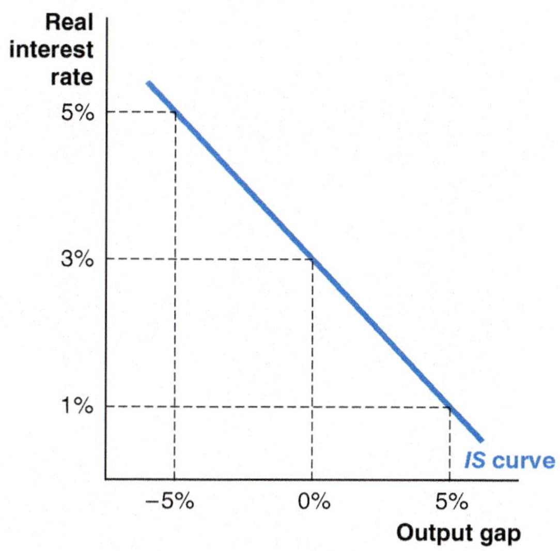

a. How does the output gap change if the real interest rate rises from 1% to 3%?

b. Explain the process by which output gap changed. How did the change in the real interest rate affect aggregate expenditure?

c. How do actual output and potential output change?

4. For each of the following, illustrate with a graph how the *IS* curve will change.

a. Poor numbers from several leading economic indicators cause businesses to become pessimistic about the future of the economy.

b. The real interest rate falls, which causes consumption spending to rise.

Learning Objective 30.3 *Use the* MP *curve to summarise how the real interest rate is determined.*

5. The cash rate set by the RBA is 4%, and inflation is 3%. The real interest rate that people can borrow money at is 1.5%.

a. Draw an *MP* curve.

b. Determine the risk premium. Label it and the risk-free interest rate on your graph.

c. Illustrate how the *MP* curve will change if the risk premium increases.

Learning Objective 30.4 *Forecast economic conditions and how they'll respond to monetary and fiscal policy.*

6. Draw an *IS-MP* graph where the macroeconomic equilibrium is at a real interest rate of 6% and actual output is 10% below potential GDP. Use this graph to answer the following questions.

a. You're a financial analyst at a regional bank. In a weekly staff meeting your department head asks your opinion on how RBA policy is going to change in the coming months. If the RBA wishes to close the output gap, how would it change the cash rate? Explain your reasoning using the graph.

b. Another analyst in the meeting argues that it's time for the government to cut government purchases in an effort to increase GDP. Would this fiscal policy suggestion cause the output gap to close? Explain using your graph.

7. To combat a recession, the Indian government enacts expansionary fiscal policy, which increases government spending by 2 trillion rupees. In response, GDP rises by 6 trillion rupees.

a. What is the multiplier?

b. The policy pushes India from producing 3% below its potential output to now producing 2% above potential output. Illustrate this change in an *IS-MP* graph assuming the real interest rate is constant at 4%.

c. If the Indian government wants to target the highest sustainable level of output, should it continue to increase government spending or pull back? Explain your reasoning.

Learning Objective 30.5 *Use the* IS-MP *framework to forecast the effects of macroeconomic shocks.*

8. Classify the following as an example of either a spending shock or a financial shock. Determine how the macroeconomic equilibrium will change by illustrating this shift in an *IS-MP* graph.

a. Lenders become less risk averse and cut the risk premium they charge when making risky loans.

b. The federal government ends a long-standing tax cut for families with small children.

c. Parliament passes a new tax law that decreases corporate taxes by 10%.

d. Due to signals from the RBA, businesses expect interest rates to rise in the next few weeks.

e. Electric power providers become more confident in the ability of wind farms to meet electricity demand. This leads to a boom in building and producing wind farms across the country.

9. Housing prices in Australia decline dramatically and remain depressed for several months. Using an *IS-MP* graph, explain what happens to the macroeconomic equilibrium in Australia. Using a separate *IS-MP* graph, explain the impact of this housing market crash on the Chinese economy, one of Australia's largest trading partners.

CHAPTER 31

The Phillips Curve and Inflation

Chapter Objective

Assess the causes of inflation.

31.1 Three Inflationary Forces
Identify the three causes of inflation: inflation expectations, demand-pull inflation, and supply shocks.

31.2 Inflation Expectations
Explore how inflation expectations lead to inflation.

31.3 The Phillips Curve
Analyse the link between the output gap and inflation.

31.4 Supply Shocks Shift the Phillips Curve
Assess how shocks to production costs shift the Phillips curve.

Fir Mamat/Alamy Stock Photo

A microcosm of the Australian economy.

The Whopper is almost as ubiquitous in Australia as the Big Mac. It's the signature burger at fast-food chain Hungry Jack's—the Australian franchise of American chain Burger King. It was brought to Australia in 1971 by now-billionaire restaurateur Jack Cowin.

It's also a microcosm of the Australian economy. In 1991 you could get a Whopper and onion rings for $2.95. In 2022 you're looking at $10.30—although they will now throw in a small Coke. The Whopper alone now costs $6.90. But it doesn't go up by the same amount every year. Some years the price doesn't rise at all, sometimes it shoots up. Most other goods have followed a similar trajectory, reflecting the macroeconomic trend toward inflation. And just as the price of the Whopper has risen in fits and starts, the broader inflation rate has fluctuated, rising and falling as economic conditions have changed.

Restaurant industry executives expect the rising cost of ingredients to pose a major challenge. They're not alone. Across the whole economy, *expectations* of ongoing inflation play a central role in pricing decisions. It's a key reason that prices for the Whopper—and many other goods—will likely continue to rise.

Overall *demand* also influences inflation. When the financial crisis of 2008 hit, Hungry Jack's management needed to keep a lid on prices to attract customers. As the economy recovered, it was possible to edge prices up to cover the rising cost of ingredients and increases in award wages for Hungry Jack's workers. The same pattern played out throughout the rest of the economy: The financial crisis caused inflation to fall, and the subsequent recovery led it to rise.

It's not just the strength of the economy that shapes inflation. Most, if not all, fast-food restaurants in Australia faced significant challenges in early 2022 as the Omicron variant of Covid-19 put pressure on supply chains, and the cost of ingredients rose. It was widely reported that the industry was facing pressures unlike anything they had experienced before. These *supply shocks* might increase production costs, which could force Hungry Jack's to raise prices. Indeed, across the whole economy, higher production costs often generate inflation.

We analysed the consequences of inflation in Chapter 24; our task in this chapter is to understand what causes it. As the Whopper illustrates, the rate of change of prices is driven by three key factors: inflation expectations, demand, and supply shocks. In this chapter, we'll develop the framework that top forecasters, executives, and government officials use to analyse inflation, assessing each of these factors separately.

31.1 Three Inflationary Forces

Learning Objective *Identify the three causes of inflation: inflation expectations, demand-pull inflation, and supply shocks.*

Three causes of inflation:
1. Inflation expectations
2. Demand-pull inflation (the Phillips curve)
3. Supply shocks and cost-push inflation

Let's begin with a brief sketch of the road ahead. Our goal is to understand what drives inflation, and how it responds to economic conditions. That'll require understanding the three causes of inflation. I'll introduce those causes to you here, and then we'll dig deeper into each of them in the following sections.

Inflationary Force One: Inflation Expectations

inflation expectations The rate at which average prices are anticipated to rise next year.

Before Hungry Jack's finalises its new menus, its executives have to decide whether to raise their prices for next year, and by how much. This is where **inflation expectations**—the rate at which average prices are anticipated to rise next year—become relevant. If Hungry Jack's top managers expect inflation to be 2% next year, then they'll probably follow suit and raise next year's prices by 2% to keep up. After all, if average prices across the whole economy will rise by 2%, then it's likely that the prices of their key inputs—beef, vegetables, bread, energy, and rent—will also rise by 2%. The only way for Hungry Jack's to maintain its profit margin will be to raise prices in line with this rate of expected inflation.

When other managers across the economy make similar calculations they'll make similar choices, each raising their prices in line with their inflation expectations. As a result, inflation expectations create inflation. We'll return to this inflationary force in greater detail later in this chapter in the section called "Inflation Expectations."

Andrew Burton/Getty Images

When there's a queue of people waiting, it's time to raise your prices.

Inflationary Force Two: Demand-Pull Inflation

When business is good, there can be a long queue at Hungry Jack's, as the demand outstrips the restaurant's capacity. In the long run, this will lead Hungry Jack's managers to consider opening new restaurants. But in the short run Hungry Jack's can't increase its supply of meals, so its best bet is to raise its prices.

Now consider what happens when the whole economy booms, so that actual output exceeds potential output. Millions of businesses are in the same situation as Hungry Jack's, with demand outstripping their productive capacity. Just as Hungry Jack's raised its prices, so will they. These widespread price increases create **demand-pull inflation,** which arises when demand exceeds the economy's productive capacity, pulling prices up. Alternatively, when demand falls short of productive capacity so that the output gap is negative, businesses are likely to moderate their price increases, leading to lower inflation. We'll dig deeper into this link between the output gap and inflation when we introduce a framework for analysing it called the Phillips curve.

demand-pull inflation Inflation resulting from excess demand.

Alexey Furman/Getty Images

Turmoil in Europe affects prices in Australia.

Inflationary Force Three: Supply Shocks and Cost-Push Inflation

The *interdependence principle* emphasises the importance of linkages between markets, and it's especially relevant to understanding how geopolitical tensions in Europe can push up the price of burgers in Australia. The war in Ukraine led to cutbacks in oil production, which pushed up oil prices, setting off a chain reaction. Moreover, with the wheat crop in Ukraine—which produces a quarter of the world supply of wheat—under pressure, global wheat prices shot up in early 2022. Initially, products made from oil—like gasoline, heating oil, and propane—become more expensive. These higher energy prices raised the production costs of many businesses, including fast-food restaurants. It cost more to truck ingredients across the country; it was more expensive to heat a restaurant; and the energy costs required to run a commercial kitchen rose. The wheat price doubled due to Russia's invasion of Ukraine, making burger buns dramatically more expensive. Eventually, these higher marginal costs forced Hungry Jack's to raise its prices.

A similar story played out across many sectors of the economy, as businesses discovered that higher oil prices led to higher prices for a range of oil-based inputs—including plastics, fertilisers, and rubber. Just as higher marginal costs led Hungry Jack's to raise its prices, millions of other businesses raise their prices when their marginal costs rise. These widespread price increases create inflation. This is an example of **cost-push inflation,** which occurs when prices rise in response to an unexpected rise in production costs. The original catalyst of all this was a *supply shock,* which is why we'll analyse cost-push inflation in more detail under the heading "Supply Shocks."

cost-push inflation Inflation that results from an unexpected rise in production costs.

Understanding Inflation

Put all the pieces together, and we've sketched out the three causes of inflation (and given you a preview of the chapter ahead): It's the result of expected inflation, demand-pull inflation, and cost-push inflation:

Inflation	=	Expected inflation	+	Demand-pull inflation	+	Cost-push inflation
		↑Inflation expectations → ↑Inflation		*↑Output gap → ↑Inflation*		*↑Production costs → ↑Inflation*

Okay, that's our brief sketch. We'll spend the rest of this chapter digging into each of these inflationary forces in more detail. Let's start with inflation expectations.

31.2 Inflation Expectations

Learning Objective *Explore how inflation expectations lead to inflation.*

Put yourself in the shoes of the executives at Hungry Jack's as they decide what prices to set for next year. You've got a sophisticated information system at your fingertips, tracking every detail of your business. It tells you that the food and beverage costs for a typical combo meal add up to about \$6 per person. Detailed supplier data break this down further into the cost of beef, produce, dairy, buns, and packaging, and this can help you figure out which dishes you'll need to charge a premium for. Labour costs—which include both front-of-the-house staff and back-of-the-house cooks—add another \$1.50 per customer, on average. Then other operating costs, including utilities, advertising, and rent, add an extra \$2. There's also overhead, such as insurance, lawyers, and the managers at the head office. The restaurant business is a tough one, and profit margins are razor thin.

You need to make sure that your prices remain competitive, which is why Hungry Jack's monitors the prices charged by McDonald's, and other fast-casual restaurants like Oporto and Mad Mex, and even the growing competition from meal-delivery services.

As you work your way through reams of spreadsheets, you realise that these data can only tell you what's happened in the past. But you want to know what's going to happen in the future, so that you can ensure your prices are appropriate for whatever the months ahead might hold. That's why your expectations matter.

Why Inflation Expectations Matter

Your inflation expectations describe the rate at which you expect prices to rise, on average, across the whole economy over the next year. They're important to your business because you'll set your prices with an eye to what you expect will happen in the months ahead. And they're important for the economy because inflation expectations are the key driver of inflation in the long run.

Set your prices to take account of inflation expectations. Two key factors drive most pricing decisions, and your inflation expectations are relevant to both of them.

First, there's your *marginal costs*. Hungry Jack's deals with dozens of suppliers who tend to raise their prices in line with the overall inflation rate. This means that if you expect inflation to be 2% next year, then it's likely that the price of your inputs will typically rise by around 2%. (Some prices will rise a bit more, and some a bit less.) If you want to maintain your profit margin, you'll have to charge higher prices to make up for the higher marginal costs you expect to pay.

Two key factors for setting prices:
1. Your marginal costs
2. Your competitors' prices

Annual Inflation and Changes in Restaurant Prices

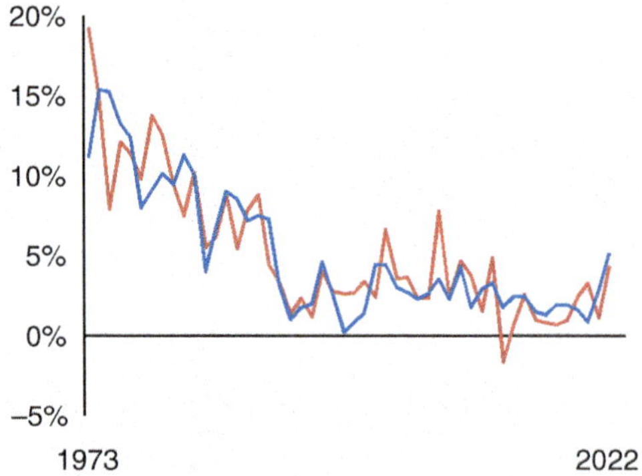

Data from: Australian Bureau of Statistics.

Second, consider your *competitors' prices*: If most prices in the economy are rising by 2%, then it's reasonable to expect that your competitors will also raise their prices by around 2%. They'll do so partly because their costs are also rising by 2%, and partly because they expect their competitors to respond to rising input costs by raising their prices by 2%. Raising your prices by the same percentage that you expect your competitors to raise their prices will maintain your competitive positioning. The reason you can reasonably expect your competitors to raise their prices is because restaurants generally raise their prices in line with overall inflation as seen in the figure in the margin.

Each of these factors suggests that—at least as a starting point—you should raise next year's prices in line with your inflation expectations. This logic gives a powerful role to expectations, suggesting that you should raise your prices for next year because you expect other businesses—both your suppliers and competitors—to raise their prices. This logic isn't specific to Hungry Jack's; it applies to just about any business.

Westend61 GmbH/Alamy Stock Photo

If she's paying more to feed her cattle, you'll pay more for burgers.

Inflation expectations create inflation. There are millions of managers across the country making similar calculations, and in each case, their inflation expectations are central to how they set next year's prices. Each manager figures that if they expect their costs to rise by 2%, and they expect the prices their competitors charge to rise by 2%, their best response is to also raise their prices by 2%. Some managers might expect inflation to be a bit higher and raise their prices a bit more; others might expect slightly lower price increases, leading them to raise their prices by less. But when millions of managers have average inflation expectations of 2%, they'll raise their prices by an average of 2%. Inflation expectations lead to inflation.

That is, *inflation occurs because we expect inflation*.

As we push this logic a bit further, you'll see how important inflation expectations really are. We've seen that expected inflation of 2% leads managers to raise their prices by 2%. The same logic says that if managers expect next year's inflation to be 3%, they should go ahead and raise their prices by 3%. If managers expect next year's inflation to be 6%, they'll raise their prices by 6%.

We've isolated the first major cause of inflation, so let's summarise:

> **Inflation Force #1: Inflation Expectations**
> Higher inflation expectations create higher inflation.
> ↑*Inflation expectations* → ↑*Inflation*

Inflation expectations create a self-fulfilling prophecy. There's something pretty extraordinary about this logic. It says that whatever rate of inflation managers expect, they'll end up raising their prices by that amount. It's a *self-fulfilling prophecy:* The widespread expectation of any particular inflation rate is enough to push suppliers to raise their prices so that they'll create that inflation.

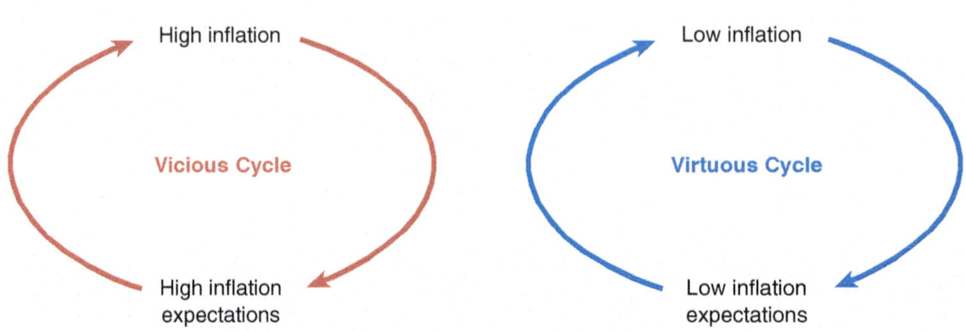

If people expect low inflation, they'll get low inflation. And if people expect high inflation, they'll get high inflation. This means that any inflation rate can become a long-run equilibrium because the rate people expect feeds through and determines the price rises that suppliers set.

Monetary policy tries to shape inflation expectations. These cycles explain why—as Figure 1 shows—some countries have persistently high inflation while others have persistently low inflation. The high-inflation countries are stuck in a vicious cycle whereby people expect high inflation, which leads to high inflation . . . which leads people to expect high inflation. By contrast, low-inflation countries, including Australia (at least over the past several decades until late 2021), enjoy a virtuous cycle whereby people expect low inflation, which leads to low inflation, which leads people to expect low inflation.

This points to an important idea for policy makers: In the long run, the key to achieving persistently low inflation is to convince people that inflation is going to be low. Once you get them to believe it, it'll turn out to be true. We'll analyse the strategies that policy makers use to ensure that the public expects low inflation in Chapter 34 on monetary policy.

Interpreting the DATA | **Inflation expectations lead actual inflation**

Our analysis so far suggests that inflation expectations play a central role in determining inflation. One way to assess this claim is to compare how actual inflation tracks expected inflation. Figure 2 shows survey data in which Australian consumers are asked about their expectations for future inflation. These inflation expectations are plotted along with the actual inflation rate. The figure shows that actual inflation closely tracks the expected inflation rate. Look carefully, and you'll see that when people expect inflation to rise, it subsequently does rise. While this is not the only explanation for this close association, it's certainly consistent with the idea that inflation expectations are a key driver of inflation. ■

Measuring Inflation Expectations

Because inflation expectations are a key driver of future inflation, it's important to track inflation expectations over time. There are three ways you can do this: by analysing surveys, by poring over economic forecasts, and by looking at financial markets.

Surveys ask people about their inflation expectations. The simplest way to find out average inflation expectations is to survey a representative group of people. Figure 3 shows inflation expectations over time from an ongoing Melbourne Institute survey that asks people about their inflation expectations. The blue line illustrates the typical response when people are asked how much inflation they expect over the next year. It's a guide to what people are thinking as they set their prices for next year.

Figure 1 | **Inflation Rates Vary Across Countries**

Average annual rise in the consumer price index, 2011–2021

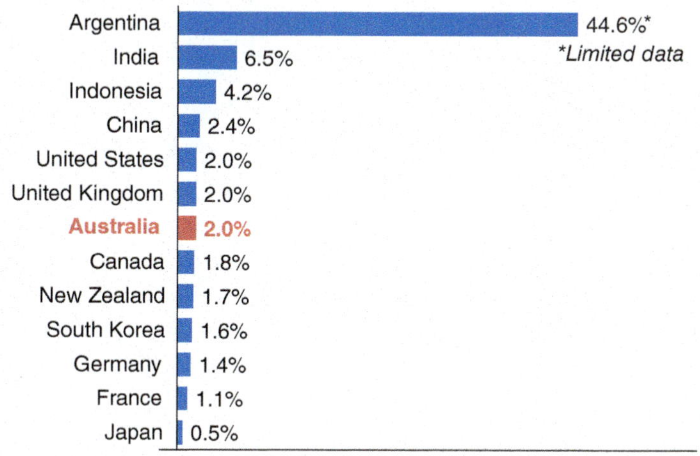

Data from: OECD.

Figure 2 | **Inflation Expectations Lead and Actual Inflation Follows**

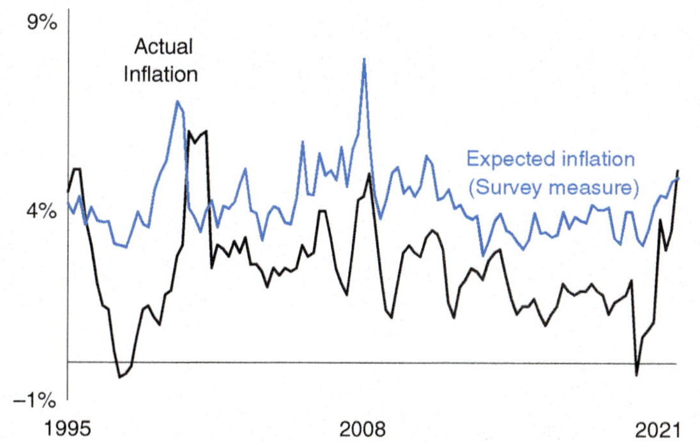

Data from: Melbourne Institute, Australian Bureau of Statistics.

Figure 3 | **Surveys Reveal the Inflation Expectations of Consumers**

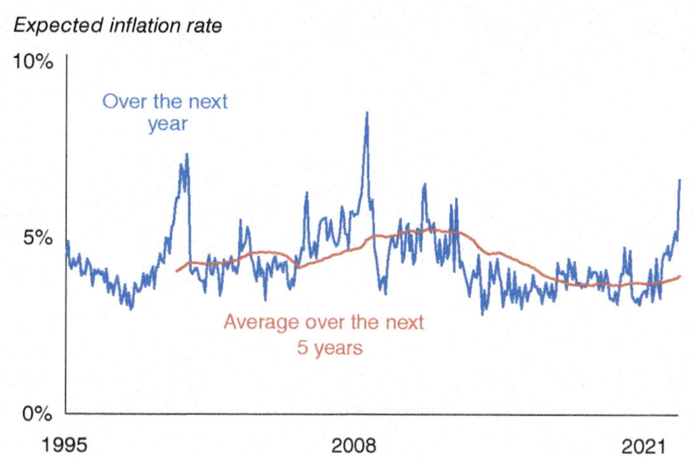

Data from: Melbourne Institute.

We can also think about what people expect inflation to be over the next 5–10 years. This is helpful for assessing whether people believe the Reserve Bank's promise that it will achieve its stated target that inflation will, on average, be around 2%. The red line shows the five-year moving average in inflation expectations, it's much less volatile than year-to-year expectations, and reveals the clear average decline in inflation expectations since the global financial crisis (until 2021).

Figure 4 | Economists' Forecasts Reveal Their Inflation Expectations

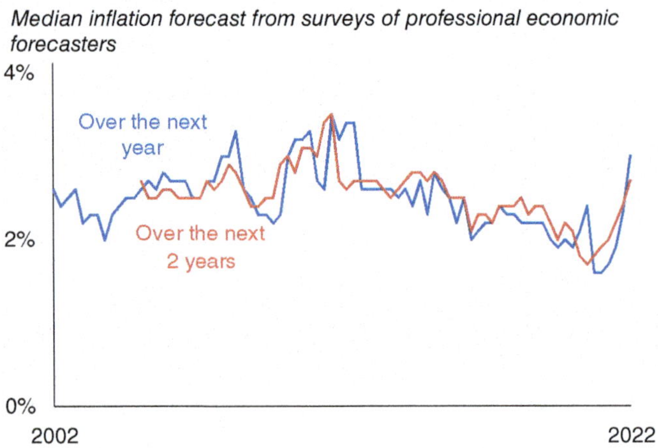

Data from: Reserve Bank of Australia.

Inflation forecasts reveal the inflation expectations of economists. Another indicator of inflation expectations relies on the inflation forecasts that professional economists publish. After all, whenever someone forecasts next year's inflation rate, they're telling you what they expect the inflation rate to be next year. Figure 4 illustrates the median inflation forecast from an ongoing survey of professional economists. It shows their inflation expectations when asked to project inflation both over the next year and over the next two years. The blue line shows what they expect inflation to be next year, while the red line shows longer-term inflation expectations. Notice that one-year inflation expectations tend to shadow two-year expectations from the previous year. In either case, most economists believe that inflation will average around 2% per year.

Figure 5 | Financial Market Inflation Expectations

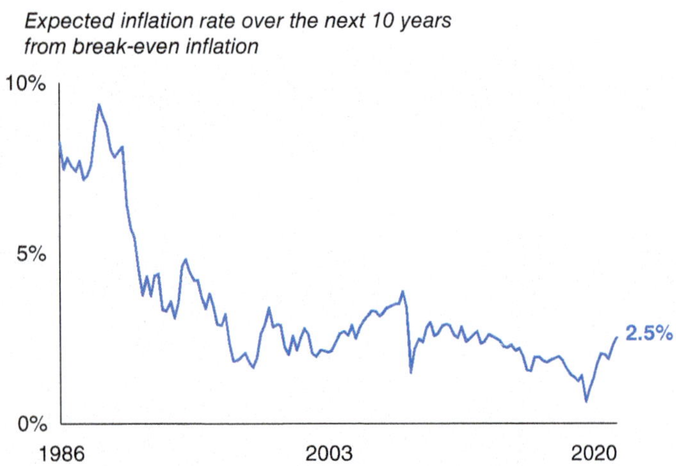

Data from: Reserve Bank of Australia.

Financial markets bet on the future path of inflation. An alternative measure of inflation expectations comes from analysing financial market data. *Break-even inflation* is a commonly used measure of financial market inflation expectations. The Australian Government issues two different types of securities: nominal and inflation indexed. The yield from inflation indexed securities (such as Treasury Indexed Bonds, which are traded on exchanges as eTIBs) is automatically adjusted for inflation, whereas the yield for nominal securities are not. As such, comparing the yield of nominal bonds with inflation indexed bonds can tell us what the market expects inflation to be. This difference of yields on 10-year bonds is called the break-even 10-year inflation rate. As you can see in Figure 5, in March 2022, the break-even 10-year inflation rate was 2.5%, suggesting that the market expects inflation to average 2.5% over the next 10 years. It's an informative measure because it summarises the collective wisdom of many sophisticated financial traders. Economists also like to track these numbers to see how these market prices respond in real time to changing economic conditions and the actions of the Reserve Bank. The downside of market-based measures is that they're an imperfect measure of expected inflation because traders may bid the price of these swaps higher or lower, depending on how risky they're perceived to be.

Inflation expectations can be adaptive, anchored, rational, or sticky. If inflation depends on inflation expectations, then you might ask: What determines people's inflation expectations? There are many possibilities. Some managers might expect recent levels of inflation to continue, which means they have *adaptive expectations*. Others might believe that the Reserve Bank will deliver on its promise to ensure that inflation will be around 2%, and so they have *anchored expectations,* anchored to the Reserve Bank's inflation target. Still others might use all available data and a deep understanding of macroeconomic relationships to come up with the most accurate forecast possible with available data, so that they have *rational expectations*. There is also evidence that people revisit their views about inflation only irregularly, and so they stick with their previous views for long periods of time, which means they have *sticky expectations*.

For most people, it's probably some combination of all of these factors. If you're a manager, the important thing is not to figure out precisely how inflation expectations are formed, but rather to form the most accurate expectations you can. Fortunately, there's a simple trick that'll help you with this.

EVERYDAY Economics **The average of many economists beats any individual**

Many managers rely on their own intuitions to guide their inflation expectations. Think about the benefits of specialisation, and you'll realise that doesn't make much sense. As with most things in life, you'll probably get better results if you depend on a specialist, which in this case would mean relying on a professional economic forecaster. Indeed, professional economists typically have more accurate expectations than either managers or the general public. That's why some managers simply call their bank's economist to ask what they predict next year's inflation rate to be.

But there's an easy way to do even better: Rather than listening to just one economist, it's better to rely on the average forecast from many expert economists. (If it's a pride of lions and a gaggle of geese, then I propose we call them a *surplus* of economists.) Studies show that the most accurate forecasts come from taking the average inflation forecast across many different professional economists. Indeed, the average of many forecasts is typically more accurate than the forecast of any individual financial whiz.

Point your browser to the Survey of Market Economists from the Reserve Bank of Australia (at https://www.rba.gov.au/statistics/tables/, under Inflation Expectations – G3.). There, you'll find the average inflation expectation across many leading economists. Rely on the average forecast of many professional economists, and you'll have access to the best inflation forecast of all. Even better, it's free! ■

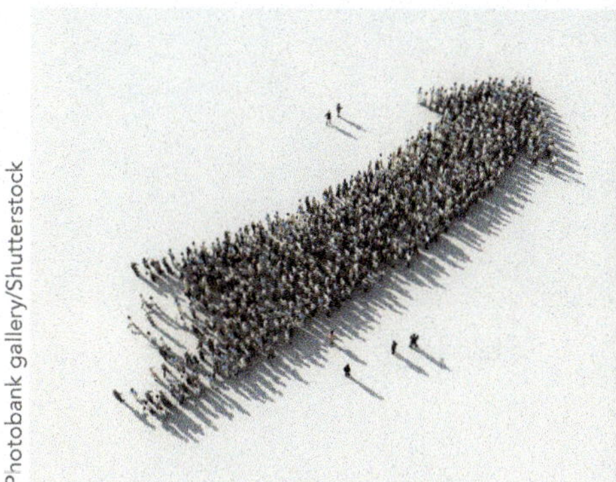

Photobank gallery/Shutterstock

Want to know if inflation will rise or fall? Don't ask one economist . . . ask a crowd of economists.

That's it. We've now identified the key long-run force driving inflation: inflation expectations. But, while inflation expectations are important, they're not the whole story. In the short run, the ups and downs that drive the business cycle might drive inflation higher or lower. That's our next topic.

31.3 The Phillips Curve

Learning Objective *Analyse the link between the output gap and inflation.*

A strong economy has created a rather pleasant dilemma for you and your fellow executives at Hungry Jack's. People are busy and have healthy incomes, and so more people are willing to grab takeaway rather than cook dinner or eat leftovers for lunch. But it's a dilemma because Hungry Jack's locations are already overflowing at peak times. Some customers give up waiting and leave. Hungry Jack's faces **excess demand** given its limited seating capacity, as the quantity demanded at the prevailing price exceeds the quantity that it can supply.

excess demand When the quantity demanded at the prevailing price exceeds the quantity supplied.

In the long run, if business continues to boom, it's worth building more restaurants. But in the short run, you're stuck with your existing capacity. In this situation, what advice would you give your fellow executives?

Demand-Pull Inflation

When demand for your product exceeds your capacity, it's time to think about raising your prices. After all, there's no point having more customers than you can serve. Hungry Jack's can raise its prices—and hence its profit margin—and still fill its restaurants. If inflation expectations would normally lead you to raise your prices by 2%, the fact that you're also facing excess demand is a reason to raise your prices a bit more. In fact, this is precisely what Hungry Jack's management has typically done, raising its prices a bit faster when its restaurants face excess demand.

Takatoshi Kurikawa/Alamy Stock Photo

Should you raise prices?

Excess demand leads inflation to rise above inflation expectations. A strong economy puts millions of businesses in a similar situation to Hungry Jack's, with customer demand exceeding what producers can supply. Each of these businesses will respond to their excess demand much as Hungry Jack's did, by raising their prices by a bit more than required just to keep pace with expected inflation. The result is *demand-pull inflation,* which occurs when excess demand pulls inflation up, so that it rises above expected inflation.

Insufficient demand leads inflation to fall below inflation expectations. Demand-pull inflation can also pull inflation below inflation expectations when demand is unexpectedly weak. To see why, let's return to the dark days following the financial crisis, when the economy was so weak that few people had extra cash to spend on restaurant meals. This cut two ways for Hungry Jack's. On the one hand people didn't have a lot of money with which to eat out. But this affected higher-end restaurants more. In fact, some people "traded down" to cheaper fast-food restaurants like Hungry Jack's.

insufficient demand When the quantity demanded at the prevailing price is below what's supplied.

The restaurant industry generally was facing a problem of **insufficient demand,** as the quantity of restaurant meals demanded at the prevailing price was below the quantity that restaurants wished to supply. In response, many restaurants cut prices or offered better deals for the same price. That's effectively the same thing.

In a weak economy, millions of businesses face insufficient demand. Like Hungry Jack's, most will find that their marginal costs are low when they're producing well below their capacity. They'll follow the same logic as restaurants during the financial crisis and respond to insufficient demand with price restraint, either raising their prices by a bit less than they otherwise would or in some cases cutting them. Across the whole economy, the result is widespread price restraint that pulls inflation below expected inflation. That is, insufficient demand leads inflation to fall below expected inflation.

Don Arnold/Getty Images

How can you bring in the crowds?

When the economy is operating at full capacity, inflation equals inflation expectations. Notice that demand-pull inflation is a separate force that operates in addition to inflation expectations. When there's excess demand, it pulls inflation to rise above inflation expectations, and when there's insufficient demand, it pulls inflation to fall below inflation expectations.

Between these two cases—of excess demand and insufficient demand—is the case where demand matches the economy's productive capacity. In this case there's no demand-pull inflation and hence no pressure for prices to rise faster or slower than expected. And so when the economy is operating at full capacity, inflation is equal to inflation expectations.

The output gap measures the imbalance between output and productive capacity. In all of this, the driver of demand-pull inflation is the imbalance between buyers' demand for output versus the productive capacity of suppliers. This suggests that demand-pull inflation is driven by the *output gap,* which measures actual output relative to potential output.

The Phillips Curve Framework

Putting these pieces together yields two key observations that form the basis of the framework we're building to analyse inflation.

Observation one: Demand-pull inflation is driven by the output gap. When output exceeds potential output—meaning the output gap is positive—there is excess demand. The more positive the output gap is, the greater the degree of excess demand, and hence the greater the pressure to raise prices. By contrast, when output falls short of potential output—meaning the output gap is negative—there is insufficient demand. The more negative the output gap is, the greater the degree of insufficient demand, and hence the greater the pressure for price restraint.

Observation two: Demand-pull inflation leads inflation to diverge from inflation expectations. Demand-pull inflation occurs in addition to inflation expectations, meaning that demand-pull factors cause inflation to either rise above inflation expectations (when there's excess demand), or fall below inflation expectations (when there's insufficient demand). That is, it drives **unexpected inflation,** which is the difference between inflation and inflation expectations:

Unexpected inflation = Inflation − Inflation expectations

unexpected inflation The difference between inflation and inflation expectations = Inflation − Inflation expectations

The Phillips curve describes how the output gap is linked to unexpected inflation. Put these two observations together, and we conclude that *the output gap causes inflation to rise above, or fall below, inflation expectations.* We can summarise this as follows:

> **Inflation Force #2: Demand-Pull Inflation**
> The output gap drives inflation to rise above or fall below inflation expectations.
> *↑Output gap → ↑Inflation (relative to inflation expectations)*

Demand-pull inflation creates a link between the output gap and unexpected inflation (the gap between inflation and inflation expectations). When you graph this link, the result is known as the **Phillips curve.** Figure 6 shows the Phillips curve, illustrating how the output gap affects unexpected inflation.

Phillips curve A curve illustrating the link between the output gap and unexpected inflation.

Figure 6 | **The Phillips Curve**

The output gap drives inflation to rise above or fall below inflation expectations.

(A) When **output exceeds potential output**, *excess demand* leads managers to raise prices more, causing **inflation to rise above expected inflation**.

(B) When **output is equal to potential output**, the absence of demand-pull inflation means that **inflation will be equal to expected inflation**.

(C) When **output is less than potential output**, *insufficient demand* leads to price restraint, causing **inflation to fall below expected inflation**.

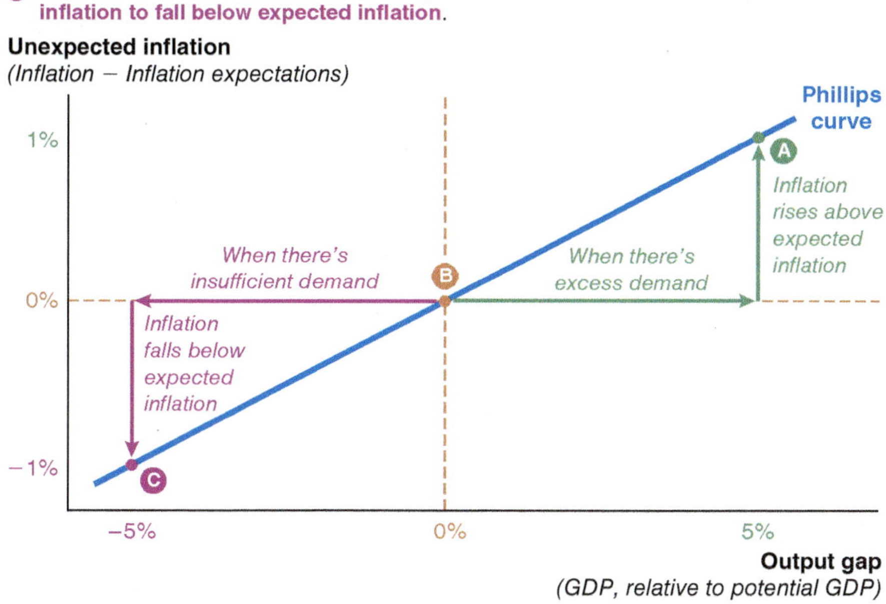

The Phillips curve is named after Bill Phillips who first discovered it. He was a bit of a character—a crocodile hunter, adventurer, and war hero, who once jerry-rigged a secret miniature radio while captured in a prisoner-of-war camp. While he only passed his economic principles class by a single point, he went on to make a major mark on the field by showing that excess demand generates inflationary pressure. His analysis of historical data unearthed the importance of demand-pull inflation.

Let's explore this graph in a bit more detail.

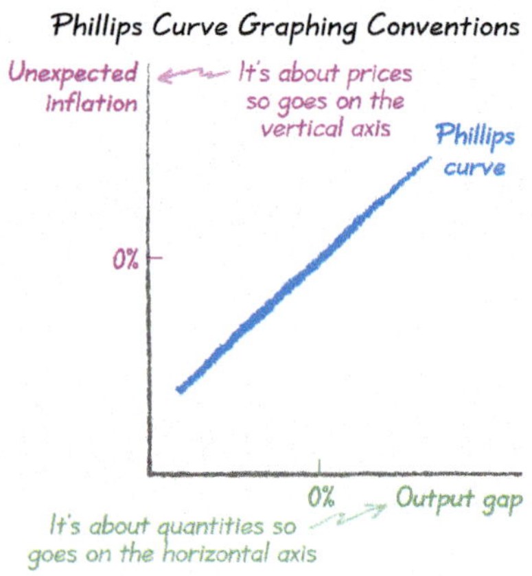

Unexpected inflation goes on the vertical axis, and the output gap goes on the horizontal axis. By now, you're pretty familiar with the graphing convention in economics of using the horizontal axis to show what's going on with quantities and the vertical axis to show what's going on with prices. The same conventions apply to the Phillips curve, so make sure you put the output gap (which is about quantities) on the horizontal axis, and unexpected inflation (which is about prices) on the vertical axis. And don't forget that the Phillips curve describes inflation above and beyond that caused by inflation expectations, which is why the vertical axis measures unexpected inflation (which is inflation less inflation expectations).

One more graphing tip: Both the output gap and unexpected inflation can be either positive or negative, so it's usually a good idea to extend both axes into negative territory. That means you draw the axes so that zero is pretty much in the middle. (This may seem unusual at first—it means the axes no longer rise from zero—but you'll see that the curve still makes sense when you draw it.)

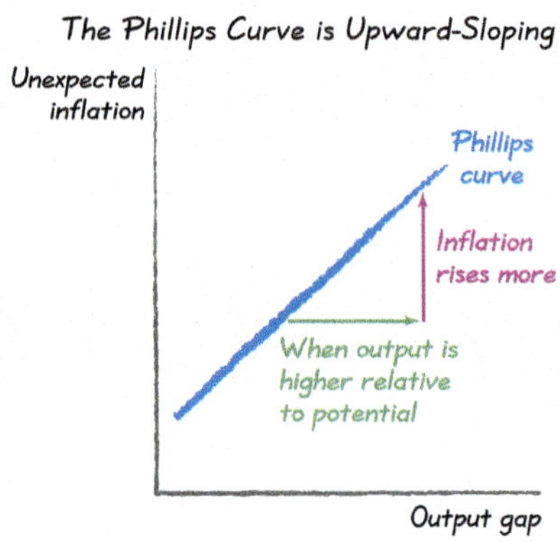

The Phillips curve is upward-sloping. The Phillips curve is upward-sloping because higher output relative to potential output—a more positive output gap—leads to greater inflationary pressure, causing inflation to rise above inflation expectations. It illustrates the idea that:

$$\uparrow \text{Output gap} \rightarrow \uparrow \text{Unexpected inflation}$$

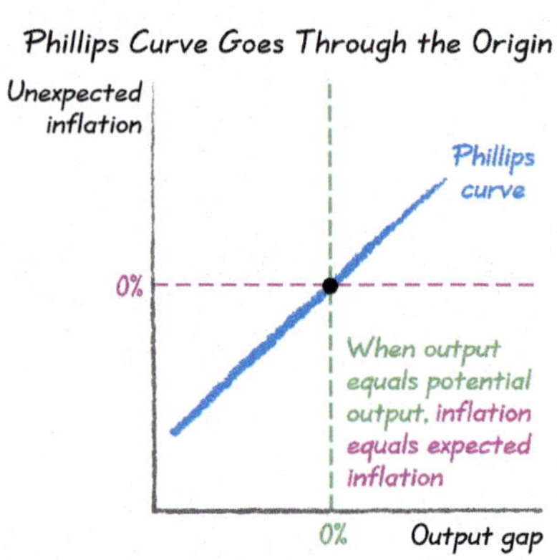

When output is equal to potential output, then inflation is equal to expected inflation. The Phillips curve passes through the origin, which is the point at which the output gap is zero and unexpected inflation is zero. At this point, output is equal to potential output and so the absence of demand-pull inflation means that inflation is pulled neither above nor below inflation expectations. As a result, when actual output is equal to potential output, actual inflation is equal to expected inflation.

The Phillips curve predicts how far inflation will diverge from expected inflation. Notice that the vertical axis of the Phillips curve suggests that unexpected inflation can be either positive or negative. This doesn't mean that actual inflation is likely to be negative (that can also happen, but it's rare). Rather, the Phillips curve is all about *unexpected inflation*. When it says that unexpected inflation will be negative, this simply means that actual inflation will be less than expected inflation. And positive rates of unexpected inflation tell you that actual inflation will be greater than expected inflation. Indeed, the Phillips curve is useful because it tells you by how much actual inflation will be above or below expected inflation.

EVERYDAY Economics **How Uber is like the Phillips curve**

As the concert ends late on a rainy Saturday night, you head outside, pull out your phone, and tap on the Uber app, hoping to summon a ride home. But the app responds that a ride that would normally cost $10 will now cost $30. You look around at the hundreds of other concert goers nearby, and your inner Bill Phillips explains what's just happened: There are more concert-goers trying to get a ride home than available Uber drivers, so there's excess demand.

Uber's surge-pricing algorithm has kicked in. It's like a turbo-charged Phillips curve, programmed to respond to excess demand by raising prices immediately. We say it's turbo-charged because it usually takes other businesses months rather than minutes to change their prices in response to a surge in demand. That's why the Phillips curve typically describes inflation rising or falling over a period of months.

There's one important difference. During that brief post-concert surge, most other prices—the price of taxis, of buses, or even of rental cars—are unchanged. As such, Uber's surge pricing is best viewed as a change in *relative prices*—it raises the price of taking an Uber relative to taking the bus. By contrast, the Phillips curve describes how a surge in demand across the whole economy leads many businesses to raise their prices, and these widespread price rises create inflation. ■

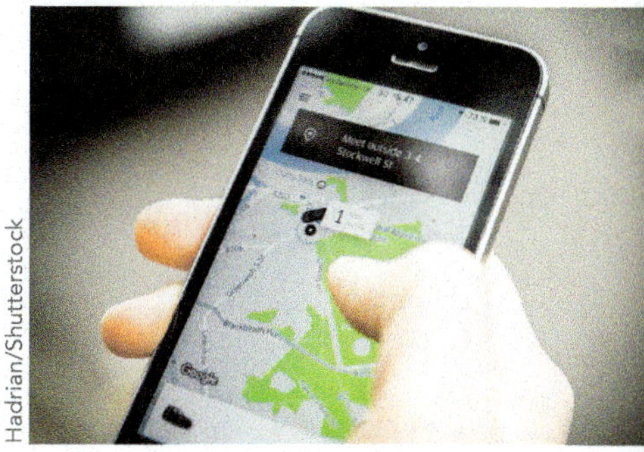

Hadrian/Shutterstock

It's like the Phillips curve.

The Phillips Curve in Australia

Bill Phillips once described his curve as a "wet weekend's bit of work." He discovered it by plotting historical data for the United Kingdom covering the period from 1861 to 1957. It's time for us to update his plots with an eye to discovering the modern Phillips curve for Australia.

Discover the Phillips curve for Australia. We begin by compiling the relevant historical data. To construct our measure of unexpected inflation, we need to collect data on both the actual inflation rate each year and expected inflation (and here, I'm relying on the measure based on forecasts of the financial market). We calculate unexpected inflation simply as actual inflation less expected inflation. Next, we plot unexpected inflation in each year against the corresponding output gap.

Figure 7 plots these data, showing the shape of the Phillips curve for Australia. You'll see that these data roughly bear out the predictions of our analysis: When the output gap is positive so that GDP is high relative to potential GDP, inflation has *typically* risen higher than inflation expectations. And when the output gap is negative so that GDP is low relative to potential GDP, inflation has typically fallen lower than inflation expectations. The upward slope of this curve reveals that the more positive the output gap, the more unexpected inflation there is.

The data also reveal that this prediction isn't always borne out, illustrating that the Phillips curve is an imprecise relationship. Even so, it remains an important tool because accounting for the output gap leads to more accurate inflation forecasts. The fact that the data do not lie exactly along this Phillips curve suggests that other factors also play a role. For example, the dot for 1992 (in the bottom left) is nowhere near the Phillips curve. That was a year in which Australia was recovering from an almost induced recession that Treasurer Paul Keating infamously described as "the recession we had to have." We'll come back to explaining why that boosted inflation shortly.

When economists try to figure out what the Phillips curve looks like, they compile data like this and compute a line that best fits the data. The line of best fit in Figure 7 is an example of this sort of analysis. You could do this with a pencil, a ruler, and a bit

Figure 7 | **Discover the Phillips Curve for Australia**

Ⓐ The grey dots show the level of unexpected inflation and the output gap in each year from 1985 to 2021.

Ⓑ These data are aligned along an upward-sloping line of best fit, confirming that—as the theory suggests—a more positive output gap leads to more unexpected inflation.

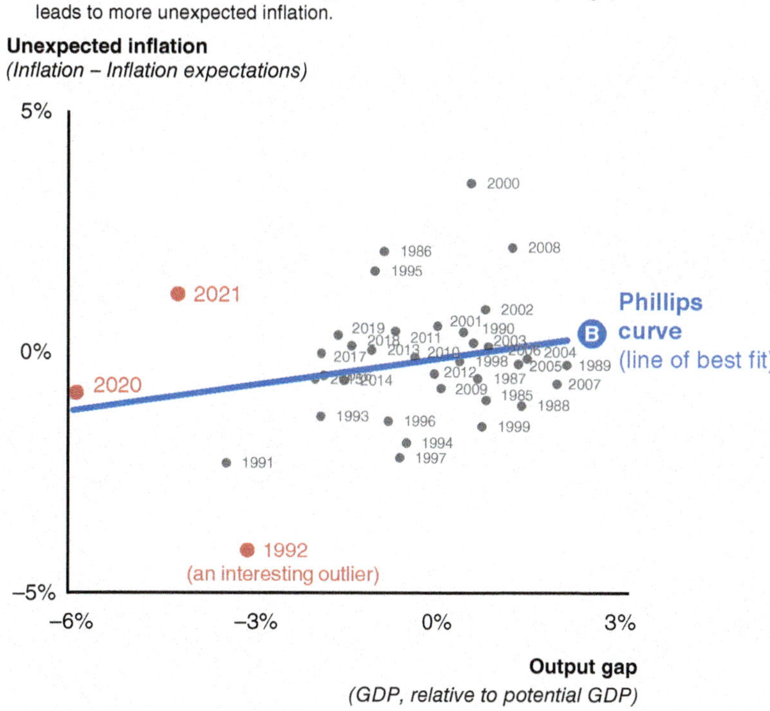

Data from: Australian Bureau of Statistics; Reserve Bank of Australia; CEIC.

of judgement, but in the example shown here, I've computed the line of best fit using a spreadsheet. (If you've taken a statistics or econometrics class, you'll recognise this as a regression line; if you haven't, all you need to know is that this line best describes the relationship on average.)

A more complete analysis would also take account of other factors that might affect inflation, such as changes in oil prices, productivity, or the exchange rate. For now, be patient—we'll incorporate these supply-side factors shortly.

Figure 8 | Use the Phillips Curve to Forecast Inflation

For any given output gap, look up until you hit the Phillips curve, then look across to forecast unexpected inflation.

(A) Locate the output gap on the horizontal axis, and look up until you hit the Phillips curve.
(B) Then look across to find your forecast of unexpected inflation.
(C) Inflation = Unexpected inflation + Inflation expectations.

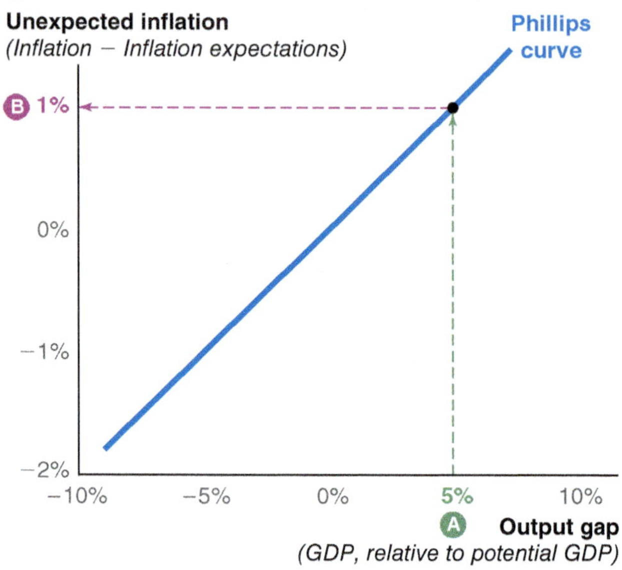

Use the Phillips curve to forecast future inflation. Investment banks, businesses, and government economists forecast inflation by using estimates of the Phillips curve that are similar to our line of best fit.

It's a two-step process:

Step one: Assess inflation expectations. You can measure inflation expectations by analysing surveys of inflation expectations, surveys of economists, or financial market-based measures.

Step two: Forecast unexpected inflation. This is where the Phillips curve is useful. Start with your estimate of what the output gap will be, look up to the corresponding point on the Phillips curve, and then look across to find your forecast for unexpected inflation. For instance, Figure 8 shows that an output gap of +5% corresponds with unexpected inflation of 1%.

Your inflation forecast, of course, should be the sum of your forecasts for expected inflation and unexpected inflation. So if inflation expectations are running at 2% and you're also forecasting demand-pull inflation to add another 1%, you should forecast inflation to be 3%.

Do the Economics

You're about to negotiate your salary for next year, and want to make sure that it adjusts for likely changes in the cost of living. The economy is doing well, and you expect GDP to be 5% above potential output. Inflation expectations are currently 2%.

a. Using the Phillips curve in Figure 8, how much of a pay raise will you need to request to be able to buy the same stuff you currently buy?

b. What if GDP is 2.5% below potential instead?

c. What if GDP is exactly equal to potential GDP? ■

Answers: a. Inflation = expected inflation + unexpected inflation = 2% + 1% = 3%. b. If the output gap is −2.5%, the Phillips curve shows unexpected inflation will be −0.5%, so inflation will be 1.5%; c. A 0% output gap corresponds with unexpected inflation of 0%, so inflation will be 2%.

An Alternative Illustration: The Labour Market Phillips Curve

So far, we've described the Phillips curve as the relationship between unexpected inflation and the output gap. We focused on the output gap because it's a measure of output relative to the economy's productive capacity, and so it describes the extent to which managers are dealing with excess demand (which leads them to raise their prices a bit more) or insufficient demand (which leads them to show price restraint). The Reserve Bank has used the output gap and the Phillips curve to forecast inflation since at least the mid-1980s.

But historically the Phillips curve was drawn a little differently—partly because Phillips' insights pre-dated modern methods to measure the output gap. This alternative version represents the same ideas, it was just sketched a little differently. Some economists even prefer this alternative version, so it's worth becoming familiar with it.

The labour market Phillips curve links unexpected inflation to the unemployment rate. This alternative approach focused on the labour market. It noted that unemployed workers are an unused resource, and so the *unemployment rate*—which is the share of the labour force without a job—provides an alternative measure of whether the economy is producing above or below its productive capacity. Indeed, in Chapter 29, we saw that *Okun's rule of thumb* describes a close link between the output gap and the unemployment rate. It says that a high unemployment rate corresponds with a negative output gap (where output is below potential output, and so insufficient demand is a problem). It also says that an especially low unemployment rate corresponds with a positive output gap (where output exceeds potential output, and so excess demand arises).

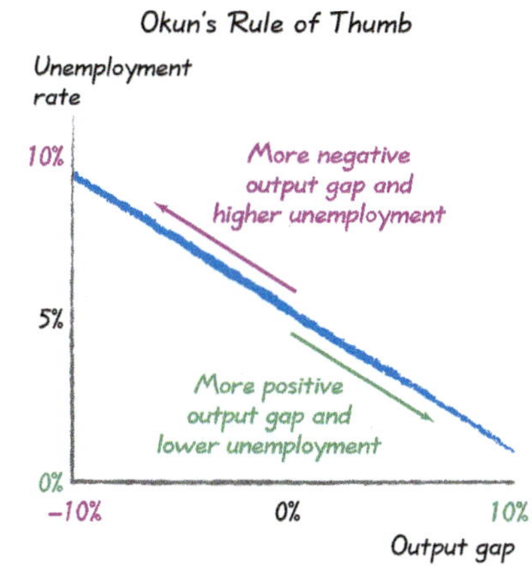

It follows that there's an alternative version of the Phillips curve that links low unemployment to higher demand-pull inflation. We can summarise it as saying:

$$\downarrow \text{Unemployment rate} \rightarrow \uparrow \text{Unexpected inflation}$$

Both versions of the Phillips curve tell the same story. This alternative version of the Phillips curve, which is illustrated in Figure 9, links inflation to unemployment. In order to keep the concepts clear, we'll call this version the **labour market Phillips curve**. It summarises the *exact* same ideas as the Phillips curve, but it relies on a different measure of excess demand. The most obvious difference—that the curves slope in different directions—is purely cosmetic. It arises only because excess demand corresponds with a *high* level of GDP relative to potential output, but a *low* unemployment rate. Both versions of the Phillips curve suggest that excess demand leads to higher inflation.

labour market Phillips curve A Phillips curve linking unexpected inflation to the unemployment rate.

Inflation is stable at the equilibrium unemployment rate. The inflation rate will only be stable when inflation is equal to inflation expectations, and this occurs at the point where unexpected inflation is 0%. The corresponding unemployment rate is called the *equilibrium unemployment rate*. (You may also hear it called the "natural rate" or the NAIRU, which stands for the "non-accelerating inflation rate of unemployment"—a bit of a mouthful that's trying to say it's the only unemployment rate that will neither nudge inflation higher nor lower.) This is the only unemployment rate that's consistent with stable inflation. The equilibrium unemployment rate is not zero because there remain potential workers who are facing frictional or structural barriers to unemployment. (Remember that we discussed why the equilibrium unemployment rate is not zero in Chapter 23.) When unemployment is lower than the equilibrium unemployment rate, inflation starts to creep up. It's hard to know with any precision what the equilibrium unemployment rate is—economists debate the matter endlessly—and so rather than emphasising a particular number, it's probably safer to say that it lies somewhere between 3% and 6%.

Figure 9 | The Labour Market Phillips Curve

The unemployment rate determines how much inflation will rise above or fall below inflation expectations.

- **A** The **unemployment rate** is an alternative indicator of **insufficient or excess demand.**
- **B** The **labour market Phillips curve** shows that **higher unemployment leads to lower unexpected inflation**, and **lower unemployment leads to higher unexpected inflation.**
- **C** At the **equilibrium unemployment rate, unexpected inflation is zero**, so inflation is equal to inflation expectations.

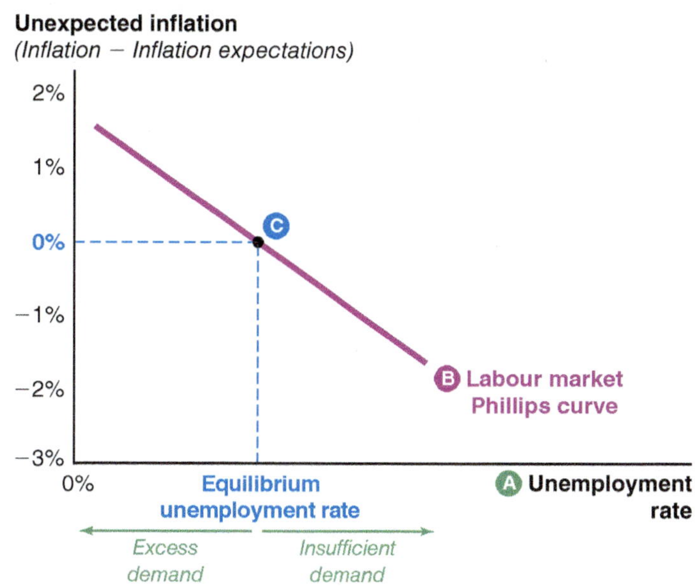

Demand-pull inflation is driven by too much demand. We started this chapter by analysing inflation expectations. We've now also analysed the demand side of the economy, finding that excess demand creates demand-pull inflation, which causes inflation to rise above inflation expectations. (And insufficient demand causes inflation to fall below inflation expectations.)

While we've analysed the role of demand in driving price changes, we've yet to explore the role of supply. Let's fix that. As we turn to analysing how changing supply conditions can produce inflation, we'll discover that supply-side shocks shift the Phillips curve. But to see why, we'll have to explore the link between Wonder Woman and geopolitics.

A victim of geopolitical tension.

31.4 Supply Shocks Shift the Phillips Curve

Learning Objective *Assess how shocks to production costs shift the Phillips curve.*

In 1974, a six-year old girl went to the toy store to buy a Wonder Woman action figure. She thought she had saved up enough to buy it, but when she arrived, she discovered that the price had risen. So she returned home, determined to keep saving her allowance. Several months later, she returned with what she now hoped was enough money. But again, the price had risen. Wonder Woman remained elusive. The six-year old's hopes were dashed by geopolitical tensions that were about to roil the global economy.

Action figures are made of plastic, and plastic is made largely from oil, and much of the world's oil comes from the Arabian Peninsula. Many oil-producing Arab nations were angered that the United States had supported Israel in the Yom Kippur War, so they retaliated by halting the sale of oil to the United States. This geopolitical disruption led to macroeconomic disruption. It caused a dramatic decrease in the supply of oil to the United States, which led the price of oil to quadruple in just a matter of months. Because oil is an internationally traded commodity, there is a global price for it. So the price also shot up in Australia.

Expensive oil constituted a sharp increase in costs for American toymakers, who responded to these higher marginal costs by raising their prices. This led to higher prices of the imported toys in Australia. Similarly, the oil price hike raised marginal costs for the millions of Australian businesses that use oil as an input. In response, these businesses also raised their prices. Inflation shot up from 5.6% in the middle of 1973 to 16.7% in late 1974.

Figure 10 | Rising Costs Shift the Phillips Curve

(A) Rising production costs lead to **rising prices** at any given output gap, **shifting the Phillips curve up**.

(B) The result can be that **inflation exceeds inflation expectations**, even when output is below potential output, as at the point shown.

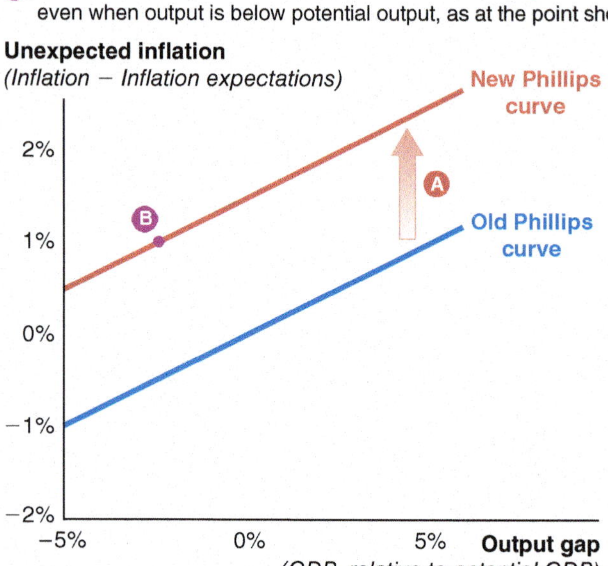

How Supply Shocks Shift the Phillips Curve

This was an example of *cost-push inflation,* where an unexpected boost to production costs pushed sellers to raise their prices.

Rising production costs create an additional reason to raise prices, above and beyond existing inflation expectations and demand-pull pressures. This means that cost-push inflation leads to more inflation at any given level of the output gap, and for any given level of inflation expectations. As Figure 10 illustrates, cost-push inflation causes the Phillips curve to shift.

Rising production costs shift the Phillips curve up. Indeed, *any factor that leads to an unexpected rise in production costs will cause the Phillips curve to shift upward.* The reverse is also true: An unexpected decline in production costs will cause the Phillips curve to shift down as sellers respond by cutting prices (or raising them less).

This brings us to our third key insight about the causes of inflation:

> **Inflation Force #3: Cost-Push Inflation**
> An unexpected rise in production costs will cause higher inflation.
> ↑*Production costs* → ↑*Inflation*

Three types of supply shocks shift the Phillips curve. This third inflationary force reflects the influence of unexpected changes in production costs, which is why it's called *cost-push inflation*. And because changes in costs shift producers' supply curves, an unexpected change in production costs that shifts the Phillips curve is called a **supply shock.**

supply shocks Any change in production costs that leads suppliers to change the prices they charge at any given level of output. Supply shocks shift the Phillips curve.

There are three key types of supply shocks that might shift the Phillips curve: shifts in input prices, shifts in productivity, and shifts in exchange rates. In each case we focus on an *unexpected* change in costs because anticipated rises or falls in input prices will have already been factored into inflation expectations. Let's explore each in turn.

The Phillips curve shifts in response to changes in:

1. Input prices
2. Productivity
3. Exchange rates

Phillips Curve Shifter One: Input Prices

Any time the price of your inputs rises, so will your marginal costs, and higher marginal costs lead sellers to raise their prices. Thus, rising input prices lead to rising prices, and because this boosts inflation at any given level of the output gap, it shifts the Phillips curve up. The same forces also operate in reverse, and declining input prices shift the Phillips curve down. The more that an input price changes, and the more important that input is in the costs of a typical firm, the more it will shift the Phillips curve.

Input Prices Shift the Phillips Curve

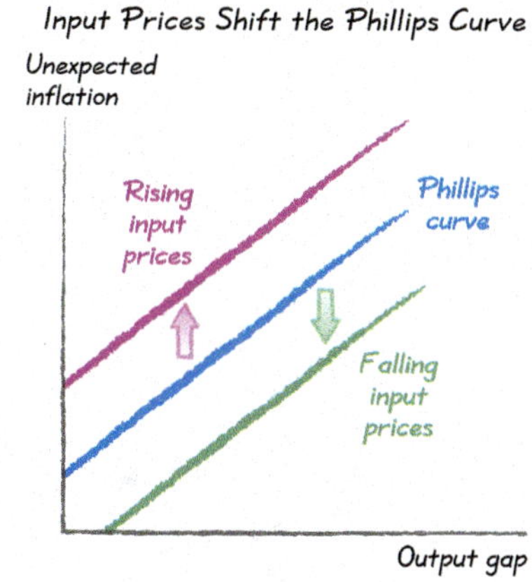

Oil and commodity prices are important input prices. Oil is a major input in many sectors of the economy, and so the changing price of oil has frequently been an important source of cost-push inflation. Oil is important because it can be burned to generate electricity, refined into gasoline or diesel fuel, or synthesised into plastic (some of which might be used to make action figures). A rise in the price of oil has ripple effects throughout the economy, leading to higher electric and heating bills, higher gasoline prices, which lead to higher transportation prices, which raises the prices of nearly everything at your local supermarket. The oil price also bears watching because it has historically been so volatile, rising and falling in response to embargoes, wars, coups, and revolutions in the politically unstable Middle East, as well as unpredictable discoveries of new energy sources.

Other commodity prices—including agricultural goods in particular—can create supply shocks, particularly when severe weather disrupts harvests. It's something that managers at Hungry Jack's plan for, and indeed, in most cases increased commodity prices can be passed through to customers through increases in menu prices. When other companies follow suit, commodity price shocks will generate widespread cost-push inflation.

Rising wages can cause a wage-price spiral. Perhaps the most important input price is the price of labour, otherwise known as the hourly wage. A sharp rise in the wages you have to pay to attract quality workers will raise your company's marginal costs, causing many managers to raise their prices. Indeed, in the past, executives at fast-casual restaurants like Hungry Jack's have reported that higher wages increase labour costs, but they counter this by increasing menu prices. Once again, as other companies follow suit, higher wages will quickly generate cost-push inflation.

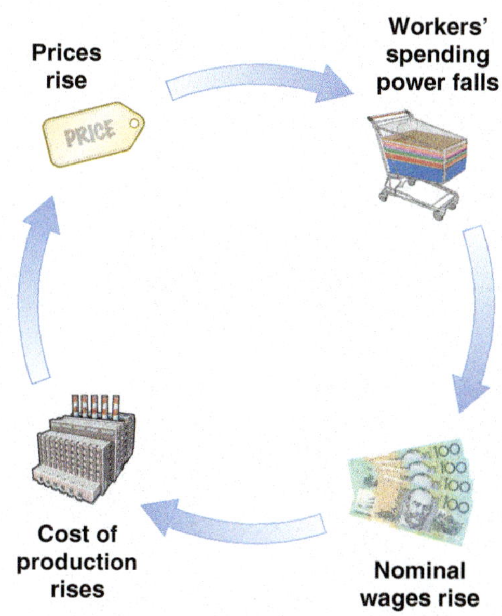

Wages are particularly important because they can *amplify* the effects of a temporary inflation shock and make it *persistent*. This is because a **wage-price spiral** can take hold, in which workers respond to inflation by demanding higher nominal wages to maintain their spending power, leading businesses to respond to higher wages by raising prices.

wage-price spiral A cycle where higher prices lead to higher nominal wages, which lead to higher prices.

Thus, an initial inflationary impulse can cause workers to seek higher nominal wages, which causes businesses to further raise their prices, which causes workers to seek higher nominal wages, and so it continues as wages chase prices, and prices chase wages. The result is higher inflation that persists long after the initial inflationary impetus has receded.

Productivity Growth Shifts the Phillips Curve

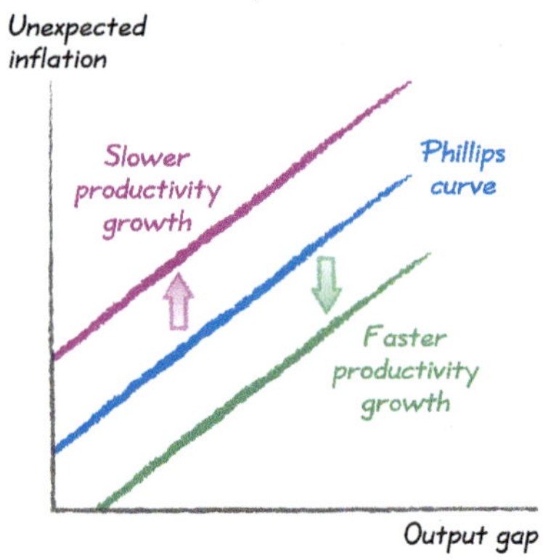

Phillips Curve Shifter Two: Productivity

Your company's productivity also changes your production costs, as a more productive firm needs less of each input to produce the same output. It follows that faster-than-expected productivity growth lowers your marginal costs, leading to greater price restraint at any given output gap. As a result, stronger productivity growth shifts the Phillips curve down—a form of negative cost-push inflation.

It also works the other way. Productivity growth through the 1960s had been quite rapid, and many businesses had gotten in the habit of giving their employees large nominal wage raises without it causing their per-unit costs to rise. But in the mid-1970s, productivity growth slowed even as wages continued to grow rapidly. The result was rising production costs that led to cost-push inflation. And so weaker productivity growth shifted the Phillips curve up.

Phillips Curve Shifter Three: Exchange Rates

The nominal exchange rate also creates cost-push inflation, thereby shifting the Phillips curve. There's both a direct effect on the price of goods made overseas and an indirect effect due to the changing prices of foreign goods putting pressure on the prices of domestically produced goods.

Direct effect: When the Australian dollar depreciates, foreign goods are more expensive. A reminder: The *exchange rate* is the price of an Australian dollar. For instance, when the exchange rate is 80 U.S. cents, that means that one Australian dollar buys 80 U.S. cents. Or, put differently, one U.S. dollar costs A$1.25. We say that the Australian dollar *depreciates* when the price of an Australian dollar falls, say to 75 U.S. cents. It means the Australian dollar becomes cheaper for foreigners to buy; it also means that foreign currency is expensive for Australians to buy because it'll cost more Australian dollars to buy a specific quantity of U.S. dollars.

This is relevant because you'll need foreign currency to buy goods from foreigners. When the Australian dollar depreciates, then each Australian dollar buys less foreign currency. In turn, that means it'll take more Australian dollars to pay for imported goods. And so a depreciating Australian dollar directly increases the price of foreign-made goods, boosting inflation.

Exchange Rates Shift the Phillips Curve

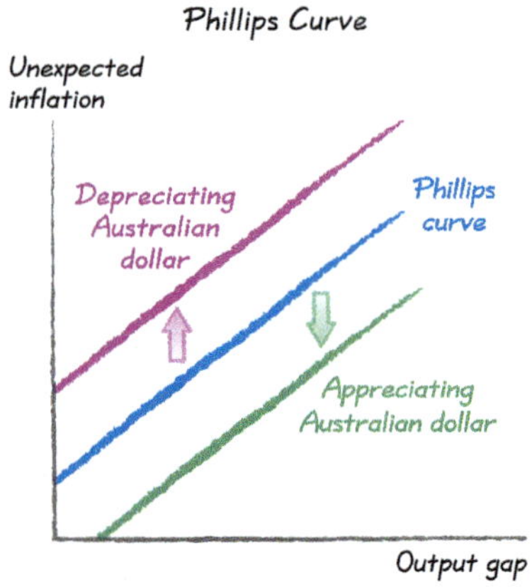

Indirect effects: More expensive foreign goods lead to higher prices on domestic goods. There are also indirect effects that lead Australian producers to raise their prices:

- *For businesses that rely on imported inputs*: A depreciating Australian dollar raises the cost (in dollars) of their imported inputs, and these higher marginal costs lead them to raise their prices.
- *For businesses that compete with imported products*: A depreciating Australian dollar raises the price (in dollars) of goods made by foreign competitors. This weakens the competitive pressure on domestic businesses, leading some of them to raise their prices.
- *For businesses that export their products*: A depreciating Australian dollar means that their foreign customers are now willing to pay more (in dollars) for their products. This increased pressure from foreign customers may lead some companies to raise the prices they charge their Australian customers.

A depreciating Australian dollar shifts the Phillips curve up; an appreciating Australian dollar shifts the Phillips curve down. Together, these direct and indirect effects mean that a depreciating Australian dollar boosts inflation at any level of the output gap, thereby shifting the Phillips curve up. When the same forces operate in reverse, a rising value of the Australian dollar—which we call an *appreciation* of the exchange rate—lowers inflation at any given output gap, shifting the Phillips curve down.

Shifts versus Movements Along the Phillips Curve

We've covered a lot of ground, so before we conclude, let's recap. We'll do so in a way that clarifies the difference between factors that cause a movement along the Phillips curve, and factors that cause a shift in the Phillips curve.

Demand-pull inflation leads to movement along the Phillips curve. The Phillips curve illustrates the impact of demand-pull factors, showing how inflation changes in response to the output gap. Thus, booms and busts—which lead to changes in the output gap—represent movements *along* the Phillips curve.

↑Output gap (↑GDP relative to potential) → Excess demand → Rising prices → Movement along the Phillips curve (upward and to the right)

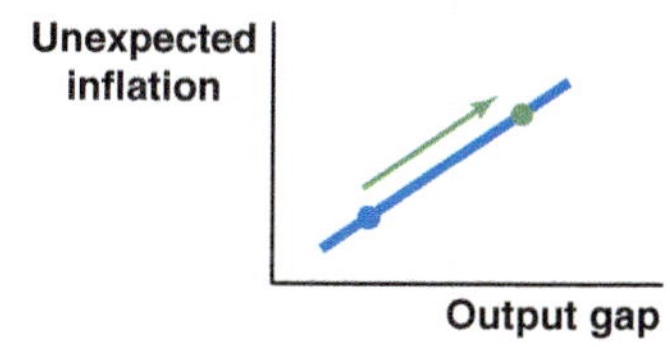

↓Output gap (↓GDP relative to potential) → Insufficient demand → Falling prices (or slower rates of increase) → Movement along the Phillips curve (downward and to the left)

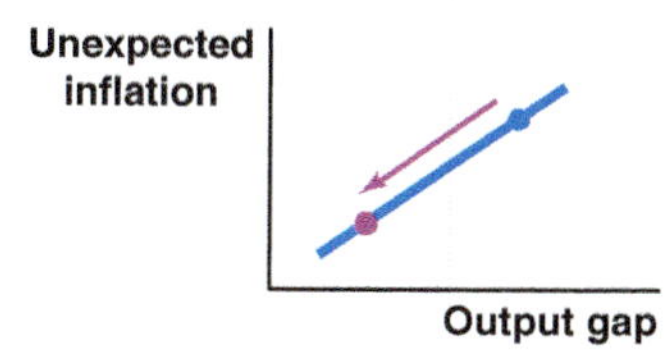

Cost-push inflation leads to a shift in the Phillips curve. In contrast, any other factor that changes producers' pricing decisions for a given output gap leads to a shift in the Phillips curve. A shift in your production costs creates pressure to shift your prices, and this occurs whatever the output gap is. We call these shifts supply shocks.

Rising production costs lead to higher marginal costs, causing businesses to raise their prices. The result will be higher inflation at any level of the output gap. Thus, rising production costs shift the Phillips curve up. On the flip side, falling production costs lead businesses to raise their prices by a bit less, or even cut them. The result will be lower inflation at any level of the output gap. Thus, falling production costs shift the Phillips curve down.

↑Input costs (oil, wages)
↓Productivity growth
↓Australian dollar
→ Rising production costs → Rising prices at each output gap → Phillips curve shifts up

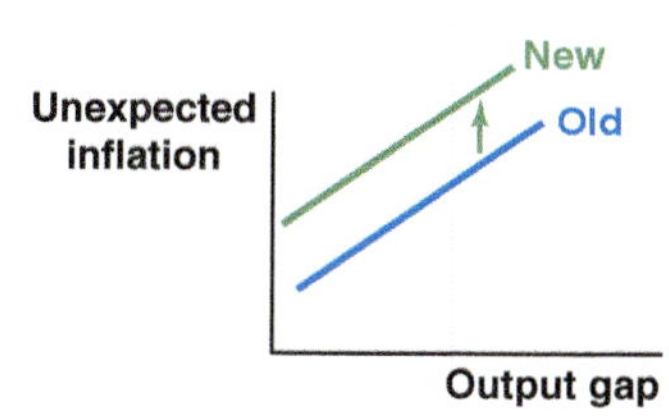

↓Input costs (oil, wages)
↑Productivity growth
↑Australian dollar
→ Falling production costs → Falling prices at each output gap (or slower rates of increase) → Phillips curve shifts down

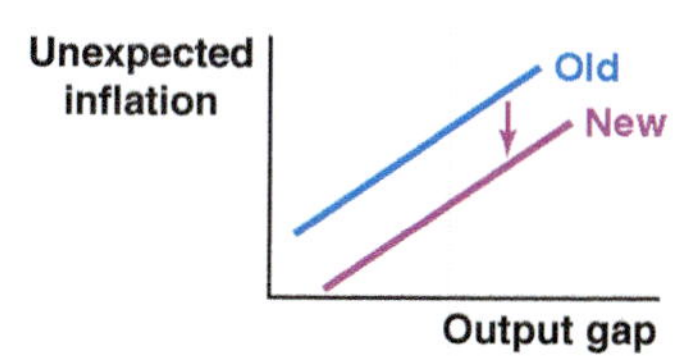

The Phillips curve is about short-run trade-offs, while inflation expectations remain relevant in the long run. We began this chapter by describing inflation expectations as the key long-run cause of inflation. Inflation expectations neither shift the Phillips curve nor cause a movement along it, but they still play an important role in driving inflation. Recall that total inflation is the sum of expected inflation and unexpected inflation. The Phillips curve focuses on the short run in which inflation deviates from inflation expectations, and so it explains *unexpected inflation.* By contrast, rising inflation expectations lead to a rise in *expected inflation.* Thus, changes in inflation expectations are an important long-run factor determining overall inflation at any given level of the output gap and for any given constellation of input costs.

Rising inflation expectations → Rising expected inflation → Rising expected inflation + No change in unexpected inflation = Rising inflation

Falling inflation expectations → Falling expected inflation → Falling expected inflation + No change in unexpected inflation = Falling inflation

Is it a demand shock or a supply shock? You can use this framework to diagnose what's going on in the economy. To see how, notice that demand-pull inflation always leads the output gap and unexpected inflation to move in the same direction: More output leads to higher inflation (for a given level of inflation expectations), while less output leads to less inflation (again, for a given level of inflation expectations). In contrast, supply shocks can lead to higher inflation, even when output has declined. This means that if you see the double-whammy of higher unexpected inflation and lower output, you can infer that there has been a supply shock. And if inflation rises in line with measures of inflation expectations, then you can infer that it's inflation expectations that have shifted.

Tying It Together

It's time to pan back to take in the big picture. The Phillips curve is central to macroeconomics because it links developments in the real economy—like the output gap or the unemployment rate—with their implications for purely nominal variables, like inflation. But that link has very different implications in the short run versus the long run, and so our final task is to spell those differences out.

Let's start with the *short run,* by which I mean the year-to-year economic fluctuations over the course of a business cycle. In the short run, the Phillips curve illustrates how developments in the real economy shape nominal variables like inflation. For instance, when output is temporarily above potential output, higher inflation will result. Likewise, it suggests that nominal variables affect the real economy. For instance, policy makers can achieve temporarily higher output by allowing inflation to temporarily rise. But this is only a short-run trade-off.

In the *long run*—over periods measured in decades rather than years—the determinants of inflation are very different. Over the long run, the ups and downs of the output gap will average out. (Sometimes the output gap will be positive, and sometimes it'll be negative, but on average, it'll be close to zero.) The ups and downs of supply shocks will also average out. So neither demand-pull nor cost-push factors matter much over the long run.

This means that in the long run *inflation expectations* determine inflation. That's a big deal. It means that in the long run, nominal variables like inflation are *not* determined by real variables like output or unemployment. And real variables like output or unemployment are not determined by nominal variables like inflation. This implies that real and nominal variables are unrelated in the long run, an insight sometimes called the **classical dichotomy** because it was first articulated by the early classical economists. This is the idea that in the long run, adding an extra zero at the end of every price tag (including wage rates, bank balances, and currency) wouldn't change how much stuff gets made, how many people work, or indeed, any real variable.

classical dichotomy A purely nominal change—like a change in the average price level—won't have any effect on real variables in the long run.

This distinction between the short- and long-run determinants of inflation lies at the heart of one of the most consequential misinterpretations of the Phillips curve. It's tempting to read the Phillips curve as presenting a trade-off between more output and higher inflation. It appears to suggest that policy makers can choose either more output paired with high inflation, or less output paired with low inflation. Indeed, for a while in the 1960s, some policy makers seemed to believe just that; they read the Phillips curve as if it were a menu of options and their job was just to choose the best macroeconomic meal—their preferred combination of inflation and output. And indeed, they often thought that a little bit of inflation wasn't too high a price to pay for a stronger economy that would raise output and lower unemployment.

It's a tempting inference to draw, but it's also mistaken. Just because high inflation is a common *consequence* of high levels of output doesn't mean that allowing high inflation will lead to sustainably higher output. The problem is that high inflation eventually feeds through to create high inflation expectations.

When policy makers push output above potential output, the immediate impact—illustrated by the Phillips curve—is to push inflation above inflation expectations. Over time, higher inflation leads to higher inflation expectations. If policy makers persist in trying to keep output above potential, the Phillips curve says that a positive output gap will cause inflation to exceed these higher inflation expectations. And in turn, this higher inflation leads to even higher inflation expectations. The result is that keeping output above potential leads to ever-rising rates of inflation. Indeed, Milton Friedman won the Nobel Prize in economics partly for this insight. In a famous address to the big annual conference of economists, he argued that:

> There is always a temporary tradeoff between inflation and unemployment; there is no permanent tradeoff. The temporary tradeoff comes not from inflation per se, but from unanticipated inflation, which generally means, from a rising rate of inflation.

Friedman made this assessment in 1968, but it's a lesson that policy makers ended up learning the hard way. Throughout the late 1960s and 1970s the government made successive attempts to boost the economy by passing tax cuts, boosting government spending, and lowering interest rates. These led to higher inflation, but no lasting effect on output. The result was a period known as the "Great Inflation," in which inflation rose sharply, and many countries got used to double-digit inflation. The problem was that once policy makers signalled that they were willing to tolerate somewhat higher inflation, people began to expect higher inflation. And so we got the self-fulfilling prophecy of higher inflation due to higher inflation expectations but no lasting improvements in output.

It was a painful lesson, and it led to a rethinking of the Phillips curve. Today, policy makers understand that the Phillips curve is a useful tool for predicting how inflation will respond to the ups and downs of the business cycle but it shouldn't be read as a menu of options. They now know that there's no long-run trade-off between inflation and output. For instance, in the 2021–22 recovery from the coronavirus pandemic, inflation started to rise sharply once again. As inflation started to rise, so did inflation expectations, as shown in Figure 11. Remembering the Great Inflation of the 1970s, the RBA were quick to try and cut off inflation by raising interest rates aggressively. We'll talk more about this in Chapter 34 when we look at monetary policy.

Figure 11 | Inflation Raises Inflation Expectations

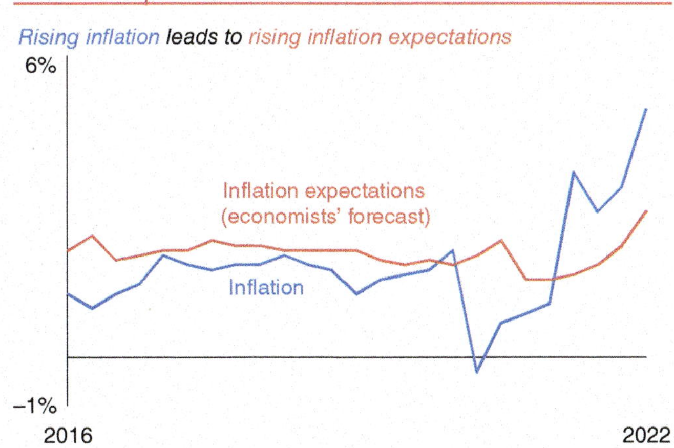

Data from: Australian Bureau of Statistics; Reserve Bank of Australia.

Chapter at a Glance

Inflation = Expected inflation + Demand-pull inflation + Cost-push inflation

↑ Inflation expectations → ↑ Inflation | ↑ Output gap → ↑ Inflation | ↑ Production costs → ↑ Inflation

The Three Causes of Inflation

Cause #1. Inflation expectations: Higher inflation expectations create higher inflation.

↑ Inflation expectations → ↑ Inflation

Inflation expectations (the rate at which you expect prices to rise, on average, across the whole economy over the next year) are a key driver of long-run inflation.

- Three ways to track inflation expectations: surveys, economists' forecasts, and financial markets.
- Monetary policy tries to shape inflation expectations.

Cause #2. Demand-pull inflation: The output gap drives inflation to rise above or fall below inflation expectations.

↑ Output gap → ↑ Inflation (relative to inflation expectations)

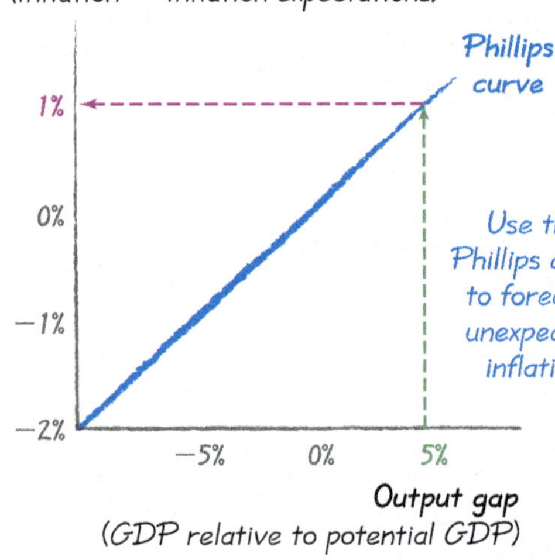

Demand-pull inflation is driven by the output gap (which measures actual output relative to potential output). It leads inflation to diverge from inflation expectations.

- **Excess demand** (when output > potential output) => inflation rises above expected inflation.
- **Insufficient demand** (when output < potential output) => inflation falls below expected inflation.
- When output is equal to potential output => inflation = inflation expectations.

Demand-pull inflation creates a link between the **output gap** and **unexpected inflation**. When you graph this link, the result is known as the **Phillips curve.**

Cause #3. Cost-push inflation: An unexpected rise in production costs will cause higher inflation.

↑ Production costs → ↑ Inflation

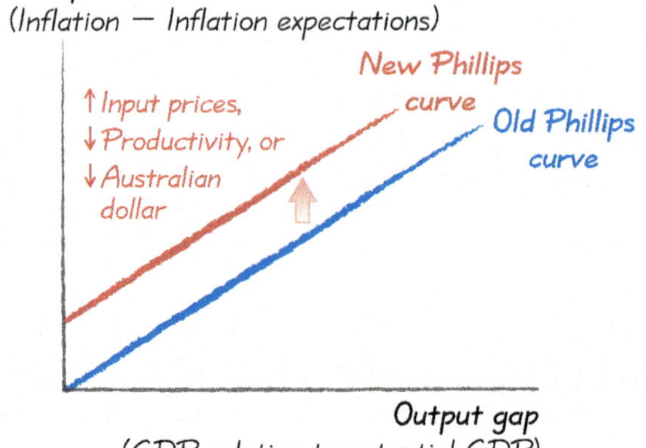

Rising production costs lead to more inflation at any given level of the output gap, and for any given level of inflation expectations.

Cost-push inflation causes the Phillips curve to shift.

Three types of supply shocks shift the Phillips curve

1. Input prices
2. Productivity
3. Exchange rates

Key Concepts

classical dichotomy, 812
cost-push inflation, 797
demand-pull inflation, 796
excess demand, 801
inflation expectations, 796
insufficient demand, 802
labour market Phillips curve, 807
Phillips curve, 803
supply shock, 809
unexpected inflation, 803
wage-price spiral, 809

Discussion and Review Questions

Learning Objective 31.1 *Identify the three causes of inflation: inflation expectations, demand-pull inflation, and supply shocks.*

1. Rare earth metals are used in the production of many of the personal electronic devices you use every day. Use the interdependence principle to discuss the impact of an unexpected increase in the price of rare earth metals on inflation.
2. You've been invited to help a foreign affiliate of your company set next year's prices. Inflation last year was 5%, the unemployment rate dropped to record lows, and GDP skyrocketed. In addition, geopolitical tensions led the price of crude oil to rise by 50%. Given these circumstances, what do you think annual inflation will be next year, and how will this affect your advice? Explain your reasoning.

Learning Objective 31.2 *Explore how inflation expectations lead to inflation.*

3. Explain how inflation expectations are like a self-fulfilling prophecy.
4. In June 2019, the average price for a cup of coffee in Venezuela was 6,500 bolivars; in June 2018 the average price was just 8 bolivars. This represents an 81,150% increase in a cup of coffee for Venezuelans, who have seen similarly dramatic increases in the prices of everything they buy. Discuss how this experience impacted the inflation expectations of the average Venezuelan during that time, and how those expectations can impact actual inflation.

Learning Objective 31.3 *Analyse the link between the output gap and inflation.*

5. Explain the difference between expected inflation and unexpected inflation.
6. Draw an example of a Phillips curve and a labour market Phillips curve. Explain how they summarise the exact same idea while using different measures of excess demand.

Learning Objective 31.4 *Assess how shocks to production costs shift the Phillips curve.*

7. If Parliament levies a new $100 per tonne tax on carbon emissions to pay for expanded Centrelink benefits, how do you think this will impact unexpected inflation?
8. The adoption of vehicle automation has exploded over the last few years: Automated tractors are already in use harvesting produce on farms, while self-driving vehicles are used to move cargo around shipping yards and warehouses. Use a Phillips curve to help explain how this technological change impacts inflation.

Study Problems

Learning Objective 31.1 *Identify the three causes of inflation: inflation expectations, demand-pull inflation, and supply shocks.*

1. For each of the following, determine whether inflation expectations, demand-pull inflation, or cost-push inflation—and hence inflation overall—will change.
   a. A rapid influx of foreign investment causes the output gap to become more positive.
   b. The government unexpectedly announces a tariff on aluminum and steel.

Learning Objective 31.2 *Explore how inflation expectations lead to inflation.*

2. In January 2019, inflation expectations in the United Kingdom fell from 2.9% to 2.6%. What effect will this have on inflation in the United Kingdom if nothing else changes in the economy? Explain your reasoning.
3. Seana owns a small pet shop and expects inflation to be 3% next year. By how much does Seana expect her marginal costs to change? By how much does she expect her competitor's prices to change?
4. You're a pricing analyst for a manufacturing firm. You are tasked with predicting how average prices will change over the next quarter to help your manager decide how to change their prices. How would you find the best estimate of the likely inflation rate? What do you tell your manager and why?

Learning Objective 31.3 *Analyse the link between the output gap and inflation.*

5. You're a junior consultant at a management consulting company and your team has been hired to help guide a struggling regional retailer. You do some research and find that the output gap is currently zero, and inflation is 4%. In an effort to boost output before the next election, the government announces an unexpected stimulus package that you expect will increase next year's output to be 5% above potential.

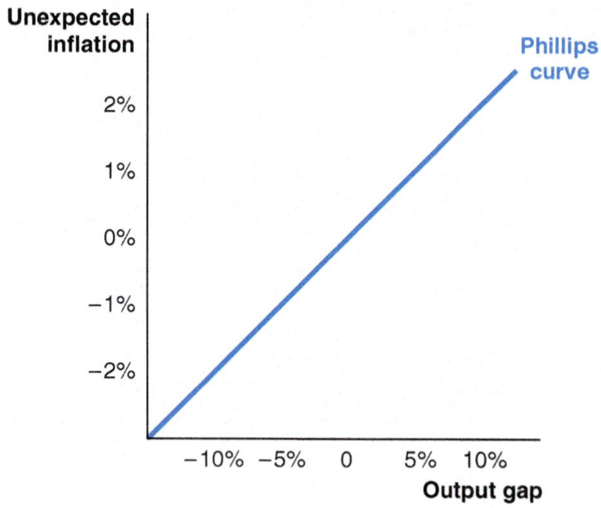

a. Use the Phillips curve to estimate unexpected inflation after the stimulus.

b. What is your forecast for actual inflation after the stimulus?

c. How do you advise the retailer when they ask you how they should change prices next year, given the stimulus will have boosted output?

6. Take the Phillips curve from the previous question and illustrate the corresponding labour market Phillips curve where the initial unemployment rate was 7.5% and the final unemployment rate is 2.5%. What is the equilibrium unemployment rate in the economy?

Learning Objective 31.4 *Assess how shocks to production costs shift the Phillips curve.*

7. In 2022, policy makers debated whether an increase in the federal minimum wage ($20.33 an hour) would be good for the economy. Use a Phillips curve to explain how inflation would change for the following scenarios. Assume that the output gap does not change.

a. Policy makers announce that starting next week, the federal minimum wage will be $25.60 an hour.

b. Policy makers announce that the federal minimum wage will increase to $25.60 an hour over the course of the next 10 years by annual increases of $1.05.

c. Explain how the initial increase in the federal minimum wage for low-wage earners could lead to a wage-price spiral throughout the economy.

8. Between 2011 and 2015, the Australian dollar depreciated relative to the Chinese yuan. What are the direct and indirect effects on inflation? Explain.

9. Identify whether the following will represent a shift in the Phillips curve or a movement along the Phillips curve. Illustrate with a graph.

a. Consumer confidence increases unexpectedly and causes the output gap to become more positive.

b. Inflation last year was far greater than even the best forecaster expected even though the output gap was zero.

c. A devastating late-spring freeze destroys crops across northern Queensland, which causes the output gap to become more negative.

The RBA Model: Putting the Pieces Together

CHAPTER 32

Chapter Objective

Put the pieces together into a complete model of business cycles.

32.1 The RBA Model
Analyse the RBA model, which puts together the *IS* curve, the *MP* curve, and the Phillips curve.

32.2 Analysing Macroeconomic Shocks
Use the RBA model to analyse the consequences of financial shocks, spending shocks, and supply shocks.

32.3 Diagnosing the Causes of Macroeconomic Changes
Use the RBA model to diagnose the causes of economic fluctuations.

Science & Society Picture Library/Getty Images

An analogue model of the economy.

It's about the size of an old refrigerator, and runs on water. The motor, scavenged from an old military plane, pumps pink-dyed water through a series of transparent plastic tubes and into a variety of tanks, at a rate determined by finely tuned valves. Built in the 1940s by New Zealand economist Bill Phillips, the Monetary National Income Analogue Computer, or MONIAC for short, was the most ambitious attempt of its time to account for all the moving parts within the economy.

The MONIAC provided a creative solution to the central challenge of macroeconomics: tracking the many forms of interdependence that make the field so interesting. The water represents flows of income. The valves are calibrated to regulate the flow of water in a way that resembles the economic relationships that determine the flow of income. The valves that determine the rate at which water flows into tanks have neat labels proclaiming that they represent consumption, investment, government purchases, imports, and exports.

Want to forecast what will happen if businesses invest more? Tweak the right valve, let the water flow, and see what happens. Paper spools atop the machine and four pens connected to floats within different tanks trace the model economy's ups and downs. Let the water run long enough, and you'll discover where it settles in equilibrium. One Cambridge professor described it as "a thing of wonder and joy." Versions of this liquid economy were used to teach economics at universities around the world, and the Ford Motor Company bought one. If you ever visit the Science Museum in London, you can see it for yourself.

Fortunately, economics has progressed since Phillips's time, so our models no longer look like Rube Goldberg contraptions. But the challenge of how to fit the pieces together to account for these interdependencies remains central to macroeconomics. And so in this chapter, we're going to do with simple graphs the same thing that the MONIAC tried to do with water: We'll combine key economic relationships to see how they interact to determine economic conditions. Think of this chapter as a capstone that draws the various threads of our study of business cycles together. The result will look less like Phillips's liquid data, and more like the sorts of analyses that power government policy decisions, financial market investments, and the strategic choices of big businesses.

Besjunior/Shutterstock

What happens when we put the pieces together?

32.1 The RBA Model

Learning Objective *Analyse the RBA model, which puts together the IS curve, the MP curve, and the Phillips curve.*

RBA model The framework that uses the *IS* curve, the *MP* curve, and the Phillips curve to link interest rates, the output gap, and inflation.

Over the past two chapters you've done something pretty amazing: You've developed all of the components necessary to construct a complete model of business cycles. You can draw links from monetary policy and financial markets to interest rates using the *MP* curve, then from the real interest rate through spending decisions to output using the *IS* curve, and then from the consequences for the output gap through to the resulting inflationary pressure using the Phillips curve.

In this chapter, we'll put these components together. The result isn't just a textbook tool, it's the actual framework that businesses, economists, and policy makers use to understand the ups and downs of the business cycle. We call it the **RBA model,** because it's the framework that policy makers at the Reserve Bank use to analyse, forecast, and tweak the economy. They use it because it represents the state of the art for understanding our economy.

The RBA Model Combines the *IS, MP,* and Phillips Curves

All that remains is to put each of the pieces of our analysis together into this whole. In Chapter 30, we analysed how the intersection of the *IS* and *MP* curves determines the output gap. And in Chapter 31, we saw how the Phillips curve illustrates the role the output gap plays in shaping inflation. Put the pieces from these two chapters together, and you'll be able to forecast interest rates, the output gap, and inflation.

You can see the connections as follows:

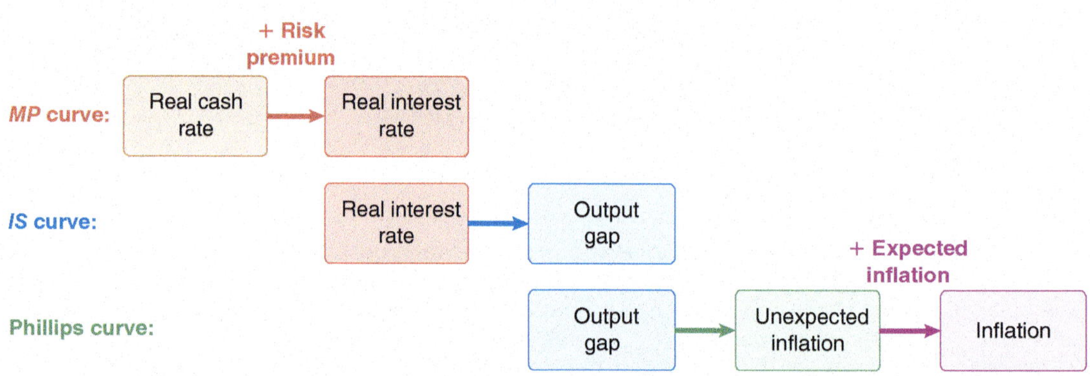

The RBA model isn't a distinct mode of analysis. Rather, it puts together the pieces you've already developed. That's why it's sometimes also called *IS-MP-PC analysis,* because it combines *IS-MP* analysis with the Phillips curve (or "PC" to its friends):

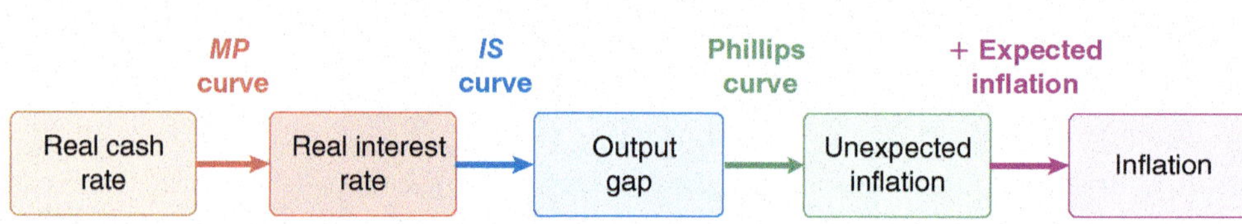

Forecasting Economic Outcomes

Putting these pieces together requires stepping through each of the basic tools we've developed in the past two chapters, in turn.

Start by finding the output gap. Begin your analysis with the *IS-MP* framework, which determines the output gap. We do this in the top panel of Figure 1, which reproduces a familiar chart from Chapter 30. Remember that the vertical axis is the real interest rate and the horizontal axis is the output gap. The *MP* curve is a horizontal line illustrating the current real interest rate, and the *IS* curve is a downward-sloping line illustrating how a lower real interest rate stimulates more spending and output.

Importantly, macroeconomic equilibrium occurs where the *MP* curve cuts the *IS* curve. You can look down from the point where the curves cross to find the resulting output gap. In the example shown in Figure 1, you would forecast an output gap of –5%.

Next, assess inflation. Use the Phillips curve to figure out the inflationary implications of this output gap. I've stacked the Phillips curve directly under the *IS-MP* curves in Figure 1, so you can trace the output gap down from the top panel to the lower panel until you hit the Phillips curve. Once you've found the Phillips curve, you just need to look across to find out what will happen to inflation. Recall the vertical axis of the Phillips curve tells you what will happen to *unexpected* inflation, and you also need to consider the influence of inflation expectations. So to forecast actual inflation, you'll add this forecast of unexpected inflation to the latest reading of inflation expectations.

In this example, an output gap of –5% leads to unexpected inflation of –1%, which means that actual inflation will be 1% below expected inflation. If inflation expectations are 2%, this says inflation will be 1%.

Figure 1 | The RBA Model

Use the IS-MP framework to find the output gap and the Phillips curve to forecast unexpected inflation.

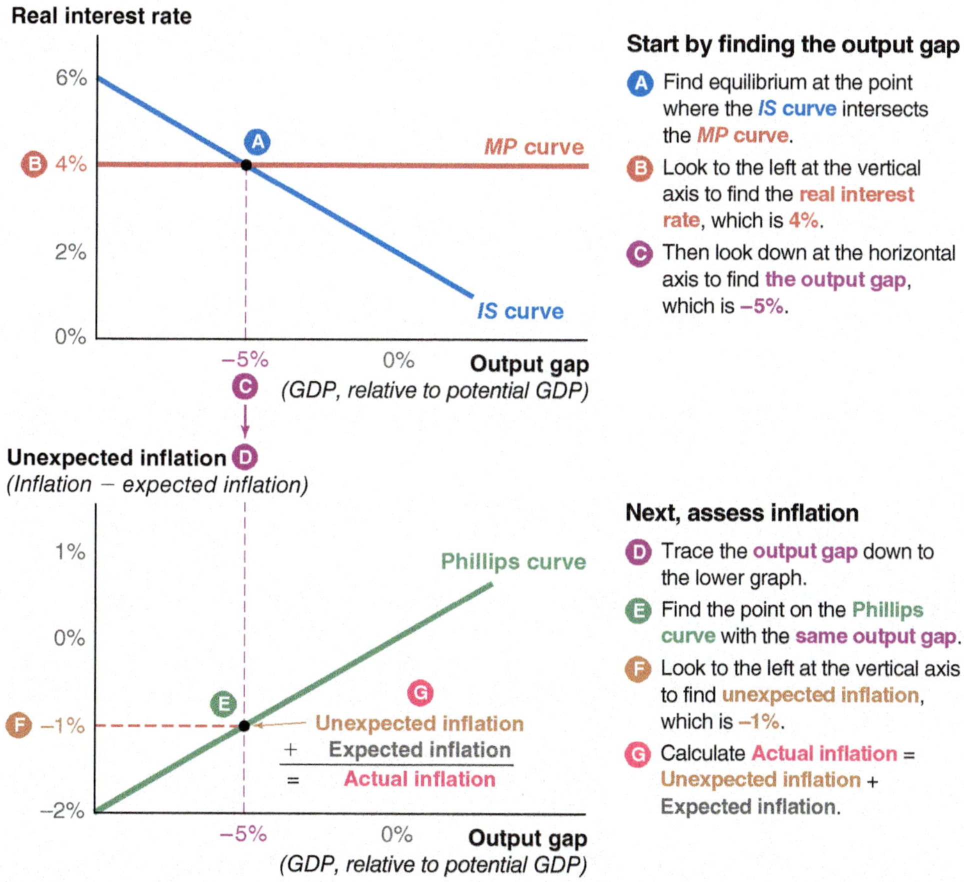

You can see why RBA economists like this style of analysis—it delivers a complete set of forecasts: the real interest rate will be 4%, the output gap will be –5%, and unexpected inflation will be –1%, and so if expected inflation is 2%, inflation will be 1%.

But what will happen if economic conditions change? That's where the RBA model really shines. So let's read on.

Warning: Potential shocks ahead.

financial shocks Any change in borrowing conditions that changes the real interest rate at which people can borrow. Financial shocks shift the *MP* curve.

spending shocks Any change in aggregate expenditure at a given real interest rate and level of income. Spending shocks shift the *IS* curve.

supply shocks Any change in production costs that leads suppliers to change the prices they charge at any given level of output. Supply shocks shift the Phillips curve.

Three Types of Macroeconomic Shocks

There are dozens of shocks that might hit the economy. You can just imagine the headlines: Stocks crater! Productivity surges! Banks fail! Confidence soars! Exports wither! Aussie Dollar plummets! RBA cuts rates! Uncertainty rocks markets! Oil prices dive! Wages boom! And so on . . . (So! Many! Exclamation points!)

There are financial shocks, spending shocks, and supply shocks. Fortunately, the RBA model categorises each of these many possibilities into one of three types of shocks, each of which is familiar from the past two chapters.

- **Financial shocks:** Any change in borrowing conditions that affects the real interest rate—whether due to the Reserve Bank shifting the cash rate, or changes in financial markets shifting the risk premium—will shift the *MP* curve.
- **Spending shocks:** Any change in aggregate expenditure at a given real interest rate and level of income—whether due to consumption, planned investment, government expenditure, or net exports—will shift the *IS* curve.
- **Supply shocks:** Any change in production costs that leads suppliers to change the prices they charge at any given level of output will shift the Phillips curve. Common supply shocks include changes in input prices, productivity, and the exchange rate.

The RBA model brings together three curves, which are shifted by the three kinds of shocks. Thus, we can summarise our complete framework—which includes the *IS*, *MP*, and Phillips curves, as well as the economic shocks that cause them to shift—as follows:

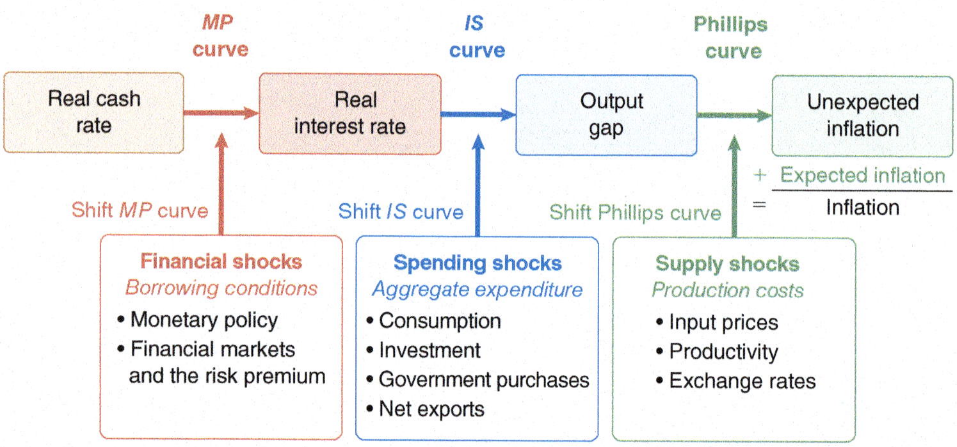

Types of shocks:
- Financial
- Spending
- Supply

This taxonomy is tremendously helpful because it means that forecasting the consequences of whichever of the zillion things that might happen next to the economy—a collapse in the banking system, plummeting consumer confidence or rising oil prices—doesn't require a zillion different kinds of analysis. Rather, you simply need to figure out if you're dealing with a financial shock (such as when the banking system collapses), a spending shock (such as when plummeting consumer confidence leads to a decrease in consumption), or a supply shock (such as when oil prices skyrocket). Then it's simply a matter of exploring how that type of shock will affect the economy.

32.2 Analysing Macroeconomic Shocks

Learning Objective *Use the RBA model to analyse the consequences of financial shocks, spending shocks, and supply shocks.*

One of the most important uses of a macroeconomic framework like the RBA model is to forecast how the economy will respond if a macroeconomic shock knocks it off its current path. That's going to be our next task.

A Recipe for Analysing Macroeconomic Shocks

This task is all about exploring the consequences of a shift in the *IS, MP,* or Phillips curve. And it'll be a lot simpler if you follow this simple three-step recipe:

Three steps for analysing macroeconomic shocks:

1. Identify the shock and shift the curve
2. Find the output gap
3. Assess inflation

Step one: Identify the shock so you can shift a curve. The first thing you need to do is to identify the shock, so you can shift the relevant curve in the appropriate direction. Is this a change in borrowing conditions (a *financial* shock, which shifts the *MP* curve), a change in aggregate expenditure (a *spending* shock, which shifts the *IS* curve), or a change in production costs (a *supply* shock, which shifts the Phillips curve)?

As you assess which direction you should shift the curve, remember the key lessons of the past two chapters:

Financial Shocks Shift the *MP* Curve

An increase in interest rates shifts the *MP* curve up, while a decrease shifts it down.

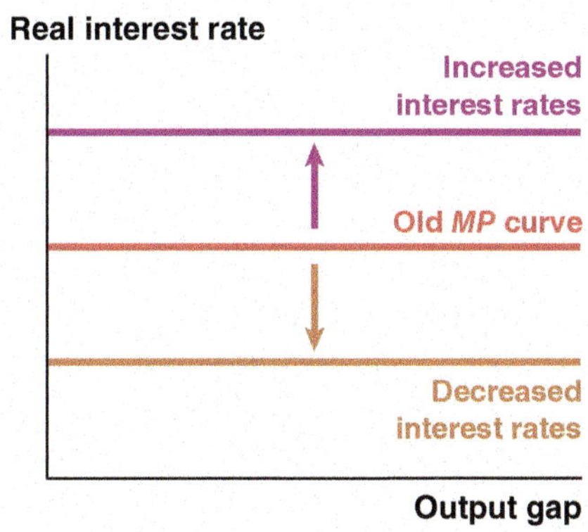

Spending Shocks Shift the *IS* Curve

An increase in aggregate expenditure shifts the *IS* curve to the right, while a decrease shifts it to the left.

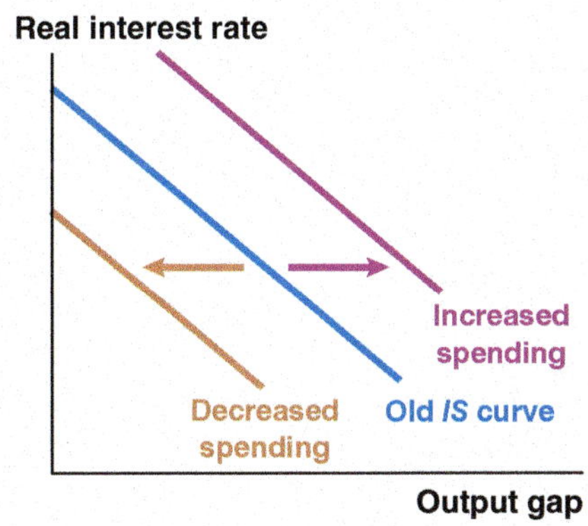

Supply Shocks Shift the Phillips Curve

Rising production costs shift the Phillips curve up, while falling production costs shift it down.

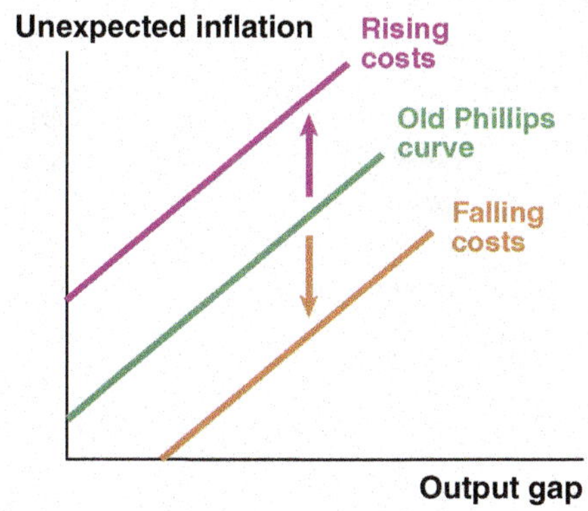

Step two: Find the output gap. Once you've shifted the appropriate curve in the appropriate direction—or multiple curves if there are multiple shocks—the rest of this process is about analysing the new equilibrium. And so the second step is familiar: Look at the intersection of the (new) *IS* and *MP* curves to find the equilibrium output gap and real interest rate.

Step three: Assess inflation. Finally, trace the output gap down from the *IS-MP* graph to the (potentially shifted) Phillips curve to find the inflationary implications of this output gap. Remember, the Phillips curve is all about *unexpected* inflation, and so to forecast actual inflation, you'll add this forecast of unexpected inflation to the latest reading of inflation expectations.

We'll use this three-step recipe to explore the likely consequences of each of the three kinds of shocks: financial shocks, then spending shocks, and finally, supply shocks.

In each of the examples that follows, we'll start with an economy at rest with an output gap of zero and with unexpected inflation of zero (so inflation equals expected inflation). Then we'll forecast how the economy will respond to a shock. Economists are often a pessimistic group, and so in each case we'll analyse adverse shocks that make economic conditions worse. To figure out the effects of a positive shock, simply move the corresponding curve in the opposite direction.

Analysing Financial Shocks

A financial shock occurs whenever borrowing conditions change the real interest rate at which you can borrow money, thereby shifting the *MP* curve. An increase in the real interest rate will shift the *MP* curve up, while a decrease will shift it down.

Changing borrowing conditions in financial markets shift the *MP* curve.

The *MP* curve shifts in response to monetary policy and financial market risks. The real interest rate is the sum of the risk-free interest rate set by the Reserve Bank and the risk premium determined in financial markets. This means that the *MP* curve will shift in response to changes in:

- *Monetary policy:* When the Reserve Bank raises or lowers the risk-free real interest rate, the rate borrowers pay also changes, shifting the *MP* curve.
- *Financial market risks:* Any change that makes banks more reluctant to lend money at a given interest rate will raise the risk premium, raising the interest rate that borrowers pay, shifting the *MP* curve. This could arise due to concerns that borrowers may not be able to repay their debt, concerns about liquidity, uncertainty about future interest rates, or rising risk aversion.

(If you feel a bit rusty on this, take a moment to review "Financial Shocks Shift the *MP* Curve" in Chapter 30.)

Higher interest rates lead to lower output and lower inflation. Okay, now it's time to figure out the consequences of an adverse financial shock that raises the real interest rate from 2% to 4%. To figure out the consequences, we'll work through our three-step recipe in Figure 2.

Figure 2 | **Financial Shocks Shift the *MP* Curve**

An upward shift of the MP curve leads to a decrease in output and lower inflation.

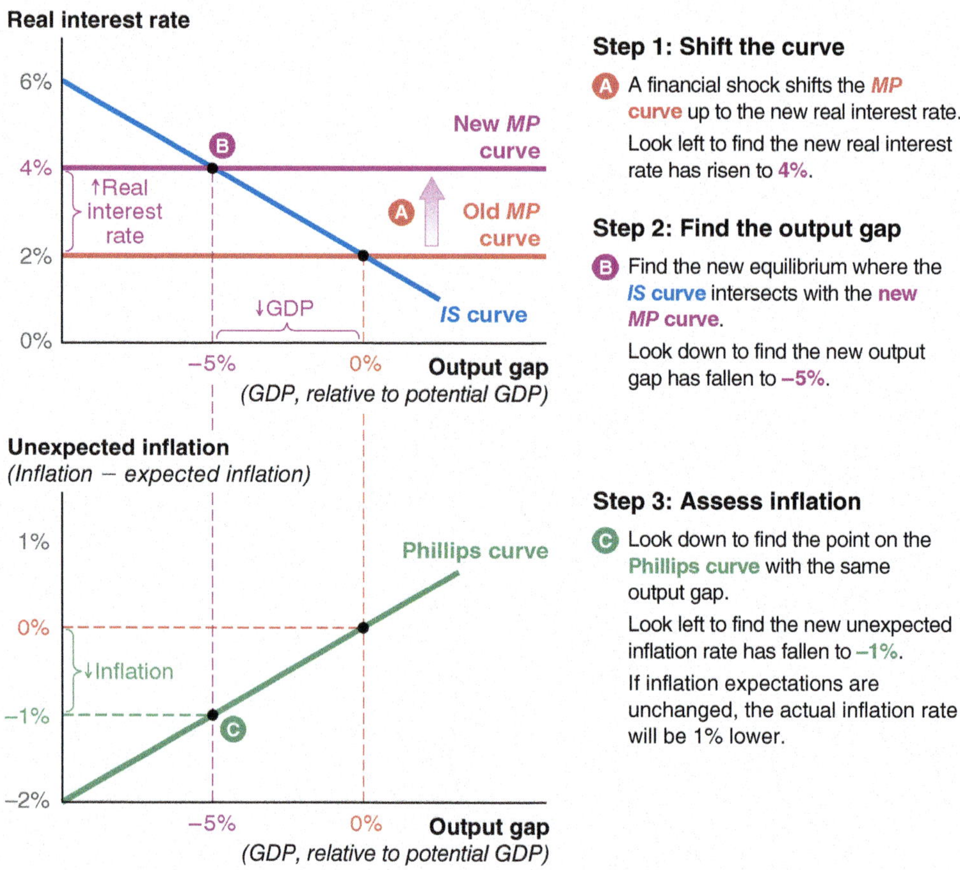

Step one: *Shift the curve.* Higher real interest rates shift the *MP* curve up by 2 percentage points to a real interest rate of 4%.

Step two: *Find the output gap.* The new equilibrium occurs where this *new MP* curve cuts the *IS* curve. In this example, this occurs when output shrinks to be 5% below potential output.

Step three: *Assess inflation.* Trace this output gap down onto the Phillips curve to assess the inflationary consequences. In this case, an output gap of –5% will cause unexpected inflation to decline to –1%. Thus, if expected inflation is unchanged at 2%, actual inflation will fall to be one percentage point lower, at 1%.

You can track the effects as follows:

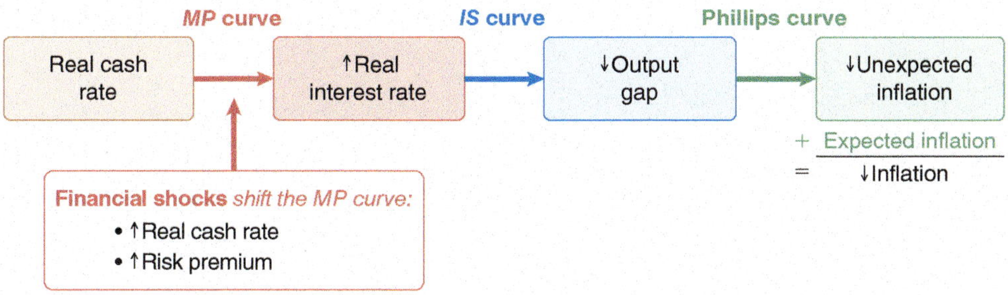

All told, we conclude that a financial shock that leads to higher real interest rates will also lead to lower output and lower inflation. Let's now turn to the effects of spending shocks.

Analysing Spending Shocks

Spending shocks occur whenever there's been a change in spending—in any element of aggregate expenditure—at a given real interest rate and level of income. An increase in spending will shift the *IS* curve to the right, while a decrease will shift it to the left.

Sandy Huffaker/Getty Images

They're shifting the *IS* curve.

The *IS* curve shifts in response to changes in aggregate expenditure. Total spending is the sum of consumption, planned investment, government purchases, and net exports. This means that the *IS* curve will shift in response to changes in:

- *Consumption,* which may be driven by changes in wealth, consumer confidence, government assistance, taxes, or inequality.
- *Planned investment,* which changes in response to changes in future economic growth, business confidence, investment tax credits, corporate taxes, lending standards, cash reserves, or uncertainty.
- *Government spending,* which reflects the government's fiscal policy, and the operation of automatic stabilisers.
- *Net exports,* which are driven by economic growth among our trading partners, trade policy, and exchange rates.

If any of this is unclear, take a moment to review the section "Spending Shocks Shift the *IS* Curve" in Chapter 30. You don't need to memorise a long list of these factors; rather, make sure you recognise the types of shocks that will lead to changes in spending and hence shift the *IS* curve. You're looking for any shock that will lead to a change in spending at a given real interest rate.

A Spending Shock Shifts the *IS* Curve

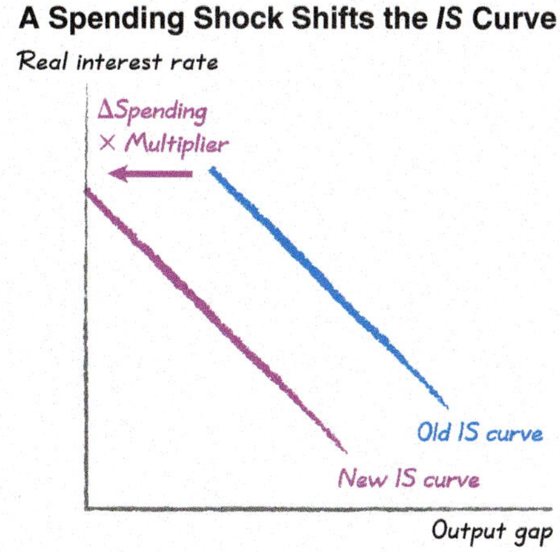

The *IS* curve shifts by the change in spending times the multiplier. Let's evaluate the consequences of an economic shock that reduces aggregate expenditure at any given real interest rate by \$50 billion. If the multiplier is 2, then this spending shock will set off a chain reaction that will lead aggregate expenditure to decline by a total of $2 \times \$50$ billion = \$100 billion. As a result, it will shift the *IS* curve to the left by \$100 billion, which is 5% of potential output (when potential output is \$2 trillion).

Decreased aggregate expenditure leads to lower output and lower inflation. We can now work through the three-step recipe in Figure 3:

Step one: *Shift the curve.* We've established that a \$100 billion cut in aggregate expenditure will shift the *IS* curve to the left by 5% of potential output.

Figure 3 | **Spending Shocks Shift the *IS* Curve**

A leftward shift of the IS curve leads to a decrease in GDP and lower inflation.

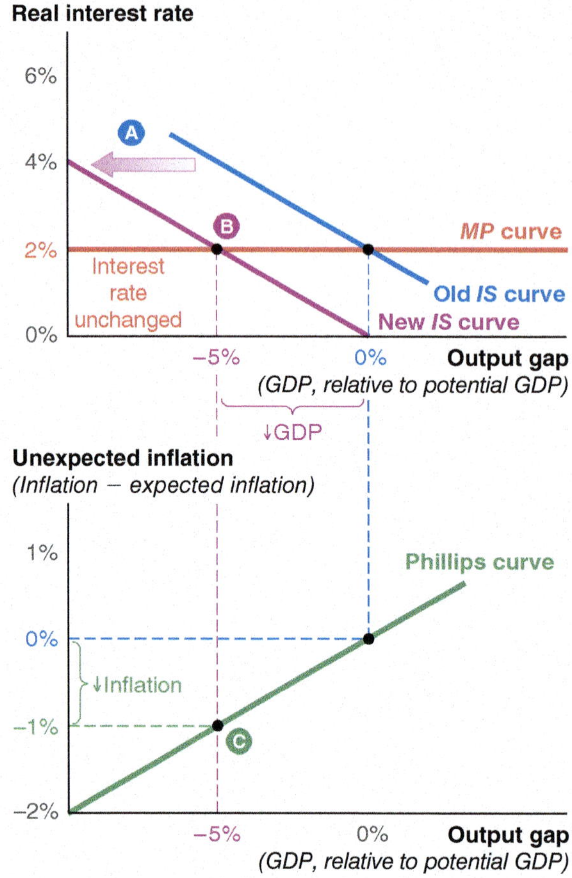

Step 1: Shift the curve

(A) A decrease in aggregate expenditure shifts the ***IS* curve** to the left. It moves left by: Δ***Spending*** × ***Multiplier***.

Step 2: Find the output gap

(B) Find the new equilibrium where the **new *IS* curve** intersects with the ***MP* curve**.

Look down to find the new output gap has fallen to **−5%**.

Step 3: Assess inflation

(C) Look down to find the point on the **Phillips curve** with the same output gap.

Look left to find the new unexpected inflation rate has fallen to **−1%**.

If inflation expectations are unchanged the actual inflation rate will be 1% lower.

Step two: *Find the output gap.* Analyse where this *new IS* curve cuts the *MP* curve. In this example, this occurs when output shrinks to be 5% below potential output.

Step three: *Assess inflation.* Trace this output gap down onto the Phillips curve to assess the inflationary consequences. In this case, an output gap of −5% will cause unexpected inflation to decline to −1%. Thus, if expected inflation is 2%, actual inflation will fall to be one percentage point lower, at 1%.

We can represent this chain of events as follows:

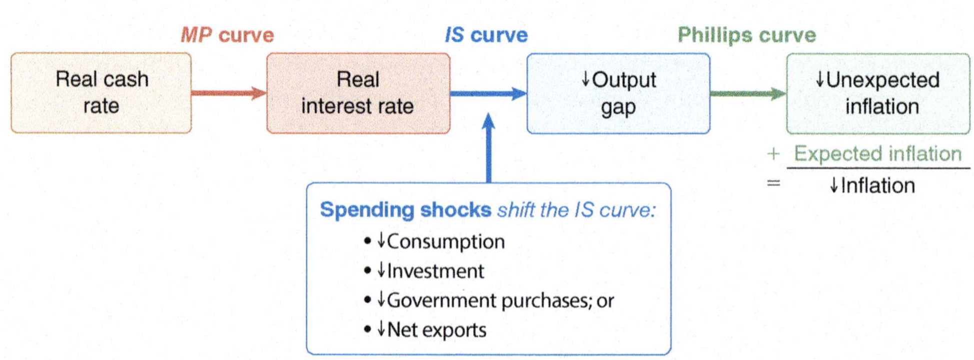

All told, we conclude that a negative spending shock will result in lower output, lower inflation, and no effect on the real interest rate.

Analysing Supply Shocks

Supply shocks occur whenever there's an unexpected change in sellers' production costs that will lead to price changes at a given output gap. An increase in production costs will shift the Phillips curve up, while a decrease in production costs will shift the Phillips curve down.

The Phillips curve shifts in response to changes in production costs. Production costs drive the pricing decisions of businesses, and hence will change the inflation rate at any given output gap. In turn, production costs shift in response to:

- *Input prices:* When the price of important inputs—such as oil and labour—rise, so will production costs, shifting the Phillips curve up.
- *Productivity:* Faster productivity growth leads to more rapid declines in production costs, shifting the Phillips curve down. When productivity growth is weaker than expected, production costs will rise more quickly than expected, shifting the Phillips curve up.
- *Exchange rates:* Top executives watch the value of the Australian dollar closely, because it determines the price of imports (including imported inputs) and hence the pressure that foreign competition puts on the pricing decisions of Australian businesses. A depreciating Australian dollar leads imported inputs to become more expensive and makes foreign competitors less competitive, both of which lead domestic prices to rise, shifting the Phillips curve up. An appreciating dollar will shift the Phillips curve down.

(You can review any of this by rereading the section in Chapter 31 on "Supply Shocks Shift the Phillips Curve.")

Rising production costs lead to rising prices and inflation, shifting the Phillips curve.

Increased production costs lead to higher inflation and no change in output. Okay, now it's time to figure out the broader consequences of a supply shock—a rise in production costs that shifts the Phillips curve up. We'll work through the three-step recipe in Figure 4:

Figure 4 | Supply Shocks Shift the Phillips Curve

An upward shift of the Phillips curve leads to a rise in unexpected inflation.

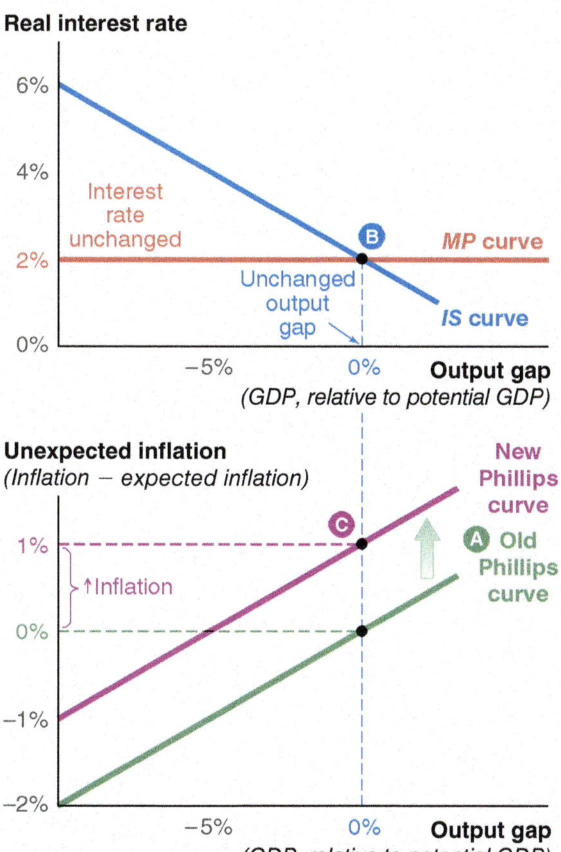

Step 1: Shift the curve

Ⓐ An increase in production costs shifts the Phillips curve up.

Step 2: Find the output gap

Ⓑ The output gap is determined by the intersection of the (unchanged) *IS* curve with the (unchanged) *MP* curve.

Look down to find the output gap is unchanged at 0%.

Step 3: Assess inflation

Ⓒ Look down to find the point on the new Phillips curve with the same output gap.

Look left to find the unexpected inflation rate has risen to +1%.

If inflation expectations are unchanged, the actual inflation rate will be 1% higher.

Step one: *Shift the curve.* We've established that higher production costs will shift the Phillips curve upward.

Step two: *Find the output gap.* The output gap is determined by the intersection of the *IS* and *MP* curves. Because a supply shock shifts neither of these curves, the output gap remains unchanged.

Step three: *Assess inflation.* Trace this output gap down to the *new* Phillips curve to assess the inflationary consequences. In this case, the unchanged output gap corresponds with higher unexpected inflation of +1%. Thus, if expected inflation is unchanged at 2%, actual inflation will rise to be one percentage point higher, at 3%.

You can summarise this chain of events as follows:

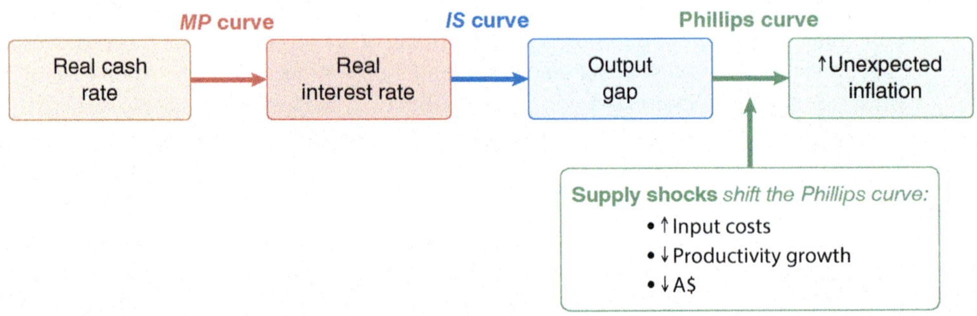

The bottom line of our analysis is that a supply shock leads to higher inflation, with no effect on the real interest rate, or the output gap.

A caveat: A supply shock can cause output to decline. It's time to add an important caveat to our analysis of supply shocks. In addition to their effect on inflation, supply shocks can disrupt both actual output and potential output. These effects are important, but they didn't show up in Figure 4, because our framework focuses on the output gap, which is the difference between actual and potential output.

To see how supply shocks can reduce both actual and potential output, consider what would happen if oil prices were to double tomorrow. Over time, businesses would shift from being energy intensive to becoming more energy efficient. We'd need more hybrid cars and fewer SUVs, and we'd shift from energy-intensive manufacturing towards more energy-efficient services. Given the change in supply conditions, this transition makes long-run sense. But in the short run, this transition creates severe disruption, as existing factories that were profitable when oil prices were low are rendered unprofitable once they're high. When these factories close, both actual and potential output fall. And so the initial effect is lower output (matched by lower potential output). Production will only return to its earlier levels once more energy efficient factories have been built.

As a result, a supply shock can cause not only higher inflation, but also short-run stagnation, as output declines. This combination of economic *stag*nation and high in*flation* is called **stagflation.** It's a reminder that when you account for the effects of a supply shock, realise that the shock can lower output by lowering potential output even if the output gap remains unaffected.

stagflation A combination of economic stagnation—or falling output—combined with high inflation.

Interpreting the DATA How a trade war can cause a supply shock

When President Trump imposed tariffs—effectively an additional sales tax—on imported goods, proponents of the policy hoped that it would lead to a spending shock that would boost output. Their thinking was that the tariffs would lead Americans to buy fewer imported goods, and buy more American-made goods instead. Lower imports mean higher net exports and thus higher aggregate expenditure. That is, their hope was that this spending shock would shift the IS curve to the right, which would lead to more output and a more positive output gap. At the time, inflation was low, so they weren't worried about the increase in inflation that would result from the more positive output gap.

What they didn't count on was that China and Europe would retaliate with their own tariffs, designed to reduce American exports in roughly equal measure. When lower imports are matched by lower exports, there's no effect on net exports, nor on aggregate expenditure. A positive spending shock was offset by a negative spending shock. As a result, the IS curve didn't really move.

But these tariffs still had an important effect: They led to an adverse supply shock. More than half of all imports to the United States are used as inputs by American businesses in the production of their output. Tariffs raised the cost of purchasing these imported inputs. When the price of imported inputs rises, so do production costs, shifting the Phillips curve up. And indeed, over the following months, those sectors of the economy most reliant on imported inputs raised their prices more rapidly, which fed higher inflation. Ultimately then, a policy designed to generate a positive spending shock may have led to a negative supply shock, and so instead of increasing output, it only boosted inflation. ■

EVERYDAY Economics What economic forecasters actually do

Kzenon/Shutterstock

She's thinking about the RBA model.

You might be thinking: Is all this curve shifting really what macroeconomists do? If you're working as a macroeconomist—perhaps at the RBA, at the Treasury, in state and local government, at a large corporation, or a major investment bank—your job will likely include generating economic forecasts. And just as the RBA model suggests, you'll probably rely on the *IS*, *MP*, and Phillips curves to assess what's likely to happen. But your job will extend beyond saying whether output, inflation, or interest rates will rise or fall. You'll have to be more precise, and say by how much. That's a task much better suited to a computer than a pencil and paper. And so you might code the relationships that each of these curves represent into a spreadsheet, or use a statistical package like R to create a fully computerised model of the economy.

Even then, the stylised graphs that we're studying remain important. It's not unusual to see a top economist poring over tables of output from their computerised model, while sketching *IS*, *MP*, and Phillips curves in the margin, to try to make sense of it all. They're using these graphs as an "intuition pump," to help them explain and understand the somewhat opaque output of their computerised models. Most forecasters have a line at the bottom of their spreadsheet that says "add factor." It's a hack. When their computer model disagrees with the intuition they've sketched in the margins, they'll use this line to add a bit to their computer-generated forecast to make it better match their curve-driven intuition. ■

Do the Economics

It's time to practice using the RBA model to predict how the economy will respond as market conditions change. Each of the dozen examples that follow is inspired by a real episode that has affected the Australian economy over recent decades. In each case, you should use the three-step recipe to forecast how real interest rates, the output gap, and inflation will respond.

Consumer confidence rose sharply following the election of a new government.

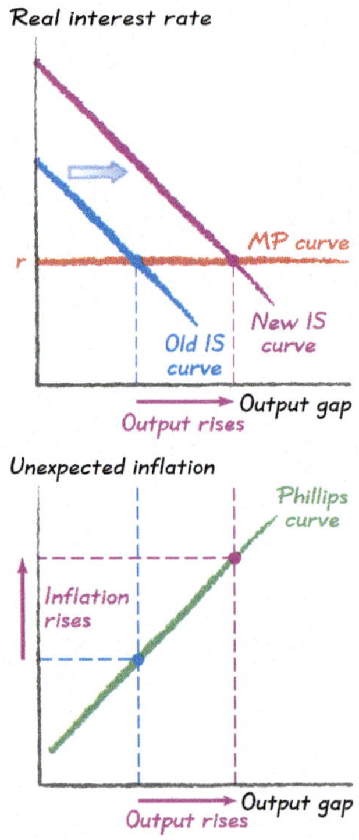

Increase in consumption
→ Shift *IS* curve to the right

Result: Unchanged real interest rate, higher output, and higher inflation.

Concern that the economy was underperforming led the RBA to cut interest rates sharply.

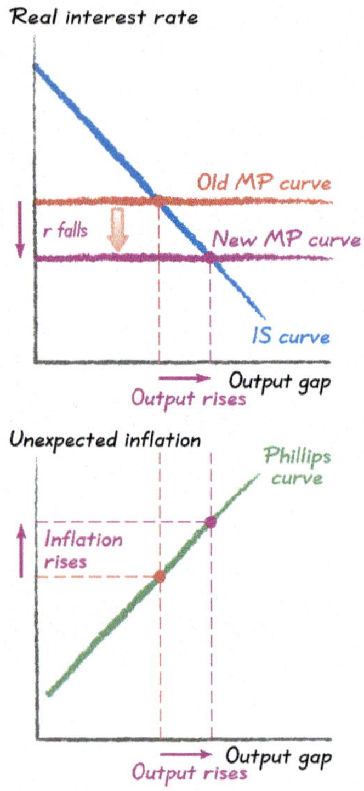

Decrease in real interest rates
→ Shift *MP* curve downward

Result: Lower real interest rate, higher output, and higher inflation.

The onset of the Gulf War with Iraq led to supply disruptions that caused oil prices to rise sharply.

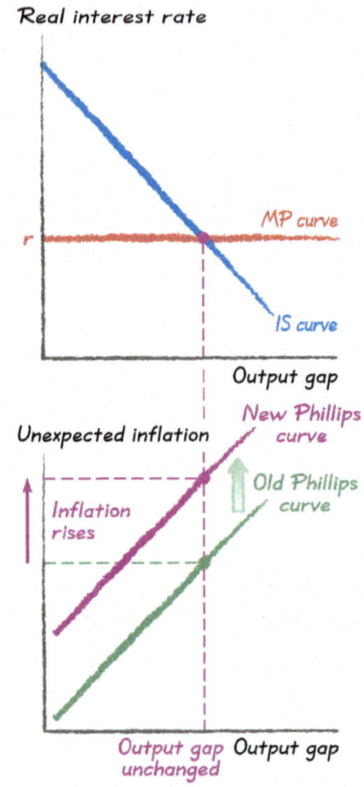

Rising production costs
→ Shift Phillips curve up

Result: Unchanged real interest rate, unchanged output gap, and higher inflation.

Rapid productivity growth due to new technology led to falling production costs.

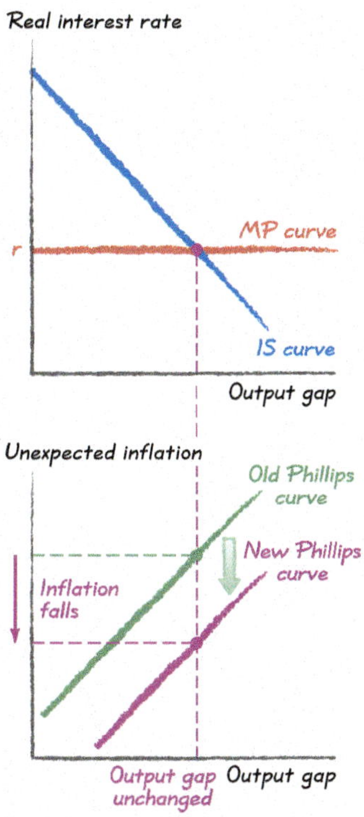

Falling production costs
→ Shift Phillips curve down

Result: Unchanged real interest rate, unchanged output gap, and lower inflation.

The end of the tech boom led businesses to rethink their investment in new technology, leading to a sharp decline in investment.

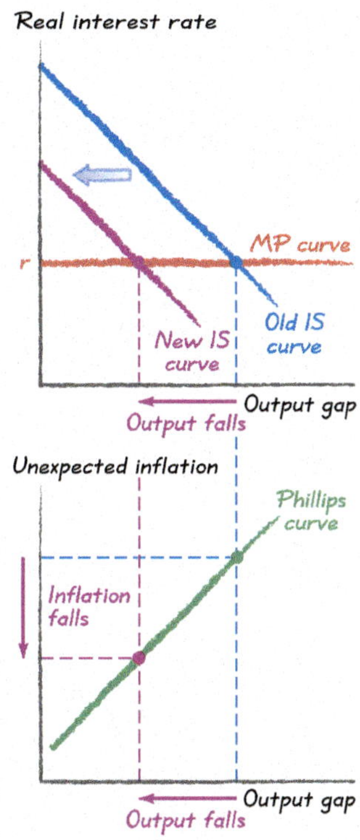

Decrease in investment
→ Shift *IS* curve to the left

Result: Unchanged real interest rate, lower output, and lower inflation.

Rapidly falling house prices meant that many homeowners could no longer afford to repay their mortgages. Given this risk of not being repaid, banks were only willing to lend if they were paid a risk premium that was 2 percentage points higher.

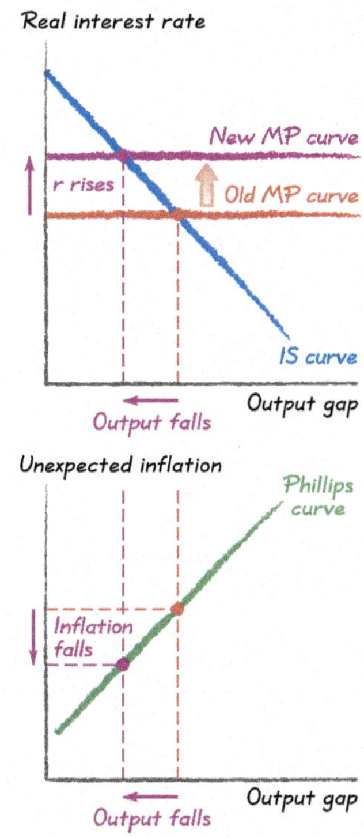

Increase in real interest rates
→ Shift *MP* curve upward

Result: Higher real interest rate, lower output, and lower inflation.

By 2022, the worst of the pandemic had passed and government fiscal support had been wound back.

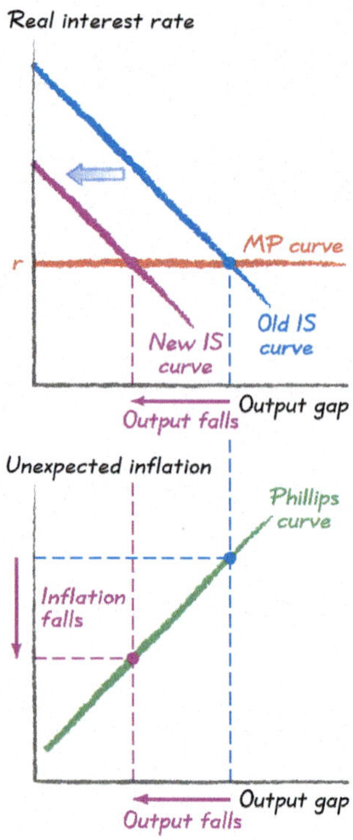

Decrease in government purchases
→ Shift *IS* curve to the left

Result: Unchanged real interest rate, lower output, and lower inflation.

As the financial bailout worked, banks became more willing to lend, lowering the risk premium they charged on new loans.

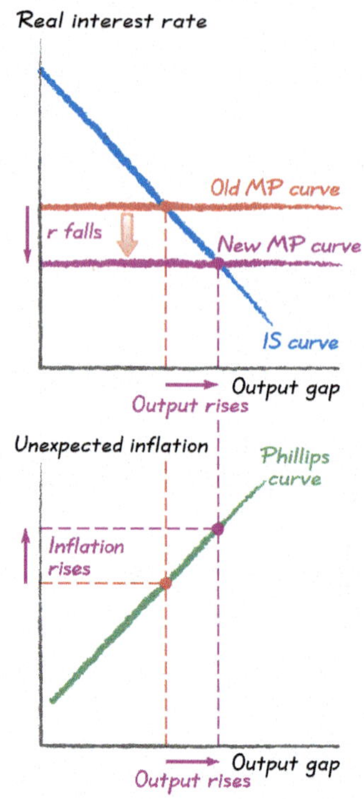

Decrease in real interest rates
→ Shift *MP* curve downward

Result: Lower real interest rate, higher output, and higher inflation.

Improvements in renewable technology and transmission led the price of energy to decline.

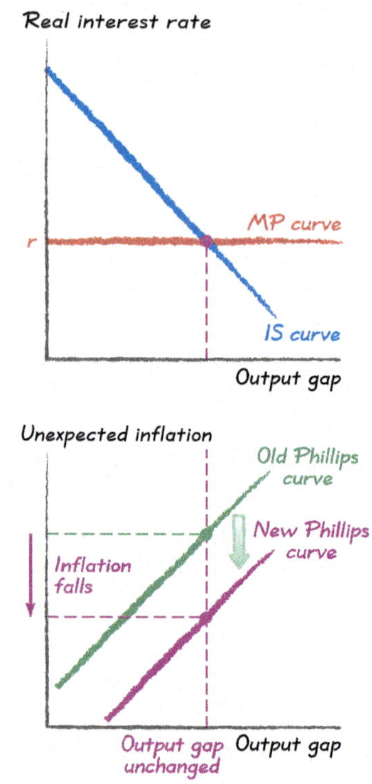

Falling production costs
→ Shift Phillips curve down

Result: Unchanged real interest rate, unchanged output gap, and lower inflation.

Rapid economic growth in China led to an increase in demand for Australian goods and services.

As the bargaining power of workers eroded, their nominal wages unexpectedly fell.

A new RBA governor, determined to reduce inflation, raised the cash rate sharply.

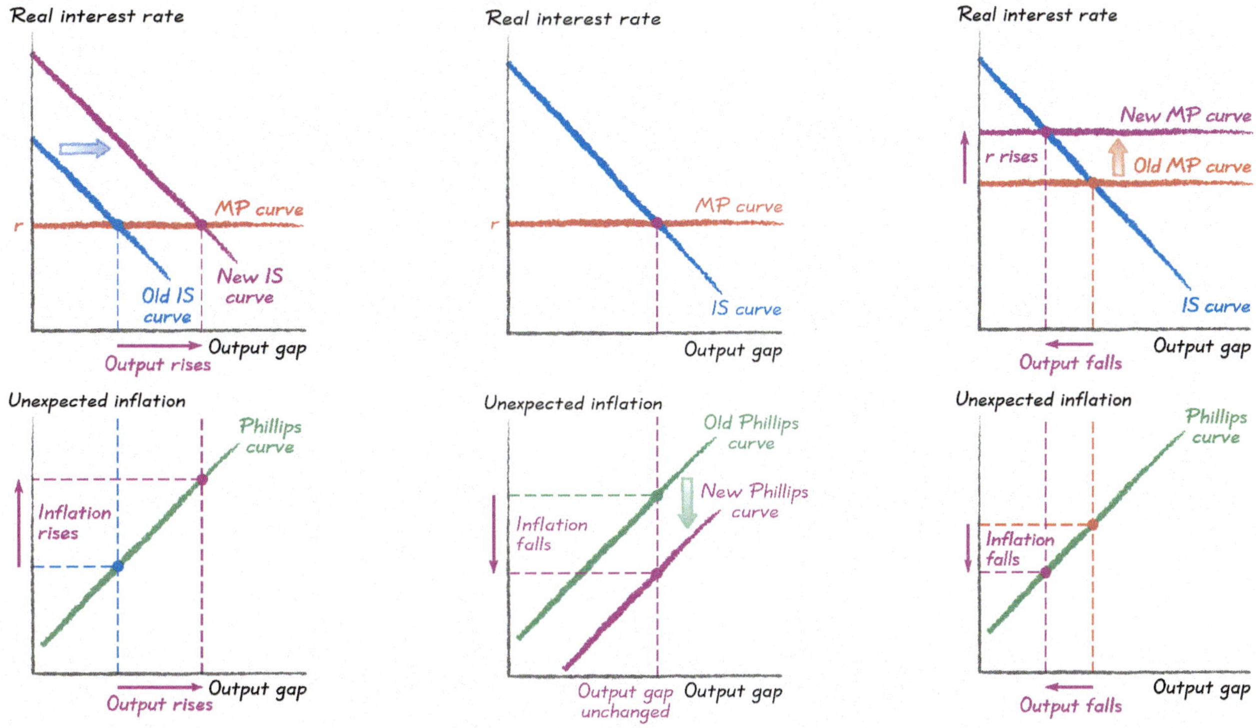

Increase in net exports
→ Shift *IS* curve to the right
Result: Unchanged real interest rate, higher output, and higher inflation.

Falling production costs
→ Shift Phillips curve down
Result: Unchanged real interest rate, unchanged output gap, and lower inflation.

Increase in real interest rates
→ Shift *MP* curve upward
Result: Higher real interest rate, lower output, and lower inflation. ■

32.3 Diagnosing the Causes of Macroeconomic Changes

Learning Objective *Use the RBA model to diagnose the causes of economic fluctuations.*

So far we've used the RBA model to *predict* the consequences of macroeconomic shocks. But there's another use for it. Economic conditions can sometimes shift sharply, and the economy—unlike a textbook—doesn't come with a big heading telling you whether that shift was caused by a financial, spending, or supply shock. And so you can use what we've learned in this chapter to *diagnose* the causes of macroeconomic fluctuations. It's an important job because the first step to solving a country's macroeconomic ills is diagnosing their cause.

A Brief Recap

But first, we'll need to draw the threads of our analysis together. Figure 5 summarises the findings from our analysis of financial, spending, and supply shocks.

Figure 5 | **The Consequences of Different Shocks**

	Step one **Shift the curve**	*Step two* **Real interest rate**	**Find the output gap**	*Step three* **Assess inflation**
Financial shocks				
↑Real interest rates	*MP* curve shifts up	↑	↓	↓
↓Real interest rates	*MP* curve shifts down	↓	↑	↑
Spending shocks				
↑Spending	*IS* curve shifts right	No change	↑	↑
↓Spending	*IS* curve shifts left	No change	↓	↓
Supply shocks				
↑Production costs	Phillips curve shifts up	No change	No change	↑
↓Production costs	Phillips curve shifts down	No change	No change	↓

A Diagnosis Tool

As we've worked to predict economic outcomes, we've read this table from left to right—observing which curves shift, and then tracing out the implications for what that will mean for the output gap, real interest rate, and inflation. But now, we want to work in reverse: Given what we've observed has happened to these economic indicators, what can we infer about the shocks that have hit the economy?

Look closely at this table, and you'll notice that financial, spending, and supply shocks each leave a different pattern of footprints behind. We can use these differences to diagnose the cause of any recent macroeconomic change. In particular, notice:

1. If the real interest rate changes, that's evidence that the economy has been hit by a *financial shock.*
2. If the output gap has shifted without much movement in the real interest rate, it suggests that there's been a *spending shock.*
3. If inflation rises in a weak economy, or if it falls in a strong economy, that points to a *supply shock* as the cause.

Armed with these rules, let's work through some examples of how this can help you make sense of changing economic conditions.

Do the Economics

In each of the following examples, use your diagnostic tools to assess what economic shock hit the economy:

a. "This makes no sense," said a private-sector economist, "why is inflation falling even though the economy remains in good shape? The Phillips curve teaches us that inflation falls when the economy is weak."

   If inflation falls but the economy remains strong, you can infer that the Phillips curve has shifted down and the economy is enjoying the sort of happy supply shock that reduces production costs, leading to lower inflation at any given output gap.

b. At a meeting of the Reserve Bank, policy makers were puzzled. They reasoned that "For some reason output is booming, despite the fact that we haven't cut interest rates at all."

   If output is rising but interest rates are unchanged, the economy has likely received a positive spending shock, where higher aggregate expenditure at a given real interest rate has shifted the *IS* curve to the right.

c. Imagine Wesfarmers' chief economist observing, "Our sales are falling as is output throughout the economy". They continue, noting that they might attribute this to higher interest rates on credit cards and personal loans, although they add that these higher interest rates were somewhat puzzling given that the RBA hadn't changed its benchmark interest rate.

Interest rates reflect both actions by the Reserve Bank and the risk premium determined in financial markets. It sounds like these higher interest rates are due to a rising risk premium. When output declines following a rise in interest rates, you can infer the economy has suffered a financial shock that shifted the *MP* curve up. ■

Tying It Together

Each chapter of this book has focused on one part of the economy, uncovering the key economic forces at work. As we've progressed, I bet you've noticed that the relationships described in any one chapter depend on other economic variables, whose determinants are described in some other chapter. This is the *interdependence principle* in action, and macroeconomics is all about understanding these interdependencies.

Our crowning achievement in this chapter is uncovering how these disparate elements fit together into a coherent whole. The result is a complete model of the macroeconomy that you can use to track the full macroeconomic implications of any change in market conditions. You can use it to forecast how economic conditions are likely to change, what the major threats are to your forecast, and how policy makers can respond.

A model is particularly valuable when you can ask it "what if" questions. And you can use the RBA model to ask: What will happen if the global economy craters, the stock market booms, or productivity growth takes off? Policy makers use the RBA model to ask "what if" questions that directly affect economic policy. At the RBA, they ask: What if we raise interest rates? What if we lower interest rates? They use a computerised version of the RBA model to figure out what sorts of economic outcomes will result from each interest rate setting, and then choose the policy that corresponds with what they judge to be the best set of outcomes. At the Treasury, they use similar models to ask: What if we raise government spending? What if we cut taxes? These analyses help guide fiscal policy. And businesses around the country use related models to game out the likely consequences of whatever economic shocks their executives see on the horizon.

The approach in this chapter puts you remarkably close to the cutting edge of how economists—both those at policy institutions like the RBA, as well as leaders in the financial sector—analyse the economy. And it has a number of features that make it particularly useful.

Our analysis of the RBA model has been *dynamic*, analysing shifts over time from one equilibrium (say, when the real interest rate is low) to another equilibrium (after the interest rate has risen). A shortcoming of our analyses so far is that they have been largely silent about the pace at which these changes will occur. These dynamics play an important role in economic forecasting, and they're an important feature of the more complicated computerised versions of the RBA model used on Martin Place and in financial markets.

A key strength of the RBA model is that it provides a coherent way to trace out the consequences of the many random (or *stochastic*) shocks that hit the economy. It provides a framework for analysing virtually any spending, financial, or supply shock.

The RBA model also takes a *general equilibrium* approach, which means that rather than analysing individual markets or variables separately, it analyses all of them jointly, paying careful attention to the ways in which choices in one domain affect those in others. In general equilibrium, everything can depend on everything else, and it's our job to sort out what will happen. The RBA model applies this approach to business cycles, jointly considering consumption, investment, government purchasing, and importing and exporting decisions; it evaluates spending decisions together with production choices; it explores the relationship between the financial sector and the broader economy; and it explores the connections between output and pricing decisions, and hence inflation. It provides a useful framework for analysing the key economy-wide prices—like the real interest rate, inflation, the exchange rate, wages, and stock prices—which can transmit shocks from one market to another.

But perhaps the real value of the RBA model is that, unlike the MONIAC, you can do all of this without getting wet.

Chapter at a Glance

The RBA Model (IS-MP-PC): A complete model of business cycles that puts together the **IS curve**, the **MP curve**, and the **Phillips curve**. Use it to analyse macroeconomic shocks using a **three-step recipe:**

Step 1—Identify the shock, and shift the relevant curve:

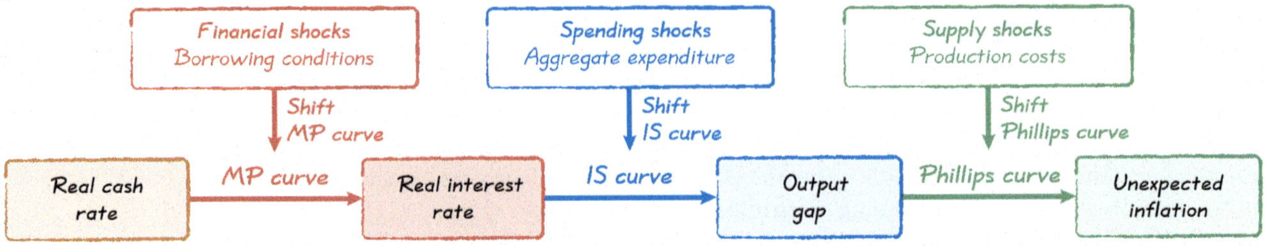

Step 2—Find the output gap: Look at the intersection of the IS and MP curves to find the **equilibrium output gap** and **real interest rate.**

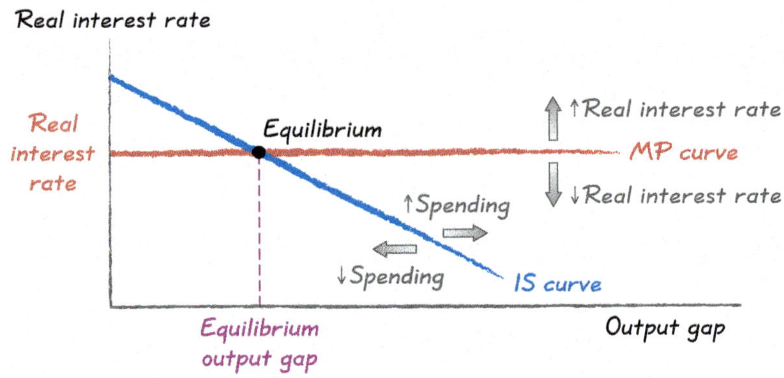

Step 3—Assess inflation: Use the **Phillips curve** to find the **inflationary implications** of this **output gap.**

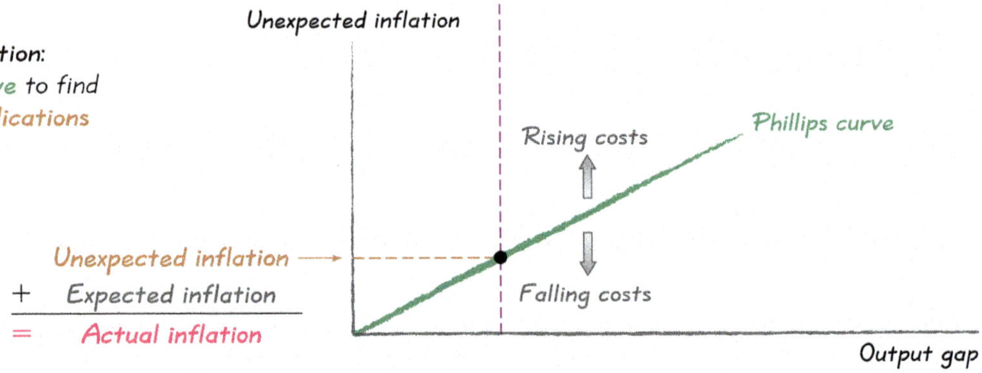

Predicting and Diagnosing the Effects of Economic Shocks

Macroeconomic shock	① Shift the curve	Real interest rate	② Find the output gap	③ Assess inflation
Financial shocks				
↑ Real interest rates	MP curve shifts up	↑	↓	↓
↓ Real interest rates	MP curve shifts down	↓	↑	↑
Spending shocks				
↑ Spending	IS curve shifts right	No change	↑	↑
↓ Spending	IS curve shifts left	No change	↓	↓
Supply shocks				
↑ Production costs	Phillips curve shifts up	No change	No change	↑
↓ Production costs	Phillips curve shifts down	No change	No change	↓

Key Concepts

RBA model, 818
financial shocks, 820
spending shocks, 820
stagflation, 826
supply shocks, 820

Discussion and Review Questions

Learning Objective 32.1 *Analyse the RBA model, which puts together the IS curve, the MP curve, and the Phillips curve.*

1. The interdependence principle says that what happens in one part of the economy will affect other parts. Use the RBA model to explain the interdependence between the real interest rate, the output gap, and inflation.
2. Compare and contrast the three different economic shocks using the RBA model, and explain which curve shifts for each type of shock.

Learning Objective 32.2 *Use the RBA model to analyse the consequences of financial shocks, spending shocks, and supply shocks.*

3. The economy is experiencing a recession. The output gap is hovering at −7%, causing higher than normal unemployment. Using the RBA model, compare and contrast how monetary policy and fiscal policy can impact the economy. What can the Reserve Bank do to stimulate greater output and hence employment? What can the federal government do? What happens if both monetary and fiscal policy are used?
4. You open the newspaper and read that Europe is headed for a recession. Use the RBA model to forecast what you expect to happen to the Australian economy. Use the three-step recipe for analysing macroeconomic shocks to explain your answer.

Learning Objective 32.3 *Use the RBA model to diagnose the causes of economic fluctuations.*

5. Consider the three types of economic shocks: financial shocks, spending shocks, and supply shocks. Discuss how each one affects the real interest rate, output gap, and the inflation rate.
6. Use your answer to the previous question as a guide to help you diagnose what kinds of shocks have hit the economy. If the real interest rate changes, what type of shock can you conclude must have occurred? Alternatively, if the output gap has shifted without much movement in the real interest rate, what does this tell you must have happened? Or what if you find that inflation has risen despite a weak economy, or inflation has fallen despite a strong economy?

Study Problems

Learning Objective 32.1 *Analyse the RBA model, which puts together the IS curve, the MP curve, and the Phillips curve.*

1. Determine if the following changes to the economy are examples of financial, spending, or supply shocks. For each case, explain whether the *IS*, *MP*, or Phillips curve will shift, and in what direction.
   a. The Chinese government eliminates the tariffs it charges on goods exported from Australia.
   b. The implementation of artificial intelligence in manufacturing has led to faster than expected productivity growth, which results in decreasing production costs.
   c. A financial crisis makes banks extremely reluctant to take on risky loans without charging an extremely high risk premium.
   d. Businesses' confidence about the future of the economy falls, which leads them to scrap planned investment projects.
   e. The Reserve Bank raises the cash rate from 4% to 5%.
   f. The federal government cuts the corporate tax rate, a move applauded by business executives who say that it will make more investment opportunities profitable.

Learning Objective 32.2 *Use the RBA model to analyse the consequences of financial shocks, spending shocks, and supply shocks.*

2. The next meeting of RBA policy makers is coming up, and the following graph summarises the state of the economy. Your boss asks you how you think the Reserve Bank should respond to these economic conditions.

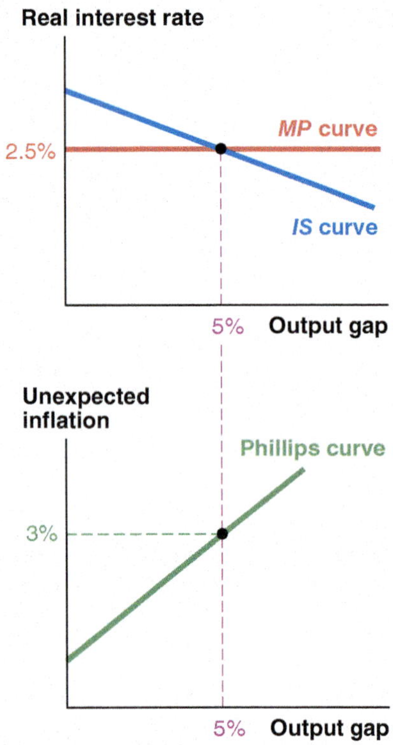

a. Would you recommend that the RBA try to increase, decrease, or not change the real interest rate? Explain your reasoning.

b. What type of shock will your policy change cause?

c. Which curve in the RBA model will shift?

d. Predict what will happen to real interest rates, output, and inflation.

3. For each of the following scenarios, use the RBA model to forecast how output, the real interest rate, and inflation will change. In each case, start with an economy with an output gap of zero, and with no unexpected inflation, and illustrate how economic conditions will change.

a. A breakthrough in solar power technology decreases the price of energy.

b. The election of a new federal government leads households to become more hopeful about their future economic prospects, which leads them to increase their consumption.

c. In response to concerns about rising national debt, the federal government passes a new bill that dramatically reduces government spending on education and the military.

d. In a shock to financial markets, the Reserve Bank announces that it will decrease the cash rate from 3% to 1.5%.

4. Now go back to Study Problem 1 and predict how each change that it lists will impact output, inflation, and the real interest rate. Illustrate your answers.

Learning Objective 32.3 *Use the RBA model to diagnose the causes of economic fluctuations.*

5. For each of the following, diagnose which type of economic shock has hit the economy:

a. On your drive to campus you hear a radio report describing how the recession appears to have ended and while output remains less than potential, the output gap has risen from –7% to –5%. The host is interviewing an economist who states, "The change in GDP isn't terribly surprising, as the Reserve Bank continues to cut the real interest rate."

b. The latest inflation report indicates an unexpected uptick in inflation even though output remains below potential output.

c. The real interest rate has been stable over the past few quarters, yet output has grown rapidly, leading to a more positive output gap.

Aggregate Demand and Aggregate Supply

CHAPTER 33

Click through to the latest business news and you can quickly become overwhelmed by reports of rising consumer confidence, corporations announcing major investment projects, rumours that Parliament may cut taxes, a speech from the RBA governor expressing concerns about productivity, or reports that geopolitical tensions in Russia are causing oil prices to spike. Bill Evans, the chief economist at Westpac, has to keep track of them all, so that he can keep his many clients in business and finance informed about the economy and help them assess where it's going.

Every week or so, he writes up his analysis along with a few choice charts in a note that he e-mails to his clients. It details why he believes the latest data suggest that the economy is stronger than previously thought, and that this strength will likely continue into the future. This is actionable information that will help his clients—including the managers of some of the economy's most important businesses—adjust their production, hiring, and purchasing plans. His analysis is also read by policy makers because they want to know what his clients are thinking so that they can get advance warning of any boom or bust cycles that might be emerging.

As Bill Evans can tell you, macroeconomic conditions are always changing, and the list of new developments that you'll have to keep track of is dizzyingly large. That's why this chapter introduces a framework for tracking, analysing, and forecasting the economy. Once you master it, you'll be equipped to track where the economy is headed, so that just like Bill's high-paying clients, you'll have the info you need to make better decisions.

He's keeping track of the economy.

PENNY BRADFIELD/The Sydney Morning Herald/Getty Images

Chapter Objective

Analyse how aggregate demand and aggregate supply determine macroeconomic outcomes.

33.1 The *AD-AS* Framework
Understand how aggregate demand and aggregate supply determine macroeconomic equilibrium.

33.2 Aggregate Demand
Evaluate the forces that shape the total quantity of goods and services that purchasers want to buy.

33.3 Aggregate Supply
Evaluate the forces that shape the total quantity of goods and services that businesses want to supply.

33.4 Macroeconomic Shocks and Countercyclical Policy
Forecast how the economy will respond to changing conditions.

33.5 Aggregate Supply in the Short Run and the Long Run
Distinguish between the immediate effects, short-run effects, and long-run consequences of economic shocks.

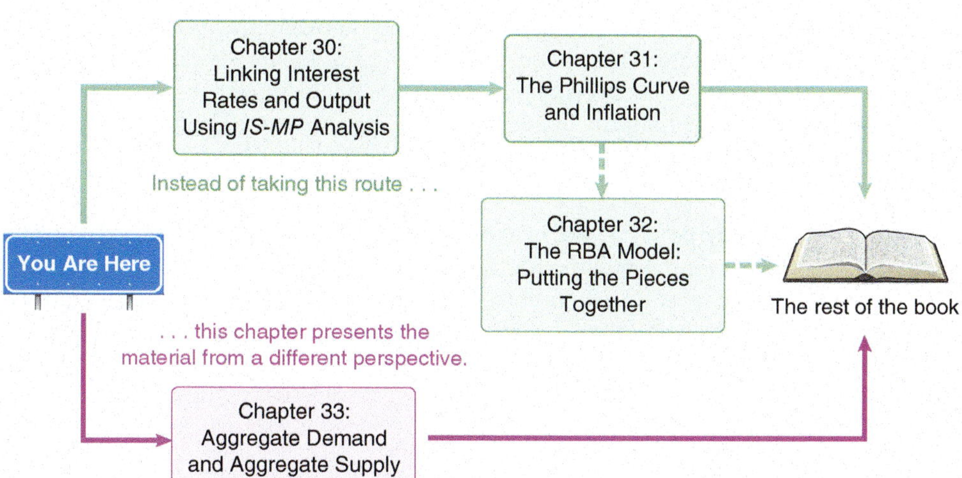

***Organisational note:** The last three chapters presented one framework for analysing business cycles, and this chapter presents a different, but closely related, framework. These aren't competing views, but rather alternative perspectives from which to analyse the same economic forces. Your time is valuable, so you should read either Chapters 30–32, or this chapter.*

33.1 The *AD-AS* Framework

Learning Objective *Understand how aggregate demand and aggregate supply determine macroeconomic equilibrium.*

As you think about whether it's a good time to buy a car; get ahead repaying your student loans; look for a new job; or pursue a graduate degree, your answers will likely depend—at least to some extent—on where you think the economy is going. That's why our task in this chapter is to develop a framework that you can use to forecast where the economy is headed.

Introducing Aggregate Demand and Aggregate Supply

Much of this framework will feel familiar from your earlier analysis of how the microeconomic forces of demand and supply determine outcomes in individual markets, like the market for petrol, coffee, or haircuts. We're going to supersize these concepts and introduce you to their macroeconomic cousins, *aggregate demand* and *aggregate supply*, which describe the forces that determine *aggregate* outcomes such as total output and average prices across the economy as a whole.

Use the *AD-AS* framework to forecast output and the average price level. This supersized version is called the *AD-AS* framework (that's short for Aggregate Demand and Aggregate Supply), and it focuses on two key macroeconomic outcomes:

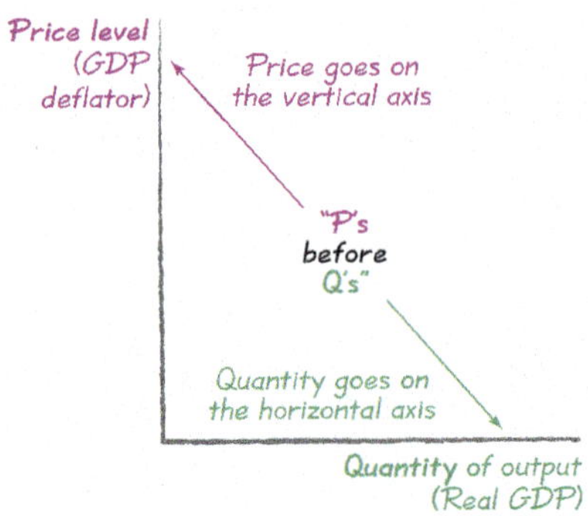

- The *quantity* of output produced across the economy as a whole, which is measured by real GDP; and
- The *price* of that output, which is measured by the GDP deflator. Think of this as the price of a basket containing the many goods and services we produce.

We'll follow the usual convention in economics of plotting price on the vertical axis and quantity on the horizontal axis. Even if this seems familiar, there's an important difference: This supersized framework isn't about explaining the price and quantity of any individual good, but rather what's happening to *total output* and *average prices* across the economy as a whole.

aggregate demand curve Shows the relationship between the price level and the total quantity of output that buyers collectively plan to purchase.

The aggregate demand curve is downward-sloping. The **aggregate demand curve** (or "*AD* curve" to its friends) summarises the purchasing plans of all buyers throughout the economy. It shows the relationship between the average price level and the total quantity of output that all buyers—consumers, businesses, the government, and overseas customers—collectively plan to purchase. A lower average price level leads buyers to demand a larger quantity of output, which means that the aggregate demand curve is downward-sloping.

aggregate supply curve Shows the relationship between the price level and the total quantity of output that suppliers collectively produce.

The aggregate supply curve is upward-sloping. The **aggregate supply curve** (or "*AS* curve") summarises the production plans of all suppliers throughout the economy. It shows the relationship between the average price level and the quantity of output that suppliers collectively produce. A higher price level leads suppliers to produce a larger quantity of output, which means that the aggregate supply curve is upward-sloping.

Macroeconomic equilibrium occurs where the curves cross. Scientists describe an equilibrium as a stable situation, with no tendency to change because opposing forces are in balance. This idea also applies to the economy as a whole: A **macroeconomic equilibrium** occurs when the quantity of output that buyers collectively want to purchase is equal to the quantity of output that suppliers collectively produce. As Figure 1 shows, macroeconomic equilibrium occurs at the point where the two curves cross.

macroeconomic equilibrium Occurs when the quantity of output that buyers collectively want to purchase is equal to the quantity of output that suppliers collectively produce.

Figure 1 | The *AD-AS* Framework

The state of the economy is determined by the intersection of the aggregate demand and aggregate supply curves.

- A The **aggregate demand** curve shows that the quantity of output that buyers collectively plan to purchase falls as the average price level rises.
- B The **aggregate supply curve** shows that the quantity of output that suppliers collectively produce rises as the average price level rises.
- C The economy will move to the point of **macroeconomic equilibrium** where the two curves intersect. This is the only point where the quantity of output demanded is equal to the quantity supplied.
- D This determines the level of **equilibrium GDP**, which in this case is $2 trillion.
- E It also determines the average **price level**.

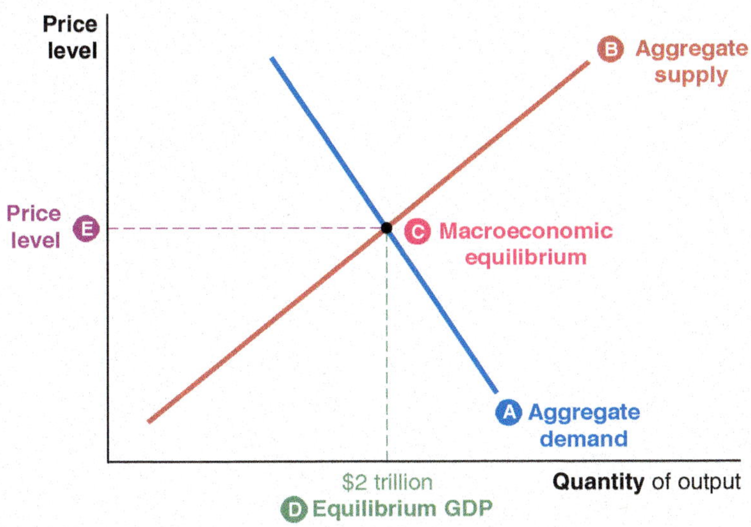

That's it! You now have a powerful framework for forecasting both the level of GDP and the average price level in the economy. As we'll discover, this framework is particularly useful for analysing the year-to-year fluctuations that make up the business cycle.

Macroeconomic versus Microeconomic Forces

All that remains is to dig deeper into understanding the macroeconomic forces that underlie the aggregate demand and aggregate supply curves and to figure out when changing market conditions lead them to shift. That's pretty much our whole agenda for the rest of this chapter.

The *AD-AS* framework looks a lot like the microeconomic supply-equals-demand framework. This approach should feel familiar from the microeconomic demand-equals-supply framework that we use to analyse individual markets. It's familiar

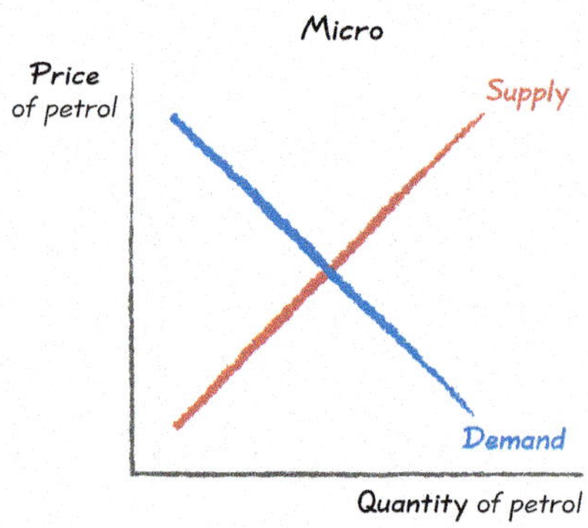

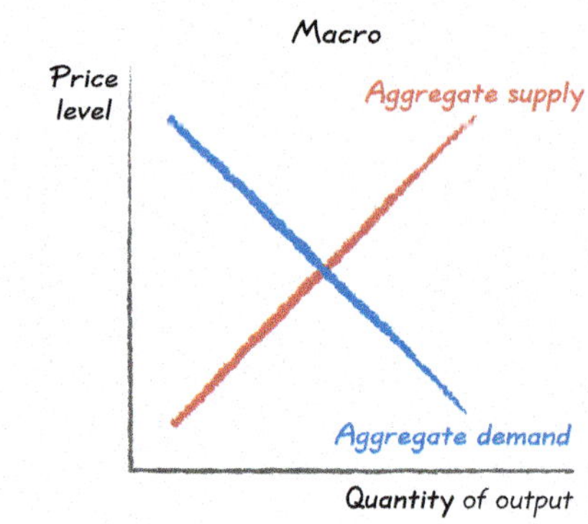

because in micro, as in macro, equilibrium occurs where the curves cross. And when market conditions change, you'll forecast what will happen next by shifting the curves and finding the new equilibrium.

But the *AD-AS* framework summarises a different set of macroeconomic forces. These different curves summarise different trade-offs. In a microeconomic context, the key opportunity cost of buying petrol is not buying something else. But in a macroeconomic context we're focused on spending on *all* goods and services, and so the relevant opportunity cost of buying output *today* is that you can't save your money so that you can buy more output in the *future*. In micro, the key trade-offs are across products, while in macro the key trade-offs are across time.

Because the forces that shape these macroeconomic trade-offs are so different, it's important that you label the curves in Figure 1 "aggregate demand" (or simply "AD") and "aggregate supply" (or "AS") rather than just "demand" or "supply." The modifier "aggregate" is there to remind you to think about aggregate or macroeconomic forces. What are those forces? Glad you asked. That's what we're going to analyse next.

33.2 Aggregate Demand

Learning Objective *Evaluate the forces that shape the total quantity of goods and services that purchasers want to buy.*

The aggregate demand curve summarises the purchasing plans of all buyers throughout the economy at each possible price level. That means it describes the effect that the average price level has on the demand for output. To understand why the aggregate demand curve is downward-sloping, we need to dig into the forces that shape the total demand for output in the economy.

Aggregate Expenditure

aggregate expenditure The total amount of goods and services that people want to buy across the whole economy.

= *Consumption*
+ *Planned investment*
+ *Government purchases*
+ *Net exports*

Aggregate expenditure refers to the total amount of goods and services that people want to buy across the whole economy—the sum of consumption, planned investment, government purchases, and net exports.

Aggregate expenditure is the sum of four components:

= *Consumption:* When households buy goods and services

+ *Planned investment:* When businesses purchase new capital

+ *Government purchases:* When the government buys goods and services

+ *Net exports:* Spending by foreigners on Australian-made exports, less spending by Australians on foreign-made imports.

Some abbreviations
AE: Aggregate Expenditure
C: Consumption
I: Planned Investment
G: Government purchases
NX: Net exports

Economists often use abbreviations to simplify things, and so you might find it easier to write it this way:

$$\underbrace{AE}_{\text{Aggregate expenditure}} = \underbrace{C}_{\text{Consumption}} + \underbrace{I}_{\text{Planned investment}} + \underbrace{G}_{\text{Government purchases}} + \underbrace{NX}_{\text{Net exports}}$$

When you're trying to assess economy-wide demand, you need to focus on how much people (including businesses) want to buy, not the unsold inventories that companies accumulate. That's why the measure of investment that's counted in aggregate expenditure is *planned investment,* which includes all the spending on new capital by businesses but excludes unplanned changes in inventories.

The aggregate demand curve illustrates the level of aggregate expenditure associated with different values of the aggregate price level. To see why this curve is downward-sloping, we'll need to visit Sydney, to sit in on one of the most economically consequential meetings on the planet.

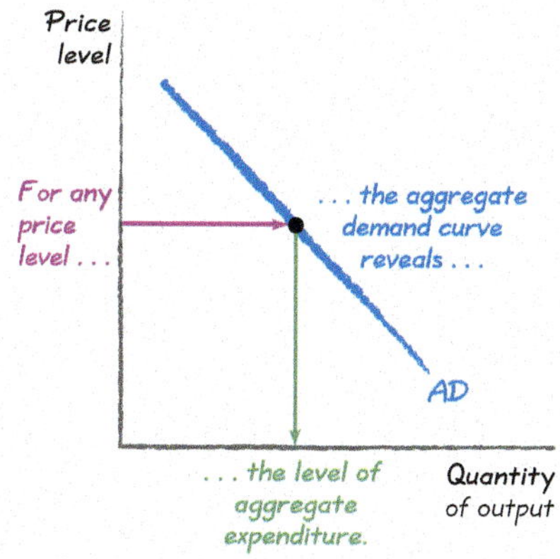

Why Aggregate Demand Is Downward-Sloping

On the first Tuesday of every month (except January), the board of the Reserve Bank—or "the RBA"—meet in Martin Place, Sydney. They consider all kinds of data about how the economy is doing, discuss trends they're seeing in different parts of the economy, debate the implications, and think through a variety of scenarios. When the meeting ends, the RBA announces its new setting for the interest rate.

This is important because the real interest rate shapes aggregate expenditure and hence *aggregate demand*. Importantly, the RBA sets that interest rate based at least partly on what's happening to the *price level*. As such, the RBA's decisions are central to the relationship between the price level and aggregate expenditure illustrated by the aggregate demand curve. To see how, let's step through each of the links in the chain connecting a higher price level to the quantity of output demanded.

A higher price level corresponds to a higher inflation rate. The first link follows from a definition: The inflation rate measures—in percentage terms—how much higher this year's price level is than last year's. Given that last year's price level is set in stone, the higher this year's price level is, the higher this year's inflation rate will be.

Inflation is the rate of change of the price level, so given last year's prices, the higher the price level this year, the higher the inflation rate.

Higher inflation leads the RBA to raise the real interest rate. Here's where the RBA comes in: The Reserve Bank tries to keep the inflation rate stable within its target band of 2–3%. When the inflation rate is either too high or too low, the Reserve Bank will adjust the real interest rate to bring inflation back towards its target level. Specifically, high inflation leads the RBA to raise the real interest rate, while low inflation leads it to lower the real interest rate. Thus, we have the next link in the chain connecting a higher price level to the quantity of output demanded:

The RBA responds to higher inflation by raising the real interest rate.

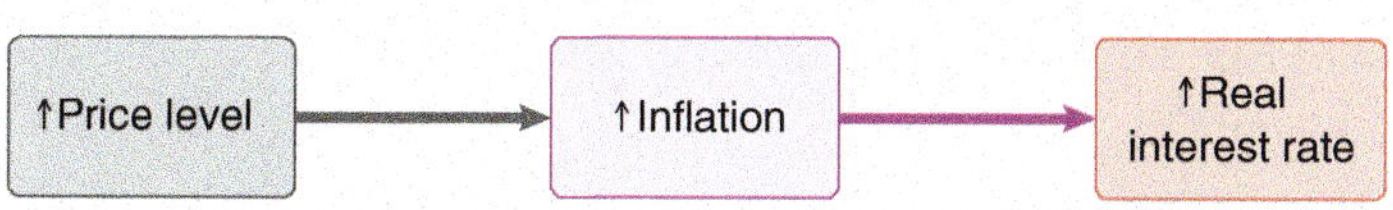

The process by which the RBA determines when to adjust interest rates, and how it goes about making those changes, is so important that we'll devote all of Chapter 34, on monetary policy, to understanding how it does this. For now, it's sufficient to note that the RBA responds to higher inflation by setting a higher real interest rate. A rough rule of thumb suggests that when the inflation rate is one percentage point higher, the RBA responds by setting the real interest rate half a percentage point higher.

A higher real interest rate leads to lower aggregate expenditure. The real interest rate is the nominal interest rate adjusted for inflation, and it matters because it represents the opportunity cost of spending. The *opportunity cost principle* tells you that before spending money, you should ask, "Or what?" You can spend money now, *or* you can save it, earn interest, and buy even more in the future. The real interest rate tells you how much more stuff you'll be able to buy if you wait until next year. A higher real interest rate corresponds to a higher opportunity cost of spending, and so it leads to less aggregate expenditure.

This is particularly true for investment because a higher real interest rate means that fewer investment projects will be profitable enough to offset the opportunity cost of keeping your money in the bank to earn interest. A higher real interest rate also reduces consumption partly because it raises the cost of borrowing to fund big-ticket items like a car. It can also cause net exports to decline through an *exchange rate effect,* in which inflows of foreign savings cause the Australian dollar to appreciate, making Australian exports more expensive for foreigners. Together, these observations give us the final link in our chain connecting a higher price level to the quantity of output demanded—higher real interest rates reduce aggregate expenditure, and hence the aggregate demand for output:

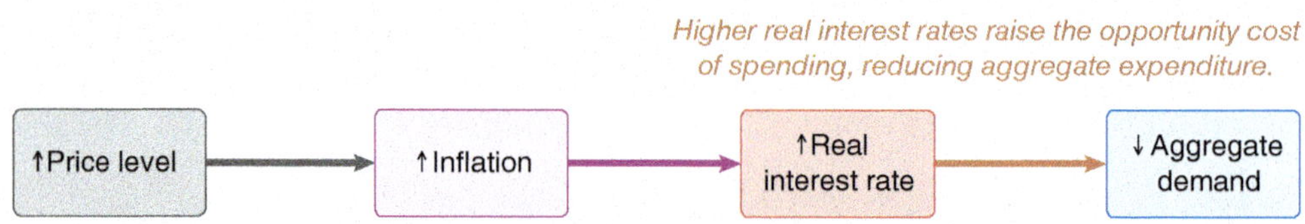

The aggregate demand curve is downward-sloping because a higher price level leads to less aggregate demand. Put the links together, and we've explained why the aggregate demand curve is downward-sloping: The higher this year's average price level, the higher is the inflation rate; the RBA responds to inflation by raising the real interest rate; and this higher interest rate leads to lower levels of spending, and hence less aggregate demand:

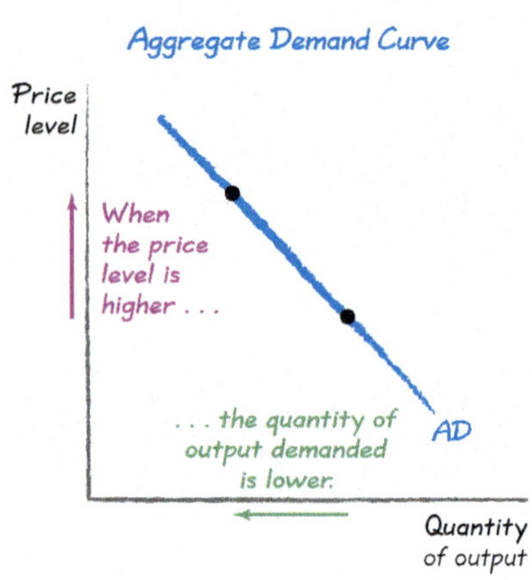

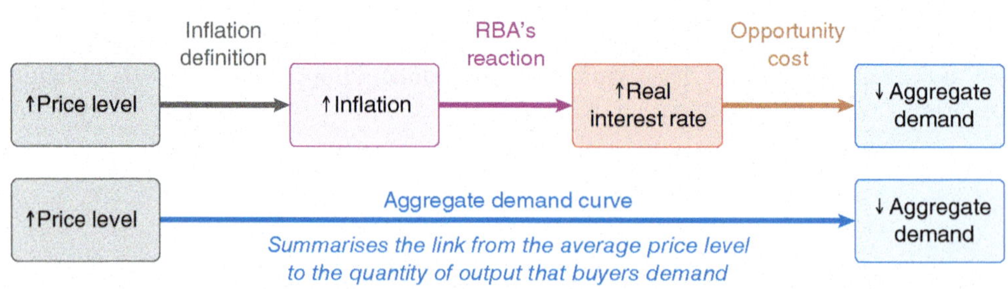

The aggregate demand curve summarises this logic, showing that a higher price level ultimately leads buyers to demand a lower quantity of output. The same forces also operate in reverse, and so they also show that a lower price level leads buyers to demand a higher quantity of output. Because monetary policy plays an important role in this process, this is sometimes called the *monetary-policy channel.*

There are other economic forces that also lead the aggregate demand curve to be downward-sloping. In addition to the *monetary-policy channel,* there's an *international trade effect,* in which a higher price level in Australia leads Australian-made products to become more expensive relative to foreign goods. Thus, a higher price level reduces net exports, and hence aggregate expenditure. Because net exports is a small component of aggregate expenditure, this effect tends to be small.

There's also a *wealth effect,* in which a higher price level reduces real wealth by reducing the purchasing power of assets whose values are fixed in nominal dollars—like the cash in your wallet. Lower real wealth leads people to spend less. This effect is likely small for two reasons. The first is that, as you learned in Chapter 25 on consumption, changes in wealth tend to lead to relatively small changes in spending. The second is because there is an offsetting *debt effect* because a higher price level reduces the real value of people's nominal debts, which leads them to spend more.

Analysing Aggregate Demand

The aggregate demand curve is useful because you can use it to forecast the consequences of changing market conditions. As you do so, be sure to distinguish between the effects of a change in the price level—which will cause a movement along the aggregate demand curve—from shifts in other factors, which shift the curve.

Changes in the price level lead to movements along the aggregate demand curve. The aggregate demand curve illustrates how different price levels lead to differences in the quantity of output demanded. It's useful because when the price level changes, you can simply consult this curve to figure out the new quantity of output demanded. The green arrow in Figure 2 illustrates how a higher price level leads to a movement along the aggregate demand curve to a new point that corresponds to a lower quantity of output demanded. The purple arrow shows that a lower price level leads to a movement along the aggregate demand curve, but this time to a point where there's a higher quantity of output demanded.

Figure 2 | The Aggregate Demand Curve

Changes in the price level lead to movements along the aggregate demand curve.

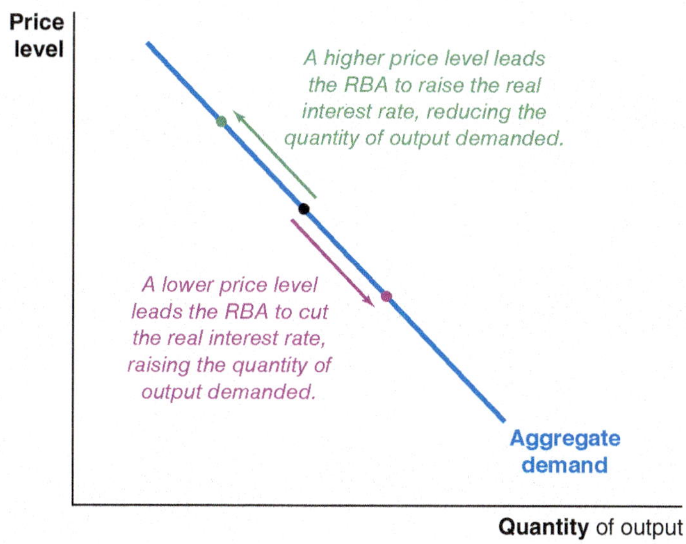

Changes in spending (at a given price level) shift the aggregate demand curve. The aggregate demand curve shows the level of aggregate expenditure at each price level. Whenever consumers, investors, the government, or foreigners change their spending plans (at a given price level), the ensuing change in aggregate expenditure will cause the aggregate demand curve to shift.

A boost in spending that raises aggregate expenditure at a given price level causes *an increase in aggregate demand,* which shifts the aggregate demand curve to the right. The new equilibrium will occur where this new aggregate demand curve intersects the aggregate supply curve. As Panel A on the left of Figure 3 shows, an increase in aggregate demand leads the economy to move to a new equilibrium which results in a rise in GDP and a rise in the price level. That means that increasing aggregate demand leads to a period of rising GDP (which we call an expansion) and rising prices (which you should recognise as inflation).

By contrast, spending cuts that decrease aggregate expenditure at a given price level will cause a *decrease in aggregate demand,* shifting the aggregate demand curve to the left. As Panel B on the right of Figure 3 shows, a decrease in aggregate demand leads the economy to move to a new equilibrium which results in a fall in GDP and a fall in the price level. It follows that decreasing aggregate demand leads to a recession (a period of declining economic activity), and deflation (in which the price level is falling). In reality, many economies experience ongoing inflation for other reasons, and so a decrease in aggregate demand might lead to a decrease in inflation, rather than outright deflation.

Figure 3 | Shifts in Aggregate Demand

The aggregate demand curve shifts due to changes in aggregate expenditure (at a given price level).

Panel A: An Increase in Aggregate Demand

- **A** An **increase in aggregate expenditure** at any price level causes the **aggregate demand curve to shift to the right**.
- **B** This leads the economy to move to a **new equilibrium**.
- **C** Leading to a **rise in GDP** (and hence an *economic expansion*).
- **D** It also leads to a **rise in prices** (and hence a burst of *inflation*).

Panel B: A Decrease in Aggregate Demand

- **A** A **decrease in aggregate expenditure** at any price level causes the **aggregate demand curve to shift to the left**.
- **B** This leads the economy to move to a **new equilibrium**.
- **C** Leading to a **fall in GDP** (and hence a *recession*).
- **D** It also leads to a **fall in prices** (and hence a burst of *deflation*, or perhaps *lower inflation*).

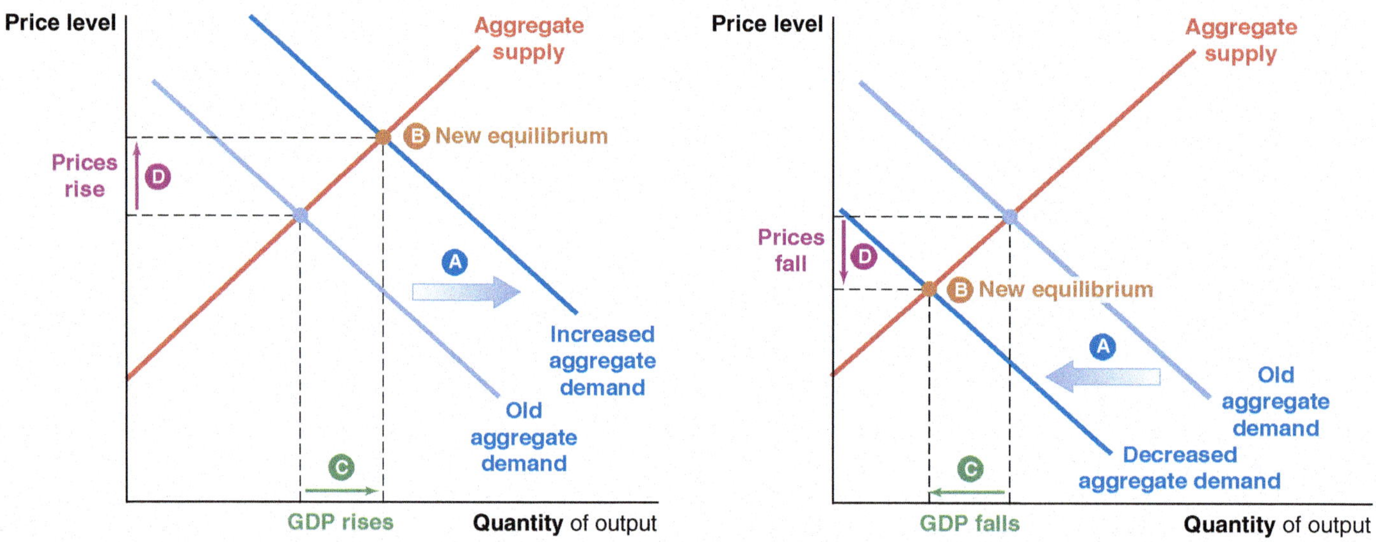

Aggregate Demand Shifters

> *Aggregate demand* shifts in response to changes in aggregate expenditure, and so responds to shifts in:
> 1. Consumption
> 2. Investment
> 3. Government purchases
> 4. Net exports

> *Consumption* increases if people feel more prosperous:
> ↑ Wealth
> ↑ Consumer confidence
> ↑ Government assistance
> ↓ Taxes
> ↓ Inequality

So far we've seen that shifts in aggregate demand have an important influence on business cycle conditions. Our next task is to identify the sorts of changes that might catalyse a shift in aggregate expenditure and hence the aggregate demand curve. Remember, *Aggregate expenditure* $= C + I + G + NX$, and so aggregate demand will increase in response to an increase in consumption, investment, government spending, or net exports.

Demand shifter one: Consumption increases when people feel more prosperous. People typically increase their spending when they have more money to spend, or are confident that they soon will. Thus, any development that makes people feel more prosperous—or more confident that they will soon be prosperous—leads to an increase in consumption, thereby increasing aggregate demand. This means that consumption will shift in response to:

Wealth: When the stock market booms or house prices rise, stockholders and homeowners feel more prosperous because their wealth has increased. As those lucky stockholders and homeowners spend some of their newfound wealth, consumption will increase.

Consumer confidence: The *interdependence principle* reminds you that the decisions you make today depend on your expectations about what's going to happen in the future. And when you feel confident that your income will grow in the future, you might ramp up your spending in advance. As a result, consumption increases when an improved economic outlook boosts consumer confidence.

Taxes and government assistance: When the government cuts taxes, or when it increases government assistance payments like JobSeeker, people have more disposable income that they can use to buy stuff. And so consumption increases when government policy puts more money in people's pockets.

Inequality: People with low incomes tend to spend a larger share of their income than do those with higher incomes. It follows that redistributing income from those with higher incomes to those with lower incomes—including through government transfer payments and changes in the tax system—tends to increase consumption.

Sarah Casillas/DigitalVision/Getty Images

They're shifting the aggregate demand curve.

Demand shifter two: Investment increases when it's profitable for businesses to expand. As a manager, you'll invest in new machinery when you believe that it will be profitable to expand your production. The *cost-benefit principle* reminds you to consider both the benefits of the extra revenue you'll earn from enhancing your production capacity, and the cost of making that investment. As a result, aggregate demand will shift when investment changes in response to:

Investment increases if it's profitable to expand production:
- ↑ GDP growth
- ↑ Business confidence
- ↑ Investment tax credits
- ↓ Corporate taxes
- ↑ Easier lending standards and more cash reserves
- ↓ Uncertainty

An expanding economy: When the economy is expanding, so is the demand for goods and services. In order to produce more, managers will need to expand their production capacity, and entrepreneurs will see an opportunity to start new businesses. As a result, investment in new equipment increases when the economy is expanding more rapidly.

Business confidence: Because capital investments tend to last for years, or even decades, your assessments about whether to buy new equipment should depend not only on today's profits, but also on your expectations about future profitability. That's why investment increases when managers are more confident about their future profitability.

Corporate taxes: Lower corporate taxes increase the after-tax profits that entrepreneurs earn from investing in new equipment. As a result, investment increases in response to a cut in corporate tax rates. Investment also increases in response to targeted investment tax credits that reduce the after-tax cost of buying new equipment.

Lending standards and cash reserves: If your business finds it hard to borrow money at a reasonable interest rate, your best alternative is to invest in new equipment only when your company has the cash on hand to do so. It follows that investment tends to increase when loans are easier to get, or businesses have large cash reserves. Cash reserves are particularly important when the financial system is not working well.

Uncertainty: If you're uncertain about the economic outlook—it could be great, it could be terrible—remember that you usually have the option to postpone breaking ground on major investment projects until the outlook is a bit clearer. Lower uncertainty leads managers to restart these shelved projects, leading to an increase in investment.

Jochen Tack/Alamy Stock Photo

It's only a worthwhile investment if the opportunity cost isn't too high.

Demand shifter three: Government purchases increase when policy makers decide to spend more on goods and services. For example, they may pass legislation that increases government spending on highways or military equipment. In some cases, these spending bills have the explicit goal of stimulating an increase in aggregate demand. In addition, some government programs—known as *automatic stabilisers*—automatically increase spending when the economy is weak.

Government purchases increase in response to:

- Spending bills
- Automatic stabilisers

. . . but not transfer payments (at least not directly)

Remember that government spending only directly increases aggregate expenditure—and hence shifts the aggregate demand curve—when the government purchases goods and services. By contrast, many government programs—such as JobSeeker or the Age Pension simply transfer money from one bank account (the government's) to another (the recipient's), and so they don't *directly* increase aggregate expenditure. There may however be an *indirect* effect, as redistributing money to people who are more likely to spend it might increase consumption.

Net exports increase in response to global factors:

↑ Global GDP growth
↓ Australian dollar
↓ Trade barriers in foreign markets
↑ Trade barriers to Australian market

Demand shifter four: Net exports increase due to global factors. Net exports rise when people in other countries want to buy a lot of Australian-made goods and services. It's the *interdependence principle* at work, as net exports link the Australian economy with economies around the world. Aggregate demand will shift when net exports rise or fall in response to:

Global economic growth: When the economies of the United States, Europe, Japan, and China do well, their consumers and businesses have more money to spend, and so they buy more goods, including more Australian-made goods, leading net exports to increase.

The exchange rate: Net exports also shift in response to changes in the exchange rate. When the Australian dollar becomes cheaper, our goods become cheaper to foreign buyers, leading exports to rise. A cheaper Australian dollar also means that foreign goods become more expensive (in Australian dollars) for Australian buyers, leading imports to fall. Both forces—rising exports and falling imports—cause net exports to increase.

Paul Street/Alamy Stock Photo

Global factors determine net exports.

Trade barriers: Exports increase when there are fewer barriers preventing Australian businesses from selling their goods in other countries, while imports increase when there are fewer barriers preventing foreign businesses from selling to buyers in Australia. Because trade agreements typically reduce barriers to both imports and exports, their effect on net exports (which is exports less imports) is unclear. Likewise trade wars—in which higher trade barriers preventing imports lead other countries to retaliate by raising barriers that prevent foreigners from buying Australian exports—will reduce both imports and exports, yielding an unclear effect on net exports.

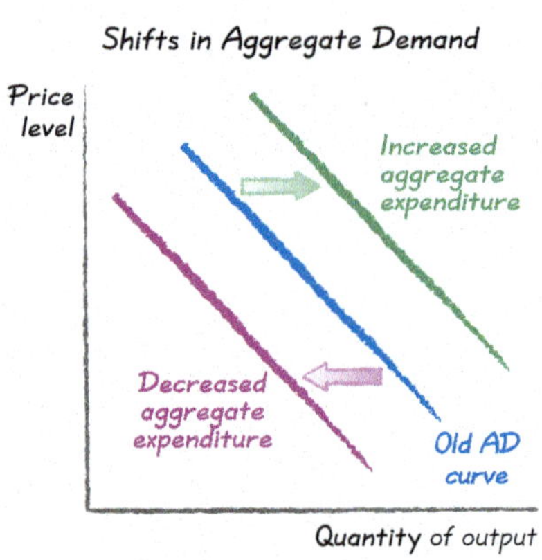

Recap: Anything that shifts any component of aggregate expenditure shifts the AD curve. At this point, this list of changes that can shift the aggregate demand curve might seem a bit exhausting. I've put it all together for you in Figure 4. But you don't need to memorise this whole list, because it's all about just one idea: The aggregate demand curve shifts in response to an increase in any component of aggregate expenditure. That's the easy way to remember this list: It's just *C, I, G,* and *NX*.

Figure 4 Factors That Shift the Aggregate Demand Curve

Aggregate demand shifter	Examples*
Consumption *rises if people feel more prosperous*	↑Wealth, ↑Consumer confidence, ↑Government assistance, ↓Taxes, ↓Inequality
Investment *rises if it's profitable to expand production*	↑GDP growth, ↑Business confidence, ↑Investment tax credits, ↓Corporate taxes, ↑Easier lending standards and more cash reserves, ↓Uncertainty
Government purchases *rise in response to expansionary fiscal policy*	Spending bills, Automatic stabilisers . . . but not transfer payments (at least not directly)
Net exports *rise in response to global factors*	↑Global GDP growth, ↓Australian dollar, ↓Trade barriers in foreign markets, ↑Trade barriers to Australian market

*These examples all increase aggregate demand. Reverse the sign of any arrow, and you'll get a change that decreases aggregate demand.

There's one more factor to consider—changes in the real interest rate. The interest rate matters because it can lead to changes in aggregate expenditure, particularly investment. But it won't always lead the aggregate demand curve to shift. (Why? Remember that the aggregate demand curve already reflects the changes in aggregate expenditure due to the RBA adjusting interest rates in response to inflation.) We'll dig into when and how changing interest rates shift aggregate demand in a few pages when we analyse monetary policy.

EVERYDAY Economics **How a recession is like a bad night's sleep**

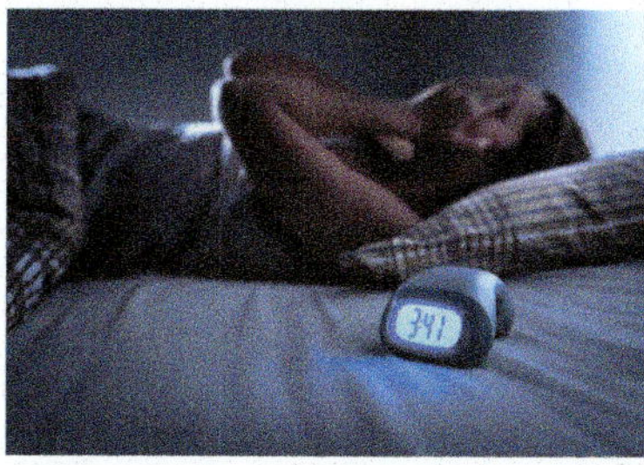

Tero Vesalainen/Shutterstock

You have nothing to fear, but fear itself.

It's the night before a major exam, a big interview, or an important recital, and your mind races as you realise how important it is that you sleep well. Perhaps you're lucky, and you fall asleep right away. But if you don't, you might start to worry that you're not yet asleep, which stresses you out . . . making it impossible to fall asleep. Essentially, your anxiety about not sleeping causes you not to sleep. I bet you know the feeling.

The thing is, if you can quiet your fear of not sleeping, you'll find it easier to fall asleep. If you believe you can fall asleep, you probably will. It's a self-fulfilling prophecy. The same kind of self-fulfilling prophecy that prevents you from getting to sleep can cause an economic boom or bust. If you fear that a recession's looming, you might spend less. The problem is that if lots of people fear that a recession is looming, then lots of people will spend less, and aggregate demand will decrease. So if people fear a recession, there will probably be a recession. Pessimistic beliefs about the economy can create a pessimistic reality. U.S. President Franklin D. Roosevelt summarised this logic towards the end of the Great Depression, famously telling Americans that "the only thing we have to fear is fear itself."

His speech was intended to help switch the economy from an equilibrium of self-fulfilling pessimism to one of self-fulfilling optimism. Roosevelt knew that if he could convince people that the economy would recover, then they would spend more. And if they spent more, the increase in aggregate demand would lead the economy to recover. A more optimistic expectation can also create a more optimistic reality. Remember FDR's lesson next time you're struggling to sleep: If you can quiet your fear of not sleeping, you'll find it easier to fall asleep. ■

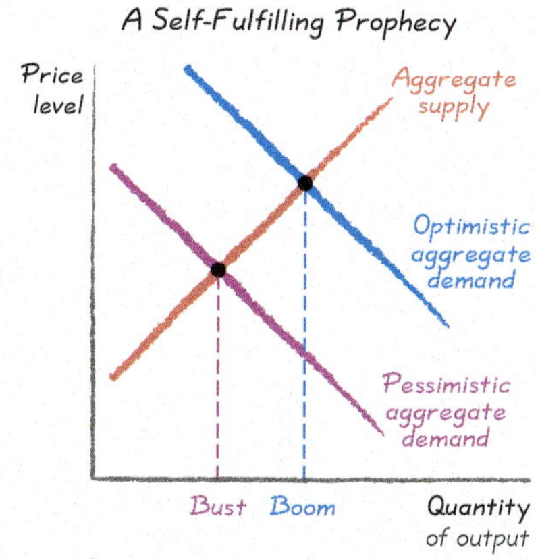

33.3 Aggregate Supply

Learning Objective *Evaluate the forces that shape the total quantity of goods and services that businesses want to supply.*

Fir Mamat/Alamy Stock Photo

What price will Hungry Jack's charge for a Whopper next year?

The aggregate supply curve describes the production and pricing decisions that suppliers make, and how they respond as macroeconomic conditions change. It's a topic so beefy that we'll need to start with a visit to Hungry Jack's.

Why Aggregate Supply Is Upward-Sloping

More precisely, we'll visit corporate headquarters. Put yourself in the shoes of the executives who have to decide what prices to print on next year's menus—what price to charge for the "Whopper", "Grill Masters Double Cowboy Angus", or "Frozen Fanta Traditional Lemonade Spider." At Hungry Jack's, like almost any other business, pricing decisions depend on the state of the economy.

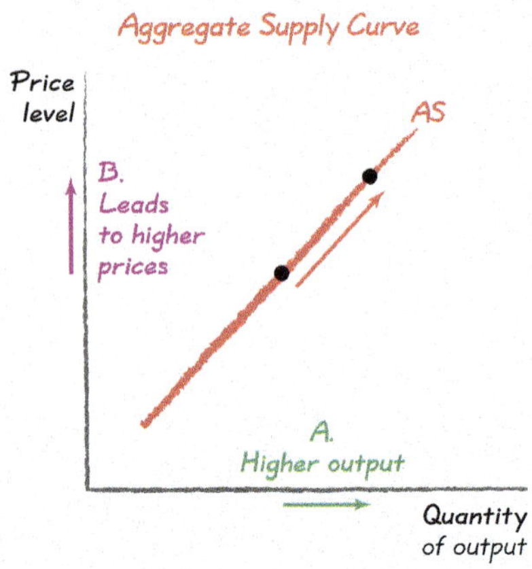

Higher output leads to higher prices. A strong economy with high GDP is good news for Hungry Jack's because when incomes are high, your customers are more willing to eat out. When the economy is doing particularly well, you'll find your restaurants have plenty of customers, and you'll need to pay your staff overtime to keep up. Even then, you might not be able to keep up, and some of your customers might leave rather than queue for too long. This is even more true of more upscale restaurants, where dining is more of a luxury than grabbing a burger from a fast-casual restaurant.

A strong economy can lead to *excess demand* given your limited capacity. In the long run, if business continues to boom, it's worth building more restaurants. But that takes years; in the short run, you're stuck with your existing capacity, which means it's time to raise your prices. After all, even with higher prices, you can still fill your restaurant. And those higher prices will help cover your overtime bill.

The aggregate supply curve describes what happens, on average, across the millions of businesses that make up the Australian economy. Hungry Jack's story is relevant, because when GDP is high, millions of businesses are in a similar situation to Hungry Jack's. Many of these businesses will respond to their excess demand much as Hungry Jack's did, by raising their prices a bit. The result is that in periods of high GDP, the average price level will be a bit higher than it would be otherwise.

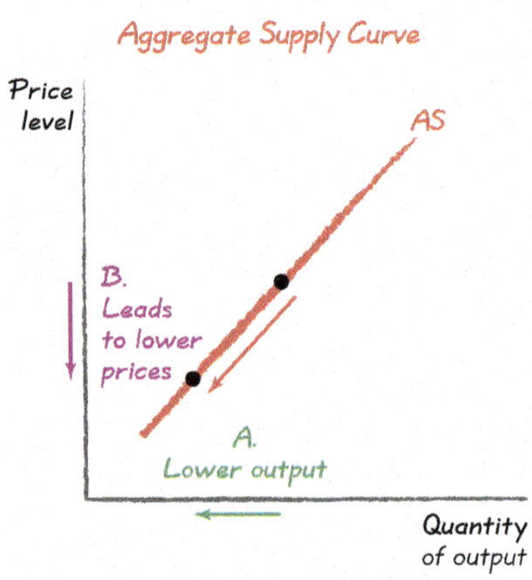

Lower output leads to lower prices. On the other hand, a weaker economy will typically lead to lower prices. To see why, let's return to the dark days of 2009, when the financial crisis loomed large. This cut two ways for Hungry Jack's. On one hand, people didn't have a lot of money with which to eat out. But this affected higher-end restaurants more. In fact, some people "traded down" to cheaper fast-food restaurants like Hungry Jack's. On balance, however, this was a negative for Hungry Jack's.

Hungry Jack's was facing a problem of *insufficient demand,* as the quantity of restaurant meals demanded at the prevailing price was below the quantity that Hungry Jack's wished to supply. In response, many restaurants like Hungry Jack's cut prices or offered better deals for the same price. That's effectively the same thing.

When GDP is low, millions of businesses face insufficient demand. Like Hungry Jack's, most will find that their marginal costs are low when they're producing well below their capacity. They'll follow the same logic and respond to insufficient demand with lower prices. The result is that in periods of low GDP, the average price level across the whole economy will tend to be a bit lower than it would be otherwise.

Richard Levine/Alamy Stock Photo

Lower GDP leads to lower prices.

The aggregate supply curve is upward-sloping because higher output leads to a higher price level. The figures in the margin show that lower output levels are associated with a lower average price level and higher output levels are associated with a higher average price level. Put the pieces together, and you've constructed the upward sloping aggregate supply curve.

Analysing Aggregate Supply

You'll find the aggregate supply curve to be helpful because you can use it to forecast how changing market conditions will affect economic conditions. As you do so, make sure to distinguish between a change in the price level (or a change in output), which causes a movement along the aggregate supply curve, from shifts in other factors that cause the price level to change at a given level of output, leading the aggregate supply curve to shift.

Changes in the price level lead to movements along the aggregate supply curve. The aggregate supply curve illustrates how different price levels are associated with suppliers producing different levels of output. You can use it to assess how the price level will respond to changes in output or how output will respond to changes in the price level. The green arrow in Figure 5 illustrates how a movement along the aggregate supply curve to a higher price level is also associated with suppliers producing a higher quantity of output.

(Alternatively phrased, it shows that higher output leads suppliers to push the price level higher.) The purple arrow shows that a lower price level leads to a movement along the aggregate supply curve, but this time to producing a lower quantity of output. (Or to say it the other way, it shows that lower output leads suppliers to nudge the price level lower.)

What causes the aggregate supply curve to shift? I'm glad you asked . . .

Changes in production costs shift the aggregate supply curve. The costs of production are central to pricing decisions. And that matters because changing production costs cause suppliers to change the prices they'll charge at any given level of output, thereby causing the aggregate supply curve to shift.

Lower production costs lead businesses to charge lower prices. As a result, lower production costs reduce the average price level across the whole economy (at any given level of output), thereby shifting the aggregate supply curve downward or to the right. Because this shift leads to an increase in the quantity of output associated with any given price, we say that *lower production costs* lead to an *increase* in aggregate supply. This increase arises because lower production costs boost the profitability of producing stuff, leading suppliers to increase the quantity of output they'll produce at any given price level. Panel A on the left of Figure 6 shows that an increase in aggregate supply—by shifting the aggregate supply curve to the right—leads to both higher GDP and a lower price level. That is, it causes an economic expansion accompanied by deflation. (In reality there are often other factors driving inflation, and so this might lead to a decrease in inflation rather than outright deflation.)

Figure 5 | The Aggregate Supply Curve

The relationship between the quantity of output supplied and the average price level.

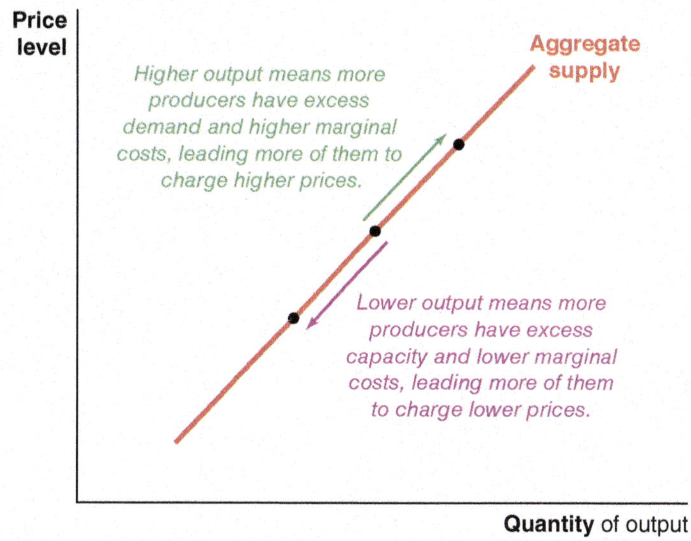

Figure 6 | Shifts in Aggregate Supply

The aggregate supply curve shifts due to changes in production costs.

Panel A: An Increase in the Aggregate Supply

- A: A fall in production costs causes the aggregate supply curve to shift to the right (or downward).
- B: This leads the economy to move to a new equilibrium.
- C: Leading to a rise in GDP (and hence an *economic expansion*).
- D: It also leads to a fall in prices (and hence a burst of *deflation*, or perhaps *lower inflation*).

Panel B: A Decrease in the Aggregate Supply

- A: A rise in production costs causes the aggregate supply curve to shift to the left (or upward).
- B: This leads the economy to move to a new equilibrium.
- C: Leading to a fall in GDP (and hence a *recession*).
- D: It also leads to a rise in prices (and hence a burst of *inflation*).

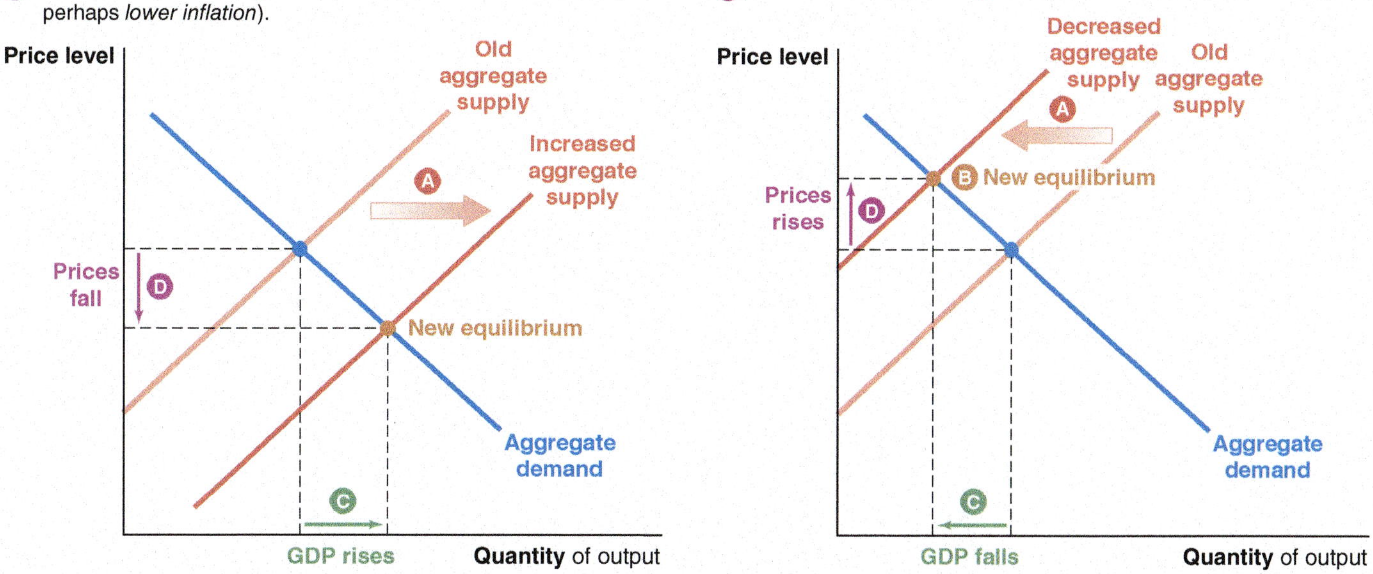

By contrast, higher production costs lead businesses to charge higher prices. The resulting rise in the average price level (at any given level of output) shifts the aggregate supply curve upward or to the left. Because this decreases the quantity of output associated with any given price, we say that *higher production costs* lead to a *decrease* in aggregate supply. Panel B on the right of Figure 6 shows that a decrease in aggregate supply—by shifting the aggregate supply curve to the left—leads to both lower GDP and a higher price level. This combination of declining GDP (and hence economic stagnation) and rising prices (and hence inflation) is sometimes called stagflation—at least when it is severe, like in the 1970s.

An aside: We usually describe curves shifting left or right, rather than up or down. But sometimes you might find it more intuitive to think about the aggregate supply curve as shifting up rather than left when higher production costs lead businesses to raise prices. Both descriptions are accurate. Likewise, it's just as accurate to say that lower production costs shift the aggregate supply curve down as it is to say they'll shift the curve to the right. What's important is that you shift your way to the right answer.

Aggregate supply shifts in response to changes in production costs, which can be caused by shifts in:
1. Input prices
2. Productivity
3. The exchange rate

Higher energy prices make everything more expensive.

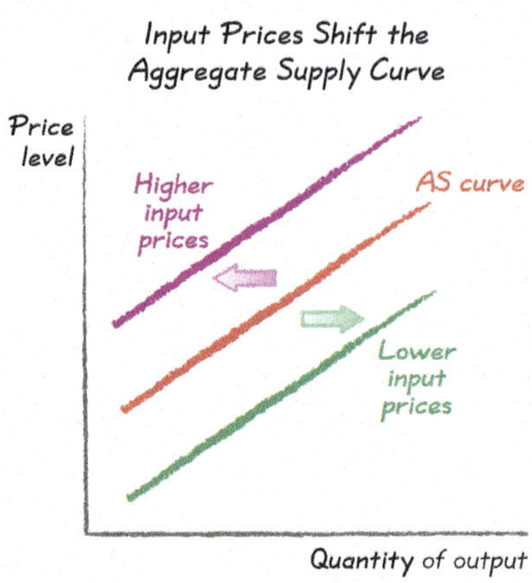

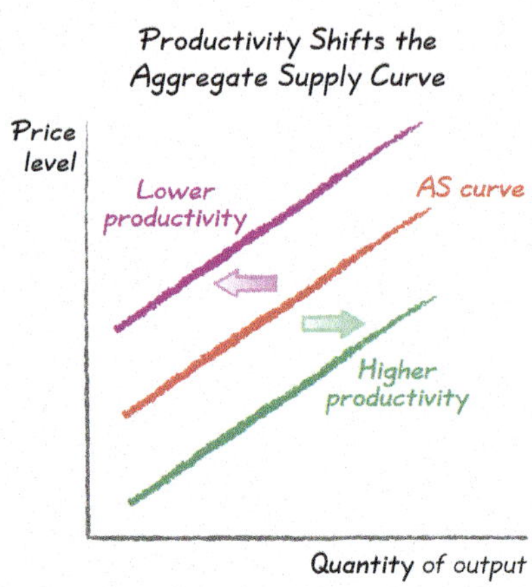

Shifts in Aggregate Supply

There are three key factors that shift production costs and hence the aggregate supply curve: shifts in input prices, productivity, and the exchange rate. Let's explore each in turn.

Supply shifter one: Higher input prices raise production costs. The *interdependence principle* emphasises the importance of linkages between markets, and it's especially relevant to understanding how geopolitical tensions in the Middle East can play a central role in the pricing decisions of many suppliers. Those tensions led to cutbacks in oil production that pushed up oil prices, setting off a chain reaction. Initially, products made from oil—like petrol and propane—become more expensive. In turn, those higher costs made it more expensive to operate a restaurant as they raised the costs of running a commercial kitchen, heating a restaurant, and trucking ingredients across the country. Eventually, these higher marginal costs forced restaurants to raise their prices.

A similar story played out across many sectors of the economy, as businesses discovered that higher oil prices led to higher prices for a range of inputs that were produced using oil—including plastics, fertilisers, and rubber. Just as higher marginal costs led restaurants to raise their prices, tens of thousands of other businesses raised their prices when their marginal costs rose. And so the average price level set by suppliers at a given level of output rose, which led to a decrease in aggregate supply.

This oil shock is a specific example of a more general phenomenon: Any time the price of your inputs rises, so will your marginal costs, and higher marginal costs lead producers to set higher prices, which shifts the aggregate supply curve to the left (or up). Indeed, labour is one of a restaurant's most important inputs (as it is for many businesses), which means that sharp wage changes can cause the aggregate supply curve to shift. When there are large rises in restaurant industry award wages—as occurred in mid 2022—restaurants like Hungry Jack's tend to raise their prices.

Supply shifter two: Weaker productivity raises production costs. Your company's productivity also changes your production costs, as a less productive company needs to buy more of each input to produce the same output. Because productivity determines marginal costs, it also impacts the prices businesses charge at any given level of GDP. For example, productivity growth slowed quite dramatically from the mid-1970s and into the 1980s, and many businesses found their production costs to be higher than they had expected them to be. Those higher costs led businesses to raise their prices. The result was a decrease in aggregate supply, shifting the curve to the left (or upward). It also works the other way, and more rapid productivity growth increases aggregate supply, thereby shifting the aggregate supply curve to the right (or downward).

Supply shifter three: A depreciating Australian dollar raises production costs and reduces competition from overseas. Changes in the nominal exchange rate also shift pricing decisions and hence aggregate supply. Remember, the *exchange rate* is the price of an Australian dollar in another currency. For instance, when the exchange rate is 100 Japanese yen per dollar, that means that one Australian dollar buys 100 Yen. We say that the Australian dollar *depreciates* when the price of an Australian dollar falls, say to 90 Yen. This means the Australian dollar becomes cheaper for foreigners to buy, but it also means that foreign currency is more expensive for Australians to buy because it'll cost more Australian dollars to buy a specific quantity of yen.

This really matters for businesses that rely on imported inputs because a depreciating Australian dollar raises the cost of their imported inputs. For example, when a high-end restaurant like Rockpool Bar & Grill offers Kobe beef imported from Japan, a depreciating Australian dollar means that it will cost Rockpool more dollars to import the same quantity of Japanese beef. These higher marginal costs lead Rockpool to raise its prices.

The exchange rate also matters to businesses such as Malvern Star bikes that compete with imported products, such as those from Trek, because a depreciating Australian dollar raises the price (in Australian dollars) of goods made by foreign competitors like Trek. This weaker competitive pressure might lead domestic producers to raise their prices. Alternatively, if your business exports its output, a depreciating Australian dollar makes your foreign customers willing to pay more (in dollars) for your products. This increased pressure from foreign customers will lead many Australian exporters to raise the prices they charge their Australian customers.

Consequently, a depreciation in the Australian dollar leads suppliers to set higher prices at any level of output, leading to a decrease in aggregate supply. By contrast, an appreciation of the Australian dollar leads suppliers to set lower prices at any level of output, leading to an increase in aggregate supply.

Exchange Rates Shift the Aggregate Supply Curve

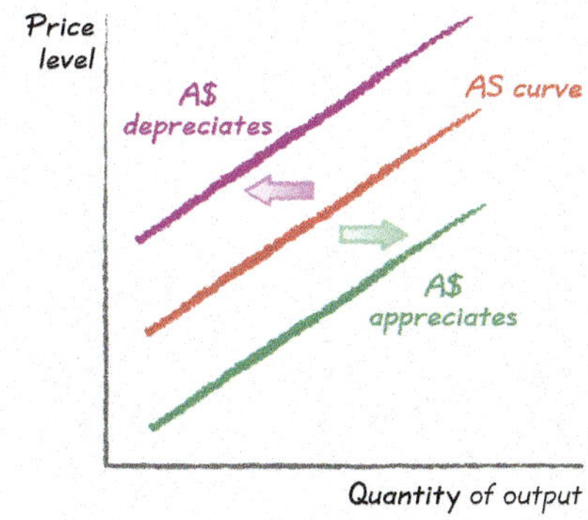

Interpreting the DATA — How a trade war shifted the aggregate supply curve

When United States President Trump imposed tariffs—effectively an additional sales tax—on imported goods, many proponents of the policy focused on the effects on aggregate demand. They hoped that these tariffs would lead to fewer imports, and hence boost net exports (which are exports less imports) and thus aggregate demand. What they didn't count on was that China and Europe would retaliate with their own tariffs, designed to reduce American exports in roughly equal measure. When lower imports are matched by lower exports, there's no effect on net exports nor on aggregate demand.

But these tariffs had a more important effect on aggregate supply. More than half of all imports to the United States are used as inputs by American businesses in the production of their goods and services. Tariffs raised the cost of purchasing these foreign inputs.

This constituted a major rise in input costs for sellers who were particularly reliant on foreign goods. For example, Jeff Starin, president of Rostar Filters, now faces hundreds of thousands of dollars in tariffs on automotive filters he imports from China. He doesn't see a better alternative than continuing to import filters because finding alternative sources also involves higher costs. He decided to pass those higher costs on to his customers. The bottom line according to Starin is that for "the owner of a vehicle, their brake job just went up by $120." Many other businesses have also said that increased tariffs mean they must increase prices for consumers. All this means that the aggregate supply curve shifted up (or left). And so a policy intended to increase aggregate demand ultimately instead decreased aggregate supply. ■

Florin Seitan/Alamy

A shock to aggregate demand, or aggregate supply?

Higher Tariffs Led to a Decrease in Aggregate Supply

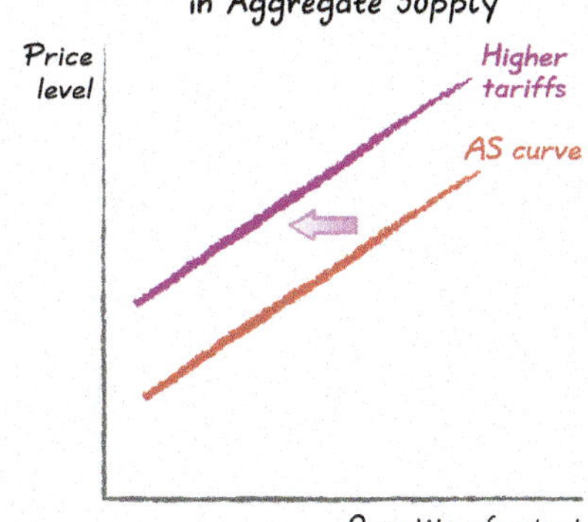

Recap: Anything that shifts production costs shifts the *AS* curve. The point of this analysis isn't to memorise a long list of factors that might shift the aggregate supply curve. Rather, focus on the bigger picture, which is that the aggregate supply curve shifts in response to changes in production costs, and we've identified three key shifters: input prices, productivity, and the exchange rate.

We're now going to explore how the tools of macroeconomic policy fit in all of this. And that's going to require a brief visit into one of the most hair-raising periods in modern economic history: the global financial crisis.

33.4 Macroeconomic Shocks and Countercyclical Policy

Learning Objective *Forecast how the economy will respond to changing conditions.*

zimmytws/Deposit Photos

Grim headlines.

Late 2008 heralded one of the most tumultuous periods in Australia's economic history. You've already seen how it impacted one business—Hungry Jack's—but the financial crisis created far more widespread economic challenges, and it was arguably the most severe economic crisis since the Great Depression (at least until the coronavirus pandemic). House prices fell, stock prices plummeted, and every day seemed to bring news of another financial institution in danger of going bust. Businesses stopped investing, consumers cut their spending, and unemployment shot up to 6% from 4%. That initial decline in spending led to job losses, and the ensuing decline in income led people to further cut their spending. The economy was confronting free fall, and no one knew how bad things could get. Was the next Great Depression just a few months away?

Officials at Treasury and the Reserve Bank knew that they needed to take rapid, decisive action. And because they had learned the lessons of the Great Depression, they had a playbook to draw on.

There was the prospect of a huge fall in aggregate demand. If you were on the Treasury or RBA team, what would you do?

Monetary Policy

The Reserve Bank responded decisively, cutting its benchmark interest rate four times over the course of 2008. It did so with the hope that lower interest rates would lead people to spend more, and this boost to aggregate expenditure would kick-start a recovery.

monetary policy The process of setting interest rates in an effort to influence economic conditions.

The RBA cuts interest rates in response to both low inflation and weak output. This process of the RBA setting and adjusting interest rates in an effort to influence economic conditions is called **monetary policy.** It's worth distinguishing between the two reasons that RBA officials cut interest rates:

- **An inflation-induced response:** Through 2008, widespread price restraint led the price level to be lower than it otherwise would be, and inflation fell sharply. When the RBA is worried that inflation is too low, it responds by cutting the real interest rate. We call this an *inflation-induced* response.
- **An output-induced response:** But the RBA cut interest rates much more dramatically than needed to offset the decline in inflation. It did so because it has another objective: promoting maximal employment and hence output. Thus, the RBA cut the real interest rate even further in an effort to combat the decline in GDP. We call this an *output-induced* response.

An Inflation-Induced Interest Rate Cut

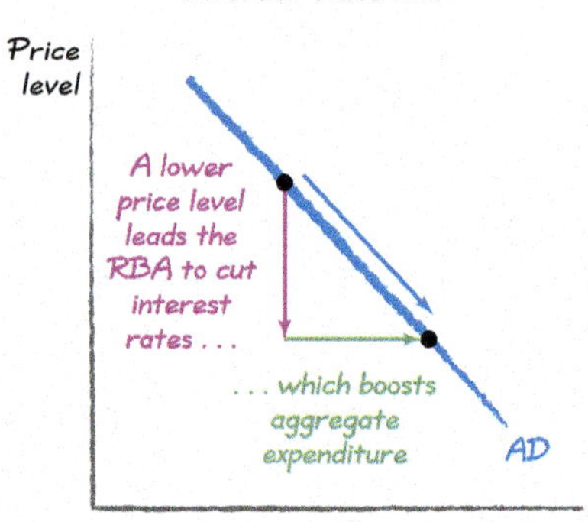

An inflation-induced change in interest rates does not shift the aggregate demand curve. This distinction matters because we evaluate them differently. An inflation-induced response by the RBA is caused by a *change in the price level,* and you should recall that a change in the price level leads to a movement along the aggregate demand curve but not a shift. The RBA's inflation-induced responses are important, and they affect the economy. But their effects are already reflected in the aggregate demand curve whose downward slope illustrates how lower prices ultimately boost aggregate expenditure (by causing lower inflation, which induces the RBA to cut the real interest rate). As a result, a change in the interest rate that's caused by the RBA's typical response to inflation—that is, an inflation-induced response—won't shift the aggregate demand curve.

Any other change in the real interest rate shifts the aggregate demand curve. By contrast, an output-induced cut in the real interest rate reduces the real interest rate at the prevailing price level. It will stimulate greater aggregate expenditure at the current price level, thereby shifting the aggregate demand curve to the right. More generally, any change in the real interest rate—other than the RBA's systematic inflation-induced response to changes in the price level—will change the amount of aggregate expenditure at a given price level, thereby shifting the aggregate demand curve.

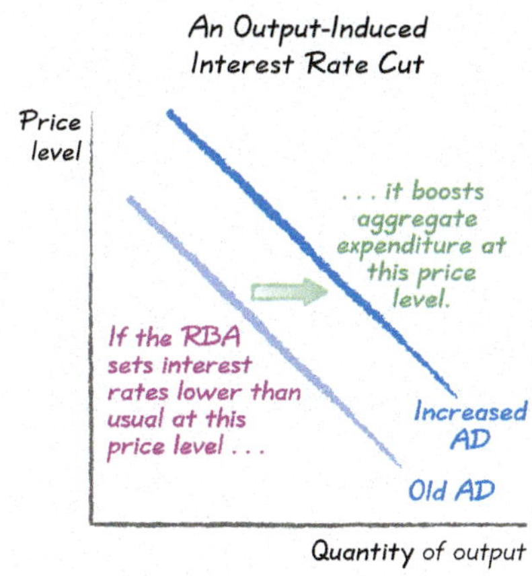

Lower real interest rates are expansionary. The RBA is said to be pursuing an *expansionary* monetary policy when it reduces the real interest rate lower than would be expected given its usual response to inflation. An expansionary monetary policy—like that pursued in 2008—leads to an increase in aggregate demand. As Figure 7 shows, it shifts the aggregate demand curve to the right, leading to a new equilibrium with a higher level of output and higher prices. On the flip side, if the RBA set a higher interest rate than would be expected given its usual response to inflation—pursuing a *contractionary* monetary policy—it would lead to less spending at any given price level, which would shift the aggregate demand curve to the left, leading to a lower level of output and prices.

This sort of analysis led many economists to forecast—correctly, as it turned out—that the RBA's expansionary monetary policy would help avoid recession or get the economy growing again. The RBA's repeated interest rate cuts provided a useful boost, but Prime Minister Kevin Rudd and Secretary of the Treasury Ken Henry knew that they couldn't rely on monetary policy alone. In fact, they realised this sooner than many policy makers overseas did.

Figure 7 | Monetary and Fiscal Policy

Expansionary fiscal or monetary policy shift the aggregate demand curve to the right.

- **A** An output-induced interest rate cut, or a boost to government purchases, will **shift the aggregate demand curve to the right**.
- **B** In response, the **quantity of output** rises.
- **C** And so does the **price level**.

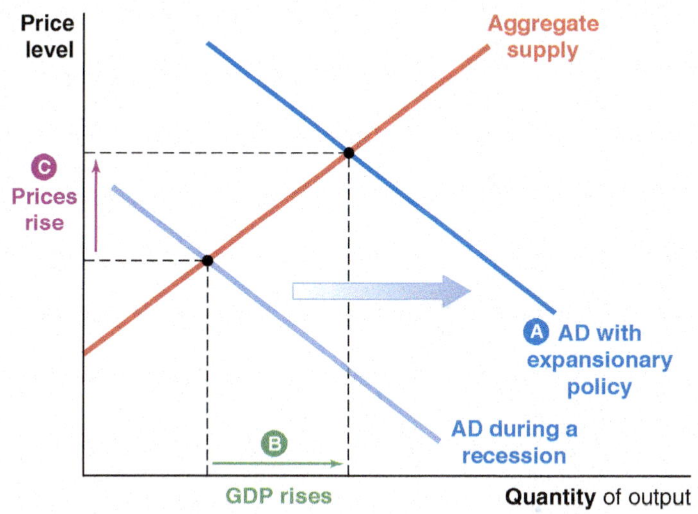

Fiscal Policy and the Multiplier

The government can also influence the economy by adjusting its own spending and tax policies—that is through **fiscal policy.** And so in mid-October 2008, the Rudd government announced a $10.4 billion stimulus package involving $1,000 or $2,000 direct payments to pensioners and low- and middle-income households. Treasury Secretary Ken Henry famously described the strategy to quickly get cash into the pockets of those most likely to spend it as "go hard, go early, go households."

In early February 2009, the government followed up with a (then) massive $42 billion additional stimulus package known as the "Nation Building and Jobs Plan," which consisted largely of infrastructure spending. To see how much this increased output, we'll need to explore an idea called the multiplier.

fiscal policy The government's use of spending and tax policies to influence economic conditions.

An increase in spending has a multiplied effect on aggregate expenditure. An initial burst of government spending will have repercussions throughout the economy. Consider the money spent building new roads. The direct effect is to put unemployed transportation engineers, construction workers, and road maintenance crews back to work. There will also be important ripple effects. For instance, a worker who spends their new paycheque buying home-improvement supplies at Bunnings boosts the incomes of Bunnings workers and Wesfarmers workers and shareholders. There are also second-round ripple effects. As Bunnings sells more gear, it will hire more workers, who might buy lunch at a local Subway, leading the franchise owner to hire more sandwich artists. There are third-round effects, too. If some of those new Subway staff members enroll their children in day care, the local child-care providers also receive a boost to their income. And so it continues.

As this initial boost in spending reverberates through the economy, it illustrates the importance of the *interdependence principle* for understanding macroeconomic developments. This interdependence arises because one person's spending is another person's

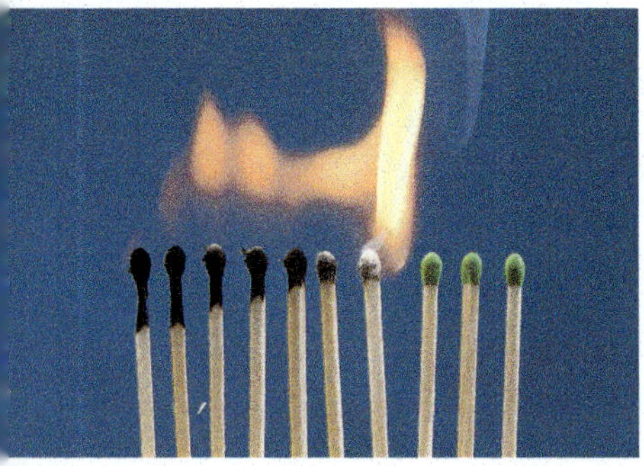

gjohnstonphoto/Deposit Photos

An initial stimulus can spark a lot of subsequent activity.

income. It means that extra spending by the government stimulates extra spending by construction workers, which stimulates extra spending in the car, food, and child-care industries. As the initial burst of government purchases ripples through the economy, it has a *multiplier effect,* leading to an even larger boost to aggregate expenditure.

A burst of government spending will crowd out some private spending. There's another dynamic however, and it tempers this multiplier effect. As spending boosts the demand for output, some businesses will run into capacity constraints. When the demand for their output exceeds their ability to supply it, they'll raise their prices, and the resulting boost to inflation might lead the RBA to raise the real interest rate. These higher interest rates reduce private-sector spending (especially investment). Thus a burst of government spending might end up *crowding out* some private spending. The overall effect on the economy depends on how much of the multiplier effect is dampened by crowding out.

The multiplier summarises the effect of an initial burst of spending on output. You can summarise the consequences of a rise in spending—including the direct impact, subsequent multiplier effects, and crowding out—with a single number called the multiplier. The **multiplier** measures how much GDP changes as a result of both the direct and indirect effects flowing from each extra dollar of spending. For instance, if the multiplier is 2, then an initial \$1 boost to spending will generate a total of \$2 in additional spending and hence output. When people have a greater propensity to spend additional income they receive, the ripple effects of an initial burst of spending will be larger, leading the multiplier to be larger. It is also larger when the absence of capacity constraints limits the extent of crowding out.

multiplier A measure of how much GDP changes as a result of both the direct and indirect effects flowing from each extra dollar of spending.

The multiplier is useful because you can use it to forecast the effects of changes in spending, as follows:

$$\Delta\text{GDP} = \Delta\text{Spending} \times \text{Multiplier}$$

You can use the multiplier to figure out the likely consequences of the 2008–09 stimulus bills. (To simplify, we'll treat the entire \$52 billion cost of the stimulus bill as if it were a rise in government purchases, which is not strictly accurate.)

Do the Economics

How much will GDP rise after a \$52 billion increase in government purchases if the multiplier is 2?

$$\Delta\text{GDP} = \underbrace{\$52\text{ billion}}_{\Delta\text{Spending}} \times \underbrace{2}_{\text{Multiplier}} = \$104\text{ billion}$$ ■

If you want to dig more deeply into the logic (and maths) of the multiplier, read the appendix, "Aggregate Expenditure and the Multiplier."

Forecasting Macroeconomic Outcomes

It's time to pull the threads of this chapter together so that you can use what you now know about aggregate demand and aggregate supply to forecast how the economy will respond to changing market conditions.

Apply the three-step recipe to forecast macroeconomic outcomes. You'll find forecasting easiest if you work your way through the following three-step recipe. To assess the likely consequences of any change in economic conditions, ask yourself:

Step one: *Is this a shift in aggregate demand or aggregate supply?*

Remember the aggregate demand curve shifts in response to changes in any element of aggregate expenditure at the current price level, whether it's due to *C, I, G,* or *NX.* By contrast, the aggregate supply curve shifts in response to changes in production costs.

Step two: *Is that shift an increase, shifting the curve to the right? Or is it a decrease, shifting the curve to the left?*

Higher aggregate expenditure will shift the aggregate demand curve to the right, while higher production costs will shift the aggregate supply curve to the left.

Step three: *How will the price level and quantity of output change in the new equilibrium?*

Compare the old equilibrium with the new equilibrium.

Forecast how the economy responds to macroeconomic shocks. It's time to apply our *AD-AS* framework to assessing real-world macroeconomic developments.

Example one: *In 2008, the government was worried that the economy was underperforming. In an effort to prevent a recession, the federal government sent stimulus cheques of more than $1,000 to pensioners and low- and middle-income households. How did this affect the economy?*

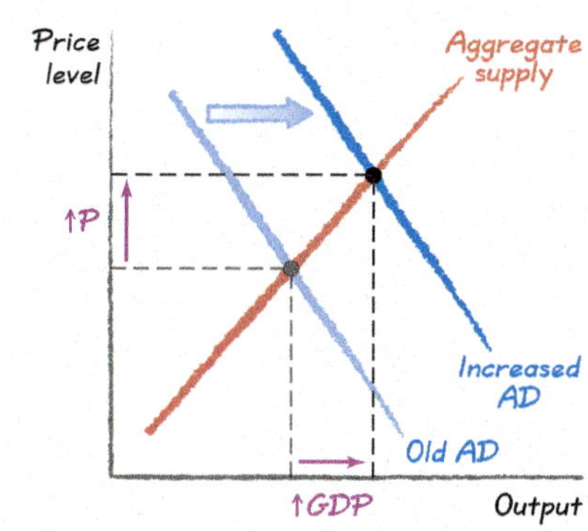

Step one: The stimulus cheques give people more after-tax income, which leads them to *spend* more—and so this will *shift the aggregate demand curve.*

Step two: Because higher after-tax income leads to more consumption spending which *increases* aggregate expenditure, it will *shift the aggregate demand curve to the right.*

Step three: At the new equilibrium, this increase in aggregate demand leads to *higher output,* and a *higher average price level.*

Example two: *The onset of the Gulf War with Iraq led to disruptions in the supply of oil from the Middle East, causing oil prices to rise sharply. How did this affect the economy?*

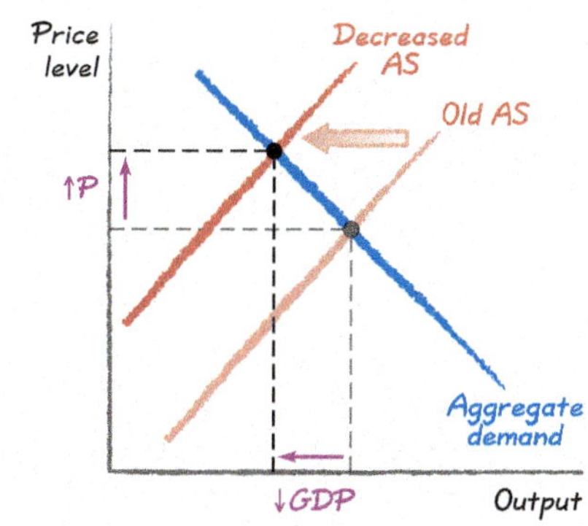

Step one: Oil is an important input into the production process for many businesses, and so changes in this important input price affect their *production costs,* which will *shift the aggregate supply curve.*

Step two: Higher input prices lead to higher production costs, which make it less profitable to produce output. This leads suppliers to *decrease* the quantity of output they produce at any given price level, *shifting the aggregate supply curve to the left.* (Alternatively phrased, higher production costs lead businesses to charge higher prices at any given level of output, *shifting the aggregate supply curve up.*)

Step three: This decrease in aggregate supply leads to *lower GDP,* and a *higher average price level.*

Example three: *Rapid advances in technology, including the widespread adoption of the internet and industrial automation, are projected to boost productivity growth. How will this affect the economy?*

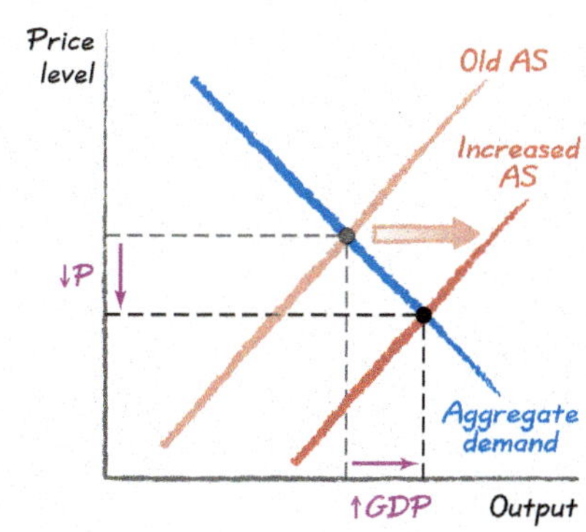

Step one: More rapid productivity growth means that businesses can produce any given level of output with fewer inputs. This change in *production costs* will *shift the aggregate supply curve.*

Step two: Lower production costs means that businesses will find it profitable to *increase* production at any given price level, which will *shift the aggregate supply curve to the right.* (Alternatively phrased, lower production costs lead businesses to charge lower prices at any given level of output, *shifting the aggregate supply curve down.*)

Step three: This increase in aggregate supply leads to *higher GDP,* and a *lower average price level.*

Example four: *In September 2008, the world's financial system froze. The grim reality for many businesses was that if they needed to borrow, they had to pay much higher interest rates than they normally would, given these economic conditions. How did this affect the economy?*

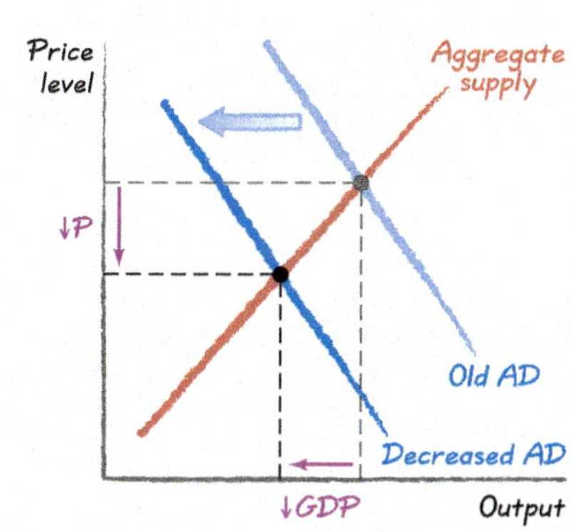

Step one: This financial shock led the real interest rate to be higher than it otherwise would be. A change in the real interest rate will affect how much money people and businesses *spend,* which will *shift the aggregate demand curve.*

Step two: A higher real interest rate leads consumers to spend less, businesses to invest less, and net exports to also decline. The resulting *decrease* in aggregate expenditure will *shift the aggregate demand curve to the left.*

Step three: At the new equilibrium, this decrease in aggregate demand leads to *lower output*, and a *lower average price level.*

Do the Economics

Think you've got the economy all figured out? Here's your chance to practice, as you work through half a dozen more examples. In each case, your job is to forecast how the economy will respond to an array of economic developments:

In an effort to balance the budget, the federal government reduced spending on the military.

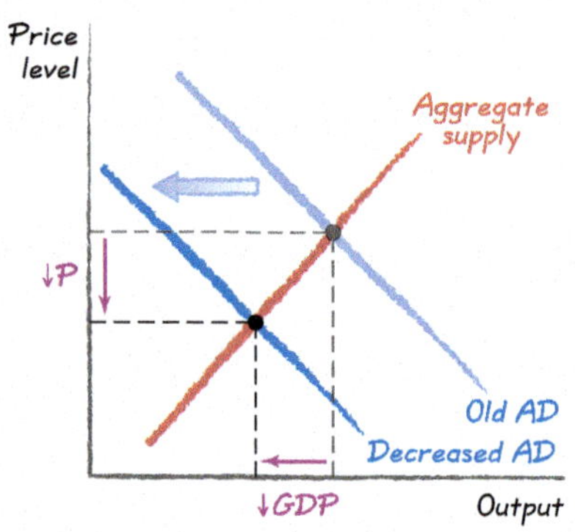

Decrease in government purchases
→ Shift *AD* curve to the left

Result: Lower GDP and lower prices

As consumer confidence boomed, people became more willing to buy cars, appliances, and furniture.

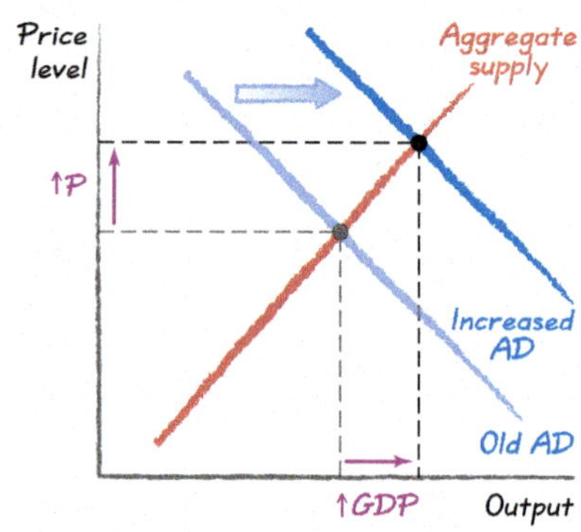

Increase in consumption
→ Shift *AD* curve to the right

Result: Higher GDP and higher prices.

A green technology boom led energy prices to decline sharply in Australia.

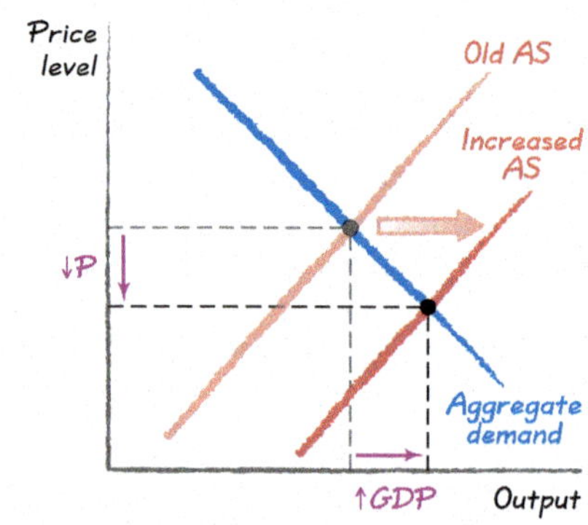

Lower input costs
→ Shift *AS* curve to the right

Result: Higher GDP and lower prices.

A decision by the Fair Work Commission led to a sharp rise in the minimum wage and award wages, raising wage costs for many businesses.

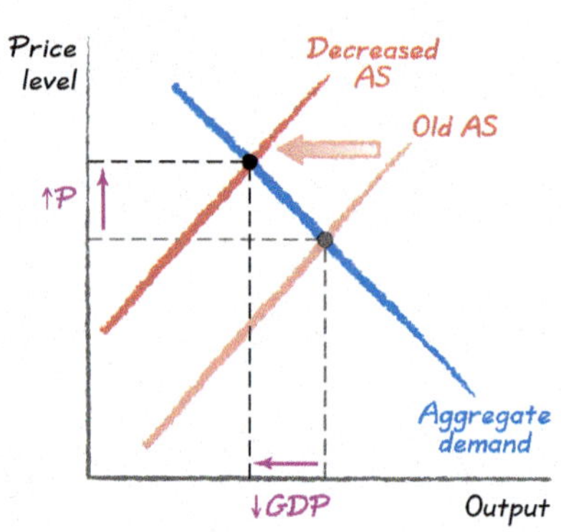

Higher input costs
→ Shift *AS* curve to the left

Result: Lower GDP and higher prices.

Rising political uncertainty led many executives to put their investment plans on hold until they could feel more certain about the business environment.

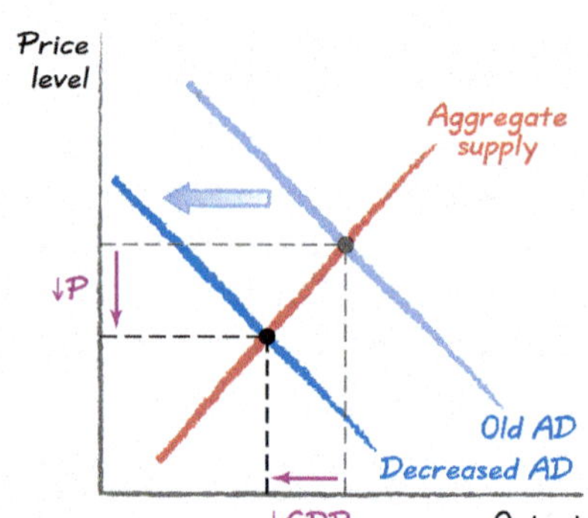

Decreased investment
→ Shift *AD* curve to the left

Result: Lower GDP and lower prices.

Worries that inflation was too high led the Reserve Bank to raise the real interest rate.

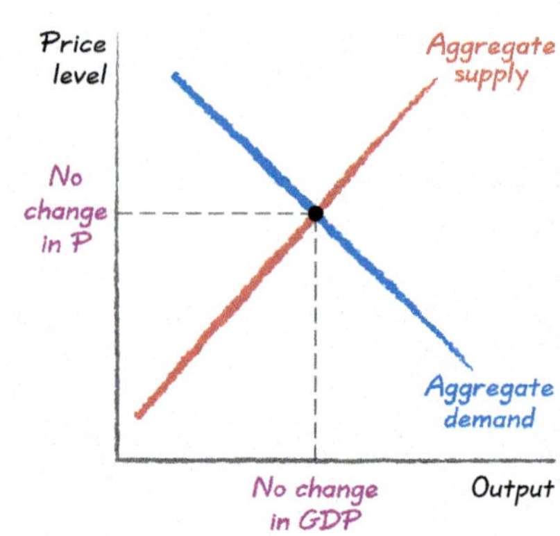

An inflation-induced interest rate change does not shift the *AD* curve

Result: No change in GDP or prices. ■

Inflation will be lower when you forecast that the price level will be lower than it otherwise would be. In many of these cases the *AD-AS* framework led us to predict that the average price level would fall, causing an episode of deflation. Don't take this too literally. In reality, deflation is rare. It's rare because inflation often has its own momentum, and so prices are often rising for other reasons. Think of your forecast as suggesting that this year's price level will be lower *than it otherwise would be.* When you conclude that this year's price level will be lower than it otherwise would be, you'll often be more accurate if you describe your forecast as likely to lead to *lower inflation,* rather than outright deflation.

Scott Houston/Alamy Stock Photo

Deflation is rare.

33.5 Aggregate Supply in the Short Run and the Long Run

Learning Objective *Distinguish between the immediate effects, short-run effects, and long-run consequences of economic shocks.*

As a forward-looking manager you'll want to be able to forecast where the economy is going not only over the next few weeks and months, but also the ensuing few years, and even in the longer term beyond that. Changes in aggregate demand often have a fairly immediate effect. But because businesses take a while to change the prices they charge and the wages they pay, supply-side responses can take a while to play out. This can really matter because when suppliers have yet to adjust their prices, they often adjust the quantity of their output instead. And so the initial impact of a macroeconomic shock may be quite different than the longer-term effect. That's why our final task in this chapter is to adapt our analysis of the aggregate supply curve so that it can generate useful forecasts over many different time horizons.

We'll begin by analysing two extreme cases: We'll start with the long run, in which all prices have adjusted, and then turn to the opposite extreme of the very short run, in which no prices have adjusted. These two cases will yield useful intuitions that will help us analyse the full set of responses over time.

Aggregate Supply in the Long Run with Flexible Prices

Let's start with the *long run,* which in this context means a period of time long enough that all businesses have had a chance to adjust the prices they charge, to tweak the wages they pay, and to adapt to any price changes from their suppliers, their rivals, and other businesses. Long-run analysis is relevant over time periods long enough for this process of adjustment to be complete—typically several years or longer. Over this time horizon you can think of all prices as responding flexibly to changing conditions.

RichVintage/E+/Getty Images

A long run.

In the long run, a change in the average price level has no effect on real variables. The question that the aggregate supply curve seeks to answer, is: How will suppliers change the quantity of output they'll produce at different average price levels? In the long run, the answer is: Not at all.

That might seem surprising, but a thought experiment might help explain why. Imagine that you go to sleep tonight, and you wake up a decade later to discover that every price in the economy is 10 times higher. This future economy looks just like the present, except every price tag in the economy has grown an extra zero on the end of it. The price of your output is 10 times higher, as is the price charged by each of your competitors. The price of your raw materials is 10 times higher, as is the price of your electricity, and the price of your monthly rent. And because the wage is 10 times higher, your customers also have 10 times as much income. After getting a quick breakfast (a decade is a long time to sleep!), you have to figure out what quantity of goods your factory should produce. Think about it for a while, and you'll realise that this future economy has a lot more zeros in it, but apart from that, nothing has changed. And if nothing has changed, there's no reason

Charles Bowes/EyeEm/Getty Images

Would adding zeros to all these price tags change anything?

for you to change the quantity of output you produce. Indeed, no one will change the physical quantities of the stuff they buy, sell, produce, or do. In the long run, a change in the price level has no effect on the quantity of goods produced.

classical dichotomy A purely nominal change—like a change in the average price level—won't have any effect on real variables in the long run.

This insight reflects an idea called the **classical dichotomy,** and it informs how economists think about the long-run effects of changes in purely nominal variables, like the price level. The *dichotomy* is that what's happening in the real economy—like the quantity of output that businesses produce—can be analysed separately from purely nominal variables like the average price level. And it's *classical* because it comes from the classical economists whose insights best apply to the long run.

Figure 8 | The Long-Run Aggregate Supply Curve

In the long run when all prices are flexible, shifts in aggregate demand affect the price level but not output.

(A) In the long run, the quantity of output supplied is unaffected by the average price level, yielding a **vertical long-run aggregate supply curve**.

(B) (C) In both the equilibrium with **strong aggregate demand** and **weak aggregate demand**, output is the same.

(D) Changes in aggregate demand have **no effect on output**.

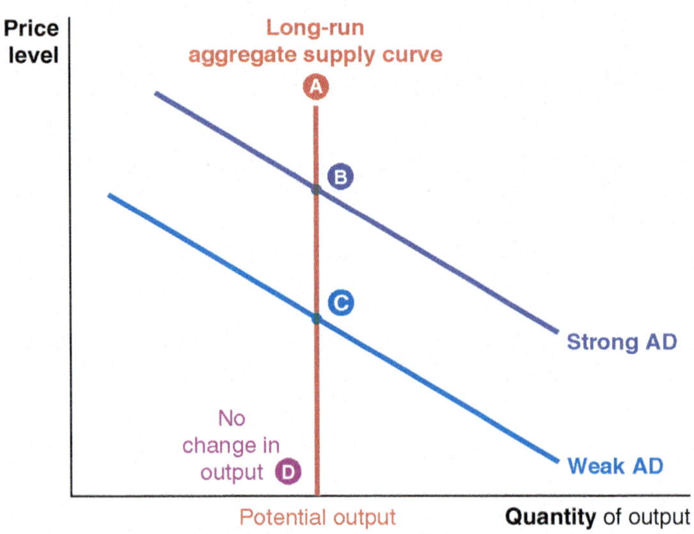

The long-run aggregate supply curve is vertical.

This thought experiment reveals that in the long run, the quantity of output that businesses supply will be the same whether the average price level stays at today's level or rises by a factor of 10. The same logic says that the quantity of output supplied will be the same whether the average price level rises by a lot, a little, or indeed, if it falls. It follows that in the long run, the aggregate supply curve must be vertical, as shown in Figure 8. This vertical **long-run aggregate supply curve** illustrates the idea that over time, the economy will return to producing its potential output—the level of output that's produced when all resources are fully employed. The economy gravitates towards its potential output because market prices adjust to ensure that the demand for labour, capital, and raw materials will be equal to the supply.

Aggregate demand is irrelevant to long-run output. Figure 8 illustrates two alternative scenarios—one in which aggregate demand is weak and another in which it is strong. In both cases, the equilibrium level of output is identical (though the price level differs). This suggests that in the long run, aggregate demand is irrelevant in determining output. This insight is the reason that most economic analyses of the long-run determinants of output—like that we conducted in Chapter 22 on economic growth—focus on supply-side factors such as the quantities of capital, labour, and human capital that are available, and the technology that producers use to combine them.

long-run aggregate supply curve The aggregate supply curve that applies to the long run when prices have fully adjusted. Because the economy will return to producing its potential output, this curve is vertical.

Aggregate Supply in the Very Short Run with Fixed Prices

Now let's turn to the opposite extreme, and consider how the economy responds to an aggregate demand shock in the *very short run*—that is, over a period of time so brief that no business has had a chance to change its price. In the very short run, all prices are effectively fixed, which means that the aggregate supply curve must be horizontal, as shown in Figure 9.

very-short-run aggregate supply curve The aggregate supply curve that applies to the very short run, in which no prices have changed. Because prices are effectively fixed, this curve is horizontal.

The very-short-run aggregate supply curve is horizontal. This **very-short-run aggregate supply curve** illustrates the idea that in the immediate aftermath of an economic shock—before managers are able to adjust their prices—the only way that businesses can respond to changing conditions is to adjust the quantity of output they produce. In this context, the very short run might be a period of several weeks. If aggregate demand suddenly weakens and people feel they can no longer afford to eat out then restaurants will sit empty and their output will decline. And if strong aggregate demand boosts incomes and leads people to eat out more, then restaurants' output will rise sharply as they sell more meals each week. Figure 9 illustrates the economy-wide implications, in which changes in aggregate demand will—in the very short run—lead to large changes in output.

The response of suppliers depends on the time horizon you're analysing. Our analysis so far yields a stark contrast: Shifts in aggregate demand lead to large changes in output in the very short run, but no change in output in the long run. These findings might sound contradictory, but they're not. Both Figure 8 and Figure 9 illustrate the response of the same economy with the same suppliers to the same economic shock, but they're showing effects over different time horizons. The immediate (very-short-run) effect of an increase in aggregate demand is that suppliers produce a lot more output, and in the longer run, that effect dissipates and there's no lasting effect on output.

These different responses over different time horizons arise because in the very short run prices don't adjust at all, leaving the burden of adjustment to quantities, while in the long run prices fully adjust, leaving none of the burden of adjustment to quantities. Let's now explore what happens in between—over the months or years that are relevant to analysing the ups and downs of the business cycle.

Figure 9 | The Very-Short-Run Aggregate Supply Curve

In the very short run when prices are fixed, aggregate demand shifts affect output, but not the price level.

A In the very short run, prices are yet to change and so the **very-short-run aggregate supply curve is horizontal**.
B If **aggregate demand is weak**, output will be low.
C If **aggregate demand is strong**, output will be high.
D Shifts in aggregate demand have a **big effect on output**.

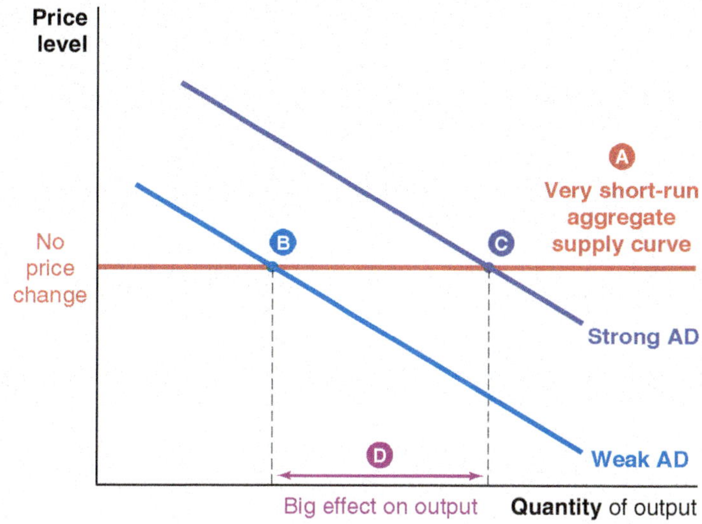

Aggregate Supply in the Short Run and Medium Run with Sticky Prices

If you ask the managers at Hungry Jack's why they don't immediately adjust their prices whenever economic conditions change, they'll tell you that changing prices can be costly, requiring them to reprint their menus, amend their advertising, and risk antagonising customers.

The *cost-benefit principle* says that it's only worth adjusting your prices if the benefits of doing so exceed these *menu costs.* This logic leads Hungry Jack's—like many businesses—to have **sticky prices,** which adjust sporadically and sluggishly to changes in market conditions. Indeed, many businesses—including Hungry Jack's—update their most important prices only once or twice per year. This really matters for assessing how aggregate supply will respond in the *short run,* which in this context means a period of a few months.

sticky prices Prices that adjust sporadically and sluggishly to changes in market conditions.

Sticky prices explain why the short-run aggregate supply curve is upward-sloping. Consider how different restaurants might respond to a few months of insufficient demand. Their restaurants will sit half empty, and because their waitstaff are underworked, their marginal costs will be low. Hungry Jack's executives might consider cutting their prices, but decide not to, figuring it's not worth incurring the cost of reprinting their menus at this time. But a rival like McDonald's might have been about to reprint its menu anyway, and so will take the opportunity to cut its prices. Across the whole economy, some businesses are like McDonald's—ready to change their prices now—while others are like Hungry Jack's, and will decide not to change their prices for now. As the purple arrow in Figure 10 shows, when output is below potential, sporadic price cutting in response to insufficient demand leads to a somewhat lower average price level.

Figure 10 | The Short-Run Aggregate Supply Curve

Some suppliers adjust their prices in the short run.

A In the **very short run**, the **price level is stuck** at its preexisting level.
But as time passes . . .
B If the economy is experiencing **insufficient demand**, some sellers will **cut prices**.
C If the economy is experiencing **excess demand**, some sellers will **raise prices**.
D The result is an upward-sloping **short-run aggregate supply curve**.

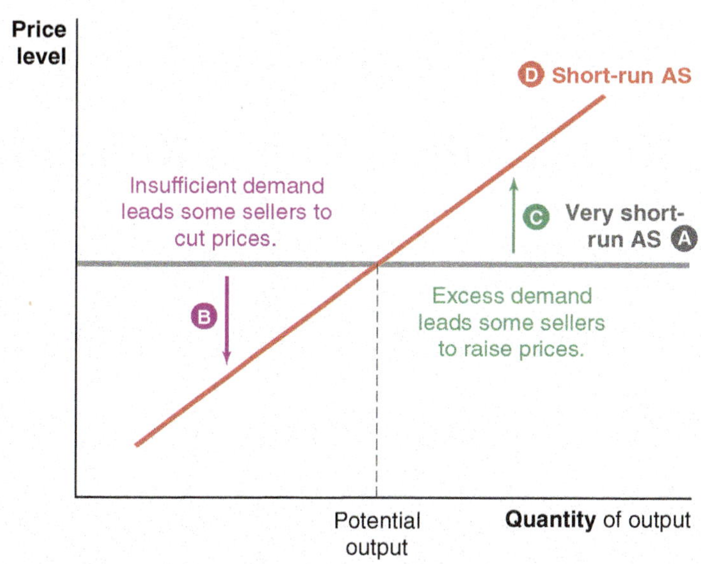

Similar dynamics apply to periods of excess demand, but in reverse: Faced with more customers than they can serve, and

short-run aggregate supply curve The aggregate supply curve that applies over a period when prices are neither fully fixed nor fully flexible. As a result, the short run aggregate supply curve is upward-sloping.

higher marginal costs due to a rising overtime bill, some suppliers will raise their prices, but others will not. As the green arrow in Figure 10 shows, when output exceeds potential, sporadic price rises in response to excess demand will lead to a somewhat higher price level.

As a result of this partial-but-incomplete adjustment of prices, the **short-run aggregate supply curve** is upward-sloping. Indeed, the upward-sloping aggregate supply curve we've analysed throughout this chapter is sometimes called the short-run aggregate supply curve.

Figure 11 | **The Medium-Run Aggregate Supply Curve**

More suppliers adjust their prices in the medium run.

(A) In the **short run**, some suppliers have adjusted their prices in response to the state of demand.

But as time passes . . .

(B) **Insufficient demand** will lead **more** sellers to **cut prices**.

(C) **Excess demand** will lead **more** sellers to **raise prices**.

(D) The result is an even steeper **medium-run aggregate supply curve**.

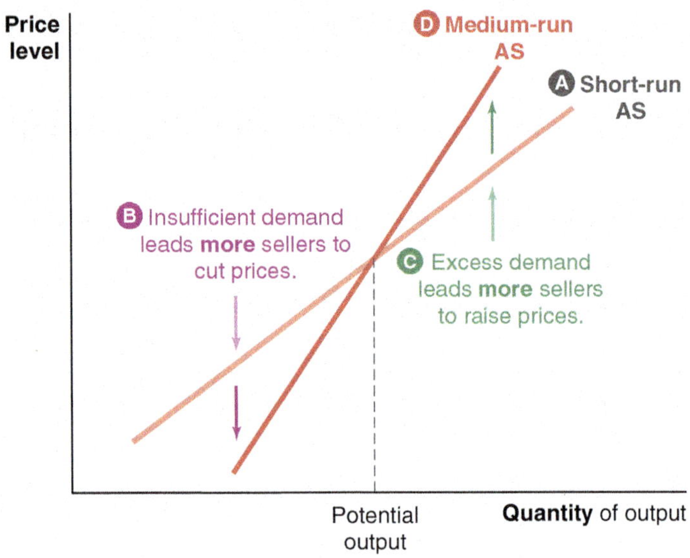

The aggregate supply curve is steeper in the medium run. Let's now fast forward a year or two to see what changes. We'll call this the *medium run*. The passage of time gives many more restaurants the opportunity to reprint their menus and change their prices. Managers are also more likely to think it's worth paying the menu cost to change their prices in response to insufficient or excess demand that persists for a year or two, rather than for just a few months. As a result, in the medium run, prices are less sticky as more sellers adjust their prices to economic conditions.

If output is below potential output, the bold purple arrows in Figure 11 show that these extra sellers cutting their prices will push the average price level down further. Alternatively, if output exceeds potential output, the bold green arrows in Figure 11 show that the extra sellers raising their prices will push the average price level up further. As a result, the medium-run aggregate supply curve is steeper than the short-run aggregate supply curve. More generally, the longer the time horizon you're analysing, the steeper the relevant aggregate supply curve will be.

Getting from the Very Short Run to the Long Run

We now have all the tools we need to map out the effects of an aggregate demand shock *over time*. The slope of the aggregate supply varies, depending on whether you're looking at the shorter- or longer-term response of suppliers. The longer the time period you're analysing, the more time managers have had to adjust their prices. Consequently over longer time periods, price adjustments will bear more of the burden of adjustment, leading to an increasingly vertical aggregate supply curve.

Let's explore what this means for how the economy responds to a decrease in aggregate demand—much like the shift that led to the 2008 downturn. You can forecast the effect of this shift over time, by evaluating this shift relative to the economy's aggregate supply curve in the very short run, short run, medium run, and long run, as follows:

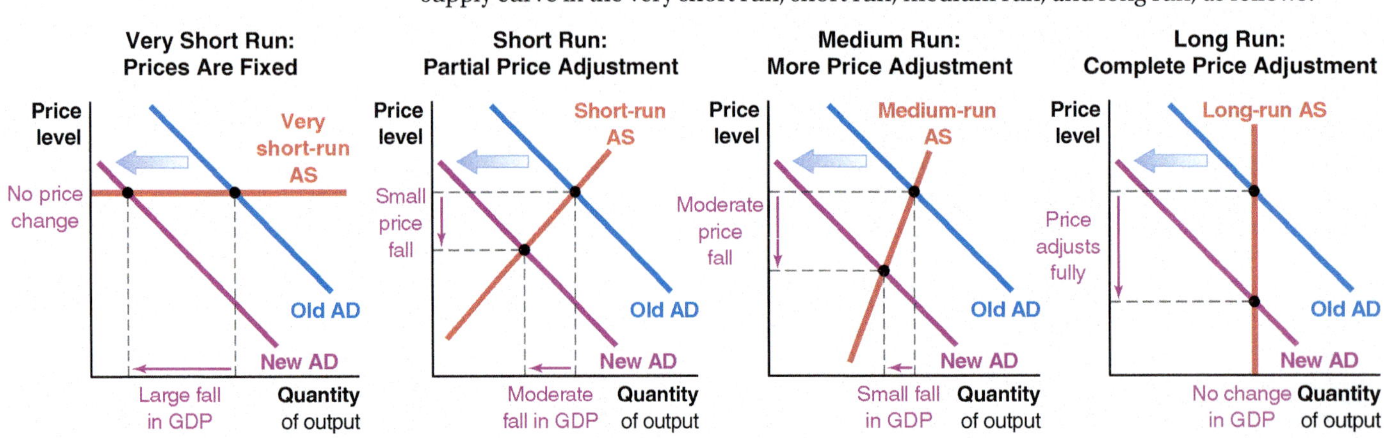

Over the first few weeks hardly any businesses will have had a chance to change their prices, and so our very-short-run analysis is relevant. It suggests the immediate effect will be a recession as output falls sharply. Over the subsequent months, the short-run aggregate supply curve becomes more relevant. It suggests that a few months later the price level will be a bit lower, and the initial decline in output will moderate. In the first year or two following this shock—that is, in the medium run—more businesses will cut their prices, and output will recover somewhat to only be a bit below its pre-recession levels. After a period of several years or more—that is, in the long run—all prices eventually adjust to restore the economy to producing at its potential.

Okay, so how well did our analysis match reality?

Figure 12 shows the path of output following a major shock to aggregate demand. Most analysts argue that an aggregate demand shock happened in the second half of 2008, following the collapse of U.S. investment firm Lehman Brothers. Our very-short-run analysis suggests that this decrease in aggregate expenditure would lead to a large fall in output. And indeed, in the United States real GDP declined by more than 3% in the final two quarters of 2008. In Australia, the huge fiscal stimulus that was enacted by the Rudd government helped the Australian economy weather the crisis far better than the U.S. Output fell, but only for one quarter, before the economy started growing again.

Our analysis also suggests that over the months and years after the aggregate demand shock, price adjustments would bear more of the burden of adjustment, and the red line in Figure 13 shows that the price level fell relative to its previous trend for several years. Consistent with our long-run analysis, which had suggested that the lower price level would persist even after the recession was over, the price level appears to have remained permanently lower as a result of this recession.

It's a testament to the value of our *AD-AS* framework you've just learned that if you had drawn a few aggregate demand and aggregate supply curves back in 2008, you might have been able to predict much of the dramatic economic change, and the policy responses, that ensued.

Figure 12 | Output Growth Slowed, Then Gradually Recovered

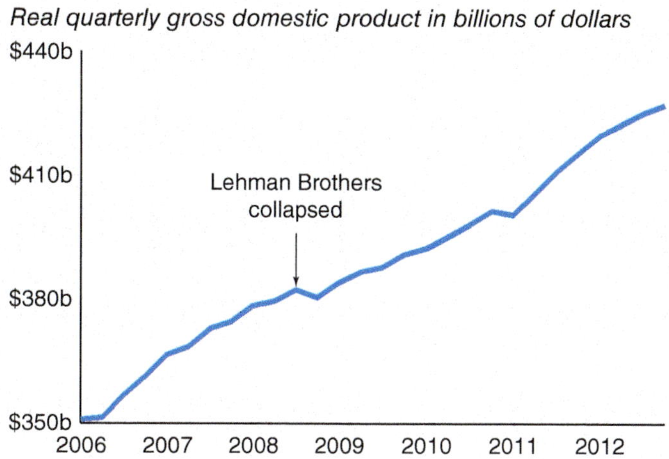

Data from: Australian Bureau of Statistics.

Figure 13 | Prices Slowly Fell, Relative to the Previous Trend

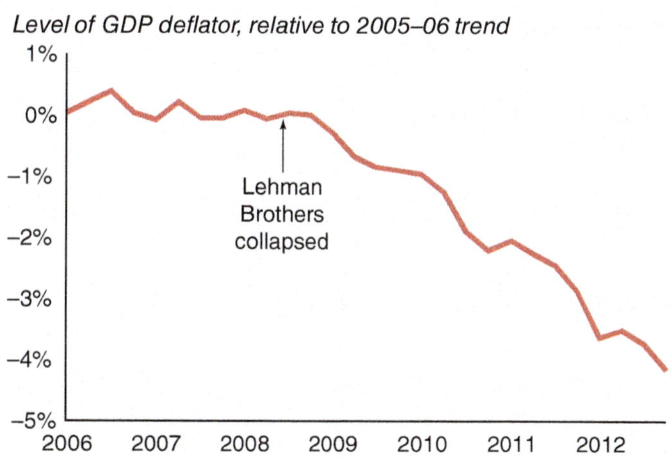

Data from: Australian Bureau of Statistics.

Tying It Together

You now have all the tools you need to join the discussion of one of the most fiercely debated questions in all of macroeconomics: What role should the government play in countering the ups and downs of the business cycle?

One argument—historically associated with the classical economists, and more recently with new-classical economists—says that the economy is self-correcting, and so there's not much reason for the government to get involved. This argument is based on our long-run analysis, which suggests that the aggregate supply curve is vertical. If the economy is going to return to potential output anyway, then it's not worth taking the risk that monetary or fiscal policy will cause other problems.

The counterargument is most closely associated with economist John Maynard Keynes and collaborators, including Joan Robinson, who wrote in the wake of the Great

Depression, the worst economic slump in modern memory. The Depression shook the faith of many economists, leaving them wondering how it was possible for the economy to perform so poorly as to leave millions of people unemployed. This experience led Keynes to argue that either the economy is not self-correcting as the classical economists had supposed, or alternatively that the process of adjustment to the long run is so slow and so costly that long-run analysis is rarely relevant. According to this perspective, monetary and fiscal policy may be the only way to push the economy back towards full employment in a reasonable fashion.

And while this debate began hundreds of years ago, it continues to this day. It's a sure bet that next time the economy goes into a recession some people will argue that the government needs to pass a major stimulus, while others will argue that the government should do nothing because the economy will recover faster on its own. Now that you are equipped to join this debate, what's your view?

Chapter at a Glance

The AD-AS Framework

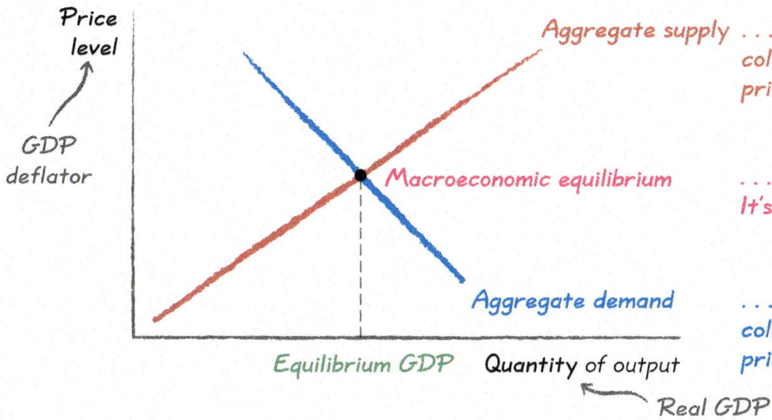

Aggregate supply . . . shows the quantity of output that sellers collectively produce rises as the average price level rises.

Macroeconomic equilibrium . . . where the two curves intersect. It's where the economy is headed.

Aggregate demand . . . shows the quantity of output that buyers collectively plan to purchase falls as the average price level rises.

Forecasting Macroeconomic Outcomes

1. Is there a shift in **aggregate demand** or **aggregate supply**?
2. Is that shift an **increase**, shifting the curve to the right? Or is it a **decrease**, shifting the curve to the left?
3. How will the **price level** and **quantity of output** change in the new equilibrium?

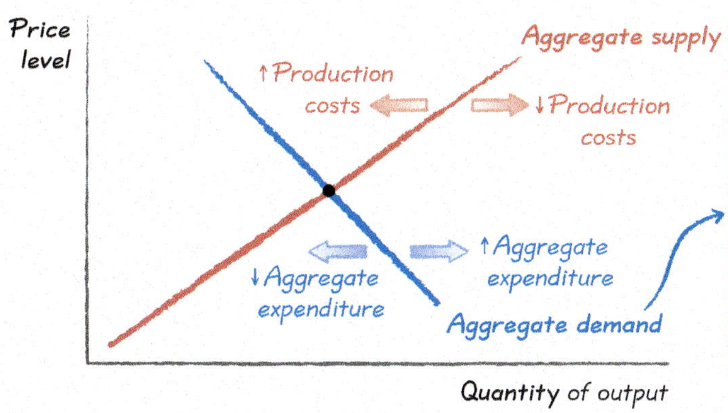

Aggregate supply . . . shifts in response to changes in production costs:
1. Input prices
2. Productivity
3. The exchange rate

Aggregate demand . . . shifts in response to changes in aggregate expenditure:
1. Consumption (C)
2. Planned investment (I)
3. Government purchases (G)
4. Net exports (NX)

Monetary and Fiscal Policy

Expansionary **fiscal** or **monetary policy** shifts the **AD curve** to the right.
The **quantity of output** rises and so does the **price level**.
**An inflation-induced cut in interest rates will not shift aggregate demand. Other interest rate cuts will.*

Multiplier effect: An initial burst of spending will ripple through the economy, leading to an even larger boost to output.

From the Very Short Run to the Long Run

Very Short Run (a few weeks) → Short Run (a few months) → Medium Run (a year or two) → Long Run (several years or more)

Very Short Run (a few weeks)	Short Run (a few months)	Medium Run (a year or two)	Long Run (several years or more)
Prices are fixed	Partial price adjustment	More price adjustment	Complete price adjustment

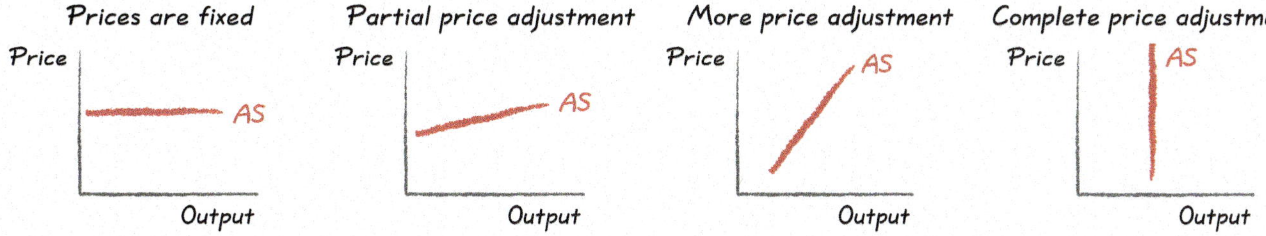

Key Concepts

aggregate demand curve, 838
aggregate expenditure, 840
aggregate supply curve, 838
classical dichotomy, 858
fiscal policy, 853
long-run aggregate supply curve, 858
macroeconomic equilibrium, 839
monetary policy, 852
multiplier, 854
short-run aggregate supply curve, 860
sticky prices, 859
very-short-run aggregate supply curve, 858

Discussion and Review Questions

Learning Objective 33.1 *Understand how aggregate demand and aggregate supply determine macroeconomic equilibrium.*

1. Compare and contrast the microeconomic forces of demand and supply with the macroeconomic forces of aggregate demand and aggregate supply. How do the opportunity costs of buyers in the micro context of a single market (for example, for buyers of petrol) compare to the opportunity costs of all buyers in the macro context of aggregate demand?

Learning Objective 33.2 *Evaluate the forces that shape the total quantity of goods and services that purchasers want to buy.*

2. Explain how the Reserve Bank plays a central role in determining the slope of the aggregate demand curve. For example, if a lower price level leads inflation to be below the RBA's target band, how will the RBA likely react and how will its actions eventually impact the quantity of goods and services people want to buy?
3. What changes to the economy will lead the aggregate demand curve to shift? What changes will lead to a movement along the aggregate demand curve? Provide a few examples to illustrate your answer.

Learning Objective 33.3 *Evaluate the forces that shape the total quantity of goods and services that businesses want to supply.*

4. How do businesses change their prices at different levels of output, and how does this lead to an upward-sloping aggregate supply curve?
5. What changes to the economy will lead the aggregate supply curve to shift? What changes will lead to a movement along the aggregate supply curve? Provide a few examples to illustrate your answer.

Learning Objective 33.4 *Forecast how the economy will respond to changing conditions.*

6. Explain how—depending on the circumstances—the RBA changing the real interest rate can lead either to a movement along the aggregate demand curve or to a shift of the aggregate demand curve. Be sure to consider the two types of responses from the RBA.
7. Illustrate in separate *AD-AS* graphs how the macroeconomic equilibrium will change when the Reserve Bank pursues an expansionary monetary policy and when it pursues a contractionary monetary policy. What macroeconomic problems might an expansionary monetary policy solve? What about a contractionary monetary policy?
8. Explain how an initial increase in government purchases can increase GDP by a greater amount than the increase in government spending.
9. Think of at least one example of a change to the economy that will lead to the following outcomes and illustrate your answers with an *AD-AS* graph.
   a. GDP increases and the price level increases.
   b. GDP increases and the price level decreases.
   c. GDP decreases and the price level decreases.
   d. GDP decreases and the price level increases.

Learning Objective 33.5 *Distinguish between the immediate effects, short-run effects, and long-run consequences of economic shocks.*

10. Explain why, in the long run, a change in prices has no impact on output. What impact does aggregate demand have in determining output in the long run?
11. One common argument against expansionary fiscal or monetary policy goes like this, "Since the economy returns to potential output in the long run, we should not react to the short-term fluctuations in the economy. If we do nothing, the economy will fix itself." Formulate a counter-argument. Which argument do you agree with and why?
12. Why does aggregate supply analysis require looking at specific time horizons to predict macroeconomic outcomes?

Study Problems

Learning Objective 33.1 *Understand how aggregate demand and aggregate supply determine macroeconomic equilibrium.*

1. Draw aggregate demand and aggregate supply curves where macroeconomic equilibrium occurs at an output

of $17 trillion. On your graph, indicate the equilibrium price level, but don't worry about assigning it an exact value. Indicate on the graph where macroeconomic equilibrium occurs. Make sure to label each part of the graph.

Learning Objective 33.2 *Evaluate the forces that shape the total quantity of goods and services that purchasers want to buy.*

2. For each of the following, use a graph to show the shift in aggregate demand.
   - **a.** Poor numbers from several leading economic indicators cause businesses to become pessimistic about the future of the economy.
   - **b.** The latest budget released by Treasury increases government purchases by 3%.
   - **c.** Housing prices have been declining in recent years, leading homeowners to feel less prosperous.
   - **d.** The Chinese government eliminates the tariffs it charges on goods exported from Australia.
   - **e.** Banks become complacent and begin taking on riskier business loans at lower interest rates.
   - **f.** A rise in the price level leads the RBA to increase the real interest rate.

Learning Objective 33.3 *Evaluate the forces that shape the total quantity of goods and services that businesses want to supply.*

3. Illustrate how each of the following will impact aggregate supply and explain your reasoning.
   - **a.** The implementation of artificial intelligence in manufacturing has led to faster than expected productivity growth.
   - **b.** Low levels of output across the entire economy leave many businesses with excess capacity, leading them to lower their prices by 3%.
   - **c.** The Fair Work Commission raises the minimum wage by 5%.
   - **d.** The Australian dollar depreciates relative to the Chinese yuan.

Learning Objective 33.4 *Forecast how the economy will respond to changing conditions.*

4. To combat a recession, the Indian government enacts expansionary fiscal policy, which increases government spending by 2 trillion rupees. In response, GDP increases by 6 trillion rupees.
   - **a.** What is the multiplier?
   - **b.** Illustrate the impact of this expansionary fiscal policy on the Indian economy using an *AD-AS* graph.
   - **c.** How will the price level change?
5. For each of the following, forecast how prices and output will change by drawing an *AD-AS* graph, and explain your answers using the three-step recipe to forecast macroeconomic outcomes.
   - **a.** The RBA decreases interest rates amid concerns of a looming recession.
   - **b.** The latest data on consumer confidence indicate that consumers have become pessimistic about the future of the economy and are therefore spending less.
   - **c.** Innovations in solar cell technology cause energy prices to decline across the country.
   - **d.** The federal government passes a new bill that dramatically increases government spending on education and the military.
   - **e.** The Japanese government eliminates the tariffs it charges on goods exported from Australia.
   - **f.** Top executives report that they're quite uncertain about the future, as trade deals with the country's largest trading partners are being renegotiated and remain in flux.
   - **g.** Automation by the largest shipping and transportation companies has significantly decreased the transportation costs for businesses across the country.

Learning Objective 33.5 *Distinguish between the immediate effects, short-run effects, and long-run consequences of economic shocks.*

6. In an effort to boost output, the government passes a large fiscal stimulus that raises government spending by $100 billion. Use the *AD-AS* framework to predict how prices and output change in the very short run, in the short run, in the medium run, and in the long run.
7. For each of the following scenarios predict how the price level and output will change over time from immediate impact to long-run impact. In each case, consider an economy that was initially producing at its level of potential output.
   - **a.** The government passes legislation that increases corporate taxes by 25%.
   - **b.** Economies around the globe are experiencing a time of prosperity and, as a result, demand for Australian exports increases.

PART IX:

Macroeconomic Policy

Part IX: Macroeconomic Policy

The Big Picture

Everything you've learned so far comes together in our final two chapters, where we'll explore how the government uses its policy tools to try to manage the economy. You'll learn to make sense of the economic news you hear during your daily commute: What's happening with interest rates? Can policy makers prevent a looming recession? Should you worry about government debt? Along the way we'll learn how to interpret the promises that politicians make when trying to court your vote.

Our tour begins when we step inside a **Reserve Bank** meeting to learn how it sets **monetary policy.** We'll explore the RBA's goals, its targets, and the tools it uses to keep the economy and financial system running smoothly. Along the way, we'll discuss how you should respond to monetary policy when managing your business and personal finances.

Next, we'll take a look at how the government shapes economic outcomes through its **spending and taxing decisions.** We'll uncover what the government spends money on and where it gets the money. Then we'll consider how it can use **fiscal policy** to smooth out business cycles. Finally, we'll take a long hard look at **government deficits and debt,** and what they mean for you now, and for the economy in the long run.

34 Monetary Policy

Understand how the Reserve Bank makes and implements monetary policy.

- What happens behind closed doors at a Reserve Bank meeting?
- How do the RBA's decisions affect you?
- Can you predict what the RBA will do next?
- Why does the RBA target inflation when it also cares about unemployment?
- How does the RBA implement monetary policy?
- What can the RBA do when it can't lower the interest rate any further?

35 Government Spending, Taxes, and Fiscal Policy

Learn about government spending, revenue, and debt.

- What does the government spend money on (and where does it get the money)?
- What do federal, state, and local governments do?
- What is fiscal policy and how can it help smooth business cycles?
- Why do governments run deficits?
- Should you worry about growing government debt?

CHAPTER

34

Monetary Policy

One of the most important meetings in Australia happens every month in Sydney. No, it's not at Kirribilli House. In fact, the Prime Minister isn't even involved. The meeting happens at the headquarters of the Reserve Bank of Australia—our nation's central bank, called the RBA for short. The attendees are the members of the Reserve Bank Board.

Simon Dawson/Bloomberg/Getty Images

Reserve Bank board member Carolyn Hewson participates in meetings that have big implications for the Australian economy.

The Reserve Bank is run by the Governor, who is appointed to a seven-year term. When the RBA acts to raise interest rates it sets off a chain of events—borrowing becomes more expensive, which encourages consumers to save today instead of spending and discourages businesses from investing. Higher Australian interest rates usually also raise the value of the Australian dollar, which makes Australian exports more expensive and imports to Australia cheaper. All of these changes mean that business decisions all over the country, and also with our trading partners, respond to the RBA's decisions. For you, it can mean higher interest rates on your credit cards, or the mortgage you might be hoping to get one day.

The RBA raises (or lowers) interest rates for a reason. You've already learned how interest rates affect spending and hence output and unemployment, which filters through to affect prices and inflation. The RBA adjusts interest rates to keep inflation stable and unemployment low. So while you'll pay more in interest when the RBA raises interest rates, its actions mean that prices won't rise as much as they otherwise would.

In this chapter, we'll dig into how the RBA actually operates—from making decisions to implementing them. You'll also learn about the current policy issues surrounding how the RBA should make decisions and the tools it should use. The financial crisis of 2008 led central banks around the world to implement new policy tools. We'll take a look at some of those tools in the last section of this chapter. Let's get started!

Chapter Objective

Understand how the Reserve Bank makes and implements monetary policy.

34.1 The Reserve Bank
Learn how the Reserve Bank makes monetary policy decisions.

34.2 The RBA's Policy Goals and Decision-Making Frameworks
Discover how the Reserve Bank assesses its goals and makes interest rate choices.

34.3 How the RBA Sets Interest Rates
Understand how the Reserve Bank implements monetary policy decisions.

34.4 Unconventional Monetary Policy
Learn about the tools the Reserve Bank uses to set monetary policy when nominal interest rates are zero.

34.1 The Reserve Bank

Learning Objective *Learn how the Reserve Bank makes monetary policy decisions.*

monetary policy The process of setting interest rates in an effort to influence economic conditions.

Central banks determine a country's **monetary policy,** which is the process of setting interest rates in an effort to influence economic conditions. In Australia, the Reserve Bank is our central bank. It was created by Parliament, which gave it instructions "to ensure that the monetary and banking policy of the Bank is directed to the greatest advantage of the people of Australia and that the powers of the Bank ... are exercised in such a manner as, in the opinion of the Reserve Bank Board, will best contribute to: a. the stability of the currency of Australia; b. the maintenance of full employment in Australia; and c. the economic prosperity and welfare of the people of Australia." The RBA interprets this to mean it should try to smooth business cycles—so that it keeps unemployment as low as is sustainable, while also keeping inflation low and stable.

GREG WOOD/AFP/Getty Images

The Reserve Bank's headquarters in Martin Place, Sydney.

The RBA can't change inflation, output, or unemployment directly. Instead, it uses interest rates as a tool to influence the economy. Interest rates determine the *opportunity cost* of spending money today. For borrowers, higher interest rates mean a higher cost of credit. For savers, higher interest rates mean forgoing more interest in order to spend money today. Thus, the RBA uses the interest rate to nudge people and businesses to spend more or less today, which in turn affects output, unemployment, and inflation. It's a task made more difficult by the imprecision of data and the difficulty of forecasting the future.

In practice, this means the RBA balances risks: The risk of setting a too-high interest rate that leads the economy to produce at a level below potential, versus the risk of setting a too-low interest rate that causes output to exceed the economy's potential output thereby sparking inflation. The RBA is basically focused on keeping unemployment low, and inflation within a target band of 2–3%. The maximum sustainable level of employment occurs when the economy's output is equal to its potential output, so the RBA will need to pay a lot of attention to GDP even though output is not in its formal mandate.

Let's explore the structure of the Reserve Bank and the process by which the RBA gathers information, weighs the risks, makes decisions, and then communicates its analysis and decisions to the public.

The Reserve Bank

The Reserve Bank was originally part of the Commonwealth Bank, which you now know as a private commercial bank. It used to be a government-owned bank that also functioned as Australia's central bank. In 1959, with the Reserve Bank Act, these two functions were separated. The Reserve Bank conducts monetary policy, is responsible for maintaining a strong financial system, issues the nation's currency, and manages Australia's gold and foreign exchange reserves. It also provides banking and registry services to various Australian government agencies and to a number of overseas central banks.

Mark Graham/Bloomberg/Getty Images

RBA Deputy Governor Michelle Bullock appears before the House of Representatives Economic Committee.

The Board of the Reserve Bank consists of the Governor (who acts as Chair), the Deputy Governor, Secretary to the Australian Treasury, and six external members who are appointed to five-year terms.

Central bank independence is important for macroeconomic stability. The Reserve Bank of Australia is an independent government agency. It's independent for a reason—to free it from short-term political pressures. A problem with political pressure is that policy makers can achieve temporarily higher output by overheating the economy, which might unleash future inflation. But this short-run choice to allow higher inflation will eventually lead to higher inflation expectations, which causes higher inflation that persists long after the temporary blip in output dissipates. As a result, in the long run output isn't any higher, but inflation is. The problem is that politicians often think too much about the short run—the next election—and may overweigh the benefit of a short-run output boost relative to its long-run inflationary cost. For example, then Treasurer Paul Keating (in)famously boasted in 1989 that "they do what I say." The next year he said he had the RBA "in his pocket."

Research shows that countries that give their central banks more independence have lower inflation rates on average. That means that if you reduce independence, you should expect higher inflation. And, as you learned in Chapter 24, higher inflation is costly.

There is a lot of government oversight of the RBA. Just because the RBA is independent, you shouldn't think that there isn't government oversight. The Governor and the Board are selected by Federal Cabinet. Within limits, this basically means that the Federal Treasurer appoints the entire board—and even has the head of the Department of Treasury as a standing member of the board.

The RBA board members are chosen for their specific perspectives or areas of expertise, all of which shape their assessments. For instance, one former board member Roger Corbett was CEO of supermarket chain Woolworths, and current board member Wendy Craik is chair of the CSIRO Oceans and Atmosphere Advisory Board.

Since the mid 1990s, the Governor and senior RBA officials have appeared twice a year before the House of Representatives Standing Committee on Economics. Often they are asked some penetrating questions. The Governor gives many speeches and the RBA releases minutes of their board meetings as well as making numerous press releases. The RBA "provides public access to records 20 years from the date of their creation, in accordance with the Archives Act 1983." Usually they do this voluntarily with 15 years.

The Reserve Bank Board

The **Reserve Bank Board** is responsible for the general oversight on the RBA, but a key purpose is to decide on Australian official interest rates. The RBA Governor chairs the board and is the most important spokesperson for the RBA. The board meetings that take place eleven times a year, and the decisions they make about interest rates—and monetary policy more generally—are hugely influential. So let's take a look inside.

Reserve Bank Board The body that decides on Australian interest rates. It consists of the Governor, Deputy Governor, Treasury Secretary, and six external members.

Step into the meeting. When you walk into an RBA board meeting, you'll see a big table with the members seated around it, and some other RBA staff members in attendance (but not voting). The RBA Governor sits in the middle and decides who's going to speak and in what order. These decisions sound minor, but they can have a bigger impact on outcomes than you might expect. At the U.S. Federal Reserve (the U.S. central bank) Former chair Alan Greenspan used to tell everyone what he thought the right monetary policy decision was first, making it awkward for other members to discuss alternatives. That's been known to happen on the RBA board as well!

So now that you know who's at the meeting, let's turn to what they talk about. To decide monetary policy, each member must be prepared to answer three questions:

1. What are your forecasts for the Australian economy?
2. What are the right policy choices given the economic outlook?
3. How should the RBA communicate its plans effectively to the public?

Each member prepares their answers to these questions in advance, and they'll often arrive at the meeting with quite different views. The meeting is a time for them to discuss their answers to these three questions, develop a consensus view, and make a decision. Let's see how.

RBA board members prepare answers to three questions:

1. What are your forecasts for the Australian economy?
2. What are the right policy choices given the economic outlook?
3. How should the RBA communicate its plans effectively to the public?

Question one: What are your forecasts for the Australian economy? The board chair asks everyone to share their views on current economic conditions and their short- and medium-term forecasts for the economy. Each member brings different information, perspectives, and backgrounds. The six external members don't have expert economists on their staff so they bring perspectives from industry. The RBA also has a "business liaison program." The program has about 15 economists who "hold regular discussions with external contacts...across a broad cross-section of the business community, and there are currently around 1000 active contacts across the country" according to the RBA. Each participant brings unique knowledge about the various factors that influence the Australian economy, from conditions in other countries to stability in the financial sector. The RBA tracks literally thousands of variables, each of which provides clues about the future path of inflation and unemployment. People arrive at the meeting with different forecasts reflecting their unique knowledge, different readings of noisy data, and what they expect to happen if their preferred monetary policy decision is implemented.

Interpreting the DATA How good are the RBA's forecasts?

Let's take a look at some of the forecasts that the RBA has made recently. Figure 1 shows their forecasts of economic growth, unemployment, and inflation in each of the next few years. These forecasts were prepared in August 2022.

Figure 1 | RBA Forecasts

	Forecasts released August 2022		
RBA forecasts for:	**December 2022**	**December 2023**	**December 2024**
Change in real GDP	3.2%	1.8%	1.7%
Unemployment rate	3.4%	3.5%	4.0%
Inflation rate (trimmed mean)	6.0%	3.8%	3.0%

Data from: Reserve Bank of Australia.

Notice that the RBA produces forecasts for the next three years. That's because it wants to identify and counter economic problems before they emerge. If the RBA forecasts trouble in a year or two, then it wants to take action today.

Even the most careful forecasts are often wrong, so if you want to find out if these RBA forecasts were right, use the RBA website to look up what economic growth, the unemployment rate, and the inflation rate really were in each of these years: www.rba.gov.au/statistics. ■

Question two: What are the right policy choices given the economic outlook? Once the board has debated projections for the economy, it's time to turn the discussion to what they should do about it. The board's primary tool is to influence the real interest rate. Recall that the real interest rate is the opportunity cost of spending and it tells you how much more you'll be able to buy if you spend your money next year, instead of this year. Similarly, businesses care about the real interest rate, since it represents the opportunity cost of making an investment. That's why the real interest rate is effectively the price that determines this year's aggregate expenditure.

The board will raise the real interest rate when it wants to induce people to spend less today and save more for later. It'll do this because reducing spending today reduces output, which lowers inflationary pressure. And the board will lower the real interest rate when it wants to stimulate greater spending, which will lead to higher output and higher employment. In the long run, stable inflation and maximum sustainable employment are both achieved when output is equal to potential output.

When recessions hit, the board has to determine whether to lower interest rates, and by how much. This isn't a decision that happens in just one meeting. Rather, it's an ongoing process in which the board constantly assesses (and re-assesses) whether it has taken sufficient action and should keep interest rates where they are, or whether even lower rates are warranted. Similarly, as the economy recovers, the board will gradually return interest rates to normal, attempting to steer the economy back to maximum employment without unduly risking higher inflation. So discussion at most meetings focuses on where the economy appears to be relative to where it was at the previous meeting, and assessing outcomes of the decisions that were made in previous meetings. Had they raised rates enough? Not enough? Too fast or too slow?

Once the members have debated the options and assessed the risks associated with each possible action, the governor typically recommends a course of action, and the board votes on it.

Question three: How should the RBA communicate effectively to the public? Market participants like bond traders hang on every word that comes out of the Reserve Bank. If they can figure out a little better than others what the RBA is going to do on interest rates, they could make tens of millions of dollars. The RBA knows that what they say can move markets, but do they want to be clear in their communication, or be somewhat vague?

So what should the central bank say? There's a term used to describe how central bankers tend to talk which gets it's name from the U.S. Federal Reserve (or "Fed"): *Fedspeak*. It's a communication style that relies on intentionally vague and bureaucratic language. The idea is that it's hard for central bankers to communicate what they know credibly. Why? Suppose a central banker says something that is both credible and precise. Markets will believe it and know what it means for future policies. But this very fact gives the central bank a reason to lie, to move markets in ways consistent with its goals. Identifying this "time-consistency problem" helped Finn Kydland and Edward Prescott win the 2004 Nobel Prize in economics. The tension often leads to central bankers being almost comically vague. Alan Greenspan, the U.S. Federal Reserve chair from 1987 to 2006, made this into an art.

Rick Rycroft/AP Photo

Philip Lowe: "This means that probabilities have shifted and the decision to adjust the approach to the yield target reflects this shift in probabilities."

Over the past few decades, the U.S. Federal Reserve (the Fed) has changed its communication policy to move away from Fedspeak and to aim for much greater transparency. Today, the Fed strives to clearly communicate its analysis, decisions, and objectives. This transparency is crucial for accountability. If you disagree with the Fed's policy decisions, you can pinpoint exactly what you are disagreeing with, if you understand why it made those choices.

The RBA hasn't embraced the Fed's approach—at least not fully. The Fed chair holds a press conference after each meeting, but the RBA governor doesn't. The Fed publishes the forecasts of the official interest rate three years into the future by each of it's board members in what it calls the "dot plot." The RBA doesn't do that. The Fed announces how each member voted, but the RBA doesn't.

Susan Walsh/AP Photo

Former U.S. Federal Reserve Chair Janet Yellen: "We've made a commitment . . . that we would do our best to communicate as clearly as we could."

But RBA officials do give regular speeches and try to influence expectations about the path of the economy. The RBA wants to convince people that it will follow through and achieve its goals. Businesses will be more likely to hire if they believe the RBA will deliver a strong economy, and they're more likely to restrain their price increases if they believe the RBA will meet its goal of price stability. Expectations are an important factor shaping economic decisions, and the RBA is trying to shape those expectations. If the RBA can convince people to expect maximum employment and stable prices, then those outcomes become more likely.

34.2 The RBA's Policy Goals and Decision-Making Framework

Learning Objective *Discover how the Reserve Bank assesses its goals and makes interest rate choices.*

You've now learned what happens during the RBA board meeting, so let's dig into how the RBA assesses its goals and determines its policy choices. The RBA's two main goals are stable prices and maximum sustainable employment. Let's start with the RBA's goals and then turn to its policy options.

The RBA's Goals: Stable Prices and Maximum Sustainable Employment

inflation target A publicly stated goal for the inflation rate.

Central bankers consider prices to be stable when the inflation rate is low and predictable enough that it doesn't play much of a role in people's decisions. If inflation is low enough not to influence or distort people's choices, it has few costs. Low and stable inflation has a precise meaning for the RBA—it means that inflation is close to its **inflation target,** a publicly stated goal for the inflation rate. Let's now turn to analysing this inflation target.

Price stability means inflation that is within the RBA's inflation target band. The RBA has an inflation target of 2–3%. In the early 1990s, RBA board members had agreed somewhat informally to aim for an inflation rate of around 2–3%. But they didn't announce a formal inflation target until 1993, when the RBA changed to an explicit target. Since then the RBA has explicitly stated that:

> *The Governor and the Treasurer have agreed that the appropriate target for monetary policy in Australia is to achieve an inflation rate of 2–3 per cent, on average, over time. This is a rate of inflation sufficiently low that it does not materially distort economic decisions in the community. Seeking to achieve this rate, on average, provides discipline for monetary policy decision-making, and serves as an anchor for private-sector inflation expectations.*

By setting an inflation target and telling the public what it is, the RBA hopes to convince price-setters that inflation will be stable at its announced low rate. It's trying to set in motion a virtuous cycle: If people believe that inflation will be low and stable, then price increases will be small, ensuring that inflation in fact remains low and stable. Thus, the more credible the RBA's commitment to low and stable inflation, the easier it will be to achieve.

Interpreting the DATA — Has the RBA succeeded in meeting its inflation target?

Take a look at actual inflation compared to the RBA's target band of 2–3% in Figure 2. Do you think that the RBA has succeeded in ensuring that inflation did not run persistently above or below its target of 2–3%?

The graph makes it clear that monetary policy isn't an exact science. When the RBA sets the interest rate to try to achieve 2–3% inflation, actual inflation may turn out to be a bit higher or a bit lower.

Critics have argued that the RBA doesn't worry enough about missing the target on the low side. The problem, as they see it, is that between 2015 and 2019 the RBA could have been more aggressive in boosting output and employment—which were below their maximum sustainable level—and that it would have improved their credibility by getting inflation back above 2%.

Other commentators worry more about high inflation than low inflation and argue that by keeping rates too low for too long during 2021, the RBA sowed the seeds of high inflation in 2022.

What do you think? ■

Figure 2 | **Has the RBA Succeeded in Hitting Its Inflation Target?**

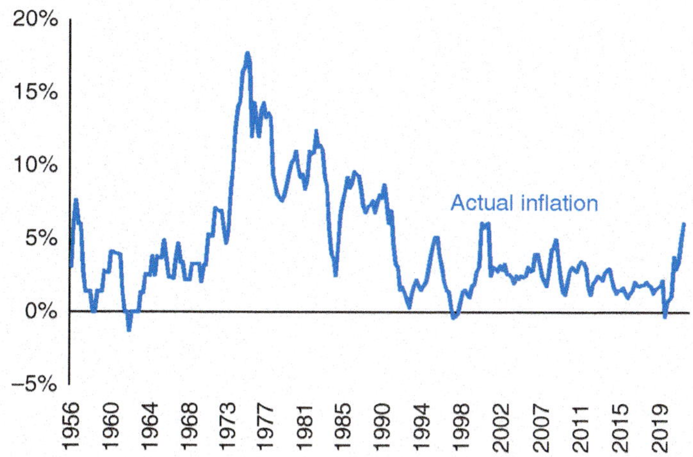

Data from: ABS and RBA.

Hitting the inflation target promotes maximum sustainable employment. You might be wondering: Why is the RBA targeting inflation instead of targeting employment? After all, it's aiming at two things: inflation and employment.

There are two answers to this question. The first is that the inflation rate over the long run is primarily determined by monetary policy, and so it's easily targeted by monetary policy. By contrast, maximum sustainable employment is the amount of employment that occurs when the economy is operating at potential. But employment can change as people decide to work more or less for reasons that have nothing to do with monetary policy (for example, retirement), or based on structural changes in the economy. That's why the RBA pays more attention to the unemployment rate than to total employment. But even the unemployment rate is influenced by factors unrelated to monetary policy. Frictional unemployment is determined by the time it takes for workers and employers to find each other, while structural unemployment is determined by structural barriers in the labour market such as minimum wage laws, unions, labour market regulations, and employers' desire to pay efficiency wages. These factors can change, and when they do, the equilibrium unemployment rate will change. Thus, an RBA target for the unemployment rate would need to change as those factors change. In contrast, many countries target low inflation and it's likely to be the inflation target in Australian for the medium to long term.

The second reason that the RBA targets inflation instead of unemployment is due to the *interdependence principle*: Inflation and unemployment are interdependent. Keeping inflation low and stable at its target also requires keeping the unemployment rate near its lowest sustainable level. When unemployment is higher than this, the economy is operating with excess capacity, leading the inflation rate to decline below the RBA's target. And if unemployment is lower than this, capacity constraints will lead inflation to rise above the RBA's target band. So targeting low and stable inflation is consistent with targeting the lowest sustainable unemployment rate. Alternatively phrased, there is no long-run trade-off between price stability and employment stability. That's not to say that the RBA can ignore the unemployment rate when targeting inflation. The RBA needs to look at all of the data available, including the unemployment rate, because each piece of data helps paint the overall picture of the state of the economy.

Why not target zero inflation? If the RBA's goal is price stability, why doesn't it aim for 0% inflation? There are four reasons not to aim for zero:

> Why the RBA doesn't target zero inflation:
> 1. Inflation greases the wheels of the labour market.
> 2. The RBA can lower real interest rates by more when inflation is above zero.
> 3. A 0% inflation target runs the risk of deflation.
> 4. Measured inflation may be overstated.

Reason one: Inflation greases the wheels of the labour market. Employers often find it difficult to cut nominal wages, even when real wage cuts are needed to save jobs. But with 2% inflation, they can do it quietly, because failing to give someone a nominal raise this year effectively cuts their real wages by 2%. If inflation were 0%, they would have to cut nominal wages by 2% in order to achieve the same real wage cut. In theory, these are the same. In practice, workers dislike nominal wage cuts much more than they dislike real wage cuts achieved through inflation. And so in order to avoid creating friction with their workers, many employers are reluctant to cut their nominal wages. This means that if inflation is zero, they'll rarely cut real wages—even during a recession. You might be thinking: That sounds great! But recessions cause a decrease in labour demand, and when employers can't cut real wages, they lay off more workers than they otherwise would. This suggests that a 0% inflation target will lead unemployment to rise more during recessions.

zero lower bound The constraint that nominal interest rates cannot be effectively set below zero.

Reason two: The RBA can lower real interest rates by more when inflation is above zero. The RBA faces an important constraint: It effectively can't set nominal interest rates below zero. Economists refer to this as the **zero lower bound.** If the RBA set a negative nominal interest rate, then savers would have to pay to keep their money in the bank. So a –1% interest rate would mean that if you put $100 in the bank, a year later you'd have $99. Why do that when you can put the money in a safe and still have $100 at the end of the year? That's why pushing the nominal interest rate below 0% doesn't actually do much—people can earn 0% by avoiding banks altogether.

This zero lower bound on the nominal interest rate constrains how low the RBA can set the real interest rate (which is what really matters). For instance, if inflation is 2%, then setting the nominal interest rate at the zero lower bound results in a real interest rate of –2%. But if inflation were 0%, this would be impossible, and the lowest the RBA could set the real interest rate would be 0%. In the last U.S. recession, the Federal Reserve was unable to cut rates as much as was needed to fight the recession. You can see this from the fact that the nominal interest rate stayed at close to 0% for seven years. If not for this constraint, the Fed would likely have set a lower interest rate, which would have provided a bigger economic boost.

deflation A generalised decrease in the overall level of prices.

Reason three: A 0% inflation rate target runs the risk of deflation. You've seen that the RBA undershot its target band of 2–3% inflation from 2015 to 2021. If it set a 0% target, it would risk inflation sometimes being below 0%. **Deflation** occurs when prices are falling on average, so that the inflation rate is negative. Deflation sounds great—things are getting cheaper! But it can cause problems because falling prices lead people to delay spending today, in favour of buying stuff in the future when prices are even lower. This decrease in aggregate expenditure will reduce output, which leads prices to fall further, setting off a vicious cycle of deflation, reducing spending, which creates yet more deflation. Worse, this cycle of deflation might lead the inflation rate to become more negative, which raises the real interest rate (which is the nominal interest rate less this negative inflation rate), which further depresses spending.

Reason four: Measured inflation may be overstated. Many economists believe that the measured inflation rate overstates the actual inflation rate. As we discussed in Chapter 24, this occurs because the measured inflation rate fails to account for reductions in the cost of living due to unmeasured quality improvements and the introduction of new products. Consequently, a measured inflation rate of zero may actually mean deflation. While the RBA targets a measure of inflation that adjusts for substitution bias, there's still likely upward bias in the measure of inflation it uses. Some estimates of these biases suggest that if the RBA were to target measured inflation of 0%, it would actually be delivering an actual inflation rate of around –1%, a mild deflation.

Not all economists agree on the optimal inflation target. Some point out that even low inflation erodes the value of a dollar and has costs, and they'd prefer the inflation rate to be zero. Others have argued for a slightly higher target, such as 3–4%, to create more room for the RBA to cut rates to counter recessions before hitting the zero lower bound. Regardless of this disagreement about the exact target, most economists agree that the RBA should aim to keep inflation low and stable near a publicly announced target rate. This agreement reflects a belief that *inflation targeting* will help the RBA keep inflation low, and also keep employment close to its highest sustainable level.

How the RBA Chooses the Interest Rate

Let's take stock. You know that the RBA is trying to keep inflation at 2–3%. You also know that the RBA examines lots of data to come up with forecasts for inflation, unemployment, and economic growth. Finally, you know that the RBA lowers the real interest rate when inflation is too low and unemployment is too high. It also raises interest rates when inflation is too high and unemployment is unsustainably low. Because inflation and unemployment are linked to output, the RBA looks for evidence of gaps between expected future output and potential output, and gaps between the current or forecasted inflation rate and its inflation target. In response to such gaps, the RBA can either lower or raise interest rates to try to steer the economy back to its inflation target and potential output.

Let's take a look at the four factors that shape the RBA's policy choices.

Factor one: The RBA starts with the neutral real interest rate. The **neutral real interest rate** is the real interest rate that operates when the economy is in neutral—producing neither above nor below its potential. The neutral real interest rate is important because it tells policy makers what real interest rate will ensure both that the economy doesn't underperform its potential, and that it won't overheat from running ahead of its capacity. Setting the real interest rate higher than the neutral real interest rate will push actual output below potential output. And setting the real interest rate lower than the neutral real interest rate will push actual output above potential output.

neutral real interest rate The real interest rate at which real GDP is equal to potential GDP, and hence the output gap is zero.

Many economists used to think of the neutral real interest rate as being roughly stable at around 2%. However, more recently economists have begun to suspect that the neutral real interest rate has fallen somewhat and may now be well below 2%. This decline in the neutral rate is the result of a trend sometimes called *secular stagnation*.

Factor two: The RBA targets the nominal interest rate when trying to influence the real interest rate. The real interest rate is the opportunity cost that the RBA is trying to shift in order to steer people's spending and businesses' investment decisions. But in practice, the RBA controls a nominal interest rate. Recall that the nominal interest rate is simply the real interest rate plus inflation. So once the RBA has decided on a real interest rate it wants to hit, it needs to add in the inflation rate to find the corresponding nominal interest rate.

The interest rate that the RBA focuses on is the **cash rate,** which is the nominal interest rate that banks pay to borrow from each other overnight in the Australian cash market. In the next section, we'll dig into why banks lend to each other overnight, how this market works, and how it affects the broader economy. But for now, we'll simply focus on the RBA adjusting this nominal interest rate.

cash rate The interest rate that the RBA uses as its policy tool, which is the nominal interest rate that banks pay to borrow from each other overnight.

Factor three: The RBA compares inflation with its inflation target. When inflation is higher than the RBA's inflation target, that signals to the RBA that it should set real interest rates higher than the neutral real interest rate in order to encourage consumers and investors to spend less, which will reduce excess demand and hence inflationary pressure. When inflation is lower than the RBA's inflation target, then setting real interest rates lower than the neutral real interest rate will encourage consumers and investors to spend more, which boosts demand and hence inflation. The key idea here is that the RBA looks at the *gap between inflation and the inflation rate target,* and uses that difference as a guideline for how much to change the real interest rate.

RBA policy makers don't just look at today's inflation, they also look ahead to forecasts of inflation. If they forecast that inflation is likely to rise or fall above or below their inflation target at some future date, they'll consider changing real interest rates today to get ahead of the problem.

Factor four: The RBA looks at the output gap. The output gap is the difference between actual and potential output, measured as a share of potential output. It is zero—or as Goldilocks would say, "just right"—when actual output is equal to potential

youngvet/E+/Getty Images

The RBA pays attention to signs like this.

output. The output gap is important to the RBA because an overheating economy can cause inflation. When the output gap is positive, output exceeds potential output. That can continue for a while—as people work overtime and factories run extra shifts and defer maintenance—but it's not sustainable. Eventually, businesses will respond to this excess demand by raising their prices, sparking higher inflation.

Conversely, if the output gap is negative so that the economy is operating below potential, then employment is likely below its maximum sustainable level, and insufficient demand will cause businesses to cut their prices (or raise them by less), which causes inflation to decline.

So the output gap hints at the future path of two variables the RBA cares a lot about: inflation and unemployment. A positive output gap occurs when unemployment is below its lowest sustainable level and it will likely spark higher inflation. That's why the RBA responds to a positive output gap by setting the real interest rate above the neutral real interest rate in an attempt to cool the economy and reduce inflationary pressure. A negative output gap corresponds to high unemployment and lower inflation. And that'll lead the RBA to respond by setting the real interest rate below the neutral real interest rate, so as to stimulate greater spending and output, which will reduce unemployment. The RBA also looks at forecasts of the future output gap so that it can get ahead of any looming problems.

RBA rule-of-thumb The recipe that describes how the RBA often sets the interest rate:

Cash rate − Inflation = Neutral real interest rate + ½ × (Inflation − 2.5%) + Output gap

Putting it all together: An RBA rule-of-thumb approximates what it does. There isn't really a recipe for monetary policy, but RBA decision making does seem to follow a standard pattern. The **RBA rule-of-thumb** shows how the RBA combines the neutral real interest rate and estimates of inflation and output in deciding how to adjust the interest rate. The RBA influences the economy by changing the real interest rate, but it sets nominal rates. So it evaluates the (nominal) cash rate by subtracting its estimate of the inflation rate so as to focus on the real interest rate. It then sets that real rate equal to the neutral real rate plus adjustments for deviations of inflation from its target and output from potential output. This formula shows the RBA rule-of-thumb:

This is the *nominal* interest rate the RBA controls

The real interest rate that would keep the economy neutral

Raise rates by the gap between actual and potential output

$$\text{Cash rate} - \text{Inflation} = \text{Neutral real interest rate} + \frac{1}{2} \cdot (\text{Inflation} - 2.5\%) + \text{Output gap}$$

The *real* interest rate is what the RBA really cares about so it adjusts for inflation

Raise rates by one half of . . .

. . . the gap between inflation and the RBA's 2.5% target

The RBA responds to the inflation gap by raising or lowering the real interest rate by an amount equal to one-half of the difference between inflation and the target rate of 2.5%. So if the inflation rate is 3%—putting it 1 percentage point above the RBA's inflation target—it will set the real interest rate half a percentage point higher. The RBA responds to the output gap by raising or lowering the real interest rate by 1 percentage point for each percentage point difference between actual output and potential output. And so if the output gap is +1%—meaning output exceeds potential output by 1%—then the RBA will set the real interest rate to be 1 percentage point higher than it would otherwise be.

Do the Economics

It's your turn to play Reserve Bank board member. Or perhaps you're a bond trader, trying to predict the RBA's next move. The neutral real interest rate is 2%, inflation is

1.5%, and the output gap is +0.5%—meaning that output is 0.5% above its potential. What does the RBA's rule-of-thumb suggest is an appropriate setting for the cash rate?

$$\text{Cash rate} - \text{Inflation} = 2\% + \tfrac{1}{2} \times (1.5\% - 2.5\%) + 0.5\% = 2.0\%$$

$$\text{Cash rate} = 2.0\% + \text{Inflation} = 2.0\% + 1.5\% = 3.5\% \blacksquare$$

Monetary policy choices are systematic but not automatic. The RBA rule-of-thumb provides a pretty good prediction of the RBA's actual interest rate decisions. Figure 3 shows the actual cash rate compared to the RBA rule-of-thumb using a neutral interest rate of 2.5%. The RBA rule-of-thumb is also known as a *Taylor Rule*, named after the economist who demonstrated that the rule did a good job of describing past monetary policy actions.

Figure 3 | The RBA Rule-of-Thumb

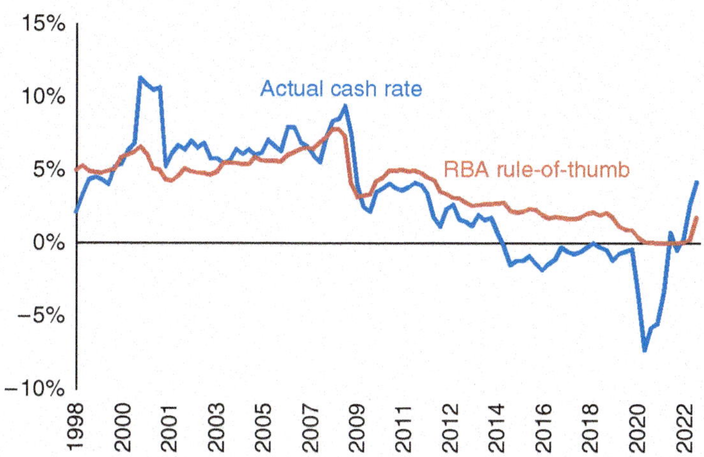

Data from: RBA, ABS.

The fact that the RBA rule-of-thumb is a good predictor of the actual cash rate doesn't mean that the RBA follows the rule-of-thumb like a recipe and it certainly isn't an argument to allow computers to set interest rates using a formula like the RBA rule-of-thumb. You've already seen that RBA board members pore over a range of measures of excess capacity in the economy to assess the output gap, as well as a range of measures of price changes to assess inflation. They also assess ways in which deeper forces—such as globalisation, automation, demographics, market power, inequality, technological change, and financial interconnectedness—might change the structure of the economy.

RBA decisions are *systematic*—meaning that the RBA responds in a reliable fashion to the state of the economy. But they are not *automatic*—meaning that they aren't simply an application of a single rule over time. RBA officials argue that their decisions depart from the rule-of-thumb when their superior information, economic insights, and decision-making abilities suggest that a different choice will help the RBA better meet its goal of price stability and maximum employment. So even though the RBA rule-of-thumb is a formula that closely tracks RBA decisions, there's a lot of judgement that goes into actual RBA decisions.

The case for rules versus discretion. Some economists worry that the RBA might be tempted to lower interest rates to create a short-term economic boom. If it were to give in to this temptation, it would risk overheating the economy, which could spark higher inflation. Even the perception that the RBA might be tempted to do this can be problematic because it might lead people to expect higher inflation, which leads managers to raise their prices, thereby causing higher inflation.

That's why some economists have suggested that the RBA should follow a strict rule when setting interest rates, arguing that it would effectively remove this temptation, and so might result in lower and more stable inflation. In addition, it would make monetary policy more predictable.

However, strict adherence to a rule has some significant downsides. Many RBA officials have argued that the prospect of being close to the zero lower bound or the possibility of financial instability means that they sometimes need to take stronger action than the RBA rule-of-thumb suggests. This partly explains why the pattern of rate changes in recent years has diverged from that predicted by the RBA rule-of-thumb.

More generally, discretion risks the folly of humans, but it also allows them to use their judgment to come to better decisions based on all available data. That's why many monetary policy discussions begin with a look at what the RBA rule-of-thumb predicts, and then proceed to assessing how officials might use their discretion to try to make a better policy choice. This approach means that you can usually predict where interest rates are going by consulting the RBA rule-of-thumb, and listening closely to speeches by RBA officials for hints about how they might diverge from it.

34.3 How the RBA Sets Interest Rates

Learning Objective *Understand how the Reserve Bank implements monetary policy decisions.*

When the RBA announces that it will raise or lower interest rates, it's announcing a new level for a specific interest rate called the *cash rate*. But it doesn't directly set the cash rate, which you'll recall is the rate that banks charge each other for overnight loans in the Australian cash market. Only banks and certain other financial entities can borrow and lend in this market. So in order to implement its new monetary policy decision to shift this interest rate, the RBA needs to create incentives for banks that shift the supply or demand for loans in this market. Let's explore how it does this.

The Overnight Market for Interbank Loans

We'll begin by thinking through why banks sometimes need to borrow from each other overnight. When your salary is deposited into your bank account the money doesn't just sit as cash in the vault. Banks make money by lending out the funds you've deposited. But when you make an electronic transfer to your landlord to pay your rent, you expect the bank to give that money to your landlord. Banks must keep cash (even if it is "digital cash") on hand—known as **reserves**—so that they can make those payments. So banks face a trade-off: If they loan more of their money out, they make more revenue from borrowers paying them interest on those loans, but they also risk not having enough cash available to make payments like the one to your landlord. When they don't have enough cash on hand, they'll need to borrow money to make those payments.

reserves The cash that banks need to keep on hand to make payments.

The RBA sets **reserve requirements:** a minimum amount of reserves—that is, available cash—that each bank must hold. They have to either hold these reserves as cash in their vaults, or on deposit at the RBA. These balances held with the RBA are in something called an "Exchange Settlement" (ES) account. ES balances are used to make payments to the RBA or other banks. Sometimes banks don't have enough ready cash to meet the reserve requirement or are short of what they need to make payments on a given day. As a result, they have a demand for funds, which they can meet by borrowing money overnight from another bank in the Australian cash market. Other banks may have more cash than they need. These banks are willing to supply funds, lending their spare cash overnight to those who need it. The forces of supply and demand determine the price in this market, which is the interest rate charged on these overnight loans. It's called the cash rate because it is the price in the Australian cash market.

reserve requirements A minimum amount of reserves that each bank must hold.

Tools the RBA uses to influence the cash rate:

1. Pays interest to banks on excess reserves
2. Sets a rate at which it is willing to lend to banks who have an Exchange Settlement (ES) account.

The RBA sets an "interest rate corridor" around the target cash rate. This corridor is comprised of a floor and a ceiling. The floor is the RBA's deposit rate. This is the rate that the RBA pays on excess reserves (i.e., ES balances). This is typically set at the cash rate minus 0.1%. The ceiling is the RBA's lending rate on ES shortfalls. This is typically the cash rate plus 0.25%.

Tool one: The RBA pays interest to banks on their excess reserves. In order to influence the cash rate, the RBA pays interest to banks on excess reserve balances—the reserves (or ES balances) they hold above the amount required. This effectively creates a minimum interest rate that a bank will charge before loaning its excess funds to other banks. (The RBA also pays interest on required reserves, but since those reserves are required, that interest doesn't affect banks' willingness to lend their extra cash.)

If you can just leave your extra cash in your own ES account and earn a 1% return with no risk of losing your money, you'll only take it out of your account and lend it to someone else if they offer a rate higher than 1%. As a result, the **interest rate on excess reserves** effectively serves as a floor on the interest rate at which banks will loan their funds. The higher this interest rate, the fewer reserves are available to loan to other banks, which will raise the interest rate on overnight loans. And so when the RBA wants to increase or decrease the cash rate, it raises or lowers the interest rate it pays on excess

interest rate on excess reserves The interest rate the RBA pays to banks on reserves that are in excess of required reserves.

reserves. The RBA does this by mechanically setting the RBA deposit rate at the target cash rate minus 0.1%.

Tool two: The RBA sets a rate at which it is willing to lend to banks who have an ES shortfall. The RBA has another way of establishing a floor for the price of borrowing money: It can borrow from financial institutions and pay them interest on the loan. By engaging in overnight borrowing, the RBA increases the demand for overnight loans, which leads to higher interest rates. When it reduces such borrowing, it decreases the demand for overnight loans, which lowers rates. It does this primarily to have a tool to set an effective floor for the cash rate target at financial institutions that aren't banks.

Sometimes banks will have a shortfall in their ES balances. Because there is opportunity cost to holding reserves, and because sometimes their customers might make big withdrawals, a bank might need to top up their reserves. They can do this by borrowing from other banks. The RBA also offers a facility from which they can borrow. The rate at which the RBA is willing to lend to banks overnight is typically set at the target cash rate plus 0.25%. Since banks can borrow from the RBA at this rate, they will not borrow from other banks at a higher rate. Thus, the RBA has created a ceiling on the actual cash rate.

Taken together, the ceiling and the floor that the RBA creates mean that the cash rate has to be within the target band. In practice, the target cash rate is a focal point and prices tend to gravitate there. But, if they wanted to, the RBA could squeeze the corridor. Instead of paying the cash rate minus 0.1%, they could offer less. And they could similarly lower the ceiling. As Figure 4 shows, the actual cash rate trades tightly within the interest rate corridor.

Figure 4 | **The Australian Cash Market**

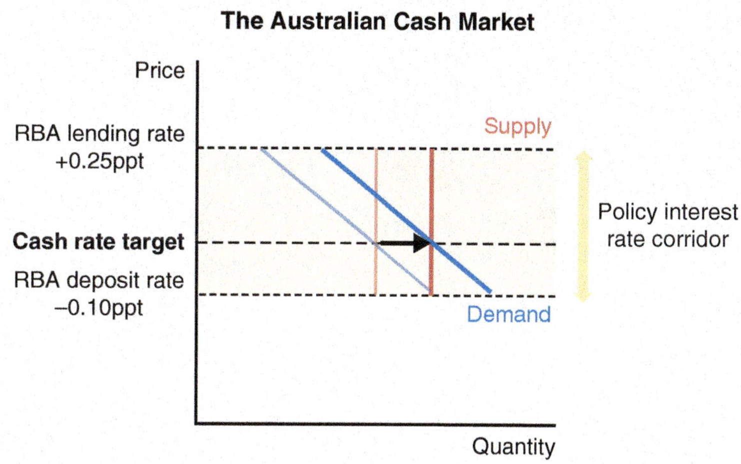

The Impact of Changing the Cash Rate on the Rest of the Economy

Ok, so now you know how the RBA adjusts its main tool—the cash rate. But how does that affect you? Once the RBA has succeeded in moving the cash rate, the effects ripple throughout the economy. Banks adjust many of their interest rates such as those on credit cards, business loans, mortgages, savings accounts, and car loans. Those interest rate changes then have broader macroeconomic effects. A lower real interest rate leads to more consumption and investment, an exchange rate depreciation, and higher net exports. This rise in aggregate expenditure leads managers to expand production, which requires them to hire more workers. Higher output leads more businesses to experience capacity constraints, leading them to raise their prices more frequently and by larger amounts, boosting higher inflation. People follow the RBA's decisions closely because they eventually affect nearly every corner of the economy. Let's see how all of this happens.

Lisa Maree Williams/Getty Images

The RBA's decisions ripple out and affect every part of the economy.

A change in the cash rate percolates through to other interest rates. When the cash rate changes, banks reset the rate they charge borrowers because the marginal costs and benefits of making loans has changed. The marginal benefit to your bank of loaning money to you is the interest you pay. Its marginal cost is the opportunity cost—the interest it could earn by leaving the money in its reserves, instead. When a lower cash rate leads this opportunity cost to fall, the *cost-benefit principle* tells banks to make more loans at any given interest rate. This increase in the supply of loans causes the interest rate that banks charge people like you to fall.

The cash rate directly impacts short-term and variable interest rates. Many variable interest rates—such as variable-rate mortgages—move directly with the cash rate. Some credit cards also have a variable rate. Your savings account may have a variable rate that adjusts with the cash rate.

Changes in short-term interest rates also percolate through to longer-term loans. To understand why, realise that a longer-term loan can be thought of as a series of short-term loans. So when you pay a fixed interest rate on a five-year car loan, the bank can think of adding up the different interest rates it would charge over each month of the five years. Since the opportunity cost for the bank of making you a five-year loan is not making a series of short-term loans, it will only do so if the interest it earns is at least as great as what it could expect to earn on a series of short-term loans. As a result, long-term interest rates move when the cash rate changes, and how much they move depends on how long banks expect the cash rate to be at its new rate.

yalcinsonat1/iStock/Getty Images

RBA decisions affect how much you will pay for your mobile phone.

Interest rates change the value of consuming today versus consuming tomorrow. For consumers and businesses, consumption and investment change with the interest rate because of the *opportunity cost principle*. When the RBA changes the cash rate, the effects filter through to change the interest rates you face on things like your savings account and credit cards, which affects your choices about how much to save or borrow. Similarly, the return on savings for businesses changes, as does the cost of borrowing. Likewise interest rates change how much the government pays to borrow, therefore potentially affecting how much the government has available to spend on other things.

Interest rates change the value of the Australian dollar. Investors are global actors, seeking the highest risk-adjusted returns they can find. When Australian interest rates fall, investing in Australia becomes less attractive. With fewer foreign investors trying to buy Australian dollars so that they can invest in Australia, the value of the dollar falls. This depreciation means that it takes fewer U.S. dollars, yen, euros, or yuan (the currencies of the United States, Japan, Europe, and China) to buy an Australian dollar.

When it takes fewer yen to buy an Australia dollar, Japanese consumers can buy Australian-made goods more cheaply. If you're exporting wine to Japan, you'll get the same number of dollars, but it costs your Japanese customers fewer yen. And that increases demand for your exported wine. Indeed, when the Australian dollar depreciates, people around the world will discover that Australian goods will be cheaper in terms of their own currency, leading them to buy more goods exported from Australia.

The flip side is that it takes more Australian dollars to buy goods priced in other currencies. In order for a U.S. phone producer to receive the same number of U.S. Dollars, you must pay more Australian dollars for an American mobile phone. That price rise leads to a decline in the quantity of imported goods that Australians demand. If the quantity of imports declines by enough to offset the higher prices, then total spending by Australians on imported goods will also fall.

All this means that low interest rates lead to a cheaper Australian dollar, causing exports to rise and imports to fall, thereby increasing net exports. The opposite happens when interest rates rise: The value of the dollar rises, making Australian goods more expensive and foreign goods cheaper, and this leads to a decrease in net exports.

The RBA's decisions, therefore, percolate through the entire global economy because of their impact on global financial flows, exchange rates, and international trade. To summarise, a change in the cash rate changes real interest rates throughout the economy, which in turn changes consumption, investment, government spending, and net exports.

atakan/E+/Getty Images

The RBA just lowered rates. Should you take out a car loan?

EVERYDAY Economics

The RBA just lowered interest rates. Does that mean it's a good time to borrow?

When the RBA lowers the cash rate, other interest rates will follow. You'll likely be able to take out a car loan for less as a result. So does this make it a good time to buy a car? The RBA hopes you think so—after all, it's trying to boost spending with the lower rates. But whether this is a good decision depends on your personal situation. In particular, it's important to realise that the RBA lowers rates when it sees the economy weakening.

That means that you should factor in the chance that you might lose your job. If that were to happen, would you still be able to make payments? Typically, young people are the most vulnerable to high rates of unemployment during an economic downturn. So be extra careful with your budget when you see the RBA lowering rates, and perhaps hold off on that car purchase until you're sure you could support yourself (and the car payment) if you lose your job. ■

34.4 Unconventional Monetary Policy

Learning Objective *Learn about the tools the Reserve Bank uses to set monetary policy when nominal interest rates are zero.*

The RBA's primary tool for affecting the economy is the cash rate, but this is not its only tool. The RBA's other tools are particularly relevant when it needs to encourage spending even after it has lowered the cash rate to zero. Additionally, the RBA has a responsibility to ensure stability in the financial system. During the coronavirus pandemic the RBA explored several new tools to help stimulate the economy. Let's explore some of these tools.

Monetary Policy Choices When Nominal Interest Rates Are Zero

In order to fight the economic fallout of the coronavirus pandemic, the RBA lowered the cash rate essentially to zero in 2020. The zero lower bound meant that the RBA thought it could not push the cash rate any lower, so it had to start exploring other instruments that might encourage additional spending. The two main approaches both reflect the same goal—to push longer-term interest rates down. In normal times, the RBA sets a short-term interest rate—recall that the cash rate is an interest rate on overnight loans. (That's pretty short term!) But when this rate has hit the lower bound, and the economy is still below potential, the RBA can still push longer-term rates even lower to encourage people and businesses to take out more long-term loans to fund more spending today.

James D. Morgan/Getty Images

Things were desperate in 2020.

Forward guidance helps push down longer-term interest rates. Communication became a more important policy tool once the cash rate was at zero. The idea is that the RBA can stimulate the economy even when short-term interest rates are as low as they can go by committing to low rates in the future. This strategy of providing information about the future course of monetary policy in order to influence market expectations of future interest rates is called **forward guidance**.

forward guidance Providing information about the future course of monetary policy in order to influence market expectations of future interest rates.

The way it works is that the RBA makes up for the fact that rates can't go lower today by promising that they will stay low in the future. This pushes down longer-term interest rates because the RBA is promising that people can count on low interest rates for longer. This promise pushes down the interest rates on longer-term loans, like home mortgages, five-year car loans, and longer-term business loans, and these lower rates will lead more people to buy houses and cars, and make business investments.

For forward guidance to work, it's crucial that people believe that the RBA is committed to keeping rates low for a while because it's those beliefs that push down the interest rate on long-term loans, and spur more spending.

Quantitative easing aims to push interest rates below zero. **Quantitative easing**, or QE, is the name given to the RBA's strategy of purchasing large quantitites of longer-term government bonds and (in principle, but not current practice) other securities in an effort to put downward pressure on long-term interest rates, including mortgage rates. During the pandemic, the RBA purchased hundreds of billions of dollars of these assets.

quantitative easing (QE) Purchasing large quantities of longer-term government bonds and other securities in an effort to lower long-term interest rates.

The RBA wasn't exactly spending billions of dollars through quantitative easing. Instead, it bought government bonds from savers like you. By buying long-term bonds, the RBA is effectively increasing the supply of long-term loans. This increase in supply pushes down interest rates on other long-term loans, allowing businesses to borrow at lower rates. Quantitative easing also helped increase lending in the housing market, and as a result, people paid historically low rates on three-year fixed-rate mortgages.

This reduction in long-term interest rates also helps the RBA convince banks that it's committed to keeping rates low for a long period.

WILLIAM WEST/AFP/Getty Images

The coronavirus pandemic meant high unemployment even with interest rates as low as they could go.

Lender of Last Resort

Finally, the RBA plays a key role in preventing bank runs and financial panics. A bank run occurs when many people want to withdraw their savings from a bank at the same time, collectively trying to withdraw more cash than the bank has on hand. The bank has enough money on the books to pay everyone, but it's not all accessible because it has lent some of it to its other customers.

The RBA can help prevent bank failures by acting as a **lender of last resort,** meaning it is the lender that financial institutions turn to when they need cash right away, but they're having trouble getting a loan elsewhere. A lender of last resort is what it sounds like—someone who gives you a loan when no one else will.

lender of last resort The RBA's role as the lender that financial institutions turn to when they're having trouble getting loans.

The lender of last resort can prevent a financial crisis. During the financial crisis of 2007–2009, the RBA acted aggressively as a lender of last resort, providing loans to financial institutions in an effort to prevent an emerging financial panic from spreading. To understand why, consider the failure of central banks in advanced economies around the world to act during the Great Depression: central banks had the capacity to bail out banks, but they opted not to help. If a handful of banks were to go bust, it probably wouldn't pose much of a problem to the whole economy. But bank runs tend to be contagious because the failure of one bank prompts savers at other banks to worry that their bank might be next; those savers race to withdraw their money, and the trouble spreads.

The RBA is a lender of last resort to a broad set of financial institutions. There was something different about the 2007–2009 financial crisis: It wasn't just banks that were in trouble. Other financial institutions known as shadow banks were also at risk of failing. Shadow banks often act like banks, but they're not officially banks, and so they can't borrow at the discount window. The collapse of a U.S. shadow bank called Lehman Brothers prompted widespread fear that others like it would fail. To prevent runs on other shadow banks, the U.S. Federal Reserve worked to expand its reach as a lender of last resort throughout the financial system including to shadow banks. In Australia, the Australian Government Guarantee Scheme was announced on 24 October 2008, and was administered by the Reserve Bank. This provided depositors with the confidence that the RBA would stand behind banks and other "Authorised Deposit-Taking Institutions" (ADIs).

The RBA's role as a lender of last resort is largely about ensuring financial stability, but as this episode demonstrated, it also serves to ensure maximum employment and stable prices by helping to prevent financial crises.

The RBA can lose money when it makes loans to failing financial institutions. When the RBA acts as a lender of last resort, it takes on some of a financial institution's risk. After all, if that financial institution can't repay its loan, then it's the RBA—and hence taxpayers—who stand to lose money. Some people argued that the RBA should not have used public money to prop up private, for-profit companies. Australia weathered the financial crisis well enough that this didn't become an issue. But in the United States it did. For example, loans from the U.S. Federal Reserve (together with help from Treasury) helped prevent AIG, an American multinational insurance company, from going bust. These actions benefited AIG's shareholders, even as they also prevented broader financial chaos, which arguably benefits the taxpayers who were putting their money on the line.

Ultimately, the Fed was fully paid back (with interest) for all the loans it made in its capacity as a lender of last resort during the financial crisis. But while these bailouts worked well—the American taxpayers made money and helped save some financial institutions—there were real risks involved. Australian taxpayers had their money put at risk as well, but they did not end up having to actually bail out any Australian banks or other financial firms.

Bailouts can lead banks to take bigger risks. There's an old joke that says that if you owe the bank $100 that's your problem, but if you owe your bank $100 million, that's the bank's problem. The RBA faces a similar problem when it acts as lender of last resort to the largest and most interconnected financial institutions: If any big financial firm were to fail, it would create widespread economic chaos, which the RBA was set up to prevent. The problem is that these financial institutions understand that—from the RBA's perspective—they're *too big to fail*. That creates incentives for these financial institutions to take on extra risk. After all, if their financial bets don't pay off, the RBA has little choice but to help them. This suggests that even as the RBA acting as lender of last resort can soften the blow of a financial crisis, it may also make future financial crises more likely.

This increase in risk taking because financial institutions know they will be bailed out is known as "moral hazard." It's the same idea that suggests if your car is fully insured you will take more risks in how you drive. The RBA and Australian government understand this, which is why there are a host of regulations that try and control bank lending and financial risk-taking more generally.

Tying It Together

The Reserve Bank is charged with steering the economy into smooth waters, avoiding costly inflation and helping foster a labour market in which unemployment is at its lowest sustainable rate. It's not an easy job, and the RBA hasn't always got it right. In the 1970s, the RBA let inflation run too high without taking enough action. It took a period of high interest rates that caused a painful recession with high unemployment in the early 1980s to bring the inflation rate back down. Some of the RBA's critics argue that low interest rates of the 2010s caused a housing bubble. And yet the RBA was seen by many as failing to do enough to push down interest rates (and thus unemployment) in 2018 and 2019, and for persistently allowing inflation to be lower than its 2–3% target band. Through 2021, commentators debated whether the RBA should have announced that it planned not to raise interest rates until at least 2024.

You learned how the RBA approaches these problems, the questions it needs to ask, the information it uses, and how it makes decisions. The real interest rate is the opportunity cost of consuming today versus saving for tomorrow, and the RBA shapes it to influence the behaviour of everyone in the economy.

The RBA's actions highlight just how important the *interdependence principle* is. The RBA can set one interest rate—the interest rate it pays on reserves—and that sets off a chain reaction throughout the economy by shifting the cost-benefit calculations of nearly everyone in the country—and some beyond. The RBA raises interest rates, and you might see a higher rate on your credit card leading you to cut back your spending. Foreign investors push up the value of the Australian dollar, since higher interest rates in Australia increase demand to invest in Australia. As you cut back your spending and look for discounts, you find more of them as the price of imports falls and businesses react to the decline in spending by lowering prices. And yet in China, a mother notices that the price of beef has risen because China imports a lot of beef from Australia. So she switches to chicken, which is produced in China, meaning that the Chinese chicken producers see an increase in sales. And so it continues, as the RBA's decision sets off a chain of interdependent decisions.

So now you know why the RBA is so important, how it does what it does, and what you can do to make good decisions when the RBA makes a change. My final tip: Now that we've studied business cycles and the RBA, combine your ability to track the economy with your new understanding of where interest rates might be headed. With this information, you'll be better placed to figure out where the economy is going, which will help you make better decisions in your own life.

Chapter at a Glance

The Reserve Bank (the RBA): the Australian central bank. Central banks determine a country's monetary policy (the process of setting interest rates in an effort to influence economic conditions).

Inflation target: A publicly stated goal for the inflation rate. The RBA has an inflation target of 2-3%.

Why doesn't the RBA target 0% inflation?

- Inflation greases the wheels of the labour market
- The RBA can lower real interest rates by more when the inflation is above zero
- The risk of deflation
- Measured inflation may be overstated

Cash rate: The interest rate that the RBA uses as its policy tool, which is the nominal interest rate that banks pay to borrow from each other overnight.

Starts with the neutral real interest rate → **Targets the nominal interest rate in order to influence the real interest rate** → **Compares inflation to its inflation target** → **Looks at the output gap**

An RBA rule-of-thumb approximates what it does:

$$\text{Cash rate} - \text{Inflation} = \text{Neutral real interest rate} + \frac{1}{2} \times (\text{Inflation} - 2.5\%) + \text{Output gap}$$

- Cash rate: This is the *nominal* interest rate the RBA controls
- Cash rate − Inflation: The *real* interest rate is what the RBA really cares about so it adjusts for inflation
- Neutral real interest rate: The real interest rate that would keep the economy neutral
- $\frac{1}{2}$: Raise rates by one half of . . .
- (Inflation − 2.5%): . . . the gap between inflation and the RBA's 2.5% target
- Output gap: Raise rates by the gap between actual and potential output

Tools the RBA uses to influence the cash rate:

Sets a floor on the cash rate:

1. Pays interest to banks on excess reserves
2. Sets a rate at which it is willing to lend banks who have an ES shortfall.

Monetary policy choices when nominal interest rates are zero:

Forward guidance	Providing information about the future course of monetary policy in order to influence market expectations of future interest rates.
Quantitative easing (QE)	Purchasing large amounts of longer-term government bonds and other securities in an effort to put downward pressure on longer-term interest rates.

Key Concepts

Discussion and Review Questions

Learning Objective 34.1 *Learn how the Reserve Bank makes monetary policy decisions.*

1. Use the opportunity cost principle to explain why the RBA uses interest rates to influence the economy. How do interest rates impact the opportunity cost of spending money today?
2. Why does the RBA pay such close attention to GDP if its objective is to promote maximum employment while keeping prices stable?
3. Explain why countries with central banks independent from the government have lower inflation on average.

Learning Objective 34.2 *Discover how the Reserve Bank assesses its goals and makes interest rate choices.*

4. What are the pros and cons of targeting a 0% inflation rate? Do you believe the RBA should target 0% inflation, its current 2–3% inflation target, or some other value? Explain your reasoning.
5. With the advent of big data and increased computing power, some people have advocated for monetary policy by algorithm. Basically, real-time data is fed into a computer program, which then determines monetary policy decisions. Discuss the benefits and potential problems with such an approach.

Learning Objective 34.3 *Understand how the Reserve Bank implements monetary policy decisions.*

6. Explain how the RBA creates a lower and upper bound for the cash rate and the incentives that drive financial institutions to move the cash rate to that target.
7. Explain how the average Australian is affected by monetary policy. How does a change in the cash rate percolate from big banks to everyday Australians?

Learning Objective 34.4 *Learn about the tools the Reserve Bank uses to set monetary policy when nominal interest rates are zero.*

8. Compare and contrast how changes in the cash rate and quantitative easing affect interest rates and the broader economy.
9. Do you think that the RBA's role as a lender of last resort leads financial institutions to make more risky investments? What problem might the economy face if these institutions were left to fail?

Study Problems

Learning Objective 34.1 *Learn how the Reserve Bank makes monetary policy decisions.*

1. For each of the following misconceptions about the RBA, identify what is wrong with the statement and why.
   a. The Reserve Bank lacks accountability because no one audits the RBA. There's no way to know what really goes on behind the scenes.
   b. The Reserve Bank just prints more money when the economy needs it and gives it to banks.
   c. A government agency should not have so much control over the economy because politicians are always just going to do anything to win the next election.
2. In recent years, the U.S. Federal Reserve has transitioned from an intentionally vague and bureaucratic communication style to a more direct and transparent approach. What is the impact on inflation expectations of each of these communication styles? Should the RBA make a similar move?

Learning Objective 34.2 *Discover how the Reserve Bank assesses its goals and makes interest rate choices.*

3. You are working at the campus bookstore earning $28.00 per hour. Your manager tells you that in the upcoming year you will get a 2% raise. How does your real wage change if inflation next year is 1%, 2%, or 3%? What flexibility does inflation provide employers, especially during prolonged economic downturns?
4. Predict how the RBA would likely respond if the output gap became more positive, so that output moved from being 0.1% above potential output to being 3% above potential output, and inflation rose above its 2.5% target rate. How would you expect unemployment to change over the next year or two in response to the RBA's actions?

5. Use the RBA rule-of-thumb to predict how the RBA would want to change the cash rate and the real interest rate targets for each of the following scenarios if its estimate of the neutral real interest rate is 2.5%.

   a. A recession hits the economy leading output to be 0.75% below potential output and inflation to fall to 1%.

   b. An increase in consumer and business confidence pushes the economy to producing output at 2% above potential output while inflation rises to 3.5%.

Learning Objective 34.3 *Understand how the Reserve Bank implements monetary policy decisions.*

6. The RBA board is presented with data and analysis that indicates the output gap has changed from being close to 0 to now being large and negative. Additionally, inflation is 1.2% instead of the target of 2.5%. Predict how the RBA is likely to change its interest rate target by changing: (1) the floor framework and (2) the discount rate. Explain how altering these rates can help close the output gap.

7. The RBA increases real interest rates. Explain how each component of GDP—consumption, investment, government spending, and net exports—changes in response, and why. What happens to output, inflation, and unemployment? What would have led the RBA to increase interest rates?

Learning Objective 34.4 *Learn about the tools the Reserve Bank uses to set monetary policy when nominal interest rates are zero.*

8. The RBA has decreased the cash rate—a nominal short-term interest rate—to 0%, and yet the economy is still struggling. Explain what tools it still has at its disposal to help spur the economy and how it could use them.

CHAPTER 35

Government Spending, Taxes, and Fiscal Policy

Chapter Objective

Analyse government spending, revenue, deficits, and debt.

35.1 The Government Sector
Assess the size and scope of the government.

35.2 Fiscal Policy
Discover how fiscal policy can smooth business cycles.

35.3 Government Deficits and Debt
Understand why governments run deficits and the implications of government debt.

Sam Mooy/Getty Images

Your economics textbook is light reading compared to the multivolume federal budget.

Every year, typically on the second Tuesday of May, the Treasurer of Australia presents a proposed budget. The budget has more pages than an entire semester's worth of textbooks. Hundreds of detailed tables outline actual and proposed spending on everything that's funded with federal government dollars.

Each department across the federal government spends months developing spending proposals. They submit these proposals to Treasury and the Expenditure Review Committee, which considers them when it authorises spending for each year. Analysts also prepare forecasts for the billions of dollars of government spending that is not authorised annually, but rather is predetermined by laws passed long ago. As the budget is prepared, there is a series of arm-wrestles between different ministers, as they struggle to get a share of the limited funding for their preferred programs.

To budget is to fight over money. And fighting over money is really about fighting over priorities. What's most important to you: increasing funding for the military, education, or health care? Wouldn't another aircraft carrier make us just a little bit safer? Wouldn't more education spending to pay for more teachers, better buildings, and fresher teaching materials increase student learning? Wouldn't spending a bit more on public health care prevent more early deaths? Deciding among these options is all about opportunity cost—if you spend a dollar on one thing, you're not spending it on another. But your sense of the relative benefits of buying another aircraft carrier versus spending more on education or health care depends on your values, preferences, and beliefs. In other words, the slew of numbers that makes up the budget lays out a vision for society.

The federal budget doesn't just lay out a vision for our country; it also tells Parliament what the government thinks will happen to the Australian economy and what role government spending and taxation will play in influencing that outcome. That means the budget is also a plan of attack for smoothing business cycles and helping the economy operate closer to its potential.

In this chapter, we'll take a close look at what the government spends money on and how it raises revenue. You'll see that the government regularly borrows money, and thus our national debt is growing. We'll also examine how the government uses spending and taxation to stabilise the economy, and how its debt affects private investment and the economy. Let's get started!

35.1 The Government Sector

Learning Objective *Assess the size and scope of the government.*

The government plays a big role in your life. The university you're attending probably gets funding from the federal government. Before you started university, your high school or TAFE institution also received state or local government support. You might be getting a HECS-HELP loan or Youth Allowance from the federal government. You probably take public transport to campus on roads or railway tracks that are built, maintained, and patrolled using federal, state, or local government dollars. And chances are that you or someone in your family has relied on JobSeeker payments, Rent Assistance, or government-provided health care at some point in their lives.

social insurance Insurance provided by the government against bad outcomes such as unemployment, illness, disability, or outliving your savings.

Together, the spending by federal, state, and local governments adds up to nearly two-fifths of GDP. Let's explore what they spend the money on, and how they raise the money they spend.

Figure 1 | Total Government Spending

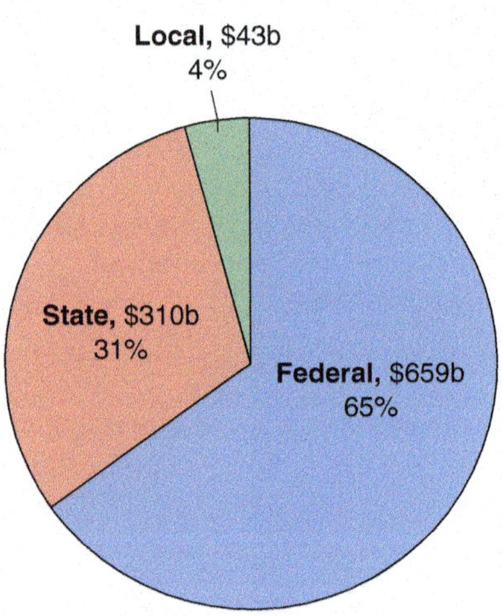

2022 Data from: Treasury.

Government Spending

The federal government spends more than state and local governments combined. Figure 1 shows that in 2021 the federal government spent $659 billion, state governments spent another $310 billion, and local governments spent $43 billion.

That adds up to almost $39,000 for each person in Australia. It's a lot of money, so let's look at what it gets spent on. Because federal, state, and local governments have different responsibilities, we'll look at each separately.

The federal government spends most of its money on social insurance programs, education and defence. **Social insurance** refers to government-provided insurance against bad outcomes such as unemployment, illness, disability, or outliving your savings. Figure 2 shows that social insurance programs—which fall mostly in the slices for social security and welfare, or health—are some of the biggest slices of the federal spending pie. Taken together, these social insurance programs, plus spending on education and defence, accounted for 60% of federal government spending in the 2020–2021 financial year—in other years it's around 65%.

Figure 2 | Federal Government Spending

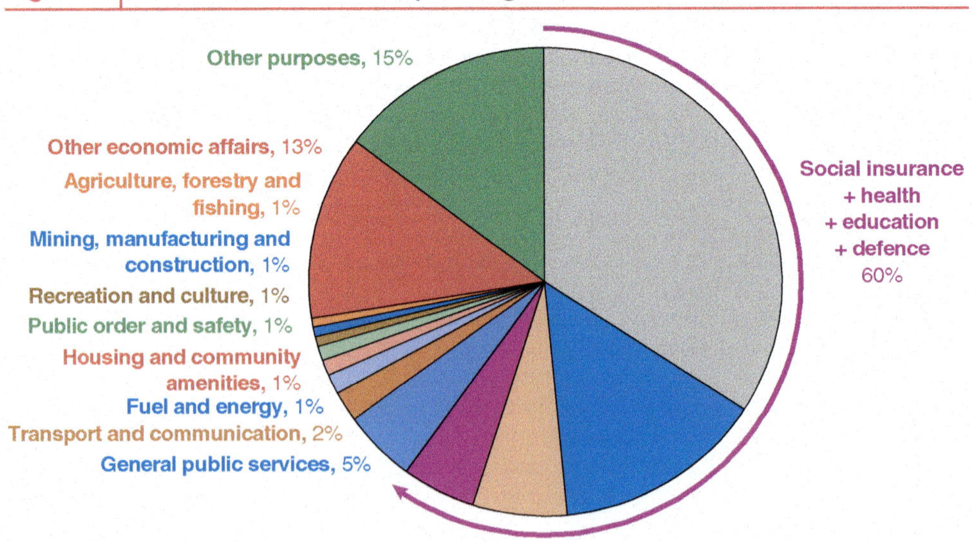

2022 Data from: Australian Bureau of Statistics.

Revenue assistance to States and Territories takes a further 13% of the overall budget, and the economic response to the coronavirus takes off another 10%, leaving just 17% to pay for everything else. That remaining money gets spread pretty thin across courts and federal law enforcement, housing, recreation and culture, transportation and communication, fuel and energy, and general public services (including things like foreign aid, courts, federal law enforcement, and research). Many people think that the government spends a lot more than it actually does on these small slivers of the federal budget.

Two out of every 10 dollars the federal government spends goes to the elderly or disabled. This is largely because the government provides the Age Pension to a majority of Australians over the age of 67. Many of these elderly Australians also receive government-funded aged care, which costs around the same amount per year as the entire National Disability Insurance Scheme—a government program supporting children with disabilities or developmental delays. The generous federal support for the elderly and disabled reflects the different responsibilities of federal, state, and local government.

States provide health care, law enforcement, and education. While there are differences across states, Figure 3 shows that on average, half of state government spending goes toward health care and education. This spending includes hospital services (about 60% of health expenditure) and pre-primary to secondary education (about 75% of education expenditure). You might recall that the federal government also spends much of their money on health care and education. The federal government is responsible for things listed under the Medicare Benefits Scheme (MBS)—for example, visits to your GP, as well as subsidised medicine under the Pharmaceutical Benefits Scheme (PBS). State governments, on the other hand, are responsible for public hospitals, community health, and mental health care (among other things). Federal and state governments jointly fund schools and vocational education.

States spend around a tenth of their budget on other social insurance, a little over a tenth on public safety, and another tenth on transport. Your state government also provides services like housing and environmental protection.

Figure 3 State Government Spending

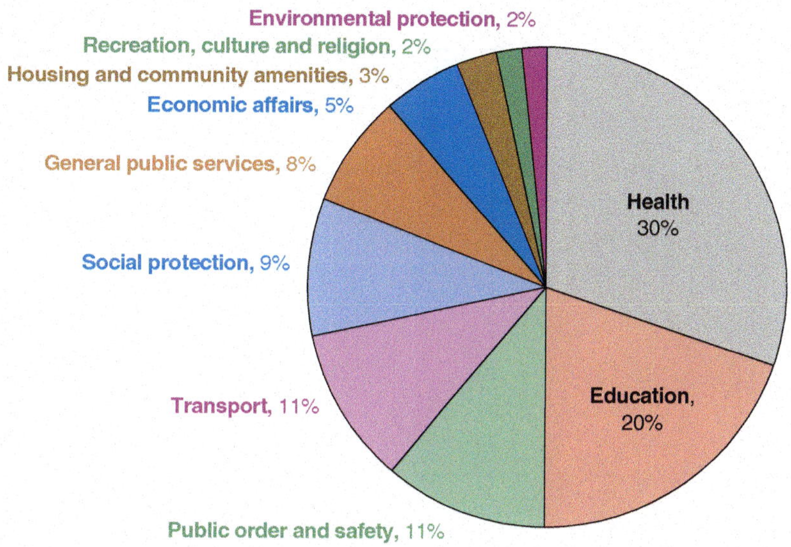

2022 Data from: Australian Bureau of Statistics.

Local government provides many of the government services you've interacted with so far in your life. Figure 4 shows that transport is the biggest chunk of local government spending, and your local government provides the local roads, street signs, and bus stops in your neighbourhood—that is, if you don't live next to a highway. Your local government also provides the community services your family might rely on—local kindergartens and preschools, local parks and playgrounds, rubbish and recycling collection, local libraries, and community health (in conjunction with your state government).

Figure 4 Local Government Spending

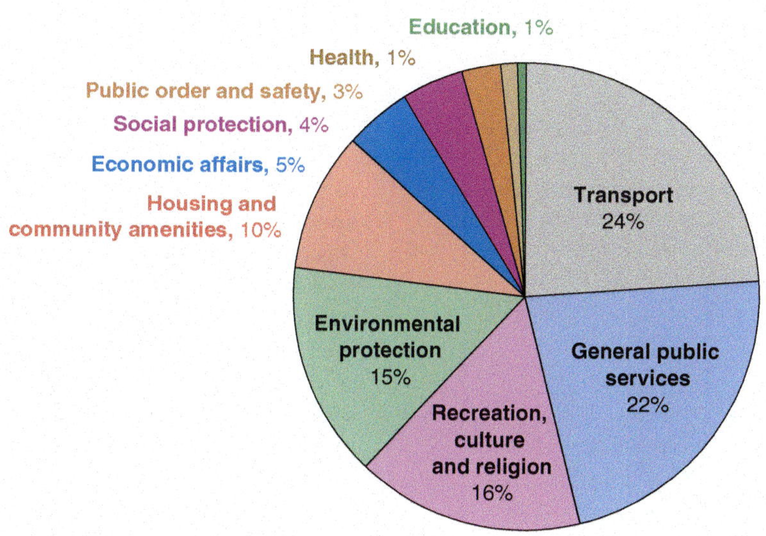

2022 Data from: Australian Bureau of Statistics.

Evaluate government spending as a share of available resources. You'll typically see government spending expressed as a percentage of GDP rather than in dollars. This allows us to make comparisons over time and across countries, because it adjusts for both price differences and differences in the size of the economy.

Figure 5 | Government Spending Over Time

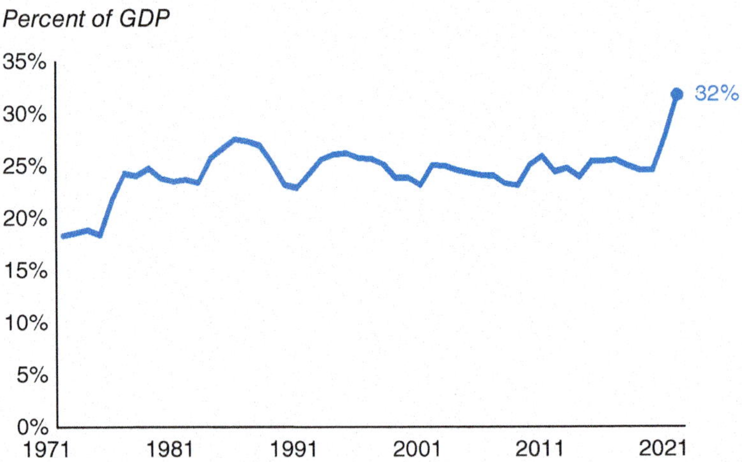

Data from: Treasury.

Figure 6 | Spending on Social Insurance Has Risen Over Time

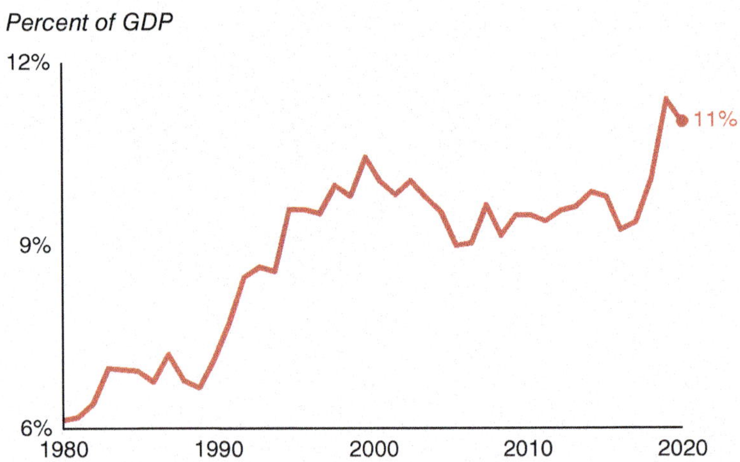

Data from: Treasury.

Federal government spending has been roughly stable over recent decades. Figure 5 shows federal government spending as a share of GDP over time. In 2021, federal government spending was 30% of GDP, higher than its average over the previous five decades due to the additional spending that was undertaken in response to the coronavirus pandemic. While there have been some noteworthy changes—spending was a tad higher in the 1980s, it fell through the 1990s, and it spiked in response to the coronavirus pandemic—the federal government's share of the economy has been remarkably stable over recent decades.

Government social insurance spending has grown over time. One of the good things about Australia is that we have a strong social safety net. This includes universal health insurance through Medicare, the Age Pension for those without sufficient superannuation savings for retirement, and the National Disability Insurance Scheme, which was introduced in 2013. Along with unemployment benefits through JobSeeker, these can be described as "social insurance" programs. The government acts as a kind of insurance provider for people who get an unlucky outcome in the lottery of life. But these programs are not cheap, and they have been growing faster than the overall size of the economy.

Figure 6 shows that spending on social insurance has grown as a share of GDP, from around 6% in 1980 to 10% in recent years. The projected growth in spending on the NDIS will likely see this number rise in coming years.

Much of future federal government spending is already determined. Most social insurance programs convey an entitlement to a certain amount of spending, which is why they're often called *entitlement programs*. The age pension guarantees retirees payments that are a function of their past savings and current income for as long as they live. Medicare guarantees health care for all Australians, regardless of the health problems they might develop. NDIS guarantees access to specialists, support workers, and resources for people with additional needs.

mandatory spending Spending on programs that does not get determined annually; instead, it is set in law.

It would be hard to plan for retirement if these programs changed much from year to year. That's why both programs are part of the federal budget called **mandatory spending,** which means that the terms of the spending are written into the legislation that created the program. Anything can become mandatory spending if Parliament passes legislation mandating it. For example, legislation known as the Farm Household Support Act spells out spending on farm subsidies. Mandatory spending can only be cut if Parliament repeals or amends this earlier legislation.

discretionary spending Spending that Parliament appropriates annually.

In contrast, funding for federal departments and most government programs is **discretionary spending.** This is spending that Parliament annually *appropriates*—that is, it provides funds for each specific purpose. By law, the government can only spend money that Parliament has appropriated.

Discretionary spending is what you most often hear about when the government fights over spending. That's because Parliament has to decide on discretionary spending each year. Yet discretionary spending is only around 30% of federal government spending. About half of discretionary spending is revenue assistance provided to state and local governments. The rest is on the smaller slices of the federal budget, such as housing, science, energy, the environment, and international affairs.

While Parliament fights over discretionary spending, most of the growth in federal spending comes from mandatory spending obligations and interest on government debt. The aging of the "baby boomer" population and growing life expectancy is increasing spending on mandatory programs for retirees like the age pension. In addition, the government's debt is growing, which is leading to higher annual interest payments.

Government spending is lower in Australia than in other rich countries. The combination of federal, state, and local spending in Australia adds up to 47% of GDP. Figure 7 shows that this is a bit lower than in many other developed countries, most of which devote half or more of their GDP to government spending.

Why are some other countries spending more? It's because their governments tend to publicly provide things that we privately pay for in Australia. For example, Australia has a universal healthcare system, but it is a system in which there are incentives for higher-income earners to buy private health insurance. Compulsory superannuation is a form of private retirement savings that also reduces government spending on the age pension.

Figure 7 | **Government Spending by Country**

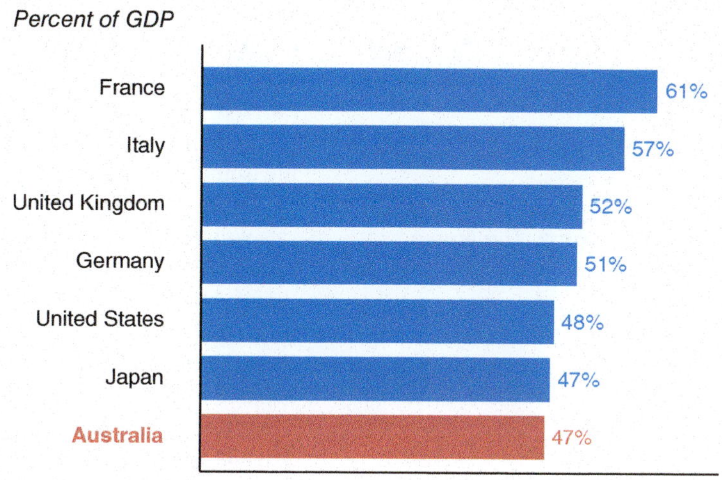

2021 Data from: OECD.

Government Revenue

Now that you've seen how much the government spends, a natural question is: Where does all the money come from to pay for it? The federal government primarily collects revenue by taxing people's incomes, while state and local governments focus more on taxing people's spending. Let's see how it breaks down.

Federal government tax revenue comes primarily from income taxes and GST. Overall, 80% of the federal government's revenue comes from either income taxes or the Goods and Services Tax (GST). The rest comes from excise and customs duty and other taxes, as shown in Figure 8. When you get your paycheque, you'll notice that income taxes have been withheld. That's because income taxes are a *direct tax*—a tax paid directly from you to the government. GST, on the other hand, is an *indirect tax*—you don't pay GST directly to the government.

Figure 8 | **Federal Revenues**

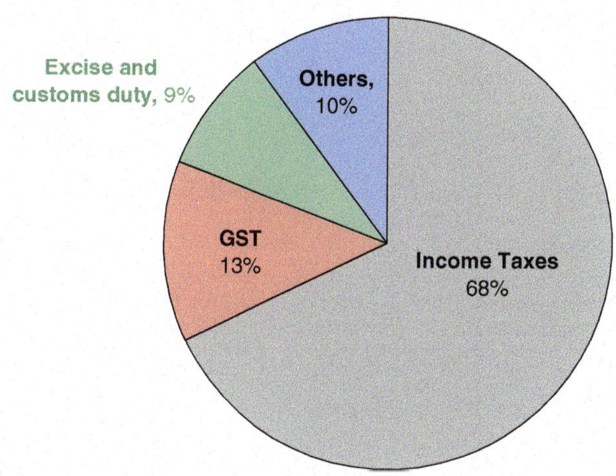

2022 Data from: Treasury.

You pay income taxes on all income. **Income taxes** are taxes collected on *all* income, regardless of its source. Income includes both the income you earn from working and unearned income such as investment income, pensions, capital gains, and inheritance or gift income. *Income* is all the money that you receive in a year, from all sources. Don't confuse this with *wealth,* which is your stock of savings and assets.

income taxes Taxes collected on all income, regardless of its source.

You pay GST only on purchases. While income taxes are taken directly from your paycheques, GST applies only when you buy things. This is why GST is an indirect tax, called a **sales tax**. A sales tax is a tax on purchases that's typically a percentage of the purchase price of goods and services. In the case of GST, it's a 10% tax on the purchase price of all goods and services, except for some essentials that are GST-free, such as fruit, medicine, and water.

sales tax A tax on purchases that's typically a percentage of the purchase price of goods and services.

The GST replaced a slew of state sales taxes when it was introduced under the Howard government in 2000. Because of this, the revenue the federal government receives from GST is actually redistributed to the states. This makes up a large portion of the "Revenue Assistance to States and Territories" that we saw in the section on government spending.

excise tax A tax on a specific product.

The other indirect taxes that the government receives a large amount of revenue from are excise taxes and customs duty. An **excise tax** is a tax on a specific product such as petrol, cigarettes, or alcohol. Unlike a regular sales tax, excise taxes are usually levied based on the quantity you buy, not the price you pay. For example, the federal excise tax on fuel is 44.2 cents per litre. Customs duties are taxes on imports and exports. Sometimes these can be excises, for example there are special duties on cigarettes and alcohol.

progressive tax A tax whereby those with more income tend to pay a higher share of their income in taxes.

Income taxes are progressive. The Australian federal income tax is a **progressive tax,** which means that those with more income tend to pay a higher share of their income in tax. A tax is progressive when the tax rate you pay increases with your income. That's why the amount you'll actually have to pay in federal income taxes will depend on how much income you receive throughout the year. So even though your employer might withhold an amount for payment of federal income taxes from your paycheque, this withholding is just a guess at how much you might owe.

taxable income The amount of your income that you pay taxes on.

Figure 9 shows you the federal income tax rate schedule for individuals in 2022. The tax rate you face depends on your **taxable income** which is the amount of your income you pay tax on. The way it works is that your first $18,200 in taxable income is tax-free. This means that if your taxable income is under the "tax-free threshold" of $18,200 then you won't have to pay any income tax. Once your taxable income exceeds $18,200, you pay 19% on every dollar of taxable income between $18,200 and $45,000. This means that if your income is $30,000, you would pay 0% tax on your first $18,200, and 19% on the remaining $11,800. Then once your taxable income exceeds $45,000, you pay 19% on every dollar between $18,200 and $45,000 and 32.5% on every dollar up until you earn $120,000, and so on.

marginal tax rate The tax rate you pay if you earn another dollar.

The tax rate you pay if you earn another dollar is your **marginal tax rate.** If your taxable income is $30,000, your marginal tax rate is 19%. If your taxable income is $60,000, then the marginal tax rate on the next dollar is 32.5%. The highest marginal tax rate is 45%, and it applies to every dollar of taxable income over $180,000 per year. Once you start earning enough, you will also have to pay the Medicare levy. The Medicare levy is an additional 2% of your taxable income used to help fund Medicare, but there are exemptions and reductions for low-income earners, and surcharges for high-income earners—so it's another progressive tax.

Figure 9 | **2019 Tax Rate Schedule for Individuals**

For taxable income over . . .	. . . but not over . . .	. . . the marginal tax rate is:
$0	$18,200	0%
$18,200	$45,000	19%
$45,000	$120,000	32.5%
$120,000	$180,000	37%
$180,000	–	45%

Figure 9 highlights the progressivity of the tax system—as you earn more, your marginal tax rate increases, which ensures that those with higher incomes will end up paying a larger share of their income in taxes.

So far it sounds pretty simple, but the real challenge is determining your *taxable income.* Here's the tricky part: It's not the same thing as the income you receive. You can subtract many possible deductions from your actual income in calculating your taxable income. For example, lots of people claim deductions for work-related expenses—if you work from home you can claim a deduction for the work-related portion of the expenses you incur, like internet, lighting, and air conditioning. We'll go over some more of these deductions later, but for now realise that when calculating each year's taxable income, most people subtract thousands of dollars off of what they actually earn. (You may be starting to understand why people complain about doing their taxes; they spend a lot of time searching for—or worrying that they missed—things to subtract from their income.)

regressive tax A tax where those with less income tend to pay a higher share of their income on the tax.

Sales and excise taxes are regressive. A **regressive tax** is one in which those with less income tend to pay a higher share of their income in taxes. Sales and excise taxes tend to be regressive because lower-income households spend a higher share of their income on things like petrol, housing, groceries, and clothing. Because they spend a higher share of their income on petrol, they also spend a higher share of their income on petrol taxes. At the other end of the distribution, higher-income households spend a much smaller share of their income on petrol; as a result, they also spend a smaller share of their income on petrol taxes. As you can see, the federal government uses a mix of both progressive and regressive taxes—though the vast majority of its revenue comes from income tax, which is progressive.

Do the Economics

You currently have a job that gives you an annual income of $85,200 a year and you have worked out that you have deductions of $5,200, leaving you with a taxable income of $80,000. A competitor offers you a similar job, and is willing to give you a $3,000 raise, but you would no longer be able to walk to work each day.

Given your current taxable income, what's your marginal tax rate?

With a taxable income of $80,000, the tax rate on the next dollar you earn is 32.5%.

Calculate how much extra you'll owe in additional federal income taxes if you accept the higher-paying job.

$$0.325 \times \$3{,}000 = \$975$$

Remember that you'll also need to pay the 2% Medicare levy on the additional income. How much more in taxes will you pay?

$$0.02 \times \$3{,}000 = \$60$$

The competitor's job is across town, which will require that you spend $120 a month on public transport. How much more will you make each year after taxes and transportation costs if you take the new job?

$$\underbrace{\$3{,}000}_{\text{Extra income}} - \underbrace{\$975}_{\text{Extra income tax}} - \underbrace{\$60}_{\text{Extra Medicare levy}} - \underbrace{12 \times \$120}_{\text{New expenses}} = \$525$$

Much of that $3,000 raise got eaten up with your new expenses and taxes. Bottom line: It's worth doing the maths before you pick among jobs because the differences in the take-home pay might not be as big as you first think. ■

Company taxes are paid by people. Sixteen percent of federal taxes are collected from companies. But what does it mean for a company to pay a tax? All taxes require someone to forgo some income. The people who ultimately pay most of the company taxes are the owners of the companies. For publicly held companies, the owners are the shareholders—the people who've invested their money and bought stock in the company. You'll probably be a shareholder one day if you aren't already, since most people hold part of their superannuation in stock.

Workers also bear some of the burden of company taxes. As taxes rise, businesses buy less capital, which makes their workers less productive. And when workers are less productive, employers aren't willing to pay them as much. Studies of the effect of corporate taxes on workers' wages vary, but the Commonwealth Treasury estimates that for every dollar of company tax, workers lose about 67 cents, and shareholders lose 33 cents.

State governments collect payroll taxes, property taxes, and stamp duties. A **payroll tax** is a tax on wages, and it's typically a percentage of the total wages paid by an employer. Payroll taxes only apply to employers whose wage bill exceeds a threshold set by the state(s) in which they operate. For example, in NSW, only employers with a total annual wage bill above $1.2 million pay the payroll tax of 5.45%.

payroll tax A tax on wages that's typically a percentage of an employer's total wage bill.

Figure 10 | **State Government Revenues**

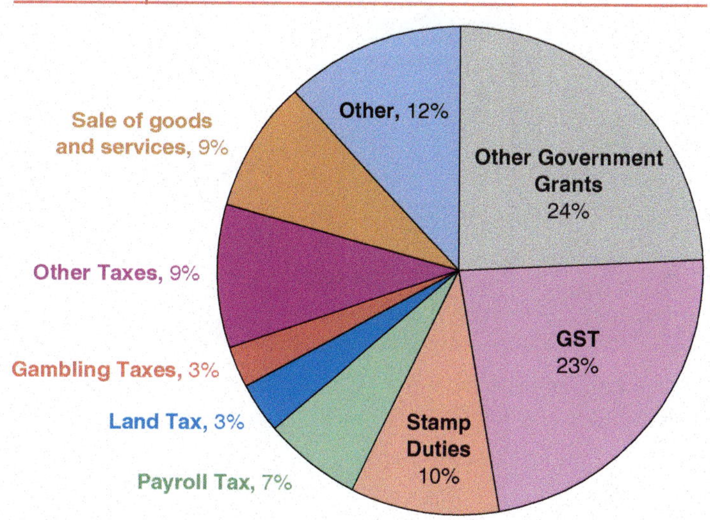

2022 Data from: Australian Bureau of Statistics.

Figure 10 shows that state governments receive 23% of their revenue through the Goods and Services Tax (GST), which is collected by the federal government. They also get 24% of the funding from federal government grants tied to specific purposes (such as for schools and hospitals). This partly reflects the fact that Australian states and territories do not levy their own income tax, unlike in some countries such as the United States. These taxes are the largest source of revenue for state and local governments on average.

property tax A tax on the value of property, usually real estate.

Property taxes, which are taxes on the value of property (usually real estate) provide another 13% of state government revenue. But state governments receive revenue from properties through another source, too—in fact, this other source is the largest source of state revenue (on average).

stamp duty A tax paid to the state government to legally register a change of ownership; sometimes called a *transfer duty.*

Stamp duties are taxes you pay to the state government to legally register a change of ownership. For example, if you buy a house or car you have to pay stamp duty (sometimes called transfer duty) to have the purchase recognised by the state. Just like income taxes, stamp duty is usually a progressive tax—it becomes marginally more expensive the larger the value of the asset being transferred. In the old days, transfer forms would literally be stamped with the amount of tax that had been paid, hence the name stamp duty. Stamp duties make up 10% of state government revenues, and they are quite inefficient taxes. Stamp duties are a tax on transactions that people want to make—buying and selling homes. This makes it less likely that people will move to get better jobs, send their children to better schools, or downsize their home when they are older. Economists generally prefer land tax as a way of raising government revenue from property holdings because it doesn't create these distortions.

State governments rely on some progressive taxes like stamp duty, but because they receive GST revenue from the federal government which makes up 23% of state revenue, most state tax systems are considered regressive.

Hidden Government Spending: Tax Expenditures

tax expenditures Special deductions, exemptions, or credits that lower your tax obligations, to encourage you to engage in certain kinds of activities.

Parliament can often implement its programs by changing the tax code, rather than directly increasing government spending. **Tax expenditures** describe the special deductions, exemptions, or credits that lower your tax obligations, and hence reduce government revenue. You may have also heard them be called write-offs, loopholes, or tax breaks.

Tax expenditures are a hidden form of government spending. To see how they're equivalent to government spending, let's consider a tax expenditure that you or someone in your family might have received before—the Low and Middle Income Tax Offset (LMITO). The idea that led to this tax expenditure was a desire to transition to a simpler progressive tax system. The LMITO was introduced as a part of the personal income tax plan, a plan to move towards an income tax system with only three brackets—removing the $120,000–$200,000 bracket and lowering the income tax rate to 30% for all individuals earning between $45,000 and $200,000 a year. The LMITO granted a tax reduction of up to $1,080 for anyone earning less than $126,000 per year from 2020–2024 in the lead up to the income tax change.

Chris Putnam/Alamy Stock Photo

Parliament is eager to hide spending in the tax code.

Parliament could have passed this program as a spending program—simply mailing each qualifying individual a $1,080 cheque each year. Instead, it implemented this program as a tax offset, and so this tax expenditure subtracts $1,080 (or less, depending on your income) from your federal income tax bill. For individuals receiving the offset, these are equivalent—you end up $1,080 better off whether you get a $1,080 cheque from the government or you pay $1,080 less in tax. And the government has $1,080 less, either way. But these otherwise-identical alternatives look quite different in the government's budget because a direct-spending program shows up as government spending, while a tax expenditure simply means there's less government revenue than there otherwise would be.

The politics of tax expenditures are different. Money that never shows up in the government's coffers is harder to trace than money it spends by sending out cheques. Some politicians implement their preferred programs as tax expenditures, rather than as increased government spending. They'll argue that they're letting people keep their own hard-earned money, rather than raising taxes to pay for more government spending. (Pause for a moment: How convincing do you find this argument?)

Importantly, because tax expenditures are part of the tax code, they don't need to be renewed or evaluated each year as part of the budget process. This really matters because it means that tax expenditures are not part of the annual fight over what to include in the discretionary budget. This lack of review has led many economists and tax experts to repeatedly urge Parliament (to little effect) to scrutinise tax expenditures more closely, rather than allowing them to persist through continued inaction. Tax expenditures are a big deal: In 2020–2021, the federal government's tax expenditures added up to $172 billion, which is close to the total amount of its discretionary spending ($198 billion).

Tax expenditures encourage spending on certain goods and services. Some of the largest tax expenditures include tax breaks offered on owner-occupied housing, voluntary superannuation contributions, and private health insurance. These tax breaks are the government's way of encouraging you to buy your own home, save more for retirement, or get private health insurance.

Hero Images/Getty Images

There's a big tax incentive to become a homeowner.

The government offers many important tax breaks for buying your own home, and we'll mention two of the most important ones here. The first is that you pay no capital gains tax when you eventually sell your home, if it is your main place of residence. The second is more subtle. When you rent your house, your landlord typically has to pay income tax on the rent you pay them. But when you buy the house and become your own landlord, you don't have to pay income tax on the rent you effectively pay yourself. This tax break—not having to pay tax on the rental value of owner-occupied housing—is one of the biggest benefits of homeownership.

The federal government has also created a number of savings programs that can reduce how much tax you pay when you stash money away for retirement. For example, you can put up to $27,500 of your salary into your superannuation fund at a tax rate of 15%, regardless of your marginal tax rate (as long as you earn less than $250,000 a year). The Government will even let you use part of your superannuation contributions to help you buy your first home under the First Home Super Saver Scheme.

EVERYDAY Economics

Should you live in, or rent out your first home?

GV Images/Alamy Stock Photo

Buying your first home is a big decision.

Buying your first home is a big financial decision. You have to save up tens or even hundreds of thousands of dollars for a deposit, and then you'll still need to take out a twenty to thirty year loan for the rest! One question that a lot of first-home buyers ask is: Should I live in, or rent out my first home? There are lots of important factors to consider when making this decision, so let's look at an example.

Let's say you've just bought a home and you're deciding whether to live in it or rent it out. The property will cost you $10,000 per year in expenses (maintenance, rates, taxes, etc.), and $20,000 per year in mortgage interest. You work out that you can rent your new home to a tenant for $25,000 per year. This means you'll have to pay the extra $5,000 per year out of your own pocket for the mortgage, and you'll also have to continue paying rent of $25,000 per year at the place where you're currently living. Alternatively, you can live in your new home, and you'll have to pay the $30,000 per year out of your own pocket. At first, it might sound like the two options are equivalent, because either way you'll end up paying $30,000 per year.

Not so fast! You need to consider your taxable income. When you rent out your property to a tenant, the income you receive is taxable. This means that you'll have to pay your marginal tax rate on the $25,000 in rental income you earn from the property. On the other hand, the $30,000 annual costs to maintain the property and pay back the interest on your mortgage are tax deductible. This means that the property will take

$30,000 – $25,000 = $5,000 off of your taxable income, equal to the annual loss you incur on the property. When a property costs you more than the rental income you make on it, this is called *negative gearing*. If your marginal tax rate is 32.5%, this means that you'll receive a tax credit of $1625. So overall if you decide to rent, it will cost you $25,000 + $5,000 – $1,625 = $28,375 per year.

On the other hand, if you live in your new home, you don't have to pay tax on the rental income you essentially pay yourself, which means you can deduct the full $30,000 cost per year off of your taxable income. If your marginal tax rate is 32.5%, this means that you'll receive a tax credit of $9,750. Moreover, almost every state and territory in the country offers a "first home owner grant," typically $10,000 to $15,000 if you live in your first home for at least six months after purchasing. If you receive a $10,000 grant, plus a $9,750 tax credit, your total cost to live in the property will be $30,000 – $10,000 – $9,750 = $10,250.

All of this means that renting out your first home involves more taxable income, and hence a higher tax bill. In this example, once you've accounted for both the cost of maintaining a house and the effect on your tax bill, you'll take home more money if you live in the house yourself. More generally, when you're comparing houses to buy your first home, you should consider not only the benefits, but also the relative costs of renting and buying, and how these are taxed. It's possible that if you're already living somewhere with very low rent, you might be better off renting out your first home. ■

Tax expenditures are often inefficient, poorly targeted, and persistent. Economists and policy makers on both sides of the political aisle tend to be against many (although not all!) of these tax expenditures. It's not that economists don't think that there are good reasons for the government to subsidise housing, retirement, or health insurance. The problem is that the budgetary cost of tax expenditures is opaque, and obscures how inefficient some programs are. They're poorly targeted because your benefit depends on your tax rate and so the biggest tax breaks are often given to those who need them least. And because spending on these programs is not debated annually, even outdated or inefficient programs tend to continue indefinitely with little scrutiny.

Regulation

You've already seen how the government can disguise spending as tax breaks. It can also disguise spending by getting someone else to do it.

Regulation allows the government to require spending, while others pay the bill. Governments often make laws or regulations requiring people or businesses to pay for things directly. For instance, when the government decided that all workers were entitled to compulsory superannuation, it could have paid for superannuation directly through a social insurance program that would be part of its budget. Instead, it required employers to provide superannuation to all workers. Making employers pay for it sounds cheaper—after all, the government doesn't pay a dollar for it. But asking employers to pay for it doesn't change the cost, it merely shifts who pays from taxpayers to employers. It's also likely that employers pass some of the costs on to workers in the form of lower wages. So the cost doesn't disappear; it's just that someone else is paying the bill.

Regulation changes incentives. Almost any government policy could be set up as a direct-spending program, a tax expenditure, or a regulation. When policy makers try to figure out the best way to design a policy, they pay careful attention to how people might adjust their behaviour in response to the policy. For instance, a regulation that requires employers to pay for parental leave may lead some employers to try to avoid the cost by not hiring parents (In fact, this is one of the reasons the government provides parental leave through a social insurance program in Australia.).

35.2 Fiscal Policy

Learning Objective *Discover how fiscal policy can smooth business cycles.*

Now that you have a good understanding of what the government spends its money on and how it raises revenue, let's turn to examining the macroeconomic consequences of its choices. We'll focus now on how it affects the year-to-year fluctuations that make up the business cycle, and then we'll conclude this chapter by studying the long-term consequences.

A Countercyclical Force

Fiscal policy refers to the government's use of spending and tax policies to attempt to stabilise the economy. It involves the government adjusting its taxes and spending in an effort to reduce output fluctuations and keep actual GDP close to potential output.

fiscal policy The government's use of spending and tax policies to attempt to stabilise the economy.

Higher spending and lower taxes will boost output. Typically, the government responds to weak output with an *expansionary fiscal policy* involving some combination of higher government spending and lower taxes. Increased government purchases directly increase aggregate expenditure. Lower taxes boost people's after-tax incomes, spurring increased consumption. And because company tax cuts both make new investments more profitable and provide the extra cash necessary to fund these new projects, they spur greater investment. The resulting boost to aggregate expenditure increases the demand for output, leading businesses to ramp up production, which raises GDP.

Lower spending and higher taxes will reduce output. On the flip side, the government can counter an overheating economy with a *contractionary fiscal policy* involving lower government purchases and higher taxes. The same mechanisms operate in reverse as lower spending or higher taxes decrease aggregate expenditure, and hence output. That's why the government will consider contractionary fiscal policy when it is worried that output in excess of potential output might spark inflationary price rises.

Government spending can add to GDP directly and indirectly. It's worth distinguishing between two types of government spending. The first is *government purchases,* in which the government directly purchases goods and services such as schools, highways, and military equipment. The second is *transfer payments*—money that's taken from the government's coffers and sent to individual households. This distinction matters because government purchases are counted directly in GDP, while transfer payments don't directly add to GDP because nothing is purchased or produced. However, when the people who receive transfer payments spend that money, they boost aggregate expenditure and hence GDP.

The multiplier effect makes fiscal policy more potent. The *interdependence principle* reminds us that in addition to these first-round effects of expansionary fiscal policy in boosting aggregate expenditure, there will be ripple effects. That's because one person's spending is another's income, and so an initial burst of spending will cause some people's incomes to rise, which may lead them to boost their spending, which in turn boosts the incomes of others, causing them to spend more also. The *multiplier effect* describes the possibility that an initial boost in spending will set off ripple effects that ultimately lead to a larger rise in GDP. The same effects also operate in reverse, such that an initial decrease in aggregate expenditure due to a contractionary fiscal policy can also have a multiplied effect that leads to a larger decline in GDP.

There's a microeconomic rationale for counter-cyclical fiscal policy. So far, we've focused on the potential for fiscal policy to affect macroeconomic outcomes. But there's an alternative microeconomic argument for countercyclical government spending that applies whenever the government can choose *when* to embark on a new project—perhaps building a new highway, bridge, or airport. The *opportunity cost principle* suggests this investment is best done during an economic slump. After all, when unemployment is high, the next best use of an engineer's time might be lower as their next best alternative might be working in a job that doesn't use their skills, or perhaps continued unemployment. Moreover because real wages tend to be lower during a slump, these projects can be completed more cheaply. Similarly, capital equipment may be idle during a recession, which means a lower opportunity cost of putting machines to work on government investment projects.

Rawpixel.com/Shutterstock

Will you shop more because of a tax refund?

Interpreting the DATA: Can a one-time tax cut boost spending during a recession?

When the financial crisis struck in 2008, one of the government's first responses was to provide $10.4 billion in cash payments to low- and middle-income earners and pensioners. The thinking behind this expansionary fiscal policy was that higher income leads to higher consumption, and so these "rebate cheques" would stimulate greater aggregate expenditure and hence output. But some economists were sceptical it would work. They noted that this income boost was temporary, and so people might save, rather than spend, their rebate cheque. Indeed, if you were worried about a looming recession, would you advise your friends to spend this windfall, or save it for a rainy day?

Careful studies estimate that the stimulus boosted retail sales by $7.5 billion and helped save about 115,000 jobs in early 2009. This estimate tells us two things. First, people spent more of the money than many of the more sceptical economists expected, suggesting that even a temporary boost to income can stimulate an immediate boost in consumption. Second, people spent less than if the government had spent the money directly on goods and services. After all, when the government spends a dollar, the whole dollar is spent, but when it mails a dollar to people, they only spend a portion of it. ■

Discretionary government spending can involve substantial time lags. If the economy starts slipping into a recession, Parliament may consider passing legislation to temporarily increase spending or cut taxes, with an eye toward boosting the economy. This is called **discretionary fiscal policy** because Parliament has to use its discretion and decide to take action. Similarly, the government may use discretionary fiscal policy to cut, spend, or raise taxes when output is above potential. One of the biggest challenges with discretionary fiscal policy is getting the timing right because there are delays at every step of the process.

discretionary fiscal policy Policy that temporarily changes government spending or taxes to boost or slow the economy.

The first step of discretionary fiscal policy is recognising that it's needed. Macroeconomic data are imperfect and often send conflicting signals, and so it can take months for policy makers to recognise that the economy has stalled or is overheating.

Once policy makers realise that the economy needs help, they have to formulate a plan. This second step can be the source of lengthy delays, as Parliament must come up with a plan and pass legislation authorising it. The more politically contentious a tax or spending idea is, the more difficult it can be to get rapid political agreement.

The third step is to actually spend the money, and with complex infrastructure projects, this can take months, or even years. The government should try to maintain a pipeline of "shovel-ready projects"—projects where much of the planning and engineering work have been done in advance—so that an increase in funding can lead to an immediate increase in spending. In practice, government doesn't do a great job of this kind of planning; shovel-ready projects are hard to find.

The delays involved in discretionary fiscal policy mean that during short downturns, it's unlikely that Parliament will be able to act quickly enough to boost aggregate expenditure when it's needed. When it acts too late, it may end up providing a boost after the economy has already recovered. At worst, this can mean that discretionary fiscal policies become procyclical instead of countercyclical, which would destabilise the economy.

Interpreting the DATA Did discretionary fiscal policy work in the 2007–2009 global financial crisis?

Philip Game/Alamy Stock Photo

In response to the global financial crisis, in mid-October 2008 the Rudd government announced a $10.4 billion stimulus package involving $1,000 to $2,000 direct payments to pensioners and low- and middle-income households. Treasury Secretary Ken Henry famously described the strategy to quickly get cash into the pockets of those most likely to spend it as "go hard, go early, go households." In early February 2009, the government followed up with a (then) massive $42 billion additional stimulus package known as the "Nation Building and Jobs Plan," which consisted largely of infrastructure spending.

It also provided an interesting laboratory for economists to study the effects of discretionary fiscal policy. Australia was one of the few countries in the world to avoid a recession during the global financial crisis, and most economists agree that the discretionary fiscal policy of the Rudd government was largely to thank for this. ■

Fiscal policy works best when it's timely, targeted, and temporary. Fiscal policy works best when it is implemented before economic conditions have severely worsened, when it targets those parts of the economy that are most affected, and when it's used for only as long as it's needed. This leads to the three *Ts* of fiscal policy: It must be timely, targeted, and temporary. *Timely* refers to the idea that policy makers must act quickly, getting ahead of looming problems. *Targeted* refers to the idea that fiscal policy—unlike monetary policy—can focus on the specific regions, industries, and groups of workers who need the most help. Fiscal stimulus is more likely to be effective when it's targeted in a way that gets money into the hands of those who are more likely to spend it. (By contrast, sending money to people who are going to save it or pay off existing debt won't raise spending and hence won't boost GDP.) Finally, *temporary* refers to the idea that extra spending is no longer required when the economy has recovered. Indeed, as we're about to see, were a rise in government spending to persist, it risks reducing private investment.

Fiscal policy works best when it's:
1. Timely
2. Targeted
3. Temporary

Government spending can crowd out investment spending. Sometimes a rise in expansionary fiscal policy will lead to a decline in private spending, and particularly investment—an effect known as **crowding out.** It's as if the government enters an already crowded store and shoves a few customers aside. More precisely, crowding out occurs when expansionary fiscal policy leads to a higher real interest rate, which reduces private spending. Because investment is particularly sensitive to the real interest rate, the main impact will be to reduce investment. The extent of crowding out depends on the time period being analysed and the state of the economy. Let's see why.

crowding out The decline in private spending—and particularly investment—that follows from a rise in government borrowing.

In the short run, expansionary fiscal policy will boost output, and (as we discussed in Chapter 34) the RBA typically responds to a more positive output gap—and the possibility that it will spark inflation—by raising the real interest rate, which reduces investment. The extent of crowding out depends on how aggressively the RBA responds to the output gap, and that in turn depends on how much excess capacity the economy has. During a deep recession—when there's a lot of excess capacity—both fiscal and monetary policy are likely working in concert, and so the RBA is unlikely to raise the real interest rate in response to an expansionary fiscal policy. As a result, there won't be much crowding out. But if politicians were to pass a fiscal stimulus when the economy is already operating close to potential (perhaps in the hope of creating a boom that'll help them get reelected), then the RBA will likely counter by raising rates, and these higher rates will lead to substantial crowding out.

In the long run, the neutral real interest rate—the rate that ensures that output is equal to potential—is determined by the supply and demand of loanable funds (we analysed

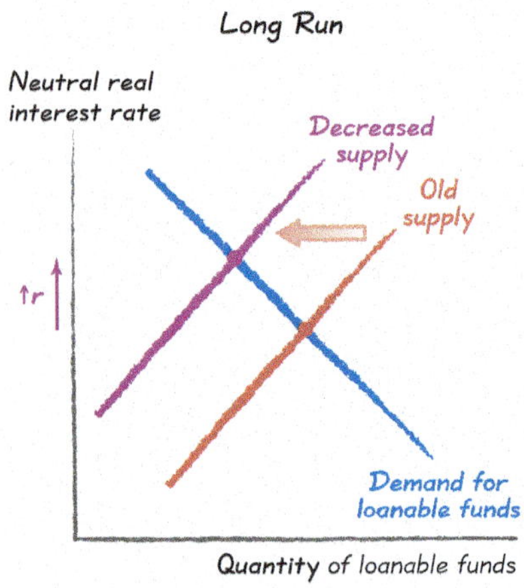

this market in Chapter 26). Expansionary fiscal policy involves the government dissaving, which decreases the supply of loanable funds. This decrease in supply will raise the neutral real interest, and these higher rates will deter investment. (You could alternatively think about the government's borrowing as increasing the demand for loanable funds, which has the same effect of raising the neutral real interest rate.)

Remember that in the long run, output cannot sustainably exceed potential output, which is determined by the supply of available labour, human and physical capital, and technological progress. Because increased government spending doesn't affect potential output, it won't affect the long-run level of output. By this view, in the long run every extra dollar of government spending will crowd out a dollar of private spending and so fiscal stimulus can only have temporary effects on output.

Automatic Stabilisers

automatic stabilisers Spending and tax programs that adjust as the economy expands and contracts, without policy makers taking any deliberate action.

An **automatic stabiliser** is a fiscal policy that adjusts as the economy expands and contracts without policy makers taking any deliberate action. It's *automatic* because no policy maker has to take any action—the adjustments are built into current law. And it's *stabilising* because these adjustments are countercyclical, boosting output during recessions and reducing it during expansions. Automatic stabilisers are built into both tax and spending programs. Let's dig into each, in turn.

Steve Helber/AP Photo

During recessions, some workers get fewer shifts.

Government revenue automatically adjusts during business cycles.

Almost everything about a recession is bad: Business profits fall, some workers lose their jobs, others have their hours cut, and average wages decline. As a result, incomes fall. But there's a silver lining to this loss of income: You'll pay less in taxes. This automatic stabiliser helps support after-tax incomes, ensuring that spending—and hence output—won't decline by as much as it otherwise might.

When incomes fall, tax payments fall for two reasons. The first one is probably obvious: You pay income taxes on your income, so if you earn less income you'll pay less tax. The second is more subtle. Because income taxes are progressive—meaning that tax rates are higher when you earn more—as your income falls, so does your tax rate. As a result, if a recession halves your pre-tax income, the amount of tax you'll pay will fall by more than half, meaning that your after-tax income falls by less than half. Progressive taxes cushion the blow of a recession.

As a result, the government takes in less tax revenue during a recession. This keeps more money in the hands of businesses and consumers, and to the extent they spend it, they'll boost aggregate expenditure, and hence output.

A similar dynamic operates—in reverse—during an economic boom. As income rises, taxes automatically start to rise, both because there's more income to tax, and because more people are bumped into higher tax brackets. As a result, federal tax revenues rise. Money that the government collects in taxes is money that people can't spend, so this reduces aggregate expenditure and hence output. As such, the tax system acts to counter both booms and busts, smoothing out business cycle fluctuations.

Bai Xuefei/Xinhua/Alamy Stock Photo

More people receive government benefits during recessions.

Government spending automatically adjusts during business cycles.

Government spending also rises automatically during a recession. When income falls, more people qualify for government benefits, such as a low-income healthcare card—providing access to subsidised medicines and additional free health care—or Youth Allowance, for which eligibility is based primarily on income. As more people lose their jobs due to the downturn, more people become eligible to receive JobSeeker payments. These additional payments support aggregate expenditure by allowing those receiving support to spend more than they would have otherwise been able to.

The reverse happens during a boom: When people earn more, they're less likely to qualify for government support programs. As a result, government spending on these programs falls automatically as the economy recovers. And so this inbuilt tendency for government spending to rise during recessions and then fall during expansions works to counter the business cycle.

Automatic stabilisers are timely, targeted, and temporary. These automatic changes in taxes and spending are *timely* because they're automatically triggered whenever people's incomes decline. They're also well *targeted* because taxes decline only for those whose income has fallen, and eligibility for income support payments depends on each person's financial or employment status. And they're *temporary* because they automatically reverse course as the economy reverses course.

This makes them quite effective, and the Treasury estimates that automatic stabilisers added around 1% to GDP in the recovery from the coronavirus pandemic, preventing a severe downturn from being much worse. As such, even those economists who are wary of discretionary fiscal policy often argue in favour of creating more automatic stabilisers. With a bit of imagination, the amount of spending on almost any government program could be tied to the state of the economy. Yet politicians often prefer discretion, because it allows them to steer tax and spending changes to benefit their preferred constituencies, and they can claim political credit for these changes.

Fiscal Policy and Monetary Policy Interactions

When the threat of a recession looms, policy makers have two main ways to respond. The RBA can adopt an *expansionary monetary policy* by lowering interest rates, which will encourage more spending. In addition—or instead—the government can adopt an *expansionary fiscal policy* by increasing government purchases and cutting taxes. In many respects these policy tools are quite similar—they each operate by boosting aggregate expenditure and hence output. So when will one tool be more effective than the other?

Monetary policy is more nimble. The RBA is constantly assessing the state of the economy, ready to act as soon as it senses an impending problem. A decision to lower interest rates can be implemented by the end of the afternoon. And so the advantage of monetary policy is that it can be implemented quickly. The disadvantage is that changes in interest rates don't immediately boost spending, and it can take a year or more before lower interest rates stimulate more spending. That's why fiscal policy through automatic stabilisers can work in concert with monetary policy to more quickly steer the economy back to potential output.

Fiscal policy can be more targeted. A big increase in the price of iron ore can cause a boom in the mines of Western Australia, but Tasmania might struggle as prices go up. Fiscal policy can target support to Tasmania or any other region of the country that is struggling, just as it can target the mining sector or other specific industries. And so while fiscal policy can be tailored to local economic conditions, monetary policy imposes a one-size-fits-all solution on the whole economy.

Fiscal policy is particularly important at the zero lower bound. When the RBA can't cut short-term nominal rates any further—and its capacity to cut long-term rates is limited—discretionary fiscal policy might be the only effective tool left to stabilise the economy. When policy makers are worried about this possibility, fiscal policy and monetary policy can work in concert to reinforce each other. That's why the RBA initially responded to the coronavirus pandemic by cutting nominal interest rates close to zero, and then the federal government passed discretionary fiscal policy to further stimulate the economy.

35.3 Government Deficits and Debt

Learning Objective *Understand why governments run deficits and the implications of government debt.*

Now that you know what the government spends money on, how it raises revenue, and how it uses spending and tax policy to stabilise the economy, it's time to talk about the longer-run implications of the government's budget.

Government Budget Deficits

budget deficit The difference between spending and revenue in a year in which spending exceeds revenue.

budget surplus The difference between spending and revenue in a year in which revenue exceeds spending.

The federal government rarely brings in enough revenue to pay for all its spending, and so it borrows a lot of money. In those years in which government spending exceeds government revenue, the government runs a **budget deficit,** and it must borrow money to fund this shortfall. On those seemingly rare occasions when government revenue exceeds spending, the result is a **budget surplus.** While budget surpluses used to be quite common in Australia, they are not so much anymore.

The government's *debt* is the total accumulated amount of money that it owes. Its budget *deficit* in a given year adds to the total debt, while a budget *surplus* can be used to repay its debt. The deficit measures the *flow* of new borrowing over a year, while the debt measures the accumulated *stock* of borrowing at a point in time.

Figure 11 | Federal Revenues and Spending

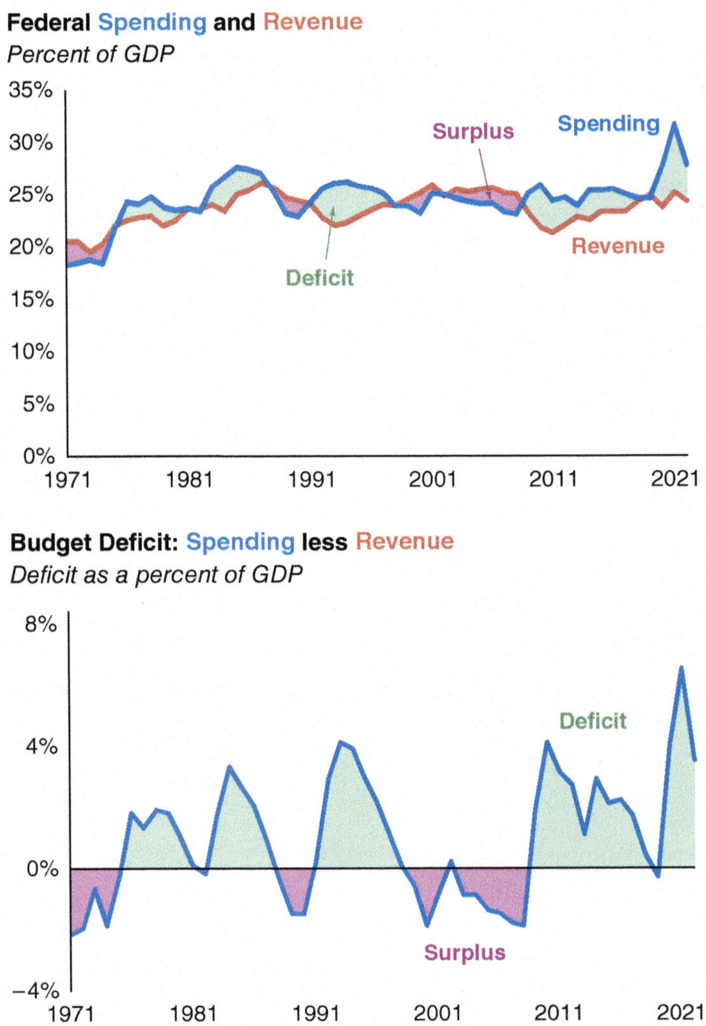

Data from: Treasury.

The federal government runs deficits. There are four things to notice about federal government spending and revenue:

1. *The federal government typically runs budget deficits.* The green areas in Figure 11 show budget deficits, and the purple areas show surpluses. You'll notice that there hasn't been any purple in the graph since 2008.
2. *Persistent large budget deficits are a relatively recent phenomenon.* In the last 50 years, Australia has had a mix of budget deficits and surpluses. Our fiscal history looks like a bit of a roller coaster. In the mid-1970s, the budget tipped into deficit, returning to surplus in the late 1980s. The early 1990s recession pushed it back into deficit. From the late 1990s until the 2008 financial crisis, large surpluses were run—so much so that all federal government debt was repaid. Since then the budget has never been in surplus, despite a small one being forecast before the coronavirus pandemic hit.
3. *Economic crises require a sudden surge of spending that results in budget deficits.* The government ran its biggest deficits during the 2020 coronavirus pandemic as it borrowed money to soften a deep recession. Periods of crisis require a quick surge in spending. Borrowing money during these times effectively means asking future generations to pay some of the cost, which makes sense given that the effects of a depression can last for generations.
4. *Business cycles create budget deficit cycles.* The federal government's budget deficit tends to rise during contractions and fall during expansions. Partly, this is due to the use of expansionary fiscal policy as Parliament tends to temporarily boost spending and cut tax rates to counter contractions. In addition, the size of the deficit or surplus reflects the influence of automatic stabilisers. During a slump, the government both takes in less tax revenue and spends more on income-support programs, raising the deficit. Likewise, a boom creates more tax revenue and reduces the number of people relying on government programs. This reduces the deficit and occasionally produces a surplus such as in the the mid 2000s.

When should the government run deficits? The usual way that people think about budget deficits is that they reflect a mismatch between *how much* the government spends and *how much* revenue it takes in. But an alternative perspective is that they reflect a mismatch between *when* the government spends money and *when* it takes in the revenue to pay for this spending. This framing suggests that deficits (or surpluses) often make sense because there's no reason to expect the pattern of *when* it's best to spend money to match the pattern of when it's best to raise revenue.

When the government spends on infrastructure like roads, highways, airports, internet connectivity, and research, the benefits of that spending will last for decades. So why should it pay for it all upfront? Just as many people borrow money to purchase a house and then pay it off over time, the government can borrow to make investments and pay for those investments over time. Moreover, government investments help spur GDP growth, making it easier for the government to subsequently repay those debts.

A related argument for deficit spending is that whenever there is a need for a surge in spending—like during a war or pandemic—it's inefficient to collect all the revenue at once. Raising taxes a lot in one year and lowering them the next creates distortions, leading people to shift income from one year to the other. People tend to change their behaviour more to avoid taxes when tax rates are higher. So smoothing taxes over time reduces economic distortions. It also reduces the burden of taxes because people prefer to smooth their consumption.

Just as you're starting to get comfortable with the government running budget deficits, it's time to discuss the problems—many of which come from the costs to the economy when the government accumulates large amounts of debt. We'll turn to the problems of government debt shortly. But for now, let's consider the political problem.

Four facts about government spending and revenue:

1. The federal government typically runs budget deficits.
2. Persistent large budget deficits are a relatively recent phenomenon.
3. Economic crises require a sudden surge of spending that results in budget deficits.
4. Business cycles create budget deficit cycles.

freedomnaruk/Shutterstock

martin berry/Alamy Stock Photo

Investments in infrastructure benefit many generations.

Budget deficits may reflect short-run political incentives. Spending programs are popular with voters, but raising taxes to pay for those programs is not. That's why election-minded politicians like to spend money on programs that make voters happy, but they don't like raising taxes to pay for them. These unbalanced incentives might explain why the federal government typically runs budget deficits.

But it's not just that deficits reflect short-run political incentives; such incentives might also lead to a bigger and more inefficient government. The problem is that if politicians can get the political benefit of spending without facing the cost, they're likely to approve more spending than they otherwise would. And so the ability to run deficits may also lead to more government spending—even on programs whose costs exceed their benefits. One proposal that is often suggested to fix these unbalanced incentives is to require the government to balance its budget. This would force politicians to consider not only the benefits of new spending programs, but also the costs of raising the revenue to pay for them.

Requiring a balanced budget would make business cycles worse. So should the government be required to balance its budget? Adopting a *balanced budget rule*—which would require the federal government to balance its budget each and every year—would cause another set of problems because the government would not be able to use fiscal policy to counteract business cycles. Indeed, balancing the budget each year would require it to implement a fiscal policy that would exacerbate economic fluctuations. Remember, a downturn leads to lower tax revenues. That means a balanced budget rule would force the government to raise tax rates or cut spending (or both) in the midst of a downturn. Further, government spending automatically rises during downturns as more people qualify for benefits. To maintain an annually balanced budget, such programs would need to be scaled back at exactly the time when more people need them. This would not only hurt those who've lost their jobs or seen their incomes decline—it would also worsen the broader economic slump. That is, balancing the budget during a recession would lead to a contractionary fiscal policy, which would reduce aggregate expenditure, causing output to decline even more.

Deficit debates reflect both economic forces and value judgements. The value judgement is whether the next generation should help pay for the spending priorities of the current generation. You might think, "No way!" But consider how much richer you are than your grandparents were at your age. Real personal incomes—meaning income adjusted for inflation—have more than doubled over the past four decades. That means that you can buy twice as much stuff as your grandparents could. In economic terms, the sacrifice from having you pay an extra dollar in taxes is likely much smaller than it would have been if your grandparents had footed the bill. Likewise, future generations will likely be richer than yours, and so the sacrifice they will need to make to pay a bit more in taxes is even smaller still. Debates about economic forces also reflect concern about debt's impact on the economy. Those concerns are what we're going to turn to now.

Government Debt

gross government debt The total accumulated amount of money the government owes.

net government debt The debt that the government owes to individuals, businesses, and other governments both here and abroad.

Government debt is the total amount the government owes. It reflects the long history of both past borrowing to fund budget deficits, and past repayments from occasional surpluses. The government borrows by selling *government bonds* to savers in both Australia and abroad. Government bonds are effectively IOUs from the government, promising to repay the amount it borrowed, plus interest. When you buy a government bond, you're loaning the government money. Your superannuation fund probably invests some portion of your retirement savings in government bonds, making you one of these lenders.

In mid-2021, the total debts of the federal government—called the **gross government debt**—added up to $830 billion. But the government also has its own set of assets—cash, deposits, investments, and even loans it has given out. What really matters is the government's financial position, taking into account both its liabilities (mostly made up of gross debt) and its assets. The difference between the government's liabilities and assets is called **net government debt,** and it amounts to about $620 billion.

Figure 12 Net Government Debt

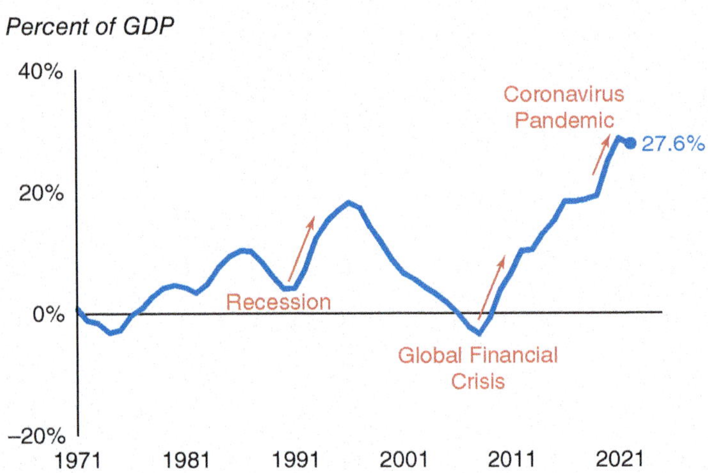

Data from: Treasury.

Evaluate the debt relative to a country's GDP. Numbers measured in the billions can be hard to make sense of, so let's try to develop a sense of scale. It makes sense to think about a country's debt relative to its capacity to repay it. That's why economists typically focus on the ratio of a country's government debt to its annual GDP, which is a measure of the resources available to make repayments. In Australia, this *debt-to-GDP ratio* in 2021 was 27.6%. This says the net government debt is equivalent to what we currently produce in 27.6% of a year (roughly 3½ months).

Figure 13 Net Government Debt by Country

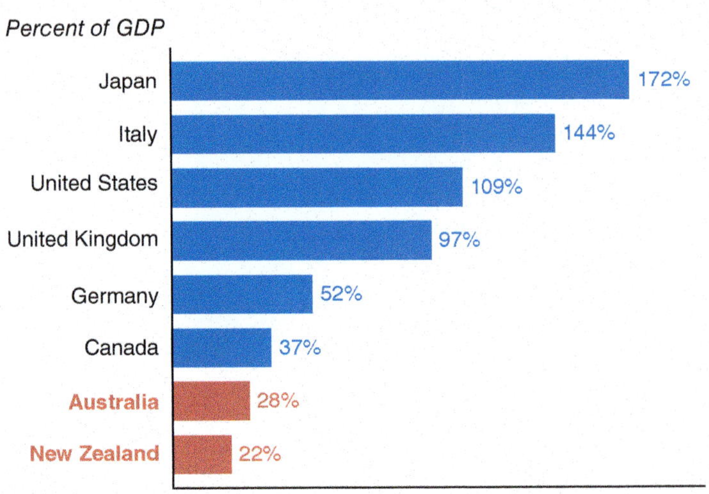

2022 Data from: IMF and Treasury.

Government debt is currently high, relative to our history. Figure 12 shows the debt-to-GDP ratio since 1970–71. It shows that government debt tends to rise sharply in times of severe economic downturns. The current level of government debt, at 31.1% of GDP, is higher than in any other period. This mostly reflects the dramatic effect of the coronavirus pandemic, in which an expansionary fiscal policy led to lower tax revenue, greater government spending, and hence more borrowing. But since then, government debt has remained high, and is expected to peak at 33.1% of GDP in 2025.

Australia's government debt is much lower than that of other leading countries. Figure 13 compares the net government debt of Australia (as a share of GDP) to that of other large advanced economies. As this figure illustrates, governments get by with a variety of debt levels, and Australia is near the bottom of the pack. And while all of the countries shown in this figure have a net government debt, a small number of countries—including Finland and Norway—have a negative debt, which means that they've put aside a stockpile of money for the future. At the opposite extreme, Japan has the highest debt-to-GDP ratio of any country in the world, much of it due to successive attempts to use expansionary fiscal policy to revive its economy, which has struggled since the 1990s. Australia's government debt is currently well above New Zealand's level of 22% of GDP. But it may not stay that way forever.

Government debt is expected to decline over the coming decade. Figure 14 shows recent projections from the Treasury, which suggest that if the government maintains its current course, the debt-to-GDP ratio is expected to fall to 26.9% over the next decade.

We have a fairly clear idea about where the debt is headed because much of the federal budget is non-discretionary spending. In particular, spending on the Age Pension, National Disability Insurance Scheme, and Medicare is projected to remain relatively stable relative to GDP growth. These benefits are an **unfunded liability**—a commitment to incur expenses in the future without a plan to pay for them. The federal government has a lot of unfunded liabilities, and they're projected to be the primary driver of rising deficits and debt over coming decades.

They're also intimately tied to the other key driver of government debt, which is interest payments. The more the government borrows, the more interest it pays. As unfunded liabilities push the debt higher, the government will have to make increasingly larger annual interest payments, which in turn will also push deficits and debt higher still. In 2022, the federal government spent 3.1% of its budget paying interest on the debt, and that is expected to grow somewhat in coming years. Interest rates were at historic lows during the late 2010s and early 2020s and are expected to rise back to more normal levels.

Figure 14 | **Projected Federal Net Government Debt**

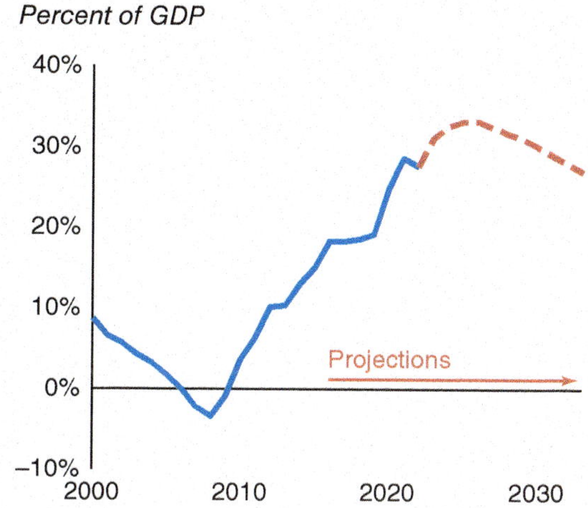

Data from: Treasury.

All of this raises the question: How worried should you be about government debt? I have good news and bad news. The good news is that in the next few pages, I'll tell you about some reasons not to be so worried. But the bad news is that the following few pages also give you some reasons to be more concerned. At the end, it will be up to you to figure out where you stand.

unfunded liability A commitment to incur expenses in the future without a plan to pay for those expenses.

Reasons Not to Worry About the Debt

People who want to stoke alarm about government debt often divide the size of the debt by the size of the population to argue that each of us owes a lot of money. Scaling big numbers is a good idea, and when you divide the net government debt of $620 billion by the total population of 26 million, you get roughly $24,000 per person. That sounds like a lot (and it might sound even worse when you add it to your HECS-HELP debt!).

But you do not owe anybody $24,000. Don't make the mistake of thinking about government debt as if it's your personal household debt. Understanding why the government's finances are not like a family's finances yields five reasons not to worry so much about the government's debt.

Reasons not to worry about government debt:

1. Most of our government debt is money owed by Australians to Australians.
2. Future generations can help shrink the debt.
3. It wouldn't take a big adjustment to repay the debt.
4. The government never really needs to repay the debt.
5. The government has options that you don't.

Reason one: Most of our government debt is money owed by Australians to Australians. When a family is in debt, the problem is that it owes money to someone else. But the government debt is different. To a large degree, it's money that we owe ourselves. That's because most—though by no means all—of the government's debt is borrowed from Australians. And so while the Australian people owe the debt, they are also owed much of the debt.

Reason two: Future generations can help shrink the debt. It's also important to remember that the government—unlike a household—can shrink its debt over many generations. And so that means that the burden of repaying $620 billion in debt can be spread over not only the current population of 26 million, but also tens of millions of people in future generations. That might even be fairer. After all, much of this debt reflects major investments by past generations building infrastructure, creating a well-functioning economy, and investing in better education. These are investments that future generations will continue to enjoy, so why not ask them to chip in to help pay the costs, too? When there are many more than 26 million Australians shrinking the debt, your personal "share" is much less than $24,000.

Reason three: It wouldn't take a big adjustment to repay the debt. Even if the current cohort of Australians decides it should repay the entire debt, the burden may not be as bad as you fear. Here's why. Recall that the government spends $25,000 a year per person on government services. So over your lifetime the government will likely spend well over a million dollars on you. Your current "share" of the debt is small relative to this. It follows that if the government decides to repay the debt, it wouldn't have to cut much of the spending it plans to do over your lifetime. So even if your generation alone had to pay back the entire debt, it might not be as bad as you think if it pays it back slowly—like over the course of your life.

Reason four: The government never really needs to repay the debt. The Australian government has been in and out of debt since its formation. Yet even if it had never repaid its debts, it wouldn't be a problem. That's because government debt doesn't have to be fully repaid to be sustainable. What matters is whether the government has the means to make the required payments. That's why economists focus on the debt-to-GDP ratio, which measures our current debt relative to our capacity to pay. Moreover, the Australian government debt is decreasing as a share of GDP, so many economists are actually advocating that the government take on more debt. Notice that a sustainable outcome requires getting the debt to be a stable share of GDP, not eliminating the debt. And there's more room in the federal budget before we reach that point.

Reason five: The government has options that you don't. People get into trouble with credit when their monthly paycheque can't cover their monthly payments. Their problem is that it's really hard to increase the amount of revenue coming into a household to cover the rising interest payments going out. But the federal government can pretty easily raise more revenue—it just has to raise taxes. Indeed, raising tax rates by a few percentage points would be enough to stabilise the debt-to-GDP ratio, if it ever looked like it was getting out of control. Remember, the federal government can tap a rather extraordinary resource that individual households cannot—the combined incomes and wealth of 26 million people (and their descendants).

Bill Bachman/Alamy Stock Photo

The government can print money. You can't.

The government has one more option that households don't: It can literally print money, and use that money to repay its debt. But as seductive as this seems, it's rarely a good idea. Printing more money to chase the same quantity of goods leads to inflation, and in some cases, it has led to chaotic hyperinflation. And lenders aren't happy because even if the government repays the nominal value of their debt, it's paying them dollars that are worth a lot less. When a government inflates away its debt like this, lenders are very reluctant to ever lend to them again.

Reasons to worry about government debt:

1. Slower economic growth
2. Future fiscal choices are constrained
3. The risk of a crisis of confidence
4. A debt crisis becomes more likely

Reasons to Worry About Government Debt

Just as you're starting to feel comfortable with government debt, it's time to turn the tables, and dig into some of the reasons you should be concerned.

Reason one: Slower economic growth. High and rising debt risks slower economic growth. The problem is that the government borrows funds that might otherwise be used to finance investments in productive capital, like new machinery. Without this funding, the private sector invests in less capital, which makes workers less productive, meaning they produce less output.

Reason two: Future fiscal choices are constrained. Higher government debt makes it harder to borrow more when the government needs funds. It won't be able to easily borrow during national emergencies, such as wars, recessions, or natural disasters. It will also find it harder to borrow for important national investments that will yield benefits for generations, such as infrastructure.

Reason three: The risk of a crisis of confidence. The Australian government pays just about the lowest interest rates of anyone, anywhere in the world. That's because investors are confident that when they loan the Australian government money, they'll be repaid in full and in a timely manner. That confidence is a valuable asset, saving the government billions of dollars in lower interest payments each year.

That confidence is also fragile. Consider the possibility that at some point investors become concerned that the government's debt is unsustainable. Perhaps they're worried that the government will miss its next scheduled loan repayment. This risk of losing money will lead lenders to charge the government a higher interest rate. The problem for a government that has borrowed a lot of money is that even a small rise in the interest rate will lead to a large rise in its annual interest bill. If its interest bill gets too large, it won't be able to make those loan repayments. And so the perception that the government debt is unsustainable can lead lenders to charge higher interest rates, and those higher interest rates create the reality that the government's debt is unsustainable. Even worse, this kind of *crisis of confidence*—where investors' fears spark a vicious cycle of higher interest rates and less sustainable debt—can happen in the blink of an eye.

Think of this as a self-fulfilling prophecy, with either a good or a bad outcome. The good outcome occurs when lenders think that the government will repay them, leading them to charge low interest rates, and because interest rates are low, the government easily makes its scheduled repayments. The bad outcome occurs when lenders think the government won't make its payments, so they charge higher interest rates. This crippling interest burden may even lead the government to miss its scheduled payments. And so the observation that Australia is currently enjoying the good outcome is no guarantee that things won't change tomorrow.

Take a look at Greece, where in 2009, investors suddenly became concerned that the government might not repay its debt. The interest rate that lenders charged the Greek government rose from 5% in 2009 to over 25% in 2012. What had been a difficult fiscal situation became untenable, as it became virtually impossible for Greece to meet its annual interest payments. Ultimately the European Union and the IMF stepped in with emergency loans and a recovery program. But along the way, this crisis led to a modern-day depression in Greece.

Milos Bicanski/Getty Images

Greece faced a debt crisis starting in 2009.

Reason four: A debt crisis becomes more likely. At its worst, high government debt can lead to a *debt crisis* in which the government simply can't repay its loans. The government stops making payments on its debt and so investors abruptly refuse to lend it any more money. When a government can't borrow money, it must immediately balance its budget either by raising taxes or cutting spending. When this occurred in many Latin American countries in the early 1980s, the abrupt shift to a contractionary fiscal policy plunged many of these countries into a sharp recession. The more recent crisis of confidence that led the interest rates Greece faced to soar also plunged it into a debt crisis in which it simply couldn't repay its loans. As of 2019, Greece was still struggling to climb out of the recession that was caused by its debt crisis. Australia is pretty far away from a debt crisis, but let this serve as an important reminder not to let the debt spin out of control.

Tying It Together

An idealised view of how government works is that a smart population will vote for smart policies and a responsive government will deliver what people most value. By this idealised view, those values will determine the government's taxing and spending priorities, how it uses fiscal policy to actively fight recessions, and how it'll manage its debts to ensure that your generation pays its fair share, but no more.

Perhaps that was once a reasonable description a century or two ago when Australians started with a nearly blank slate. Back then, the federal government's only real tasks were national defence and delivering the mail, and so earlier generations essentially invented the government they wanted. But today, your generation has inherited a mature government with a long history of passing mandatory spending and tax bills in which future plans for government taxing and spending priorities are already largely spelled out.

All of our past decisions can be changed if we decide that our priorities for government taxing and spending have shifted. The challenge is that it's harder to enact change when you have to scrap the choices made by previous generations. Eliminating or even reducing promised spending (and tax expenditures) is politically difficult, even if we can all agree that there are better ways to spend our money. The task of shaping the government to serve your generation has been made even harder because past generations can make spending plans without accompanying plans to raise enough revenue to pay for them. In 2022–23, the federal government planned to spend $626 billion, while it planned to bring in revenue of only $548 billion. Economists estimate that the "structural" or steady-state budget deficit is about $40 billion, or 2% of GDP. The good news is that with Australia's relatively low debt levels, this deficit can be sustained for many years. The bad news is that sooner or later something has to be done to eliminate that gap between revenues and expenditures. This will require tax and spending reforms.

Chapter at a Glance

The Government Sector: Government spending has grown over time as the role of the government in providing social insurance and education has expanded.

Social insurance: Government-provided insurance against bad outcomes such as unemployment, illness, disability, or outliving your savings.

Federal Spending
- Social insurance programs
- Defence
- Education

State Spending
- Social insurance programs
- Education
- Hospitals
- Law enforcement

Local Spending
- Garbage collection and recycling
- Community services

Federal government revenue sources:
- Income taxes
- Company taxes
- Goods and services tax
- Excise and customs duty

State and local government revenue sources:
- Commonwealth government grants
- Property taxes
- Other levies

Hidden Government Spending: The government has other ways to effectively spend money without any spending showing up on their books. These are not counted as government spending but they have the same effect.

1. **Tax expenditures:** Parliament can implement programs through the tax code. These are special deductions, exemptions, or credits that lower your tax obligations to encourage you to engage in certain kinds of activities.
2. **Government regulation:** The government can mandate that citizens or businesses engage in certain behaviour that costs money.

Fiscal Policy: The government's use of spending and tax policies to attempt to stabilise the economy. Fiscal policy is more important at the zero lower bound and works best when it's timely, targeted, and temporary.

Discretionary fiscal policy: Policy that temporarily changes spending or taxes to boost or slow the economy.

Automatic stabilisers: Spending and tax programs that adjust as the economy expands and contracts, without policy makers taking any deliberate action.

Budget Deficits

Budget deficit: The difference between spending and revenue when spending exceeds revenue over a year.

Budget surplus: The difference between spending and revenue when revenue exceeds spending over a year.

Four facts about government budget deficits:

1. The federal government typically runs budget deficits.
2. Persistent large budget deficits are a relatively recent phenomenon.
3. Economic crises require a sudden surge of spending that results in budget deficits.
4. Business cycles create government budget deficit cycles.

Government Debt

Gross government debt: The total accumulated amount of money the government owes.

Net government debt: The debt that the government owes to individuals, businesses, and other governments both here and abroad.

Reasons not to worry about government debt

1. Most of our government debt is money owed by Australians to Australians.
2. Future generations can help shrink the debt.
3. It wouldn't take a big adjustment to shrink the debt.
4. The government never really needs to repay the debt.
5. The government has options that you don't.

Reasons to worry about government debt

1. Slower economic growth.
2. Future fiscal choices are constrained.
3. The risk of a crisis of confidence.
4. A debt crisis becomes more likely.

Key Concepts

automatic stabilisers, 902
budget deficit, 904
budget surplus, 904
crowding out, 901
discretionary fiscal policy, 900
discretionary spending, 892
excise tax, 894
fiscal policy, 899
gross government debt, 906
income taxes, 893
mandatory spending, 892
marginal tax rate, 894
net government debt, 906
payroll tax, 895
progressive tax, 894
property tax, 896
regressive tax, 894
stamp duty, 896
sales tax, 893
social insurance, 890
tax expenditures, 896
taxable income, 894
unfunded liability, 907

Discussion and Review Questions

Learning Objective 35.1 *Assess the size and scope of the government.*

1. Explain what the federal government's biggest expenditures are on. Why do you think this is so?
2. Some federal government spending is said to be "mandatory." What does this mean and how does it differ from discretionary spending?
3. How do federal, state, and local government spending differ in focus?
4. How is a tax expenditure similar to government spending? How is it different?
5. You're working for a member of Parliament from your state. They are looking to co-sponsor a bill to provide assistance to low-wage workers who want to pursue higher education. They ask you to brief them on how they might implement it as (a) a direct-spending program, (b) a tax expenditure, or (c) using regulation. Describe the implications, as well as some of the pros and cons of each approach.

Learning Objective 35.2 *Discover how fiscal policy can smooth business cycles.*

6. Use the three *T*s of fiscal policy to explain the challenges of using discretionary fiscal policy to counter a recession.
7. Explain how different types of government spending add to GDP directly and indirectly, and how a rise in government spending can have a multiplied effect on GDP.
8. Explain how increases in government spending can crowd out investment spending. Is crowding out a major concern when the economy's output is below its potential?
9. Describe how automatic stabilisers respond when output is above potential output. Assess the extent to which these responses are timely, targeted, and temporary.
10. The RBA has conducted expansionary monetary policy to combat a recession but is running up against the zero lower bound, and the economy is still not recovering. What other steps could the government take in order to try to stabilise the economy?

Learning Objective 35.3 *Understand why governments run deficits and the implications of government debt.*

11. Explain why requiring the federal government to balance its budget each year would limit its ability to respond to an economic downturn. Why might a policy of requiring balanced budgets exacerbate an economic downturn in a state?
12. How is government debt different from personal debt?

Study Problems

Learning Objective 35.1 *Assess the size and scope of the government.*

1. A friend of yours argues that federal government spending is out of control and significant cuts in spending are needed to reduce the size of the government. They tell you that if we cut federal government spending on science and international affairs, it will really reduce the size of the government. Do you agree? Why or why not?
2. Spending on Medicare, the Age Pension, and NDIS is expected to grow over the next few decades as the share of the population who are elderly grows. Explain why an aging population increases government spending on these programs. How might future spending change if Medicare, the Age Pension, and NDIS were discretionary spending programs instead?
3. Marissa just got hired at a new job for an annual salary of $112,200. After deductions, her taxable income will be $100,000. Use the marginal tax rates shown in Figure 9 to calculate how much she will owe in income taxes if she has no other income and no additional deductions. What share of her income would she be paying in taxes?
4. In an effort to encourage people to purchase electric cars, the federal government proposes a tax credit of $2,500 for each new electric car that is bought in Australia. Who

do you think would benefit from this tax expenditure? What do you think the government's goal is with such a tax expenditure? Do you think that the tax expenditure is likely to achieve this goal?

5. A politician says, "We could help low-wage workers by offering them tax credits like the earned income tax credit, but it would be cheaper to do it by raising the minimum wage because that would cost the government nothing." Evaluate this argument.

Learning Objective 35.2 *Discover how fiscal policy can smooth business cycles.*

6. Which of the following are examples of expansionary fiscal policy, and which are examples of automatic stabilisers?
   a. The government paid an extra $5 million in JobSeeker claims last month.
   b. New legislation temporarily extends JobKeeper benefits for an additional 26 weeks.
   c. The Australian Tax Office collected $5 billion more in taxes last year, even though tax rates were unchanged.
   d. Parliament appropriates an additional $20 million in funds to help states pay teachers during a recession.

7. If the economy slides into recession next year, and Parliament does nothing to adjust existing tax and spending programs, how will government spending and government revenue change? Do any of these adjustments help stabilise the economy?

8. Now consider what happens if the federal government introduces new government spending to combat the recession. How will this affect the economy in the short run? As the economy recovers, political pressures lead the government to keep this spending in place. What are some possible long-run consequences of making the increased government spending permanent?

Learning Objective 35.3 *Understand why governments run deficits and learn about government debt.*

9. In 2020, the federal government spent $578 billion and brought in revenue of $486 billion.
   a. Is this a budget deficit or surplus, and what is its size?
   b. If net government debt in 2019 was $374 billion, what will it be in 2020?
   c. GDP was $1.95 trillion in 2019 and $1.98 trillion in 2020. How has the debt-to-GDP ratio changed from 2019 to 2020?

10. Parliament has just passed a new budget that drastically cuts taxes without decreasing government spending. When asked how the government plan to address the dramatic increase in deficits that will occur due to the tax cuts, the Prime Minister responds, "We're going to see some amazing economic growth because of this new policy, so much growth that we're going to grow our way out of any short-term increases to government debt." If this extra economic growth doesn't materialise, what are some of the risks to the Australian economy?

APPENDIX A

A Closer Look at Aggregate Expenditure and the Multiplier

Stocks tanked. A typical investment in the stock market worth $100 just a few years prior quickly fell to be worth only $13. Bankruptcies soared and more than a third of all banks failed, erasing families' savings. The U.S. economy shrank by nearly 30%, having global ripple effects, and roughly one in four people who wanted to work couldn't find jobs. The Great Depression began in 1929 and launched a dark decade in U.S. history. It didn't just reshape the American economy, it reshaped society. Poverty and malnourishment rose. Evictions led to widespread homelessness. The birth rate fell and the suicide rate spiked. Australia suffered a similar fate, even though the Great Depression began with the 1929 Wall Street stock market crash. In 1932, unemployment in Australia reached a straggering 32%. It took a decade for the Australian economy to recover, and, as in the United States, the Depression led to dramatic changes in economic thinking and policy-making in Australia.

Library of Congress, Prints & Photographs Division.

Photographer Dorothea Lange documented the dire circumstances of the Depression.

This extraordinary episode also changed economics forever. It exposed the mistakes of an earlier generation of economic thinkers who had argued that the economy would quickly repair itself. This period saw the introduction of the term macroeconomics, and it led to the development of a new approach to understanding broad economic trends. John Maynard Keynes and colleagues such as Joan Robinson created a macroeconomic framework that explains the painful reality that recessions and depressions can be common, costly, and persistent.

This chapter outlines the framework they built. We'll start by analysing the central role that spending decisions play in determining economic outcomes. Then we'll explore how it's possible for the economy to get stuck in a bad equilibrium in which joblessness and misery can persist. Finally, we'll investigate the possibility that changes in spending can have a multiplied effect on the broader economy.

Together, these insights suggest that a determined government can halt an economic slump by boosting spending. This prescription was tested as the government scrambled to counter the Great Depression. President Roosevelt's New Deal boosted government spending and appeared—at least for a while—to halt the economic decline. As Hitler rose to power in Europe, nervous investors sent their funds to the United States, which lowered interest rates and stimulated greater spending. The U.S. government's heavy investment in the war effort also helped to boost spending. Ultimately economic growth resumed, the Depression ended, and this new field of macroeconomics had proved its worth. Australia did not develop a "New Deal" like the United States. In fact, the government led by Prime Minister Joseph Lyons reduced spending and kept paying interest on debt owed to British banks. It wasn't until World War II and the government spending it involved that Australia really pulled out of the Great Depression. The insights we'll explore in this chapter have since been built into the foundations of modern macroeconomics.

Objective

Explore the influence of aggregate expenditure and the multiplier on the business cycle.

A.1 Aggregate Expenditure and Income
Measure aggregate expenditure and analyse how it varies with income.

A.2 Macroeconomic Equilibrium and the Keynesian Cross
Find the macroeconomic equilibrium and analyse how it changes as economic conditions change.

A.3 The Multiplier
Analyse how moderate changes in spending can have bigger consequences through the multiplier effect.

A.1 Aggregate Expenditure and Income

Learning Objective *Measure aggregate expenditure and analyse how it varies with income.*

When businesses assess how macroeconomic conditions are likely to shape the demand for their products, they focus on the total amount of goods and services that people want to buy. That is, they focus on **aggregate expenditure,** which refers to the total amount of goods and services that people want to buy across the whole economy. Let's dig a little deeper into aggregate expenditure to better understand how it is measured.

aggregate expenditure The total amount of goods and services that people want to buy across the whole economy.
= Consumption
+ Planned investment
+ Government purchases
+ Net exports

Some abbreviations
AE: Aggregate Expenditure
C: Consumption
I: Planned Investment
G: Government purchases
NX: Net exports

Aggregate Expenditure

Aggregate expenditure is the sum of four components:

= *Consumption:* When households buy goods and services
+ *Planned investment:* When businesses purchase new capital
+ *Government purchases:* When the government buys goods and services
+ *Net exports:* Spending by foreigners on Australian-made exports, less total spending by Australians on foreign-made imports

Aggregate Expenditure = *C* + *I* + *G* + *NX*. Economists often use abbreviations to simplify things, and so you might find it easier to write it this way:

$$\underbrace{AE}_{\text{Aggregate expenditure}} = \underbrace{C}_{\text{Consumption}} + \underbrace{I}_{\text{Planned investment}} + \underbrace{G}_{\text{Government purchases}} + \underbrace{NX}_{\text{Net exports}}$$

planned investment Spending on machinery, software, and buildings used to produce goods and services. Unlike total investment, it excludes changes in inventories.

Whichever way you write it, the point is simply that aggregate expenditure is the sum of spending on Australian-made goods by all economic actors: consumers, businesses, governments, and those engaged in international trade.

Stephen Dwyer/Alamy Stock Photo

A planned investment.

Chris Helgren/Reuters/Alamy Stock Photo

An unplanned investment.

Aggregate expenditure includes planned investment, but excludes inventories. Notice that aggregate expenditure depends on *planned investment,* rather than *total investment.* Let me explain the distinction. **Planned investment** refers to the investments that a business intentionally makes when it buys capital goods such as buildings, machinery, and software. We use the modifier "planned" to distinguish this from *total investment,* which—because of an accounting convention—also includes unplanned changes in inventories.

When Cochlear buys equipment to open a new production line, that's a planned investment, and it counts as aggregate expenditure. But when Cochlear can't sell all the hearing implants it produces, it stockpiles the extra implants as inventories. While accountants classify this increase in inventories as investment, they're not a planned investment and hence we don't count them in aggregate expenditure. That's because when you're trying to assess economy-wide demand, you want to focus on the stuff that consumers, businesses, and governments purchase, not the unsold inventories they accumulate. Unsold inventories are also the key to seeing the difference between GDP—which measures total *output* including unplanned investment—and aggregate expenditure.

Now that you know how to measure aggregate expenditure, let's analyse its key determinant: income.

Aggregate Expenditure Rises with Income

When business analysts forecast aggregate expenditure, they pay special attention to income because it plays an important role in shaping people's spending decisions. We're going to follow their lead.

Higher income leads to higher consumption and hence higher aggregate expenditure. To see why income matters, let's focus on consumers (like you!). Most people tell me that if their income were higher, they would spend more. If so, then higher individual income leads to higher individual consumption. And because millions of people respond this way, when income across the whole economy is higher—that is, when GDP is higher—then total consumption also tends to be higher.

Figure 1 summarises this idea with the **consumption function,** a curve plotting the level of consumption associated with each level of income. It illustrates the insight that higher GDP leads to higher total consumption. (You might recognise this idea from Chapter 13 on consumption.)

Figure 1 | The Consumption Function

Ⓐ The consumption function shows how consumption rises with the level of income (GDP).

Ⓑ The slope of the consumption function is equal to the **marginal propensity to consume**, which describes the extra consumption that arises from each dollar of extra income.

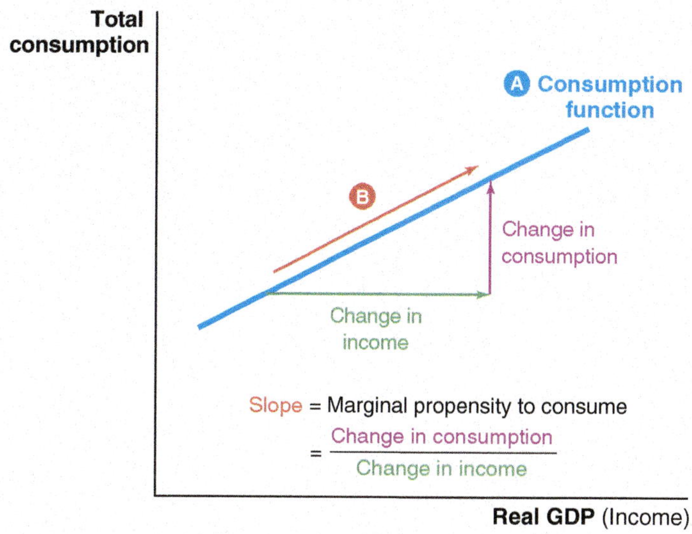

The marginal propensity to consume determines how much consumption rises when income rises. Typically, when your income rises, you'll spend a fraction of it today and save the rest. The fraction of each extra dollar of income that a typical household spends is called the **marginal propensity to consume** (or "*MPC*," for short). You can measure the fraction of each dollar someone spends as the ratio of the change in consumption to the change in income. Most people don't immediately spend all of the extra income they get, suggesting that the marginal propensity to consume is less than one. The slope of the consumption function (remember, slope is "rise over run") is the ratio of the change in consumption to the change in income. That is, the slope is equal to the marginal propensity to consume.

consumption function A curve plotting the level of consumption associated with each level of income.

marginal propensity to consume The fraction of each extra dollar of income that households spend on consumption.

The marginal propensity to consume is useful because it tells you how much consumption—and hence aggregate expenditure—rises with income. For instance, if the marginal propensity to consume is 0.5, then each extra dollar of income will lead to 50 cents of extra spending this year. It tells the government that if it were to send each Australian a $100 cheque in an effort to stimulate the economy, this year's spending will rise on average by $50 per person. At the level of the whole economy, it says that if income were to rise by $100 billion, you should forecast consumption will rise by $50 billion.

The aggregate expenditure line shows how aggregate expenditure rises with income. We now have all the pieces we need to graph the relationship between aggregate expenditure and total income. Let's start with consumption, and build up from there. The lower line in Figure 2 is the consumption function, which illustrates the tendency for consumption to rise with income (or equivalently, it shows how consumption rises with GDP).

Aggregate expenditure is consumption plus planned investment, government purchases, and net exports. As a result, the aggregate expenditure line lies above the consumption function, and the distance between them is equal to the sum of these other components. If these other components of spending are unaffected by income, then the aggregate expenditure line lies a fixed distance above the consumption function. This means that the slope of the aggregate expenditure line is the same as the slope of the consumption function, and is equal to the marginal propensity to consume. For now, we're holding planned investment, government purchases, and net exports constant, but in a few pages, we'll see what happens when they shift.

Figure 2 | **Aggregate Expenditure Rises with Income**

Aggregate expenditure is the sum of consumption, planned investment, government purchases, and net exports.

(A) Higher income leads people to spend more, and so **consumption rises with GDP**.

(B) **Aggregate expenditure** also includes **planned investment, government purchases, and net exports**, and so it lies above the **consumption function**.

(C) As a result, **aggregate expenditure rises with income** (even if planned investment, government purchases, and net exports don't change).

(D) The **aggregate expenditure line** has the same slope as the **consumption function**: Its **slope** is the **marginal propensity to consume**.

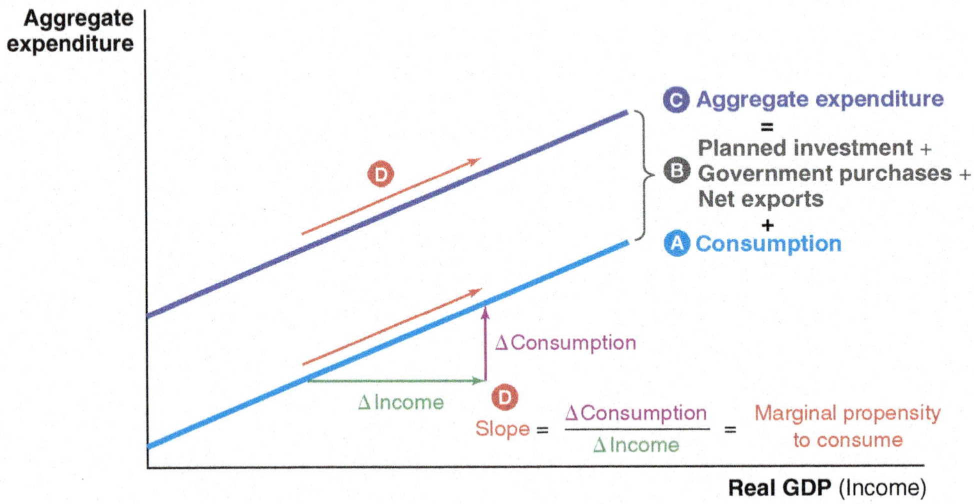

Figure 3 | **Use the Aggregate Expenditure Line to Forecast Spending**

(A) Locate the **level of GDP** on the horizontal axis, and **look up** until you hit the **aggregate expenditure line**.

(B) Then **look left** to find the level of **aggregate expenditure** associated with this level of GDP.

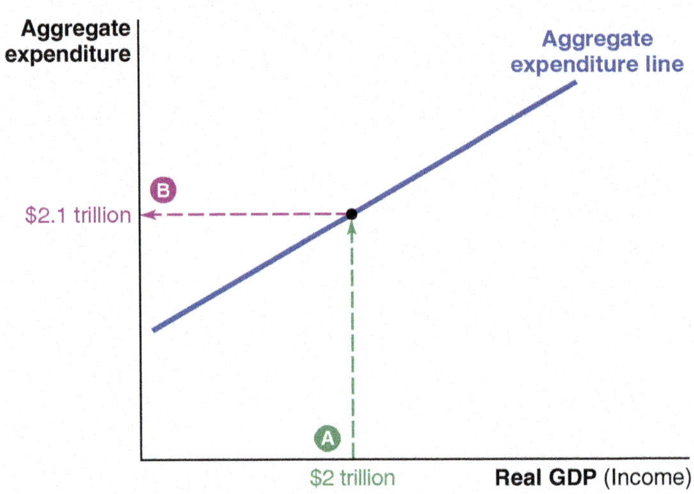

How to Use the Aggregate Expenditure Line

The aggregate expenditure line is a valuable tool for managers, and you can use it to assess how robust spending is likely to be next year. For instance, you can forecast what aggregate expenditure will be if total income—that is, GDP—is $2 trillion next year. Figure 3 illustrates how to figure this out. First, locate your GDP forecast on the horizontal axis, then look up until you hit the aggregate expenditure line. Now look across to discover that the corresponding level of aggregate expenditure is $2.1 trillion.

If other things change, so should your forecast. Economists often talk about their forecasts as holding other things constant. If other factors change, then so should your forecast. You can use the aggregate expenditure line to forecast the consequences of changing economic conditions. As you do so, it's important to distinguish between:

- *Changes in income,* which cause a *movement along* the aggregate expenditure line; and
- *Changes in other factors that change aggregate expenditure at any given income level,* which cause the aggregate expenditure line to *shift*.

Let's see how this works in practice.

A change in income leads to a movement along the aggregate expenditure line. What happens when income changes? For instance, what will aggregate expenditure be if GDP rises to $2.4 trillion?

In Figure 4, locate this new income level on the horizontal axis, and look up until you hit the aggregate expenditure line. Look left, and you'll see that it corresponds to an aggregate expenditure of $2.3 trillion. You can conclude that increasing income by $400 billion will lead aggregate expenditure to rise by $200 billion.

Notice that this change in income led spending to move from one point on the aggregate expenditure line to another point on the same line. This makes sense: This line shows how aggregate expenditure responds to a change in income, and so therefore changes in income do not shift this line. Instead, *a change in income leads to a movement along the aggregate expenditure line.*

Figure 4 | A Change in Income Causes Movement Along the Aggregate Expenditure Line

(A) When GDP is $2 trillion, aggregate expenditure is $2.1 trillion.
(B) When GDP is $2.4 trillion, aggregate expenditure is $2.3 trillion.
(C) Changes in income lead to movement along the aggregate expenditure line.

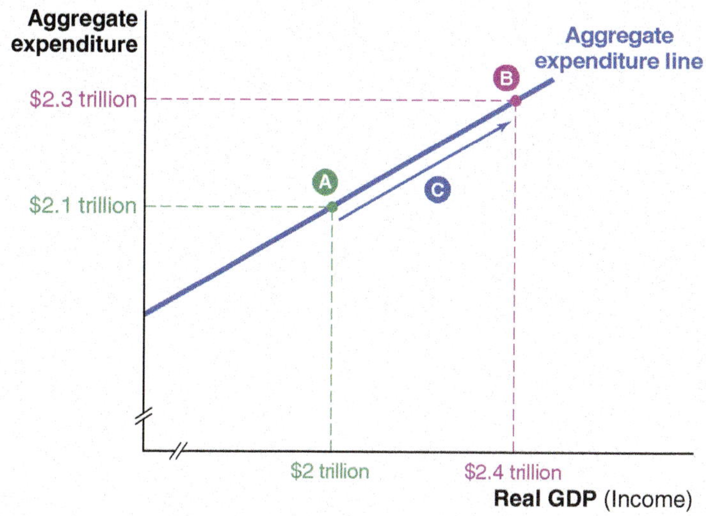

A.2 Macroeconomic Equilibrium and the Keynesian Cross

Learning Objective *Find the macroeconomic equilibrium and analyse how it changes as economic conditions change.*

Ask a business owner how much they plan on producing, and they'll say that it depends on how much people plan on spending. Ask people how much they plan to spend, and they'll say it depends on how much income they expect to earn. Ask them how much income they expect to earn, and they'll tell you it depends on how much work they have, which depends on how much businesses produce.

If this all feels a bit circular, that's because it is. As Figure 5 shows, spending depends on income, income depends on production, and production depends on spending. This is the *interdependence principle* at work, and it arises because one person's spending creates a demand for others to produce more output, which boosts their income. When those people spend that extra income, they'll kick-start further cycles of interdependence as their spending stimulates greater production, more income, and yet more spending.

Figure 5 | Macroeconomic Interdependence

You'll need to focus on the equilibrium in order to resolve the interdependence between income, spending, and production.

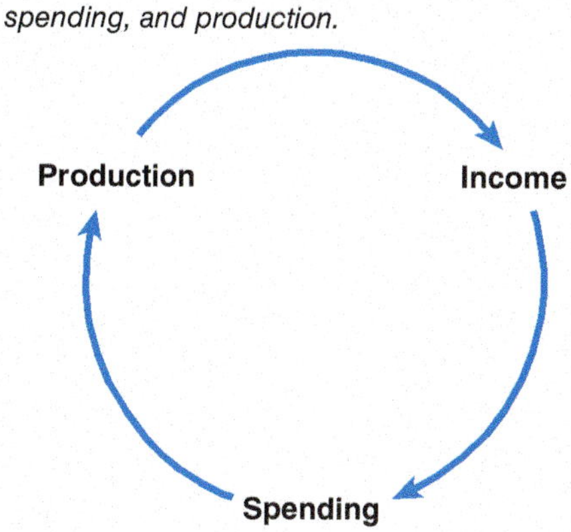

Aggregate Expenditure in Macroeconomic Equilibrium

This interdependence makes macroeconomics seem harder than it really is. The secret to resolving this apparent circularity is to look for the equilibrium that results from the interaction of income, spending, and production.

Scientists describe an equilibrium as a stable situation with no tendency to change. In microeconomics, an individual market has a tendency to move to the equilibrium where the quantity of a product that's supplied is equal to the quantity demanded. The idea of macroeconomic equilibrium is similar, but rather than analysing an individual market, it involves thinking about the economy as a whole.

Macroeconomic equilibrium occurs when aggregate expenditure matches total production. **Macroeconomic equilibrium** is the point at which the total quantity of output that buyers collectively want to purchase is equal to the total quantity of output that suppliers collectively produce. As such, it happens when aggregate expenditure (a measure of the total demand for stuff) equals GDP (a measure of total production, or the total supply of stuff):

macroeconomic equilibrium Occurs when the quantity of output that buyers collectively want to purchase is equal to the quantity of output that suppliers collectively produce.

$$\text{Aggregate expenditure} = \text{GDP}$$

When total spending and total production are in balance, there's no tendency for total output to change. That's why you can forecast that an economy that's in macroeconomic equilibrium is likely to stay there—at least until something else intervenes.

Macroeconomic equilibrium doesn't mean that every single market for each individual product is in supply-equals-demand equilibrium. Supply might exceed demand in some markets (leading those suppliers to cut back on production), while in others, demand might exceed supply (leading those suppliers to expand production). In a macroeconomic equilibrium, these effects offset and, across the economy as a whole, businesses are producing as much stuff as people are willing to buy. As a result, there's no reason for *total* production to either increase or decrease.

Figure 6 | **Macroeconomic Equilibrium Occurs on the 45-Degree Line**

Equilibrium occurs when: ***Aggregate expenditure = GDP***.
The 45-degree line shows all possible points of macroeconomic equilibrium.

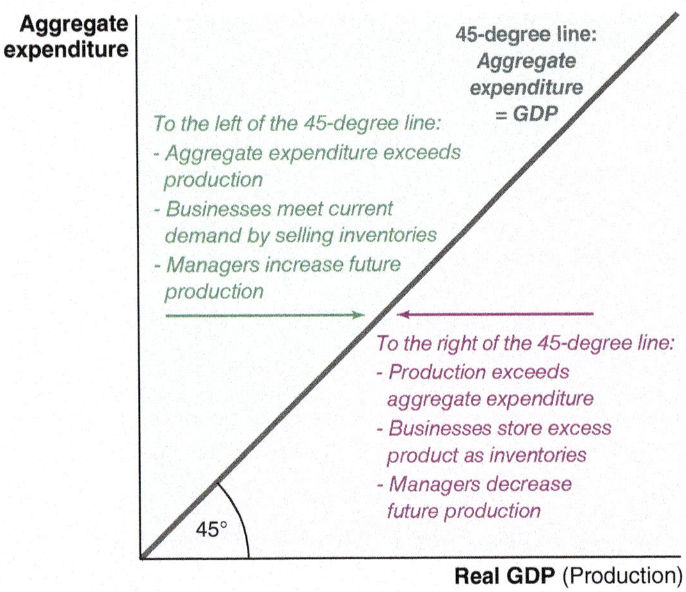

Macroeconomic equilibrium occurs on the 45-degree line. Figure 6 illustrates a simple graphical trick to find all the points that are consistent with a potential macroeconomic equilibrium: When you graph aggregate expenditure against GDP, the set of points where the two are equal is simply the 45-degree line. That's because a 45-degree line shows all the points where the value on the vertical axis (that is, aggregate expenditure) is equal to the value on the horizontal axis (which is GDP). Thus, the 45-degree line illustrates all the possible points of macroeconomic equilibrium.

Production will adjust toward the 45-degree line. At points to the right of the 45-degree line, GDP exceeds aggregate expenditure, which is not an equilibrium. At these points—shown in purple—suppliers are producing more than people want to buy. Initially, they'll store this excess supply as inventories. But producers don't want to keep accumulating warehouses full of unsold inventories, and so eventually they'll adjust by cutting production. This tendency to cut production when it exceeds aggregate expenditure will push the level of output back toward a macroeconomic equilibrium where aggregate expenditure and production are in balance—which occurs on the 45-degree line.

Alternatively, at points to the left of the 45-degree line, GDP is less than aggregate expenditure, which also is not an equilibrium. At these points—shown in green—suppliers are producing less than people want to buy. Initially, they'll meet this excess demand by selling inventories, but that can't continue forever. Rather than risk forgoing profitable sales if their inventories run out, they'll ramp up production. This tendency to raise production when it's less than aggregate expenditure will push the level of output back toward macroeconomic equilibrium, once again bringing them into balance along the 45-degree line.

Put the pieces together, and you'll see that as managers adjust their production levels to better match aggregate expenditure, they'll push GDP back toward macroeconomic equilibrium and the 45-degree line. It follows that any point along the 45-degree line can be a macroeconomic equilibrium.

Equilibrium occurs where aggregate expenditure crosses the 45-degree line. Okay, so the 45-degree line tells you that there are many possible points of macroeconomic equilibrium where GDP could come into balance with aggregate expenditure. To figure out which of these possible outcomes will be next year's actual outcome, you'll need to figure out which one coincides with next year's actual level of aggregate expenditure. And so it's time to bring the aggregate expenditure line back into our analysis.

Macroeconomic equilibrium occurs at the point where the aggregate expenditure line meets the 45-degree line. As Figure 7 illustrates, at this point the level of aggregate expenditure is equal to GDP.

Figure 7 | Macroeconomic Equilibrium

Equilibrium occurs where the aggregate expenditure line meets the 45-degree line.
Ⓐ The **45-degree line** shows the set of possible equilibria where ***aggregate expenditure = GDP***.
Ⓑ The **aggregate expenditure line** shows how total spending varies with the level of GDP.
Ⓒ **Macroeconomic equilibrium** occurs where the **aggregate expenditure line** crosses the **45-degree line**, ensuring that spending and production plans are consistent with each other.

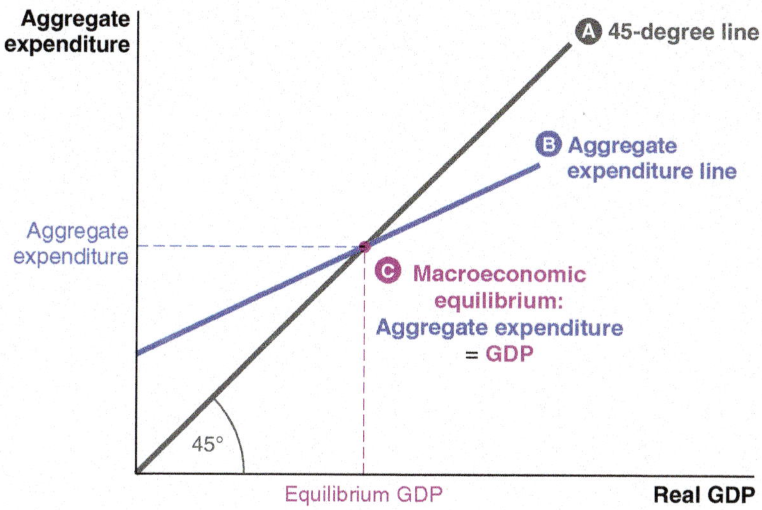

That's it! Now you know how to find the point of macroeconomic equilibrium: It occurs where the aggregate expenditure line crosses the 45-degree line. This framework is often called the *Keynesian cross* and you can probably see why. It's a *cross* because it suggests that the economy will move to the level of output where the two lines cross. And it's *Keynesian* because it illustrates the central insight of John Maynard Keynes, that spending plays a key role in determining macroeconomic outcomes.

Equilibrium GDP can fall short of potential GDP. A macroeconomic equilibrium describes where we expect the economy to come to rest. But that doesn't necessarily mean that it's a good outcome—merely that it's a stable one. Just as you can come to rest in a good place or a bad one, so too can the economy. A macroeconomic equilibrium can occur at a high level of GDP or at a low one—it really depends on the position of the aggregate expenditure curve. For instance, during the coronavirus pandemic, equilibrium GDP was far below potential GDP.

Luke Sharrett/Bloomberg Creative Photos/Getty Images

A low-GDP equilibrium.

Shifts in Aggregate Expenditure

So far we've focused mainly on the effects of changes in *income,* which lead to *movement along the aggregate expenditure line.* Let's now expand our analysis to also include factors that might cause a change in aggregate expenditure *at any given income level* causing a *shift in the aggregate expenditure line.*

It's important to distinguish between two forces that change spending: income and everything else. As you evaluate changes in spending, simply ask yourself: What caused this change? If it's a change in income, the aggregate expenditure line won't shift. But if it's any other factor, then it shifts the aggregate expenditure line. As we're about to see, any shift in the aggregate expenditure line leads to a new level of equilibrium GDP.

A decrease in spending will shift the aggregate expenditure line down. Let's start by considering the effects of a decrease in aggregate expenditure. This would occur if consumers cut back on their spending, businesses reduce investment in new equipment, governments reduce their purchases, foreigners spend less on our exports, or Australians import more of their purchases from abroad. Any factor that leads to a decrease in aggregate expenditure *at any given income level*—whether due to a change in *C*, *I*, *G*, or *NX*—will shift the aggregate expenditure line downward, as shown by the purple line in Panel A on the left of Figure 8.

This lower level of aggregate expenditure yields a new macroeconomic equilibrium at a lower level of GDP. As the economy adjusts to this new equilibrium, GDP declines, causing a recession, or in a severe case, a depression. In this new equilibrium, output is much lower, and so businesses need fewer workers. As a result, this low-GDP equilibrium corresponds with widespread unemployment. Think of this as the equilibrium during the latest recession. Even worse: Because this economic slump is a macroeconomic equilibrium, it's likely to persist until something changes.

Figure 8 | Shifts in Aggregate Expenditure Can Cause Recessions and Expansions

Panel A: A Decrease in Spending

(A) A **decrease in aggregate expenditure** at any given level of income causes the **aggregate expenditure line to shift down**.

(B) This leads the economy to move to a **new equilibrium**, with a lower level of GDP, and hence lower income and employment.

(C) Because **GDP decreases**, it follows that a decrease in aggregate expenditure causes a **recession**.

Panel B: An Increase in Spending

(A) An **increase in aggregate expenditure** at any given level of income causes the **aggregate expenditure line to shift up**.

(B) This leads the economy to move to a **new equilibrium**, with a higher level of GDP, and hence higher income and employment.

(C) Because **GDP increases**, it follows that an increase in aggregate expenditure causes an economic **expansion**.

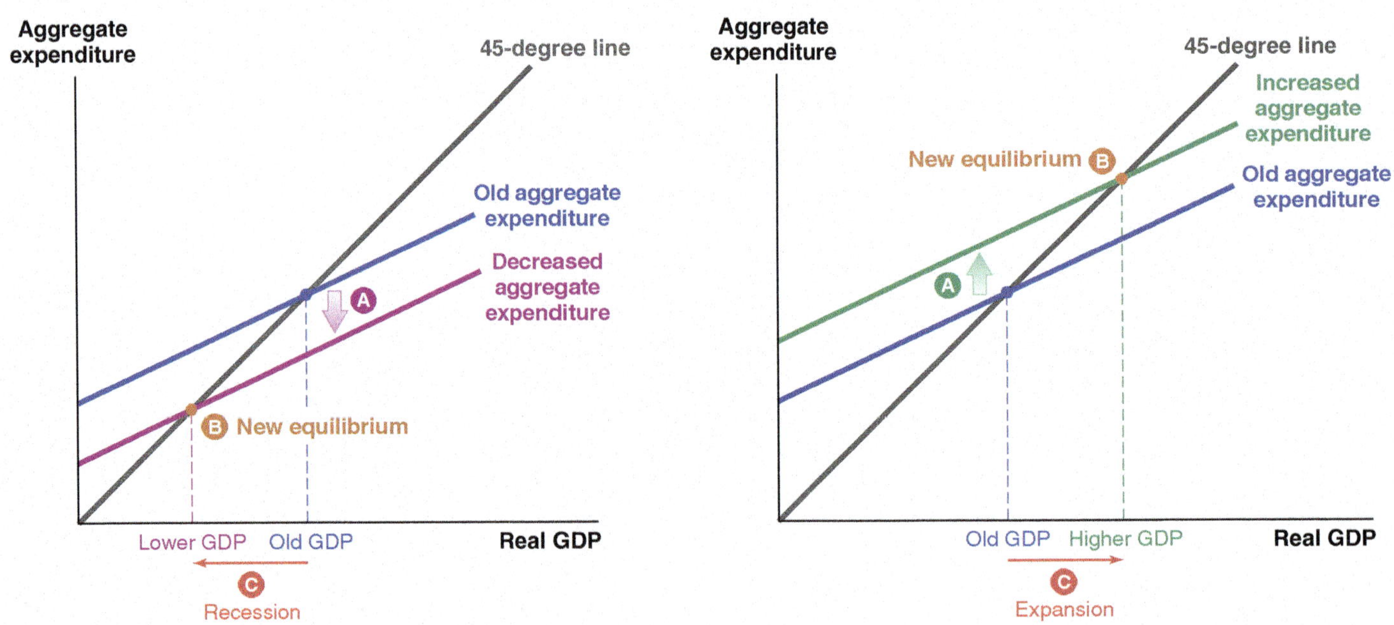

A positive spending shock will shift the aggregate expenditure line up. Following similar logic in the opposite direction suggests that an increase in aggregate expenditure can spark an economic boom. In this case, we'll evaluate an increase in aggregate expenditure. Again, this increase in spending could reflect a rise in *C*, *I*, *G*, or *NX*. Whatever the cause, any factor that leads to an increase in aggregate expenditure *at any given income level* will shift the aggregate expenditure line upward, as shown by the green line in Panel B on the right of Figure 8.

This boost to spending yields a new macroeconomic equilibrium at a higher level of GDP. As the economy adjusts to this new equilibrium, GDP rises, causing an economic expansion. In this new equilibrium, output is much higher, and so businesses need more workers. As a result, this high-GDP equilibrium corresponds with low unemployment. Think of this as the equilibrium during an economic boom.

Predicting the State of the Economy

She's looking into the future.

Congratulations! You've now developed a framework that you can use to forecast how the economy will respond to changing economic conditions.

Follow the three-step recipe to forecast how the economy will respond. All you need to do is answer the three questions:

Step one: *Have spending plans changed?*

The question here is whether aggregate expenditure will change at any given income level. That means asking whether consumers will alter their spending, businesses will change how much they invest, policy makers will adjust government purchases, foreigners will shift their spending on exports from Australia, or Australians will change whether they make their purchases from abroad. (Make sure you remember to think about each of the components of aggregate expenditure—including *C, I, G,* and *NX.*)

Step two: *Shift the aggregate expenditure line*

Is this an *increase* in spending at any given income level (shifting the aggregate expenditure line upward) or a *decrease* (shifting it down)?

Step three: *Analyse the new equilibrium*

How does the equilibrium level of GDP change in the new equilibrium? And how does it compare to potential output, which is the level of GDP at which all resources are fully employed?

Let's practice using this framework to forecast where the economy is going.

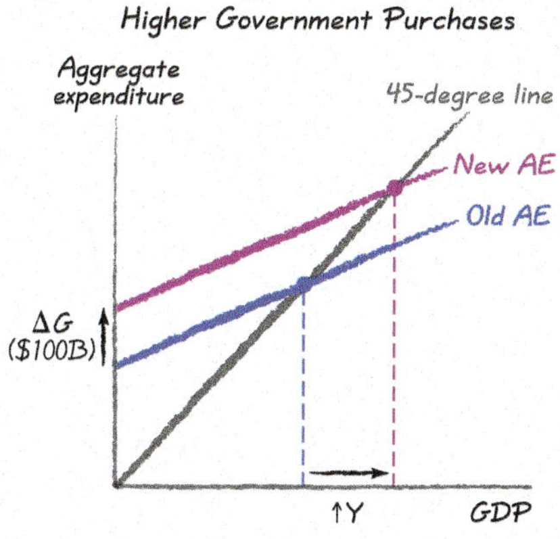

Example one: *Parliament passes a fiscal stimulus bill that raises the level of government purchases by $100 billion. How will this affect GDP?*

Let's follow our three-step recipe:

Step one: This fiscal stimulus bill leads to an increase in government purchases—and hence aggregate expenditure—at any given income level.

Step two: This increase in government purchases will increase aggregate expenditure, thereby shifting the aggregate expenditure line up by $100 billion.

Step three: As the figure in the margin illustrates, the new equilibrium level of GDP is higher than the previous level.

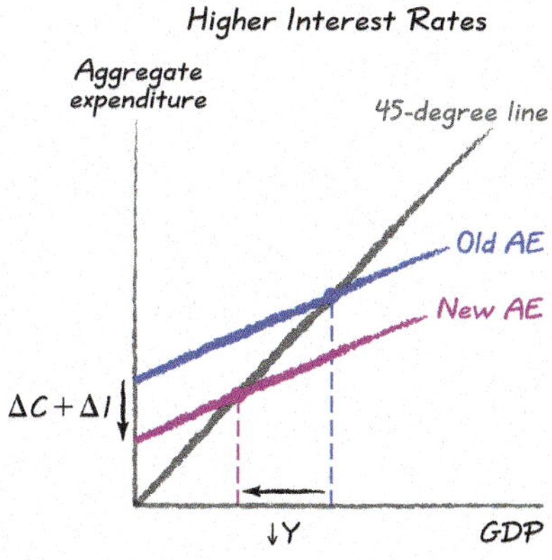

Example two: *The Reserve Bank raises interest rates.*

Let's follow our three-step recipe:

Step one: An increase in real interest rates leads households to consume less and businesses to invest less at any given income level.

Step two: This decrease in consumption and investment will decrease aggregate expenditure, thereby shifting the aggregate expenditure line down.

Step three: As the figure in the margin illustrates, this leads to a new equilibrium level of GDP that's lower than the previous level.

Do the Economics

Think you've got this business of economic forecasting all figured out? Here are a half-dozen more examples for you to work through.

The invention of new pharmaceuticals will increase Australian exports.

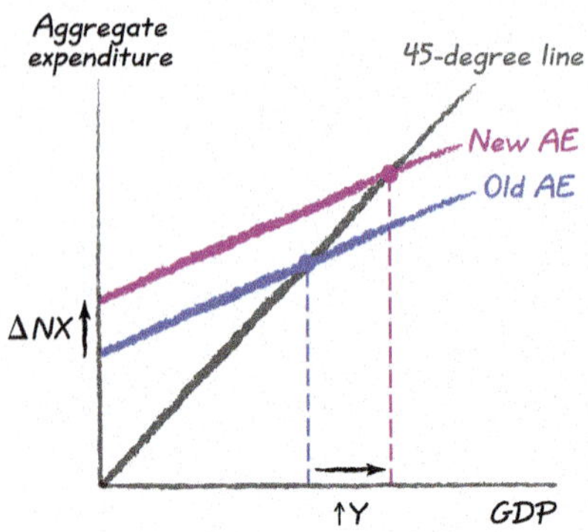

An increase in net exports
→ Shift aggregate expenditure up
Result: Higher GDP.

A fall in stock market wealth makes consumers willing to spend less at each level of income.

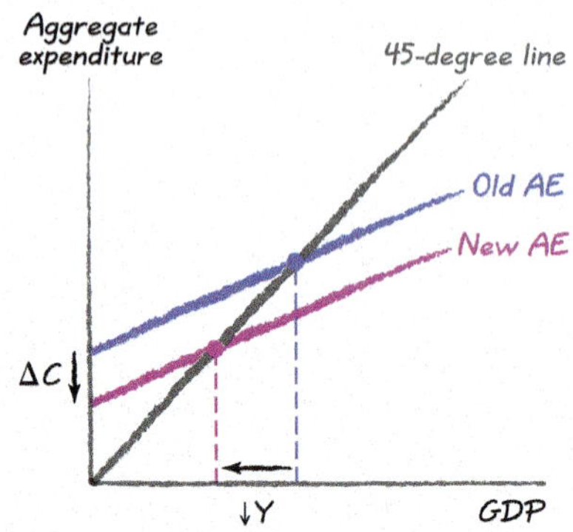

A decrease in consumption
→ Shift aggregate expenditure down
Result: Lower GDP.

An investment tax credit leads businesses to spend an extra $200 billion on machinery.

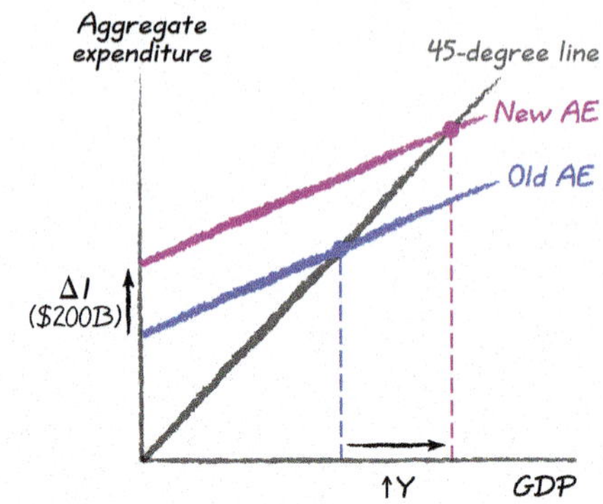

An increase in investment
→ Shift aggregate expenditure up
Result: Higher GDP.

As uncertainty rose, many managers decided to postpone major investment projects.

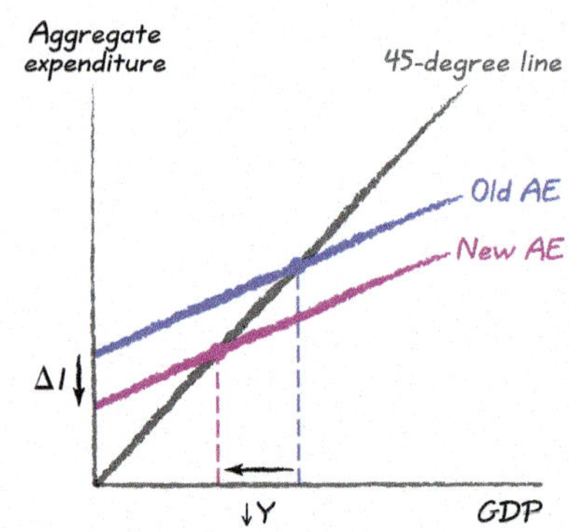

A decrease in investment
→ Shift aggregate expenditure down
Result: Lower GDP.

A decrease in the value of the Australian dollar makes Australian exports more attractive to foreigners.

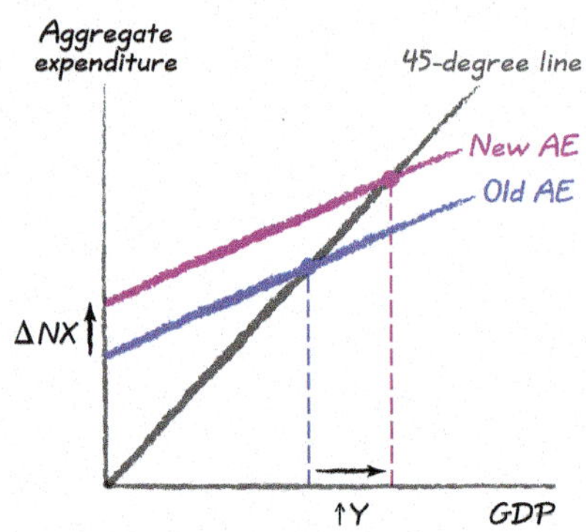

An increase in net exports
→ Shift aggregate expenditure up
Result: Higher GDP.

The government invested $200 billion modernising Australian military equipment.

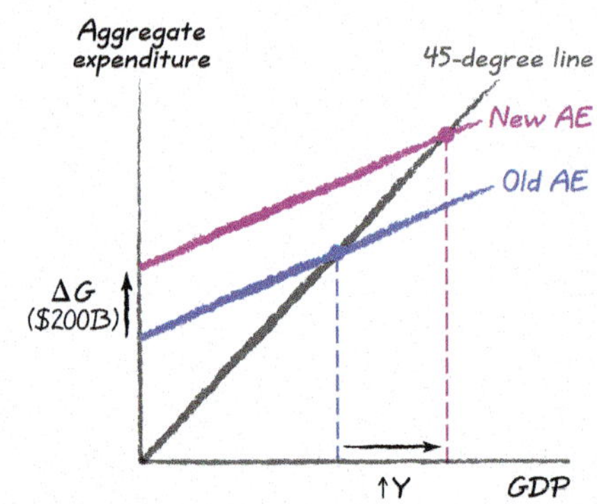

An increase in government purchases
→ Shift aggregate expenditure up
Result: Higher GDP. ■

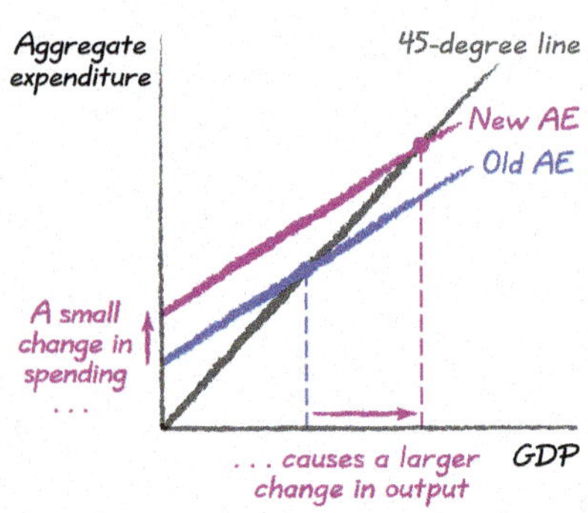

Moderate changes in spending can have large effects on output. There's one final point to notice, and it's evident in each of the examples you've just worked through: The shift in the aggregate expenditure line (the change in spending noted along the vertical axis) is small relative to the resulting change in real GDP (the shift along the horizontal axis). This suggests that even small or moderate changes in aggregate expenditure can have quite large effects—effectively multiplied effects—on GDP. These multiplied effects further reinforce the idea that moderate shifts in aggregate expenditure can drive the large changes in output that occur over the business cycle. This insight also suggests that government policy can have a sizeable effect on GDP, as moderate changes in government purchases might have a multiplied effect on output. Let's dig deeper into understanding how these multiplier effects work.

A.3 The Multiplier

Learning Objective *Analyse how moderate changes in spending can have bigger consequences through the multiplier effect.*

Jim Snyders/Alamy Stock Photo

Where stimulus goes, will growth follow?

As the U.S. recession deepened through 2009, the Australian Labor Party, led by Prime Minister Kevin Rudd, was desperate to make sure the Australian economy did not succumb to the same fate. The Rudd government's response was a stimulus bill called the Nation Building and Jobs Plan, which authorised $42 billion in extra government spending, tax cuts, and other forms of assistance. The goal was to shift the aggregate expenditure line upward, which would stimulate an increase in GDP. It was a big policy change, leading managers everywhere to ask: How will this stimulus affect my business?

The Multiplier Effect

Caroline owns a construction company in Melbourne, and she asked her top analysts to evaluate the likely effects of the stimulus for her business. Digging into the details, they noted that the government planned to spend billions of dollars on new construction projects. Caroline immediately directed her staff to look for the best contracts to bid on and to make plans to hire extra workers to work on those projects. Think of this boost as the direct effect of the stimulus.

An initial increase in spending boosts incomes, leading to more spending. There are also ripple effects. Even though the stimulus contained no direct spending on hearing implants, economists still projected it would boost sales at Cochlear. By their thinking, some of the workers Caroline hired would spend some of their new earnings on new hearing implants. There are also second-round ripple effects. For instance, when Cochlear hires workers so that it can expand production, some of those new workers will buy lunch at a nearby Subway, leading the franchise owner to hire more sandwich artists. And there are third-round effects, too. If the newly hired sandwich artists spend some of their pay on child care, then local day-care providers will also see higher incomes. And so it continues, showing the power of the *interdependence principle*, as an initial burst of spending in the construction sector reverberates through the medical, food prep, and child-care sectors, and out to the broader economy.

Add up the ripple effects to find the total effect on GDP. How far does this process go, and how much does an extra dollar of spending raise GDP? Let's zoom in and track a single dollar of extra spending as it percolates through the economy.

Initially, the government spends a dollar, perhaps on a construction contract with Caroline. Then the ripple effects begin. In the first round, the government's extra spending also counts as extra income for Caroline, and she'll spend some of it. If her marginal propensity to consume is 0.5, she'll increase her spending by $0.5\times\$1=50$ cents. There's a second-round effect: Caroline's extra spending raises someone else's income by 50 cents, and they'll spend a fraction of this extra income. If the typical marginal propensity to consume is 0.5, then Caroline's spending generates an additional 0.5×50 cents $=25$ cents of spending. The third-round effects follow the same pattern, with the people whose income just rose by 25 cents deciding to spend an extra 0.5×25 cents $=12.5$ cents. And so it goes on, with each further round of ripple effects yielding yet another boost to spending, although these ripples are successively smaller.

Alex Staroseltsev/Shutterstock

Beyond the initial impact, there are ripple effects.

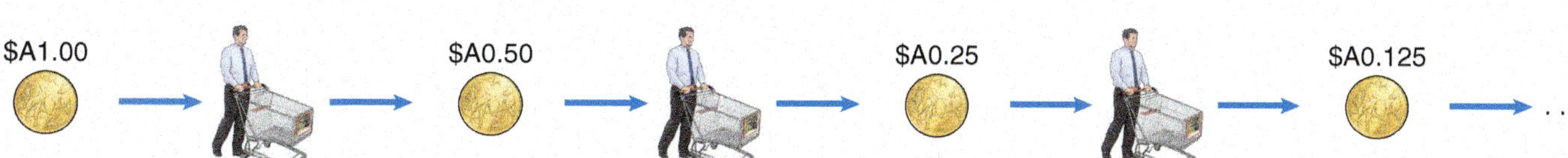

Add it all up, and you'll discover that the initial \$1 increase in spending generates a total rise in GDP of: \$1 + \$0.5 + \$0.25 + \$0.125 + \$0.061 + \$0.031 + \$0.016 + \$0.008 + ··· = \$2.00.

Don't get too wrapped up in the math for now (we'll come back to it). Focus on the bigger picture and you'll see that a one-dollar increase in aggregate expenditure has a larger effect—a multiplied effect—on GDP. This is a pretty extraordinary insight because it suggests that moderate changes in spending can have much larger macroeconomic effects. This *multiplier effect* is the reason many economists believe that the governments can counter large swings in GDP by making moderate changes in the pattern of government purchases, which then have a multiplied effect offsetting these swings.

The Size of the Multiplier

multiplier A measure of how much GDP changes as a result of both the direct and indirect effects flowing from each extra dollar of spending.

You can summarise the consequences of a rise in spending—including both the direct impact and the many rounds of subsequent ripple effects—with a single number called the multiplier. The **multiplier** measures how much GDP changes as a result of both the direct and ripple effects flowing from each extra dollar of spending. In our simple example, the multiplier is 2 because a \$1 boost to spending generated a total of \$2 in extra GDP.

The multiplier is useful because you can use it to forecast the effects of changes in aggregate expenditure, as follows:

$$\Delta\text{GDP} = \Delta\text{Spending} \times \text{Multiplier}$$

Do the Economics

How much will GDP rise after a new program of renewable energy credits—effectively an incentive for businesses to invest in renewable energy—leads to an additional \$10 billion increase in investment in the sector, if the multiplier is 2?

$$\Delta GDP = \underbrace{\$10\text{ billion}}_{\Delta\text{Spending}} \times \underbrace{2}_{\text{Multiplier}} = \$20\text{ billion}$$ ■

The multiplier is larger if the marginal propensity to consume is larger. How big is the multiplier in practice? As you're about to see, it all depends on the marginal propensity to consume (*MPC*), which you'll recall is the fraction of each dollar of extra income that gets spent. The *MPC* matters because the size of each subsequent ripple effect depends on the extent to which extra income translates into extra spending.

To see this, let's work through the implications of a rise in spending in Figure 9. The initial rise in spending is $\Delta Spending$. In the first-round ripple effect, the recipient of that spending will increase their spending by $\Delta Spending \times MPC$. In the second round, the recipient of that extra spending will spend a proportion of it, yielding a further increase in spending of $(\Delta Spending \times MPC) \times MPC$. In the third round, the recipient of that extra income will increase their spending by $(\Delta Spending \times MPC \times MPC) \times MPC$, and so it goes on.

Figure 9 | Multiplier Effects

Initial change	$= \Delta Spending$
First-round ripple effect	$= \Delta Spending \times MPC$
Second-round ripple effect	$= \Delta Spending \times MPC \times MPC$
Third-round ripple effect	$= \Delta Spending \times MPC \times MPC \times MPC$
...	...
Total change in GDP	$= \Delta Spending \times \underbrace{(1 + MPC + MPC^2 + MPC^3 + \cdots)}_{Multiplier}$

Add it all up, and you'll find that the total effect of a rise in spending on GDP is: $\Delta Spending \times (1 + MPC + MPC^2 + MPC^3 + \cdots)$, where the expression in brackets is the multiplier. The expression in brackets is the sum of a geometric series, and the beautiful thing is that because the MPC is less than 1, it all adds up to $1/(1 - MPC)$. That's it. As a result, the multiplier is equal to:

$$\text{Multiplier} = \frac{1}{1 - MPC}$$

For instance, when the marginal propensity to consume is 0.5, then the multiplier is $1/(1 - MPC) = 2$. More generally, the larger the marginal propensity to consume, the larger the ripple effects from an initial boost to spending, and hence the larger the multiplier.

The multiplier applies to all increases in spending. There's one final thing to note: While we've focused on the effects of an increase in government purchases, the multiplier applies with equal force to any increase or decrease in aggregate expenditure. Just as increasing government purchases will have ripple effects, so too will changes in consumption, investment, or net exports.

Interpreting the DATA How big is the multiplier?

Economists have conducted hundreds of studies attempting to answer the question: How big is the multiplier? In most cases they try to assess how effectively fiscal policy—changes in government spending and taxes—can stimulate a weak economy.

This turns out to be a surprisingly difficult question to answer. The problem is that the relationship between government purchases and output reflects (at least) three different forces. The first is the *multiplier effect,* in which greater government purchases boost future output. The second is called the *fiscal policy reaction function,* which reflects the reality that policy makers implement fiscal stimulus—increasing government purchases—when they anticipate weaker future output. The third is the *monetary policy reaction function,* which describes the Reserve Bank's tendency to cut interest rates when it anticipates weak future output. The multiplier effect creates a link from higher government purchases to higher future output. The fiscal policy reaction function creates a link from lower future output to higher government purchases. And the monetary policy reaction function creates a link from lower future output to lower interest rates, which boosts aggregate expenditure. All of this means that the correlation between government purchases and future output reflects a mishmash of these three forces.

In response, researchers have devised some ingenious studies to measure the multiplier effect. They first isolate and then track the effects of changes in government purchases that aren't caused by the state of the economy (and hence don't reflect the fiscal policy reaction function), and that don't cause the RBA to respond (and hence don't reflect the monetary policy reaction function). Some studies examine changes in government spending on the military caused by geopolitical tensions, finding that these lead to higher output. Others examine the historical record, finding that changes in tax rates, which were motivated by long-run considerations unrelated to the business cycle, also subsequently boosted output.

So, you might ask, what is the multiplier? Figure 10 illustrates an attempt by non-partisan economists at the International Monetary Fund (IMF) to estimate the multiplier effect. There are three key things we should be aware of:

- The estimate of the multiplier is different depending on where the government increases expenditure. The multiplier is largest for government investment, and much smaller for things like tax cuts.

Figure 10 | Estimates of the Multiplier Effect

The average 2-year response of real GDP to a 2-year, 1% of GDP change in the relevant fiscal instrument.

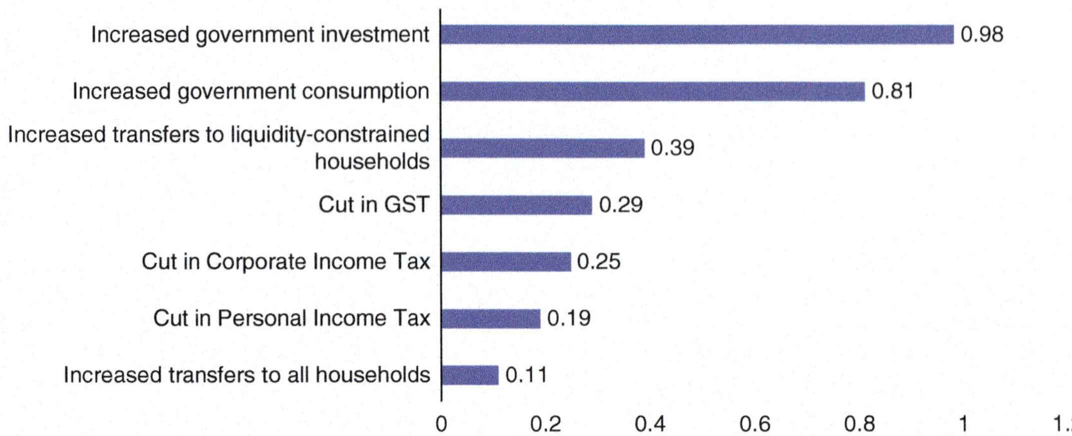

Data from: International Monetary Fund.

- The ripple effects that create the multiplier effect *play out over time* and may take time to become fully evident—this is why the time horizon in Figure 10 is 2 years.
- There is *tremendous uncertainty* about the multiplier. Other reports by the IMF put the multiplier at somewhere between 0.5 and 1.8, which illustrates that even today, economists don't think they know the size of the multiplier with any certainty. ■

Tying It Together

Our analysis in this chapter is all about one big idea: Aggregate expenditure is a major factor shaping macroeconomic outcomes. It matters because if people don't want to buy much stuff, then businesses won't produce much stuff. As a result, the economy can get stuck in the sort of depressed low-spending, low-production equilibrium that leads to recessions.

Fortunately, there's also a happier outcome in which people buy a lot of stuff, and so businesses produce a lot of stuff, leading to a high-output equilibrium in which there are jobs for everyone. There are also many other possible outcomes between these extremes of depression and full employment.

Sina Schuldt/picture alliance/Getty Images

The more stuff people demand, the more stuff the economy will produce . . . and deliver.

Aggregate expenditure focuses on the demand side of the economy. The key lesson of our analysis is that the demand side of the economy—that is, aggregate expenditure—really matters. Moreover, the multiplier effect reinforces this point. When the effects of any change in consumption, planned investment, government purchases, or net exports have multiplied effects on GDP, the economy is susceptible to being knocked off course. As a result, even modest changes in aggregate expenditure can lead to economic booms and busts. The same insights suggest that government policy really matters because changes in government purchases can help push the economy back on course.

These ideas are all important. And indeed, each of them has been built into the foundations of the modern frameworks economists use to understand the economy. Equally, it's worth emphasising that our analysis of aggregate expenditure doesn't yield a complete account of the macroeconomy. Income is not the only driver of aggregate expenditure—interest rates also play a major role. And that, in turn, suggests a more complete analysis needs to also account for the role of the financial sector in shaping interest rates and therefore spending decisions.

The supply side is important when the economy is close to capacity. Our focus on the role that buyers and the demand side of the economy play means that we've yet to say much about the sellers and the supply side of the economy. Implicitly, we've been assuming that when the demand for stuff rises, businesses are willing to supply more of that stuff at the current price. This is why extra spending translates into extra production, rather than shortages or higher prices.

But when the economy is close to full capacity, businesses cannot easily increase production, or they wouldn't want to do so without raising their prices. Perhaps their production lines are already overloaded, or maybe key inputs like skilled workers are hard to come by. When these supply-side constraints are binding—which can occur when output exceeds *potential output*—it's no longer appropriate to assume that extra spending will translate into extra production. Rather, it may spark higher prices and inflation. This suggests that it's important to integrate this chapter's demand-side emphasis on aggregate expenditure with an understanding of how supply constraints can lead inflation to emerge.

Economists emphasise demand in the short run and supply in the long run. Finally, this distinction between demand- and supply-side analysis can help you integrate your understanding of the determinants of the state of the economy in the short and long run. In Chapter 10, we analysed the long-run determinants of the level of potential GDP, emphasising that it reflects the number of workers, their skill levels, the number of machines they have to work with, and the technology for combining them. This emphasis on the supply side—the quantity and quality of inputs to production—is appropriate for analysing the economy's *potential output,* which is the level that occurs when all resources are fully employed.

But in the short run, the economy may fail to meet this potential. Indeed, a shortfall in aggregate expenditure will lead the economy to produce below its full-employment potential. This explains why economists tend to emphasise demand factors in the short run and supply factors in the long run. Fluctuations in demand are the source of many of the short-run disruptions that make up the business cycle, while supply factors determine the economy's long-run potential. Of course, in the real world, distinctions are never quite as sharp as in textbooks. Sometimes changes on the supply side can also cause short-run disruptions. And sometimes short-run demand disruptions—like the Great Depression in the United States—can last for so long and do so much damage that they have long-run consequences.

Chapter at a Glance

Aggregate expenditure = **C** Consumption + **I** Planned investment + **G** Government purchases + **NX** Net exports

The total amount of goods and services people want to buy across the whole economy.

Aggregate expenditure rises with income (and hence real GDP), since **consumption** rises with income.

Macroeconomic Equilibrium

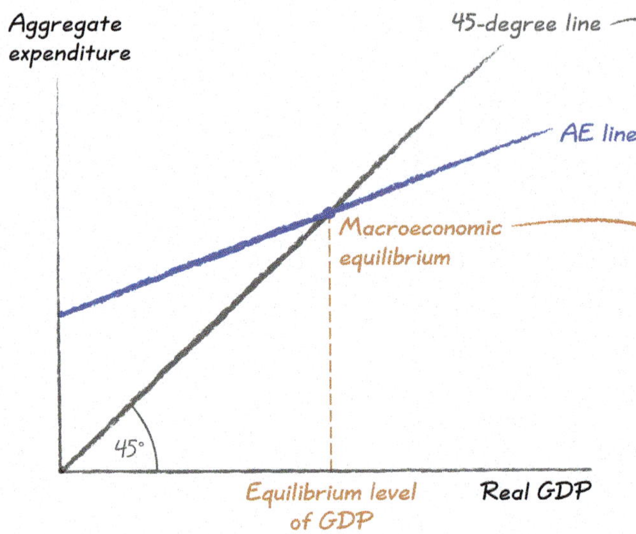

The **45-degree line** shows all possible points of macroeconomic equilibrium.

The **aggregate expenditure** line shows how aggregate expenditure rises with income.

Macroeconomic equilibrium occurs when:
Aggregate expenditure = GDP
(where the **AE line** intersects the 45-degree line)

The economy can be in macroeconomic equilibrium in both booms and busts.

Shifts in Aggregate Expenditure

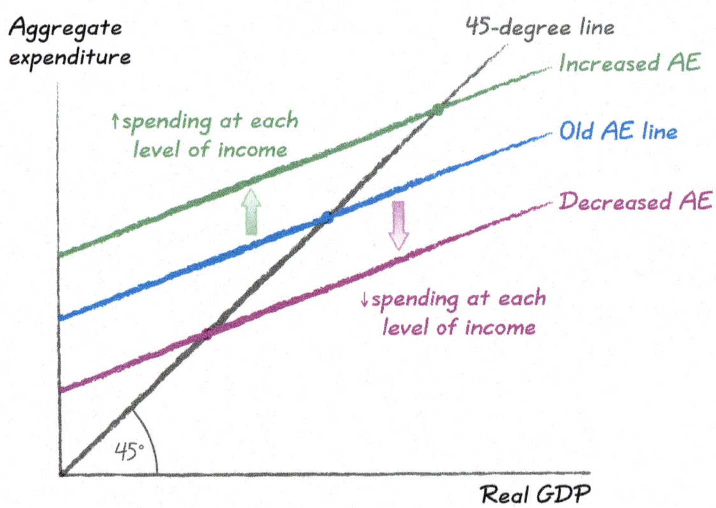

Step one: Did spending plans change?

- Is there a change in how much consumers spend, businesses invest, governments purchase, or importers and exporters trade at each level of income?

Step two: Shift the aggregate expenditure line

- An increase in spending shifts the aggregate expenditure line up.
- A decrease in spending shifts the aggregate expenditure line down.

Step three: Analyse the new equilibrium

- How does the **equilibrium level of GDP** change in the new equilibrium?

The Marginal Propensity to Consume (MPC) and the Multiplier

Marginal propensity to consume	Multiplier	Total change in GDP
The fraction of each extra dollar of income that you spend.	A measure of how much GDP changes as a result of both the direct and indirect effects flowing from each extra dollar of spending.	The larger the multiplier, the more GDP increases when spending increases.
$MPC = \frac{\Delta Consumption}{\Delta Income} < 1$	$Multiplier = \frac{1}{1 - MPC}$	$\Delta GDP = \Delta Spending \times Multiplier$

Key Concepts

aggregate expenditure, A-2	macroeconomic equilibrium, A-5	multiplier, A-12
consumption function, A-3	marginal propensity to consume, A-3	planned investment, A-2

Discussion and Review Questions

Learning Objective A.1 *Measure aggregate expenditure and analyse how it varies with income.*

1. Explain why unplanned inventory changes are not considered part of aggregate expenditure.
2. You receive $1,000. How much of it will you spend this year and how much of it will you save? What is your marginal propensity to consume?

Learning Objective A.2 *Find the macroeconomic equilibrium and analyse how it changes as economic conditions change.*

3. Spending depends on income, income depends on production, and production depends on spending. Explain how this circular interdependence is resolved at the macroeconomic equilibrium.
4. Explain why the 45-degree line represents all the possible points of macroeconomic equilibrium. Why would production tend to change if it is to the left or right of the 45-degree line?
5. Use the Keynesian cross to illustrate how changes in aggregate expenditure can lead to changes in output. Provide an example of something that would lead to a recession and something that would lead to an expansion. Illustrate each example with a small graph showing the shift in aggregate expenditure and the subsequent change in output.

Learning Objective A.3 *Analyse how moderate changes in spending can have bigger consequences through the multiplier effect.*

6. If everyone has the same marginal propensity to consume as you indicated in your answer to question 2, determine the multiplier. Explain why the marginal propensity to consume determines the multiplier.
7. Your state legislators and premier are debating whether they should use state funds to encourage motion picture studios to shoot and produce films in your state. The premier's office issues a report that includes the following statement:

   "The average budget for a movie is $70 million but our consultants estimate that this will have broader ripple effects across many industries and will boost state output by about $210 million dollars."

   What multiplier is the premier's office using to come to this conclusion? Do you think the multiplier is realistic for this scenario?

Study Problems

Learning Objective A.1 *Measure aggregate expenditure and analyse how it varies with income.*

1. In 2021, Real GDP in Australia increased by $94.4 billion relative to 2020 and consumption spending increased by $71.7 billion.
   a. What do these data suggest was the marginal propensity to consume?
   b. If real income increases by $80 billion in 2022, use this estimate of the marginal propensity to consume to predict how consumption spending will change in 2022.
2. Use the graph to answer the following questions.

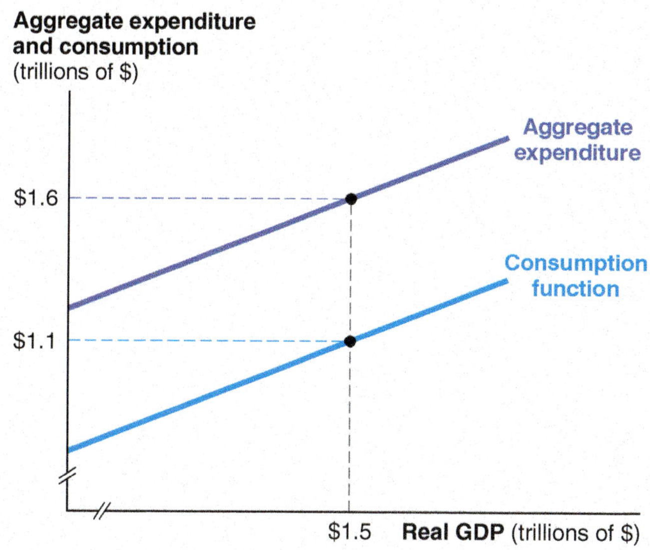

   a. What is consumption spending if income is $1.5 trillion?
   b. What is aggregate expenditure if income is $1.5 trillion?
   c. What is the sum of planned investment, government purchases, and net exports when income is $1.5 trillion?
   d. If income rises, will consumption rise, fall, or stay the same? Will this cause the consumption function to shift? Explain your reasoning.
   e. If income falls, will aggregate expenditure rise, fall, or stay the same? Will this cause the aggregate expenditure line to shift? Explain your reasoning.

Learning Objective A.2 *Find the macroeconomic equilibrium and analyse how it changes as economic conditions change.*

3. If aggregate expenditure in Thailand this year is on track to be $500 billion and output is $400 billion, is the economy currently at a macroeconomic equilibrium? Predict how unplanned inventories will change. How will producers respond to this imbalance? Do you anticipate GDP will rise or fall in response?
4. Draw an aggregate expenditure graph and label the macroeconomic equilibrium on it, which occurs when real GDP is $7 trillion. Then illustrate how a decrease in aggregate expenditure will lead the economy to experience a recession as it shifts to a new macroeconomic equilibrium where real GDP is $5 trillion.
5. Forecast how aggregate expenditure and real GDP will change in each of the following scenarios. Indicate which component of aggregate expenditure changes and illustrate your answers with a graph.
   a. A sharp uptick in stock prices increases consumer wealth and makes consumers willing to spend more at each level of income.
   b. China imposes tariffs on all goods imported from Australia, which causes Australian exports to fall.
   c. Parliament passes a new tax law that removes a business investment tax credit. In response to this change, businesses spend $50 billion less on new machinery and building projects.
   d. Parliament passes a fiscal stimulus package that devotes $40 billion to improving infrastructure across the country.
   e. Bolstered by reassurances from the RBA, businesses become confident that historically low interest rates will continue for the foreseeable future and begin to plan large investment projects.

Learning Objective A.3 *Analyse how moderate changes in spending can have bigger consequences through the multiplier effect.*

6. In response to a $24 billion increase in government purchases, GDP increased by $36 billion.
   a. What is the multiplier?
   b. Use this estimate to predict how GDP will change if businesses invest an additional $10 billion in capital investment projects.
   c. What is the marginal propensity to consume?
7. The federal government is expected to pass a new spending bill that increases government purchases by $5 billion. Predict how GDP will change if the multiplier is 1.2. Explain why the change in GDP is not exactly equal to the change in government spending.

Glossary

A

absolute advantage The ability to do a task using fewer inputs.

absolute poverty Judges the adequacy of resources relative to an absolute standard of living.

accounting profit The total revenue a business receives, less its explicit financial costs.

actively managed When a fund is managed by stock pickers.

actuarially fair An insurance policy that, on average, is expected to pay out as much in compensation as it receives in premiums.

adverse selection of buyers The tendency for the mix of buyers to be skewed toward more high-cost buyers when sellers don't know buyers' type.

adverse selection of sellers The tendency for the mix of goods to be skewed toward more low-quality goods when buyers can't observe quality.

aggregate demand curve Shows the relationship between the price level and the total quantity of output that buyers collectively plan to purchase.

aggregate expenditure The total amount of goods and services that people want to buy across the whole economy.
= *Consumption*
+ *Planned investment*
+ *Government purchases*
+ *Net exports*

aggregate supply curve Shows the relationship between the price level and the total quantity of output that suppliers collectively produce.

anchoring bias The tendency to begin with an anchor, or starting point, and insufficiently adjust from there.

annualised rate Data converted to the rate that would occur if the same growth rate had occurred throughout the year.

anti-coordination game When your best response is to take a different (but complementary) action to the other player.

appreciation When the price of a currency rises.

automatic stabilisers Spending and tax programs that adjust as the economy expands and contracts, without policy makers taking any deliberate action.

availability bias The tendency to overestimate the frequency of events that are easily recalled, and to underestimate the frequency of less memorable events.

average cost Cost per unit, calculated as your firm's total costs (including fixed and variable costs) divided by the quantity produced.

average revenue Revenue per unit, calculated as total revenue divided by the quantity supplied. Average revenue is equal to the price, if you charge everyone the same price.

B

bank run When many bank customers try to withdraw their savings at the same time.

bargaining power Your ability to negotiate a better deal.

barriers to entry Obstacles that make it difficult for new firms to enter a market.

behavioural economics Economic analysis that includes psychological factors in assessing how people make economic decisions.

best response The choice that yields the highest payoff given the other player's choice.

bilateral trade balance How much we buy from a specific country compared to how much they buy from us.

binding price ceiling A price ceiling that prevents the market from reaching the market equilibrium price, meaning that the highest price sellers can charge is set below the equilibrium price.

binding price floor A price floor that prevents the market from reaching the equilibrium price, meaning that the lowest price that sellers can charge is above the equilibrium price.

bond An IOU. Specifically, a promise to pay back a loan with interest.

budget deficit The difference between spending and revenue in a year in which spending exceeds revenue.

budget surplus The difference between spending and revenue in a year in which revenue exceeds spending.

bundling Selling different goods together as a package.

business cycle Short-term fluctuations in economic activity.

business investment Spending by businesses on new capital assets.

C

cap and trade A quantity regulation implemented by allocating a fixed number of permits, which can then be traded.

capital stock The total quantity of capital at a point in time.

cash rate The interest rate that the RBA uses as its policy tool, which is the nominal interest rate that banks pay to borrow from each other overnight.

catch-up growth The rapid growth that occurs when a relatively poor country invests in its physical capital.

change in the quantity demanded The change in quantity associated with movement along a fixed demand curve.

change in the quantity supplied The change in quantity associated with movement along a fixed supply curve.

classical dichotomy A purely nominal change—like a change in the average price level—won't have any effect on real variables in the long run.

club good A good that is excludable, but nonrival in consumption.

Coase Theorem If bargaining is costless and property rights are clearly established and enforced, then externality problems can be solved by private bargains.

collusion An agreement to limit competition; an agreement by rivals to not compete with each other, but to all charge high prices instead.

common resource A good that is rival and also nonexcludable.

comparative advantage The ability to do a task at a lower opportunity cost.

compensating differential The differences in wages required to offset the desirable or undesirable aspects of a job.

complementary goods Goods that go together. Your demand for a good will decrease if the price of a complementary good rises.

complements-in-production Goods that are made together. Your supply of a good will increase if the price of a complement-in-production rises.

compounding formula Future value in t years = Present value × $(1 + r)^t$

congestion effect When a good becomes less valuable because other people use it. If more people buy such a product, your demand for it will decrease.

constant returns to scale Increasing all inputs by some proportion will cause output to rise by the same proportion.

consumer price index (CPI) An index that tracks the average price consumers pay over time for a representative "basket" of goods and services.

consumer surplus The economic surplus you get from buying something; Consumer surplus = Marginal benefit – Price.

consumption function A curve plotting the level of consumption associated with each level of income.

consumption Household spending on final goods and services.

consumption smoothing Maintaining a steady or smooth path for your consumption spending over time.

coordination game When all players have a common interest in coordinating their choices.

corrective subsidy A subsidy designed to induce people to take account of the positive externalities they cause.

corrective tax A tax designed to induce people to take account of the negative externalities they cause.

cost-benefit principle Costs and benefits are the incentives that shape decisions. You should evaluate the full set of costs and benefits of any choice, and only pursue those whose benefits are at least as large as their costs.

cost-push inflation Inflation that results from an unexpected rise in production costs.

credit constraints Limits on how much you can borrow.

cross-price elasticity of demand A measure of how responsive the demand of one good is to the price changes of another. It measures the percent change in quantity demanded that follows from a 1% change in the price of another good.

crowding out The decline in private spending—and particularly investment—that follows from a rise in government borrowing.

current account balance Measures the difference between the income that Australians receive from abroad and the income that Australians pay to people abroad.

cyclical unemployment Unemployment that is due to a temporary downturn in the economy.

D

deadweight loss How far economic surplus falls below the efficient outcome; Deadweight loss = Economic surplus at the efficient quantity – Actual economic surplus.

decrease in demand A shift of the demand curve to the left.

decrease in supply A shift of the supply curve to the left.

default risk The risk that your loan won't be repaid.

deflation A generalised decrease in the overall level of prices.

demand-pull inflation Inflation resulting from excess demand.

deposit insurance A guarantee that you won't lose the money you deposit in the bank.

depreciation rate The proportion of an investment's remaining productive capacity you lose each year due to depreciation.

depreciation The decline in capital due to wear and tear, obsolescence, accidental damage, and aging; when the price of a currency falls.

derived demand The demand for an input derives from the demand for the stuff that input produces.

diminishing marginal benefit Each additional item yields a smaller marginal benefit than the previous item.

diminishing marginal product The marginal product of an input declines as you use more of that input.

diminishing marginal utility Each additional dollar yields a smaller boost to your utility—that is, less marginal utility—than the previous dollar.

discounting Converting *future values* into their equivalent *present values*.

discounting formula Present value $= \text{Future value in } t \text{ years} \times \frac{1}{(1+r)^t}$

discouraged worker Someone who wants a job, but isn't looking for work because they don't think there are jobs available for them.

discretionary fiscal policy Policy that temporarily changes government spending or taxes to boost or slow the economy.

discretionary spending Spending that Parliament appropriates annually.

discrimination Treating people differently based on characteristics such as their gender, race, ethnicity, sexual orientation, religion, disability, social class, or other factors.

disposable income Your after-tax income.

dissaving The excess amount you consume above your income in a given period that you therefore must pay for by either withdrawing money from your savings or borrowing money.

distributional consequences Who gets what.

diversification Reducing risk by combining a large number of small risks whose outcomes are not closely related.

dividends A share of profits that a company pays to its shareholders.

domestic demand curve Shows the quantity of a good that all domestic consumers added together plan to buy, at each price.

domestic supply curve Shows the quantity of a good that all domestic suppliers added together plan to sell, at each price.

E

economic burden The burden created by the change in after-tax prices faced by buyers and sellers.

economic efficiency An outcome is more economically efficient if it yields more economic surplus.

economic profit The total revenue a firm receives, less both explicit financial costs and the entrepreneur's implicit opportunity costs.

economic surplus The total benefits minus total costs flowing from a decision. It measures how much a decision has improved your well-being.

effective marginal tax rate The amount of each extra dollar you earn that you lose to higher taxes and lower government benefits.

efficiency wage A higher wage paid to encourage greater worker productivity.

efficient allocation Allocating goods to create the largest economic surplus, which requires that each good goes to the person who'll get the highest marginal benefit from it.

efficient markets hypothesis The theory that at any point in time, stock prices reflect all publicly available information.

efficient outcome The efficient outcome yields the largest possible economic surplus.

efficient production Producing a given quantity of output at the lowest possible cost, which requires producing each good at the lowest marginal cost.

efficient quantity The quantity that produces the largest possible economic surplus.

elastic When the absolute value of the percent change in quantity is larger than the absolute value of the percent change in price, which means that the absolute value of the price elasticity is greater than 1.

employed Working-age people who are working.

equilibrium The point at which there is no tendency for change. A market is in equilibrium when the quantity supplied equals the quantity demanded.

equilibrium price The price at which the market is in equilibrium.

equilibrium quantity The quantity demanded and supplied in equilibrium.

equilibrium unemployment rate The long-run unemployment rate to which the economy tends to return.

equity An outcome yields greater equity if it results in a fairer distribution of economic benefits.

excess demand When the quantity demanded at the prevailing price exceeds the quantity supplied.

excise tax A tax on a specific product.

expansion A period of increasing economic activity.

expected utility What your utility will be, on average, if you make a particular choice.

export To sell goods or services to foreign buyers.

exports Goods or services produced domestically and purchased by foreign buyers.

external benefit A benefit accruing to bystanders.

external cost A cost imposed on bystanders.

externality A side effect of an activity that affects bystanders whose interests aren't taken into account.

extrinsic motivation The desire to do something for its external rewards such as higher pay.

F

fair bet A gamble that, on average, will leave you with the same amount of money.

final goods and services Finished goods or services.

financial account balance The difference between financial inflows and financial outflows.

financial inflows Investments by foreigners in Australia.

financial outflows Investments by Australians in foreign countries.

financial shocks Any change in borrowing conditions that changes the real interest rate at which people can borrow. Financial shocks shift the *MP* curve.

finitely repeated game When you face the same strategic interaction a *fixed* number of times.

firm demand curve An individual firm's demand curve, summarises the quantity that buyers demand from an individual firm as it changes its price.

first-mover advantage The strategic gain from an anticipatory action that can force a rival to respond less aggressively.

fiscal policy The government's use of spending and tax policies to attempt to stabilise the economy.

Five Forces framework The structure of competition in your market can be described in terms of five forces.

fixed costs Those costs that don't vary when you change the quantity of output you produce.

focal point A cue from outside a game that helps you coordinate on a specific equilibrium.

focusing illusion The tendency to mis-predict your utility by focusing on a few factors at the expense of others.

foreign exchange market The market in which currencies are bought and sold.

foreign saving Funding that comes from foreigners lending to Australians.

forward guidance Providing information about the future course of monetary policy in order to influence market expectations of future interest rates.

framing effect When a decision is affected by how a choice is described, or framed. You should avoid letting framing effects alter your own decisions.

free entry When there are no factors making it particularly difficult or costly for a business to enter or exit an industry.

free-rider problem When someone can enjoy the benefits of a good without bearing the costs.

frictional unemployment Unemployment due to the time it takes for employers to search for workers and for workers to search for jobs.

fundamental analysis A framework for assessing an asset's fundamental value.

fundamental value The present value of the future profits that a company will earn.

future value The amount that your money will grow into by a future date, as a result of earning interest.

G

gains from trade The benefits that come from reallocating resources, goods, and services to better uses.

game tree Shows how a game plays out over time, with the first move forming the trunk, and then each subsequent choice branching out, so the final leaves show all possible outcomes.

GDP deflator A price index that tracks the price of all goods and services produced domestically.

GDP per person Total GDP divided by the population.

general skills Skills useful to many employers.

globalisation The increasing economic, political, and cultural integration of different countries.

government failure When government policies lead to worse outcomes.

government purchases Government purchases of goods and services.

government saving Saving by the government.

"greater fool" theory The idea that people buy an investment because they expect other people to buy it from them at a higher price.

Grim Trigger strategy If the other players have cooperated in all previous rounds, you will cooperate. But if any player has defected in the past, you will defect.

gross domestic product (GDP) The market value of all final goods and services produced within a country in a year.

gross government debt The total accumulated amount of money the government owes.

group pricing Price discrimination by charging different prices to different groups of people.

H

hedge Acquire an offsetting risk.

"holding other things constant" A commonly used qualifier noting your conclusions may change if some factor that you haven't analysed changes. (In Latin, it's *ceteris paribus*.)

hold-up problem Once you have made a relationship-specific investment, the other side may try to renegotiate so that they get a better deal (and you get a worse one).

housing investment Spending on building or improving houses or apartments.

human capital The accumulated knowledge and skills that make a worker more productive.

hurdle method Offer lower prices only to those buyers who are willing to overcome some hurdle, or obstacle.

hyperinflation Extremely high rates of inflation.

hysteresis When a period of high unemployment leads to a higher equilibrium unemployment rate.

I

imperfect competition When you face at least some competitors and/or you sell products that differ at least a little from your competitors. Monopolistic competition and oligopoly are examples.

implicit bias Judgements shaped by the unconscious attribution of particular qualities to specific groups.

import To buy goods or services from foreign sellers.

imports Goods or services produced in a foreign country and purchased by domestic buyers.

import quota A limit on the quantity of a good that can be imported.

income The money you receive in a period of time, such as a year.

income effect Measures how people's choices change when they have more income. A higher wage increases your income, leading you to choose more leisure and hence less work.

income elasticity of demand A measure of how responsive the demand for a good is to changes in income. It measures the percent change in quantity demanded that follows from a 1% change in income.

income taxes Taxes collected on all income, regardless of its source.

increase in demand A shift of the demand curve to the right.

increase in supply A shift of the supply curve to the right.

indefinitely repeated game When you face the same strategic interaction with no definitive endpoint.

index fund A mutual fund that consists of a broad market index; an investment that automatically invests in a predefined portfolio of stocks.

indexation Automatically adjusting wages, benefits, tax brackets, and the like to compensate for inflation.

individual demand curve A graph, plotting the quantity of an item that someone plans to buy, at each price.

individual supply curve A graph plotting the quantity of an item that a business plans to sell at each price.

inelastic When the absolute value of the percent change in quantity is smaller than the absolute value of the percent change in price, which means that the absolute value of the price elasticity is less than 1.

inferior good A good for which higher income causes a decrease in demand.

inflation A generalised rise in the overall level of prices.

inflation expectations The rate at which average prices are anticipated to rise next year.

inflation fallacy The (mistaken) belief that inflation destroys purchasing power.

inflation rate The annual percentage increase in the average price level.

inflation target A publicly stated goal for the inflation rate.

informative advertising Advertising that provides information about a product and its attributes.

initial public offering When a company first sells stock directly to the public.

insufficient demand When the quantity demanded at the prevailing price is below what's supplied.

insurance A promise of compensation if a specified bad thing happens.

interdependence principle Your best choice depends on your other choices, the choices others make, developments in other markets, and expectations about the future. When any of these factors change, your best choice might change.

interest rate on excess reserves The interest rate the RBA pays to banks on reserves that are in excess of required reserves.

intergenerational mobility The extent to which the economic status of children is independent of the economic status of their parents.

intermediate goods and services Goods or services used as inputs in the production of other products.

internal markets Markets within a company to buy and sell scarce resources.

intrinsic motivation The desire to do something for the enjoyment of the activity itself.

investment Spending on new capital assets that increase the economy's productive capacity.

investment line The line that shows how the quantity of investment increases as the real interest rate falls.

involuntarily part time Someone who wants full-time work and is working part time because they haven't found a full-time job.

***IS* curve** Illustrates how lower real interest rates raise spending and hence GDP, leading to a more positive output gap.

J

job-specific skills Skills that are only useful in a job with one particular employer.

K

knowledge problem When knowledge needed to make a good decision is not available to the decision maker.

L

labour force The employed plus the unemployed.

labour force participation rate The percentage of the working-age population that is either employed or unemployed.

labour market Phillips curve A Phillips curve linking unexpected inflation to the unemployment rate.

labour productivity The quantity of goods and services that each person produces per hour of work.

labour supply The time you spend working in the market.

lagging indicators Variables that follow the business cycle with a delay.

law of demand The tendency for quantity demanded to be higher when the price is lower.

law of diminishing returns When one input is held constant, increases in the other inputs will, at some point, begin to yield smaller and smaller increases in output.

law of supply The tendency for the quantity supplied to be higher when the price is higher.

leading indicators Variables that tend to predict the future path of the economy.

lender of last resort The RBA's role as the lender that financial institutions turn to when they're having trouble getting loans.

liquidity The ability to quickly and easily convert your investments into cash, with little or no loss in value.

liquidity risk The risk that if you need to sell an asset quickly, you may not be able to get a good price for it.

long run The horizon over which you, or your rivals, may expand or contract production capacity and new rivals may enter the market or existing firms may exit.

long-run aggregate supply curve The aggregate supply curve that applies to the long run when prices have fully adjusted. Because the economy will return to producing its potential output, this curve is vertical.

long-term unemployed People who have been unemployed for twelve consecutive months or longer.

look forward In games that play out over time, you should look forward to anticipate the likely consequences of your choices.

loss aversion Being more sensitive to losses than to gains.

M

macroeconomics The study of the economy as a whole.

macroeconomic equilibrium Occurs when the quantity of output that buyers collectively want to purchase is equal to the quantity of output that suppliers collectively produce.

mandate A requirement to buy or sell a minimum amount of a good.

mandatory spending Spending on programs that does not get determined annually; instead, it is set in law.

marginal benefit The extra benefit from one extra unit (of goods purchased, hours studied, etc.).

marginal cost The extra cost from one extra unit.

marginal external benefit The extra external benefit accruing to bystanders from one extra unit.

marginal external cost The extra external cost imposed on bystanders from one extra unit.

marginal principle Decisions about quantities are best made incrementally. You should break "how many" questions into a series of smaller, or marginal decisions, weighing marginal benefits and marginal costs.

marginal private benefit The extra benefit enjoyed by the buyer from one extra unit.

marginal private cost The extra cost paid by the seller from one extra unit.

marginal product The increase in output that arises from an additional unit of an input, like labour.

marginal product of labour The extra production that occurs from hiring an extra worker.

marginal propensity to consume The fraction of each extra dollar of income that households spend on consumption.

marginal revenue The addition to total revenue you get from selling one more unit.

marginal revenue product Measures the marginal revenue from hiring an additional worker. The marginal revenue product is equal to the marginal product of labour multiplied by the price of that product.

marginal social benefit All marginal benefits, no matter who gets them = Marginal private benefit + Marginal external benefit.

marginal social cost All marginal costs, no matter who pays them = Marginal private cost + Marginal external cost.

marginal tax rate The tax rate you pay if you earn another dollar.

marginal utility The additional utility you get from one more dollar.

marginally attached Someone who wants a job, and who has looked for a job within the past year, but who isn't counted as unemployed because they aren't currently searching for work.

market A setting bringing together potential buyers and sellers.

market demand curve A graph plotting the total quantity of an item demanded by the entire market, at each price.

market economy Each individual makes their own production and consumption decisions, buying and selling in markets.

market failure When the forces of supply and demand lead to an inefficient outcome.

market for loanable funds The market for the funds used to buy, rent, or build capital.

market power The extent to which a seller can charge a higher price without losing many sales to competing businesses.

market supply curve A graph plotting the total quantity of an item supplied by the entire market, at each price.

maturity transformation Using short-term loans to make long-term loans.

means-tested programs Programs for which eligibility is based on income and sometimes wealth.

menu costs The marginal cost of adjusting prices.

monetary policy The process of setting interest rates in an effort to influence economic conditions.

money Any asset regularly used in transactions.

money illusion The (mistaken) tendency to focus on nominal dollar amounts instead of inflation-adjusted amounts.

monopolistic competition A market with many small businesses competing, each selling differentiated products.

monopoly When there is only one seller in the market.

monopsony power A business using its bargaining power as a major buyer of labour to pay lower prices, including lower wages.

moral hazard The actions you take because they are not fully observable and you are partially insulated from their consequences.

movement along the demand curve A price change causes movement from one point on a fixed demand curve to another point on the same curve.

movement along the supply curve A price change causes movement from one point on a fixed supply curve to another point on the same curve.

***MP* curve** Illustrates the current real interest rate, which is shaped by monetary policy and the risk premium.

multiple equilibria When there is more than one equilibrium.

multiplier A measure of how much GDP changes as a result of both the direct and indirect effects flowing from each extra dollar of spending.

mutual fund A fund that buys a portfolio of stocks (and sometimes bonds) on your behalf.

N

Nash equilibrium A profile of choices such that the choice that each player makes is a best response to the choices other players are making.

natural monopoly A market in which it is cheapest for a single business to service the market.

negative externality An activity whose side effects harm bystanders.

net exports Spending on exports minus spending on imports; also referred to as the trade balance.

net government debt The debt that the government owes to individuals, businesses, and other governments both here and abroad.

net wealth The amount by which your assets exceed your debts.

network effect When a good becomes more useful because other people use it. If more people buy such a good, your demand for it will also increase.

neutral real interest rate The interest rate that operates when the economy is in neutral—producing neither above nor below its potential.

next best alternative The value of your best option.

nominal exchange rate formula

$$\text{Nominal exchange rate} = \frac{\text{Number of units of a foreign currency}}{\text{Number of dollars}}$$

nominal exchange rate The price of a country's currency (in terms of another country's currency).

nominal GDP GDP measured in today's prices.

nominal interest rate The stated interest rate without a correction for the effects of inflation.

nominal variable A variable measured in dollars (whose value may fluctuate over time).

nominal wage rigidity Reluctance to cut nominal wages.

nonexcludable When someone cannot be easily excluded from using something.

non-price competition Competing to win customers by differentiating your product.

nonrival good A good for which one person's use doesn't subtract from another's.

normal good A good for which higher income causes an increase in demand.

normative analysis Prescribes what *should* happen, which involves value judgements.

not in the labour force Those in the working-age population who are neither employed nor unemployed.

O

Okun's rule of thumb For every percentage point that actual output falls below potential output, the unemployment rate is around half a percentage point higher.

oligopoly A market with only a handful of large sellers.

one-shot game A strategic interaction that occurs only once.

opportunity cost The true cost of something is the next best alternative you have to give up to get it.

output gap The difference between actual and potential output, measured as a percentage of potential output.

overconfidence The tendency to overrate the accuracy of your forecasts.

P

pay-for-performance Linking the income your workers earn to measures of their performance. Examples include commissions, piece rates, bonuses, or promotions.

payoff table A table that lists your choices in each row, the other player's choices in each column, and so shows all possible outcomes, listing the payoffs in each cell.

payroll tax A tax on wages that's typically a percentage of an employer's total wage bill.

peak A high point in economic activity.

perfect competition Markets in which 1) all businesses in an industry sell an identical good; and 2) there are many sellers and many buyers, each of whom is small relative to the size of the market.

perfect price discrimination Charging each customer their reservation price.

perfectly elastic When any change in price leads to an infinitely large change in quantity.

perfectly inelastic When quantity does not respond at all to a price change.

permanent income hypothesis The idea that consumption is driven by permanent income rather than current income.

permanent income Your average lifetime income; your best estimate of your long-term average income.

personal saving Saving by households of whatever money they don't either spend or pay as taxes.

persuasive advertising Advertising that tries to persuade or manipulate you into believing that you'll enjoy a particular product.

Phillips curve A curve illustrating the link between the output gap and unexpected inflation.

physical capital Tools, machinery, and structures.

planned economy Centralised decisions are made about what is produced, how, by whom, and who gets what.

planned investment Spending on machinery, software, and buildings used to produce goods and services. Unlike total investment, it excludes changes in inventories.

positive analysis Describes what *is* happening, explaining why, or predicting what will happen.

positive externality An activity whose side effects benefit bystanders.

potential output The level of output that occurs when all resources are fully employed.

poverty line An income level, below which a family is defined to be in poverty.

poverty rate The percentage of people whose family income is below the poverty line.

precautionary saving Saving to be prepared for a financial emergency.

prediction markets Markets whose payoffs are linked to whether an uncertain event occurs.

prejudice A preconceived bias against a group that's not based on reason or experience.

premium The price of insurance.

present value The amount of money that you would need to invest today in order to produce an equivalent benefit in the future.

price ceiling A maximum price that sellers can charge.

price competition Competing to win customers by offering lower prices.

price discrimination Selling the same good at different prices.

price elasticity of demand A measure of how responsive buyers are to price changes. It measures the percent change in quantity demanded that follows from a 1% price change.

price elasticity of supply A measure of how responsive sellers are to price changes. It measures the percent change in quantity supplied that follows from a 1% price change.

price floor A minimum price that sellers can charge.

price-taker Someone who decides to charge the prevailing price and whose actions do not affect the prevailing price.

principal-agent problem The problems that arise when a principal hires an agent to do something on their behalf, but the principal cannot perfectly observe the agent's actions.

private information When one party to a transaction knows something the other doesn't.

producer price index (PPI) A price index that tracks the prices of inputs into the production process.

producer surplus The economic surplus you get from selling something; Producer surplus = Price − Marginal cost.

product differentiation Efforts by sellers to make their products different from those of their competitors.

production function The methods by which inputs are transformed into output which determines the total production that's possible with a given set of ingredients.

production possibility frontier Shows the different sets of output that are attainable with your scarce resources.

profit margin Profits per unit sold.

progressive tax A tax where those with more income tend to pay a higher share of their income in taxes.

property rights Control over a tangible or intangible resource.

property tax A tax on the value of property, usually real estate.

prune the tree method A method for solving game trees: Start by looking forward to the final period and highlighting your rival's best responses, then prune the options the rival would never choose—the "dead leaves"—off your game tree.

public good A nonrival good that is nonexcludable and hence subject to the free-rider problem.

Q

quantitative easing (QE) Purchasing large quantities of longer-term government bonds and other securities in an effort to lower long-term interest rates.

quantity discount When the per-unit price is lower when you buy a larger quantity.

quantity regulation A minimum or maximum quantity that can be sold.

quota A limit on the maximum quantity of a good that can be sold.

R

random walk When a price follows an unpredictable path.

Rational Rule for Consumers Consume more today if the marginal benefit of a dollar of consumption today is greater than (or equal to) the marginal benefit of spending a dollar plus interest in the future.

Rational Rule for Employers Hire more workers if the marginal revenue product is greater than (or equal to) the wage.

Rational Rule for Entry You should enter a market if you expect to earn a positive economic profit, which occurs when the price exceeds your average cost.

Rational Rule for Exit Exit the market if you expect to earn a negative economic profit, which occurs if the price is less than your average costs.

Rational Rule for Investors Pursue an investment opportunity if the present value of future revenues exceeds the up-front cost.

Rational Rule for Markets Produce more of a good if its marginal benefit is greater than (or equal to) its marginal cost.

Rational Rule for Sellers in Competitive Markets Sell one more item if the price is greater than (or is equal to) the marginal cost.

Rational Rule for Society Produce more of an item if its marginal social benefit is greater than (or equal to) the marginal social cost.

Rational Rule for Workers Work one more hour as long as the wage is at least as large as the marginal benefit of another hour of leisure.

Rational Rule If something is worth doing, keep doing it until your marginal benefits equal your marginal costs.

RBA model The framework that uses the *IS* curve, the *MP* curve, and the Phillips curve to link interest rates, the output gap, and inflation.

RBA rule-of-thumb The recipe that describes how the RBA often sets the interest rate: Cash rate – Inflation = Neutral real interest rate + ½ × (Inflation – 2.5%) + Output gap

real exchange rate The domestic price divided by the foreign price, expressed in the domestic currency. Calculated as:

$$\frac{\text{Domestic price}}{\text{Foreign price/Nominal exchange rate}}$$

real GDP GDP measured in constant prices.

real interest rate The interest rate in terms of changes in your purchasing power; ≈ Nominal interest rate – Inflation rate

real variable A variable that has been adjusted to account for inflation.

reason backward Start by analysing the last period of the game. Use this to figure out what will happen in the second-to-last period, and keep reasoning backward until you can see all the consequences that follow from today's decision.

recession A period of declining economic activity.

regressive tax A tax where those with less income tend to pay a higher share of their income on the tax.

relationship-specific investment An investment that is more valuable if the current business relationship continues.

relative poverty Judges poverty relative to the material living standards of your contemporary society.

relative valuation An assessment of the value of an asset by comparing it to similar assets.

repeated game When you face the same strategic interaction with the same rivals and the same payoffs in successive periods.

representativeness bias The tendency to assess the likelihood that something belongs in a category by judging how similar they are to that category.

reservation price The maximum price a customer will pay for a product. It is equal to their marginal benefit.

Reserve Bank Board The body that decides on Australian interest rates. It consists of the Governor, Deputy Governor, Treasury Secretary, and six external members.

reserve requirements A minimum amount of reserves that each bank must hold.

reserves The cash that banks need to keep on hand to make payments.

retained earnings The profits that a company chooses not to give as dividends to shareholders.

revisions Updates to earlier estimates.

risk averse Disliking uncertainty.

risk loving Liking uncertainty.

risk neutral Indifferent to uncertainty.

risk premium The extra interest that lenders charge to account for the risk of loaning money.

risk spreading Breaking a big risk into many smaller risks so that it can be spread over many people.

risk-free interest rate The interest rate on a loan that involves no risk.

rival good A good for which your use of it comes at someone else's expense.

Rule of 70 Divide 70 by the annual growth rate to get the number of years until the original amount doubles.

S

sales tax A tax on purchases that's typically a percentage of the purchase price of goods and services.

saving The portion of income that you set aside, rather than spending on consumption.

scarcity The problem that resources are limited.

search good A good that you can easily evaluate before buying.

seasonally adjusted Data stripped of predictable seasonal patterns.

second-mover advantage The strategic advantage that can follow from taking an action that adapts to your rival's choice.

shadow banks Financial firms that are similar to banks, but are not regulated like banks.

shift in the demand curve A movement of the demand curve itself.

shift in the supply curve A movement of the supply curve itself.

shoe-leather costs The costs incurred trying to avoid holding cash.

short run The horizon over which the production capacity, and the number and type of competitors you face, cannot change.

short-run aggregate supply curve The aggregate supply curve that applies over a period when prices are neither fully fixed nor fully flexible. As a result, the short run aggregate supply curve is upward-sloping.

shortage When the quantity demanded exceeds the quantity supplied.

signal A costly action taken to credibly convey private information, or information that is hard for someone else to verify.

social insurance Government-provided insurance against bad outcomes such as unemployment, illness, disability, or outliving your savings.

social safety net The cash assistance, goods, and services provided by the government to better the lives of those at the bottom of the income distribution.

socially optimal outcome The outcome that is most efficient for society as a whole, including the interests of buyers, sellers, and bystanders.

someone else's shoes technique By mentally "trading places" with someone so that you understand their objectives and constraints, you can forecast the decisions they will make.

specialisation Focusing on specific tasks.

speculative bubble When the price of an asset rises above what appears to be its fundamental value.

spending shocks Any change in aggregate expenditure at a given real interest rate and level of income. Spending shocks shift the *IS* curve.

stagflation A combination of economic stagnation—or falling output—combined with high inflation.

stamp duty A tax paid to the state government to legally register a change of ownership; sometimes called a transfer duty.

statistical discrimination Using observations about the average characteristics of a group to make inferences about an individual.

statutory burden The burden of being assigned by the government to send a tax payment.

sticky prices Prices that adjust sporadically and sluggishly to changes in market conditions.

stock market The market where people buy and sell existing stocks.

strategic interaction When your best choice may depend on what others choose, and their best choice may depend on what you choose.

strategic plan A list of instructions that describes exactly how to respond in any possible situation.

structural unemployment Unemployment that occurs because wages don't fall to bring labour demand and supply into equilibrium.

subsidy A payment made by the government to those who make a specific choice.

substitute goods Goods that replace each other. Your demand for a good will increase if the price of a substitute good rises.

substitutes-in-production Alternative uses of your resources. Your supply of a good will decrease if the price of a substitute-in-production rises.

substitution bias The overstating of inflation that occurs because people substitute toward goods whose prices rise by less.

substitution effect Measures how people respond to a change in relative prices. A higher wage increases the returns to work relative to leisure, leading you to work more.

sunk cost A cost that has been incurred and cannot be reversed. A sunk cost exists whatever choice you make, and hence it is not an opportunity cost. Good decisions ignore sunk costs.

supply shocks Any change in production costs that leads suppliers to change the prices they charge at any given level of output. Supply shocks shift the Phillips curve.

surplus When the quantity demanded is less than the quantity supplied.

switching costs An impediment that makes it costly for customers to switch to buying from another business.

systematic risk Risks that are common across the whole economy.

T

tariff A tax on imported products.

tax expenditures Special deductions, exemptions, or credits that lower your tax obligations, to encourage you to engage in certain kinds of activities

tax incidence The division of the economic burden of a tax between buyers and sellers.

taxable income The amount of your income that you pay taxes on.

technological progress New methods for using existing resources.

term risk The risk that arises from uncertainty about future interest rates.

The Rational Rule for Buyers Buy more of an item if the marginal benefit of one more is greater than (or equal to) the price.

The Rational Rule for Sellers Sell one more item if the marginal revenue is greater than (or equal to) marginal cost.

tick method If you put a tick next to each player's best response, then an outcome with a tick from each player is a Nash equilibrium.

total revenue The total amount you receive from buyers, which is calculated as price × quantity.

trade costs The extra costs incurred as a result of buying or selling internationally, rather than domestically.

tragedy of the commons The tendency to overconsume a common resource.

transfer payments Payments that transfer income from one person to another.

trough A low point in economic activity.

U

underemployed Someone who has some work but wants more hours, or whose job isn't adequately using their skills.

unemployed Working-age people without jobs who are trying to get jobs.

unemployment rate The percentage of the labour force that is unemployed.

unexpected inflation The difference between inflation and inflation expectations = Inflation − Inflation expectations

unfunded liability A commitment to incur expenses in the future without a plan to pay for those expenses.

user cost of capital The extra cost associated with using one more machine next year $= (r+d) \times C$

utilitarianism The political philosophy that government should try to maximise total utility in society.

utility Your level of well-being.

V

valuation formula Present value of an ongoing stream of payments $= \dfrac{\text{Next year's revenue}}{r+d}$

value added The amount by which the value of an item is increased at each stage of production. = Total sales − Cost of intermediate inputs

variable costs Those costs—like labour and raw materials—that vary with the quantity of output you produce.

vertical integration When two (or more) companies along a production chain combine to form a single company.

very-short-run aggregate supply curve The aggregate supply curve that applies to the very short run, in which no prices have changed. Because prices are effectively fixed, this curve is horizontal.

voluntary exchange Buyers and sellers exchange money for goods only if they both want to.

W

wage-price spiral A cycle where higher prices lead to higher nominal wages, which lead to higher prices.

wealth All the assets—including savings, cars, a home—that you currently have.

willingness to pay In order to convert nonfinancial costs or benefits into their monetary equivalent, ask yourself: "What is the most I am willing to pay to get this benefit (or avoid that cost)?"

working-age population Those age 15 or older who are not in the military or institutionalised.

world price The price that a product sells for in the global market.

Z

zero lower bound The constraint that nominal interest rates cannot be effectively set below zero.

Index

Note: **Boldface** type indicates key terms.

D

F

T